Handbook of Research on Bullying in Media and Beyond

Gülşah Sarı
Aksaray University, Turkey

IGI Global
PUBLISHER of TIMELY KNOWLEDGE

A volume in the Advances in Social Networking and Online Communities (ASNOC) Book Series

Published in the United States of America by
IGI Global
Information Science Reference (an imprint of IGI Global)
701 E. Chocolate Avenue
Hershey PA, USA 17033
Tel: 717-533-8845
Fax: 717-533-8661
E-mail: cust@igi-global.com
Web site: http://www.igi-global.com

Library of Congress Cataloging-in-Publication Data

Names: Sarı, Gülşah, 1984- editor.
Title: Handbook of research on bullying in media and beyond / Gülşah Sarı, editor.
Description: Hershey, PA : Information Science Reference, [2023] | Includes bibliographical references and index. | Summary: "Bullying, which includes the repeated aggressive behavior of the strong against the weak, is a condition seen in both children and adults and in this book, the types of bullying (physical, verbal, social, cyber) will be discussed with the approaches of different disciplines and their reflections in the media will be examined"-- Provided by publisher.
Identifiers: LCCN 2022021822 (print) | LCCN 2022021823 (ebook) | ISBN 9781668454268 (hardcover) | ISBN 9781668454275 (ebook)
Subjects: LCSH: Bullying. | Cyberbullying. | Social media and society.
Classification: LCC BF637.B85 I658 2023 (print) | LCC BF637.B85 (ebook) | DDC 302.34/3--dc23/eng/20220712
LC record available at https://lccn.loc.gov/2022021822
LC ebook record available at https://lccn.loc.gov/2022021823

This book is published in the IGI Global book series Advances in Social Networking and Online Communities (ASNOC) (ISSN: 2328-1405; eISSN: 2328-1413)

British Cataloguing in Publication Data
A Cataloguing in Publication record for this book is available from the British Library.

All work contributed to this book is new, previously-unpublished material. The views expressed in this book are those of the authors, but not necessarily of the publisher.

For electronic access to this publication, please contact: eresources@igi-global.com.

Advances in Social Networking and Online Communities (ASNOC) Book Series

Hakikur Rahman
Ansted University Sustainability Research Institute, Malaysia

ISSN:2328-1405
EISSN:2328-1413

Mission

The advancements of internet technologies and the creation of various social networks provide a new channel of knowledge development processes that's dependent on social networking and online communities. This emerging concept of social innovation is comprised of ideas and strategies designed to improve society.

The **Advances in Social Networking and Online Communities** book series serves as a forum for scholars and practitioners to present comprehensive research on the social, cultural, organizational, and human issues related to the use of virtual communities and social networking. This series will provide an analytical approach to the holistic and newly emerging concepts of online knowledge communities and social networks.

Coverage

- Networks and Knowledge Communication in R&D Environments
- Broadband Infrastructure and the New Wireless Network Solutions
- E-capacity Building Programmes to Ensure Digital Cohesion and Improved E-Government Performance at Local Level
- Supporting Virtual Communities of Practice and Interest Networks
- Flourishing Knowledge Creation Environments
- Epistemology of Knowledge Society
- Generation of Municipal Services in Multi-Channel Environments
- Knowledge Communication and the Role of Communities and Social Networks
- Introduction to Mobile Computing
- Networks as Institutionalized Intermediaries of KC

IGI Global is currently accepting manuscripts for publication within this series. To submit a proposal for a volume in this series, please contact our Acquisition Editors at Acquisitions@igi-global.com or visit: http://www.igi-global.com/publish/.

The Advances in Social Networking and Online Communities (ASNOC) Book Series (ISSN 2328-1405) is published by IGI Global, 701 E. Chocolate Avenue, Hershey, PA 17033-1240, USA, www.igi-global.com. This series is composed of titles available for purchase individually; each title is edited to be contextually exclusive from any other title within the series. For pricing and ordering information please visit http://www.igi-global.com/book-series/advances-social-networking-online-communities/37168. Postmaster: Send all address changes to above address.

Titles in this Series

For a list of additional titles in this series, please visit: http://www.igi-global.com/book-series/advances-social-networking-online-communities/37168

Handbook of Research on Technologies and Systems for E-Collaboration During Global Crises
Jingyuan Zhao (University of Toronto, Canada) and V. Vinoth Kumar (Jain University, ndia)
Information Science Reference • © 2022 • 461pp • H/C (ISBN: 9781799896401) • US $295.00

Information Manipulation and Its Impact Across All Industries
Maryam Ebrahimi (Independent Researcher, Germany)
Information Science Reference • © 2022 • 234pp • H/C (ISBN: 9781799882350) • US $215.00

E-Collaboration Technologies and Strategies for Competitive Advantage Amid Challenging Times
Jingyuan Zhao (University of Toronto, Canada) and Joseph Richards (California State University, Sacramento, USA)
Information Science Reference • © 2021 • 346pp • H/C (ISBN: 9781799877646) • US $215.00

Analyzing Global Social Media Consumption
Patrick Kanyi Wamuyu (United States International University – Africa, Kenya)
Information Science Reference • © 2021 • 358pp • H/C (ISBN: 9781799847182) • US $215.00

Global Perspectives on Social Media Communications, Trade Unionism, and Transnational Advocacy
Floribert Patrick C. Endong (University of Calabar, Nigeria)
Information Science Reference • © 2020 • 300pp • H/C (ISBN: 9781799831389) • US $195.00

Electronic Hive Minds on Social Media Emerging Research and Opportunities
Shalin Hai-Jew (Kansas State University, USA)
Information Science Reference • © 2019 • 358pp • H/C (ISBN: 9781522593690) • US $205.00

Hidden Link Prediction in Stochastic Social Networks
Babita Pandey (Lovely Professional University, India) and Aditya Khamparia (Lovely Professional University, India)
Information Science Reference • © 2019 • 281pp • H/C (ISBN: 9781522590965) • US $195.00

Cognitive Social Mining Applications in Data Analytics and Forensics
Anandakumar Haldorai (Sri Eshwar College of Engineering, India) and Arulmurugan Ramu (Presidency University, India)
Information Science Reference • © 2019 • 326pp • H/C (ISBN: 9781522575221) • US $195.00

IGI Global
PUBLISHER of TIMELY KNOWLEDGE

701 East Chocolate Avenue, Hershey, PA 17033, USA
Tel: 717-533-8845 x100 • Fax: 717-533-8661
E-Mail: cust@igi-global.com • www.igi-global.com

Editorial Advisory Board

List of Contributors

Table of Contents

Detailed Table of Contents

This chapter focuses on bullying of youth within the D/deaf community. D/deaf students often struggle with mental health and the development of emotional intelligence, both of which are critical to an individual to be successful and happy. The goal of this chapter is to provide original insight to highlight the negative impact of bullying in the D/deaf community while offering promising points of consideration so that teachers, parents, guardians, and other adults who are prominently featured in a child's life may be better prepared to help. This is a topic important to all, as one in three babies is born with hearing loss and by 2050 nearly 2.5 billion people will have some degree of hearing loss.

In the film, which attempts to make sense of the inner world of a young woman named Adrien, the aspect of violence is elevated to the central theme. The audience's perspective on the main character, concerns of identification with her, and the main female protagonist's cyborg status are all discussed in conjunction with the patriarchal world order. The study's fundamental themes are drawn from Donna Haraway's Cyborg Manifesto (1991). The study raises questions on discussions about the role of violence in film narratives by referencing these discourses and the opinions of sociologist and political science theoreticians.

However, little research pays attention to cyberbullying on Chinese social media. This research uses the content analysis method to analyze cyberbullying on one of the biggest social media platforms in China, Weibo, focusing on language features and factors that influence the frequency of cyberbullying language in comments on key opinion leaders' (KOLs) posts. The findings reveal that most cyberbullying language on Weibo appears in the form of mildly offensive or ordinary words with special meanings and offensive references, rather than directly offensive words. In addition, this research found that KOL type and post content type interact to affect the frequency of cyberbullying language on Weibo. Overall, this research has made a valuable contribution to cyberbullying research.

For decades, cyberbullying has been acknowledged as a social phenomenon that poses adverse effects on victims. Scholarship generally defines cyberbullying as repeated behaviors that intend to harm the victims. Prior studies aimed at investigating cyberbullying and victimization patterns among juveniles. Furthermore, risk factors, which increase the likelihood of cyberbullying engagement, had been revealed in several different studies. While there are consistent findings regarding the negative outcomes of cyberbullying, the trends are somewhat obscure due to inconsistent methodology. Furthermore, despite cyberbullying being a domestic and international issue, prior research practices have limited generalizability across samples. These limitations led to inherent gaps in the literature, which ultimately hinders a comprehensive understanding of cyberbullying. Thus, the ultimate purpose of this chapter is to provide both domestic and international reviews regarding cyberbullying engagement. By doing so, this chapter will navigate an in-depth analysis of cyberbullying worldwide.

The development of new information technologies has led to new forms of violence between adolescents and young people, frequent users of social networks, chats, and e-messages. Thus, this chapter aims to clarify the concept of cyberbullying and characterize this problem by reflecting on similarities and differences of traditional bullying and its typologies and presenting some prevalence data in different countries, namely during pandemic situation. The authors intend to characterize the participants and roles played in this problem, also reflecting on the consequences for them in the short and long term with an emphasis in the consequences on mental health. The main risk and protection factors of a biopsychosocial nature will be explored considering that this phenomenon is complex and dynamic. Subsequently, preventive strategies will be presented at school and family levels to foster more proactive than reactive responses to the fight against cyberbullying. Finally, some empirically validated intervention strategies stand out.

The author of this chapter provided a comparison of cyberbullying-related issues across the diverse cyber laws of countries. A definition and distinction between cybercrime and cyberbullying and the impact of cyberbullying on individuals of various ages, socioeconomic, and sociocultural backgrounds were discussed. The cyberbullying provisions in national cyber laws of the top five cyberbullying victim countries were reviewed. Then they were compared to Bangladesh's Information and Communication Technology Act, 2006, and the Digital Security Act, 2018. The final section of the chapter compares the legislation governing cyberbullying in India, Brazil, the United States of America, Belgium, and South Africa to Bangladesh's acts. The comparisons of the crimes demonstrate why the acts are more infamous in Bangladesh than in other nations with a higher rate of cyberbullying victims. Some future recommendations for the Bangladeshi government by examining the country's legislation with the international community and identifying new research possibilities for the future were recommended.

The rapid progress of technological developments and their opening to the use of societies has brought with it various problems. Although the internet makes our lives easier, bullying has started to be seen in this area. The subject of cyberbullying, which should be addressed in a wide area from economy to politics, from social life to culture, has also manifested itself in the metaverse area. This study examines how the Turkish national press handles cyberbullying in the metaverse area. News about Metaverse has been published in many publications. The news that deals with cyberbullying and solution suggestions are only included in this study. In the Turkish national press, a total of six stories about cyberbullying in the metaverse area were reached. The news usually consists of harassment, precautionary, and solution suggestions. They were analyzed by the discourse analysis method. While performing discourse analysis, both macro and micro analyses were made.

With the inclusion of the internet in life, changes and transformations have occurred in almost every field at different points and continue to be experienced. This change and transformation can be seen in a positive way as well as in a negative way. The structure, which is equipped with new communication

Sexual harassment is a concept that has become a growing concern globally as it occurs in all areas of life and also in the workplace. In the workplace it is described as any undesirable sexual behavior that is perceived as a threat, border violation, and attack by the exposed person, negatively affecting the employee's ability to do his/her job. This problem disproportionately affects women and can negatively affect their economic and career outcomes. Studies show that sexual harassment cases in health institutions are quite pervasive. Studies examining the sexual harassment of nurses in Turkey determined that the rate of exposure to sexual harassment ranged from 1.5% to 75%. Sexual harassment incidents in health institutions usually occur by relatives of patients, patients, physicians, other healthcare professionals, and colleagues. In this chapter, the definitions, causes, frequency, effects, and consequences of sexual harassment will be discussed.

Bullying is an important problem that concerns children, families, and society. In this chapter, the effects of bullying on children's health are discussed. The aim of the chapter is to reveal the effects of bullying on the health of children and adolescents in all aspects and to determine the measures that can be taken to prevent these effects. The chapter focuses on the definition of bullying; its types, prevalence; physical, psychological, and long-term effects; and preventive approaches. It is thought that the information in the chapter will contribute to all professionals working with children.

Physical abuse is the state of harming the child's body by the people around him. Scars of unknown cause, traces resulting from burning, spots due to impact on any part of the body, traces caused by a bite by another person, bruises and stains caused by squeezing with any tool, burns and scars caused by smoking cigarettes on the victim reflect physical abuse. Problems such as rumination disorders, problems in socialization, lack of self-respect, depression, fear of all situations, withdrawal behaviors, incompatibility, colic, problems in mental perception processes, and decreased academic achievement are observed in these children.

Schools are indispensable institutions of society. Necessary measures should be taken to ensure that children can continue their education in safety in schools that concern almost all society. For this reason, the importance given to school health and safety is increasing day by day. Bullying is an important

Bullying is the intentional harming and humiliation of others, particularly those who are smaller, weaker, younger, or more vulnerable than the bully. Cyberbullying is defined as bullying that happens via the use of modern technologies. The anonymous internet propagation of nasty remarks about a person is referred to as cyberbullying. Cyberbullying is a burning issue, and it's important to evaluate the implications of cyber aggression on individuals of all ages, particularly adolescents and emerging adults, and to provide some insight into how individuals cope with or handle cyberbullying. The aim of this chapter is to explore and discuss the idea of cyberbullying including its various forms and methods. The reasons for cyberbullying, cyberbullying consequences, prevalence of cyberbullying, and gender disparities in cyberbullying are also discoursed. Different prevention and intervention strategies are also be explored and discussed in order to combat cyberbullying.

Cyberbullying, which internet users have faced especially in recent years, is a new type of bullying that has emerged with the widespread use of the internet. It is expressed as bullying using technological platforms with internet access. It includes repetitive behaviors aimed at intimidating, angering, or embarrassing target individuals. Since the number of victims of cyberbullying is increasing day by day, it is an important social problem that should be detected early, and precautions should be taken with protective strategies. In this chapter, there is information about cyberbullying, cyberbullying behaviors, cyberbullying tools, types of cyberbullying, the frequency of cyberbullying, the causes of cyberbullying, the roles of cyberbullying, the effects of cyberbullying, what to do when faced with cyberbullying, and precautions to be taken.

Foreword

In today's society, where everything is becoming more and more digital, it is seen that crimes and bullying are on the rise and pose a threat to both the digital and physical worlds. In contrast to real life, the risks in the digital realm are predictable and our digital footprints are more specific. Therefore, it is crucial that the participants in the digital world are aware of these risks and well-informed before they are exposed to them. Contrarily, it is important to organize thoughtful and responsible people, parents, and institutions that know what to do when confronted with any negativity.

The book consists of 28 chapters with the goal of addressing issues related to cyberbullying from all perspectives. Each section's specific goal is to structure the bullying difficulties into a specific point so that it can be related to other issues. Thus, the book covers a wide range of academic disciplines and topics including but not limited to: Body image, bullying, child abuse, cyber harassment, cyberbullying, media, metaverse, peer bullying, sexual harassment, social media, violence.

Cyberbullying brings in many different perspectives and consequences might involve the handicapped ones as well. Chapter 1 handles the silent struggles of adolescent deaf focusing on bullying of youth within the deaf community who often struggle with mental health and the development of emotional intelligence, both of which are critical for an individual to be successful and happy. Thus, the goal of this chapter is to provide original insight to highlight the negative impact of bullying in the deaf community, while offering promising points of consideration so that teachers, parents, guardians, and other adults who are prominently featured in a child's life. The chapter underlines this important topic to all, as one in three babies is born with hearing loss and, by 2050, nearly 2.5 billion people will have some degree of hearing loss, and cyberbullying of the handicapped ones would become a more important topic.

How cyberbullying is portrayed in movies is covered in Chapter 2. Focused on the discourse of Titan Tracking Violence With Cyborg Women: Cyborg Alexia: A Picture of Violence in the Digital Age and how the movie elevates the topic of violence become the main issue in an effort to understand the inner world of a young woman named Adrien. The primary female protagonist's status as a cyborg, audience perceptions of her, and issues with identifying with her are all examined in relation to the patriarchal system of society. The study's main topics are taken from Donna Haraway's Cyborg Manifesto, but it also makes reference to discourses on the use of violence in narratives as well as the views of sociologists and political scientists to pose questions regarding these discourses.

There is a kind of misunderstanding that minimizes the cyberbullying environment into computer games or in times of enjoyment only. However, due to the fact that cyberbullying also involve sexual harassment and workplace bullying, these could affect both working people and institutionalized contexts. Chapter 3 focuses on the problematic modern workplace communication and examines the fundamental components of sexual harassment and workplace bullying. It also conceptualizes sexual bullying and explores its potential effects on both employees and the company. Cyberbullying as it occurs in the workplace puts the concept into a part of understanding this phenomenon as an embryonic stage that the victims of sexual bullying who are targets of cyberbullying are another consideration worth exploring. Sexual bullying is when employees are subjected to bullying tactics that are sexual and/or gender-related in nature. and this classification is novel in its application to the workplace setting.

In the past two decades, bullying in all of its forms has become easier to find, and Chapter 4 examines the psychological and media effects of sexual harassment. The purpose of this chapter is to explore what sexual harassment is, theoretical models that are founded on it, the societal and personal impacts of sexual harassment, and its place in the media. In the chapter, the term "sexual harassment" was defined in relation to relevant theoretical models, gender variations in sexual harassment, and global statistics on sexual harassment. The psychological ramifications of sexual harassment at the individual level are studied from the perspective of psychology in the chapter's discussion of the repercussions of sexual harassment on society and the individual. The chapter also examines the impact of sexual harassment on society and the individual from a psychological perspective. The effects of sexual harassment on an individual level were looked at from a clinical psychology standpoint. The chapter also discusses the impact of sexual harassment on the media, as well as how it is represented there and on social media.

Since identity issues appear to be the century's top concern, Chapter 5 focuses on bullying's new frontiers toward body image during adolescence, when the self-image takes on greater significance and influences practically all life events. This section discusses adolescent bullying, body image, and body dissatisfaction, bullying related to appearance among peers, bullying related to body image as a mediator of socio-cultural effects, bullying related to body image as a mediator of media effects, the results of peer bullying related to body image in adolescents, solutions and suggestions.

One other geography, the case of Nigeria is handled in Chapter 6 as the utilization of social media for child abuse prevention. The study's goal may be summed up as looking at how social media affects child abuse prevention in Nigeria. The goals were to find out how much awareness social media has raised about the problem of child abuse, how to prevent child abuse, and whether social media is indeed useful in preventing child abuse in Nigeria. According to research findings, social media has had little to no impact on child abuse prevention in Nigeria, even though the information provided regarding child abuse on social media platforms is credible and accepted. According to research findings, social media has had little to no impact on child abuse prevention in Nigeria, even though the information provided regarding child abuse on social media platforms is credible and accepted. In order to do this, the researcher suggested that there be public education campaigns that are accessible to the general public in order to raise knowledge of child abuse prevention, its impacts on children, and its legal repercussions.

Chapter 7 discusses a tough question like if Sharenting is Apart of Bully? By using examples from the Malaysian context, this section focuses on how the sharenting phenomenon occurs and functions in an effort to develop a perspective among parents over their children's social media activity. It comes to the conclusion that even if parents are eager to provide a lot of information about their children, especially when they are pleased with their accomplishments, it could have negative consequences and hurt both the children and parents. It also offers hints about the parents' lack media literacy, making it easier to predict potential misuse of social media data.

As cyberbullying occurs in different ways in different societies, different implications occur. Chapter 8 address the problem of cyberbullying in Chinese Social Media settings probing its language features and the influence factors in comments on key opinion leaders' posts. Previous studies have analyzed the prevalence and consequences of cyberbullying and the detection and prevention of it. However, little research pays attention to cyberbullying on Chinese social media. This research makes use of content analysis to analyze cyberbullying on one of the biggest social media platforms in China, Weibo, focusing on language features and factors that influence the frequency of cyberbullying language in comments on Key Opinion Leaders' (KOLs) posts. The findings reveal that most cyberbullying language on Weibo appears in the form of mildly offensive or ordinary words with special meanings and offensive references, rather than directly offensive words. Besides, this research reveals that KOL type and post content type interact to affect the frequency of cyberbullying language on Weibo.

For decades, cyberbullying has been acknowledged as a social phenomenon that poses adverse effects on victims and scholarship generally defines cyberbullying as repeated behaviors that intend to harm the victims. Prior studies aimed at investigating cyberbullying and victimization patterns among juveniles. Yet, Chapter 9, handles cyberbullies and cyberpunks, examining cyberbullying through a domestic and international lens. It is known that risk factors, which increase the likelihood of cyberbullying engagement, had been revealed in several different studies whereas there are consistent findings regarding the negative outcomes of cyberbullying, the trends are somewhat obscure due to inconsistent methodology. Furthermore, despite cyberbullying being a domestic and international issue, prior research practices have limited generalizability across samples. These limitations led to inherent gaps in the literature, which ultimately hinders a comprehensive understanding of cyberbullying. Thus, the ultimate purpose of this chapter is to provide both domestic and international reviews regarding cyberbullying engagement and provide an in-depth analysis of cyberbullying worldwide.

The focus of Chapter 10 is on cyberbullying, which is arguably the most significant form of bullying and a form of peer aggression in the digital age. Due to the limitless potential of new information technologies, frequent users of social networks, chat rooms, and e-messages are typically teenagers and young adults. It is stated that urgent precautions and preventive measures are needed due to the rise in cyberbullying cases and its implications during pandemic. Finally, a few intervention tactics that have received empirical validation stand out.

Chapter 11, "Revisiting the Cyberbullying Legislation in Bangladesh: A Comparative Study with Global Scenario," is another chapter that discusses the global perspective in contrast to the national one. As implied by the chapter's title, it compares cyberbullying-related issues across the various cyberlaws of nations, laying out the definition of and differences between cybercrime and cyberbullying as well as the effects of cyberbullying on people from different ages, socioeconomic backgrounds, and sociocultural backgrounds. The chapter focuses on the cyberbullying provisions in national cyber laws of the top five nations that experience cyberbullying. These provisions are studied and compared to Bangladesh's Information and Communication Technology Act of 2006 and the Digital Security Act of 2018. The conclusions also include some recommendations for the Bangladeshi government's future actions, such as evaluating the nation's legislation with the assistance of the international community and establishing fresh research opportunities.

The rapid progress of technological developments and their opening to the use of societies has brought with it various problems and even if the internet makes our lives easier, bullying has started to be seen in this area. Chapter 12 portrays a discourse analysis of news containing cyberbullying in metaverse both macro and micro perspectives. Whereas the subject of cyberbullying, which should be addressed in a wide area from economy to politics, from social life to culture, has also manifested itself in the metaverse area, this study examines how the Turkish national press handles cyberbullying in the metaverse area. News about Metaverse has been published in many publications and most of these deal with cyberbullying usually consisting of harassment, precautionary and solution suggestions.

Chapter 13 concentrates on a critical look at cyberbullying and cyber harassment in the digital area within the scope of social media literacy, with the inclusion of the internet in life, changes and transformations have occurred in almost every field at different points and the transformations continue in the last decades. As in all areas, these changes could be interpreted in both ways as in a positive and a negative way. The chapter enlightens the issues such as cyberbullying, cyber harassment, cyber humiliation, cyber victim, and cyber victimization.

Chapter 14 focuses on a serious issue needing not just social awareness but also anger management, namely bullying of healthcare personnel. The chapter discusses several forms of bullying among healthcare professionals to provide better understanding of its occurrence, causes, and effects. Even though it is well recognized that bullying among healthcare employees has a bad impact on both organizations and the victims, the problem tends to spread throughout society and has a significant negative impact on both healthcare institutions and the individuals who work in them. It is necessary to create and implement prevention strategies as well as raise awareness about workplace bullying in order to regulate this social problem.

As a growing and complex public health issue that affects both children and adults of all ages, bullying is introduced in Chapter 15 along with the public health approach as a remedy. While the chapter argues that it is both humane and cost-effective to identify risk groups that may be bullying victims and perpetrators and to develop intervention programs to reduce risks, it also asserts that policies and programs aimed at providing multifaceted community education should be developed and put into place in order to lessen or even eliminate bullying in society.

The focus of Chapter 17 is sexual harassment in Turkish healthcare institutions. Since it occurs in many spheres of life, including the workplace, it primarily gives information about the causes, frequency, impacts, and consequences of the concept, which is becoming a significant source of worry worldwide. Sexual harassment occurrences in healthcare facilities typically include patients, patients' family, doctors, other healthcare professionals, and coworkers, despite studies showing that these incidents are fairly common and can range from 1.5 percent to 75 percent.

Chapter 18 focuses on the negative impact of bullying on children's health as a significant issue that affects kids, families, and society. The chapter's main goal is to show how bullying affects kids' overall health and to establish the steps to be taken to prevent these consequences.

Chapter 19 discusses the concept of physical bullying toward children. Physical abuse is defined as the act of causing bodily harm to a kid by those around. This definition emphasizes the possibility that this kind of abuse could result in issues like rumination disorders, socialization issues, low self-esteem, depression, and withdrawal tendencies. Beyond that, the effects could result in child incompatibility, colic, issues with mental perception, and decreased academic achievement.

The discussion of bullying in schools is covered in Chapter 20, with a focus on prevention strategies and practices. The chapter serves as an example of the various forms of bullying that occur at school as a significant issue that concerns school health and safety and has a detrimental impact on a person's physical, emotional, and spiritual growth. In the end, it is important to address bullying in schools from all angles and implement policies that will help to stop it.

The main focus of Chapter 21 is on emotional bullying against children, which includes mental cruelty, mental harm, verbal or emotional abuse, emotional maltreatment, mental deprivation, and emotional assault. Emotional bullying is one of the terms that is frequently used today, especially now that digital media is more widely available. It is defined as a type of behavior in which a person is purposefully and repeatedly subjected to non-physical acts by another person that harms their behavioral, emotional, and mental functioning. The chapter focuses on various definitions, signs, impacts and types of emotional bullying as well as mitigation strategies.

Chapter 22 delves into peer bullying, and what bullying makes an appearance in various manners starting from the first years of life. Regardless of whether it is direct or relational, bullying negatively affects the bullies and the victims and has destructive effects on societies as well. In this respect, it is highly important to know what bullying, the types of bullying, characteristics of bullies and victims, bullying statuses, factors that affect bullying, and the short and long-term effects of bullying are. In this sense, it can be seen that all kinds of research, activities, studies, and programs which might be effective against bullying are necessary.

Chapter 23 explores the role of teachers in peer bullying and it emphasizes the importance of teachers also play a critical role in the prevention and intervention plans for peer bullying in addition to the school, family, and community. The chapter concentrates on the arrangements that teachers should make in the prevention and intervention phases of peer bullying and the components that teachers can apply to prevent peer bullying; education programs, classroom environments, and what needs to be done at the individual level are explained.

In Chapter 24 peer bullying is handled as an increasing problem in schools. Peer bullying is when an individual is exposed to negative actions on his/her property, body, emotions, relationships, reputation, or digital presence by a stronger peer or peers, and in peer bullying, there are different roles such as bully, victim, bully/victim, bystander, and even these roles can change over time, whereas, bullying is examined under five headings as physical, verbal, relational, sexual and cyber bullying.

With the advancement of technology, social networks, and online social media, cyberbullying has become a cultural reality. Chapter 25 encompasses the issue with definitions and examples. While the increased usage of digital media presents many opportunities in the modern day when the real world and the virtual world can be experienced simultaneously, the increased time spent online also brings with it unwanted situations like cyberbullying. By defining cyberbullying as an act of online aggression intended to harass or humiliate, and by taking into account that it is the behavior that interferes with the social relationships of those chosen as victims and seeks to elicit negative emotions, it may be possible to compare and contrast the variety of ways that cyberbullying occurs. The chapter contributes to the redefining of the acts and concepts of cyberviolence, cyberbullying, traditional bullying, and cyber victimization.

Cyberbullying researchers point out that females tend to be more cyber victims than males. And chapter 26 concentrates on different prevention methods which can be grouped into three categories firstly, laws, rules, and policies to control the use of media; secondly, education programs about using safe internet for children and youths and teaching them how to avoid these kinds of situations on the internet, and lastly, technological approaches.

Cyberbullying issues ranges from bullying is the intentional harming and humiliation of others, particularly those who are smaller, weaker, younger, or more vulnerable than the bully. The aim of chapter 27 is to explore and discuss the idea of cyberbullying including its various forms and methods. Thus, the chapter discusses, the reasons for cyberbullying, its consequences, its prevalence, and gender disparities in cyberbullying are also discussed. Different prevention and intervention strategies are also explored and discussed in order to combat cyberbullying.

Chapter 28 concentrates on cyberbullying, which internet users have faced especially in recent years, as a new type of bullying that has emerged with the widespread use of the internet used to be expressed as bullying using technological platforms with internet access. Somewhat different from the general tendency to handle bullying as an outcome, this chapter includes the analysis of repetitive behaviors aimed at intimidating, angering, or embarrassing target individuals. Since the number of victims of cyberbullying is increasing day by day, it is an important social problem that should be detected early and precautions should be taken with protective strategies.

Ultimately, the goal of this handbook is to know more about the research that addresses issues having an impact on society and individuals and meanwhile, contributing to societies negatively or positively into a vogue but problematic digital future. Individuals all over the world may be forced to move to digital and make risky decisions. In that instance, the role of digital media could serve as a catalyst for overcoming the immediate threat and raising public awareness.

I believe that in the future, this collection of research papers, will be serving as a fundamental handbook as a reliable source and guidance for researchers, governmental and non-governmental organizations seeking to avoid the negative consequences of crises.

Nilüfer Pembecioğlu
Istanbul University, Turkey

Nilüfer Pembecioğlu *is Professor of Istanbul University Faculty of Communication Radio Television Cinema Department. She conducted many EU projects as well as other international projects and has many articles on a national and international basis, regarding education, communication, citizenship, journalism, peace journalism, new media, digitalization, children, women and advertising fields. Specialized in Media Literacy, Digital Literacy, Social Discrimination and Exclusion, Cyber Bullying, Systemic Family Therapy, Film Therapy and Family Coaching, she works with a variety of governmental institutions and ministries. She is the director of 8 long feature documentary films, 30 short films and 8 animations. Graduated from IU Faculty of Literature, Department of Foreign Languages Education, English Language Teaching Department she is specialized in Teacher Training and completed her MA in Marmara University, Atatürk Faculty of Education, Foreign Languages Education on TESL/TEFL Testing and Evaluation. After finishing Cambridge University Royal Society of Arts DOTE (Diploma for Overseas Teachers of English) Course, Pembecioğlu, continued to her Ph.D. in Istanbul University Faculty of Communication, Radio Television Cinema Department and pursued an associate degree from European Union Department of IU as well as an associate degree Health Institutions Management Program of IU. She is the member of ESSI: European School of Social Innovation and Smart Cities World, attending the educational and innovative meetings and webinars and specifically researching regarding the mobility issues.*

Preface

Bullying which consists of repetitive, aggressive behaviors that occur intentionally, harm the individual exposed to the act and cause stress, and occur in situations where there is a power imbalance. (Kara and Kaçar, 2017: 115). "Bullying can involve verbal acts, such as threats, insults, or use of nicknames, or it can encompass physical acts such as assault or theft. In addition, social acts such as exclusion from the peer group are considered to manifest bullying" (Markkanen et al., 2019, 24). If we need to talk about some types of bullying, we can talk about sexual harassment, physical bullying, verbal bullying, peer bullying, cyber bullying, the effects of which reach the longest and serious dimensions with the development of communication technologies. Studies show that bullying has the highest prevalence, occurring between the ages of 12 and 18. (Khasanah and Sirodj, 2019: 211).

xThis book will deal with bullying in all its forms, with a particular focus on its relationship with the children who are most exposed to bullying and its reflection in the media.

ORGANIZATION OF THE BOOK

The book has 28 chapters. In the first chapter, entitled "Silent Struggles of D/Deaf Youth," author touches bullying of youth within the D/deaf community.

The second chapter titled "Titane Tracking Violence with Cyborg Women: *Cyborg Alexia* – A Picture of Violence in the Digital Age" raises questions about the debates about the role of violence in film narratives.

The third chapter titled "Leave Me Alone! Sexual Bullying at Work" focuses on sexual harassment and workplace bullying.

In the fourth chapter titled "Reflections of Sexual Harassment on Psychology and Media," the author discusses sexual harassment, its social and individual effects, and its place in the media.

The fifth chapter titled "Bullying Towards Body Image During Adolescence" deals with children who are bullied about body image during adolescence.

In the sixth chapter titled "Utilisation of Social Media for Child Abuse Prevention in Nigeria," the authors examine the impact of social media on child abuse prevention in Nigeria.

The seventh chapter titled "Is Sharenting Apart of Bully? A Perspective among Parents Towards Their Social Media Activities" deals with the social media shares of parents about their children.

In the eighth chapter titled "Cyberbullying on Chinese Social Media: Language Features and Influence Factors in Comments on Key Opinion Leaders' Posts," the authors discuss cyberbullying on Weibo, one of the largest social media platforms in China.

Chapter 9, titled "Cyberbullies and Cyberpunks, Oh My: Examining Cyberbullying Through a Domestic and International Lens," provides an in-depth analysis of cyberbullying worldwide.

The tenth chapter titled "Cyberbullying: A Form of Peer Violence in the Digital Era" focuses on the effects of cyberbullying on mental health.

In the eleventh chapter titled "Revisiting the Cyberbullying Legislation in Bangladesh: A Comparative Study With Global Scenario," the author makes a comparison of cyberbullying issues in various cyber laws of countries.

The twelfth chapter titled "An Analysis of News Containing Cyberbullying in Metaverse" examines how the Turkish national press deals with cyberbullying in the metaverse.

In the thirteenth chapter titled "A Critical Look on Cyberbullying and Cyber Harassment in the Digital Area Within the Scope of Social Media Literacy," the concepts of cyber bullying and cyber harassment are evaluated with various examples and the importance of being conscious and having a high level of awareness in social media is emphasized.

In the fourteenth chapter titled "Bullying Among Healthcare Workers," the authors evaluate bullying among health care workers with its causes and consequences.

In the fifteenth chapter titled "Bullying and Public Health Approach," public health programs to combat bullying are discussed.

Chapter 16, titled "Bullying Due to Dentofacial Features and Its Relationship With Quality of Life in View of Oral Health," deals with the issue of bullying between dentists and their patients.

In the seventeenth chapter, titled "Sexual Harassment in Health Institutions in Turkey: Causes, Frequency, Effects, and Consequences," the authors discuss the definitions, causes, frequency, effects and consequences of sexual harassment and sexual harassment in health institutions.

Chapter 18, titled "Effects of Bullying on Child Health," addresses the approaches to preventing bullying by revealing all aspects of the effects of bullying on child and adolescent health.

In the nineteenth chapter titled "Physical Bullying Towards Child," types of physical abuse, the effects of physical bullying on children, risk factors of physical bullying against children and the prevalence of physical bullying against children are mentioned.

In the twentieth chapter titled "Bullying in Schools: Behaviors and Principles of Prevention," studies on bullying at school, types of bullying behavior, risk factors and prevention are included.

In the twenty-first chapter titled "Emotional Bullying Towards Child," the definition and categories of emotional bullying, behaviors considered as emotional bullying, the causes and consequences of emotional bullying are discussed in line with the findings of the relevant studies.

In the twenty-second chapter titled "Peer Bullying," bullying, risk factors and characteristics of victims are mentioned.

In the twenty-third chapter titled "The Role of Teachers in Peer Bullying," teachers' attitudes towards peer bullying and the components that teachers can implement to prevent bullying are discussed.

In the twenty-fourth chapter titled "An Increasing Problem in Schools Peer Bullying," the relationship between peer bullying, the actors of peer bullying, family, school and social environment with peer bullying is mentioned.

In the twenty-fifth chapter titled "A New Problem Emerging with the Internet and Digital Media: Cyberbullying," the concepts of cyber violence, cyber bullying, traditional bullying and cyber victimization are explained.

In the twenty-sixth chapter titled "Cyberbullying: An Overview of Cyberbullying," the features that distinguish cyberbullying from traditional bullying, the theoretical framework of cyberbullying, gender differences in cyberbullying and the consequences of cyberbullying are mentioned.

The twenty-seventh chapter titled "Cyberbullying Issues" includes the causes and consequences of cyberbullying and a case study.

In the last chapter titled "What is Cyberbullying?" cyberbullying tools, the frequency of cyberbullying, the effects of cyberbullying, what to do when faced with cyberbullying and precautions are included.

As a result, this book, which deals with its types and different aspects of bullying, aims to be a source book in terms of providing interdisciplinary data for professionals, researchers, experts, and students who are interested in the subject.

Gülşah Sarı
Aksaray University, Turkey

REFERENCES

Kara, H., & Kaçar, M. (2017). Peer Bullying and its Social Importance: Two Case Reports [Akran zorbalığı ve toplumsal önemi: İki olgu sunumu]. *Anatomia Clinica, 22*(2), 114–118.

Khasanah, A. N., & Sirodj, D. A. N. (2019, March). Types of bullying in junior high school students. In *Social and Humaniora Research Symposium (SoRes 2018)* (pp. 211-214). Atlantis Press. 10.2991ores-18.2019.50

Markkanen, I., Välimaa, R., & Kannas, L. (2021). Forms of bullying and associations between school perceptions and being bullied among Finnish secondary school students aged 13 and 15. *International Journal of Bullying Prevention, 3*(1), 24-33.

Acknowledgment

As an editor, I owe a great debt of gratitude to my dear academics who wrote chapters for this book. This book will shed light on researchers, students and academics interested in the field thanks to the contributions of valuable authors. I would also like to express my gratitude to the academics of the editorial advisory board who provided full support in the constitution of the book.

Finally, I would like to thank the IGI Global publishing house for helping me to publish this edited book.

Chapter 1
Silent Struggles of D/deaf Youth

Tamara Leigh Wandel
University of Evansville, USA

ABSTRACT

This chapter focuses on bullying of youth within the D/deaf community. D/deaf students often struggle with mental health and the development of emotional intelligence, both of which are critical to an individual to be successful and happy. The goal of this chapter is to provide original insight to highlight the negative impact of bullying in the D/deaf community while offering promising points of consideration so that teachers, parents, guardians, and other adults who are prominently featured in a child's life may be better prepared to help. This is a topic important to all, as one in three babies is born with hearing loss and by 2050 nearly 2.5 billion people will have some degree of hearing loss.

"The handicap of deafness is not in the ear; it is in the mind." —Marlee Matlin

PURPOSE

In a 1984 national convention address, civil rights activist and politician Jesse Louis Jackson said, "America is not like a blanket—one piece of unbroken cloth, the same color, the same texture, the same size. America is more like a quilt—many patches, many pieces, many colors, many sizes, all woven and held together by a common thread."

That quilt – bursts of colors and textures and seams that are more like veins running in different directions – is indicative of America's melting pot. As a society, we are fond of the idea of celebrating differences. However, equally true is that our society possesses a tendency to target those individuals who have distinguishing characteristics and who are different in some way. This targeting can manifest in stereotyping, scrutinization and shunning, and it can be disheartening at any age or stage. For youth, it can be particularly heart-wrenching. According to the National Bullying Prevention Center, one out of five children reports having been bullied, and 41% of these children report that they believe the bullying will be repeated. These experiences and feelings have been linked to depression and anxiety in young adults.

DOI: 10.4018/978-1-6684-5426-8.ch001

This chapter focuses on bullying within a particular community of individuals – those who are deaf. Deaf individuals bring beautiful color and texture to our patchwork quilt, but in allowing them to become victims of bullying, we are diminishing their value and place in the fabric of our society. The result of this is that D/deaf students often struggle with mental health and the development of emotional intelligence, both of which are critical to an individual to be successful and happy. The goal of this chapter is to provide data and original insight to highlight the negative impact of bullying in the deaf community, while offering points of consideration so that teachers, parents, guardians, and other adults who are prominently featured in a child's life may be better prepared to help.

The topic should be important to all of us. One in three babies is born with hearing loss and, by 2050, nearly 2.5 billion people will have some degree of hearing loss. Hearing loss effects many aspects of an individual's life, including cognition, education, employment, and social interaction. The perceived differences surrounding these factors contribute to the negative stigma that surrounds deafness and can lead to actions of bullying (WHO, 2021).

This chapter will share data and original stories from numerous interviews to illuminate the topic and encourage awareness and inclusivity as related to school, media, sports and more, allowing the research to show real people facing real struggles who have real insight to offer. The interview design is used to obtain "thick, rich data utilizing a qualitative investigational perspective (Creswell, 2007). According to Turner (2010), the strength of the general interview guide approach – used in this chapter – is the ability of the researcher "…to ensure that the same general areas of information are collected from each interviewee; this provides more focus than the conversational approach, but still allows a degree of freedom and adaptability in getting information from the interviewee". Interviews with deaf individuals and those who work with programs associated with deaf culture were conducted, with over 10 original interviews taking place.

Figure 1. Deaf Culture Sign

DISTINCTIONS OF D/DEAF

When discussing the D/deaf community, it is important to first establish the difference between the terms "deaf," "Deaf," and "hard of hearing", as they are used in a variety of ways and seen in an equally variety of acronyms: D, d, D/d, D/HH, D/d/HH. The National Organization of the Deaf cites Carol Padden and Tom Humphries, two Deaf authors, and their book, *Deaf in America: Voices from a Culture*, to distinguish the terms from each other. The suggested guidelines are to "use the lowercase deaf when referring to the audiological condition of not hearing, and the uppercase Deaf when referring to a particular group of deaf people who share a language – American Sign Language – and a culture" (Padden and Humphries, 1988).

This definition denotes a key difference between the two cohorts. Whereas a deaf person is an individual unable to hear, a person who is Deaf is a member of a larger group of other Deaf people that have their own culture. Just as any other culture, Deaf culture has been established over generations and possesses its own traditions and characteristics. Another key separator is the use of American Sign Language (ASL). ASL is intertwined deeply with Deaf culture, as "members of the group have inherited their sign language [and] use it as a primary means of communication." (Padden and Humphries, 2009). The Deaf and deaf communities are vastly different in one specific way. As deaf individuals adapt to the hearing world, Deaf culture continually spreads awareness about Deafness extending beyond physical limitations and into aspects of social life.

The Deaf Health Network in the UK defines the wording a bit differently. The Network uses the word deaf to identify anyone who has a severe hearing problem, and then uses Deaf with a capital D when referring to people "who have been deaf all their lives or since before they started to learn to talk."

Another added complexity to the nuances of the phraseology and the topic of Deaf and deaf cultures was introduced when, in the 1980s, cochlear implants were introduced to treat hearing loss in adults. Although a cochlear implant does not restore normal hearing, it does provide a sense of sound to a deaf person that helps them understand sounds around them, including speech.

As of December 2019, the U.S. Department of Health and Human Services estimates that 739,900 devices have been implanted worldwide, including 183,100 in the United States. In addition, since 2000, they have been used for children starting at 12 months of age (U.S. Department of Health and Human Services).

As reported by Skelton and Valentine (2003), deafness is "used by people who tend not to present a strong Deaf identity… rely on oral styles of communication (lip-reading, speaking); and by deaf people who identify themselves as disabled." This broadly refers to all people who experience total hearing loss. It is not tied to a social construction of identity, but rather to a burden to cope with.

Conversely, Deafness recognizes that Deaf people are excluded from the hearing world. Instead of conforming, Deaf individuals focus on empowering themselves. "For people who place themselves firmly within Deaf culture then there is a definite rejection of the notion of impairment – 'hearing impaired' is a detested term." (p.453). Additionally, members of Deaf culture are strongly against the use of cochlear implants and giving them to children because they believe it infringes upon the child's right to decide what happens to their own body. However, Deaf people do not deny their hearing impairments, rather they seek to acknowledge the social attitudes that exist towards Deaf people.

Opponents to cochlear implants argue that implants are an assault on Deaf culture, as they interfere with the right of deaf children to acquire sign language (Valente, Bahan and L. Bauman, 2011).

Just like spoken languages, different cultures and countries have their own sign language, and sign language is deeply entrenched within Deaf culture. According to the World Federation of the Deaf, there are 70 million people who use sign language worldwide. American Sign Language is used in the United States, and estimates show that about 500,000 people in the United States use ASL (Ross, Young, Bachelda and Karchmer, 2006).

The last phrase of categorization to reference is that of "hard of hearing", being seen as "HH" in many printed resources. Simply put, hard of hearing can denote a person with a mild-to-moderate hearing loss. Hard of hearing can also denote somebody who is deaf but does not affiliate with the Deaf community and culture. According to the World Health Organization, about 5% of the world's population suffers from disabling hearing loss. However, many of those 430 million people would be considered hard of hearing.

Together, these three phrases create a delicate balance. It is possible for somebody to be deaf but not Deaf. It can also be possible to be hard of hearing and be a member of both the hearing and Deaf communities. Deciding how to identify oneself is a personal decision, and one that others should respect, particularly in a society priding itself on the melting pot theory. Each phrase – Deaf, deaf and hard of hearing – has its own definition and implications, and the distinct differences between them mean that the decision is an important one. It's also written in various formats, allowing for confusion, and the National Association of the Deaf has not taken a definitive stand on the issue. For this chapter, we recognize various distinctions but will utilize all lowercase "d" henceforth for a focus on the audiological condition. The exception will be when discussing specific organizations or programs which have a capital "D" in its title.

BULLYING

This battle for equality has been fought for decades by the deaf community. In ancient Greece, it was believed that deaf people were not capable of ideas or language. In the Middle Ages, deaf adults were subject to ridicule, serving as court jesters or sent to asylums. However, over time, deaf people began to become more accepted and appreciated by society. The first school for the deaf in the United States was opened in 1817, and the first institution of higher learning for deaf people was established in 1864 with the opening of Gallaudet University. However, the "quilt" remains frayed and, today, higher rates of mental health issues are reported in the deaf population compared to hearing individuals (Fellinger, Holzinger, & Pollard, 2012).

Bullying is formally defined as "repetitive verbal teasing, threatening, physical intimidation, demeaning others, violent acts, torture, and other forms of verbal and physical aggression." (Weiner, 2006, p. 61). Bullies thrive off their own insecurities as they seek power, and abuse may happen at any time or any place to anyone, but in the context of this chapter, it is important to recognize that "bullying happens when children are thrown together with others they would not ordinarily choose to spend time with." (Weiner, 2013, p. 335).

When differences are recognized, bullying oftentimes begins, stemming from the bully's own personal insecurities. However, its effects on those who are bullied can be detrimental. "Students may come to regard students with differences as unpopular or less important, a perception that results in a dehumanization of the child that makes bullying easier for peers. Additionally, unpopular students may have fewer close friendships, and, therefore, less protection from bullying, than students without the differences." (p. 341).

Perpetrators of bullying are also more likely to select the withdrawn or timid students as victims because deafness has been associated with withdrawal and anxiety disorders (Shoham, Lewis, Favarato, & Cooper, 2019).

The anxiety stems from experiences like Katie Timm had as a child. She was not born with hearing loss, but became sick as a baby and the illness left her deaf. At two years old, her parents made the decision to get her cochlear implants, considered a new and revolutionary procedure at the time. As Katie grew up, she went to speech therapy to work on her voice. Even with cochlear implants, she explained, it's challenging to hear her own voice which makes it difficult to improve upon speaking. Despite her hard work at therapy, she recalls many of her peers teasing her.

"They would make fun of how I pronounced words and mock me for it, said Katie." When she would speak in class, "the other students would often snicker in the background because I pronounced a few words wrong here and there."

This greatly affected her self-esteem, and surprisingly to her, it was not just hearing individuals who would mock her. She expressed she was also bullied by Deaf people for her cochlear implants, being called a "hearing wannabe". This hurt Katie because she just wanted to fit into both of her worlds – hearing and deaf – and she wound up not feeling welcomed in either.

Katie is able to talk on the phone and have other verbal conversations, and she said she has felt that some deaf people see this and think that she thinks that she is better than them for being able to do this along with signing, perhaps as if she is not honoring her culture which she says is not the case. She said she was also bullied early on when her "signs weren't up to par."

"Deaf people are ruthless and will tell you their honest opinion without thinking of the repercussions," said Katie, when they were frustrated at her for not being "deaf enough." Katie is now 37 years old and is quick to point out that, while seemingly insensitive, some deaf people behave this way for an understandable reason. That reason is that they are constantly having to prove that they are just as capable as hearing people. She said it is a lifelong battle, something they work their whole lives to prove.

In addition to the cochlear debate, the classification of deafness as a disability provides conflicting and strong opinions. Disabilities come in all forms, including physical and mental, so the topic of deafness being a disability or not is a recurring debate even with the deaf community. SignStation, a blog dedicated to deafness, said, "The basic answer to this question is that while people who aren't deaf mostly assume that being deaf is a disability, a lot of deaf people will disagree. Some deaf people will agree. Some deaf people are insulted by the terms "hearing impairment/impaired", and thus are insulted by being characterized as "disabled". It's complex. Legally speaking, deafness is considered a disability according to laws across the United States and the world. However, these laws are often seen as outdated and ignorant" (SignStation, 2022).

The blog is correct. It is complex. In countries where deaf people have access to funded interpreters, the services are organized under a disability umbrella. The same goes for receiving monies from the government for being disabled or deaf children can get schooling only under the disability classification. "The dilemma is that deaf people want access and as citizens in a democracy have a right to access—access to public events, government services, and education—but when they sub scribe to the disability definition in order to gain access, they undermine their struggle for other rights—such as an education for deaf children using their best language, an end to implant surgery on those children, and an end to efforts to discourage deaf births in the first place" (Lane, 2002).

A sophomore at the University of Wisconsin-Madison, Emily Phillips is hard of hearing due to a rare genetic condition called an Enlarged Vestibular Aqueduct. She has worn hearing aids her whole life. However, even with her hearing aids, she believes learning in the classroom still provides her challenges. In order to learn effectively, it is important for her to sit where she can clearly see the instructor. "It helps tremendously with lip reading, and I can pick up so much more information. She also wears a microphone that connects to my hearing aid via Bluetooth. That helps me focus on her voice rather than all the background noise."

Although these accommodations, specifically her hearing aids, help Emily learn effectively, they have also made her a target for bullying and mistreatment. She says that her hearing aids and hearing difficulties have caused people to make "assumptions about my intelligence." Since she could not hear as well as other kids, they made assumptions that she was not as smart as them. "It put immense pressure on me to portray myself as intelligent and capable so people cannot assume anything negative about my intelligence based on my disability," she said.

Furthermore, Emily experienced mistreatment in social environments while she was growing up. For instance, when she was in a louder environment, she would speak louder because she "couldn't hear myself or anybody else talk due to the background noise." In response, some of her peers would make fun of her. Additionally, she said she was bullied when she was younger and had her hearing aid out to clean it or change the battery.

Katie recognized many of these challenges, as well, and made the point that when it comes to the difference between being bullied by deaf people and being bullied by hearing people, it's still bullying and fueled from ignorance.

School Setting and Emotional Intelligence

Bullying is the most prevalent form of school-based violence among adolescents in schools (Bauman & Pero, 2011). The academic failings and education dropout rates of deaf and hard of hearing children has been called a national scandal (McCrone, 2004). Add to that the fact bullying is the most prevalent form of school-based violence among adolescents in schools (Bauman & Pero, 2011), and it's clear that more progress is needed in this area.

To adequately understand the needs of deaf individuals within social settings, it is crucial to identify the role of educators and guardians in the success of these individuals. Children typically discover their preferred way of communicating in infancy when the parent or guardian adapts to caring for a deaf child. Approximately 90-95% of deaf children are born to non-deaf parents (Moores, 2001), so most of these parents must learn to navigate this barrier and learn skills to adapt to their children's development. If gaps exist, weaknesses in abstract thinking and problem-solving skills, limited peer relationships and self-esteems issues can be seen, predisposing them to increased psychological distress and academic issues (Brown and Cornes, 2015).

After the influence of parents and guardians, it is often schools which hold a significant impact to children. These can be positives or, as researchers Hutzell and Payne found, there are "bully-prone locations" such as school playgrounds and athletic fields (2012). Specifically, bullied students reported that bullying occurred in the school hallways 43% of the time, in the classroom 42% of times in the cafeteria 27% of the time, school grounds 22%, online or by text 15%, in the locker room or bathroom 15%, and on the school bus 8% of the time (National Center for Educational Statistics, 2019).

Given the amount of time young people spend at school, the school setting is critical to be as safe as place as possible for all students, and especially those who are targeted negatively. According to the research conducted by Wolke and others from the University of Warwick and Duke University, victims of bullying and victims of bullying who also bullied others are more likely to suffer from poor health and wealth in the future and have difficult social relationships with others. This was found even after the researchers controlled for other external issues, including family issues and other mental health struggles. What may seem like short-term bullying-related issues, such as reduced academic achievement, can easily set off a chain of dominos that result in lower incomes later in life. Not only lower incomes, but psychological and physical health problems can follow individuals far into the future as well, impacting social, physical, and emotional well-being (Wolke et al, 2013). Students who are targeted are often those perceived as "weak" or "different" in some way. Because our society is conditioned to adhere to hearing individuals, deaf individuals stand out as being "different." Therefore, in addition to the struggles of trying to survive and thrive in a world simply not built for them, many deaf students find themselves dealing with bullies as well. Bullies often target deaf individuals by mocking sign language by making fake gestures with their hands or mimicking the deaf student's "distinctive vocal quality and speech production" (Miller et al., 2006).

According to a study performed by Weiner and Galvin, there is much work to be done when it comes to making school settings safer and more equitable for deaf students. These students are bullied at a much higher rate than hearing students; in fact, they are two to three times more likely to experience bullying while in school (Weiner et al., 2013). This is consistent regardless of the type of school, but the authors did find that it is even more likely in school areas where the same children are going to school with one another for most of their grade school careers. When this is the case, a sort of "hierarchy" is likely to form, and those who are "different" will fall to the bottom of the food chain.

One way this impacts deaf children is social and emotional development. Weiner and Galvan found that deaf children who are bullied will often grow up to be less empathetic than the average hearing individual because their social and emotional growth was stunted by the bullying. Additionally, the barriers they may have when attempting to understand and communicate with their teacher, who is addressing a hearing majority in the classroom, bring even more of a challenge to that growth (Weiner et al., 2013). However, both hearing and deaf students feel empathy for other students who are bullied, which shows that deaf students have the potential to feel empathy and develop those social and emotional skills when given equitable care (Weiner et al., 2013).

The development of emotional intelligence is critical to thriving in modern society. There are countless books describing the benefits emotional intelligence provide an individual in the workforce as well as their personal lives. Emotional intelligence is important at all ages and stages of life, and it is crucial during transitions. In a school setting, this can be seen in transitions between grades where a student suddenly has new teachers and classmates. Irvin and Richardson researched the specific timing of transitions from elementary to middle school. These researchers defined emotional intelligence as having the three parts of "understanding and expressing emotions in oneself and others, regulating emotions in self and others and using emotions in thinking, reasoning, problem-solving, and creativity" (Irvin et al., 2002).

Another helpful definition comes from Danvila del Valle and others: "Emotional intelligence is a subset of social intelligence that involves the capacity to control one's own feelings and emotions, and those of others, to discriminate between them and use this information to guide thinking and actions" (Danvila del Valle et al., 2013). Irvin and Richardson believe that one's emotional intelligence is what controls—or at the very least, strongly influences – an individual's response to new situations and conflict. Furthermore, the study found, relative to this context, emotional intelligence also helps control reactions to new environments, such as a new classroom and school. According to the teachers interviewed by Irvin and Richardson, the transition to middle school requires students to be able to tackle a variety of social challenges, and given that strong emotional intelligence assists problem solving, it is critical to the success of these students.

Typically, hearing students can develop emotional intelligence in school as they work with their peers and teachers through conflict and transitions. This ability, according to Irvin and Richardson, allows students to "to cope, to develop their emotional autonomy, and to behave in socially appropriate and responsible ways" (Irvin et al., 2002). This enables them to accept the social challenges of transitions more readily. Additionally, the duo found that emotional intelligence and capacity impacts learning. In their study, they found a direct correlation that students with higher emotional intelligence scores had a stronger academic performance. The researchers concluded that this is because students with high emotional intelligence were able to tolerate frustration better and were, therefore, less impulsive and more focused.

Emotional intelligence is critical to a young person's life. Therefore, because deaf students are targeted by bullies more often than their hearing counterparts, they are more likely to have lower emotional intelligence. Not only are they not getting the opportunity to fully develop their emotional intelligence in a school system that is not built for them, but many are also having their emotional intelligence growth stunted by bullies, as discussed above. Weiner and Galvan found that a lack of empathy and emotional intelligence is common because of the emotionally taxing attacks these students are facing due to their bullies (Weiner et al., 2013).

Not having a strong foundation in emotional intelligence as a child often impacts one's life as an adult, as well, indicating that being bullied as a child can have a long-term impact. Emotional intelligence is becoming increasingly critical in the workplace. According to a study done by Danvila del Valle and others, emotional intelligence has a direct influence over leadership and communication skills. Emotional intelligence includes the ability to empathize well with others, which in turn makes for a strong leader who can rally and value those who work beneath them. This makes for a positive, productive, and therefore valuable working environment (Danvila del Valle et al., 2013). Therefore, by not having the opportunity to develop these skills from an early age at the same rate as hearing students, Deaf and hard of hearing students are likely to be at a disadvantage in the workplace. This is an example of not only inequality, but also inequity, which, for the purpose of this chapter, is defined as the state where all individuals are given the unique resources they need to meet the unique challenges they face so that they are all able to thrive. If bullying in deaf students was prevented or at least lessened, society would be taking a large step in the right direction when it comes to the deaf community.

Of course, society had to adjust in many respects during the pandemic, the deaf community included. "Right now, in the middle of a global pandemic, the combination of masks and being hard of hearing is really making it more difficult for me in school than it is has been in the past," said Emily PHillips. I never realized just how much I relied on lip reading until everybody began wearing masks. Especially in loud, crowded rooms, it's bad. Even when an instructor is wearing the microphone that connects to my hearing aid, it's still difficult for me to hear the teacher if I cannot read their lips." In addition, masks make it hard to understand sign language, as facial expressions are a crucial part of sign language (National Association of the Deaf, 2020). In response to these challenges, the deaf community has advocated for the use of clear masks. These masks allow the lips of the user to be seen, allowing others to read their lips as well as see facial expressions.

Interpreters, Parent Guides and Mentors

When you think of those resources in a school setting, it seems logical that an interpreter would play an obvious role. But even forgoing financial considerations of the costs of hiring interpreters, and even when interpreters are formally trained, a school setting is a special one in which they might not be trained or prepared for jobwise. The Commission on Education of the Deaf observed that only two interpreter training programs were involved specifically in preparing interpreters for work in an educational setting (Antia & Kreimeyer, 2001). When they are present and trained, it has been shown that bullying is far less likely to occur (Weiner, 2006, p.65).

In addition to interpreters, some schools are pairing hearing students with deaf students through special programming. Layla Leigh Wandel, a 2022 senior at Castle High School, said she has learned a great deal from the student she is paired with for one period once a day, a young woman named Trinity. “Getting to work with Trinity has taught me so much. I am so grateful to have learned all I have from her, and I enjoy learning ASL through her.” Layla Leigh emphasized that people often don’t understand that when you’re talking to an individual with an interpreter, you don’t need to talk any differently. “Don’t change the way you word your sentences and avoid saying things like, ‘can you tell them that …’. Just look at who you are talking to and say what you want to stay.”

Much discrimination within the deaf community is not in a bullying capacity but simply a lack of awareness which is, of course, still hurtful. In American culture, the negative stigmas toward deaf people can manifest in voicing pity toward the deaf and hard of hearing.

Ana Brooks, a bilingual parent guide for Hands and Voices, notices that shame culture is real. For her daughter, Kaylyn, the mindset is, “’Oh, she has those hearing aids, we need to cover them up.’ It’s kind of a double whammy. This is what my daughter has to deal with on a daily or weekly basis,” said Brooks. “They’ll say, ‘Oh, she’s your little angel. And she came to you because you were the perfect parent for her.’ It’s those stigmas that you want to break. There’s nothing wrong with saying she’s deaf, there’s nothing wrong with saying she’s disabled.”

People need to realize that deaf and hard of hearing individuals are perfectly capable of engaging in conversation, reading, and doing regular tasks. What they need assistance with is their relation between others and themselves. This is where a large struggle exists. There is a shortage of available interpreters, and without an interpreter there is a separation between that individual and the rest of the world.

“Trinity gets extremely excited when someone learns a sign to communicate with her,” said Layla Leigh, “and it shows how disconnected being deaf has made her. She misses out on a lot of small talk that isn’t interpreted to her.”

In addition to school programs, there are parent unions such as Hands and Voices that assists those who have deaf and hard of hearing children. Liliana Herrara, a parent guide for Hands and Voices, says she is there for parents, “if they have any questions or concerns, if they need to vent to somebody, or if they want to know about what it’s like to have a child who is deaf or hard of hearing.”

At two years old, her son, Yovani, was diagnosed with hearing loss. “When I found out, I knew nothing. I didn’t know where to go or where to turn. It was a lot of trial and error, and a lot of lessons learned,” said Herrera. “It’s really hard trying to manage the health system, the education system, and all the therapies.”

“Parents tend to shy away and just stick to their lane. I encourage parents to speak up and let them know they have a say and a proper seat at the table,” said Brooks.

Figure 2. Stephanie Nogueras introduces herself to kids at the Bohol Deaf Academy in Bohol, Philippines in November 2019]

Stephanie Nogueras, a deaf actress and active mentor to those in the deaf community, feels economic status can hinder the ability for children to more easily grow and interact with others. As a result, not all deaf children have the chance to learn in the supportive environments found in schools for the deaf. "A deaf school was much easier for me so I could socialize and make friends," she said. "I was fortunate enough that my dad had a good job that allowed me to transfer to a deaf school, because it was out of the state."

That social integration in an academic setting is one of the major challenges for deaf children in inclusive settings, according to Stinson and Antia (1999). They define social integration as the ability to interact with, make friends with, and be accepted by peers. From the studies available, it appears that deaf children in mainstream education often have few friends, have less interaction with hearing peers, and are more often rejected or neglected than their hearing peers (Wauters & Knoors, 2008).

With about 90% of babies born with hearing loss being born to hearing parents who oftentimes need medical and other guidance (National Institute on Deafness and Other Communication Disorders), much pressure falls on their parents. Nogueras said, "My mom was self-taught to learn ASL - she went to the library! She found a VHS to learn ASL."

While we have discussed the school setting and the importance of self-esteem and emotional intelligence, this importance of this aspect of parenting and the role played in a deaf's child life cannot be over-emphasized. It circles back to the idea that to lesson bullying aspects or even simply improve quality of life, the first thing that needs to happen is that deaf children need to have a strong sense of identity from a very young age (Weiner, 2006). This begins with their parents, whether they are born to hearing or deaf parents (Weiner, 2006). These parents need assistance and resources, as many adults at school or at home tend to ignore or minimally respond to bullying and teasing witnessed or reported to them. Parents have been reported to view teasing as being benign and harmless, and they often underestimate the negative impact on children (Miller, 1982). They also may view bullying as a rite of passage by which children will become tougher and more confident adults if they learn to stand up to it, even when the physical and psychological odds of this happening are overwhelming.

"Parents tend to shy away and just stick to their lane. I encourage parents to speak up and let them know they have a say and a proper seat at the table," said Brooks.

Of the 70 million deaf people worldwide, only 10 percent are born to deaf parents (Mitchell and Karchmer, 2004). Since most deaf people are born to hearing parents, they grow up in a different linguistic, cultural, and social environment than their parents.

"Personally, it took some time for my family to be accepting of the fact that this isn't going away. This is permanent. It's not like a Band-Aid that's going to heal. In their head, it was like a wound. You have surgery and you're going to get fixed. No, this is a long-term lifetime thing. And she is going to deal with it. But, if we support her if we rally around her, then she's going to be successful," said Brooks.

Barb Witte, mother of a deaf child, is direct about the difficulties and beauties of raising a child with a disability. "Be prepared to grieve over the whole thing," she advised, and then "be open to anything and enjoy your child." Witte's daughter, Karen Tidd, is now 58 years old and can "swim, drive and do anything anyone else can do," said Witte.

Witte had Rubella during her pregnancy, which led to Tidd's deafness at birth. Witte was a young mother at 18 years old, and resources were limited. Witte referenced Spencer Tracy as one of the only people she knew of at the time who was a parent to a deaf child. The American actor of the Golden Age of Hollywood utilized a teaching method for his own son that Witte described as "see, say". Inspired by this teaching method, Witte utilized pictures and words to help Tidd learn from a young age. "I had thousands of 3x5 cards with pictures," said Witte. "They were taped all over our house, and it became like a game." The initial efforts were also a wild guess, Witte admitted, given she had no collaboration with other deaf individuals or teachers in the early years of Tidd's life.

Educational resources would have been helpful, but even knowing about something as simple as lighted fire alarms and other resources available for deaf individuals, is crucial, Witte said. Also, not being afraid to be an advocate for your child, no matter the age. Fairly recently, Witte and Tidd were at a grocery store when a miscommunication occurred and resulted in the check-out clerk suggesting Tidd wear a sign noting her deafness. A manager was eventually involved, who offered to fire the clerk. Instead, Witte suggested sensitivity training as it was a learning moment.

Tidd's own daughter, Chyane, has experienced bullying for using sign language. Chyane, whose hearing is fine, grew up in the deaf community. "Learning to sign is the same thing as learning to talk. In fact, I signed before I spoke my first word. When I was younger, my peers were fascinated with learning sign, but as I got older, I sometimes got bullied for signing." Better understanding of sign language, and teachings within schools, could help push toward the inclusivity of the deaf community with benefits for all. As Chyane said, in both hearing and deaf children, signing is an effective way to communicate and express themselves in circumstances where verbal speech isn't possible. Babies being able to sign before they are able to produce speech enables them to more accurately and quickly express desires and needs.

Mirror Images and the Media

As discussed in various ways in the interviews for this chapter, perhaps the most organic way of eradicating the issue of bullying is to work harder at inclusivity and normalize being comfortable with our differences. Media has the ability influence beliefs, attitudes and behaviors. Prior research shows media influencing through either the individual, direct effect or the social or indirect effect. In the individual effect, media information about new norms persuade individuals to accept them. In the social effect, the information creates common knowledge of a norm and enhances social coordination as individuals more readily accept the information if they believe others have also accepted it (Arias, 2019).

Research also shows that a lack of representation in media can lead to negative psychological outcomes for those with identities that are underrepresented or negatively portrayed (Tukachinsky, Mastro, & Yarchi, 2017). For this chapter, we considered a sampling of children's books, TV shows and movies.

Children's books provide a source from which children draw to understand themselves, their culture, their language and that of others to the point that "… literary characters can provide children with a mirror image of themselves and their own culture or a "window" into the cultural lives of others" (Golos & Moses, 2011). In early childhood development, the relationship between pictures and certain meanings can be understood much more before the relationship between words and their meanings. "Picture books are powerful and popular in the world of educating and caring for young children. Beyond skill development, the words and illustrations in children's books can serve as a means for developing children's identity and sense of self as well as their understanding of other people and cultures." (Golos, 2012).

The messages portrayed in these books should be positive and accurate as they help shape the way children see the world. In children's literature, deaf characters are often described as disabled. Since deaf children have few deaf role models around, the deaf characters they are exposed to can affect the way they view themselves. In books, deaf characters are rarely seen interacting with other deaf individuals. A commonality surrounding these characters in children's literature is that they are often depicted as being isolated or in danger. Rather than inaccurately portraying deafness as something that can be possibly cured through medical intervention, books could serve as a positive influence to provide deaf children with role models."

Deaf Unity, a charity for the deaf, recommends these seven books for children:

1. Dad and Me in the Morning – Patricia Lakin, illustrated by Robert G. Steele
2. Ranvir Cannot Hear – Genevieve Yusuf, illustrated by Shermain Phillip
3. Freddie and the Fairy – Julia Donaldson, illustrated by Karen George
4. Let's Hear it for Almigal – Wendy Kupfer, illustrated by Tammie Lyon
5. El Deafo – Cece Bell, illustrated by Cece Bell and Kate Fitch
6. All the Ways I Hear You – Stephanie Marrufo, illustrated by Priscila Soares
7. Proud to Be Deaf – Ava, Lilli and Nick Beese, illustrated by Romina Marti

Children base their impressions via direct contact, indirect experience through things such as books, social groups such as peers and teachers (Ostrosky 33). Since book reading is a popular pastime of many children and a prominent activity in classrooms, how disabilities are portrayed can have a strong influence.

Equally strong are what young people see and hear on traditional media platforms. Young people, in 2019, spent an average of two hours per day watching television shows (Rideout, 2019). Unfortunately, negative examples abound, such as the depiction of bullying of the deaf on the TV show *My name is Earl*. The character of Ruby, a successful lawyer, enters her office to the cast of main characters who immediately disrespect her. She speaks some and signs some, with the help of her interpreter, and a main character named Joy begins mocking her over the way her voice sounds. The main characters refer to Ruby as "my deaf lawyer" instead of "Ruby" or "my lawyer".

Rather than running through a litany of other negative stereotype examples, such as "The Witches" which has been met with negative feedback from the deaf community, this chapter will intentionally focus on a few positive representations. The year 2022 was an exciting one for this, with *CODA* (Child of a Deaf Adult) winning an Oscar for Best Motion Picture of the Year and, equally notable, Best Performance by an Actor in a Supporting Role. The latter was won by Troy Kotsur, the first deaf actor to win this award. Another current standout is Stephanie Nogueras, a deaf actress starring as Natalie Pierce on ABC Family's *Switched at Birth* from 2011-2017 and now starring in *Killing It*. In addition to acting, she dedicates her time to helping deaf youth learn ASL (American Sign Language.) Communicating via Zoom chat in spring 2022, Nogueras shared that acting is her career, but when she has free time, she mentors for the deaf youth and teaches all ages ASL 1-3 and deaf culture.

"Acting is not my dream career," she said. "It basically was an accident. I was originally planning to be a counselor. My ex was following his dream to be a professional actor, so I supported him and helped him. However, his formal manager found an audition that she thought was perfect for me. I told her I was not interested. That was for *Switched At Birth*. She insisted, so I gave it a try for FUN, and the rest is history. I am stuck in this flowing path, so I stick with it for now."

Nogueras said, "Many people in this Hollywood industry are not ready for deaf actors and actors with a disability so accommodations are not always available for us. We have to work harder and educate them. There's a lot of discrimination along the way. The challenges are patience and brushing off those discriminations. There are extremely limited roles for us. We have to push and keep going."

Switched at Birth was met with more than 100 episodes, and the overall story line is of two teen girls who discover that they were accidentally switched at birth. One grew up in an affluent family with two parents and a sibling, while the other grew up with a single mother and grandmother in a poor neighborhood. After the discovery, the two families come together to spend time with both girls. Through the TV show, we see the delicate line of learning how to work through differences, overcome confusion and awkward situations, and sometimes clashes between well-intentioned cultures. We gain insight from the character Daphne's experiences at the Carlton School for the Deaf as well as her classmates.

As one viewer commented on the IMDb site, "I rarely begin to follow a television show while it is in its first for fear that it will be canceled. Yet this one drew me in, and I cannot get enough of it. The idea of being switched at birth is so bizarre, and the dynamics of both families are so real. The raw emotion and feelings portrayed by these characters makes me feel sorry for and sometimes resent them all at the same time. The drama always keeps me eager to see what will happen on the next episode. The writers may have struck gold with this one."

It's the raw, real quality that makes this TV series a prime example of an accurate portrayal – of complicated family dynamics and, particular to this paper, of deaf representation. Other examples with positive takeaways exist, including in movies such as *Children of a Lesser God* and even individual scenes such as one from *The Sandlot2*.

As this chapter is focused on the struggles of the deaf, it's worthwhile to note that the 2017 movie *A Silent Voice* addresses head-on the bullying that can occur within that community. This movie, winner of the Japanese Movie Critics Awards for Best Animated Feature Film, centers around a young girl who is hard of hearing. A student at a new school, she was excited to encounter her hearing peers. She brought a notebook as a way for her to communicate if they did not know sign language. Not long after a boy in her class began to bully her, he would tease how she would read and how she would talk and even at a point in the movie take out her hearing aid and throw them around in the classroom. After basically being tortured by her classmate the girl left schools. After the girl left the school the boy who was bullying her would eventually begin to get bullied himself. After seeing what it was like to be bullied, he was traumatized for what he did to the girl and would go and try to find her years later even trying to learn sign language so that he is able to communicate with her to apologize. This was a great movie that gave a little representation of what deaf children may have to deal with while they are in school. This is also rare because in traditional media this is not a topic that is represented a lot.

Finally, one last example to share is the documentary *Sound and Fury*, directed by Josh Aronson and produced by Roger Weisberg, shares the difficult challenges a family faces when it comes to the decision whether to utilize medical technology with a cochlear implant. The Artinian family from Long Island is showcased as they have heated disagreements with family members over whether to allow their son to undergo the surgery. They receive both support and opposition. The father, Chris, has a brother whose wife and three children are all deaf. We learn the brother, Peter, strongly opposes cochlear implants. Another twist arises when one of Peter's children requests the surgery. Many deaf people feel one of their biggest difficulties is the hearing culture that treats them as though they are people to be pitied or changed. The documentary highlights the point that a large percentage of deaf people would opt out of the hearing world given a choice, particularly those born deaf.

Schools and programs could select a variety of these and other positive depictions to watch, review, discuss and normalize the questions and confusion surrounding deaf culture. And parents of young children can seek out shows such as *Sesame Street* which has programming depicting characters with a wide variety of representation and has "continuously evolved with social topics over time, introducing Muppets and human characters dealing with diverse and real-life experiences such as autism, incarcerated parents, homelessness, substance use, and HIV" (Levinson, 2020).

It was *Sesame Street*, in fact, which helped encourage understanding of deafness and sign language to many in the 1970s with its character Linda, a librarian on the show. The part was played by Linda Bove, who is HH in real life.

Much like puppetry, dolls have a place in the normalization of differences in young children. Amy Jandrisevits, associated with the nonprofit organization "A Doll Like Me", creates dolls that resemble their owners, particularly children with disabilities. These disabilities range from cleft lips to missing limbs to hearing loss. Other diverse dolls exist, thanks to people like Clare Tawell, who started Bright Ears UK after her daughter Matilda was born deaf. The popular American Girl company also introduced a doll with a hearing aid. Since 2012, the company has been selling hearing aids as one of hundreds of accessory options for dolls, but the Joss Kendrick doll is the first doll to have an actual story surrounding her hearing loss. Hailing from Huntington Beach, California, the 10-year-old surfer and competitive cheerleader provides a strong role model as independent and fierce.

As Jandrisevits said, "Every kid should see themselves on the store shelves." (Ability Magazine, 2022). If preschool programs and other early childhood settings could incorporate dolls and discussions about differences, similarities and disabilities, normalization may occur at an earlier, more natural stage (This & Foster, 1991).

SPORTS AND SPECIAL PROGRAMMING

The Centers for Disease Control and Prevention states that children and adolescents from age 6 – 17 should participate in a minimum of 60 minutes of moderate to vigorous physical activity each day. It's more than just a health issue, though, as it also impacts mental health, socialization and more. "Sports can provide excellent educational opportunities for social development because many of the social and moral requirements for participation in sports are parallels to how individuals must function in a law-abiding society" (Seefeldt & Ewing, 1997).

Of course, the development is only beneficial when the sports foster positive experiences and minimize negative experiences. When it does, cultural bonding can occur and sports can become a great equalizer. Isaac, age 9, and Salim, age 11, are good examples of how sports can play a helpful role in the social growth of interesting, active youth.

Isaac Roof and Salim El Abdellaoui don't share the same type of deafness, as Isaac was born with continuous hearing loss as opposed to Salim who was born completely deaf. But the two do share the traits of perseverance and ambition … and a love of sports.

Isaac's mom Sarah, a graduate of the University of Evansville with a degree in science and psychology, said, "Isaac has always loved sports from a young age. Football is his favorite sport to play and watch. He's currently a Kansas City Chiefs fan but also loves the Eagles and Bengals." In addition to football, Isaac plays golf, baseball, soccer, and is on the local YMCA swim team.

Salim, originally from the Netherlands, has always been interested in sports. His mom, Lina, said, "He has done all types of sports, but his biggest love is soccer, which he is pretty good at as well. It literally looks like he is not aware of his disability when he's playing, which is awesome."

Even with the positive moments, there are naturally some obstacles. Sarah explained it's helpful to try and utilize these as learning experiences for all. "Baseball creates challenges as a helmet is difficult while wearing cochlear implants (which Isaac does). In addition, coaches often yell instructions from the dugout, which is nearly impossible for Isaac to hear if he's in the outfield or playing on the opposite side of his dugout. Coaches are asked to be sure to get his attention when they need to communicate to him and then face him while talking."

Lina shared how the learning experiences can extend to handling challenging situations. "Salim is a very quiet and shy kid. He tends to isolate himself when he notices that something went wrong or when he thinks something is his fault. I remember when he went to sit down on the sideline once because one of his teammates had made a gesture toward him after something had gone wrong in a soccer game." For her and for Salim, her reaction – or lack thereof – was important.

"The way I handled it was to not make a big deal out of it, because if I did this would strengthen his thought that him being different is a bad thing." She wanted to address it, but to do so in a calming way. "I told him that everybody makes mistakes and that all kids mess up sometimes during a game. In the next game, he scored two goals, and I'm pretty sure he didn't even remember the previous game anymore."

Overall, sports have provided a positive outlet. "Sometimes I believed that Salim's cochlear implants caused him to feel ashamed which resulted in him avoiding contact with others," said Lina. "But his talents in soccer seemed to have boosted his confidence as I now have to drag him out of the locker room when he is joking around with his teammates after practice."

Both Sarah and Lina stressed the importance of strong role models. For Isaac, one of his biggest inspirations is found in Mason Gooch, who cannot detect any sound without his cochlear implant. He received the implant when he was 20 months old and went on to be part of the Gallaudet University Bison football team. Sarah said that Isaac seeing others with the same disability as his make it to a high level in athletics gave him the confirmation he needed to believe in his own goals.

The story of Isaac getting to meet Mason is a special one. "The local news had done a story on Mason," said Sarah, "so I reached out to Mason's mom via Facebook and asked if he would be willing to send an autographed photo to Isaac. He did!" Then, about a year after the initial request, Isaac and Mason were able to meet face-to-face at a SuperHEARo 5k event.

Figure 3. Mason and Isaac

''Sports have a positive impact for any young child," said Sarah. "For Isaac, they give him a place to belong and make friends. He is very social, so he loves to be a part of something and to interact with friends. It also teaches him the concept of being part of a team as well as working hard to achieve something."

Sports has helped him learn to be an advocate for himself, explained Sarah.

DHH Heroes

Like-minded, mirror imaging, and inspiring individuals in media or sports can promote a healthy mindset for what young people believe they can achieve. Working from this platform, a unique program called *DHH Heroes: Inspiring Connections* is making tremendous strides. The Kentucky chapter of Hands & Voices created the program in 2019 to help forge better connectivity with families of children who are deaf or hard of hearing and deaf adults.

The DHH Heroes are deaf and hard of hearing adults who want to support others children and families by answering questions, attending community events and serving as inspiration. Each DHH Hero has their unique superhero persona on a trading card that the children attempt to collect. While other kids trade baseball cards, these kids trade cards of a different kind of hero. From 'Captain Green Thumb' to 'Valegro' to 'Silent Sleuth,' the Heroes have cards which showcase their powers and accomplishments, and hobbies and interests. With a basic introduction of the Hero already established, the cards make it easier for the kids to approach the heroes and start conversations at events.

One of the original Heroes, Blake Noland – aka Captain Green Thumb – chose his persona based on the sheer number of plants filling his home. He typically shows up at events dressed in bright green clothing to represent his Hero name. Another Hero is Holly Evans – aka Silent Sleuth. "You know Deaf people are silent. I'm not silent at all. Don't even think that, but sleuth is like detecting, and I like finding information and investigating."

Brooke Montgomery, the Assistant Director with Kentucky Hands & Voices, knew from her son's own needs that the DHH Hero program would be a beautiful way for him to make new connections. With each new encounter, her hope for Luke's future well-being increased. Montgomery said she and the other board members saw that these connections had a duality of benefit: both for the parents' education and also for the children's self-esteem.

Montgomery recalled the story of her and Luke's lunch meeting with Anita Dowd, the President of Kentucky Hands & Voices. In doing so, Montgomery signed one word: "same". The hand placement involves curling the pointer, middle and ring finger into the palm of the hand while the thumb and pinky finger extend to the side. The hand then moves back and forth pointing to the two like things: so, in this case Luke and Dowd. It's the word Luke, then only a toddler, signed as Dowd had pulled back the curtain of her hair to reveal her ears to be adorned with hearing aids.

Figure 4. DHH Trading Cards

With chapters around the world and in most U.S. states, Hands & Voices has as its pillar of philosophy that any communication method, whether orally or through sign language, is acceptable if it is the right for that individual. When it comes to hearing parents making choices about their kids' communication method, there are a lot of outside opinions fighting to be heard, which can be isolating for all involved. Hands & Voices operates with a non-judgmental approach, believing that each situation is different and the parents and children must work together to understand their best fit. Upon learning of this unique perspective, Jena White, one of the DHH Heroes, said, "When I heard the philosophy of Hands & Voices,

I was like it really matches my philosophy, and at that point I decided I needed to get involved." White, also known as Valegro, chose her name after a famous dressage horse of the same name. According to White, the weirdness and foreign nature of the name were other deciding factors.

An addition to the D/HH Heroes program is the DHH Sidekick program. It is still in the planning stages, but the kids seem enthusiastic for this to become a reality. Luke had asked for his own superhero card, and when Montgomery made it for him, they realized the Sidekick program could greatly impact the kid's involvement. Not only will they have the cards of the adults to look up to, but they can collect the cards of their peers so they can learn more about them. The whole program spans the state of Kentucky, so the children only see each other at the larger events. Having the cards of their peers will help them feel connected when they do see each other. White said, "The goal is to make trading cards for those kids so they can become their own hero."

As Luke said, "I am a fan of the DHH Heroes… a BIG fan."

Figure 5. Sidekick Program

FUTURE RESEARCH AND DIRECTIONS

This chapter began with a reference to Jesse Louis Jackson's quote of America being somewhat like a quilt, with its many patches, pieces, colors and sizes. If we look at this from the standpoint deaf community, we can see positive outcomes from educational programming to eradication of bias, from media inclusion to clear masks, that we together can sew for a stronger, multi-layered society. While endless possibilities for encouraging acceptance and understanding of deafness exist, it is the central theme of normalization and inclusivity which seems to hold most promise, whether that's in school, media, sports, or programming. This must be the guiding focus of all future research – normalizing the differences and finding ways to encourage more meaningful interaction between hearing and deaf individuals beginning at a young age.

In 2006 (Weiner & Miller), it was stated that "Measures to describe and quantify bullying factors in this population should be developed and validated that address characteristics of deaf victims and bullies, various types of school settings deaf children attend, bullying dynamics that may be unique to this population and its peers, and other environmental factors." It was accurate then and still applicable today. Studying the successful components of progressive programs such as the DHH Hero program are necessary in moving forward. By ultimately learning and repurposing pieces that have worked and creating more programming and events, integrated school and sporting activities, and mirrored images within pop culture and mainstream media, we can recognize our similarities while celebrating our differences.

REFERENCES

A Doll Like Me – Every Child Should Feel Included. (2022). *Ability Magazine*. Retrieved February 24, 2022, from https://abilitymagazine.com/a-doll-like-me-every-child-should-feel-included/

Antia, S. D., & Kreimeyer, K. H. (2001). The role of interpreters in inclusive classrooms. *American Annals of the Deaf, 146*(4), 355–365. doi:10.1353/aad.2012.0142 PMID:11816860

Arias, E. (2019). How Does Media Influence Social Norms? Experimental Evidence on the Role of Common Knowledge. *Political Science Research and Methods*, *7*(3), 561–578. doi:10.1017/psrm.2018.1

Bargh, J. A., & McKenna, K. Y. A. (2004). The Internet and social life. *Annual Review of Psychology*, *55*(1), 573–590. doi:10.1146/annurev.psych.55.090902.141922 PMID:14744227

Bauman, S., & Pero, H. (2011). Bullying and cyberbullying among deaf students and their hearing peers: An exploratory study. *Journal of Deaf Studies and Deaf Education*, *16*(2), 236–253. doi:10.1093/deafed/enq043 PMID:20855432

Creswell, J. W., Hanson, W. E., Clark Plano, V. L., & Morales, A. (2007). Qualitative research designs: Selection and implementation. *The Counseling Psychologist*, *35*(2), 236–264. doi:10.1177/0011000006287390

Danvila, I., Sastre, M.A., & Marroquin, E. (2013). The importance of professional competencies in the development of emotional intelligence. *Revista Internacional De Organizaciones*, (10), 157. . doi:10.17345/rio10.157-179

Fellinger, J., Holzinger, D., & Pollard, R. (2012). Mental health of deaf people. *Lancet*, *379*(9820), 1037–1044. doi:10.1016/S0140-6736(11)61143-4 PMID:22423884

Golos, D. B., & Moses, A. M. (2011). Representations of deaf characters in children's picture books. *American Annals of the Deaf, 156*(3), 270–282. doi:10.1353/aad.2011.0025 PMID:21941877

Golos, D. B., Moses, A. M., & Wolbers, K. A. (2012). Culture or disability? Examining deaf characters in children's book illustrations. *Early Childhood Education Journal*, *40*(4), 239–249. doi:10.100710643-012-0506-0

Lane, H. (2002). Do deaf people have a disability? *Sign Language Studies*, *2*(4), 356–379. doi:10.1353ls.2002.0019

Levinson, J. (2020, March 5). Why Diversity in Children's Media is so Important. *Psychology in Action*. https://www.psychologyinaction.org/psychology-in-action-1/2020/3/5/why-diversity-in-childrens-media-is-so-important

Margaret Brown, P., & Cornes, A. (2015). Mental health of deaf and hard-of-hearing adolescents: What the students say. *Journal of Deaf Studies and Deaf Education, 20*(1), 75–81. doi:10.1093/deafed/enu031 PMID:25237152

McCrone, W. P. (2004). School Bullying: A Problem for Deaf and Hard of Hearing Students? Insights and Strategies. Odyssey. *New Directions in Deaf Education, 5*(2), 4–9.

Mitchell, R.E., & Karchmer, M. (2004). Chasing the Mythical Ten Percent: Parental Hearing Status of Deaf and Hard of Hearing Students in the United States. *Sign Language Studies, 4*(2), 138-163. https://www.jstor.org/stable/26190985

Moores, D. (2001). *Educating the deaf: Psychology, principles and practices* (5th ed.). Houghton Mifflin.

National Center for Education. (2019). *Student Reports of Bullying Results from the 2017 School Crime Supplement to the National Victimization Survey*. Author.

National Deaf Children's Society. (2014, June). *Bullying Advice for Parents of Deaf Children*. Author.

Norwich, B., & Kelly, N. (2004). Pupils' views on inclusion: Moderate learning difficulties and bullying in mainstream and special schools. *British Educational Research Journal, 30*(1), 43–65. doi:10.1080/01411920310001629965

Ostrosky, M. M., Mouzourou, C., Dorsey, E. A., Favazza, P. C., & Leboeuf, L. M. (2015). Pick a Book, Any Book: Using Children's Books to Support Positive Attitudes Toward Peers with Disabilities. *Young Exceptional Children, 18*(1), 30–43. doi:10.1177/1096250613512666

Padden, C., Humphries, T., & Padden, C. (2009). *Inside deaf culture*. Harvard University Press. doi:10.2307/j.ctvjz83v3

Rideout, V., & Robb, M. B. (2019). *The Common Sense Census: Media Use by Tweens and Teen*. Academic Press.

Seefeldt, V. D., & Ewing, M. E. (1997). Youth sports in America: An overview. *President's Council on Physical Fitness and Sports Research Digest*.

Shoham, N., Lewis, G., Favarato, G., & Cooper, C. (2019). Prevalence of anxiety disorders and symptoms in people with hearing impairment: A systematic review. *Social Psychiatry and Psychiatric Epidemiology, 54*(6), 649–660. doi:10.100700127-018-1638-3 PMID:30547211

SignStation. (2022). https://signstation.org

Skelton, T., & Valentine, G. (2003). 'It Feels Like Being Deaf is Normal.': An Exploration into the Complexities of Defining D/deafness and Young D/deaf People's Identities. *The Canadian Geographer. Geographe Canadien, 47*(4), 451–466. doi:10.1111/j.0008-3658.2003.00035.x

Statistics, B. (n.d.). *PACER Center – Champions for Children with Disabilities*. Retrieved February 10, 2022, from https://www.pacer.org/bullying/info/stats.asp

Stinson, M. S., & Kluwin, T. N. (2003). Educational consequences of alternative school placements. In M. Marschark & M. E. Spencer (Eds.), *Deaf studies, language, and education* (pp. 52–64). Oxford University Press.

Thios, S. J., & Foster, S. B. (1991). *Changing Preschoolers' Attitudes toward Children with Disabilities.* Academic Press.

Tukachinsky, R., Mastro, D., & Yarchi, M. (2017). The Effect of Prime Time Television Ethnic/Racial Stereotypes on Latino and Black Americans: A Longitudinal National Level Study. *Journal of Broadcasting & Electronic Media, 61*(3), 538–556. doi:10.1080/08838151.2017.1344669

Turner, D. W. III. (2010). Qualitative interview design: A practical guide for novice investigators. *Qualitative Report, 15*(3), 754.

Wauters, L. N., & Knoors, H. (2008). Social integration of deaf children in inclusive settings. *Journal of Deaf Studies and Deaf Education, 13*(1), 21–36. doi:10.1093/deafed/enm028 PMID:17573356

Weiner, M. T., Day, S. J., & Galvan, D. (2013). Deaf and hard of hearing students' perspectives on bullying and school climate. *American Annals of the Deaf, 158*(3), 334–343. doi:10.1353/aad.2013.0029 PMID:24133958

Weiner, M. T., & Miller, M. (2006). Deaf children and bullying: Directions for future research. *American Annals of the Deaf, 151*(1), 61–70. doi:10.1353/aad.2006.0021 PMID:16856647

Wolke, D., Copeland, W. E., Angold, A., & Costello, E. J. (2013). Impact of bullying in childhood on adult health, wealth, crime, and social outcomes. *Psychological Science, 24*(10), 1958–1970. doi:10.1177/0956797613481608 PMID:23959952

ADDITIONAL READING

Broekhof, E., Bos, M., Camodeca, M., & Rieffe, C. (2018). Longitudinal Associations Between Bullying and Emotions in Deaf and Hard of Hearing Adolescents. *Journal of Deaf Studies and Deaf Education, 23*(1), 17–27. doi:10.1093/deafed/enx036 PMID:28977584

Cheng, A. W., Chou, Y. C., & Lin, F. G. (2019). Psychological Distress in Bullied Deaf and Hard of Hearing Adolescents. *Journal of Deaf Studies and Deaf Education, 24*(4), 366–377. doi:10.1093/deafed/enz014 PMID:31089728

Flynt, S. W., & Morton, R. C. (2004). Bullying and children with disabilities. *Journal of Instructional Psychology, 31*(4), 330–333.

Grushkin, D. (2016, November 9). *How do deaf people live day-to-day life?* Retrieved February 11, 2022, from https://www.quora.com/How-do-deaf-people-live-day-to-day-life

Hutzell, K. L., & Payne, A. A. (2012). The impact of bullying victimization on school avoidance. *Youth Violence and Juvenile Justice, 10*(4), 370-385.

Lee, W. Y., Tan, J., & Kok, J. K. (2022). The Struggle to Fit in: A Qualitative Study on the Sense of Belonging and Well-being of Deaf People in Ipoh, Perak, Malaysia. *Psychological Studies*, 1–16. Advance online publication. doi:10.100712646-022-00658-7 PMID:35529704

KEY TERMS AND DEFINITIONS

Bullying: The use of force, coercion, hurtful teasing or threat, to abuse, aggressively dominate or intimidate. The behavior is often repeated and habitual. One essential prerequisite is the perception (by the bully or by others) of an imbalance of physical or social power. This imbalance distinguishes bullying from conflict.

Deafness: Condition of extreme hearing loss.

Emotional Intelligence: The capacity to be aware of, control, and express one's emotions, and to handle interpersonal relationships judiciously and empathetically.

Inclusivity: The practice or policy of providing equal access to opportunities and resources for people who might otherwise be excluded or marginalized, such as those having physical or intellectual disabilities or belonging to other minority groups.

Lip Reading: The interpreting of speech by watching the speaker's lip and facial movements without hearing the voice.

Normalization: The process of bringing or returning something to a normal condition or state.

Sign Languages: Languages that use the visual-manual modality to convey meaning. Sign languages are expressed through manual articulations in combination with non-manual elements.

Victimization: The action of singling someone out for cruel or unjust treatment.

Chapter 2
Titane Tracking Violence With Cyborg Women: *Cyborg Alexia* – A Picture of Violence in the Digital Age

Berceste Gülçin Özdemir
İstanbul University, Turkey

ABSTRACT

In the film, which attempts to make sense of the inner world of a young woman named Adrien, the aspect of violence is elevated to the central theme. The audience's perspective on the main character, concerns of identification with her, and the main female protagonist's cyborg status are all discussed in conjunction with the patriarchal world order. The study's fundamental themes are drawn from Donna Haraway's Cyborg Manifesto (1991). The study raises questions on discussions about the role of violence in film narratives by referencing these discourses and the opinions of sociologist and political science theoreticians.

INTRODUCTION

Donna Haraway Cyborg Manifesto: What Does She Say about Science, Technology, and Socialist-Feminism in the Late Twentieth Century

Women's stories have started to diversify as stories that not only female viewers but also male viewers want to watch. Instead of thinking about how to identify with whom, the female viewer can watch the types of identification in different stories, with different female characters. However, in the cinema where male domination has been present for centuries, it is not an immediate situation that the female perspective gains momentum as much as the male perspective. At the same time, all the steps necessary for this state to be realized continue to be taken by women. The 2010s were challenging male-dominated cinema narratives. Instead of stereotyped female characters categorized by feminist film theorists, radical female characters breaking these stereotypes are now categorized. Female characters that are promising, strong,

DOI: 10.4018/978-1-6684-5426-8.ch002

able to raise their voices in the public sphere, make their voices heard, and who can talk about realities against the face of society are represented as women replacing the compassionate mother, punished woman, and beautiful, femme-fatale woman. Going out of the beauty judgments of the social order has a very important role in breaking the male-dominant view.

Haraway, who works on feminism and techno-science, contributes to women's studies, social gender studies, and the field of new media. Saying, "I would rather be a cyborg than a goddess", Haraway's thought enables philosophy to open its doors to the readers who follow her.

Haraway starts her work with the title of "An Ironic World of Creating a Common Language for Women in the Integrated Circuit". She mentions that she wrote the text on the way to an ironic political myth that believes in feminism, socialism, and materialism. Saying that irony has a relationship with humor and serious play, Haraway states that the cyborg image lies at the root of her ironic belief. Haraway defines the cyborg as: "A cyborg is a cybernetic organism, a hybrid of machine and organism, a creature of social reality as well as a creature of fiction." Cyborgs are defined as those who prevent sexuality, heterosexism and do not reproduce as a result of organic reproduction. Saying that we are all chimeras, Haraway states that based on the combination of machine and organism, humans are made-up hybrids and emphasizes that our ontology is cyborgs. The cyborg is stated as the creature of the post-gender world. In a postmodernist, non-naturalistic fashion, Haraway imagines a world without gender, without birth, and the end of the world. An ultimate self, freed from all addictions is important to her. The cyborg is firmly attached to partiality, irony, intimacy, and perversion. Therefore, the cyborg is oppositional and has nothing to do with innocence. The dream of establishing a family based on the organic family model is not found in the cyborg. They also present the possibility that humans may have close matches with other living beings in a way that is both disturbing and pleasurable. The boundary between the physical and the non-physical becomes blurred based on cyborgs and in questioning the boundaries between the human and animal. "They are like ether," Haraway says of cyborgs. Ether is a colorless, volatile liquid with a distinctive odor. Therefore, cyborgs are not ubiquitous and they have invisible qualities. Cyborgs, who are related to consciousness or its simulation, are beings with the ability to read the power network well. Referring to Herbert Marcuse's *One-Dimensional Man: Studies in the Ideology of Advanced Industrial Society* (1964) and Carolyn Merchant's *The Death of Nature: Women, Ecology and the Scientific Revolution* (1980), Haraway states that these works emphasize the domination brought by the technique mandatorily and indicates that there is an effort to return to an imaginary organic body that will integrate people's resistance. The cyborg world is about situations where people are afraid of being related to animals and machines and do not hesitate to have fragmented identities.

Sexual objectification is seen as the result of gender/social gender structure. At this point, it is the woman who becomes the sexual object. Likewise, Haraway underlines that the dualities within some concepts are ideologically problematic. Like mind/body, animal/human, organism/machine, public/private, nature/culture, man/woman, primitive/civilized... They are the ones that create a structure of the things that are imagined about personal and social possibilities in gender, sexuality, reproduction, and high-tech myth systems. Feminists such as Luce Irigaray and Monique Wittig are also thinkers who write about the body and question eroticism, cosmology, and politics based on images of embodiment, fragmentation, and reconstitution of bodies. Cyborgs in feminist science fiction make problematic the status of the human being, whether male or female, as a member of a race, as a singular being, or as a body.

Stating that the cyborg body is not innocent and has adopted irony from the beginning, Haraway underlines that people are now becoming machines. She adds that the people responsible for the machines cannot be dominated or threatened by the machines. While it is pointed out that gender is not a global identity, it is thought that cyborg gender may be a local possibility that attempts to take revenge on a global scale. The regrowing limb may come out as a freak, or it may be a copy of the old one. For this reason, Haraway, who believes in rebirth, argues that this possibility includes a utopian dream such as the hope of a monstrous world that does not recognize social gender. The cyborg's imagination, bodies, and tools can show people the way out of the labyrinth of dualities that is explained by them. This state is seen by Haraway as a heteroglossia. This imagination means both constructing and destroying machines, identities, categories, relationships, and stories of space. Therefore, Haraway emphasizes that she prefers to be a cyborg rather than a goddess (Haraway, 2006).

BACKGROUND

This study presents the events that the female protagonist of the movie experiences by using violence. The presentation of the use of violence by the female character in the film shot by a female director is interesting. Violence is not a phenomenon that can only be attributed to men, but in the patriarchal social order, it is generally men who increase violence in every field and put it into practice. The fact that women are more distant in their practice of violence makes it interesting that such a film that focuses on violence was shot by a female director. For this reason, the discourses of some theorists and thinkers discussing violence provide the diversification of discussions on violence. At the same time, this study tries to reveal the importance of making sense of the phenomenon of violence, which increases its momentum and diversity in the digital age, in a versatile way.

FILM ANALYSIS:

Cyborg Alexia – A Picture of Violence in the Digital Age

The movie begins with close-up images made of automobile accessories and the sounds of its metallic material. Along with these images, the increase in the tension music prioritizes that the film will tense the spectators. The transition to the movie world is made with the sound of a child sitting in the back of the car as if imitating the speed of the car. The child is making noises in the back seat of the car and continues to make noises despite her father's warnings. Then, as a reaction to the father who turned up the volume of the music, the child starts kicking the chair where her father is sitting. When the father looks back to stop her, a serious traffic accident occurs. The part of the body where the child's brain is operated on is presented to the spectators. The hard blows to the skull and the bloody, vivid image of the inside of the brain cause the spectator to question what to watch. The little girl will have to continue to live with a titanic plate inside her head and a permanent scar on her head for the rest of her life. It is informed to the spectators that the child named Alexia is a stubborn character who likes to attract attention and resists doing what she wants at a young age. In this flashback, the experience of Alexia and her family in the past is conveyed. Likewise, this issue is very important in terms of making sense of Alexia's inner world and psychological state. Some images are also important in terms of making sense of the film. Contrary to conventional productions, movies that think with images are full of elements that constantly emphasize that what is watched is a movie (İpek, 2019: 22).

Figure 1. Alexia with Titane Plaque.

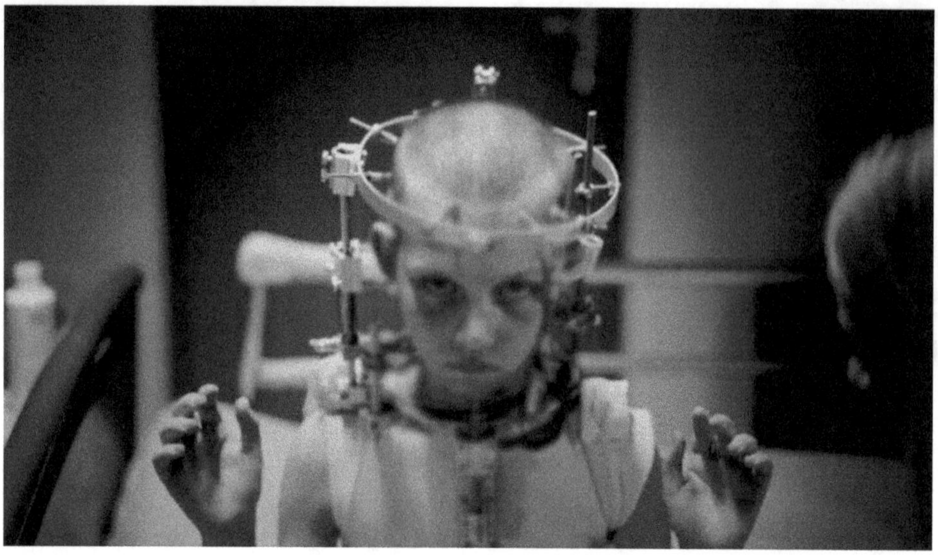

In front of a moving camera, we see Alexia as a young woman, accompanied by harsh music, and a stitch mark behind her ear. The camera follows Alexia. She enters a place where women perform erotic performances in a large area full of cars. The design of each car is unique and different; the camera close-ups the interior design and details of the cars. In each car, sexy-dressed women are performing seductive dances. In sexy, fetish clothes, erotic dances are performed on sports cars. Men watch and enjoy women in this area. The female characters are objects of desire in this space, while the male characters are scopophilic and voyeuristic. Men who get excited by watching women and desire them, regard women as commodities. Women who are paid per show try to earn money in this way while maintaining their lives. In most parts of the world, the fact that women are commodity-like objects of desire is presented in the narrative of the film as if it were a common rule.

The main female character of the movie, Alexia, has decided to return home after the show is over, and as she proceeds to her car, she encounters a fan who insists on kissing her. Although Alexia gets in her car, her fan wants to kiss her and forces her to do so. Alexia unexpectedly pulls a long, thin hairpin out of her hair and sticks it in the man's ear. The movie, which starts with serious tension, causes the spectators to be nailed to their seats. The presentation of both the sound and the images is both remarkable and tense at the beginning of the movie, immersing the spectators in the movie. With this move of Alexia, the spectators do not know what to watch and with this scene, where violence is presented very harshly, think about the distance between them and the movie. Returning to the area to clean up the dead man's vomit, Alexia sees that there is no one in the area and there is only one car left. She gets into the car and has a sexual experience with it. This scene opens the doors to Alexia's sexual world. While the spectators think that there is another person in the car, they are informed that there is no other person in the car. Feeling sexual feelings in her contact with the car, Alexia satisfies herself and takes pleasure by touching it. In this scene where she gets close to the car, it is understood that the car also takes pleasure from Alexia. At this point, it is seen that the sexual intercourse between the human and non-human seen in science fiction movies takes place. The fact that Alexia enjoys the car starts the process of questioning how human-like she is, in this scene.

It is remarkable that Alexia does not talk to her parents at home, is distant from them, and even looks at them with hatred. Alexia, who befriends another girl she met in the show area, goes to her house and spends time. Alexia and her friend develop intimacy. However, Alexia, who has black fluid coming from her phallic, concludes that she is pregnant and even takes a pregnancy test. Alexia is portrayed with an imagination of a human-looking, non-human creature that contains violence, enjoys sexual pleasure with cars, and becomes pregnant from a car after intercourse. Alexia, who meets Haraway's cyborg definitions, is a cyborg that makes feminist theories' debates about women possible again. With her image of social reality, which does not allow people to suspect her, and the titan plate she carries inside, her transcendent characteristics make it possible for her to exist as a cyborg.

While trying to leave the house of her newly met female friend, Alexia, who encounters a few people staying at home, kills all the people she sees at home in violent ways because rather than getting harmed, she does not want to be in close contact with people and she does not have any feelings other than hatred towards them. After killing and damaging people in horrific ways, she makes her way to her home. Thinking that her father guessed the violence she has done, Alexia sets fire to her mother and father's house while they are sleeping and lets them burn to death, leaving her house in flames and running away. Learning that she is wanted all over the country when she enters public places, Alexia sets out to deceive her family by posing as a missing child. Her purpose is to take shelter in a house. Breaking her nose to disguise herself as the missing child, Alexia inflicts serious damage to her body and goes to the police to state that she is the missing child, Adrien Legrand. The violence that Alexia inflicts on herself shows that she is not in a healthy mood, which must exist in a human, and reveals the lack of states such as compassion, love, and self-respect. As Haraway points out, cyborgs are good analysts with deviance and the skill to read the web of power well. Alexia uses practical ways to find a solution to the dangerous situation she is in and creates strategies to save herself, for which she follows deviant ways, both spiritually and concretely. Hannah Arent, in her work *On Violence* (1969), emphasizes the intertwining of power and violence (Arent, 2018: 57). According to Arendt, those who oppose violence with pure power will understand that they are struggling not only with people but also with tools made by human hands (Arent, 2018: 63). In this context, considering that cyborgs are beings created at the hands of a human, the human again takes himself on violence. In this dialectic, the human is the one who allows the creation of violence, and when confronted with it, he is the one who struggles; in fact, the human is the main source of violence. This philosophical inference reveals the critique of the patriarchal social order from the feminist theme in the context of the perception of Alexia's existence.

The father of the missing child perceives Alexia as his child upon notice from the police and opens up his house to her. This fire chief named Vincent is not a healthy person. He is a person who hurts his body to gain muscle by constantly giving himself injections. Vincent, who cannot talk to Alexia from the moment he meets her, does not force her. Even if he realizes that she is not his child, she does not speak up, because she, like Alexia, is a character lacking in love and care. Alexia, whose belly has grown during this time, wraps her belly and breasts tightly in cloth to hide them. By recruiting Alexia to work alongside the firefighters, Vincent wants her to mature and join life. Alexia's incomprehensible, strange image causes ridicule among firefighters.

From time to time, Vincent's relationship with fire is shown, as he exercises with a fire simulation. Vincent's relationship with life is as dangerous and distant as his relationship with fire. Living alone with his muscle-strengthening pills and injections, Vincent's only concern is to look muscular. He is alone, helpless, and single in his private sphere. Just as he is alone, helpless, and single when he goes to meet fire... Alexia, who is attempting to escape from Vincent's house, is unable to do so, and although she has a chance to kill him, she cannot. The emotional states that pregnancy brings to a woman are experienced by Alexia. Alexia, who does not even call 'dad' to her biological father, tries to help Vincent in his desperate moment and calls him 'dad'.

Alexia tries to harm her body by making harsh movements from time to time to get rid of the baby in her belly but cannot be successful. Every time she tries to miscarry, her face turns red, the veins in her belly become prominent, and black fluid comes out of her womb. The clothes she wraps to hide her belly leave deep scars on her upper body. Alexia is someone who is not afraid of harming not only others but also her own body. Violence is one of the basic concepts that Alexia internalizes in life. As she can easily harm and kill others, she also has the psychology of harming herself. According to Byung-Chul Han, the situation in which an act of violence takes place is often embedded in the system, and in a fabric that is inherent in the system. According to Slavoj Žižek, ideology, which generates social and symbolic violence, is like a natural condition of consent before every conscious decision. Stating that violence is exclusion and building a wall, Žižek says that the victims of violence are not only homines sacri, who are outside the welfare zone, but also other groups such as minorities and the unemployed. In his explanation of homines sacri, Giorgio Agamben indicates that the city of the dead and the dying, inhabited by people excluded from the civilized order, constitutes the post-apocalyptic death zone. Pierre Bourdieu and Johan Galtung, on the other hand, argue that both structural violence and symbolic violence will take place without the need for hierarchy. Therefore, the subject here becomes the system itself. There is no criminal subject that can be held responsible for oppression or exploitation (Han, 2018: 83- 87). Han's references to thinkers reveal the fact that ideology, which is the source of social, structural, and symbolic violence, harms all humanity. If we deepen the perspective of Bourdieu and Galtun more philosophically, it is remarkable that violence can exist everywhere and does not recognize hierarchy, so that the crime subject cannot be found. Likewise, we can argue that in the violence that Alexia inflicts on herself, the subject of the crime is not her because it is not only the ideological leaks in the power mechanism but also humanity itself that brings Alexia into society and makes her violence prone.

Vincent wants Alexia to participate in life while asking her to understand life by comparing it to real events. Taking Alexia with him while helping people, Vincent teaches her what to do in an emergency. The spectator sees Alexia, who has communicated with Vincent and did not communicate with her real father in the past while doing a favor. She tries to help a woman who is having trouble breathing. She tries to wake Vincent up in his difficult moment. Alexia wants to love Vincent sometimes with paternal warmth, sometimes with her desire for a man, wavering between mixed feelings because the fact that she did not grow up in a healthy development process, neither in the communication she established with her family for years nor in her adulthood, is presented understandably. Lack of communication, lack of love, the process of finding an unhealthy sexual identity, and friendlessness are the realities that Alexia has internalized throughout her life. Even her family, who could understand that she was in an unhealthy psychological state, did not help her, therefore, the foundations for serial murder were laid. Perhaps for the first time, she encounters concepts such as benevolence, finding love for love, kindness, and friendship, thanks to Vincent.

While having fun with her firefighter friends, Alexia's supporter, who was watched in surprise by her friends with her erotic dance show, was again Vincent. Remembering her femininity after her dance show, Alexia has sexual intercourse with a fire truck after this show. This scene is important for feminist film theories and practice because the male characters, who have ambiguous feelings and thoughts about Alexia's gender and sexual identity, do not enjoy her sexy dance show, and even the feeling of awkwardness and not understanding is at the forefront in their gaze. For the spectator, who knows Alexia's gender, the sense of identifying with or watching Alexia also includes complex situations because, for the female spectator, Alexia is a violent and spiritually tragic character. In her work *Film and The Masquerade: Theorizing the Female Spectator* (1992), Mary Ann Doane examines the concept of mask in detail with psychoanalytic explanations, along with identification in terms of female characters and spectators. According to Doane, the mask opens the door to thinking of those different from the identifications suggested by classical narrative cinema in terms of identification between the character and spectators.

"While the desire of the female spectator allows Doane to make a narcissistic identification through the mask, the transvestite glance comes with it when the female spectator becomes a male spectator. Tragic events and emotions in the film narrative, which are followed by masochistic sentiments through masks, also clarify why women use the mask. In this context, female spectators feel an excessive identification of masculinity as they identify themselves with female characters. On the other hand, the female spectator can feel narcissism by making herself an object of desire at the time of identification" (as cited in Özdemir, 2018: 113).

At this point, no character offers the female spectator to watch the movie with pleasure from the woman. In terms of the male spectator, Alexia's masculine appearance and non-sexual appearance do not show her as an enjoyable character. Alexia is not an object of desire, but she also has an ambiguous visual and sexuality about how to look at her and feel about her from the spectator's point of view. Therefore, Alexia's appearance and behavior that deconstructs sexuality categories reveal the inference that sexualities are given as patriarchal codes and opens the door to discussion of heteronormative social gender indicators.

Towards the end of the movie, Alexia, who is in the last stages of her pregnancy, goes into physical trouble giving birth to her child. Vincent tries to help her give birth to her baby as Alexia suffers black fluids coming out of her belly, mouth, and womb. The labor pain of Alexia, whose skin on the navel is gradually torn, metallic images appear from each torn part, and the veins in her body become quite evident and the movie tries to present it as both a painful and an unbearable experience. It is seen that a metallic material, i.e. titan, begins to appear in the ear area of Alexia, whose stitch scar behind the ear is torn during birth. All these scenes remind us of the existence of non-human, strange-looking creatures in the human body, or the emergence of frightening creatures that suddenly appear on earth in David Cronenberg's cinema. Cronenberg also makes the spectators think about the possibility of "unintelligible, strange" creatures with incomprehensible and violent situations in which there is the human body.

Vincent spreads the legs of Alexia, who has difficulties in giving birth to her baby and enables the baby to come out with the normal delivery method. The titanium plate on the spinal cord of the baby and the skin color of the baby indicate that a normal human baby was not born. Alexia has given birth to a human-like creature but not a fully human being. Alexia has not had sexual intercourse with a man but has had intercourse with automobiles throughout the film narrative. The born baby is a baby born after having intercourse with an automobile. During the birth, Alexia died, giving birth to a non-human cyborg being. Alexia, who has experienced and felt the types of violence in different ways, feels the self of hers in different physical violence while giving birth to her baby, and passes away with the last severe pain she feels. It is as if she has a one-on-one encounter with the god of violence. In his work *Der Antichrist* (1895), Friedrich Wilhelm Nietzsche explains that wars were fought in the name of the god of war, who was prone to violence in the Aztecs, and tries to explain the use of violence: "A people who still have not lost faith in themselves also have their own god. … They project the pleasure of being

Figure 2. Alexia while giving birth.

themselves, the feeling of power.... What good would a god do if it did not know anger, revenge, jealousy, ridicule, deceit, violence, and even did not taste the pleasures of victory and destruction?" (Han, 2018: 24). Alexia is a cyborg who declared herself her god during her life on earth, brutally murdered people as if fighting, and suppressed her feelings of anger, revenge, and jealousy with violence. As Han stated, killing protects from death and violence serves as a thanatological method against the approaching death threat. As violence is used, the sense of power increases (Han, 2018: 25). From the moment she feels that a baby is developing in her womb, Alexia starts to commit murders by increasing the momentum of violence. For Alexia, who prioritizes that the baby to be born will lead her to death, violence has become both inevitable and a kinetic act that reminds her of her power. In this context, Han's thoughts coincide with Alexia's practice of using violence. Adam Phillips indicates that "the subject of fear is the future in the past" (Phillips, 1998: 69). This thought epitomizes Alexia's fear of her inner world. In David Lynch's presentation of violence, the inner world of the characters is one of the subjects that the spectator makes sense of. In Lynch's cinema, violence is a transition from outside to inside, it penetrates the body of the world, and life and violence are the same and one thing (Atayman, 2006: 209). What is also seen in Titane is the fact that the force that pushes Alexia to violence comes from outside and it embodies deeply inside by taking over her body and soul. This fact is so real that it reveals the perception that people have normalized the violence that is constantly encountered in life.

Another viewpoint supporting Haraway, who states that Irigaray and Wittig claim thoughts that question the body, is that of Judith Butler. Irigaray reverses Simone de Beauvoir's claim that the woman is the gender, and argues that woman is not the gender attributed to her, but the masculine gender disguised as otherness. By marking the female gender in this way, phallogocentrism produces dreams about its self-stimulating desire (Butler, 2012: 60). Alexia is a character who, for a long part of the movie, tries to get rid of all her feminine features with her male appearance. Having female biology, disguised as a man, whose gender is not easily understood, perceived as strange in the social order, Alexia actually puts forward a stance that questions the basic idea of phallogocentrism. Even if she is pregnant, her pregnancy is not perceived as a normal pregnancy process by the spectator. It is possible to indicate that those of the female spectator who have experienced pregnancy have distances in identification with Alexia. The sexy, beautiful Alexia at the beginning of the movie has turned into a physically ugly, skinny, passive male character after the breaking point of the movie. This transformation is represented so close to reality that the spectator cannot perceive Alexia as Alexia that they saw at the beginning of the movie, but the female spectator has to distance herself in the process of identification with her. Rather than perceiving Alexia as an object of desire because of her ambiguous and ugly image, the male spectator may also experience the feeling of dislike for her, perhaps because of the black liquid coming from her, and because of the frightening wounds and deformity on her body.

FUTURE RESEARCH DIRECTIONS

Studies on violence have been carried out in every field of social sciences for years. The presentation of violence in the cinema confronts the spectators with different narrative styles. Making sense of violence with cinema allows more concrete thoughts to be generated. In the digital age, the appearances and contents of violence continue to change. By sharing every changing and transforming concept with the spectators, cinema allows them to think again about every subject it presents. The concept of cyborgs started to exist in violence, which is one of the most important issues of the digital age and creates the perception that violence will no longer come only from humans. Therefore, future studies in the field of cinema need to rethink how futuristic concepts are presented in films, in what contexts they are represented, and how the spectator makes sense of these presentations and representations. Futurist perspectives, which prioritize the proliferation of non-human beings, have many ideas about what these beings will add to the world. However, at this point, the fact that non-human beings lack human emotions is worrying for the future of humanity. Especially if we assume that the phenomenon of violence has frightening dimensions even in humans, it will not even be possible to predict the extent of violence in non-human beings. If issues such as the ontological approach to violence in the presentation of violence in films, and the identification relationship that the spectators establish with violence in their receptions of violence are examined in more detail, some questions about the representation of violence can be brought. In the context of this study, more detailed research can be conducted with scientific focus groups on the presentation of female characters as non-human beings and whether female spectators feel human in character identification. These suggestions will be important in determining the approach of the human to the non-human and may pave the way for humanity to develop defense strategies to protect itself from its own productions.

CONCLUSION

Alexia is a creature of the post-gender world, as Haraway claims for cyborgs. Titane brings forward the presentation mechanism that makes sexualities questioned and many emotions about Alexia's sexuality such as pleasure, desire, sexual intercourse, emotional intimacy, etc. In the movie, the titanium plate on Alexia's body and the biological and physical features that are not seen in humans do not make it possible to directly describe her as human. This study claims that Alexia is a cyborg. Features that Haraway attributes to the cyborg-like dissent, being irrelevant to innocence, not dreaming of starting a family based on the organic family model, not having an innocent body, embracing irony, being ethereal, and her gender being a local possibility to take revenge on a global scale are features that overlap and parallel with Alexia's presentation. Avoiding close contact with people, let alone starting a family, Alexia is a character far from bodily innocence, who can appear whenever she wants and can take on an invisible form like ether when she wants. Therefore, the fact that Alexia is a cyborg, which contains dangers for humanity, concretely represents one of the most violent possibilities that arise as a result of human mechanization. Alexia, who creates love and lack of communication inside her, more or less shows what humanoid robots, which may appear in the coming years, can do to the humanity that produces them if they are designed to be devoid of human characteristics. The world that Haraway imagines in the context of cyborgs draws an ontologically more positive planet because her cyborg imagery, bodies, and tools are capable of showing people the way out of the labyrinth of dualities explained with their help. Even though Alexia displaces gender codes and makes one think about all existing dual-gender frameworks, she also shows that non-human beings point to danger with the violence phenomenon that exists in them.

REFERENCES

Arendt, H. (2018). On violence (B. Peker, Trans.). İstanbul, Turkey: İletişim Yayınları.

Atayman, V. (2006). Şiddetin Mitolojisi. İstanbul, Turkey: Donkişot Güncel Yayınlar.

Butler, J. (2012). Gender trouble: Feminism and the subversion of identity (B. Ertür, Trans.). İstanbul, Turkey: Metis Yayınları.

Han, C.-B. (2018). Topologie der gewalt (D. Zaptçıoğlu, Trans.). İstanbul, Turkey: Metis Yayınları.

Haraway, D. (2006). A cyborg manifesto: Science, technology, and socialist-feminism in the late twentieth century," in simians, cyborgs and women: The reinvention of nature (O. Akınhay, Trans.). İstanbul, Turkey: Agora Yayınları.

İpek, Ö. (2019). İmgeler Arasında: Yeni Türkiye Sinemasının Düşünen İmgeleri Üzerine. İstanbul, Turkey: Doruk Yayınları.

Özdemir, B. G. (2018). *A Film Toz Bezi Criticized by Within The Scope of Identification and Representation Facts Associated With Masquerade and Space in Academic Research in Social, Human and Administrative Sciences II*. Gece Kitaplığı.

Phillips, A. (1998). Terrors and experts (T. Erdem, Trans.). İstanbul, Turkey: Metis Yayınları.

KEY TERMS AND DEFINITIONS

Cyborg: A person whose body contains mechanical or electrical devices and whose abilities are like a post-human.

Female Characters: They are the ones who perform the representation of women's roles in film narratives.

Representation: Presenting an event, person, or situation to the spectators with certain narrative strategies.

Violence: Physical force used so as to injure, damage, or destroy.

Chapter 3
Leave Me Alone!
Sexual Bullying at Work

Shalini Ramdeo
The University of the West Indies, St. Augustine, Trinidad and Tobago

Riann Singh
The University of the West Indies, St. Augustine, Trinidad and Tobago

ABSTRACT

The contemporary work environment is plagued with many problems. Two such issues are the occurrence of sexual harassment and workplace bullying. These pervasive behaviors continue to proliferate, with attempts to curtail such acts from occurring. Interestingly, when employees are subjected to bullying tactics that are sexual and/or gender-related in nature, sexual bullying is occurring. This classification is novel in its application to the workplace setting. The authors seek to shed light on the issue, as within the workplace setting understanding this phenomenon is at an embryotic stage. This chapter considers the key elements of workplace bullying, sexual harassment, and conceptualizes sexual bullying. The possible consequences of sexual bullying on employees and the organization are explored. Further, victims of sexual bullying who are targets of cyberbullying is another consideration worthy of exploration. Possible solutions and recommendations are advanced as are areas for further research.

INTRODUCTION

Within the contemporary workplace, bullying and sexual harassment are pervasive issues that workers continue to experience at an alarming rate. According to the Workplace Bullying Foundation, a survey on workplace bullying from the United States of America (USA) in 2021 revealed that "39% suffer abusive conduct at work, another 22% witness it, 61% are affected by it, and 73% are aware that workplace bullying happens" (WBI 2021, 6). It was further projected that in the USA alone, workers who have been directly bullied are around 48.6 million and those who witnesses bullying is another 30.6 million. Another prevalent workplace issue is sexual harassment. In Canada, the Survey on Sexual Misconduct at Work revealed that in 2020, one in four women and one in six men have experienced inappropriate

DOI: 10.4018/978-1-6684-5426-8.ch003

sexualized behaviors (Burczycka, 2021). Further, more than one in five employees targeted indicated that an individual with organizational authority perpetrated sexual behavior towards them. In the United Kingdom, sexual harassment research conducted in 2016 revealed that more than half (52%) of women, and nearly two-thirds (63%) of women aged 18-24 years old have experienced sexual harassment at work (Trades Union Congress 2016). Further, in many of the reported cases of sexual harassment the perpetrator was male (88%), and nearly one in five (17%) women reported that it was someone with direct authority over them, or their line manager. Findings are consistent in Australia where it was estimated that one in every three persons experienced workplace sexual harassment over the last five years, that is, 2017 to 2022 (Safe Work Australia, 2022).

In organizations, the fundamental principles and rights of workers promote equality of opportunity and treatment in employment and occupation (International Labor Organization, 2022). Employees' psychological contracts are shaped by organizational principles, work conditions, and intra-office relationships conflict. When an employee experiences a breach in the psychological contract, the result is a toxic work environment, which damages the long-term viability of the organization (Harder, Rash, & Wagner 2014, 207). Workplace bullying and sexual harassment are toxic events which violates the fundamental rights of workers as they are subjected to degrading and dehumanizing behaviors at the 'hands' of their perpetrator (s). When the victim is exposed to continued sexual mistreatment, this can have a detrimental effect, not only on the victim, but also bystanders, and the organization. The question arises, what happens when the bully uses tactics that are sexual in nature towards the target? While both phenomena have been explored under the umbrella of workplace aggression, but often investigated separately, in this article the researchers explore a hybrid of both, that is, sexual bullying.

OBJECTIVES

Given the ever-evolving business environment and work dynamics, workplace issues are also mutating with sexual bullying becoming more apparent. It is against this backdrop that this chapter seeks to achieve the following objectives:

1) Describe the key elements of workplace bullying, workplace sexual harassment, and workplace sexual bullying.
2) Discuss the consequences of workplace sexual bullying on employees and the organization.
3) Evaluate how victims of workplace sexual bullying can be targets of cyberbullying.
4) Propose approaches that organizations can adopt to deter workplace sexual bullying from occurring.

BACKGROUND

Workplace Bullying and Sexual Harassment

Within the contemporary workplace, hostile work environments and cultures continue to permeate and flourish. Increasing pressures to survive and thrive are promoting the deployment of more intense and goal-oriented performance management systems whose ends justify the means (Harrington, Warren, and Rayner, 2011). In many instances, this is fostering a breeding ground for aggressive workplace behaviors to proliferate. Aggression in the workplace comes from multiple sources and causes some form of stressor for the target. The following sections provide insights into two widespread workplace issues, that is, workplace bullying and workplace sexual harassment.

Workplace Bullying

In the past, the term bullying was synonymous to children in school yards. Today, when applied to the organization's setting, bullying continues to be a pervasive issue that is evolving and adversely impacting workers and the organizational climate. Over the last three decades there has been a proliferation of research on this issue, drawing attention to its antecedents and consequences. In conceptualizing workplace bullying, much of the current debate revolves around the inconsistencies in coherent terminologies used within the academic literature. In reviewing the terminology used to describe this phenomenon around the world, it is referred to as incivility (Andersson and Pearson 1999), victimization (Aquino & Bradfield, 2000), workplace psychological harassment (Crawshaw, 2009), social undermining (Duffy, Ganster & Pagon, 2002), mobbing (Leymann, 1996) and bullying (Einarsen et al., 2003). While there are varying terminologies, there is growing agreement among academics regarding the significant features that define workplace bullying.

For this chapter, in analyzing the constituents, workplace bullying is defined as "an escalating process in which one or more employees are subjected to negative psychological and physical abuse recurring over an extended period of time (usually 6 months or more), where the target is reduced to a psychologically inferior state, and it creates a hostile work environment to those exposed" (Ramdeo et al., 2020). Within this definition, there are certain key aspects that delineates this phenomenon. Firstly, there is a psychological imbalance that occurs where the target is reduced to a psychologically inferior state. Secondly, both the target and the perpetrator are from the same organization. Thirdly, the perpetrator may target one employee or a group of employees. Fourthly, there is a time element involved as the individual is exposed to such repeated abuse over a period of time, for instance usually 6 months or more. The subjective interpretation of behaviors directed to individuals must be considered as well. For instance, an employee may classify an experience as bullying after one occurrence.

Notably, there are different tactics that the perpetrator may use towards the target. These can be classified as person-related bullying and/or work-related bullying (Glasø, Nielsen, & Einarsen, 2009). The behaviors related to person-related bullying include aspects such as humiliation or ridicule in front of others, making offensive remarks, spreading malicious rumors and gossip, intentionally ignoring someone, constant criticism, direct criticism, and physical threats. Excessive monitoring of work, ignoring views and opinions, assigning meaningless tasks, withholding information which can affect a worker's performance, setting unreasonable or impossible deadlines, unmanageable workloads, misuse of power or supervision (for instance, intentionally blocking promotion and/or training opportunities) are all behaviors associated with work-related bullying. Traditional bullying occurs in the face-to-face, in-person setting where the target is exposed to such behaviors while at the physical workplace. However, with technological advancements, bullying has evolved beyond the physical workplace to limitless possibilities, referred to as cyberbullying.

The question arises, why engage in bullying behaviors? A bully may direct bullying actions and behaviors towards others for several reasons (Salin, 2003). For instance, the bully may be dissatisfied with the work environment, there is a power imbalance between the perpetrator and target, and within the workplace there is diminutive or no consequence for exhibiting such behaviors. Studies have supported hypotheses regarding positional power as a precondition to creating a favorable bullying situation. Tehrani (2012, p. 5) refers to positional power as the "power derived from the person's role or position. Managers and supervisors can abuse their power to impose unfair restrictions or rules affecting one or more people". Therefore, the action of the perpetrator is a partial reflection of their job position as the manipulation of power takes place between the supervisor/manager and the subordinate or employees of equal standing in the organization (Tepper, 2000; Wheeler, Halbesleben, & Shanine, 2010). Another factor that needs to be considered is the personality of the perpetrator. The personality and presence of some persons makes it difficult for others to challenge them where such behaviors can be used to intimidate and bully others. This inability to identify as a bully can hinder attempts to effectively mitigate bullying situations by confronting the bully (Crawshaw, 2012). It should be noted that national cultures and societal influences affect tolerance and prevalence rates of bullying (Jacobson, Hood, & Van Buren III, 2014). Therefore, in some cultures bullying behaviors are considered 'normal' where policies are developed for compliance and public relation, however, enforcement is lacking.

Sexual Harassment

Another prevalent workplace issue that employees may experience is sexual harassment. Sexual harassment refers to "perceived implicit or explicit unwelcomed sex-related behaviors that can take the form of gender harassment, unwanted sexual attention, and/or sexual coercion" (Balwant et al., 2019, p. 440). From this definition, there are multiple dimensions to sexual harassment. *Firstly*, gender harassment includes a variety of degrading behaviors directed to the target where these behaviors can be grouped into two categories, that is, sexist hostility and sexual hostility. Sexist hostility refers to discriminatory experiences because of one's gender (for instance, insulting or derogatory gender-related remarks). Further, sexual hostility refers to sexually explicit experiences (for instance, sexual jokes). *Secondly*, unwanted sexual attention refers to actions directed to the target that is not reciprocated and gestures that are unwelcomed where there are sexual verbal and/or non-verbal acts (for instance, sending intrusive letters, calls of a sexual nature, touching, and grabbing). *Thirdly*, sexual coercion, also known as *quad pro quo*, occurs when organizational rewards are offered by one person to another in exchange for sexual favors (for instance, a promotion or an increase in one's salary/pay). Therefore, sexual harassment can be classified as sexual discrimination and can be a one-time occurrence to be classified as sexual harassment. From the dimensions, it is apparent that individuals experience many forms of harassment. Verbal harassment may appear less threatening to the target than if the harassment involves physical contact. However, the psychological and emotional abuse may cause higher levels of post-traumatic stress disorder (McDonald, 2012). Similar to the perpetrator in workplace bullying, with sexual harassment, the harasser can be an organizational agent (for instance, supervisor, manager, employer) or it can be someone of equal standing (for instance, coworker/s). Interestingly, in most instances, the harasser is a male.

Further, according to Cortina and Berdahl (2008) sexual harassment can be viewed from three perspectives: the legal perspective, the social-psychological perspective, and the lay or public perspective. From a *legal perspective*, the term sexual harassment emerged in the 1970s, where lawmakers recognized the pervasive act as discrimination. The United States of America Equal Employment Opportunity Commission (EEOC) in 1980 defined sexual harassment as "Unwelcome sexual advances, requests for sexual favors, and other verbal or physical conduct of a sexual nature constitute sexual harassment when this conduct explicitly or implicitly affects an individual's employment, unreasonably interferes with an individual's work performance, or creates an intimidating, hostile, or offensive work environment" (p.

74617). Therefore, under state law it is illegal in most countries where an individual can face legal action as a consequence for sexual harassment behaviors being directed to another individual. From the *social-psychological* perspective, this is based upon women's experiences where sexual harassment is defined as "unwanted sex-related behavior at work that is appraised by the recipient as offensive, exceeding her resources, or threatening her well-being" (Fitzgerald et al., 1997, p. 15). This perspective advances that individuals' perceptions of specific behaviors rather than work outcomes would determine one's perceptions of sexual harassment. Since men are also subjected to sexual harassment in the workplace, this perspective has been expanded to include all genders. From the *lay or public perspective*, the general opinions of the public must be considered as it can influence how employees and management perceive this phenomenon. According to this perspective, sexual harassment is defined according to the society's changing perceptions of sexual harassment with variations over time (Cortina & Berdahl 2008; Quick & McFadyen, 2017). While there are differing perspectives advanced to delineate this phenomenon, these variations should not detract the pervasive nature of such sexual acts within the work environment.

MAIN FOCUS OF THE CHAPTER

What is Sexual Bullying? Exploring the Concept

Interestingly, these toxic workplace phenomena have evolved where bullying and sexual harassment can be associated, rather than being viewed in silos. Here both phenomena are a person performing the pervasive act and a person on the receiving end of that act. Therefore, sexual bullying is similar in nature (Turner-Moore et al., 2021). While often attributed to children and young adults where sexuality or gender is used to degrade someone, sexual bullying can also occur in the workplace. Within the context of children and adolescents, sexual bullying refers to "a dyadic process in which one individual is the recipient of (repeated) unpleasant teasing, taunting, harassing, or threatening behavior inflicted by another individual. The instigator of said behavior acts with a conscious malicious intent and at least one party has a sexual interest in the other. The instigator's behavior may appear 'romantic' in nature, yet there is a lack of consideration or appreciation for the recipient, and a power imbalance exists. The social environment allows this behavior" (Fredland, 2009, p. 101). Here, the harassment experienced is related to sexuality, sexualized, and/or related to a gender expression. In the work environment, a power imbalance may not exist as an individual may experience sexual bullying by a coworker or subordinate.

Sexual harassment and bullying are different ways that a perpetrator inflicts harm on a victim. In the literature, there is an ongoing discussion on whether sexual harassment and bullying are distinct or related. Here it should be noted that while sexual harassment and bullying are similar, they are not the same, rather, sexual harassment can be considered a form of workplace bullying. The main difference is the time element in defining both concepts, as with workplace bullying the target is exposed over a period of time where the behaviors are recurrent, however, with sexual harassment it can be a one-time occurrence (Nabe-Nielsen et al., 2016). With a plethora of definitions advanced for each, there are key overlapping dimensions to their conceptualizations. With sexual harassment, the power dynamics is one of the main factors fueling such behaviors being directed to the target. Stemming from this discussion, the concept of sexual bullying is explored.

For this chapter, the authors operationalize workplace sexual bullying as *an escalating process in which one or more employees are subjected to negative psychological and/or physical abuse, where the intention is sexual and/or gender-related, and recurring over an extended period of time (usually 6 months or more). This reduces the target to a psychologically inferior state and creates a hostile work environment.* The differentiating characteristic of workplace bullying and sexual bullying in the workplace is the intent. Furthermore, it is important to understand what constitutes sexual bullying. *Firstly*, the abuse directed to the target is sexual in nature, where the target is subjected to sexual language, gestures, and/or physical abuse, that is unwanted sexual attention. Such behaviors create a sexually hostile work environment. With workplace bullying, it may not be sexually motivated. When the acts directed to the target is sexually motivated, then it will be classified as sexual bullying. Therefore, the bullying tactics used by the perpetrator include unwelcomed sexual behaviors to reduce the individual to a psychologically inferior state. *Secondly*, with sexual bullying, the individual may be targeted because of their gender, similar to gender harassment. Therefore, from a social-psychological perspective, any gender can be targeted. However, with workplace bullying, the individual's gender may not be the primary motive driving the bullying behaviors of the perpetrator. Further, as with bullying, classifying behaviors as sexual bullying is challenging as the perceptions of the target much be considered. For instance, an individual may perceive an act as sexual bullying after one occurrence. *Thirdly*, the time frame suggested considers the severity of the issue. With workplace bullying for classification purposes, a period of 6 months is identified when viewing bullying from a general perspective. However, with sexual bullying, given the sexual nature of the behaviors where it can be direct or indirect, psychological and/or physical, the proposed time-period is relative for classification purposes. It should be reiterated that the perceptions of the target must be considered. For instance, frequent physical gestures may be perceived as more severe and direct, than verbal acts, for instance, sexual jokes.

Since sexual harassment is considered illegal, in instances where the organization fails to address claims of sexual bullying, the victim can report this to the authorities as there are national and international standards, and country/state laws protecting individuals from sexual harassment. Further, the perpetrator bullies the victim with sexual acts and comments that can occur in person or using some form of technology. Aggression in the workplace can come from various sources, that is vertical (that is, superior subordinate) and horizontal (that is, a coworker). Within the workplace bullying literature, an employee may experience supervisory bullying, referred to as abusive supervision. Abusive supervision refers to the "subordinates' perceptions of the extent to which supervisors engage in the sustained display of hostile verbal and nonverbal behaviors excluding physical contact" (Tepper, 2000, p. 178). This operationalization introduced subjective assessment on the proposition that an individual can view the supervisor's behavior as abusive in one context and as non-abusive in another context. Therefore, an individual can experience sexual bullying where the perpetrator is a superior. In such instances, the vulnerability of the target is intensified due to the lack of status, power, or a formal process. However, the victim can report such claims to the authorities, thereby initiating legal proceedings against the perpetrator and/or the organization. Further, coworkers may engage in sexual bullying tactics as well. Here, both the perpetrator and the target are at the same level of power and organizational status within the reciprocal exchange. In such instances, the victim can initiate legal proceedings against the perpetrator if the organization fails to address the claim.

Consequences of Sexual Bullying on Employees and The Organization

Building on the workplace aggression literature, sexual bullying has far-reaching consequences for the workforce and the organization. The urgency and significance in addressing these adverse consequences are important as they distract from the development and maintenance of a healthy workplace and corporate reputation. Given the nature of this phenomenon, there are implications for employees and the organization. However, empirical evidence on the consequences of sexual bullying in the workplace is sparce.

Employees

When employees are exposed to sexual bullying the effects of those exposed can be classified as work-related, person-related, and health and well-being related outcomes. The discrepancy experienced ranges along a continuum where on one end the created discrepancy is manageable while on the other end it is extreme. When the bullying behavior is sustained, the employee may experience cognitive dissonance, which impacts their productivity and adversely affects employee health and well-being. In this chapter, these two consequences are explored.

Employee Productivity: When employees experience sexual bullying, it is anticipated that various negative work-related consequences will occur. Drawing from research on sexual harassment and workplace bullying, some attitudinal and behavioral consequences are explored. Research findings suggest that sexual harassment experiences are associated with negative job outcomes such as decreased job satisfaction, lower organizational commitment, withdrawing from work (Willness, Steel, & Lee, 2007) and employees who were sexually harassed reported a decrease in job satisfaction, greater turnover intentions, and a higher rate of absenteeism (Markin & Shah, 2014). Reasonably consistent research findings have classified the work-related outcomes of workplace bullying into two categories. The attitudinal/affective category includes job satisfaction, turnover intentions and organizational commitment, while the behavioral category includes performance and absenteeism (Nielsen & Einarsen, 2012; Tepper, 2007). According to Hershcovis and Barling (2010, p. 24) workplace aggression is defined as "negative acts that are perpetrated against an organization or its members and that victims are motivated to avoid". Within the workplace aggression frameworks, the findings by Hershcovis and Barling (2010) provide meta-analytic evidence in support of varying attitudinal, behavioral, and health reactions to workers for different sources of aggression. Supervisor aggression had the strongest negative relationships on job satisfaction, affective commitment, intentions to quit and organizational deviance, followed by co-worker aggression and these workplace attitudes and behaviors. Their findings provide support for the variations in outcomes to aggression from different sources as evidenced in the magnitude of the effects. Since sexual bullying can be classified as workplace aggression, one can anticipate that the resulting work-related consequences will be similar to those experienced by targets and victims of workplace bullying and sexual harassment. Therefore, employees who experience sexual bullying may exhibit decreases in job satisfaction, organizational commitment, and increases in turnover intentions and organizational deviance.

Employee Health and Well-Being related outcomes: The dissonance experienced by targets and victims can increase the risk of psychological and psychosomatic health complaints. Further, an employee's physical health and physiological health may also be adversely affected. This is similar to research findings for workplace bullying (Lewis, Sheehan, & Davies, 2008; Vartia, 2001, Nielsen & Einarsen, 2012). Further, sexual harassment has been associated with poor physical and mental health, and even symptoms of post-traumatic stress disorder (Willness, Steel &, Lee 2007). Research conducted by Nabe-Nielsen et al. (2016) with 7650 individuals from Denmark where observations were collected over a two-year observation period, found that bullying and unwanted sexual attention were prospectively associated with long-term sickness absence. Drawing on the similarities of the health and well-being related outcomes of both workplace bullying and sexual harassment, it is anticipated that with exposure to sexual bullying, similar effects may occur. Research further suggests that employees who experience verbal sexual harassment are at a higher risk of suffering from post-traumatic stress disorder due to the prolonged psychological impact that it has on the victim than with physical abuse (McDonald, 2012).

Organization

When sexual bullying occurs, there are various issues that the organization must consider. In this chapter, three areas are explored, that is, the liability to the employer/organization, the corporate reputation, and the financial impact.

Liability to employer/organization: Sexual harassment is illegal and can result in lawsuits being brought against the organization when the perpetrator is a supervisor. In determining the liability of the employer, two conditions must be considered, that is, the employer knew about the sexual harassment and the employer failed to take the appropriate corrective action. In the USA, Supreme Court ruling on the matter of Burlington Industries, Inc. v. Ellerth and Faragher v. City of Boca Raton, established the rule that "[a]n employer is subject to vicarious liability to a victimized employee for an actionable hostile environment created by a supervisor with immediate (or successively higher) authority over the employee" (as cited in Bankers 2013, p. 1786). Therefore, when the perpetrator is a supervisor, then the organization can be liable. With sexual bullying, these conditions also apply as the employer can be held liable for creating a hostile environment. In such hostile environments, the employer may know of sexual bullying if a complaint is filed to management about a supervisor or manager, and if it is openly practiced or known among employees.

Corporate Reputation: The possibility of tainting an organization's reputation through public exposure is always possible where the public backlash from bullying and sexual harassment claims can have dire consequences for organizations. For instance, a single sexual harassment claim can dramatically affect the public perceptions on gender equity for the entire organization. With sexual bullying, this can also have serious repercussions as the organization may be viewed as less equitable than when other transgressions are made. This can affect the ability to recruit top talent as well as retaining talented employees. Therefore, organizations need to be responsive and proactive when claims are made that contain a sexual component, as this benefit alleged victims and enhances public perception as well.

Financial Impact: In the USA, for 2019, the Equal Employment Opportunity Commission (EEOC) received over 7,514 claims of sexual harassment, which resulted in $68 million in direct settlements (U.S. Equal Employment Opportunity Commission, 2021). When claims are made, the legal expenses and costs of settlements can adversely affect the organization's financial standings. Further, organizations may incur higher insurance costs as the fear of potential legal risks associated with sex-based harassment would lead to selecting plans with greater coverage. Therefore, when sexual bullying occurs, the action or inaction of the organization will determine the financial impact that such behaviors can have.

Victims Of Sexual Bullying as Targets of Cyberbullying

Technology continues to revolutionize the workplace as it is the primary communication medium for organizational success. The proliferation and use of the internet, virtual communication platforms, the use of electronic mail and the increasing accessibility and use of electronic devices such as computers and cellular phones are required to create a virtual workspace for employees. There are instances where the perpetrator may not limit their advances to the face-to-face setting but extend this through technological means. With the rise in alternative work arrangement options available to workers (Ramdeo & Singh, 2021), remote work has provided an opportunity for cyberbullying to proliferate as 'work' is no longer a well-defined activity with clear boundaries. In the face-to-face, physical environment, the victim of sexual bullying is able to 'escape' their perpetrator when they leave the organization on a daily basis. However, cyberbullying is not restricted by time, tools, or location as the perpetrator continues to direct advances toward the victim on a continuous basis using technological means. The blurring of boundaries with work and technology, fueled with social media and mobile platforms are changing the interaction among employees. In such instances, the trapped feeling experienced by the victim is never ending as the perpetrator can establish contact at any time.

It has become apparent that bullying and sexual harassment are not confined to face-to-face work environments but has evolved to the perpetrator using some form of technology to target their victims. This is referred to as cyberbullying where it can be direct or indirect, and the perpetrator uses electronic means to taunt, harass or intimidate the target by communication via messages, pictures, and webpages to target their peers (Ramdeo & Singh, 2020). With sexual bullying, there are many behaviors of a sexual nature that are directed to the target, for example, the perpetrator may share sexual content with the target in person or via electronic means, engage in emotional blackmail, spreading rumors of a sexual nature, and inappropriate sexual innuendos constantly directed to the target. As many persons continue to work remotely where technology facilitates employee communication and interactions, victims of sexual bullying being targeted through cyberbullying may be more widespread than before. There is the ongoing humiliation and distress experienced by the victim as images may be circulated virtually that have the potential to adversely affect the victim's reputation and career.

There are many different forms of cyberbullying tactics used by perpetrators. These include flaming, exclusion, outing, masquerading, denigration, and harassment (Ramdeo & Singh, 2021). Of particular interest is harassment where the cyberbully repeatedly sends an individual or group of individuals malicious and offensive messages. Here cyberstalking can emerge where the bully sends inappropriate messages and continuous threats which can then manifest into physical harassment. With victims of sexual bullying who are targets of cyberbullying, the messages sent can include sexual jokes, inappropriate pictures, and messages that are sexual. Further, inappropriate gender-related messages can also be shared with the target (s).

While some have argued that cyberbullying is a type of bullying, there are key differentiators. For sexual bullying, certain differentiators apply. Firstly, with cyberbullying there is anonymity. Therefore, the target may be subjected to sexual and gender-based content from an anonymous source, that is shared via a virtual platform. Secondly, the personal power of the victim is diminished as the power of technology may fuel the powerlessness of the target. With face-to-face bullying, the victim is able to regain his/her power upon leaving the organization after work. However, with cyberbullying the target is at the mercy of technology and the ability of the perpetrator to reach the target. While research on cyberbullying is sparce, research findings suggest that victims experience lower job satisfaction, organizational commitment, and higher turnover intentions (Lim & Teo 2009; Coyne et al., 2017; Muhonen et al., 2017). Therefore, it is important for employers and employees to become aware of this phenomenon of sexual bullying where preventative and corrective measures can be developed and implemented to protect workers especially when the employee is also a target of cyberbullying.

Approaches That Organizations Can Adopt to Deter Sexual Bullying from Occurring

Within the work environment, developing and implementing preventative measures are necessary to deter this pervasive act from occurring. Further, formulating awareness and intervention strategies are necessary as this phenomenon can spiral beyond the individual to the wider organization. The failure of organizations to address this issue can result in victims retaliating by engaging in deviant behaviors and legal ramifications as incidents can be reported to the authorities. In such instances, the reputation of the organization may be adversely affected. To deter and manage sexual bullying, various measures are advanced and discussed below.

Internal Policy: Within recent times, organizations are moving towards developing policies on sexual harassment and workplace bullying. Sexual bullying should also be contained within these policies. Within the policy, sexual bullying should be clearly defined, the behaviors that constitute sexual bullying should be outlined, and the grievance process should be specified. The grievance process should include guidelines for lodging a complaint, the process to be followed when a complaint is made, the agent/s who is/are responsible for the process (whether assigned organizational agents or an external party), and the report that is submitted upon completion of the investigation. Further, to curtail sexual bullying the redress mechanisms needs to be enforced. Since there are also legal implications, organizations must ensure that each reported incident is investigated as a target or victim may seek legal redress via the courts of the country if the individual perceives that the organization is not thoroughly investigating the report. Organizations may also couple the sexual bullying policy with a behavioral code of conduct. By establishing clear expectations of how employees should behave and act, this would set the values and standards that employees must adhere to. To ensure access, this should be embedded into the company's website where employees can easily access information on grievance procedures, handbooks, and informational brochures.

Zero-tolerance approach: Organizations need to communicate with all employees, regardless of status and position, that sexual bullying will not be tolerated. The internal policy, upon development, must be disseminated throughout the organization where employees are sensitized of the issue, and the measures that have been implemented to deter and address such. Like anti-bullying and anti-sexual harassment campaigns, anti-sexual bullying initiatives should also be advanced. Periodic reminders must also be circulated to continue to sensitize employees of the evolving nature of sexual harassment and workplace bullying. As part of the onboarding activities, new employees should be informed of the policy and the process for reporting incidents.

Training: All employees, including managers and supervisors, should engage in training to sensitize persons throughout the organization about sexual bullying, and the behaviors that are considered acceptable and unacceptable (a behavioral code of conduct). In some instances, perpetrators may be unaware that their actions are being perceived as sexual bullying. Further, since the organization can be liable in instances where the perpetrator is an organizational agent, proactive measures must be taken to minimize the risk of such situations from arising.

FUTURE RESEARCH DIRECTIONS

With the growing interest among researchers and practitioners on such pervasive issues, sexual bullying within the workplace setting is not a 'new' phenomenon. However, research in this area is limited, thereby providing researchers with an opportunity to further explore this phenomenon. While research in the areas of sexual harassment and workplace bullying is gaining momentum, exploring sexual bullying requires empirical research to advance its understanding as it can certainly be categorized under the umbrella of workplace aggression (Hershcovis, 2011). It is necessary to consider the unique aspects for policy development and effective management as concise differentiations would allow targets to easily identify and determine the nature of the behavior directed to them. The dearth of research is alarming as there are opportunities to understand the antecedents and consequences of this phenomenon on individuals, the organization, and wider society. Further, exploring the status of the perpetrator and the varying impacts on the victim is certainly worthy of investigation as the severity of the impact may differ. Future research should also focus on the role of technology where victims of sexual bullying may also experience cyberbullying. Employees may be subjected to such acts beyond working hours where the perpetrator uses another medium beyond face-to-face interactions to direct sexual acts towards the target.

CONCLUSION

In conclusion, workplace sexual bullying is a very serious issue that requires special consideration. As a form of workplace bullying, the sexual intention differentiates this phenomenon since sexual harassment is considered illegal. Therefore, the implications are far-reaching as the target can take legal action against the perpetrator, when the individual is a coworker, and against the organization, when the individual is a supervisor or manager. The severity of sexual bullying in the workplace and associated litigation can present dire consequences for organizations. Organizations should not remain idle on this matter as the actions or inactions can shape employees' perception of fairness in the process and outcomes, thereby shaping the psychological contract of employees. By being proactive, instituting sound policy, adopting a zero-tolerance approach, and offering comprehensive sexual bullying prevention training programs, organizations can reduce the likelihood of workplace sexual bullying from occurring and becoming part of the organization's culture.

REFERENCES

Andersson, L. M., & Pearson, C. M. (1999). Effect of Tit for Tat? The Spiraling in the Workplace Incivility. *Academy of Management Review*, *24*(3), 452–471. doi:10.2307/259136

Aquino, K., & Bradfield, M. (2000). Perceived Victimization in the Workplace: The Role of Situational Factors and Victim Characteristics. *Organization Science*, *11*(5), 525–537. doi:10.1287/orsc.11.5.525.15205

Australia, S. W. (2022). *Workplace sexual harassment statistics and What to do if you are sexually harassed at work– new infographics*. Available at https://www.safeworkaustralia.gov.au/media-centre/news/workplace- sexual-harassment-statistics-and- what-do-if-you-are-sexually-harassed-work-new-infographics#:~:text=Social%20media-, Workplace%20sexual%20harassment%20statistics%20and%20What%20to%20do%20if%20you,harassed%20at%20work%E2%80%93%20new%20infographics&text=One%20in%20three%20people%20 (33,in%20the%20last%20five%20years.

Balwant, P. T., Odell, J., & Ramdeo, S. (2019). I've had enough!" Mental health as a mechanism in the relationship between sexual harassment and organizational commitment. *Work (Reading, Mass.)*, *64*(3), 1–13. doi:10.3233/WOR-193006 PMID:31683497

Bankers, C. J. (2013). Identifying Employers' Proxies in Sexual-Harassment Litigation. *Iowa Law Review*, *99*, 1785–1815.

Cortina, L. M., & Berdahl, J. L. (2008). Sexual harassment in organizations: A decade of research in review. Handbook of Organizational Behavior, 1, 469-497.

Coyne, I., Farley, S., Axtell, C., Sprigg, C., Best, L., & Kwok, O. (2017). Understanding the Relationship Between Experiencing Workplace Cyberbullying, Employee Mental Strain and Job Satisfaction: A Disempowerment Approach. *International Journal of Human Resource Management*, *28*(7), 945–972. doi:10.1080/09585192.2015.1116454

Crawshaw, L. (2009). Workplace Bullying? Mobbing? Harassment? Distraction by a Thousand Definitions. *Consulting Psychology Journal*, *61*(3), 263–267. doi:10.1037/a0016590

Duffy, M. (2009). Preventing Workplace Mobbing and Bullying with Effective Organizational Consultation, Policies, and Legislation. *Consulting Psychology Journal*, *61*(3), 242–262. doi:10.1037/a0016578

Einarsen, S., Hoel, H., Zapf, D., & Cooper, C. L. (2003). *Bullying and Emotional Abuse in the Workplace: International Perspectives in Research and Practice*. Taylor and Francis. doi:10.4324/9780203278734

Equal Employment Opportunity Commission. (1980). Guidelines on discrimination because of sex (Sect. 1 604.1 1) Federal Register, 45,7 4676-1 4611.

Fitzgerald, L. F., Swan, S., & Magley, V. J. (1997). But was it really sexual harassment? Legal, behavioral, and psychological definitions of the workplace victimization of women. In W. T. Donohue (Ed.), *Sexual Harassment: Theory, Research, and Treatment*. Allyn and Bacon.

Glasø, L., Nielsen, M. B., & Einarsen, S. (2009). Interpersonal Problems Among Perpetrators and Targets of Workplace Bullying. *Journal of Applied Social Psychology*, *39*(6), 1316–1333. doi:10.1111/j.1559-1816.2009.00483.x

Harder, H. G., Rash, J., & Wagner, S. (2014). *Mental Illness in the Workplace: Psychological Disability Management*. Gower Publishing Limited.

Herschcovis, M. S. (2011). Incivility, Social Undermining, Bullying…oh My!: A Call to Reconcile Constructs within Workplace Aggression Research. *Journal of Organizational Behavior*, *32*(3), 499–519. doi:10.1002/job.689

Hershcovis, M. S., & Barling, J. (2010). Towards a Multi-Foci Approach to Workplace Aggression: A Meta-Analytic Review of Outcomes from Different Perpetrators. *Journal of Organizational Behavior, 31*(1), 24–44. doi:10.1002/job.621

International Labour Organization. (2016). *Fundamental Rights at Work.* Accessed January 29, 2022. http://www.ilo.org/caribbean/areas-of-work/ils/rights-at-work/lang--en/index.htm

Jacobson, K. J. L., Hood, J. N., & Van Buren, H. J. III. (2014). Workplace Bullying across Cultures: A Research Agenda. *International Journal of Cross Cultural Management, 14*(1), 47–65. doi:10.1177/1470595813494192

Lewis, D., Sheehan, M., & Davies, C. (2008). Uncovering Workplace Bullying. *Journal of Workplace Rights, 13*(3), 281–301. doi:10.2190/WR.13.3.e

Leymann, H. (1996). The Content and Development of Mobbing at Work. *European Journal of Work and Organizational Psychology, 5*(2), 165–184. doi:10.1080/13594329608414853

Lim, V. K. G., & Teo, T. S. H. (2009). Mind your E-manners: Impact of cyber incivility on employees ' work attitude and behavior. *Information & Management, 46*(8), 419–425. doi:10.1016/j.im.2009.06.006

McDonald, P. (2012). Workplace Sexual Harassment 30 Years on: A Review of the Literature. *International Journal of Management Reviews, 14*(1), 1–17. doi:10.1111/j.1468-2370.2011.00300.x

Merkin, R. S., & Shah, M. K. (2014). The impact of sexual harassment on job satisfaction, turnover intentions, and absenteeism: Findings from Pakistan compared to the United States. *SpringerPlus, 3*(1), 1–13. doi:10.1186/2193-1801-3-215 PMID:24851198

Muhonen, T., Jönsson, S., & Bäckström, M. (2017). Consequences of cyberbullying behaviour in working life: The mediating roles of social support and social organizational climate. *International Journal of Workplace Health Management, 10*(5), 376–390. doi:10.1108/IJWHM-10-2016-0075 PMID:29721038

Nabe-Nielsen, K., Grynderup, M. B., Lange, T., Andersen, J. H., Bonde, J. P., Conway, P. M., & Hansen, Å. M. (2016). The role of poor sleep in the relation between workplace bullying/unwanted sexual attention and long-term sickness absence. *International Archives of Occupational and Environmental Health, 89*(6), 967–979. doi:10.100700420-016-1136-4 PMID:27137811

Nielsen, M. B., & Einarsen, S. V. (2012). Outcomes of Exposure to Workplace Bullying: A Meta-Analytic Review. *Work and Stress, 26*(4), 309–332. doi:10.1080/02678373.2012.734709 PMID:23236220

Nielsen, M. B., & Einarsen, S. V. (2018). What we know, what we do not know, and what we should and could have known about workplace bullying: An overview of the literature and agenda for future research. *Aggression and Violent Behavior, 42*, 71–83. doi:10.1016/j.avb.2018.06.007

Quick, J. C., & McFadyen, M. (2017). Sexual harassment: Have we made any progress? *Journal of Occupational Health Psychology, 22*(3), 286–298. doi:10.1037/ocp0000054 PMID:27732009

Ramdeo, S., Balwant, P. T., Cowell, N., & Persadie, N. (2020). The moderated mediation model of bullying, support, justice, and organizational outcomes. *International Journal of Employment Studies., 28*(1), 48–81.

Ramdeo, S., & Singh, R. (2020). Cyberbullying in the Workplace. In Encyclopedia of Criminal Activities and the Deep Web. IGI Global. doi:10.4018/978-1-5225-9715-5.ch047

Ramdeo, S., & Singh, R. (2021). Out with the Old, in with the New: Innovative Work Practices for Navigating the Unknown. In B. Mehta (Ed.), *The Impact of COVID-19 on Human Resource Management* (pp. 57–67). Proud Pen. doi:10.51432/978-1-8381524-4-4_5

Salin, D. M. (2003). Ways of Explaining Workplace Bullying: A Review of Enabling, Motivating and Precipitating Structures and Processes in the Work Environment. *Human Relations*, *56*(10), 1213–1232. doi:10.1177/00187267035610003

Tehrani, N. (2012). *Workplace Bullying: Symptoms and Solutions*. Routledge.

Tepper, B. J. (2000). Consequences of Abusive Supervision. *Academy of Management Journal*, *43*(2), 178–190. doi:10.2307/1556375

Tepper, B. J. (2007). Abusive Supervision in Work Organizations: Review, Synthesis, and Research Agenda. *Journal of Management*, *33*(3), 261–289. doi:10.1177/0149206307300812

Trades Union Congress. (2016). *Report on Sexual Harassment in the Workplace*. Available at https://www.tuc.org.uk/news/nearly-two-three-young-women-have-experienced-sexual-harassment-work-tuc-survey-reveals

Turner-Moore, T., Milnes, K., & Gough, B. (2021). Bullying in Five European Countries: Evidence for Bringing Gendered Phenomena Under the Umbrella of 'Sexual Bullying' in Research and Practice. *Sex Roles*, *86*(1-2), 89–105. doi:10.100711199-021-01254-1

U.S. Equal Employment Opportunity Commission. (2022). *Charges Alleging Sex-Based Harassment (Charges filed with EEOC) FY 2010-FY 2021*. Available at https://www.eeoc.gov/statistics/charges-alleging-sex-based-harassment-charges-filed-eeoc-fy-2010-fy-2021

Vartia, M. A.-L. (2001). Consequences of Workplace Bullying with Respect to the Well-Being of Its Targets and the Observers of Bullying. *Scandinavian Journal of Work, Environment & Health*, *27*(1), 63–69. doi:10.5271jweh.588 PMID:11266149

WBI. (2021). *U.S. Workplace Bullying Survey.* The Workplace Bullying Institute. https://workplacebullying.org/wp-content/uploads/2021/04/2021-Full-Report.pdf

Wheeler, A. R., Halbesleben, J. R. B., & Shanine, K. (2010). Eating Their Cake and Everyone Else's Cake, Too: Resources as the Main Ingredient to Workplace Bullying. *Business Horizons*, *53*(6), 553–560. doi:10.1016/j.bushor.2010.06.002

Willness, C. R., Steel, P., & Lee, K. (2007). A meta-analysis of the antecedents and consequences of workplace sexual harassment. *Personnel Psychology*, *60*(1), 127–162. doi:10.1111/j.1744-6570.2007.00067.x

ADDITIONAL READING

Cheung, H. K., Goldberg, C. B., King, E. B., & Magley, V. J. (2018). Are they true to the cause? Beliefs about organizational and unit commitment to sexual harassment awareness training. *Group & Organization Management, 43*(4), 531–560. doi:10.1177/1059601117726677

Coyne, I., Gopaul, A. M., Campbell, M., Pankász, A., Garland, R., & Cousans, F. (2019). Bystander responses to bullying at work: The role of mode, type and relationship to target. *Journal of Business Ethics, 157*(3), 813–827. doi:10.100710551-017-3692-2

Heatherington, W., & Coyne, I. (2014). Understanding individual experiences of cyberbullying encountered through work. *International Journal of Organization Theory and Behavior, 17*(2), 163–192. doi:10.1108/IJOTB-17-02-2014-B002

McDonald, P., Charlesworth, S., & Graham, T. (2016). Action or inaction: Bystander intervention in workplace sexual harassment. *International Journal of Human Resource Management, 27*(5), 548–566. doi:10.1080/09585192.2015.1023331

Namie, G., & Namie, R. (2018). Risk factors for becoming a target of workplace bullying and mobbing. *Workplace Bullying and Mobbing in the United States, 1*, 53–74.

Pallesen, S., Nielsen, M. B., Magerøy, N., Andreassen, C. S., & Einarsen, S. (2017). An Experimental Study on the Attribution of Personality Traits to Bullies and Targets in a Workplace Setting. *Frontiers in Psychology, 8*, 1–7. doi:10.3389/fpsyg.2017.01045 PMID:28690574

Tepper, B. J., Simon, L., & Park, H. M. (2017). Abusive supervision. *Annual Review of Organizational Psychology and Organizational Behavior, 4*(1), 123–152. doi:10.1146/annurev-orgpsych-041015-062539

Vranjes, I., Baillien, E., Vandebosch, H., Erreygers, S., & De Witte, H. (2017). The dark side of working online: Towards a definition and an Emotion Reaction model of workplace cyberbullying. *Computers in Human Behavior, 69*, 324–334. doi:10.1016/j.chb.2016.12.055

KEY TERMS AND DEFINITIONS

Cyberbully: A person who directly or indirectly uses technology to reduce another person to a psychologically inferior state.

Cyberstalking: A form of harassment where the cyberbully makes continuous threats and sends inappropriate messages to an individual in the form of text messages, instant messaging, social media, emails.

Gender Harassment: Includes a variety of degrading behaviors directed to the target where these behaviors can be grouped into two categories, that is, sexist hostility and sexual hostility. Sexist hostility refers to discriminatory experiences because of one's gender (for instance, insulting or derogatory gender-related remarks). Further, sexual hostility refers to sexually explicit experiences (for instance, sexual jokes).

Sexual Bullying: An escalating process in which one or more employees are subjected to negative psychological and/or physical abuse, where the intention is sexual and/or gender-related and recurring over an extended period of time (usually 6 months or more). This reduces the target to a psychologically inferior state and creates a hostile work environment.

Sexual Coercion: Also known as *quad pro quo*, occurs when organizational rewards are offered by one person to another in exchange for sexual favors (for instance, a promotion or an increase in one's salary/pay).

Sexual Harassment: Unwelcomed sex-related behaviors that can take the form of gender harassment, unwanted sexual attention, and/or sexual coercion that is perceived as implicit or explicit.

Unwanted Sexual Attention: Actions directed to the target that is not reciprocated and gestures that are unwelcomed where there are sexual verbal and/or non-verbal acts (for instance, sending intrusive letters, calls of a sexual nature, touching, and grabbing).

Workplace Aggression: Negative acts that are perpetrated against an organization or its members and that victims are motivated to avoid.

Workplace Bullying: An escalating process in which one or more employees are subjected to negative psychological and physical abuse recurring over an extended period of time (usually 6 months or more), where the target is reduced to a psychologically inferior state, and it creates a hostile work environment to those exposed.

Chapter 4 Reflections of Sexual Harassment on Psychology and Media

Umut Çıvgın
Bursa Technical University, Turkey

ABSTRACT

In this chapter, the aim is to discuss what sexual harassment is, theoretical models based on sexual harassment, social and individual effects of sexual harassment, and the place of sexual harassment in the media. This chapter consists of three main sections. Firstly, sexual harassment is defined, and the theoretical models related to sexual harassment, gender differences in sexual harassment, and world statistics on sexual harassment are introduced. In the second part, the effects of sexual harassment on the society and the individual are examined from the perspective of psychology. In addition, the psychological consequences of sexual harassment at the individual level are examined from the perspective of clinical psychology. The last section covers the impact and visibility of sexual harassment on the media and the social media visibility examples of sexual harassment.

INTRODUCTION

Sexual harassment is a phenomenon that has been studied by many researchers and different disciplines until today. Although it is considered as a joint work of psychology and legal disciplines, it is now taking its place in the media quite often. Fitzgerald, Swan, and Magley (1997), drawing attention to the distinction made in terms of the definition of sexual harassment, stated that there is a need for different definitions in terms of psychological and legal aspects. In order to the definition to be more explanatory, theoretical models have been created. In this sense, four models examining the issue of sexual harassment will be introduced in this chapter. These are Single Factor Theory, Natural/Biological Theory, Social-cognitive Theory of Sexual Harassment, Multi-factor Theory of Sexual Harassment.

According to the World Population Report (2021), it is stated that the probability of women being sexually harassed by men is 35% during their lifetime. Although 141 countries have laws on sexual

DOI: 10.4018/978-1-6684-5426-8.ch004

harassment, it is understood that this number is still low and although there are laws, they are not sufficient in terms of implementation (UN Women, 2021). Although researches show that women frequently come face to face with sexual harassment, it is stated that the frequency of sexual harassment by young men and LGBTIQ+ groups is increasing (Promundo & UN Women, 2017). Some social theorists regard sexual harassment as a reflection of the patriarchal system (Pryor, 1987; Vaux, 1993). Therefore, sexual harassment is frequently seen in societies where the perception that social beliefs legitimize male dominance is prominent. In such societies, women may appear to play a passive role, avoiding confusion, attractive, taking responsibility for distrusting their own judgment (Sokoloff, 1980). According to Welsh, Carr, MacQuarrie and Huntley (2006), citizenship status can also be a visible and complex component of women's definitions of sexual harassment. In societies that value women's rights, the existence of more sensitive and educated individuals against sexual harassment and the existence of legally strong systems also bring about social change.

Beside that the other impact of sexual harassment, its individual effects are also very destructive and threaten the physical and psychological health of the harassed individual. PTSD (Larsen and Fitzgerald, 2011), eating disorders (Harned & Fitzgerald, 2002), concentration problems, and depression (Chan, Lam, Chow & Cheung, 2008) would often be experienced by individual after being harassed. Amongst the long-term effects, people who have experienced this condition may experience a decrease in their self-esteem (Harned & Fitzgerald, 2002), decrease in work efficiency and even job losses (Welsh & Gruber, 1999). It is understood that reporting and not reporting the event can cause significant differences in the life of abused individual. The literature indicates that the consequences of reporting and non-reporting of sexual harassment are complex (Bell, Street, & Stafford, 2014). It shows that reporting can have both positive and negative consequences in terms of social/work life and psychological health (Campbell, 2008). It is also stated that this consequences depending on how the laws work in the region where they live.

SEXUAL HARASSMENT

The term "sexual harassment" is a term that emerged in North America in the mid-1970s to address the conceptual problem that posed the work of various researchers (Farley, 1978; MacKinnon, 1979). In the most general sense, sexual harassment is defined as inappropriate behavior in the sexual dimension. But whether there is a power difference in the realization of harassment; the necessity of specifying the location; whether the victim's behavior is problematic; It is seen that there are discussions in terms of whether sexist behavior is a kind of sexual harassment (O'Donohue, Downs, & Yeater, 1998). Fitzgerald, Swan, and Magley (1997) defined sexual harassment on a psychological basis as sexually related behavior in the workplace, offensive by the recipient, exceeding resources, threatening bodily integrity, and undesirable behavior. The most common and most severe types of violence against women are rape, sexual coercion, sexual abuse, forced prostitution and exploitation of labor (Watts & Zimmerman, 2002). As can be understood from here, it can be predicted that sexual harassment is an umbrella topic and is related to many fields.

The problems faced by individuals in their social and business life can affect individuals socially, economically and psychologically. Especially with the 1900s, with the increasing visibility of women in business life, the phenomenon of sexual harassment has become a frequently encountered problem.

It has begun to attract attention globally, and the devastating consequences of sexual harassment, which is a frequently discussed topic in social sciences, have started to be seen more clearly over the years.

From the past to the present, the position of women in business life can be a controversial topic. This is illustrated by examples such as receiving a lower salary than a male employee working at the same level or not being promoted to higher seniority (Davidson & Cooper, 1992). Similarly, gender discrimination draws attention in relationships in business life. Unequal interpersonal attitudes and behaviors in business life can be defined as harassment in general (Sbraga & O'donohue, 2000). It is understood that the important sub-title under the title of harassment, the definition of which is still being discussed, is sexual harassment. Behavior spectrum ranging from sexist jokes to rape behavior can be defined as sexual harassment.

The work of Fitzgerald and her colleagues (1985, 1987) laid the groundwork for establishing a model that categorizes sexual harassment. The legal categories of hostile environment and quid pro quo are two types of harassment. Sexual coercion means engaging in sexual behavior through promise or threat at work. Although it was seen as the least common type of sexual harassment in the early 1990s (Gruber, 1990), it is a situation frequently encountered in the new century. Other types can be unwanted sexual attention, refers to intimidating, hostile sexual behavior, both verbally and in behavior. Hostile environment harassment (in legal contexts) includes repeated date requests, inappropriate comments and insinuations about an individual's clothing. Fitzgerald et al. (1997) has defined gender harassment as a new type of sexual harassment. Gender harassment includes sexist words and behaviors belonging to the sexes.

As can be understood from the theoretical definitions, sexual harassment is a situation that can negatively affect individuals in many ways. It can create social, economic and psychological grievances. Although it is observed that the sanctions related to sexual harassment increase in both working life and social life, the increase in sexual harassment victimization makes one think that the determined sanctions should be questioned. In the next section, it is aimed to provide a social and psychological perspective to sexual harassment by explaining the frequency of sexual harassment, its effects and its visibility in the media.

Prevalence of Sexual Harassment

In the World Population Report (2021), it is stated that women are more likely to be sexually harassed during their lifetime. Considering the judicial systems of the countries, it is understood that despite the high number of countries with laws on sexual harassment, there are inadequacies in terms of implementation of the laws (UN Women, 2021).

Spitzberg (1999), who made a systematic review of studies including statistics on the prevalence of sexual harassment, emphasized that sexual harassment and sexually coercive behaviors are among the most physically severe forms of sexual aggression. Sexual harassment is often seen as an act committed by men against women (Pryor, 1995). It is understood that the results of current statistical studies and the results of outdated studies do not differ much from each other in terms of the direction of this sexual harassment. For example, the results of the U.S. Merit Systems Protection Board (1988) survey showed that almost all (93%) of women who reported sexual harassment were harassed by men. Similarly, according to the WHO 2021 Report, it is understood that women are more exposed to violence in this relationship in terms of intimate partner violence (affecting around 641 million).

According to the results of the 2020 Sexual Harassment Survey conducted in the UK, almost 72% of people living in the UK have experienced sexual harassment at least once in their lifetime. In addition, compared to men, 51% of women reported that they had been sexually harassed (Government Equalities Office, 2020). Looking at the United States statistics, the lifetime experience of sexual harassment among women there is seen as one in six women. Sexual harassment women can be seen in private areas (such as homes) as well as in public areas. According to US- Equal Employment Opportunity Commission, %25 of women experience sexual harassment in the workplace (Kearl, 2018). When the rates in the Middle East are examined, it is seen that the numbers have increased dramatically. In a study where 548 women working in Africa were used as a sample, it was determined that one out of every two women had been subjected to verbal or physical sexual abuse at work (Women in News, 2021). Finally, similar rates can be encountered according to current statistics in Turkey. It is reported that some of the existing cases are not reflected in the legal institutions, as is the case all over the world, and Forensic Statistics of the Ministry of Justice for 2019 showed that the crime of sexual abuse in Turkey has set a record for the last 8 years.

In the light of data, the statistics of sexual harassment in the last 40 years show that there has been a significant numerical change from the past to the present, and even point to an increasing range. This statistical information, which shows that the frequency of sexual harassment is increasing, also shows that the need for increasing scientific knowledge in this sense is increasing. The dramatic increase in sexual harassment cases has attracted the attention of many researchers from social sciences to law, and an increase in the number of studies in this field has been observed. It is seen that this issue has been discussed frequently in the 1990s and many theoretical models have been created based on the causes of sexual harassment.

Theoretical Models of Sexual Harassment

The different theoretical explanations have emerged with the studies conducted in the field of sexual harassment. It is understood that the theories are grouped as single factor or multi factor according to the factors they focus on (Pina, Gannon, & Saunders, 2009). In this chapter, four theories will be summarized. These are Single Factor Theory, Natural/Biological Theory, Social-cognitive Theory of Sexual Harassment, Multi-factor Theory of Sexual Harassment.

Single Factor Theory includes Sociocultural and Organizational Theories. *Social-Cultural Theories* consider sexual harassment in a social and cultural context. Interpretations are mostly made from a feminist perspective. The feminist approach sees sexual harassment as the result of gender inequality and sexism in society (Thomas & Kitzinger, 1997). In addition, this situation is associated with the ideology that advocates male hegemony and sexist male dominance (Matchen & DeSouza, 2000). Perception of women's low status in society and in the workplace should not result in or be the cause of sexual harassment. However, the fact that accepted gender norms, especially the denial of the status of women in business life and/or their lower status compared to men, may reveal the perception that sexual harassment can also be justified. The upbringing and life experiences of individuals within this perspective also reminds us that sexual harassment is presented as a result of cultural experiences. However, according to Bem (1983), Bem (1983), this perspective was superficial. Gender role behaviors have changed over the years, and all aspects of behavior have come to be considered normal for the genders. On the other hand, although sexual harassment is frequently seen in society, it is not a normative behavior specific to men. Most men do not commit sexual harassment, and the Feminist perspective is unable to provide a comprehensive explanation due to empirical shortcomings (Pina, Gannon, & Saunders, 2009). *Organizational Theory* states that the structure of the organization, hierarchical structure and authority relations in the organization determine the power level of the employees in the organization. The distorted perception of power that may arise in this way also creates a suitable ground for the harasser (Terpstra & Baker, 1989). In fact, this model does not predict the sex of the harasser to be just a particular gender. However, due to the fact that women's status in organizations is kept lower, they are more likely to be victims. Thus, the harasser becomes the party that has more power and is more protected and concealed. The structure of the workplace can also pave the way for sexual harassment. For example, inequalities in gender distribution, expectation of overtime, lack of clear employee rights, expectations of sexy behavior in the workplace / expectations of wearing sexy clothes make sexual harassment more common in the workplace (O'Donohue, Downs, & Yeater, 1998).

Secondly, The Biological Theory which has been criticized in many ways, explains sexual harassment only in terms of biological and evolutionary processes. From the biological point of view, sexual harassment is associated with mate selection (which stems from the theory of evolution). In this approach, it is stated that men have stronger motives to be aggressive and to choose a mate. But that doesn't justify the man's sexual harassment. In other words, this strong motive in men can sometimes create conflict and reveal inappropriate behaviors (Tangri & Hayes, 1997). There is no empirical data showing cause and effect these relational inferences established by researchers. Therefore, this approach has been criticized in many ways. First, the developed idea is very simple. On the other hand, it is quite difficult to test the basic assumptions of the theory. In this sense, the assumptions remain unfounded. A final point of criticism is the small number of empirical studies testing biological explanations of sexual harassment (O'Donohue, Downs, & Yeater, 1998).

Although *The Social-Cognitive Theory* plays an important role in understanding and explaining rape (Pryor, 1987), it is thought that this theory makes an important contribution to the explanation of sexual harassment (Pina, Gannon, & Saunders, 2009). The components of social cognitive theory (Hollon & Kriss, 1984) are long-term memory, social-cognitive processing (attention, recall, etc.), and cognitive products (beliefs, thoughts, and attributions). The relationships between these components can provide empirical information on the cause of sexual harassment (Pryor & Stoller, 1994; Polaschek & Ward, 2002). For example, according to DeJudicibus & McCabe (2001), in their research with sexual harassers, it was seen that the cognitive processes that lead to harassment-type behaviors (they are automatic and unconscious) have content that supports harassment. In addition, in another study, it was found that there are prejudiced attitudes in the beliefs and schemas in long-term memories that support the behavior of men who engage in anti-social behavior. That is, it can be seen that social-cognitive theory reveals important findings in explaining the link betw een them. On the other hand, it should be noted that this theory is not sufficient on its own to explain all the components, and it should not be forgotten that it has limitations.

Fourthly, The Four Factor Theory which includes more than one single factor theory, predicted to explain sexual harassment by bringing together the key factors. O'Hare and O'Donohue (1998), one of the leading researchers of the theory, argued that 4 conditions must be met for sexual harassment to occur. These are (1) the individual is motivated to abuse, (2) the internal barriers to the abuse have been overcome, (3) the external barriers have been overcome, and (4) the victim's resistance has been broken. When the research findings were analyzed, it was understood that the sexual harassment explanation variance of the four-factor structure was superior to the single factor. In addition, other factors explaining the high rate of sexual harassment are ignorance of complaint procedures, unprofessional working environment and sexist attitudes. As with other theories, this model also has limitations. However, like other theories, it contains important findings for new theories and researches to be made. These theories, which were derived to explain sexual harassment, have been the source of many new researches. One aspect of the research focused on understanding the effects of sexual harassment, while another focused on gender differences in sexual harassment.

Gender Differences in Sexual Harassment

Reflections of sexual harassment, which is an important problem in working life and social life, on gender can be different. The majority of studies show that women experience sexual harassment more than men (Larsen, Nye, & Fitzgerald, 2019; Rotundo, Nguyen, & Sackett, 2001; Street, Gradus, Stafford, & Kelly, 2007). It has been observed that since the early 2000s, studies on sexual harassment consequences of men have increased. The study by Street, Gradus, Stafford, & Kelly (2017) had a fairly large number of participants (n= 3946). With this study, researchers wanted to examine gender differences in sexual harassment experiences. According to the analysis, it was understood that the percentage of women reporting sexual harassment is higher. In addition, it has been reported that women experience almost all subtypes of sexual harassment. Being a woman can be seen as a risk factor for experiencing the most severe forms of sexual harassment.

When the sub-types of sexual harassment are examined in terms of gender, it is seen that the difference between the genders is large. In the study, in which the uncommon types of sexual harassment are examined, the differences between the sexes are widened more and it is understood that women report these uncommon types more (Cortina, Lonsway, Magley, Freeman, Collingsworth, Hunter, et al., 2002). What men experience in terms of sexual harassment is more often exposed to sexual jokes and bad comments (Stockdale, Visio, & Batra, 1999). Another factor where sexual harassment can differ between men and women is the gender of the harasser. While men are mostly harassed by their own gender; women can be sexually harassed by the opposite sex (Stockdale et al., 1999).

The reasons of men sexual harassment may differ from women's. The power imbalances that exist between men and women in work environments can create the perception that men are more open to pressure and harassment towards women. On the other hand, sexual harassment against men can be based on "femininity" or being feminine. Such behaviors can be interpreted as resulting from the social devaluation of femininity and the complementary valuation of male heterosexuality and masculinity (Waldo, Berdahl, &Fitzgerald, 1998).

Another difference in terms of gender is seen in the characteristics of sexual harassment. From the past to the present, the vast majority of those who sexually harassed are men. Establishing sociodemographic profiles of sexual abusers based on some research results can be misleading (Brown, 1998; Neibuhr & Boyles, 1991). Existing statistics show that sexual abusers can be of any social status, age and occupation (Pina, Gannon, & Saunders, 2009). As a result, the meaning, severity and existence of sexual harassment for women and men can change in terms of many factors. It is understood that there are significant differences between men and women for all related parameters.

EFFECTS OF SEXUAL HARASSMENT

The results and effects of sexual harassment, which people are exposed to both in work life and in social life, are being used more and more as a research topic day by day. In this section, the effects of sexual harassment on psychological and social life will be examined.

Psychological Effects of Sexual Harassment

Sexual harassment is defined as a situation that causes a high level of psychological stress. There are theoretical studies that state that sexual harassment also negatively affects mental health (Street, Gradus, Stafford, & Kelly, 2007). Previous and current studies indicate that learned helplessness and feeling loss of resources are among the prominent psychological effects (Bell, Street, & Stafford; 2014; Charney & Russel, 1994; Hobfoll, 1989; Kilpatrick, Veronen, & Resnick, 1982; Min, 2014). In addition, low self-esteem and high depressive symptoms are among the psychological effects reported by survivors of sexual harassment (Harned & Fitzgerald, 2002).

It seems that many factors play a mediating and regulatory role in the relationship between sexual harassment and psychological impact, and can explain this relationship more. Stress coping strategies, gender, perceived social support levels and perception of sexual harassment level can be effective on psychological symptoms (Bulger, 2001; Cortina, 2004). In the meta-analysis study conducted by Chan, Chow, Lam, and Cheung (2008), the relationship between sexual harassment and psychological well-being was investigated. It is seen that many studies dealing with this subject have been examined in terms of age, psychological status, physical condition, and attitudes towards work life. According to the results of the study, it was understood that there was a moderate negative relationship between sexual harassment and psychological well-being. In addition, it has been reported that there is a positive relationship between the level of stress and sexual harassment.

Most of the research emphasized that there is a strong link between physical health and psychological state. The difficulties and obstacles faced from source affect psychological health, so there may be changes in terms of physical health. Although the human body shows stronger physiological reactions when the stress level is high, an increased level of inflammation can be observed in the suppressed immune system (Smith, 2006). From this point of view, the frequency of sleep disturbance, headache and gastrointestinal disorders may increase. In a review study, significant relationships were found between sexual harassment and physical health. It has been reported that the physical health levels of those who have been sexually abused have decreased. At the same time, gender, stress level and age were found to have a moderator effect (Chan, Chow, Lam, & Cheung, 2008).

Victims of sexual harassment perceive this phenomenon as unexpected and undesirable. Therefore, the relationship between sexual harassment and trauma is not unexpected. Studies have shown that individuals no longer only show signs of trauma as a result of sexual harassment; emphasizes that they were diagnosed with post-traumatic stress disorder (Palmieri & Fitzgerald, 2005). PTSD symptom level in sexual harassment survivors is also related to perceived control over the situation. The level of perceived control may be related to the course of symptoms and is associated with self-blame (Frazier, Berman, & Steward, 2002). The level of self-blame may also have a positive relationship with the course of PTSD. In other words, as individuals blame themselves, more PTSD symptoms may appear (Najdowski & Ullman, 2009). It is understood that this result is repeated in the study by Larsen and Fitzgerald (2011). According to the results of the research, the level of self-blame and blaming the abuser is positively related to the level of PTSD. When the effect of the perception of control is added to this relationship, the presence of thoughts that the person cannot control the harassment situation can be a factor that reduces the PTSD symptom level.

In addition to being associated with traumatic experiences, it is understood that eating disorders are highly associated with rape and sexual harassment. As some studies have stated that sexual harassment and rape in childhood are associated with having an eating disorder in later life (Neunmark- Sztainer et al., 2000); some studies show that being exposed to sexual harassment at an earlier age increases the risk of having an eating disorder more (Kinzl, Mangweth, Traweger, & Bielb, 1997). In a study, female university graduates were accepted as participants and various eating disorder symptoms of the participants were found to be associated with sexual harassment. In addition, it has been found that the level of eating restriction and behavioral eating disorder symptom level are directly related (Harned, 2000). According to other analyzes of the study, it was found that the use of eating behavior as a coping mechanism, depression and anxiety levels played a mediating role in the relationship between sexual harassment and eating disorder symptoms. According to the results of another study conducted by Harned and Fitzgerald (2002) with female and male military service and female non-military groups, sexual harassment experienced at work was positively related to the symptom of eating disorder. However, it was noted that there was no such relationship in the unemployed female participant group. Therefore, it can be seen that the occupational group and gender may also indicate different findings in terms of the consequences of sexual harassment.

Sexual harassment literature indicates that sexual harassment may have different psychological consequences for men and women. It is understood that depression and anxiety related to sexual harassment are more common in female victims of sexual harassment than male victims (DeSouza & Fansler, 2003). Similarly, PTSD and eating disorder symptoms are more common in female victims (Murdoch et al., 2006). However, there are debates as these findings may also be due to the numerical disproportion of male and female sexual abuse victims. In another study conducted with a large number of participants, it is stated that women and men show similar characteristics in terms of sexual harassment and mental health (Magley, Waldo, Drasgow, & Fitzgerald, 1999). On the other hand, victims of male-military sexual harassment may show more serious psychological problems due to both sexual harassment and war trauma (Vogt, Pless, King, & King, 2005). In another study examining data collected from the male-dominated environment, it was found that male sexual harassment victims had more pronounced mental health disorders than females (Street, Gradus, Stafford, & Kelly, 2007).

As a summary, the psychological effects of sexual harassment can be very diverse and related to many fields. Although the victimized individual exhibits psychological withdrawal characteristics on one hand; on the one other hand, the individual does not cut off their interaction with the environment. Therefore, the interaction and communication with the environment can also affect the psychological state of the victims and their way of coping with this situation. In the next section, it is aimed to present holistic information about the effects of sexual harassment by discussing sexual harassment and its socially effective relationship.

Social Effects of Sexual Harassment

The concept of social support, which is associated with psychological processes, is very important for individuals' social lives. Social support has a function that strengthens the individual in terms of coping with challenging life events. Social support has been defined as important by Cohen and McKay (1984), as a buffer zone that protects the individual against stressful life events. When sexual harassment victims are considered, it can be quite difficult to express this experience. Accordingly, reporting the event of harassment may also mean that the individual is labeled by the people around them, and social losses are experienced. On the other hand, not reporting this compelling situation can also make the individual lonely and reveal the inability to receive the social support they need. It has both direct and indirect effects on the mental health and social life of the individual (Holahan & Moos, 1994). It is thought that the way individuals perceive social support and their level of perception are also important. This perceived social support can affect psychological state positively. (Chan, Limoges, & Fung, 2010; Cohen & McKay, 1984; Cortina, 2004; Lazarus & Folkman, 1984). When it is considered in terms of the sexual harassment victim, the need for perceived social support arises. This social support can be provided by the relatives of the victims, institutions, some unions and the state (Cortina, 2004).

The direct and indirect form of support can be important in terms of affecting the victim. With the support provided by institutions or organizations, this situation of the victim can be announced. As a result, unfortunately, job loss, financial losses due to job loss, and emotional support from the social environment can also be experienced. Workplaces with undeveloped organizational systems may not evaluate such grievances within the framework of the required ethical codes and may add a psychological burden such as labeling to the victim in addition to the event they have experienced. In the study conducted by Cortina (2004) with Spanish women victims of sexual harassment, it is understood that the victims rely more on the social support they perceive from their families and friends. It has been observed that they do not trust the social support that can be perceived from the institutions. In addition, increased perceived social support was found to indicate reducing the psychological effects of sexual harassment.

An important area that constitutes the social life of adult individuals is working life. Working life that supports individuals socially and financially, can become cluttered due to a situation such as sexual harassment which cause many devastating effects on individuals. After such a victimization, the career development and working life of individuals may be damaged (Buchanan & Fitzgerald, 2008). The most common effect of sexual harassment in business life can be burnout (Hu, Elis, Hewitt, et al., 2019). Low job satisfaction, job loss, low job commitment, low concentration, low workforce can be seen in people with burnout (Bakaç, Chen, Zyberaj, Kehr, & Quirin, 2022; Cheng & Yi, 2018).

Studies in the literature claim that both social support and the social support mechanisms that organizations provide for sexual harassment have different consequences. For example, in a study examining the relationships between psychological states, job satisfaction levels and both social and organizational support processes of tour guides who have experienced sexual harassment, it is seen that organizational support has more effective results than social support. For this sample, it is concluded that organizational support positively influences the effects of sexual harassment (Alrawadieh, Demirdelen Alrawadieh, Olya, Erkol Bayram, & Kahraman, 2021).

Another negative effect of sexual harassment can be the exclusion of victims from social life and self-isolation. There may be prejudice, exclusion and accusations against victims in the environment. Especially in male-dominated societies, it can be seen that women cannot defend their rights and do not share their experiences of sexual harassment. However, despite these, the perception of power brought by being visible and demanding rights can also provide social support resources to women in this sense. In Adikaram's study (2017), it is stated that sharing this situation with the victim's own social environment, colleagues and even managers makes people more functional as socially and psychologically. In addition, it is understood that sharing the bad experience provides emotional support, support in terms of information (related to legal application) and a social network.

Nevertheless, sexual harassment encountered in all areas of life has started to be seen in the digital world as well. Although the virtual social environment has positive and negative effects on individuals; the real-life reflections of sexual harassment through virtual tools are not different from those mentioned above. McLean and Griffiths (2019) conducted a remarkable qualitative study examining online harassment and other related factors of women playing online games. In this study, data of 271 women playing online games were collected through various discussion forums. According to the results of the thematic analysis, women who were victims of virtual sexual harassment reported that they perceived less social support, felt anxious and lonely on the surface, could not tell their relatives about their online experience, left the game groups and continued to play alone. In the light of this information, it is understood that sexual harassment can occur to individuals in both real and digital fields, and the psychological and social consequences of these experiences in both areas are similar.

With the digitalized world, people's daily experiences and social bonds with other people may differ from the past. In this sense, digital applications and media tools make people more visible and enable individuals to be heard more. Especially for bad life experiences such as sexual harassment, victims become more vocal and have easier access to social, psychological and legal support mechanisms. On the other hand, with today's media channels, the rapid spread of information and the ease of manipulation, individuals become more vulnerable. In the next section, a more detailed evaluation is presented by considering the relationship between sexual harassment and media.

SEXUAL HARASSMENT AND MEDIA

Media is seen as a resource where individuals are informed, shared and used to meet various social needs of individuals in social life (Kocadaş, 2005). Although the main purpose is the same over time, it is understood that the media tools and the sources of the media have changed. Traditional media consists of content that is followed by a passive audience or reader, produced in a film studio with the source or by an editorial staff. It is understood that with the digitalizing world, the way of use and sources of media has changed. It is observed that the media user, who used to be passive, now takes a more interactive role that produces content and is a resource for the media (Reid Chassiakos, 2016). The media, which produces content and is a news source, has become more powerful in terms of attracting attention, making their voice heard and raising awareness. It is now easier for a person who has been exposed to a negative life event anywhere in the world to announce their situation very quickly and to create social awareness. In particular, it has become easier to raise a voice about discrimination and misbehavior based on children, women, LGBTIQ+, ethnic identity, through these new media. In this sense, the subject that has been on the agenda of the media recently is sexual harassment.

In television, which is one of the most important visual media tools, the content and the way the content is presented changes every year. Grauerholz and King (1997) examined the role of women in prime time programs and the contents of the programs in their qualitative study. In these programs, it was stated that sexual harassment has visible and invisible dimensions. In these programs, some situations that can be considered as sexual harassment are expressed through jokes and this situation can show sexual harassment as if it is not a serious enough issue. Although sexual harassment is presented as an important issue in some programs today, the way in which sexual harassment is conveyed and the way the program owners approach the victims they bring to the program may not be correct and ethical. Considering Turkey in particular, although these programs are a tool that gives courage to the victims and helps to make their voices heard, the victim's exposure and the revival of the traumas caused by the way the program was handled can actually cause significant harm to the victims.

As mentioned above over the years, the media audience has become not only a viewer, but also a content producer and a voice. It is understood that social media applications (Twitter, Facebook, Instagram, etc.) pave the way for this. Therefore, when individuals are in a negative situation, they can easily spread it, gather support and form public opinion about the situation. The #metoo movement is a social media phenomenon that was created to show sexual harassment and to draw attention to its frequency, where individuals can share their sexual harassment experiences (Chowdhury, Sawhney, Mathur, Mahata, & Shah, 2019). Widespread sexual abuse allegations against Harvey Weinstein were a major news item in October 2017. After a while, the #metoo movement started to become more remarkable with Alyssa Milano's statement that sexual abuse was more common than is actually known (Milano, 2017). The #metoo movement, which first appeared in 2006, flared up again with this current spread (me too, 2020). This viral #metoo movement, which started the interaction related to sexual violence globally and developed to support speaking and making a voice heard, is still an important and active movement today. This developing social media trend has also started to be the subject of scientific publications. In particular, the ways in which the news of sexual harassment started to be the subject of, and the way the media handled sexual harassment in the sense of before and after the trend were examined. In a study, it was stated that a global interaction started with just one tweet, awareness and transformation in the social context were emphasized, and the way other media channels talked about sexual harassment was affected (Noetzel, Mussalem Gentile, Lowery, Zemanova, Lecheler, & Peter, 2022).

This awareness about sexual harassment has also brought other viral trends. The #deleteUber trend, which includes many economic, political and social factors, is an important trend that not only makes the voice of Uber employees heard, but also shows that the company is punished with the deletion and non-use of the application by the society for wrong applications. Another sweeping #deleteUber trend has also been interpreted as a digital boycott. With this trend, in which experiences of sexual harassment and sexist attitudes are shared, the awareness of individuals has actually improved and company owners have been informed about changing the negative aspects of the company in this sense (Illia, Colleoni, Ranvidran, & Ludovico, 2022). Researchers have pointed out that these viral sexual harassment experiences can have some harms as well as benefits. Sharing individual memories about sexual harassment through social media channels can also cause unauthorized use and dissemination of this information (Şimşek, 2019). It is seen that the relationship between sexual harassment and the media has been examined in terms of many factors. Considering the well-being of individuals, it is known that sharing a traumatic situation such as harassment has positive effects. It is stated that the ability of individuals to make their voices heard freely and with their own expressions is also an important variable. In a study, it was understood that people who share with #metoo hashtag and communicate with other individuals report more positive psychological development (Chowdhury, Sawhney, Shah, & Mahata, 2019).

Blog posts, tweets, personal videos and photos have become important sources of information today. On the other hand, these shares are also used as a means of socialization. Socialization without time and place restrictions allows individuals to communicate with a large number of people. The rapid dissemination of information, of course, can lead to bad results, on the other hand, revealing traumatic experiences such as harassment and abuse has also shown positive results in terms of being able to hear the voices of the victims. Sharing and reporting traumatic experiences such as sexual harassment, abuse and neglect can be challenging in many ways. The positive and negative results of sharing are both observed and revealed through scientific studies. In recent years, the personalization of media tools and the expansion of their sphere of influence can have a positive impact on victims, especially in challenging issues such as sexual harassment, and increase their support opportunities both socially and legally. In this sense, it is underlined that especially digitalized personal media tools provide social, psychological and legal benefits to individuals.

CONCLUSION

Studies on sexual harassment examine this phenomenon from many perspectives. In social, psychological, societal, media and biological sense, the victim is negatively affected by this phenomenon and the results of sexual harassment can be devastating. Although it is almost impossible for the victim to return to her/his previous routines, there are legal systems, health systems and empowering social systems that support the victim.

When viewed more socially, media tools change over time and it is observed that the side of providing unilateral communication has changed. Individuals can now both receive information and function as a source of information with digitalized media tools. Thus, it is observed that the opportunities of individuals to make their voices heard faster and uncensored increase. It has become easier in this way for adverse events such as sexual harassment to be disclosed or for individuals to report it. Although this has both positive and negative consequences, it can be seen as an important development and change that the victims can make their voices heard without any obstacles, especially in terms of closed societies.

FUTURE RESEARCH AND DIRECTIONS

In this chapter, it is aimed to discuss what sexual harassment is, theoretical models based on sexual harassment, social and individual effects of sexual harassment, and the place of sexual harassment in the media. Within the scope of this study, studies in the social and communication sciences literature were examined and compiled. With the 19th century, it has been understood that sexual harassment works in many areas. It is understood that the definition of sexual harassment, the creation of a theoretical framework, the understanding of its frequency and forms of sexual harassment, the effect of legal processes, and the individual and social reflections of sexual harassment are the subjects of studies. For future studies, it may be beneficial to focus on what kind of restructuring will be made for the psychological recovery of the victims and their re-adaptation to their social lives, and how to create protocols for the re-empowerment of individuals after victimization. At the same time, it is thought that theoretical and practical examples may be needed on how actions can be taken at the individual, organizational and state levels in order to prevent sexual harassment. In addition, it is predicted that the effective treatment of sexual harassment in media and the conduct of studies on how the expression of such sensitive issues in social media affects the psychological states of individuals will make significant contributions to the literature.

REFERENCES

Adikaram, A. (2016). Not So Silent: How Social Support is Given and Received in Dealing with Sexual Harassment in Sri Lankan Work-Places. *NSBM Journal of Management*, *1*(2), 94–126. doi:10.4038/nsbmjm.v1i2.13

Alrawadieh, Z., Demirdelen Alrawadieh, D., Olya, G.T., Erkol Bayram, G., & Kahraman, O. C. (2021). Sexual harassment, psychological well-being, and job satisfaction of female tour guides: the effects of social and organizational support. *Journal of Sustainable Tourism*, 1 – 20. doi:10.1080/09669582.2021.1879819

Bakaç, C., Chen, Y., Zyberaj, J., Kehr, H. M., & Quirin, M. (2022). Perceived intrinsic motivation mediates the effect of motive incongruence on job burnout and job satisfaction. *The Journal of Psychology*, *156*(1), 12–32. doi:10.1080/00223980.2021.1980758 PMID:34762556

Bell, M. E., Street, A. E., & Stafford, J. (2014). Victims' psychosocial well-being after reporting sexual harassment in the military. *Journal of Trauma & Dissociation*, *15*(2), 133–152. doi:10.1080/15299732.2014.867563 PMID:24410254

Bell, M. E., Street, A. E., & Stafford, J. (2014). Victims' psychosocial well-being after reporting sexual harassment in the military. *Journal of Trauma & Dissociation*, *15*(2), 133–152. doi:10.1080/15299732.2014.867563 PMID:24410254

Bem, S. L. (1983). Gender schema theory and its implications for child development: Raising gender-aschematic children in a gender-schematic society. *Signs (Chicago, Ill.)*, *8*(4), 598–616. doi:10.1086/493998

Brown, J. M. (1998). Aspects of discriminatory treatment of women police officers serving in forces in England and Wales. *British Journal of Criminology*, *38*(2), 265–282. doi:10.1093/oxfordjournals.bjc.a014235

Buchanan, N. T., & Fitzgerald, L. F. (2008). Effects of racial and sexual harassment on work and the psychological well-being of African American women. *Journal of Occupational Health Psychology*, *13*(2), 137–151. doi:10.1037/1076-8998.13.2.137 PMID:18393583

Bulger, C. A. (2001). Union resources and union tolerance as moderators of relationships with sexual harassment. *Sex Roles*, *45*(11/12), 723–741. doi:10.1023/A:1015684202115

Campbell, R. (2008). The psychological impact of rape victims. *The American Psychologist*, *63*(8), 702–717. doi:10.1037/0003-066X.63.8.702 PMID:19014228

Chan, D. K., Chow, S. Y., Lam, C. B., & Cheung, S. F. (2008). Examining the job-related, psychological, and physical outcomes of workplace sexual harassment: A meta- analytic review. *Psychology of Women Quarterly*, *32*(4), 362–376. doi:10.1111/j.1471-6402.2008.00451.x

Chan, E. K. H., Lımoges, K. M., & Fung, T. S. (2010). Functional Social Support and Major Depression in Cancer Patients. *Psychology Journal*, *7*(2), 46–50.

Charney, D. A., & Russel, R. C. (1994). An overview of sexual harassment. *The American Journal of Psychiatry*, *151*(1), 10–17. doi:10.1176/ajp.151.1.10 PMID:8267106

Cheng, J. C., & Yi, O. (2018). Hotel employee job crafting, burnout, and satisfaction: The moderating role of perceived organizational support. *International Journal of Hospitality Management*, *72*, 78–85. doi:10.1016/j.ijhm.2018.01.005

Chowdhury, A. G., Sawhney, R., Mathur, P., Mahata, D., & Shah, R. R. (2019, June). Speak up, fight back! detection of social media disclosures of sexual harassment. In *Proceedings of the 2019 conference of the North American chapter of the Association for Computational Linguistics: Student research workshop* (pp. 136-146). 10.18653/v1/N19-3018

Chowdhury, A. G., Sawhney, R., Shah, R., & Mahata, D. (2019, July). # YouToo? detection of personal recollections of sexual harassment on social media. In *Proceedings of the 57th Annual Meeting of the Association for Computational Linguistics* (pp. 2527-2537). 10.18653/v1/P19-1241

Cohen, S. V., & McKay, G. (1984). Social Support, Stress and the BufferingHypothesis: A Theoretical Analysis. Handbook of Psychology and Health, 253-267.

Cortina, L. M. (2004). Hispanic perspective on sexual harassment and social support. *Personality and Social Psychology Bulletin*, *30*(5), 570–584. doi:10.1177/0146167203262854 PMID:15107157

Cortina, L. M., Lonsway, K. A., Magley, V. J., Freeman, L. V., Collingsworth, L. L., & Hunter, M. (2002). What's gender got to do with it? Incivility in the federal courts. *Law & Social Inquiry*, *27*(2), 235–270. doi:10.1111/j.1747-4469.2002.tb00804.x

Davidson, M. J., & Cooper, C. L. (1992). *Shattering the glass ceiling: The woman manager*. Paul Chapman Publishing.

De Judicibus, M., & McCabe, M. P. (2001). Blaming the target of sexual harassment: Impact of gender role, sexist attitudes, and work role. *Sex Roles*, *44*(7/8), 401–417. doi:10.1023/A:1011926027920

DeSouza, E., & Fansler, A. G. (2003). Contrapower sexual harassment: A survey of students and faculty members. *Sex Roles*, *48*(11/12), 529–542. doi:10.1023/A:1023527329364

Farley, L. (1978). *Sexual shakedown: The sexual harassment of women on the job*. McGraw-Hill.

Fitzgerald, L. F., Swan, S., & Magley, V. J. (1997). But was it really sexual harassment? Legal, behavioral, and psychological definitions of the workplace victimization of women. In W. O'Donohue (Ed.), *Sexual harassment: Theory, research and therapy* (pp. 5–28). Allyn & Bacon.

Forensic Statistics of the Ministry of Justice. (2020). *Judicial Statistics 2020.* Turkish Republic Ministry of Justice. https://adlisicil.adalet.gov.tr/Home/SayfaDetay/adalet-istatistikleri-yayin-arsivi

Frazier, P., Berman, M., & Steward, J. (2002). Perceived control and posttraumatic stress: A temporal model. *Applied & Preventive Psychology*, *10*(3), 207–223. doi:10.1016/S0962-1849(01)80015-9

Government Equalities Office. (2020). *2020 Sexual Harassment Survey*. IFF Research. https://assets.publishing.service.gov.uk/government/uploads/system/uploads/attac hment_data/file/1002873/2021-07-12_Sexual_Harassment_Report_FINAL.pdf

Grauerholz, E., & King, A. (1997). Prime time sexual harassment. *Violence Against Women*, *3*(2), 129–148. doi:10.1177/1077801297003002003 PMID:12294811

Gruber, J. E. (1990). Methodological problems and policy implications in sexual harassment research. *Population Research and Policy Review*, *9*(3), 235–254. doi:10.1007/BF00162837

Harned, M. S. (2000). Harassed bodies: An examination of the relationships among women's experiences of sexual harassment, body image, and eating disturbances. *Psychology of Women Quarterly*, *24*(4), 336–348. doi:10.1111/j.1471-6402.2000.tb00216.x

Harned, M. S., & Fitzgerald, L. F. (2002). Understanding a link between sexual harassment and eating disorder symptoms: A mediational analysis. *Journal of Consulting and Clinical Psychology*, *70*(5), 1170–1181. doi:10.1037/0022-006X.70.5.1170 PMID:12362967

Hobfoll, S. E. (1989). Conservation of resources: A new attempt at conceptualizing stress. *The American Psychologist*, *44*(3), 513–524. doi:10.1037/0003-066X.44.3.513 PMID:2648906

Hollon, S. D., & Kriss, M. R. (1984). Cognitive factors in clinical research and practice. *Clinical Psychology Review*, *4*(1), 35–76. doi:10.1016/0272-7358(84)90036-9

Hu, Y.-Y., Ellis, R. J., Hewitt, D. B., Yang, A. D., Cheung, E. O., Moskowitz, J. T., Potts, J. R. III, Buyske, J., Hoyt, D. B., Nasca, T. J., & Bilimoria, K. Y. (2019). Discrimination, abuse, harassment, and burnout in surgical residency training. *The New England Journal of Medicine*, *381*(18), 1741–1752. doi:10.1056/NEJMsa1903759 PMID:31657887

Illia, L., Colleoni, E., Ranvidran, K., & Ludovico, N. (2022). Mens rea, wrongdoing and digital advocacy in social media: Exploring quasi-legal narratives during #deleteuber. *Journal of Public Affairs*, 1 – 16. doi:10.1002/pa.2805

Kearl, H. (2018). *The facts behind the #metoo movement: A national study on sexual harassment and assault*. Stop Street Harassment. https://www.nsvrc.org/sites/default/files/2021-04/full-report-2018-national-study-on-sexual-harassment-and-assault.pdf

Kilpatrick, D. G., Veronen, L. J., & Resnick, P. A. (1982). Psychological sequelae to rape: Assessment and treatment strategies. In D. M. Doleys, R. L. Meredith, & A. R. Ciminero (Eds.), *Behavioral medicine: Assessment and treatment strategies* (pp. 473–497). Plenum Press. doi:10.1007/978-1-4684-4070-6_19

Kinzl, J. F., Mangweth, B., Traweger, C. M., & Biebl, W. (1997). Eatingdisordered behavior in males: The impact of adverse childhood experiences. *International Journal of Eating Disorders*, *22*(2), 131–138. doi:10.1002/(SICI)1098-108X(199709)22:2<131::AID-EAT3>3.0.CO;2-G PMID:9261650

Kocadaş, B. (2005). Kültür ve medya. *Bilig*, *34*, 1–13.

Larsen, S. E., & Fitzgerald, L. F. (2011). PTSD symptoms and sexual harassment: The role of attributions and perceived control. *Journal of Interpersonal Violence*, *26*(13), 2555–2567. doi:10.1177/0886260510388284 PMID:21156692

Larsen, S. E., Nye, C. D., & Fitzgerald, L. F. (2019). Sexual harassment expanded: An examination of the relationships among sexual harassment, sex discrimination, and aggression in the workplace. *Military Psychology*, *31*(1), 35–44. doi:10.1080/08995605.2018.1526526

Lazarus, R. S., & Folkman, S. (1984). Coping and adaptation. In W. D. Gentry (Ed.), *Handbook of Behavioral Medicine* (pp. 282–325). Guilford Press.

MacKinnon, C. A. (1979). *Sexual harassment of working women: A case of sex discrimination*. Yale University Press.

Magley, V. J., Waldo, C. R., Drasgow, F., & Fitzgerald, L. F. (1999). The impact of sexual harassment on military personnel: Is it the same for men and women? *Military Psychology*, *11*(3), 283–302. doi:10.120715327876mp1103_5

Matchen, J., & DeSouza, E. (2000). The sexual harassment of faculty members by students. *Sex Roles*, *42*(3–4), 295–306. doi:10.1023/A:1007099408885

McLean, L., & Griffiths, M. D. (2019). Female gamers' experience of online harassment and social support in online gaming: A qualitative study. *International Journal of Mental Health and Addiction*, *17*(4), 970–994. doi:10.100711469-018-9962-0

me too. (2020). Available at: https://metoomvmt.org/about/

Milano, A. (2017). *Twitter.com*. Retrieved from: https://twitter.com/alyssa_milano/status/919659438700670976?lang=en

Min, J. (2014). The relationships between emotional intelligence, job stress, and quality of life among tour guides. *Asia Pacific Journal of Tourism Research*, *19*(10), 1170–1190. https://doi.org/10.1080/10941665.2013.839459

Murdoch, M., Bradley, A., Mather, S. H., Klein, R. E., Turner, C. L., & Yano, E. M. (2006). Women and war: What physicians should know. *Journal of General Internal Medicine*, *21*, 5–10.

Najdowski, C. J., & Ullman, S. E. (2009). PTSD symptoms and self-rated recovery among adult sexual assault survivors: The effects of traumatic life events and psychosocial variables. *Psychology of Women Quarterly*, *33*, 43–53.

Neumark-Sztainer, D., Story, M., Hannan, P. J., Beuhring, T., & Resnick, M. D. (2000). Disordered eating among adolescents: Associations with sexual/physical abuse and other familial/psychosocial factors. *International Journal of Eating Disorders*, *28*, 249–258.

Noetzel, S., Mussalem Gentile, M. F., Lowery, G., Zemanova, S., Lecheler, S., & Peter, C. (2022). Social campaigns to social change? Sexual violence framing in US news before and after# metoo. *Journalism*, 1 – 32. doi:10.1177/14648849211056386

O'Donohue, W., Downs, K., & Yeater, E. A. (1998). Sexual harassment: A review of the literature. *Aggression and Violent Behavior*, *3*(2), 111–128.

O'Hare, E., & O'Donohue, W. (1998). Sexual harassment: Identifying risk factors. *Archives of Sexual Behavior*, *27*(6), 561–579.

Palmieri, P. A., & Fitzgerald, L. F. (2005). Confirmatory factor analysis of posttraumatic stress symptoms in sexually harassed women. *Journal of Traumatic Stress*, *18*, 657–666.

Pina, A., Gannon, T. A., & Saunders, B. (2009). An overview of the literature on sexual harassment: Perpetrator, theory, and treatment issues. *Aggression and Violent Behavior*, *14*(2), 126–138.

Polaschek, D. L. L., & Ward, T. (2002). The implicit theories of potential rapists: What our questionnaires tell us. *Aggression and Violent Behavior*, *7*(4), 385–406.

Promundo & UN Women. (2017). *Understanding Masculinities: Results from the International Men and Gender Equality Survey (IMAGES) – Middle East and North Africa, UN Women Headquarters*. https://www.unwomen.org/en/digital-library/publications/2017/5/understanding-masculinities-results-from-the-images-in- the-middle-east-and-north-africa

Pryor, J. B. (1987). Sexual harassment proclivities in men. *Sex Roles*, *17*(5), 269–290.

Pryor, J. B. (1995). The phenomenology of sexual harassment: Why does sexual behavior bother people in the workplace. *Consulting Psychology Journal*, *47*, 160–168.

Pryor, J. B., & Stoller, L. M. (1994). Sexual cognition processes in men who are high in the likelihood to sexually harass. *Personality and Social Psychology Bulletin*, *20*, 163–169.

Reid Chassiakos, Y. L., Radesky, J., Christakis, D., Moreno, M. A., Cross, C., Hill, D., ... Swanson, W. S. (2016). Children and adolescents and digital media. *Pediatrics*, *138*(5), 1–18.

Rotundo, M., Nguyen, D. H., & Sackett, P. R. (2001). A meta-analytic review of gender differences in perceptions of sexual harassment. *The Journal of Applied Psychology*, *86*(5), 914–922.

Russell, D. E. H. (1984). *Sexual exploitation: Rape, child sexual abuse, and workplace harassment*. Sage.

Sbraga, T. P., & O'donohue, W. (2000). Sexual harassment. *Annual Review of Sex Research*, *11*(1), 258–285.

Şimşek, T. (2019). Sosyal medyada mahremiyetin ifşası "instagram örneği". *Sosyolojik Düşün*, *4*(1), 10–24.

Spitzberg, B. H. (1999). An analysis of empirical estimates of sexual aggression, victimisation and perpetration. *Violence and Victims*, *14*, 241–260.

Stark, S., Chernyshenko, O. S., Lancaster, A. R., Drasgow, F., & Fitzgerald, L. F. (2002). Toward standardized measurement of sexual harassment: Shortening the SEQ–DoD using item response theory. *Military Psychology*, *14*, 49–72.

Stockdale, M. S., Visio, M., & Batra, L. (1999). The sexual harassment of men: Evidence for a broader theory of sexual harassment and sex discrimination. *Psychology, Public Policy, and Law*, *5*, 630–664.

Street, A. E., Gradus, J. L., Stafford, J., & Kelly, K. (2007). Gender differences in experiences of sexual harassment: Data from a male-dominated environment. *Journal of Consulting and Clinical Psychology*, *75*(3), 464–474.

Tangri, S., & Hayes, S. (1997). Theories of sexual harassment. In W. O'Donohue (Ed.), *Sexual harassment: Theory, research, and treatment* (pp. 112–128). Allyn & Bacon.

Terpstra, D. E., & Baker, D. D. (1989). The identification and classification of reactions to sexual harassment. *Journal of Organizational Behavior*, *10*, 1–14.

Thomas, A. M., & Kitzinger, C. (1997). *Sexual harassment. Contemporary feminist perspectives*. Open University Press.

UN Women. (2021). *Research Brief - Intimate Partner Violence in Five CARICOM Countries: Findings from National Prevalence Surveys on Violence Against Women*. UNICEF. https://www.unicef.org/easterncaribbean/media/2926/file/Gen-U%20Trinidad%20Fact%20Sheet.pdf

U.S. Merit Systems Protection Board. (1988). *Sexual harassment in the federal Government: An update*. Government Printing Office.

Vogt, D., Pless, A. P., King, L. A., & King, D. W. (2005). Deployment stressors, gender, and mental health outcomes among Gulf War I veterans. *Journal of Traumatic Stress*, *18*, 272–284.

Waldo, C. R., Berdahl, J. L., & Fitzgerald, L. F. (1998). Are men sexually harassed? If so, by whom? *Law and Human Behavior*, *22*(1), 59–79.

Watts, C., & Zimmerman, C. (2002). Violence against women: Global scope and magnitude. *Lancet*, *359*(9313), 1232–1237.

Welsh, S., Carr, J., MacQuarrie, B., & Huntley, A. (2006). "I'm not thinking of it as sexual harassment" understanding harassment across race and citizenship. *Gender & Society*, *20*(1), 87–107.

Welsh, S., & Gruber, J. E. (1999). Not taking it any more: Women who report or file complaints of sexual harassment. *Canadian Review of Sociology/Revue canadienne de sociologie, 36*(4), 559-583.

WHO. (March 9, 2021). *Younger women among those most at risk: WHO.* https://www.who.int/news/item/09-03-2021-devastatingly-pervasive-1-in-3-women-globally-experience-violence#

Women in News. (2021). *Sexual Harassment in the Media: African Report.* WAN-IFRA. https://womeninnews.org/wp-content/uploads/2021/07/20210712-Low-Res-Sexual-Harassment-Report.pdf

World Population Record. (April 14, 2021). *UNFPA Launches the State Of World Population Report, 2021: My Body Is My Own*. UNFPA. https://in.one.un.org/news/unfpa-launches-the-state-of-world-population-report-2021-my-body-is-my- own/#:~:text=Is%20My%20Own,UNFPA%20Launches%20the%20State%20Of%20Wor ld%20Population%20Report%2C%202021,My%20Body% 20Is%20My%20Own&text=Nearly%20half%20of%20all% 20women,Wednesday%2C%20April%2014%2C%202021

ADDITIONAL READING

Ceccato, V., & Loukaitou-Sideris, A. (2022). Fear of sexual harassment and its impact on safety perceptions in transit environments: A global perspective. *Violence Against Women*, *28*(1), 26–48. doi:10.1177/1077801221992874 PMID:33656953

Evans, A. E., Currin, J. M., Garos, S., Stokes, A., Cox, K., & Meyer, C. L. (2022). 'Wasn't This Already Considered Sexual Harassment?': Exploring the Confusion Around the Law Mandating Consent to Receive a Nude Sext Message. *American Journal of Sexuality Education*, *17*(3), 1–25. doi:10.1080/15546128.2021.2025181

Galdi, S., Maass, A., & Cadinu, M. (2014). Objectifying media: Their effect on gender role norms and sexual harassment of women. *Psychology of Women Quarterly*, *38*(3), 398–413. doi:10.1177/0361684313515185

McDonald, P., & Charlesworth, S. (2013, March). Framing sexual harassment through media representations. *Women's Studies International Forum*, *37*, 95–103. doi:10.1016/j.wsif.2012.11.003

KEY TERMS AND DEFINITIONS

Media: It is the general name given to communication channels that allow access to areas such as news, music, education, and information. It enables to receive information from the society and to give information to the society.

Perceived Social Support: It is defined as the perception of financial, moral and psychological support from friends, family members or others as appropriate when needed.

Post-Traumatic Stress Disorder (PTSD): It is a psychiatric disorder that can be seen in individuals who have faced or experienced natural disaster, serious accident, terrorist attack, war, harassment or threat of death, rape, or injury.

Self-Esteem: It is the individual's subjective values of one's own values. It can include beliefs about one's self and emotional states such as victory, pride, and shame.

Self-Isolation: It is defined as a reluctance to communicate with other individuals and generally a desire to stay indoors.

Sexual Coercion: It is all unwanted sexual activities that occur under psychological pressure, deception, threat, or coercion.

Sexual Harassment: Sexual approach, sexual demands and/or other verbal/physical behaviors with sexual content against the will of the individual.

Chapter 5
Bullying Towards Body Image During Adolescence

Kadriye Özyazıcı
Sivas Cumhuriyet Üniversitesi, Turkey

ABSTRACT

In this chapter, children who are bullied about body image during adolescence are discussed. Adolescent bullying, body image and body dissatisfaction, appearance-related bullying among peers, body image bullying as a mediator of sociocultural effects, body image bullying as a mediator of media effects, results of peer bullying related to body image in adolescents, and solutions and suggestions are presented. Having difficulty in adapting to the physical changes that come with development, the adolescent also faces bullying caused by environmental stress factors and needs to regulate their relations with their peers. During this difficult period of development, it becomes more important to understand the stressors that result from closely changing the adolescent in the way of supporting them socially. Bullying and negative perception of body image is becoming more common. It poses a major threat to the well-being and health of adolescents worldwide. Therefore, this chapter aims to explain body image bullying towards adolescents.

INTRODUCTION

In this section, the children being bullied about their body image during adolescence are discussed. Adolescents' bullying, body image, and body dissatisfaction, appearance-related bullying among peers, body image bullying as a mediator of sociocultural effects, body image bullying as a mediator of media effects, observed results of peer bullying about body image on the adolescents, solutions, and suggestions are presented. Adolescence is known as a period, in which significant changes occur at each developmental stage and when the adaptation could be very compelling. Changes in the body can sometimes cause dissatisfaction and negative perceptions about its appearance. Children who are underweight and overweight in relation to their body parts may be at risk of being bullied about their appearance. Seemingly non-bullying conversations with peers about appearance put pressure on body image and can contribute significantly to body dissatisfaction. Sometimes, it can be seen that the expression used

DOI: 10.4018/978-1-6684-5426-8.ch005

by the family member unconsciously or criticizing the body shape and weight at home, suggesting a diet affect the adolescent's perception of body image. The physical attractiveness and beauty criteria of the living culture for men and women may cause the internalization of attractiveness ideals and results such as body dissatisfaction and irregular nutrition. In addition to all these factors, in the historical time we live in, the mass media constantly creates a perception about what is attractive to adolescents, how important it is for them to look, and how to achieve this appearance. For this reason, the individuals might face various difficulties or problems especially during the adolescence period. An adolescent, who struggles with adaptation to physical changes coming with development, also faces the bullying arising from environmental stressors and need to arrange his/her relationships with peers. In this difficult period of development, understanding the stressors originating from close modifying them in the way socially supporting the adolescent becomes more important. In order to protect children from bullying towards body image, it is necessary to make a planning that includes all inter-system relations such as family, friends, teachers, mass media, cultural approach, which indirectly affect the development of the individual, starting from the closest social environment. Adolescents exposed to body image bullying do not create a perception that they are not attractive by their peers and are labeled as unpopular youth. The victimized adolescent internalizes this perception attributed to them due to the bullying and finds themselves less attractive. They behave more passively in many areas of their lives such as social relations, sports and academics, and they think that they are less competent. They perceive their mocking thoughts about their appearance by their peers as worse than the current situation. Victims of bullying experience a great deal of deprivation, especially unhealthy eating behavior, in the face of difficulties and anxiety-inducing situations in their lives. For these reasons, adolescents want to change the view of their body more and more every day. Bullying and negative perception towards body image are becoming more and more common.It poses a major threat to adolescent well-being and health worldwide. For this reason, this section aims to explain the body image bullying toward adolescents. This section begins with the definition of the concepts of Adolescence, Body Image, and Body Dissatisfaction. After the definitions, the possible sources of bullying addressing the body image of adolescent will be discussed.

BULLYING

Bullying refers to behaviors causing pain, distress, and sorrow by one or more students towards others without an obvious motivation. It is accepted as a series of intentional, offensive, and repetitive behaviors creating negative effects on the victims (Gilbert & Irons, 2009). Bullies want to harm others by using force or through offensive behaviors (Arseneault, Bowes & Shakoor, 2010). In general, they make their victims feel bad, feared, and defenseless (Pegis, 2013).

Bullying is categorized into four classes as physical, verbal, relational, and cyber-bullying (Migliaccio & Raskauskas, 2016). It can be performed through various ways such as direct or indirect physical contact, verbal abuse, social exclusion, and misuse of social or cyber networks (Arseneault, Bowes & Shakoor, 2010). Physical bullying includes the physical attack to peers or their belongings by children, especially during the early childhood period (Pegis, 2013). Relational bullying is categorized as causing problems in peer relations, exclusion, or manipulation of relationships. It includes psychological attacks such as humiliation, spreading rumors, and damaging self-respect or social status and it can generally be related with other types of bullying. Especially verbal aggression and relational aggression are among the types of bullying observed together. Cyberbullying can be considered relational and verbal bullying via media tools and social networks. Insult, threatening, and bad-naming the victim are among the common cyberbullying behaviors (Migliaccio & Raskauskas, 2016).

ADOLESCENCE

Adolescence is a process of rapid growth, in which childhood is left behind, before adulthood. Between the ages of 12 and 18 in general, various cultural, social, physical, and psychological changes characterizing the adolescence uniquely interact with each other (Voelker, Reel & Greenleaf, 2015). Including the inner turmoils, many changes emerge in this period of development. Besides the unforeseen differentiations in emotions and behaviors occurring suddenly, one of the necessities for the adolescent is the adaptation to a developing and growing body (Ricciardelli & Yager, 2015). Adolescence can be defined as a period playing a determinant role in the development of body image. Important social, cognitive, and physical changes occurring in this period might cause anxieties about the body and weight of adolescents (Ata, Ludden & Lally, 2007). The rapid growth attack occurring in this phase of development might bring adaptation problems with it (Wood, Lane & Cheetham, 2019). Because of the personal differences, the timing of the growth attack might differ individually. Because of the growth, height, weight, and pubertal growth attack, the changes in the appearance of children might reach a level that can be observed physically (Roelants & Cameron, 2022).

BODY IMAGE AND BODY DISSATISFACTION

Body image is a multidimensional phenomenon regarding the physical appearance of a person including subjective satisfaction, appreciating one's own body, and cognitive perceptions and behaviors about the body (Grogan, 2021). Body image is our way of seeing our body. Our feelings towards our bodies and our beliefs and thoughts about our bodies constitute our body image (Ricciardelli & Yager, 2015). Body dissatisfaction refers to the negative perceptions toward general appearance related with body size, shape, and weight. It means that a person had subjectively negative assessments about one's body regarding the body parts. The level of dissatisfaction might vary from slight discomfort to very extreme levels such as repulsion, disgust, and event hatred (Ricciardelli & Yager, 2015). During the transition to adulthood, the remarkable changes in the body shape refer to an important phase in the development of positive or negative body image (Voelker, Reel & Greenleaf, 2015).

Girls put on approximately 7-25 kg weight during the adolescence period and, consequently, their body fat increases aprroximately by 120%. However, boys put on aprroximately 7-30 kg; a minority of this weight increase is in fat mass but it generally occurs as an increase in muscle mass. Previous researches showed that, for many men, adolescence was considered a positive experience because of approaching the shape that is considered ideal by society. Muscle mass in the bodies of boys increases, shoulder-width expands and, thus, they approach more to the physical appearance idealized by the society (Ricciardelli & Yager, 2015). In this parallel, boys, who are not satisfied with their bodies because of leanness, become more inclined to mental and behavioral problems and it was observed that they might exhibit aggressive behaviors. The risk of being bullied because of physical weaknesses also increases and they are under the risk of becoming bully-victim (Holubcikova, Kolarcik, Madarasova Geckova, Van Dijk & Reijneveld, 2015). This process occurs less positively for girls. Normative increases in body fat cause enlargements in hips and curved body contour and they might deviate from the body shape idealized by society for women (Ricciardelli & Yager, 2015). It might cause body image concerns and negative eating attitudes and behaviors among adolescent girls. Although negative body image is more frequently observed among girls, overweight/obese boys and lean boys are also under the risk of bullying behaviors (Lawler & Nixon, 2011). For both genders, adolescence occurs as a critical phase for body image but the girls and boys have different anxieties and concerns (Ata, Ludden & Lally, 2007).

During adolescence, thin and overweight/obese children are under the risk (Holubcikova, Kolarcik, Madarasova Geckova, Van Dijk & Reijneveld, 2015). Regardless of their demographic characteristics such as gender, race, socioeconomic status, social skills, and academic achievements, overweight or obese children are under a higher risk of being bullied. Being overweight or obese is the main parameter in terms of getting bullied (Farhat, Iannotti & Simons-Morton, 2010). Overweight adolescents are vulnerable to bullying. Although different appearances of adolescents cause lack of self-respect, it can also make them easy targets for aggressive behaviors of others (Sentenac, Arnaud, Gavin, Molcho, Gabhainn & Godeau 2012). Considering the relationships between body image and bullying experiences varying depending on the obesity status among adolescents, the bodyweight for becoming a victim of bullying becomes more important (Fowler, Kracht, Denstel, Stewart & Staiano, 2021). The adolescents reporting negative body image and those considering themselves fat can more likely be a victim or bully-victim. It was also reported that boys considering themselves thin might be bully-victim (Sentenac, Arnaud, Gavin, Molcho, Gabhainn & Godeau 2012).

The false perception about the bodyweight is more commonly observed among thin, normal-weight, and overweight children and adolescents. Emotional and physical outcomes of misperception vary depending on the gender and the direction of misperception (Lee, Dale, Guy & Wolke, 2018). In the adolescence period, which is called a period of storms and stress, identity formation continues and the abstract reasoning causing self-comparison with others might cause further body image anxieties (Ricciardelli & Yager, 2015). Such bullying experiences might have an adolescent feel non-attractive and it might lead them to ignore the identity of others, tyrannize them, or harm them (Gilbert & Irons, 2009). It is thought that bullying victimhood is an important risk factor for childhood and adolescence psychopathology (Arseneault, Bowes & Shakoor, 2010). Among the adolescents having low level of self-respect, weight-related pressures from family and friends further increase the negative eating behaviors and body weight anxieties (Ata, Ludden & Lally, 2007). Body image dissatisfaction is an important risk factor for the beginning of eating pathology and depression. Understanding the determinants of negative body image becomes gradually more important. Both overweight/obese and thin boys are under the risk of low quality of life (Lawler & Nixon, 2011). Among the adolescents who have been bullied regarding their appearance in the period, when body changes and takes shape, and had suffered, it causes a higher level of body image concern, appearance anxiety, and sometimes dysmorphic symptoms (Zimmer-Gembeck & Webb, 2017).

During adolescence, weight-related bullying concepts cause overemphasis on body weight and appearance and they may also cause the development of body images and dissatisfaction regarding specific parts of the body. During adolescence, body image bullying is influenced by many factors including the characteristics of development period affecting the body shape, weight, and appearance (Voelker, Reel & Greenleaf, 2015).

Peers and Appearance Talks

Participating daily life talks with peers about appearance, image, and attractiveness, adolescents nearly receive appearance training. During their talks about physical appearance, their talks expressing their emotions and thoughts about appearance and image provide an environment, where their physical appearances are interpreted and their appearances are valued. These talks based on long and detailed analyses regarding their body images during daily routines might become a point of focus in their lives. Further internalizing the norms and ideals related with the appearance they create, they also encourage other individuals in their circle to adopt these norms. Together with their peers, they discuss the image and seek after getting a better image. The adolescents, for whom the subject of those talks is only the body image, develop more body dissatisfaction when compared to those discussing this subject less (Jones, 2004). Even the talks of peers not incorporating a body image bullying and seeming like completely harmless focus on this subject and cause pressure related with the body image, as well as significantly contributing to body dissatisfaction. Talking with friends about physical appearance causes the formation of ideal appearance norms and adaptation of these norms. The ideal appearance perception causes individuals to evaluate his/her physical appearance by comparing it to others and it creates body dissatisfaction. Ideal appearance creates similar results among boys and girls through similar peer experiences. For this reason, the peer group obviously acts as an important instrument for transmitting the sociocultural messages of appearance ideals. During the daily talks with peers, the talks incorporating humiliation addressing the physical appearance lead them to pay more importance to physical appearance and they might turn it into idealized images (Lawler & Nixon, 2011).

Although girls tend more to speak to their friends about physical appearance and to be dissatisfied with their bodies when compared to boys, being bullied by their peers regarding their physical appearance is among the most important sources of the pressure of adolescence for both girls and boys. Appearance criticisms by peers seem to be an important predictor of body dissatisfaction for both girls and boys and, in the adolescence period, peer bullying plays a central role in body dissatisfaction. As a result of adolescents being bullied by their peers about their physical appearance, their body dissatisfaction is affected (Lawler & Nixon, 2011).

Peers are important social support sources, especially during the adolescence period. Communication with peers increases in this period but it also stratifies among different groups. Adolescents' efforts for achieving social acceptance might cause the development of problems such as competition to gain a place in peer groups, as well as popularity, competition, and social status among adolescents (Gilbert & Irons, 2009). In the adolescence period, adolescents desire to achieve the social acceptance and approval of their peers. Not being accepted and not being approved might cause pressure on them and it may sometimes cause them to bully (Pegis, 2013). Social interactions with peers are of vital importance for bullying dynamics. Being subjected to bullying and damaged peer relationships in a social circle might cause severe deterioration of development (Smokowski & Evans, 2019). How adolescents get involved in these competitive fields and how a process they have there are affected by a series of factors related with groups' stability and ecology, as well as the character of adolescents (Gilbert & Irons, 2009). Contrary to what is believed, bullies might have high skills from the aspects of social skills and social intelligence. In parallel with these skills they have, they make social manipulation and regulate their social circle in favor of themselves. As a natural outcome of this process, it can be seen that more than half of bullies have a strong and good social status. Considering these skills of bullies, it is considered very likely that adolescents, who have low levels of body image and lack of social competence, would be socially excluded (Hymel, Schonert-Reıchl, Bonanno, Vaıllancourt & Henderson 2010).

Peer Appearance Bullying

Peers are children or adolescents, who are at the same age or level of maturity. While the level of being affected by the peers is low between the ages of 10 and 14, it peaks between the ages of 14 and 18. Directly or indirectly guiding about what is acceptable and appropriate, peers can establish subjective emotions about various norms. Peer group defines expectations, norms, and ideal image and determines parameters about which is acceptable and which isn't (Ricciardelli & Yager, 2015). Peer appearance can be thought as an instrument, with which the culture is defined, shared, and accepted between the adolescents. Girls and boys not meeting the qualities accepted to be attractive are subjected to negative peer comments and they are criticized in various ways. Adolescent's exposure to a criticism about his/her body and a direct negative criticism by another one about the personal appearance of a person might affect the psychological processes (Jones, Vigfusdottir & Lee, 2004). It can be stated that peer norms are learned and internalized through two main ways according to Social Learning Hypothesis (Bandura, 1989). First of them is the model, in which the attitudes and behaviors of peers are directly observed and then mimicked. Positive and negative attitudes towards specific body shapes and weights regarding the body image are observed in the social circle. As a result of these observations, the ideal norms are adopted by the adolescent. They avoid attitudes towards the body ideal that is not accepted by the peers. In this case, while mimicking one of the body ideals of role models, adolescent avoid the non-accepted situations. Another way of learning is the social consolidation including prizes for complying with the group norms and pressure and undesired outcomes for those now complying. Adolescent would try to fit the idealized body image in order to be approved and appreciated. Besides that, they would avoid the situations that are criticized (Ricciardelli & Yager, 2015).

Although the idealized appearance is different for boys and girls, they are both affected similarly by the ideal appearance and body image satisfaction. The students, who frequently talk to their friends about physical appearance, highly internalize it in both genders. It causes the individual to be more dissatisfied with his/her body (Jones, Vigfusdottir & Lee, 2004). Adolescent girls, who are humiliated by their peers about their weight, physical appearance, and body shape, tend more exhibit weaker body image and seek for solutions in their own ways. They possibly make effort in order to achieve the ideal and approved status (Lieberman, Gauvin, Bukowski & White, 2001). Critical approach toward physical appearance also causes body dissatisfaction and a decrease in emotional wellbeing among boys. In a longitudinal study on secondary school and high school students, it was concluded that the reason for low self-respect and body dissatisfaction was the humiliation (Eisenberg, Neumark-Sztainer, Haines & Wall, 2006). Being overweight is a socially undesired situation for both boys and girls (Jones, Vigfusdottir & Lee, 2004). The pressure of being thin perceived from the circle results in increasing body dissatisfaction. Pressures about the ideal body stereotype from friends and family might occur directly as a result of humiliation about weight but it can also occur through a friend expressing his/her concerns (Stice, Maxfield & Wells 2003). The humiliation experienced during the adolescence period may also be related with facial characteristics, in addition to bodyweight. Humiliations addressing hair, breasts, abdomen, hips, and height predict low self-esteem (Jeong-Ju & Johnson, 2007). Humiliation addressing specific body parts such as nose, general face, skin, teeth, feet, legs/thighs, ears, general deformations, breasts, eyebrows, nails, lips, muscle mass, and shoulders are positively related with the dysmorphic deformations (Buhlmann, Cook, Fama & Wilhelm, 2007). The individuals having congenital facial differences were found to be subjected to humiliation during the adolescence period. It can be very effective on the body image related with the levels of physical appearance and depressive symptoms among women (Feragen & Stock, 2016).

The adolescents being bullied about their body image are rated as less popular and less attractive by their peers. Victim adolescents internalize this perception, consider themselves less attractive, and think they are less competent in sports and academic field. The thoughts of their peers about their physical appearance are perceived as worse than the actual situation (Zimmer-Gembeck & Webb, 2017). For these reasons, more than half of adolescents want to change their physical appearance. Girls are more vulnerable to the social pressure arising from the talks idealizing the appearance and they perceive more pressure towards complying with the cultural ideal (Lawler & Nixon, 2011). Their perceptions about weight and appearance during the adolescence period also bring the highly externalized self-perception. Peer humiliation towards the appearance of adolescents also causes social results such as inability to be popular and the lack of flirt requests from the opposite gender (Lieberman, Gauvin, Bukowski & White, 2001).

In a study carried out on 51,192 students aiming to determine the extent of bullying and analyze its relationship with body perception in Brazilian schools, it was determined that boys were subjected to humiliation more than girls (7.2%) and they bullied more than girls did (Garcia, Sousa & Varela Monteiro, 2021). The prevalence of negative perception about the body image gradually increases and it poses a significant threat to the adolescent health around the world (Chisuwa & O'Dea 2011). Peer bullying is one of the reasons for problems about body image and eating during the adolescence period, especially among girls. For this reason, it becomes important to understand how the victimization experiences during this important developmental phase can be related to the body image and eating psychopathology (Duarte, Pinto-Gouveia & Stubbs, 2017; Voelker, Reel & Greenleaf, 2015). Among adolescents, the relationship between humiliation and bullying, irregular eating, and body image disorder is very complex. When compared to non-victim adolescents, the ones being humiliated or bullied tend more to have an eating disorder and negative body image problem. Being overweight causes exposure to bullying, but getting bullied also causes eating disorders (Day, Bussey, Trompeter & Mitchison, 2021). Victims of bullying may prefer calming themselves down via unhealthy eating behavior against the difficulties and the situations causing anxiety. It suggests that body image is closely related with body image shame and eating psychopathology. It also shows that shame experiences including bullying are related with weaker emotional regulation and negative psychological outcomes during the adolescence period (Duarte & Pinto-Gouveia, 2017).

BODY IMAGE: BULLYING AS A MEDIATOR IF SOCIOCULTURAL EFFECTS

Sociocultural models come to the forefront in explaining the development of body image dissatisfaction among young individuals. Society supports an appearance culture emphasizing the desirability of physical beauty and attractiveness for both women and men (Keery, Van den Berg & Thompson, 2004). Internalization of social attractiveness towards body is one of the most important risk factors for body dissatisfaction and irregular eating. It causes the social ideals imposed on women and men to be internalized and adopted as personal goals. Every individual, who has been subjected to this pressure of ideal appearance, cannot reach the target and, thus, they are under a risk. When they compare themselves to the ideals, they feel less attractive and are not pleased with their appearance (Ricciardelli & Yager, 2015).

Appearance-oriented culture generally addresses young individuals as potential buyers. It especially shapes their ideal body image perception. These cultural ideals and beliefs are reinforced by adolescents' close circle including family, friends, and romantic partners. While gaining primary and secondary sexual characteristics, adolescents are subjected to culturally idealized beauty comparisons. Growing and developing adolescents might remain in between socially idealized body image and his/her appearance not complying with this image (Voelker, Reel & Greenleaf, 2015). Among the young individuals, sociocultural structure plays a non-negligible intermediary role in the development of body image dissatisfaction. It causes adolescents to establish body image models in parallel with society's ideals. These models support an appearance emphasizing the desirability of physical attractiveness and beauty for both men and women (Keery, Van den Berg & Thompson, 2004). The main characteristic of female beauty and the key to physical attractiveness are related to the low body weight. Despite the thinness idealized for women, men are expected to have a muscular or mesomorphic appearance. Sociocultural ideals constructed for girls and boys cause body image dissatisfaction among adolescents (Knauss, Paxton & Alsaker, 2007).

At very young ages, girls realize that they are assessed on how they look. Before how they feel or what they can do, they start understanding how their bodies are perceived by other individuals. It causes young girls to have low respect for their own bodies and to have less and irregular eating behavior. Cultural context causing women to criticize their bodies causes women (from all age groups) to develop negative body perceptions. As it becomes difficult to achieve the cultural context standards and to have ideal body weight, it strains individuals further and becomes a problem. When the perception of cultural body standards are internalized by individuals and women cannot achieve these standards, they may feel ashamed. When these standards about physical appearance are not achieved, rather than questioning the pressure of cultural image, they feel bad. As a result, limited and irregular eating behavior and a higher body-shame develop (McKinley, 1999).

Appearance-related Domestic Bullying

Negative body image, eating problems, and problematic eating behaviors can also be related with familial pressure. One of the factors playing determinant role in adolescents' body weight perceptions is the family (Ata, Ludden & Lally, 2007). Mostly, there might be an older sibling or even a parent intentionally or unintentionally bullying a family member (Tarshis & Tarshis, 2010). Parents' criticisms about the body shape and weight are observed to possibly affect the adolescent's perception of body image. Structurally having a high level of anxiety, adolescents might be more sensitive towards the messages of their parents and it might make them to be affected more even by the sincere messages. Besides that, daughters might warp the messages coming from their parents. These exaggerated or wrong messages they perceive might be further reinforced by the peer messages and further internalized. Through their own behaviors and attitudes, parents may cause pressure by indirectly transmitting implicit messages about the ideal body (Ricciardelli & Yager, 2015). The relationship between girls' body experiences and messages from their families has a bidirectional determinant effect. Through the messages they have received from their families since the early ages, girls learn the acceptability criteria for the female body. They have knowledge about the ideal female body through direct and indirect messages. Girls' respect for their body and perceptions about their appearance are closely related with the approval by the family (McKinley, 1999).

This pressure made by the closest ones to adolescents deeply influences them. Perceiving the pressure from the family, adolescents think that their body was different from the ideal figure and it might cause them to develop negative eating behaviors. Thinking that he/she was way far from the ideal body, adolescents might develop inappropriate dietary habits, excessive eating, and vomiting behaviors (Ata, Ludden & Lally, 2007). Humiliations and criticisms made by families about physical appearance would increase the body dissatisfaction of adolescents (Jones, Vigfusdottir & Lee, 2004).

Another aspect of family, which might be related with bullying, is the character of the parent-child relationship. A gradually increasing number of studies focus on the role of the parent-child relationship in bullying. It was reported that vast majority of children bullying their peers had an insecure bond with their primary caregivers. Children bullying their peers were observed to have a history of avoider bonding style. Moreover, bullies might generally have damaged relationships with their parents and they mostly perceive a very low level of social support from their parents (Nıckerson, Mele & Osborne-Olıver, 2010). It is known that bully kids were generally grown in inconsistent families exhibiting non-functional discipline. Bullying kids may sometimes have been physically, mentally, or sexually abused by family members (Pegis, 2013).

Body Image Bullying as a Mediator of Media Effects

Mass communication instruments constantly create a perception about what is attractive, how important looking like this is, and how to achieve this appearance. In the last two centuries, young individuals have been subjected to pressures motivating them into a specific image consciousness. Young people use multiple media platforms at the same time and they spent a significant amount of time on these platforms. The images of muscular men and thin women on the media are considered the reason for internalizing these unrealistic standards as norms by young individuals (Ricciardelli & Yager, 2015). Intense exposure to media does not necessarily lead to image dissatisfaction but social media culture can generally create body image dissatisfaction (Ata, Ludden & Lally, 2007; McCabe & Ricciardelli, 2005).

TV, movies, and journals explicitly and implicitly transmit messages about body image perceptions. The body image accepted and represented on the media is almost soaked by the mind. The perceptions internalized by a person would be open to a complex comparison from a different perspective. A person would idealize the media figures presented as role models. Considering the perception idealized on the body image regarding the personal defects in the real-life, an incompliance would cause a negative self (Wickman, 2000). Appearance journals are among the most significant predictors of body dissatisfaction among girls (Jones, Vigfusdottir & Lee, 2004). Watching TV is a stronger predictor of body ideals and irregular eating when compared to reading. Since the early ages, watching TV causes girls to develop unrealistic body ideals in adolescence and adulthood periods (Harrison and Hefner, 2006).

Through the media, the unrealistically thin female bodies and unrealistically muscular male bodies are internalized and it significantly affects the body image (Carlson Jones, 2004). Media has a remarkable effect on the formation of ideal body perception and is an important source for body image perception concerns. Standard ideal appearance may cause depressing perception of insufficiency in the course of time. Young individuals' appearances that do not comply with the standards may lead them to prefer wrong methods (Wickman, 2000). Both psychological theories and research results show that media might cause development and continuity of eating problems among women. Despite the emphasis on a person's perfect physical appearance, most women might not be able to achieve that appearance despite all the efforts. Hence, it would cause pressure on them. For instance, after seeing those images, the adolescents having anorexia and bulimia problems would further exaggerate their body size and exhibit more unhealthy limiting eating attitudes. Such media images affect a wide population including pregnant women, besides the adolescents (Gaskill & Sanders, 2000).

The remarkable effects on the body image also include the media addressing adolescents and their peers contributing to construction of the beliefs about perceived body ideal. The internalization of socially determined body ideals and the pressures towards complying with them help explaining the relationships between body weight and body image (Voelker, Reel & Greenleaf, 2015). In addition, situations, where people's appearances are stereotyped or ridiculed by the characters in the media, are often reflected on the screen. For instance, beautiful and blond characters are generally described as stupid or less intelligent on the screen. Overweight characters can be presented as more negative in comparison to the thin ones. Such messages are important since they lead society, especially the youth, to encourage prejudice and intolerance. Such stereotypes about the body image cluster individuals into groups via simplified images or beliefs (Murphy, 2009).

Three strict standards were set for the body image model constructed by the mass communication instruments; beauty, youth, and perfect body. Although there are 3 billion women on earth, only 8 women (Naomi Campbell, Cindy Crawford, etc.) have the idealized perfect body. These 8 supermodels are considered concrete examples of perfect body image. It results in the development of negative body image among women not fitting the definition of ideal woman. Besides the personal problems it causes among women, it also influences their social acceptability. It leads women to be dissatisfied with their "imperfect" bodies and to seek for various solutions (Ring, 2000). The status of a woman in a society is determined mainly by her physical appearance, whereas the status of a man is determined mainly by his physical and intellectual skills (Sanders, Gwynne & Gaskill, 2000). This perception of physical appearance leads women to options such as plastic surgery since the period of adolescence. Plastic surgery is a procedure performed in order to re-shape the normal. It refers to enhancing body structures or body parts in order to improve the appearance and self-esteem of consumer. Improvements can be carried out on the appearance of almost every part of the body in accordance with the ideal body perception, so that people feel better (Ring, 2000).

It can be seen that especially the media has a significant effect on the society's beauty perceptions. Media is an important source of information and socialization for children. It is known that 90% of young individuals access the information about the world through various media instruments; thus, anything on the media would be very important (Sanders, Gwynne & Gaskill, 2000). It can be seen that 92% of young individuals use Internet on daily basis, 77% use social media, and social media is an instrument that is becoming more and more popular every day. Especially the visual social media platforms increase the levels of increasing anxiety and depression. It became very important to receive likes in photo- or video-based applications such as Facebook and Instagram. In order to draw the attention of followers' interest, filters assist the content creators. The images that are not fitting to the perceived ideal do not yield likes but they might cause humiliations. Humiliations and criticisms through social media influence the negative body image and self-respect (Kennedy, 2019). It can be seen that media is the predictor of body dissatisfaction among boys and girls in idealization and internalization of body and in perceiving the pressure. An adolescent aiming to achieve more approval on media would perceive more pressure. Although boys perceive less pressure from the media in comparison to girls, media still is the most important predictor of body dissatisfaction for men. For this reason, it becomes important to educate both boys and girls the skills of accurately assessing and managing their body ideals reflected on the media (Knauss, Paxton & Alsaker, 2007).

OBSERVABLE RESULTS OF BULLYING ON BODY IMAGE AMONG ADOLESCENTS

The effects of peer bullying on the health and wellbeing of children are commonly investigated. Among the victims of bullying, the most common stressors are the negative mental conditions and/or emotions and they consist of external stressors constructed by portions such as the rings of a chain (Eisenstadt, Stapley, Deighton & Wolpert, 2020). Bullying addressing the body image might be related with depression (Chen, Luo & Chen, 2020), high level of anxiety and depressive symptomatology, low developmental level (Patte, Livermore, Qian & Leatherdale, 2021), mental health problems negatively influencing the daily life (Krusell, Hohwü, Bjereld, Madsen & Obel, 2019), less interest in academic phenomenon, leaving the school, lower level of social integration (Stamate, Aimé, Gagnon & Villatte, 2021), muscle dysmorphic disorder (Fabris, Badenes-Ribera & Longobardi, 2021), increasing motivation for surgery (Milothridis, 2020), substance abuse (Klinck, Vannucci, Fagle & Ohannessian, 2020), body image shame, self-criticism, low self-esteem, eating psychopathology (Duarte, Pinto-Gouveia & Rodrigues, 2015), skipping meals, use of non-prescribed diet medications, intentionally vomiting, use of laxatives in order to lose or control body weight, and such irregular weight control behaviors (Levinson, Sarda, Sonneville, Calzo, Ambwani & Austin, 2020). When get bullied and especially when it remained unsolved or children remained defenseless, it might even cause suicide. Especially in adolescence period, the risk of suicide might increase when they feel unresolved (Englander, 2020). Getting bullied in childhood is related with lack of social relationships, economic problems, and low level of perceived quality of life up to the age of 50 years (Takizawa, Maughan & Arseneault, 2014). In the long-term, bullying causes victims to develop problems in body development and eating disorders in the further parts of life. In a 14-year longitudinal study, it was determined that body image development and irregular eating behaviors of those, who got bullied during childhood, began in childhood and body dissatisfaction continued even in adulthood (Gattario, Lindwall & Frisén, 2020). In a meta-analysis carried out by Lie et al., it was observed that, in 71% of 22 studies examined, the individuals having eating disorders were the victims of appearance bullying more than those in control. It was found that there was a more clear relationship between victimhood and bulimia nervosa and binge eating syndrome when compared to anorexia nervosa (Lie, Ro & Bang, 2019).

The victims having increased level of exposure to bullying have more mental health disorders when compared to their non-victim peers. On the other hand, the children with decreasing level of suffering might show similar mental health development in comparison to non-suffered children. Victimization in adolescence is related to the permanent defects in mental health (Sharpe, Fink, Duffy & Patalay, 2021). Assessment of a person's body image by others affects the self-concept of the person. In case that the body image of a person is appreciated by others, it might contribute to the self-image positively. Exclusion or denial of a person from the social circle might have them feel invaluable (Duarte, Pinto-Gouveia & Rodrigues, 2015). As a result of the denial of a person's physical appearance by others, the disorders such as pushing the level of self-criticism and hating oneself, damaging oneself, or self-abuse can be observed (Gilbert, Clarke, Hempel, Miles & Irons, 2004).

Bodyweight is also related with social behaviors. Women having standard bodyweight report more positive results in their social relationships. Being physically active ad fit is related with more positive and less victim. All these findings corroborate the models imposed to women and men by the society (Fernández-Bustos, Pastor-Vicedo, González-Martí & Cuevas-Campos, 2020).

Suggestions for Adolescents

Body image should be defined more positively and healthily among young individuals. For adolescents, comparing one's body to those of others and deciding to be insufficient are widely observed phenomena. However, the perfect body is a non-real perception. Instead, it is necessary to remain healthy and establish a more realistic and accurate goal. Appreciating one's body and not comparing to others would be an important step (Murphy, 2009). Overweightness, obesity, and unhealthy diet are among the increasing social problems. Nowadays, the rate of obese individuals gradually increases and such that it can be stated that one of every three young individuals is overweight. These individuals are under high risk of disorders including high blood pressure, high cholesterol level, diabetes, and even cardiac disorders. Feeling unhealthy decreases the self-esteem of young individuals. Some of the concrete steps to be taken can be listed as eating several small snacks during the day, taking the calories that do not offer nutritional value under control, controlling the amount of unhealthy foods called junk food, and preparing a workout plan (Tarshis, 2010).

Establishing friendships is one of the best methods of protection from bullying. Having at least one friend while walking to school or bus stop, eating lunch, or spending time during breaks might be a protective factor. Even if one had a history of getting bullied, not being alone would decrease the risk of another bullying. Moreover, a good friend might increase self-respect and it might remind the person of the fact that he/she is a person deserving respect (Murphy, 2009).

SOLUTIONS AND SUGGESTIONS

Within the scope of Bronfenbrenner's classical ecological theory (1979), a solution can be produced by adopting an approach that covers the entire social environment from near-to-far in parallel with the components of the ecological environment influencing human behavior. Starting with the family and close circle that constitutes the microsystem of a child, a plan that includes all the relationships between the systems indirectly influencing the development of an individual should be prepared. A child's family, friends, and teachers constitute his/her microsystem. Parents' friends and occupations and teachers' activities at school constitute the exosystem. As a whole, the consistency of micro, meso, and exo systems, which are present in culture, in the macro-system constitutes the final environment. Bronfenbrenner's social-ecological frame indicates the complexity of human behavior. Theories and researches corroborate the hypothesis that bullying and peer victimization are mutually affected by individual, family, peer group, school, community, and society (Espelage & Swearer, 2010). For this reason, the steps to be taken in order to struggle with bullying should incorporate the cooperation between all the systems around the child and adolescent.

- Obesity poses a severe risk for adolescent health and wellbeing from both physical and psychological aspects. Being obese or overweight increases bullying among adolescents. For this reason, the focus should be directed on increasing the awareness of the importance of weight-caused victimization (Gunn & Goldstein, 2017).
- Health-related behaviors might be important risk factors for both bullying and victimhood. Consuming healthy foods is related to a significant decrease in the risk of committing bullying.

Healthy eating should be supported for all children and adolescents (Waasdorp, Mehari, Milam & Bradshaw, 2019).

- Encouraging the physical activity is related with social health. body weight is also related to the social behaviors (Fernández-Bustos, Pastor-Vicedo, González-Martí & Cuevas-Campos, 2020).
- Highly positive body satisfaction can have protective effects. Body satisfaction is related to better eating habits and healthier physical activity levels. Adolescents and young individuals should be provided with opportunities to reduce the risk of being overweight (Berg & Neumark-Sztainer, 2007).
- Adolescents' coping skills, which can be defined as skills of managing, improving, and continuing the situations testing or even exceeding the limits of adolescents, should be developed and improved. Improving the strength of adolescents plays an important role in struggling with bullying and increasing the level of welfare. Improving the strengths, social skills, and self-esteem of young individuals would contribute to their socio-emotional moods, as well as their mental health (Slee & Skrzypiec, 2016).
- Social support acts as a buffer against bullying victimization. Development of relationship-oriented prevention and intervention strategies to be implemented since the early periods of young individuals' lives is a must (Mishna, Khoury-Kassabri, Schwan, Wiener, Craig, Beran & Daciuk, 2016).
- Regarding the body weight, supportive relationships should be provided in the family. Families should be made aware of how implications, miscommunications, and pressures in the family affect adolescents. Familial support is a necessity for adolescents to improve their health and wellbeing (Ricciardelli & Yager, 2015).
- As shareholders, parents should undertake sufficient responsibility. As role models, families should exhibit no behavior incorporating any bullying activity (Gunn and Goldstein, 2017).
- Peer conciliation between children might be useful. Especially in the high school period, conflict resolution skills can be improved by creating suitable environments (Gunn & Goldstein, 2017).
- At every level of the education process, starting with the elementary school period, exercises and activities addressing the toleration and the respect to differences can be given importance. School administrations and teachers might increase the interventions aiming to determine the students labeled for their weight. Coping skills can be developed for the victims of bullying within the borders of school. School-based education can be offered in order to minimize the humiliating behaviors addressing the physical appearance. In the school, teachers can prepare environments requiring children to cooperate making use of cooperative learning strategies (Chisuwa-Hayami & Haruki, 2017).
- A positive school climate encouraging the desired behaviors can be created. A school having a positive climate is an inviting factor. Students and teachers motivate themselves to do their bests. Such an environment would increase the commitment to peers and school and decrease the risk of offensive behaviors (Orpınas & Horne, 2010).
- In general, media creates a negative body image. It is almost impossible to completely avoid the negative effect of media on young individuals but the damage can be minimized.

REFERENCES

Arseneault, L., Bowes, L., & Shakoor, S. (2010). Bullying victimization in youths and mental health problems: 'Much ado about nothing'? *Psychological Medicine*, *40*(5), 717–729. doi:10.1017/S0033291709991383 PMID:19785920

Ata, R. N., Ludden, A. B., & Lally, M. M. (2007). The effects of gender and family, friend, and media influences on eating behaviors and body image during adolescence. *Journal of Youth and Adolescence*, *36*(8), 1024–1037. doi:10.100710964-006-9159-x

Buhlmann, U., Cook, L. M., Fama, J. M., & Wilhelm, S. (2007). Perceived teasing experiences in body dysmorphic disorder. *Body Image*, *4*(4), 381–385. doi:10.1016/j.bodyim.2007.06.004 PMID:18089284

Carlson Jones, D. (2004). Body image among adolescent girls and boys: A longitudinal study. *Developmental Psychology*, *40*(5), 823–835. doi:10.1037/0012-1649.40.5.823 PMID:15355169

Chen, X., Luo, Y. J., & Chen, H. (2020). Body image victimization experiences and disordered eating behaviors among Chinese female adolescents: The role of body dissatisfaction and depression. *Sex Roles*, *83*(7), 442–452. doi:10.100711199-020-01122-4

Chisuwa, N., & O'Dea, J. (2011). Historical Perspective of Body Image and Body Image Concerns among Male and Female Adolescents in Japan. In Body image: Perceptions, interpretations and attitudes içinde (pp. 1-27). Nova Science Publishers.

Chisuwa-Hayami, N., & Haruki, T. (2017). Associations of body-related teasing with weight status, body image, and dieting behavior among Japanese adolescents. *Health Promotion Perspectives*, *7*(2), 80–87. doi:10.15171/hpp.2017.15 PMID:28326288

Day, S., Bussey, K., Trompeter, N., & Mitchison, D. (2021). The impact of teasing and bullying victimization on disordered eating and body image disturbance among adolescents: A systematic review. *Trauma, Violence & Abuse*. Advance online publication. doi:10.1177/1524838020985534 PMID:33461439

Duarte, C., & Pinto-Gouveia, J. (2017). Can self-reassurance buffer against the impact of bullying? Effects on body shame and disordered eating in adolescence. *Journal of Child and Family Studies*, *26*(4), 998–1006. doi:10.100710826-016-0624-1

Duarte, C., Pinto-Gouveia, J., & Rodrigues, T. (2015). Being bullied and feeling ashamed: Implications for eating psychopathology and depression in adolescent girls. *Journal of Adolescence*, *44*(1), 259–268. doi:10.1016/j.adolescence.2015.08.005 PMID:26318063

Duarte, C., Pinto-Gouveia, J., & Stubbs, R. J. (2017). The prospective associations between bullying experiences, body image shame and disordered eating in a sample of adolescent girls. *Personality and Individual Differences*, *116*, 319–325. doi:10.1016/j.paid.2017.05.003

Eisenberg, M. E., Neumark-Sztainer, D., Haines, J., & Wall, M. (2006). Weight-teasing and emotional well-being in adolescents: Longitudinal findings from Project EAT. *The Journal of Adolescent Health*, *38*(6), 675–683. doi:10.1016/j.jadohealth.2005.07.002 PMID:16730595

Eisenstadt, M., Stapley, E., Deighton, J., & Wolpert, M. (2020). Adolescent stressors and their perceived effects on mental well-being: A qualitative study. *Mental Health in Family Medicine, 16*, 992–1001.

Englander, E. K. (2020). *25 Myths about Bullying and Cyberbullying*. John Wiley & Sons. doi:10.1002/9781118747957

Espelage, D. L., & Swearer, S. M. (2010). A Social-Ecological Model for Bullying Prevention and Intervention: Understanding the Impact of Adults in the Social Ecology of Youngsters. In The Handbook of Bullying in Schools: An International Perspective Shane (pp. 61-72). Roultredge.

Fabris, M. A., Badenes-Ribera, L., & Longobardi, C. (2021). Bullying victimization and muscle dysmorphic disorder in Italian adolescents: The mediating role of attachment to peers. *Children and Youth Services Review, 120*, 105720. doi:10.1016/j.childyouth.2020.105720

Farhat, T., Iannotti, R. J., & Simons-Morton, B. G. (2010). Overweight, obesity, youth, and health-risk behaviors. *American Journal of Preventive Medicine, 38*(3), 258–267. doi:10.1016/j.amepre.2009.10.038 PMID:20171527

Feragen, K. B., & Stock, N. M. (2016). A longitudinal study of 340 young people with or without a visible difference: The impact of teasing on self-perceptions of appearance and depressive symptoms. *Body Image, 16*, 133–142. doi:10.1016/j.bodyim.2016.01.003 PMID:26828822

Fernández-Bustos, J. G., Pastor-Vicedo, J. C., González-Martí, I., & Cuevas-Campos, R. (2020). Physical fitness and peer relationships in Spanish preadolescents. *International Journal of Environmental Research and Public Health, 17*(6), 1890. doi:10.3390/ijerph17061890 PMID:32183282

Fowler, L. A., Kracht, C. L., Denstel, K. D., Stewart, T. M., & Staiano, A. E. (2021). Bullying experiences, body esteem, body dissatisfaction, and the moderating role of weight status among adolescents. *Journal of Adolescence, 91*(1), 59–70. doi:10.1016/j.adolescence.2021.07.006 PMID:34333320

Franklin, J., Denyer, G., Steinbeck, K. S., Caterson, I. D., & Hill, A. J. (2006). Obesity and risk of low self-esteem: A statewide survey of Australian children. *Pediatrics, 118*(6), 2481–2487. doi:10.1542/peds.2006-0511 PMID:17142534

Garcia, A. C., Sousa, R., Varela, A., & Monteiro, L. (2021). Bullying, physical activity, and body image among Brazilian students. *Journal of Health Psychology, 26*(10), 1661–1673. doi:10.1177/1359105319884598 PMID:31674842

Gaskill, D., & Sanders, F. (2000). The Encultured Body: Policy Implications for Healthy Body Image and Disordered Eating Behaviours. Queensland University of Technology.

Gattario, K. H., Lindwall, M., & Frisén, A. (2020). Life after childhood bullying: Body image development and disordered eating in adulthood. *International Journal of Behavioral Development, 44*(3), 246–255. doi:10.1177/0165025419877971

Gilbert, P., Clarke, M., Hempel, S., Miles, J. N., & Irons, C. (2004). Criticizing and reassuring oneself: An exploration of forms, styles and reasons in female students. *British Journal of Clinical Psychology, 43*(1), 31–50. doi:10.1348/014466504772812959 PMID:15005905

Gilbert, P., & Irons, C. (2009). Shame, self-criticism, and self-compassion in adolescence. *Adolescent Emotional Development and The Emergence of Depressive Disorders*, *1*, 195–214.

Grogan, S. (2021). *Body Image: Understanding Body Dissatisfaction in Men, Women and Children*. Routledge. doi:10.4324/9781003100041

Gunn, J. F. III, & Goldstein, S. E. (2017). Bullying and suicidal behavior during adolescence: A developmental perspective. *Adolescent Research Review*, *2*(2), 77–97. doi:10.100740894-016-0038-8

Harrison, K., & Hefner, V. (2006). Media exposure, current and future body ideals, and disordered eating among preadolescent girls: A longitudinal panel study. *Journal of Youth and Adolescence*, *35*(2), 146–156. doi:10.100710964-005-9008-3

Holubcikova, J., Kolarcik, P., Madarasova Geckova, A., Van Dijk, J. P., & Reijneveld, S. A. (2015). Is subjective perception of negative body image among adolescents associated with bullying? *European Journal of Pediatrics*, *174*(8), 1035–1041. doi:10.100700431-015-2507-7 PMID:25708851

Hymel, S., Schonert-Reıchl, K. A., Bonanno, R. A., Vaıllancourt, T., & Henderson, N. R. (2010). Bullying and Morality: Understanding How Good Kids Can Behave Badly. In The Handbook of Bullying in Schools: An International Perspective Shane (pp. 101-118). Roultredge.

Jeong-Ju, Y., & Johnson, K. K. (2007). Effects of appearance-related testing on ethnically diverse adolescent girls. *Adolescence*, *42*(166), 353. PMID:17849941

Jones, D. (2004). Body image among adolescent girls and boys: A longitudinal study. *Developmental Psychology*, *40*(5), 823–835. doi:10.1037/0012-1649.40.5.823 PMID:15355169

Jones, D. C., Vigfusdottir, T. H., & Lee, Y. (2004). Body image and the appearance culture among adolescent girls and boys: An examination of friend conversations, peer criticism, appearance magazines and Internalization of appearance ideals. *Journal of Adolescent Research*, *19*(3), 323–329. doi:10.1177/0743558403258847

Keery, H., Van den Berg, P., & Thompson, J. K. (2004). An evaluation of the Tripartite Influence Model of body dissatisfaction and eating disturbance with adolescent girls. *Body Image*, *1*(3), 237–251. doi:10.1016/j.bodyim.2004.03.001 PMID:18089156

Kennedy, K. (2019). *Positive and negative effects of social media on adolescent well-being* [Master of Science]. Minnesota State University.

Klinck, M., Vannucci, A., Fagle, T., & Ohannessian, C. M. (2020). Appearance-related teasing and substance use during early adolescence. *Psychology of Addictive Behaviors*, *34*(4), 541–548. doi:10.1037/adb0000563 PMID:32039619

Knauss, C., Paxton, S. J., & Alsaker, F. D. (2007). Relationships amongst body dissatisfaction, internalization of the media body ideal and perceived pressure from media in adolescent girls and boys. *Body Image*, *4*(4), 353–360. doi:10.1016/j.bodyim.2007.06.007 PMID:18089281

Krusell, M. K., Hohwü, L., Bjereld, Y., Madsen, K. B., & Obel, C. (2019). The impact of childhood bullying on the daily lives of Nordic children and young adolescents. *Acta Paediatrica (Oslo, Norway)*, *108*(6), 1096–1102. doi:10.1111/apa.14642 PMID:30421832

Lawler, M., & Nixon, E. (2011). Body dissatisfaction among adolescent boys and girls: the effects of body mass, peer appearance culture and internalization of appearance ideals. *Journal of Youth And Adolescence*, *40*(1), 59-71. doi:10.1007/s10964-009-9500-2

Lee, K., Dale, J., Guy, A., & Wolke, D. (2018). Bullying and negative appearance feedback among adolescents: Is it objective or misperceived weight that matters? *Journal of Adolescence*, *63*(1), 118–128. doi:10.1016/j.adolescence.2017.12.008 PMID:29289824

Levinson, J. A., Sarda, V., Sonneville, K., Calzo, J. P., Ambwani, S., & Austin, S. B. (2020). Diet pill and laxative use for weight control and subsequent incident eating disorder in US young women: 2001–2016. *American Journal of Public Health*, *110*(1), 109–111. doi:10.2105/AJPH.2019.305390 PMID:31751147

Lie, S. O., Ro, O., & Bang, L. (2019). Is bullying and teasing associated with eating disorders? A systematic review and meta-analysis. *International Journal of Eating Disorders*, *52*(5), 497–514. doi:10.1002/eat.23035 PMID:30706957

Lieberman, M., Gauvin, L., Bukowski, W. M., & White, D. R. (2001). Interpersonal influence and disordered eating behaviors in adolescent girls: The role of peer modeling, social reinforcement, and body-related teasing. *Eating Behaviors*, *2*(3), 215–236. doi:10.1016/S1471-0153(01)00030-7 PMID:15001032

Maxfield J, Wells T (2003) Adverse effects of social pressure to be thin on young women: An experimental investigation of the effects of "fat talk". *Int J Eat Disord, 34*(1), 108–117. doi:10.1002/eat.10171

McCabe, M. P., & Ricciardelli, L. A. (2005). A prospective study of pressure from parents, peers, and the media on extreme weight change behaviours among adolescent boys and girls. *Behaviour Research and Therapy*, *43*(5), 653–668. doi:10.1016/j.brat.2004.05.004 PMID:15865919

McKinley, N. M. (1999). Women and objectified body consciousness: Mothers' and daughters' body experience in cultural, developmental, and familial context. *Developmental Psychology*, *35*(3), 760–769. doi:10.1037/0012-1649.35.3.760 PMID:10380866

Migliaccio, T., & Raskauskas, J. (2016). *Bullying as a social experience: Social factors, prevention and intervention*. Ashgate Publishing Company. doi:10.4324/9781315570525

Milothridis, P. (2020). Bullying About Someone's Appearance and Interest in Cosmetic Surgery. In *Cosmetic Patient Selection and Psychosocial Background* (pp. 33–39). Springer. doi:10.1007/978-3-030-44725-0_4

Mishna, F., Khoury-Kassabri, M., Schwan, K., Wiener, J., Craig, W., Beran, T., Pepler, D., & Daciuk, J. (2016). The contribution of social support to children and adolescents' self-perception: The mediating role of bullying victimization. *Children and Youth Services Review*, *63*, 120–127. doi:10.1016/j.childyouth.2016.02.013

Murphy, A. G. (2009). *Dealing with bullying*. Infobase Publishing.

Nıckerson, A. B., Mele, D., & Osborne-Olıver, K. M. (2010). Parent-Child Relationships and Bullying. In The Handbook of Bullying in Schools: An International Perspective Shane (pp. 187-198). Routledge.

Orpınas, P., & Horne, A. M. (2010). Creating a Positive School Climate and Developing Social Competence. In The Handbook of Bullying in Schools: An International Perspective Shane (pp. 49-60). Routledge.

Patte, K. A., Livermore, M., Qian, W., & Leatherdale, S. T. (2021). Do weight perception and bullying victimization account for links between weight status and mental health among adolescents? *BMC Public Health, 21*(1), 1–16. doi:10.118612889-021-11037-8 PMID:34088278

Pegis, J. (2013). *Straight Talk About Bullyıng*. Crabtree Publishing Company.

Ricciardelli, L. A., & Yager, Z. (2015). *Adolescence and body image: From development to preventing dissatisfaction*. Routledge., doi:10.4324/9781315849379

Ring, A. (2000a). Advertising and the Body as Ideal Image. In *The Encultured Body: Policy Implications for Healthy Body Image and Disordered Eating Behaviours*. Queensland University of Technology.

Ring, A. (2000b). Cosmetic Surgery and the Body as Work-in-Progress. In *The Encultured Body: Policy Implications for Healthy Body Image and Disordered Eating Behaviours*. Queensland University of Technology.

Roelants, M., & Cameron, N. (2022). Adolescent growth. In *Human Growth and Development* (pp. 101–123). Academic Press., doi:10.1016/B978-0-12-822652-0.00015-8.

Sanders, F., Gwynne, E., & Gaskill, D. (2000). Barbie Magazine: The First 12 Months. In *The Encultured Body: Policy Implications for Healthy Body Image and Disordered Eating Behaviours*. Queensland University of Technology.

Sentenac, M., Arnaud, C., Gavin, A., Molcho, M., Gabhainn, S. N., & Godeau, E. (2012). Peer victimization among school-aged children with chronic conditions. *Epidemiologic Reviews, 34*, 120–128. doi:10.1093/epirev/mxr024

Sharpe, H., Fink, E., Duffy, F., & Patalay, P. (2021). Changes in peer and sibling victimization in early adolescence: Longitudinal associations with multiple indices of mental health in a prospective birth cohort study. *European Child & Adolescent Psychiatry*, 1–10. doi:10.100700787-020-01708-z PMID:33432402

Slee, P. T., & Skrzypiec, G. (2016). *Well-being, positive peer relations and bullying in school settings*. Springer. doi:10.1007/978-3-319-43039-3

Smokowski, P. R., & Evans, C. B. (2019). *Bullying and victimization across the lifespan*. Springer International Publishing. doi:10.1007/978-3-030-20293-4

Stamate, I. F., Aimé, A., Gagnon, C., & Villatte, A. (2021). Association between Weight-and Appearance-related Bullying in High School and Postsecondary Academic Adaptation in Young Adults. *Journal of School Violence, 20*(4), 1–12. doi:10.1080/15388220.2021.1952079

Stice, E., Maxfield, J., & Wells, T. (2003). Adverse effects of social pressure to be thin on young women: An experimental investigation of the effects of "fat talk". *International Journal of Eating Disorders, 34*(1), 108–117. doi:10.1002/eat.10171 PMID:12772175

Takizawa, R., Maughan, B., & Arseneault, L. (2014). Adult health outcomes of childhood bullying victimization: Evidence from a five-decade longitudinal British birth cohort. *American Journal of Psychiatry, 171*(7), 777-784. doi:10.1176/appi.ajp.2014.13101401

Tarshis, T. P. (2010). *Living with peer pressure and bullying*. Infobase Publishing.

Tarshis, T. P., & Tarshis, T. P. (2010). *Living with peer pressure and bullying*. Infobase Publishing.

Van den Berg, P., & Neumark-Sztainer, D. (2007). Fat¢ n happy 5 years later: Is it bad for overweight girls to like their bodies? *The Journal of Adolescent Health, 41*(4), 415–417. doi:10.1016/j.jadohealth.2007.06.001 PMID:17875468

Voelker, D. K., Reel, J. J., & Greenleaf, C. (2015). Weight status and body image perceptions in adolescents: Current perspectives. *Adolescent Health, Medicine and Therapeutics, 6*, 149. doi:10.2147/AHMT.S68344 PMID:26347007

Waasdorp, T. E., Mehari, K. R., Milam, A. J., & Bradshaw, C. P. (2019). Health-related risks for involvement in bullying among middle and high school youth. *Journal of Child and Family Studies, 28*(9), 2606–2617. doi:10.100710826-018-1260-8

Wickman, L. J. (2000). *A correlational study of the impact of media influence on the body image of adolescent females* [Master of Science Degree]. Wisconsin-Stout Üniversitesi.

Wood, C. L., Lane, L. C., & Cheetham, T. (2019). Puberty: Normal physiology (brief overview). *Best Practice & Research. Clinical Endocrinology & Metabolism, 33*(3), 101265. doi:10.1016/j.beem.2019.03.001 PMID:31000487

Zimmer-Gembeck, M. J., & Webb, H. J. (2017). Body image and peer relationships: Unique associations of adolescents' social status and competence with peer-and self-reported appearance victimization. *Journal of Adolescence, 61*(1), 131–140. doi:10.1016/j.adolescence.2017.10.002 PMID:29080408

ADDITIONAL READING

Franklin, J., Denyer, G., Steinbeck, K. S., Caterson, I. D., & Hill, A. J. (2006). Obesity and risk of low self-esteem: A statewide survey of Australian children. *Pediatrics, 118*(6), 2481–2487. doi:10.1542/peds.2006-0511 PMID:17142534

Garcia-Hermoso, A., Oriol-Granado, X., Correa-Bautista, J. E., & Ramírez-Vélez, R. (2019). Association between bullying victimization and physical fitness among children and adolescents. *International Journal of Clinical and Health Psychology, 19*(2), 134–140. doi:10.1016/j.ijchp.2019.02.006 PMID:31193131

Pytash, K. E. (2013). Using YA literature to help preservice teachers deal with bullying and suicide. *Journal of Adolescent & Adult Literacy, 56*(6), 470–479. doi:10.1002/JAAL.168

Shetgiri, R. (2015). *Practical strategies for clinical management of bullying*. Springer. doi:10.1007/978-3-319-15476-3

Taylor, N. (2015). *Schooled on Fat: What Teens Tell Us About Gender, Body Image, and Obesity* (1st ed.). Routledge. doi:10.4324/9781315684505

Wilson, M. L., Viswanathan, B., Rousson, V., & Bovet, P. (2013). Weight status, body image and bullying among adolescents in the Seychelles. *International Journal of Environmental Research and Public Health, 10*(5), 1763–1774. doi:10.3390/ijerph10051763 PMID:23644826

KEY TERMS AND DEFINIONS

Adolescence: It generally describes the period of life between childhood and adulthood. It typically covers the ages of 12 to 18 years. Puberty is often a biological phenomenon driven by increases in hormones, including the development of secondary sex characteristics and modulations in muscle and fat.

Body Dissatisfaction: Dissatisfaction with the physical size, shape and proportions of persons, normative discontent. Criticism about his physical body is associated with hatred and disgust.

Body Image: It is a multidimensional structure that encompasses how we perceive, think, feel and act our body. These dimensions include cognitive, emotional, evaluative and behavioral aspects of physical appearance.

Bullying: It is a subtype of aggressive behavior by an individual or a group of individuals, such as repeatedly attacking, humiliating and/or ostracizing a relatively weak person.

Family Relationships: Present and future body image of parent-adolescent relationships are related. The negative message about weight and shape by family members can cause verbal criticism adolescents to feel bullied towards their body image.

Media: Influences body image through the presentation of an unnaturally unattainable ideal of appearance. The media exerts great influence with famous models and high-status figures. It mediates the social learning of followers about standard beauty and body image.

Peer Bullying: Physical, verbal, indirect and emotional negative actions by a person or a group of students repeatedly to create victimization against their peers.

Chapter 6
Utilisation of Social Media for Child Abuse Prevention in Nigeria

Desmond Onyemechi Okocha
https://orcid.org/0000-0001-5070-280X
Bingham University, Nigeria

Sienne Ozioma Okpor
Bingham University, Nigeria

ABSTRACT

The purpose of this study was to examine the influence of social media on child abuse prevention in Nigeria. The objectives were to discover the level of cognizance social media has created on the issue of child abuse, child abuse prevention, and if social media is really a tool in preventing child abuse in Nigeria. The study was anchored on technology determinism theory. Using the purposive sampling technique, 30 discussants were selected for focus group discussion on the subject matter. The study found that social media alone is not effective enough in preventing child abuse in Nigeria. Research findings further revealed that although the information given about child abuse on social media platforms are believable and acceptable, there has been no significant influence of social media on child abuse prevention in Nigeria. To this end, the researcher recommended that there should be public enlightenment programs that reach the grassroots to create public awareness on child abuse prevention, its effects on children, and the legal consequences.

INTRODUCTION

Globally it is estimated that up to 1 billion children, ages 2-17 years old, have experienced different forms of emotional, physical, and sexual abuse over the last year (Hillis, Mercy, Amobi, and Kress, 2016). In 1979, the United Nations declared the year as the 'international year of the child' and went ahead to develop a list of children's rights. Among the rights as articulated by the United Nations are that every

DOI: 10.4018/978-1-6684-5426-8.ch006

child is entitled to the rights to be loved and understood, to be provided with adequate food and healthcare, free education, play, and an identity, however many people are not aware or rather nothing is done to offenders that is why child abuse is still very rampant in most countries of the world including Nigeria.

In Nigeria today, many children are being used to beg for alms, exposing them to harmful and inhuman circumstances at incredibly early ages. The Child Right Acts of 2003 was made to end the menace but sadly, it has not been effectively enforced by our legal system. The lapses are clearly observable by the number of children that are seen on the streets hawking items and being exposed to dangers of all kinds and to assume that they are responsible for themselves at that tender and vulnerable age calls for serious concerns. With the number of children on the streets begging or hawking instead of going to school, one still wonders if these children are the ones, we call leaders of tomorrow. It is obvious that Parents/guardians and relatives of these children most times are not aware of the legal implications of their actions, Section 30 (3) of the Child's Right Act provides that a person who contradicts the provisions of Subsection (1) of this section commits an offence and is liable on conviction to imprisonment for a term of ten years. Parents/guardians of such children have disrespected the law and yet the legal system has failed to enforce the required punishment to end this menace.

The effects of child abuse may include increased fear, guilt, self-blame, distrust of adults or difficulty in forming relationships with others, mental health disorders, learning disorders, drug, and alcohol abuse, etc. Despite the attention and the interest, it has won from the media, the hassle nonetheless has remained a largely forgotten area wherein proper steps that may be taken to fight it hasn't been agreed upon (Carballo, 1995).

Anuoluwapo (2018) expressed that the world of Information and Communication Technology is yet to experience something more phenomenal than social media. She added that social media has indeed become a trend in media study such that many researchers have turned towards researching and assessing its influence and impact on society. This is so as several decades saw the dominance of the traditional media in society especially in exercising the responsibility of information, education, and entertainment. But with the turn of events in the new century, the evolution of technology and the ubiquitous power of the information and communication technology (ICT) has converged the world so much so that Marshall McLuhan's global village philosophy is no longer a mere expression but a startling reality. (Ikpe & Olise, 2010) have observed that "social media are new communication technologies which are used as means of information dissemination to diverse audiences without time crunch, space or distance". With social media, one can easily send or receive information to or from anyone and at any time regardless of geographical location.

In recent times there has been lots of social media campaigns directed towards child abuse, these campaigns are to increase the public knowledge of child's rights and child's abuse, to influence people's attitudes towards children positively, and to change behaviors that contribute to the problems of child abuse in Nigeria.

STATEMENT OF THE PROBLEM

Child abuse has become one of the social epidemics disturbing the global society in Nigeria. UNICEF reported in 2015 that six out of ten children in Nigeria have experienced emotional, physical, or sexual abuse before the age of eighteen with half experiencing physical violence. Despite all of the provisions of extant legal guidelines, many Nigerian children are still subjected to various forms of child abuse even while with parents and guardians. Social media platforms especially Twitter, TikTok, Facebook, YouTube, and Instagram have been in the forefront of the efforts to combat this social malaise. Thus, this study sets out to evaluate the influence of these social media campaigns at preventing child abuse.

RESEARCH OBJECTIVES

1. To evaluate the influence of social media on child abuse prevention
2. To find out the level of awareness created by social media on the issue of child abuse.
3. To determine the level of awareness created by social media on the issue of child abuse prevention in Nigeria

RESEARCH QUESTIONS

1. What is the influence of social media on child abuse prevention?
2. What is the level of awareness created by social media on the issue of child abuse?
3. What the level of awareness created by social media on the issue of child abuse prevention in Nigeria?

THEORETICAL FRAMEWORK

This research work is anchored on technological determinism theory. Technological Determinism theory believes that media technology affects how people in the society think, feel, and even act. The idea essentially explains that we act the manner we do due to the messages we via the contemporary available technology. The theory was proposed by Marshal McLuhan, a Canadian communication scholar who believed that the new media technologies in communication would soon determine social and cultural changes in the society and end up turning the world into a global village. He believed that the socio-political, economic, and cultural changes are inevitably based on development and diffusion of technology and that the new media would soon have an impact on societal modifications. This study adopts technological determinism theory because it supports the belief that the new media has an influence/ impact in our lives.

LITERATURE REVIEW

Child Abuse - An Overview

Over the years, the term child abuse has been discussed and defined by many researchers and authors. the Oxford Advanced Learners Dictionary describes a child as a young human who is not yet an adult. Child abuse or child maltreatment is the physical, sexual, and/or psychological maltreatment or neglect of a child or children, especially by a parent or a caregiver. Child abuse may include any act or failure to act by a parent or a caregiver that results in actual or potential harm to a child and can occur in a child's home, or in the organizations, schools, or communities the child interacts with. According to Owolabi (2012), the legally and acceptable definition of a "child" is a minor, a person younger than the age of majority. As cited in (Umobong, 2010), the African Network for Prevention and Protection against Child Abuse and Neglect (ANPPCAN) defines child abuse as "the intentional, unintentional, or well intentional acts which endangers the physical health, emotional, moral and the educational welfare of a child. Child abuse can be seen as any act of omission or commission, physical or psychological mistreatment or neglect of a child by its parents, guardians, caregiver, or other adults that may endanger the child's physical, psychological, or emotional health and development. Child abuse is also seen as the "physical or emotional mistreatment and neglect of children or the sexual exploitation in circumstances for which the parents can be held responsible through acts of commission or omission" (Doye, 1990).

According to the National Child Abuse and Neglect Data System (NCANDA, 2006) reported by Gelles (2009) more than 900,000 children in the United States suffer severe injury, some 1,000 to 2,000 children die because of abuse and those who survive often suffer emotional trauma that may take long for the bruises to be healed. The statistics of abused children have continued to increase over the years and yet nothing has been done by the government to end this menace. Child abuse will in the long run affect the economy of the nation as it continues to have long term effects on children.

Types of Child Abuse

The World Health Organization in 2006 identified four types of child abuse: physical abuse, sexual abuse, emotional abuse, and neglect.

Physical Abuse

Physical abuse can be defined as any deliberate act to harm a child thereby causing injury, pain or trauma to a child by way of physical contact. Physical abuse sometimes involves more than one abuser, and more than one victim. Sometimes, it comes in form of beating, Punching, Kicking, Shaking, Suffocating, Pinching, Biting, Scalding, or burning someone. Physical abuse is sometimes prevalent in homes, schools, and sometimes in public places.

Emotional Abuse

Emotional abuse can be in from of verbal abuse or consistent criticism, intimidation, manipulation, and refusal to ever be pleased sometimes by parents or guardians. Emotional abuse sometimes involves Blaming, shaming, and manipulating. At an early age, the child's self-confidence and emotional well-being is altered and even diminished resulting to an emotionally abused child. Emotionally abused children sometimes grow to become detached from friends and family.

Sexual Abuse

Child sexual abuse, also called child molestation, is a form of child abuse in which an adult or older adolescent uses a child for sexual stimulation and forcefully has sexual intercourse with a child. This is one of the worst forms of child abuse as it most times leaves children depressed and leaves a lifelong emotional scar on them. Some children never get to recover from this act, sometimes they develop serious fear an even hatred for the gender. Child sexual abuse can occur anywhere sometimes its home, school, church, mosques, relatives house etc. sexual abuse mostly has adverse effects on children, it includes depression, Post traumatic stress disorder, anxiety, and sometimes high sexual drive.

Neglect

Cambridge English dictionary defines neglect as to not give enough care or attention to people or things that are your responsibility. Neglect in the context of child abuse simply means depriving a child of the basic needs and leaving the welfare of the child for the child. Child neglect is one of the prevalent forms of child abuse and it is very common in Nigeria. Many parents in Nigeria give birth to children and send them to beg or to live with relatives, why give birth these children if you cannot take care of them?

Child Marriage

Child marriage is a formal or informal union between anyone under 18 with an individual. Majority of child marriages in Nigeria are the ones between a girl and man. Child marriage infringes the rights of children and has long term effects for children who're pressured into the act. For girls, in addition to post mental stress disorder (Ptsd), lack of access to education and career opportunities, early pregnancy and childbirth, these young girls are constantly exposed to VVF (Vestico Vaginal Fistula). This lethal sickness has taken, and it is nonetheless still taking the lives of many girls. The report by the United Nations Children Fund (UNICEF) revealed that over 0.4 million women suffer from obstetric Fistula in Nigeria, ranking the country as the highest prevalence of obstetric fistula in the world. This brings us to another question, which is, how well are the Child's Right Acts being enforced. The reality on ground is that our legal system seems to aid this menace called Child Abuse as the wrath of the law seems to only be regarded in books and movies than in its implementation in Nigeria. There are penalties for offenders of the laws in Nigeria, why are these child abuse perpetuators not being dealt with? Why has the government chosen to be quiet? There is a need for the Nigerian Government to indulge the legal system to implement enacted laws as it seems like the only solution to changing the narratives of child abuse in Nigeria.

Child Abuse Cases in Nigeria

Nigerian children continue to suffer in the hands of so-called ward/guardians (Cynthia, 2017) disclosed in her article on child abuse cases that made it to court that Kingsley Philip was caught fingering his neighbors five-year-old daughter in his apartment in Lagos, he was charged too court and he pleaded not guilty. She continued, Magaji Dansele allegedly raped his baby. He drugged his new wife in order to be able to carry out the act while she slept at their apartment in Musawa, Katsina State. Dansale tried to convince his wife that pile was the culprit, but a visit to the hospital proved otherwise, making him the prime suspect in the baby's rape. it is disheartening to note that some of children are molested and sexually assaulted by their parents.

Nelson @kanuelsonmirag on twitter shared that he was abused at five, though he did not understand what was going on. "When I was 4 or 5, our neighbor's daughter who was already more than 30 at that time would bring me inside her room and strip me, she would carry me on top of herself and be pushing me up and down, I didn't know much about what she was doing to me. It continued for years; eventually told my mom and she beat me up so much, I then kept quiet. and she continued abusing me till we relocated. Those past events affected my emotions, sexual life, and relationships generally, but I thank God things are getting better,". Recently, a horrendous case of child abuse was just uncovered in Kebbi state, a 10-year-old boy was found in a pen with domestic animals and after some interrogation, it was discovered that he had been there for two years and had been surviving on food remnants left by the animals.

In Nigeria today, it is obvious that many children are subjected to sexual assault, the above stories are to mention but a few out of the millions of child abuse cases in Nigeria. There is need now than ever before, to put in place great awareness and effective legal protection for the abused children and also implement policies that ensures that perpetuators of these horrible acts are brought to book. It is strongly believed that the legal system will have a far more reaching effect if proper measures are put in place and the enforcement of appropriate laws.

Social Media as a Tool for Child Abuse Prevention

In recent times, social media has proven to be key for disseminating information and enlightening the public about the importance of preventing child abuse and neglect. Soola (1998) describes social media as communication technologies with impressive array of sophistication, increasing efficiency, reliability, speed, accuracy, cheapness, and portability. He observed that social media provides near limitless possibilities of increasing the quantity and enhancing the quality, speed, and availability of information in a complex but increasingly interdependent world. Social media campaigns have been shown to increase awareness and knowledge of abuse prevention. These campaigns may also have an effect on primary prevention behaviors if the message is reinforced over time (Darkness to Light, 2012; Rheingold, et al, 2007).

Social Media has rapidly grown in importance as a forum for social activism in its different forms in Nigeria. Social media platforms, such as Twitter, and Facebook, WhatsApp, Instagram and Tik Tok have provided new ways to stimulate citizen engagement in contemporary issues and challenges. As of January 2021, Nigeria had approximately 33 million active social media users. It is a tool that has proven to be effective at reaching a global audience and therefore exerts tremendous influence on behavioral changes. this statement is in total alignment with the views of Nwanchor and Nkwuda (2021: 40) that "media of all forms and sizes have primary roles to inform, educate, sensitize and entertain the masses and bring to the knowledge of the public what goes on in all areas of life in the right dosages and proportion".

Many NGOs like StopS-CAN, Feedthekidsng, Hfucharity, YobeMeToo, and hskinitiative in Nigeria today utilize social media campaigns in their vision to protect children from abuse. These NGOs have come up with different means to create awareness of child abuse prevention in Nigeria. the likes of #heretohelppod and WACOL have been hosting online campaigns on twitter though the use of slides, fliers, podcasts and even through twitter spaces.

RESEARCH METHOD

This study adopts the qualitative research approach, this can be defined as a research method that focuses on obtaining data through open-ended and conversational communication. Data was generated using primary and secondary sources. Using the purposive sampling technique, 30 discussants (identified as discussant 1 to 30) were selected for focus group discussion on the subject matter which held on WhatsApp. Discussions were collated and narratively analyzed while the demographic distribution of the respondents was manually tabulated in a frequency distribution table.

DATA ANALYSIS AND FINDINGS

Table 1. Distribution of Discussants by sex. Source field survey,2022

Characteristics	Frequency	Percentage (%)
Male	14	46.7
Female	16	53.3
Total	30	100

Table 1 indicates that 14 participants representing 46.7% were Male, while 16, representing 53.3% were female.

Table 2. Distribution of Discussants by age. Source field survey,2022

Characteristics	Frequency	Percentage (%)
20-25	13	43.3
25-30	15	50
30-35	2	6.7
Total	30	100

Table 2 reveals that people between the ages of 25-30 were more than other age brackets among the discussants, this was followed by the 20-25, the least was 30-35.

Table 3. Distribution of Discussants by occupation. Source field survey,2022

Characteristics	Frequency	Percentage (%)
Employed	23	76.7
Self-employed	4	13.3
Students	2	6.7
Unemployed	1	3.3
Total	**30**	**100**

Table 3 shows that 23 of the discussants, representing 76.7% were employed,4 participants representing 13.3% were self-employed, 2 participants representing 6.7% were students, while 1 person representing 3.3 percent was unemployed.

Q1: Level of Awareness of Social Media

All the discussants agree that they are aware of social media, and they use social media platforms every day. Discussant 14 affirmed by saying "I definitely know what social media is, I'm not sure anyone born in this age doesn't". social media has become a very important part of our lives. According to Anuoluwapo (2017), it is important to note that through the use of social media, people are kept up dated on issues or events taking place anywhere in Nigeria. This is particularly possible because these social websites are interactively accessible with mobile phones. The use of WhatsApp and Facebook on phones for instance, makes this easier, as one can send either images or snapped shots alongside information on the most current event or issues as the case may be, on minute interval.

Q2: Commonly Used Social Media Platforms

Common examples of social media platforms identified by the discussants are Facebook, Snapchat, Instagram, Telegram, WhatsApp, and Tiktok.

Q3: Awareness of Child Abuse

All the discussants affirm that they familiar with child abuse as it is a reoccurring phenomenon in almost every locality. This is agreed through the different ways by which the discussants responded to the question. All of the discussants simply answered by saying "yes"

Q4: Child Abuse Experiences

Discussants shared personal child abuse experiences. discussant 15 stated:

"I was just 5 when I was raped by my uncle, he was my dad's worker and he lived with us. I had just gotten back from school. I was in the living room, he asked me to take off my school uniform then he zipped down and asked me to have oral sex with him, I did for a while then he told me to lie down, and he started raping me, I was in pains and screaming but no one really heard me, he threatened to kill me if I told anyone. After that day, I became withdrawn and really stopped talking to people including my family members, it has always been so for me. Till this day, my parents wonder how I suddenly became a quiet person. Somedays I wonder where Uncle Hassan is.''

Discussant 3 added that:

"my mum died while giving birth to me, so I never really knew her, and I grew up cursing myself every slightest chance I got because I blamed myself for her death. Things got though for my dad, so I had to go stay with a relative. I suffered; you know the whole wicked stepmother character we see portrayed in Nigerian movies? I had that exact experience, and it wasn't a funny one. I couldn't even call my dad because there were no phones then. The truth is many Nigerian children are going through hell, at least regardless of my experiences, I had a place to sleep, many of these children don't which makes it easier for them to be abused".

Q5: Frequency of Child Abuse Messages on Social Media

Majority of the discussants affirm that they come across child abuse cases very often. Discussant 25 agrees by saying “very often”. This appears to be the common answer among the discussants as others simply said: 'often'. Discussant 18 disclosed that ‘’ you can hardly go a month without seeing a child abuse case, on at Facebook and even twitter. Discussant 4 agrees to seeing child abuse cases very often by saying “Child Abuse is the most common form of abuse in Nigeria, it is so common that it has been normalized in our society and every time I go on Facebook, I see something related to abuse, either rape, child abuse, molestation, it is a pity that children are subjected to this inhumane treatment.”

Q6: Use of Social Media on Promotion of Child Abuse Experiences

From the discussion, it is believed that social media promotes child abuse cases in Nigerian discussant 13 clearly stated that:

I believe that social media plays a huge role in promotion of child abuse cases in Nigeria. in recent times, social media has helped expose child abusers in Nigeria. the case 14-year-old Karen-Happuch Aondodoo, a student of Premier Academy in Lugbe, who was allegedly raped in her school and died few days later on 22 June 2021 as a result of complications has been on the lips of Nigerians on social media. Nigerian's allover took to Twitter and Facebook with the hash tag #justiceforKaren demanding that proper investigation be carried out and the abuser made to face the wrath of the law.

Nigerians on social media have been on the forefront in fighting and ensuring that child abuse cases are not suppressed.

Q7: Impact of Social Media on Child Abuse Prevention in Nigeria

Majority of the discussants believed that the social media has not influenced child abuse prevention. One of the discussants, discussant 11 said:

“It hasn't particularly helped prevention it has just brought to the limelight child abuse cases and has helped showcase the level of evil that child abusers perpetuate therefore appealing the emotions of the public. To an extent it has helped create awareness and disillusioned the perpetrators from thinking they can go Scott free”

Discussant 24 added that:

“It is said that social media is an effective tool for whistleblowing hence it has helped publicize child abuse cases, but it has not really brought about any revolution or really prevented child abuse from occurring in Nigeria. There are thousands of child abuse cases that are being promoted on social media yet, we still find more and more every day.”

Again, Discussant 13 stated:

"I believe social media has its role to play which is the constant publicity of these child abuse cases, but the truth is that it has not really prevented it from happening. And a lot of these children still continue to suffer in silence."

DISCUSSION OF FINDINGS

This paper has found out certain facts about the subject matter of study. The work was set to find out the influence of social media on child abuse prevention.

For the first objective, the outcome of the discussion indicated that social media has created awareness on child abuse in Nigeria. Significantly, social media has been essential to the growth of society's awareness of child abuse and neglect. The case of 14-year-old Karen-Happuch Aondodoo, the secondary school student that was raped and died afterwards is one among the several cases discussed. This is in agreement with Silverman and Wilson (2002), they believed the explosion in media interest in child offences has also helped to fuel a moral panic. It can therefore be said that social media has undoubtedly played a key role in raising awareness of child abuse.

The second objective was to find out the level of awareness social media has created on child abuse prevention and the study showed that the likes of Facebook, Instagram, Twitter, WhatsApp, TikTok and Blogs have been at the forefront of promoting child abuse cases. it was discovered that there have been different campaigns against child abuse on different social media platforms at different times. As earlier asserted under literature review in this study, Social Media has rapidly grown in importance as a forum for social activism in its different forms in Nigeria. Social media has become a primary communication medium in the developed world over the past decade. Due to increased globalization, facilitated by the widespread use of the internet and social media, this medium allows for the widespread and fast dissemination of ideas and can also serve as a means to change norms about child abuse.

The third objective which was to determine if social media is really a tool in preventing child abuse in Nigeria. From the data obtained, the influence of social media on child abuse prevention has been factually established. The study found out that social media alone is not effective enough in preventing child abuse In Nigeria. It is believed that social media has its role to play which is the constant publicity of these child abuse cases as it helps to inform and sensitize people on its implication on both the abuser and the child. "At best, the media are effective at building citizen awareness of an issue, but more complex attitudinal or behavioral change requires more direct forms of citizen contact and intervention". (O'Keefe & Reed, 1990: 215)

The paper proves that the information given about child abuse on social media are believable and acceptable, however, for several reasons, the effectiveness of these campaigns remains contentious rough. Burrows (1988: 16) reveals that "a media campaign can be effective, but it means nothing unless the campaign is integrated into an overall approach dealing with the various aspects." He adds that, "whatever happens at the mass level must be complemented and supported at a grassroots level for any long-term behavioral change to occur," (Julie Urquhart cited in Wood, 1994: 18).

RECOMMENDATIONS

Based on the findings, the study recommends as follows:

1. There should be public enlightenment programs that reaches the grassroot to create awareness on child abuse and its legal implications for offenders.
2. Fights against child abuse should be taken down to the family level where parents and guardians are found. By this, it means that discussions on child abuse should take place in churches, women groups, marketplaces, and other social gatherings.
3. The Nigeria government should Make available childcare homes and services or empower already existing organizations to cater for the welfare of child abuse victims and also children that lack parental care.
4. The Nigerian government should ensure through appropriate authorities that the child rights laws are enacted.

CONCLUSION

Social media has become quite pervasive in our everyday lives and has also been proven to have an influence on our lives. This study therefore sought to examine if the level of awareness created by social media on the issue of child abuse has helped in its prevention. While the results are not necessarily generalizable because of the limited sample size, the findings offer significant insight into the role of social media in child abuse prevention in Nigeria and would be a trigger for further studies into the phenomenon. The results showed that although there are numerous discussions and campaigns against child abuse on social media, it is not effective enough in the prevention of child abuse in Nigeria.

REFERENCES

Alade Anuoluwapo. (2017, June). *The social media and the Nigerian society*. Academic Press.

Carballo-Diéguez & Dolezal. (1995, May 19). *Association between history of childhood sexual abuse and adult HIV-risk sexual behavior in Puerto Rican men who have sex with men*. Academic Press.

Chiemela, Q. A., Ovute, A. O., & Obochi, C. I. (2015). The Influence of the Social Media on the Nigerian Youths: Aba residents experience. *Journal of Research in Humanities and Social Science*, *3*(3), 12–20.

Gelles, R. J. (2001). Child Abuse as Psychopathology: A Social Critique and Reformulation. *The American Journal of Orthopsychiatry*, *43*(4), 611–621. doi:10.1111/j.1939-0025.1973.tb00830.x PMID:4736790

Gelles, R. J. (2009). Child abuse. *Microsoft Encarta Online encyclopedia*. Retrieved from http://encarta.msn.com

McLuhan. (2008). Marshall McLuhan's Theory of Communication. Global Media Journal.

National Legislative Bodies / National Authorities. (2003). Nigeria Act No. 26 of 2003, Child's Rights Act, 2003 Refworld | Nigeria: Act No. 26 of 2003, Child's Rights Act, 2003

Nche, G. C. (2012). The Social Media Usage Among Nigerian Youths: Impact on National Development. *International Journal of Advancement in Development Studies,* *7*(5), 18-23.

Ndinojuo, Gbeneka, Diegbegha, & Eludu. (2016). Challenges in using contemporary Digital Tools in media relations practice in Nigeria. *Research on Humanities and Social Sciences*.

UNICEF. (2016). Ending violence against children in Nigeria: A multi-sectoral response to the 2014 Nigeria Violence Against Children Survey. In *Ending violence against children in Nigeria*. UNICEF Nigeria.

ADDITIONAL READING

Chiemela, Q. A., Ovute, A. O., & Obochi, C. I. (2015). The Influence of the Social Media on the Nigerian Youths: Aba residents experience. *Journal of Research in Humanities and Social Science*, *3*(3), 12–20.

KEY TERMS AND DEFINITIONS

Child Abuse: Or child maltreatment is the physical, sexual, and/or psychological maltreatment or neglect of a child or children, especially by a parent or a caregiver.

Child Marriage: Is a formal or informal union between anyone under 18 with an individual. Majority of child marriages in Nigeria are the ones between a girl and man.

Cyberbullying: Is bullying which uses e-technology as a means of victimizing others". It is the usage of internet media or mobile technologies like email, chat rooms, and discussion groups on the internet, mobile phones, mobile phone cameras, web pages, text messages, with the intention of harming other persons.

Neglect: In the context of child abuse simply means depriving a child of the basic needs and leaving the welfare of the child for the child.

Physical Abuse: Can be defined as any deliberate act to harm a child thereby causing injury, pain, or trauma to a child by way of physical contact.

Prevention: The act of stopping something from happening or of stopping someone from doing something.

Social Media: Are interactive technologies and digital channels that allow people to create and share information, ideas, hobbies, and other kinds of expression via virtual communities and networks.

Utilisation: The act of making practical and effective use of something.

Chapter 7
Is Sharenting Apart From Bullying?
A Perspective Among Parents Towards Their Social Media Activities

Nor Hazlina Hashim
University Malaya, Malaysia

Muhammad Emeer Nor Azhar
University of Malaya, Malaysia

Marshina Juliza Mohd Hasim
University of Malaya, Malaysia

Zaridah Abdullah
Universiti Teknologi MARA, Malaysia

ABSTRACT

Pictures, videos, and written information about children have become overwhelmed by digital content on many social media platforms. This phenomenon is known as sharenting. Attitude and trust have been identified as two variables that predict parents sharing behaviour in social media. Results from a survey among 303 parents across Malaysia indicated that attitude and trust are good predictors of parents' sharenting behaviour on social media among Malaysian parents. By applying the theory of reasoned action, this study concludes that parents in Malaysia are willing to disclose much information about their children when they believe there is nothing wrong with sharing that information, especially when they feel proud of their children's achievements. In addition, parents also highly trust that social media users might not misuse information that they share, and they believe the law would protect the information from being abused by users.

DOI: 10.4018/978-1-6684-5426-8.ch007

INTRODUCTION

Sharing pictures, video, and written information about kids become a typical sight on the social media feed at the current moment. This kind of activities known as sharenting, it's an amalgamation of two words: sharing and parenting (Marasli, Suhendan & Yilmazturk, 2017). The parents are enthusiastic to share and display information, picture, and video of their children on social media platforms (Blum-Ross & Livingstone, 2017; Otero, 2017). Albeit there is no big day or special event, but these contents randomly pop up in other users' social media timeline. The social media is usually a forum for parents to express their personal opinions, such as parenting joy or happiness, skills, advice, and sometimes they share how proud and adorable their kid is with online contacts. The digital content could be a family gathering, outing with friends, funny moments, happy moments, daily routine activities, holiday, and a big day like a birthday party (Brosch, 2016; Kumar & Schoenebeck, 2015). Unlike the traditional albums, relatives and friends across the states and worldwide are accessing the moments with the kids using the social media platforms.

The sharenting activities nowadays are getting worse when parents share information excessively (oversharenting) and leave digital footprints about their children on the social media (Blum-Ross & Livingstone, 2017; Brosch, 2016; Davidson-Wall, 2018; Kumar & Schoenebeck, 2015). The impact of oversharenting and digital footprints would result in several negative consequences toward the children's future life. As stated in the study by Blum-Ross & Livingstone (2017), the digital footprints would create a permanent record of the presence of children on the internet web. The digital footprints also are known as digital tattoos which portray negative impact to the children, for instance, embarrassment (Brosch, 2016; Hall, 2018; Steinberg, 2017), low self-esteem, depression (Davidson-Wall, 2018), cyberbully (Elsaesser et al., 2017b; Martínez et al., 2019), and children identity theft (Fox & Hoy, 2019; Hall, 2018; Mascheroni et al., 2018; Otero, 2017).

According to a study in the Czech Republic (Kopeckya, Szotkowskia, Aznar-Díazb, & Romero-Rodríguez, 2020), parents are abusing their children's rights by using them as commercial tools. Moreover, children are used as an attention magnet to attract new followers, and even as a monetization tool. For instance, Ryan Kaji is the most successful and influential YouTuber. His video mostly reviewing toys and hit more than 20 million YouTube subscribers. This kind of exposure can be seen positive but the videos, pictures, home and living of the kid is being disclosed excessively or over exploit by parents, social media channels and blogs.

In addition to this matter, The DaddyOFive channel can be considered as a worse case of sharenting (Kopeckya et al., 2020). Some of the videos in The DaddyOFive channel were about parents bullying their children by the prank, abuse, lie, and even destroy things. All the reactions of their kids were recorded and posted on the internet. After the controversial issue, the parents had to stop creating a new video for their channel by using the kids as main actors and got probation supervision for 5 years.

In Malaysia context, back in early 2020, an influential cosmetic individual was arrested on charges that he assaulted his adopted daughter (Farik, 2020). In a police report, the housekeeper of the suspect claims that the suspect abused the two-year-old girl. Where the suspect slapped his two-year-old adopted daughter with his hand because he wanted to film the child crying for content for his social media channel. The suspect's Instagram account was riddled with comments by people who demand for clarification. However, the case was classified as child abuse under Section 31(1)(a) of the Child Act 2001.

Nevertheless, we have to admit that sharenting phenomenon is being accepted and integral part of parenthood (Sivak & Smirnov, 2019) and some people are not aware that this is an issue that can affect the child's privacy rights. In the present day, we can see the identity of children is exploited by parents through online disclosure to the public (Steinberg, 2017). Unfortunately, children will be exposed to online danger and misuse (Hammond, 2019) without their consent and intention. On the other hand, Sharenting also might attract paedophiles to use the items uploaded on predatory websites, putting them at risk of being preyed upon, harmed, or kidnapped by cyber predators (The Star, 2020) and leads to identity theft which can make it easier for fraudsters to steal their children's identity. (Md. Salleh & Mohd Noor, 2019; Haley, 2020).

In Malaysia, the present policy is not clear and strong enough to protect children's online presence (Anis Shuhaiza & Nor Azlina, 2019). According to Anis Shuhaiza and Nor Azlina (2019), it is a necessary for a government to investigate this sharenting issues more seriously and improvement to existing laws are vital in order to provide more comprehensive children's protection, especially on their online presence.

In short, this research is fairly needed as it gives a good insight of parents on the current trend, pattern and behaviour in sharenting on social media. Previous research in 2021 was focused on qualitative study of an open-ended questionnaires on sharenting activities on social media platform among forty mothers in Penang and Kuala Lumpur, Malaysia (Nor Hazlina, Yusniza, Marshina & Nur Atikah, 2021). Hence, this study focusses on quantitative research method in identifying factors that significantly contribute to 'sharenting', the sharing behaviour among local parents within their social media activities.

LITERATURE REVIEW

Sharenting apparently happened when parents were involved and had been involved in practically disclosing and sharing information about their children, specifically on social media platforms (Marasli, Suhendan & Yilmazturk, 2017). Sharenting does not seem dangerous to the one who practices it, since the sharenting purpose may be positive and beneficial to one's own. However, the definition of sharenting can be varied from one author to another author based on their comprehension of this matter. For example, Choi & Lewallen (2018) identified sharenting as an overuse of social media by parents who post content for children and increase digital social media exposure for their children. While Lipu & Siibak (2019) defined as the moment of parents felt at ease exchanging images and details about their children and were not worried about the possible threats to their children's identification and privacy, Lazard, Capdevila, Dann, Locke, & Roper (2020) describe sharenting as a combination of parenting, routine posting and a form of parental digital sharing practices on social networking sites. Currently the most common social media platforms are Instagram, Facebook, YouTube and TikTok.

According to Ouvrein & Verswijvel (2019), parents perform sharenting activity on social media due to several sharenting motives: information-archiving motive, impression management motives, social motive, and parental advice motive. In the online world, approximately 80% of parents post photographs of their children with captions and share them with their friends through the online forum, e-mail, instant messaging, MMS, and SNSs (Kopeckya, et. al., 2020). According to Lipu & Siibak (2019), most parents are comfortable posting information about their children on social media and do not knowingly or subconsciously understand that their actions will lead to new threats to the identification and privacy of their children.

On the other side, children's information provided by parents on social media may serve as an outlet for parents to connect with online contacts, i.e., family members and friends. This could be the motivation of self-representation, where parents take part in sharenting activities on social media. According to

Holiday, Norman and Densley (2020), parents know that children can draw attention and use their kids as supplementary in their post to extend themselves virtually. Furthermore, parents, especially mothers, want to show that they are practicing "good mothering", and this would lead to communicative activities within the digital world (Lazard et al., 2019).

Meanwhile, Wagner and Gasche (2018), mentioned that parents also eager in received comments, reviews, and number of 'likes' from the online viewers each time they post pictures or videos of their children. According to the authors, one of the motivations that drive parents to participate in sharenting activities are social participations. Parents who engage in sharenting activities on social media can be considered as an extension of self-disclosure. Showing pride can be one of the motivations for the parents to participate in the sharenting activities. Most parents are very proud of their children and therefore would want to show off their children to the world. On the other hand, by showing pride and too much of self-disclosure can create other parents' jealousy and covetousness feelings.

In the Malaysian context, the understanding of Malaysian parents on threats and digital practices is healthy (Zulfadli et al., 2019). The online threats include excessive Internet use, adult content exposure, cyber bullying, privacy issues, online predators and harmful content exposure. In Malaysia, 60% of sexual abuse case are among children that have been reported to Royal Malaysia Police, more 70% of commercial crime are from cybercrime, 50% of secondary school students are use social media as a channel for them to interact with their friends, one out of four children facing threats and harassment on the net, one out of four of children are willing to meet people from the net and 94% of children in Malaysia are expose to online pornography (CyberSecurity Malaysia, 2019).

The CyberSecurity Malaysia showed data on children and adolescent that using internet and social media for communication channel were exposed to threats and negative consequences. As parents, they should understand and be informed clearly about the risks and try to guide them to behave and exercise a good practice on the net. The risks and threats include sexual threats, scam, cyberbully, identity theft, aggressive games that might influence the behaviour, online gambling, internet addiction, and negative influence from the internet. The law on sharenting must consider in order to set a guideline that able to control the sharenting activities on social media. According to Anis Shuhaiza and Nor Azlina (2019), to avoid the negative consequences on children, the law on sharenting must be created. In addition, Malaysia government takes very serious on cyber threat toward children especially on child grooming. For instance, Child Act 2001 dan Sexual Offences against Children Act 2017. According to Anis Shuhaiza and Nor Azlina (2019) the improvement on these laws needs to be improvised, i.e., the need of consent from two parties between parents and children. In conclusion, if there's no specific law that able to address the sharenting problems, this would lead to negative consequences like cyberbully, kidnap, and sexual crime (Shuhaiza & Nor Azlina, 2019).

Developing Theoretical Framework

The Theory of Reasoned Action has become a widely recognized method for predicting individual's behaviour. Introduced by Fishbein and Azjen (1975) in which interpret the actions of an individual to be a positive function of their meaningful intention to perform that behaviour. This behaviour relies on two independent factors: the attitude of an individual towards behaviour performance, and subjective norms of an individual. This theory was used to measure the impact of social media on consumer behaviour (Bigne et al. 2018) and the sharing behaviours across social media platforms (Ham, Lee, Hayes, & Bae, 2019). Next is a study from Germany, showed that attitude and subjective norms contribute positively to news-sharing intention and turn it into positive actual news-sharing behaviour (Karnowski, Leonhard, & Kümpel, 2018). Based on the findings previously mentioned, it shows that TRA is a suitable theory that capable to measure the behaviour of an individual in the digital environment including sharenting.

Attitude towards sharing information is associated with perceived motives or intention to use social media. According to Lin et al (2013), social presence and commitment are two variables that positively impact users' attitude towards information sharing on social media. Social presence can act to create more approachable and comfortable environment which users are more willing to interact with each other under high social presence environment. On the other hand, users are more likely to be involved in the social media sites when they feel more committed to the social media community.

In addition, a research study by Lee, Periyayya, & Nair (2017) showed that young adults aged between 18 to 24 have positive intrinsic and extrinsic motivations correlations with online photo sharing behaviours on Facebook. The intrinsic motivations showed a stronger connection to online photo sharing behaviours and there were no differences between genders in their online photo sharing behaviours. The results indicate a strong attitude towards sharing information that is associated with intention to use social media.

In the context of sharenting, parents performing sharenting activities for the reason of collecting the memories and informing their online contacts about their family activities (Blum-Ross & Livingstone 2017), parents also exchange information about their children because they feel proud of the accomplishments of their children (Verswijvel et al., 2019; Lazard et al. 2018), to seek and share parenting advice (Clark et al. (2015), to stay in touch with distance relatives (Lazard et al., 2018; Goodwin, 2017), for the need of self-realization and social approval (Brosch, 2016), and also because of the desire to perform models of "good" parenting and receive external validation (Ammari & Schoenebeck, 2015; Kumar & Schoenebeck, 2015). However, there's no available research that has been conducted to examine parents' attitudes toward sharenting in Malaysia.

Another variable besides attitude is trust. Based on Cambridge Dictionary, trust can be a noun or a verb, which means the belief that you can trust someone or something (https://dictionary.cambridge.org/dictionary/english/trust). In this sharenting context, the trust of parents sharing information in social media platforms. According to Krasnova & Veltri (2010), trust toward social media can be divided into three groups: (1) trust in social media platforms, (2) trust in online contact, and lastly (3) trust in legal assurance. Researchers have divided trust into three groups to be measured in this study: trust in social media platform (TSMP), trust in online contacts (TOC) and trust in legal assurance (TLA). These three groups of trust are suggested by Krasnova & Veltri (2010).

First is trust in social media platform. The researchers would like to explore trust belief toward the social media platforms, and this includes the benevolence, integrity and competence as suggested by Cho et al. (2017) and Krasnova & Veltri, 2010). This is aligned with study by Benbasat and Wang (2005), where internet users have shown to be influence by perceived competence, benevolence, and integrity. This was supported by Porter et al. (2013), social media users make effort in building trust in social media platform by performing post activities.

Second is trust in online contact. Based on the result, many parents trust their online contacts or followers. They believe that they will not misuse or embarrass them with the information they shared on social media. This also aligns with the study from Ouvrein and Verswijvel (2019), where parents don't mind sharing information with their followers. In order to show that parents trust their online contact, an article written by Mayer (2022) stated that parents sometimes tend to share their struggles and not everyone is trying to show that they have a picture-perfect life. Some parents are reclaiming social media as a tool to show that behind many smiling family photos was a meltdown leading up to it.

Lastly, trust in legal assurance, all the legal assurance items meant to measure the parents' confidence level toward the legal framework to protect their information privacy on social media (Krasnova & Veltri, 2010). Surprisingly, the finding indicated that many parents are assured that current legislation protects their privacy and information on social media. They still feel more confident using social media, as they believe that the current regulatory body addresses data privacy appropriately. In achieving the research objective, this study focuses on analyzing the framework model based on the parents' perspectives of their social media activities regards to sharenting; therefore, Figure 1 is the proposed conceptual framework, and the following hypotheses are proposed as:

Hypothesis one: Attitude is positively correlated to sharenting behaviour
Hypothesis two: Trust is positively correlated to sharenting behaviour
Hypothesis three: Trust is positively correlated to attitude
Hypothesis four: Attitude and trust significantly contributed to sharenting behaviour

Figure 1. Proposed Conceptual Framework

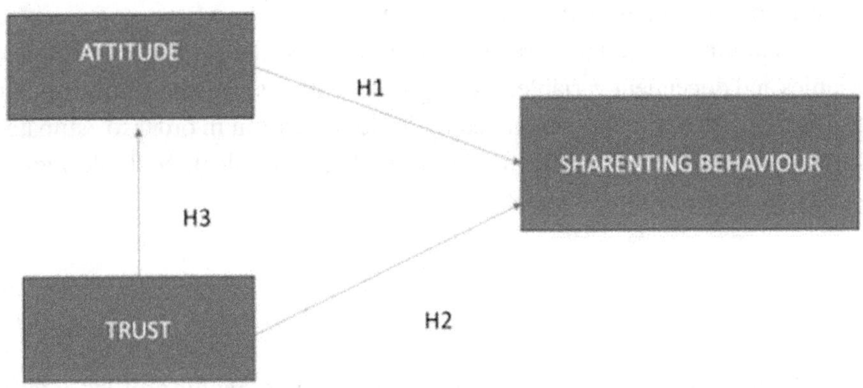

METHODOLOGY

Previous research in 2021 has done but only focused on qualitative study of an open-ended questionnaires on sharenting activities on social media platform among forty mothers in Penang and Kuala Lumpur, Malaysia (Nor Hazlina, et al. 2021). This time, this research is more extensive by using a quantitative approach and the data collected using Google form of online survey. Regards to Movement Control Order (MCO) during the COVID-19 pandemic, snowball technique sampling was used. Questionnaires were distributed by sharing at social media platforms and instant messages application (Telegram, What's App, WeChat), Instagram, LinkedIn, Facebook, and Twitter. This study used the formula based on Krejcie, & Morgan, (1970) and suggestions by DeVellis, (2017) and Tabachnick & Fidell, (2013) on sample size calculation. Three hundred and three respondents were involved in the study. The factors involved in the study were attitude and trust, while the dependent variable was sharenting behaviour among parents in social media. The researchers have adopted items to measure attitude, trust and sharenting behaviour from Verswijvel et al. (2019). Data was analysed by using IBM Statistical Package for the Social Sciences (SPSS) statistical software version 26.

There are three sub-concepts to measure attitude as another factor or independent variable which contribute to sharenting behaviour. The instruments were attitude towards written information, attitude toward pictures, and attitude toward video. (e.g.: "What do you think about sharing written information about your kids on social media?" and "What do you think about sharing pictures of your kids on social media?". For attitude variable, it were measured in a semantic differential scale ranging from "useful" (1) to "useless" (5), "not embarrassing" (1) to "embarrassing" (5), "good" (1) to "bad" (5), "fair" (1) to "unfair" (5), "not harmful" (1) to "harmful" (5), and "acceptable" (1) to "unacceptable" (5).

According to Verswijvel et al. (2019), there are 16 items to examine trust among parents towards social media that motivate them to share pictures and information of their children on online platform (e.g In general, social media platform is open to the needs of its members; Generally, I trust that social media users will not misuse my sincerity; As a parent, I feel confident that existing laws protect me against abuse of my information on social media.).The scale used for these instruments was semantic differential scales. While six items were identified to assess Sharenting Behaviour as a dependent variable in this study (e.g., As a parent, I normally share social pictures of my kids on social media; As a parent, I normally share videos of my kids on social media). The items are measured by 5-points Likert Scale ranging from 1 (totally disagree) to 5 (totally agree).

Subsequently, correlation has been performed in order to assess the strength of relationship between independent variables and dependent variable. The high correlation score, the stronger relationship with one and another. Finally, researcher has conducted multiple regression in order to estimate the association between variables (dependent variables and independent variables). Multiple regression helped researcher to predict the value of the dependent variable.

FINDINGS

In this research, the descriptive analyses were performed on the demographic profiles of the respondents. Table 1 shows that majority of the parents were female (71.3%) followed by male (28.7%). Majority of them were Malay (88.4%), while the balance about 12% were a combination of Chinese, Indian and other race. Most of the respondents (31%) were between 25 to 34 years old and many of them (52%) hold a bachelor's degree (refer Table 1). In addition, majority works in private sectors (47.2%). They were also married and has between 1 to children. The social media which were popular among them was WhatsApp (97%), followed by Facebook (79%) and YouTube and Instagram (72%). Most of them spent between 2.1 to 4 Hours a day on social media (45.2%).

Multiple regression was performed to identify whether attitude and trust would contribute to social media sharenting behaviour among parents. Table 2 describes the means and standard deviations for all the three variables involved in the study. In addition, the correlation analysis found that attitude and trust significantly correlated to sharenting behaviour ($r_{attitude}=0.624, p<0.05; r_{trust}=0.589, p<0.05$). Detail information as per below table (Table 2).

Table 1. Demographic profiles of the respondents (n=303)

Demography	Number of Respondents	Percentage
Gender: Male Female	87 216	28.7 71.3
Race: Malay Chinese India Others	268 11 11 13	88.4 3.6 3.6 4.3
Age: Below 25 years 25 – 34 35 – 44 45 – 54 55 years and above	58 94 54 58 39	19.1 31.0 17.8 19.1 12.9
Education: PMR/SPM STPM/Matric/Foundation/Certificate Diploma Bachelor's Degree Master's Degree PhD	30 12 44 158 51 8	9.9 4.0 14.5 52.1 16.8 2.6
Occupation: Student Unemployed Private Sector Public Sector Own Business Housewife Others	55 5 143 52 13 15 20	18.2 1.7 47.2 17.2 4.3 5.0 6.6
Status: Married Widowed	290 13	95.7 4.3
No. of children: 1 to 2 3 to 4 5 and above	199 80 24	65.7 26.4 8
Social media used: YouTube WhatsApp Facebook Instagram Twitter	228 293 239 228 101	75.2 96.7 78.9 75.2 33.3
Average hours spent on social media in a day: Less than 2 hours 2.1 to 4 hours More than 4 hours	93 137 73	30.7 45.2 24.1

The multiple linear regression analyses involved two independent variables to predict the significant factors that contributed to sharenting behaviour. Two models were developed in which model one involved attitude and sharenting behaviour, while model 2 involved attitude and trust. The researchers had also run the multicollinearity test and found that there was no multicollinearity between the independent variables (VIF = 1.229). Refer to Table 3 for detail information.

Table 2. Descriptive statistics and bivariate correlation

Variable	1	2	3	Mean	Std. D
1. Attitude	-	0.431*	0.624*	54.9	11.9
2. Trust		-	0.589*	48.5	10.2
3. Sharenting behaviour			-	16.3	4.9

*p<0.05, N=303

Table 3. Regression model 1 and 2 in predicting sharenting behaviour

	Variable	B	SE	β	t	p
Model 1	Constant Attitude	2.334 0.255	1.031 0.018	0.624	2.263 13.871	0.024 0.000
Model 2	Constant	-2.971	1.101		-2.699	0.007
	Attitude	0.186	0.018	0.455	10.216	0.000
	Trust	0.187	0.187	0.392	8.801	0.000

Model 1: $F(2,301) = 192.408$; $p<0.05$; $R=0.624$; $R^2=0.390$; Adj. $R^2=0.388$
Model 2: $F(2,300)=159.372$; $p<0.05$; $R=0.718$; $R^2=0.515$; Adj. $R^2=0.512$

In Table 3, Model 1 found that attitude contributed significantly to sharenting behaviour ($F(2,301) = 192.408$, $p<0.05$ with an $R^2=0.390$). It shows that 39% of sharenting behaviour can be explained by parents' attitude. While for Model 2 of the analysis was found that attitude and trust significantly contributed to sharenting behaviour ($F(2,300) = 159.372$, $p<0.05$ with an $R^2 = 0.515$ (Table 3). The results also indicated that when combined, parents' attitude and trust contributed 51.5% to parents' sharenting behaviour. The analysis shows that when trust was included in the analysis, it contributes 12.5% more towards sharenting behaviour among parents. Thus, attitude and trust are significant good predictors towards sharenting behaviour.

In answering to the research objective of this study which focused on analyzing the framework model based on the parents' perspectives of their social media activities regarding sharenting as proposed framework reflected in Figure 1. The results reflected in Figure 2 shows that attitude is positively and strongly correlated to sharenting behaviour ($r=0.624$) while trust is positively and moderately correlated to sharenting behaviour ($r=0.589$). Trust also moderately correlated to attitude ($r=0.431$). When parents have positive attitude towards social media function, they are more willing on sharing information and pictures of their kids on social media.

Similarly, when parents put their trust towards social media, they will be actively posting and updating stories of their kids on social media. Trust is another variable which significantly contribute to parents' attitude to share information and stories of their kids.

Figure 2. Correlations between attitude, trust and sharenting behaviour

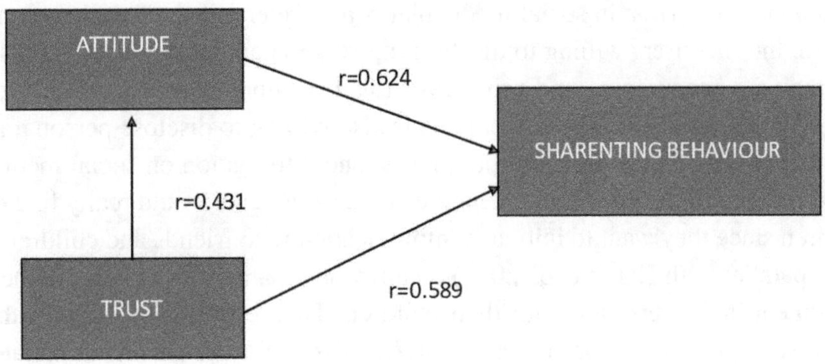

DISCUSSION

This research study focuses on parents' perspectives regards to sharenting behaviour towards their social media activities. The researchers have applied attituded from TRA model and trust as the main variables towards parents sharenting behaviour. The results showed that attitude and trust are significant good predictors towards sharenting behaviour. In supporting these results, the first variable is attitude, which it was divided into three sub-concepts as suggested by Verswijvel et al. (2019): written information, pictures, and videos. Most of parents feel that the written information, pictures, and videos that they have shared on social media is not embarrassing, acceptable, useful, fair, and not harmful to themselves and their children. Based on the sharenting behaviour as dependent variable, parents normally share social photos, children's hobbies activities, children's sport performance, video, children's education record and statuses. Parents would like to improve their online presence by sharing information about their children on social media.

This finding is similar with the study conducted in Belgium, which parents use their children for self-representation and impression management (Verswijvel et al., 2019). According to Blum-Ross and Livingstone (2017), parents are uncertain and worry about self-representation they encounter on social media. Usually, parents would love to share cute and funny contents of their children on social media (Blum-Ross & Livingstone, 2017; Brosch, 2016, Brosch, 2018; Kumar & Schoenebeck, 2015; Wagner & Gasche, 2018) to show that there are good and better. Parents like to portray a better impression and present themselves in a favourable way to their online contacts via sharing virtual contents (written information, picture, and video) on social media. This is happening because parents would like to show that they have a "good parenting skill" via their sharing behaviours to indicate a happy and healthy family (Kumar & Schoenebeck, 2015).

Next is parents in Malaysia performing sharenting activities for the reason of collecting the memories and informing their online contacts about their family activities. One of the key reasons of parents' exchange knowledge about their children is because they feel proud of the accomplishments of their children (Verswijvel et al., 2019). Parents also have a high degree to share information on social media because they like to share and seek parenting advice from their online contacts, especially family members and friends. This result is supported by Aggarwal et al. (2016), in their study, social media platforms can be a very important platform for internet user to seek advice from their online contacts. The finding indicates that attitude is positively related to sharenting behaviour (H1).

Second variable is trust. Trust in social media platform is referring to the online contacts and trust in legal assurance. Internet users willing to disclose information and post activities on social media to build trust and they are encouraging and primed for this behaviour (Porter et al, 2013; Thompson & Brindley, 2020). According to Brosch (2018), parents also willing to disclose personal information on social media platform, personal feeling, opinion, ideas, and information on social media because they want to maintain their relationship with their online contacts. Parents would really like to share details about their children since they want to initiate communication with friends and children.

This result is parallel with Hammond (2019) result, where parents especially mothers have shown a greater involvement in conversation with their children. This result would support the children are being featured in social media be considered as intermediaries for the parents stimulate conversation with their online contacts (Holiday et al., 2020). Parents also feel more confident using social media, as they believe that the current regulatory body addresses data privacy appropriately. This is in line with a study in Estonia by Lipu and Siibak (2019). Results from the research indicated that this privacy concern (comfortable to share) is acceptable due to easy-going culture in Europe countries and make parents have lack of general concern about the potential privacy risk. The overall findings in this study indicate that trust is positively related to sharenting behaviour (H2).

Trust and attitude are the important factors why parents want share info of their kids via social media platforms. According to Tucker (2022) whenever parents overshared their social media activities, kids will be vulnerable for cyberbully. Besides that, kid's mental health and well-being especially self-esteem will significantly impact as they constantly need to be ready on-camera for photos and videos shots as part of their parents' social media content. Nowadays, virtual kidnapping or stolen identity is by stealing kids' photos to make fake pass entries. Hence, parents would need to be precautious on their social media activities on not to oversharing information on their kids.

FUTURE RESEARCH AND CONCLUSION

This research has presented a clearer understanding of sharenting behaviour of the Malaysian parents. Unambiguously, this study has contributed factor that can stimulate sharenting, namely: (1) trust and (2) attitude. This study has contributed on theory: Theory of Reasoned Action, to investigate the sharenting behaviour among parents in Malaysia. In relation to theory of reasoned action, in this study, the theory has contributed to a strong relationship between independent variables (attitude, and trust) and the dependent variable of sharenting behaviour. Thus, the researchers recommend this theory to be used in the future study on sharenting. Additionally, this study also contributes to literature review from Malaysia perspective on sharenting behaviour.

Future research should be conducted specifically on sharenting among four main races in Malaysia, using sample that represents diversity (i.e., Malay, Chinese, and Indian) to represent Malaysian parents. Secondly, a qualitative survey needs to be conducted in future study to capture the insight and better viewpoint of sharenting phenomenon in Malaysia. Thirdly, a study on sharenting among mothers in Malaysia should be conducted as mothers have more tendency to participate, disclose, share, and display information about their children to family and friends. It would be interesting to see the comparison of sharenting behaviour among mothers from Malaysia perspective and other countries perspectives.

For the marketing view, marketer need to concentrate on informative advertising to increase awareness on sharenting issue. Marketers need to design informative regarding attitude and trust of sharenting, which the target audience is millennial parents in Malaysia. For example, an infographic with an up-to-date statistic and information that very helpful to parents to make a posting decision on social media. Additionally, marketers can use this opportunity, to understand parents' behaviour on social media. Marketers can use the result from this study to create a campaign to penetrate parents' market in Malaysia.

The result showing that parents in Malaysia would spend 2-3 hours a day on social media, specifically on WhatsApp, Facebook, and Instagram. They believe that social media platform is a trusted platform, convenient and a place for them to archive their children moment and sweet memory. This would help marketers to do product advertisement based on the study result. For instance, marketers using social appeal advertising on Facebook to increase product awareness and engagement.

This study indicates that attitude and trust sharenting behaviours in Malaysian perspective. Based on Amira Nur Diana & Safinaz (2020) study, found that Malaysia still does not have adequate provision of privacy protections for children and recommends exposure to parents regarding the dangers of sharenting their children as well as privacy protections in laws protecting children in Malaysia. Therefore, not only government but also the Non- Governmental Organization (NGOs), social bodies, associations, and society should play important roles to educate Malaysian parents about sharenting behaviour. Government agencies for example, Malaysian Communication and Multimedia Commission (MCMC) and Ministry of Welfare, Community Wellbeing, Women, Family and Childhood Development should consider implementing some initiatives to educate parents about good governance of sharenting guidelines and highlight some potential negative impacts of sharenting. The sharenting guidelines should cover children's privacy violation, oversharenting phenomenon and cyberbully. Government can launch a campaign on social media regarding sharenting issue, for example, "Do Not Sure, Do Not Post" or "Reduce Digital Footprint Campaign" or "Say No to Digital Tattoo".

REFERENCES

Aggarwal, S., Rai, S., Jaiswal, M. P., & Sorensen, H. (2016). Norm of reciprocity –Antecedent of trustworthiness in social media. In *Social media: The good, the bad and the ugly*. Springer.

Amira Nur Diana, A. H., & Safinaz, M. H. (2020). The effects of sharenting on children and its implications on a child's privacy rights in Malaysia. *Current Legal Issues*, *2*, 21–52.

Ammari, T., & Schoenebeck, S. (2015) Understanding and supporting fathers and fatherhood on social media sites. In *Proceedings of the 33rd Annual ACM Conference on Human Factors in Computing Systems* (pp.1905-1914). New York, NY: Association for Computing Machinery Press. 10.1145/2702123.2702205

Benbasat, I., & Wang, W. (2005). Trust in and adoption of online recommendation agents. *Journal of the Association for Information Systems*, *6*(3), 72–101. Advance online publication. doi:10.17705/1jais.00065

Bigne, E., Andreu, L., Hernandez, B., & Ruiz, C. (2018). The impact of social media and offline influences on consumer behaviour. An analysis of the low-cost airline industry. *Current Issues in Tourism*, *21*(9), 1014–1032. doi:10.1080/13683500.2015.1126236

Blum-Ross, A., & Livingstone, S. (2017). "Sharenting," parent blogging and the boundaries of the digital self. *Popular Communication*, *15*(2), 110–125. doi:10.1080/15405702.2016.1223300

Brosch, A. (2016). When the child is born into the internet: Sharenting as a growing trend among parents on facebook. *The New Educational Review*, *43*(2), 225–235. doi:10.15804/tner.2016.43.1.19

Brosch, A. (2018). Sharenting – Why do parents violate their children's privacy? *The New Educational Review*, *54*(4), 75–85. doi:10.15804/tner.2018.54.4.06

Cho, S., Park, C., & Kim, J. (2017). Leveraging consumption intention with identity information on sharing economy platforms. *Journal of Computer Information Systems*, *00*(00), 1–10. doi:10.1080/08874417.2017.1326295

Choi, G. Y., & Lewallen, J. (2018). "Say Instagram, Kids!": Examining Sharenting and Children's Digital Representations on Instagram. *The Howard Journal of Communications*, *29*(2), 140–160. doi:10.1080/10646175.2017.1327380

Clark, S. J., Davis, M. M., Singer, D. C., Matos-Moreno, A., Kauffman, A. D., & Hale, K. (2015). *'Parents on social media: Likes and dislikes of sharen-ting: C. S. Mott children's hospital national poll', National poll on children's health.* Retrieved January 3, 2022, from https://mottpoll.org/sites/default/files/docu-ments/031615_sharenting_0.pdf

CyberSecurity Malaysia. (2019). *CyberSafe Parenting: Ke Arah Kesejahteraan Siber* [Towards Cyber Wellness]. Cyberjaya, Selangor Darul Ehsan.

Davidson-Wall, N. (2018). *"Mum, seriously!": Sharenting the new social trend with no opt-out.* Paper presented at the 9th Debating Communities and Social Networks 2018 OUA Conference. Online Conference.

DeVellis, R. F. (2017). *Scale development: Theory and applications* (4th ed.). Sage.

Dictionary, C. (2022). *Cambridge University Press.* Retrieved May 24, 2022, from https://dictionary.cambridge.org/dictionary/english/

Farik, Z. (2020). *Cosmetics businessman arrested over child abuse allegations.* Retrieved January 6, 2020, from https://www.thestar.com.my/news/nation/2020/03/06/cosmetic-businessman-arrested-over-child-abuse-allegations?fbclid=IwAR27Svkdq-BTz_rhtxd-TisbZZcA52J5N6eDXDvMcbtAWABzqa-fpAqgHNsU

Fishbein, M. A., & Azjen, I. (1975). *Belief, attitude, intention and behaviour: An introduction to theory and research.* Addison-Wesley.

Fox, A. K., & Hoy, M. G. (2019). Smart devices, smart decisions? Implications of parents ' sharenting for children ' s online privacy : An investigation of mothers. *Journal of Public Policy & Marketing*, *38*(4), 414–432. doi:10.1177/0743915619858290

Goodwin, K. (2017). *Sharenting- What parents need to consider before sharing pictures of their kids.* Retrieved January 3, 2022, from https://drkristygoodwin.com/sharenting-what-parents-need-to-consider-before-sharing-pictures-of-their-kids/

Haley, K. (2020). Sharenting and the (potential) right to be forgotten. *Indiana Law Journal, 95*(3), 1006-1020. https://www.repository.law.indiana.edu/ilj/vol95/iss3/9

Hall, H. K. (2018). Oversharenting : Is it really your story to tell ? 33 oversharenting: Is it really. *The John Marshall Journal of Information Technology & Privacy Law, 33*(3).

Ham, C. D., Lee, J., Hayes, J. L., & Bae, Y. H. (2019). Exploring sharing behaviors across social media platforms. *International Journal of Market Research, 61*(2), 157–177. doi:10.1177/1470785318782790

Hammond, J. W. (2019). *Parenting and working in the digital age: A qualitative examination of intensive parenting and ideal worker norms* (Doctoral dissertation). Washington State Univesity. https://research.libraries.wsu.edu/xmlui/bitstream/handle/2376/16735/Hammond_wsu_0251E_12635.pdf?sequence=1&isAllowed=y

Holiday, S., Norman, M. S., & Densley, R. L. (2020). Sharenting and the extended self: Self-representation in parents' Instagram presentations of their children. *Popular Communication, 18*(3), 1–15. doi:10.1080/15405702.2020.1744610

Karnowski, V., Leonhard, L., & Kümpel, A. S. (2018). Why users share the news : A Theory of Reasoned Action-based study on the antecedents of news- sharing behavior. *Communication Research Reports, 35*(2), 91–100. doi:10.1080/08824096.2017.1379984

Kopeckya, K., Szotkowskia, R., & Inmaculada Aznar-Díazb, J.-M. R.-R. (2020). The phenomenon of sharenting and its risks in the online environment. Experiences from Czech Republic and Spain. *Children and Youth Services Review, 110*, 104812. Advance online publication. doi:10.1016/j.childyouth.2020.104812

Krasnova, H., & Veltri, N. F. (2010). *Privacy calculus on social networking sites : Explorative evidence from Germany and USA.* Paper presented at 43rd Hawaii international conference on system sciences. 10.1109/HICSS.2010.307

Krejcie, R. V., & Morgan, D. W. (1970). Determining sample size for research activities. *Educational and Psychological Measurement, 30*(3), 607–610. doi:10.1177/001316447003000308

Kumar, P., & Schoenebeck, S. (2015). The modern day baby book. *Proceedings of the 18th ACM Conference on Computer Supported Cooperative Work & Social Computing- CSCW '15.* 10.1145/2675133.2675149

Lazard, L., Locke, A., Dann, C., Capdevila, R., & Roper, S. (2018). *Sharenting: Why mothers post about their children on social media.* Retrieved January 4, 2022, from https://theconversation.com/sharenting-why-mothers-post-about-their-children-on-social-media-91954

Lee, W. C., Periyayya, T., & Nair, G. V. (2017). Advent of the new media: The influence of intrinsic and extrinsic motivation in online photo sharing behaviours on facebook among young Malaysian adults. *SHS Web of Conferences 33,* 59. doi: 10.1051/ 73300059

Lin, X., Featherman, M., & Sarker, S. (2013). Information Sharing in the Context of Social Media: An Application of the Theory of Reasoned Action and Social Capital Theory. *SIGHCI 2013 Proceedings*, 17. https://aisel.aisnet.org/sighci2013/17

Lipu, M., & Siibak, A. (2019). 'Take it down!': Estonian parents' and pre-teens' opinions and experiences with sharenting. *Media International Australia, 170*(1), 57–67. doi:10.1177/1329878X19828366

Marasli, M., Suhendan, E., Yilmazturk, N. H., & Cok, F. (2017). Parents ' shares on social networking sites about their children : Sharenting. *The Anthropologist, 24*(2), 399–406. doi:10.1080/09720073.2016.11892031

Martínez, I., Murgui, S., Garcia, O. F., & Garcia, F. (2019). Parenting in the digital era: Protective and risk parenting styles for traditional bullying and cyberbullying victimization. *Computers in Human Behavior*, *90*, 84–92. doi:10.1016/j.chb.2018.08.036

Mascheroni, G., Ponte, C., & Jorge, A. (2018). *The challenges for families in the digital age. In The International Clearinghouse on Children, Youth and Media at Nordicom (Nordic Information Centre for Media and Communication Research)*. University of Gothenburg.

Mayer, B. A. (2022). *Why parents overshare on social media and when it might be dangerous*. Retrieved February 5, 2022 from https://www.parents.com/parenting/better-parenting/sharenting-meaning-and-when-it-might-be-dangerous/

Muhd. Zulfadli Hafiz, I., Nik Daliana, N. F., Rafzah, A. Z., Ramona Susanty, A. H., Elina, A. M. Edwan, M. A., & Aida, T. (2019). *Towards good cyber parenting- Exploring stakeholders' views in understanding parental digital security practice and online threat concerns in Malaysia*. doi:10.13140/RG.2.2.14431.30884

Nor Hazlina, H., Yusniza, K., Marshina, M. H. J., & Nur Atikah, A. R. (2021). "Sharenting": A study of Malaysian parents' use of social media platforms. SEARCH. *Journal of Media and Communication*, *13*(3), 125–140.

Otero, P. (2017). Sharenting... should children's lives be disclosed on social media? *Archivos Argentinos de Pediatria*, *115*(5), 412–413. PMID:28895685

Ouvrein, G., & Verswijvel, K. (2019). Sharenting: Parental adoration or public humiliation? A focus group study on adolescents' experiences with sharenting against the background of their own impression management. *Children and Youth Services Review*, *99*, 319–327. doi:10.1016/j.childyouth.2019.02.011

Porter, C., Devaraj, S., & Sun, D. (2013). A test of two models of value creation in virtual communities. *Journal of Management Information Systems*, *30*(1), 261–292. doi:10.2753/MIS0742-1222300108

Md. Salleh, A. S., & Mohd Noor, N. A. (2019). Sharenting: Implikasinya dari perspektif perundangan Malaysia. *Kanun: Jurnal Undang-undang Malaysia*, *31*(1), 121-156.

Shuhaiza Md Salleh, A., & Azlina Mohd Noor, N. (2019). Sharenting: Implikasinya dari perspektif perundangan Malaysia (Sharenting: Its implications from the Malaysian legal perspective). *Kanun: Jurnal Undang-undang Malaysia*, *31*(1), 121–156. doi:10.1108/13522751111163245

Sivak, E., & Smirnov, I. (2019). Parents mention sons more often than daughters on social media. In *Proceedings of the National Academy of Sciences of the United States of America* (vol. 116, pp. 2039–2041). 10.1073/pnas.1804996116

Star. (2020a). *Are you sharenting your children?* Retrieved May 25, 2022, from https://www.thestar.com.my/lifestyle/health/2020/06/12/are-you-sharenting-your-children

Star. (2020b). *Entrepreneur accused of abusing his two-year-old to create social media content*. Retrieved May 22, 2022, from https://www.thestar.com.my/news/nation/2020/03/05/report-lodged-alleging-entrepreneur-abused-adopted-child-2-for-online-content

Steinberg, S. B. (2017). Sharenting : Children 's Privacy in the Age of Social Media. *Emory Law Journal, 66*(839).

Tabachnick, B., & Fidell, L. (2013). *Using multivariate statistics.* Pearson Education Inc.

Thompson, N., & Brindley, J. (2020). Who are you talking about? Contrasting determinants of online disclosure about self or others. *Information Technology & People.* Advance online publication. doi:10.1108/ITP-04-2019-0197

Tucker, J. (2022). *How parental oversharing on social media harms kids.* Retrieved May 23, 2022, from https://www.moms.com/how-parental-oversharing-on-social-media-harms-kids/

Verswijvel, K., Walrave, M., Hardies, K., & Heirman, W. (2019). Sharenting, is it a good or a bad thing? Understanding how adolescents think and feel about sharenting on social network sites. *Children and Youth Services Review, 104*, 104401. Advance online publication. doi:10.1016/j.childyouth.2019.104401

Wagner, A., & Gasche, L. A. (2018). *Sharenting: Making decisions about other's privacy on social networking sites.* Retrieved February 10, 2020, from https://mkwi2018.leuphana.de/wp-content/uploads/MKWI_81.pdf

ADDITIONAL READING

Abdul Syukor, S., Abd. Rahman Shah, H., & Musa, N. A. (2017). Regulating children's safety on the internet: A Malaysian perspective. *International Journal for Studies on Children, Women, Elderly and Disabled, 1*, 152–156.

Latipah, E., Adi Kistoro, H. C., Hasanah, F. F., & Putranta, H. (2020). Elaborating motive and psychological impact of sharenting in millennial parents. *Universal Journal of Educational Research, 8*(10), 4807–4817. doi:10.13189/ujer.2020.081052

Siibak, A., & Traks, K. (2019). The dark Sides of sharenting. *Catalan Journal of Communication & Cultural Studies, 11*(1), 115–121. doi:10.1386/cjcs.11.1.115_1

KEY TERMS AND DEFINITIONS

Attitude: A complex mental state involving beliefs and feelings and values and dispositions to act in certain ways.

Cyberbullying: The use of electronic communication to bully a person, normally by sending messages of an intimidating or threatening nature.

Sharenting: Parents' habitual use of social media to share news, images, or videos of their children.

Social Media: Websites and other online means of communication that are used by large groups of people to share information and to develop social and professional contacts.

Trust: Reliance on the integrity, strength, ability, surety, etc., of a person or thing.

Chapter 8

Cyberbullying on Chinese Social Media:

Language Features and Influence Factors in Comments on Key Opinion Leaders' Posts

Jin Liu
City University of Hong Kong, Hong Kong

Yuantao Peng
City University of Hong Kong, Hong Kong

Caiwei Wang
City University of Hong Kong, Hong Kong

Jingyi Guo
City University of Hong Kong, Hong Kong

Yinyu Chen
City University of Hong Kong, Hong Kong

Michael Prieler
Hallym University, South Korea

ABSTRACT

The rapid development of information and communication technologies contributes to the growth of social media channels, which also bring some problems such as cyberbullying. Previous studies have analyzed the prevalence and consequences of cyberbullying and the detection and prevention of it. However, little research pays attention to cyberbullying on Chinese social media. This research uses the content analysis method to analyze cyberbullying on one of the biggest social media platforms in China, Weibo, focusing on language features and factors that influence the frequency of cyberbullying language in comments on key opinion leaders' (KOLs) posts. The findings reveal that most cyberbullying language on Weibo appears in the form of mildly offensive or ordinary words with special meanings and offensive references, rather than directly offensive words. In addition, this research found that KOL type and post content type interact to affect the frequency of cyberbullying language on Weibo. Overall, this research has made a valuable contribution to cyberbullying research.

DOI: 10.4018/978-1-6684-5426-8.ch008

INTRODUCTION

With the rapid development of information and communication technologies, computer-mediated communication made a revolutionary leap in the late 20th century (Romiszowski & Mason, 1996; Steinmueller, 2000). At the same time, social media platforms have continuously emerged and developed providing more comprehensive, faster, and richer information (Kaplan & Haenlein, 2010).

However, there are pros and cons of the Internet development. There is no doubt that the emergence and development of social media has brought different kinds of benefits. But at the same time, social media also provides a platform for people to conduct challenging and negative behavior such as cyberbullying (Sari & Camadan, 2016; Walrave & Heirman, 2011). Cyberbullying is aggressive, intentional, harmful behavior carried out by individuals or groups through electronic or digital media which inflict harm or discomfort on others (Patchin and Hinduja, 2006; Smith et al., 2008; Tokunaga, 2010). In recent years, cyberbullying occurs frequently on social media, which not only causes psychological harm to the victims but also "pollute" the network environment (Alim, 2017).

In the network era, humans have acquired an infinitely large new space — cyberspace, through the activities of text transmission. At the same time, online writing has become an important way for Chinese people to communicate or record in writing with the rapid expansion of the number of internet users (Wang, 2004). In the virtual cyberspace, communication has gained greater freedom than ever, and the mode of verbal communication has also changed. The cooperation of them results in the emergence of network language. Network language is a tool for Internet users to communicate in the virtual space, as well as a form of language to express their feelings and explain their views (Liu, 2008). This kind of language is not only the carrier of information in the network context but also the variant of social language (Li, 2020). Besides, the network language has been widely used and become popular because of its conciseness, convenience, innovation, liveliness, humor, and other advantages (Liu & Ning, 2004). However, there are no restrictions on the form and content of network language, and netizens are free to create, comment, and spread. As a result, cyberbullying language appeared at the same time with the function to insult, abuse, and slander other people on social media platforms.

Halliday (2011) argues that "it has become increasingly clear that language has the power to convince, deceive and, in fact, control." (p.141) As a result, we "must choose our words carefully, and one day we will be able to measure the power of good and evil in our words" (Angelou, 2014). In other words, cyberbullying language and the bad consequences brought by it undoubtedly fully reflect the harm of malicious words.

The widespread language of cyberbullying has gained the attention of societies and scholars around the world. As early as 2012, The People's Daily published an article, which pointed out that our spiritual world is suffering from the ravages of cyberbullying, and there is no time to set aside the governance of language cyberbullying (Xu, 2021). According to the nationwide survey in the UK, nearly 56 percent of young people had witnessed cyberbullying and 42 percent of the interviewees felt unsafe on the internet (Family lives, 2020). In China, Sina Chongqing also did a survey on cyberbullying language. From the survey data, it can be seen that about 84 percent of the interviewees have been attacked by vulgar or abusive language on the internet, and 65 percent of them admitted that they had used violent language to others online. Moreover, a survey of college students in Shanxi Province in 2014 showed that more than 50 percent of the students had engaged in language cyberbullying (Mao & Liang, 2014).

In this paper, we will take cyberbullying language as the research object and focus on the posts and comments on Weibo, one of the mainstream social media platforms in China, to study the features and characteristics of cyberbullying language on Weibo. Besides, it is necessary to analyze the factors which contribute to the appearance of cyberbullying language. Content analysis is used to analyze the phenomenon of language cyberbullying on Weibo, including the content, language features, target group, and frequency. Based on the research data and findings, the analysis of the phenomenon is more comprehensive, which is helpful to the discussion on reducing the cyberbullying language and building a better network environment. This study has focused on comments on KOL posts since Weibo users spend the most time reading the posts of KOLs.

In the subsequent sections, the paper is organized as follows. In the next section, we first looked at the definition of cyberbullying by different scholars. Then we made a summary and review of the previous studies related to cyberbullying. Based on the existing research, we also outlined the limitation of language cyberbullying. After that, we reported the methodology, which describes the sample selection, data collection, coding, and the results and analysis. In the final part, the paper made a discussion about the new trend of cyberbullying language on Weibo, refinement of media regulation and governance guidelines, and the limitations of this research.

LITERATURE REVIEW

Definitions and Features of Cyberbullying

Cyberbullying is not a new issue in academia. It derives from traditional bullying during the progress of information and communications technologies (Olweus, 2012; Smith et al., 2008). However, there is no consensus on the definition of cyberbullying which can be distinguished from traditional bullying in academia (Alipan et al., 2015; Berne et al., 2013; Langos, 2012; Peter & Petermann, 2018). Generally, researchers tend to understand the concept of cyberbullying through the approach of separating "cyber" and "bullying" and merging the two meanings into a new integration (Langos, 2012). In this regard, "cyber" refers to the context of cyberspace through which bullying behaviors occur, while "bullying" follows the criteria of defining traditional bullying (Peter & Petermann, 2018). The pioneer of research on bullying, Owleus, also known as the creator of the Owleus Bullying Prevention Program (OBPP), defined "a person is bullied when he or she is exposed, repeatedly and over time, to negative actions on the part of one or more other persons, and he or she has difficulty defending himself or herself" (Olweus, 1993, p. 8). This definition contains three important components: negative (aggressive) action, repetition, and power imbalance, which have long been adopted by many researchers as the key criteria of traditional bullying (e.g., Smith & Brain, 2000; Smith et al., 2013). Cyberbullying was considered as one of the forms of bullying and shared these primary features with it (Kowalski & Limber, 2007; Kowalski et al., 2012). In 2012, Owleus responded to the rising attention on cyberbullying from the media and educators and simply defined it as "bullying performed via electronic means" (Olweus, 2012, p. 521). But he also admitted that the definition of cyberbullying is still under debate and needs further refinements (Olweus & Limber, 2018).

In general, there are three definitions of cyberbullying cited most often. The first one is by Patchin and Hinduja (2006) and adopted by the Cyberbullying Research Center, defining cyberbullying as "willful and repeated harm inflicted through the medium of electronic text" (p. 152). The second one is developed by Smith et al. (2008), defining cyberbullying as "an aggressive, intentional act carried out by a group or individual, using electronic forms of contact, repeatedly and over time against a victim who cannot easily defend him or herself" (p. 376). And the last one is from Tokunaga (2010) suggesting that "cyberbullying is any behavior performed through electronic or digital media by individuals or groups that repeatedly communicates hostile or aggressive messages intended to inflict harm or discomfort on others" (p. 278). Overall, we can see that these definitions are developed mainly based on the bullying definition of Olweus (1993). However, it should be noted that the unique features of cyberbullying that differentiate it from traditional bullying are not included, such as anonymity, infinite audiences, technological skills, and 24-hour presence, etc., which can be seen quite often in the cyberbullying literature (Dooley et al., 2009; Görzig & Ólafsson, 2013; Kowalski et al., 2014).

In the context of Chinese academia, research on cyberbullying is still at an early stage, and the lack of a clear consistent definition of cyberbullying is more distinct. Some researchers regard it as a particular type of cyber-attack that infringes upon the rights of other people from the perspective of law (Zhang, 2010), others define it as a kind of cyber anomalous behavior (Jiang, 2011). According to the China Internet Network Information Center (2020), there were 0.94 billion internet users in China by June 2020, accounting for over 20% of the internet users worldwide. And according to the statistics of two leading Chinese social media platforms up to 19 October 2020 (Kemp, 2020), WeChat has 1.206 billion monthly active users, nearly half of the Facebook users worldwide (2.701 billion), while Sina Weibo's monthly active users reaches 523 million, exceeding its counterpart, Twitter's potential advertising reach worldwide (roughly 353 million). Apparently, there is not enough attention being brought to the cyberbullying issues displayed on Chinese social media platforms compared to its large figures.

Previous Studies: Overview and Limitations

The amount of research on cyberbullying has increased over the past decade (Li, 2020; Olweus & Limber, 2018), but these studies also have limitations. In general, previous studies on cyberbullying mainly use research methods like surveys and interviews to analyze the prevalence and consequences of cyberbullying, with the help of machine learning techniques for detection (Berne et al., 2013; Xu, 2021). However, there is a lack of theoretical models in the cyberbullying literature to date. Current models used by many researchers to understand bullying behaviors are mainly from theories of aggression (Dooley et al., 2009; Kowalski et al., 2014; Vannucci et al., 2012), such as the general aggression model (GAM) developed by Anderson and Bushman (2002) and the social information processing (SIP) model proposed by Crick and Dodge (1994). According to Barlett (2017), the only published theory that is specific to cyberbullying is by Barlett and Gentile (2012). According to Barlett and Gentile's Cyberbullying Model (BGCM), the positive attitudes toward cyberbullying are formed by two main factors: anonymity and strength differential. Given that these two are unlikely to be the only determinants pertaining to the cyberbullying process (Ooi et al., 2019), it still needs some improvements to reach a relatively mature theoretical model.

Second, teenagers are the focus of most of the studies on cyberbullying due to their impressionable characteristics (Kowalski et al., 2014; Wang et al., 2019; Xu, 2021). Subsequently, little is known about adults who are also the target of cyberbullying. A study based on a national sample of New Zealand adults revealed that nearly 14.9% of respondents have experienced cyberbullying, with young adults reporting the highest levels of cyberbullying experiences (Wang et al., 2019). Moreover, even these studies, which have focused on cyberbullying targeted at adults, mostly pay a great deal of attention to cyberbullying in the workplace (Forssell, 2016; Privitera & Campbell, 2009). However, it should be noted that compared to ordinary people, celebrities and social media influencers can be exposed to exponential cyberbullying behaviors in the contemporary social media era. Since social media create an illusion of equality for everyone to be heard. But in fact, it is very hard for ordinary people to gain attention. People then get mad when the result has failed to meet expectations (Leslie, 2021). This partially explains why the cyber discourse today is flooded with bad temper, especially when it comes to celebrities and social media influencers. Furthermore, studies have shown that moral-emotional messages and content that triggers anger are more likely to be shared (Berger & Milkman, 2012; Brady et al., 2017), which in turn amplifies the adverse effect of cyberbullying.

In addition, as mentioned above, most previous studies on cyberbullying are based on English-language-based social media like Twitter, YouTube, and Myspace (Rosa et al., 2019). Thus, there is a limited number of studies on cyberbullying in the context of Chinese social media, in contrast to its vital weight and significance that should not be neglected. Furthermore, research on cyberbullying commonly resorts to automatic detection approaches like machine learning techniques for large-scale data collection, which leads to a state of uncertainty regarding the accuracy of cyberbullying detection. This problem becomes more salient and challenging when it applies to the context of the Chinese language, because Chinese is a rather complex language, with numerous newly emerging words to be created by Chinese netizens constantly (Li, 2020).

Finally, little attention has been given to the linguistic features of cyberbullying. Although there are various means to perform cyberbullying including cyber manhunt, spreading unauthorized nude photos of private individuals, etc., language violence is the most common means of cyberbullying. Li (2020) found that Chinese netizens "prefer strong or directly offensive words to mild or indirectly offensive language when the intention is to attack others or to express anger online". As the Chinese government is moving to tighten laws by adding new regulations for social media platforms, we are curious to know the latest situation about the cyberbullying phenomenon in contemporary China, given the fact that cyberbullying had caused real-life tragedies that took lives in recent years and studies have shown a clear association between being the target of bullying or cyberbullying and the risk of suicide (Bauman et al., 2013; Hinduja & Patchin, 2010; Kim & Leventhal, 2008). For example, Chinese singer and actor Kimi Qiao was found dead in his apartment following a suicide on September 16, 2016. According to the statement released by his agency, he had suffered from severe depression since a series of assaults from disinformation and language violence one year earlier. After his death, celebrities who had been friends with him but not have shown "proper regret" on social media were also insulted by netizens on Weibo. More recently, a 25-year-old influencer on the leading Chinese video-sharing website, Bilibili, who shared her experiences of fighting against lung cancer, died of the disease in December 2020, after being cyberbullied for 10 months for "feigning illness".

Research Questions

Given the above limitations, our research aims to fill the gap and analyze features of cyberbullying language targeted at celebrities and social media influencers (or key opinion leaders in the context of Weibo) on one of the leading Chinese social media platforms, Sina Weibo. Considering that Weibo had adopted a new regulation towards its comment section in June 2020 (Weibo, 2020), it seemed desirable to analyze whether cyberbullying word categories have been different after that change. Accordingly, in the study presented here, we sought to examine the relation of key opinion leader (KOL) type and post content type to the emergence of cyberbullying language.

Specifically, we examine these questions:

RQ1: What are the features of cyberbullying language on Weibo?
RQ2: What is the connection between the type of post content and the frequency of cyberbullying language?
RQ3: What is the connection between the type of KOL and the frequency of cyberbullying language?

METHOD

In order to answer the research questions, this research used quantitative content analysis to analyze the comments of KOLs' posts on Weibo which may contain cyberbullying language, and the relation of KOL type and post content type to the frequency of cyberbullying language.

Sample

First, we randomly chose 5 areas from the official KOL hot list on Weibo, namely 5 types of KOL. From each area, 2 KOLs were chosen randomly, so 10 KOLs were chosen by using the random sampling method. Second, on November 12th, 2020, the three most popular posts on each KOL's page were selected. Lastly, from the total of 30 posts extracted, the researchers analyzed the top 500 most popular comments for each post, which means that the research had totally analyzed 15,000 comments and obtained the number of comments with different types of cyberbullying language word categories that each KOL suffered under the equal number of comments.

Coding

Trained coders coded the KOL types, post content types, and word categories of cyberbullying language that appeared in comments. First, KOLs from the five most popular areas on the Weibo platform were coded by 1-Military KOL, 2-Fashion and Cosmetic KOL, 3-Public Intellectual KOL, 4-Funny KOL, and 5-Entertainment Celebrity KOL. Second, we examined the content of 10 posts selected and coded the post content type by the following coding method: (1) Selfie post, (2) Advertising post, (3) Opinion sharing about others post, (4) Statement/PR management post, (5) Opinion sharing about themselves post, and (6) Daily life post. The last step was to code the word categories of comments that contain cyberbullying language on Weibo. We adopt the classification of cyberbullying word category proposed by Li (2020). Li (2020) classified word category as cyberbullying word and sensitive cyberbullying word. Cyberbullying words refer to directly or strongly offensive words, including cursing, sexual and abusive words. Sensitive cyberbullying words refer to mildly offensive or ordinary objects with offensive references in the context, including emotional, emphatic and cathartic words, newly-emerging words, idiomatic set phrases, and some ordinary words with special meanings.

According to the coding rules, this research divided the word categories into 8 types: (1) Idiomatic set phrases and ordinary words with special meanings, (2) Newly-emerging words, (3) Emphatic and cathartic words, (4) Emotional words, (5) Cursing words, (6) Sexual words, (7) Abusive words.

Intercoder Reliability

We had five coders to code the KOL type, post content type, and word category. The Krippendorff's Alpha values for word category ($\alpha = 0.946$), content category ($\alpha = 1.000$), and KOL type ($\alpha = 1.000$)

indicate that the intercoder reliability was very high. To make the coding more accurate and reliable, we discussed the word category coding of some comments that different coders have different views, we referred to the classification of cyberbullying word category and made further modifications.

RESULTS

Cyberbullying Language on Weibo

In total, out of a total number of 15,000 comments, we found 605 comments involving cyberbullying language with different word categories. According to the cyberbullying language word categories data, Table 1 was drawn to show the frequency of different word categories to answer the first research question.

Table 1. Frequency of cyberbullying language word categories

Word categories of cyberbullying language	Abusive words	Sexual words	Cursing words	Emphatic and cathartic words	Newly-emerging words	Emotional words	Idiomatic set phrases and ordinary words with special meanings
Frequency	2.31%	5.62%	9.42%	3.97%	12.23%	3.47%	63.47%

From Table 1, it can be clearly seen that among the seven types of cyberbullying language word categories, idiomatic set phrases and ordinary words with special meanings account for 63.47%, which is the most frequent one among all categories. The second most frequent category is the newly-emerging word category, about 12.23% of cyberbullying comments appeared in this form. Relatively speaking, the frequency of the other five categories is relatively low and close, generally in the range of 2% to 10%.

In summary, sensitive cyberbullying words constituted 83.14% of all cyberbullying language. Therefore, we can answer the first research question. Rather than directly and strongly offensive language, cyberbullying language on Weibo generally appears in the form of mildly offensive or ordinary words but with special meanings and offensive references.

Effect of Post Content and KOL Type on the Frequency of Cyberbullying Language

For RQ2 and RQ3, Table 2 and Table 3 were drawn to show the frequency of comments of cyberbullying language for every post content type and KOL type. The frequency of cyberbullying language showed the average number of comments containing cyberbullying language per post and the percentage.

Table 2 shows that the majority of posts were statements/PR management posts or advertising posts. Table 3 shows that most cyberbullying comments were made for public intellectual and entertainment celebrity KOLs.

Table 2. Post content type and frequency of cyberbullying language

Post content type	Selfie post	Advertising post	Opinion sharing about others post	Statement/PR management post	Opinion sharing about themselves post	Daily life post
Number of posts	5	4	9	4	5	3
Average number(frequency) of comments with cyberbullying language per post	16.4 (3.28%)	25.5(5.1%)	10.89(2.18%)	49.5(9.9%)	25(5%)	0

Table 3. KOL Type and frequency of cyberbullying language

KOL type	Military KOL	Fashion and cosmetic KOL	Public intellectual KOL	Funny KOL	Entertainment celebrity KOL
Number of posts	6	6	6	6	6
Average number(frequency) of comments with cyberbullying language per post	0	13.67(2.73%)	31.67(6.33%)	21.83(4.37%)	33.67(6.73%)

In the following, the Analysis of Variance (ANOVA) tests between KOL type and the frequency of cyberbullying language, and post content type on the frequency of cyberbullying language were conducted. Table 4 shows the ANOVA results which indicate that the effect of post content type on the frequency of cyberbullying language was not statistically significant, $F(4, 25) = 1.768$, $p = .167$, and the effect of KOL type on the frequency of cyberbullying language was also not statistically significant, $F(5, 24) = 1.559$, $p = .21$.

So, we considered that post content type and KOL type may have an interaction effect on the frequency of cyberbullying language. The ANOVA test showed that the interaction effect of post content and KOL type on the frequency of cyberbullying language was significant, $F(4, 16) = 4.256$, $p = .0156$.

In summary, neither the post content nor the KOL type can affect the frequency of cyberbullying language independently. However, the two variables, post content type, and KOL type can interact to affect the frequency of cyberbullying language.

Table 4. ANOVA results

	sum of squares	df	mean square	F	sig.
post content type	4597	4	1149.3	1.768	0.167
KOL type	5111	5	1022.3	1.559	0.21
post content type *KOL type	5633	4	1408.3	4.256	0.0156

Table 5 showed the frequency of cyberbullying language under two variables, post content type, and KOL type.

Table 5. Post Content/KOL Type and frequency of cyberbullying language

Post content type/ KOL type and Average number of comments with cyberbullying language per post	Military KOL	Fashion and cosmetic KOL	Public intellectual KOL	Funny KOL	Entertainment celebrity KOL
Selfie post	0	27.33(5.47%)	0	0	0
Advertising post	0	0	0	0	51(10.2%)
Opinion sharing about others post	0	0	32.67(6.53%)	0	0
Statement/PR management post	0	0	0	32.67(6.53%)	100(20%)
Opinion sharing about themselves post	0	0	30.67(6.13%)	33(6.6%)	0
Daily life post	0	0	0	0	0

The data showed that when entertainment celebrity KOLs publish statement/PR management posts, the frequency of cyberbullying language is the highest, reaching the frequency of 20% (see Table 5). Entertainment celebrities often publish statement/PR management posts when they encounter controversial events or face crises. Besides, they receive more attention and have more influence as public figures, so the public holds stricter standards for their words and deeds. This may explain why this type received most cyberbullying language.

Entertainment celebrity KOLs' advertising posts are the second most frequent type of receiving comments with cyberbullying language. Sometimes KOLs themselves and the content of advertising are controversial which may draw cyberbullying language. For example, in our sample, one post was Guojingming advertising his new film The Yin-Yang Master: Dream Of Eternity, this film only has a score of 5.1/10 on Douban.com, a Chinese movie review website (Douban, 2021). Besides this film, other films directed by Guo all have scored no more than 5.0. In the comments of this post, people criticize this film as a bad film and Guo as a bad director.

Public intellectual KOLs' opinion sharing about themselves or others posts, funny KOLs' statement/ PR management, and opinion sharing about themselves posts also receive cyberbullying language with the frequency of around 6%. Opinion sharing posts are likely to have comments with cyberbullying language because Weibo users are very likely to have different opinions with KOLs. In contrast, Military KOL with different post types least suffered by cyberbullying language.

DISCUSSION

New Trend of Cyberbullying on Chinese Social Media

Cyberbullying is a growing global problem and is also becoming increasingly prevalent in Chinese media platforms. Data show that the form of cyberbullying language on Weibo platform presents some new trends.

The frequency of the use of different cyberbullying language on Weibo has changed a lot in recent years. Comparing the previous data (Li, 2020) (posts from 2015-2018) with our data, abusive words accounted for 29.02% and now (2020) for only 2%. Sexual words previously accounted for 21.7% and now (2020) for 6%. Newly emerging words previously accounted for 5.78% and now (2020) for 12%. Emotional words changed from 11.46% to 3%, and emphatic and cathartic words changed from 11.77% to 4%. Finally, the most significant changes are in the idiomatic set phrases and ordinary words with special meanings, which previously accounted for only 5.78%, have grown rapidly to 64% in just a few years. Thus, idiomatic words and ordinary words with special meanings have become dominant in online cyberbullying, while abusive words and sexual words appeared less and less frequently in cyberbullying.

In the research database, the proportion of abusive words and sexual words is only 8%, showing a significant decrease. The most widely used words of abusive words are逼 (refers to cunt), 操 (refers to fuck) and sex words are 贱 (refers to bitch or slut), 婊 (refers to whore), 骚 (refers to coquettish). However, on the Weibo platform, these comments are gradually decreasing. This may be related to two reasons: 1. Weibo has increasingly sophisticated and intelligent keyword filtering mechanisms, and the filtering causes such comments to be automatically deleted by the system. 2. Feminist issues have been hotly discussed on Weibo in recent years.

After several years of network technology development, the language purification function of Weibo has become more intelligent. It can automatically identify abusive words through big data monitoring and delete such comments in large quantities. The rise of the female economy has allowed the topic of feminism to spread widely on new media platforms (Wei, 2018). Comments related to gender violence and sexism can also be opposed by feminist Weibo users. The more feminist users speak out on new media platforms, the number of abusive words and sexual words comments is decreasing. At the same time, the "me too" movement in China in the past two years and various women's equal rights topics have enabled women's discourse and feminism to be also widely spread on Weibo (Wu, 2019). With the development of the "me too" movement, female users on the Weibo platform began to pay attention to their own subjectivity and know how to use legal means to protect their rights. The diverse views of feminism have also been continuously converging and merging (Xiu, 2019). Through the power of social media, the "Me Too" movement has empowered women. On Weibo, the discourse of the "MeToo" movement also includes the fight against "slut shaming" (Wu, 2019). The sexual words comments are also seen as a form of slut-shaming to a certain extent. Therefore, the women's movements in the new media environment have greatly reduced the frequency of the use of sexual words used to attack women.

Moreover, the frequency of newly emerging words and ordinary words with special meanings increased significantly. Network languages have always been popular among Weibo users, and netizens often create new words and give new meanings to some ordinary words. These newly emerging words and ordinary words with special meanings have been spread on a large scale in cyberbullying. In the past research data, the newly emerging words and ordinary words with special meanings accounted for only 18% (Li, 2020), and the current data show that these two types of words account for 76% of cyberbullying words, showing a rapid growth trend. The essence of these words is a public discourse in the form of entertainment, which expresses netizens' concern for reality and builds up the cultural identity and discourse consensus among netizens (Zhou, 2019). The newly emerging words and ordinary words with special meanings express complex psychological feelings that the original words cannot convey. Because of the convenience of broadcasting channels, the interactivity of the network environment, the convenience of the storage environment, the ease of use of communication tools, and the richness of communication content, network languages are more likely to be imitated, copied, and distributed by network users (Cao & Jin, 2016). Also, these words are not easily recognized by Weibo's intelligent filtering system, so they will not be deleted by the platform. This is the reason why these two types of words have been widely spread and used in cyberbullying comments in recent years.

The research also noticed that the strong or directly offensive attacking words have become mild or indirectly offensive words in recent years. In the classification of cyberbullying words, emphatic and cathartic words, emotional words, cursing words, abusive words, and sexual words with strong or directly offensive attacking account for only about 24%. However, in previous research, the proportion of these categories was about 80% (Li, 2020). Nowadays, a large number of cyberbullying comments are newly emerging words and ordinary words with special meanings, and this kind of strong or directly offensive comments has been greatly reduced. This is directly related to the growth of network language, and the new guidelines (Weibo, 2020) for comment management on the Weibo platform.

The Refinement of Media Regulation and Governance Guidelines

In order to establish a harmonious, civilized, and polite online social environment, Weibo has continuously improved its keyword filtering mechanism and updated user guidelines in recent years. In order to reduce personal injury caused by cyberbullying, Weibo does not allow users to upload, display or spread harassing, slanderous, offensive, abusive, intimidating, racially discriminatory, defamatory, or privacy disclosure, obscene, malicious plagiarism, violence, or other illegal comments (Weibo, 2020). Regarding such comments, Weibo uses an intelligent filtering system to delete them in large quantities. In addition, Weibo also allows KOLs to block users who make offensive comments about themselves, which also eases the level of cyberbullying to a certain extent. These increasingly sophisticated and intelligent keyword filtering mechanisms and Weibo's rules have also led to a different network environment in recent years.

Limitations

As with every research, this research has its limitations. Because of the sample size limitation of human coding, we only looked at 5 KOL types we randomly selected in this research, however, there are 34 areas in total in Weibo's official KOL hotlist. So, this research cannot provide a full view of cyberbullying language on Weibo. However, the overall analysis of these comments can still provide valuable data. Besides, user habits and Weibo's keyword filtering mechanism and rules are changing rapidly, so the findings might not be accurate in the near future.

CONCLUSION

This research considered cyberbullying language targeted at Key Opinion Leaders on Sina Weibo, the leading social media platform in China. Using content analysis, this research found that "idiomatic set phrases and ordinary words with special meanings" and "newly-emerging word" were the two most frequent cyberbullying language word categories in our sample posts from 2020. In comparison, in Li's (2020) sample posts from 2015 to 2018, the two most frequent cyberbullying language word categories were "abusive words" and "sexual words". The reason for his change might be that the keyword filtering mechanism of Weibo is increasingly sophisticated, and network language is growing rapidly on Weibo these years. Another finding is that KOL type and post content type interact to affect the frequency of cyberbullying language on Weibo.

FUTURE RESEARCH DIRECTIONS

Future studies can use machine learning techniques to detect content that contains cyberbullying language and identify the word category. Machine learning techniques can overcome the sample size limitation of human coding, so that further studies can cover more KOLs, posts, and comments, in order to provide results that are closer to the full view of Weibo.

REFERENCES

Alim, S. (2016). Cyberbullying in the world of teenagers and social media: A literature review. *International Journal of Cyber Behavior, Psychology and Learning*, *6*(2), 68–95. doi:10.4018/IJCBPL.2016040105

Alipan, A., Skues, J., Theiler, S., & Wise, L. (2015). Defining cyberbullying: A multiple perspectives approach. *Studies in Health Technology and Informatics*, *219*, 9–13. https://ebooks.iospress.nl/publication/42114 PMID:26799870

Anderson, C. A., & Bushman, B. J. (2002). Human aggression. *Annual Review of Psychology*, *53*(1), 27–51. doi:10.1146/annurev.psych.53.100901.135231 PMID:11752478

Barlett, C. P. (2017). From theory to practice: Cyberbullying theory and its application to intervention. *Computers in Human Behavior*, *72*, 269–275. doi:10.1016/j.chb.2017.02.060

Barlett, C. P., & Gentile, D. A. (2012). Attacking others online: The formation of cyberbullying in late adolescence. *Psychology of Popular Media Culture*, *1*(2), 123–135. doi:10.1037/a0028113

Bauman, S., Toomey, R. B., & Walker, J. L. (2013). Associations among bullying, cyberbullying, and suicide in high school students. *Journal of Adolescence*, *36*(2), 341–350. doi:10.1016/j.adolescence.2012.12.001 PMID:23332116

Berger, J., & Milkman, K. L. (2012). What makes online content viral? *JMR, Journal of Marketing Research*, *49*(2), 192–205. doi:10.1509/jmr.10.0353

Berne, S., Frisén, A., Schultze-Krumbholz, A., Scheithauer, H., Naruskov, K., Luik, P., Katzer, C., Erentaite, R., & Zukauskiene, R. (2013). Cyberbullying assessment instruments: A systematic review. *Aggression and Violent Behavior*, *18*(2), 320–334. doi:10.1016/j.avb.2012.11.022

Brady, W. J., Wills, J. A., Jost, J. T., Tucker, J. A., & Van Bavel, J. J. (2017). Emotion shapes the diffusion of moralized content in social networks. *Proceedings of the National Academy of Sciences of the United States of America*, *114*(28), 7313–7318. doi:10.1073/pnas.1618923114 PMID:28652356

Cao, J., & Jin, Y. (2016). Theoretical interpretation on the communication power of internet strong language memes. *Chinese Journal of Journalism & Communication*, *2*, 37–56.

China Internet Network Information Center. (2020). *The 46th China statistical report on Internet development.* https://cnnic.net.cn/hlwfzyj/hlwxzbg/hlwtjbg/202009/P020200929546215182514.pdf

Crick, N. R., & Dodge, K. A. (1994). A review and reformulation of social information-processing mechanisms in children's social adjustment. *Psychological Bulletin, 115*(1), 74–101. doi:10.1037/0033-2909.115.1.74

Dooley, J. J., Pyżalski, J., & Cross, D. (2009). Cyberbullying versus face-to-face bullying. *Zeitschrift für Psychologie. The Journal of Psychology, 217*(4), 182–188. doi:10.1027/0044-3409.217.4.182

Family Lives. (2020). *What is cyber bullying? Being bullied online and advice on what to do.* Retrieved from https://www.bullying.co.uk/cyberbullying/what-is-cyberbullying/

Forssell, R. (2016). Exploring cyberbullying and face-to-face bullying in working life – Prevalence, targets and expressions. *Computers in Human Behavior, 58*, 454–460. doi:10.1016/j.chb.2016.01.003

Görzig, A., & Ólafsson, K. (2013). What makes a bully a cyberbully? Unravelling the characteristics of cyberbullies across twenty-five European countries. *Journal of Children and Media, 7*(1), 9–27. doi:10.1080/17482798.2012.739756

Hinduja, S., & Patchin, J. W. (2010). Bullying, cyberbullying, and suicide. *Archives of Suicide Research, 14*(3), 206–221. doi:10.1080/13811118.2010.494133 PMID:20658375

Jiang, F. (2011). Cyberbullying: Concept, origin and solutions—An analytical perspective based on risk society. *Zhejiang Academic Journal, 6*, 181–187.

Kaplan, A. M., & Haenlein, M. (2010). Users of the world, unite! The challenges and opportunities of social media. *Business Horizons, 53*(1), 59–68. doi:10.1016/j.bushor.2009.09.003

Kemp, S. (2020). *Digital 2020: October Global Statshot.* Data Reportal. https://datareportal.com/reports/digital-2020-october-global-statshot?rq=global%20social%20media%202020

Kim, Y. S., & Leventhal, B. (2008). Bullying and suicide: A review. *International Journal of Adolescent Medicine and Health, 20*(2), 133–154. doi:10.1515/IJAMH.2008.20.2.133 PMID:18714552

Kowalski, R. M., Giumetti, G. W., Schroeder, A. N., & Lattanner, M. R. (2014). Bullying in the digital age: A critical review and meta-analysis of cyberbullying research among youth. *Psychological Bulletin, 140*(4), 1073–1137. doi:10.1037/a0035618 PMID:24512111

Kowalski, R. M., & Limber, S. P. (2007, December). Electronic bullying among middle school students. *The Journal of Adolescent Health, 41*(6), S22–S30. doi:10.1016/j.jadohealth.2007.08.017 PMID:18047942

Kowalski, R. M., Limber, S. P., & Agatston, P. W. (2012). *Cyberbullying: Bullying in the digital age* (2nd ed.). Wiley-Blackwell.

Langos, C. (2012). Cyberbullying: The challenge to define. *Cyberpsychology, Behavior, and Social Networking, 15*(6), 285–289. doi:10.1089/cyber.2011.0588 PMID:22703033

Li, W. (2020). The language of bullying: Social issues on Chinese websites. *Aggression and Violent Behavior, 53*, 101453. doi:10.1016/j.avb.2020.101453

Liu, C. D. (2008). Current situation and development trend of network language research in China. *Shandong Social Science*, *9*, 155–158.

Liu, Y. C., & Ning, F. M. (2004). Study on network language. *Journal of Armed Police Medical College*, *4*, 75–79.

Olweus, D. (1993). *Bullying at school: What we know and what we can do*. Blackwell.

Olweus, D. (2012). Cyberbullying: An overrated phenomenon? *European Journal of Developmental Psychology*, *9*(5), 520–538. doi:10.1080/17405629.2012.682358

Olweus, D., & Limber, S. P. (2018). Some problems with cyberbullying research. *Current Opinion in Psychology*, *19*, 139–143. doi:10.1016/j.copsyc.2017.04.012 PMID:29279213

Ooi, K. B., Lee, V. H., Hew, J. J., & Lin, B. (2019). Mobile social cyberbullying: Why are keyboard warriors raging? *Journal of Computer Information Systems*, *61*(4), 371–382. doi:10.1080/08874417.2019.1679685

Patchin, J. W., & Hinduja, S. (2006). Bullies move beyond the schoolyard: A preliminary look at cyberbullying. *Youth Violence and Juvenile Justice*, *4*(2), 148–169. doi:10.1177/1541204006286288

Peter, I.-K., & Petermann, F. (2018). Cyberbullying: A concept analysis of defining attributes and additional influencing factors. *Computers in Human Behavior*, *86*, 350–366. doi:10.1016/j.chb.2018.05.013

Privitera, C., & Campbell, M. A. (2009). Cyberbullying: The new face of workplace bullying? *Cyberpsychology & Behavior*, *12*(4), 395–400. doi:10.1089/cpb.2009.0025 PMID:19594381

Romiszowski, A., & Mason, R. (2013). Computer-mediated communication. In D. Jonassen & M. Driscoll (Eds.), *Handbook of research on educational communications and technology* (pp. 402–436). Routledge.

Rosa, H., Pereira, N., Ribeiro, R., Ferreira, P. C., Carvalho, J. P., Oliveira, S., Coheur, L., Paulino, P., Veiga Simão, A. M., & Trancoso, I. (2019). Automatic cyberbullying detection: A systematic review. *Computers in Human Behavior*, *93*, 333–345. doi:10.1016/j.chb.2018.12.021

Sari, S. V., & Camadan, F. (2016). The new face of violence tendency: Cyber bullying perpetrators and their victims. *Computers in Human Behavior*, *59*, 317–326. doi:10.1016/j.chb.2016.02.027

Smith, P. K., & Brain, P. (2000). Bullying in schools: Lessons from two decades of research. *Aggressive Behavior*, *26*(1), 1–9. doi:10.1002/(SICI)1098-2337(2000)26:1<1::AID-AB1>3.0.CO;2-7

Smith, P. K., del Barrio, C., & Tokunaga, R. (2013). Definitions of bullying and cyberbullying: How useful are the terms? In S. Bauman, J. Walker, & D. Cross (Eds.), *Principles of cyberbullying research: Definition, measures, and methods* (pp. 26–40). Routledge.

Smith, P. K., Mahdavi, J., Carvalho, M., Fisher, S., Russell, S., & Tippett, N. (2008). Cyberbullying: Its nature and impact in secondary school pupils. *Journal of Child Psychology and Psychiatry, and Allied Disciplines*, *49*(4), 376–385. doi:10.1111/j.1469-7610.2007.01846.x PMID:18363945

Steinmueller, W. (2000). Will new information and communication technologies improve the 'codification' of knowledge? *Industrial and Corporate Change*, *9*(2), 361–376. doi:10.1093/icc/9.2.361

Tokunaga, R. S. (2010). Following you home from school: A critical review and synthesis of research on cyberbullying victimization. *Computers in Human Behavior*, *26*(3), 277–287. doi:10.1016/j.chb.2009.11.014

Vannucci, M., Nocentini, A., Mazzoni, G., & Menesini, E. (2012). Recalling unpresented hostile words: False memories predictors of traditional and cyberbullying. *European Journal of Developmental Psychology*, *9*(2), 182–194. doi:10.1080/17405629.2011.646459

Walrave, M., & Heirman, W. (2011). Cyberbullying: Predicting victimisation and perpetration. *Children & Society*, *25*(1), 59–72. doi:10.1111/j.1099-0860.2009.00260.x

Wang, B. C. (2004). Network language and the new trend of current social and cultural development. *Zhejiang Academic Journal, 6.*

Wang, M. J., Yogeeswaran, K., Andrews, N. P., Hawi, D. R., & Sibley, C. G. (2019, November). How common is cyberbullying among adults? Exploring gender, ethnic, and age differences in the prevalence of cyberbullying. *Cyberpsychology, Behavior, and Social Networking*, *22*(11), 736–741. doi:10.1089/cyber.2019.0146 PMID:31697598

Weibo. (2020). *Weibo Community Convention.* http://service. weibo.com/roles/gongyue

Wu, Z. (2019). In search of the "middle ground": Rethinking the politics of othering in the "MeToo" movement. *Press Circles*, *3*, 51–61. doi:10.15897/j.cnki.cn51-1046/g2.2019.03.007

Xu, Y. (2021). The invisible aggressive fist: Features of cyberbullying language in China. *International Journal for the Semiotics of Law - Revue internationale de Sémiotique juridique, 34*, 1041-1064. doi:10.1007/s11196-020-09746-1

Zhang, R. (2010). Legal analysis of the characteristics of cyberbullying subject. *Seeker*, *12*, 140–142.

Zi, W. (2018). *The discourse research of Feminist we media—based on sample analysis of Sina microblog* (Master's degree thesis). Guangxi Normal University. https://kns.cnki.net/KCMS/detail/detail.aspx?dbname=CMFD201901&filename=1018851076.nh

ADDITIONAL READING

Bauman, S., Cross, D., & Walker, J. (Eds.). (2013). *Principles of cyberbullying research: Definitions, measures, and methodology*. Routledge.

Santre, S. (2022). Cyberbullying in adolescents: A literature review. *International Journal of Adolescent Medicine and Health*, *0*(0). Advance online publication. doi:10.1515/ijamh-2021-0133 PMID:35245420

KEY TERMS AND DEFINITIONS

Abusive Words: This kind of word category is very similar to swear or slang words in English, which is always considered obnoxious and rude when used to intimidate or humiliate an individual. Each single word or its portmanteau formations can be regarded as direct cyberbullying language due to its meaning and function.

Cursing Words: Cursing words in Chinese society the most commonly used term of abuse is the expression meaning 'die' or 'death' to initially act as powerfully threatening utterances expressing a wish to punish, injure or destroy something or someone.

Cyberbullying: Cyberbullying is any behavior performed through electronic or digital media by individuals or groups that repeatedly communicates hostile or aggressive messages intended to inflict harm or discomfort on others.

Cyberbullying Words: In the context of this paper, cyberbullying words refer to directly or strongly offensive words, including cursing, sexual and abusive words.

Emotional Words: Emotional words express emotions, emotional processes, or functions, in order to either describe something or to express emotion directly.

Emphatic and Cathartic Words: Emphatic and cathartic words are used to emphasize emotions in a negative or positive way.

Idiomatic Set Phrases and Ordinary Words With Special Meanings: They are neutral words which appear in the dictionary and are normally used in daily communication. When they are used in the context of cyberbullying or sensitive cyberbullying, they always have abusive, sexual or cursing meanings.

KOL Type: There is an official KOL hot list on Weibo, Weibo classifies all KOLs into 25 types based on KOLs' area of expertise.

Newly Emerging Word: This type of word is always created by netizens, or words which have changed their meaning based on social culture or specific events. They appear and disappear quickly and have individualized meanings in certain situations or for certain groups.

Post Content Type: In this research, the content of 10 posts selected is examined, and classified into 6 types: selfie post, advertising post, opinion sharing about others post, statement/PR management post, opinion sharing about themselves post, and daily life post.

Sensitive Cyberbullying Words: They refer to mildly offensive or ordinary objects with offensive references in the context, including emotional, emphatic and cathartic words, newly emerging words, idiomatic set phrases, and some ordinary words with special meanings.

Sexual Words: This type of word category is the most commonly used sexual words, which are always relevant to rudely suggestive anatomical or sexual matters with obscenity or sexual features in language to describe, satirize or insult the targets.

Chapter 9
Cyberbullies and Cyberpunks, Oh My:
Examining Cyberbullying Through a Domestic and International Lens

Songyon Shin
Southeast Missouri State University, USA

Joshua T. Shadwick
Southeast Missouri State University, USA

Kristen N. Sobba
Southeast Missouri State University, USA

Monica Radu
Southeast Missouri State University, USA

ABSTRACT

For decades, cyberbullying has been acknowledged as a social phenomenon that poses adverse effects on victims. Scholarship generally defines cyberbullying as repeated behaviors that intend to harm the victims. Prior studies aimed at investigating cyberbullying and victimization patterns among juveniles. Furthermore, risk factors, which increase the likelihood of cyberbullying engagement, had been revealed in several different studies. While there are consistent findings regarding the negative outcomes of cyberbullying, the trends are somewhat obscure due to inconsistent methodology. Furthermore, despite cyberbullying being a domestic and international issue, prior research practices have limited generalizability across samples. These limitations led to inherent gaps in the literature, which ultimately hinders a comprehensive understanding of cyberbullying. Thus, the ultimate purpose of this chapter is to provide both domestic and international reviews regarding cyberbullying engagement. By doing so, this chapter will navigate an in-depth analysis of cyberbullying worldwide.

DOI: 10.4018/978-1-6684-5426-8.ch009

INTRODUCTION

For decades, cyberbullying has been acknowledged as a social phenomenon that poses adverse effects on victims (Patchin & Hinduja, 2022). Scholarship generally defines cyberbullying as repeated behaviors that intend to harm the victims. The magnitude of cyberbullying is relatively high in the United States. For instance, Patchin (2019) revealed that 37 percent of high school students in the United States experienced cyberbullying victimization in 2019. The harms of cyberbullying victimization include various negative consequences, which may affect teenagers' development, including depression (Perren, Dooley, Shaw, & Cross, 2010), low self-esteem (Patchin, & Hinduja, 2010), or suicide at an extreme level (Van Geel, Vedder, & Tanilon, 2014).

Prior studies aimed at investigating cyberbullying and victimization patterns among juveniles (Hinduja & Patchin, 2010; 2011; 2015; 2018; Patchin & Hinduja, 2010). Furthermore, risk factors, which increase the likelihood of cyberbullying engagement, had been revealed in several different studies (Barlett, Rinker, & Roth, 2021; Lazuras, Barkoukis, Ourda, & Tsorbatzoudis, 2013; Kowalski, Morgan, & Limber, 2012; Li, Holt, Bossler, & May, 2016; Lianos, & McGrath, 2018; Hinduja & Patchin, 2010; Hoff & Mitchell, 2009; Zhou, Tang, Tian, Wei, Zhang, & Morrison, 2013). While there are consistent findings regarding the negative outcomes of cyberbullying, the trends are somewhat obscure due to inconsistent methodology. Furthermore, despite cyberbullying being a domestic and international issue, prior research practices have limited generalizability across samples. These limitations led to inherent gaps in the literature, which ultimately hinders a comprehensive understanding of cyberbullying. Thus, the purpose of this chapter is to provide both domestic and international reviews regarding cyberbullying engagement. Additionally, this chapter will navigate an in-depth analysis of cyberbullying occurrences worldwide.

To prevent or reduce the harms of cyberbullying, it is crucial to recognize the causes and consequences associated with this phenomenon. Therefore, the current chapter advocates for a comprehensive viewpoint that captures both domestic and international cyberbullying trends. Moreover, a thorough review of cross-sectional and longitudinal research will provide a more holistic lens on cyberbullying. The net result will be a more robust understanding for both academics and practitioners.

What is Cyberbullying? The Meaning is Not Singular in Literature

Cyberbullying refers to repeated acts using electronic forms that inflicts harm on victims (Hinduja & Patchin, 2015). The series of acts primarily includes communication that hurts or embarrasses others through messages, images, or posts on social media, gaming platforms, or text messages (Hinduja & Patchin, 2011; Sobba, Paez, & Bensel, 2017). However, inconsistencies have been pointed out when defining online bullying behaviors in literature (Corcoran, Guckin, & Prentice, 2015) (See Table 1).

Many terms have been applied (i.e. cyberbullying, online harassment, cyberstalking, etc.) referring to the definition of aggressive behavior in any online or media-based setting. In addition, many different platforms have been used to cyberbully, including electronic devices, digital media, websites, emails, texts, etc. According to prior research, the term, cyber aggression, is a wide range of behaviors bearing a purpose that humiliates others (Corcoran et al., 2015). The terminology is described as aggressive behaviors (Hosseinmardi et al., 2015; Pornari & Wood, 2010), bullying behavior (Wright, 2013), or inflicted harm based on moral implications of perpetrators (Grigg, 2012). In comparison, Li (2005) insisted that the terms, cyberbullying and cyber harassment, are interchangeable. Cyber harassment can also refer

Table 1. Examples: Various forms of perpetration

Types	Authors	Definition
Cyber Aggression	Grigg (2010).	*"...intentional harm delivered by the use of electronic means to a person or a group of people irrespective of their age, who perceive(s) such acts as offensive, derogatory, harmful, or unwanted..."*
	Pornari & Wood (2010)	*"...aggressive behaviors (e.g., rumor spreading, gossiping, saying mean things to someone) through a broad range of information and communication technologies, including social networking sites, email, chat programs, and text messages..."*
	Wright (2013).	*"...consists of cyberbullying behaviors, such as threats, insults, and rumor spreading, but it does not necessarily have to include an imbalance of power or repetition, making cyber aggression a broader form of aggressive behaviors via information and communication technologies..."*
	Hosseinmardi et al., (2015)	*"...Aggressive online behavior that uses digital media in a way that is intended to cause harm to another person..."*
Cyber Harassment	Beran et al., (2012).	*"....Cyber-harassment occurs through communications devices such as cell phones and the internet where threatening or excluding messages are sent as emails, text messages, or posted on social media or other websites..."*
	Li (2005)	*"...A new method of peer harassment has emerged, known as cyberharassment, or, cyber-bullying. These terms are used interchangeably to refer to harassment that is directed at a peer through the use of information and communication technology..."*
	Winkelman et al. (2015).	*"...Cyber harassment has found to be linked closely with cyber stalking. It is more partner or relationship focused that encompasses a range of activities such as sending abusive, threatening or obscene emails, text messages, posts on to social networking and blog sites, and phone calls..."*
	Hazelwood & Koon-Magnin, (2013).	*"...typically involves engaging in an act or behavior that torments, annoys, terrorizes, offends, or threatens an individual via email, instant messages, or other means with the intention of harming that person..."*
Cyberstalking	D'Ovidio & Doyle (2003)	*"...The repeated use of the Interne, e-mail, or related digital electronic devices to annoy, alarm, threaten a specific individual or groups of individuals..."*
	Kaur et al., (2021)	*"...Cyberstalking is understood as repetitive and unwanted communication or contact that is directed toward an individual through electronic means (e.g., Internet, social media, email or other forms of technology)..."*
	Wilson et al. (2020).	*"...This study puts forth the recommendation that cyberstalking should be identified as experiencing 10 or more repetitions of unwanted behavior/s through technology over a period of at least two weeks..."*
	Marcum, et al. (2017).	*"...Cyberstalking is an adapted definition of physical stalking as applied to technology and electronic devices..."*
	Begotti & Acquadro Maran (2019)	*"...The motive that determines the beginning of cyberstalking behavior differs from other forms of misconduct. For example, cyberharassment is a more general term that refers to the involvement of engaging in an act to torment, terrorize, or offend an individual online with the intention of harming that person..."*

to a series of acts threatening, terrorizing, excluding, or offending others (Beran, Rinaldi, Bickham, & Rich, 2012). Winkelman and colleagues (2015) found that cyber harassment occurs in relationships. However, online bullying led by relationships is more reviewed in cyberstalking studies. For instance, Begotti & Acquadro Maran (2019) asserted that the extent of misconduct in cyberbullying is narrower than cyber harassment. It is viewed as physical stalking using technology (Marcum, Higgins, & Nicholson, 2017), unwanted repeated communication (Wilson, Sheridan, & Garratt-Reed, 2020), or alarming, threatening, or annoying behaviors targeting a specific individual (D'Ovidio, & Doyle, 2003). Based on the depiction, how to define online bullying behaviors shows a gradation that links each definition and shares common aspects regarding the extent of the behaviors.

Scholars also mentioned different tools or methods that are used for perpetration. The majority of studies used terms such as electronic devices (D'Ovidio & Doyle, 2003; Marcum et al., 2017), means (Grigg, 2010; Kaur, Dhir, Tandon, Alzeiby, & Abohassan, 2021), or digital media (Hosseinmardi et al., 2015). Another approach emphasized information and communication (Beran et al., 2012; Li, 2005; Pornari & Wood, 2010; Wright, 2013). A narrowed-down definition includes some types of tools which deliver messages via social media, websites, e-mails, or texts to victims (Beran et al., 2012).

CYBERBULLYING TRENDS: STATISTICS AT NATIONAL LEVELS

The United States

The trends of cyberbullying and victimization vary by definition. For instance, Hinduja (2021) revealed that approximately 23 percent of U.S. juveniles were cyberbullied, whereas 5 percent of the entire sample were perpetrators. Beran and colleagues (2012) found that 33 percent of Northern American college students were cyber-harassed, and 8.6 percent of the sample cyber harassed while in high school. An extreme case reported that 7 out of 10 teenagers were cyber-victimized in Malaysia (Johanis, Bakar, & Ismail, 2020). Despite the inconsistency, the studies indicated that the frequency of victimization is much higher than the perpetration. According to Sobba et al. (2017), cyberbullying tends to be witnessed by unlimited users due to the network's circulation. Thus, these electronic-based acts of aggression echo across time and cyberspace.

Unfortunately, a thorough investigation regarding cyberbullying perpetration is limited in the United States. First, the National Crime Victimization Survey (NCVS) collects a supplementary dataset called "The School Crime Supplement (SCS)" (Bureau of Justice Statistics, 2020). The survey is primarily conducted by the Bureau of Justice Statistics and co-sponsored by the Department of Education's National Center for Education Statistics (NCES) (Bureau of Justice Statistics, 2020). Their research target is juveniles aged between 12 and 18 in the United States. The survey instrument measures juveniles' victimization experiences, including physical violence, gun violence, gang activities, and school bullying. Since the survey's primary focus is not cyberbullying, there is limited information on this topic. The instrument asks students about bullying victimization experiences via text or the Internet. As a result, the survey response is rephrased as electronic bullying victimization during the previous 12 months. For instance, as a part of results in 2019, 15.6 percent of students reported that they were electronically victimized during the last 12 months. Unfortunately, the dataset does not indicate juveniles' cyberbullying perpetration.

Patchin & Hinduja (2019) collected juveniles' cyberbullying victimization data since the year of 2002 (i.e., Check their website: https://cyberbullying.org/). The survey targeted juveniles in middle and high school in the United States, especially those who were aged between 12 and 17. They select approximately 25,000 juvenile participants based on a random sampling strategy every year. According to their research summary published in 2019, there was no significant increase or decrease in cyberbullying victimization and perpetration (Patchin & Hinduja, 2019). They measured the U.S. juveniles' cyberbullying, which had been defined as "repeatedly and intentionally harasses, mistreats, or makes fun of another person online or while using cell phones or other electronic devices" (Patchin & Hinduja, 2019). The finding indicated that 5.6 percent in 2016 and 6.3 percent in 2019 in the sample perpetrated cyberbullying for the

Figure 1. "Percentage of students in grades 9–12 who reported having been electronically bullied during the previous 12 months, by selected student characteristics: 2019" (The School Crime Supplement (SCS) to the National Crime Victimization Survey, 2019)
(Source: https://nces.ed.gov/programs/coe/pdf/2021/a10_508c.pdf, pp 8)

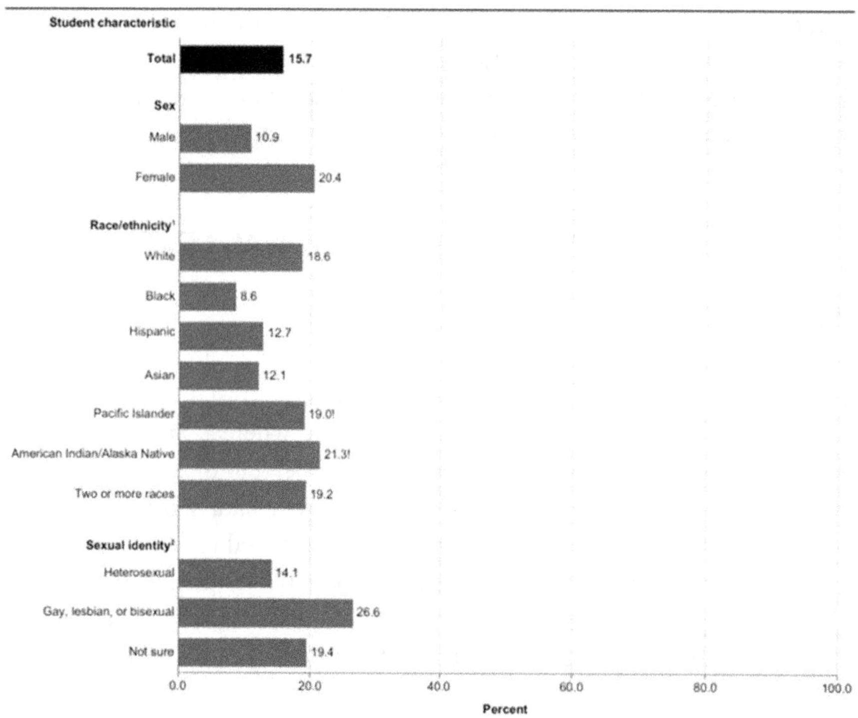

previous 30 days. Additionally, 11.4 percent in 2016 and 14.8 percent in 2019 in the sample perpetrated cyberbullying for a lifetime. Victimization rates are higher than perpetration rates. For instance, 16.5 percent in 2016 and 17.4 percent in 2019 in the sample had been victimized for the previous 30 days. Also, 33.6 percent in 2016 and 36.5 percent in 2019 in the sample had been victimized for a lifetime. They also conducted online surveys in 2004 and in 2005, where the outcome showed inflated results. 20.1 percent in 2004 and 14.4 percent in 2005 in the sample reported cyberbullying perpetration. Also, 40.6 percent in 2004 and 36.5 percent in 2005 in the sample had victimization experiences. The gap between those time frames might be a result of methodological gaps. Despite the limitations, the percentage of victimization outweighs perpetration, as suggested in Sobba and colleagues' study (2017).

Figure 2. Life time cyber bullying experienes presented by Patchin & Hinduja's research (2019)
(Source: https://cyberbullying.org/Cyberbullying-Research-In-Review.pdf)

Justin Patchin and Sameer Hinduja Cyberbullying Research Center www.cyberbullying.org (2019)	National 2019	National 2016	District G 2015	District F 2014	District E 2013	District D 2011	District A 2010	District C 2009-10	District A 2009	District B 2009	District A 2007	Online 2005	Online 2004	TOTAL/AVERAGE (since 2007)
30 day victim %	17.4	16.5	15.0	12.2	8.1	7.3	7.5	8.7	7.0	8.3	10.4		30.5	10.1
variety scale victim (mean)	1.23	1.155	0.81	0.727	0.451	n.a.	0.683	0.499	0.647	0.698				0.7
lifetime victim %	36.5	33.6	34.4	34.6	24.1	29.2	20.8	28.7	21.5	24.2	18.8	36.7	40.6	27.0
30 day offender %	6.3	5.6	6.3	4.4	2.6	4.2	8.6	4.5	6.6	8.7	9.0		11.5	6.1
variety scale offender (mean)	0.467	0.391	0.228	0.310	0.150	n.a.	0.572	0.243	0.444	0.568				0.4
lifetime offender %	14.8	11.4	14.6	17.0	12.9	18.7	19.4	11.5	14.2	18.6	19.1	14.4	20.1	15.7
Data collection dates	April 2019	Aug-Oct 2016	Feb 2015	Jan 2014	Oct 2013	Nov-Dec 2011	Jan-Feb 2010	Nov 2009/ Feb 2010	June 2009	June 2009	May 2007	Dec 2004 - Jan 2005	April - June 2004	
Sample ages	12-17	12-17	11-15	11-14	11-14	12-18	10-18	11-14	12-16	11-18	11-14	10-18	10-18	
Sample size (adolescents)	4,972	5,593	457	661	366	1,426	4,441	356	700	930	1,800	3,840	370	20,940
Population size (district)		national			1,811		181,000	2,600	181,000	18,000	181,000	n.a.	n.a.	
Number of schools	n.a.	n.a.	1	1	1	12	37	1	7	8	30	n.a.	n.a.	98
Region	U.S.	U.S.	Midwest	Northeast	Midwest	Southwest	Southwest	Midwest	Southwest	Southwest	Southwest	all online adolescents	all online adolescents	
Method	Email survey	Email survey	classroom based online survey	classroom based online survey	classroom based online survey	classroom based online survey	classroom based online survey	classroom based online survey	classroom based online survey	classroom based online survey	classroom paper based	online	online	
Selection	random	random	population	population	population	random	random	random	random	random	random	convenience	convenience	
Scale alpha (victim)	0.916	0.933	0.876	0.892	0.905	n.a.	0.942	0.831	0.926	0.934				
Scale alpha (offender)	0.939	0.965	0.793	0.965	0.935	n.a.	0.968	0.962	0.956	0.969				

WHAT MAKES THE TROUBLEMAKERS?: CAUSES OF CYBERBULLYING

Individuals' personal or psychological traits

Low Self-Esteem

Low self-esteem is a critical area addressed in cyberbullying literature. As Hinduja and Patchin (2010) found, low self-esteem can be directly associated with cyberbullying perpetration. Self-esteem means individuals' positive or negative evaluation on themselves (Rosenberg, 1965). When one's self-esteem is low, the individual perceives himself/herself as a deficient or unworthy person. When evaluating, individuals' objectivity is weakened, and thus negative self-evaluation becomes predominant (Owens, 1994). Rosenburg and colleagues (1989) insisted that self-esteem results from social interactions. For instance, when individuals compare themselves with others, the information that they accept is less objective, leading to subjective judgement toward themselves. The relationships between low self-esteem and delinquency have been thoroughly reviewed in criminological research. Kaplan's self-derogation theory (1975) indicated that delinquency might occur when perpetrators rebuild self-esteem through delinquent behaviors. In conventional society, unsuccessful youths have trouble with satisfying standards supported by reference groups. It leads to peer rejection, so youths outside the reference groups tend to choose delinquent peer association to reconstruct self-evaluation. In this case, delinquency is chosen as the alternative. Mason (2001) insisted that delinquency can be viewed as either defensive acts to the reference groups or adaptive acts to antisocial peers. Additionally, the effects of low self-esteem on antisocial behaviors are long-lasting. In Trzesniewski and colleagues' study (2006), low self-esteem during adolescence is associated with low economic status and criminal convictions during young adulthood. Therefore, serious long-term effects can also be associated with low self-esteem and cyberbullying.

The relationship between cyberbullying and self-esteem is widely supported in the literature. Hinduja and Patchin's research (2010) on juveniles' self-esteem and cyberbullying supports the linkage. They conducted a survey targeting 1,963 juveniles in 30 middle schools in the United States and found that low self-esteem increased both bullying perpetration and victimization. In Brewer and Kerslake's study (2015), the relationship can be explained based on how cyberbullies perceive others' viewpoints on the perpetrators. The authors speculated that low self-esteem perpetrators might choose online as a tool since they would feel it relatively safe due to anonymity. Fan and colleagues (2019) pointed out that narcissism may potentially cause both low self-esteem and cyberbullying perpetration. They mentioned covert narcissism, which can be represented as self-admiration, entitlement, and vulnerability. For instance, youths with covert narcissism are likely to want attention from others but have a less grandiose sense of self-importance. Their findings indicated that covert narcissism leads to low self-esteem and online bullying perpetration. Also, the relationship between cover narcissism and cyberbullying is partially mediated by low self-esteem.

Low Self-Control

The effect of low self-control is also widely supported in criminological theories. Low self-control affects crimes and delinquency which s based on the general theory of crime (Gottfredson & Hirschi, 1990). Gottfredson and Hirschi's theory (1990) started with an assumption posing that criminals' behavior is not different from ordinary people's since humans are creatures that pursue pleasure. According to the theory, a difference contributing to the occurrence of crime is people's different propensity of crime. The propensity can be represented as being vulnerable to the temptation of crime since individuals with low self-control are less likely to consider negative consequences followed by criminal acts. In other words, crimes occur when individuals have low self-control. Low self-control is represented as a series of traits such as high impulsivity, shortsightedness, or seeking risk behaviors. Self-control is constructed around the age of 7 and stably maintained for a lifetime (Gottfredson and Hirschi, 1990).

The consequences of low self-control are also widely addressed in cyberbullying literature (Bayraktar, Machackova, Dedkova, Cerna, & Ševčíková, 2015; Holt, Bossler, & May, 2012; Lianos & McGrath, 2018; Kim, Lee, & Jennings, 2022; Li et al., 2016; Peker & Nebioğlu-Yıldız, 2021; Shadmanfaat, Howell, Muniz, Cochran, Kabiri, & Richardson, 2018). Some scholars found direct effects of low self-control (Bayraktar et al., 2015; Kim et al., 2022; Holt et al., 2012), but the majority of studies indicated indirect effects of low self-control being associated with juveniles' surroundings. For instance, effective parenting is a primary source that constructs children's self-control at early age, and thus ineffective parenting may increase the likelihood of delinquent behaviors (Gottfredson & Hirschi, 1990; Unnever, Cullen, & Pratt, 2003). This assumption is supported by Shadmanfaat and colleagues' study (2018), indicating that low self-control mediates a relationship between ineffective parenting (e.g., a lack of supervision) and cyberbullying perpetration. On the other hand, the effect of self-control is mediated by other factors. For example, when delinquent peer association presents, juveniles tend to engage in online bullying behaviors (Holt et al., 2012; Bayraktar et al., 2015). Hole and colleagues (2012) explained that juveniles having low self-control tend to coalesce. It implies more exposure to deviant behaviors on the web as a process where individuals virtually imitate other's behaviors or share favorable values toward deviant acts. Li and colleagues' study (2016) supported the relationship by arguing that the social learning factors mediate the effects of low self-control on cyberbullying. Lastly, self-control may moderate the effects of psychological causes on cyberbullying. Peker and Nebioğlu-Yıldız (2021) found that individuals' self-control mediates the relationship between aggressiveness and cyberbullying. In the study, both aggressiveness and low self-control were directly associated with cyberbullying. However, the aggressiveness lessened when individuals' self-control was high. In turn, it reduced the occurrence of cyberbullying perpetration (Peker & Nebioğlu-Yıldız, 2021).

Strain or Stress

A high level of strain (Barlett et al., 2021; Lianos, & McGrath, 2018) was also pointed out as the cause of cyberbullying. Agnew (1992) posited that individuals commit a crime when they cannot deal with strain in daily life. In his theory, the sources of strain were defined as a failure to achieve positively valued goals (e.g., financial success), a presence of negative stimuli (e.g., being abused by family members), and a loss of positive stimuli (e.g., a loss of loved one). The influence of strain is moderated by negative emotions such as anger, depression, or anxiety. When individuals feel negative emotions after experiencing the daily strain, they commit a crime as a corrective action. Agnew and colleagues (2002) developed the theory indicating that how individuals perceive daily strain and react to it is based in their traits. Personal traits, such as low self-control or constrain, work as conditional factors which determine how individuals accept and deal with impulses led by strain. Also, the relationship between strain and a crime is influenced by individuals' surroundings, such as family or neighborhood environments (Agnew, Brezina, Wright, & Cullen, 2002). For instance, as a family environment factor, parental supervision plays a role that reduces the influence of strain, which eventually deters a crime (Agnew et al., 2002).

The relationships between general strain and cyberbullying have been tested in various contexts (Barlett, Rinker, & Roth, 2021; Hay, Meldrum, & Mann, 2010; Jang, Song, & Kim, 2014; Lee, Kim, & Song, 2021; Lianos, & McGrath, 2018; Paez, 2018; Patchin & Hinduja, 2011; Wang & Jiang, 2021). From a broad perspective, scholars found a positive relationship between general strain and cyberbullying perpetration (Paez, 2018; Patchin & Hinduja, 2011). Some studies identified sources of strain that increase the risk of perpetration. For instance, Jang and colleagues (2014) found that cyberbullying victimization can be a source of general strain, and thus, being bullied in online spaces may increase the possibility of cyberbullying perpetration. Types and levels of negative emotions may differentiate the influence of cyberbullying victimization. Lee and colleagues (2021) found that depression showed no effects on cyberbullying perpetration, but anger matters. In this study, negative emotion led by cyberbullying victimization undertakes an intrapersonal process. So, if individuals fail to cope with the adverse emotions, it leads to cyberbullying perpetration. This process supports Agnew's basic assumption proposed in 1992.

Not limited to cyberbullying victimization, other stressful daily events also can be sources of the strain. Jang and colleagues (2014) revealed that Korean adolescents' daily strain, including family strain, financial strain, and study strain, may increase the likelihood of cyberbullying perpetration. However, Wang and Jiang (2021) found that the relationship between the study strain and cyberbullying is negative among Chinese juveniles. It means that cyberbullying perpetration is more likely among juveniles who have less study strain. The reverse relationship can occur in different cultural settings. The influence of strain is effective even in adult groups. According to Lianos and McGrath (2018), young adults also perceive general strain led by a lack of social support, financial strain, study strain, or victimization experiences. Their research sample included young adults in the United States, the United Kingdom, and India, and they tend to engage in bullying behaviors when the level of strain increases. Temporarily historical events can cause strain. For instance, as a recent case, COVID-19 might be an adverse event for the majority of people around the world. Barlett and colleagues' findings (2021) indicated that both personal (e.g., Catching COVID-19) and secondhand experiences with COVID-19 (e.g., Knowing someone who caught COVID-19) increased the likelihood of cyberbullying perpetration especially, personal experiences with COVID 19 increase a level of adverse emotion. Based on the prior studies, it seems the sources of strain are various.

INTERPERSONAL LEVEL: CONFLICTS BETWEEN INDIVIDUAL CAUSE CYBERBULLYING.

Traditional Bullying Experiences

Traditional bullying perpetration or physical violence is also linked to perpetration in cyberspace (Cappadocia, Craig, & Pepler, 2013; Kowalski, et al., 2012; Mishna, Khoury-Kassabri, Gadalla, & Daciuk, 2012; Modecki, Minchin, Harbaugh, Guerra, & Runions, 2014; Zhou et al., 2013). Modecki and colleagues (2014) found a similarity between traditional- and online bullying perpetration in their meta-analysis. They also found the overlap between traditional aggression and cyber aggression, which implies that individuals tend to repeat their offline behavior in online spaces. The overlap can be explained by youths' perception that they think cyberspaces are just an extension of physical places (Kowalski et al., 2012). Based on the assumption, social interaction can be copied, and it produces cyberbullying perpetration when bullies and victims know each other. Otherwise, the overlap is led by perpetrators' psychological or behavioral issues. Robson and Witenberg (2013) investigated predictors of traditional bullying and cyberbullying. The results indicated that moral disengagement and diffusion of responsibility are storing predictors of traditional and cyberbullying. Kim and colleagues (2022) pointed out that the association between traditional and cyberbullying perpetration can be seen as parts of problematic behavior syndrome, indicating multiple behavioral issues observed by an individual. It means that bullies do not specify or prefer a particular space or mode when perpetrating. This result may look similar to Kowalski and colleagues' findings (2012), but Kim and colleagues (2022) did not limit the victim-offender relationship to acquaintances.

Another perspective suggests that traditional bullying victimization causes cyberbullying perpetration (Jang et al., 2014; Jose, Kljakovic, Scheib, & Notter, 2012; Kowalski et al., 2012). The theoretical approaches to explain the path are various. For instance, in Jang and colleagues' study (2014), the path was addressed based on the general strain perspective. For instance, considering the social settings where Korean juveniles' daily strain is high, traditional bullying victimization leads to cyberbullying perpetration by causing psychological issues, such as anger, anxiety, or depression (Jang et al., 2014). This path implies that cyberbullying is a type of corrective action to cope with emotional problems led by traditional bullying. On the other hand, Jose and colleagues (2012) insisted that the relationship can be addressed based on a social learning process. What they speculated was, cyberbullying victimization and perpetration create a vicious cycle where victims become bullies and vice versa. When victims are bullied, they learn about bullies' behavior and perceive perpetration as an indirect compensation. For victims, especially when they are physically weak, cyberspaces are considered attractive places for retaliation (Jose et al., 2012).

Romantic Relationship

Current romantic relationships or prior romantic relationships may cause online bullying behaviors (Calvete, Gámez-Guadix & Borrajo, 2019; Cava, Tomás, Buelga, & Carrascosa, 2020; Chakraborty, Zhang, & Ramesh, 2018; Crosslin & Crosslin, 2014; Deiss & Savage, 2010; Marcum & Higgins, 2019; Pyżalski, 2013; Roberto, Eden, Savage, Ramos-Salazar, & Deiss, 2014; Segura & Pecino,2015). If a romantic relationship turns into negative situation, this event will influence potential adverse behavior. According to Crosslin and colleagues (2014), approximately 32.4 percent of their survey participants have been cyberbullied at least twice after a relationship ended. Deiss and Savage (2010) indicated that verbal aggression might occur as a form of cyberbullying against an ex-partner. This aggression might occur due to immaturity where young adults cannot properly cope with their emotions after a breakup. This phenomenon takes place more often among adolescents. Pyżalski (2012; 2013) found that 20 percent of Polish juvenile participants reported cyberbullying perpetration experiences toward their ex-partner. The author stipulated that adolescents may perpetrate destructive electronic aggression when the romantic relationship is the first serious one (Pyżalski, 2013). Not limited to aggressive behaviors, technology is used when perpetrators try to control an ex-partner's behaviors (e.g., checking his/her locations) (Marcum & Higgins, 2019).

Cyberbullying has also been discussed in regard to finding romantic relationships. According to Segura & Pecino (2015), 46 percent of their survey participants in a college in Spain reported that they bullied their romantic partner using a phone. A current romantic partnership is deeply associated with online aggression or harassment since young people use technology when they seek romance. For instance, people use technology such as online apps when they want to find a partner, initiate a relationship, or communicate with a partner (Marcum & Higgins, 2019). Calvete and colleagues (2019) specified the behaviors as "cyber abuse in romantic relationships (CARR)," where a person attempts to threaten, humiliate, or control his / her partner electronically. The form is also view form of cyberstalking (Marcum & Higgins, 2019). Similarly, Cava and colleagues (2020) defined the form as cyber dating violence (CDV), and they found the most frequent form included cyber control and cyber-aggression. The concept of bullying in a romantic partnership is described based on different terms, but it seems there are shared characteristics among the terminology. Unfortunately, abusive behaviors can be observed when the romance is one-sided. For instance, Chakraborty and colleagues (2018) argued that unwanted communication indicating romantic interests is conveyed without victims' preference or intent.

Group level Factors

Situational Factor: Temporal Circumstances cause Cyberbullying

Situational factors, such as specific characteristics or surroundings, affect the perpetrators' choice of bullying behaviors. From a theoretical perspective, perpetrators' behavior can be explained based on choice theory.

To start, the rational choice perspective assumes that criminals estimate gain and loss followed by criminal activities (Cornish & Clarke, 1987). The economic approach, which undertakes estimation of pros and cons, stemmed from the deterrence doctrine of classical school in criminology (Akers, 1990). From a utilitarian viewpoint, individuals are creatures who are rational and seek maximized pleasure. Thus, individuals are able to calculate a pain of punishment. If the pain outweighs benefits of crimes, the individual will not choose criminal activities (Cullen, Agnew, & Wilcox, 2006). Clarke and Cornish (1985) proposed situational crime prevention techniques and classified situations and criminal decisions to design criminal causation (Clarke, 2013). With the development of the model, Cornish and Clarke (2003) introduced 25 classifications of crime prevention techniques such as increasing offenders' effort, increasing security levels, limiting values of targets, reducing provocation of offenders, and removing excuses. Another perspective that explains the effects of situational factors is routine activity theory. Routine activity theory assumed that crime issues can be addressed at a macro level, which led to a drastic change in social settings (Cohen & Felson, 1979). The theory focused on the change of individuals' life patterns based on economic development in western societies. For instance, with the development of economic status and human rights, individuals began to spend more time outside their residence for various reasons (e.g., employment or outside activities). Also, technology has developed, leading to an increase in the value of products. The situation may seem attractive from motivated offenders' viewpoints and will give them more opportunities to access their targets. Thus, Cohen and Felson (1979) specified the environmental aspects where crimes may easily occur in terms of situational settings, including a suitable target, a motivated offender, and a lack of guidance.

Cohen and Felson's perspective (1979) have been applied to cyberbullying perpetration studies that investigated the effects of situational factors. For example, cyberbullies' accessibility to online space may increase the possibility of perpetration. It can be routine activities of perpetrators who spend more time online (Mishna et al., 2012; Zhou et al., 2013). Anonymity may increase the likelihood of cyberbullying perpetration. Barlett (2015) found that cyberbullying is more prevalent when the users can shield their identities. Also, Cotler and colleagues (2017) argued that characteristics of the Internet, such as anonymity, contribute to more cyberbullying perpetration by making bullies less hesitant to perpetrate. As classical theory suggested, the perception may decrease fear of apprehension or punishment. Based on Cohen and Felson's assumption (1979), anonymity may be viewed as a lack of guardianship since the perpetrators are less likely to be detected. The lack of guardianship and cyberbullying perpetration can be linked in Zhou and colleagues' study in 2013. They found that juveniles are more likely to bully others online when they access the Internet in personal spaces without surveillance (Zhou et al., 2013). In sum, if there is any missing element of crime prevention, cyberbullying will be likely observed.

Cultural Backgrounds

Unfortunately, there are several causes that may not be controlled or changed by individuals' decisions. Cultural traits and certain atmospheres in particular countries are examples. Those factors obviously play a role that provokes cyberbullying perpetration (Park, Golden, Vizcaino-Vickers, Jidong, & Raj, 2021; Zhou and colleagues, 2013). The current study assumes that the relationship can be addressed by Olweus' argument (1993) regarding power imbalance. According to Olweus (1993), bullying behaviors is originated from an imbalance of power which can be led by a physical gap, social status in a group, or predominant power of subgroup targeting a single person (Olweus 2013; Pepler & Craig 2009; Thomas, Connor, & Scott, 2015). As bullying behaviors are repeated, perpetrators feel more power, whereas victims feel helpless (Thomas et al., 2015). Butler and colleagues (2009) pointed out that the imbalance of power is observed in cyberbullying as well as in traditional bullying. Also, the power imbalance is consolidated as bullying behaviors are repeated (Thomas et al., 2015).

In regard to gender, women are harassed in online spaces in some cultural backgrounds due to relationships. For instance, Magsi and colleagues (2017), in a study regarding female college students' cyberbullying victimization in Pakistan, reported that approximately 45 percent of young college students were cyberbullied after ending a romantic relationship or refusing to date a male. Furthermore, these females were reluctant to report the incidents even to their families since they were worried about being considered immoral (Magsi et al., 2017). One possible explanation can be speculated based on a different gender socialization process in cyberbullying (Park et al., 2021). They explained that aggressive manners by males might be led by a cultural influence that encourages males' masculinity and females' docile attitudes (Park et al., 2021). The approach can be addressed by Hagan and colleagues' perspective (1988), which argued that a gender gap in delinquency is led by social structure rather than biological differences between males and females. To be specific, they indicated that traditional patriarchal family emphasizes different gender roles that educate kids in different ways by gender (Hagan, Simpson, & Gillis, 1988). For instance, a mother will teach her daughter to be docile or silent, whereas her son to be masculine. However, the empirical studies in Asian countries will demand further explanation regarding gender gaps since there will be more reasons for differences from western society. The disrespectful attitude towards women can be observed even in higher education environments in western society. According to Cassidy and colleagues (2016), female faculty members are more likely to be targeted in cyberbullying incidents that intend to humiliate them by delivering aggressive language or spreading a rumor.

Cyberbullying against LGBTQ is also prevalent in online spaces (Hinduja & Patchin, 2020). In Abreu and Kenny's meta-analysis (2018), the LGBTQ's cyberbullying victimization is ranged from 10 to 70 percent in their target studies. Considering their marginality in terms of population number (Espinoza &Wright, 2018), Olweus' perspective (1993) on the power imbalance can be applied in this case. Additionally, Putri and Satvikadewi (2017) suggested that cyberbullying perpetration against LGBQ can be addressed based on a natural logic of perpetrators. To be specific, the bullying behavior is led by perpetrators' mindsets where they feel threatened by different people outside normality. The mindset is constructed through individuals' surroundings such as politics, religions, education, law, governmental actions, socializing, etc. The values obtained by experiences are internalized, and these causes individuals' belief that defines LGBQ populations as abnormal (Putri & Satvikadew, 2017).

VICTIMS SUFFER FROM CYBERBULLYING EXPERINCE: IMPACTS ON VICTIMS

There are a plethora of studies that reported negative impacts of cyberbullying (DePaolis & Williford, 2019; Dredge, Gleeson, & De la Piedad Garcia, 2014; Goebert, Else, Matsu, Chung-Do, & Chang, 2011; Khine et al. 2020; Kim, Kimber, Boyle, & Georgiades, 2019; Lee & Chun, 2020; Lee, Chun, Kim, & Lee, 2020; Nikolaou, 2017; Nixon, 2014; Oksanen, Oksa, Savela, Kaakinen, & Ellonen, 2022; Patchin & Hinduja, 2022; Rivituso, 2014; Smokowski, Evans, & Cotter, 2014). Unfortunately, victims of cyberbullying have suffered from various adverse outcomes that may threaten the victims' daily life psychologically and physically. Especially some studies reviewed juveniles' victimization outcomes which affect their developmental stages in the long run. Psychologically, cyberbullying victimization is associated with anxiety (Nixon, 2014; Smokowski et al., 2014), depression (DePaolis & Williford, 2019; Nixon, 2014; Smokowski et al., 2014), avoidance (Lee, & Chun, 2020), low self-esteem (DePaolis & Williford, 2019; Smokowski et al., 2014), or loneliness (Nixon, 2014). The range of psychological effects is vast, from a mild- to a severe level. For instance, some victims felt bad about themselves (Goebert et al., 2011), felt less optimistic about their future (Smokowski et al., 2014), sought social support (Lee & Chun, 2020), or had intent to drop out of the school (Lee et al., 2022). The negative emotion is amplified and may lead to suicidal thoughts of juveniles (Nikolaou, 2017). Furthermore, the emotional issues can be linked to physical reactions such as external behaviors (e.g., being aggressive) (Smokowski et al., 2014) or poor somatic health (Patchin & Hinduja, 2022), substance use (Kim et al., 2019), or suicidal attempts (Nikolaou, 2017). Not only juveniles but adults may also face hardship followed by cyberbullying victimization. For instance, Khine and colleagues (2020) reported that college students experienced poor concentration on lectures after victimization experiences. Additionally, Rivituso (2014) observed several symptoms from college student victims, including fear, feeling vulnerable, self-blame, stress, depression, frustration, embarrassment, distrust in people and technology, and a lack of self-control. Especially, when young people are exposed to social media frequently, they tend to feel technostress and exhaustion (Oksanen, 2020).

Need Protection: What are the possible approaches?

It is obvious that cyberbullying poses various harms to the victims, but there have also been controversies over possible reactions followed after cyberbullying perpetration. Unfortunately, some victim populations are reluctant to report the incidents to formal or informal institutions (Dredge et al., 2014; Li, 2010; Magsi et al., 2017). For instance, from the individual level, victims justify the perpetration by interpreting the situation as joking, and also they believe that the situations happen to others often (Dredge et al., 2014). In addition, individuals are less likely to believe that situations will be much improved even after reporting (Li, 2010). Thus, cyberbullying occurrence in statistics may be underestimated due to various reasons. According to Katz and colleagues' study (2014), there is a vast discrepancy between police and social agencies in terms of cyberbullying incident reports.

It may result from different personal expectations regarding the police's reaction (Magsi et al., 2017) or scrutiny of policies or laws when addressing cyberbullying issues (Katz, Keeley, Spears, Taddeo, Swist, & Bates, 2014). In fact, the legal definition of cyberbullying is sometimes vague or not very thorough, which may require further interpretation. For instance, in Qatar, cyberbullying is defined as a crime in the penal code that may be punishable by the government (Foody, Samara, El Asam, Morsi, & Khattab, 2017). "Immoral and Disgraceful Actions" specified that anyone who disturbs or inconveniences others through a wire, wireless or electronic methods will receive imprisonment or a fine penalty (Foody et al., 2017). Additionally, in Australia, the Criminal Code Acts 1995 can be a basis which addressed that misuse of telecommunication services, including the Internet, with the purpose of threatening, hoaxing, killing, or posing harm to others will lead to criminal liability (Butler et al., 2011). In the United States, the approach to legislation is more intensive. For instance, in Florida, legislative parties proposed that bullying, through computer systems and or data, committed by students and school employees should be prohibited (Hinduja & Patchin, 2009). However, the code or laws may demand related parties in the criminal procedure to conduct a thorough review of contexts to figure out the applicability of the laws. Also, Hinduja and Patchin (2009) pointed out that the parties may need additional effort to avoid violation of constitutional rights (e.g., a right to free speech). For instance, in 2009, in the United States, a bill named "Megan Meier Cyberbullying Prevention Act" was introduced for an amendment to the federal criminal code, indicating punishment against "those who transmits in interstate or foreign commerce a communication intended to coerce, intimidate, harass, or cause substantial emotional distress to another person, using electronic means to support severe, repeated, and hostile behavior." (111th Congress, 2009). However, the bill was not passed by Congress due to the possibility of undermining the right to free speech (Murrhee, 2010).

The strategies can be prepared in less formal ways in other social agencies. For instance, some colleges have policies such as students' codes of conduct, discrimination prohibition on campus, or electronic communication (Faucher, Jackson, & Cassidy, 2015). Not limited to policies or rules by the authorities, preventative actions on cyberbullying would be effective. For instance, Cassidy and colleagues (2013) found that educational programs or activities may promote healthy internet environments. The non-punitive action may create benign school/home atmospheres or students' attitudes that ultimately improve emotional problems, social skills, learning experiences, or perceptions toward others. Additionally, some approaches can provide specific knowledge by focusing on cyberbullying primarily to educate students on coping strategies, such as recommended responses, avoidance, or seeking support when confronting bullying perpetration (Perren et al., 2012).

CONCLUSION

The current chapter reviewed cyberbullying perpetration, victimization, definition, trends, the causes, victim impacts, and policies. A plethora of studies contributed to the development of cyberbullying research. However, further research will be required to address cyberbullying issues.

Given the diversified circumstances, scholars may face a challenge when identifying cyberbullying issues. The current study found inconsistencies in definition and various trends based on different methodologies. The causes of cyberbullying perpetration can be derived from individuals' problems, such as personal traits, but also the causes encompass a broader extent, including interpersonal conflicts, temporal situations, or cultural aspects. Based on all these reasons, cyberbullying can be a devastating experience for the victims. To reduce the adverse consequences, the government, school authorities, and various social agencies suggested strategies. However, some grounds of the law may seem doubtable due to its characteristic that violates human rights.

FUTURE RESEARCH AND DIRECTIONS

Through the lens, the current study found that there are commonly shared aspects when addressing cyberbullying issues, but also a specific approach is essential in the future to prepare strategies that fit into a certain circumstance. For instance, many studies succeeded in finding a single cause when addressing what factor increases the risk of bullying perpetration at individual or group levels. However, considering the fact that an individual is affected by various factors simultaneously, a comprehensive approach which describes a big picture of bullying incidence would be crucial. Additionally, with the development of technology, the form of cyberbullying is continuously emerging. For instance, in D'Ovidio and Doyle study (2003), the extent of cyberbullying was a little bit narrow (i.e. the Internet, e-mail, or electronic devices), but these days research on bullying in social media has drastically developed due to its influence on individual's life. Thus, longitudinal examination on cyberbullying may contribute to catching time-sensitive issues in research.

REFERENCES

111th Congress (2009-2010). H.*R.1966 - Megan Meier Cyberbullying Prevention Act.* https://www.congress.gov/bill/111th-congress/house-bill/1966

Abreu, R. L., & Kenny, M. C. (2018). Cyberbullying and LGBTQ youth: A systematic literature review and recommendations for prevention and intervention. *Journal of Child & Adolescent Trauma*, *11*(1), 81–97. doi:10.100740653-017-0175-7 PMID:32318140

Agnew, R. (1992). Foundation for a General Strain Theory of Crime and Delinquency. *Criminology*, *30*(1), 47–88. doi:10.1111/j.1745-9125.1992.tb01093.x

Agnew, R., Brezina, T., Wright, J. P., & Cullen, F. T. (2002). Strain, Personality Traits, and Delinquency: Extending general strain theory. *Criminology*, *40*(1), 43–72. doi:10.1111/j.1745-9125.2002.tb00949.x

Akers, R. L. (1990). Rational Choice, Deterrence, and Social Learning Theory in Criminology: The Path Not Taken. *The Journal of Criminal Law & Criminology*, *81*(3), 653–676. doi:10.2307/1143850

Barlett, C. P. (2015). Predicting Adolescent's Cyberbullying Behavior: A Longitudinal Risk Analysis. *Journal of Adolescence*, *41*(1), 86–95. doi:10.1016/j.adolescence.2015.02.006 PMID:25828551

Barlett, C. P., Rinker, A., & Roth, B. (2021). Cyberbullying Perpetration in the COVID-19 Era: An Application of General Strain Theory. *The Journal of Social Psychology*, *161*(4), 466–476. doi:10.1080/00224545.2021.1883503 PMID:33543673

Bayraktar, F., Machackova, H., Dedkova, L., Cerna, A., & Ševčíková, A. (2015). Cyberbullying: The Discriminant Factors Among Cyberbullies, Cybervictims, and Cyberbully-victims in a Czech Adolescent Sample. *Journal of Interpersonal Violence*, *30*(18), 3192–3216. doi:10.1177/0886260514555006 PMID:25411234

Begotti, T., & Acquadro Maran, D. (2019). Characteristics of Cyberstalking Behavior, Consequences, and Coping Strategies: A Cross-sectional Study in a Sample of Italian University Students. *Future Internet*, *11*(5), 120–131. doi:10.3390/fi11050120

Beran, T. N., Rinaldi, C., Bickham, D. S., & Rich, M. (2012). Evidence For the Need to Support Adolescents Dealing with Harassment and Cyber-harassment: Prevalence, Progression, and Impact. *School Psychology International*, *33*(5), 562–576. doi:10.1177/0143034312446976

Brewer, G., & Kerslake, J. (2015). Cyberbullying, self-esteem, empathy and loneliness. *Computers in Human Behavior*, *48*, 255–260. doi:10.1016/j.chb.2015.01.073

Bureau of Justice Statistics. (2020). *Criminal Victimization.* https://bjs.ojp.gov/library/publications/criminal-victimization-2020

Butler, D., Kift, S., Campbell, M., Slee, P., & Spears, B. (2011). School policy responses to cyberbullying: An Australian legal perspective. *International Journal of Law and Education*, *16*(2), 7–28.

Calvete, E., Gámez-Guadix, M., & Borrajo, E. (2019). Cyberbullying in Romantic Relationships: Cross-Cultural Issues. In Cyberbullying in Schools, Workplaces, and Romantic Relationships (pp. 150-183). Routledge.

Cappadocia, M. C., Craig, W. M., & Pepler, D. (2013). Cyberbullying: Prevalence, Stability, and Risk Factors During Adolescence. *Canadian Journal of School Psychology*, *28*(2), 171–192. doi:10.1177/0829573513491212

Cassidy, W., Faucher, C., & Jackson, M. (2013). Cyberbullying among Youth: A Comprehensive Review of Current International Research and Its Implications and Application to Policy and Practice. *School Psychology International*, *34*(6), 575–612. doi:10.1177/0143034313479697

Cassidy, W., Jackson, M., & Faucher, C. (2016). Gender Differences and Cyberbullying Towards Faculty Members in Higher Education. *Cyberbullying Across the Globe*, 79-98.

Cava, M. J., Tomás, I., Buelga, S., & Carrascosa, L. (2020). Loneliness, Depressive Mood and Cyberbullying Victimization in Adolescent Victims of Cyber Dating Violence. *International Journal of Environmental Research and Public Health*, *17*(12), 4269. doi:10.3390/ijerph17124269 PMID:32549276

Chakraborty, A., Zhang, Y., & Ramesh, A. (2018). Understanding Types of Cyberbullying in an Anonymous Messaging Application. *Companion Proceedings of the The Web Conference 2018*, 1001-1005. 10.1145/3184558.3191530

Clarke, R. V. (2013). Situational Crime Prevention. In R. Wortley & L. Mazerolle (Eds.), *Environmental Criminology and Crime Analysis*. Willan., doi:10.4324/9780203118214

Clarke, R. V., & Cornish, D. B. (1985). Modeling offenders' decisions: A framework for research and policy. *Crime and Justice*, *6*, 147–185. doi:10.1086/449106

Cohen, L. E., & Felson, M. (1979). Social Change and Crime Rate Trends: A Routine Activity Approach. *American Sociological Review*, *44*(4), 588–608. doi:10.2307/2094589

Corcoran, L., Guckin, C. M., & Prentice, G. (2015). Cyberbullying or Cyber Aggression?: A Review of Existing Definitions of Cyber-based Peer-to-peer Aggression. *Societies (Basel, Switzerland)*, *5*(2), 245–255. doi:10.3390oc5020245

Cornish, D. B., & Clarke, R. V. (1987). Understanding Crime Displacement: An Application of Rational Choice Theory. *Criminology*, *25*(4), 933–948. doi:10.1111/j.1745-9125.1987.tb00826.x

Cornish, D. B., & Clarke, R. V. (2003). Opportunities, Precipitators and Criminal Decisions: A Reply to Wortley's Critique of Situational Crime Prevention. In Theory for Practice in Situational Crime Prevention, Crime Prevention Studies, Vol. 16. Criminal Justice Press.

Cotler, J. L., Fryling, M., & Rivituso, J. (2017). Causes of Cyberbullying in Multi-player Online Gaming Environments: Gamer Perceptions. *Journal of Information Systems Applied Research*, *10*(1), 4–14.

Crosslin, K., & Crosslin, M. (2014). Cyberbullying at a Texas University-A Mixed Methods Approach to Examining Online Aggression. *Texas Public Health Journal*, *66*(3), 26–31.

Cullen, F. T., Agnew, R., & Wilcox, P. (2006). *Criminological Theory: Past to Present: Essential Readings*. Oxford University Press.

D'Ovidio, R., & Doyle, J. (2003). A Study on Cyberstalking: Understanding Investigative Hurdles. *FBI Law Enforcement Bulletin*, *72*(3), 10–17.

Deiss, D. M., Jr., & Savage, M. W. (2010). *Bridging the Gap in the Study of Cyberbullying: Placing the Study of Cyberbullying within the Dark Side of Interpersonal Communication Research.* Paper presented at the Annual Conference of the National Communication Association, San Francisco, CA.

DePaolis, K. J., & Williford, A. (2019). Pathways from Cyberbullying Victimization to Negative Health Outcomes among Elementary School Students: A longitudinal investigation. *Journal of Child and Family Studies, 28*(9), 2390–2403. doi:10.100710826-018-1104-6

Dredge, R., Gleeson, J. F., & De la Piedad Garcia, X. (2014). Risk Factors Associated with Impact Severity of Cyberbullying Victimization: A qualitative study of adolescent online social networking. *Cyberpsychology, Behavior, and Social Networking, 17*(5), 287–291. doi:10.1089/cyber.2013.0541 PMID:24611734

Espinoza, G., & Wright, M. (2018). Cyberbullying Experiences among Marginalized Youth: What do we know and where do we go next? *Journal of Child & Adolescent Trauma, 11*(1), 1–5. doi:10.100740653-018-0207-y PMID:32318132

Fan, C. Y., Chu, X. W., Zhang, M., & Zhou, Z. K. (2019). Are Narcissists More Likely to be Involved in Cyberbullying? Examining the Mediating Role of Self-esteem. *Journal of Interpersonal Violence, 34*(15), 3127–3150. doi:10.1177/0886260516666531 PMID:27565705

Faucher, C., Jackson, M., & Cassidy, W. (2015). When online exchanges byte: An Examination of the Policy Environment Governing Cyberbullying at the University Level. *Canadian Journal of Higher Education, 45*(1), 102–121. doi:10.47678/cjhe.v45i1.184215

Foody, M., Samara, M., El Asam, A., Morsi, H., & Khattab, A. (2017). A Review of Cyberbullying Legislation in Qatar: Considerations for policy makers and educators. *International Journal of Law and Psychiatry, 50*, 45–51. doi:10.1016/j.ijlp.2016.10.013 PMID:27837914

Goebert, D., Else, I., Matsu, C., Chung-Do, J., & Chang, J. Y. (2011). The Impact of Cyberbullying on Substance Use and Mental Health in a Multiethnic Sample. *Maternal and Child Health Journal, 15*(8), 1282–1286. doi:10.100710995-010-0672-x PMID:20824318

Gottfredson, M. R., & Hirschi, T. (1990). *A General Theory of Crime.* Stanford University Press. doi:10.1515/9781503621794

Grigg, D. W. (2010). Cyber-aggression: Definition and Concept of Cyberbullying. *Journal of Psychologists and Counsellors in Schools, 20*(2), 143–156. doi:10.1375/ajgc.20.2.143

Grigg, D. W. (2012). Definitional Constructs of Cyber-bullying and Cyber-aggression From a Triangulatory Overview: A Preliminary Study into Elements of Cyber-bullying. *Journal of Aggression, Conflict and Peace Research, 4*(4), 202–215. doi:10.1108/17596591211270699

Hagan, J., Simpson, J., & Gillis, A. R. (1988). Feminist Scholarship, Relational and Instrumental Control, and a Power-control Theory of Gender and Delinquency. *The British Journal of Sociology, 39*(3), 301–336. doi:10.2307/590481 PMID:3179640

Hay, C., Meldrum, R., & Mann, K. (2010). Traditional Bullying, Cyber Bullying, and Deviance: A General Strain Theory Approach. *Journal of Contemporary Criminal Justice, 26*(2), 130–147. doi:10.1177/1043986209359557

Hinduja, S. (2021, October 21). Bullying During the COVID-19 Pandemic. *Cyberbyllying Research Center*. https://cyberbullying.org/cyberbullying-statistics-age-gender-sexual-orientation-race

Hinduja, S., & Patchin, J. W. (2009). *Cyberbullying Fact Sheet: A brief review of relevant legal and policy issues*. Cyberbullying Research Center.

Hinduja, S., & Patchin, J. W. (2010). Cyberbullying Research Summary: Cyberbullying and Self-Esteem. *The Journal of School Health, 80*(12), 614–621. doi:10.1111/j.1746-1561.2010.00548.x PMID:21087257

Hinduja, S., & Patchin, J. W. (2011). High-tech Cruelty. *Educational Leadership, 68*(5), 48–52.

Hinduja, S., & Patchin, J. W. (2015). *Bullying Beyond the Schoolyard: Preventing and Responding to Cyberbullying* (2nd ed.). Sage Publications.

Hinduja, S., & Patchin, J. W. (2018). Connecting Adolescent Suicide to the Severity of Bullying and Cyberbullying. *Journal of School Violence, 18*(3), 333–346. doi:10.1080/15388220.2018.1492417

Hinduja, S., & Patchin, J. W. (2020). *Bullying, Cyberbullying, and LGBTQ Students*. Cyberbullying Research Center.

Hoff, D. L., & Mitchell, S. N. (2009). Cyberbullying: Causes, Effects, and Remedies. *Journal of Educational Administration, 47*(5), 652–665. doi:10.1108/09578230910981107

Holt, T. J., Bossler, A. M., & May, D. C. (2012). Low Self-control, Deviant Peer Associations, and Juvenile Cyberdeviance. *American Journal of Criminal Justice, 37*(3), 378–395. doi:10.100712103-011-9117-3

Hosseinmardi, H., Mattson, S. A., Rafiq, R. I., Han, R., Lv, Q., & Mishr, S. (2015). *Prediction of Cyberbullying Incidents on the Instagram Social Network*. arXiv preprint arXiv:1508.06257.

Jang, H., Song, J., & Kim, R. (2014). Does the Offline Bully-victimization Influence Cyberbullying Behavior among Youths? Application of General Strain Theory. *Computers in Human Behavior, 31*, 85–93. doi:10.1016/j.chb.2013.10.007

Johanis, M. A., Bakar, A. R. A., & Ismail, F. (2020, April). Cyber-Bullying Trends Using Social Media Platform: An Analysis through Malaysian Perspectives. [). IOP Publishing.]. *Journal of Physics: Conference Series, 1529*(2), 022077.

Kaplan, H. B. (1975). *Self-Attitudes and Deviant Behavior*. Goodyear.

Katz, I., Keeley, M., Spears, B., Taddeo, C., Swist, T., & Bates, S. (2014). *Research on Youth Exposure to, and Management of, Cyberbullying Incidents in Australia*. Synthesis report.

Kaur, P., Dhir, A., Tandon, A., Alzeiby, E. A., & Abohassan, A. A. (2021). A systematic literature review on cyberstalking. An analysis of past achievements and future promises. *Technological Forecasting and Social Change, 163*, 120426. doi:10.1016/j.techfore.2020.120426

Khine, A. T., Saw, Y. M., Htut, Z. Y., Khaing, C. T., Soe, H. Z., Swe, K. K., Thike, T., Htet, H., Saw, T. N., Cho, S. M., Kariya, T., Yamamoto, E., & Hamajima, N. (2020). Assessing Risk Factors and Impact of Cyberbullying Victimization among University Students in Myanmar: A cross-sectional study. *PLoS One, 15*(1), e0227051. doi:10.1371/journal.pone.0227051 PMID:31967998

Kim, J., Lee, Y., & Jennings, W. G. (2022). A Path from Traditional Bullying to Cyberbullying in South Korea: Examining the roles of self-control and deviant peer association in the different forms of bullying. *Journal of Interpersonal Violence, 37*(9-10). doi:10.1177/0886260521 1067022 PMID:35259313

Kim, S., Kimber, M., Boyle, M. H., & Georgiades, K. (2019). Sex Differences in the Association Between Cyberbullying Victimization and Mental Health, Substance Use, and Suicidal Ideation in Adolescents. *Canadian Journal of Psychiatry, 64*(2), 126–135. doi:10.1177/0706743718777397 PMID:29783849

Kljakovic, M., Scheib, E., & Notter, O. (2012). The Joint Development of Traditional Bullying and Victimization With Cyber Bullying and Victimization in Adolescence. *Journal of Research on Adolescence, 22*(2), 301–309.

Kowalski, R. M., Morgan, C. A., & Limber, S. P. (2012). Traditional Bullying as a Potential Warning Sign of Cyberbullying. *School Psychology International, 33*(5), 505–519. doi:10.1177/0143034312445244

Lazuras, L., Barkoukis, V., Ourda, D., & Tsorbatzoudis, H. (2013). A Process Model of Cyberbullying in Adolescence. *Computers in Human Behavior, 29*(3), 881–887. doi:10.1016/j.chb.2012.12.015

Lee, J., Chun, J., Kim, J., & Lee, J. (2020). Cyberbullying Victimisation and School Dropout Intention among South Korean Adolescents: The moderating role of peer/teacher support. *Asia Pacific Journal of Social Work and Development, 30*(3), 195–211. doi:10.1080/02185385.2020.1774409

Lee, S., & Chun, J. (2020). Conceptualizing the Impacts of Cyberbullying Victimization among Korean Male Adolescents. *Children and Youth Services Review, 117*, 105275. doi:10.1016/j.childyouth.2020.105275

Lee, Y., Kim, J., & Song, H. (2021). Do Negative Emotions Matter? Paths From Victimization to Cyber and Traditional Bullying From a General Strain Theory Perspective. *Crime and Delinquency*. Advance online publication. doi:10.1177/00111287211052439

Li, C. K., Holt, T. J., Bossler, A. M., & May, D. C. (2016). Examining the Mediating Effects of Social Learning on the Low Self-control-Cyberbullying Relationship in a Youth Sample. *Deviant Behavior, 37*(2), 126–138. doi:10.1080/01639625.2014.1004023

Li, Q. (2010). Cyberbullying in high schools: A Study of Students' Behaviors and Beliefs About This New Phenomenon. *Journal of Aggression, Maltreatment & Trauma, 19*(4), 372–392. doi:10.1080/10926771003788979

Li, T. B. Q. (2005). Cyber-harassment: A Study of a New Method for an Old Behavior. *Journal of Educational Computing Research, 32*(3), 265–277. doi:10.2190/8YQM-B04H-PG4D-BLLH

Lianos, H., & McGrath, A. (2018). Can the General Theory of Crime and General Strain Theory Explain Cyberbullying Perpetration? *Crime and Delinquency, 64*(5), 674–700. doi:10.1177/0011128717714204

Magsi, H., Agha, N., & Magsi, I. (2017). Understanding Cyber Bullying in Pakistani Context: Causes and Effects on Young Female University Students in Sindh Province. *New Horizons (Baltimore, Md.)*, *11*(1), 103–110.

Marcum, C. D., & Higgins, G. E. (2019). Examining the Effectiveness of Academic Scholarship on the Fight Against Cyberbullying and Cyberstalking. *American Journal of Criminal Justice*, *44*(4), 645–655. doi:10.100712103-019-09482-8

Marcum, C. D., Higgins, G. E., & Nicholson, J. (2017). I'm Watching Uou: Cyberstalking behaviors of university students in romantic relationships. *American Journal of Criminal Justice*, *42*(2), 373–388. doi:10.100712103-016-9358-2

Mason, W. A. (2001). Self-esteem and Delinquency Revisited (again): A test of Kaplan's self-derogation theory of delinquency using latent growth curve modeling. *Journal of Youth and Adolescence*, *30*(1), 83–102. doi:10.1023/A:1005276905961

Mishna, F., Khoury-Kassabri, M., Gadalla, T., & Daciuk, J. (2012). Risk factors for involvement in cyber bullying: Victims, bullies and bully–victims. *Children and Youth Services Review*, *34*(1), 63–70. doi:10.1016/j.childyouth.2011.08.032

Modecki, K. L., Minchin, J., Harbaugh, A. G., Guerra, N. G., & Runions, K. C. (2014). Bullying prevalence across contexts: A meta-analysis measuring cyber and traditional bullying. *The Journal of Adolescent Health*, *55*(5), 602–611. doi:10.1016/j.jadohealth.2014.06.007 PMID:25168105

Murrhee, K. C. (2010). Squelching Student Speech in Florida: Cyberbullying and the First Amendment. *U. Fla. JL & Pub. Pol'y*, *21*, 307.

Nikolaou, D. (2017). Does Cyberbullying Impact Youth Suicidal Behaviors? *Journal of Health Economics*, *56*, 30–46. doi:10.1016/j.jhealeco.2017.09.009 PMID:28968528

Nixon, C. L. (2014). Current Perspectives: The impact of cyberbullying on adolescent health. *Adolescent Health, Medicine and Therapeutics*, *5*, 143–158. doi:10.2147/AHMT.S36456 PMID:25177157

Oksanen, A., Oksa, R., Savela, N., Kaakinen, M., & Ellonen, N. (2020). Cyberbullying victimization at work: Social media identity bubble approach. *Computers in Human Behavior*, *109*, 106363. doi:10.1016/j.chb.2020.106363

Olweus, D. (1993). *Bullying at School: What we know and what we can do*. Blackwell.

Olweus, D. (2013). School bullying: Development and some important challenges. *Annual Review of Clinical Psychology*, *9*(1), 751–780. doi:10.1146/annurev-clinpsy-050212-185516 PMID:23297789

Owens, T. J. (1994). Two Dimensions of Self-esteem: Reciprocal effects of positive self-worth and self-deprecation on adolescent problems. *American Sociological Review*, *59*(3), 391–407. doi:10.2307/2095940

Paez, G. R. (2018). Cyberbullying Among Adolescents: A general strain theory perspective. *Journal of School Violence*, *17*(1), 74–85. doi:10.1080/15388220.2016.1220317

Park, M. A., Golden, K. J., Vizcaino-Vickers, S., Jidong, D., & Raj, S. (2021). Sociocultural Values, Attitudes and Risk Factors Associated with Adolescent Cyberbullying in East Asia: A systematic review. *Cyberpsychology (Brno)*, *15*(1), 5. doi:10.5817/CP2021-1-5

Patchin, J. W. (2019, July 9). 2019 Cyberbullying Data. *Cyberbyllying Research Center.* https://cyberbullying.org/2019-cyberbullying-data

Patchin, J. W., & Hinduja, S. (2010). Cyberbullying and Self-esteem. *The Journal of School Health*, *80*(12), 614–621. doi:10.1111/j.1746-1561.2010.00548.x PMID:21087257

Patchin, J. W., & Hinduja, S. (2011). Traditional and Nontraditional Bullying Among Youth: A test of general strain theory. *Youth & Society*, *43*(2), 727–751. doi:10.1177/0044118X10366951

Patchin, J. W., & Hinduja, S. (2019). *Life time cyber bullying experiences.* https://cyberbullying.org/Cyberbullying-Research-In-Review.pdf

Patchin, J. W., & Hinduja, S. (2022). Cyberbullying Among Tweens in the United States: Prevalence, Impact, and Helping Behaviors. *The Journal of Early Adolescence*, *42*(3), 414–430. doi:10.1177/02724316211036740

Peker, A., & Nebioğlu-Yıldız, M. (2021). Mediating Role of Self-control in the Relationship Between Aggressiveness and Cyber Bullying. *Psychiatry and Behavioral Sciences*, *11*(1), 40–49. doi:10.5455/PBS.20210114051215

Pepler, D., & Craig, W. (2009). Responding to Bullying and Harassment: An issue of rights. In W. Boyce, J. Roche, & D. Davies (Eds.), *Adolescent health: Policy, science, and human rights* (pp. 173–196). McGill-Queen's University Press.

Perren, S., Corcoran, L., Cowie, H., Dehue, F., Mc Guckin, C., Sevcikova, A., ... Völlink, T. (2012). Tackling cyberbullying: Review of Empirical Evidence Regarding Successful Responses by Students, Parents, and Schools. *International Journal of Conflict and Violence*, *6*(2), 283–292.

Perren, S., Dooley, J., Shaw, T., & Cross, D. (2010). Bullying in School and Cyberspace: Associations with depressive symptoms in Swiss and Australian adolescents. *Child and Adolescent Psychiatry and Mental Health*, *4*(1), 1–10. doi:10.1186/1753-2000-4-28 PMID:21092266

Pornari, C. D., & Wood, J. (2010). Peer and Cyber Aggression in Secondary School Students: The role of moral disengagement, hostile attribution bias, and outcome expectancies. Aggressive Behavior. *Official Journal of the International Society for Research on Aggression*, *36*(2), 81–94. doi:10.1002/ab.20336 PMID:20035548

Putri, S. A. R., & Prihandari Satvikadewi, A. A. I. (2017). A Critical Discourse Analysis Study of Cyberbullying in LGBTQ's Instagram Account. In *SHS Web of Conferences* (Vol. 33). Academic Press.

Pyżalski, J. (2013). Beyond Peer Cyberbullying: Involvement of Polish adolescents in different kinds of electronic aggression. *Studia Edukacyjne.*, *28*, 147–167.

Rivituso, J. (2014). Cyberbullying Victimization Among College Students: An interpretive phenomenological analysis. *Journal of Information Systems Education*, *25*(1), 71.

Roberto, A. J., Eden, J., Savage, M. W., Ramos-Salazar, L., & Deiss, D. M. (2014). Prevalence and Predictors of Cyberbullying Perpetration by High School Seniors. *Communication Quarterly*, *62*(1), 97–114. doi:10.1080/01463373.2013.860906

Robson, C., & Witenberg, R. T. (2013). The influence of Moral Disengagement, Morally Based Self-esteem, Age, and Gender on Traditional Bullying and Cyberbullying. *Journal of School Violence*, *12*(2), 211–231. doi:10.1080/15388220.2012.762921

Rosenberg, M. (1965). Rosenberg self-esteem scale. *Journal of Religion and Health*.

Rosenberg, M., Schooler, C., & Schoenbach, C. (1989). Self-esteem and Adolescent Problems: Modeling reciprocal effects. *American Sociological Review*, *54*(6), 1004–1018. doi:10.2307/2095720

Segura, M. D., & Pecino, R. M. (2015). Cyberbullying Trough Mobile Phone and the Internet in Dating Relationships Among Youth People. *Comunicar. Media Education Research Journal, 23*(1).

Shadmanfaat, S. M. S., Howell, C. J. M., Muniz, C. N., Cochran, J. K., Kabiri, S., & Richardson, D. A. (2018). The Predictive Ability of Self-control and Differential Association on Sports Fans' Decision to Engage in Cyber Bullying Perpetration Against Rivals. *International Journal of Cyber Criminology*, *12*(2), 362.

Smokowski, P. R., Evans, C. B., & Cotter, K. L. (2014). The Differential Impacts of Episodic, Chronic, and Cumulative Physical Bullying and Cyberbullying: The effects of victimization on the school experiences, social support, and mental health of rural adolescents. *Violence and Victims*, *29*(6), 1029–1046. doi:10.1891/0886-6708.VV-D-13-00076 PMID:25905143

Sobba, K. N., Paez, R. A., & Ten Bensel, T. (2017). Perceptions of Cyberbullying: An assessment of perceived severity among college students. *TechTrends*, *61*(6), 570–579. doi:10.100711528-017-0186-0

Thomas, H. J., Connor, J. P., & Scott, J. G. (2015). Integrating Traditional Bullying and Cyberbullying: Challenges of definition and measurement in adolescents–a review. *Educational Psychology Review*, *27*(1), 135–152. doi:10.100710648-014-9261-7

Trzesniewski, K. H., Donnellan, M. B., Moffitt, T. E., Robins, R. W., Poulton, R., & Caspi, A. (2006). Low Self-esteem During Adolescence Predicts Poor Health, Criminal Behavior, and Limited Economic Prospects During Adulthood. *Developmental Psychology*, *42*(2), 381–390. doi:10.1037/0012-1649.42.2.381 PMID:16569175

Unnever, J. D., Cullen, F. T., & Pratt, T. C. (2003). Parental Management, ADHD, and Delinquent Involvement: Reassessing Gottfredson and Hirschi's general theory. *Justice Quarterly*, *20*(3), 471–500. doi:10.1080/07418820300095591

Van Geel, M., Vedder, P., & Tanilon, J. (2014). Relationship between peer victimization, cyberbullying, and suicide in children and adolescents: A meta-analysis. *JAMA Pediatrics*, *168*(5), 435–442. doi:10.1001/jamapediatrics.2013.4143 PMID:24615300

Wang, L., & Jiang, S. (2021). The effects of strain and negative emotions on adolescent cyberbullying perpetration: An empirical test of general strain theory. *Current Psychology (New Brunswick, N.J.)*, 1–11. doi:10.100712144-021-02426-8

Wilson, C., Sheridan, L., & Garratt-Reed, D. (2020). What is Cyberstalking? A review of Measurements. *Journal of Interpersonal Violence*, 1–21. PMID:33403888

Winkelman, S., Oomen-Early, J., Walker, A. D., Chu, L., & Yick-Flanagan, A. (2015). Exploring Cyber Harassment Among Women Who Use Social Media. *Universal Journal of Public Health, 3*(5), 194–201. doi:10.13189/ujph.2015.030504

Wright, M. F. (2013). The Relationship Between Young Adults' Beliefs About Anonymity and Subsequent Cyber Aggression. *Cyberpsychology, Behavior, and Social Networking, 16*(12), 858–862. doi:10.1089/cyber.2013.0009 PMID:23849002

Zhou, Z., Tang, H., Tian, Y., Wei, H., Zhang, F., & Morrison, C. M. (2013). Cyberbullying and its Risk Factors Among Chinese High School Students. *School Psychology International, 34*(6), 630–647. doi:10.1177/0143034313479692

ADDITIONAL READING

Campbell, M., & Bauman, S. (Eds.). (2018). *Reducing Cyberbullying in Schools: International evidence-based best practices*. Academic Press.

Horowitz, M., & Bollinger, D. M. (2014). *Cyberbullying in Social Media Within Educational Institutions: Featuring student, employee, and parent information*. Rowman & Littlefield.

Joosten, T. (2012). *Social Media for Educators: Strategies and best practices*. John Wiley & Sons.

McQuade, S. C., Colt, J. P., Meyer, N. B., & Meyer, N. B. (2009). *Cyber Bullying: Protecting kids and adults from online bullies*. ABC-CLIO.

Milosevic, T. (2018). *Protecting Children Online? Cyberbullying policies of social media companies*. The MIT Press. doi:10.7551/mitpress/11008.001.0001

Ramos Salazar, L. (Ed.). (2020). *Handbook of Research on Cyberbullying and Online Harassment in the Workplace*. IGI Global. doi:10.4018/978-1-7998-4912-4

Smith, P. K., Steffgen, G., & Sittichai, R. R. (2013). The Nature of Cyberbullying, and an International Network. In *Cyberbullying through the new media* (pp. 3–19). Psychology Press. doi:10.4324/9780203799079

KEY TERMS AND DEFINITIONS

Comparative Criminology: Studies that examine differences in crimes or criminal justice systems in different cultural backgrounds.

Cyber Aggression: Aggressive behaviors using online tools to threaten, humiliate, attack, or insult others psychologically.

Cyber Harassment: Harassment using electronic devices based on communication that annoys, threats, insults, or terrorizes victims.

Cyber Stalking: Repeated and unwanted online contact, communication, tracking targeting an individual or a group of people.

Cyberattack: Online behaviors that lead to negative consequences by destroying victims or their properties, stealing information, exposing harm to victims, or spreading adverse information against victims.

Cyberbullying: Repeated harm with intents to harass victims using technologies or electronic methods.

Cyberbullying Victimization: Being victimized by bullies in online spaces.

International Study: Studies about culture, language, politics, economy, or societies in different countries.

Juvenile Delinquency: Anti-social behaviors committed by people under certain ages that may violate laws in some circumstances.

Social Media: Online spaces being built by users that share various contents such as music, images, videos, or opinions.

Chapter 10
Cyberbullying:
A Form of Peer Violence in the Digital Era

Ines Carvalho Relva
https://orcid.org/0000-0003-3718-8142
University of Trás-os-Montes and Alto Douro, Portugal & Research Center in Sports Sciences, Health Sciences and Human Development, Vila Real, Portugal & Faculty of Psychology and Education Sciences, University of Porto, Portugal

Margarida Simões
University of Trás-os-Montes and Alto Douro, Portugal & Research Center in Sports Sciences, Health Sciences and Human Development, Vila Real, Portugal & Faculty of Psychology and Education Sciences, University of Porto, Portugal

Ana Paula Monteiro
University of Trás-os-Montes and Alto Douro, Portugal & Research Center in Sports Sciences, Health Sciences and Human Development, Vila Real, Portugal & Faculty of Psychology and Education Sciences, University of Porto, Portugal

ABSTRACT

The development of new information technologies has led to new forms of violence between adolescents and young people, frequent users of social networks, chats, and e-messages. Thus, this chapter aims to clarify the concept of cyberbullying and characterize this problem by reflecting on similarities and differences of traditional bullying and its typologies and presenting some prevalence data in different countries, namely during pandemic situation. The authors intend to characterize the participants and roles played in this problem, also reflecting on the consequences for them in the short and long term with an emphasis in the consequences on mental health. The main risk and protection factors of a biopsychosocial nature will be explored considering that this phenomenon is complex and dynamic. Subsequently, preventive strategies will be presented at school and family levels to foster more proactive than reactive responses to the fight against cyberbullying. Finally, some empirically validated intervention strategies stand out.

DOI: 10.4018/978-1-6684-5426-8.ch010

INTRODUCTION

The increasing use of technologies has been changing young people's relationships, offering them the opportunity to communicate with both known and unknown people (Sari & Camadan, 2016), which adds a different dimension to peer relationships between adolescents and young people. This factor allows for faster and anonymous communication, which can lead to less positive issues (Sari & Camadan, 2016) and negative behaviours such as cyberbullying (Huang & Chou, 2010). Also, Zhou et al. (2013) refer that with the increasing use of various electronic resources, a new form of bullying has been increasing and social phenomena that were only seen offline, also began to take place online, as is the case with the transfer of traditional bullying to the Internet – cyberbullying.

Cyberbullying is currently a global problem aggravated by the constraints generated by the pandemic COVID-19 pandemic. In this sense, leaders of international organizations (e.g., ONU, WHO, UNICEF - Board Chair, end Violence Against Children African Child Policy Forum), committed to the protection of children, they signed a document in which they share the concern about this type of violence, appealing for action and promising support to protect children from violence and reduce the impact of COVID-19 on children in all countries and communities.

This chapter intend to bring new information toward this phenomenon exploring definitions, prevalence, also during pandemic time, the different roles toward cyberbullying but also the warning signs of the presence of cyberbullying. Finally, the authors suggest future research and some recommendations toward intervention/ prevention strategies in both contexts (school and family).

BACKGROUD

Definition

Cyberbullying can be defined as a bullying behaviour practiced by one or more individuals using digital communication tools, requiring the presence of three main elements: intention, repetition, and power imbalance (Seixas, Fernandes, & Morais, 2016). The use of technology to harass, threaten, harm, humiliate and intimidate or socially exclude someone in a repetitive and intentional way (OPP, 2020). In turn, Del Rey et al. (2015) defines cyberbullying as an intentional, repeated, and harmful aggression perpetrated through electronic devices, with an imbalance of power between the aggressor and the victim persisting. Regarding the definition of cyberbullying, recent qualitative research (Jacobs, Goossens, Dehue, Völlink, & Lechner, 2015) using focus group realized with low-educated Dutch adolescents between 12 and 15 cyberbullying victims stressed the distinct perspective on perceiving certain behaviors as cyberbullying. For example, victims agreed as cyberbullying talking negatively about family as cyberbullying but not agreed about calling name, received mail bombs as cyberbullying.

At present, the debate about the differences and similarities between bullying and cyberbullying persists (Garaigordobil, 2018). Cyberbullying retains some of the characteristics of traditional bullying and can be considered a new form of bullying, but with unique features granted by technology. Cyberbullying is like bullying in that it represents premeditated and intentional stalking or violent behaviour; there is an asymmetrical relationship of control and power between the aggressor and the victim, and it occurs in a repetitive or continuous way (Garaigordobil, 2018). However, it is a more complex phenomenon and with more serious consequences for being practiced online or through any technological devices.

Thus, the main differences are the anonymity of the aggressor, the public potential becomes uncontrollable, the constant nature of victimization through the constant presence of ICTs in everyday life, the increased difficulty in identifying the perpetrator and the imbalance of power created for the anonymity (O'Higgins Norman, 2020; Patchin & Hinduja, 2006; Smith, 2013). In addition, the aggressor does not observe the victim's immediate reactions, which facilitates his "moral disengagement", resulting in less remorse and lack of empathy for the victim's suffering (Smith, 2013). Additionally, comparing both tradition bullying and online bullying, although some behaviors are similar, power imbalance it is not necessary a precondition to cyberbullying perpetration according with Dennehy et al. (2020). The same it happens with the aspect of repetition that have more difficulty to applicate to cyberbullying (Slonje, Smith, & Frisén, 2013). Indeed, the author argued that "the nature of the cyber world alters the distribution of power and within cyberbullying power relations can be identified as fluid and changeable. Features such as anonymity, ambiguity, accessibility, and public exposure are experienced as disempowering by victims and empowering by perpetrators" (p. 9). Waasdorp and Bradshaw (2015) argue that in fact, one incident can be repeated when several persons viewed the same issue posted online.

The forms that cyberbullying adopts are very varied, giving rise to the development of different typologies. Thus, Vandebosh and Van Cleemput (2009), starting from the classification of traditional bullying, categorize cyberbullying into direct and indirect. In direct cyberbullying, the victim is directly involved and includes the following types: physical: against property (sending a virus to damage a computer); verbal (using the Internet or cell phone to insult or threaten); nonverbal (sending obscene or threatening images) and social (excluding someone from an online group). As for indirect cyberbullying, it can occur without the victim's (immediate) knowledge. Examples of this type of Cyberbullying are sending emails with confidential information; dissimulation (impersonating someone); spread rumours via mobile phone, email, or chat; election on a web page dedicated to defaming someone. It should be noted that the internet and mobile phone offer numerous possibilities for the practice of indirect cyberbullying.

One of the most complete and consensual typologies is the classification proposed by Willard (2007), based on the types of technological aggression: i) Flaming - repeatedly sending offensive, threatening or intimidating messages to someone, via email, SMS, MMS or others; ii) Denigration / humiliation - sending or publishing false, harmful and cruel messages, images or videos that harm someone's honour; iii) Impersonation - impersonating the victim online and sending or posting material to cause trouble or danger, or harm reputation or friendships; iv) Outing - sharing someone's embarrassing secrets, events or videos on the network (e.g., blogs, social networks or chat rooms); *v*) Exclusion - intentionally excluding someone from an online group or activity; vi) Deceive - approach someone, in order to obtain secrets or embarrassing information, in order to disclose them later on the network; and vii) Cyberstalking - repeated, intense harassment and defamation that includes threats and generates significant fear (Willard, 2007).

Willard's taxonomy inspired many later categorization approaches, for example Nocentini et al. (2010) synthesized the categories to four, focusing on the nature of the incident: written verbal (sending messages), visual (sending photos), impersonation (using someone else's profile or information), and exclusion (excluding someone from groups and online networks). Another potentially serious form of cyberbullying is Happy Slapping, which consists of the dissemination of videos containing situations of physical and/or verbal aggression towards a victim, with the aim of humiliating him (Casper, 2021).

The different types of cyberbullying presented allow us to understand the complexity of the phenomenon, so a multidimensional categorization can be useful to classify the individuals involved in this problem. The various classification approaches entail different strengths and weaknesses, so depending on the objective with which cyberbullying is approached (e.g., prevention strategies, research projects), researchers and technicians can adopt one or a combination of classification typologies to capture the dimensions of cyberbullying (Casper, 2021).

The severity of cyberbullying has been considered as dependent of its visibility. In a recent study conducted by Macaulay, Betts, Stiller, and Kellezi (2022) with 990 students with ages between 11 and 20, young people were more likely to perceive as more severe cyberbullying when occurred in public scenarios (e.g., they and everybody else could see this).

Finally, it has been reported in the literature that adolescents with reduced self-esteem and self-confidence, emotionally and verbally abused and overly criticized have a great propensity to develop over time critical thoughts about themselves promoting self-aggressive behaviors giving rise to the concept of self-cyberbullying, which through the use of social networks anonymously promotes psychological damage to oneself (e.g., publishes hostile content), with the purpose of attracting the attention of adults and peers, gaining positive reinforcements, sympathy and admiration from online observers (Figueiredo, 2015).

PREVALENCE

The variability in prevalence results from the disagreement between researchers in defining cyberbullying (Peter & Peterman, 2018). Research has sought to know the prevalence of cyberbullying in different countries; however, the use of different methodologies, instruments and analysis criteria makes it difficult to draw consistent conclusions. In the international study carried out by the EU Kids Online project (Livingstone, Haddon, Görzig, & Ólafsson, 2011), in which 25,142 children from 25 European countries were surveyed, it was found that 6% said they had been a victim of cyberbullying (while 13% considered they had been cyberbullied). victim of face-to-face bullying). The results show the presence of high-risk countries such as Poland and Romania and low-risk countries such as Belgium. Data related to the age of those involved point to a higher prevalence between 12 and 14 years old (Livingstone et al., 2011).

In an investigation carried out by Buelga, Martínez-Ferrer, and Cava (2017) with 1062 adolescents of both sexes (51.4% boys and 48.5% girls) aged between 12 and 18 years, it was observed that many adolescents and young people are involved in cyberbullying. 28.4% of the young teenagers involved are cyberbullying aggressors, 18.64% are cyberbullying aggressors and victims and 9.3% are cyberbullying victims. In a systematic review by Brochado, Soares, and Fraga (2017) based on 159 studies (mostly from North America and Europe) a prevalence between 1% and 61.1% is reported, while reports of aggression vary between 3% and 39%. Lee and Shin (2017) investigated 4000 Korean adolescents with the aim of knowing the prevalence and factors of cyberbullying perpetration. The results showed that approximately one in three students surveyed were involved in cyberbullying as a bully (6.3%), victim (14.6%) or bully and victim (13.1%). The authors mention that despite the difficulty in establishing a comparison between countries, the pattern of the prevalence rate seems identical to that of other countries in which the percentage of victims is higher than that of perpetrators (Lee & Shin, 2017).

Prevalence data in some studies also show some overlap between bullying and cyberbullying, and in the investigation by Wachs, Junger, and Sittichai (2015) with 1,928 German, Dutch and Thai adolescents, the data showed that 2.4% said they were aggressors, 5.7% said they were victims and 1.8% said they were both victims and aggressors in face-to-face and online contexts. In turn, the investigation by Cosma et al. (2020) analysed transnational trends in the period from 2002 to 2014 in the occurrence of bullying victimization in 37 countries and the overlap between cybervictimization and traditional bullying in adolescents. The results obtained indicated a prevalence of cyber-victimization tending to be lower than that of traditional victimization. The results also showed that in all countries, 45.8% of those who reported suffering from cyber victimization also reported being victims of traditional bullying (46.5% of male adolescents and 45.3% of female adolescents), having large variations were observed between countries.

In Portugal, the EU Kids Online report (2019), which presents data from 1974 participants between 9 and 17 years of age, revealed that cyberbullying predominates over bullying. Victims of this type of aggression indicated that it occurs several times a month, through calls, messages or otherwise, and one in six children and young people who experienced cyberbullying (16%) had to do things they did not want to do (Ponte & Batista, 2019).

Cyberbullying in a university context is a less studied reality compared to research carried out in previous educational stages (Cara & Moya, 2022). In the study by Méndez et al. (2019) with 765 Spanish university students from various scientific areas, the data showed that 14.4% were victims of cyberbullying, 7.3% exercised cyberbullying and 17.4% observed this problem. The results of the study also showed that women, under 20s and undergraduate students in the areas of Humanities, Social Sciences and Health Sciences obtained higher values as aggressors, victims, and bystanders of this problem. However, current literature describes an increase in cyberbullying among university students with very variable prevalence rates ranging from 10% to 60% in different countries (Khine et al., 2020).

A reduce number of studies have focus on prevalence of cyberbullying regarding children and young with disability. However, results of one (Kowalski & Toth, 2018) those studies that have been conducted with young with disabilities (e.g., ADHD, Autism Spectrum Disorder, Physical Disability) found that although both groups (young's with and without disabilities) show high rates of cybervictimization, young with disabilities displayed high levels of cybervictimization. The authors argued that this rate could be related with high rate of time spend online per day when compared with those without disability.

Due to the COVID-19 pandemic, Information and Communication Technologies (ICT) have become indispensable to satisfy a set of needs (e.g., education, entertainment, interpersonal relationships), leading many adolescents and young people to spend a lot of time on social networks, which may increase the number of cyberbullying cases (Babvey et al., 2020; Yahya, Khawaja, & Chukwuma, 2020).

According to UNICEF (United Nations Children's International Emergency Fund), one in three children say they have been victims of cyberbullying and one in five children have stopped going to school because of it. Cyberbullying can lead a person to end their own life (UNICEF, 2020). Given the conditions created by the pandemic, the lack of face-to-face contact with friends and companions can lead children and young people to take more risks, for example, by sending more sexualized content. The increase in time spent online in an unstructured way can expose children and young people to potentially harmful and violent content, as well as increase the risk of being cyberbullied (UNICEF, 2020).

In this sense, the investigation by Barlett, Simmers, Roth, and Gentile (2021) examined whether cyberbullying processes and frequency were affected by the COVID-19 pandemic, comparing results obtained with adult US participants before the start of the pandemic (July 2019; $n = 181$) with data collected during the pandemic (May 2020; $n = 173$) to determine whether there were significant differences in perceptions of anonymity, belief in the irrelevance of muscularity for online bullying, attitudes of accepting cyberbullying, and perpetrating cyberbullying. The results showed that there were significant increases regarding belief in the irrelevance of muscularity/physical strength in online bullying, attitudes of acceptance of cyberbullying and perpetration of cyberbullying during the pandemic, but there was no significant change in perceptions of anonymity. In addition, the association between some predictors of cyberbullying perpetration variables (e.g., anonymity, cyberbullying attitudes) was stronger during the pandemic period.

In Portugal within the pandemic context António, Guerra and Moleiro (2020) carried out a survey with 485 students (aged between 16 and 34 years old) from primary, secondary and higher education from all districts in the country and found that 61.4% of their participants had been victims of cyberbullying. The results also showed that male students, those from families with lower family incomes and gay or lesbian students were the main victims.

In turn, in the investigation by Babvey et al. (2020), the authors found that the number of abusive messages increased in all countries except Sweden. Growth was significant in Indonesia, the Philippines, Portugal, and Brazil, with an increase of over 30% comparing 2020 to 2019 (Babvey et al., 2020).

PARTICIPANT ROLES

Giumetti and Kowalski (2022) considers that could seems to exist three participant roles in cyberbullying: the victim, the perpetrator and being a bystander or witness of cyberbullying. The line between cyberbullying and cybervictimization seems to be very tenue. Due to their specific characteristics, that are distinct from offline bullying, made the distinction of roles of aggressor and victims a difficult task. In study conducted by Barlettt and Gentile (2012) with university students found an association between cyber-victimization and cyberbullying, suggesting a retaliation as motivation.

The witnesses of cyberaggression also called as "hybrid bystander", when occurred a change from offline to online bullying (Price et al., 2014) but also cyber-bystanders have seen increased attention in research (Machackova, 2020) According with Moxey and Bussey (2020) bystanders may have an important a role in either reducing or in escalating of cyberbullying, being constructive or aggressive when intervening in cyberbullying incidents. In their study with Australian adolescents aged 12–17 years were who completed a self - bystander intervention was analyzed, females reported higher constructive intervention behaviours when compared with males. Bystanders can have an important role, since they have the "capacity to morally engage in cyberbullying incidents; however, there are various barriers to their active positive engagement" (Price et al., 2014; p. 1). These difficulties could be related with the heterogeneity that this role present and their several types that this role could assume (cf. Polanco-Levincán & Salvo-Garrido, 2021).

WARNING SIGNS OF THE PRESENSE OF CYBERBULLYING

In Cyberbullying, the anonymity of the aggressor causes in the victims a substantial increase in the levels of fear, anxiety, pressure, and stress, with victims often having the impression that they are continuously being observed and persecuted (Seixas et al., 2016), causing feelings of unprotection and impotence, infecting those who are present, peers and adults, due to the difficulty in discovering and facing these attacks. These attacks can occur at anytime and anywhere, without any limit, and the spread of aggression can reach dimensions worldwide, without the aggressor having to directly face the clash of his behavior, gaining the cyberbullying very disturbing contours (Patrão & Sampaio, 2016). Thus, victims of cyberbullying exhibit warning signs that contribute to the awareness of the problem: absenteeism, school phobia, low school performance, avoiding home leaving, self-blaming, school disinterest, worsening physical health, general disinterest, tendency to social isolation, decreased socialization capacity, which will eventually affect the relationship with peers (Dobry, Braquehais, & Sher, 2013; Fisher et al., 2012; Seixas et al., 2016; Wendt & Lisboa, 2013); increase in psychological problems (e.g., hopelessness, impotence and fear) (Sticca & Perren, 2013), depression, anxiety, frustration low self-esteem, helplessness, social anxiety, reduced concentration, self-mutilation and suicidal ideation (Kowalski, Giumetti, Schroeder, & Lattanner, 2014), psychosomatic symptoms (e.g., headaches, abdominal pain and sleep and feeding disorders (Hansen, Hasselgard, Undheim, & Indredavik, 2013; Patchin & Hinduja, 2010), behavior problems (e.g., increased alcohol consumption, smoking and poor academic performance) (Mitchell, Ybarra, & Finkelhor, 2007).

Risk and Protector Factors

Regarding risk and protector factors, it is important to explore the distinct roles that young assume. However, there are personal variables that together seems to predict both cyberbullying perpetration and victimization forms such loneliness, empathy, and self-esteem (Brewer & Kerslake, 2015).

According to Lee et al. (2021) considered that protective factors are not only associated with a lower risk for cyberbullying perpetration mut can also contribute as a buffering effect in some negative behaviors. In a recent systematic review conducted by Zich, Farrington, and Ttofi (2019) with eighteen meta-analyses they found that have self-oriented personal competencies, parental monitoring and supervision and positive peer-interaction were protector factors of any cyberbullying role. Additionally, both school climate and safety, and perceived support (Kowalski et al., 2014), morality and self-control (Lee, Song, & Park, 2021) have been considered a protector factor of cyberbullying victimization.

Looking for risk factors, several factors have been associated with cyberbullying victimization, namely high levels of family conflict, low satisfaction levels (Rodriguez-Rivas, Varela, González, & Chuecas, 2022), negative communication pattern with both parents (Pereira, Fernandes, & Relva, *submitted*) intimate partner violence, child maltreatment, and elder abuse (QiQi, Lo, Zhu, Cheung, Chan, & Ip, 2018) aggressor-perceived anonymity (Barlett et al., 2016) and perceived difficulties, feelings of unsafe at school and uncared by teachers, and headaches (Sourander et al., 2010).

Regarding cyberaggression, positive attitudes toward cyberbullying, associated with both positive attitudes toward strength differential and anonymity (Barlett & Gentile, 2012) impulsivity and callous unemotional traits have identified as predictors of aggression in cyberbullying (Pascual-Sanchez et al., 2021) conduct problems, hyperactivity, and prosocial deficits behavior (Sourander et al., 2010) have been identified as risk factors. Personality traits also seems to be related with cyberbullying perpetration. In a recent study conducted by Xu and Zheng (2022) with a sample of 549 university students found that conscientiousness, agreeableness, and openness were significantly negatively correlated with cyberbullying perpetration.

Although there are already several factors identified as being associated with this phenomenon, research still need it, technology is also changing across the time, with bullies also improving the way they attack the victims.

THEORETICAL PERSPECTIVES

Although the importance of theory for better understand the phenomenon in study, the fact is that it is scarce the research of theory-driven applied to the cyberbullying perpetration (Barlett, 2017). In 2012, Barlett and Gentile developed the Barlett and Gentile Cyberbullying Model that it is considered by the authors the first psychological model that offers theoretical predictions of the cyberbullying. This model "posits that each time an individual cyber-attacks another, the provocateur likely perceives themselves to be anonymous and believes that they can cyber-attack anybody independent of their own or others' muscularity" (Barlett et al., 2019; p. 250-251). Although recent, this model has been used in some research's that helps to validated him (Barlett, Madison, Heath, & DeWitt, 2016; 2019; Barlett & Chamberlin, 2017).

In 2004, Suler presented the "online disinhibition effect" toward the internet user and that can have opposite directions, either benign or toxic disinhibition that can help in cyberbullying understanding. "For example, hostile words in a chat encounter could be a therapeutic breakthrough for some people. In an increasingly intimate e-mail relationship, people may quickly reveal personal information, then later regret their self-disclosures - feeling exposed, vulnerable, or shameful" (Suler, 2004; p. 321-322). The causes presented by the author for this disinhibition could be six: dissociative anonymity; invisibility; asynchronicity; solipsistic introjection; dissociative imagination and minimization of status and authority.

Althout the existence of some theories the research exploring theoretical aproches are scarce so some theories are needed it in order to better understand this specific phenomen.

CONSEQUENCES OF CYBERBULLYING

Regarding consequences, "a number of positive relationships were found between cyberbullying victimization and psychosocial and behavioral variables, including stress, anxiety, depression, loneliness, conduct problems, emotional problems, somatic symptoms, and drug and alcohol use" in a review and meta-analysis of cyberbullying conducted by Kowalski et al. (2014; p. 1124). Additionally self-harm and suicidal attempts were also high prevalent in adolescents (Yang et al., 2021) and non-suicidal self-injury (Wiguna et al., 2021). Kim, Kimber, Boyle, and Georgiades (2019) with a sample of adolescents with a mean age of 15.1 years, victims of cyberbullying found that females when compared with males reported high levels of psychological distress, suicidal ideation, and delinquency. In young with disabilities victims of cybervictimization both low self-esteem and depression were present (Kowalski, Morgan, Drake-Lavelle, & Allison, 2016). However, both cyberbullies and cybervictims present harmful consequences, "the most troubled are those who are both bullies and victims" (Sourander et al., 2010; p. 727).

Regarding bystanders, some authors (Obermaier, Fawzi, & Koch, 2016; Rafferty & Vander Vem, 2014) show that when they do not feel any connection and feeling of security with the victim do not intervene, remaining inactive, presenting a greater propensity to perpetuate cyberbullying. In addition, bystanders, when united of the aggressors, can encourage them to behave even more aggressively with the victim (Bastiaensens et al., 2014; Brody &Vangelisti 2016). Bystanders learn to be indifferent citizens, adopting attitudes of distancing and non-intervention in situations that cause suffering to others, with evident repercussions on their sociomoral development (Amado & Freire, 2002).

CYBERBULLYING EVALUATION

According with González-Cabrera et al. (2017) regarding the occurrence of cyberbullying, instead of the focus on electronic media used should be the type of intimidating behaviors. There are few measures regarding cyberbullying, one of them it is the Cyber Victimization Questionnaire for Adolescents (CYVIC; Álvarez-García, Núñez, Barreiro-Collazo, & García, 2017) used to evaluate to five types of cyber-victimization: verbal cyber-victimization; online exclusion; visual-sexual cyber-victimization; visual cyber-victimization – teasing/happy slapping and impersonation. Like the CYVIC, the Cyber-Aggression Questionnaire for Adolescents (CYBA; Álvarez-García et al., 2016) with the same indicators and response format as the CYVIC but used to evaluate cyberaggression.

Another measure it is the European Cyberbullying Intervention Project Questionnaire (ECIPQ) scale consists of 22 items, of which 11 items assess aggressive behaviours (e.g., "Said nasty/insulting words about someone to other people on the internet or in messages") and 11 items assess bullying victimization behaviours (e.g.," "Someone made nasty/insulting comments about me using the internet or messaging"). It was developed as part of the European project "Cyberbullying in Adolescence: Investigation and Intervention in Six European Countries'" – ECIPQ (Brighi et al., 2012), was subsequently validated in six European countries with excellent psychometric results (Del Rey et al., 2015). It was also used in Portugal (Monteiro, Fonseca, & Correia, submitted). Finally, the Cyberbullying-Victimization Questionnaire – CBQ -V (Estévez, Villardón, Calvete, Padilla, & Orue, 2010) is a self-response instrument that assesses the frequency of different forms of victimization caused by cyberbullying, and which showed good internal consistency.

Finally, a more specific measure it is the Styles of Bystander Intervention Scale developed by Moxey and Bussey (2020) based on Luo and Bussey's (2019) work to assess styles of bystander intervention. with three subscales (each with five items): aggressive, constructive victim-focused and constructive bully-focused intervention, to evaluate bystander responses to cyberbullying occurrences.

As already mentioned, the differences in measures used in cyberbullying evaluation also contribute to the variability in prevalence (Peter & Peterman, 2018).

PREVENTION AND INTERVENTION

Given the destructive effects of cyberbullying, strategies and prevention, intervention and combating cyberbullying should be a priority. The authors start by addressing school-level preventive strategies, focus on four of the main aspects: Cyberbullying and curriculum; Creation of a team; Assessment of the situation; Development of an action plan (Seixas et al., 2016). Cyberbullying and curriculum, cyberbullying can fall into a violation of human rights and more specifically in the rights of the child. In the school context, this theme could be framed in different curricular units, but so far it has not been framed in any of them. The authors argue that combating cyberbullying is not a priority for education policies or teacher training. This applies in several countries, where recently there has been a movement to include the theme of cyberbullying in the school curriculum and in the training of teachers.

The creation of a team is understood as a fundamental action to combat cyberbullying, involving all actors of the school community, the surrounding health networks, municipalities, and other existing informal groups (Seixas et al., 2016). These authors argues that its constitution is to jointly analyze the phenomenon, to create methodologies, policies, procedures, and strategies to prevent and combat cyberbullying. Assessment of the situation by the team constituted above will be to understand the size of the problem and make the diagnosis of the needs existing in the school community. To do this, data collection will have to be carried out using qualitative and/or quantitative methods. The implementation of an action plan will be developed from the analysis of the collected data, which is recommended to include: training and awareness raising (at the level of the entire school community, such as students of different levels of school, teachers, staff, parents and parents and guardians, enhancing the change of beliefs, behaviors, social norms, establishing supportive and trust relationships and transforming the school environment in order to cyberbullying is seen as unacceptable behavior); policies and procedures (schools will have to establish policies for the use of different information technologies, it is also advisable that schools start by defining objective rules and their consequences, which include disciplinary procedures that should be known not only to students but also to parents. In the policies defined, victim reporting systems and bystanders should also be included to prevent Cyberbullying from being reported); incident response plan (subsequent reporting it is necessary to support the victim, as well as his family, implementing an intervention program with the victim, the aggressor, and the bystander) (Seixas et al., 2016).

Regarding prevention, one of the things according to Diamanduros, Downs, and Jenkins (2008) that should be done it is to "have a thoughtful and detailed prevention plan that should be based on the assessment findings conducted in the school. School psychologists can help schools develop an anti-cyberbullying prevention plan in coordination with other schools in the district so that all schools are consistent in their efforts to prevent cyberbullying" (p. 698). At home, the role of parental control in cyberbullying (Zhu, Huang, Evans, & Zhang, 2021) it is also an important issue.

Research on effective intervention regarding cyberbullying is scarce. In a recent systematic and meta-analytical review conducted by Gaffney, Farrington, Espelage, and Ttofi (2019) 24 publications were included. The authors concluded that both cyberbullying perpetration (in approximately 10% to 15%) and victimization (in approximately 14%) can be reduced by the implementation of effective cyberbullying intervention programs, however more intervention programs are need it.

Therefore, cyberbullying interventions must cover different skills promotion, and cover different approaches different from those used to reduce bullying in their traditional form (Pascual-Sanchez et al., 2021). For example, based on the assumption that "cyberbullying is motivated by jealousy the promotion of alternative avenues for building self-esteem may be of benefit, while training in conflict resolution and positive coping skills may serve to mitigate the risks of cyber-revenge" (Dennehy et al., 2020; p. 10), additionally self-esteem or empathy-based interventions are also recommended (Brewer & Kerslake, 2015), with these intervention starting as earlier as soon as possible (Pascual-Sanchez et al., 2021). More specifically, and due to pandemic situation that the world faced in the last two years some authors proposed the develop of programs toward adolescent that may help reduce stress toward cyberbullying and increase coping strategies (Wiguna et al., 2021) but also useful in others life stressful events were the screen time has an increase.

Although, and according with Sourander et al. (2010; p. 727) the "rapid technological changes, the anonymity of the perpetrator, and the potentially large audience make cyberbullying more complicated to prevent than traditional bullying". However more interventions that involve all community school members should be implement.

Another important level of intervention it is at family, where some empirically validated strategies will be highlighted. Hutson, Kelly and Militello (2018) developed a study with the objective of doing a systematic review (where seventeen cyberbullying intervention programs were found in 23 articles) to analyze intervention studies for young people (under 18 years of age) involved in cyberbullying (aggressor and victim); evaluate the impact of parents' inclusion in the intervention and provide recommendations on effective intervention components to formulate clinical practice guidelines. The main conclusions of the study were:

- Implement cyberbullying interventions that contain evidence-based intervention components.
- Most intervention programs included primary and secondary prevention with the purpose of preventing the occurrence of cyberbullying or minimizing the impact after its occurrence.
- The programs have been applied exclusively in schools, focusing only on primary and secondary prevention, putting aside tertiary prevention or chronic conditions, i.e., young people involved in cyberbullying (victim and aggressor) and with mental health problems.
- Training in empathy (training young people to put themselves in the perspective of the victim or spectator) was present in nine of the programs.
- Digital citizenship (use of technology responsibly or being a good online citizen) was found in thirteen of the programs.
- Parent education was included in seven of the successful programs in reducing cyberbullying and cybervictimization. As recommendations for practice, the authors believe that the intervention in Cyberbullying should not only take place in the school context but extend to other contexts, namely the health context. It is also advised by the same authors to follow recommendations from the American Academy of Pediatrics to address bullying and cyberbullying.

Finally, to prevent cyberbullying more information toward the consequences of cyberbullying should be directed to educational agents (school staff, parents, educators) but also young.

FUTURE RESEARCH DIRECTIONS

Future studies should explore the prevalence of cyberbullying toward children and young with disabilities to better defined suitable strategies. It is also important to take in count the different roles that bystanders can assume to plan and develop interventions (Polanco-Levicán & Salvo-Garrido, 2021). Despite others risk factors, the anonymity should also be explored in intervention programs. In fact, Barlett, Gentile, and Chew (2016) suggest that "we can inform internet users that they are not anonymous and show them evidence of IP address tracking and how history folders operate, then perhaps cyberbullying will decrease" (p. 178). Therefore, this should be an issue integrated in intervention programs to clarify the wrong idea of anonymity in internet. Additionally, more studies where bullying and cyberbullying could be compared there still a lack of knowledge.

However, the authors suggest transnational studies since "the internet provides enormous opportunities to connect young people from all over the world, cyberbullying perpetrators may come from transnational networks" (Zhu et al., 2021).

CONCLUSIONS

Cyberbullying it is a worldwide problem, and therefore transversal, having increased the prevalence with the emergence of the pandemic, necessarily reflecting in terms of mental health.

For all those involved in the problem, there are consequences with implications in the different areas of the individual (family, school, inter and intrapersonal). The role of the victim has aroused greater scientific interest, and the role of aggressor, observer and aggressor-victim is less studied. This finding opens new lines of research that seek to characterize each of the roles involved in this problem and contribute to the development of prevention and intervention programs that consider the specificities of all those involved in Cyberbullying.

The focus should be mainly on prevention, instrument development and emphasis on intervention. This problem must be intervened in a global way (school, family, community, primary health care), with both safe, responsible, and respectful internet habits – digital citizenship. It is important that the school develops programs at the level of socio-emotional competence at the level of the first cycle.

More clinical interventions in chronic situations of cyberbullying are need it since it appears that there a scarce investment by the states in health policies. As internet usage is increasing, the authors defend that internet can be a vehicle of sensibilization of its dangers and the impact that some online behaviors have in others, namely in young.

ACKNOWLEDGMENT

National funds support the author Inês Relva' s work through the FCT—Portuguese Foundation for Science and Technology under the project the Scientific Employment Stimulus - Institutional Call – CEECINST/00127/2018.

REFERENCES

Álvarez-García, D., Barreiro-Collazo, A., Núñez, J. C., & Dobarro, A. (2016). Validity and reliability of the Cyber-aggression Questionnaire for Adolescents (CYBA). *The European Journal of Psychology Applied to Legal Context*, *8*(2), 69–77. doi:10.1016/j.ejpal.2016.02.003

Álvarez-García, D., Núñez, J. C., Collazo, A., & García, T. (2017). Validation of the Cybervictimization Questionnaire (CYVIC) for adolescents. *Computers in Human Behavior*, *70*, 270–281. doi:10.1016/j.chb.2017.01.007

Amado, J., & Freire, I. (2002). *Indisciplina e violência na Escola. Compreender para prevenir* [Indiscipline and violence at school. Understand to prevent]. Edições Asa.

António, R., Guerra, R., & Moleiro, C. (2020). *Cyberbullying em Portugal durante a pandemia do Covid-19* [Cyberbullying in Portugal during the Covid-19 pandemic]. Centro de Investigação e de Intervenção Social (CIS-IUL, ISCTE-IUL).

Babvey, P., Capela, F., Cappa, C., Lipizzi, C., Petrowski, N., & Ramirez-Marquez, J. (2021). Using social media data for assessing children's exposure to violence during the COVID-19 pandemic. *Child Abuse & Neglect*, *116*, 104747. doi:10.1016/j.chiabu.2020.104747 PMID:33358281

Barlett, C. (2017). From theory to practice: Cyberbullying theory and its application to intervention. *Computers in Human Behavior*, *72*, 269–275. doi:10.1016/j.chb.2017.02.060

Barlett, C., & Chamberlin, K. (2017). Examining cyberbullying across the lifespan. *Computers in Human Behavior, 71*, 444–449. doi:10.1016/j.chb.2017.02.009

Barlett, C., & Gentile, D. A. (2012). Attacking others online: The formation of cyberbullying in late adolescence. *Psychology of Popular Media Culture, 1*, 123-135. doi:10.1037/a0028113

Barlett, C., Madison, C. J., Heath, J., & DeWitt, C. (2019). A correlational examination of technology access and time spent online in the Barlett Gentile Cyberbullying Model. *Computers in Human Behavior, 92*, 250–255. doi:10.1016/j.chb.2018.11.013

Barlett, C. P., Gentile, D. A., & Chew, C. (2016). Predicting cyberbullying from anonymity. *Psychology of Popular Media Culture, 5*(2), 171–180. doi:10.1037/ppm0000055

Barlett, C. P., Simmers, M. M., Roth, B., & Gentile, D. (2021). Comparing cyberbullying prevalence and process before and during the COVID-19 pandemic. *The Journal of Social Psychology, 161*(4), 408–418. doi:10.1080/00224545.2021.1918619 PMID:34128768

Bastiaensens, S., Vandebosch, H., Poels, K., Cleemput, K., Desmet, A., & Bourdeaudhuij, I. (2014). Cyberbullying on social network sites. An experimental study into bystanders' behavioural intentions to help the victim or reinforce the bully. *Computers in Human Behavior, 31*, 259–271. doi:10.1016/j.chb.2013.10.036

Brewer, G., & Kerslake, J. (2015). Cyberbullying, self-esteem, empathy, and loneliness. *Computers in Human Behavior, 48*, 255–260. doi:10.1016/j.chb.2015.01.073

Brighi, A., Ortega, R., Pyzalski, J., Scheithauer, H., Smith, P. K., & Tsormpatzoudis, H. (2012). *European cyberbullying intervention project questionnaire – ECIPQ* [Unpublished questionnaire]. bullyingandcyber.net

Brochado, S., Soares, S., & Fraga, S. (2017). A scoping review on studies of cyberbullying prevalence among adolescents. *Trauma, Violence & Abuse, 18*(5), 523–531. doi:10.1177/1524838016641668 PMID:27053102

Brody, N., & Vangelisti, A. L. (2016). Bystander intervention in cyberbullying. *Communication Monographs, 83*(1), 94–119. doi:10.1080/03637751.2015.1044256

Buelga, S., Martínez-Ferrer, B., & Cava, M. J. (2017). Differences in family climate and family communication among cyberbullies, cybervictims, and cyber bully victims in adolescents. *Computers in Human Behavior, 76*, 164–173. doi:10.1016/j.chb.2017.07.017

Cara, M. J., & Moya, E. (2022). Cyberbullying in university students before and after COVID-19 lockdown. *Educación XX1, 25*(1), 67-91. doi:10.5944/educxx1.30525

Casper, D. M. (2021). Types of traditional (offline) bullying. In P. K. Smith & J. O. Norman (Eds.), *The Wiley Blackwell handbook of bullying: A comprehensive and international review of research and intervention* (pp. 96–119). Wiley Blackwell. doi:10.1002/9781118482650.ch6

Chen, Q. Q., Lo, C. K. M., Zhu, Y., Cheung, A., Chan, K. L., & Ip, P.QiQi. (2018). Family poly-victimization and cyberbullying among adolescents in a Chinese school sample. *Child Abuse & Neglect, 77*, 180–187. doi:10.1016/j.chiabu.2018.01.015 PMID:29407606

Cosma, A., Walsh, S. D., Chester, K. L., Callaghan, M., Molcho, M., Craig, W., & Pickett, W. (2020). Bullying victimization: Time trends and the overlap between traditional and cyberbullying across countries in Europe and North America. *International Journal of Public Health*, *65*(1), 75–85. doi:10.100700038-019-01320-2 PMID:31844919

Del Rey, R., Casas, J. A., Ortega-Ruiz, R., Schultze-Krumbholz, A., Scheithauer, H., Smith, P., & Guarini, A. (2015). Structural validation and cross-cultural robustness of the European Cyberbullying Intervention Project Questionnaire. *Computers in Human Behavior*, *50*, 141–147. doi:10.1016/j.chb.2015.03.065

Dennehy, R., Meaney, S., Walsh, K., Sinnott, C., Cronin, M., & Arensman, E. (2020). Young people's conceptualizations of the nature of cyberbullying: A systematic review and synthesis of qualitative research. *Aggression and Violent Behavior*, *51*, 101379. doi:10.1016/j.avb.2020.101379

Diamanduros, T., Downs, E., & Jenkins, S. J. (2008). The role of school psychologists in the assessment, prevention, and intervention of cyberbullying. *Psychology in the Schools*, *45*(8), 693–704. doi:10.1002/pits.20335

Dobry, Y., Braquehais, M. D., & Sher, L. (2013). Bullying, psychiatric pathology and suicidal behavior. *International Journal of Adolescent Medicine and Health*, *25*(3), 295–299. doi:10.1515/ijamh-2013-0065 PMID:24006324

Estévez, A., Villardón, L., & Calvete, E., Padilla, P., & Orue, I. (2010). Adolescentes víctimas de cyberbullying: Prevalência y características [Adolescents viral from cyberbullying: Prevalence and characteristics]. *Psicología Conductual*, *18*, 73–89.

Figueiredo, F. (2015). Redes sociais: Um suporte para a prática do self-cyberbullying [Social networks: A support for the practice of self-cyberbullying]. *Educação Sociedade & Culturas*, *44*, 107–129.

Fisher, H., Moffitt, T., Houts, R., Belsky, D., Arseneault, L., & Caspi, A. (2012). Bullying victimization and risk of self-harm in early adolescence: Longitudinal cohort study. *British Medical Journal*, *344*, 1–9. PMID:22539176

Gaffney, H., Farrington, D., Espelage, D., & Ttofi, M. (2019). Are cyberbullying intervention and prevention programs effective? A systematic and meta-analytical review. *Aggression and Violent Behavior*, *45*, 34–153. doi:10.1016/j.avb.2018.07.002

Giumetti, G. W., & Kowalski, R. (2022). Cyberbullying via social media and well-being. *Current Opinion in Psychology*, *45*, 101314. doi:10.1016/j.copsyc.2022.101314 PMID:35313180

Hansen, H., Hasselgard, C., Undheim, A., & Indredavik, M. (2013). Bullying behaviour among Norwegian adolescents: Psychiatric diagnoses and school well-being in a clinical sample. *Nordic Journal of Psychiatry*, *68*(5), 355–361. doi:10.3109/08039488.2013.845689 PMID:24161252

Huang, Y., & Chou, C. (2010). An analysis of multiple factors of cyberbullying next term among junior high school students in Taiwan. *Computers in Human Behavior*, *26*(6), 1581–1590. doi:10.1016/j.chb.2010.06.005

Hutson, E., Kelly, S., & Militello, L. K. (2018). Systematic review of cyberbullying interventions for youth and parents with implications for evidence-based practice. *Worldviews on Evidence-Based Nursing, 15*(1), 72–79. doi:10.1111/wvn.12257 PMID:28859246

Jacobs, N., Goossens, L., Dehue, F., Völlink, T., & Lechner, L. (2015). Dutch cyberbullying victims' experiences, perceptions, attitudes, and motivations related to (coping with) cyberbullying: Focus group interviews. *Societies (Basel, Switzerland), 5*(1), 43–64. doi:10.3390oc5010043

Khine, A.T., Saw, Y. M., Htut Z. Y., Khaing C. T., Soe H. Z., Swe K. K., Thike, Th., Htet, H., Saw, T. N., Cho, S. M., Kariya, T., Yamamoto, E., & Hamajima, N. (2020). Assessing risk factors and impact of cyberbullying victimization among university students in Myanmar: A cross sectional study. *PLoS ONE, 15*(1), 1-16. doi:10.1371/journal.pone.0227051

Kim, S., Kimber, M., Boyle, M. H., & Georgiades, K. (2019). Sex differences in the association between cyberbullying victimization and mental health, substance use, and suicidal ideation in adolescents. *Canadian Journal of Psychiatry, 64*(2), 126–135. doi:10.1177/0706743718777397 PMID:29783849

Kowalski, R., Morgan, C., Drake-Lavelle, K., & Allison, B. (2016). Cyberbullying among college students with disabilities. *Computers in Human Behavior, 57*, 416–427. doi:10.1016/j.chb.2015.12.044

Kowalski, R. M., Giumetti, G. W., Schroeder, A. N., & Lattanner, M. R. (2014). Bullying in the digital age: A critical review and meta-analysis of cyberbullying research among youth. *Psychological Bulletin, 140*(4), 1073–1137. doi:10.1037/a0035618 PMID:24512111

Kowalski, R. M., & Toth, A. (2017). Cyberbullying among youth with and without disabilities. *Journal of Child & Adolescent Trauma, 11*(1), 7–15. doi:10.100740653-017-0139-y PMID:32318133

Lee, C., & Shin, N. (2017). Prevalence of cyberbullying and predictors of cyberbullying perpetration among Korean adolescents. *Computers in Human Behavior, 68*, 352–358. doi:10.1016/j.chb.2016.11.047

Lee, S.-S., Song, H., & Park, J. H. (2021). Exploring risk and protective factors for cyberbullying and their interplay: Evidence from a sample of South Korean college students. *International Journal of Environmental Research and Public Health, 18*, 13415.

Livingstone, S., Haddon, L., Görzig, A., & Ólafsson, K. (2011). *Risks and safety on the internet: The perspective of European children*. Full Findings. EU Kids.

Luo, A., & Bussey, K. (2019). The selectivity of moral disengagement in defenders of cyberbullying: Contextual moral disengagement. *Computers in Human Behavior, 93*, 318–325. doi:10.1016/j.chb.2018.12.038

Macaulay, P., Betts, L., Stiller, J., & Kellezi, B. (2022). Bystander responses to cyberbullying: The role of perceived severity, publicity, anonymity, type of cyberbullying, and victim response. *Computers in Human Behavior, 131*. doi:10.1016/j.chb.2022.107238

Machackova, H. (2020). Bystander reactions to cyberbullying and cyberaggression: Individual, contextual, and social factors. *Current Opinion in Psychology, 36*, 130–134. doi:10.1016/j.copsyc.2020.06.003 PMID:32668382

Mitchell, K. J., Ybarra, M., & Finkelhor, D. (2007). The relative importance of online victimization in understanding depression, delinquency, and substance use. *Child Maltreatment*, *12*(4), 314–324. doi:10.1177/1077559507305996 PMID:17954938

Monteiro, A. P. (submitted for publication). Propriedades psicométricas da escala ECIPQ] [European Cyberbullying Intervention Project Questionnaire]. *Numa Amostra de Adolescentes Portugueses.*

Moxey, N., & Bussey, K. (2020). Styles of bystander intervention in cyberbullying incidents. *Int Journal of Bullying Prevention*, *2*(1), 6–15. doi:10.100742380-019-00039-1

Nocentini, A., Calmaestra, J., Schultze-Krumbholz, A., Scheithauer, H., Ortega, R., & Menesini, E. (2010). Cyberbullying: Labels, behaviours and definition in three European countries. *Australian Journal of Guidance & Counselling*, *20*(2), 129–142. doi:10.1375/ajgc.20.2.129

O'Higgins Norman, J. (2020). Tackling bullying from the inside out: Shifting paradigms in bullying research and interventions. *International Journal of Bullying Prevention*, *2*(3), 161–169. doi:10.100742380-020-00076-1 PMID:33005874

Obermaier, M., Fawzi, N., & Koch, T. (2016). Bystanding or standing by? How the number of bystanders affects the intention to intervene in cyberbullying. *New Media & Society*, *18*(8), 1491–1507. doi:10.1177/1461444814563519

Ordem dos Psicólogos, P. (2020). *Recomendações para pais, cuidadores e professores - Cyberbullying e segurança online*. Disponível em: https://www.ordemdospsicologos.pt/ficheiros/documentos/covid_19_cyberbullying_pais.pdf

Pascual-Sanchez, A., Hickey, N., Mateu, A., Martinez-Herves, M., Kramer, T., & Nicholls, D. (2021). Personality traits and self-esteem in traditional bullying and cyberbullying. *Personality and Individual Differences*, *177*, 110809. doi:10.1016/j.paid.2021.110809

Patchin, J., & Hinduja, S. (2010). Cyberbullying and self-esteem. *The Journal of School Health*, *80*(12), 614–621. doi:10.1111/j.1746-1561.2010.00548.x PMID:21087257

Patrão, I., & Sampaio, D. (2016). *Dependências online. O poder das tecnologias* [Online dependencies. The power of technology]. Pactor.

Pereira, M., Fernandes, O. M., & Relva, I. C. (submitted). *Ciberbullying, ideação suicida e comunicação parental-filial em adolescentes e jovens adultos* [Cyberbullying, suicidal ideation and parent-affiliate communication in adolescents and young adults]. Academic Press.

Peter, I.-K., & Petermann, F. (2018). Cyberbullying: A concept analysis of defining attributes and additional influencing factors. *Computers in Human Behavior*, *86*, 350–366. doi:10.1016/j.chb.2018.05.013

Polanco-Levicán, K., & Salvo-Garrido, S. (2021). Bystander roles in cyberbullying: A mini-review of who, how many, and why. *Frontiers in Psychology*. https://www.frontiersin.org/article/10.3389/fpsyg.2021.676787

Ponte, C., & Batista, S. (2018). *EU Kids Online Portugal - 2018: Usos, competências, riscos e mediações da internet reportados por crianças e jovens (9 -17 Anos)* [EU Kids Online Portugal - 2018: Uses, competencies, risks and internet mediations reported by children and young people (9 -17 Years)]. EU Kids Online; NOVA FCSH. Disponível em: http://www.fcsh.unl.pt/eukidsonline/documentos/

Price, D., Green, D., Spears, B., Scrimgeour, M., Barnes, A., Geer, R., & Johnson, B. (2014). A qualitative exploration of cyberbystanders and moral engagement. *Australian Journal of Guidance & Counselling*, *24*(1), 1–17. doi:10.1017/jgc.2013.18

Rafferty, R., & Vander Ven, T. (2014). I hate everything about you: A qualitative examination of cyberbullying and on-line aggression in a college sample. *Deviant Behavior*, *35*(5), 364–377. doi:10.1080/01639625.2013.849171

Rodriguez-Rivas, M. E., Varela, J., González, C., & Chuecas, M. J. (2022). The role of family support and conflict in cyberbullying and subjective well-being among Chilean adolescents during the Covid-19 period. *Heliyon*, *8*(4). doi:10.1016/j.heliyon.2022.e09243

Sari, S. V., & Camadan, F. (2016). The new face of violence tendency: Cyber bullying perpetrators and their victims. *Computers in Human Behavior*, *59*, 317–326. doi:10.1016/j.chb.2016.02.027

Seixas, S., Fernandes, L., & Morais, T. (2016). *Cyberbullying – Um guia para pais e educadores* [A guide for parents and educators]. Plátano Editora.

Slonje, R., Smith, P., & Frisén, A. (2013). The nature of cyberbullying, and strategies for prevention. *Computers in Human Behavior*, *29*(1), 26–32. doi:10.1016/j.chb.2012.05.024

Smith, P. K. (2013). Cyberbullying y ciberagresión. In A. Ovejero, P. K. Smith, & S. Yubero (Eds.), *El acoso escolar y su prevención: Perspectivas internacionales* [School bullying and its prevention: International perspectives] (pp. 173–190). Biblioteca Nueva.

Sourander, A., Klomek, B., Ikonen, M., Lindroos, J., Luntamo, T., Koskelainen, M., ... Hlenius, H. (2010). Psychosocial risk factors associated with cyberbullying among adolescents: A population-based study. *Archives of General Psychiatry*, *67*(7), 720–728. doi:10.1001/archgenpsychiatry.2010.79 PMID:20603453

Sticca, F., & Perren, S. (2013). Is cyberbullying worse than traditional bullying? Examining the differential roles of medium, publicity, and anonymity for the perceived severity of bullying. *Journal of Youth and Adolescence*, *42*(5), 739–750. doi:10.100710964-012-9867-3 PMID:23184483

Suler, J. (2004). Psychology of cyberspace – The online disinhibition effect. *Cyberpsychology & Behavior*, *7*(3), 321–326. doi:10.1089/1094931041291295 PMID:15257832

UNICEF. (2020). *Recomendações da Unicef têm como objetivo ajudar governos, empresas de TIC, educadores e pais a proteger as crianças em confinamento* [Unicef's recommendations aim at governments, ICT companies, educators and parents to protect children in people at the same time]. Disponível em: https://www.unicef.pt/actualidade/noticias/criancas-correm-maior-risco-desofrer abusos-online-durante-a-pandemia-global-de-covid-19/

Vandebosch, H., & Van Cleemput, K. (2009). Cyberbullying among youngsters: Profiles of bullies and victims. *New Media & Society*, *11*(8), 1349–1371. doi:10.1177/1461444809341263

Waasdorp, T., & Bradshaw, C. (2015). The overlap between cyberbullying and traditional bullying. *The Journal of Adolescent Health, 56*(5), 483–488. doi:10.1016/j.jadohealth.2014.12.002 PMID:25631040

Wachs, S., Junger, M., & Sittichai, R. (2015). Traditional, cyber and combined bullying roles: Differences in risky online and offline activities. *Societies (Basel, Switzerland), 5*(1), 109–135. doi:10.3390oc5010109

Wendt, G., & Lisboa, C. (2013). Agressão entre pares no espaço virtual: Definições, impactos e desafios do cyberbullying [Peer-to-peer aggression in virtual space: Definitions, impacts and challenges of cyberbullying]. *Psicologia Clínica, 25*(1), 73–87. doi:10.1590/S0103-56652013000100005

Wiguna, T., Minayati, K., Kaligis, F., Ismail, I., Wijaya, E., Murtani, J., & Pradana, K. (2021). The effect of cyberbullying, abuse, and screen time on non-suicidal self-injury among adolescents during the pandemic: A perspective from the mediating role of stress. *Frontiers in Psychiatry, 12*, 743329. Advance online publication. doi:10.3389/fpsyt.2021.743329 PMID:34867535

Xu, W., & Zheng, S. (2022). Personality traits and cyberbullying perpetration among Chinese university students: The moderating role of internet self-efficacy and gender. *Frontiers in Psychology, 13*, 779139. Advance online publication. doi:10.3389/fpsyg.2022.779139 PMID:35391948

Yahya, A. S., Khawaja, S., & Chukwuma, J. (2020). COVID-19 and a potential rise in bullying behaviors. *The Primary Care Companion for CNS Disorders, 22*(3). doi:10.4088/PCC.20com02642

Yang, B., Wang, B., Sun, N., Xu, F., Wang, L., Chen, J., Yu, Z., Zhang, Y., Zhu, Y., Dai, T., Zhang, Q., & Sun, C. (2021). The consequences of cyberbullying and traditional bullying victimization among adolescents: Gender differences in psychological symptoms, self-harm, and suicidality. *Psychiatry Research, 306*, 114219. doi:10.1016/j.psychres.2021.114219 PMID:34614443

Zhou, Z., Tang, H., Tian, Y., Wei, H., Zhang, F., & Morrison, C. M. (2013). Cyberbullying and its risk factors among Chinese high school students. *School Psychology International, 34*(6), 630–647. doi:10.1177/0143034313479692

Zhu, C., Huang, S., Evans, R., & Zhang, W. (2021). Cyberbullying among adolescents and children: A comprehensive review of the global situation, risk factors, and preventive measures. *Frontiers in Public Health, 9*, 634909. doi:10.3389/fpubh.2021.634909 PMID:33791270

Zich, I., Farrington, D., & Ttofi, M. M. (2019). Protective factors against bullying and cyberbullying: A systematic review of meta-analyses. *Aggression and Violent Behavior, 45*, 4–19. doi:10.1016/j.avb.2018.06.008

KEY TERMS AND DEFINITIONS

Auto Cyberbullying: Use of social networks promotes psychological harm to oneself.

Cyberbullying: Cyberbullying is bullying through digital technologies. Repeated behavior intended to frighten, infuriate, or embarrass those who are victims.

Digital Citizenship: Use of technology responsibly or being a good online citizen.

Hybrid Bystander: When occurred a change in the role from traditional bullying to cyberbullying toward the bystander.

Prevalence: Refers to the number of cases of involvement in cyberbullying found in an investigation.

Prevention: Preventing something wrong happen.

Warning Signs: Indicators that something is wrong.

Chapter 11
Revisiting the Cyberbullying Legislation in Bangladesh:
A Comparative Study With the Global Scenario

Aftab Hossain
Daffodil International University, Bangladesh & Universiti Sains Malaysia, Malaysia

ABSTRACT

The author of this chapter provided a comparison of cyberbullying-related issues across the diverse cyber laws of countries. A definition and distinction between cybercrime and cyberbullying and the impact of cyberbullying on individuals of various ages, socioeconomic, and sociocultural backgrounds were discussed. The cyberbullying provisions in national cyber laws of the top five cyberbullying victim countries were reviewed. Then they were compared to Bangladesh's Information and Communication Technology Act, 2006, and the Digital Security Act, 2018. The final section of the chapter compares the legislation governing cyberbullying in India, Brazil, the United States of America, Belgium, and South Africa to Bangladesh's acts. The comparisons of the crimes demonstrate why the acts are more infamous in Bangladesh than in other nations with a higher rate of cyberbullying victims. Some future recommendations for the Bangladeshi government by examining the country's legislation with the international community and identifying new research possibilities for the future were recommended.

INTRODUCTION

Our lives have been transformed in ways that were unimaginable even a decade ago. While this technology enables rapid and easy contact between individuals worldwide, it has also enabled offenders to commit atrocities and resulted in the emergence of new forms of Internet-related crime. Cybercrime is a term that refers to any criminal conduct committed with the use of computers, networked devices, or a network that occurs entirely within cyberspace (Babanina et al., 2021; H. Wang, 2021).

DOI: 10.4018/978-1-6684-5426-8.ch011

Because the Internet transcends traditional constraints of physical location and identity, it provides an excellent platform for stalkers and bullies to harass, abuse, and threaten people (Collier, 2021). According to Symantec (2012), up to one million people around the world were victims of cybercrime in 2012. About 34% of cybercrime victims had been cyberbullied at some point in their lives.

Bullying is a widespread occurrence and a hot topic of discussion in the academic environment. It is not restricted to children in schoolyards; hostility and violent behavior toward others have spread to adolescents, young people, and young adults as well (Tammam, 2022). Traditional bullying is largely believed to have a variety of detrimental consequences. This involves psychological distress and several types of physical concerns. Physical violence and verbal abuse are two examples, as are related activities such as gossiping and spreading rumors (Chen et al., 2018; Yoon et al., 2021).

Due to the widespread use of the internet, this issue has been dubbed "cyberbullying" in the world of the World Wide Web. Despite the growing global acknowledgment of cyberbullying, Bangladesh's lack of proper legislation has remained a significant obstacle (Hossain et al., 2022; Hossen, 2021). This article will suggest that new legislation should be drafted in Bangladesh to ensure the safety of children and adolescents. There are numerous misunderstandings between laws and policies among the populace. From the infamous "Article 57" of the "ICT Act" (Mogumder, 2022; Riaz, 2022) to the contentious "Digital Security Act," none of the laws were drafted with children and adolescents in mind (The Business Standard, 2022; The Daily Star, 2022).

The policy for cyberbullying varies by country's legislation and encompasses a variety of legal issues. However, it appears as though the legal process is universal in some countries and age-specific in others. Bangladesh's policy is categorical and based on age and occupation. Additionally, there is no explicit law prohibiting cyberbullying; rather, cybercrime is defined as cyberbullying. The "ICT Act, 2006," the "Pornography Control Act, 2012," and the "Digital Security Act, 2018" all address certain aspects of cyberbullying.

The rules governing the aforementioned acts and their changes will be thoroughly studied in this study and then compared to the laws of various countries. This literature study will look for flaws in Bangladesh's laws by comparing them to international legal precedents from other countries.

CYBERBULLYING

Cyberbullying sometimes begins as a joke, with young people hacking accounts (email, social media, and network profiles) for humor, but the repercussions are far from entertaining. However, cyberbullying occurs when the perpetrator's intent is adversarial or destructive to others (Kumar & Goldstein, 2020; Zhang et al., 2021). Additionally, the perpetrator's hostile purpose can be repeated, because cyberbullying requires anonymity. Wong & McBride (2018) found that cyberbullying requires enjoyment seeking. The degree of fun-seeking was much more predictive of cyberbullying than one of the strongest current predictors, cyberbullying normative values.

Cyberbullying has a detrimental effect on children's mental and physical health. Numerous studies have found that victims of cyberbullying can experience bodily symptoms such as sleep deprivation and decreased vitality. Bedwetting, inability to eat, pain, skin problems, and stomach/abdominal problems (Albdour et al., 2019; S. Lee & Chun, 2020; Mateu et al., 2020).

Online bullying is described as "threats or other inappropriate behavior (other than sexual solicitation) directed toward or posted about a minor on the Internet." As Allington (2020) indicates, here, aggressive behavior is ubiquitous, with ICT technologies being the primary cause of concern. Hatred is defined by Patchin & Hinduja, (2006, p.152). Cyberbullying is not related to gender, sexual orientation, color, or socioeconomic status. Contrary to popular belief, anyone may bully someone online (Mishna et al., 2020; Wachs et al., 2022).

According to some academicians, the higher class intimidated the lower class online. Others, on the other hand, concentrated on the repetitive nature of the hostile behavior (Bedrosova et al., 2022; Hall et al., 2022; L. Wang & Ngai, 2021). Experts, on the other hand, cite violent online behavior, the use of ICT technology, the repetition of bullying behavior, and power imbalances between the parties as critical components of cyberbullying (Chan et al., 2021; Chang, 2021; V. Jain, 2021; Strohmeier & Gradinger, 2022).

Four critical components were identified to describe cyberbullying. Aggressive behavior, repetition, power imbalance, and the usage of information and communication technologies. Cyberbullying can then occur. The urge to cause harm to another person is referred to as aggression (Lorenz et al., 2005; Meter et al., 2021). Rather than reacting to annoyance or provocation, proactive aggressiveness refers to unpleasant behaviors performed towards another person to obtain an advantage or accomplish a goal. Aggression should be associated with cyberbullying, as it is a manifestation of overall aggression. Cyberbullying has been associated with an increase in both reactive and proactive violence (Ang, 2022).

Aggression toward the victim is a common occurrence. The aim of injury persists in this case. Using technology, any phrase, symbol, or image can be replicated and communicated to another using technology. This propagation may be beyond the ability or desire of the original sender (Vranjes et al., 2021). Additionally, the question of repetition measurement and homogeneity presents a difficulty. Researchers, politicians, and academics continue to debate the extent to which repeated assaultive language and behavior constitute a pattern. Even a single episode of cyberbullying has the potential to be detrimental (Longobardi et al., 2021; Varela et al., 2022).

The majority of cyberbullying scholars emphasize the power imbalance between the perpetrator and victim. The bully's power is determined by their physical characteristics, socioeconomic level, and physical ability. However, with cyberbullying, the bully's power is concealed and has nothing to do with physical strength (Novitasari et al., 2021; Smith, 2019). It is becoming more and more reliant on the internet. Cyberbullying is becoming increasingly reliant on anonymity, internet access, and time spent online (G. Lee & Sanchez, 2018).

Traditional bullying, is separate from cyberbullying (Jadambaa et al., 2019; Kim et al., 2022). Several factors contribute to this. Namelessness, disinhibition, power imbalance, and observers are just a few. Bullies may feel 'anonymous' as a result of technology. The digital footprint of that identity can be corrupted or disguised. All of this is possible even if you possess ICT skills (Polanin et al., 2022). Individuals use this service to conceal their identity on online social media platforms by using a pseudonym, a sham email address, and a false name.

Difference between Cyberbullying and Cyber Crime

Cybercrime does not have a broadly accepted definition. 7 This is because numerous researchers have attempted to examine the notion from their perspective, informed by their own experiences and knowledge of what it is. As previously said, this is based on their frame of reference. However, while trying to come up with a definition, it is worth noting that cybercrime is a mashup of two terms: cyber and crime. 8 So, when we look at a definition, we need to look at the dynamic terms' definitions.

According to the literal meaning, both the words 'cyber' means online and 'crime' define criminal activities. So, in short, it means online criminal activities. In addition, The 2011 Council of Europe Convention on Cybercrime (Clough, 2012; Cruz, 2020), the first international convention on cybercrime, does not contain an express definition of the term "cybercrime," even though the Treaty classifies cybercrime. Egypt's Anti-Cyber and Information Security Though Technology Law 13 defined computers, it did not define cybercrime, computer crime, or cybercrime. Even cybercrime. The Nigerian Cybercrime (Prohibition), the Cybercrime (Prevention, etc.) Act, 2015 omitted the term "cybercrime" from Section 58 of the Act, which is the Act's interpretation section, omitting any definition of the crime (S.C. IFEMEJE, 2020). A close examination of following Section 17 of the UK's Computer Misuse Act, Section 14, which is the Act's interpretation portion, demonstrates that the Act contains no definition of cybercrime (Robert, 2021). The same is true for the United States. In 1986, Congress enacted the Computer Fraud and Abuse Act (CFAA) (amended in 1994, 1996, and 2001) (Milligan, 2022).

The true distinction between cybercrime and cyberbullying is that cybercrime is criminal behavior that is prosecuted by law enforcement authorities. On the other hand, cyberbullying frequently begins with casual banter or a fun activity designed to purposely embarrass someone (Hughes, 2022; Petric, 2022). Cyberbullying is mostly a psychological attack intended to harm another person. Another important distinction is that cyberbullying is not considered an act of bullying unless the victim asserts their victimhood. Otherwise, it may be considered "friendly banter." Although cyberbullying is also a crime, people in many countries classify cyberbullying and cybercrime together when they steal someone's identity, make threats, or stalk them, among other things (Arif, 2021; Bozyiğit et al., 2021).

Impact of Cyberbullying

For more than a decade, researchers have been examining the effects of cyberbullying on victims. However, the effect of cyberbullying on victims remains unknown. Cyberbullying is defined as the act of transmitting or posting harmful material or employing the internet or other digital technologies to engage in other forms of social aggression. While occurrences vary, research from North America, Europe, and Australia demonstrates that a sizable proportion of young people engage in or witness cyberbullying. Tokunaga, (2010) discovered in an analysis of 25 peer-reviewed publications on cyber victimization that between 20% and 40% of young people have been victims of cyberbullying.

Researchers have also examined the emotional impact of cyberbullying (Anwar et al., 2020). Thus far, the outcomes have been a shambles. In some instances, males are overrepresented as cyberbullies and victims; in others, girls are overrepresented as cyberbullies and victims; and in some instances, no gender disparity exists (Forssell, 2020;Song et al., 2020). Additionally, an emotional influence is debatable. Numerous research studies have discovered that all children who participated in the studies had symptoms such as depression and suicidal thoughts. Apart from providing aggressors with increased anonymity, cyberbullying has a vast potential audience and a lengthy history. A YouTube video, for example, can be viewed for weeks, months, or even years.

Cyberbullying has a detrimental effect on the mental health of those targeted (Romito et al., 2019). More precisely, cyber victimization has been linked to depression, surpassing traditional forms of victimization of young people's well-being, regardless of gender. Individual contextual elements, such as social support, have varying effects on different victims (Carvalho et al., 2021; Ngo et al., 2021). Anxiety appears to be a mechanism via which cyber-victimization affects women's mental health concerns

(Kircaburun et al., 2020). Long-term consequences include health problems and career dissatisfaction in adults (Loh & Snyman, 2020).

Non-fatal (health loss) and lethal suicidal attempts are increasing at an alarming rate (Kedar, 2021; Zwickl et al., 2021). While the number of victimization complaints has decreased as a result of various nations and states enacting legislation, the number of attempted suicides as a result of cyberbullying has not. Additionally, cyberbullying victims are more prone to self-harm or committing suicide than non-victims. John et al. (2018) found individuals who have been cyberbullied are more likely to act on suicidal thoughts than those who have not been cyberbullied.

LEGISLATION IN DIFFERENT COUNTRIES

Cyberbullying legislation varies by country. The issue is perceived differently in different parts of the country or even states (Barlett et al., 2021; Chudal et al., 2021). As a result, it is impossible to define cyberbullying universally. Additionally, it is more challenging to create a general punishment that encompasses all components of cyberbullying. For example, cyberbullying is a misdemeanor in the United States but an offense in the United Kingdom (Hosani et al., 2019). As a result, cyberbullying legislation, enforcement, and punishment may vary by jurisdiction. Additionally, it is more challenging to create a general punishment that encompasses all components of cyberbullying. In the United States, for example, cyberbullying is punishable by up to two years in prison (Hosani et al., 2019). However, in other nations, the penalty can be significantly harsher.

According to reports, the strongest cyberbullying regulations in the world are found in Canada, where individuals who engage in cyberbullying face suspension from school and, for repeat offenders, expulsion from school and possible jail time under the Education Act (BC Gov News, 2022; Villegas & Aberman, 2019). Cyberbullying is punishable in the United Kingdom by up to six months in prison and a fine under the Malicious Communications Act (Herring, 2021). Certain states in the United States of America are also considered to have strong cyberbullying legislation, with penalties ranging from monetary fines to misdemeanor charges or jail time, although other states in the United States have laxer or no particular cyberbullying legislation (Espelage et al., 2018; Marzano, 2019).

Whereas in Europe, where the majority of countries lack explicit cyberbullying legislation, a variety of existing laws might be enforced in incidents of cyberbullying. Certain countries have enacted legislation to penalize certain online behaviors (for example, cyberstalking is illegal in Poland) (Cheng et al., 2020; Research Service Member, 2018). International law encompasses several contentious areas: Cyberbullying, online harassment, and identity theft are now being addressed through the application of the Cybercrime Convention and European Data Protection Legislation. It also has agreements with 17 of the world's biggest social networks, like Facebook and MySpace. These agreements will help fight online abuse and better protect young people (Council of Europe, 2021; European Data Protection Supervisor, 2022).

According to the findings of (Dhiraj, 2018), the top five countries facing the highest number of cyberbullying are India, Brazil, the United States of America, Belgium, and South Africa. The number of average cyberbullying victims in these countries varies from 26 to 37 per hundred users.

On the other hand, these countries have developed or taken initiative to support their cyberbullying victims legally either from the state level, local government, schools, or federal level. According to *Table 1,* the legislation regarding cyberbullying in these countries is discussed below briefly.

India

India primarily has two distinct cyberbullying laws. As defined by the Indian Penal Code 1860 (IPC), "cyberbullying" is the use of information and communication technology (ICT) to hurt another person, or to hurt someone else's reputation. Provision 507 states that anyone who anonymously frightens or threatens another person on the internet or through social media is punishable under this section. The term is up to two years in prison. Additionally, section 509 makes it a crime to offend a woman's modesty, whether in person or online. While photographing a lady in her private place without her knowledge or consent is illegal, if the accused continues to commit the offense, he faces a 3-year prison sentence under Section 354 (C), and Section 354 (D) punishes someone who stalks or monitors another person's internet activities without their knowledge with the intent to injure or harm them. Three years is the maximum penalty. Additionally, section 499 is concerned with internet defamation.

The 2000 Indian Information Technology Act was enacted to safeguard citizens from cyberbullying incidents such as online harassment and stalking. The Act was passed by the Indian Parliament in 2000 and took effect on January 1, 2001 (C., 2020). Cyberbullying is defined under the act as the intentional use of information and communication technology (ICT) to harass, intimidate, threaten, defame, stalk, or otherwise injure another person. Cyberbullying is punishable by a fine or imprisonment for a term of up to seven years and/or a term of imprisonment for not less than six months but not more than five years and/or a fine of up to INR ten lakh (one million) fine. Fake profiles, fake identities, and the unauthorized posting of any personal images on the internet are all against the law, so don't do them.

Brazil

According to Brazil's government, cyberbullying occurs in their country, and they are aware of the importance of protecting cyber victims. They are unsure, however, how to defend the victims (Neto & Barbosa, 2018). The country's government is likewise aware of cyberbullying but has no idea how to prevent it. As a result, the government has taken steps to combat cyberbullying through anti-bullying and anti-cyberbullying legislation (Neto & Barbosa, 2018). These regulations are intended to curtail cyberbullying and other types of harassment. Additionally, the government has taken steps to safeguard youngsters against cyberbullying. As a result, the government has taken steps to combat cyberbullying through anti-bullying and anti-cyberbullying legislation.

According to article 5 of Law No. 13,185, educational institutions, clubs, and recreational organizations are responsible for promoting awareness, preventing, diagnosing, and combating violence and bullying. Article 5 emphasizes that the school community is responsible for preventing and combating bullying across society. This includes parents, siblings, and guardians.

According to Neto & Barbosa (2018) an important part of the act is that it emphasizes civic duty (cidadania), empathy, and consideration for others, all in the context of a peaceful and tolerant culture. In addition, the law wants to avoid using harsh punishments as much as possible, preferring other ways to hold people accountable and change their behavior. It also wants to make sure that bullying is known and that it is stopped, especially when students, teachers, or other professional school members engage in a pattern of bullying or physical and psychological embarrassment.

Table 1. Legislation on cyberbullying on the top five affected countries

Country	The act/ law	National or State Policy	Legislation Details and punishments	Punishment
India	The Indian Penal Code, 1860 ("IPC") (Government of India, 2022; Myadvo, 2021)	National	***Section 507:*** Threatens on the internet or Social Media to do anything against the victim's will.	- Up to 2 years of imprisonment.
			Section 509: Insulting modesty of a women	- Up to one year with/ without fine.
			Section 354(C): Capturing women's private image without consent	- Minimum 1 to 3 years of imprisonment and additionally up to 7 years imprisonment if still the accused continue to do so.
			Section 354(D): Stalking online with an intention to harm	- Up to 3 years of imprisonment
			Section 499: Any person intending to harm, or knowing or having reason to believe that such imputation will harm, the reputation of such person, is said, except in the cases hereinafter expected, to defame that person.	- Up to 2 years of imprisonment with/ without fine
	Information Technology Act, 2000 ("IT Act") (Bhushan, 2019; India Code, 2021)	National	***Section 66(D):*** Fake Identity or using someone else's image	Up to 3 years of imprisonment and/INR 1 Lakh fine.
			Section 66(E): Intentionally putting someone's private pictures on the internet and social media	Up to 3 years of jail and/or INR. 3 Lakh fine
			Section 67): Uploading or spreading any vulgar or improper content on the internet or social media	Up to 5 years of jail with/ without INR 10 lakh fine.
Brazil	13.185/2015 "Systematic Intimidation Control Program" (Library of Congress, 2015; Neto & Barbosa, 2018)	National	Systematic intimidation (*intimidação sistemática*) program consists of verbal insults, sexual harassment, stalking, threats, false identity, and social isolation along with traditional or real-life bullying.	Prevention through social practices and norms, training teachers, promoting civic responsibilities, and psychological and legal aid to the offenders and the victims.
USA	Federal Law proposed 44 State laws are available (Cyberbullying Research Center, 2021; Marzano, 2019)	- Federal Law/National Law proposed - 44 states have their laws	A total number of 48 states included cyberbullying in their bullying laws and 44 of them consider cyberbullying a criminal offense. However, 45 states included schools to implement their policies.	The punishment varies from state to state. Such as in some states punishes up to one year in jail and/ or a USD2500 fine. On the other hand, states like Florida involve school policy and sanctions.
Belgium	550 *bis* of the Belgian Criminal Code BCC (legislationline, 2020; Pennell et al., 2022)	National	Laws are included with the cybercrime laws. Such as stalking, phishing, identity theft, sexual harassment.	Six months to three years in prison and/or up to 200,000 Euro fine.
South Africa	CYBERCRIMES ACT NO. 19 OF 2020 (Eboibi, 2020; Government, 2021)	National	Cyberbullying acts are included in the act. Activities like stalking, transmitting threats, inappropriate sexual photographs	Up to three years in jail. But if a child is involved (aged between 10 to 18 years) then sending them to jail is the last possible solution.

United States

The United States of America is one of the most vulnerable countries in the world to cyberbullying. From schoolchildren to office professionals, celebrities to everyday people, cyberbullying effects all socioeconomic categories, people of diverse cultures, and people of dynamic ethnicity (S. Jain & Agrawal, 2020). The largest quantity of research occurs in the United States. According to McCarthy (2021) The United States, one of the most affected countries in the world, has failed to enact a federal law prohibiting cyberbullying. However, several states have enacted legislation prohibiting cyberbullying. The number of states passing legislation prohibiting cyberbullying has grown.

According to Cyberbullying Research Center (2021) Bullying laws differ by the state in the United States. California, Florida, Illinois, New York, and Texas are just a few of the states that have anti-bullying legislation. In addition, 48 states in the United States have passed anti-bullying laws. Alaska and Wisconsin do not include cyberbullying and cyber harassment in their anti-bullying laws. Similar to the UK, the majority of states in the United States have criminalized cyberbullying. Additionally, the United States of America passed the 2011 Cyberbullying Prevention and Response Act. The US Senate enacted this measure in 2011 and the US House of Representatives passed it in 2012.

Additionally, several states in the United States have enacted "sexting legislation," as well as other bullying and cyberbullying statutes. In the United States, the penalties for cyberbullying vary by state. In certain states, the penalty is the same as the penalty for bullying. In some states, the penalties for bullying are more severe. Additionally, a $2,500 fine and up to one year in jail may be imposed. The penalty may be increased in the amended laws (Marzano, 2019).

Belgium

Although the European Union is united in its opposition to bullying and cyberbullying, several countries still do not recognize cyberbullying as a crime and do not have anti-bullying legislation. In the instance of Belgium, no distinction has been made between cybercrime and cyberbullying. The anti-cyberbullying law, or the penalty for cyberbullying, is currently being drafted (legislationline, 2020).

Belgium's most current cybercrime law was enacted at the end of 2011, which implies that the anti-cyberbullying legislation is still in the works. Pennell et al. (2022) stated Belgium's cybercrime law includes some aspects of cyberbullying but not all of the categories. It doesn't apply to things like cyberstalking, cyber harassment, or cyberbullying that happens outside of a computer or electronic device, like when they happen outside of the computer.

In the event of identity theft or hacking in Belgium, for example, if someone hacks into another person's computer or email account to shame him or her sexually, this is not considered cyberbullying but cyberstalking. This is not cyberbullying, but cyberstalking, if someone hacks into another person's computer or email account intending to sexually embarrass him or her. Six months to three years in prison and/or a fine of between 208 EUR and 200,000 EUR is the possible penalty. If actual harm is done to the information technology system, the maximum sentence is enhanced to five years in prison and the maximum fine to 600,000 EUR (legislationline, 2020).

Phishing may also be punished under Article 145, 3, 1° of the Electronic Communications Act of June 13, 2005 (ECA), which prohibits the fraudulent start of electronic communications via an electronic communications network in order toe an illegal economic benefit (for oneself or another). This criminal offense carries a maximum sentence of one to four years in prison and/or a fine of between 4,000 and 400,000 euros.

Identity theft is often used as a way to start another crime, like theft, fraud, computer fraud, hacking, or computer sabotage, with the stolen identity. People who try to use someone else's identity to get government or military jobs, noble titles, the attorney-at-law title, or the public use of a fake family name are all guilty of identity fraud, but only if it happens in public (articles 227–231).

Generally, penalties are confined to fines (up to 8,000 EUR). Belgium's laws make it quite clear that they place a higher premium on cybercrime than on cyberbullying, deserve though cyberbullying is not a crime in Belgium (legislationline, 2020).

South Africa

South Africa is one of the countries with a high percentage of cyberbullying, with young people being the primary victims. In South Africa, cyberbullying is defined as "the purposeful and repeated use of information and communication technologies (ICTs) to cause injury or distress to another person." (Government, 2021) In South Africa, about half of all adult internet users are victims of cyberbullying.

South Africa has a high rate of cyberbullying, with children and adolescents being the primary targets. Cyberbullying is defined in South Africa as "the intentional use of ICTs to cause hurt or distress to another person." (Government, 2021) Nearly half of adult internet users in South Africa are victims of cyberbullying (Cilliers, 2021).

The South African government and law enforcement agencies moved fast to eliminate cyberbullying. After forming the cyberbullying task team, the SAPS and the NPA began investigating cyberbullies. They also started working with the SABC on a cyberbullying awareness campaign. Cyberbullying is prohibited by the Electronic Communications and Additional Protocols to the Inter-American Convention on the Prevention, Punishment, and Eradication of Violence against Women (Pennell et al., 2022).

So the Cyberbullying Act was passed in South Africa. The South African Cyberbullying Act was the world's first and the Southern Hemisphere's first. South Africa's National Assembly passed the cyberbullying bill in April 2013. Later, under ACT 19 of 2020, these new cybercrimes will help reduce cyberbullying because transmitting violent threats or inappropriate sexual photographs of someone has direct criminal implications. A person convicted of any of the aforementioned crimes may be subject to a fine and/or a maximum of three years in prison.

The Act also allows a person who files a police report for certain types of cybercrimes to seek a protection order from a magistrate's court. A Magistrate may direct that a message or image be removed or disabled from the service provider's servers (Hlazo, 2018).

Fouché et al. (2020) mentioned The Child Justice Act, 75 of 2008, controls how children are treated when accused of crimes and the repercussions they face. Children between the ages of 10 and 18 can be sent to prison, but only as a last resort and for the shortest time possible. If someone has been cyberbullied, it is critical to keep track of the evidence. Take a screenshot of the post, text message, or image. Cyberbullying-related texts or emails may be removed. To file a criminal or civil lawsuit against the person who cyberbullied you, you must have proof of the abuse.

Bangladeshi Laws on Relevant Issues

The ICT Act 2006

The Act authorizes the use of digital certificates for document authentication and signatures. The Act also contains provisions governing the establishment and licensing of competent authorities. Designated authorities determine the validity of digital certificates (Murad, 2012). The Act's rules, dubbed "Information Technology (Certifying Authorities"), have been promulgated. This framework is meant to make sure that the work of the Designated Authorities is done the same way every time (Babu & Ullah, 2021).

The modified ICT Act 2006 now recognizes law enforcement officials' authority to arrest individuals without a warrant. Due to the Act's insufficient provisions, experts said that it could not be used to combat cybercrime (Shaon, 2018). Additionally, political exploitation is a possibility. As there are insufficient cyber tribunals established around the country, only the capital has the authority to impose the suspect's bail. People who study law and human rights have said that this kind of activity can be misused (Adhikary Shubhra Tuhin, 2021). This means that the defendant can be arrested in a non-bail-able case.

Despite widespread criticism, Section 57 of the Information and Communication Technology (ICT) Act, 2006, continues to cause concern due to its frequent misapplication. Since its introduction, the law has been widely criticized by human rights advocates, journalists, legal experts, and free thinkers for the way it could be interpreted and used to harass inhabitants. This is a criminal offense under Section 57, which carries a maximum sentence of fourteen years in prison and/or a BDT fine of one crore (Shaon, 2018).

The Digital Security Act 2018

Bangladesh has yet to pass legislation to address cyberbullying. Bangladesh's government is considering enacting anti-cyberbullying legislation shortly. The administration intends to criminalize cyberbullying.

Although the country lacks specific cyberbullying legislation, it has introduced the "Digital Security Act 2018"(Bangladesh Computer Council, 2019). The legislation encompasses legal proceedings, including the use of information and communication technologies.

According to Section 21 (Bangladesh Computer Council, 2019), which relates to the cyberbullying issues of the law, anybody who uses digital devices to propagate bad propaganda against the Liberation War or the Father of the Nation, or who instigates others to do so, faces up to ten years in prison or a fine of up to BDT 1 crore (10 million), or both. If the offender commits the offense a second time or repeatedly, he faces life imprisonment or a fine of up to three crores, or both. Section 25 provides that any person who intentionally or knowingly sends offensive or fear-inducing information, who publishes or propagates any information with the intent of annoying, insulting, humiliating, or denigrating a person, or who publishes or propagates any information with the intent of tarnishing the nation's image or spreading confusion, or who does so despite knowing it is false, shall be prosecuted.

According to Runa (2019) a person who commits the offense for the second time faces up to five years in prison or a fine of BDT. ten lakh (1 million) or both. According to Section 28, if any person or group intentionally or knowingly publishes or broadcasts anything that injures religious sentiments or values, or with the intent to provoke, via any website or electronic format, such activity is considered an offense, and the offender faces a maximum sentence of seven years in prison or a maximum fine of ten lac taka or both. The person who repeatedly commits the offense faces a maximum sentence of 10 years in prison or a fine of BDT 20 lakh (2 million) or both.

Reaction to the ICT and Digital Security Acts

Both acts, according to civil society, intellectuals, and journalists, infringe on free expression. According to experts and the media, these activities are directed against those who advocate for the rights of Bangladeshi citizens. According to the Bangladeshi media, the Bangladeshi government is incapable of protecting free speech and expression. There have been times when the Bangladeshi government hasn't been able to protect journalists and the media from political pressure groups.

However, the DSA 2018 offers a negligible contribution to safeguarding Bangladesh's children and females from cyberbullying, even though protecting children and females from cyberbullying is critical. Chapters 2 and 3 of the Digital Security Act 2018 are devoted to safeguarding the government's and government-regulated companies' and institutions' reputations (Bangladesh Computer Council, 2019). Additionally, chapters 6 and 9 discuss various aspects of computer-related crimes, or cybercrime, as well as the dissemination of misinformation or misleading information. They mostly deal with religious feelings, defamation, compromising government information, hacking, and undermining public order through the use of ICT equipment.

However, none of the laws protecting Bangladeshi people from various forms of cyberbullying currently exist (Mogumder, 2022; The Business Standard, 2022). All of these instances share one feature: they were all brought under Bangladesh's 2018 Digital Security Act (DSA). The law, which took effect on October 1, 2018, has become the preferred tool of the government and ruling party activists for silencing dissidents and stifling their freedom of expression, particularly on the internet. Even before parliament passed the bill, human rights advocates and organizations decried it as a threat to free expression. The Editors' Council, Bangladesh's top body comprised of the country's prominent newspaper editors, objected and asked that the government repeal nine provisions of the law. While cabinet ministers met with editors and assured them that the information would not be misused, such assurances proved to be hollow. The act has a maximum sentence of 14 years in prison and a maximum fine of BDT 1 crore (10 million).

Bangladesh's media characterize the activities as a means of blackmailing people and harassing their right to freedom of expression. As a result, the statute does not provide for the protection of free speech and expression. It is against the law to harass and blackmail someone (Mogumder, 2022; The Business Standard, 2022).

Discussion

According to the research cited above, various countries have enacted legislation addressing cybercrime, cyber harassment, and cyberstalking. On the other hand, cyberbullying was briefly discussed. According to Indian law, cyberbullying is not properly defined as a crime comparable to cyberstalking or cybercrime. While the United States of America hasn't passed a law against cyberbullying, individual states see online bullying as an extension of schoolyard bullying and bullying that happens outside of school grounds.

Belgium and South Africa enacted legislation to penalize cybercrime, but did not include cyberbullying categories such as flaming, social isolation, and sharing awkward images or videos. However, substantial online bullying in the context of cybercrime was deemed a criminal act. According to the literature, the Brazilian government's "Systematic Intimidation (intimidaço sistemática) program" aims to include schools, teachers, and social standards to alter the perpetrators' conduct, while also providing psychological support to the victims. Schools, teachers, and society all play a role in preventing cyberbullying, as seen by the United States of America's policies. Thus, the countries with the highest number of cyberbullying instances have regulations aimed at completely or partially preventing cyberbullying.

Whereas the ICT Act and the Digital Security Act of Bangladesh do not explicitly address cyberbullying, Bangladesh's legislation is primarily concerned with the government's and its affiliated organizations' images. The policies prohibit personal cyberbullying, such as flaming, masquerading, identity theft, online insulting statements directed at specific individuals, or social exclusion. In the context of Bangladesh, and based on a review of the research, it appears that Bangladesh's youth and women are more susceptible to cyberbullying situations (Nabi, 2019; Sraboni, 2021; United News Bangladesh, 2020). Due to the rising prevalence of mental problems and suicide cases in Bangladesh, the government failed to implement any legislation to prohibit cyberbullying in favor of maintaining the country's and government's image. Although the activities have been roundly criticized by civil society and freedom of expression has been severely harmed by the laws' wrongdoing,

CONCLUSION

This study identifies a gap in the laws and legislation of the top five countries where cyberbullying is a significant issue and people, particularly young people, are being victimized by various forms of cyberbullying, but their governments have not been able to define cyberbullying or distinguish cyberbullying from cybercrime on an official level. As a result of this study, it is clear that governments must work together to develop a simple definition and standards for cyberbullying.

According to the research, countries have been impacted by cyberbullying issues and their growing prevalence. However, the top countries with cyberbullying attacks have failed to agree on a definition of cyberbullying or on appropriate punishments. Additionally, it is a moment for governments to demand labor, as their countries have an alarming rate of cyberbullying. On the other hand, Bangladesh's leadership is more concerned with protecting the government's image, even though their citizens, particularly women and children, are victims of cyberbullying.

They are attempting to draft regulations in the country with the largest number of cyberbullying attacks. They have attempted to engage their school administrations, teachers, civil society organizations, and legislators in addressing the challenges, but the situation is quite different in Bangladesh. Legislation designed to protect people from internet harassment is acting like a boomerang, and the law's abuse is readily seen in the media. In addition, even though they don't have legal help, they are more vocal about freedom of expression, objective journalism, and fear of police.

After examining and comparing the laws of India, Brazil, the United States of America, Belgium, and South Africa, it is clear that they attempted to include some aspects of cyberbullying into their legislation, but Bangladesh took the opposite approach. The various acts must be amended to benefit the people of Bangladesh rather than persecute them for exercising their right to freedom of expression.

FUTURE RESEARCH AND DIRECTION

Future research can be conducted on a greater scale. The number of participating countries may be raised, and the legal ramifications of cyberbullying and cybercrime could be thoroughly examined. Additionally, nations such as Sweden can be examined in the future because they have fair cyberbullying laws and have placed a greater emphasis on behavior-changing communication to lower the number of cyberbullying cases. Thus, the research can show why and how the problems should be fixed for a generation that spends most of its time online.

Future research can also focus on the legislation of countries such as Bangladesh, where the cybersecurity law is more contentious, and why the majority of people have a negative attitude towards it. These studies can help define the legal definition of cyberbullying on a national and international level, as well as provide punishment, psychological assistance, and guidance for perpetrators and victims, as the majority of cyberbullying perpetrators do so without their knowledge or consent.

REFERENCES

Adhikary Shubhra Tuhin. (2021). Bangladesh ICT Act: The trap of Section 57. *Dhaka Tribune*. https://www.thedailystar.net/frontpage/bangladesh-ict-act-the-trap-section-of-57-1429336

Al Hosani, H., Yousef, M., Al Shouq, S., Iqbal, F., & Mouheb, D. (2019). A comparative analysis of cyberbullying and cyberstalking laws in the UAE, US, UK and Canada. *Proceedings of IEEE/ACS International Conference on Computer Systems and Applications, AICCSA*. 10.1109/AICCSA47632.2019.9035368

Albdour, M., Hong, J. S., Lewin, L., & Yarandi, H. (2019). The Impact of Cyberbullying on Physical and Psychological Health of Arab American Adolescents. *Journal of Immigrant and Minority Health, 21*(4), 706–715. doi:10.100710903-018-00850-w PMID:30603837

Allington, W. (2020). *Antisemitic Memes and Naïve Teens: Qualitative and Quantitative Impacts of the Internet on Antisemitism, the Evolution of Antisemitism 2.0, and Developing Adaptable Research Methodologies into Online Hate, Abuse, and Misinformation*. The University of Sydney. https://ses.library.usyd.edu.au/handle/2123/22444

Ang, R. P. (2022). Bullying Among Children and Youth in the Digital Age. In *Child Safety, Welfare and Well-being* (pp. 31–45). Springer. doi:10.1007/978-981-16-9820-0_3

Anwar, A., Kee, D. M. H., & Ahmed, A. (2020). Workplace Cyberbullying and Interpersonal Deviance: Understanding the Mediating Effect of Silence and Emotional Exhaustion. *Cyberpsychology, Behavior, and Social Networking, 23*(5), 290–296. doi:10.1089/cyber.2019.0407 PMID:32282237

Arif, M. (2021). A Systematic Review of Machine Learning Algorithms in Cyberbullying Detection: Future Directions and Challenges. *Journal of Information Security and Cybercrimes Research, 4*(1), 1–26. doi:10.26735/GBTV9013

Babanina, V., Tkachenko, I., Matiushenko, O., & Krutevych, M. (2021). Cybercrime: History of formation, current state and ways of counteraction. *Revista Amazonia Investiga, 10*(38), 113–122. doi:10.34069/AI/2021.38.02.10

Babu, K. E. K., & Ullah, M. A. (2021). Cyber legislation and cyber-related legal issues in Bangladesh: Inadequacies and challenges. *International Journal of Electronic Security and Digital Forensics, 13*(2), 180–196. doi:10.1504/IJESDF.2021.113379

Bangladesh Computer Council. (2019). *BGD e-GOV CIRT | Bangladesh e-Government Computer Incident Response Team*. Bangladesh Computer Council. https://www.cirt.gov.bd/

Barlett, C. P., Seyfert, L. W., Simmers, M. M., Hsueh Hua Chen, V., Cavalcanti, J. G., Krahé, B., Suzuki, K., Warburton, W. A., Wong, R. Y. M., Pimentel, C. E., & Skowronski, M. (2021). Cross-cultural similarities and differences in the theoretical predictors of cyberbullying perpetration: Results from a seven-country study. *Aggressive Behavior*, *47*(1), 111–119. doi:10.1002/ab.21923 PMID:32853436

BC Gov News. (2022). *B.C. makes changes to better support francophone students, families*. BC Gov News. https://news.gov.bc.ca/releases/2022ECC0029-000644

Bedrosova, M., Machackova, H., Šerek, J., Smahel, D., & Blaya, C. (2022). The relation between the cyberhate and cyberbullying experiences of adolescents in the Czech Republic, Poland, and Slovakia. *Computers in Human Behavior*, *126*, 107013. doi:10.1016/j.chb.2021.107013

Bhushan, A. (2019). Understanding of Information Technology Act for E-Governance in India. *IIBM'S Journal of Management*, *4*(2), 1–6. doi:10.33771/iibm.v4i1-2.138

Bozyiğit, A., Utku, S., & Nasibov, E. (2021). Cyberbullying detection: Utilizing social media features. *Expert Systems with Applications*, *179*, 115001. doi:10.1016/j.eswa.2021.115001

C., K. (2020). Social and Legislative Issues in Handling Cyberbullying in India. In *Research Anthology on Combating Cyber-Aggression and Online Negativity* (pp. 447–466). IGI Global. doi:10.4018/978-1-7998-4912-4.ch021

Carvalho, M., Branquinho, C., & de Matos, M. G. (2021). Cyberbullying and Bullying: Impact on Psychological Symptoms and Well-Being. *Child Indicators Research*, *14*(1), 435–452. doi:10.100712187-020-09756-2

Chan, T. K. H., Cheung, C. M. K., & Lee, Z. W. Y. (2021). Cyberbullying on social networking sites: A literature review and future research directions. *Information & Management*, *58*(2), 103411. doi:10.1016/j.im.2020.103411

Chang, V. (2021). Inconsistent Definitions of Bullying: A Need to Examine People's Judgments and Reasoning about Bullying and Cyberbullying. *Human Development*, *65*(3), 144–159. doi:10.1159/000516838

Chen, G., Kong, Y., Deater-Deckard, K., & Zhang, W. (2018). Bullying Victimization Heightens Cortisol Response to Psychosocial Stress in Chinese Children. *Journal of Abnormal Child Psychology*, *46*(5), 1051–1059. doi:10.100710802-017-0366-6 PMID:29196916

Cheng, L., Hu, X., Matulewska, A., & Wagner, A. (2020). Exploring cyberbullying: A socio-semiotic perspective. *International Journal of Legal Discourse*, *5*(2), 359–378. doi:10.1515/ijld-2020-2042

Chudal, R., Tiiri, E., Brunstein Klomek, A., Ong, S. H., Fossum, S., Kaneko, H., Kolaitis, G., Lesinskiene, S., Li, L., Huong, M. N., Praharaj, S. K., Sillanmäki, L., Slobodskaya, H. R., Srabstein, J. C., Wiguna, T., Zamani, Z., & Sourander, A. (2021). Victimization by traditional bullying and cyberbullying and the combination of these among adolescents in 13 European and Asian countries. *European Child & Adolescent Psychiatry*, 1–14. doi:10.100700787-021-01779-6 PMID:33884501

Cilliers, L. (2021). Perceptions and experiences of cyberbullying amongst university students in the Eastern Cape province, South Africa. *The Journal for Transdisciplinary Research in Southern Africa, 17*(1), 6. doi:10.4102/td.v17i1.776

Clough, J. (2012). The Council of Europe Convention on Cybercrime: Defining "Crime" in a Digital World. *Criminal Law Forum, 23*(4), 363–391. doi:10.100710609-012-9183-3

Collier, B. (2021). Infrastructural Power: Dealing with Abuse, Crime, and Control in the Tor Anonymity Network. In Cybercrime in Context (pp. 283–301). Springer. doi:10.1007/978-3-030-60527-8_16

Council of Europe. (2021). *Full list.* Council of Europe. https://www.coe.int/en/web/conventions/full-list?module=treaty-detail&treatynum=185

Cyberbullying Research Center. (2021). *Bullying and Cyberbullying Laws Across America.* Cyberbullying Research Center. https://cyberbullying.org/bullying-laws

deArimatéiadaCruz, J. (2020). The legislative framework of the European Union (EU) convention on cybercrime. In *The Palgrave Handbook of International Cybercrime and Cyberdeviance* (pp. 223–237). Palgrave Macmillan. doi:10.1007/978-3-319-78440-3_5

Dhiraj, A. B. (2018). *Countries Where Cyber-bullying Was Reported The Most In 2018.* CEOWORLD Magazine. https://ceoworld.biz/2018/10/29/countries-where-cyber-bullying-was-reported-the-most-in-2018/

Eboibi, F. E. (2020). Concerns of cyber criminality in South Africa, Ghana, Ethiopia and Nigeria: Rethinking cybercrime policy implementation and institutional accountability. *Commonwealth Law Bulletin, 46*(1), 78–109. doi:10.1080/03050718.2020.1748075

Espelage, D. L., Hong, J. S., & Valido, A. (2018). Cyberbullying in the United States. In *International Perspectives on Cyberbullying* (pp. 65–99). Palgrave Macmillan. doi:10.1007/978-3-319-73263-3_4

European Data Protection Supervisor. (2022). *Interoperability.* https://edps.europa.eu/data-protection/our-work/subjects/international-standards/cybercrime-convention_en

Forssell, R. C. (2020). Gender and organisational position: Predicting victimisation of cyberbullying behaviour in working life. *International Journal of Human Resource Management, 31*(16), 2045–2064. doi:10.1080/09585192.2018.1424018

Fouché, A., Fouché, D. F., & Theron, L. C. (2020). Child protection and resilience in the face of COVID-19 in South Africa: A rapid review of C-19 legislation. *Child Abuse & Neglect, 110*, 104710. doi:10.1016/j.chiabu.2020.104710 PMID:32938531

Government, S. A. (2021). *Cybercrimes Act 19 of 2020 (English / Afrikaans).* South African Government. https://www.gov.za/documents/cybercrimes-act-19-2020-1-jun-2021-0000

Government of India. (2022). *Home | Legislative Department | Ministry of Law and Justice | GoI.* https://legislative.gov.in/

Hall, D. L., Silva, Y. N., Wheeler, B., Cheng, L., & Baumel, K. (2022). Harnessing the Power of Interdisciplinary Research with Psychology-Informed Cyberbullying Detection Models. *International Journal of Bullying Prevention, 4*(1), 47–54. doi:10.100742380-021-00107-5

Herring, J. (2021). Malicious Communications Act 1988. In Criminal Law Statutes 2011-2012 (pp. 103–105). doi:10.4324/9780203722763-40

Hlazo, N. I. (2018). *The legal remedies to protect minors against cyberbullying in South Africa*. Nelson Mandela University. http://vital.seals.ac.za:8080/vital/access/manager/Repository/vital:30914?site_name=GlobalView

Hossain, A., Abdul Wahab, J., Islam, M. R., Khan, M. S. R., & Mahmud, A. (2022). *Cyberbullying Perception and Experience Among the University Students in Bangladesh.* IGI Global. doi:10.4018/978-1-7998-9187-1.ch012

Hossen, S. (2021). Nature and Aftermath of Cyberbullying with Female University Students in Bangladesh. *Journal of the Humanities and Social Sciences, 26*(10), 45–53. doi:10.9790/0837-2610074553

Hughes, A. A. (2022). Cyberbullying: A qualitative analysis of perceptions of high school principals' mediation and intervention strategies. *Dissertation Abstracts International. A, The Humanities and Social Sciences*. https://www.proquest.com/dissertations-theses/cyberbullying-qualitative-analysis-perceptions/docview/2640072416/se-2?accountid=14744%0Ahttps://cbua-us.primo.exlibrisgroup.com/discovery/openurl?institution=34CBUA_US&vid=34CBUA_US:VU1&lang=es?url_ver=Z39.88

Ifemeje, N. M. O. (2020). Protecting the privacy of data: Search and seizure of computer devices under the cybercrime (prohibition, prevention, etc.). *International Journal of Law and Clinical Legal Education, 1*. https://nigerianjournalsonline.com/index.php/IJOLACLE/article/view/2164

India Code. (2021). *India Code: Home*. https://www.indiacode.nic.in/

Jadambaa, A., Thomas, H. J., Scott, J. G., Graves, N., Brain, D., & Pacella, R. (2019). Prevalence of traditional bullying and cyberbullying among children and adolescents in Australia: A systematic review and meta-analysis. *The Australian and New Zealand Journal of Psychiatry, 53*(9), 878–888. doi:10.1177/0004867419846393 PMID:31067987

Jain, S., & Agrawal, S. (2020). Perceived vulnerability of cyberbullying on social networking sites: Effects of security measures, addiction and self-disclosure. *Indian Growth and Development Review, 14*(2), 149–171. doi:10.1108/IGDR-10-2019-0110

Jain, V. (2021). Bullying and cyberbullying descriptions. *Asian Journal of Multidimensional Research, 10*(10), 854–859. doi:10.5958/2278-4853.2021.00970.8

John, A., Glendenning, A. C., Marchant, A., Montgomery, P., Stewart, A., Wood, S., Lloyd, K., & Hawton, K. (2018). Self-harm, suicidal behaviours, and cyberbullying in children and young people: Systematic review. Journal of Medical Internet Research, 20(4). doi:10.2196/jmir.9044

Kedar, T. (2021). Suicide and Suicide risk factors: A Literature Review. *Asian Journal of Nursing Education and Research, 11*(3), 441–446. doi:10.52711/2349-2996.2021.00107

Kim, J., Lee, Y., & Jennings, W. G. (2022). A Path from Traditional Bullying to Cyberbullying in South Korea: Examining the Roles of Self-Control and Deviant Peer Association in the Different Forms of Bullying. *Journal of Interpersonal Violence*, (9-10), 5937–5957. Advance online publication. doi:10.1177/08862605211067022 PMID:35259313

Kircaburun, K., Demetrovics, Z., Király, O., & Griffiths, M. D. (2020). Childhood Emotional Trauma and Cyberbullying Perpetration Among Emerging Adults: A Multiple Mediation Model of the Role of Problematic Social Media Use and Psychopathology. *International Journal of Mental Health and Addiction*, *18*(3), 548–566. doi:10.100711469-018-9941-5

Kumar, V. L., & Goldstein, M. A. (2020). Cyberbullying and Adolescents. *Current Pediatrics Reports*, *8*(3), 86–92. doi:10.100740124-020-00217-6 PMID:33552702

Lee, G., & Sanchez, M. (2018). Cyber Bullying behaviors, anonymity, and General Strain Theory: A study of undergraduate students at a South Eastern University in the United States. *International Journal of Cyber Criminology*, *12*(1), 84–96. doi:10.5281/zenodo.1467846

Lee, S., & Chun, J. S. (2020). Conceptualizing the impacts of cyberbullying victimization among Korean male adolescents. *Children and Youth Services Review*, *117*, 105275. doi:10.1016/j.childyouth.2020.105275

legislationline. (2020). *Belgium - Criminal codes - Legislationline*. https://www.legislationline.org/documents/section/criminal-codes/country/41/Belgium/show

Library of Congress. (2015). *Brazil: New Law Creates Program to Combat Bullying Nationwide*. Library of Congress. https://www.loc.gov/item/global-legal-monitor/2015-11-13/brazil-new-law-creates-program-to-combat-bullying-nationwide/

Loh, J., & Snyman, R. (2020). The tangled web: Consequences of workplace cyberbullying in adult male and female employees. *Gender in Management*, *35*(6), 567–584. https://doi.org/10.1108/GM-12-2019-0242

Longobardi, C., Gullotta, G., Ferrigno, S., Jungert, T., Thornberg, R., & Settanni, M. (2021). Cyberbullying and cybervictimization among preadolescents: Does time perspective matter? *Scandinavian Journal of Psychology*, *62*(2), 259–266. https://doi.org/10.1111/sjop.12686

Lorenz, K., Wilson, M. K., & Huxley, J. (2005). On aggression. In On Aggression. Routledge. https://doi.org/10.4324/9780203994269.

Marzano, G. (2019). *Setting Anti-Cyberbullying Legal Policies*. IGI Global. https://services.igi-global.com/resolvedoi/resolve.aspx?doi=10.4018/978-1-5225-8076-8.ch002

Mateu, A., Pascual-Sánchez, A., Martinez-Herves, M., Hickey, N., Nicholls, D., & Kramer, T. (2020). Cyberbullying and post-traumatic stress symptoms in UK adolescents. *Archives of Disease in Childhood*, *105*(10), 951–956. https://doi.org/10.1136/archdischild-2019-318716

McCarthy, M. (2021). Social Media, Students, and the Law. *Laws*, *10*(4), 81. https://doi.org/10.3390/laws10040081

Meter, D. J., Budziszewski, R., Phillips, A., & Beckert, T. E. (2021). A Qualitative Exploration of College Students' Perceptions of Cyberbullying. *TechTrends*, *65*(4), 464–472. https://doi.org/10.1007/s11528-021-00605-9

Milligan, B. (2022). Van Buren v. United States: Rogue Employees Avoiding Prosecution Under the CFAA Because the Court Said "So." *SSRN Electronic Journal*. doi:10.2139/ssrn.4030017

Mishna, F., Sanders, J. E., McNeil, S., Fearing, G., & Kalenteridis, K. (2020). "If Somebody is Different": A critical analysis of parent, teacher and student perspectives on bullying and cyberbullying. *Children and Youth Services Review*, *118*, 105366. https://doi.org/10.1016/j.childyouth.2020.105366

Mogumder, A. (2022). Infringing upon our basic freedoms. *Dhaka Tribune*. https://www.dhakatribune.com/op-ed/2022/04/25/infringing-upon-our-basic-freedoms

Murad, M. H. (2012). A Study of Digital Signature and Its Legal Implications in Context of Bangladesh. *IIUC Studies, 6*(6), 111–122. doi:10.3329/iiucs.v6i0.12252

Myadvo. (2021). *What is Cyber Bullying or Anti-Bullying Laws in India*. https://www.myadvo.in/blog/must-read-what-is-cyber-bullying-or-anti-bullying-laws-in-india/

Nabi, M. S. (2019). Unicef: 32% kids at risk of cyberbullying in Bangladesh. *Dhaka Tribune*. https://archive.dhakatribune.com/bangladesh/dhaka/2019/02/05/unicef-prevent-online-bullying-harassment-of-children-in-bangladesh

Neto, A. P., & Barbosa, L. (2018). Bullying and cyberbullying: Conceptual controversy in Brazil. In The Internet and Health in Brazil: Challenges and Trends (pp. 225–249). Springer. https://doi.org/10.1007/978-3-319-99289-1_12.

Ngo, A. T., Tran, A. Q., Tran, B. X., Nguyen, L. H., Hoang, M. T., Nguyen, T. H. T., Doan, L. P., Vu, G. T., Nguyen, T. H., Do, H. T., Latkin, C. A., Ho, R. C. M., & Ho, C. S. H. (2021). Cyberbullying Among School Adolescents in an Urban Setting of a Developing Country: Experience, Coping Strategies, and Mediating Effects of Different Support on Psychological Well-Being. *Frontiers in Psychology*, *12*, 930. https://doi.org/10.3389/fpsyg.2021.661919

Novitasari, N. F., Irma, N., & Hia, A. (2021). Cyberbullying in Movie Cyberbully : an Analysis From the Psychological Perspective. *Celtic: A Journal of Culture, English Language Teaching. Literatura y Lingüística*, *8*(1), 44–64. https://doi.org/10.22219/CELTIC.V8I1.16393

Patchin, J. W., & Hinduja, S. (2006). Bullies Move Beyond the Schoolyard: A Preliminary Look at Cyberbullying. *Youth Violence and Juvenile Justice*, *4*(2), 148–169. https://doi.org/10.1177/1541204006286288

Pennell, D., Campbell, M., & Tangen, D. (2022). The education and the legal system: Inter-systemic collaborations identified by Australian schools to more effectively reduce cyberbullying. *Preventing School Failure*, *66*(2), 175–185. https://doi.org/10.1080/1045988X.2021.2007835

Petric, D. (2022). Psychology of Abusive Human Behavior. *Open Journal of Medical Psychology*, *11*(02), 29–38. https://doi.org/10.4236/ojmp.2022.112003

Polanin, J. R., Espelage, D. L., Grotpeter, J. K., Ingram, K., Michaelson, L., Spinney, E., Valido, A., El Sheikh, A., Torgal, C., & Robinson, L. (2022). A Systematic Review and Meta-analysis of Interventions to Decrease Cyberbullying Perpetration and Victimization. *Prevention Science*, *23*(3), 439–454. https://doi.org/10.1007/s11121-021-01259-y

Research Service Member. (2018). *Victims Of Cyberbullying*. European Parliamentary Research Service Blog. https://epthinktank.eu/2018/10/28/victims-of-cyberbullying-what-europe-does-for-you/

Riaz, A. (2022). *How Bangladesh's Digital Security Act Is Creating a Culture of Fear - Carnegie Endowment for International Peace*. Carnegie Endowment for International Peace. https://carnegieendowment.org/2021/12/09/how-bangladesh-s-digital-security-act-is-creating-culture-of-fear-pub-85951

Robert, E. (2021). Attempting a definition of cyber crime. *SSRN Electronic Journal*. doi:10.2139/ssrn.3830589

Romito, P., Cedolin, C., Bastiani, F., & Saurel-Cubizolles, M. J. (2019). Disordered Eating Behaviors and Sexual Harassment in Italian Male and Female University Students. *Journal of Interpersonal Violence*, *34*(14), 2960–2974. https://doi.org/10.1177/0886260516664315

Runa, S. J. (2019). The Challenges of Freedom of Expression and the Digital Security Act 2018. *BiLD Law Journal*, *4*(2), 75–92. https://bildbd.com/index.php/blj/article/view/20

Shaon, A. I. (2018). The question of Section 57. *Dhaka Tribune*. https://www.dhakatribune.com/bangladesh/law-rights/2018/08/10/the-question-of-section-57

Smith, P. K. (2019). Research on Cyberbullying: Strengths and Limitations. In *Narratives in Research and Interventions on Cyberbullying among Young People* (pp. 9–27). Springer International Publishing. doi:10.1007/978-3-030-04960-7_2

Song, H., Lee, Y., & Kim, J. (2020). Gender Differences in the Link Between Cyberbullying and Parental Supervision Trajectories. *Crime and Delinquency*, *66*(13–14), 1914–1936. https://doi.org/10.1177/0011128720912371

Sraboni, S. I. (2021). *Cyber Bullying is an alarming issue during Covid-19 situation in Bangladesh*. Lawyers Club Bangladesh. http://lawyersclubbangladesh.com/en/2021/08/03/cyber-bullying-is-an-alarming-issue-during-covid-19-situation-in-bangladesh/

Strohmeier, D., & Gradinger, P. (2022). Cyberbullying and Cyber Victimization as Online Risks for Children and Adolescents. *European Psychologist*, *27*(2), 141–150. https://doi.org/10.1027/1016-9040/a000479

Symantec. (2012). *Norton Cybercrime Report*. https://icma.org/documents/2012-norton-cybercrime-report

Tammam, A. H. (2022). Cyberbullying through social media And its relationship to achievement motivation among adolescent students. *International Journal of Instructional Technology and Educational Studies*, *3*(3), 1–10. https://doi.org/10.21608/IHITES.2022.106649.1077

The Business Standard. (2022). Most DSA cases filed by ruling party people: Study. *The Business Standard*. https://www.tbsnews.net/bangladesh/most-dsa-cases-filed-ruling-party-people-study-408398

The Daily Star. (2022). Digital Security Act: 147 sued, 67 arrests a month. *The Daily Star*. https://www.thedailystar.net/news/bangladesh/news/detentions-under-dsa-recent-average-spikes-67-month-3010906

Tokunaga, R. S. (2010). Following you home from school: A critical review and synthesis of research on cyberbullying victimization. *Computers in Human Behavior, 26*(3), 277–287. https://doi.org/10.1016/j.chb.2009.11.014

United News Bangladesh. (2020). 80% of cyberbullying victims are women. *United News Bangladesh*. https://www.unb.com.bd/category/Bangladesh/80-of-cyberbullying-victims-are-women/61781

Varela, J. J., Hernández, C., Berger, C., Souza, S. B., & Pacheco, E. (2022). To ignore or not to ignore: The differential effect of coping mechanisms on depressive symptoms when facing adolescent cyberbullying. *Computers in Human Behavior, 132*, 107268. https://doi.org/10.1016/j.chb.2022.107268

Villegas, P. E., & Aberman, T. (2019). A double punishment: Post-secondary access for racialized migrant youth with precarious status in Toronto, Canada. *Refuge: Canada's Periodical on Refugees, 35*(1), 72–82. https://doi.org/10.7202/1060676ar

Vranjes, I., Farley, S., & Baillien, E. (2021). Harassment in the Digital World: Cyberbullying - Bullying and Harassment in the Workplace: Theory, Research and Practice. In *Developments in theory, research, and practice* (pp. 409–432). https://ebrary.net/131645/psychology/harassment_digital_world_cyberbullying

Wachs, S., Bilz, L., Wettstein, A., Wright, M. F., Krause, N., Ballaschk, C., & Kansok-Dusche, J. (2022). The Online Hate Speech Cycle of Violence: Moderating Effects of Moral Disengagement and Empathy in the Victim-to-Perpetrator Relationship. *Cyberpsychology, Behavior, and Social Networking*. doi:10.1089/cyber.2021.0159

Wang, H. (2021). Big Data Security Management Countermeasures in the Prevention and Control of Computer Network Crime. *Journal of Global Information Management, 30*(7), 1–16. https://doi.org/10.4018/jgim.295450

Wang, L., & Ngai, S. S. (2021). Cyberbullying Perpetration Among Chinese Adolescents: The Role of Power Imbalance, Fun-seeking Tendency, and Attitude Toward Cyberbullying. *Journal of Interpersonal Violence*. doi:10.1177/08862605211062988

Wong, N., & McBride, C. (2018). Fun over conscience: Fun-seeking tendencies in cyberbullying perpetration. *Computers in Human Behavior, 86*, 319–329. https://doi.org/10.1016/j.chb.2018.05.009

Yoon, D., Shipe, S. L., Park, J., & Yoon, M. (2021). Bulling patterns and their associations with child maltreatment and adolescent psychosocial problems. *Children and Youth Services Review, 129*, 106178. https://doi.org/10.1016/j.childyouth.2021.106178

Zhang, Z., Xiao, H., Zhang, L., & Zheng, J. (2021). Linking Cyberbullying to Job Strain: Roles of Ego Depletion and Self-Efficacy. *Journal of Aggression, Maltreatment and Trauma*. doi:10.1080/10926771.2021.1933288

Zwickl, S., Wong, A. F. Q., Dowers, E., Leemaqz, S. Y. L., Bretherton, I., Cook, T., Zajac, J. D., Yip, P. S. F., & Cheung, A. S. (2021). Factors associated with suicide attempts among Australian transgender adults. *BMC Psychiatry, 21*(1), 1–9. https://doi.org/10.1186/s12888-021-03084-7

ADDITIONAL READINGS

Adorjan, M., & Ricciardelli, R. (2018). *Cyber-risk and youth: Digital citizenship, privacy, and surveillance*. Routledge. doi:10.4324/9781315158686

Babu, K. E. K., & Ullah, M. A. (2021). Cyber legislation and cyber-related legal issues in Bangladesh: Inadequacies and challenges. *International Journal of Electronic Security and Digital Forensics, 13*(2), 180–196. doi:10.1504/IJESDF.2021.113379

Casas, J. A., Ortega-Ruiz, R., & Monks, C. P. (2020). Cyberbullying: A changing phenomenon. In Online peer engagement in adolescence (pp. 71-84). Routledge.

Hinduja, S., & Patchin, J. W. (2008). Cyberbullying: An exploratory analysis of factors related to offending and victimization. *Deviant Behavior, 29*(2), 129–156. doi:10.1080/01639620701457816

Özsungur, F. (Ed.). (2022). *Handbook of Research on Digital Violence and Discrimination Studies*. IGI Global. doi:10.4018/978-1-7998-9187-1

Schmitt, M. (2018). International cyber norms: Reflections on the path ahead. *Militair Rechtelijk Tijdschrift, 111*, 12–23.

KEY TERMS AND DEFINITIONS

Aggressive Behavior: Aggression, according to social psychology, describes any behavior or act aimed at harming a person or animal or damaging physical property.

Cyberbullying: Cyberbullying includes sending, posting, or sharing negative, harmful, false, or mean content about someone else. It can include sharing personal or private information about someone else causing embarrassment or humiliation.

Cybercrime: The use of a computer as an instrument to further illegal ends, such as committing fraud, trafficking in child pornography and intellectual property, stealing identities, or violating privacy.

Federal Law: Federal laws are bills that have passed both houses of Congress, been signed by the president, passed over the president's veto, or allowed to become law without the president's signature. Individual laws, also called acts, are arranged by subject in the United States Code.

Hate Speech: Hate speech is any form of expression through which speakers intend to vilify, humiliate, or incite hatred against a group or a class of persons on the basis of race, religion, skin color sexual identity, gender identity, ethnicity, disability, or national origin.

Legislation: Legislation is a law or a set of laws that have been passed by Parliament. The word is also used to describe the act of making a new law.

Perpetration: The act of committing a crime or a violent or harmful act. In cyberbullying, the act of intentionally hurt, insult, criminal or violent behavior online is considered as the 'cyberbully' or 'perpetrator'.

Systematic Intimidation: Any act of physical or psychological violence, intentional and repetitive, that occurs with no obvious motivation, practiced by individuals or groups against one or more persons, in order to intimidate or attack the person(s), causing pain and distress to the victim(s) in a relationship of imbalance of power between the parties involved.

Chapter 12
An Analysis of News Containing Cyberbullying in the Metaverse

İlkay Yıldız
Bingöl University, Turkey

Nural İmik Tanyıldızı
https://orcid.org/0000-0002-9177-759X
Fırat Unıversıty, Turkey

ABSTRACT

The rapid progress of technological developments and their opening to the use of societies has brought with it various problems. Although the internet makes our lives easier, bullying has started to be seen in this area. The subject of cyberbullying, which should be addressed in a wide area from economy to politics, from social life to culture, has also manifested itself in the metaverse area. This study examines how the Turkish national press handles cyberbullying in the metaverse area. News about Metaverse has been published in many publications. The news that deals with cyberbullying and solution suggestions are only included in this study. In the Turkish national press, a total of six stories about cyberbullying in the metaverse area were reached. The news usually consists of harassment, precautionary, and solution suggestions. They were analyzed by the discourse analysis method. While performing discourse analysis, both macro and micro analyses were made.

INTRODUCTION

With the rapid developments in communication and computer technologies, the more widespread use of these technologies by societies brings with it various negative situations as well as positive. The Internet has many positive features, such as enabling fast communication, eliminating time and space limitations, and being used in all areas of society, from education to health, from politics to the economy. However, the increasingly aggressive behavior on the internet, violations of personal rights and freedoms, and the idea that everyone has the right to say what they want on the internet have also revealed a new concept defined as cyberbullying. Although bullying is as old as human history, cyberbullying has become an area

DOI: 10.4018/978-1-6684-5426-8.ch012

that people are exposed to with the spread of the internet in societies. Despite being similar to traditional bullying, cyberbullying only manifests itself through the use of electronic devices and communication networks (Maftei, Holman, & Merlici, 2022, p.2). The impact of cyberbullying, whose origins are not very old, on society and individuals has reached significant dimensions. The communication skills of individuals who are exposed to swearing, insulting, abusive messages, comments, images, and videos are damaged, and their psychology is impaired.

Cyberbullying is generally the wrong use of this medium by individuals with the advancement of technological developments. The consequences of this misuse are defined as cyberbullying (Bhat, Chang, & Linscott, 2010, p. 36). Cyberbullying is generally accepted as a broad category of deliberate, aggressive behaviors targeting specific individuals or groups whose primary purpose is to harm or damage their reputation (Maftei, Holman, & Merlici, 2022, p.2). Narin and Ünal (2016, p.10) point out that cyberbullying is a special type of aggression, define cyberbullying as a form of bullying carried out through mobile phones, computers, in short, all electronic technologies and networks such as social media. Bozkanat (2020, p.44), on the other hand, stated that cyberbullying is usually done to someone who cannot defend himself easily, and she defined it as aggression that is carried out intentionally and repeatedly in the electronic environment. Belsey (2007, p.8) defined cyberbullying as the use of information and communication technologies to support the intentional, repeated, and hostile behavior of a person or group aimed at harming others. On the other hand, Bhat (2008, p. 54) defined cyberbullying with a view close to Belsey's definition: "Cyberbullying is the use of information and communication technologies to intimidate, harass, victimize or bully an individual or group of individuals". The developments in information and communication technologies have been highlighted in the definitions of cyberbullying. Champell (2005, p.1) draws attention to the negative aspect of the internet by saying that cyberbullying becomes the 'dark side' of technology with the use of technology to harm others.

The main difference that distinguishes cyberbullying from traditional bullying is that the perpetrator thinks that it is possible to hide his identity by hiding behind the internet. This is why cyberbullying is more strict. It leads to the use of harsher and more brutal words. This hiding makes it easier for the perpetrator to strike the victim without seeing the victim's physical reaction (Donegan, 2012, p.34). The increasing number of users, as today's society adapts more easily to technological developments, also increases cyberbullying.

TYPES OF CYBERBULLYING

As the usage areas of the internet have developed, the type and scope of cyberbullying experienced in this area have also expanded. Any negative situation on the Internet is not much different from a negative situation in real life. Especially, the recent attempts to create virtual universes such as the metaverse make us think again about the bullying in these areas. "Adult Online Hate, Harassment, and Abuse:" published by The London School of Economics and Political Science (LSE) in 2019: In the report called "A Rapid Evidence Assessment", today's diversity of cyberbullying was approached from a broader perspective. In this report (2019, p. 3,4,5), online harassment and trolling (phishing) constitute the most prominent cybercrimes. Of course, the important part here is that the online harassment phenomenon is at the forefront. Online harassment and other forms of cyberbullying can have as much impact on people as real-life bullying and can cause extensive damage to people's mental health. Studies on trolling are very few. For this reason, there is no information about whether trolling behavior is as effective as online harassment or what kind of effect its results have. The main types of harassment, apart from online harassment, are Nickname calling, Intentional embarrassment, Physical Threats, Continuous Harassment, Online Tracking, Sexual Harassment (2020, Bozkanat, p.45).

Cyberstalking a person is another example of cyberbullying. It is a repetitive electronic communication method in order to cause uneasiness in the person being followed and to ensure the realization of undesirable behaviors. Akça and Sayımer (2017, p. 6) defined cyber tracking as follows: "Consistent sending of offensive, frightening and extremely offensive messages that threaten to harm a targeted person. The cyberstalker may try to damage the reputation of the victim and disrupt friendship relations". Here, the follower usually adopts an obsessive attitude towards the person being followed.

Cyber Pornography is another type of cyberbullying. In this type, it is the taking or secretly broadcasting unwanted images of the person, usually for revenge or sexual satisfaction. Although pornographic content occurs at the request of the person, recording and publishing this behavior is independent of the person's will. Hekim and Başıbüyük (2013, p. 141) stated that the factor that makes cyber pornography more widespread is that it does not require face-to-face contact, and they stated that this type of material also gives their consumers a sense of being secret and hiding their identity.

Online hate speech comes in many forms. While creating hate speech, it can also be done with visual content or accompanied by songs and music. Especially after the statements of politicians, the most common hate speech is taking sections from those statements and making them caricatured.

Reymond, Lock, and Smart (2020, p.4) listed the types of cyberbullying as follows: Online stalking: Harassment to threaten or intimidate the person. Scribble: Bringing someone up with unpleasant behavior, words, or untrue material. Most of the time, these materials are also sent to the person himself, creating a threat. Exclusion: Specifically and deliberately not including a person in an event, situation, or study. Enraged: Behavior that will make someone angry, send insulting or rude messages as a result of getting angry. Impersonation: Concealing one's own identity by pretending to be someone else and sending materials that negatively affect that person based on that identity. Disclosure: Spreading private or embarrassing information or images such as pictures/videos that a person does not want to be shared. Deception: cheating to obtain private or embarrassing data that the person does not want to be shared.

It is very difficult to determine whether any behavior on the Internet falls within the scope of cyberbullying. Especially in the types of verbal cyberbullying, people often justify themselves by saying, "you misunderstood me". Veiga Simao et al. (2018, p.10) examined the types of verbal attacks against cyberbullying under nine subheadings. 1) Threatening... 2) Harassment... 3) Making fun of... 4) Pretending to be someone else... 5) Disclosure of someone's information... 6) Indicating that you have information about a person's life... 7) Using the photo without authorization... 8) To devalue someone's life... 9) To insult someone... In this context, it is possible to increase the types of verbal cyberbullying, which are examined under nine sub-headings.

THE NEW DOMAIN OF CYBERBULLYING: METAVERSE

In the metaverse, the combination of the prefix "meta" (implying transcending) with the word "universe" defines a hypothetical synthetic environment connected with the physical world (Nalbant, Uyanık, 2021, p.9). On the other hand, Kuş (221, p.245), by introducing a broad definition of the Metaverse, "offers a new reality, the world of meaning and cooperation opportunities; providing infrastructure and interaction opportunities for cultural, intellectual and economic production; different advanced technologies are used simultaneously and in an integrated manner; "Cyber is a social plane". Metaverse is the transfer of signals received from people's bodies in the real world to the virtual world (Ağralı, Aydın, 2021, p. 25). While the exact definition seems to depend on who is speaking, it is basically a new version of the internet with more emphasis on virtual worlds (Nesbo, 2021). This multi-virtual world is computer-generated and goes beyond the physical universe (Lee et al., 2021,p, 1). According to Smart et al. (2007, p.4), the metaverse should not be thought of as just a virtual universe. In addition, in the metaverse area, there is no race, gender, or physical disability (Duan, Li, Fan, Lin, Wu & Cai, 2021, p.154).

Kunz et al. (2003, p.3-4) explained the main purpose of Metaverse as follows: "to provide users with an open, borderless, immersive environment that makes them believe that traditional barriers of time and space have been removed by manipulating their visual senses". Users of this virtual universe gain access to this world in several ways. The first of these is visually immersive, the second is self-configuring and monitoring, the third is interaction, and the fourth is a portal called "Metaverse Viewing Portal" (Kunz et al. 2003, p.4).

The first person to use the word metaverse conceptually is Neal Stephenson. Stephenson used this concept in his novel Snow Crash, published in 1992 and later translated into Turkish as "parasite". In this novel, Stephenson designed the metaverse as a space where people exist and interact with their avatars (Nalbant, Uyanık, 2021, p.9). The metaverse in Snow Crash is an urban setting developed along a 100-meter-wide road called the Street of a featureless, black, perfectly spherical planet with a circumference of 65,536 kilometers. Here, people can buy virtual lands and set up their buildings (Doko, 2022). In this book, the word "metaverse" was used for the first time, and this concept was translated into Turkish as "metaverse". In addition, while this concept was used 119 times in the original of the book, it was used 117 times in the Turkish translation (Demir, Tokgöz, 2022, p.70). This book later became the subject of the computer simulation game Second Life. It has been particularly interesting because it contains unique concepts and predictions for the future, as well as psychology, history, linguistics, anthropology, archaeology, religion, computer science, politics, cryptography, portable information, and philosophy (Torun, Torun, 2021).

Another important issue in the metaverse field is the subject of "avatar". It is wrong to describe the metaverse space without avatars. In this context, Girvan defined the metaverse (2018, p. 1099) as follows: "Common, simulated spaces inhabited and shaped by its inhabitants, represented as avatars". Based on this definition, it would not be wrong to say that avatars represent a user in the metaverse. The existence of avatars is an issue that needs to be addressed in terms of cyberbullying. Because the avatars in the metaverse actually represent an individual in the real world. This individual is in the position of emphasizing how he should behave in the metaverse. Thanks to avatars, each user can define himself with a unique character and can be defined as a virtual self through which all his activities in the world are channeled (Demir, Tokgöz, 2022, p. 85). It can be said that an avatar is a digital entity that is controlled by users in the real world and mediates their movements and actions in the virtual world in real-time (Nevelsteen, 2018: 10). Although it is defined as digital, avatars can also act in the metaverse area by including many bullying since they are directed by individuals from the real world. The presence of artificial intelligence in the metaverse area, the realization of deep learning, the realization of the act of seeing through computers, and the technologies that add visual effects can create a real human face (Ko et al. 2021, p. 336). This situation can cause various effects on individuals in the real world.

RESEARCH METHODOLOGY

Subject and Importance of the Research

Cyberbullying is becoming an increasingly important field today. In this context, the subject of the research is cyberbullying in the metaverse area, which has become popular recently. The reflection of cyberbullying in the metaverse to the news texts is discussed within the scope of this study. After cyberbullying has become widespread in the metaverse, it is important to examine the news published on this subject. Contextual analyzes such as the way the news is handled, the level of informing the public, and the reliability of its sources reveal whether the necessary importance is given to cyberbullying. Moving the internet, which is widely used all over the world, to different dimensions with the metaverse requires considering the regulations to be made on cyberbullying as an area to be considered. It is expected that the news analysis and the results obtained from the study will set an example for future studies.

Method of Research

The method of this research is discourse analysis within the qualitative research design. Teun Van Dijk's critical discourse analysis was used in the study. Dijk's critical discourse analysis is concerned with discursive consequences such as any inequality, injustice, or abuse of power arising from the discourse on the subject matter. For this purpose, in Dijk's model, news texts are analyzed in two ways: semantic and syntactic. In semantic technique, words, sentences, and a general meaning formed by them are emphasized. In the syntactic technique, the grammar of the sentences is discussed. The compatibility of the sentences with the grammatical structures is analyzed. While making these analyzes, Dijk first deals with the general structure of the text and calls it macro analysis. Then it goes to the private and analyzes the sentences and words one by one. Dijk also calls this micro-examination. Headlines, news entries, the main event, news sources, background and context information, comments/evaluations of the parties of the event, photographs, etc., are analyzed within the framework of the macrostructure (Özer, 2001, p. 83). The news texts handled in micro-analysis are handled with the syntactic technique. Answers are sought to questions such as whether words are simple or complex, have an active sentence structure, or have a passive structure. In addition, whether the words in the news contain an ideology is another issue that needs to be analyzed. According to Van Dijk (1988, p. 15), the news production process is carried out continuously by the professionals who do this job, and these news productions are organized according to these two frameworks.

Problems of the Research

In the research, news about cyberbullying were analyzed, and answers were sought to the following questions in general:

- In what context was the news covered?
- Has cyberbullying been discussed in the news?
- Who is accused of being a cyberbully in the news?

In the research, attention was paid to the fact that the studies were in the nature of seeking answers to these questions.

Population and Sample of the Research

The universe of this research consists of all the news dealing with cyberbullying. The sample of the study, on the other hand, is only the news that deals with cyberbullying in the metaverse area. The metaverse field has not yet become widespread all over the world. Therefore, the metaverse is not within the knowledge of many people. The number of people using this area is quite limited compared to the number of people using the internet. Due to such limitations, the number of news published is also limited. For this reason, no publication was specified, and all news dealing with cyberbullying in the metaverse area were included in the study. Another important issue here is that news is covered on all news channels. The fact that the same news is covered in different news channels does not mean that there is a lot of cyberbullying in the metaverse area. For this reason, the media organ that deals with the same news in the most detailed way were included in the study. Other publications were not included in the study. In short, an event in the metaverse was included in the study through the most detailed publication. From this point of view, the harassment incident so far has taken place in the metaverse. These two events were covered in all news organs. After these events, news about cyberbullying within the scope of the metaverse were made, and in the same way, the publication that gave this news in the most detailed way was examined. The aim of the analyzed news is to reveal generalizable results.

Data Collection and Analysis

The data of the study were obtained by Van Dijk's discourse analysis method. For the scope of the study, the content of the news was examined as macrostructure and micro structure. In this research, it is important to analyze the news in order to find the reflection on the cyberbullying issue in the news.

Findings and Interpretation

In the findings and comment section, the analysis of the data obtained from the research is given. In this context, the analyzed news are discussed in detail within the framework of the frequency of publication, the subject of cyberbullying, the person responsible for cyberbullying, and the way the news is delivered. When the news about the metaverse was examined, there was not much cyberbullying news. In addition, there is no news about this issue involving Turkey.

Macro Analysis

In macro analysis, the title of the news, the flash of the news, the main plot, the sources of the news, the background and context information in the news, the comments and evaluations made for the event, the photographs, the spots are analyzed. In this research, these criteria of the news are discussed within the framework of macro analysis. Comments and evaluations made for the event from these criteria are not included in this study. Because the comments and evaluations about the event constitute wide and comprehensive data that should be handled within the scope of another study. However, a statement made by the expert or experts about the news was also considered as news because the information was newsworthy.

News Headlines

The headlines of the news are the most important element in terms of conveying the plot of the news to the reader. For this reason, it is also important to examine the news headlines. The news headlines that are the subject of the research are listed below according to the publication dates of the news:

1. Hidden Danger! Facebook Has Become Metaverse But... (Milliyet, news dated 01.11.2021)
2. Harassment Scandal in the Metaverse (Haber Global, news dated 19.12.2021)
3. Facebook Informant Frances Haugen: I'm Extremely Afraid of Project Metaverse (En Son Haber, News dated 23.12.2021)
4. It Happens Every 7 Minutes, The Virtual World Is Confused! Harassment Scandal in Metaverse... (Milliyet, news dated 12.01.2022)
5. "Metaverse May Cause Chaos in the World" (Habertürk, news dated 19.01.2022)
6. Sexual Harassment of Women in Metaverse: They Attacked the Avatar. (NTV, news dated 31.01.2022)
7. Metaverse Plot Scam: Your Money Can Be Vapor. (En Son Haber, news dated 01.02.2022)
8. New Measure to Prevent Harassment in the Metaverse Universe. (En Son Haber, news dated 06.02.2022)
9. Metaverse Alert from Russia: There May Be Illegal Actions (En Son Haber, news dated 07.02.2022)
10. A Fight Has Happened In The Metaverse. (Tele 1, news dated 23.02.2022)
11. Dangers Awaiting Children in the Metaverse Universe (En Son Haber, news dated 24.02.2022)

The subject covered in the news texts is correctly reflected in the news headlines. The subject of the news is to state a "negative situation in the metaverse". Looking at the news headlines on this subject, the news pattern is understood.

It is seen that there is no lack of information in the titles of the news. In general, the title has been handled as descriptive and sentence. This caused the titles to belong. However, it would be a mistake to deduct information on a subject like a metaverse, which the society does not yet know precisely what it is. In general, it has been tried to explain the question of "what happened" from the 5 W 1K, which is the news writing rule in news headlines. Other features are not included in the title.

It has been observed that generalizable expressions are generally included in the news headlines. Events that take place anywhere in the metaverse or in the domain of different companies are generalized to the entire metaverse.

News Entries

News entries are called flash. The flash of the news is the part that constructs the main event according to the 5W1K rule, which is the news writing rule and emphasizes the most critical element. News entries are very important in conveying the main theme of the event and understanding it correctly. In addition, these entries should not be written in very long sentences. The news entries that are the subject of the research are listed below according to the publication dates of the news:

1. "Facebook has changed its name! The CEO of the company, Mark Zuckerberg, announced Metaverse, which is called the social media of the future, to the whole world....Academic Seçkin Canan believes that all these questions should be looked at from a very different perspective. . "There are companies that invest a lot in the meta part of the business," says Canan, adding that Facebook stands out simply because it puts its name on it, and draws attention to the hidden danger. (Milliyet, news dated 01.11.2021)
2. "A scandalous incident occurred in the virtual world called Horizon Worlds, prepared by Facebook's parent company Meta for Metaverse." (Haber Global, news dated 19.12.2021)
3. "Facebook whistleblower Frances Haugen expressed extreme fear and concern about metaverse technologies." (En Son Haber, news dated 23.12.2021)
4. "The Metaverse started to make a name for itself more and more every day. While the majority are talking about the benefits and capabilities of this technology, with the Metaverse world, cybercrime can be taken to a different dimension." (Milliyet, news dated 12.01.2022)
5. "The President of the Association for Combating Digital Addiction, Prof. Dr. Tuncay Dilci mentioned the negativities that Metaverse, the most popular discussion topic of recent days, could cause and said that it could cause chaos in the world. (Habertürk, news dated 19.01.2022)
6. "British Jane Patel announced that her avatar on the "metaverse", the virtual platform Meta introduced as "the world of the future", was sexually harassed by the avatars of male users. The incident, which was reflected in the press, caused discussions on the safety of women and children on online platforms in the country. (NTV, news dated 31.01.2022)
7. "Experts warn against fraud that may occur in land sales made in Metaverse projects." (En Son Haber, news dated 01.02.2022)
8. "Facebook parent company Meta has announced a 1.2-meter boundary between avatars to prevent harassment in the metaverse universe." (En Son Haber, news dated 06.02.2022)
9. "Russia has warned that illegal activity may take place in the recently popular metaverse universes." (En Son Haber, news dated 07.02.2022)
10. "There has been a fight in the virtual world of Metaverse, which has been making a name for itself lately and has started to enter our lives as the world of the future..." (Tele 1, news dated 23.02.2022)
11. "The metaverse universe allows children to enter virtual strip clubs and interact with adults. Here are the problems waiting for children…" (En Son Haber, news dated 24.02.2022)

In all news entries, the "what" question, which is a 5W1K element, was answered. When the answer to the question "What" is discussed at the beginning of the news, it makes the text of the news more understandable. For this reason, all news entries gave information about the news text and were designed to summarize the event. The news entry of the first news is presented in such a way that it is much longer than necessary. News entries should be short. In the third, fifth, and sixth news entries, besides the "what" question, the answer to the "who" question is also given clearly.

The introduction of the second news, on the other hand, reduced the generalization made in the headline to even more specific and stated that there was a scandal in "Horizon Worlds". This situation is also in line with the rules of journalism. It shows that the news entry is structured to support the title.

Figure 1.

Photo Usage

Photos are an element that supports news texts and makes the news easier to read. The photographs used in the analyzed news were not created from the shooting of any reporter. Usually, the photos used are in the form of images copied and pasted from the internet. It is seen that only in the interviews with the experts on the subject, the photograph of the expert is taken and published. In the remaining photographs, an avatar symbolizing the virtual environment is generally used. Some photos show people wearing virtual reality glasses.

When we look at the distribution of news photos in the news, it is seen that the news medium where the most images and photos are shared is "Milliyet Newspaper". Milliyet newspaper used four visuals in its news dated 01.11.2021. In addition, it shared five images in his news dated 12.01.2022. One of these images consists of a portrait photograph of people who are experts in their field. A single image was shared on all the remaining news channels. No visuals were used in the news of "En Son Haber" dated 01.02.2022 and 23.12.2021. Another news channel that does not use visuals is "Tele 1".

When the photographs are evaluated in terms of cyberbullying, it is seen that no image that negates the subject is shared. Images are usually given as people using virtual reality glasses. There are two remaining images. The following image of Milliyet Newspaper can be shown as an example of cyberbullying. The image shows a female silhouette. A hidden hand is seen recording this female silhouette with a mobile phone. With this image (Figure 1), it is given the impression that people can be followed more easily in the metaverse area.

Another example image is the image used in the same news. In the image below (Figure 2) published by Milliyet Newspaper, it is seen that a hand is making secret speeches at the computer. Presenting texts as if secret passwords are flowing on the image shows that cyberbullying can also be done by speaking.

Figure 2.

Presenting the Main Event and Its Consequences

The news texts of all news are generally designed to describe a negative situation in the metaverse field.

The "Enson Haber" site usually started its news texts by giving information about the metaverse and relevant to its subject. The "Haber Global" website also entered the news by defining the metaverse and mentioned that Facebook changed its name to meta. As a result of a one-paragraph article in which it described these, it was informed that there was an incident of harassment in the metaverse area. "Habertürk Newspaper", on the other hand, referred to Dilci's work on this issue before going on with his meeting with Prof. Dr. Tuncay Dilci, President of the Association for Combating Digital Addiction. It is seen that the news of "Milliyet Newspaper" dated 12.01.2022 and the news of NTV directly emphasize sexual harassment.

The general conclusion to be drawn from the news is as follows: Metaverse is not yet a reliable and accepted area by the whole society in Turkey. For this reason, it was emphasized that a cautious approach should be taken to entering this field. In particular, the occurrence of sexual harassment and fighting in various news channels conditions the society against this area. News texts were created in a way that supports the short information given both in the headlines of the news and in the flashes of the news. The texts are generally designed to include the negativities of the metaverse field and the violence in this field. In addition, an image has been drawn about the people exposed to harassment in the metaverse area that they do not have enough information and do not approach it cautiously.

Background and Context

In communication, the background is not considered independent of the social and cultural structure. Van Dijk (1988, p.20) also emphasizes the socio-cultural and political aspects of the backgrounds in the news and states that they are structural and historical. . In the analyzed news, it is seen that the background and context for the metaverse are not sufficiently emphasized. Since the metaverse area is a very new formation, there is no clarity yet about why the harassment incidents occur, how they are done or how they can be prevented. This affects the background and context of the news. Although the reason for the cyberbullying is not included in the news, the solution proposals or the issues about the way to be followed in the future are included in almost every news.

"...You will lose most of your deposited numbers. In order to reduce this loss, it is necessary to make the right investments by researching from the right sources and meeting with the right people." (En Son Haber, February 1, 2022)

"Experts are of the opinion that ... through cryptocurrencies, systems can be designed that are more transparent, based on governance and mutual benefit, freed from the chains of traditional markets, where users can have control over their data and production without fear of manipulation, and do not have to be alienated from their work and life." (Milliyet, November 1, 2021)

News Sources and Evaluations of Event Parties

Second-hand news sources were generally used in the analyzed news. The reason why the news source is second-hand is usually due to the negative situations experienced abroad. After the events in the metaverse area are news, the news sources that evaluate the event are examples of first-hand news sources. Some of the news that will be an example of first-hand news sources are given below.

"...Metaverse Expert Can Kazancıoğlu said, "The probability of a real-life deed being fake may also be in land sales in metaverse projects." (En Son Haber, February 1, 2022.) In this news, the source is introduced as a metaverse expert. However, there is no information about where this person works. Also, it is among the questions to be asked whether there is a specialty called metaverse expertise. The reporter added a field of expertise to add credibility to his news.

"This is an important step forward, and there is more work to be done. We will continue to test and explore new ways to help people feel comfortable in virtual universes," said Vivek Sharma, Meta's vice president of Horizon. used the phrases. (En Son Haber, 6 February 2022). The source of this news is a more reliable source. Both the name of the person and the institution were explained, and the sentences were communicated from the mouth of the person making the statement.

"The UK-based Society for the Prevention of Torture of Children (NSPCC) has announced that virtual reality universes endanger children." The source of this news is the Child Torture Prevention Association. The news source is the primary source of news. The information given in the continuation of the news is based on the statement of this association.

In the news texts, the supporters of the event are the people who experience negativity in the metaverse area and the people who are authorized in this area. The statements made by the experts on the subject after a negative situation were determined as another party in the news. Thus, it was ensured that the readers had more control over the metaverse field. The fact that the event parties generally address the negative aspects of the metaverse and explain accordingly is proof that the metaverse area is intended to be shown as a very insecure area.

Micro Analysis

The subject covered in news texts is done in various ways in microanalysis. These pathways are listed as follows: syntactic analysis, regional cohesion, word choices, and rhetorical analysis. In all these ways explained, the sentences are analyzed both in terms of grammar and analysis in terms of meaning.

Syntactic Analysis

Syntactic analysis is about the analysis of the sentences in the news text. The structure of the sentence is looked at, and attention is paid to how the subject and the predicate are placed, which are among the elements of the sentence. The subject is especially important in this regard. The position of the person who is affected by the event or who does the event himself in the sentence also determines the emphasis placed on it. For this reason, the position of the subject should be considered first while performing the syntactic analysis. Then, the sentence structures are examined. It is important to find an answer to the question of whether the sentences are written simple or complex. In addition, it is examined whether the sentences are active or passive in the sentence structure. Since the active sentence structure is more understandable and creates sentences by giving the news source, it is necessary to use active sentences in news texts. In passive sentences, since the source of the news is usually unclear, such sentences should be avoided in news texts.

It is seen that the sentence structures in the analyzed news are generally written in a way that is effective. The number of sentences written in a passive form is very few. In addition, the subject is generally positioned at the beginning of the sentence in accordance with Turkish rules. Examples of news texts are as follows:

A 43-year-old mother of four in London, England, told Nina Jane Patel that she was sexually assaulted by a mob within minutes of entering Facebook's metaverse universe." (En Son Haber, 6 February 2022)

"Prof. Dr. Tuncay Dilci defined Metaverse as a new world order designed beyond the universe and said, "Metaverse is one of the most talked-about groves at the moment. It refers to a new World designed beyond the universe..." (Haberturk, 19 January 2022)

"Zuckerberg, whose video recording was published at the conference, made statements about Metaverse." (Milliyet, November 1, 2021)

"Within 60 seconds of entering the platform, three male avatars came towards me and inappropriately touched my avatar," said Patel, who joined Horizon with an avatar that looked like him. (NTV, 31 January 2022)

Regional Compliance

The sentences that make up the news texts in regional harmony are evaluated in terms of causal, referential, and functional relationships (Doruk, 2013, p.124). In the causal relationship, it is checked whether the sentences formed in the news texts are connected to each other with casual ties. In referential relations, it is checked whether the sentences formed in the news texts are related to the previous sentence.

In functional relations, it is checked whether the sentences formed in the news texts are better expressed in the next sentence.

It is seen that the news sentences in the analyzed news are connected to each other in terms of causality and functionality.

"Facebook's parent company, Meta Platforms, has imposed a personal space limit for people using virtual reality platforms due to growing concerns about user safety and sexual harassment in the metaverse universe." (En Son Haber, 6 February 2022). In this news text published by En Son Haber, it is seen that the event is connected with a causal link. In particular, the measure taken for sexual harassment, which is cyberbullying, is clearly stated.

"Russia also addressed concerns about the consequences of virtual interaction on human behavior. Experts warned that this could particularly affect children, the "most vulnerable group" in virtual universes, and said social behavior could change. (En Son Haber, 7 February 2022). Again, in this news text published by En Son Haber, it is seen that the event is presented together with the functionality relationship. First of all, the effect of the metaverse field on human behavior was emphasized, and then its effects on children were explained in terms of being more explanatory.

"After the incident, Meta launched an internal investigation. The investigation concluded that the user did not enable a security feature designed to prevent harassment." (Haber Global, 19 December 2021). In this news published by Haber Global, it is seen that the event in the news text is presented with a referential relationship. Who initiated the investigation in the text was explained in the first sentence, and then the text of the news was expanded by referring to the investigation. Such sentences are also evaluated in the context of functionality-relationship.

"This concept, which entered our lives very quickly, opened the door to new security breaches. The only thing that can be done against the crimes that may be committed in the Metaverse is to report a complaint through the applications used on this basis." (Milliyet, 12 January 2022). In the news published by Milliyet Newspaper, the news text is presented with the functionality relationship. It is stated in the first sentence that the metaverse field is very new in our lives. In the second sentence, it is emphasized that the actions to be taken in case of security breaches are very limited since it is a new concept.

Word Selection

The words used while editing the news text are usually made up of conscious choices. For this reason, it is important to examine the news texts in terms of words and to reveal whether the words reflect the meaning behind them. The news text also reflects the ideological, political, and religious views of both the journalist who wrote the news and the institution where the journalist works. With elements such as the clarity and clarity of the words used in news texts, the level of understanding of the reader also increases.

The news included in the research were evaluated separately as the headline, the flash of the news, and the news text. The words used in the news headlines usually contain words that emphasize cyberbullying. It is seen that the word "metaverse" is used very frequently, especially in the majority of the titles, along with the word that emphasizes cyberbullying.

When the news headlines are examined, it is seen that in the news of Milliyet Newspaper dated November 1, 2021, "Hidden Danger! Facebook Has Become the Metaverse, But..." In the title, the word "danger" is used by referring to the word "metaverse". In the news of Haber Global dated December 19, 2021, in the news of Milliyet Newspaper dated January 12, 2022, in the news of NTV dated January 32, 2022, the words "metaverse" and "harassment" were used together. Various words expressing cyberbullying were used together with the word "metaverse" in the remaining news headlines. Some of these words are as follows: "Fear", "fraud", "chaos", "illegal action", "fight".

When news entries are examined, the words "metaverse" and "Facebook" usually come to the fore. The fact that sexual harassment incidents are experienced in the virtual world prepared by Facebook makes Facebook even more important. The words to be emphasized in the news entries have also been carefully selected. The words aiming to introduce the metaverse as a field of cyberbullying were tried to be conveyed by the experts on the subject. For example, Milliyet Newspaper's news entry on November 1, 2021, continued with a statement by a person named Academician Seçkin Canan, after giving brief information about the metaverse. In the statement made, it was emphasized that this was a "hidden danger". Likewise, in the introduction of the news published by Latest News on December 23, 2021, Facebook whistleblower Frances Haugen took a sentence from the statement. Haugen stated that he was afraid and worried about this by using the word metaverse. The news published by Habertürk Newspaper on January 19, 2022, included the comments of Prof. Dr. Tuncay Dilci, President of the Association for Combating Digital Addiction. Dilci, on the other hand, used the word metaverse as well as the word chaos in his explanation. In the news entry published by NTV on January 31, 2022, British Jane Patel stated that she made a statement. In her statement, Patel used the words metaverse avatar and sexual harassment together. In particular, emphasizing the sexual harassment incident makes the issue important. In general, when the news entries are analyzed, it draws the image that the metaverse area of the selected words is not a safe area and that it is a place to be exposed to cyberbullying.

The most frequently used words in news texts are words that emphasize bullying, such as "metaverse", "security-insecurity", "danger", sexual harassment", "attack", "precaution", "complaint". When the news texts are examined one by one, it is seen that each news conveys the subject with almost the same words. The most used words in all the news published by Latest News are the words "metaverse" and "Facebook". The word "metaverse" was used 15 times in total in the news. The word "Facebook" was used 13 times in the news. Referring to the word metaverse, the word virtual universe is another word in the news. Another word in the news is "sexual harassment-assault". In total, this word was used in 6 places in the news. In addition, the word "incident" was used in a few places, referring to the word sexual harassment-assault, in order not to repeat the word. The words used to prevent cyberbullying are mostly "personal border", "safe area". While the word "personal boundary" was used four times, the word "safe area" was used twice. In addition, the words "warning", "fear", "concern", "illegal" are among the words used twice. The words "racist movement" and "rape" were also used once in the news.

In the news published by Haber Global on December 19, 2021, the text of the news was not constructed over the word "metaverse". Instead of using the word "metaverse", which only expresses a general concept, the word "Horizon Worlds", which is the name of the area where the sexual harassment event took place, was used more. The word metaverse was not used consciously in order not to lead the society to bad thoughts about the metaverse area and to prevent the metaverse from being shown as an area open to sexual assaults.

In the news published by Habertürk Newspaper on January 19, 2022, the text of the news was fictionalized with the statements made by the expert on the subject. The most used word in the news text is "metaverse". This word is used 11 times in the news text. In addition, it has been stated that various threats will be experienced by referring to the issue of cyberbullying. In the part where this situation is explained, the word "threat" is used twice. In addition, again referring to the subject of cyberbullying, the words "chaos" and "turmoil" were used once. The word Facebook was not used in this news text. In general, when the news text is evaluated, a negative field image is drawn for the metaverse.

The news published by Milliyet Newspaper on November 1, 2021, and January 12, 2022, constitute the longest news analyzed within the scope of the study. For this reason, these two reports were evaluated separately. The first news was published on November 1, 2021. The word choice in this article is the word "metaverse". This word is used 25 times throughout the news text. In addition, the word "Facebook" was used seven times in the news text. The predominant use of the metaverse word in the news text is due to the fact that the experts on the subject make general evaluations about this field. In other words, whether it is the metaverse areas established by Facebook or the areas established by other companies, the positive and negative features of the metaverse area are explained. Words containing cyberbullying include words such as "problem", "security", and "stolen-stealing". The words "problem" and "stolen-stealing" are used twice in the news text. The word "security" is used ten times. Throughout the news text, the words dominate the idea that even more important security measures should be taken against cyberbullying.

The second news of Milliyet Newspaper was published on January 12, 2022. This news text is more detailed. In addition, the news was carried out by consulting the opinions of two experts. In general, the word used in the news text is the word "metaverse". This word is used 17 times. In addition, the word "Facebook" was used only twice, and it was put forward to transfer the subject to Facebook. The words emphasizing cyberbullying are more in this news. For example, the words "harassment", "violence", "crime", and "security" 5 times, "danger", "threat" 2 times, "violation" 7 times, "cyberbullying" 6 times, and "privacy" The word is used once.

In the news published by NTV on January 31, 2022, the word "virtual platform" was preferred to be used instead of the word "metaverse". The word "Facebook" was used only once. This was done in order to denigrate both the metaverse field and Facebook, and to prevent a false perception in society. The word "Horizon" is often used instead of the word Facebook. This word has appeared five times in the news text. In addition, only the word "platform" was used in 3 places, referring to Horizon. The use of words for cyberbullying is less. The word "harassment" was used six times in the news, as the news text conveyed the incident of sexual harassment. The use of "sexual assault" was emphasized twice in the news text.

In the news published by Tele 1 on February 23, 2022, the number of words used for cyberbullying is quite low. In the news, the word "metaverse" was used three times, the word "virtual universe" was used once, referring to the metaverse, and the word "fight" was used three times. The reason why the word fight is used a lot is due to the fact that it turns a fight in the metaverse area into a news text.

The Rhetoric of the News

The news has a wide range of uses, from rhetorical photographs to images, from quotations to numerical data. The purpose of using this data is to enable the reader to understand the news more deeply and easily. In addition, the question marks in the mind of the reader are eliminated by clearly stating these data. In this context, the photographs will not be reviewed here again, as they are discussed in the macro analysis part of the study. No numerical data or statistical information was found in the news analyzed. However, quoting is used a lot in news texts. In particular, when seeking the opinions of experts on the subject, direct expression is generally preferred instead of indirect expression. The reason for applying an expert on the subject is to increase the credibility of the reader about the news.

CONCLUSIONS AND RECOMMENDATIONS

This study deals with the reflection of cyberbullying events in the metaverse area on news texts. In this context, news channels broadcasting on the internet were examined. The news channels examined approached the event impartially. The most important conclusion drawn from the study is as follows: Some news channels especially emphasized the metaverse area in their news texts, thus causing the area to be mentioned negatively. Some news channels, on the other hand, especially avoided using the word metaverse, instead of attempting to write the name of the area where cyberbullying is experienced. It has been determined that cyberbullying, which is experienced in a new field such as the Metaverse, is widely included in the news. The number of news published in this context is quite high. It is seen that the news of cyberbullying in the metaverse are included in the study has been discussed at length. In addition, many newspapers conducted interviews with the experts on the law and conveyed the issue to the public in a way that they could give both positive and negative perspectives. The words used in the news are designed to refer to cyberbullying. In particular, the words used are words that refer to cyberbullying, such as “sexual harassment”, “security”, “violence”, “crime”, and “violation”. The reason for the overuse of these words is sexual harassment in the metaverse area. It is not known whether there is another type of cyberbullying experienced because the metaverse area is not used by a large audience, and there is little known about this area. It is likely that other types of cyberbullying will emerge as the metaverse is used more and more by societies. However, the cyberbullying incidents that have emerged at the moment necessitate the necessary arrangements to be made in this area. Horizon Worlds, which is used especially under the ownership of Facebook, has introduced a new security measure in which each user has a certain limit in order to prevent sexual harassment. Even this situation may prevent the occurrence of cyber sexual harassment incidents.

Both the headlines and news entries of the news are written in a way that the reader can understand, easily understandable, and clear. Generally, the purpose of the news written in accordance with the news rules was not to manipulate the news or to deflect the subject. Instead, the event in the news was conveyed to the reader in an impartial and up-to-date manner. In the news texts, the plot is given according to certain regulations, and confusion is avoided.

The images used in the news are not designed for cyberbullying. The images of people using virtual reality glasses and emphasizing the virtual universe are included. Any visual describing a danger or a negative situation has not been used within the framework of the news.

Answers are also given to the problem questions determined in the study. In the study, “What is the subject of the news?” The answer to the question is usually the metaverse and sexual harassment incidents in this area. News channels have often focused on this issue. “Has cyberbullying been covered in the news?” The answer to the question has been sought. In this context, sexual harassment incidents were considered as cyberbullying by experts. “Who is accused of being a cyberbully in the news?” The answer to the question is not very clear. This is because the metaverse is a virtual universe, and people can join it as they wish. For this reason, the perpetrator of sexual harassment can be a woman or a man in real life. It could even be a child. For this reason, it is seen that the news texts avoid accusing someone or someone of cyberbullying. This is entirely due to uncertainty.

It is possible to offer various suggestions in the face of negative situations. First of all, the media literacy level of people from all age groups in society should be increased. For this, the scope and time of the education given at young ages should be expanded. Beginning in primary schools, people should be encouraged to look critically at the news and other media. Subjects and practices such as safe use of the internet and self-protection should be added to the curriculum within the media education to be given. Thus, new generations will be able to use the internet more consciously. This training should not be given only theoretically. If necessary, the opportunities will be increased, and each school should have classrooms equipped with more than one computer. Students should be able to see the topics they hear and process theoretically on the internet. The education given in schools should not be limited to children only, but also studies should be carried out for the parents of the students because students should reinforce what they see at school with their parents at home. Otherwise, the studies can not go beyond being seen only as a lesson for students. The education to be given to the parents should not only cover the internet or cyberbullying issues. When appropriate, it is important to provide education on issues such as intra-family communication, child-parent communication, etc., in raising the child. Because most of the people who are cyberbullies see violence, swearing, and devaluation from their family first. The school cannot cope with this alone. Family and school should cooperate.

Another suggestion is to ensure that students who are exposed to such cyberbullying are informed about what to do. For example, ensuring that he or she has material on hand as soon as he realizes that he has been cyberbullied. If this is done verbally, training should also be given, such as making it necessary to take a voice recording, and if it is done in writing, recording a copy of that text. Ensuring that more advanced issues such as cyberbullying are discussed with the family, or school guidance services can minimize such negative situations.

This study is expected to be a guide and resource in the field of cyberbullying.

REFERENCES

Ağralı, Ö., & Aydın, Ö. (2021). Tweet Classification and Sentiment Analysis on Metaverse Related Messages. *Journal of Metaverse, 1*(1).

Akça, E.B., & Sayımer, İ. (2017). Siber Zorbalık Kavramı, Türleri ve İlişkili Olduğu Faktörler: Mevcut Araştırmalar Üzerinden Bir Değerlendirme. *AJIT-e: Online Academic Journal of Information Technology, 8*(30).

Belsey, B. (2007). *Cyber bullying: An emerging threat to the 'always on' generation*. Retrieved June 11, from www.cyberbullying.ca

Bhat, C. S. (2008). Cyber Bullying: Overview and Strategies for School Counsellors, Guidance Officers, and All School Personnel. *Australian Journal of Guidance & Counselling, 18*(1), 53–66. doi:10.1375/ajgc.18.1.53

Bhat, C. S., Chang, S. H., & Linscott, J. A. (2010). Addressing Cyberbullying as a Media Literacy Issue. *New Horizons in Education, 58*(3).

Bozkanat, E. (2020). Dijital İletişimin Karanlık Yüzü Siber Zorbalık: Kavramsal Bir Çerçeve. In Y. Akman (Ed.), *Dijital Dönüşüm ve Yenilik Yönetimi*. İskenderiye Book.

Campbell, M. A. (2005). Cyber bullying: An old problem in a new guise? *Australian Journal of Guidance & Counselling, 15*(1), 68–76. doi:10.1375/ajgc.15.1.68

Demir, M., & Tokgöz, E. (2022). Snow Crash'ten Meta'ya, Metaverse'ün Kavramsal Ve Teknolojik Gelişimi. In N. Göker & G. Göker (Eds.), *İletişim ve Medya Alanında Uluslararası Araştırmalar IV*. Eğitim Publishers.

Dijk, T. A. V. (1988). *New Analysis: Case Studies of International and National News in the Press*. Lawrence Erlbaum Associates Publishers.

Doko, E. (2022). *Alternatif Bir Dünya Arayışı: Metaverse*. https://www.lacivertdergi.com/dosya/2022/01/12/alternatif-bir-dunya-arayisi-metaverse

Donegan, R. (2012). Bullying and Cyberbullying: History, Statistics, Law, Prevention and Analysis. Elon Journal of Undergraduate Research in Communications, 3(1).

Doruk, Ö. (2013). Disiplin Toplumu Ve Haber Söylemi: Gökkuşağı Derneği'nce Yapılması Planlanan Yürüyüşün Engellemesine İlişkin Haberlerin Çözümlenmesi. *e-GİFDER, 2*(1).

Duan, H., Li, J., Fan, S., Lin, Z., Wu, X., & Cai, W. (2021). Metaverse for social good: A university campus prototype. *Proceedings of the 29th ACM International Conference on Multimedia*. 10.1145/3474085.3479238

Girvan, C. (2018). What is a virtual world? Definition and classification. *Educational Technology Research and Development, 66*(5), 1087–1100. doi:10.100711423-018-9577-y

Hekim, H., & Başıbüyük, O. (2013). Siber Suçlar ve Türkiye'nin Siber Güvenlik Politikaları. *International Journal of Security and Terrorism, 4*(2).

Ko, S. Y., Chung, H. K., Kim, J. I., & Shin, Y. (2021). A Study on the Typology and Advancement of Cultural Leisure-Based Metaverse. *KIPS Transactions on Software and Data Engineering, 10*(8), 331–338.

Kunz, J., Jaynes, A., Seales, C., Calvert, W. B., Fei, K., & Griffioen, Z. (2003). The Metaverse - A networked collection of inexpensive, self-configuring, immersive environments. *Proceedings of the Workshop on Virtual Environments, EGVE'03*.

Kuş, O. (2021). Metaverse: 'Dijital Büyük Patlamada' Fırsatlar Ve Endişelere Yönelik Algılar. *Intermedia International e-Journal, 8*(15). doi:10.21645/intermedia.2021.109

Lee, L. H., Braud, T., Zhou, P., Wang, L., Xu, D., Lin, Z., . . . Hui, P. (2021). *All one needs to know about metaverse: A complete survey on technological singularity, virtual ecosystem, and research agenda*. arXiv preprint arXiv:2110.05352.

Maftei, A., Holman, A. C., & Merlici, I. A. (2022). Using fake news as means of cyber-bullying: The link with compulsive internet use and online moral disengagement. *Computers in Human Behavior, 127*, 127. doi:10.1016/j.chb.2021.107032

Nalbant, K.G., & Uyanık, Ş. (2021). Computer Vision in the Metaverse. *Journal of Metaverse, 1*(1).

Narin, B., & Ünal, S. (2016). Siber Zorbalıkla İlgili Haberlerin Türkiye Yazılı Basınında Çerçevelenişi. *The Journal of Akdeniz University's Faculty of Communication, 26*.

Nesbo, E. (2021). *The Metaverse vs. Virtual Reality: 6 Key Differences*. https://www.makeuseof.com/metaverse-vs-virtual-reality/

Nevelsteen, K. J. (2018). Virtual world, defined from a technological perspective and applied to video games, mixed reality, and the Metaverse. *Computer Animation and Virtual Worlds*, *29*(1), e1752. doi:10.1002/cav.1752

Özer, Ö. (2001). *Haber Söylem İdeoloji: Eleştirel Haber Çözümlemeleri*. Literatürk Publishers.

Smart, J., Cascio, J., Paffendorf, J., Bridges, C., Hummel, J., Hursthouse, J., & Moss, R. (2007). *A Cross-Industry Public Foresight Project. Metaverse roadmap 2007: Pathways to the 3DWeb*. Academic Press.

Torun, N. K., & Torun, T. (2021). *Metaverse Kavramının İlk Çıkış Noktası: Snow Crash (Parazit) İncelemesi*. 14th International Conference of Strategic Research on Scientific Studies and Education, Antalya, Turkey.

Veiga Simao, A. M. V., Ferreira, P., Francisco, S. M., Paulino, P., & de Souza, S. B. (2018). Cyberbullying: Shaping the use of verbal aggression through normative moral beliefs and selfefficacy. *New Media & Society*, (12), 4787–4806. Advance online publication. doi:10.1177/1461444818784870

ADDITIONAL READING

Olweus, D. (2012). Cyberbullying: An overrated phenomenon? *European Journal of Developmental Psychology*, *9*(5), 520–538. doi:10.1080/17405629.2012.682358

Redmond, P., Lock, J. V., & Smart, V. (2020). Developing a cyberbullying conceptual framework for educators. *Technology in Society*, *60*, 101223. doi:10.1016/j.techsoc.2019.101223

Vandebosch, H., & Van Cleemput, K. (2009). Cyberbullying Among Youngsters: Profiles of Bullies and Victims. *New Media & Society*, *11*(8), 1349–1371. doi:10.1177/1461444809341263

KEY TERMS AND DEFINTIONS

Analysıs: Analysis is the way to get to a conclusion by breaking a topic down into its essential parts, then describing the parts and their relationships.

Cyberbullying: Cyberbullying is generally the wrong use of this medium by individuals with the advancement of technological developments.

Metaverse: While the exact definition seems to depend on who is speaking, it is basically a new version of the internet with more emphasis on virtual worlds.

News: Information conveyed to the public by mass media about events.

Turkish National Press: The Turkish national press are the media organs broadcasting in Turkey.

Chapter 13

A Critical Look on Cyberbullying and Cyber Harassment in the Digital Area Within the Scope of Social Media Literacy

Hicabi Arslan
Aydin Adnan Menderes University, Turkey

Aslıhan Topal
Aydin Adnan Menderes University, Turkey

ABSTRACT

With the inclusion of the internet in life, changes and transformations have occurred in almost every field at different points and continue to be experienced. This change and transformation can be seen in a positive way as well as in a negative way. The structure, which is equipped with new communication technologies, has affected the traditional habits and forms of communication. Different elements and concepts have been articulated with digital life into the types of violence. Cyberbullying, cyber harassment, cyber humiliation, and cyber victimization are among these concepts. In today's conditions, social media usage habits are increasing, and individuals naturally recognize different faces of these channels.

INTRODUCTION

With the inclusion of the Internet in life, changes and transformations have occurred in almost every field at different points and continue to be experienced. This change and transformation can be seen in a positive way as well as in a negative way. The structure, which is equipped with new communication technologies, has affected the traditional habits and forms of communication.

Different elements and concepts have been articulated with digital life into the types of violence. Cyberbullying, cyber harassment, cyber humiliation, cyber victim, cyber victim are among these concepts. In today's conditions, especially social media usage habits are increasing, and individuals naturally

DOI: 10.4018/978-1-6684-5426-8.ch013

recognize different faces of these channels. In today's world, some transactions carried out through the so-called virtual world accounts used only by real individuals find a place as harassment and bullying by malicious people.

This harassment and bullying becomes inevitable in social media, which is so close. In this study, the concepts of cyber bullying and cyber harassment will be evaluated with various examples, and the importance of being conscious and having a higher level of awareness in social media will be emphasized.

Figure 1. We Are Social 2021 World Internet, Social Media and Mobile Usage Statistics (Dijilopedi, 2021)

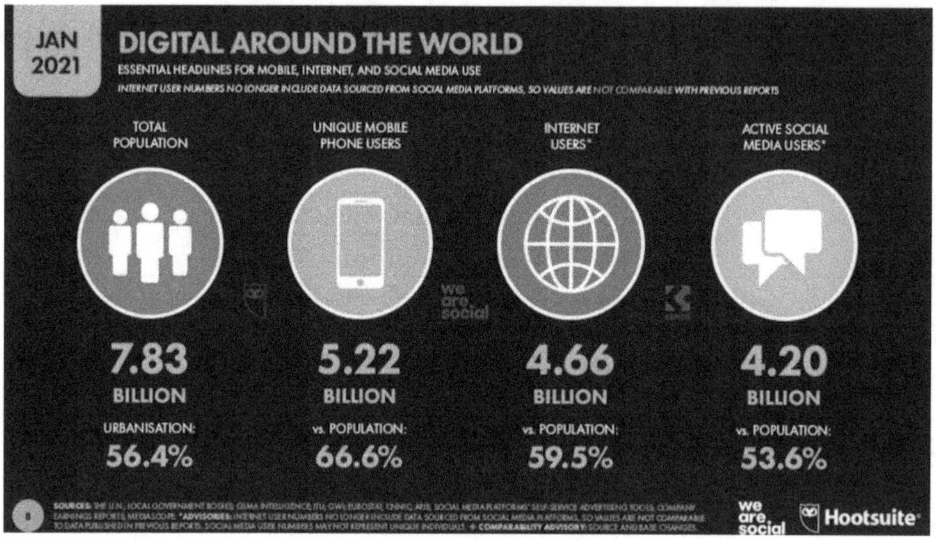

In today's conditions, where the world's population is almost 8 billion, the fact that an individual is informed about an event that takes place anywhere in the world, especially through social media tools with an internet connection, makes these channels indispensable and highlights the need to take very careful steps in these areas. presents it.

The individual, who has settled in a passive position in the traditional structure, has now risen to an active position. Its new location provides the individual with the opportunity to access the content they want whenever and wherever they want, as well as the opportunity to produce their own content, giving them privileges not given in the traditional structure. The individual in an active position can sometimes use this freedom given to him in ways that will harm himself.

It is important in many respects to increase the use of the internet and social media tools by individuals and to know which tools they use for what purposes. The internet, which is the basis of social media, offers people an environment of communication, sharing, communication and socialization that they have not had before (Dingin, 2021, p. 149). The Internet has provided new platforms for risk taking, including adolescent participation in online interpersonal violence (Elsaesser, Russell, Ohannessian, & Patton, 2017, p. 62).

Figure 2. We Are Social 2021 World Internet Usage Statistics (Dijilopedi, 2021)

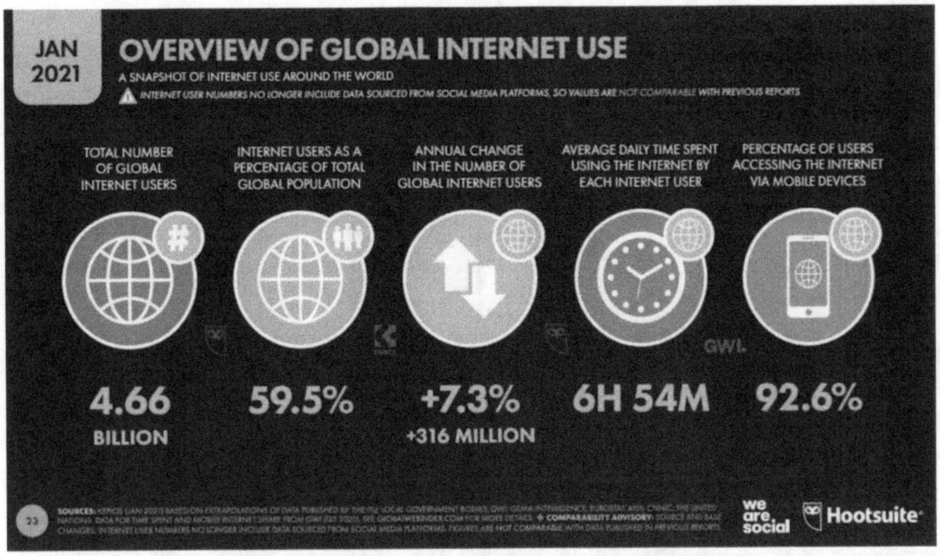

Figure 3. We Are Social 2021 — Reasons for Internet Usage (Dijilopedi, 2021)

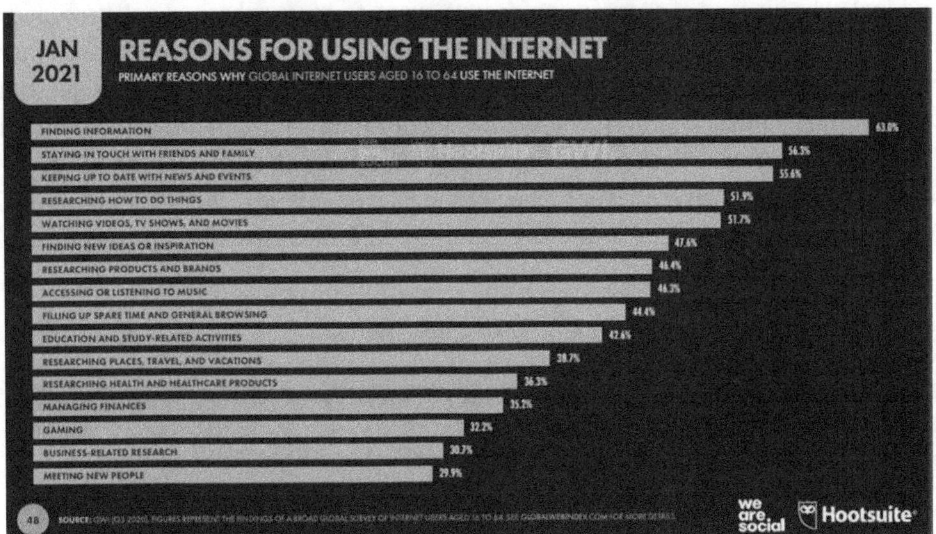

Individuals use the internet for various reasons such as accessing information, communicating with friends and family, playing games, listening to music, financial management, education, and commerce. It can access and create content. While every shared content reaches countless people and every age group is likely to be aware of this content, details such as taking screenshots and recording are important details to be careful about. The memorability of every shared content is now as high as the possibility of encountering the individual anytime, anywhere, through new media tools.

Figure 4. We Are Social 2021 – Daily Mobile Internet Usage Statistics Based on Age and Gender (Dijilopedi, 2021)

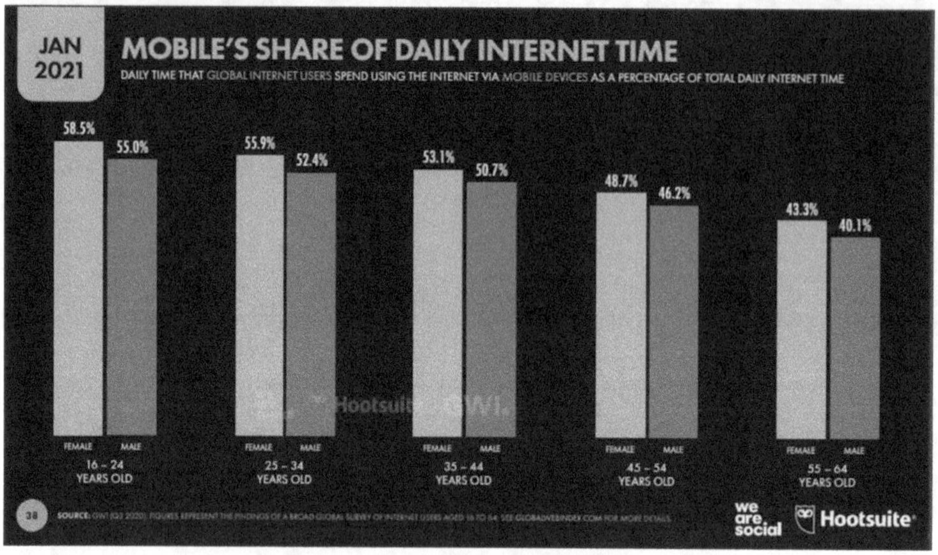

The individual, who is aware of every instantaneous event, from anywhere, at any time, and does what he wants with his smart phones, searches for more as he consumes, and this search can be answered in some way, but it is not emphasized that every answer found can be a source for other questions.

As can be seen in the image, it covers the highest rate of internet use in the world between the ages of 16-24. Since digital natives are born into technology in this field, they act without being alienated like an individual moving in their homeland. The individual, who meets technology almost in the womb, feels comfortable in this area, and it can be said that this comfort causes him to act fearlessly.

Figure 5. We Are Social 2021– Age Distribution of Social Media Users (Dijilopedi, 2021)

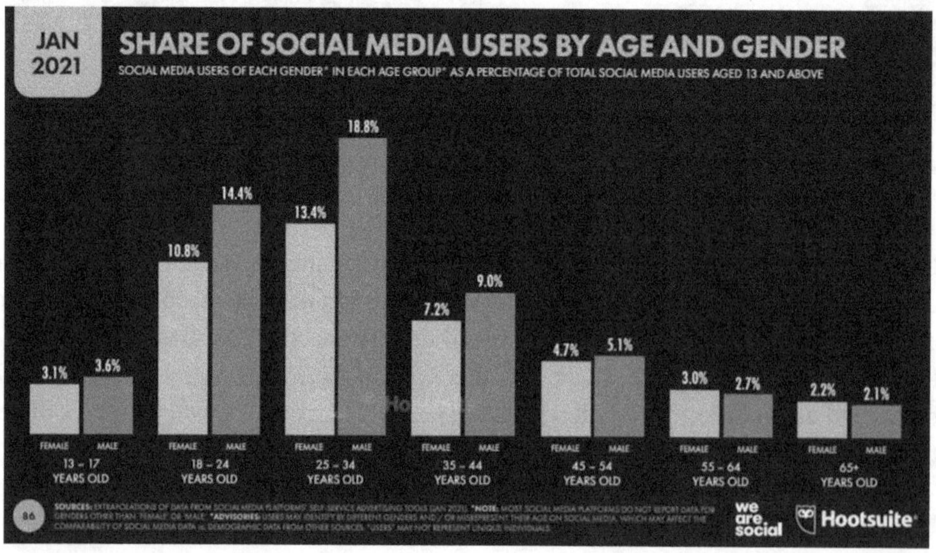

Here again, it is seen that especially the under-middle-aged group uses it more frequently. Social media networks are described as the new communication environments of the internet age, and it is very easy to communicate with people in social networks, in this regard, it is thought that it will strengthen interaction and ties (Dingin, 2020, pp. 285-289).

The dominance of those born after 1985 in this area takes its place in the image number 5 above. According to the data, it is seen that men use more than women in this field. The fact that the converted users of social media use these channels regardless of social values causes behaviors such as rejoicing, sadness, and bullying to find a new medium of expression here (Bölükbaş & Kırık, 2020, p. 948).

When the visual is examined, when the time spent in the context of age groups is evaluated, it is seen that the 16-24 age group is the segment that spends the most time in these channels.

Figure 6. We Are Social 2021– Age Distribution of Daily Time Spent on Social Media (Dijilopedi, 2021)

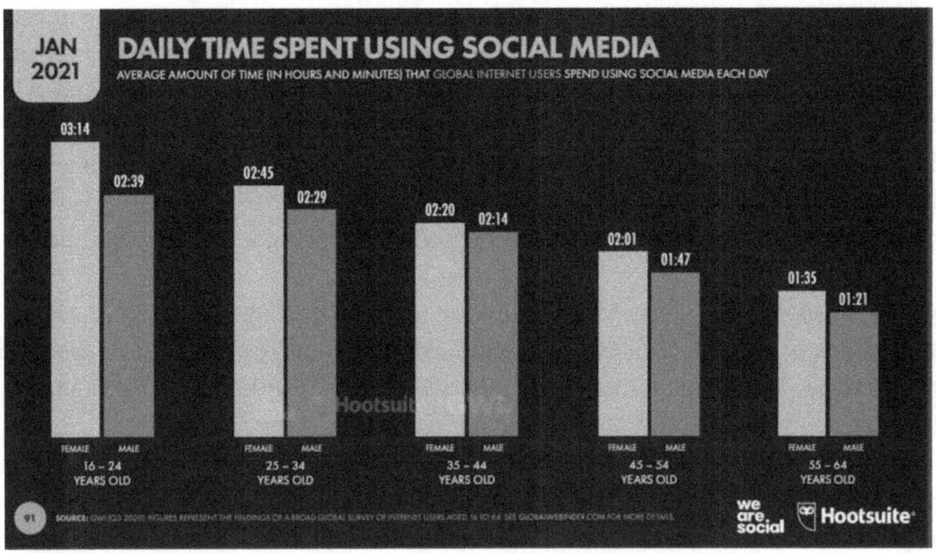

BACKGROUND

The act of violence that takes place in real life can be exhibited in the digital space anytime and anywhere without a physical closeness or contact with the person who will be exposed to violence. In today's conditions, the increasing connection between digital natives and the opportunities offered in the social media channel and the opportunities and dreams offered by this channel cause this channel to be more attractive and usable.

Through these channels, people in different places can become friends without requiring closeness or contact. The communication situation in these media, which takes place outside of traditional communication habits, brings with it some problems with its different dimension. In the traditional structure, the parent has become worried about the friend whose identity consists of a profile, which stems from the friendship relations that the child meets face-to-face.

In the traditional social structure, face-to-face friends are sometimes described as more innocent because they are at least visible. The existence of a large number of individuals who are blindfolded and groping for progress in these channels, where the state of being controllable is weakening, is full of indications that the necessity for keeping awareness at a high level on behalf of these channels is increasing.

The changes that occur in the lives of individuals with the developing technological structure have covered not only one or two areas, but almost the whole area. The opportunities offered by new communication technologies touch the individual from many points that come to mind, from education to health, from trade to cultural areas, from economy to politics.

Although individuals who are later included in new communication technologies try to act more cautiously in the face of these changes in their lives, digital natives act more fearlessly. In this area, where they act fearlessly, sometimes they live and keep alive in this new area, similar to what they experienced in the traditional structure.

While the point reached by the use of technology is always evaluated from different perspectives, it should not be overlooked how individuals use this development. The presence of a smart phone, ready for use anytime and anywhere, makes many things accessible.

This accessibility brings with it the feeling of being able to do what one wants, and it is thought that the individual may be able to act with a sense of unlimited freedom in these areas. Information technologies designed to make life easier bring along problems such as internet addiction and cyberbullying (Özözen Danacı, Kavaklı, & Tıkız, 2018, p. 87)

In particular, concepts such as cyberbullying, cyber harassment, and digital kidnapping make us think that the individual considers himself/herself as free as if he/she finds an area of action in real life, and even considers this area as a freer area. In the digital age we live in, we see that violence manifests itself in various ways.

Social media, as an area that has not been fully explored, is a medium that emphasizes the necessity of being aware of the negative aspects experienced in addition to its positive aspects, as an area where violence is experienced in different forms and under different names without any discrimination between women, men, children, adults and the elderly. shouts.

This violence experienced in the digital field is not limited to a specific area, just like other types of violence, but is actually a problem that concerns the whole world. The Digital Courtesy Research 2020 research carried out by Microsoft since 2016 was conducted in more than 30 countries with more than 58 thousand interviews. Four out of 10 people who participated in the study stated that they were exposed to cyberbullying (teknosafari.net, 2021)

In many parts of the world, facts about cyberbullying appear in the press from time to time (Aksaray, 2011, p. 407). When traditional and cyber bullying are compared, since it is easier to hide the identity on the internet, it may be more difficult to find the perpetrator of this violence and it can happen all the time, and there are factors such as the victim cannot get rid of this bullying even if the environment changes (Demir & Seferoğlu, 2016, p. 6).

Cyberbullying; means that individuals send each other written and visual messages with the aim of enmity, intimidation, threat, intimidation, harassment through information and communication technologies (Akca, Sayımer, Tuesday, & Başak, 2014, p. 18)

Cyberbullying or electronic aggression, harmful material, participating in other forms of social aggression by using the Internet or different digital technologies (Willard, 2005, p. 1), threatening by an individual or group to a different individual or group through information and communication technologies,

It is expressed as the deliberate and regular sending of frightening, insulting, slanderous, embarrassing messages and/or images (General Directorate of Special Education and Guidance Services). It is also defined as sending or publishing harmful and cruel material using the Internet or different digital technologies (E.Willard, 2007).

Cyberbullying is an umbrella term for similar constructs such as online bullying, electronic bullying, and Internet harassment (Tokunaga, 2010, p. 278). The anonymity provided by cyberbullying gives bullies a sense of power and control that they would not otherwise be able to find face-to-face with their victims (Watts, Wagner, Velasquez, & Behrens, 2017, p. 269).

While young people are involved in many forms of online interpersonal violence (e.g., cyber dating violence, cyber flashing), cyberbullying, both as a victim and perpetrator, is the most noted form of online interpersonal violence (Elsaesser, Russell, Ohannessian, & Patton, 2017, p. .62).

The roles in cyberbullying are similar to the roles in traditional peer bullying, the victim is called the victim, the person who torments the victim is called a cyberbully, and sometimes the person can be both the victim and the bully (Aksaray, 2011, p. 409). Three different segments are mentioned within the concept of cyberbullying; victims (victims), cyberbullies (bullies), and potential victims (Tanrikulu, Kınay, & Arıcak, 2013, p. 45).

The psychological, emotional and physical effects of online bullying are seen, and in some extreme cases, cyberbullying can even lead people to end their lives (UNICEF). Exposure to cyberbullying increases the rates of depression, substance use and crime, and young people who practice it are found to be more prone to behavioral problems such as breaking the rules and aggression (Aksaray, 2011, p. 418).

The victim does not tell their parents about the problem they are experiencing, so parents should be informed about this issue and should guide their children about how they should use the internet and other electronic communication tools in accordance with their children's developmental level, set limitations and supervise their children frequently (Yaman & Sönmez, 2015, p. 27).

Taştekin and Bayhan (Taştekin & Bayhan, 2018, p. 41) stated in their study that cyberbullying and victimization are an important problem among adolescents, that some segments may create more risky groups at this point, that internet usage characteristics are an important factor in terms of cyberbullying and victimization.

He stated that it is seen that it can create negative behavioral and emotional effects on people. Even if the victims of this violence have actually changed the environment they are in, there is a situation where they cannot get rid of this situation, and the fact that the victims do not have a place to take shelter by protecting themselves in the face of the trauma may cause them to worry at a higher level.

While information technologies should be used in the event in order for an act to be considered cyberbullying, it is also important to aim to humiliate the person exposed to the act by insulting/threatening or blackmailing (Doğan, Ertürk, & Aslan, 2018, p. 38).

The individual, who acts as a space where he can express what he wants with fake identities by hiding his real identity in the digital environment, exhibits violence with different dimensions in these media. Individuals who feel freer in this environment can express their feelings and thoughts more clearly because they feel more comfortable (Suler, 2004, p. 321).

When we look at the examples of cyber bullying behaviors, the bully threatens the victim using electronic communication tools or sends messages containing bad words towards the victim, sometimes gossiping about the victim on the internet or spreading pictures and private information that will embarrass the victim, presenting himself as a victim on the internet and bullying others on his behalf. (Özdemir & Akar, 2011, p. 609), leaking someone else's private or private information, using insulting expressions, harassing anonymous accounts, causing discomfort, taking over someone else's accounts, making inappropriate posts from these accounts, following someone persistently. making negative comments on someone's posts (SİBERAY, 2020), reading other people's e-mails without permission or using their personal passwords (Baker & Kavşut, 2007, p. 33).

It should also be noted that it is seen that the bully carries out such behaviors via the victim's mobile phone or e-mail account (Özdemir & Akar, 2011, p. 609).

Table 1. Psychological, social and academic effects of being exposed to cyberbullying. (Korkmaz, 2016, p. 79)

Psychological Effects	Social Effects	Academic Effects
Being sad	Low self-esteem	Fear of going to school
Experiencing intense stress	Conflict in peer relationships	Having trouble learning
Feeling worthless	Not trusting others	Skipping school
Being ashamed of knowing information about herself	Difficulty establishing friendships	Decreased course performance

Among the important points to be considered at the point of how to understand cyberbullying, there are some points that individuals will pay particular attention to; If abusive, sad, disturbing and insulting messages, comments are received, threatened, constantly and intentionally exposed to offensive behavior on the Internet, a photo or video of one's own is used for malicious purposes on the Internet without the consent of the person, ugly, fat, stupid, and similar nicknames, if the person is isolated by his friends, if photos and videos of the person are secretly taken and shared on the internet (Safe Child, 2022), cyber bullying is mentioned.

Among the things to do when faced with such a situation are; ending communication with the offending person, making the accounts in these channels safe, not making them accessible to everyone, explaining the situation to the trusted persons/parents if the bullying persists, making the necessary complaints to the bullied platforms, reporting these accounts or persons, deleting the accounts on the bullied platforms or freezing, making necessary complaints to the official authorities if it is felt in danger, remembering that bullying is not just a problem that happens to the person who is exposed, taking necessary precautions by being aware of the seriousness of the situation, talking to the parents about this issue with their children, providing information about safe internet use, providing support, following the control of their access, knowing their rights, and examining the anti-bullying policies of social media (SİBERAY, 2020).

The most important regulation regarding the measures to be taken regarding cyberbullying is the Convention on the Rights of the Child; States parties guarantee the protection of the child against all forms of sexual exploitation and sexual abuse, in particular; tricking or coercing the child to engage in illegal sexual activity; exploitation of children in prostitution or other unlawful sexual activity; It is the 34th article that requires all necessary measures to be taken at the national level and in bilateral and multilateral relations in order to prevent the exploitation of children by using them in pornographic performances and materials (Yetim, 2015, p. 361).

Among the ways to cope with cyberbullying, in various studies, it has come to the fore with titles such as "empathy-based interventions, gaining anger control skills, values education, implementing cyberbullying intervention programs, providing media use training, in-school interventions, and family interventions and support". (Yiğit & Seferoğlu, 2017, p. 26)

It is aimed to accelerate the fight against social media tools such as Twitter, cyber bullying and cyber harassment, with an application that has not yet been opened to general use in order to provide measures in the use of the Internet, which has become widespread with the Security Mode application (Doğan F., 2022)

Internet harassment is an open, deliberate act of aggression directed at another person in the online environment (Ybarra & Mitchell, 2004, p. 1308) and negative behaviors are revealed in the online environment (Bayram & Saylı, 2013, p. 108).

While cyber harassment manifests itself with persistent behaviors, cyberbullying is an interaction based on power imbalance (Dilmaç, 2020, p. 1096).

The methods that can be tried to get rid of cyber harassment, which is defined as harassing individuals about real or unfounded issues, threatening them, and providing financial or psychological "benefit" by using social media networks; Physical Access, Password Method, Internet Remains, Physical Tracking, Limitation of Sharing, Security Software (Çelik & Tekin, 2015, p. 346-347).

The frequency and number of cyber harassment cases are increasing gradually, with the increase in the rate of internet use by harassers, the possibility of exposure of children to these acts increases. 425).

In cyberbullying or cyber harassment, in both types of behavior, the individual is in one or more of the positions that apply, monitor, and victimize. The possibilities offered by new communication technologies have been adopted by the new generation. He socializes through his smart phone, computer, tablet, and can do most of his work through these tools.

Using 2003 data from the Program for International Student Assessment (PISA) in 30 countries, in a study that focused on the social divides in the access and use of digital technologies by middle adolescents, taking into account both individual and country-level effects, a country's level of modernization only affected the presence or absence of digital applications in the family home, it was concluded that they do not affect how they are used (Notten, Peter, Kraaykamp, & Valkenburg, 2009).

In a study on cyber-aggression, 30.1% of adolescents declared that they had experienced some form of cyber-aggression, a higher prevalence was observed among girls than boys, and the victims reported a significantly lower self-esteem than adolescents who had not been exposed to any form of cyber-aggression. have a higher level of respect and depression symptoms, abusive cognitions, and exposure to violence (Estévez, Villardón, Esther Calvete, & Orue, 2010, pp. 73-74).

Cyberbullying or cyber harassment are concepts that have been included in our lives with the opportunities provided by new communication technologies, and at this point, they clearly show the place and importance of social media literacy in the life of the individual.

It can be expressed as the ability to access content through social media environments, evaluate and interpret these content, create their own content and transfer them, and make their existence safe in these environments.

Within the scope of media literacy as an umbrella concept, social media literacy will play an active role in the individual's ability to continue his life away from the concepts of cyber bullying and cyber harassment, where the positive sides can be added to his life for his own benefit, he can include them in his life as safe channels, and he can live safely without being far away.

The concepts of cyber harassment and cyberbullying should be kept on the agenda frequently, not just as cyber victims come to the fore, and social media literacy should be provided with trainings to increase the awareness level of individuals with trainings for the whole society in this context.

Bhat, Chang and Linscott make the following suggestions within the scope of media literacy education;

- Defining cyberbullying and the behavioral example actions that compose it,

Providing information and understanding about information and communication technologies used for cyberbullying,

- Learning about each role, including roles in cyberbullying, active cyberbully, secondary cyberbully, observer, and target, and what actions can be taken for each to prevent cyberbullying (example making a clear list of dos and don'ts)
- Creating special security and reporting features for each technology type,
- Identifying the actions that students can take in case of encountering cyberbullying (screenshots, printing evidence, talking to and trusting adults, not retaliating, usually in a way that escalates cyberbullying)
- Behavioral examples of the types of actions to be taken to prevent cyberbullying,
- Understanding the social and academic damage and psychological impact experienced by the targets of such attacks,
- establishing reporting procedures for cases of cyberbullying and encouraging observers to take action to stop the harassment,
- Taking clear precautions for cyberbullies (Bhat, Chang, & Linscott, 2010, pp. 38-39)

MAIN FOCUS OF THE CHAPTER

Evalution of the Issue with Example News

Both cyberbullying and cyber harassment are a school from start to finish. There are also events that can not be spoken about events that can happen at any time, which can be experienced in a way related to people who are famous or not. In fact, it is important to inform our relatives without fear in such events and to be certain about this issue. In the events described, in the cases where they can come with the future in life, a small case is experienced by guessing. In fact, the ways that this child will be delivered and resolved.

Actress Mine Tugay filed a complaint against the person who sent insults, profanity and harassment messages on social media in 2019. The actress stated in the lawsuit that she was harassed by this person she did not know, through social media, and then came to the set where she was working.

In the case, it was concluded that the accused committed the crime of 'sexual harassment by taking advantage of the convenience provided by electronic communication tools' and the accused was sentenced to a judicial fine.

A 22-year-old university student in Istanbul stated that he was afraid to go out on the street, that he was psychologically worn out and started to use psychological drugs, while describing the difficult time he experienced due to cyber harassment.

Stating that he has been systematically harassed for 7 months, D. K. stated that his own photo has been montaged using the deepfake method and uploaded to inappropriate sites, and that his personal information has started to be shared, and that he has lodged the necessary complaint with the prosecutor's office.

Figure 7. The sentence of the accused who harassed Mine Tugay on social media has been determined (cumhuriyet.com, 2021)

Figure 8. Cyber pervert! She has been harassed every day for 7 months (sabah.com, 2022)

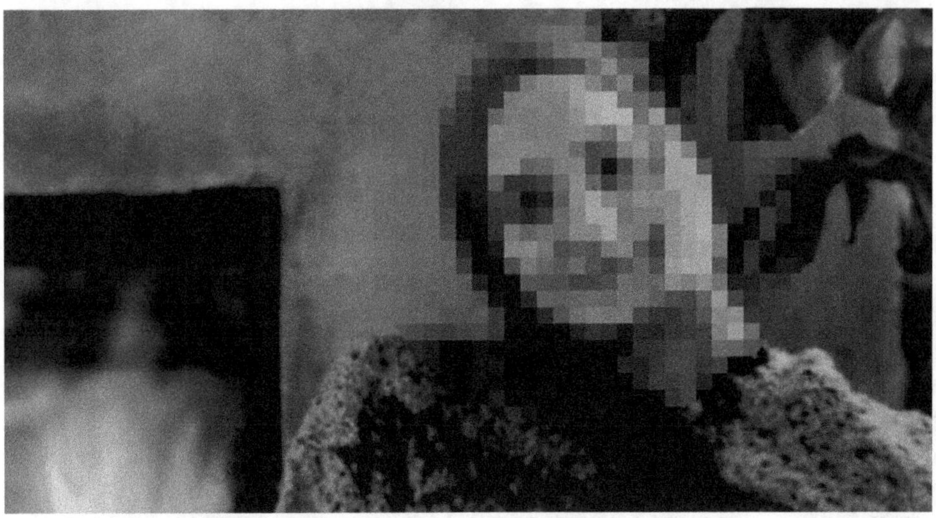

Stating that action was taken against profiles that threatened him, D. K. stated that he still had difficulty continuing his social life, and that he could not trust anyone, and that he started to question whether the person next to him was the person who harassed him wherever he went.

Cyber harassment through social media, sending obscene images by unfamiliar people live on all the face of the person who is harassing a lot of people it had blocked itself in the cyber environment has met up with harassment in the past 10 years and has asked to be heard by for exposed to such attacks, he says.

Figure 9. Jess Davies, who works as a presenter at the BBC and is also a social media phenomenon, shared the harassment she experienced on the internet. (onedio.com, 2021)

Figure 10. Turkish girl Seniz is a victim of a virtual bully (hurriyet.com, 2012)

A 14-year-old young girl named Seniz Erkan, who lives in Melbourne, Australia, has ended her life by logging into her social media account and not being able to bear what she has experienced due to the virtual bullies who make threats and attacks. The family also stated that they were not aware of this situation experienced by their daughter and that there was no change in behavior in their daughter that they would suspect. As mentioned earlier in the study, cyber bullying and cyber harassment sometimes have severe psychological consequences, while sometimes, as here, individuals end their lives in the face of this violence they experience.

Figure 11. The case of 'setting up' suicide is solved (fox19.com, 2012)

An 18-year-old teenage girl named Jessica Logan committed suicide because of her experiences after photos she shared with her ex-boyfriend were forwarded to some of her friends at the high school she was studying at. It is stated that she was the victim of bullying and harassment of other students after photos of the young girl began to be seen at school.

SOLUTIONS AND RECOMMENDATIONS

In the current digital age has created the identity safer at their points of origin to live in terms of the psychological characteristics of individuals who have experienced cyber bullying and cyber harassment with a comparative evaluation of the features of the perpetrator also for measures to be taken in this regard is important.

The provision of social media literacy in a widespread educational network throughout the world from a young age group is of great importance from the point of view of all societies and is becoming increasingly important. Within the scope of social media literacy and new media literacy, it is thought that it can raise awareness of individuals at the point where they are exposed to cyber bullying and cyber harassment.

It can also be presented as another point that media organizations pay attention to their news and shares at the point of awareness of individuals of structures in the social sphere. Trainings can be given to students, families and the whole society in order to gain responsibility and awareness about communication technologies at the point of use. Detailed studies on victims of cyber across the globe in the same physical location is found by a cyber bully or harasser, even if that creates serious difficulties to get rid of the effects of awareness of the problem and what can be done by examining the characteristics of these victims important data in the dimension of the solution can be achieved, it is believed that.

Social media tools, these tools are made to take over more of the responsibilities for sharing on government receivables measures in use in the fulfillment of individual security responsibility in the social sphere will raise the level of awareness in this area of education that the individual potential violence that may occur, will be important steps in the point of taking action against victimization. But none of them alone is not enough. It can be said that acting as a whole is vital for later periods, especially considering the developments in communication technologies.

It is necessary to evaluate cyber bullying and cyber harassment with a holistic understanding. Proceeding from this point, neither only schools, nor only parents, nor only children can be the solution. In this case, there are important tasks that also fall to all segments and the media to increase awareness and act consciously.

FUTURE RESEARCH DIRECTIONS

In order to determine the common point of action through a clear and common definition of cyber bullying and cyber harassment, it is important to investigate the studies on the role of the relevant media at this stage in order to determine the common point of action. Quoted in the news media of the concepts of the language used here, studies on the visuals, especially in our communication of the Covid-19 Pandemic that has changed in today's climate with the process of the internet, new media, increasingly widespread use of social media at this time, the period brought about by the use of the concept of areas in the social sphere is completed to ensure the visibility of the concept is necessary. The approach of the media has an impact on the way individuals view concepts. It is thought that more work is needed at the stage of determining at what point the media is in framing the news by highlighting the noteworthy elements.

CONCLUSION

The point of internet usage rates in the community, notice of time and place of the individuals by means of widely used smart phones and other technological devices in the cyber environment under the influence of the vital fields with getting all of the assets, they are recognized by concepts such as cyber bullying individuals, having known the necessity of also increasing.

As the use of social media tools and the discovery of the possibilities offered by this medium increases, it is clear that new concepts will enter our lives. It is important for individuals to maintain their presence in this area with a high level of awareness in order to protect themselves from the dangers that exist. In this sense, it is very important that joint academic studies on social media literacy are carried out widely in the world and awareness trainings for parents, especially for young age groups, are carried out with joint projects to be created.

As can be seen from the Internet news, it is seen that the consequences of violent acts that take place through these channels can also go as far as suicides. It should be noted that violence that occurs through digital media, such as bullying that occurs with physical proximity, causes devastating damage to individuals.

The examples discussed in the scope of the study also show that cyber bullying and cyber harassment can sometimes cause victims to end their lives, while sometimes they can also cause serious psychological problems. It can be seen that this violence, which turns the lives of victimized individuals upside down, can hide the traces formed on their bodies when individuals are exposed to physical violence, as well as hide this violence from their relatives or cannot explain it. For this reason, it is of great importance to transfer both the legal and psychological dimension to all individuals in schools in order to increase the awareness levels of individuals. In the sense of deterrence, it is important to express the legal dimension in a precise language in the trainings given for the whole society.

Along with new communication technologies, almost every area in the traditional structure is somehow affected by the development, change and transformation that has taken place, and it seems that it will continue to be affected. Social media literacy is a necessity for the whole world, not on the basis of individual countries, for the purposes of using these environments, which an individual does in a cyber environment to make himself visible and to be noticed.

The concepts that new communication technologies such as cyber bullying, cyber victimization and cyber victimization have added to our lives show the traces of the change experienced in the individual field very clearly. In a world where the pace of developments cannot be kept up with, many new concepts seem to take their place in life.

When cyberbullying is mentioned, it is mentioned that bullying takes place in digital environments. In the face-to-face bullying that society is used to hearing, elements such as contact, proximity to space, exclusion, verbal violence are taking place in digital environments without distance, without the need for contact and proximity this time.

The use of the Internet and the increasing prevalence of social media tools are causing the concepts of digital violence and digital violence to become more important. Now the situations that require schools, families, young people, children to act even more carefully are increasing due to the dominant qualities of digital natives in terms of taking part in this world.

Cyber bullying or cyber harassment, the dimensions of the hostility that both of them harbor should not be underestimated in terms of the destruction that they will cause to the victim compared to the physical in digital environments, but rather the existence of the effects of the permanent traces that these violence experienced in these environments will leave should be accepted.

It is also important to understand the issue and increase awareness about the issue of how media coverage of cyber bullying and cyber harassment is framed. In general, the definitions, effects, types of these concepts and their distinctions with traditional bullying are mentioned in the studies, while the way these issues are evaluated in terms of the way they are reflected in the media is not much included in the way they are handled. It is thought that suggestions can be made for further studies on this subject in terms of the importance of the subject.

Cyber bullying and cyber harassment are destructive effects for the individual in the cyber environment where the individual has gained a place for himself/herself widely in the social field. It shows that it is imperative to be careful and conscious to find a solution to the problem by noticing the individual in this situation, to convince the individual that he is not alone in the face of the violence he has been subjected to, and to be aware. Individual awareness should be able to act at a high level in the field of new opportunities, many possibilities, as well as anxiety and fear. However, the responsibility in this field falls not only on the individual, but also on many institutions and organizations in society from a holistic point of view.

Harassment that occurs with persistent tracking through computers, mobile phones, social media channels through communication tools can cause consequences such as damage caused by physically tracking an individual. In the same way, the application of physical violence through these tools also has very serious traces of psychological violence, such as the traces left by the violence applied to the bodies of individuals, and sometimes individuals can even end their lives for this reason.

For this reason, in order to use social media effectively and carefully on an individual basis, individuals have a multifaceted task in the context of security on official channels, schools, parents, and these platforms legally in order to have serious sanctions of the legal dimension of digital violence and harassment applied to individuals in these media.

The increase in the use of the Internet and computers, smartphones and social media channels shows how important security is in these areas, and the developments that have taken place also signal that we will meet new concepts in these areas. Social media literacy is a very important concept that should be raised more for the whole world in the name of safe life in a cyber environment.

REFERENCES

Akca, E. B., Sayımer, İ., Salı, J. B., & Başak, B. E. (2014). The Causes, Types And Media of Cyber Bullying in School. *Electronic Journal of Professional Development and Research (EJOIR),* 17-30.

Aksaray, S. (2011). Cyberbullying. *C. Finish. Journal of the Institute of Social Sciences*, 405-432.

Baker, Ö. E., & Kavşut, F. (2007). The New Face of Peer Bullying: Cyberbullying. *Eurasian Journal of Educational Research*, 31-42 .

Bayram, N., & Saylı, M. (2013). *Cyberbullying behavior among university students. İÜHFM.*

Bhat, B. (n.d.). *The World's First Definition of "Cyberbullying"*. https://cyberbullying.ca/

Bhat, C. S., Chang, S.-H., & Lınscott, J. A. (2010). Addressing Cyberbullying as a Media Literacy Issue. *New Horizons in Education, 58*(3), 34–43.

Bölükbaş, K., & Kırık, A. M. (2020). Twitter Phenomena in the Context of Cyberbullying. *Kahramanmaraş Sütçü Imam University Journal of Social Sciences, 17*(2), 944–966.

Bozbayındır, G. B. (2019). Cyberbullying and Criminal Law. *İstanbul Hukuk Mecmuası*, 425-450.

Çelik, T., & Tekin, Y. (2015). An Example of the Negative Effects of Social Media on Individuals: Cyberbullying. *The Journal of Academic Social Science Studies International Journal of Social Science*, 343-355.

cumhuriyet.com. (2021). *The sentence of the accused who harassed the Mine Brigade on social media has been announced.* Life News: https://www.cumhuriyet.com.tr/yasam/mine-tugayi-sosyal-medyadan-taciz-eden-sanigin-cezasi-belli-oldu-1891586

Demir, Ö., & Seferoğlu, S. S. (2016). Investigation of the Relationship between Information Literacy, Internet Addiction, Virtual Loitering and Various Other Variables with Virtual Bullying. *Online Journal of Technology Addiction & Cyberbullying, 3*(1), 1–26.

Dijilopedi. (2021). *2021 World Internet, Social Media and Mobile Usage Statistics*. https://dijilopedi.com/2021-dunya-internet-sosyal-medya-ve-mobil-kullanim-istatistikleri/

Dilmaç, J. A. (2020). Deviance in the Digital Environment: Cyber Bullying. *Turkish Studies - Social Sciences*, 1087–1099.

Dingin, A. E. (2020). The Political Aspects of Identities Formed in the Face of Social Media. He. In *Kutlu, Decoupling from Advertising to Political Communication is an Interdisciplinary Study* (pp. 283–299). Detay Anatolia Akademik Yayıncılık Ltd. Şti.

Dingin, A. E. (2021). *The new Social Media Application is the "Tiktok" Application and Popular Culture. In A Calm, Critical View of Social Media 2- From Violence to Addiction, From Discrimination to Popular Culture*. Literatürk Academia.

Doğan, B. Ö., Ertürk, Y. D., & Aslan, P. (2018). The Transformation of Bullying-Oriented Cyber Harassment Directed at Facebook User Girls into Sexual Harassment: A Descriptive Evaluation via Newspaper News. *Journal of Interaction Üsküdar University Faculty of Communication*, 36-55.

Doğan, F. (2022). *Twitter has expanded the scope of its anti-cyberbullying Security Mode feature*. Social Media: https://shiftdelete.net/twitter-siber-zorbalik-karsiti-guvenlik-modu-ozelliginin-kapsamini-genisletti

Elsaesser, C., Russell, B., Ohannessian, C. M., & Patton, D. (2017). Parenting in a digital age: A review of parents' role in preventing adolescent cyberbullying. *Aggression and Violent Behavior*, *3*, 62–72.

Estévez, A., Villardón, L., Esther Calvete, P. P., & Orue, I. (2010). Adolescentes víctimas de cyberbullying: Prevalencia, y características. *Behavioral Psychology. Psicología Conductual*, *18*(1), 73–89.

fox19.com. (2012). *Lawsuit over 'sexting' suicide settled*. https://www.fox19.com/story/19766203/lawsuit-over-sexting-suicide-of-jessica-logan-has-been-settled/

hurriyet.com. (2012). *A Turkish girl is a victim of a virtual bully*. https://www.hurriyet.com.tr/gundem/turk-kizi-seniz-sanal-zorba-kurbani-19693094

Karaca, M., Mutlu, T., & Gencer, G. (2021). Cyber victimization: A conceptual study. *Anadolu Akademi Journal of Social Sciences*,77-191.

Korkmaz, A. (2016). Cyberbullying: The new violence from physical to art. *Fiction*, *24*(2), 74–85.

Narin, B., & Ünal, S. (2016). Framing of News About Cyberbullying in the Turkish Print Media. *Akdeniz Journal of Communication*, 9 - 23.

Oned, N., Peter, J., Kraaykamp, G., & Valkenburg, P. M. (2009). Research Note: Digital Divide Across Borders--A Cross-National Study of Adolescents' Use of Digital Technologies. *European Sociological Review*, *25*(5), 551–560.

onedio.com. (2021). *Jess Davies, who works as a presenter at the BBC and is also a social media phenomenon, shared an incident of harassment she experienced over the internet*. https://onedio.com/haber/sosyal-medya-uzerinden-mustehcen-goruntulerle-taciz-edilen-bbc-sunucusunun-siber-saldirilara-karsi-isyani-1025414

Özdemir, M., & Akar, F. (2011). An Investigation of the Opinions of High School Students About Cyberbullying in Terms of Some Variables. *Educational Administration: Theory and Practice*, 605-626.

Özözen Danacı, M., Kavaklı, N., & Tıkız, G. (2018). The Effect of Narcissism Levels on Cyberbullying Sensitivity and Internet Addiction Levels of Pre-Service Teachers Studying at the Faculty of Education. *Journal of the National Academy of Education*, *2*(2), 86–98.

Peter, I.-K., & Petermann, F. (2018). Cyberbullying: A concept analysis of defining attributes and additional influencing factors. *Computers in Human Behavior*, 350–366.

sabah.com. (2022). *Cyber pervert! he has been harassed every day for 7 months.* https://www.sabah.com.tr/yasam/universite-ogrencisi-derya-kusa-sapik-kabusu-5860717

Tanrıkulu, T., Kınay, H., & Arıcak, O. T. (2013). The Scale of Sensitivity to Cyber Bullying: A Validity and Reliability Study. *Journal of the Faculty of Education of Trakya University*, 38-47.

Taştekin, E., & Bayhan, P. (2018). Onl The Investigation of Cyber Bullying and Victimization among Adolescents. *Dec.ine Journal of Technology Addiction & Cyberbullying, 5*(2), 21-45.

teknosafari.net. (2021). *Turkey is the 5th in the World in Terms of Digital Kindness. Next up!* https://teknosafari.net/turkiye-dijital-nezaket-konusunda-dunyada-5-sirada retrieved from/

Tokunaga, R. S. (2010). Following you home from school: A critical review and synthesis of research on cyberbullying victimization. *Computers in Human Behavior*, 277–287.

UNICEF. (n.d.). *Cyberbullying: what is it and how to prevent it.* UNICEF. https://www.unicef.org/turkey/siber-zorbal%C4%B1k-nedir-ve-nas%C4%B1l-%C3%B6nlenir retrieved from

Vural, Z. B., & Bat, M. (2010). Social media as a new communication medium: A study for the faculty of communication of Ege University. *Journal of Yasar University*, 3348-3382.

Watts, L. K., Wagner, J., Velasquez, B., & Behrens, P. I. (2017). Cyberbullying in higher education: A literature review. *Computers in Human Behavior, 69*, 268-274.

Willard, N. (2007). The authority and responsibility of school officials in responding to cyberbullying. *The Journal of Adolescent Health*, *41*, 64–65.

WillardN. (2005). https://cdn.ymaws.com/www.safestates.org/resource/resmgr/imported/educatorsguide.pdf

Yaman, E., & Sönmez, Z. (2015). Cyberbullying Tendencies of Adolescents. *Online Journal of Technology Addiction & Cyberbullying*, 18-31.

Ybarra, M. L., & Mitchell, K. J. (2004). Online aggressor/targets, aggressors, and targets: A comparison of associated youth characteristics. *Journal of Child Psychology and Psychiatry, and Allied Disciplines*, *45*(7), 1308–1316.

Yetim, S. (2015). Cyberbullying, Comparison of Turkey and the USA ABD v. Drew Dosyası. *TBB Dergisi*.

Yiğit, M. F., & Seferoğlu, S. S. (2017). A Review on the Factors Related to Cyberbullying and Possible Solutions. *Online Journal of Technology Addiction & Cyberbullying*, 13-49.

ADDITIONAL READING

Peter, I.-K., & Petermann, F. (2018, September). Cyberbullying: A concept analysis of defining attributes and additional influencing factors. *Computers in Human Behavior*, *86*, 350–366. doi:10.1016/j.chb.2018.05.013

Tokunaga, R. S. (2010, May). Following you home from school: A critical review and synthesis of research on cyberbullying victimization. *Computers in Human Behavior*, *26*(3), 277–287. doi:10.1016/j.chb.2009.11.014

Yiğit. (2017). *Mehmet Fatih*. Seferoğlu, Süleyman Sadi.

KEY TERMS AND DEFINITIONS

Cyber Victim: Is a victim who has been subjected to violence in various ways in a cyber environment.

Cyber Victimization: The bully who exhibits threatening, harassing, insulting behaviors using information and communication technologies disturbs the victim physically and spiritually and negatively affects the life of the victim due to this (Karaca, Mutlu, & Gencer, 2021, p. 177).

Internet: Is a communication network that is widespread throughout the world and is constantly evolving, where technically many computers or computer systems are connected to each other (Bulmaz, 2014, p. 24).

Metaverse: A new reality, the world of meaning and cooperation opportunities; cultural, intellectual and economic infrastructure and recognize the possibilities of interaction for production; advanced technologies for simultaneous and integrated in a manner that is different is used; a cyber social plane (Bird, 2021, p. 245).

New Media: Is a two-way hybrid media, one part of which contains operations specific to computers (information-processing), and another part contains structures specific to communication tools (communication-telecommunications and broadcasting) (Ceremonial, 2005, p. 88).

Social Media: Is a form of human communication in which sharing and discussion are the main ones, without time and space limitations (mobile-based) (Vural & Bat, 2010, p. 3351).

Social Media Literacy: Can be defined as the ability to access the content transmitted through the social media channel, the ability to analyze and evaluate this content, the ability to produce their own content in these media, the ability to use these media with awareness, a high level of consciousness, aware of their own security.

Virtual Harassment: Harassing individuals related to real or unreal issues through social media networks, threatening them, providing material or psychological "interests" (Çelik & Tekin, 2015, p. 346).

Chapter 14
Bullying Among Healthcare Workers

Özge Tonbuloğlu Altıner
Gazi University, Turkey

Asiye Ugraş Dikmen
Gazi University, Turkey

ABSTRACT

In this chapter, the authors comprehensively evaluate the phenomenon of bullying among healthcare workers, along with its prevalence, causes, and consequences. Bullying, which tends to become widespread in society, also seriously affects health institutions and healthcare workers. The high prevalence of bullying in the healthcare sector indicates that it is a problem that needs to be taken into account in organizational life. It is known that bullying in healthcare workers negatively affects both organizations and the victim. Bullying in the healthcare sector has a negative impact not only on the professional and personal lives of healthcare professionals, but also on the quality and scope of patient care provided. Therefore, it is important for authorities to review manpower, workplace design, policies, and organizational structures to identify factors that encourage bullying. In order to control this social phenomenon, there is a need to raise awareness about workplace bullying and to develop and implement prevention programs.

INTRODUCTION

Bullying, like all forms of violence, has increased dramatically around the world in recent years (Kingma, 2001). Leymann and Gustafsson (1996) described bullying as a type of psychological terror and defined it as "a type of psychological terror that includes sad, hostile and unethical attitudes systematically perpetrated by a person or group against a single person". Galletta et al. (2014) stated that it should be applied at least once a week and spread over a long period of time for at least six months. Although there are many studies on bullying in the literature, the fact that bullying is dependent on the emotions,

DOI: 10.4018/978-1-6684-5426-8.ch014

perceptions and reactions of the target person and is also affected by the context causes the subject to continue to be complex (Bayrakci & Dinc, 2020).

Studies have shown that verbal abuse and bullying are quite common, although physical violence is reported less frequently in the workplace. Studies on workplace bullying have attracted the attention of researchers who examine many abusive behaviors under numerous terms such as workplace violence, mobbing, aggression, abuse and harassment (Branch, 2008 Fox and Stallworth (2005) showed in their study that a certain group of employees they followed had been exposed to workplace bullying at least once in the previous five years. According to a study by Einarsen & Nielsen (2015), 11% of the global working population identified themselves as victims of bullying. In the emergence of this situation, various factors have been put forward that can lead to negative work behaviors such as personal factors and organizational factors. It has been argued that while leadership, working conditions, organizational support, job content and working environment are counted under the organizational factors that create negative work behaviors, personality traits of bullies and victims also play a role in the emergence of workplace bullying incidents (Matthiesen & Einarsen, 2010).

Studies on this subject have shown that bullying is more common in the service sector such as health, public service, finance and education services compared to other sectors. Leymann (1996) argued that bullying most commonly occurs in the healthcare sector. The healthcare sector is a sector that requires long working hours, full teamwork and cooperation as a requirement of the work done, and where the human factor still maintains its importance despite the advancing technology (Yilmaz, 2013). Today, bullying in healthcare workers has become an epidemic-sized public health problem with comprehensive consequences for both healthcare providers and healthcare users. Previous research has shown that one out of every four workplace violence incidents occurs in the health sector, and more than half of those working in this sector have experienced at least one incident of work violence (psychological or physical) during their career (Talas et al., 2011; Torshizi & Ahmadi, 2011). In a study conducted in recent years, it has been shown that 61.1% of healthcare workers have been subjected to violence at least once in their professional life, and 39.3% have been subjected to violence in the last year (Er et al., 2021). In another study, it was stated that 52.3% of healthcare workers were exposed to any type of violence at least once during their entire career (Pinar et al., 2017). Studies on this subject report that the prevalence of workplace bullying varies between 6 and 52% for healthcare workers with different levels of experience and different medical specialties (Al-Hussain et al., 2008; Askew et al., 2012; Cheema et al., 2005; Cohen et al., 2008; Daugherty et al., 1998; Gadit & Mugford, 2008; Heponiemi et al., 2014; Keeley et al., 2005; Launer, 2013; Nabi et al., 2013; Quine, 2002). It is thought that the intensity of interpersonal and emotional relationships inherent in the health sector and the hierarchical structure in health institutions may have an effect on the emergence of this situation (Awai et al., 2021). Considering the prevalence of bullying in healthcare workers, it is imperative to determine the causes of the problem and evaluate its scope, and to plan the necessary preventive actions by considering the negative consequences that may arise at the individual and organizational level (Norton et al., 2017).

DEFINITIONS

Bullying

When looking at the studies on bullying, it is noteworthy that there is no generally accepted common definition and different concepts such as mobbing, psychological terror, intimidation, psychological pressure, psychological harassment are used instead of the concept of bullying. It is considered that this situation is due to the absence of a clear, identifiable negative action that is valid in all situations and conditions that affect every individual at the same rate. Additionally, it was concluded that bullying is a situation that changes according to the perception, reaction, and emotion of the target, and the fact that the context is very effective in the perception of bullying contributes to this situation (Bayrakci & Dinc, 2020). Bullying, caused by an imbalance of power between the parties, in which the perpetrator(s) repeatedly engage in negative behavior to threaten or harm the targeted person or persons, can also be defined as the systematic abuse of power (Rigby, 2002).

Workplace Bullying

Bullying, defined as a 'major public health problem' by the World Health Organization (WHO) and also referred to as a 'silent epidemic' around the world; has also become an increasing problem in workplaces (McAvoy & Murtagh, 2003; Srabstein & Leventhal, 2010; D. Zapf et al., 2011). Workplace bullying relates to repetitive undesirable actions and practices against employees that may affect the victim's job performance and/or cause an unpleasant work environment (Einarsen et al., 2011). Although the definitions and concepts used in this subject vary, it is possible to say that researchers working on bullying agree on when negative interpersonal behaviors observed in the workplace can be characterized as bullying (Matthiesen & Einarsen, 2004). According to the researchers, a one-time or occasional negative interpersonal behavior does not qualify as bullying; for bullying to be mentioned, the relevant behaviors must be negative and hostile, it should be repeated systematically and should continue for a certain period with a certain frequency (Einarsen et al., 2002). The most important point here is the negative impact of the psychological and emotional pressure on the person's working life, and as a result, the person's being unable to do his/her job (Bayrakci & Dinc, 2020). Workplace bullying encompasses a wide range of negative actions, including work-related, personal, and physically threatening behavior. While work-related bullying involves persistently criticizing a person's work, as well as giving too many, too few, or too simple tasks; includes bullying, slander, social isolation, and gossiping about a person. Bullying including physical threats covers physical violence or the threat of physical violence (Ko et al., 2020). When evaluated in this context, excessive intimidation, verbal and nonverbal negative behaviors, belittling, humiliation, disturbing, inhibiting, angry behaviors, stressful changes in the employee's job, work and time pressure, and dangerous working conditions are some of the actions related to bullying (Einarsen et al., 2011; Einarsen & Nielsen, 2015; Fox & Stallworth, 2005; Parzefall & Salin, 2010; Samnani & Singh, 2014). Leymann (1990) suggested that to qualify as a victim of bullying, a person must be exposed to such behaviors at least once a week for six months.

According to the position of the bullied person in working life workplace bullying is divided into horizontal and vertical. Vertical bullying is also classified as bottom-up and top-down, depending on whether the person being bullied is the top (managers/supervisors) or subordinate in the work hierarchy. In horizontal bullying, the person who is bullied and the person who commits this act are in the same hierarchy. The term is also often used when an employee is exposed to negative or inappropriate behavior from third parties. Therefore, it is recognized that bullying can occur 'between colleagues', 'between supervisors and subordinates' or 'by third parties such as customers and patients' (Hoel & Vartia, 2018; Tutar, 2004; Uysal, 2016).

Leymann (1996) divides workplace bullying into five stages. In the first stage, disagreement and similar critical events trigger the existence of conflicts. Then, an active bullying situation begins to be observed through intimidation attacks under the name of psychological harassment. In the third stage, if the bullied person cannot be understood by the managers, the solution becomes difficult with misunderstanding and the victim starts to be labeled with various adjectives. In the last stage, the victim, who quit his job and ended his career, struggles with various psychological disorders as well as emotional tension (Akca & Kucukoglu Tepe, 2020).

Bullying For Healthcare Workers

The healthcare team is a union where different professional groups come together in order to provide detailed health services to the individuals in public and private health institutions, each member of the profession does his/her own duty, and their knowledge and experiences are constantly shared and transferred. Expressions such as "healthcare personnel, healthcare worker, healthcare workforce" are generally used for all occupational groups taking part in the healthcare team. Healthcare workers are considered as the main factor in the continuation of health services. Healthcare workers mean "personnel who provide all kinds of healthcare services in the public and private sectors" (Ucak, 2009). The World Health Organization (WHO) defines healthcare workers as those who work with the goal of promoting health. With a general approach, WHO has included in the definition all kinds of preventive, protective, encouraging and curative healthcare workers such as doctors, nurses, midwives, laboratory technicians, specialists dealing with public health, community health workers, pharmacists (WHO, 2006).

WHO has recognized the vital role that healthcare workers play as "the most valuable resource for health". However, workers in this industry are constantly exposed to a variety of complex health and safety hazards during their work (Joseph & Joseph, 2016). Healthcare professionalism is seen as one of the professions with the highest levels of workplace bullying (Farouque & Burgio, 2013). In the literature, it is stated that health care workers (especially nurses and doctors) are exposed to negative behaviors 16 times more than other service sector workers (Kingma, 2001). As a matter of fact, according to researches, workplace bullying in health institutions affects the health of employees, job satisfaction and patient care outcomes (Alcantara et al., 2017). In addition, the costs of bullying appear to be higher for organizations made up of healthcare professionals performing complex tasks in direct contact with patients (Giorgi et al., 2016).

EPIDEMIOLOGY

Workplace bullying, which is seen as a serious and growing problem today, affects a significant part of health professionals. Although a number of tools have been developed to detect the prevalence and determinants of workplace bullying, and these measurement tools have been validated for different regions, cultures and geographical settings; given the varying definitions of workplace bullying across societies, this has led to varying prevalences between populations and countries studied, and inconsistent estimates of the magnitude of bullying in occupational settings (Awai et al., 2021). When the different studies on this subject are examined, the prevalence of workplace bullying is shown to be 75.8% in Bulgaria, 85.2% in Turkey, 67.2% in Australia, 89.6% in Egypt, 54% in Thailand and 61% in South Africa (Abbas et al., 2010). Also, workplace bullying among healthcare workers differs between and within countries in terms of its prevalence and characteristics (Al-Surimi et al., 2020). In a study from European countries, it was reported that the prevalence of bullying in workplaces where healthcare services are provided is 0.3%-85.5% (Kirilmaz et al., 2016).

Bullying in healthcare workers has reached particularly troubling dimensions today. According to the data of the World Health Organization; between 8% and 38% of healthcare workers have experienced physical violence at least once in their career, and many more have been subjected to verbal aggression or threats(WHO, 2017). When the studies investigating the prevalence of bullying in healthcare workers are examined, it has been shown that 31.9% of doctors, 30.8% of nurses, 12.4% of allied health personnel and 2.3% of administrative personnel are exposed to bullying in any way (Lever et al., 2019). Unfortunately, the manifestation of violence against the professional workforce is often viewed as just part of the job and not taken seriously. One study showed that 70% of attacks against social workers and other agency personnel are never investigated (Fink-Samnick, 2016).

Studies to investigate the frequency and antecedents of bullying among healthcare workers are mostly carried out among nurses. In one review, data of 151.347 nurses were evaluated by examining 136 articles. In the results, it was stated that 25% of the nurses were exposed to sexual harassment, 36.4% to physical violence, 39.7% to bullying and 66.9% to non-physical violence. It has been observed that the type of violence experienced shows interesting geographical differences. The highest rates of non-physical violence and bullying were reported in the Middle East, while the highest rates for physical violence and sexual harassment were found in the Anglo region (Spector et al., 2014). Yildirim (2009) stated that the most common bullying behaviors faced by nurses are putting pressure on their work and attacking their professional status and personality. Chipps & McRury (2012) stated that the most common bullying behavior faced by nurses is verbal abuse. In a survey conducted in The UK, 97% of nurses reported that they physically knew a nurse who had been assaulted in the past year, 72% of nurses did not feel safe from being attacked in their workplace, and up to 95% of nurses reported that they had been bullied at work (Kingma, 2001).

However, organizational structures and power imbalances in health care services can pave the way for bullying for all healthcare workers (Norton et al., 2017). In a study of junior doctors at The UK, 37% of doctors said they had been bullied in the past year and 84% said they had encountered bullying at some point in their career (Quine, 2002). In a study among surgeons; It has been reported that 40% of the assistants and consultants have been exposed to bullying, while 54.3%–58.5% have witnessed bullying (Pei et al., 2020). It has been shown that one in four ambulance personnel has been assaulted on the job in one year in Australia (Kingma, 2001). Er et al. (2021) reported that 66.0% of nurses, 64.2% of research assistants, 63.6% of specialist physicians, 41.0% of other health workers, 39.4% of technicians are being exposed to violence at least once. Rowell (2005) states that especially in the healthcare sector, workplace bullying has increased and this type of behavior is 4 times more common than sexual harassment in this sector.

CAUSES

Bullying in the workplace is a multifactorial phenomenon. While there is little awareness of workplace bullying and why it persists in healthcare circles, it is vital to understand the causes that drive the emergence and development of this societal phenomenon. Many studies conducted to date have shown that; workplace bullying is a dynamic and complex process preceded by many individual, organizational and many possible combinations (Francioli, 2015).

As early as the 1980s, Leymann mentioned the importance of organizational factors as one of the antecedents of workplace bullying. Leynmann (1996) was the first to emphasize that a poor psychosocial work environment predisposes to bullying. In the 1990s and early 2000s, limited studies were conducted on this topic. Subsequently, many studies in this area have focused on the role of poor psychosocial work environment as one of the main antecedents of workplace bullying (Francioli, 2015). Michelson (2001) argued that bullying should be seen as a problem of organizations rather than a problem of individuals. The phenomenon of bullying; cannot be considered independently of organizational policies, activities, pressures, and reward systems. The European Parliament (2001) reported that negative factors such as excess competition among employees, deficiencies in job security and precarious employment, which are stress factors in the workplace, are effective in the emergence of bullying events. Also, in a recent study among healthcare professionals in Canada, the main causes of inter-nurse bullying were found to be organizational dimensions such as excessive workload, lack of control, inadequate rewards, and lack of communication with management (Giorgi et al., 2016). In many studies from The UK, Australia, New Zealand and the USA, it has been reported that leadership characteristics, which is one of the organizational factors, are generally the source of bullying behaviors (Hutchinson et al., 2005; Lewis, 2006; McKenna et al., 2003; Rowe & Sherlock, 2005). Under a strong authoritarian leader, employees are compelled to obey the orders of their superiors, regardless of the underlying reality. This causes excessive pressure and stress on employees. There is a strong causal link between stress and bullying, as demonstrated by Folkman (2013) and Delongis et al. (1999). On the other hand, a weak leader profile may cause employees to perceive the probability of intervening in workplace bullying as low and to have low belief that the aggressor will be caught and punished for bullying. As a result, this increases the possibility of perpetrators to engage in bullying behaviors in the workplace (Salin, 2003).

Hierarchical organizational structures of health institutions are seen as one of the reasons why bullying occurs more frequently in the healthcare sector than in other industries (Awai et al., 2021).

As in the model shown in Figure 1, C-suite administrators and physicians bully clinical professionals (e.g. nurses, pharmacists, rehabilitation staff, social workers), while clinical professionals bully paraprofessionals (e.g. certified nursing assistants), associate professionals bully nonclinical support staff (e.g.cleaning staff) (Fink-Samnick, 2016). Leymann (1996) argued that excessive workloads and double supervision (by doctors and head nurses) cause bullying to be common, especially among nurses. The study by Yildirim (2009) confirms that 87% of nurses in Turkey, especially those in the public sector, are exposed to some form of bullying. Norton et al. (2017) reported in a study among healthcare professionals that bullying was predominantly vertical and more frequent among nurses.

It can be mentioned that nurses have a high tendency to encounter bullying behavior due to their close relationship with patients and their relatives, the fact that most of the members of the profession are women, there is no homogeneity in the profession due to different education levels, and their dependent functions based on physician requests. Unfortunately, in nursing, those who witness such acts also face a difficult dilemma. Although they usually do not get the support of their colleagues, they are

Figure 1. Hierarchical stratification in health care (Nesbitt, 2012)

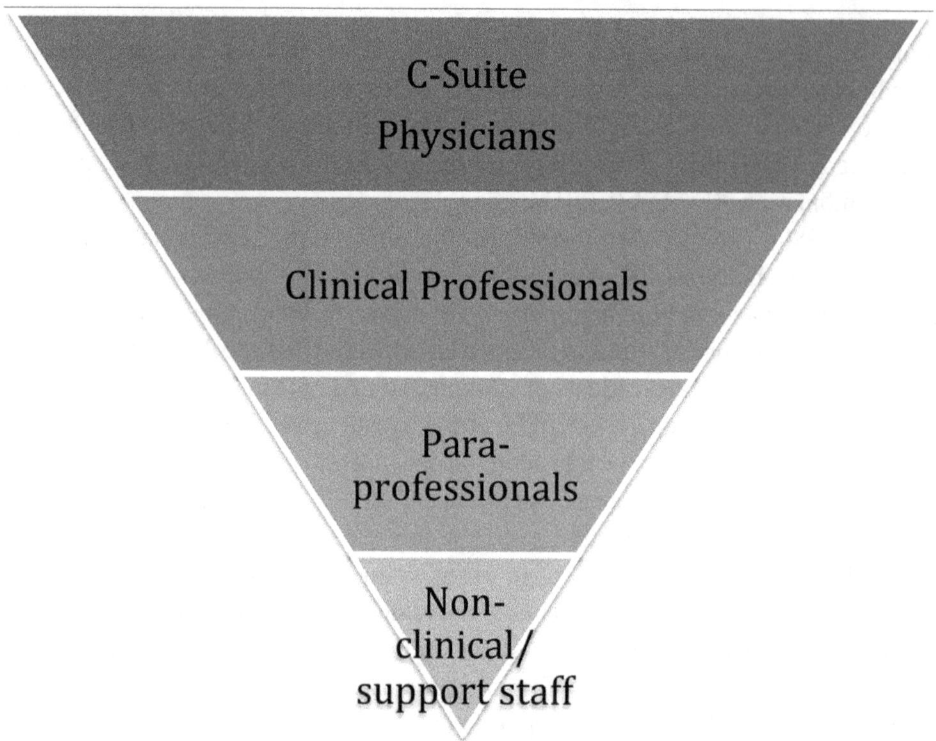

also worried about their own position and career development because they do not want to be seen as troublemakers (Lewis, 2006). Thus, it is seen that nurses who consider bullying as a part of the job do not complain about bullying by ignoring negative behaviors (Giorgi et al., 2016). When nurses accept bullying behaviors as normal, they allow such behaviors to continue (Szutenbach, 2013). Ko et al. (2020) showed that unmarried nurses are more frequently exposed to workplace bullying than married nurses. In other studies, it has been emphasized that unmarried nurses have less family support and less social support causes more workplace bullying exposure (Tai et al., 2014; Tian, 2008). It has been determined that many nurses in Taiwan quit their jobs after marriage due to the shift work system. This has commonly resulted in less night shifts and less paperwork and responsibilities for married nurses. Thus, unmarried nurses who work more night shifts, serve as emergency support personnel, and perform more non-patient activities, as a result, are at greater risk of being bullied (Wang et al., 2007). These findings showed that nurses can sometimes be evaluated according to non-work-related standards such as marital status, instead of being evaluated fairly according to their job performance.

On the other hand, doctors/pharmacists tend to work in rotation between various hospital departments. They communicate more with patients and their families, especially for the purpose of informing about medical diagnosis, clinical prognosis and vital critical decisions. For this reason, workplace bullying incidents faced by physicians and pharmacists may be caused by reasons such as lack of communication with patients and their relatives, interruptions or misinterpretation of messages by patients. In addition, experts state that traditional and often outdated vocational training models are among the factors that affect the existence of bullying throughout the sector. In a study conducted among surgeons, it was shown that surgical assistants are more bullied than consultant surgeons, and that some consultant surgeons see threats and harassment as a functional tool in surgical training, which is effective in the emergence of this result (Ling et al., 2016).

Considering the working conditions and environment in the healthcare sector; the reasons such as the fact that this sector is a labor-intensive sector, the number of female employees, long working hours, and high job stress contribute to the high frequency of bullying in this sector (Kirilmaz et al., 2016). Previous research has shown that women face a higher risk of experiencing workplace bullying than men (Ling et al., 2016; WBI, 2015). In a study involving doctors, it was found that women were exposed to more bullying than men (Quine, 2002). It has been thought that the fact that the victims of bullying in the workplace are generally women, may be due to the fact that men are more frequently in managerial positions in organizations and that women are more inclined to report bullying incidents (Einarsen et al., 2011; Salin, 2005). In some studies, it has been suggested that women are more likely to face verbal threats, while men are reported to be more exposed to physical violence (Andrews et al., 2012; Flannery et al., 2011). In addition, sleep deprivation caused by night work and long shifts leads to a decrease in self-control and tolerance, resulting in increased workplace violence (Christian & Ellis, 2011).

However, temporary workers are also seen as a group with a higher risk of experiencing workplace bullying, as they fear that their contracts will not be renewed or canceled if they experience any conflict at work (Baron & Neuman, 1996). In a study conducted by Ozen Col, S. (2008), it was found that the attackers were doctors, nurses, administrative personnel and managers with a high level of education, while the groups that were thought to have the least tendency to aggression were subcontracted workers and temporary personnel.

It has been shown that workplace violence occurs mostly in waiting rooms, emergency services, geriatric units and psychiatry services (Kwok et al., 2006). It has been shown that in a medical center in Iran, 34.5% of the emergency room workers are exposed to physical abuse, 71.6% to verbal abuse and 44.4% to bullying every year (Saleh et al., 2020). Liu et al. (2020) showed that healthcare personnel working in outpatient clinics and emergency services have a higher risk of experiencing both physical and psychological violence than other healthcare professionals. Similar results were found in other studies (Chen et al., 2019; P. Li et al., 2018; Lu et al., 2020; Xing et al., 2015). Emergency services are considered to be more risky among all departments due to reasons such as being accessible 24 hours a day, lack of security and stressful environments (Najafi et al., 2014). The uncertain nature of acute illnesses, trauma and patients with pain, the stress and strain of patients and their families and unexpected consequences such as death; lack of privacy, intense interpersonal interactions and long waiting times are the factors that prepare the environment for this situation. Patients, family members and visitors constitute a significant portion of the perpetrators of violence in emergency services (Talas et al., 2011). In a study conducted at Kartal Training and Research Hospital in Turkey, 70.4% of healthcare workers who were exposed to violence stated that they were subjected to violence by the relatives of the patients (Eker et al., 2011). In a study conducted with the participation of nurses serving in the emergency department, 60.2% of the nurses who were exposed to violence stated that they were subjected to violence by the relatives of the patients, and 33.6% by the patients (Bahar et al., 2015).

Al-Surimi et al. (2020) stated that among individual factors, age and professional experience are also effective factors on the probability of being bullied by healthcare workers. In this study, workplace bullying was found to be more common among younger (<30 years) and less experienced workers (<10 years). In another study, it was found that 70.5% of those with 6-10 years of work in the profession and 71.4% of those with 11-15 years of work were exposed to violence, and the exposure to violence of these two groups was higher than the health workers in the other group (Er et al., 2021). On the other hand, Pinar et al. (2017) stated that being younger (£29 years old) and lack of professional experience (1-4 years) increased the risk of exposure to workplace violence. It was thought that this result might be due to the lack of interpersonal work relations and communication skills of recent graduates and young practitioners (Awai et al., 2021). So that special trainings organized by health institutions and managers for health workers, especially inexperienced workers, may be important in dealing with difficult patients and their relatives (Pinar et al., 2017).

A recent study among healthcare professionals found that a significant proportion (17.1%) of respondents experienced workplace bullying or patient aggression related to coronavirus disease 2019 (COVID-19). In addition, in this study, fear and anxiety about COVID-19 infection and any experience of workplace bullying or patient attack related to COVID-19 were found to be effective risk factors on psychological stress (Asaoka et al., 2021). On the other hand, Shigemura et al. (2020) argued that exaggerated and sensational news headlines and images add anxiety and fear to the current situation during the COVID-19 pandemic, thus feeding rumors and false information. It was thought that this situation may have caused the healthcare workers to be exposed to discrimination or stigmatization because they were close to the patient infected with COVID-19. In other studies, it is mentioned that during the COVID-19 pandemic, harmful social reactions caused by communication technologies can lead to COVID-19-related bullying and harassment against healthcare workers. It is important to popularize the use of reliable and official sources of information as one of the strategies to reduce bullying and harassment related to COVID-19 among healthcare professionals professionals (Dye et al., 2020). The worsening mental health of healthcare professionals is not only dependent on responding to COVID-19 patients, as reported in previous studies, but also on patient aggression and workplace bullying related to COVID-19 (Greenberg, 2020; Imai, 2020; Li et al., 2021; Pappa et al., 2020). Actions planned to improve the mental health of healthcare workers during the COVID-19 pandemic must include measures to prevent workplace bullying and patient aggression. Indeed, a previous study revealed that subgroups, such as healthcare workers, who are at greater risk of exposure to stigma and discrimination in public health emergencies, need special attention and protection(WHO, 2020).

CONSEQUENCES

Individual Consequences

Bullying mostly occurs when there is a real attributed power imbalance between the parties, and where the strong dominate the weak. Studies have shown that victims of bullying experience severe psychological symptoms such as self-hatred, depression, and anxiety, as well as psychosomatic disorders. Bullying not only harms the psychological and physical health of its victims, but also negatively affects the welfare and effectiveness of employees. Lever et al. (2019) showed that both the mental and physical health of healthcare personnel who are exposed to bullying are adversely affected, and their absenteeism from work is higher.

It is observed that the levels of anxiety and depression generally increase in individuals who are bullied, and therefore their coping strategies are weakened (Yildiz & Yildiz, 2009). In the research findings of Zapf (1999), it was stated that those who were bullied showed higher depression scores than those who did not.

According to Yildirim (2009), it was found that 45% of nurses showed symptoms of depression and that the behaviors involving psychological violence that nurses were exposed to had a significant effect on their depression. In a study conducted with the participation of 1179 nurses in Quebec, the effects of workplace bullying on the mental health of employees were investigated. It has been shown that exposure to bullying increases burnout in nurses (Trépanier et al., 2013). In another study examining the relationship between bullying and nurses' burnout symptoms, it was found that burnout (emotional exhaustion and depersonalization) was more common among nurses who reported being bullied(Sa & Fleming, 2008).

Physiological symptoms of bullying include distress, headache, dizziness, memory loss, inability to concentrate and insomnia (Paksoy, 2007).

The Workplace Bullying Institute (2015) has listed some symptom frequencies as follows:

- Debilitating Anxiety—80%
- Panic Attacks— 52%
- Clinical Depression (newly diagnosed or exacerbated in existing)—49%
- Post Traumatic Stress Disorder —30%

The first-stage effects of the bullying process on the victims are generally seen as crying for no reason, sleep disturbances, irritability and difficulty concentrating in all kinds of situations. In the second stage, symptoms such as stomach complaints, high blood pressure, depression, being late for work and not wanting to go to work are added to the symptoms in the first stage. In the third stage, the severity of depression increases, panic attacks happen and anxiety occurs. Accidents and suicidal tendencies are mostly seen in the last phase of the mobbing process (Davenport et al., 2003). In another study, it was found that one out of every 7 suicides is a result of emotional bullying at work (Rayner & Hoel, 1997).

Organizational Consequences

Studies on workplace bullying show that this phenomenon not only concerns the bullies and the victims of bullying, but also may have negative effects at the organizational level (Matthiesen & Einarsen, 2001). Chaos and uneasiness in a workplace where there is bullying can be reflected in the image of the organization and cause the organization to be recognized in a negative way. Employees seek to escape from the growing uneasiness and conflict in the organization. The decrease in employees' sense of belonging to their jobs and organizations causes them to look for opportunities to move to workplaces with a better working atmosphere. The loss of experience gained in the organization with the departure of trained individuals results in an increase in the cost of retraining. There is also an increase in the leaves used due to the diseases caused by the bullying process. Intention to leave of both the victims of the process and the other employees of the organization who want to get away from the negative environment by using leave also affect the productivity of the (Yildiz & Yildiz, 2009). Pallas et al. (2006) argued that the problems experienced by nurses in their relationships with their colleagues and superiors and the lack of communication negatively affect their motivation and job performance. Considering the importance of nurses collaborating with their colleagues and managers while caring for patients, it can be said that bullying behaviors not only create a negative working environment, but also reduce the effectiveness and efficiency of the health care provided to patients (Yildirim, 2009). Specifically, it can be mentioned that nurses who are bullied affect the continuity of patient care by showing low job performance, while doctors who are victims of bullying are more prone to make mistakes while making decisions in the diagnosis and treatment processes of patients. In another study, according to the opinions of healthcare professionals, the three most common changes in the patient's approach after exposure to violence are; decrease in tolerance to patient demands, decrease in verbal communication and decrease in explaining (Er et al., 2021). Combined with high absenteeism, turnover and decreased productivity in healthcare settings, these consequences result in significant institutional-level costs (Awai et al., 2021).

Royal College of Nursing (Great Britain) (2000) stated that one-third of nurses faced with bullying became alienated from their profession, resigned and turned to other professions. Similarly, Simons (2008) states that bullying is an important determinant of intention to leave the organization. Johnson & Rea (2009) reported that 30% of bullied and newly graduated nurses left the profession in the first year and 57% in the second year.

FUTURE RESEARCH DIRECTIONS

Bullying and workplace violence are unwelcome visitors to all healthcare delivery settings. Due to the sensitive nature of this issue, the frequency and severity of workplace bullying reported in studies to date likely reflect less of the actual exposure. Other outcome measures should be considered in the future to better understand the impact of bullying on healthcare workers. It is important to conduct studies evaluating the effectiveness of anti-bullying intervention programs developed with increasing awareness on this issue. In addition, there seems to be an important need to work on countermeasures through the collaboration of various institutions and communities to prevent healthcare workers from being bullied and harassed related to public health emergencies such as COVID-19.

CONCLUSION

Bullying in healthcare workers has consequences that no one can ignore individually, organizationally and socially. All hospital administrators have important responsibilities to ensure a safe working environment that is free from all kinds of harassment and bullying, which is the right of all healthcare workers and patients. In this context, action plans can be initiated for the education of vulnerable groups and for closely monitoring their working environments. Establishing, reporting, and resolving early warning signs of workplace bullying are important steps in identifying high-risk work environments in healthcare workplaces. Strategies for the prevention of workplace bullying need to be developed in order to promote safe psychosocial working environments.

REFERENCES

Abbas, M. A., Fiala, L. A., Abdel Rahman, A. G., & Fahim, A. E. (2010). Epidemiology of workplace violence against nursing staff in Ismailia Governorate, Egypt. *The Journal of the Egyptian Public Health Association*, *85*(1-2), 29–43. PMID:21073846

Akca, M., & Kucukoglu Tepe, M. (2020). Relations Between Workplace Bullying, Conscientiousness And Counterproductive Work Behaviours: A Study At Logistics Company. *Beykoz Akademi Dergisi, 8*(1), 117–136. doi:10.14514/BYK.m.26515393.2020.8/1.117-136

Al-Hussain, S. M., Al-Haidari, M. S., Kouri, N. A., El-Migdadi, F., Al-Safar, R. S., & Mohammad, M. A. (2008). Prevalence of mistreatment and justice of grading system in five health related faculties in Jordan University of Science and Technology. *Medical Teacher, 30*(3), e82–e86. doi:10.1080/01421590801938845 PMID:18484446

Al-Surimi, K., Al Omar, M., Alahmary, K., & Salam, M. (2020). Prevalence of Workplace Bullying and Its Associated Factors at a Multi-Regional Saudi Arabian Hospital: A Cross-Sectional Study. *Risk Management and Healthcare Policy, 13*, 1905–1914. doi:10.2147/RMHP.S265127 PMID:33061722

Alcantara, G. M., Claudio, E. G., & Gabriel, A. G. (2017). Prognosis of Workplace Bullying in Selected Health Care Organizations in the Philippines. *Open Journal of Social Sciences, 5*(9), 154–174. doi:10.4236/jss.2017.59012

Andrews, M. E., Stewart, N. J., Morgan, D. G., & D'Arcy, C. (2012). More alike than different: A comparison of male and female RNs in rural and remote Canada. *Journal of Nursing Management, 20*(4), 561–570. doi:10.1111/j.1365-2834.2011.01195.x PMID:22591157

Asaoka, H., Sasaki, N., Kuroda, R., Tsuno, K., & Kawakami, N. (2021). Workplace Bullying and Patient Aggression Related to COVID-19 and its Association with Psychological Distress among Health Care Professionals during the COVID-19 Pandemic in Japan. *The Tohoku Journal of Experimental Medicine, 255*(4), 283–289. doi:10.1620/tjem.255.283 PMID:34897160

Askew, D. A., Schluter, P. J., Dick, M. L., Régo, P. M., Turner, C., & Wilkinson, D. (2012). Bullying in the Australian medical workforce: Cross-sectional data from an Australian e-Cohort study. *Australian Health Review, 36*(2), 197–204. doi:10.1071/AH11048 PMID:22624642

Awai, N. S., Ganasegeran, K., & Abdul Manaf, M. R. (2021). Prevalence of Workplace Bullying and Its Associated Factors among Workers in a Malaysian Public University Hospital: A Cross-Sectional Study. *Risk Management and Healthcare Policy, 14*, 75–85. doi:10.2147/RMHP.S280954 PMID:33447111

Bahar, A., Sahin, S., Akkaya, Z., & Alkayis, M. (2015). Acil Serviste Calisan Hemsirelerin Siddete Maruz Kalma Durumu ve Is Doyumuna Etkili Olan Faktörlerin İncelenmesi [Investigation of the Factors Affecting the Exposure to Violence and Job Satisfaction of the Nurses Working in the Emergency Service]. *Psikiyatri Hemsireleri Dernegi, 6*(2).

Baron, R. A., & Neuman, J. H. (1996). Workplace violence and workplace aggression: Evidence on their relative frequency and potential causes. *Aggressive Behavior, 22*(3), 161–173. doi:10.1002/(SICI)1098-2337(1996)22:3<161::AID-AB1>3.0.CO;2-Q

Bayrakci, E., & Dinc, M. (2020). Tersine Zorbalik (Mobbing) Eylemleri ve Tersine Zorbalikla Basa Cikma Stratejileri Uzerine Nitel Bir Arastirma [A Qualitative Study on Acts of Reverse Bullying(Mobbing) and Strategies for Coping with Reverse Bullying]. *Süleyman Demirel Üniversitesi Vizyoner Dergisi, 11*(27), 403–418.

Branch, S. (2008). You say Tomatoe and I say Tomato: Can we differentiate between Workplace Bullying and other Counterproductive behaviours? *International Journal of Organisational Behaviour*, 13.

Cheema, S., Ahmad, K., Giri, S. K., Kaliaperumal, V. K., & Naqvi, S. A. (2005). Bullying of junior doctors prevails in Irish health system: A bitter reality. *Irish Medical Journal*, *98*(9), 274–275. PMID:16300107

Chen, N., Zhang, M., Li, R., Wang, P., & Wang, Y. (2019). Investigation on workplace violence in a Grade 2A hospital - - A survey using the investing tool for workplace violence in hospitals developed by the World Health Organization. *China Occupational Medicine*, 157-162.

Chipps, E. M., & McRury, M. (2012). The development of an educational intervention to address workplace bullying: A pilot study. *Journal for Nurses in Staff Development*, *28*(3), 94–98. doi:10.1097/NND.0b013e31825514bb PMID:22617778

Christian, M. S., & Ellis, A. P. J. (2011). Examining the Effects of Sleep Deprivation on Workplace Deviance: A Self-Regulatory Perspective. *Academy of Management Journal*, *54*(5), 913–934. doi:10.5465/amj.2010.0179

Cohen, J. S., Leung, Y., Fahey, M., Hoyt, L., Sinha, R., Cailler, L., & Patten, S. (2008). The happy docs study: A Canadian Association of Internes and Residents well-being survey examining resident physician health and satisfaction within and outside of residency training in Canada. *BMC Research Notes*, *1*(1), 105. doi:10.1186/1756-0500-1-105 PMID:18957136

Daugherty, S. R., Baldwin, D. C. Jr, & Rowley, B. D. (1998). Learning, satisfaction, and mistreatment during medical internship: A national survey of working conditions. *Journal of the American Medical Association*, *279*(15), 1194–1199. doi:10.1001/jama.279.15.1194 PMID:9555759

Davenport, N., Distler, R. S., & Elliott, G. P. (2003). Mobbing, İşyerinde Duygusal Taciz [Mobbing, Emotional Harassment at Work] (O. C. Önertoy, Trans.). Istanbul: Sistem Yayincilik.

DeLongis, A., Folkman, S., & Lazarus, R. S. (1988). The impact of daily stress on health and mood: Psychological and social resources as mediators. *Journal of Personality and Social Psychology*, *54*(3), 486–495. doi:10.1037/0022-3514.54.3.486 PMID:3361420

Dye, T. D., Alcantara, L., Siddiqi, S., Barbosu, M., Sharma, S., Panko, T., & Pressman, E. (2020). Risk of COVID-19-related bullying, harassment and stigma among healthcare workers: An analytical cross-sectional global study. *BMJ Open*, *10*(12), e046620. doi:10.1136/bmjopen-2020-046620 PMID:33380488

Einarsen, S., Hoel, H., Zapf, D., & Cooper, C. (2010). *Bullying and harassment in the workplace: Developments in theory, research, and practice*. CRC Press. doi:10.1201/EBK1439804896

Einarsen, S., Hoel, H., Zapf, D., & Cooper, C. L. (2002). The concept of bullying at work: the European tradition. In *Bullying and Emotional Abuse in the Workplace* (pp. 21–48). CRC Press. doi:10.1201/9780203164662-6

Einarsen, S., Hoel, H., Zapf, D., & Cooper, C. L. (2011). The concept of bullying and harassment at work: The European tradition. *Bullying and harassment in the workplace: Developments in theory, research, and practice, 2*, 3-40.

Einarsen, S., & Nielsen, M. B. (2015). Workplace bullying as an antecedent of mental health problems: A five-year prospective and representative study. *International Archives of Occupational and Environmental Health, 88*(2), 131–142. doi:10.100700420-014-0944-7 PMID:24840725

Eker, H. H., Topcu, İ., Sahinoz, S., Ozder, A., & Aydin, H. (2011). Bir Egitim ve Arastirma Hastanesindeki Siddet Sikligi [Frequency of Violence in a Training and Research Hospital]. *Bidder Tıp Bilimleri Dergisi, 3*(3), 16–22.

Er, T., Ayoglu, F., & Acikgoz, B. (2021). Saglik calisanina yonelik siddet: Risk faktorleri, etkileri, degerlendirilmesi ve önlenmesi [Violence against healthcare workers: Risk factors, effects, assessment and prevention]. *Turkish Journal of Public Health, 19*(1), 69–78.

Farouque, K., & Burgio, E. (2013). *The impact of bullying in health care*. The Royal Australasian College of Medical Administrators.

Fink-Samnick, E. (2016). The New Age of Bullying and Violence in Health Care: Part 2: Advancing Professional Education, Practice Culture, and Advocacy. *Professional Case Management, 21*(3), 114–126. doi:10.1097/NCM.0000000000000146 PMID:27035082

Flannery, R. Jr, LeVitre, V., Rego, S., & Walker, A. (2011). Characteristics of Staff Victims of Psychiatric Patient Assaults: 20-Year Analysis of the Assaulted Staff Action Program. *The Psychiatric Quarterly, 82*(1), 11–21. doi:10.100711126-010-9153-z PMID:20821050

Folkman, S. (2013). *Stress: Appraisal and Coping*. Springer.

Fox, S., & Stallworth, L. E. (2005). Racial/ethnic bullying: Exploring links between bullying and racism in the US workplace. *Journal of Vocational Behavior, 66*(3), 438–456. doi:10.1016/j.jvb.2004.01.002

Francioli, L. (2015). Workplace Bullying, Antecedents and Mechanisms. Università degli studi di Milano.

Gadit, A. A., & Mugford, G. (2008). A pilot study of bullying and harassment among medical professionals in Pakistan, focussing on psychiatry: Need for a medical ombudsman. *Journal of Medical Ethics, 34*(6), 463–466. doi:10.1136/jme.2007.021832 PMID:18511621

Galletta, D. (2014). Mobbing: From a Social Phenomenon to Psychopathology: Preliminary Data. *Journal of Psychiatry, 17*(5). Advance online publication. doi:10.4172/Psychiatry.1000137

Giorgi, G., Mancuso, S., Fiz Perez, F., Castiello D'Antonio, A., Mucci, N., Cupelli, V., & Arcangeli, G. (2016). Bullying among nurses and its relationship with burnout and organizational climate. *International Journal of Nursing Practice, 22*(2), 160–168. doi:10.1111/ijn.12376 PMID:25825025

Greenberg, N. (2020). Mental health of health-care workers in the COVID-19 era. *Nature Reviews. Nephrology, 16*(8), 425–426. doi:10.103841581-020-0314-5 PMID:32561871

Heponiemi, T., Kouvonen, A., Virtanen, M., Vänskä, J., & Elovainio, M. (2014). The prospective effects of workplace violence on physicians' job satisfaction and turnover intentions: The buffering effect of job control. *BMC Health Services Research, 14*(1), 19. doi:10.1186/1472-6963-14-19 PMID:24438449

Hoel, H., & Vartia, M. (2018). Bullying and sexual harassment at the workplace, in public spaces, and in political life in the EU. In European, Parliament Directorate-General for Internal Policies of the, Union. European Parliament.

Hutchinson, M., Vickers, M. H., Jackson, D., & Wilkes, L. (2005). "I'm gonna do what i wanna do." Organizational change as a legitimized vehicle for bullies. *Health Care Management Review*, *30*(4), 331–336. doi:10.1097/00004010-200510000-00007 PMID:16292010

Imai, H. (2020). Trust is a key factor in the willingness of health professionals to work during the COVID-19 outbreak: Experience from the H1N1 pandemic in Japan 2009. *Psychiatry and Clinical Neurosciences*, *74*(5), 329–330. doi:10.1111/pcn.12995 PMID:32105381

Johnson, S. L., & Rea, R. E. (2009). Workplace bullying: Concerns for nurse leaders. *The Journal of Nursing Administration*, *39*(2), 84–90. doi:10.1097/NNA.0b013e318195a5fc PMID:19190425

Joseph, B., & Joseph, M. (2016). The health of the healthcare workers. *Indian Journal of Occupational and Environmental Medicine*, *20*(2), 71–72. doi:10.4103/0019-5278.197518 PMID:28194078

Keeley, P. W., Waterhouse, E. T., & Noble, S. I. (2005). Prevalence and characteristics of bullying of trainees in palliative medicine. *Palliative Medicine*, *19*(1), 84–85. doi:10.1191/0269216305pm968xx PMID:15690873

Kingma, M. (2001). Workplace violence in the health sector: A problem of epidemic proportion. *International Nursing Review*, *48*(3), 129–130. doi:10.1046/j.1466-7657.2001.00094.x PMID:11558684

Kirilmaz, H., Yorgun, S., & Atasoy, A. (2016). Saglik Calisanlarinda Psikososyal Risk Faktörlerini Belirlemeye Yonelik Bir Arastirma [A Study on Determining Psychosocial Risk Factors in Healthcare Professionals]. *Uluslararasi Kulturel ve Sosyal Arastirmalar Dergisi (UKSAD)*, *2*(1), 66-82.

Ko, Y. Y., Liu, Y., Wang, C. J., Liao, H. Y., Liao, Y. M., & Chen, H. M. (2020). Determinants of Workplace Bullying Types and Their Relationship With Depression Among Female Nurses. *The Journal of Nursing Research*, *28*(3), e92. doi:10.1097/JNR.0000000000000367 PMID:31972730

Kwok, R. P., Law, Y. K., Li, K. E., Ng, Y. C., Cheung, M. H., Fung, V. K., & Leung, W. C. (2006). Prevalence of workplace violence against nurses in Hong Kong. *Hong Kong Medical Journal*, *12*(1), 6–9. PMID:16495582

Launer, J. (2013). Bullying in the health service. *Postgraduate Medical Journal*, *89*(1051), 307–308. doi:10.1136/postgradmedj-2013-131983 PMID:23596258

Lever, I., Dyball, D., Greenberg, N., & Stevelink, S. A. M. (2019). Health consequences of bullying in the healthcare workplace: A systematic review. *Journal of Advanced Nursing*, *75*(12), 3195–3209. doi:10.1111/jan.13986 PMID:30816567

Lewis, M. A. (2006). Nurse bullying: Organizational considerations in the maintenance and perpetration of health care bullying cultures. *Journal of Nursing Management*, *14*(1), 52–58. doi:10.1111/j.1365-2934.2005.00535.x PMID:16359446

Leymann, H. (1996). The content and development of mobbing at work. *European Journal of Work and Organizational Psychology*, *5*(2), 165–184. doi:10.1080/13594329608414853

Leymann, H., & Gustafsson, A. (1996). Mobbing at work and the development of post-traumatic stress disorders. *European Journal of Work and Organizational Psychology*, *5*(2), 251–275. doi:10.1080/13594329608414858

Li, L., Sun, N., Fei, S., Yu, L., Chen, S., Yang, S., & Li, H. (2021). Current status of and factors influencing anxiety and depression in front-line medical staff supporting Wuhan in containing the novel coronavirus pneumonia epidemic. *Japan Journal of Nursing Science*, *18*(2), e12398. doi:10.1111/jjns.12398 PMID:33258559

Li, P., Xing, K., Qiao, H., Fang, H., Ma, H., Jiao, M., & Liu, M. (2018). Psychological violence against general practitioners and nurses in Chinese township hospitals: Incidence and implications. *Health and Quality of Life Outcomes*, *16*(1), 117. doi:10.118612955-018-0940-9 PMID:29871642

Ling, M., Young, C. J., Shepherd, H. L., Mak, C., & Saw, R. P. (2016). Workplace Bullying in Surgery. *World Journal of Surgery*, *40*(11), 2560–2566. doi:10.100700268-016-3642-7 PMID:27624759

Liu, Y., Zhang, M., Li, R., Chen, N., Huang, Y., Lv, Y., & Wang, Y. (2020). Risk assessment of workplace violence towards health workers in a Chinese hospital: A cross-sectional study. *BMJ Open*, *10*(12), e042800. doi:10.1136/bmjopen-2020-042800 PMID:33371045

Lu, L., Dong, M., Wang, S. B., Zhang, L., Ng, C. H., Ungvari, G. S., & Xiang, Y. T. (2020). Prevalence of Workplace Violence Against Health-Care Professionals in China: A Comprehensive Meta-Analysis of Observational Surveys. *Trauma, Violence & Abuse*, *21*(3), 498–509. doi:10.1177/1524838018774429 PMID:29806556

Matthiesen, S. B., & Einarsen, S. (2001). MMPI-2 configurations among victims of bullying at work. *European Journal of Work and Organizational Psychology*, *10*(4), 467–484. doi:10.1080/13594320143000753

Matthiesen, S. B., & Einarsen, S. (2004). Psychiatric distress and symptoms of PTSD among victims of bullying at work. *British Journal of Guidance & Counselling*, *32*(3), 335–356. doi:10.1080/03069880410001723558

Matthiesen, S. B., & Einarsen, S. (2010). Bullying in the workplace: Definition, prevalence, antecedents and consequences. *International Journal of Organization Theory and Behavior*, *13*(2), 202–248. doi:10.1108/IJOTB-13-02-2010-B004

McAvoy, B. R., & Murtagh, J. (2003). *Workplace bullying: The silent epidemic* (Vol. 326). British Medical Journal Publishing Group.

McKenna, B. G., Smith, N. A., Poole, S. J., & Coverdale, J. H. (2003). Horizontal violence: Experiences of Registered Nurses in their first year of practice. *Journal of Advanced Nursing*, *42*(1), 90–96. doi:10.1046/j.1365-2648.2003.02583.x PMID:12641816

Michelson, G. (2001). Whether victor or vanquished, we all lose to the office bully. *Sydney Morning Herald*, p. 1.

Nabi, H., Harley, S., & Murphy, E. (2013). The perils and triumphs of night surgical residents across South Australia. *Journal of Surgical Education*, *70*(2), 265–272. doi:10.1016/j.jsurg.2012.09.004 PMID:23427975

Najafi, F., Fallahi-Khoshknab, M., Dalvandi, A., Ahmadi, F., & Rahgozar, M. (2014). *Workplace violence against Iranian nurses: A systematic review* [خشونت محل کار علیه پرستاران در ایران: مرور نظام مند]. Retrieved from http://jhpm.ir/article-1-243-en.html

Nesbitt, W. (2012). *Workplace bullying in the healthcare setting. SMSI Online Newsletter: The Hospital Reporter*. Security Management Services International and The Hospital Reporter.

Norton, P., Costa, V., Teixeira, J., Azevedo, A., Roma-Torres, A., Amaro, J., & Cunha, L. (2017). Prevalence and Determinants of Bullying Among Health Care Workers in Portugal. *Workplace Health & Safety*, *65*(5), 188–196. doi:10.1177/2165079916666545 PMID:28061740

O'Brien-Pallas, L., Duffield, C., & Hayes, L. (2006). Do we really understand how to retain nurses? *Journal of Nursing Management*, *14*(4), 262–270. doi:10.1111/j.1365-2934.2006.00611.x PMID:16629840

Ozen Col, S. (2008). Isyerinde psikolojik siddet: hastane calisanlari uzerine bir arastirma [Psychological violence at work: a study on hospital workers]. *Calisma ve Toplum Dergisi*, *4*(19), 107–134.

Paksoy, N. (2007). Isyerinde Psikolojik Taciz-Yildirma (Mobbing) [Psychological Harassment-Intimidation (Mobbing) at Work]. Isletme Yuksek Lisans Projesi, Sosyal Bilimler Enstitusu, Kahramanmaras Sutcu Imam Universitesi.

Pappa, S., Ntella, V., Giannakas, T., Giannakoulis, V. G., Papoutsi, E., & Katsaounou, P. (2020). Prevalence of depression, anxiety, and insomnia among healthcare workers during the COVID-19 pandemic: A systematic review and meta-analysis. *Brain, Behavior, and Immunity*, *88*, 901–907. doi:10.1016/j.bbi.2020.05.026 PMID:32437915

Parzefall, M.-R., & Salin, D. M. (2010). Perceptions of and reactions to workplace bullying: A social exchange perspective. *Human Relations*, *63*(6), 761–780. doi:10.1177/0018726709345043

Pei, K. Y., Hafler, J., Alseidi, A., Slade, M. D., Klingensmith, M., & Cochran, A. (2020). National Assessment of Workplace Bullying Among Academic Surgeons in the US. *JAMA Surgery*, *155*(6), 524–526. doi:10.1001/jamasurg.2020.0263 PMID:32236505

Pinar, T., Acikel, C., Pinar, G., Karabulut, E., Saygun, M., Bariskin, E., & Cengiz, M. (2017). Workplace Violence in the Health Sector in Turkey: A National Study. *Journal of Interpersonal Violence*, *32*(15), 2345–2365. doi:10.1177/0886260515591976 PMID:26124224

Quine, L. (2002). Workplace bullying in junior doctors: Questionnaire survey. *BMJ (Clinical Research Ed.)*, *324*(7342), 878–879. doi:10.1136/bmj.324.7342.878 PMID:11950736

Rayner, C., & Hoel, H. (1997). A Summary Review of Literature Relating to Workplace Bullying. *Journal of Community & Applied Social Psychology*, *7*(3), 181–191. doi:10.1002/(SICI)1099-1298(199706)7:3<181::AID-CASP416>3.0.CO;2-Y

Rigby, K. (2002). *New perspectives on bullying*. Jessica Kingsley Publishers.

Rowe, M. M., & Sherlock, H. (2005). Stress and verbal abuse in nursing: Do burned out nurses eat their young? *Journal of Nursing Management*, *13*(3), 242–248. doi:10.1111/j.1365-2834.2004.00533.x PMID:15819837

Rowell, P. A. (2005). Being a "target" at work: Or William Tell and how the apple felt. JONA. *The Journal of Nursing Administration, 35*(9), 377–379. doi:10.1097/00005110-200509000-00002 PMID:16200000

Royal College of Nursing (Great Britain). (2000). *Bullying and harassment at work: a good practice guide for RCN negotiators and health care managers*. Royal College of Nursing.

Sa, L., & Fleming, M. (2008). Bullying, burnout, and mental health amongst Portuguese nurses. *Issues in Mental Health Nursing, 29*(4), 411–426. doi:10.1080/01612840801904480 PMID:18382918

Saleh, L., Niroumand, S., Dehghani, Z., Afshari Saleh, T., Mousavi, S. M., & Zakeri, H. (2020). Relationship between workplace violence and work stress in the emergency department. *Journal of Injury & Violence Research, 12*(2), 183–190. doi:10.5249/jivr.vol12i2.1526 PMID:32653889

Salin, D. (2003). Ways of Explaining Workplace Bullying: A Review of Enabling, Motivating and Precipitating Structures and Processes in the Work Environment. *Human Relations, 56*(10), 1213–1232. doi:10.1177/00187267035610003

Salin, D. (2005). Workplace bullying among business professionals: Prevalence, gender differences and the role of organizational politics. *Perspectives interdisciplinaires sur le travail et la santé*.

Samnani, A.-K., & Singh, P. (2014). Performance-enhancing compensation practices and employee productivity: The role of workplace bullying. *Human Resource Management Review, 24*(1), 5–16. doi:10.1016/j.hrmr.2013.08.013

Shigemura, J., Ursano, R. J., Morganstein, J. C., Kurosawa, M., & Benedek, D. M. (2020). Public responses to the novel 2019 coronavirus (2019-nCoV) in Japan: Mental health consequences and target populations. *Psychiatry and Clinical Neurosciences, 74*(4), 281–282. doi:10.1111/pcn.12988 PMID:32034840

Simons, S. (2008). Workplace bullying experienced by Massachusetts registered nurses and the relationship to intention to leave the organization. *Advances in Nursing Science, 31*(2), E48–E59. doi:10.1097/01.ANS.0000319571.37373.d7 PMID:18497581

Spector, P. E., Zhou, Z. E., & Che, X. X. (2014). Nurse exposure to physical and nonphysical violence, bullying, and sexual harassment: A quantitative review. *International Journal of Nursing Studies, 51*(1), 72–84. doi:10.1016/j.ijnurstu.2013.01.010 PMID:23433725

Srabstein, J. C., & Leventhal, B. L. (2010). Prevention of bullying-related morbidity and mortality: A call for public health policies. *Bulletin of the World Health Organization, 88*(6), 403–403. doi:10.2471/BLT.10.077123 PMID:20539848

Szutenbach, M. P. (2013). Bullying in nursing: Roots, rationales, and remedies. *Journal of Christian Nursing, 30*(1), 16–23. doi:10.1097/CNJ.0b013e318276be28 PMID:23495431

Tai, S.-Y., Lin, P.-C., Chen, Y.-M., Hung, H.-C., Pan, C.-H., Pan, S.-M., & Wu, M.-T. (2014). Effects of Marital Status and Shift Work on Family Function among Registered Nurses. *Industrial Health, 52*(4), 296–303. Advance online publication. doi:10.2486/indhealth.2014-0009 PMID:24909112

Talas, M. S., Kocaoz, S., & Akguc, S. (2011). A survey of violence against staff working in the emergency department in ankara, Turkey. *Asian Nursing Research, 5*(4), 197–203. doi:10.1016/j.anr.2011.11.001 PMID:25030520

Tian, J. (2008). *A correlational study among workplace bullying and job vigor of cabin crew by using social support as moderating variable* [Unpublished master's thesis]. University of Technology Institute of Technical and Vocational Education and Human Resource Development.

Torshizi, L., & Ahmadi, F. (2011). Job stressors from clinical nurses 'perspective. *Iran Journal of Nursing*, *24*(70), 49–60.

Trépanier, S.-G., Fernet, C., & Austin, S. (2013). Workplace bullying and psychological health at work: The mediating role of satisfaction of needs for autonomy, competence and relatedness. *Work and Stress*, *27*(2), 123–140. doi:10.1080/02678373.2013.782158

Tutar, H. (2004). Is yerinde psikolojik siddet sarmali: Nedenleri ve sonuclari [The spiral of psychological violence at work: Causes and consequences]. *Yönetim Bilimleri Dergisi*, *2*(2), 85–108.

Ucak, A. (2009). *Saglik personelinin maruz kaldigi is kazalari ve geri bildirimlerinin değerlendirilmesi [Evaluation of occupational accidents and feedbacks of healthcare personnel] [Master]*. Afyon Kocatepe University, Institute of Health Sciences.

Uysal, H. T. (2016). Calisanlarin liderlik algisi ve ters mobbing egilimi: Isgoren odakli liderligin etkisi [Employees' perception of leadership and reverse mobbing tendency: The effect of employee-oriented leadership]. *Journal of International Social Research*, *9*(47), 933–943. doi:10.17719/jisr.2016.1441

Wang, C. L., Huang, C. Y., Lu, K. Y., & Ho, M. Y. (2007). A study of the social support and job stress among nursing staff. *VGH Nursing*, *24*(1), 59–68.

WBI. (2015). *Mental health harm from workplace bullying*. Retrieved from https://www.workplacebullying.org/individuals/impact/mental-health-harm/

WHO. (2006). The world health report: 2006: working together for health. World Health Organization.

WHO. (2017). *Violence and injury prevention - violence against health workers*. Retrieved from https://www.who.int/violence_injury_prevention/violence/workplace/en/

WHO. (2020). *Mental health and psychosocial considerations during the COVID-19 outbreak*. Retrieved from Geneva: https://apps.who.int/iris/handle/10665/331490

Xing, K., Jiao, M., Ma, H., Qiao, H., Hao, Y., Li, Y., & Wu, Q. (2015). Physical Violence against General Practitioners and Nurses in Chinese Township Hospitals: A Cross-Sectional Survey. *PLoS One*, *10*(11), e0142954. doi:10.1371/journal.pone.0142954 PMID:26571388

Yildirim, D. (2009). Bullying among nurses and its effects. *International Nursing Review*, *56*(4), 504–511. doi:10.1111/j.1466-7657.2009.00745.x PMID:19930081

Yildiz, S., & Yildiz, S. E. (2009). Bullying ve depresyon arasindaki iliski: Kars ilindeki saglik calisanlarinda bir arastirma [The relationship between bullying and depression: A study among healthcare workers in Kars province]. *Istanbul Ticaret Universitesi Sosyal Bilimler Dergisi*, *8*, 133–150.

Yilmaz, E. (2013). *Mobbing davranisi ve Bandirma Ili kamu hastaneleri calisanlarina yonelik bir arastirma [A research on mobbing behavior and public hospital employees in Bandirma] [Master]*. Okan University Institute of Health Sciences.

Zapf, D. (1999). Organisational, work group related and personal causes of mobbing/bullying at work. *International Journal of Manpower, 20*(1/2), 70–85. doi:10.1108/01437729910268669

Zapf, D., Escartin, J., Einarsen, S., Hoel, H., & Vartia, M. (2011). Empirical findings on prevalence and risk groups of bullying in the workplace. In S. Einarsen, D. Hoel, D. Zapf, & C. Cooper (Eds.), *Bullying and Harassment in the Workplace* (pp. 75–106). Taylor and Francis.

ADDITIONAL READING

Saleh, L. A., Niroumand, S., Dehghani, Z., Saleh, T. A., Mousavi, S. M., & Zakeri, H. (2020). Relationship between workplace violence and work stress in the emergency department. *Journal of Injury & Violence Research, 12*(2), 183. PMID:32653889

Warshawski, S., Amit Aharon, A., & Itzhaki, M. (2021). It takes two to tango: public attitudes toward prevention of workplace violence against health care staff: a mixed-methods study. *Journal of Interpersonal Violence, 36*(15-16), NP8724–NP8746. doi:10.1177/0886260519846865 PMID:31046535

KEY TERMS AND DEFINITIONS

Bullying: It is a form of aggressive behavior in which the stronger intentionally and repetitively causes physical harm or emotional distress to the victim.

COVID-19: The novel coronavirus disease (COVID-19) is a contagious respiratory disease caused by the SARS-CoV-2 virus, which emerged in late 2019 and affects different people in different ways (from mild symptoms such as sore throat, cough to severe illness and death).

Health Personnel: All personnel with or without vocational training working in the provision of health services within health institutions or as individual practitioners.

Healthcare Sector: The economic sector concerned with the provision, distribution and consumption of goods and services to meet the health needs of individuals and communities. The healthcare sector encompasses a wide variety of industries, with activities ranging from research to manufacturing to the management of institutions.

Occupational Stress: Negative physical, mental, and emotional reactions caused by the pressure and demands of the employer or customers, or by other factors such as the physical infrastructure of the workplace, psychological factors such as violence in the workplace.

Turkey: Turkey, officially known as the Republic of Turkey, is a transcontinental country in Southeast Europe and Southwest Asia, bordering the Black Sea. The capital city is Ankara.

Workplace Violence: Any physical or psychological threat, action or event carried out in the workplace with the aim of harming another individual in the working environment.

Chapter 15
Bullying and Public Health Approach

Seçil Özkan
Gazi University School of Medicine, Turkey

ABSTRACT

Bullying, which is an important public health problem, is a complex problem that affects children and adults of all ages. It is both humane and inexpensive to identify risk groups that may be victims and perpetrators of bullying and to develop intervention programs to reduce risks. Primordial and primary protection in view of public health is the most important form of prevention; policies and programs aimed at provision of multifaceted community education, development, and improvement should be implemented in order to reduce or even prevent bullying in society.

INTRODUCTION

The World Health Organization has defined health as "not only the absence of illness and disability, but also a state of complete well-being physically, spiritually and socially". The disease is a "state created by structural and functional and abnormal changes in tissues and cells" (WHO, 2020). But the disease is not just a biological process. It is also a social and cultural phenomenon. A condition that is considered a disease in one society may not be considered a disease in another society. The reason as to why Hippocrates is considered the founder of scientific medicine is that he did not attribute the causes of disease to supernatural forces. Accordingly, diseases are either a violation of the balance between blood, yellow bile, black bile and phlegm within the body or external factors. The causes of the disease can be briefly listed as follows (McWhinney, 1987):

1. Individual reasons
    a. Disorders of genes, hormones and metabolism, etc.
2. Environmental reasons
    a. Physical causes: heat, cold, rays, traumas
    b. Chemical causes: poisons, carcinogens, etc.

DOI: 10.4018/978-1-6684-5426-8.ch015

   c. Deficiencies of essential substances: vitamins, essential amino acids, minerals
   d. Biological factors: microorganisms, parasites, fungi
3. Psychological reasons
4. Social, cultural and economic reasons

Psychological, social and cultural reasons greatly affect the formation of health problems. Bullying, which affects the health of individuals in society, is caused by social, cultural and moral structure of society. For this reason, bullying and prevention strategies and intervention measures have been examined in this section with a public health perspective.

DETERMINANTS OF HEALTH

There are four different and overlapping perspectives in regards to determinants of health from a Public Health Perspective (Wilkinson & Marmot, 2003);

1. Biomedical Perspective: Microorganisms and genetic factors are at the heart of diseases. Currently, this perspective continues to dominate the field with the development of molecular genetics as a science.
2. Lifestyle Perspective: Obesity, sedentary lifestyle, alcohol and cigarette addiction being important determinants especially for chronic diseases had resulted in development of lifestyle perspective.
3. Broad Socio-Economic Perspective: In view of poor countries being more susceptible to diseases, the existence of a broad socio-economic perspective can be argued. The research efforts that became the agenda with the economic crisis have also revealed this perspective.
4. Community Health Perspective: Health policies and practices constitute the main roof in the community health perspective, which is integrated with the health promotion model.

This model was updated in 2021 by adding omni-directional arrows to the four determinant layers in Figure 1a. The importance of these vertical connections in academic and practical fields has become more relevant today. Along with the importance of developing policies aimed at lifestyle and individual behavior alteration strategies, multisectoral structural interventions have become more urgent than ever.

BULLYING AND PREVENTION STRATEGIES

Bullying, which has been described in various forms by many researchers over time, is an original and complex form of interpersonal aggression and is recognized as a serious public health problem affecting children and adolescents all over the world. In order for a behavior to be considered bullying, it has been reported that the behavior has to be done repeatedly with the intention of hurting or offending and there has to be an imbalance between the powers of the parties (Aleem, 2016). Researchers have expressed the definition of bullying by combining the common points of different definitions as: a) Bullying is in a sub-group of violent behaviors; b) A variety of actions such as physical, emotional and/or socially negative behaviors are performed repeatedly within a time frame, causing the victim harm; c) Is performed intentionally; d) Generally not prompted by the victim; e) Although a single victim is

Figure 1. The Main Determinants of Health (Dahlgren & Whitehead, 1991)

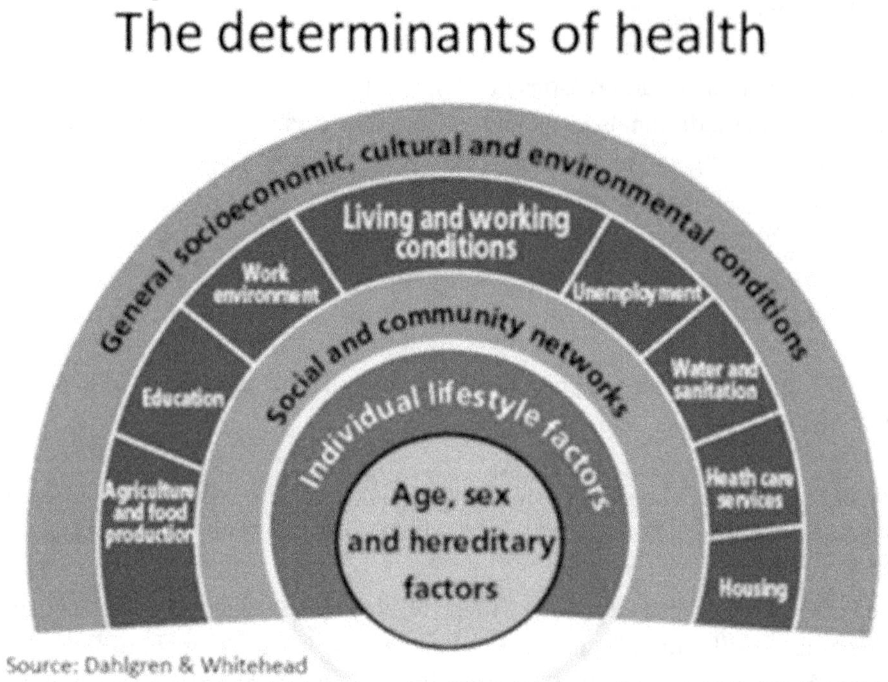

Figure 2. The Main Determinants of Health (Dahlgren & Whitehead, 2021)

expressed, the bullying may be initiated by a singular person or a group and may cause harm to one or more than one people (Carrera et al., 2011).

UNESCO's 2011 Global Education Digest report on the Prevalence of Bullying informs that 20% of students in the world were bullied. There are many types of bullying such as emotional, physical and social. Direct and indirect behaviors of bullying comprise hitting, kicking, threatening, name-calling, spreading gossip and exclusion from the group. Bullying behaviors serve different functions and manifest themselves in different relationship patterns. Bullying is not just about the relationship between the bully and the victim. It is a group phenomenon that occurs in a social environment that stimulates, facilitates or suppresses bullying (Olweus, 1993b; S. Swearer & Hymel, 2015). Theory of ecological systems claims that the human development occurs through the mutual interaction that takes place between individuals and many systems such as house, school, neighborhood, culture and society in which they live (Bronfenbrenner, 1979). Within the view of which, it is possible to say that bullying is not a result of the individual characteristics of the bully and the victim, but a result of the interaction of environmental variables such as families, friends, neighbors, teachers, media, technology. In other words, bullying is an interaction that takes place in a socio-ecological environment between the victim and the bully. This interaction is a dynamic process determined by the personality characteristics of the victim and the bully, the peculiarity of the interactions of this duo, the presence of friends, teachers, the school environment and social norms (Aleem, 2016). We can sort these variables as follows:

1. The influence of individual characteristics (S. Swearer & Hymel, 2015)
2. The influence of friends (Bacchini et al., 2009; Barboza et al., 2009; Bauman & Del Rio, 2006; S. Swearer & Hymel, 2015; Thornberg et al., 2013).
3. The impact of school/environment
4. The impact of social environment (Barboza et al., 2009; S. M. Swearer et al., 2014)

Exposure to bullying has been associated with psychological pressure, psychosomatic diseases, physical disorders, depression that can lead to suicide, deterioration in social adaptation, social isolation and substance use, which can also be effective in adulthood. Bullying affects the academic achievement, positive social skills and psychological well-being of both victims and bullies (Arnarsson & Bjarnason, 2018) .Therefore, the traumatic effect of bullying during school years can continue throughout life and negatively affect public health. For this reason, bullying in the school environment is a public health problem that should be considered in great detail (Craig et al., 2007).

- Children who bully others are more likely to become addicted to alcohol and drugs in adolescence and adulthood, exhibit violent/quarrelsome/aggressive behavior, and drop out of school (Hurley, 2019).
- Children who are subjected to bullying (victims) experience mental, psychological and academic problems. Typically, these problems are low academic achievement, chronic depression, self-esteem, loss of self-harm a tendency to suicidal thoughts, suicide plans and suicide attempts, Post-Traumatic Stress Disorder, general poor health, substance abuse, mental health disorders and lifelong difficulties with interpersonal relationships (Gini & Pozzoli, 2009; Hurley, 2019; Lereya et al., 2015; Nansel et al., 2004; Ttofi & Farrington, 2011).

- Similarly, children (observers) who witness bullying become afraid of the power of bullies and avoid intervening due to the fear of becoming victims. These children may experience an increase in mental health problems, including depression and anxiety.

With the increasing awareness of the effects of bullying on the society as a whole, it is understood how important it is to prevent bullying. In this context, the number of studies related to bullying prevention programs has increased significantly. All over the world, the interest and need for bullying prevention programs are increasing every day. In many meta-analysis studies, it is emphasized that bullying can be reduced with preventive programs (Evans et al., 2014; S. Lee et al., 2015; Salmivalli et al., 2013). Quite a few experimental studies have been conducted that measure the effectiveness of programs designed to prevent the onset of peer bullying or reduce bullying (Bradshaw, 2015). In meta-analyses conducted on bullying prevention programs, it was concluded that the common features of the most effective bullying prevention programs are (a) those that target different environments, (b) multi-faceted and (c) school-wide bullying and aggression reduction programs (Farrington & Ttofi, 2009) (1) KiVa and (2) Olweus Peer Bullying Prevention Program stand out as the two most successful programs in the literature (Ttofi & Farrington, 2011).

DEVELOPING PUBLIC HEALTH INTERVENTION PROGRAMS TO COMBAT BULLYING

Public health interventions have to be based on community. Community-based practice is a professional activity that covers community health assessment, policy planning and development (Stanhope & Lancaster, 2019). There are five basic criteria for community-based intervention (Schoon et al., 2018):

1. The intervention has to focus on all populations with similar health problems or characteristics,
2. It has to evaluate and analyze the health status of the entire population, identify priorities and plan programs and strategies based on the state of the population
3. It has to consider the factors that establish, support and improve health (income, social status, housing, nutrition, education, ethnicity, etc.)
4. It has to consider all levels of prevention, mainly the primary level of prevention
5. It has to consider all levels of application (individual/family, community and system)

If an intervention considers all of these steps, it can be regarded as community based. These considerations are reflected on intervention wheel in three different sections from the center out; individual/family, society, and system (Figure 2). The intervention wheel bases its operations at these three levels (Keller, Strohschein, Lia-Hoagberg, et al., 2004; Keller, Strohschein, Schaffer, et al., 2004)

- Individual/family focus: An individual-oriented application based on society changes the information, attitudes, beliefs, skills, practices and behaviors of the individual or family. This level of application is intended for individuals or family members alone. The practice with individuals and families is community-based only in cases where an identified public health problem is addressed and contributes directly to the improvement of the general health status of the community.

Figure 3. Public Health Intervention Wheel (Keller, Strohschein, Schaffer, et al., 2004)

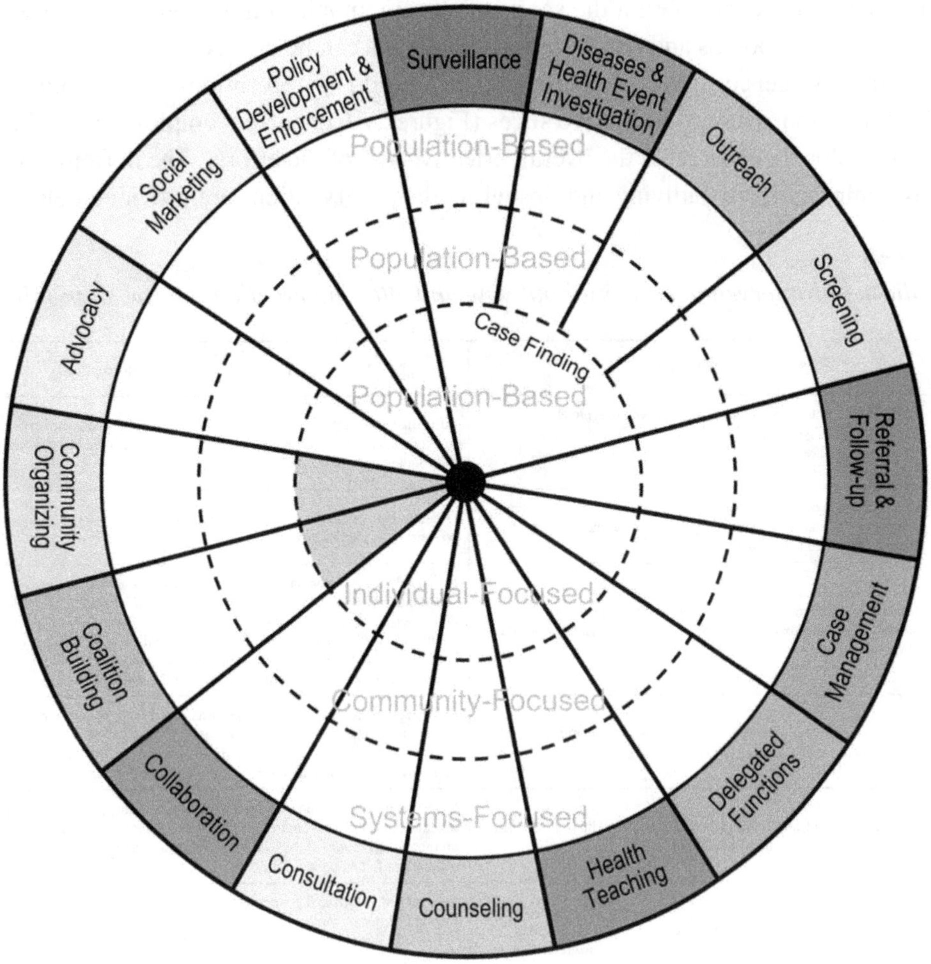

- Community focus: Community-based practice alters community health by changing community norms, attitudes, awareness, practices, and behaviors. This level of application is aimed at the entire population within a particular community or specific groups within that population. Community-oriented practice is measured by how much the population under consideration has changed.
- System focus: A community-based system-oriented application changes organizations, organizations, policies, laws, and power structures. The focus is not on individuals and communities directly, but on systems that affect health. Changing systems involves everyone, without requiring a change in community norms or each individual in a community, in influencing public health; it is more long-lasting and effective.

For the case of bullying, through individual focus, those who might bully or be subjected to bulling may be taken into training programs based on bullying and its effects on health which aim at changing their attitudes towards bullying, improve their blocking skills and managing stress. Within the scope of society, norms on prevention of bullying and social campaigns can be established. Education on such matters can be incorporated into schools and students' attitudes towards bullying can be changed by increasing their knowledge. Within the scope of system, monitoring systems can be established by cooperating with school boards and anti-bullying campaigns can be carried out.

The intervention wheel consists of a colored outer ring and 17 interventions. Similar interventions are combined by color groups, constituting five slices (Figure 2). Concurrent employment of interventions within the same color slice increases the overall effectiveness of the efforts. The definitions of these 17 interventions, their relation to bullying and ties with other interventions are provided below.

Table 1. Public health intervention areas for bullying and inter-intervention relationships (Health, 2019)

Areas of intervention	Definition	Connection with other interventions
Surveillance	Systemic and continuous collection, analysis and interpretation of health data on bullying and areas related to bullying with the aim of planning public health interventions; explaining/monitoring health issues/situations.	Surveillance and interventions for the study of diseases and health events are considered together. Surveillance by public health professionals is used to assess the health status of the community.
Investigation of bullying incidents	It systematically collects, analyzes, determines the source of the threat, identifies cases and other issues that pose a risk, defines the control measures that need to be taken.	Often applied together with surveillance intervention; these two interventions are usually considered as a single process.
Social help	It determines the general condition of the relevant society or individuals at risk; provides information about what can be done and how to obtain services.	Social help intervention on community level follows almost the same principles with social marketing. Effective implementation of social marketing principles creates an effective social help intervention. This intervention is combined with efforts in informing people or societies on existing threats and aiding them with initiatives under health education intervention, aiming to enhance their health. Social help is often used as a precursor to other interventions in red slice of the wheel.
Screening (identification of risk groups)	It identifies individuals with unrecognized/unknown/unnoticed health risk factors in society, or those who have been bullied.	Screening intervention is usually used after social help and social marketing interventions; together with health education and consultation interventions; before the referral and follow-up interventions, in which those who might be subjected to bullying in places such as school and work are referred to related authorities.
Finding a Case of Bullying	It identifies individuals/families with risk factors and makes establishes connections to the relevant resources.	Case-finding intervention is connected with surveillance, examination of disease and other health phenomena, outreach and screening interventions and occurs as a result of all these interventions at the individual level and usually requires the implementation of referral and follow-up interventions.
Referral and Follow-up	It helps individuals, families, groups, institutions and/or communities identify and access the necessary resources to prevent and/or solve problems or alarming situations with referral. The results related to the use of the resources determined by the monitoring are evaluated.	Referral and follow-up intervention is most often involved before or after the implementation of another intervention, such as health education, counseling, transfer of powers, consultation, screening, case finding. They are also an important component of case management intervention and are mostly implemented together as the attempts made for the case and the subsequent referral also require follow-up.
Case management	This refers to the coordination and provision of services and includes research, planning, care evaluation and advocacy processes based on collaborative work for the services needed to meet the needs of individuals/families. It optimizes the capacities of systems and communities to improve safety, quality of care and cost-effective outcomes.	When the services needed in the community are not available during the case management intervention, it often becomes necessary to implement advocacy and collaboration interventions at the community and system level.
Health Teaching and Counseling	This refers to sharing of information and experiences on bullying and its health effects through educational activities designed to develop relevant knowledge, attitudes, behaviors and skills. Counseling involves building an interpersonal relationship on an emotional level.	Health teaching is used together or in turn with counselling services for bullies and/ or to create alternative solutions to the problems. Health teaching and social marketing interventions similarly focus on altering a behavior; however, health teaching does not involve commercial marketing principles. Besides, while planning health teaching interventions, it is possible to cooperate with persons and establishments in view of collaboration intervention.
Consultation	Interactively searches for information and creates ideal solutions for problems or issues that are perceived through problem solving. It determines and acts on the best option appropriate for the issue.	Consultation intervention can also be applied in combination with health teaching and/or counseling intervention, or all of them in turn.
Collaboration	It is a coming together of two or more people/institutions with one or more members for the development/protection of health with a common benefit and purpose. Its effectiveness includes sharing information, resources, in a harmonious way.	Coalition-building and collaboration interventions, which are in the same slice as cooperation interventions, require joint work. Many initiatives, especially at the community level, are related to all three interventions and share the practices made. The difference of the collaboration intervention from the other two interventions is that in order to achieve common goals, one or more members require working above their own capacity. If it is desired to change how the way people or systems in a community work, norms, attitudes, beliefs; policy development and enforcement can be applied together with cooperation intervention. Cooperation is also a common intervention that is preferred in conjunction with authorized functions and requires the use of advocacy. At the individual/family level, it is usually used in conjunction with health teaching, counseling, consultation and case management interventions.

continues on following page

Table 1. Continued

Areas of intervention	Definition	Connection with other interventions
Coalition building	It supports and develops cooperation between institutions or associations for a common purpose; establishes connections, solves problems and/or develops local leadership to deal with health problems.	Coalition-building interventions, similarly with community organization and cooperation interventions, also require finding partners and working together. All practices, especially at the community level, cover all three interventions. In order to change how systems or people work in a society, their norms, attitudes and beliefs, coalition building intervention can be jointly used with policy development and enforcement intervention. Coalition building require the implementation of advocacy intervention, which is necessary for any issue on community or system level. Coalition building intervention can also be used jointly with social help intervention on system level and social marketing intervention on community level to ensure reach or establishing connection with the target audience.
Community organizing	It refers to the process in which people come together and determine common issues or goals, mobilize resources, develop and implement strategies in order to solve said issues.	Community organizing, coalition building and collaboration interventions all involve partnering and working together. For this reason, they are involved together in many initiatives, especially in community-level applications. Community organizing intervention takes place with the successful implementation of outreach intervention at the system and community levels. Advocacy and social marketing are often used as auxiliary interventions in community organizing intervention to raise awareness in a community or change health behavior. Community organizing is applied together with policy development and enforcement intervention, especially when a system-level policy is wanted to be changed.
Advocacy	It is the action to improve and protect the health of individuals/ communities by cooperating with relevant third parties to support/ legislate policies to improve social health outcomes, facilitating access to health and social services, and actively implementing solution decisions.	Counseling and health education at the system and community level are used to raise public awareness before implementing an advocacy intervention. In addition, public health nurses can collaborate and use advocacy intervention in initiatives such as evaluating an individual's needs, promoting and protecting health during a case management intervention.
Social marketing	A process that uses marketing principles and techniques to change the behavior of the target audience in a manner that benefits both society and the individual.	In a similar manner with health education intervention, social marketing intervention aims to change attitudes and behavior. That is why it is often seen as an application of health education. Social marketing intervention employed at the social level usually employs advocacy implementation as well.
Policy development and enforcement	It communicates health problems to decision-makers, creates a solution plan, determines the necessary resources and concludes with laws, rules, regulations, decrees and policies. Laws, rules, regulations, legislation established by policy development oblige people to comply with decrees and policies.	Policy development and enforcement intervention mostly requires cooperation in society and system application levels, coalition building and community organizing as health issues are brought to the attention of the decision makers and that it provides technical assistance aiding the change of laws, rules, legislations and policies. Advocacy intervention is generally used at the system level. Depending on the protocol between Ministry of National Education and Ministry of Health, bullying can be fought against in schools throughout the country.

Bullying prevention programs can be examined as general prevention programs and target group-specific prevention programs;

1. **General precautionary programs:** The most frequently studied and used approaches to bullying prevention are aimed at developing positive behavior and teaching social emotional skills throughout the school and at the classroom level. There are also intervention approaches that focus specifically on bullying behavior (Nickerson, 2019). In the USA and most of the European and Scandinavian countries, free support lines also provide services for peer bullying (Erk, 2019). All school programs are usually complex, consist of several components aimed at different levels of influence (students, parents, classes, schools) and include a variety of methods. The different components are typically evaluated in combination rather than separately. As a result, the contribution of each component to the overall effects of a particular program is unknown, but they have a combined greater effect (Menesini & Salmivalli, 2017).
    a. Positive Behavioral Intervention and Support Programs: Positive behavioral intervention and support programs developed to prevent peer bullying cover both staff and students and are applied school-wide. They focus on improving the quality of life through strategies that help develop appropriate social behavior and cover all the students in the school. Small group activities are held especially for disadvantaged people about how they should behave. The aim

of these applications is to support, correct and assist students in the elimination of behavioral problems rather than the application of punitive methods (Caldarella et al., 2011)

b. Social-Emotional Support Programs: The social-emotional support programs developed to prevent peer bullying are based on the fact that teaching and learning have strong social, emotional and academic components. Students usually learn alongside their peers with the help of their teachers and the support of their families. Emotions can facilitate or hinder children's academic participation, work ethic, commitment, and school success. Unfortunately, many students lack social and emotional competencies and become less connected to school as they progress from primary to secondary education, and this lack of connection negatively affects the academic performance, behavior and health of children (Nickerson, 2019). These programs promote students the social-emotional developments of students by creating a safe, caring environment that encapsulates peer and family initiatives, improved classroom management and teaching practices, school community building activities. In turn, students feel more valuable and are subjected to greater intrinsic motivation experiences; achieving better academical performances and exhibiting a broadly-applicable social-emotional competence that mediates improved health behaviors and being an exemplary citizen (Durlak et al., 2011; Nickerson, 2019)

c. Olweus Bullying Prevention Program: The most well-known is the Olweus Bullying Prevention Program. It is the most comprehensive and systematically evaluated bullying prevention program implemented on a large scale in Norway, following several bullying-related suicides (Erk, 2019; Nickerson, 2019) The program aims to reduce existing bullying, prevent the development of new bullying problems, and improve peer relationships in schools (Wójcik & Hełka, 2018). The program, designed by Dan Olweus for use at all grade levels, consists of four components. School-level components focus on the introduction of school rules against bullying, as well as creating committee meetings, staff training and discussion groups. At the classroom level, the components focus on the implementation of school rules against bullying and regular classroom meetings to discuss in-group relationships. The individual level components are aimed at supervising students who participate in on-site bullying and staff interventions when bullying occurs. Community-level components include community engagement and partnership to support the school program (Olweus, 1993a; Wójcik & Hełka, 2018).

KiVa: It is an effective intervention program in reducing the victimization of peer bullying in students throughout grades 1-9 (Garandeau et al., 2014; Haataja et al., 2014; Williford et al., 2012).

2. **Special Prevention Programs for the Target Group:** These programs are structured within specific goals for groups involved in the bullying cycle. It has been stated that the parents, school employees and medical personnel attending to the bullying child exhibit a negative attitude, do not approach them empathetically and criticize them. The mental health needs and frailties of these children should not be ignored. In order to establish healthy relationships in the future, it is important for bullied children to establish positive friendship relationships in school life (Cowie & Colliety, 2016). Prevention Program for Perpetrators *and* Prevention Programs for Victims should be planned.

All of these programs require multi-sectoral work together with basic, primary, secondary and tertiary protection strategies (Table 2). Basic protection of the public is a multi-sectoral endeavor which aims to prevent the emergence of social, economic and cultural life patterns that are known to have a role in the formation of health problems. It is not included in the table below.

Table 2. Recommendations for an approach to primary, secondary and tertiary protection in bullying prevention programs (Cooper et al., 2012; Lee, 2018; Pigozi & Jones Bartoli, 2016; Raskauskas & Stoltz, 2004; S, 2011; Wolke & Lereya, 2015)

Level	Primary protection Preventing the emergence of bullying behavior	Secondary protection Reducing the discomfort or long-term effects of bullying, Intervening early, Stopping bullying	Tertiary protection Improve and provide rehabilitation for people who are bullied and victimized
Individual	It aims to prevent bullying generally by organizing educational programs for individuals, parents (and other related persons) and risk groups who may be victims or perpetrators of bullying; By organizing different events such as literature, drama, discussions and educational audiovisual materials And by encouraging individuals to take responsibility and make efforts to not exhibit bullying behavior	Conducting observations and screenings to catch bullying victims and perpetrators early Collecting the necessary information about the incident (what happened, where, why and how it happened, who was involved, how it was reacted, etc.), and record keeping If there is an injury, providing care	Providing long-term monitoring, psychosocial support, etc. to victims and perpetrators of bullying Providing consultancy
Relationships	Encouraging positive peer relationships by providing education to school children Providing health education to support individuals to improve their social skills, problem solving and coping skills, learn conflict resolution techniques, develop positive self-perception (revealing the feeling that they are valuable as a person, that they are important)	Efforts to identify and correct relationships that may cause bullying	Strengthening relationships through family, school therapies, group therapies Supporting perpetrators and victims to share their feelings with their families and express their problems
Community	Protective environmental planning that include adequate lightning and security cameras in places where there may be bullying incidences such as schools and workplaces. Providing people with a safe and comfortable environment where they can talk about bullying and keeping records	Making arrangements to ensure that the perpetrators and victims do not experience the bullying incident again and to ensure their safety	Conducting programs that will ensure the perception of stress-related conditions so that the victims and the perpetrators of bullying can express their requests for treatment
Society	Disciplinary and criminal sanctions Ensuring the formation of an understanding that does not tolerate bullying	Providing early diagnosis and treatment services to perpetrators and victims	Developing public health interventions and policies

FUTURE RESEARCH DIRECTIONS

Research supports implementing effective anti-bullying programs as essential public health and crime prevention strategies. Most anti-bullying programs are located in schools and use ecological approaches that address both individual and environmental dimensions of bullying, including individual traits, family experiences, parental involvement, school climate, and community characteristics.

Public health departments have expertise and the ability to make a difference in preventing bullying because of their knowledge working with a broad range of people, including different state and local agencies, community groups, and families and youth themselves. As a field, public health deals with complex issues that require multipronged, sustained interventions/strategies and public health understands the need to adapt strategies over time. It also appreciates the need to select and implement evidence-informed/ promising practices and supports policy change that promotes a healthy and safe climate.

Public health programs can use the following five strategies to help prevent bullying:

- Assess relevant state law and policies related to bullying
- Develop, implement, and evaluate interventions
- Collect, analyze, and disseminate data
- Provide training and technical assistance to public health and other professionals
- Facilitate collaborations between relevant organizations and professionals

A public health approach includes a strong emphasis on larger social factors that might influence outcomes. Such macro-determinants have been little considered, although, recent work has shown the strong effect of economic inequality on both bullying and victimization. A public health approach should balance promotion and prevention. An emphasis on building skills to reduce and prevent bullying in those youth with identified individual and social risk profiles has been a staple of interventions in the Europe and the USA. However, programs to promote social–emotional development may be an important strategy as well. Finally, a successful public health approach requires coordination across abroad range of systems and sectors to create policy and program strategies to protect young people. A comprehensive and coordinated strategy informed by knowledge of bullying determinants is needed to engage multiple sectors.

CONCLUSION

Identifying and intervening with individuals involved in bullying is extremely important, so increasing screening and early identification by people who live and work with young people is a priority strategy. Prevention of bullying among young people working to reduce a four step model is guided by the public health. The first step of the model involves revealing the "who", "what", "when", "where" and "how" associated with bullying. Data on the magnitude, scope, characteristics and consequences of the problem at the local, state and national levels are systematically collected to show how often bullying behavior occurs, where it occurs most often, who are the victims and perpetrators, and its impact on victims, families and communities. It is important that public health problems are identified in a way that allows for consistent measurement, so that the change in the level of the problem identified in a community is more likely to be attributed to the underlying problem, and not to different definitions of the problem. Therefore, consistent with the first step of the public health model, this document provides a uniform description of bullying among young people. Therefore, assessment of bullying should be integrated into broader routine monitoring systems (e.g., surveillance of health or multiple types of youth violence) when possible. The identification of risk and protective factors is the second step in the public health model. With a better understanding of the factors that put young people at risk of bullying, we can begin to develop and test prevention strategies that try to change the relevant factors that increase a teenager's risk of experiencing bullying. In this third step of the public health model, programs and policies are implemented and decisively evaluated to determine what "works" to prevent bullying among young people. The last step of the public health model is to ensure the dissemination and adoption of anti-bullying programs.

REFERENCES

Aleem, S. (2016). Bullying behavior among school students: A review. *Indian Journal of Health & Wellbeing*, *7*(10).

Arnarsson, A., & Bjarnason, T. (2018). The Problem with Low-Prevalence of Bullying. *International Journal of Environmental Research and Public Health*, *15*(7), 1535. Advance online publication. doi:10.3390/ijerph15071535 PMID:30036943

Bacchini, D., Esposito, G., & Affuso, G. (2009). Social experience and school bullying. *Journal of Community & Applied Social Psychology*, *19*(1), 17–32. doi:10.1002/casp.975

Barboza, G. E., Schiamberg, L. B., Oehmke, J., Korzeniewski, S. J., Post, L. A., & Heraux, C. G. (2009). Individual characteristics and the multiple contexts of adolescent bullying: An ecological perspective. *Journal of Youth and Adolescence*, *38*(1), 101–121. doi:10.100710964-008-9271-1 PMID:19636795

Bauman, S., & Del Rio, A. (2006). Preservice teachers' responses to bullying scenarios: Comparing physical, verbal, and relational bullying. *Journal of Educational Psychology*, *98*(1), 219–231. doi:10.1037/0022-0663.98.1.219

Bradshaw, C. P. (2015). Translating research to practice in bullying prevention. *The American Psychologist*, *70*(4), 322–332. doi:10.1037/a0039114 PMID:25961313

Bronfenbrenner, U. (1979). Contexts of child rearing: Problems and prospects. *The American Psychologist*, *34*(10), 844–850. doi:10.1037/0003-066X.34.10.844

Caldarella, P., Shatzer, R. H., Gray, K. M., Young, K. R., & Young, E. L. (2011). The Effects of School-wide Positive Behavior Support on Middle School Climate and Student Outcomes. *RMLE Online: Research in Middle Level Education*, *35*(4), 1–14. doi:10.1080/19404476.2011.11462087

Carrera, M. V., DePalma, R., & Lameiras, M. (2011). Toward a more comprehensive understanding of bullying in school settings. *Educational Psychology Review*, *23*(4), 479–499. doi:10.100710648-011-9171-x

Cooper, G. D., Clements, P. T., & Holt, K. E. (2012). Examining childhood bullying and adolescent suicide: Implications for school nurses. *The Journal of School Nursing: the Official Publication of the National Association of School Nurses*, *28*(4), 275–283. doi:10.1177/1059840512438617 PMID:22333524

Cowie, H., & Colliety, P. (2016). Who cares about the bullies? *Pastoral Care in Education*, *34*(1), 24–33. doi:10.1080/02643944.2015.1119880

Craig, W., Pepler, D., & Blais, J. (2007). Responding to bullying: What works. *School Psychology International*, *28*(4), 465–477. doi:10.1177/0143034307084136

Dahlgren, G., & Whitehead, M. (1991). *Policies and strategies to promote social equity in health*. Institute for Futures Studies.

Dahlgren, G., & Whitehead, M. (2021). The Dahlgren-Whitehead model of health determinants: 30 years on and still chasing rainbows. *Public Health*, *199*, 20–24. doi:10.1016/j.puhe.2021.08.009 PMID:34534885

Durlak, J. A., Weissberg, R. P., Dymnicki, A. B., Taylor, R. D., & Schellinger, K. B. (2011). The impact of enhancing students' social and emotional learning: A meta-analysis of school-based universal interventions. *Child Development*, *82*(1), 405–432. doi:10.1111/j.1467-8624.2010.01564.x PMID:21291449

Erk, A. (2019). *Peer bullying, peer bullying prevention studies in schools and applications for children in the bullying cycle*. Equinox Publishing House.

Evans, C., Fraser, M., & Cotter, K. (2014). The effectiveness of school-based bullying prevention programs: A systemic review. *Aggression and Violent Behavior*, *19*(5), 532–544. doi:10.1016/j.avb.2014.07.004

Farrington, D. P., & Ttofi, M. M. (2009). School-Based Programs to Reduce Bullying and Victimization. *Campbell Systematic Reviews*, *5*(1), i-148. doi:10.4073/csr.2009.6

Garandeau, C. F., Poskiparta, E., & Salmivalli, C. (2014). Tackling acute cases of school bullying in the KiVa anti-bullying program: A comparison of two approaches. *Journal of Abnormal Child Psychology*, *42*(6), 981–991. doi:10.100710802-014-9861-1 PMID:24615005

Gini, G., & Pozzoli, T. (2009). Association between bullying and psychosomatic problems: A meta-analysis. *Pediatrics*, *123*(3), 1059–1065. doi:10.1542/peds.2008-1215 PMID:19255040

Haataja, A., Voeten, M., Boulton, A. J., Ahtola, A., Poskiparta, E., & Salmivalli, C. (2014). The KiVa antibullying curriculum and outcome: Does fidelity matter? *Journal of School Psychology*, *52*(5), 479–493. doi:10.1016/j.jsp.2014.07.001 PMID:25267170

Health, M. D. o. (2019). *Public health interventions: Applications for public health nursing practice* (2nd ed.). Public Health. Retrieved from https://www.health.state.mn.us/communities/practice/research/phncouncil/wheel.html

Hurley, K. (2019). *Short Term and Long Term Effects of Bullying*. Remedy Health Media, LLC.

Keller, L. O., Strohschein, S., Lia-Hoagberg, B., & Schaffer, M. A. (2004). Population-based public health interventions: Practice-based and evidence-supported. Part I. *Public Health Nursing (Boston, Mass.)*, *21*(5), 453–468. doi:10.1111/j.0737-1209.2004.21509.x PMID:15363026

Keller, L. O., Strohschein, S., Schaffer, M. A., & Lia-Hoagberg, B. (2004). Population-based public health interventions: Innovations in practice, teaching, and management. Part II. *Public Health Nursing (Boston, Mass.)*, *21*(5), 469–487. doi:10.1111/j.0737-1209.2004.21510.x PMID:15363027

Lee, J. H. (2018). Victimization by Bullying and Physical Symptoms Among South Korean Schoolchildren. *The Journal of School Nursing: the Official Publication of the National Association of School Nurses, 34*(2), 149–155. doi:10.1177/1059840517696962 PMID:29512433

Lee, S., Kim, C. J., & Kim, D. H. (2015). A meta-analysis of the effect of school-based anti-bullying programs. *Journal of Child Health Care, 19*(2), 136–153. doi:10.1177/1367493513503581 PMID:24092871

Lereya, S. T., Copeland, W. E., Costello, E. J., & Wolke, D. (2015). Adult mental health consequences of peer bullying and maltreatment in childhood: Two cohorts in two countries. *The Lancet. Psychiatry, 2*(6), 524–531. doi:10.1016/S2215-0366(15)00165-0 PMID:26360448

McWhinney, I. R. (1987). Health and disease: Problems of definition. *Canadian Medical Association Journal, 136*(8), 815. PMID:3567791

Menesini, E., & Salmivalli, C. (2017). Bullying in schools: the state of knowledge and effective interventions. *Psychol Health Med, 22*(sup1), 240-253. doi:10.1080/13548506.2017.1279740

Nansel, T. R., Craig, W., Overpeck, M. D., Saluja, G., & Ruan, W. J. (2004). Cross-national consistency in the relationship between bullying behaviors and psychosocial adjustment. *Archives of Pediatrics & Adolescent Medicine, 158*(8), 730–736. doi:10.1001/archpedi.158.8.730 PMID:15289243

Nickerson, A. B. (2019). Preventing and intervening with bullying in schools: A framework for evidence-based practice. *School Mental Health, 11*(1), 15–28. doi:10.100712310-017-9221-8

Olweus, D. (1993a). Bully/victim problems among schoolchildren: Long-term consequences and an effective intervention program. In Mental disorder and crime (pp. 317-349). Academic Press.

Olweus, D. (1993b). Bully/victim problems among schoolchildren: Long-term consequences and an effective intervention program. In P. Hodgins (Ed.), *Mental disorder and crime*. Sage Publications, Inc.

Pigozi, P. L., & Jones Bartoli, A. (2016). School Nurses' Experiences in Dealing With Bullying Situations Among Students. *The Journal of School Nursing: the Official Publication of the National Association of School Nurses, 32*(3), 177–185. doi:10.1177/1059840515613140 PMID:26502929

Raskauskas, J., & Stoltz, A. D. (2004). Identifying and intervening in relational aggression. *The Journal of School Nursing: the Official Publication of the National Association of School Nurses, 20*(4), 209–215. doi:10.1177/10598405040200040501 PMID:15283614

S, C. (2011). *Developing a framework for public health law in Europe*. Retrieved from http://www.euro.who.int/__data/assets/pdf_file/0004/151375/e95783.pdf

Salmivalli, C., Poskiparta, E., Ahtola, A., & Haataja, A. (2013). The Implementation and Effectiveness of the KiVa Antibullying Program in Finland. *European Psychologist, 18*(2), 79–88. doi:10.1027/1016-9040/a000140

Schoon, P. M., Porta, C. M., & Schaffer, M. A. (2018). Population-based public health clinical manual: The Henry Street model for nurses (3rd ed.). Sigma Theta Tau International Society of Nursing.

Stanhope, M., & Lancaster, J. (2019). *Public health nursing e-book: Population-centered health care in the community*. Elsevier Health Sciences.

Swearer, S., & Hymel, S. (2015). Bullying and Discrimination in Schools: Exploring Variations Across Student Subgroups. *School Psychology Review, 44*(4), 504–509. doi:10.17105/15-0133.1

Swearer, S. M., Wang, C., Berry, B., & Myers, Z. R. (2014). Reducing bullying: Application of social cognitive theory. *Theory into Practice, 53*(4), 271–277. doi:10.1080/00405841.2014.947221

Thornberg, R., Halldin, K., Bolmsjö, N., & Petersson, A. (2013). Victimising of school bullying: A grounded theory. *Research Papers in Education, 28*(3), 309–329. doi:10.1080/02671522.2011.641999

Ttofi, M. M., & Farrington, D. P. (2011). Effectiveness of school-based programs to reduce bullying: A systematic and meta-analytic review. *Journal of Experimental Criminology, 7*(1), 27–56. doi:10.100711292-010-9109-1

WHO. (2020). Basic documents. World Health Organization.

Wilkinson, R. G., & Marmot, M. (2003). *Social determinants of health: the solid facts.* World Health Organization.

Williford, A., Boulton, A., Noland, B., Little, T. D., Kärnä, A., & Salmivalli, C. (2012). Effects of the KiVa anti-bullying program on adolescents' depression, anxiety, and perception of peers. *Journal of Abnormal Child Psychology, 40*(2), 289–300. doi:10.100710802-011-9551-1 PMID:21822630

Wójcik, M., & Hełka, A. M. (2018). Meeting the Needs of Young Adolescents: ABBL Anti-Bullying Program During Middle School Transition. *Psychological Reports, 122*(3), 1043–1067. doi:10.1177/0033294118768671 PMID:29652220

Wolke, D., & Lereya, S. T. (2015). Long-term effects of bullying. *Archives of Disease in Childhood, 100*(9), 879–885. doi:10.1136/archdischild-2014-306667 PMID:25670406

ADDITIONAL READING

Einarsen, S., & Nielsen, M. B. (2015). Workplace bullying as an antecedent of mental health problems: A five-year prospective and representative study. *International Archives of Occupational and Environmental Health, 88*(2), 131–142. doi:10.100700420-014-0944-7 PMID:24840725

KEY TERMS AND DEFINITIONS

Primary Prevention: To prevent health problems before they occur by controlling the risk and causal factors of health problems. It can be aimed at individuals and society.

Primordial Prevention: This level of protection is the stage of preventing the occurrence of risk factors. In other words, it is the prevention of the emergence of social, economic and cultural life patterns that are known to have a role in the formation of health problems. An example of such prevention is the regulation of social and environmental conditions for high-risk children, adolescents and adults.

Secondary Prevention: Detection and treatment of health problems at an early stage and the reduction of their serious consequences. Serious progress is prevented, minimized, or slowed down. It is suitable for health problems that can be diagnosed at an early stage and have an effective treatment.

Tertiary Prevention: It is the prevention of progression and complications of existing health problems and reduction of the mental, social hardships, disability or pain caused by a health problem.

Chapter 16
Bullying Due to Dentofacial Features and Its Relationship With Quality of Life in View of Oral Health

Nevra Karamüftüoğlu
Cyprus International University, Cyprus

ABSTRACT

Bullying is defined as the aggressive behavior or intentional harm to which an individual is repeatedly subjected in a relationship characterized by instability, usually triggered by social, religious, and physical characteristics that distinguish the victim from other members of the group. Deviation from normal dentofacial aesthetics leads to increased incidences of bullying in children and teenagers with a reported worldwide prevalence of 5% to 58%, causing both physiological and psychological harm with both long-term and short-term effects, affecting an individual's psychosocial status and causing social disadvantage. The purpose of this chapter is to analyze the effect of dentofacial deviations on bullying and quality of line in view of oral health-related quality of life (OHRQoL) matrix and highlight the importance of informing the public via public health policies, anti-bullying policies in schools, and dental professionals as they are likely to have bullied patients among their clients.

INTRODUCTION

Bullying is defined as intentional harm to which an individual is repeatedly exposed in a relationship characterized by the practice of aggressive behavior or imbalance (Olweus, 1994). Bullying can be in form of aggression that cause direct (hitting, kicking, insults and threats) or indirect (gossip, spreading rumors and social exclusion) harm (Boulton & Underwood, 1992; Solberg et. al., 2007; Nansel et. al., 2004; van der Wal et. al. 2003). It has been observed for a long time and its prevalence varies depending on the location and age, and it is stated that it has become a global concern at a rate of occurence as high as 88% (Carney & Merrel, 2001; Chikaodi et. al., 2017; Ometeso, 2010).

DOI: 10.4018/978-1-6684-5426-8.ch016

Prominent physical characteristics and aesthetical concerns in society are observed more intensively in both childhood and adolescence (Scheffel, 2014). The factors that trigger bullying are usually social, religious, and physical characteristics that distinguish the victim from other members of the group (Malta et. al., 2014). The most commonly observed physical characteristics for nicknames are related to weight, height and facial appearance (Kolawole et. al., 2009). In view of which, dentofacial features are associated with increased incidents of bullying in children and adolescents (Baldo Moraes et. al., 2021). Deviation of normal dentofacial aesthetics can affect the individual's psychosocial status and cause social disadvantage (Shaw et. al., 1980). Since the dentofacial region contributes significantly to the overall facial appearance and a harmonious smile plays an important role in conforming to the normative standards; the existence of untreated dental caries, bleeding gingiva, misaligned teeth and/or malocclusion or lack of alignment between the maxillary bones and mandible could lead to one being bullied (Barasuol et. al., 2017; Baldo Moraes et. al., 2021; Shaw, 1981; Shaw et. al., 1980). Severe facial disfigurement evokes feelings of sympathy and compassion, but lighter disfigurements result in ridicule; creating greater psychological distress in individuals. Individuals with high facial attractiveness receive a more positive reaction from society than those with a low level of facial attractiveness. In addition, the importance of having a good dentofacial appearance is recognized as an important trait that affects friendships, career advancement, and flirting (Macgregor, 1970). Although the relationship between malocclusion and psychosocial well-being is complex, there is a clear connection between the presence of malocclusion, bullying, self-esteem and quality of life in view of oral health. Certain dental features that increase the risk of ridicule, which disrupts a normal psychological development, including dento-alveolar trauma, cleft palate or lip, maxillary crowding, increased overjet and deep overbite have been identified (Agou et. al., 2008; Fekkes et. al., 2005; Kim et. al., 2004; Lyznicki et. al., 2004; Solberg & Olweus, 2003; Thomson et. al., 2001).

The effects of bullying can be both short-term and long-term, causing both physiological and psychological symptoms (Seehra et. al., 2011). As a result of bullying, children and adolescents may become afraid of school, have difficulty concentrating in lessons and a decrease in the perception of school attendance and academic performance may be observed (Al-Bitar et. al., 2013; Chikaodi et. al., 2017; Glew et. al., 2005). In addition, the reported harmful effects also include increased suicidal thoughts, suicidal risk and the rate of self-harm (Kim et. al., 2005). As long-term effects of bullying, victims of bullying are more likely to remain anxious and depressed for life (Bond et. al., 2001; Rigby, 1999). The psychological effects of peer victimization in school-aged children may also persist during the transition to high school and adulthood (Rigby, 1999). Children who were severely bullied during the adolescent period had low self-esteem and depression as young adults (Olweus, 1994).

Malocclusion is a fairly common public health problem, and many studies have shown that it has a negative effect on quality of life, self-esteem, and social perceptions (Dimberg et. al., 2015; Eslamipour et. al., 2018; Jung, 2010; Kolawole et. al., 2009; Pithon et. al., 2014; Shen et. al., 2018). The relationship between orthodontic treatment and better self-esteem is still open to discussion (Bernstein & Watson, 1997; Seehra et. al., 2013). It is observed that children with untreated malocclusion are at greater risk of bullying (Barasuol et. al., 2017).

Dentofacial features in childhood and adolescence, undergoing orthodontic treatments are defined as conditions associated with bullying (Cunningham & Hunt, 2001; Seehra & Fleming et.al., 2011; Seehra & Newton et. al., 2011; Tristão et. al., 2020;). This age group is repeatedly exposed to negative actions over time, especially in the school environment (Olweus, 1994). Bullying is widespread among schoolchildren with worldwide prevalence ranging from 5% to 58%, its effects can be long-lasting and devastating (Barasuol et. al., 2017; DiBiase & Sandler, 2001; Fleming & Jacobsen, 2010; Spriggs et. al., 2007). It has been shown that dentofacial characteristics and various treatments related to oral health in children exposed to bullying have a great impact on their quality of life (Seehra et. al., 2010; Whitney & Smith, 1993). The most commonly reported conditions of being targeted by the bullies are dentofacial features, gaps between teeth or missing teeth, the shape or color of teeth, pronounced maxillary anterior teeth (Al-Bitar et. al., 2013).

Oral Health-related Quality of Life (OHRQoL) is defined as the effect of oral conditions on social life and the formation of a positive dentofacial self-esteem and the absence of negative effects (Inglehart & Bagramian, 2002; Kiyak, 2008). Recently, oral health and diseases, the appearance of teeth, malocclusion, and the effect on psychological and functional well-being of the treatment of these cases are increasingly attracting the attention of clinicians and researchers (Inglehart & Bagramian, 2002; Whitney & Smith, 1993). When malocclusion and orthodontic treatments are examined in view of the variables that affect QHRQoL (ethnicity, gender, age), enhanced aesthetics is found to be a great source of motivation for young patients to receive said treatments (Chan et. al., 2017; de Oliveira & Sheiham, 2004; Johal et. al., 2007; O'Brien et. al., 2007; Zhang et. al., 2006).

Social media provides an accessible resource for gaining valuable information about the social culture of bullying. An analysis of Twitter posts reveals four main categories relating to dentofacial features, braces and bullying; (i) morphological features, (ii) psychological and psychosocial impact, (III), coping mechanisms, and (IV) the role of the family. Individuals who have been bullied have reported various psychological effects and coping mechanisms. Social media can provide new and valuable information about the causal factors and social problems related to oral health and bullying. It is also stated that some coping mechanisms can reduce the negative effects of bullying (Chan et. al., 2017).

In general, social media, forums, blogs and daily digital applications are widely used not only in adults but also in the daily lives of children and adolescents. Studies have shown that communicating and providing information visually to children and adolescents is more effective during adolescence (Patel et. al., 2008; Thomson et. al., 2001). Internet has a large footprint on modern life. Most traditional means of communication, including phones, television, newspapers, radios are being redefined and reshaped; bearing new services such as e-mails, online TV, video and music streaming services, means of communication similar to phones and digital newspapers. Newspapers, books, and other print publishing are adapting to online technologies or are being reshaped as blogs and online news services. By means of instant messaging, forums and social networks, internet has enabled and accelarated new shapes of personal interaction; effectively becoming a common tool to transfer information (Pricewaterhouse Coopers (PwC) Health Research Institute, 2012). An important point on that is how the doctor-patient relationship has changed with the development of the internet. Traditionally, the doctor has been the main source of information on the diagnosis and treatment of the patient. However, this principle is subject to change as patients search for information on the internet; in many cases, this endeavor leads to unreliable information, causing hardships to doctors on treating patients who believe the information they have read online to be true. In order to ensure the delivery of trusted information, patients must be directed to foundation websites and blogs, online journals and trusted websites.

Teasing and Bullying: Are They the Same?

Both teasing and bullying are considered aggressive behaviors, but they are located at opposite ends of the spectrum. Teasing is considered a mild form of aggressive behavior, usually cheerful in nature, which takes place among peers who do not cause significant harm to the receiver. In turn, bullying, no matter what form it takes, harms a person. It should be remembered that bullying should be considered bullying if it results in harm and distress (Pearce, 2002).

PREVALENCE OF BULLYING IN SCHOOL: AGE CHILDREN

The reported prevalence of bullying in school-age children varies between 10-26%. These differences are influenced by factors such as age, cultural differences, and time. With increasing psychological and physiological development, children become less vulnerable and less tolerant of aggressive behavior (Pearce, 2002). In the school environment, 71% of bullying occurs in the playground, followed by classes with 46%, physical education classes with 40%, cafeteria with 39%, corridors and stairs with 33% and buses with 28% (Macgregor, 1970). Both at school and at home, children can freely communicate with each other through various multimedia applications and devices. Recently, the concept of 'cyberbullying' has been documented (Pearce, 2002).

GENDER DIFFERENCES AND THE TYPE AND LOCATION OF BULLYING

Both boys and girls can be exposed to direct and indirect forms of bullying. Among studies in literature, it is noted that gender differences cause differences on the frequency of bullying. Although it is not common all over the world, it has been reported that boys tend to be bullied more than girls (Al-Bitar et. al., 2013; Baldry & Farrington, 1999; Boulton & Underwood, 1992; Dawkins, 1995; Department for Education. Bullying webpage.; Nansel et. al., 2001; Pearce, 2002; Pricewaterhouse Coopers (PwC) Health Research Institute., 2012). Current research reports that this finding is not true (Tristão et. al., 2020). There are slight differences between boys and girls: boys are more likely to endure direct forms of aggression such as physical attacks, but, in contrast, girls are exposed to more indirect types of bullying, such as gossip and isolation (Baldry & Farrington, 1999; Boulton & Underwood, 1992; Olweus, 1994). The prevalence of indirect aggression is likely to be underestimated due to the fact that both children and teachers do not perceive it as a form of bullying (Carney & Merrel, 2001; Ometeso, 2010). The most common form of direct aggression is verbal abuse with a derogatory nickname (Pearce, 2002).

THE ROLE OF DENTAL PROFESSIONALS IN BULLYING

It is probable that among the patients of dental professionals, there are those who are subjected to bullying (Pearce, 2002; Seehra & Newton et.al., 2011).

The role of a clinician who has encountered this condition should include:

1. Identification of children at risk
2. Counseling for families
3. Screening for psychiatric comorbidities
4. Defense for prevention (Lyznicki, 2004).

Children at risk can be difficult to identify. Some personality traits are common to both victims and bullies; however, care should be taken not to stereotype children by dividing them into groups. Unexplained physical and psychological symptoms and behavioral changes may be the first presentation of peer victimization. If a child acknowledges that he or she has been bullied, it is very important that child should be believed and reassured that he/she is doing the right thing by reporting it (Dawkins, 1995; Lyznicki, 2004). The families of children who have been bullied should be informed about the severity and possible consequences of the bullying. They should be encouraged and requested to contact the school about the situation, to meet with teachers, principals or parents (Department for Education. Bullying webpage.). If psychological symptoms such as depression and anxiety are evident, a referral for psychological evaluation should be requested after consulting with the patient's family doctor (Pearce, 2002). In terms of dental treatment, guidelines for dentists are nonexistent, and more information is needed on this issue.

QUALITY OF LIFE RELATED TO ORAL HEALTH (OHRQoL)

Due to the fact that the concept of quality of life is embraced by many different disciplines ranging from economics to health, politics to social sciences, making a general definition for this concept becomes harder (Farquhar, 1994; Testa & Simonson, 1996). In 1946, when the World Health Organization (WHO) defined health as not only the absence of illness and disability, but also the presence of physical, mental and social well-being, the concept of 'quality of life' became important for health practices and research (Engel, 1992). Over the past 30 years, the research on concept of quality of life have been increasing in the medical literature (Sischo & Broder, 2001). WHO also defines quality of life as ''the way individuals perceive their positions in life in accordance with their goals, expectations, interests and living standards within the culture and value system in which they live'' (Görgünbaran, 2008; The Whoqol Group, 1998). Oral health affects aspects of social life such as self-esteem, social interaction, school and work performance, etc.

The impact of diseases on the quality of life is becoming increasingly accepted and is taken into account when assessing the treatment of the disease and its consequences. Clinical indicators alone are not enough to describe the state of health, and it has been reported that people with chronic disabilities can perceive their quality of life as better. This also applies to oral diseases and their consequences on the quality of life related to oral health (OHRQoL) (Farquhar, 1994). OHRQoL is the interaction of health variables such as biological and physiological functional status, as well as personal characteristics such as role function, social and psychological functionality representing multidimensional and individual perception of oral language and health-related verbal communication. In line with this, healthy instruments which enable an individual to eat and talk, being able to socialize without an active illness, discomfort or embarrassment contribute to the overall well-being (Sischo & Broder, 2001). Caries and periodontal diseases, oral cancer patients, children with cleft lip and palate, early childhood caries (ECC), patients with craniofacial malformations affect the quality of life in view to oral health in patients of all age groups (Broder, 2007; Filstrup, 2003; Gerritsen et. al., 2010; Ship, 2002). Although it has been revealed in recent years, OHRQoL has significant implications for the clinic (Petersen et. al., 2005). The two most common oral diseases, caries and periodontal disease usually do not cause symptoms in the early stages. The presence of clinical indicators of carious or periodontal involvement, such as the number of carious teeth, tooth mobility and periodontal pocket depth strongly correlate with deterioration in OHRQoL (Gerritsen et. al., 2010). However, caries and periodontal disease are progressive and, if not treated adequately, lead to tooth loss. Loss of teeth will lead to functional impairment in relation to chewing and aesthetics. OHRQoL models and measurements have been developed to evaluate the impact of oral diseases (Allen, 2003). The Oral Health Impact Profile (OHIP) has been developed based on this model, which is one of the most popular criteria (Allen, 2003; Locker, 1988; Slade & Spencer, 1994). Many studies conducted today provide quite strong evidence of the relationship of tooth loss with a deterioration in OHRQOL. In addition, not only the number, but also the location and distribution of missing teeth affect the severity of OHRQoL defects (Allen, 2003; Gerritsen et. al., 2010; Hultin, 2012; Locker, 1988; Petersen et. al., 2005).

OHRQoL research is widely used in pediatric dentistry and orthodontics. Although not considered a disease, malocclusion is considered important and is regarded as a public health issue due to the high prevalence in the community, requiring orthodontic treatment, causing the patient to develop oral diseases such as periodontitis and trauma, affects oral functions such as chewing, swallowing and speech in time (Görgünbaran, 2008; Kiyak, 2008; Sischo & Broder, 2011; The Whoqol Group, 1998). Malocclusions in children, especially in adolescents aged 8 to 18 years, are associated with decreased OHRQoL. However, this effect increases especially for children over the age of 14 (Locker, 1988). The high severity of malocclusion is associated with the effect of OHRQOL on some physical areas and all psychosocial areas (Slade & Spencer, 1994). There is a relationship between bullying and OHRQoL. Adolescents are three times more likely to have reduced OHRQOL caused by negative consequences of bullying incidents (Hultin, 2012).

Congenital anomalies are the most common cause of death among newborns (Petersen, 2003). Cleft lip and/or palate is considered to be the most common congenital craniofacial malformation (Abreu, 2016; Almeida et. al., 2014). One of the most common anomalies in dentistry is the absence of maxillary lateral incisors in cleft lip and palate patients (Kragt et. al., 2016; Sun et. al., 2017). Supernumerary teeth are seen especially in the maxillary central and lateral teeth (Gatto et. al., 2019; Kragt et. al., 2016). In patients with cleft lip and palate, the teeth that are more prone to tooth decay due to enamel hypoplasia are the central teeth (Francine, 2014; Kragt et. al., 2016). Microdontia and wedge-shaped maxillary lateral incisors are other dental anomalies and are more common in affected patients (Francine, 2014; Sun et. al., 2017). Cleft lip and/or palate malformation is usually diagnosed at a late age, which can be disappointing for the treatment of young patients and can affect speech, aesthetics, and their daily lives (Hosseini, 2017).

OHRQoL effects are important due to oral health inequalities and access to care due to socioeconomic and racial/ethnic factors (The Whoqol Group, 1998). Developing countries often do not have facilities that provide dental services. Access to treatment in developed countries is disrupted due to high costs and sometimes transportation difficulties (Menezes et. al., 2018). In recent years, OHRQoL assessments have been used in observational clinical trials to measure the effectiveness of treatment in order to improve oral care. OHRQoL research can be used to inform society and also helps eliminate oral health inequalities. There are significant relationships between bullying and dentofacial characteristics, self-esteem and OHRQoL (Rajion & Alwi, 2007; Vaiciunaite et. al., 2020).

CONCLUSION

It is necessary to promote public health policies aimed at reducing oral health inequalities, thereby improving the well-being and quality of life of the targeted population, and to develop anti-bullying policies in schools. Peer victimization in the school setting is a complex process of social interaction between parents, peer groups, and teachers. The primary goal should be to change behavior and the environment among these three groups of individuals. Clinicians should be aware that children with dentofacial problems such as malocclusion, dental caries and gingival problems may be subjected to constant peer victimization resulting in a negative impact on both their self-esteem and their oral health-related quality of life.

REFERENCES

Al-Bitar, Z. B., Al-Omari, I. K., Sonbol, H. N., Al-Ahmad, H. T., & Cunningham, S. J. (2013). Bullying among Jordanian schoolchildren, its effects on school performance, and the contribution of general physical and dentofacial features. *American Journal of Orthodontics and Dentofacial Orthopedics, 144*(6), 872–878. doi:10.1016/j.ajodo.2013.08.016 PMID:24286910

Allen, P. F. (2003). Assessment of oral health related quality of life. *Health and Quality of Life Outcomes, 1*(1), 1–8. doi:10.1186/1477-7525-1-40 PMID:14514355

Almeida, A. B. D., Leite, I. C. G., Melgaço, C. A., & Marques, L. S. (2014). Dissatisfaction with dentofacial appearance and the normative need for orthodontic treatment: Determinant factors. *Dental Press Journal of Orthodontics, 19*(3), 120–126. doi:10.1590/2176-9451.19.3.120-126.oar PMID:25162576

Baldo Moraes, R., Knorst, J. K., Brondani, B., Baldo Marques, B., de Sousa Reis, M., Henriqson, D., & Ardenghi, T. M. (2021). Relationship between gingival bleeding and associated factors with reports of verbal bullying in adolescents. *Journal of Periodontology, 92*(2), 225–233. doi:10.1002/JPER.19-0745 PMID:32716571

Baldry, A. C., & Farrington, D. P. (1999). Brief report: Types of bullying among Italian school children. *Journal of Adolescence, 22*(3), 423–426. doi:10.1006/jado.1999.0234 PMID:10462433

Barasuol, J. C., Soares, J. P., Castro, R. G., Giacomin, A., Gonçalves, B. M., Klein, D., Torres, F. M., Borgatto, A. F., Ramos-Jorge, M. L., Bolan, M., & Cardoso, M. (2017). Untreated dental caries is associated with reports of verbal bullying in children 8-10 years old. *Caries Research, 51*(5), 482–488. doi:10.1159/000479043 PMID:28954260

Bernstein, J. Y., & Watson, M. W. (1997). Children who are targets of bullying: A victim pattern. *Journal of Interpersonal Violence, 12*(4), 483–498. doi:10.1177/088626097012004001

Bond, L., Carlin, J. B., Thomas, L., Rubin, K., & Patton, G. (2001). Does bullying cause emotional problems? A prospective study of young teenagers. *BMJ (Clinical Research Ed.), 323*(7311), 480–484. doi:10.1136/bmj.323.7311.480 PMID:11532838

Boulton, M. J., & Underwood, K. (1992). Bully/victim problems among middle school children. *The British Journal of Educational Psychology, 62*(1), 73–87. doi:10.1111/j.2044-8279.1992.tb01000.x PMID:1558813

Broder, H. L. (2007). Children's oral health-related quality of life. *Community Dentistry and Oral Epidemiology, 35*(1), 5–7. doi:10.1111/j.1600-0528.2007.00400.x PMID:17615045

Carney, A. G., & Merrell, K. W. (2001). Bullying in schools: Perspectives on understanding and preventing an international problem. *School Psychology International, 22*(3), 364–382. doi:10.1177/0143034301223011

Chan, A., Antoun, J. S., Morgaine, K. C., & Farella, M. (2017). Accounts of bullying on T witter in relation to dentofacial features and orthodontic treatment. *Journal of Oral Rehabilitation, 44*(4), 244–250. doi:10.1111/joor.12487 PMID:28128466

Chikaodi, O., Abdulmanan, Y., Emmanuel, A. T., Muhammad, J., Mohammed, M. A., Izegboya, A., Donald, O. O., & Balarabe, S. (2019). Bullying, its effects on attitude towards class attendance and the contribution of physical and dentofacial features among adolescents in Northern Nigeria. *International Journal of Adolescent Medicine and Health, 31*(2). Advance online publication. doi:10.1515/ijamh-2016-0149 PMID:28731856

Cunningham, S. J., & Hunt, N. P. (2001). Quality of life and its importance in orthodontics. *Journal of Orthodontics, 28*(2), 152–158. doi:10.1093/ortho/28.2.152 PMID:11395531

Dawkins, J. (1995). Bullying in schools: Doctors' responsibilities. *BMJ (Clinical Research Ed.), 310*(6975), 274–275. doi:10.1136/bmj.310.6975.274 PMID:7866165

De Oliveira, C. M., & Sheiham, A. (2004). Orthodontic treatment and its impact on oral health-related quality of life in Brazilian adolescents. *Journal of Orthodontics, 31*(1), 20–27. doi:10.1179/146531204225011364 PMID:15071148

Department for Education. (n.d.). *Bullying webpage*. http://www.education.gov.uk/schools/pupilsupport/behaviour/bullying

DiBiase, A. T., & Sandler, P. J. (2001). Malocclusion, orthodontics and bullying. *Dental Update, 28*(9), 464–466. doi:10.12968/denu.2001.28.9.464 PMID:11806190

Dimberg, L., Arnrup, K., & Bondemark, L. (2015). The impact of malocclusion on the quality of life among children and adolescents: A systematic review of quantitative studies. *European Journal of Orthodontics, 37*(3), 238–247. doi:10.1093/ejo/cju046 PMID:25214504

Engel, G. L. (1977). The need for a new medical model: A challenge for biomedicine. *Science, 196*(4286), 129–136. doi:10.1126cience.847460 PMID:847460

Eslamipour, F., Afshari, Z., & Najimi, A. (2018). Prevalence of malocclusion in permanent dentition of Iranian population: A review article. *Iranian Journal of Public Health, 47*(2), 178. PMID:29445627

Farquhar, M. (1994). Quality of life in older people. In R. Fitzpatrick (Ed.), *Advances in Medical Sociology*. JAI Press Inc.

Fekkes, M., Pijpers, F. I., & Verloove-Vanhorick, S. P. (2005). Bullying: Who does what, when and where? Involvement of children, teachers and parents in bullying behavior. *Health Education Research, 20*(1), 81–91. doi:10.1093/her/cyg100 PMID:15253993

Filstrup, S. L., Briskie, D., da Fonseca, M., Lawrence, L., Wandera, A., & Inglehart, M. R. (2003). Early childhood caries and quality of life: Child and parent perspectives. *Pediatric Dentistry*, *25*(5), 431–440. PMID:14649606

Fleming, L. C., & Jacobsen, K. H. (2010). Bullying among middle-school students in low and middle income countries. *Health Promotion International*, *25*(1), 73–84. doi:10.1093/heapro/dap046 PMID:19884243

Francine, R., Pascale, S., & Aline, H. (2014). Congenital anomalies: prevalence and risk factors. *Mortality, 1*, 2.

Gatto, R. C. J., Garbin, A. J. Í., Corrente, J. E., & Garbin, C. A. S. (2019). The relationship between oral health-related quality of life, the need for orthodontic treatment and bullying, among Brazilian teenagers. *Dental Press Journal of Orthodontics*, *24*(2), 73–80. doi:10.1590/2177-6709.24.2.073-080.oar PMID:31116290

Gerritsen, A. E., Allen, P. F., Witter, D. J., Bronkhorst, E. M., & Creugers, N. H. (2010). Tooth loss and oral health-related quality of life: A systematic review and meta-analysis. *Health and Quality of Life Outcomes*, *8*(1), 1–11. doi:10.1186/1477-7525-8-126 PMID:21050499

Glew, G. M., Fan, M. Y., Katon, W., Rivara, F. P., & Kernic, M. A. (2005). Bullying, psychosocial adjustment, and academic performance in elementary school. *Archives of Pediatrics & Adolescent Medicine*, *159*(11), 1026–1031. doi:10.1001/archpedi.159.11.1026 PMID:16275791

Görgünbaran, A. (2008). Socialization and Quality of Life in Old Ages [Yaşlılıkta sosyalizasyon ve yaşam kalitesi]. *Yaşlı Sorunları Araştırma Dergisi*, *1*(2), 86–97.

Hosseini, H. R., Kaklamanos, E. G., & Athanasiou, A. E. (2017). Treatment outcomes of pre-surgical infant orthopedics in patients with non-syndromic cleft lip and/or palate: A systematic review and meta-analysis of randomized controlled trials. *PLoS One*, *12*(7), e0181768. doi:10.1371/journal.pone.0181768 PMID:28742129

Hultin, M., Davidson, T., Gynther, G., Helgesson, G., Jemt, T., Lekholm, U., ... Tranaeus, S. (2012). Oral rehabilitation of tooth loss: A systematic review of quantitative studies of OHRQoL. *The International Journal of Prosthodontics*, *25*(6). PMID:23101034

Ingelehart, M. R., & Bagramian, R. A. (2002). Oral health-related quality of life: an introduction. *Oral Health-Related Quality of Life*, 1-6.

Johal, A., Cheung, M. Y. H., & Marcenes, W. (2007). The impact of two different malocclusion traits on quality of life. *British Dental Journal*, *202*(2), E6–E6. doi:10.1038/bdj.2007.33 PMID:17260428

Jung, M. H. (2010). Evaluation of the effects of malocclusion and orthodontic treatment on self-esteem in an adolescent population. *American Journal of Orthodontics and Dentofacial Orthopedics*, *138*(2), 160–166. doi:10.1016/j.ajodo.2008.08.040 PMID:20691357

Kim, Y. S., Koh, Y. J., & Leventhal, B. (2005). School bullying and suicidal risk in Korean middle school students. *Pediatrics*, *115*(2), 357–363. doi:10.1542/peds.2004-0902 PMID:15687445

Kim, Y. S., Koh, Y. J., & Leventhal, B. L. (2004). Prevalence of school bullying in Korean middle school students. *Archives of Pediatrics & Adolescent Medicine*, *158*(8), 737–741. doi:10.1001/archpedi.158.8.737 PMID:15289244

Kolawole, K. A., Otuyemi, O. D., & Adeosun, O. D. (2009). Nicknames and name calling among a population of Nigerian schoolchildren. *European Journal of Paediatric Dentistry*, *10*(3), 115. PMID:19761284

Kragt, L., Dhamo, B., Wolvius, E. B., & Ongkosuwito, E. M. (2016). The impact of malocclusions on oral health-related quality of life in children—A systematic review and meta-analysis. *Clinical Oral Investigations*, *20*(8), 1881–1894. doi:10.100700784-015-1681-3 PMID:26635095

Locker, D. (1988). Measuring oral health: A conceptual framework. *Community Dental Health*, *5*, 3–18. PMID:3285972

Lyznicki, J. M., McCaffree, M. A., & Robinowitz, C. B. (2004). Childhood bullying: Implications for physicians. *American Family Physician*, *70*(9), 1723–1728. PMID:15554490

MacGregor, F. C. (1970). Social and psychological implications of dentofacial disfigurement. *The Angle Orthodontist*, *40*(3), 231–233. PMID:5269955

Malta, D. C., Porto, D. L., Crespo, C. D., Silva, M. M. A., Andrade, S. S. C. D., Mello, F. C. M. D., Monteiro, R., & Silva, M. A. I. (2014). Bullying in Brazilian school children: Analysis of the national adolescent school-based health survey (PeNSE 2012). *Revista Brasileira de Epidemiologia*, *17*(suppl 1), 92–105. doi:10.1590/1809-4503201400050008 PMID:25054256

Menezes, C., de Arruda, J. A., Silva, L. V., Monteiro, J. L., Caribé, P., Álvares, P., ... Bueno, D. F. (2018). Nonsyndromic cleft lip and/or palate: A multicenter study of the dental anomalies involved. *Journal of Clinical and Experimental Dentistry*, *10*(8), e746. doi:10.4317/jced.54926 PMID:30305871

Nansel, T. R., Craig, W., Overpeck, M. D., Saluja, G., & Ruan, W. J. (2004). Cross-national consistency in the relationship between bullying behaviors and psychosocial adjustment. *Archives of Pediatrics & Adolescent Medicine*, *158*(8), 730–736. doi:10.1001/archpedi.158.8.730 PMID:15289243

Nansel, T. R., Overpeck, M., Pilla, R. S., Ruan, W. J., Simons-Morton, B., & Scheidt, P. (2001). Bullying behaviors among US youth: Prevalence and association with psychosocial adjustment. *Journal of the American Medical Association*, *285*(16), 2094–2100. doi:10.1001/jama.285.16.2094 PMID:11311098

O'Brien, C., Benson, P. E., & Marshman, Z. (2007). Evaluation of a quality of life measure for children with malocclusion. *Journal of Orthodontics*, *34*(3), 185–193. doi:10.1179/146531207225022185 PMID:17761802

Olweus, D. (1994). Bullying at school: Basic facts and effects of a school based intervention program. *Journal of Child Psychology and Psychiatry, and Allied Disciplines*, *35*(7), 1171–1190. doi:10.1111/j.1469-7610.1994.tb01229.x PMID:7806605

Omoteso, B. A. (2010). Bullying behaviour, its associated factors and psychological effects among secondary students in Nigeria. *Journal of International Social Research*, *3*(10).

Patel, J. H., Moles, D. R., & Cunningham, S. J. (2008). Factors affecting information retention in orthodontic patients. *American Journal of Orthodontics and Dentofacial Orthopedics, 133*(4), S61–S67. doi:10.1016/j.ajodo.2007.07.019 PMID:18407022

Pearce, J. (2002). What can be done about the bully. *Bullying a practical guide to coping for schools*, 74-91.

Petersen, P. E. (2003). The World Oral Health Report 2003: Continuous improvement of oral health in the 21st century–the approach of the WHO Global Oral Health Programme. *Community Dentistry and Oral Epidemiology, 31*, 3–24. doi:10.1046/j..2003.com122.x PMID:15015736

Petersen, P. E., Bourgeois, D., Ogawa, H., Estupinan-Day, S., & Ndiaye, C. (2005). The global burden of oral diseases and risks to oral health. *Bulletin of the World Health Organization, 83*, 661–669. PMID:16211157

Pithon, M. M., Andrade, D., Fernandes, I., Mendes, J., Nunes, K., Michele, L., Ribeiro, A. V., & da Silva Coqueiro, R. (2014). Influence of malocclusion on social perceptions of adolescents at public and private schools. *European Archives of Paediatric Dentistry; Official Journal of the European Academy of Paediatric Dentistry, 15*(1), 37–43. doi:10.100740368-013-0050-7 PMID:23797925

Pricewaterhouse Coopers (PwC). (2012). *Health Research Institute. 2012. Social media "Likes" healthcare. From marketing to social business.* https://www.pwc.com/us/en/health-industries/health-research-institute/publications/pdf/health-care-social-media-report.pdf

Rajion, Z. A., & Alwi, Z. (2007). Genetics of cleft lip and palate: A review. *The Malaysian Journal of Medical Sciences: MJMS, 14*(1), 4. PMID:22593645

Rigby, K. (1999). Peer victimisation at school and the health of secondary school students. *The British Journal of Educational Psychology, 69*(1), 95–104. doi:10.1348/000709999157590 PMID:10230345

Scheffel, D. L. S., Jeremias, F., Fragelli, C. M. B., dos Santos-Pinto, L. A. M., Hebling, J., & de Oliveira, O. B. Jr. (2014). Esthetic dental anomalies as motive for bullying in schoolchildren. *European Journal of Dentistry, 8*(01), 124–128. doi:10.4103/1305-7456.126266 PMID:24966759

Seehra, J., Fleming, P. S., Newton, T., & DiBiase, A. T. (2011). Bullying in orthodontic patients and its relationship to malocclusion, self-esteem and oral health-related quality of life. *Journal of Orthodontics, 38*(4), 247–256. doi:10.1179/14653121141641 PMID:22156180

Seehra, J., Newton, J. T., & DiBiase, A. T. (2011). Bullying in schoolchildren–its relationship to dental appearance and psychosocial implications: An update for GDPs. *British Dental Journal, 210*(9), 411–415. doi:10.1038j.bdj.2011.339 PMID:21566605

Seehra, J., Newton, J. T., & DiBiase, A. T. (2013). Interceptive orthodontic treatment in bullied adolescents and its impact on self-esteem and oral-health-related quality of life. *European Journal of Orthodontics, 35*(5), 615–621. doi:10.1093/ejo/cjs051 PMID:22843555

Shaw, W. C. (1981). The influence of children's dentofacial appearance on their social attractiveness as judged by peers and lay adults. *American Journal of Orthodontics, 79*(4), 399–415. doi:10.1016/0002-9416(81)90382-1 PMID:6939333

Shaw, W. C., Addy, M., & Ray, C. (1980). Dental and social effects of malocclusion and effectiveness of orthodontic treatment: A review. *Community Dentistry and Oral Epidemiology*, *8*(1), 36–45. doi:10.1111/j.1600-0528.1980.tb01252.x PMID:6989548

Shen, L., He, F., Zhang, C., Jiang, H., & Wang, J. (2018). Prevalence of malocclusion in primary dentition in mainland China, 1988–2017: A systematic review and meta-analysis. *Scientific Reports*, *8*(1), 1–10. doi:10.103841598-018-22900-x PMID:29549346

Ship, J. A., Inglehart, M. R., & Bagramian, R. A. (2002). Oral health-related quality of life in patients with oral cancer. *Oral Health-Related Quality of Life*, 153-168.

Sischo, L., & Broder, H. (2011). Oral health-related quality of life: What, why, how, and future implications. *Journal of Dental Research*, *90*(11), 1264–1270. doi:10.1177/0022034511399918 PMID:21422477

Slade, G. D., & Spencer, A. J. (1994). Development and evaluation of the oral health impact profile. *Community Dental Health*, *11*(1), 3–11. PMID:8193981

Solberg, M. E., & Olweus, D. (2003). Prevalence estimation of school bullying with the Olweus Bully/Victim Questionnaire. *Aggressive Behavior: Official Journal of the International Society for Research on Aggression*, *29*(3), 239–268. doi:10.1002/ab.10047

Solberg, M. E., Olweus, D., & Endresen, I. M. (2007). Bullies and victims at school: Are they the same pupils? *The British Journal of Educational Psychology*, *77*(2), 441–464. doi:10.1348/000709906X105689 PMID:17504556

Spriggs, A. L., Iannotti, R. J., Nansel, T. R., & Haynie, D. L. (2007). Adolescent bullying involvement and perceived family, peer and school relations: Commonalities and differences across race/ethnicity. *The Journal of Adolescent Health*, *41*(3), 283–293. doi:10.1016/j.jadohealth.2007.04.009 PMID:17707299

Sun, L., Wong, H. M., & McGrath, C. P. (2017). Relationship between the severity of malocclusion and oral health related quality of life: A systematic review and meta-analysis. *Oral Health & Preventive Dentistry*, *15*(6), 503–517. PMID:28944350

Testa, M. A., & Simonson, D. C. (1996). Assessment of quality-of-life outcomes. *The New England Journal of Medicine*, *334*(13), 835–840. doi:10.1056/NEJM199603283341306 PMID:8596551

Thomson, A. M., Cunningham, S. J., & Hunt, N. P. (2001). A comparison of information retention at an initial orthodontic consultation. *European Journal of Orthodontics*, *23*(2), 169–178. doi:10.1093/ejo/23.2.169 PMID:11398554

Tristão, S. K. P., Magno, M. B., Pintor, A. V. B., Christovam, I. F., Ferreira, D. M. T., Maia, L. C., & de Souza, I. P. R. (2020). Is there a relationship between malocclusion and bullying? A systematic review. *Progress in Orthodontics*, *21*(1), 1–13. doi:10.118640510-020-00323-7 PMID:32869136

Vaiciunaite, R., Mitalauskiene, A., & Vasiliauskas, A. (2020). The relationship between congenital cleft lip and palate malformation, skeletal and dental occlusal anomalies, and the influence of its treatment on affected patients' oral health-related quality of life (OHRQoL). *Stomatologija*, *22*(4), 116–119. PMID:33847283

Van der Wal, M. F., De Wit, C. A., & Hirasing, R. A. (2003). Psychosocial health among young victims and offenders of direct and indirect bullying. *Pediatrics, 111*(6), 1312–1317. doi:10.1542/peds.111.6.1312 PMID:12777546

Whitney, I., & Smith, P. K. (1993). A survey of the nature and extent of bullying in junior/middle and secondary schools. *Educational Research, 35*(1), 3–25. doi:10.1080/0013188930350101

Whoqol Group. (1998). The World Health Organization quality of life assessment (WHOQOL): Development and general psychometric properties. *Social Science & Medicine, 46*(12), 1569–1585. doi:10.1016/S0277-9536(98)00009-4 PMID:9672396

Zhang, M., McGrath, C., & Hägg, U. (2006). The impact of malocclusion and its treatment on quality of life: A literature review. *International Journal of Paediatric Dentistry, 16*(6), 381–387. doi:10.1111/j.1365-263X.2006.00768.x PMID:17014535

ADDITIONAL READING

Abreu, L. G., Melgaço, C. A., Abreu, M. H., Lages, E. M. B., & Paiva, S. M. (2016). Perception of parents and caregivers regarding the impact of malocclusion on adolescents' quality of life: A cross-sectional study. *Dental Press Journal of Orthodontics, 21*(6), 74–81. doi:10.1590/2177-6709.21.6.074-081.oar PMID:28125143

Agel, M., Marcenes, W., Stansfeld, S. A., & Bernabé, E. (2014). School bullying and traumatic dental injuries in East London adolescents. *British Dental Journal, 217*(12), E26–E26. doi:10.1038j.bdj.2014.1123 PMID:25525032

Agou, S., Locker, D., Streiner, D. L., & Tompson, B. (2008). Impact of self-esteem on the oral-health-related quality of life of children with malocclusion. *American Journal of Orthodontics and Dentofacial Orthopedics, 134*(4), 484–489. doi:10.1016/j.ajodo.2006.11.021 PMID:18929265

Al-Bitar, Z. B., Hamdan, A. M., Al-Omari, I. K., Naini, F. B., Gill, D. S., & Al-Omiri, M. K. (2022). Is self-harm among orthodontic patients related to dislike of dentofacial features and oral health-related quality of life? *The Angle Orthodontist, 92*(2), 240–246. doi:10.2319/060421-448.1 PMID:34878532

Al-Omari, I. K., Al-Bitar, Z. B., Sonbol, H. N., Al-Ahmad, H. T., Cunningham, S. J., & Al-Omiri, M. (2014). Impact of bullying due to dentofacial features on oral health–related quality of life. *American Journal of Orthodontics and Dentofacial Orthopedics, 146*(6), 734–739. doi:10.1016/j.ajodo.2014.08.011 PMID:25432254

Kiyak, H. A. (2008). Does orthodontic treatment affect patients' quality of life? *Journal of Dental Education, 72*(8), 886–894. doi:10.1002/j.0022-0337.2008.72.8.tb04564.x PMID:18676797

KEY TERMS AND DEFINITIONS

Bullying: Bullying is defined as intentional harm to which an individual is repeatedly exposed in a relationship characterized by the practice of aggressive behavior or imbalance.

Dentofacial Features: Dentofacial features are associated with increased incidents of bullying in children and adolescents.

Oral Health: In terms of oral health, there is a clear link between the presence of malocclusion, bullying, self-esteem and quality of life.

Quality of Life: Dentofacial characteristics and various oral health-related treatments greatly affect the quality of life of bullied children.

Chapter 17
Sexual Harassment in Health Institutions in Turkey:
Causes, Frequency, Effects, and Consequences

Hatice Ulusoy
Sivas Cumhuriyet University, Turkey

Sinem Sarıçoban
Sivas Cumhuriyet University, Turkey

ABSTRACT

Sexual harassment is a concept that has become a growing concern globally as it occurs in all areas of life and also in the workplace. In the workplace it is described as any undesirable sexual behavior that is perceived as a threat, border violation, and attack by the exposed person, negatively affecting the employee's ability to do his/her job. This problem disproportionately affects women and can negatively affect their economic and career outcomes. Studies show that sexual harassment cases in health institutions are quite pervasive. Studies examining the sexual harassment of nurses in Turkey determined that the rate of exposure to sexual harassment ranged from 1.5% to 75%. Sexual harassment incidents in health institutions usually occur by relatives of patients, patients, physicians, other healthcare professionals, and colleagues. In this chapter, the definitions, causes, frequency, effects, and consequences of sexual harassment will be discussed.

INTRODUCTION

Definition of Sexual Harassment

Sexual harassment is a concept that has become a growing concern globally as it occurs in all areas of life and also in the workplace (Chaudhuri, 2007). Sexual harassment can take many different forms, overt or covert, and behavior perceived as sexual harassment may be characterized differently by every-

DOI: 10.4018/978-1-6684-5426-8.ch017

one. Therefore, it is difficult to make a precise and common definition of sexual harassment (Sarmaşık, 2009). However, in general sexual harassment is defined as unwelcome sexual advances, requests for sexual favors, and other verbal or physical conduct of a sexual nature (Scholcoff et al., 2020). Although sexual harassment may seem like a situation that only concerns the abused person, it is actually a social phenomenon. It is because sexual harassment shows that there is a situation arising from inequality between the sexes (Durmuş, 2013).

Sexual harassment, which could be seen on the street, on travel and even in the family and which could be exposed by people whom the person knows or does not know, may also be perpetrated by colleagues or managers in the workplace. With the continuation of sexual harassment cases in different sectors for the last 30 years, more women are exposed to sexual harassment as more women join the workforce nowadays (National Academies of Sciences, Engineering and Medicine, 2018). In the United States, more than a quarter of women reported having been sexually harassed at work (Edison Research, 2018).

On the other hand, sexual harassment in the workplace is any undesirable sexual behavior that is perceived as a threat, border violation and attack by the exposed person, negatively affecting the employee's ability to do his/her job (Adams et al., 2019; Çelik & Şenol Çelik, 2007). Sexual harassment is a term often used to describe the unwanted sexual attitudes and behaviors of men towards women in the workplace. Unwanted touching, speaking, insinuation, actions and attitudes are considered within the scope of sexual harassment. However, it is also possible for women, albeit to a lesser extent, to perpetrate passive sexual harassment by provoking men at a disturbing level (Arslan, 2001). Sexual harassment in the workplace has been handled from different perspectives by different countries and has been accepted as gender discrimination, violation of personal rights or abuse of power (authority) in order to gain sexual interest (Bakırcı, 2000). However, fundamentally, workplace violence and harassment are violations of basic human rights (International Labour Organization, 2019).

There are some elements for a behavior to be defined as sexual harassment in the workplace. These are listed below:

- The behavior in question must occur in the workplace or in a work-related environment. Harassment that occurs while away from the workplace for business is also considered as sexual harassment in the workplace.
- The behavior must be about the person's gender, sexuality or sexually suggestive subjects. A word expressing gender discrimination or anecdotes containing sexuality can be evaluated within this scope.
- The behavior must be done without the will or consent of the person was harassed.
- It must affect the person's working conditions or working environment. The behavior of a manager who dismisses or does not promote the employee that does not accept his offer of sexual intercourse or the decrease in the work efficiency of an employee due to the behaviors can be given as examples for these matters.
- For some behaviors, it must be a continuous behavior. Sometimes a single behavior can be considered as sexual harassment, and for some behavior to be considered as sexual harassment, it must be a repetitive behavior such as a colleague who persistently invites to a dinner/coffee date despite being rejected.

If these elements occur in the workplace, they are described as "sexual harassment in the workplace". However, in order for a behavior to be qualified as sexual harassment, it does not need to meet all the elements (Yeşiltaş, 2005).

Sexual assault is different from sexual harassment in that it "covers a range of unwanted behaviors – up to but not including penetration – that are attempted or completed against a victim's will or when a victim cannot consent because of age, disability, or the influence of alcohol or drugs (United States Department of Justice, 2010). Sexual assault and sexual harassment in the workplace are global problems (Kearl, 2018; Shafran- Tikva et al., 2021; Smith & Ortiz 2021; Ulusoy et al., 2011; World Health Organization, 1997) that disproportionately affect women and can negatively affect their economic and career outcomes (Dougherty et al., 1996; McLaughlin et al., 2017). Approximately 40% of women in the United States, for example, indicated they received unwanted sexual advances or experienced sexual harassment in a professional or work setting (Graf, 2018). In studies examining the sexual harassment of nurses in Türkiye, it was determined that the rate of exposure to sexual harassment ranged from 1.5% to 75%.

Sexual harassment and related behaviors are intended to insult and humiliate the person (Berdahl, 2007) and at the same time, it is a show of power that is frequently used to intimidate or pressure the employee (Güngör, 1999 as cited in Sarmaşık, 2009). It is possible to evaluate this show of power as a product of the power of the manager to reward and punish, especially when one of the parties is in the position of manager (usually male) and the other in the position of employee (usually female). The fact that women are harassed by their subordinates even when they are in a managerial position can be explained by subordinates' traditional gender role perceptions of women and their efforts to "justify" these perceptions, as well as an attempt to "provide equality" (Solmus, 2005).

Toker and Sümer (2010), in their study to determine the perception of sexual harassment of female employees in Türkiye, revealed five different dimensions of sexual harassment in the workplace. These dimensions show parallelism with the results of studies conducted in the USA (Toker & Sümer, 2010). However, one of these dimensions, the "insinuation of interest" dimension, which does not explicitly include sexuality but includes an insinuation of interest towards women, is not found in studies conducted in the USA (Toker, 2016). The result of this study can be considered as an example of cultural differences in the interpretation of sexual harassment. In a study carried out with 49 female residents the most frequent act of harassment, "gazing at the physician in a lewd manner", was reported by 51% of participants (Ulusoy et al., 2011). Similarly, in another study, 61.4% of the nurses reported that they were exposed to "gazing in a lewd manner" (Erdemir et al., 2011).

Sexual Harassment in Healthcare Institutions

While sexual harassment continues to be a permanent problem in society and in the workplace, health institutions are also one of the stakeholders of the same problem. Sexual harassment is a type of violence that is frequently seen in addition to many types of violence encountered in health institutions (Draucker, 2020). Studies show that sexual harassment cases in health institutions are quite pervasive (Hammoud et al., 2020; Shafran- Tikva et al., 2021; Smith & Ortiz 2021). A study conducted in Pakistan revealed that 80% of nurses had a history of sexual harassment in the hospital (Khan et al., 2015). In the study conducted by Pitot et al., (2021), 60.3% of female radiologists and trainee radiologists reported that they had been sexually harassed at work. According to the results of a systematic review study conducted in 2014, it was stated that 25% of the nurses were sexually harassed (Spector et al., 2014). According to another systematic review study conducted in 2020, the rate of sexual harassment against female nurses is between 10% and 87.30% (Kahsay et al., 2020). Bahji and Altomare (2020), in their meta-analysis study to determine the prevalence of mobbing, harassment and discrimination reported by resident physicians during training, found that sexual harassment reported by resident physicians was 52%. Although sexual harassment in health institutions is common among female employees, male healthcare workers are also exposed to sexual harassment. In a qualitative study with 16 male physicians, male physicians stated that they were exposed to sexual harassment, including physical harassment (Farkas et al., 2020). The literature on sexual harassment in the workplace indicates that sexual harassment incidents are common in health institutions.

Reasons for Sexual Harassment in Health Institutions

Sexual harassment is commonly associated with the exercise of power (Phillips & Schneider 1993). Sexual harassment in the workplace is often associated with actions of supervisors; however, sexual harassment may occur in peer relationships, or can be targeted at someone of higher status. Additionally, sexual harassment may involve a non-employee such as a volunteer worker, patients or their family members (Çam & Üstüner- Top, 2021; Çelik & Şenol Çelik, 2007; Kısa & Dziegielewski, 1996; Kısa et al., 2002; Pınar et al., 2017; Robinson et al., 2005; Sabak et al., 2021; Talas et al., 2011; Tekin & Bulut, 2014; Ulusoy et al., 2011; Ünlüsoy Dinçer, 2012;).

Employees in health institutions frequently encounter violence due to the distinctive working conditions of health institutions and the natural structure of their environment. In addition to physical, verbal and psychological violence, sexual harassment is one of the types of violence encountered in health institutions due to the high number of female employees. Situations such as being a woman, young and single, working in the evening, being alone in the working environment or in the patient's room are among the causes of violence in health institutions. In a study conducted to determine sexual harassment against female nurses, it was found that single nurses aged 30-34 were exposed to more sexual harassment (Çelik & Şenol Çelik, 2007). In another study, it was observed that among the emergency service workers, physicians, women, and 28-34 years old health workers were the most likely to be subjected to sexual harassment (Talas et al., 2011). One of the important factors of sexual harassment in health institutions is the working hours and the working environment. In many studies, it has been determined that health workers are more exposed to sexual harassment during the evening or night shift (Kısa & Dziegielewski, 1996; Kısa et al., 2002; Talas et al., 2011). In addition, it was determined that the harassment occurred mostly in clinics and patient rooms (Çelik & Şenol Çelik, 2007; Kısa & Dziegielewski, 1996; Kısa et al., 2002; Ünlüsoy Dinçer, 2012).

In the studies conducted, the reasons for sexual harassment were listed as sexuality and male-dominated discourse and culture, conservative social structure, lack of communication and education, work and working conditions, inadequate security measures, unresponsiveness of the victims with the feeling of being blamed and not reporting the harassment, administrative inadequacies, legal inadequacies (Ulusoy et al., 2011; Ünlüsoy Dinçer, 2012). In a study carried out with emergency service workers, health workers reported that there were no rules preventing patients and visitors from being in the emergency room unnecessarily. In addition, it was determined that the security personnel in the emergency clinic do not carry weapons and do not intervene sufficiently when they were exposed to sexual harassment. Almost all of the health workers (95.5%) who have been sexually harassed think that the security personnel or the police do not protect them enough against violence (Sabak et al., 2021). Healthcare professionals take individual measures to avoid sexual harassment due to the above-mentioned inadequacies that do not protect healthcare personnel from harassment. These include maintaining modesty of clothing, changing verbal and non-verbal communication, and maintaining physical distance for self-protection (Ulusoy et al., 2011).

Frequency and Type of Sexual Harassment

The rate and frequency of sexual harassment in health institutions varies. In a study conducted in Türkiye by Kısa and Dziegielewski (1996), determined that 75% of female nurses have been exposed to sexual harassment at least once during their careers. Erdemir et al., (2011) found that most of the nurses (71.7%) indicated that they had been sexually harassed by patients. When the relevant literature is examined, it is seen that various sample groups are discussed in studies examining violence (physical, verbal, psychological, sexual) including sexual harassment in health institutions. Some studies focused on specific departments, such as emergency services, while others focused on occupational groups. Considering the studies examining the violence in the emergency room, it is seen that the rates of sexual harassment in the emergency room are between 1.8% and 15.9% (Aydemir et al., 2020; Talas et al., 2011;). Sabak et al., (2021) found the rate of sexual harassment among emergency physicians to be 6.1% in their study. Contrary to other studies conducted in Türkiye, in a study, male physicians reported that they experienced more sexual harassment than female physicians in this study (Sabak et al., 2021). In studies examining harassment among nurses, the rate of nurses being exposed to sexual harassment varies between 1.5% and 75% (Çam & Üstüner- Top, 2021; Çelik & Şenol Çelik, 2007; Dinçer 2006; Erdemir et al., 2011; Kısa & Dziegielewski, 1996; Kısa et al., 2002; Tekin & Bulut, 2014; Ünlüsoy Dinçer, 2012). Tekin and Bulut (2014), on the other hand, examined sexual harassment incidents in operating rooms and found that 32.6% of nurses were exposed to sexual harassment while working in the operating room.

Sexual harassment occurs at a high rate not only in nurses but also in physicians. Ulusoy et al. (2011), 67.3% of resident physicians stated that they were sexually harassed at some point in their careers. In studies examining all incidents of violence against healthcare professionals, the rate of sexual harassment is relatively lower than other types of violence. In studies conducted for this purpose, the rate of sexual harassment was found to be between 1.0% and 6.2% (Aytaç & Dursun, 2013; Dursun, 2012; Dursun & Aytaç, 2021; Pınar et al., 2017;). While the rate of health workers who stated that they were exposed to sexual harassment once is between 26.8% and 77.8% (Aytaç & Dursun, 2013; Dursun, 2012; Dursun & Aytaç, 2021; Ünlüsoy Dinçer, 2012), The rate of those who state that they have experienced sexual harassment 1-4 times or occasionally varies between 39.0% and 69.4% (Aytaç & Dursun, 2013; Kısa et al., 2002; Ünlüsoy Dinçer, 2012;).

The type of sexual harassment experienced by healthcare professionals also varies. Sexual harassment usually occurs as verbal or physical abuse. Ünlüsoy Dinçer (2012) found that nurses were subjected to verbal, physical and both verbal and physical sexual harassment, respectively. Healthcare workers are frequently subjected to verbal sexual harassment, such as unsolicited innuendos and remarks, sexually explicit jokes, stories or questions, coercion to go on a date, private (obscene) questions, undesired e-mails or phone calls, sexual threats and profanity (Çelik & Şenol Çelik, 2007; Erdemir et al., 2011; Kısa & Dziegielewski, 1996; Kısa et al., 2002; Talas et al., 2011; Tekin & Bulut, 2014; Ulusoy et al., 2011). In addition to this, physical sexual harassment such as staring disturbingly (lewd gaze), touching obscene parts of the body, brushing, or grabbing are also experienced (Erdemir et al., 2011; Kısa & Dziegielewski, 1996; Kısa et al., 2002; Talas et al., 2011; Ulusoy et al., 2011).

Individual and Organizational Consequences of Sexual Harassment

Sexual harassment in health institutions can have emotional, physical and social effects. Health workers who are exposed to sexual harassment have health problems such as headache, tiredness, nausea/vomiting, dizziness, trouble sleeping as well as anger, fear, self-blame, helplessness, disappointment, sadness, powerlessness, low self-esteem, hostility, hatred, anxiety, hopelessness, humiliation, disgust, depression, headache, fatigue, nausea/vomiting (Çelik & Şenol Çelik, 2007; Kısa & Dziegielewski, 1996; Talas et al., 2011). Sexual harassment also negatively affects social life and family relationships (Çelik & Şenol Çelik, 2007; Tekin & Bulut, 2014).

Sexual harassment also has important organizational consequences for healthcare workers. A significant portion of the employees exposed to sexual harassment stated that their productivity at work decreased (Çelik & Şenol Çelik, 2007; Kısa & Dziegielewski, 1996; Kısa et al., 2002;) and they were considering quitting their job (Çelik & Şenol Çelik, 2007; Tekin & Bulut, 2014). Kırlıoğlu and Toygar (2020) determined that sexual harassment in nurses negatively affects the quality of work life and their intention to quit. In addition, it is stated that the depression and stress levels of those who are exposed to violence are higher (Aytaç & Dursun, 2013) and their job satisfaction levels are lower than those who are not exposed to violence (Dursun & Aytaç, 2021). According to a study, the emotional exhaustion and desensitization levels of employees who are exposed to any type of violence were found to be statistically significantly higher than those who were not exposed to violence (Dursun, 2012).

Reactions After Exposure to Sexual Harassment

Health workers who are exposed to sexual harassment give various reactions from 'doing nothing' to 'notifying the manager' after the incident. However, health workers who have been sexually harassed mostly exhibit the behavior of 'ignoring the behavior' and 'doing nothing' (Çelik & Şenol Çelik, 2007; Erdemir et al., 2011; Kısa et al., 2002; Ulusoy et al., 2011; Ünlüsoy Dincer, 2012). Avoiding the person, telling the person to stop, remaining unresponsive and silent, moving away from the scene and making jokes about the event are other reactions (Çam & Üstüner- Top, 2021; Çelik & Şenol Çelik, 2007; Erdemir et al., 2011; Kısa et al., 2002; Talas et al., 2011; Ulusoy et al., 2011). Although efforts to change policies and report the incident to management are the most effective methods to prevent harassment, this type of behavior of healthcare personnel is less common than other reactions (Çam & Üstüner- Top, 2021; Çelik & Şenol Çelik, 2007; Kısa et al., 2002; Talas et al., 2011; Ünlüsoy Dinçer, 2012).

CONCLUSION

All kinds of violence occur in health institutions. In addition to verbal, physical and psychological abuse, sexual abuse is also common. Some characteristics of both the victim and the work and healthcare work environment are among the factors that make the health worker open to violence. According to the studies, the fact that the health workers who are female, single, and young may be exposed to violence more. In addition, working in the evening or night shift and being alone in the working environment can also cause exposure to violence. The rates of sexual harassment against healthcare workers are quite high. Among health workers, nurses are the most exposed ones to sexual harassment. Violence against healthcare professionals is mostly perpetrated by patients and their relatives, but healthcare professionals are also exposed to violence in various ways by their co-workers (physician, nurse, other healthcare personnel). When evaluated in terms of sexual harassment, the most common types of sexual harassment are unwanted sexual words and innuendo, obscene-implied looks, coercion to go on a date and touching obscene parts of the body.

After the violence experienced, health workers experience emotional effects such as anger, guilt, fear, humiliation, and helplessness, as well as physical effects such as headaches, sleep problems, nausea and vomiting. However, in response to the sexual harassment experienced, avoidant behaviors such as ignoring, being unresponsive and moving away from the environment are exhibited the most, and they generally do not report the harassment they experience to the institution management.

Work-related productivity of health workers who are exposed to sexual harassment decreases and organizational level results occur. Sexual harassment negatively affects the quality of work life and intention to quit the job. In addition, results such as burnout, decreased job satisfaction, increased depression and stress levels are seen in healthcare workers who are exposed to any type of violence.

Future Research and Directions

As against all forms of violence, health institutions should adopt a "zero tolerance" approach to sexual harassment and aim to prevent such incidents from happening. In particular, sexual harassment is not easily shared because it can make the victim feel guilty. However, both institutional level administrators and political administrators should create a working environment that will enable reporting of sexual harassment incidents and take necessary security measures and implement policies that will prevent all incidents of violence, including sexual harassment. Today, the "health police" practice, which is considered among the measures to be taken against violence, is one of the recommended practices.

REFERENCES

Adams, E.A., Darj, E., Wijewardene, K., & Infanti, J.J. (2019). Perceptions on the sexual harassment of female nurses in a state hospital in Sri Lanka: a qualitative study. *Global Health Action*, *12*(1). doi: 10.1080/16549716.2018.1560587

Arslan, M. (2001). *İş ve Meslek Ahlâkı*. Nobel Yayınları.

Aydemir, İ., Üçlü, R., & Aydoğan, A. (2020). Acil servis personeline göre şiddetin nedenleri [According to the emergency room staff the reasons for violence]. *Journal of Istanbul Faculty of Medicine*, *83*(1), 60–68. doi:10.26650/IUITFD.2019.0018

Aytaç, S., & Dursun, S. (2013). Çalışma hayatında kadına yönelik şiddet: sağlık sektöründe bir uygulama [Violence against women in working life: an application in the health sector]. *Journal of Istanbul University Law Faculty*, *71*(1), 67–78.

Bahji, A., & Altomare, J. (2020). Prevalence of intimidation, harassment, and discrimination among resident physicians: A systematic review and meta-analysis. *Canadian Medical Education Journal*, *11*(1), e97. doi:10.36834/cmej.57019 PMID:32215147

Bakırcı, K. (2000). *İş yerinde cinsel taciz ve Türk iş hukukuna ilişkin çözüm önerileri* [Suggestions for sexual harassment in the workplace and Turkish labor law]. http://www.turkhukuksitesi.com/makale_25.htm

Berdahl, J. L. (2007). Harassment based on sex: Protecting social status in the context of gender hierarchy. *Academy of Management Review, 32*(2), 641–658. doi:10.5465/amr.2007.24351879

Çam, H. H., & Ustuner Top, F. (2021). Workplace violence against nurses working in the public hospitals in Giresun, Turkey: Prevalence, risk factors, and quality of life consequences. *Perspectives in Psychiatric Care*, 1–11. doi:10.1111/ppc.12978 PMID:34860413

Chaudhuri, P. (2007). Experiences of Sexual Harassment of Women Health Workers in Four Hospitals in Kolkata, India. *Reproductive Health Matters, 15*(30), 221–229. doi:10.1016/S0968-8080(07)30319-4 PMID:17938090

Dinçer, Ç. (2006). *İşyerinde cinsel tacizin bayan doktorlar ve hemşireler tarafından algılanmasına yönelik karşılaştırmalı bir alan araştırması [An empirical research about female doctors and nurses perception of sexual harassment at workplace]. Yayımlanmamış yüksek lisans tezi.* Hacettepe Üniversitesi.

Dougherty, T. W., Turban, D. B., Olson, D. E., Dwyer, P. D., & Lapreze, M. W. (1996). Factors affecting perceptions of workplace sexual harassment. *Journal of Organizational Behavior, 17*(5), 489–501. doi:10.1002/(SICI)1099-1379(199609)17:5<489::AID-JOB780>3.0.CO;2-6

Draucker, C. B. (2019). Responses of nurses and other healthcare workers to sexual harassment in the workplace. *Online Journal of Issues in Nursing, 24*(1), 9. doi:10.3912/OJIN.Vol24No01Man03

Durmuş, E. (2013). Cinsel taciz: Üniversite öğrencilerinin algı ve tepkileri [Sexual harassment: university students' perceptions and reactions]. *İnönü Üniversitesi Eğitim Fakültesi Dergisi, 14*(1), 15-30.

Dursun, S. (2012). İşyeri şiddetinin çalışanların tükenmişlik düzeyi üzerine etkisi: Sağlık sektöründe bir uygulama [The effect of workplace violence on employees' level burnout: an application on health sector]. *Çalışma İlişkileri Dergisi, 3*(1), 105-115.

Dursun, S., & Aytaç, S. S. (2021). The prevalence of violence against healthcare workers in Turkey and employee job satisfaction. *Pakistan Journal of Medical & Health Sciences, 15*(6), 1607–1620. doi:10.53350/pjmhs211561607

Edison Research. (2018). *Sexual harassment in the workplace: A marketplace survey.* https://www.edisonresearch.com/sexualharassmentworkplace/

Erdemir, F., Çıtak, E. A., Ulusoy, H., & Geçkil, E. (2011). Hemşirelerin hastalar tarafından cinsel tacize uğrama durumlarının belirlenmesi [Determination of sexual harassment of nurses by patients]. *Hacettepe Üniversitesi Hemşirelik Fakültesi Dergisi, 18*(2), 27–35.

Farkas, A. H., Scholcoff, C., Machen, J. L., Kay, C., Nickoloff, S., Fletcher, K. E., & Jackson, J. L. (2020). The experience of male physicians with sexual and gender-based harassment: A qualitative study. *Journal of General Internal Medicine, 35*(8), 2383–2388. doi:10.100711606-020-05695-4 PMID:32076981

Graf, N. (2018). *Sexual harassment at work in the era of #MeToo.* Pew Research Center. Social and demographic trends. https://www.pewresearch.org/social-trends/2018/04/04/sexual-harassment-at-work-in-the-era-of-metoo/

Hammoud, M. M., Appelbaum, N. P., Wallach, P. M., Burrows, H. L., Kochhar, K., Hemphill, R. R., Daniel, M., Clery, M. J., & Santen, S. A. (2021). Incidence of resident mistreatment in the learning environment across three institutions. *Medical Teacher, 43*(3), 334–340. doi:10.1080/0142159X.2020.1845306 PMID:33222573

International Labour Organization. (2019). *Sexual harassment at work: Insights from the global garment industry.* ILO.

Kahsay, W. G., Negarandeh, R., Dehghan Nayeri, N., & Hasanpour, M. (2020). Sexual harassment against female nurses: A systematic review. *BMC Nursing, 19*(1), 1–12. doi:10.118612912-020-00450-w

Kearl, H. (2018). *The facts behind the #Metoo movement: A national study on sexual harassment and assault.* https://web.archive.org/web/20201127111900/https://ncvc.dspacedirect.org/handle/20.500.11990/790

Khan, N., Begum, S., & Shaheen, A. (2015). Sexual harassment against staff and student nurses in tertiary care Hospitals Peshawar KP Pakistan. *International Journal of Innovative Research and Development, 4*(1), 285–292.

Kirlioğlu, M., & Toygar, Ş. A. (2020). The effects of sexual harassment on quality of nurses' work life and turnover intentions: A sample of Ankara province. *OPUS Uluslararası Toplum Araştırmaları Dergisi, 16*(29), 1613–1627. doi:10.26466/opus.775992

Kisa, A., & Dziegielewski, S. F. (1996). Sexual harassment of female nurses in a hospital in Turkey. *Health Services Management Research, 9*(4), 243–253. doi:10.1177/095148489600900404 PMID:10162521

Kisa, A., Dziegielewski, S. F., & Ates, M. (2002). Sexual harassment and its consequences: A study within Turkish hospitals. *Journal of Health & Social Policy, 15*(1), 77–94. doi:10.1300/J045v15n01_05 PMID:12212934

McLaughlin, H., Uggen, C., & Blackstone, A. (2017). The economic and career effects of sexual harassment on working women. *Gender & Society, 31*(3), 333–358. doi:10.1177/0891243217704631 PMID:29056822

National Academies of Sciences, Engineering, and Medicine. (2018). *Sexual harassment of women: climate, culture, and consequences in academic sciences, engineering, and medicine.* Author.

Phillips, S. P., & Schneider, M. S. (1993). Sexual harassment of female doctors by patients. *The New England Journal of Medicine, 329*(26), 1936–1939. doi:10.1056/NEJM199312233292607 PMID:8247058

Pınar, T., Açıkel, C., Pınar, G., Karabulut, E., Saygun, M., Barışkın, E., Guidotti, T. L., Akdur, R., Sabuncu, H., Bodur, S., Egri, M., Bakir, B., Acikgoz, E. M., Atceken, I., & Cengiz, M. (2017). Workplace violence in the health sector in Turkey: A national study. *Journal of Interpersonal Violence, 32*(15), 2345–2365. doi:10.1177/0886260515591976 PMID:26124224

Pitot, M. A., White, M. A., Edney, E., Mogensen, M. A., Solberg, A., Kattapuram, T., & Kadom, N. (2022). The current state of gender discrimination and sexual harassment in the radiology workplace: A survey. *Academic Radiology*, *29*(3), 416–425. doi:10.1016/j.acra.2021.01.002 PMID:33495074

Robinson, R. K. (n.d.). Sexual harassment in the workplace: Guidelines for educating healthcare managers. *Journal of Health and Human Services Administration*, *27*(4), 501–530. PMID:16318016

Sabak, M., Al-Hadidi, A., Oktay, M. M., Al, B., Kazaz, T., Kowalenko, T., & Hakmeh, W. (2021). Workplace violence in emergency departments in Turkey. *Avicenna Journal of Medicine*, *11*(03), 111–117. doi:10.1055-0041-1732284 PMID:34646787

Sarmaşık, Ş. (2009). *İşyerinde cinsel taciz algılaması ve yönetim ilişkilerine etkisi hakkında bir araştırma [Detection of sexual harassment at work and the research about it effects on management relations].* Yayımlanmamış Yüksek Lisans Tezi, Pamukkale Üniversitesi.

Scholcoff, C., Farkas, A., Machen, J. L., Kay, C., Nickoloff, S., Fletcher, K. E., & Jackson, J. L. (2020). Sexual harassment of female providers by patients: A qualitative study. *Journal of General Internal Medicine*, *35*(10), 2963–2968. doi:10.100711606-020-06018-3 PMID:32700219

Shafran-Tikva, S., Gabay, G., & Kagan, I. (n.d.). Sexual harassment of religious Jewish nurses by patients and its relation to the ward's listening climate, care avoidance and quality of nursing care. *Journal of Nursing Management*, 1-10. doi:10.1111/jonm.13515

Smith, A. M., & Ortiz, R. R. (2021). # Metoo social media engagement and perceived hypersensitivity in the workplace. *Communication Studies*, *72*(4), 531–546. doi:10.1080/10510974.2021.1953091

Spector, P. E., Zhou, Z. E., & Che, X. X. (2014). Nurse exposure to physical and nonphysical violence, bullying, and sexual harassment: A quantitative review. *International Journal of Nursing Studies*, *51*(1), 72–84. doi:10.1016/j.ijnurstu.2013.01.010 PMID:23433725

Talas, M. S., Kocaöz, S., & Akgüç, S. (2011). A survey of violence against staff working in the emergency department in Ankara, Turkey. *Asian Nursing Research*, *5*(4), 197–203. doi:10.1016/j.anr.2011.11.001 PMID:25030520

Tekin, Y. E., & Bulut, H. (2014). Verbal, physical, and sexual abuse status against operating room nurses in Turkey. *Sexuality and Disability*, *32*(1), 85–97. doi:10.100711195-014-9339-7

Toker, Y. (2016). İşyerlerinde cinsel taciz: kapsamı, öncülleri, sonuçları, kurumsal baş etme yöntemleri [Sexual Harassment in the Workplace: Scope, Antecedents, Consequences, Institutional Coping Methods]. *Türk Psikoloji Yazilari*, *19*(38), 1–19.

Toker, Y., & Sümer, H. C. (2010). Workplace sexual harassment perceptions in the Turkish context and the role of individual differences. *Applied Psychology*, *59*(4), 616–646. doi:10.1111/j.1464-0597.2010.00420.x

Ulusoy, H., Swigart, V., & Erdemir, F. (2011). Think globally, act locally: Understanding sexual harassment from a cross-cultural perspective. *Medical Education*, *45*(6), 603–612. doi:10.1111/j.1365-2923.2010.03918.x PMID:21501219

United States Department of Justice. (2010). *Sexual assault definition*. https://web.archive.org/web/20191007043843/https://www.justice.gov/ovw/sexual-assault

Ünlüsoy Dinçer, N. (2012). *Hemşirelerin İşyeri Şiddetine Maruz Kalma Durumları ile İş Doyumları ve İşten Ayrılma Eğilimleri [The violence on nurses at workplace and the tendency to leave the job and job satisfaction of nurses]. Yayımlanmamış doktora tezi*. Hacettepe Üniversitesi.

World Health Organization. (1997, July). *Violence against women: A priority health issue*. https://web.archive.org/web/20201205103604/https://apps.who.int/iris/bitstream/handle/10665/63553/WHO_FRH_WHD_97.8.pdf

Yeşiltaş, M. (2005). İnsan kaynakları yönetimi açısından bir sorun olarak işyerinde cinsel taciz [Sexual harassment in the workplace as a problem for human resources management]. *Manas Üniversitesi Sosyal Bilimler Dergisi*, *7*(13), 147–153.

ADDITIONAL READING

Boland, M. L. (2005). *Sexual harassment in the workplace*. Sphinx Legal.

Celik, Y., & Çelik, S. Ş. (2007). Sexual harassment against nurses in Turkey. *Journal of Nursing Scholarship*, *39*(2), 200–206. doi:10.1111/j.1547-5069.2007.00168.x PMID:17535323

Chan, D. K., Chow, S. Y., Lam, C. B., & Cheung, S. F. (2008). Examining the job-related, psychological, and physical outcomes of workplace sexual harassment: A meta-analytic review. *Psychology of Women Quarterly*, *32*(4), 362–376. doi:10.1111/j.1471-6402.2008.00451.x

Cortina, L. M., & Wasti, S. A. (2005). Profiles in coping: Responses to sexual harassment across persons, organizations, and cultures. *The Journal of Applied Psychology*, *90*(1), 182–192. doi:10.1037/0021-9010.90.1.182 PMID:15641899

Hoff, L. A. (2009). *Violence and abuse issues: Cross-cultural perspectives for health and social services*. Routledge. doi:10.4324/9780203875629

Hunt, C. M., Davidson, M. J., Fielden, S. L., & Hoel, H. (2010). Reviewing sexual harassment in the workplace – an intervention model. *Personnel Review*, *39*(5), 655–673. doi:10.1108/00483481011064190

Kabat-Farr, D., & Crumley, E. T. (2019). Sexual harassment in healthcare: A psychological perspective. *Online Journal of Issues in Nursing*, *24*(1), 1–12. doi:10.3912/OJIN.Vol24No01Man04

Solmuş, T. (2005). İş yaşamında travmalar: Cinsel taciz ve duygusal zorbalık/taciz (mobbing). *ISGUC The Journal of Industrial Relations and Human Resources*, *7*(2), 1–14. doi:10.4026/1303-2860.2005.0016.x

KEY TERMS AND DEFINITIONS

Harassment: Disturbing behavior that does not contain an offensive element.
Health Institutions: Institutions where inpatient or outpatient health services are provided.
Health Police: Police trained and assigned for violence in health institutions.
Healthcare Workers: Employees involved in health service provision.

Sexual Harassment: Undesirable behavior that neglects sexual privacy but does not include sexual assault.

Violence: Harmful acts performed physically, mentally, or verbally.

Zero Tolerance: Strict and uncompromising rejection of behavior.

Chapter 18
Effects of Bullying on Child Health

İlknur Yıldız
Sivas Cumhuriyet University, Turkey

ABSTRACT

Bullying is an important problem that concerns children, families, and society. In this chapter, the effects of bullying on children's health are discussed. The aim of the chapter is to reveal the effects of bullying on the health of children and adolescents in all aspects and to determine the measures that can be taken to prevent these effects. The chapter focuses on the definition of bullying; its types, prevalence; physical, psychological, and long-term effects; and preventive approaches. It is thought that the information in the chapter will contribute to all professionals working with children.

INTRODUCTION

Bullying, which is widespread among children and adolescents and has serious lasting consequences, is an important public health problem. Preventing and recognizing bullying and developing solutions for its consequences are important to a child's healthy growth and development. Early action and intervention can prevent or minimize the serious negative consequences of bullying. Families, educators, health professionals, and society play a crucial role in this regard. This section discusses the definition, types, prevalence, effects, and prevention of bullying.

Definition of Bullying

Bullying is defined as aggressive behavior by a stronger person or persons toward a less strong person intended to cause harm and often recurs over time (APA Resolution on Bullying Among Children and Youth, 2004; Gürhan, 2017). Dan Olweus (1994), who conducted the first studies on bullying, stated that three criteria must be met for a behavior to be judged as bullying:

1. Aggressive behavior with the intent to cause harm,

DOI: 10.4018/978-1-6684-5426-8.ch018

2. Continuous behavior,
3. An imbalance of power between the bully and victim.

In addition, Dan Olweus (1994) stated that bullying behavior usually occurs without overt provocation and can be considered peer abuse.

Until the 1970s, bullying was accepted as normal in child development. However, bullying drives children to suicide in Norway, which has led to this situation being considered an abnormal and important problem. Studies on bullying started in Norway and then continued in many different countries such as England, America, Japan, Austria, Ireland, Canada, Israel, Italy, Greece, and the Netherlands (Pişkin, 2002; Kartal & Bilgin, 2007; Karataş & Öztürk, 2009).

Aggression, violence, and bullying are related terms. Bullying is a subset of aggression and is considered a specific type of violent behaviour (Kartal & Bilgin, 2012). For an act to be considered bullying, it must not only be offensive but also have a purpose, be ongoing, and there must be an imbalance of power between the parties (Pişkin, 2002; Gürhan, 2017; Dolgun, 2018; Süner et.al.,2021).

Many factors can play a role in the aggressive behavior of bullies. These are as follows;

- In the early years, the caregivers', especially the mother's, emotional attitude toward the child is very important. Negative emotional attitudes, such as warmth and lack of interest, can increase the child's risk of being aggressive and hostile toward others later in life.
- If the caregiver tolerates the child's aggressive behavior toward peers, siblings, and adults and does not set clear boundaries, this can increase the child's level of aggression.
- Parents who use parenting methods that involve physical punishment and violent emotional responses to the child may cause the child to become more aggressive.

It is said that children who get angry quickly may be more aggressive in the future compared to calm children (Olweus, 1994).

TYPES OF BULLYING

Bullying is mostly seen in schools and workplaces in all areas of life, and it is experienced in various forms and a wide range such as physical, verbal, sexual, homophobic, religious, racial, or cyberbullying (APA Resolution on Bullying Among Children and Youth, 2004; Dolgun, 2018). Physical bullying is seen in the form of pushing, punching, kicking, harming people and their belongings; direct verbal bullying is seen in the form of mocking, slandering, name-calling, insulting, and threatening; and indirect and emotional bullying is seen in the form of covert behaviors that harm peer relationships, self-esteem, or social status (Dolgun, 2018; Armitage, 2021). Bullying can be direct or indirect. While direct bullying takes the form of overt attacks such as hitting, pushing, teasing, and threatening, indirect bullying takes the form of behaviors such as exclusion from the group, spreading gossip, and embarrassment (Kartal &Bilgin 2007). The peer relationships and resulting peer bullying are defined as the constant negative actions of one or more students against another student (Süner et.al., 2021; Avşar & Ayaz-Alkaya 2018). Bullying is widespread among children. According to the UNICEF (2019) report, half of the students between the ages of 13-15 around the world (approximately 150 million students) are exposed to peer bullying in and around the school. In addition to the traditional types of bullying, including peer bullying, cyberbullying has become a problem as another type of bullying with the advance in technology that draws attention and needs to be addressed urgently due to the increase in its prevalence and severity (Meral & Çağlar, 2021).

Cyberbullying is defined as intentional, harmful, and repeated behavior toward one or more individuals via digital technologies such as email, instant messaging and social media, and the Internet, using smartphones, computers, and other electronic devices (Taştekin &Bayhan, 2018; Kavurucu &Küçük, 2021; Meral & Çağlar, 2021). Because cyberbullying can reach a larger audience anonymously at any time, it can have more negative consequences than traditional types of bullying (Kavurucu & Küçük, 2021). Considering that children and young people widely use digital technologies, the risk of cyberbullying or victimization is quite high. According to the study results on the use of information technologies among children (2021), in 2013, it was 50.8% for children in the age group of 6-15 years, while it was 82.7% in 2021 (Information Technologies Use in Children Research, 2021). It is noted that cyberbullying is especially prevalent among adolescents and that adolescents attempt to harm the relationships or status of their peers through cyberbullying (Meral & Çağlar, 2021). According to the U-Report, a youth engagement tool, one in three teens in 30 countries is bullied online (UNICEF, 2019). A study comparing the rates of traditional and cyberbullying concluded that the victimization rate for traditional bullying was 25.13%, and the use rate was 5.27%. In comparison, the victimization rate for cyberbullying was 7.02%, and the use rate was 3.45%, and it was concluded that bullying is widespread among children and adolescents (Jadambaa et.al.,2019).

Prevalence

Bullying is a global and common problem that results from a complex interaction of both environmental and individual factors (Demir & Küçük, 2020; Armitage, 2021). The United Nations Educational, Scientific and Cultural Organization (UNESCO) report states that nearly one in three children around the world is exposed to bullying. According to the data from the Global School-based Student Health Survey (GSHS), the prevalence of bullying is 31.7% in North America, 25% in Europe, 41% in the Middle East, and 48.2% in sub-Saharan Africa (UNESCO, 2019). According to the report by the Organization for Economic Cooperation and Development (OECD), 19% of students at the age of 15 in Turkey are exposed to physical or verbal violence by their peers at least a few times a month (Demir & Küçük, 2020). It is estimated that about 20% of adolescents were bullied at school, and about 16% were affected by cyberbullying (Stephens et.al., 2018). In the study conducted to determine the victimization by traditional bullying and cyberbullying among high school students in the U.S., the results of the Youth Risk Behavior Survey 2011-2019 were examined, and it was found that the prevalence of victimization by bullying is 19.74% for traditional bullying and 15.38% for cyberbullying (Li et.al.,2020). This result shows that the victimization rates for both types of bullying are very close. In examining the relationship between bullying and age, it was found that bullying generally increases in middle school and decreases in high school (Nansel et.al., 2001; Hong & Espelage, 2012; Kartal & Bilgin, 2007). In middle school and early adolescence, aggressive behavior may occur due to children's discovery of new social roles and their search for status within their peer groups. In high school, bullying is at a lower level due to the development of social skills (Pellegrini, 2002 as cited in Hong & Espelage, 2012; Kartal & Bilgin 2007). In general, the incidence of bullying increases with age, while the incidence of being victimized decreases with age (Olweus, 1994; Pişkin, 2002). In addition, the type of bullying is found to change with age. Physical bullying is more common among students in small classes, and verbal bullying is more common among students in large classes (Pişkin, 2002). In a study conducted with 1221 primary school students in Australia, it was found that one in three children experience verbal bullying, physical bullying, or both verbal and physical bullying at least once a week (Bayer et.al., 2018). It was found that 22.7% of children and adolescents ages 6-17 in the U.S. are bullied, and 6.4% bully others, with slightly higher victimization rates among children ages 6-11 than among children ages 12-17 (Lebrun-Harris et.al., 2019). When bullying is examined by gender, it is found that both bullying and victimization rates are higher for boys than girls, although the study findings differ (Nansel et.al., 2001; Pişkin, 2002; Karataş & Öztürk, 2009; Hong & Espelage, 2012). It was found that boys are mostly exposed to direct physical bullying in hitting, kicking, and pushing by boys. At the same time, girls mostly experience indirect bullying with verbal content such as name-calling, taunting, mocking, and rumors about both genders (Olweus, 1994; Pişkin, 2002). A study conducted to determine the prevalence of bullying among secondary school students in Turkey found that female students are bullied verbally, and male students are bullied by spreading rumors (Gökkaya & Tekinsav Sütçü, 2020). It is found that bullying mainly affects girls who tell it to their close environment, while boys do not tell anyone about the bullying (Pişkin, 2002).

In bullying behavior, the bullies are the people who exhibit and continue to exhibit the bullying behaviors; the bully-victims are the people who are sometimes the victim and sometimes the bully, hence at greater risk since it is uncertain when they will be the victim and when they will be the bully; and the victims are the generally powerless, and vulnerable people who have been harmed by the actions, behaviors, or words of other person or persons (Pişkin, 2002; Gürhan, 2017; Dolgun, 2018).

If we examine the characteristics of bullies, we can see that they are aggressive towards adults and their peers, do not follow the rules and have a positive attitude towards violence (Olweus, 1994). Most of them are unaware of their aggression; they do not feel uncomfortable in this situation, and they have a positive attitude towards themselves. They have a quick temper, act reactively and have a low level of self-control. They feel the need to control others and events. They are not uncomfortable with the victim's suffering but rejoice when the victim suffers and argue that the victim provokes them. They have little empathy for their victims. In addition, bullies have low anxiety levels and high self-esteem. Their problem-solving skills are inadequate (Pişkin, 2002; Gökler, 2009). In a study conducted to determine risk and protective factors as predictors of adolescent bullying roles, the predictors of bullying were gender, substance use, truancy, attention deficit hyperactivity disorder (ADHD), moral neutralization, self-control, parental monitoring, physical punishment, preference for school, commitment to teachers, and classmates (Zych et.al.,2021).

Victims are anxious, insecure, reserved, introverted, and quiet. They have low self-esteem and perceive themselves as unsuccessful and shy. They generally have poor social skills, have difficulty making friends, have few friends, and are ostracized by their peers. Victims do not exhibit aggressive behavior; they have negative attitudes toward violence. It is stated that they cannot defend themselves when confronted with bullying; the younger ones cry and withdraw, especially males appearing physically weak (Pişkin, 2002; Gökler, 2009). Although physical appearance is the most common trigger of childhood bullying, it is stated that children who are perceived as different from others in any way have a high risk of being victimized (Armitage, 2021). In a study conducted to determine elementary school students' perceptions of the causes of bullying, it was found that the most commonly cited reason for bullying was physical weakness (Kartal & Bilgin, 2012). In youth people, differences in sexual orientation, any illness or disability, or outliers in height and weight can be risk factors for being a victim of bullying (Stephens et.al., 2018).

Both the bully and the bully-victim have low self-esteem and social skills, exhibit impulsive behavior, are easily provoked and provoke others. In addition to the bully, the victim, and the bully-victim, there are also bystanders/witnesses (Pişkin, 2002; Dolgun, 2018). In a study conducted to determine bullying among peers in secondary school, it was found that 2.8% of 1740 students were bullies, 34.9% were victims, 27% were bully-victims, and 35.3% were bystanders. Male students and eighth-graders were more likely to be bully-victims (Gökkaya & Tekinsav Sütçü, 2020). In another study conducted with secondary students, it was found that 3.4% of 340 students were bullies, 26.9% were victims, 60.8% were bullies/victims, and 8.6% were non-bullies (Siyez & Kaya, 2011). In a study conducted with 5183 elementary school students in seven European countries, 14.3% of children were defined as bullies, 18.2% as victims, and 19.0% as both bullies and victims (Husky et.al.,2020).

THE EFFECTS AND RESULTS OF BULLYING

Childhood bullying has serious effects on physical and mental health and may lead to significant consequences (Stephens et.al., 2018; Armitage, 2021). These effects are felt by everyone in the bullying cycle, including bullies, victims, and victims of bullying, and continue into adulthood (Arslan et.al., 2012; Armitage, 2021). Considering that those who witness bullying are also physically and emotionally affected, it is reasonable to assume that the rate and impact of children and youth exposed to bullying are higher than expected. When a child experiences bullying in any form, they exhibit physiological and psychosomatic responses to stress (Demir & Küçük, 2020). It is also stated that there is a significant relationship between the frequency and intensity of bullying and the severity of the health problems it causes (Armitage, 2021).

Physical Effects

It is found that most of the physical effects of bullying are psychosomatic problems, including insomnia, dizziness, headaches, stomach aches, and digestive problems (Stephens et.al., 2018; Hansson et.al., 2020; Armitage, 2021). It was found that about eight out of ten students who were bullied in Iceland reported weekly pain, and the frequency of pain, including neck, shoulder, head, stomach, and back pain, was higher among bullied students than among their non-bullied peers (Garmy et al., 2019). Children and adolescents exposed to bullying are more likely to suffer from health problems such as depression, difficulty falling asleep, and dizziness than those who have not been bullied (Hansson et.al., 2020). Children and adolescents with health problems such as asthma and obesity are highly likely to be bullies, victims, or bullies/victims, both in-person and online. Healthy eating habits and regular physical activity reduce bullying and bullying victimization (Jennings et.al., 2019; Waasdorp et.al., 2019). Being a victim of bullying in the traditional sense has exacerbated physical and psychological problems for obese and overweight adolescents (Lee et.al., 2018).

Psychological Effects

In general, the negative psychological consequences of childhood bullying are experienced most by bullying victims, followed by victims and bullies. In the studies on the effects of bullying, it has been found that those who have been bullied suffer from crying, anger, restlessness, irritability, sadness, emotional distress, depression, anxiety, social isolation, low self-esteem, internalizing problems, externalizing problems, and alexithymic symptoms (Karataş & Öztürk, 2011; Stephens et.al., 2018; Livingston et.al., 2019; Prino et. al., 2019). In addition, school bullying victims have weak relationships with parents, teachers, and peers and exhibit low personal health perceptions and life satisfaction (Chai et.al., 2020). School bullying and cyberbullying are associated with anxiety, depression, psychosocial difficulties, and self-injurious behaviors among secondary and high school students in Turkey, decreasing their subjective well-being and causing them to experience more emotional and behavioral problems (Arslan et.al., 2021; Eyuboğlu et. al., 2021). In a study conducted in European countries, bullying was associated with psychological problems in elementary school students, the bully-victims suffer from externalizing disorder and victims suffer from a generalized anxiety disorder, and bullies suffer from separation anxiety (Husky et.al., 2020). In Pakistan, both victims and perpetrators of bullying were found to experience negative emotional and social consequences (Naveed et.al., 2019). In addition, bullying has been found to reduce the quality of life of children, and there is a negative relationship between the level of bullying and quality of life (Hidalgo-Rasmussen et.al., 2018; Xiao et.al., 2021). The association between childhood bullying and suicidal thoughts and behaviors has been recognized worldwide (Armitage, 2021). It is found that especially in children who are victims of bullying, depression and suicidal thoughts are strong, and they are more likely to attempt suicide (Katsaras et.al 2018; Zhang et.al 2019; Cao et.al. 2020).

Bullying also adversely impacts the educational life of children and adolescents. Bullying can affect the continuity of educational participation and lead to truancy, reluctance to go to school, and poorer academic performance. It is claimed that children frequently bullied are twice as likely to drop out of school as children who are not bullied (Armitage, 2021).

EFFECTS OF CYBERBULLYING

Traditional bullying is considered the main form of bullying that affects the mental health of children and adolescents. However, cyberbullying, which has been on the rise in recent years, causes negative physical and mental health problems for both victims and bullies. It is found that nine out of ten adolescents who report being victims of cyberbullying are also victims of traditional bullying, meaning cyberbullying creates very few additional victims (Armitage, 2021). Various physical and psychological problems such as sleep disturbances, stomachaches, headaches, anxiety, fear, depression, suicidal thoughts, and lowered self-esteem are more common in children and adolescents exposed to cyberbullying (Armitage, 2021; Kavurucu & Küçük, 2021). Studies conducted with adolescents have found that psychological cyberbullying is most strongly associated with mental health problems in both genders compared to other types of bullying. In addition, victims of cyberbullying are more likely to have suicidal thoughts and attempts than victims of traditional bullying (Katsaras et.al., 2018).

Long-term Effects

The effects of bullying on children and adolescents are found to last into adulthood and have the potential to lead to long-term negative consequences (Wolke & Lereya, 2015; Demir & Küçük, 2020). It is stated that childhood bullying can lead to three main problems in adulthood: psychopathology, suicide and delinquency in the victim, bully and bully-victims (Armitage, 2021). Childhood bullying victimization has had surprising effects on mental health in adulthood, with young adults and people in middle adulthood (18-50 years) consistently at higher risk for internalizing problems, particularly diagnoses of anxiety disorders and depression. It is stated that there is a strong relationship between the frequency of bullying in childhood and adolescence and the problems experienced in adulthood, and its effects continue until at least the age of fifty (Stapinski et.al., 2014; Wolke & Lereya, 2015; Armitage, 2021).

PREVENTING BULLYING

Bullying was considered a normal situation for children until recently. However, when its effects and consequences are considered, it should be accepted as an urgent problem that requires attention (Armitage, 2021). It is accepted that family relationships are an important factor in bullying behavior and being exposed to bullying, and family also plays an important role in preventing bullying (Özada & Duyan, 2018; Süner et.al., 2021). For this reason, the family should be included when preparing and implementing interventions in order to prevent and reduce bullying behaviour (Özada & Duyan, 2018). The American Academy of Pediatrics recommends that parents be interviewed about bullying in the follow-up of healthy six-year-old children (Committee on Injury, Violence, and Poison Prevention,2009). Interventions that focus on helping young parents whose children are at high risk to acquire effective parenting skills can reduce bullying and violent behaviors. Providing parents with accurate and open information about bullying and its effects can directly impact their ability to better participate in shared decision-making and improve their children's overall health (Stephens et.al., 2018; Armitage, 2021).

It is stated that school-based interventions significantly reduce bullying behavior in children and adolescents. School-based approaches that involve a high level of participation from multiple disciplines are approaches to teaching positive behavior and social-emotional skills in the school and classroom environment (Demir &Küçük, 2021). The best-known approach is the Olweus Bullying Prevention Program (OBPP), which aims to develop peer relationships in schools, reduce bullying, and prevent the development of new bullying behaviors (Demir & Küçük, 2021; Armitage, 2021). Another approach is the Positive Behavioral Intervention and Support Programs, which aim to improve quality of life with approaches that engage all students in the school and enable them to acquire social behavior skills. On the other hand, social-emotional support programs focus on interpersonal processes in peer bullying, such as recognizing and managing social-emotional skills, respecting others' perspectives, and establishing and maintaining positive relationships (Demir & Küçük, 2021).

It is very important to develop effective interventions for cyberbullying because it is less prevalent than traditional bullying but has higher suicide rates. Children and adolescents may be more reluctant to admit or disclose that they have been cyberbullied for fear that their online time will be restricted, or their digital devices will be confiscated (Stephens et.al., 2018). It is said that developing problem-solving skills, peer support, and family and teacher training can effectively prevent cyberbullying among children and adolescents (Kavurucu & Küçük, 2021). Cyberbullying intervention programs are typically school-based interventions that can reduce the impact of the short-term consequences of bullying. Therefore, it is emphasized that interventions should be developed to address the long-term consequences (Hutson et.al.,2018).

Considering the short and long-term effects of bullying on the health of the child, it is an issue that must be addressed by health professionals (Wolke & Lereya 2015). However, there are no clear information and referral pathways showing how to manage bullying and where to direct it for health professionals who encounter childhood bullying. For this reason, there is a need to educate health workers about the consequences of childhood bullying, recognize such cases, and raise their awareness. Some anti-bullying organizations offer counselling and training opportunities for children affected by bullying, their families, teachers, and health professionals (Armitage, 2021).

Prevention, detection, and intervention of bullying require teamwork from various disciplines such as teachers, nurses, psychologists, psychological counsellors, and physicians (Avşar & Ayaz-Alkaya, 2018; Süner et.al., 2021). As a link between the primary care and education systems, school nurses should follow the signs by observing the students who are at higher risk or who have the characteristics of a victim or a bully (Avşar & Ayaz-Alkaya, 2018). Local and national prevention and intervention programs should be developed and implemented widely. High-risk groups can be identified by performing regular screenings. Children affected by bullying and their families should be followed up and supported regardless of their side in the bullying situation (Stephens et.al., 2018; Süner et.al., 2021).

Once bullying is uncovered, it is important to assess its physical, psychological, and educational effects comprehensively. A comprehensive, multi-faceted approach that includes family, school, and community can help address bullying. Children affected by bullying may feel anxious or guilty about disclosing the bullying and fear that the violence and intensity of the bullying will increase. In this situation, it can be helpful to explain to children that disclosing the bullying can help end the cycle of bullying, not only for themselves but also for others. (Stephens et.al., 2018). At the 40th General Conference of UNESCO, 193 Member States unanimously declared the first Thursday of November of every year as the International Day against School Violence, Bullying, and Cyberbullying.

FUTURE RESEARCH DIRECTIONS

Bullying impacts every aspect of children's health. Even its effects last for many years. Although there are several studies in the literature on the health effects of bullying, more research can be conducted on the short and long-term consequences. Comprehensive intervention programs can be developed to prevent bullying and resolve bullying cases. Because bullying is long-lasting, screening and follow-up studies to determine these effects are beneficial.

CONCLUSION

Bullying is an important problem that affects the health and development of children and adolescents. Children are exposed to bullying in various ways, either directly or indirectly. In recent years, cyberbullying has been added to the traditional forms of bullying and is becoming more common. All types of bullying harm a child's health, leading to health problems with both short and long-term effects. To prevent bullying, it is recommended that the risk factors are identified, screenings are conducted for the detection and results, and intervention programs are developed. All professionals working with families, society, and children should be trained on this topic. The children affected by bullying and their families should be monitored and supported concerning the effects of bullying.

REFERENCES

APA Resolution on Bullying Among Children and Youth. (2004). Available from https://www.apa.org/about/policy/bullying.pdf

AraştırmasıÇ. B. T. K. (2021). Available from https://data.tuik.gov.tr/Bulten/Index?p=Cocuklarda-Bilisim-Teknolojileri-Kullanim-Arastirmasi-2021-41132

Armitage, R. (2021). Bullying in children: Impact on child health. *BMJ Paediatrics Open*, *5*(1), e000939. doi:10.1136/bmjpo-2020-000939 PMID:33782656

Arslan, G., Allen, K. A., & Tanhan, A. (2021). School bullying, mental health, and wellbeing in adolescents: Mediating impact of positive psychological orientations. *Child Indicators Research, 14*(3), 1007–1026. doi:10.100712187-020-09780-2

Arslan, S., Hallett, V., Akkaş, E., & Akkaş, O. A. (2012). Bullying and victimization among Turkish children and adolescents: Examining prevalence and associated health symptoms. *European Journal of Pediatrics, 171*(10), 1549–1557. doi:10.100700431-012-1782-9 PMID:22735980

Avşar, F., & Ayaz-Alkaya, S. (2018). Akran zorbalığının önlenmesinde okul sağlığı hemşiresinin rolü [The role of school health nurses in the prevention of peer bullying]. *Journal of Hacettepe University Faculty of Nursing*, *5*(1), 78–84.

Bayer, J. K., Mundy, L., Stokes, I., Hearps, S., Allen, N., & Patton, G. (2018). Bullying, mental health and friendship in Australian primary school children. *Child and Adolescent Mental Health*, *23*(4), 334–340. doi:10.1111/camh.12261 PMID:32677138

Cao, Q., Xu, X., Xiang, H., Yang, Y., Peng, P., & Xu, S. (2020). Bullying victimization and suicidal ideation among Chinese left-behind children: Mediating effect of loneliness and moderating effect of gender. *Children and Youth Services Review*, *111*, 104848. doi:10.1016/j.childyouth.2020.104848

Chai, L., Xueb, J., & Hanc, Z. (2020). School bullying victimization and self-rated health and life satisfaction: The mediating effect of relationships with parents, teachers, and peers. *Children and Youth Services Review*, *117*, 105281. doi:10.1016/j.childyouth.2020.105281

Committee on Injury, Violence, and Poison Prevention. (2009). Role of the pediatrician in youth violence prevention. *Pediatrics, 124*(1), 393–402.

Demir, K., & Küçük, S. (2020). Akran zorbalığı önleme ve müdahale programlarında güncel yaklaşımlar ve hemşirelik rolleri [Current approaches and nursing roles in peer bullying prevention and intervention programs]. *Türkiye Sağlık Bilimleri ve Araştırmaları Dergisi*, *3*(2), 87–102.

Dolgun, G. (2018). Akran zorbalığını önlemede hemşirenin rolü [Role of nurse in peer bullying prevention]. *Sağlık Bilimleri ve Meslekleri Dergisi*, *5*(1), 95–101. doi:10.17681/hsp.335312

Eyuboğlu, M., Eyuboğlu, D., Pala, S. C., Oktar, D., Demirtaş, Z., Arslantaş, D., & Ünsal, A. (2021). Traditional school bullying and cyberbullying: Prevalence, the effect on mental health problems and self-harm behavior. *Psychiatry Research*, *297*, 113730. doi:10.1016/j.psychres.2021.113730 PMID:33486274

Garmy, P., Hansson, E., Vilhjálmsson, R. & Kristjánsdóttir, G. (2019). Bullying and pain in school-aged children and adolescents: a cross-sectional study. *SAGE Open Nursing. 10*, 5.

Gökkaya, F., & Tekinsav Sütcü, S. (2020). Akran zorbalığının ortaokul öğrencileri arasındaki yaygınlığının incelenmesi [An investigation of the prevalence of peer bullying among middle school students]. *Hacettepe University Journal of Education, 35*(1), 40–54.

Gökler, R. (2009). Okullarda akran zorbalığı [Peer bullying in schools]. *International Journal of Human Sciences, 6*(2), 511–537.

Gürhan, N. (2017). Her yönü ile akran zorbalığı [All aspects of the bullying]. *Türkiye Klinikleri J Psychiatr Nurs-Special Topics, 3*(2), 175–181.

Hansson, E., Garmy, P., Vilhjálmsson, R., & Kristjánsdóttir, G. (2020). Bullying, health complaints, and self-rated health among school-aged children and adolescents. *The Journal of International Medical Research, 48*(2), 1–9. doi:10.1177/0300060519895355 PMID:32054367

Hidalgo-Rasmussen, C. A., Ramírez-López, G., Rajmil, L., Skalicky, A., & Martín, A. H. (2018). Bullying and health-related quality of life in children and adolescent Mexican students. *Ciencia & Saude Coletiva, 23*(7), 2433–2441. doi:10.1590/1413-81232018237.16392016 PMID:30020395

Hong, J. S., & Espelage, D. L. (2012). A review of research on bullying and peer victimization in school: An ecological system analysis. *Aggression and Violent Behavior, 17*(4), 311–322. doi:10.1016/j.avb.2012.03.003

Husky, M. M., Delbasty, E., Bitfoi, A., Carta, M. G., Goelitz, D., Koç, C., Lesinskiene, S., Mihova, Z., Otten, R., & Kovess-Masfety, V. (2020). Bullying involvement and self-reported mental health in elementary school children across Europe. *Child Abuse & Neglect, 107*, 104601. doi:10.1016/j.chiabu.2020.104601 PMID:32570185

Hutson, E., Kelly, S., & Militello, L. K. (2018). Systematic review of cyberbullying interventions for youth and parents with implications for evidence-based practice. *Worldviews on Evidence-Based Nursing, 15*(1), 72–79. doi:10.1111/wvn.12257 PMID:28859246

Jadambaa, A., Thomas, H. J., Scott, J. G., Graves, N., Brain, D., & Pacella, R. (2019). Prevalence of traditional bullying and cyberbullying among children and adolescents in Australia: A systematic review and meta-analysis. *The Australian and New Zealand Journal of Psychiatry, 53*(9), 878–888. doi:10.1177/0004867419846393 PMID:31067987

Jennings, W. G., Song, H., Kim, J., Fenimore, D. M., & Piquero, A. R. (2019). An examination of bullying and physical health problems in adolescence among South Korean youth. *Journal of Child and Family Studies, 28*(9), 2510–2521. doi:10.100710826-017-0885-3

Karataş, H., & Öztürk, C. (2009). Sosyal bilişsel teori ile zorbalığa yaklaşım [Approach to bullying with social cognitive theory]. *Dokuz Eylül Üniversitesi Hemşirelik Yüksekokulu Elektronik Dergisi, 2*(2), 61–74.

Karataş, H., & Öztürk, C. (2011). Relationship between bullying and health problems in primary school children. *Asian Nursing Research, 5*(2), 81–87. doi:10.1016/S1976-1317(11)60016-9 PMID:25030257

Kartal, H., & Bilgin, A. (2007). İlköğretim öğrencilerine yönelik bir zorbalık karşıtı program uygulaması: Okulu zorbalıktan arındırma programı [An implementation of an anti-bullying program for elementary school students: bully proofing your school]. *Journal of Theory and Practice in Education*, *3*(2), 207–227.

Kartal, H., & Bilgin, A. (2012). İlköğretim öğrencilerinin zorbalığın nedenleri ile ilgili algıları [The perceptions of elementary students about the reasons for bullying]. *Gaziantep Üniversitesi Sosyal Bilimler Dergisi*, *11*(1), 25–48.

Katsaras, G. N., Vouloumanou, E. K., Kourlaba, G., Kyritsi, E., Evagelou, E., & Bakoula, C. (2018). Bullying and suicidality in children and adolescents without predisposing factors: A systematic review and meta-analysis. *Adolescent Research Review*, *3*(2), 193–217. doi:10.100740894-018-0081-8

Kavurucu, Ö., & Küçük, L. (2021). Çağın gelişen sorunu siber zorbalık: çocuk ve ergenlerde siber zorbalığı önleme [Cyberbullying, the emerging problem of the age: prevention of cyberbullying in children and adolescents]. *Medical Research Reports*, *4*(3), 50–56.

Lebrun-Harris, L., Sherman, L. J., Limber, S. P., Miller, B. D., & Edgerton, E. A. (2019). Bullying victimization and perpetration among U.S. children and adolescents: 2016. National Survey of Children's Health. *Journal of Child and Family Studies*, *2*(9), 2543–2557. doi:10.100710826-018-1170-9

Lee, B., Jeong, S. & Roh, M. (2018). Association between body mass index and health outcomes among adolescents: the mediating role of traditional and cyber bullying victimization. *BMC Public Health*, *18*(1), 674.

Li, R., Lian, Q., Su, Q., Li, L., Xie, M., & Hu, J. (2020). Trends and sex disparities in school bullying victimization among U.S. youth, 2011–2019. *BMC Public Health*, *20*(1), 1583. doi:10.118612889-020-09677-3 PMID:33087087

Livingston, J. A., Derrick, J. L., Wang, W., Testa, M., Nickerson, A. B., Espelage, D. L., & Miller, K. E. (2019). Proximal association among bullying, mood, and substance use: A daily report study. *Journal of Child and Family Studies*, *28*(9), 2558–2571. doi:10.100710826-018-1109-1 PMID:32269466

Meral, B., & Çağlar, S. (2021). Siber zorbalık: çocuklarda zorbalığın yeni dönemi ve hemşirelik yaklaşımları [Cyber bullying: the new period of childhood and nursing approaches in children]. *Dokuz Eylül Üniversitesi Hemsirelik Fakültesi Elektronik Dergisi*, *14*(3), 261–267.

Nansel, T. R., Overpeck, M., Pilla, R. S., Ruan, W. J., Simons-Morton, B., & Scheidt, P. (2001). Bullying behaviors among US youth: Prevalence and association with psychosocial adjustment. *Journal of the American Medical Association*, *285*(16), 2094–2100. doi:10.1001/jama.285.16.2094 PMID:11311098

Naveed, S., Waqas, A., Aedma, K. K., Tayyaba Afzaal, T., & Majeed, M. H. (2019). Association of bullying experiences with depressive symptoms and psychosocial functioning among school going children and adolescents. *BMC Research Notes*, *12*(1), 198. doi:10.118613104-019-4236-x PMID:30940177

Olweus, D. (1994). Annotation: bullying at school: basic facts and effects of a school based intervention program. *Child Psychology & Psychiatry & Allied Disciplines*, *35*(7), 1171–1190. doi:10.1111/j.1469-7610.1994.tb01229.x PMID:7806605

Özada, A., & Duyan, V. (2018). Ebeveyn-çocuk ilişkisi ve zorbalık [Parent-child relationships and bullying]. *Turkish Journal of Family Medicine and Primary Care*, *12*(1), 49–55. doi:10.21763/tjfmpc.399941

Pişkin, M. (2002). Okul zorbalığı, tanımı, türleri, ilişkili olduğu faktörler ve alınabilecek önlemler [School bullying: Definition, types, related factors, and strategies to prevent bullying problems]. *Educational Sciences: Theory and Practice*, *2*, 531–562.

Prino, L. E., Longobardi, C., Fabris, M. A., Parada, R. H., & Settanni, M. (2019). Effects of bullying victimization on internalizing and externalizing symptoms: The mediating role of alexithymia. *Journal of Child and Family Studies*, *28*(9), 2586–2593. doi:10.100710826-019-01484-8

Siyez, D., & Kaya, A. (2011). Akran zorbalığı gruplarında empatik eğilim [Empathic tendency in the peer bullying groups]. *Inonu University Journal of the Faculty of Education*, *12*(2), 23–43.

Stapinski, L. A., Bowes, L., Wolke, D., Pearson, R. M., Mahedy, L., Button, K. S., Lewis, G., & Araya, R. (2014). Peer victimization during adolescence and risk for anxiety disorders in adulthood: A prospective cohort study. *Depression and Anxiety*, *31*(7), 574–582. doi:10.1002/da.22270 PMID:24788688

Stephens, M. M., Cook-Fasano, H. T., & Sibbaluca, K. (2018). Childhood bullying: Implications for physicians. *American Family Physician*, *97*(3), 187–192. PMID:29431974

Süner, A. F., Emli Alpay, E., & Ünal, B. (2022). Akran zorbalığına kısa bir bakış: birinci basamak sağlık çalışanlarına tavsiyeler [A brief overview of peer bullying: Recommendations to primary care workers]. *Sürekli Tıp Eğitimi Dergisi*, *30*(6), 444–450.

Taştekin, E., & Bayhan, P. (2018). Ergenler arasındaki siber zorbalığın ve mağduriyetin incelenmesi [Examination of cyber bullying and victimization among adolescents]. *Online Journal of Technology Addiction & Cyberbullying*, *5*(2), 21–45.

UNESCO. (2020). *International day against violence and bullying at school including cyberbullying 2020*. Available from https://www.unesco.org/en/days/againts-school-violence-and-bullying-day

UNICEF. (2019) Available from https://www.unicef.org/turkey/bas%C4%B1n-b%C3%BCltenleri/unicef-d%C3%BCnyadaki-gen%C3%A7lerin-yar%C4%B1s%C4%B1-okulda-ve-okul-%C3%A7evresinde-akran-%C5%9Fiddetine-maruz

UNICEF. (2019). Available from https://www.unicef.org/turkey/bas%C4%B1n-b%C3%BCltenleri/unicef-anketi-30-%C3%BClkedeki-gen%C3%A7lerin-%C3%BC%C3%A7te-birinden-fazlas%C4%B1-%C3%A7evrimi%C3%A7i-zorbal%C4%B1k

United Nations Educational, Scientific and Cultural Organization (UNESCO). (2019). *Behind the numbers: ending school violence and bullying*. Available from https://unesdoc.unesco.org/ark:/48223/pf0000366483

Waasdorp, T. E., Mehari, K. R., Milam, A. J., & Bradshaw, C. P. (2019). Health-related risks for involvement in bullying among middle and high school youth. *Journal of Child and Family Studies*, *28*(9), 2606–2617. doi:10.100710826-018-1260-8

Wolke, D., & Lereya, S. T. (2015). Long-term effects of bullying. *Archives of Disease in Childhood*, *100*(9), 879–885. doi:10.1136/archdischild-2014-306667 PMID:25670406

Xiao, H., Gong, Z., Ba, Z., Doolan-Noble, F., & Han, Z. (2021). School bullying and health-related quality of life in Chinese school-aged children and adolescents. *Children & Society, 35*(6), 885–900. doi:10.1111/chso.12465

Zhang, H., Chi, P., Long, H., & Ren, X. (2019). Bullying victimization and depression among left-behind children in rural China: Roles of self-compassion and hope. *Child Abuse & Neglect, 96*, 104072. doi:10.1016/j.chiabu.2019.104072 PMID:31319239

Zych, I., Farrington, D. P., Llorent, V. J., Ribeaud, D., & Eisner, M. P. (2021). Childhood risk and protective factors as predictors of adolescent bullying roles. *International Journal of Bullying Prevention, 3*(2), 138–146. doi:10.100742380-020-00068-1

ADDITIONAL READING

Fraguas, D., Díaz-Caneja, C. M., Ayora, M., Durán-Cutilla, M., Abregú-Crespo, R., Ezquiaga-Bravo, I., Martín-Babarro, J., & Arango, C. (2021). Assessment of School Anti-Bullying Interventions: A Meta-analysis of Randomized Clinical Trials. *JAMA Pediatrics, 175*(1), 44–55. doi:10.1001/jamapediatrics.2020.3541 PMID:33136156

Moore, S. E., Norman, R. E., Suetani, S., Thomas, H. J., Sly, P. D., & Scott, J. G. (2017). Consequences of bullying victimization in childhood and adolescence: A systematic review and meta-analysis. *World Journal of Psychiatry, 7*(1), 60–76. doi:10.5498/wjp.v7.i1.60 PMID:28401049

KEY TERMS AND DEFINITIONS

Aggression: Intentional behavior and actions aimed at hurting or harming others.

Bully: Individuals who deliberately and constantly act in a way that causes discomfort to their peers who are physically or psychologically weaker than themselves.

Bully-Victim: Individuals who are both bully and victim who are bullied while being bullied.

Cyberbullying: It is bullying that takes place in a virtual environment using digital technologies.

Health: A state of complete physical, social, and mental well-being, not the absence of disease or infirmity.

Traditional Bullying: Bullying that takes place in face-to-face settings.

Victim: Individuals who are constantly exposed to the words and actions of their peers who are stronger than themselves, with the aim of harming them.

Violence: All kinds of attitudes and behaviors that result in or are likely to result in physical, sexual, psychological or economic loss and harm by applying the power to another person, self, a group or a society.

Chapter 19
Physical Bullying Towards Children

Mehmet Kanak
Sivas Cumhuriyet University, Turkey

Serpil Pekdoğan
İnönü University, Turkey

ABSTRACT

Physical abuse is the state of harming the child's body by the people around him. Scars of unknown cause, traces resulting from burning, spots due to impact on any part of the body, traces caused by a bite by another person, bruises and stains caused by squeezing with any tool, burns and scars caused by smoking cigarettes on the victim reflect physical abuse. Problems such as rumination disorders, problems in socialization, lack of self-respect, depression, fear of all situations, withdrawal behaviors, incompatibility, colic, problems in mental perception processes, and decreased academic achievement are observed in these children.

INTRODUCTION

Bullying is defined as repetitive aggressive behaviors that cause stress and pain to the victim, which are applied psychologically, socially, physically, and verbally against those who have no power to oppose, for their own pleasure and interests (Besag, 1989). Physical bullying is the intentional and persistent harassment of the weak by the physically strong, such as kicking, beating, pushing, slapping, pulling ear or hair, hitting, taking or threatening to take their belongings by force, exacting or intimidate to take their money (Alper, 2008).

Since the concept of bullying is an act of attack against those who have no power, the concept of physical abuse is also discussed as a whole with the concept of physical bullying throughout present study. In this context, physical bullying is violence that causes tissue damage to the child, whether it leaves a mark on the child's body or not, such as hitting, pushing, or beating, burning or biting in anger for any reason (Heyman et al., 2020; Koç et al. 2014; Tıraşçı et al., 2007). Torturing a child includes ac-

DOI: 10.4018/978-1-6684-5426-8.ch019

tions such as throwing any harmful substance on the child, sticking and throwing sharp objects to harm his/her body (Yalçın, 2011). Sun and Cao (2020) conducted a study on explaining physical bullying in Chinese secondary schools and found that there was a social relationship between those who reported being a victim of bullying and those who bulliedin the past 6 months. In other words, according to the results of the research, bullies are generally people who know the child.

TYPES OF PHYSICAL ABUSE

Bullying behaviors towards children are divided into various classifications according to the way they are practiced and form the types of physical abuse. According to the studies examined, the types of physical abuse are listed as follows.

Yalçın (2011) classified physical abuse under seven headings according to the way it is applied in his thesis named Child Abuse and Solution Suggestions in Turkey. These headings are respectively non-instrumental aggressions, instrumental aggressions, poisoning, water intoxication, Munchausen by Proxy Syndrome, and shaken baby syndrome.

- **Non-instrumental aggressions** are direct attacks without using any tools. In these cases, the abuser makes attacks such as slapping, jostling, rumpling, hitting (Soyer, 2018). In addition to these, behaviors such as pinching, forcefully stuffing food into the mouth, closing the mouth with hands, throttling, kicking are also indicators of non-instrumental aggressions.
- **Instrumental aggression** are the use of any tool in a physical attack. For example, it is the application of tools such as hose, pillow, iron, stick to the child's body in a harmful way. Likewise, actions such as hitting with slippers, damaging with household items, beating with a belt, extinguishing cigarettes on the body can be examples of instrumental aggressions (Hançerli Ekdal, 2011; Polat, 2014).
- **Poisoning** is toxication of a child with a harmful substance knowingly and willingly. The consumption of inappropriate drugs and chemicals. is an example for this.
- **Water poisoning** is when a child is forced to drink large amounts of water (Yalçın, 2011).
- **Munchausen by Proxy syndrome** is when the individual who takes care of the child produces disease scenarios about the child, even though the child is not sick, takes him to hospitals and exposes him to a lot of unnecessary examinations (Jakobi et al, 2010).
- **Shaken baby syndrome (SBS)** usually occurs when an infant aged less than 6 months up to the age of two is held by the shoulders or arms and shaken violently. May cause injury to the brain and neck area. It is a syndrome that occurs when babies shake too fast while they are put to sleep. It can cause serious brain damage (Christian, 2009; Jakobi et al, 2010).

In addition to this classification, Jakobi et al (2010) considered the following types as physical bullying. These are:

- **Blunt trauma** consists of bruises and crushes on the body. It does not consist of cutting and driller tools. Injuries due to impact are seen on the lips, mouth and teeth. There are bruises caused by holding too tight. Fractures or bites may occur. Abdominal trauma due to hit may be seen.

- **Thermal injuries** consist of abuse such as scalding and burns. There are cigarette burns on the hands and burns caused by heating various tools.

Berkowitz (2017) classified physical bullying under four headings. These are head trauma due to bullying, abdominal trauma, skin and intraoral findings and fractures.

- It has been stated that babies younger than one year of age are more at risk for **head trauma due to bullying.** Babies may have symptoms such as lameness, vomiting, and swelling of the scalp. Retinal bleedings have been observed in approximately 85% of children with head trauma.
- It has been observed that 3% to 4% of children with **abdominal traumas** have increased liver or pancreatic enzymes. It has been shown that it affect toddlers more.
- **Skin and oral findings** are seen in children as bruising, handprint, belt welt on any part of the body or scalding with boiling water.
- **Fractures** usually occur by tightening the baby, mostly rib fractures occur. Skull fractures are very rare.

The manifestations of physical bullying are quite diverse.

- **Skin injuries:** It consists of ecchymoses, pole scars, fractures, visceral injuries, and head trauma.
- **Skeletal system lesions:** Fractures, luxations.
- **Visceral organ injuries:** types of abuse such as chest, abdominal trauma, head trauma, and growth retardation have been observed (Koç et al, 2014).

In a study, it was seen that ecchymoses on the arms and legs are caused by the adult holding the child tightly to shake it, those on the hips are caused by hitting, face and mouth wounds are caused by slapping, and the wounds on the abdomen are caused by finger pressure by adults (Wang, Baz, & Berchtel, 2007). In addition, in cases of abuse skull fractures, head traumas, visceral organ injuries, rib fractures, internal bleeding in the abdomen, ingestion of toxic substances, bruising on the skin, bite marks, burns (scalding, hot metal etc.), eye and endaural bleeding are seen (Kara et al., 2004). For example, spanking a child on the hip for touching a prohibited or liked object (Straus, 1994). Physical bullying behaviors that parents apply to their children are mostly in the form of spanking or hitting with a belt (Lawson et al., 2020).

EFFECTS OF PHYSICAL BULLYING TOWARDS CHILDREN

Early childhood is an important period in which children's social emotional skills develop and their cognitive thinking skills are shaped. Children interact positively and negatively with their peers by shaping their social skills. In this direction, children may be exposed to bullying by their peers. Considering that children have not yet developed a sense of conscience as a characteristic of this period, children may not be aware that their behavior is bullying. At this point, the most important role falls upon parents and teachers. In order to diagnose and prevent bullying, we must first know what bullying is. Olweus (1996) has defined bullying as a repetitive action that intentionally harms another person by including a power imbalance. The power imbalance between the bully and the victim can be physical strength or psychological strength (Perren & Alsaker 2006).

Physical bullying, as a direct attack on the victim, which is one of the types of direct bullying, and can be observed more easily compared to other types of bullying, involves hitting, damaging their belongings, kicking, pushing, pinching, pulling hair, slapping, throwing, tripping, hitting, taking their belongings without permission and punching (Olweus, 1996). Salmivalli (2010) identified six roles of bullying as bully, victim, helper, supporter, outsider, and defender. While the bullying child is defined as the bully, the bullied child is defined as the victim.

Gender and age bullying behaviors also affect peer relations differently. In some studies, it is stated that boys display more physical and verbal bullying behavior than girls do, while girls use relational bullying more (Monks et al., 2009). Some of the researchers examining the change in bullying behaviors according to age have stated that physical bullying decreases as children get older. Sapouna examined the issue of bullying in Greek primary and secondary schools from various perspectives in 2008 and found that significant gender differences in types of victimization occur only for physical bullying, which is more common in boys. Temel et al. (2018) also stated that as a result of their research, boys are more commonly bullied and exposed to physical bullying than girls.

When the literature studies on physical bullying, which causes extremely negative experiences on children in the physical, mental and academic sense, are examined, there are studies examining the effects on the psychosocial adaptation of the child (Bulut Serin,2016; Gürhan, 2017; Hawker & Boulton, 2000; Silverman vd., 1996; Vanderbilt &Augustyn, 2010; Weiler & Widom, 1996), its long-term effects on the person (Schwartz, 1999 et al.; Wolke & Lereya, 2015; Beitchman et al., 1992; Smokowski et al., 2009), its effects on various health problems (Akduman, 2012; Beitchman et al., 1992; Schacter et al., 2021; (Wolke & Lereya, 2015), and its effects on school success (Uysal & Dinçer, 2012; Nakamoto & Schwartz, 2010; Jan & Husain, 2015; Al-Bitar et al., 2013).

When the literature is examined, the psychosocial problems caused by physical bullying are summarized as follows.

Akduman (2012) concluded in his study that children who are exposed to physical bullying have different effects in the future, such as bedwetting, introversion, irregular sleep, aggression, loneliness and submissiveness. Gürhan (2017) stated in a study,in which he investigated peer bullying in all aspects, that bullied children cause effects such as fatigue, social alienation, low self-esteem and stress disorder, as well as mental problems.

Bulut Serin (2016) argues in his study that children exposed to violence experience different emotions and behaviors such as feelings of guilt, outbursts of anger, deterioration in social relations, lack of attention, loss of self-esteem, hatred towards authority, feelings of worthlessness, disrupting classroom discipline and risk-taking behaviors.Wolke and Lereya (2015) stated in their study that they examined the long-term effect of bullying, that children who were bullied experiencedheadaches, stomachaches or sleep problems, internalization problems, hatred of authority, lack of attention, loss of self-esteem, poor peer relationships, psychosis, poor self-perception, and depression problems. They also stated that victimized children who have been bullied have more problems in making or keeping friends compared to their peers even in their adult years, and they need social support.

Vanderbilt and Augustyn (2010) found in their study that victims had more depression, psychosomatic complaints, drug use, poor peer relationships, and suicidal tendencies. Long-term adulthood consequences of being bullied as a child include psychosis, depression, and poor self-image.

The psychological effects of bullying can be summarized as fear of school, school hatred in children, children who are bullied have more negative thoughts and low self-esteem than their peers who are not, experience anxiety and depression problems, and tend to suicidal behavior (Olweus, 1993; Hawker &

Boulton, 2008; Kapcı, 2004). It has been observed that children who are both bullied and who engage in bullying behavior (bully-victim) have higher rates of depression, loneliness, alcohol use, carrying a gun, and weaker peer relationships, and they find it justified to bring guns to school. Bully-victims have higher rates of anxiety and antisocial personality disorders (Vanderbilt & Augustyn, 2010).

When the effect of being bullied on children's characteristics is examined, it is seen that the victims are more obedient, have less leadership skills, are more introverted, more isolated, less cooperative, and less social (Perren & Alsaker, 2006). It has been concluded that victims are characterized by features such as submissiveness-withdrawal, low level of assertiveness-prosociability, and poor academic functioning (Tom et al., 2010).

When we examine the consequences of childhood bullying in adulthood, namely the long-term effects, it was seen that these children's depression rates, anxiety levels and suicidal tendencies in adulthood were higher than their peers who were not bullied. Being bullied makes it difficult to stay in emotional well-being in adulthood. Being bullied also affects social relationships in adulthood. It has been found that children who are bullied are more likely to live without a spouse or partner at age 50, have poor social relationships, and are less likely to access social support when they are sick. In summary, being bullied in childhood affects victims not only in terms of mental health, but also socially and economically (Takizawa et al., 2014; Camodeca & Nava, 2022).

The effects of bullying on social cognition can be summarized as victims' becoming more sensitive to threats, focusing on negative or threatening social cues, recording cues less accurately in general, perceiving their peers more negatively and attributing more hostile intentions to them, and being more sensitive to rejection (Kellij et al., 2022).

Ma, Han, and Kang (2022) in their study on corporal punishment, physical abuse and child behavior problems in South Korea found that parental physical abuse of the child was associated with child behavior problems. They also concluded that exposure to corporal punishment and physical abuse was associated with high levels of aggression, depression, and low levels of academic achievement. Temel et al. (2018) in their study, which aimed to examine the relationship between witnessing or being exposed to physical violence and their self-perceptions of 5-6 year old children, they found that as the frequency of mild violence witnessed or exposed by children increased, their self-efficacy and self-esteem levels decreased.

In studies examining the effects in terms of health;

When we look at the effects of exposure to violence on the child's body, it is understood that the telomeres of the children who are exposed to two or more types of violence are shortened, they have an eating disorder with limbic system dysfunction, they experience sleep problems at a higher rate, and they have a shorter sleep duration (Shalev et al., 2013; Mercurio. et al., 2020; Pei et al., 2022).

Litwiller and Brausch (2013), in their study investigating the role of violent behavior and substance use in cyberbullying and physical bullying in adolescent suicides, examined whether three behavioral outcomes most often associated with bullying and suicidal behavior, substance use, violent behavior, and unsafe sexual behavior mediate the frequently observed relationship between being a victim of bullying and adolescent suicidal behavior.In present study, two types of bullying, cyber bullying and bullying with physical violence, were examined. Overall, the results revealed that both types of bullying, cyber and physical, positively predicted suicidal behavior, substance use, violent behavior, and unsafe sexual behavior.

On the other hand, Schacter et al. (2021) has argued in his study that victimized children and adolescents are at risk of experiencing physical health problems. These health problems are caused by somatization and are symptoms that children themselves can notice (eg, headaches and stomachaches).

Others turned out to be symptoms that could only be identified through biological sampling (eg, cortisol dysregulation, inflammation).

It has been understood that being bullied causes many negative effects in terms of both physical and psychological health of the person. It has been observed that individuals with a history of bullying show blunted cardiovascular responses to social stress, have more physiological responses to rejection, and experience symptoms of bedtime fears, night terrors, and insomnia (Newman, 2014; Donoghue & Meltzer, 2018).

In addition, social exclusion caused sleep problems in some of them, as well as loss of appetite (Skarstein et al., 2020). Tharp-Tylor et al (2009)., in their study on mental and physical bullying and exposure to substance use in early adolescence, examined the relationship between exposure to mental and physical bullying and the use of alcohol, cigarettes, marijuana, and volatile substance abuse among secondary school students. It was seen that the results supported the relationship between bullying and victimization caused by substance use.

Bullying also negatively affects the education life of the child. It has been understood that bullying reduces the educational performance in high school, causes children to skip classes and drop out of high school, the educational performance of those who are exposed to bullying at high school is also negatively affected, and the rate of graduation from university decreases (Nikolaou, 2022).

RISK FACTORS OF PHYSICAL BULLYING TOWARDS CHILDREN

There are many risk factors that affect physical bullying against children. At the beginning of these risks are factors such as low socioeconomic level according to the information obtained from mothers, being exposed to violence by their spouse, having a history of violence from their families in childhood, and low self-esteem (Altıparmak et al. 2013). In a study examining the attitudes towards violence in terms of different variables, the reasons for children's inclination to violence (without specifying the order of importance) are listed as follows: being male in terms of gender, being under the influence of the media and friend groups, ascribing some meanings to violence within the framework of social relations, a sense of belonging to school and low self-efficacy perception. (Balkıs et al., 2005). Risk factors for physical bullying can be listed as having a child at a young age, an unhappy marriage, substance use, domestic violence, living with a divorced mother/father, presence of a stepparent, and low-income level. In addition, inadequate social environment, psychological well-being of family members and a history of abuse may also cause negative behaviors (Sunday et al., 2003). In a study examining bullying behaviors in terms of family characteristics, the causes of bullying behaviors of children were stated as living in a broken family, being an only child, socioeconomic level, education level of parents, environment, number of siblings and exposure to violence (Çetin & Danacı, 2016). Different family characteristics such as emotional structure and migration history are highly influential in the formation of bullying and victim roles. Bully children grew up in a disciplined and authoritative home environment with strict rules (Perren et al., 2008).

Children may be exposed to undesirable situations such as neglect and abuse. They may experience restlessness in the home environment for various reasons. Such negativities may cause children to reflect them in different ways at school. Children who are exposed to violence may use violence, and some may display an introverted attitude by internalizing their parents who are exposed to violence. This often causes them to become victims for bullying children (Uysal & Dinçer, 2012). The causes of school bullying are grouped under two headings as those arising from the child's family and environment due to physical and psychological reasons arising from the child himself. It is possible to state that the reasons arising from the child's self-esteem are high/low self-esteem, anger level and other personality traits (Koç, 2007). Children who have not been able to establish close friendships and do not feel part of the school are more likely to engage in risky behaviors (Thomas, Sandra & Smith, 2004).

In a study examining the causes of bullying in primary schools, it was stated that children who were bullied sought revenge and tried to act like a bully. In addition, it was observed that girls who were bullied were more absent than boys (Jan & Husain, 2015). A significant portion of the victims of bullying reported that they skipped school, did not want to be in the classroom, and did not like school more than those who were not bullied. In addition, in this study, it was determined that children are more likely to be bullied by bullies due to their dentofacial characteristics (jaw and dental disorders) (Al-Bitar et al., 2013).

Güçlü and Acemioğlu (2020) examined physical abuse experienced in early childhood in terms of physical abuse of children aged 3-17, gender, education level of parents, and the number of children in the family. According to the findings of the study, it was seen that the most frequently abused children were 12 years old and the majority of them were boys. They found a decrease in the rate of physical abuse as the child's age progressed. They stated that as the education level of the parents increased, they used less violence. They also found that the rate of abuse of first children was higher than the others. When the results of the research are examined, it can be counted among the main risk factors that the child's gender, being young and being the first child of the family. It has been determined that the testosterone hormone secreted in males due to the Y chromosome is associated with aggressive behavior. General nervousness, irregular eating and sleeping habits, negative mood states, difficulties in adapting to the new situation cause aggression and behavioral disorders (Pearce, 1992). In an example of a child's age being a risk factor, Naidoo (2000) aimed to profile head, face and neck injuries in child abuse cases on the Cape Peninsula in Cape Town, South Africa. It has been determined that children younger than 2 years of age are at the highest risk of abuse and that physical abuse is experienced at a high rate in the child's own home. He stated that the face was the most frequently injured part of the body, and the cheek was the most frequently injured part. He stated that oral-facial injuries generally include skull fractures, cerebral hemorrhage, retinal hemorrhages, bruises, burns and ruptures.

Dukes, Stein, and Zane (2010) examined the relationship between gender differences in the relative impact of physical and relational bullying on adolescent injuries and carrying a gun and conducted a study evaluating the simultaneous relationships between physical bullying, relational bullying, physical victimization, relational victimization, injury, and carrying a gun. It was found that relational bullying was a significantly stronger predictor of carrying a gun than physical bullying for both genders, and both types of bullying were significant predictors of carrying more guns. In addition, it was concluded that being a victim of physical bullying, being a victim of relational bullying or being a relational bully predicted significantly more injury for both genders. In hidden mean comparisons, adolescent girls reported more relational victimization and adolescent boys reported more physical bullying and victimization. Again, the conclusion of this study that male gender is a higher risk factor for physical bullying is clearly observed.

Berger (2005), in his study titled income, family characteristics and physical violence against children, stated that the presence of depression in the mother, alcohol consumption and domestic violence history of the mother had a great effect on the exposure of children to bullying behaviors. In addition, it has been concluded that income has a significant share in terms of domestic violence in physical abuse of children in single-parent families compared to two-parent families.

PREVALENCE OF PHYSICAL BULLYING TOWARDS CHILDREN

It is seen that physical bullying towards children is very common today. Under this heading, research findings on the prevalence of physical bullying have been shared in the literature. It is stated that approximately 250 million children in the 2-4 age group are beaten at home. This means that two out of every three children in that age group in the world are beaten (UNICEF, 2017).

Tsur, Katz, and Klebanov (2021) in their study titled "I have no fur to protect me": The painful experience reported by children in forensic interviews following parental physical abuse, found as a result of the thematic analysis of the interviews with children that while children emphasized the intense pain they experienced during bullying, they ignored this pain and ignored it in their statements.

In their study of the increasing rate of physical child abuse injuries at a level I pediatric trauma center during the Covid-19 outbreak, Kovler et al. (2021) found an increase in the rate of traumatic injuries caused by physical abuse of children at home due to mandatory social distancing measures to reduce the spread of the coronavirus, with children averaging 11,5 months old.

Güçlü and Acemioğlu conducted a study in 2020 aimed at examining physical abuse experienced in early childhood. In this direction, the physical abuse of children and the variables of age, gender, family ranking and parental education level were tried to be examined with the scientific method. As a result of the research, it was determined that 10.94% of the children who were subjected to physical abuse were 12 years old, and 10.45% were 5 years old and 8 years old. 0.90% of the children are in the 17 age group. It was observed that 45.77% of the children who experienced physical abuse were the first child in the family, 27.3% were the second child, and 18.4% were the third child. Within the scope of the education level variable, it was concluded that the education levels of the parents of the children in the 3, 4, 5, 6 and 7 age groups were closer to each other. Parents of children aged 7 and 12 showed concentration at the undergraduate education level.

In the study conducted by Petska et al. (2019), 7.9% of children between 2 weeks and 59 months of age who were suspected of being physically abused stated that they were also exposed to hidden drugs. They found that the detected drug substance was mostly cocaine.

Aslan and Tuğrul investigated the content analysis of bullying and victimization behaviors in preschool children's games in 2014. In present study, it is aimed to reveal the content of bullying and victimization behaviors that occur during the games of children attending kindergarten. As a result of the research, more physical and relational bullying behaviors emerged in the games of children with high relational bullying scores. On the other hand, it was revealed that children with high physical bullying scores were exposed to more physical bullying behaviors. Among the physical bullying and victimization behaviors, the behaviors of forcibly taking the toy or object from the friend's hand and pushing the friend emerged. While it was determined that threatening one's friend and excluding him/her from the game/group emerged the most among relational bullying behaviors, it was determined that ignoring/disregarding one's friend and exclusion from the game/group mostly emerged from relational victimization behaviors.

Damashek, McDiarmid Nelson, and Bonner (2013) examined the characteristics of victims, families, and alleged perpetrators of fatal maltreatment of children in 685 cases identified by child welfare services in the US state of Oklahoma over a 21-year period. The children are mostly younger than 5 years old and the most alleged perpetrators are their parents. It has been determined that men are more likely to commit physical abuse among alleged perpetrators. It has been determined that 51% of the cases resulting in death are due to neglect, and the perpetrators of neglect are more likely to be women and to be biologically related to the victim.

Friedman, Sheppard, and Friedman (2012) examined cases of suspected child maltreatment admitted to hospitals in Illinois, USA, over a 10-year period. They found that maltreated children were significantly more likely to die during hospitalization than their non-maltreated peers. The primary cause of death in maltreated children was from severe traumatic brain injuries, accounting for the majority of Shaken Baby Syndrome cases included in this study.

Çankaya conducted a study on peer bullying in primary education in 2011. The aim of this research is to determine the bullying behaviors of the students attending the eighth grade of primary education from their peers. It has been determined that the most common bullying behaviors students encounter are verbal and physical bullying behaviors. It was determined that boys were exposed to more bullying behaviors than girls were. They shared the conclusion that the prevalence is higher in boys.

Kepenekçi and Çınkır conducted a study on child abuse and neglect in 2006. The aim of this study is to investigate school bullying among public high school students in Turkey. All of the students participating in the research stated that they had been bullied at least once, and the result of the research was that they were exposed to physical bullying the most with 35.5%.

Starling, Heller and Jenny (2002) aimed to determine whether pelvic fractures in infants were defined as suspicious for child physical abuse in the literature. They found that the most common fractures in abused children were metaphysis, rib, skull and long bone fractures. Pelvic fractures in children are relatively rare and were not among the fractures considered to be abuse-specific in children. Based on the case and the literature, they stated that pelvic fractures should be considered highly suspicious in terms of child physical abuse.

CONCLUSION

Physical bullying behavior towards children has become one of the main problems of today. Bullying is defined as a weak child being subjected to painful violence by someone stronger than himself/herself, and many reasons are considered as a risk factor for this bullying against the child. Springer et al., (2007) stated in their study that physical bullying behaviors by parents in childhood negatively affect mental and physical health in middle age, and these effects can be reduced according to age, gender, family history and childhood adversities, but they cannot be eliminated.

A child who has been bullied may not be able to explain the situation to his family immediately (Pişkin, 2002). That's why we need to pay attention to behaviors that indicate bullying. For example, they may be frightenedon the way to or from school, cry and make excuses not to go to school, avoid school or insist on being taken to school by us, come home with damaged clothes or belongings, not want to do homework, or start to stutter introvertedly, lose self-confidence and loss of appetite can be seen, crying in his/her sleep, and even exhibiting persistently anxious behaviors such as behaving irritably to family members - constantly asking for money - stealing (Kepenekci & Çınkır, 2003).

As a result, when the literature is examined, it is seen that physical bullying affects the child negatively in every aspect. Since physical bullying is more visible than other types of bullying, it allows parents or teachers to take preventive measures to prevent children from being exposed to this bullying or to make quicker decisions and practices to prevent bullying from turning into a chronic form.

FUTURE RESEARCH AND DIRECTIONS

Physical bullying is the easiest to spot because it leaves visible scars. Unfortunately, starting from the pre-school period, it is seen that people frequently encounter physical bullying in every developmental period. Sometimes this bullying can be done by parents, sometimes by teachers, and sometimes by peers and partners in our relationships. Physical bullying is a method generally used by people who have problems with emotion regulation. Fighting physical bullying is primarily possible with primary prevention efforts. It is an important requirement to make more scientific publications in this field for primary prevention studies to be more effective.

REFERENCES

Akduman, G. (2012). Okul öncesi dönemde akran zorbaliğin incelenmesi [Examination of peer bullying in preschool period]. *Gazi Üniversitesi. Toplum ve Sosyal Hizmet Dergisi, 23*(1), 121–138.

Al-Bitar, Z. B., Al-Omari, I. K., Sonbol, H. N., Al-Ahmad, H. T., & Cunningham, S. J. (2013). Bullying among Jordanian school children, its effects on school performance, and the contribution of general physical and dentofacial features. *American Journal of Orthodontics and Dentofacial Orthopedics, 144*(6), 872–878. doi:10.1016/j.ajodo.2013.08.016 PMID:24286910

Alper, S. İ. (2008). *İlköğretimde zorbalık* [Bullying in primary education] [Unpublished master's thesis]. Uludağ Üniversitesi, Sosyal Bilimler Enstitüsü, Bursa.

Altiparmak, S., Yildirim, G., Yardimci, F., & Ergin, D. (2013). Annelerden alınan bilgilerle çocuk istismarı ve etkileyen etkenler [Child abuse and influencing factors with information obtained from mothers]. *Anatolian Journal of Psychiatry, 14*(4), 354–361. doi:10.5455/apd.39819

Balkıs, M., Duru, E., & Buluş, M. (2005). Şiddete yönelik tutumların özyeterlik, medya, şiddete yönelik inanç, arkadaş grubu ve okula bağlılık duygusu ile ilişkisi [The relationship of attitudes towards violence with self-efficacy, media, belief towards violence, friendship group and sense of commitment to school]. *Ege Eğitim Dergisi, 6*(2), 81–97.

Beitchman, J. H., Zucker, K. J., Hood, J. E., DaCosta, G. A., Akman, D., & Cassavia, E. (1992). A review of the long-term effects of child sexual abuse. *Child Abuse & Neglect, 16*(1), 101–118. doi:10.1016/0145-2134(92)90011-F PMID:1544021

Berger, L. M. (2005). Income, family characteristics, and physical violence toward children. *Child Abuse & Neglect, 29*(2), 107–133. doi:10.1016/j.chiabu.2004.02.006 PMID:15734178

Berkowitz, C. D. (2017). Physical abuse of children. *The New England Journal of Medicine, 376*(17), 1659–1666. doi:10.1056/NEJMcp1701446 PMID:28445667

Besag, V. E. (1989). *Bullies and victims in schools. A guide to understanding and management.* Open University Press.

Bulut Serin, N. (2012). Erkek ergenlerin anne-baba ve genç yetişkinlerine yönelik duygusal istismar algıları [Perceptions of emotional abuse by male adolescents towards their parents and young adults]. *Türk Uluslararası Özel Eğitim ve Rehberlik ve Danışmanlık Dergisi, 1*(2), 18–26.

Camodeca, M., & Nava, E. (2022). The long-term effects of bullying, victimization, and by stander behavior on emotion regulation and its physiological correlates. *Journal of Interpersonal Violence, 37*(3-4), NP2056–NP2075. doi:10.1177/0886260520934438 PMID:32597723

Cetin, Z., & Danaci, M. O. (2016). A multivariate examination of the child-abuse potential of parents with children aged 0-6. *Eurasian Journal of Educational Research, 16*(66), 71-86.

Christian, C. W., & Block, R. (2009). Abusive head trauma in infants and children. *Pediatrics, 123*(5), 1409–1411. doi:10.1542/peds.2009-0408 PMID:19403508

Damashek, A., Nelson, M. M., & Bonner, B. L. (2013). Fatal child maltreatment: Characteristics of deaths from physical abuse versus neglect. *Child Abuse & Neglect, 37*(10), 735–744. doi:10.1016/j.chiabu.2013.04.014 PMID:23768940

Donoghue, C., & Meltzer, L. J. (2018). Sleep it off: Bullying and sleep disturbances in adolescents. *Journal of Adolescence, 68*(1), 87–93. doi:10.1016/j.adolescence.2018.07.012 PMID:30067959

Dukes, R. L., Stein, J. A., & Zane, J. I. (2010). Gender differences in the relative impact of physical and relational bullying on adolescent injury and weapon carrying. *Journal of School Psychology, 48*(6), 511–532. doi:10.1016/j.jsp.2010.08.001 PMID:21094396

Friedman, L. S., Sheppard, S., & Friedman, D. (2012). A retrospective cohort study of suspected child maltreatment cases resulting in hospitalization. *Injury, 43*(11), 1881–1887. doi:10.1016/j.injury.2012.07.192 PMID:22901423

Güçlü, D. M., & Acemioğlu, R. (2020). Erken çocukluk döneminde yaşanan fiziksel istismar: Nitel bir çalışma [Physical Abuse in the Early Childhood: A Qualitive Study]. *Uluslararası Anadolu Sosyal Bilimler Dergisi, 4*(4), 97–111.

Gürhan, N. (2017). Her yönü ile akran zorbalığı [Bullying in every aspect]. *Turkiye Klinikleri J Psychiatr Nurs-Special Topics, 3*(2), 175–181.

Hançerli Ekdal, S. (2011). *Çocuğun fiziksel istismari: Kuzey Kıbrıs Türk Cumhuriyeti örneği* [Physical abuse of the child: The case of the Turkish Republic of Northern Cyprus] [Unpublished master's thesis]. Polis Akademisi.

Hawker, D. S., & Boulton, M. J. (2000). Twenty years' research on peer victimization and psychosocial maladjustment: A meta-analytic review of cross-sectional studies. *Journal of Child Psychology and Psychiatry, and Allied Disciplines, 41*(4), 441–455. doi:10.1111/1469-7610.00629 PMID:10836674

Heyman, R. E., Snarr, J. D., Slep, A. M. S., Baucom, K. J., & Linkh, D. J. (2020). Self-reporting DSM–5/ICD-11 clinically significant intimate partner violence and child abuse: Convergent and response process validity. *Journal of Family Psychology, 34*(1), 101–111. doi:10.1037/fam0000560 PMID:31328945

Jakobi, A. P., Martens, K., & Wolf, K. D. (Eds.). (2009). *Education in political science*. Routledge. doi:10.4324/9780203873311

Jan, A., & Husain, S. (2015). Bullying in elementary schools: Its causes and effects on students. *Journal of Education and Practice*, *6*(19), 43–56.

Kapçı, E. G. (2004). İlköğretim öğrencilerinin zorbalığa maruz kalma türünün ve sıklığının depresyon, kaygı ve benlik saygısıyla ilişkisi [The relationship between the type and frequency of being bullied in primary school students with depression, anxiety and self-esteem]. *Ankara Üniversitesi Eğitim Bilimleri Fakültesi Dergisi*, *37*(1), 1–13. doi:10.1501/Egifak_0000000087

Kara, B., Biçer, Ü., & Gökalp, A. S. (2004). Çocuk istismarı [Child abuse]. *Çocuk Sagligi ve Hastaliklari Dergisi*, *47*(2), 140–151.

Kellij, S., Lodder, G., van den Bedem, N., Güroğlu, B., & Veenstra, R. (2022). The social cognitions of victims of bullying: A systematic review. *Adolescent Research Review*, *7*(3), 1–48. doi:10.100740894-022-00183-8

Kepenekci, Y.K., & Çınkır, Ş. (2006). Türk lise öğrencileri arasında zorbalık [Bully Among Turkish High School Students]. *Çocuk istismarı ve ihmali, 30*(2), 193-204.

Koç, F., Halıcıoğlu, O., & Akşit, S. (2014). Hangi bulgular fiziksel istismarı düşündürür? [Which findings suggest physical abuse?]. *The Journal of Pediatric Research*, *1*(1), 1–5.

Kovler, M. L., Ziegfeld, S., Ryan, L. M., Goldstein, M. A., Gardner, R., Garcia, A. V., & Nasr, I. W. (2021). Increased proportion of physical child abuse injuries at a level I pediatric trauma center during the Covid-19 pandemic. *Child Abuse & Neglect*, *116*, 104756. doi:10.1016/j.chiabu.2020.104756 PMID:33004213

Lawson, M., Piel, M. H., & Simon, M. (2020). Child maltreatment during the COVID-19 pandemic: Consequences of parental job loss on psychological and physical abuse towards children. *Child Abuse & Neglect*, *110*, 104709. doi:10.1016/j.chiabu.2020.104709 PMID:32893003

Litwiller, B. J., & Brausch, A. M. (2013). Cyber bullying and physical bullying in adolescent suicide: The role of violent behavior and substance use. *Journal of Youth and Adolescence*, *42*(5), 675–684. doi:10.100710964-013-9925-5 PMID:23381779

Ma, J., Han, Y., & Kang, H. R. (2022). Physical punishment, physical abuse, and child behavior problems in South Korea. *Child Abuse & Neglect*, *123*, 123. doi:10.1016/j.chiabu.2021.105385 PMID:34800844

Mercurio, A. E., Hong, F., Amir, C., Tarullo, A. R., Samkavitz, A., Ashy, M., & Malley-Morrison, K. (2022). Relationships among childhood maltreatment, limbic system dysfunction, and eating disorders in college women. *Journal of Interpersonal Violence*, *37*(1-2), 520–537. doi:10.1177/0886260520912590 PMID:32228345

Monks, C. P., Smith, P. K., Naylor, P., Barter, C., Ireland, J. L., & Coyne, I. (2009). Bullying in different contexts: Commonalities, differences and the role of theory. *Aggression and Violent Behavior*, *14*(2), 146–156. doi:10.1016/j.avb.2009.01.004

Naidoo, S. (2000). A profile of the oro-facial injuries in child physical abuse at a children's hospital. *Child Abuse & Neglect*, *24*(4), 521–534. doi:10.1016/S0145-2134(00)00114-9 PMID:10798841

Nakamoto, J., & Schwartz, D. (2010). Is peer victimization associated with academic achievement? A meta-analytic review. *Social Development, 19*(2), 221–242. doi:10.1111/j.1467-9507.2009.00539.x

Newman, M. L. (2014). Here we go again: Bullying history and cardiovascular responses to social exclusion. *Physiology & Behavior, 133*, 76–80. doi:10.1016/j.physbeh.2014.05.014 PMID:24858188

Nikolaou, D. (2022). Bullying, cyberbullying, and youth health behaviors. *Kyklos, 75*(1), 75–105. doi:10.1111/kykl.12286

Olweus, D. (1993). *Bullying at school: What we know and what we can do understanding children's worlds*. Blackwell Publishing Ltd.

Pearce, J. (1992). What can be done about the bullying. In M. Elliot (Ed.), Bullying. A practical guide to coping for schools. Longman.

Pei, F., Yoon, S., Maguire-Jack, K., & Lee, M. Y. (2022). Neighborhood influences on early childhood behavioral problems: Child maltreatment as a mediator. *Child Abuse & Neglect, 123*, 105391. doi:10.1016/j.chiabu.2021.105391 PMID:34768072

Perren, S., & Alsaker, F. D. (2006). Social behavior and peer relationships of victims, bully-victims, and bullies in kindergarten. *Journal of Child Psychology and Psychiatry, and Allied Disciplines, 47*(1), 45–57.

Petska, H. W., Porada, K., Nugent, M., Simpson, P., & Sheets, L. K. (2019). Occult drug exposure in young children evaluated for physical abuse: An opportunity for intervention. *Child Abuse & Neglect, 88*, 412–419.

Pişkin, M. (2002). Okul zorbalığı: Tanımı, türleri, ilişkili olduğu faktörler ve alınabilecek önlemler (School bullying: Definition, types, related factors and measures to be taken). *Kuram ve Uygulamada Eğitim Bilimleri, 2*(2), 531–562.

Polat, O. (2016). Şiddet [Violence]. *Marmara Üniversitesi Hukuk Fakültesi Hukuk Araştırmaları Dergisi, 22*(1), 15–34.

Salmivalli, C. (2010). Bullying and the peer group: A review. *Aggression and Violent Behavior, 15*(2), 112–120. doi:10.1016/j.avb.2009.08.007

Schacter, H. L., Lessard, L. M., Kiperman, S., Bakth, F., Ehrhardt, A., & Uganski, J. (2021). Can friendships protect against the health consequences of peer victimization in adolescence? A systematic review. *School Mental Health, 13*(3), 578–601. doi:10.100712310-021-09417-x

Schwartz, D., McFadyen-Ketchum, S., Dodge, K. A., Pettit, G. S., & Bates, J. E. (1999). Early behavior problems as a predictor of later peer group victimization: Moderators and mediators in the pathways of social risk. *Journal of Abnormal Child Psychology, 27*(3), 191–201. doi:10.1023/A:1021948206165 PMID:10438185

Shalev, I., Moffitt, T. E., Sugden, K., Williams, B., Houts, R. M., Danese, A., Mill, J., Arseneault, L., & Caspi, A. (2013). Exposure to violence during childhood is associated with telomere erosion from 5 to 10 years of age: A longitudinal study. *Molecular Psychiatry, 18*(5), 576–581. doi:10.1038/mp.2012.32 PMID:22525489

Silverman, A. B., Reinherz, H. Z., & Giaconia, R. M. (1996). The long-term sequelae of child and adolescent abuse: A longitudinal community study. *Child Abuse & Neglect, 20*(8), 709–723. doi:10.1016/0145-2134(96)00059-2 PMID:8866117

Skarstein, S., Helseth, S., & Kvarme, L. G. (2020). It hurts inside: A qualitative study investigating social exclusion and bullying among adolescents reporting frequent pain and high use of non- prescription analgesics. *BMC Psychology, 8*(1), 1–9. doi:10.118640359-020-00478-2 PMID:33115532

Smokowski, P. R., David-Ferdon, C., & Stroupe, N. (2009). Acculturation and violence in minority adolescents: A review of the empirical literature. *The Journal of Primary Prevention, 30*(3), 215–263. doi:10.100710935-009-0173-0 PMID:19387835

Soyer, C. (2018). Okul yöneticisi ve öğretmenlerinin görüşlerine göre çocukların cinsel istismar ve ihmalinin değerlendirilmesi [Evaluation of children's sexual abuse and neglect according to the opinions of school administrators and teachers]. *Turkish International Journal of Special Education and Guidance & Counselling, 7*(2), 14-28.

Springer, K. W., Sheridan, J., Kuo, D., & Carnes, M. (2007). Long-term physical and mental health consequences of childhood physical abuse: Results from a large population-based sample of men and women. *Child Abuse & Neglect, 31*(5), 517–530. doi:10.1016/j.chiabu.2007.01.003 PMID:17532465

Starling, S. P., Heller, R. M., & Jenny, C. (2002). Pelvic fractures in infants as a sign of physical abuse. *Child Abuse & Neglect, 26*(5), 475–480. doi:10.1016/S0145-2134(02)00323-X PMID:12079085

Straus, M. A. (1994). State-to-state differences in social inequality and social bonds in relation to assaults, on wives in the United States. *Journal of Comparative Family Studies, 25*(1), 7–24. doi:10.3138/jcfs.25.1.7

Sunday, S., Labruna, V., Kaplan, S., Pelcovitz, D., Newman, J., & Salzinger, S. (2008). Physical abuse during adolescence: Gender differences in the adolescents' perceptions of family functioning and parenting. *Child Abuse & Neglect, 32*(1), 5–18. doi:10.1016/j.chiabu.2007.03.025 PMID:18082259

Takizawa, R., Maughan, B., & Arseneault, L. (2014). Adult health outcomes of childhood bullying victimization: Evidence from a five-decade longitudinal British birth cohort. *The American Journal of Psychiatry, 171*(7), 777–784. doi:10.1176/appi.ajp.2014.13101401 PMID:24743774

Temel, Z. F., Ekicİ, K. B. K., Kanat, K., & Şahin, E. N. (2018). 5-6 Yaş çocuklarinin fiziksel şiddete maruz kalma ya da tanik olmalari ile benlik algilari arasindaki ilişkinin incelenmesi [Examination of the relationship between 5-6 year old children being exposed to or witnessing physical violence and their self-perceptions]. *Sakarya Üniversitesi Eğitim Fakültesi Dergisi*, (35), 109-122.

Tharp-Taylor, S., Haviland, A., & D'Amico, E. J. (2009). Victimization from mental and physical bullying and substance use in early adolescence. *Addictive Behaviors, 34*(6-7), 561–567. doi:10.1016/j.addbeh.2009.03.012 PMID:19398162

Thomas, S. P., & Smith, H. (2004). School connectednes, anger behaviors and relationships of violent and nonviolet American Youth. *Perspectives in Psychiatric Care, 40*(4), 219–228. doi:10.1111/j.1744-6163.2004.tb00011.x PMID:15739755

Tıraşçı, Y., & Gören, S. (2007). Çocuk istismarı ve ihmali [Child abuse and neglect]. *Dicle Tıp Dergisi, 34*(1), 70–74.

Tom, S. R., Schwartz, D., Chang, L., Farver, J. A. M., & Xu, Y. (2010). Correlates of victimization in Hong Kong children's peer groups. *Journal of Applied Developmental Psychology, 31*(1), 27–37. doi:10.1016/j.appdev.2009.06.002

Tsur, N., Katz, C., & Klebanov, B. (2021). "I don't have fur to protect me": Children's experience of pain as communicated in forensic interviews following parental physical abuse. *Children and Youth Services Review, 120*, 105420. doi:10.1016/j.childyouth.2020.105420

Uysal, H., & Dinçer, Ç. (2012). Okul öncesi dönemde akran zorbalığı [Peer bullying in the preschool period]. *Journal of Theoretical Educational Science, 5*(4), 468–483.

Uysal, H., & Dinçer, Ç. (2012). Okul öncesi dönemde akran zorbalığı [Peer bullying in the preschool period]. *Kuramsal Eğitimbilim Dergisi, 5*(4), 468-483.

Vanderbilt, D., & Augustyn, M. (2010). The effects of bullying. *Paediatrics & Child Health, 20*(7), 315–320. doi:10.1016/j.paed.2010.03.008

Wang, N. E., Baz, B., & Bechtel, K. (2007). Physical abuse of children: Identification. Evaluation, and management in the emergency department setting. *Emergency Medicine, 12*(9), 97–108.

Weiler, B. L., & Widom, C. S. (1996). Psychopathy and violent behaviour in abused and neglected young adults. *Criminal Behaviour and Mental Health, 6*(3), 253–271. doi:10.1002/cbm.99

Wolke, D., & Lereya, S. T. (2015). Long-term effects of bullying. *Archives of Disease in Childhood, 100*(9), 879–885. doi:10.1136/archdischild-2014-306667 PMID:25670406

Yalçın, N. (2011). *Türkiye'de çocuk istismari ve çözüm önerileri* [Child abuse and solution proposals in Turkey] [Unpublished master's project]. Beykent Üniversitesi.

Zhang, X., Sun, J., Wang, J., Chen, Q., Cao, D., Wang, J., & Cao, F. (2020). Suicide ideation among pregnant women: The role of different experiences of childhood abuse. *Journal of Affective Disorders, 266*, 182–186. doi:10.1016/j.jad.2020.01.119 PMID:32056874

ADDITIONAL READING

Cadzow, S. P., Armstrong, K. L., & Fraser, J. A. (1999). Stressed parents with infants: Reassessing physical abuse risk factors. *Child Abuse & Neglect, 23*(9), 845–853. doi:10.1016/S0145-2134(99)00063-0 PMID:10505899

Crouch, J. L., & Behl, L. E. (2001). Relationships among parental beliefs in corporal punishment, reported stress, and physical child abuse potential. *Child Abuse & Neglect, 25*(3), 413–419. doi:10.1016/S0145-2134(00)00256-8 PMID:11414399

Zhang, X., Sun, J., Wang, J., Chen, Q., Cao, D., Wang, J., & Cao, F. (2020). Suicide ideation among pregnant women: The role of different experiences of childhood abuse. *Journal of Affective Disorders*, *266*, 182–186. doi:10.1016/j.jad.2020.01.119 PMID:32056874

KEY TERMS AND DEFINITIONS

Beating: It is the harming of children by any tool or physical beating. Scars and bruises are seen in different parts of the body.

Non-Instrumental Aggressions: It is a type of bullying that is not used by any means such as slapping or kicking the child, biting him/her.

Physical Bullying: It is a situation where the child's body is harmed by people stronger than herself around him/her.

Polle Syndrome-Munchausen by Proxy Syndrome: In this syndrome, the child's family acts as if the child has a disease. In this way, the doctor takes his child around. In this way, the child is included in the medical history and the child is harmed.

Shaken Baby Syndrome: It is a negative condition applied to babies under the age of 2 and younger than 6 months. It is the situation where the child is shaken quickly and uncontrollably by the angry and angry family members who want to silence the crying baby.

Chapter 20
Bullying in Schools:
Behaviors and Principles of Prevention

Hülya Şirin
https://orcid.org/0000-0001-8489-5005
University of Health Sciences Gulhane School of Medicine, Turkey

ABSTRACT

Schools are indispensable institutions of society. Necessary measures should be taken to ensure that children can continue their education in safety in schools that concern almost all society. For this reason, the importance given to school health and safety is increasing day by day. Bullying is an important problem that threatens school health and safety and negatively affects the physical, emotional, and spiritual development of the individual. Schools constitute the most important environment where children with different cultural, social, economic, physical, and emotional characteristics come together. Bullying negatively affects the development of children. For this reason, bullying at school should be handled in every aspect, and school policies should be established to prevent it.

INTRODUCTION

Human beings continue their lives together with other people in a structure called society from the moment of birth, which has its own rules in order to continue its existence (Myers & Twenge, 2021). While society helps people to meet their needs and survive, people also contribute to society by assuming different roles and responsibilities. These roles are transferred to individuals by social structures such as school as well as the family (Deb, 2018; Jakes & Debord, 2010).

Schools are one of the most important institutions of the social structure in which individuals gain the culture of socialization and coexistence with others, as well as knowledge and talents. Every individual in the school system has the right to obtain education in a safe school atmosphere (Leach, 2003). The existence of all kinds of bad behavior, bullying and violence at school is against this most basic human right. On the other hand, the reason why schools are seen as risky in terms of bullying is related to the structure of the schools. Schools are places where individuals with different characteristics (physical, social, economic etc.). It is known that individuals who are bullied in schools are also exposed to bul-

DOI: 10.4018/978-1-6684-5426-8.ch020

lying due to their different characteristics (Sullivan et al., 2021). No parent wants their child to face bullying. In this context, it would be appropriate to provide preventive services that prepare children for life in schools so that children with different characteristics can continue their education life safely (Sullivan et al., 2021).

BULLYING IN SCHOOL

School bullying has been emphasized for nearly half a century. It is already known that bullying is a very damaging form of violence, in which some students intentionally attack and harm those who are unable to protect themselves. The definition of bullying has been defined in many way. Bullying is a pattern of behavior that repeatedly and intentionally harms and humiliates others, particularly those that are younger, weaker, younger, or in any way more vulnerable than a bully. Bullying is a form of aggression, but the deliberate targeting of those with less power is what separates bullying from aggression (Dodge & Coie, 1987; D. Olweus, Limber, & Mihalic, 1999; Smith et al., 1999; Olafsen & Viemerö, 2000; Espelage, Bosworth, & Simon, 2000; Pellegrini, 2002; Pellegrini & Long, 2002;).

Following the pioneering work of Olweus (D. Olweus et al., 1999; Dan Olweus, 2001), bullying has been described as a subcategory of interpersonal aggression illustrated by intentionality, repetition, and an imbalance of power, with abuse of power being a primary distinction between bullying and other forms of aggression (Smith et al., 1999; Vaillancourt, Hymel, & McDougall, 2003; Hymel & Swearer, 2015).

According to American Psychological Association, bullying is a form of aggressive behavior in which someone intentionally and repeatedly causes another person injury or discomfort. Bullying can take the form of physical contact, words or more subtle actions. (https://www.apa.org/topics/bullying)

To be considered bullying, the behavior must include aggression, and also include:

- **The Power Imbalance:** The perpetrator of bullying is stronger and use their power to control or harm others in many way (physically stronger, more popular, high socioeconomic status etc).
- **Repetition:** Bullying behaviors are repeated or have the possibility to occur more than once. Also bullying could be perpetrated via computer as a cyberbullying and cannot be observed easily by others.

Types of Bullying Behavior

School bullying is the activity of repetitive, aggressive behavior aimed at harming another individual physically, mentally, or emotionally. It turns out to be a very complex phenomenon. It can take many different forms. It can occur among different student groups.

Bullying can be classified direct or indirect. Direct bullying includes hitting, taunting, name calling etc. Indirect bullying includes rumors, exclusion, cyberbullying etc.

There are types of bullying that can be experienced at school; (NCAB, n.d.)

1. **Physical bullying:** Physical bullying includes pushing, kicking, hitting, biting, tripping, pinching or damaging property. Short- and long-term effects may be encountered after physical bullying.

2. **Verbal bullying:** Verbal bullying includes name calling, insults, humiliation, teasing, intimidation, homophobic or racist remarks, or verbal abuse. While verbal bullying can start off harmless, it can escalate to levels which start affecting the individual target.
3. **Social bullying:** Also, it is a repeated behavior intended to intimidate, anger or embarrass the targeted persons. Social bullying (sometimes referred to as covert bullying or relational bullying) is often harder to recognize and can be carried out behind the bullied person's back. It is designed to harm someone's social reputation or social standing and/or cause humiliation. Social bullying includes ostracizing someone, lying and spreading rumors, making ugly facial expressions or physical gestures, threatening or insulting looks, making bad jokes to embarrass or humiliating, unkindly imitating, encouraging others to socially exclude someone, may involve damaging someone's social reputation or damaging someone's social reputation.
4. **Cyber bullying:** Intentional and repeated harm inflicted using computers, phones, and other electronic devices via social media, instant messaging, texts, websites, and other online platforms. It can happen anytime and anywhere. Cyber bullying can include abusive or hurtful texts, emails or posts, images or videos, deliberately excluding others online, nasty gossip or rumors, and imitating others online or using their log-in.

Bullying can occur during school time or after school time. Students may also encounter bullying outside of school, on their way to and from school, in school yards, playgrounds and bus stops. While most reported bullying happens in the school building, a significant percentage also happens in places like on the playground or on the Internet. Roles in school bullying can appear in many different ways and not limited to two; those who bully others and those who are bullied. Olweus talks about the "circle of bullying" to define both those directly involved in bullying and those who actively or passively assist the behavior or defend against it (Olweus, 1999; Olweus, 2013). Most kids can play more than a role in bullying over time. At least, they can be directly associated in bullying as the one bullying others or being bullied and in others they may witness bullying and play an assisting or defending role. Each condition differs in itself. There are some children who both bully and have been bullied others It is important to pay attention to the various roles children play, because who are both bully and have been bullied others may carry more risk for unwanted results, such as depression or suicidal thoughts.

To prevent bullying, which can be seen in different forms, it is necessary to understand the roles related to bullying. It is not possible for a person to be a bully or bully alone, so there are shared roles in bullying (Jimerson, Annan, Skokut, & Renshaw, 2009). Although there are at least two people, the bully and the victim, in bullying events, more people may be involved in bullying depending on the situation (Gordon, 2018). Attitudes and behaviors of people other than the bully and the victim about the bullying determine the other roles in bullying (Zych et al., 2020). In recent years, Olweus emphasized that using the words bully and victim should be avoided, it would be more appropriate to use the concepts of " the child who was bullied " instead of victim, "the child who bullied" instead of bully, and labeling students should be avoided. (https://olweus.sites.clemson.edu). Olweus has listed the roles in the bullying event as follows, although he defines the people who are not the bully and the victim as the audience in a general framework (Dan Olweus, 2001; (Dan Olweus, 2013); (Rivara, Le Menestrel, & Victimization, 2016) (Figure 1):

A. **Student who bullies:** These students want to bully, start the bullying and play the leader role.

B. **Followers or henchmen:** These students are positive toward the bullying and take an active role but don't usually initiate it and don't play a lead role.
C. **Supporters or Passive bullies:** These students actively and openly support the bullying but they don't join in.
D. **Passive supporters or Possible Bullies:** These students like the bullying but don't Show outward sign of support.
E. **Disengaged onlookers:** These students don't involve, don't take a stand or participate actively.
F. **Possible Defender:** These students don't approve the bullying and think they should support the student being bullied but do nothing.
G. **Defenders:** These students don't like the bullying and help or try to help the student who is being bullied.

Figure 1. The Bullying Circle: Students' modes of reaction/roles in an acute bullying situation (D. Olweus, Limber, & Mihalic, 1999)

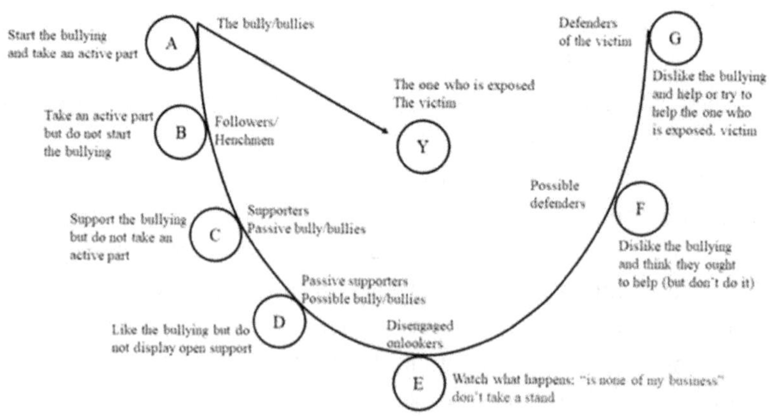

Bullying in schools also exhibits different dimensions according to grades, bullying in elementary school, middle school and high school. This classification is especially important in terms of school bullying diversity and prevention/prevention strategies. Studies show that bullying unfortunately starts from the pre-school period (Moeller, 2001). In addition, it is seen that bullying is mostly seen in primary schools (primary and secondary schools) and bullying gradually decreases with the increase in the age and class levels of the students. Those involved in bullying/victimization are not fixed in their roles as bully or victim, moving in and out of these roles appears to be the norm. It's clear consensus that bullying increased during the middle school. However, the students who are aggressive in elementary school tend to be the same students who are aggressive in middle and high school (Ozdemir & Stattin, 2011).

There is a decrease in physical bullying with increasing age. However, bullying continues verbally. In addition, although there is a numerical decrease in physical bullying with the advancement of age and class, it is seen that there is an increase in its severity (Craig et al., 2009). With the spread of social networks, people of all ages and groups may be exposed to cyberbullying even if they are not physically bullied. For this reason, taking developmental and preventive measures for each place group is of vital importance in minimizing the incidents and effects of bullying.

Risk Factors of Bullying

In particular, identifying problematic behaviors in childhood is of great importance in preventing future problems. It is also an important parameter for the formation of healthy individuals and societies. Schools, teachers, and parents play an important role in observing school-age children, correcting undesirable behaviors and guiding the behaviors accordingly (Akman, 2021; Mental health and behavior in schools, 2018).

Figure 2. Risk Factors for bullying (Resource: https://www.stopbullying.gov/bullying/at-risk)

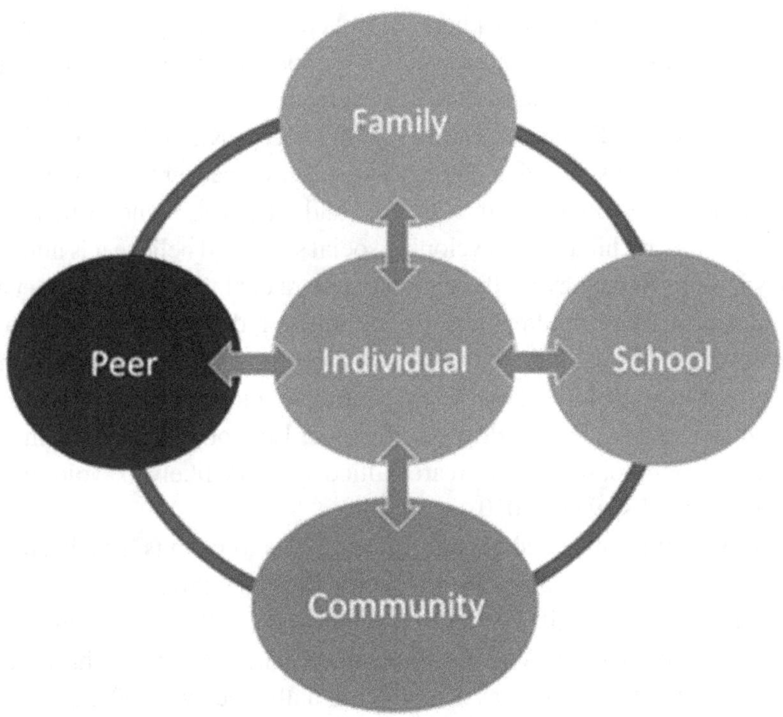

Bullying risk factors can be classified as:

1. **Personal risk factors:** Girls and boys can be both bullies and victims of bullying. Studies have found that boys are more bullied than girls. Especially, this fact in bullying is more significant for direct acts of bullying, such as physical attack or threats (Zych, Farrington, Llorent, & Ttofi, 2017; Cook, Williams, Guerra, Kim, & Sadek, 2010). Generally, bullying hadbegun at around 10 years of age (Eslea & Rees, 2001). From primary to high school, the rate of bullying decreases as children

ages (Due et al., 2005). Bullying is most common in secondary school and decrease with high school. The younger and weaker students are most exposed (Dan Olweus, 1993; Smith, Madsen, & Moody, 2006; Smith et al., 2006). Although a significant relationship was found between body weight and bullying in male students, this relationship was not found in female students. These results suggest that underweight and obese kids are more likely to be bullied than their average-weight peers. This reflects the conflict theory, in which the victim of bullying is often different from the majority (Greenleaf, Petrie, & Martin, 2014). Victims, bully-victims, and some bullies have different, particularly inadequate, social skills. (Cook et al., 2010). Kids with emotional and behavior disorders are more likely to be bullied (Rose, Swearer, & Espelage, 2012). Also, some studies show that bullies and aggressive peers are popularly accepted by their peers in elementary and middle school (Rodkin, Farmer, Pearl, & Van Acker, 2006). Research has shown that school students who belong to an ethnic minority are more likely than an ethnic majority to be harassed (S. Jimerson, Swearer, & Espelage, 2010). Higher levels of victimization have increased in socio-economic inequality within one country (Due et al., 2009).

2. **School Risk Factor:** School environment refers to the overall quality and relationship of school activities. Bullying and school atmosphere are linked to student's academic achievement, learning and development if the school environment is not good and unhealthy, bullying and related problems are general (such as lower academic achievement, lower self-esteem, higher level of anxiety etc.) (Glew, Fan, Katon, Rivara, & Kernic, 2005; Rigby, K., 2003. One of the most important roles in the struggle against bullying belongs to teachers. Teachers' reactions to bullying will vary depending on their individual thoughts, beliefs, and attitudes. Some of them think bullying as a normal act may support children in developing social skills and believe it is unnecessary to interfere because they have no sympathy for the victim (Romera et al., 2021; Boulton et al., 2021). Schools have many classrooms and children, and it's possible to reduce bullying in a class setting. A study showed some key points that foresee bullying in class: poor teacher student relationships, insufficient peer-to-peer relationship, a lack of self-control, and inadequate problem-solving capabilities among students (Marengo, Fabris, Prino, Settanni, & Longobardi, 2021; Sentse, Veenstra, Kiuru, & Salmivalli, 2015). Also, students who are bullied are more likely to avoid school and to drop out of school (Swearer & Espelage, 2010).
3. **Family Risk Factor:** Positive and negative attachments to parents have been found important of bullying behaviour and victimization. Parents' control over the child, controlling attitudes were found to be linked to the status of bully or victim (Dan Olweus, 1993; Cook et al., 2010; Papanikolaou, Chatzikosma, & Kleio, 2011. Raising in a environment where the parents have alcohol or drug abuse problems, domestic violence and physically or sexually abusive predicted bullying and bullying victimization in children (Swearer & Espelage, 2010). Insufficient parental guidance and conflict in the home are typical points among bullies (Cook et al., 2010).
4. **Community risk factors:** Neighborhood characteristics significantly affect bullying attitude (Cook et al., 2010). Research carried out many years to determine whether exposure to vicious computer games, TV, and movies is linked to higher levels of anger. Surely, meta-analyses of these studies indicate that media violence is linked with aggressive and antisocial behavior (Holt, Greif Green, Tsay-Vogel, Davidson, & Brown, 2017).

School climate defines to the quality and characteristics of school life. School climate is based on the school life experiences of students, parents, teachers and other school staffs and reflects aims, norms, values, relationships of students and teachers, educational practices, and schools'organizational structures (Kochenderfer & Ladd, 1996). Positive school atmosphere can be built with strong curriculum, effective teachers, safe environment. In a positive school climate, students should feel respected as individuals, their learning difficulties should be supported, and courses should be interesting.

PREVENTING BULLYING IN SCHOOL

Failure to respond to bullying in a timely and appropriate manner means supporting the risk of recurrence. In order for students to feel safe in the school climate, they need to be aware of the zero-tolerance approach to be heard and noticed by adults such as teachers and principals. Also, interventions by students (peer influence) can be a successful way to prevent bullying.

Nowadays, bullying in school is an important public health problem and new research are being added dây by day. Preventing bullying should be seen as a team effort, and all stakeholders involved in the education of the child, especially school administrators, should work together. It is thought that focusing on positive studies such as prevention-oriented tolerance, democracy, peace and empathy education instead of problem-oriented studies will be beneficial in order to prevent bullying (Lipsitz, 2019; Zych et al., 2017).

The most well-known of the programs used to reduce bullying in schools is the "Olweus Bullying Prevention Program (OBPP)" (Olweus & Limber, 2019). The Olweus Program is a comprehensive method that includes schoolwide, classroom, individual, and community parts. The program is concentrated on long-term change that creates a safe and positive school climate. It is designed and evaluated for use in elementary, middle, junior high and high schools. In the program, students' perception of bullying is evaluated anonymously with scales. After the scales are applied, a bullying prevention committee is established consisting of teachers, school management and parents. In this program, regular in-house training is provided to school personnel. School-based decisions are taken to prevent bullying and these decisions are posted in various parts of the school. In the execution of the program, the school administration and the teachers work in cooperation. Class meetings are held as part of the program. Individual interviews are also conducted with students who display bullying behaviors (Olweus, 2013). Olweus, who has many research on bullying, reported his 20 years of experience with bullying in schools. According to the findings of the research based on the scanning model conducted with more than 150,000 Scandinavian students aged 8-16 in the 1980s; It has been determined that approximately 15% of the students encounter bully/victim problems. In addition, 9% of the students were victims and 6-7% were bullies. About 20 years after this research, Olweus and his colleague Solberg investigated bullying in 2001 by applying a scale to 11,000 primary and secondary school students. In this study, the victim rate increased by 50% compared to the research conducted in the 1980s. According to Olweus (2003), this situation is a result of negative developments in society. According to the research findings, bullying is seen as an important problem worldwide.

In turkey, research aimed at preventing direct bullying have been developed and their effectiveness has been investigated. A researcher developed a program (Bullying Prevention Program) to prevent bullying in primary education (grades 1-8) and investigated its effectiveness. As a result of the research, it has been determined that the BPP developed by the researcher is effective in reducing the subject's being victim and bully (Karatas, 2011). Another researcher, who wanted to test the effect of peer help, developed a peer support program for coping with bullying in her research and examined the effects of this program on middle school students (6th and 7th grades) coping skills in the study, the majority of the students stated that the peer support program was effective in improving their coping skills with bullying (Turktan, 2013). One of the methods used to combat bullying is peer support. In turkey, projects such as "don't be a bully, become a bro" (zorba olma, kanka ol) which are supported by people who are known from the media at the national level, are carried out. (https://www.cartoonnetwork.com.tr/show/zorba-olma-kanka-ol)

FUTURE RESEARCH DIRECTIONS

Bullying behavior is a significant public health problem. Bullying is not just a school and parents' problem. Solving the problem of bullying in school, first of all, requires community awareness and sensitivity. To solve the problem parents, educators and school administrators, health care providers, academicians, policymakers, families, and others need to work together.

CONCLUSION

Preventing bullying in schools helps the individual's not only academic but also emotional, psychological and social development. Psychological counselors working in school Psychological Counseling and Guidance (PDR) services take an active role in developmental and preventive studies applied in schools (Gordon, 2018). From this point of view, it is thought that efforts to strengthen interpersonal communication skills and prevent bullying within the scope of counseling services in schools will help solve possible problems that children may encounter in their lives. Considering that individuals with different characteristics coexist in schools today, how important a problem bullying should be coming to the fore once again. Also, it is a known fact that a positive school environment plays an important role in preventing bullying (Gordon, 2018; Lipsitz, 2019; Dan Olweus & Limber, 2019).

REFERENCES

Akman, Y. (2021). The Relationship between School Climate and Students' Aggressive Behaviors. *International Journal of Progressive Education, 17*(2), 430–448. doi:10.29329/ijpe.2021.332.26

Boulton, M. J., Macaulay, P. J. R., & Atherton, S. (2021). *Promoting Junior School Students' Anti-bullying Beliefs with the CATZ Cross-age Teaching Zone Intervention. Int Journal of Bullying Prevention.* doi:10.100742380-021-00111-9

Cook, C. R., Williams, K. R., Guerra, N. G., Kim, T. E., & Sadek, S. (2010). Predictors of Bullying and Victimization in Childhood and Adolescence: A Meta-analytic Investigation. *School Psychology Quarterly, 25*(2), 65–83. doi:10.1037/a0020149

Craig, W., Harel-Fisch, Y., Fogel-Grinvald, H., Dostaler, S., Hetland, J., Simons-Morton, B., Molcho, M., de Mato, M. G., Overpeck, M., Due, P., & Pickett, W. (2009). A cross-national profile of bullying and victimization among adolescents in 40 countries, the HBSC Violence & Injuries Prevention Focus Group* and the HBSC Bullying Writing Group. *International Journal of Public Health, 54*(S2), 216–224. doi:10.100700038-009-5413-9 PMID:19623475

Deb, S. (2018). *Positive schooling and child development: International perspectives. In Positive Schooling and Child Development: International Perspectives*. Springer Singapore. doi:10.1007/978-981-13-0077-6

Dodge, K. A., & Coie, J. D. (1987). Social-Information-Processing Factors in Reactive and Proactive Aggression in Children's Peer Groups. *Journal of Personality and Social Psychology, 53*(6), 1146–1158. doi:10.1037/0022-3514.53.6.1146 PMID:3694454

Due, P., Holstein, B. E., Lynch, J., Diderichsen, F., Gabhain, S. N., Scheidt, P., ... Health, T. (2005). Bullying and symptoms among school-aged children: International comparative cross sectional study in 28 countries Behaviour in School-Aged Children Bullying Working Group. *European Journal of Public Health, 15*(2), 128–132. doi:10.1093/eurpub/cki105 PMID:15755782

Due, P., Merlo, J., Harel-Fisch, Y., Damsgaard, T., Scient Soc, M., Holstein, B. E., ... Lynch, J. (2009). Socioeconomic Inequality in Exposure to Bullying During Adolescence: A Comparative, Cross-Sectional, Multilevel Study in 35 Countries. *American Journal of Public Health, 99*(5), 907–914. doi:10.2105/AJPH.2008.139303 PMID:19299676

Eslea, M., & Rees, J. (2001). At what age are children most likely to be bullied at school? *Aggressive Behavior, 27*(6), 419–429. doi:10.1002/ab.1027

Espelage, D. L., Bosworth, K., & Simon, T. R. (2000). Examining the social context of bullying behaviors in early adolescence. *Journal of Counseling and Development, 78*(3), 326–333. doi:10.1002/j.1556-6676.2000.tb01914.x

Glew, G. M., Fan, M.-Y., Katon, W., Rivara, F. P., & Kernic, M. A. (2005). Bullying, Psychosocial Adjustment, and Academic Performance in Elementary School. *Archives of Pediatrics & Adolescent Medicine, 159*(11), 1026–1031. doi:10.1001/archpedi.159.11.1026 PMID:16275791

Gordon, J. U. (2018). *Bullying prevention and intervention at school: Integrating theory and research into best practices.* Academic Press.

Greenleaf, C., Petrie, T. A., & Martin, S. B. (2014). Relationship of Weight-Based Teasing and Adolescents' Psychological Well-Being and Physical Health. *The Journal of School Health, 84*(1), 49–55. doi:10.1111/josh.12118 PMID:24320152

Holt, M. K., Greif Green, J., Tsay-Vogel, M., Davidson, J., & Brown, C. (2017). Multidisciplinary Approaches to Research on Bullying in Adolescence. *Adolescent Research Review, 2*(1), 1–10. doi:10.100740894-016-0041-0

Hymel, S., & Swearer, S. M. (2015). *Four Decades of Research on School Bullying An Introduction.* Academic Press.

Jakes, S. S., & Debord, K. (2010). The Interface of Family, School, and Community Factors for the Positive Development of Children and Youth. *Journal of Prevention & Intervention in the Community, 38*(3), 177–182. doi:10.1080/10852352.2010.486293 PMID:20603756

Jimerson, S., Swearer, S., & Espelage, D. (2010). *Handbook of bullying in schools: An international perspective*. Taylor&Francis/Routledge.

Jimerson, S. R., Annan, J., Skokut, M., & Renshaw, T. L. (2009). Educational Psychology in New Zealand: Results of the 2006 International School Psychology Survey. *School Psychology International, 30*(5), 443–455. doi:10.1177/0143034309341617

Karatas, H. (2011). *Examining the effect of the program developed for bullying in primary schools* [Unpublished doctoral dissertation]. Dokuz Eylul University, Izmir, Turkey.

Kochenderfer, B. J., & Ladd, G. W. (1996). Peer Victimization: Cause or Consequence of School Maladjustment? *Society for Research in Child Development, 67*(4), 1305–1317. doi:10.2307/1131701 PMID:8890485

Leach, F. (2003). Learning to be violent: The role of the school in developing adolescent gendered behaviour. *Compare: A Journal of Comparative Education, 33*(3), 385–400. doi:10.1080/03057920302587

Lipsitz, J. (2019). *Successful schools for young adolescents. Successful Schools for Young Adolescents* (1st ed.). Taylor and Francis. doi:10.4324/9781351318327

Marengo, D., Fabris, M. A., Prino, L. E., Settanni, M., & Longobardi, C. (2021). Student-teacher conlict moderates the link between students' social status in the classroom and involvement in bullying behaviors and exposure to peer victimization. *Journal of Adolescence*, 87. PMID:33545582

Moeller, T. G. (2001). *Youth aggression and violence : a psychological approach*. Lawrence Erlbaum Associates. doi:10.4324/9781410606488

Myers, D. G., & Twenge, J. M. (2021). *Social psychology* (14th ed.). McGraw-Hill Education.

Olafsen, R. N., & Viemerö, V. (2000). Bully/victim problems and coping with stress in school among 10- to 12-year-old pupils in Åland, Finland. *Aggressive Behavior, 26*(1), 57–65. doi:10.1002/(SICI)1098-2337(2000)26:1<57::AID-AB5>3.0.CO;2-I

Olweus, D. (1993). *Bullying at School: what we know and what we can do*. Blackwell Publishing.

Olweus, D. (2001). Bullying at school: Tackling the problem. *The OECD Observer. Organisation for Economic Co-Operation and Development*, 24.

Olweus, D. (2013). School bullying: Development and some important challenges. *Annual Review of Clinical Psychology, 9*(1), 751–780. doi:10.1146/annurev-clinpsy-050212-185516 PMID:23297789

Olweus, D., & Limber, S. P. (2019). The olweus bullying prevention program (OBPP): New evaluations and current status. *Making an Impact on School Bullying: Interventions and Recommendations*, 23–44.

Olweus, D., Limber, S., & Mihalic, S. F. (1999). Blueprints for violence prevention, book nine: Bullying prevention program. Center for the Study and Prevention of Violence, 12(6), 256–273.

Ozdemir, M., & Stattin, H. (2011). Bullies, victims, and bully-victims: A longitudinal examination of the effects of bullying-victimization experiences on youth well-being. *Journal of Aggression, Conflict and Peace Research, 3*(2), 97–102. doi:10.1108/17596591111132918

Papanikolaou, M., Chatzikosma, T., & Kleio, K. (2011). Bullying at School: The role of family. *Procedia: Social and Behavioral Sciences, 29*, 433–442. doi:10.1016/j.sbspro.2011.11.260

Pellegrini, A. D. (2002). Bullying, victimization, and sexual harassment during the transition to middle school. *Educational Psychologist, 37*(3), 151–163. doi:10.1207/S15326985EP3703_2

Pellegrini, A. D., & Long, J. D. (2002). A longitudinal study of bullying, dominance, and victimization during the transition from primary school through secondary school. *British Journal of Developmental Psychology, 20*(2), 259–280. doi:10.1348/026151002166442

Rivara, F., & Le Menestrel, S. (2016). Preventing Bullying Through Science, Policy, and Practice - NCBI Bookshelf. National Academies Press (US).

Rodkin, P. C., Farmer, T. W., Pearl, R., & Van Acker, R. (2006). They're cool: Social status and peer group supports for aggressive boys and girls. *Social Development, 15*(2), 175–204. doi:10.1111/j.1467-9507.2006.00336.x

Romera, E. M., Ortega-Ruiz, R., Runions, K., & Camacho, A. (2021). Bullying perpetration, moral disengagement and need for popularity: Examining reciprocal associations in adolescence. *Journal of Youth and Adolescence, 50*(10), 2021–2035. doi:10.100710964-021-01482-4 PMID:34331660

Rose, C. A., Swearer, S. M., & Espelage, D. L. (2012). Bullying and students with disabilities: The untold narrative. *Focus on Exceptional Children, 45*(2), 1–10. doi:10.17161/foec.v45i2.6682

Sentse, M., Veenstra, R., Kiuru, N., & Salmivalli, C. (2015). A Longitudinal Multilevel Study of Individual Characteristics and Classroom Norms in Explaining Bullying Behaviors. *Journal of Abnormal Child Psychology, 43*(5), 943–955. doi:10.100710802-014-9949-7 PMID:25370007

Smith, P. K., Madsen, K. C., & Moody, J. C. (2006). What causes the age decline in reports of being bullied at school? Towards a developmental analysis of risks of being bullied. *Educational Research, 41*(3), 267–285. doi:10.1080/0013188990410303

Smith, P. K., Morita, Y., Junger-Tas, J., Olweus, D., Catalano, R. F., & Slee, P. (Eds.). (1999). *The nature of school bullying: A cross-national perspective*. Taylor & Frances/Routledge.

Sullivan, T. N., Farrell, A. D., Sutherland, K. S., Behrhorst, K. L., Garthe, R. C., & Greene, A. (2021). Evaluation of the Olweus Bullying Prevention Program in US Urban Middle Schools Using a Multiple Baseline Experimental Design The OBPP focuses on the prevention of bullying, which encompasses acts of aggression repeatedly directed toward. *Prevention Science, 22*(8), 1134–1146. doi:10.100711121-021-01244-5

Swearer, S., & Espelage, D. (2010). *Expandıng The Socıal–Ecologıcal Framework Of Bullyıng Among Youth: Lessons Learned from the Past and Directions for the Future. Bullying in North American Schools*. Routledge.

Turktan, S. (2013). *The effects of peer support program for coping with bullying on middle school 6th and 7th grade students' ability to cope with bullying* [Unpublished doctoral dissertation]. Anadolu University, Eskisehir, Turkey.

Types of bullying. National Centre Against Bullying [NCAB]. (n.d.). Retrieved from https://www.ncab.org.au/bullying-advice/bullying-for-parents/types-of-bullying/

Vaillancourt, T., Hymel, S., & McDougall, P. (2003). Bullying is power: Implications for school-based intervention strategies. *Journal of Applied School Psychology*, *19*(2), 157–176. doi:10.1300/J008v19n02_10

Zych, I., Farrington, D. P., Llorent, V. J., & Ttofi, M. M. (2017). *Protecting Children Against Bullying and Its Consequences*. Academic Press.

Zych, I., Ttofi, M. M., Llorent, V. J., Farrington, D. P., Ribeaud, D., & Eisner, M. P. (2020). A Longitudinal Study on Stability and Transitions Among Bullying Roles. *Child Development*, *91*(2), 527–545. doi:10.1111/cdev.13195 PMID:30566232

ADDITIONAL READING

Ahmed, G. K., Metwaly, N. A., Elbeh, K., Galal, M. S., & Shaaban, I. (2022). Risk factors of school bullying and its relationship with psychiatric comorbidities: A literature review. *The Egyptian Journal of Neurology, Psychiatry and Neurosurgery*, *58*(1), 1–11. doi:10.118641983-022-00449-x PMID:35645553

Cook, C. R., Williams, K. R., Guerra, N. G., Kim, T. E., & Sadek, S. (2010). Predictors of Bullying and Victimization in Childhood and Adolescence: A Meta-analytic Investigation. *School Psychology Quarterly*, *25*(2), 65–83. doi:10.1037/a0020149

Olweus, D. (1993). *Bullying at School: what we know and what we can do*. Blackwell Publishing.

Swearer, S. M., Espelage, D. L., & Napolitano, S. A. (2009). *Bullying Prevention & Intervention: Realistic Strategies for School*. The Guilford Press.

KEY TERMS AND DEFINITIONS

Bullying: Bullying is unwanted, aggressive behavior among school aged children that involves a real or perceived power imbalance.

Bullying Prevention: Bullying prevention is a multilevel school-based program to prevent or reduce bullying in elementary, middle, and junior high schools, both at school and off campus. It is essential for schools to develop a positive culture and to guide social-emotional learning.

School Climate: School climate refers to the quality and character of school life. School climate is based on patterns of students', parents' and school personnel's experience of school life and reflects norms, goals, values, interpersonal relationships, teaching and learning practices, and organizational structures

Chapter 21
Emotional Bullying Towards Children

Mehmet Kanak
Sivas Cumhuriyet University, Turkey

Seda Sakarya
Kırıkkale University, Turkey

ABSTRACT

In the literature, the concept of emotional bullying is mental cruelty, mental injury, emotional or verbal abuse, emotional maltreatment, mental deprivation, emotional assault. Emotional bullying is one of the commonly used concepts related to emotional abuse. Emotional abuse has been defined as a form of behavior in which a person is deliberately and repeatedly subjected to non-physical acts by another person that harms their behavioral, emotional, and mental functioning. Although it is more harmful than other types of abuse, it is difficult to notice. This type of bullying can be seen alone, or it is more common because it accompanies other types of bullying. Using the child, forcing the child to take a side in domestic problems, isolating him from the society for fear of being harmed, leaving him alone, dressing the child in a way that is not suitable for the society and place in which he lives in a way that is ridiculed by his friends and environment are also considered as emotional bullying.

INTRODUCTION

It is noteworthy that the concept of childhood is defined in different ways in different societies and even in different segments within these societies. As a result of the changing perspectives on the development and education of the child, the different approaches discussed, and the increasing interest in issues such as children's rights with an interdisciplinary approach, different perspectives on childhood and child development have emerged, and the concept of child has begun to be discussed in a multi-faceted context (Sağlam & Aral, 2016). For instance, in this regard, the Turkish child protection law addresses the child as a juvenile; and Juvenile Protection Law No. 5395 defines the juvenile as "*Any individual that has not yet completed age eighteen, regardless of whether they have reached full legal age earlier*" (mevzuat.gov.

DOI: 10.4018/978-1-6684-5426-8.ch021

tr). In line with various social, economic, and cultural developments, the concept of the child includes the characteristics of being an individual with their own rights, separate from adults. All segments of society, especially families, have serious responsibilities in the protection and care of children. There is no doubt that having more individuals who are aware of these responsibilities will contribute to the welfare of the society (Çetin, 2020).

Any kind of behavior involving violence against children is defined as child bullying. The World Health Organization reports that the cause of death of 31000 children under the age of fifteen every year is bullying and addresses the fact that bullying of children can occur in every country, at every socioeconomic level and in every cultural class. In general, since the concept of bullying has an interdisciplinary nature and cultural/social values, it is difficult to express its definition with clear lines. For this concept, which is included in law, health and many different disciplines with different content, the definition of legal discipline is built on the intention of the person who performs the action, while the definition of health discipline is built on the effects of the action on the child. When some cultural influences are added to this formula, the perception on behaviors to be considered as bullying can be shaped within the framework of different views (WHO, 2006).

The types of bullying experienced in childhood are generally classified as physical bullying, sexual bullying, emotional bullying and neglect. Actions or inactions that are not in compliance with and are considered damaging in social and professional norms directed to the child by parents or by any other person who provides primary care to children, and that negatively affect the development of the child, are described as child bullying and neglect (Taner & Gökler, 2004).

Emotional bullying occurs in the form of being exposed to behaviors involving psychological pressure by the bully. Although emotional bullying may occur separately, cases accompanied by physical and sexual bullying are often possible. In general, it manifests itself in forms such as an expectation of success above the individual's capacity, aggressive-violent behaviors, judgment, unfulfillment of the need for loving relations, and excluding the individual (denial) by the people around the individual (Görener, 2010, Ersanlı, Yılmaz, & Özcan, 2013; as cited in Hürler, 2018). Emotional bullying encompasses all other forms of ill-treatment and accompanies all acts that can be considered ill-treatment, the resulting effects are often covert and destructive; therefore, it is a more difficult type of bullying to diagnose and detect than other types of bullying due to its characteristics (Sneddon, Iwaniec, & Stewart, 2010). Often there is a superficial impression that children who are emotionally bullied are well cared for; in order to eliminate this factor, growth and development patterns should be carefully evaluated by examining in detail whether there are findings causing delay in emotional development (Romeo, 2000; Schöt & Frank, 1989).

Within the concept of bullying, especially emotional bullying can negatively affect the psychological and mental development of individuals and can cause some destructive undesirable effects on individuals in all developmental periods of life. There is no doubt that children who are exposed to emotional bullying especially at early ages will encounter some situations that may harm their development. The issue of emotional bullying should be discussed in detail and explained with the support of the literature, since emotional bullying has challenges in terms of understanding its findings compared to other types of bullying, and creates undesirable effects that are likely to occur in developmental areas. From this point of view, in this section, the definition and categories of emotional bullying, the behaviors accepted as emotional bullying, the causes and consequences of emotional bullying will be presented in line with the findings of relevant studies.

DEFINITION AND CATEGORIES OF EMOTIONAL BULLYING

The era we live in stands out as a period in which the child is accepted as an individual and researches on early childhood period are intensified. Early childhood is expressed as the critical years of life in terms of development; and it is known that cognitive, emotional and social thoughts and behaviors of adults are an output of their experiences in early childhood. In this context, it is an inevitable result that the traumas experienced by children who were bullied in early childhood will be effective in their future life. In order for any action to be characterized as bullying, there must be a disproportionate power relationship between the bully and the victim, and the child who has been bullied must have difficulty defending himself/herself against the perpetrator (Eriksen et al., 2012). Berenson and Andersen (2006), in a study examining the effects of childhood bullying on the interpersonal relationships of adults, revealed that the participants experienced more rejection expectations, insecurity, dislike, and emotional indifference.

Bullying is defined as repetitive and aggressive behaviors that are used by strong and powerful individuals for their own pleasure and interests, psychologically, socially, physically and verbally against those who do not have the strength to resist (Besag, 1989). Bullying can occur in different ways. These can be listed as behaviors such as beating, pushing, pulling, poking, kicking, intimidation, harassment, humiliation, false rumors, exclusion, attack on property, forcibly taking money and insulting (Pişkin, 2002). When the characteristics of bullies are examined, it is noteworthy that these people are more prone to violence, impulsive and stronger (Eriksen et al., 2012). Whether an individual is acting as a bully or a victim may depend on the experiences at school, along with other factors. Bullying among children and adolescents usually occurs at school or while commuting to school (Al-Bitar et al., 2013). The group in which the bullying occurs differs from many social groups in one important respect; the membership here is involuntary, which means that the victim cannot easily escape from the negative conditions (Salmivalli, 2010).

There are many researchers who argue that the concept of bullying has different types. In the classification made by Mynard and Joseph (2000), peer bullying was examined under four categories as verbal, physical, social manipulation and attacks on property. Olweus (1993), on the other hand, divided the concept of bullying into two groups as direct and indirect. While direct bullying is classified as acts such as pushing, hitting, damaging things, threatening, picking nicknames, indirect bullying is classified as acts such as spreading gossip, exclusion, and lying. According to Olweus (1996), physical and verbal bullying is defined as direct bullying because of observable and open attacks, while emotional and social bullying is described as indirect bullying for the opposite.

In the literature, it is also noteworthy that the concept of emotional bullying is often classified as relational, indirect and social bullying (Archer & Coyne, 2005). Relational aggression is defined as the intention to harm another by abusing a relationship (Remillard & Lamb, 2005). The concept of aggression is a broader concept that includes bullying; therefore, in order for aggressive behaviors to be considered as bullying, there must be some characteristics such as intentional and continuous behavior and an imbalance of power between the parties (Acar, 2009). Emotional bullying includes expressions and behaviors such as unfulfilling the needs of the child for the sake of punishment, forcibly keeping the child in a place, scolding, shouting, leaving alone, throwing the child out of the house or threatening with beating, insulting, and offending in front of others (Salmivalli, 2010). Norman et al. (2012) stated that individuals who have been emotionally abused have depressive symptoms and anxiety disorders three times more than those who have not been abused, and that there is an increase in drug use and suicidal behavior of these people. In addition, it is among the findings that emotional abuse increases the risk factors affecting the lifestyle such as the risk of chronic disease and smoking.

Behaviors that cause stagnation and regression in the child's physical, mental and psychosocial development are accepted as emotional bullying behavior. Such behaviors are negative behaviors such as overprotecting the child, threatening, defaming, scapegoating, manipulation, excessive punishment, and rejection (Rees, 2009). Garbarino et al. (1986) mentioned in their book "*The Psychologically Battered Child*" that cruel caregiver behaviors such as intimidation, humiliation, torment, exploitation, ignoring, and destructive criticizing can be listed among the types of emotional abuse (Iwaniec, Larkin, and Higgins, 2006). Hart and Brassard (1991), on the other hand, stated that emotional bullying can occur in many forms; accordingly, the most common emotional bullying behaviors can be shouting, rejecting, swearing, leaving alone, deceiving, intimidating, discouraging, threatening, ignoring emotional needs, expecting responsibilities beyond the capacity of child's age, discriminating between siblings, bias, underestimating, humiliating, taunting, picking nicknames, an excessive pressure and authority.

Wagner and Mongan (1998) stated that the effects of emotional bullying on health indicators are health problems such as difficulty in sleeping and losing weight, excessive sweating, feeling tired, muscle tension, and weakness. In addition, it was stated that those who were bullied experienced negative health problems such as feeling hot or cold, arm or leg pain, chills and swelling of the arms, hands, legs or feet, regardless of the weather conditions. In the book "Child Abuse: Causes and Consequences", Kars (1996) stated that persistent denigration of the child's qualities, capacity, and desires, deprivation from social contact, repeated threats with supernatural powers, severe social harm or abandonment, making demands that are not appropriate for the child's age or strength, raising the child with childcare methods that are contrary to social norms are the types of emotional bullying (as cited in Öztürk, 2007).

Categories of emotional unavailability, unresponsiveness, and neglect; negative and wrong attributions to the child (such as rejection, humiliation and hostility, making the child believe that he/she is not worthy of love); inappropriate or inconsistent interactions in terms of development (unrealistic expectations, overprotection, and exposure to traumatic events); not recognizing or accepting the child's individuality and psychological limits (such as use of child for the parent's psychological needs, not understanding the dead-end situations that the child experience, and determination of beliefs); failure to promote the child's social cohesion (such as missocialization, degeneration and failure to provide cognitive stimulation and experiential learning, and involving children in criminal activities) are addressed under emotional bullying (Glaser & Prior, 1997).

In the World Health Organization's (2006) "*Preventing Child Maltreatment: A Guide to Taking Action and Generating Evidence*", restriction of freedom of movement, humiliation, blame, threats, intimidation, discrimination, teasing, exclusion and other forms of hostile approaches that do not involve physical use of force are listed as types of emotional bullying. From another point of view, behaviors that can be considered as emotional bullying are classified according to the level of violence. According to this classification, shouting, scolding, threatening to harm are low-level emotional bullying behaviors while swearing, insulting, humiliating in front of others, threatening to leave are high-level emotional bullying behaviors (Benice, 2013). In their study, Krugman and Krugman (1984) examined emotional bullying in the context of school and observed 17 primary school students. According to the findings obtained from the research; verbal humiliation, labeling, inconsistent behavior, threatening, belittling, and yelling at children until they cry are more frequently performed by teachers as emotional bullying behaviors. Some sources describe three different types of bullying that fall under the category of emotional bullying. First, harmful parental characteristics, including behaviors such as violence, alcohol, drugs, suicide, and schizophrenia; secondly, negative behaviors such as not being able to check on the child, overprotecting the child, unresponsiveness, and negligence; and the third is the behaviors that cause deteriorations or delays in the development of the child (Glaser & Prior, 1997). According to the study of Kara et al. (2004); children exposed to emotional bullying develop dependent personality, perform maladaptive behaviors, distance themselves from the family, have feelings of worthlessness, are constantly tense, and perform aggressive behaviors.

The American Professional Society on the Abuse of Children (APSAC) lists rejection, denial, terrorization, abetment, exploitation, corruption, denial of emotional sensitivity, and mental, medical or educational neglect as emotional bullying types that the child may experience (ASPAC, 1995). Children have the right to grow up in environments where they are protected and cared for. From this point of view, one of the most important issues in developed and developing countries is the protection and promotion of the rights provided to children. When considered in terms of the historical process, it is obvious that the value attributed to children by the societies is related to the welfare and development of the societies. The point that should be taken as a basis here is the fact that the child is not a belittled adult, but rather an independent individual with his/her own personal characteristics. Regarding the protective environments that should be provided to children in the context of children's rights; opportunities focused on supporting children's care, nutrition, education and all development areas, awareness of children's rights created in the society, guaranteeing children's rights by law, neglect-abuse follow-up and the creation of necessary intervention programs are remarkable in terms of content. Evaluating such content all together and ensuring sustainability is very important for the fight against child neglect and bullying (Uğurlu & Gülsen, 2014).

Emotional bullying is defined as behavioral patterns that can cause serious damage to the emotional development of the child, such as systematic humiliation, ignoring, and devaluation. Behavior patterns that can be seen as the determinants of emotional abuse can be listed as follows (as cited in Gözün-Kahraman & Şahin, 2018).

- **Rejecting with contempt:** Belittling the child, tarnishing the child's honor, putting the child in a situation that will make him/her feel ashamed, making a mockery of the child, criticizing and humiliating the child by choosing the child amongst others in a group.
- **Terrorizing:** Making the child feel insecure, putting the child in dangerous situations, forcing unrealistic expectations with the threat that the child will be harmed if the expectations are not fulfilled.
- **Supporting the child in performing inappropriate behaviors:** Encouraging the child to inappropriate behaviors in terms of his/her development and being a bad role model in this regard.
- **Lack of emotional reactions:** Depriving the child of emotionally needed responses such as love and affection.
- **Refusing:** Detaining or ignoring the child.
- **Isolating:** Forcing unreasonable restrictions on the freedom that the child needs in terms of his/her development.
- **Being inconsistent:** Constantly behaving in different ways and being inconsistent in expectations for the child.
- **Neglecting mental health and medical-educational needs:** Ignoring the child's educational needs for all developmental areas, failing to provide the necessary treatment for the health prob-

lems he/she experiences. Ignoring the child's care and treatment needs or delaying or failing to meet these needs.

- **Exposure to spousal violence:** The child's witnessing all kinds of violence in the household, even if the child is not directly subjected to violence.

The number of research results showing that children who are exposed to emotional bullying are adversely affected by such undesirable experiences in the short and long term is increasing. In the literature on emotional bullying, there are studies examining the effects on the child's psychosocial adaptation (Smokowski et al., 2014; Berzenki & Yates, 2010; Berenson & Andersen, 2006; Lee, 2015; Aktay, 2020; Kara et al., 2004; Kepenekci & Çınkır, 2003; Dias et al., 2015; Burns et al., 2010 ; Riggs & Kaminski, 2010), its long-term effects on the person (Moeller et al., 1993; Spertus et al., 2003), its implications on various health problems (Wagner & Mongan, 1998; Norman et al., 2012; Kent & Waller, 2000), and its effects on success at school (Al-Bitar et al., 2013). Aktay (2020) listed the effects of abuse on the child as low self-esteem, hopelessness, fear of rejection and abandonment, self-blame, urinary incontinence, insomnia and sore throat in her study examining the effects of abuse on children; on the other hand, Kepenekci and Çınkır (2003) stated that a child who is bullied may not be able to tell his/her family about the situation, may exhibit intimidated and anxious behaviors, may run away from school or lie to avoid going to school, may behave ill-tempered towards family members, may repeatedly ask the family for money to give it to the bully later, or may attempt to steal money.

EMOTIONAL BULLYING AT SCHOOL

Studies on bullying started more than 50 years ago, and researchers defined bullying behavior as a stronger peer behaving in a way that could negatively affect their less powerful peer or peers (Olweus, 1994; as cited in Atış Akyol et al., 2018). Bullying can involve various forms of behavior. There is a general consensus on what physical bullying is (hitting, pushing); however, a general agreement has not yet been reached on the classification of non-physical bullying (Underwood & Rosen, 2011). The vast majority of non-physical bullying can be direct such as insults or mockery; however, it may manifest itself with indirect patterns of behavior such as spreading rumors about the person. Physical or direct bullying can be in the form of harming a person in a way that is easily noticed when observed from the outside. Indirect actions, such as taking the person's belongings without permission, damaging the things that are important to the person, can be behaviors that result in emotional harm to the bullied person, even if they are not easily noticed from the outside. A similar result can also be observed in the type of verbal bullying, which evokes ridicule or contempt (Crick & Grotpeter, 1995; as cited in Smith, 2014). In addition, relational/social aggression includes forms of behavior such as social exclusion and spreading rumors (Monks & Smith, 2006: Olweus 1993; Smith 2014). There is a difference between direct physical and verbal bullying from relational bullying (Crick & Grotpeter, 1995). Unlike physical and verbal aggression (which is face-to-face), relational aggression can be both overt and covert; here, harm to the person arises from the harm done to one's relationships or social status, and often includes behaviors such as rumors, gossip, and social exclusion (Boulton & Hawker, 1997). According to Ross (2002), considering the literature on bullying, it can be seen that bullying usually occurs in schools and many bullying cases occur in different educational settings (such as boarding schools). In addition, some groups related to being bullied were found to be more at risk and more vulnerable to harm. The literature on the physical characteristics of students involved in bullying behaviors presents varying results (as cited in Sandres, 2004). Olweus revealed that variables such as physical disabilities (hearing/vision disability, problems related to hearing/speech), obesity, personal hygiene, facial expression, and clothing are not related to being a victim of bullying; on the contrary, Lowenstein stated that the victims of peer bullying have a less attractive physical appearance, have more strange attitudes or have physical disabilities compared to non-victim students (as cited in Dake et al., 2003). Kent and Waller (2000) argued that abuse imposes a risk on multifactorial models of eating disorders and predisposes individuals to psychopathology (including eating disorders) by damaging children's self-concept and reducing their quality of life. Spertus et al. (2003), on the other hand, associated emotional bullying with increased anxiety, depression, post-traumatic stress, and physical symptoms as well as lifelong exposure to trauma.

Bullying at school can be examined under two categories. The first of these is the teacher's bullying against the child and the other is peer bullying.

BULLYING BEHAVIORS OF TEACHERS AGAINST CHILDREN

Bullying behaviors have been extensively studied to date; however, there are not many studies on school victimization from teacher to child or foreigner to child (Benbenishty & Astor, 2007). Although there are extensive studies on peer bullying, teacher bullying has been perceived and investigated as a problem quite recently. In the few studies addressing this issue, some behaviors related to teacher bullying have been defined and according to the results of these studies, it has been accepted by teachers, students and administrators that these are partially common (McEvoy, 2005; Twemlow et al., 2006; as cited in Whitted & Dupper, 2008). Twemlow et al. (2006) examined teacher behaviors and identified two types of bullying. Sadistic bullying consists of behaviors such as the teacher punishing children repeatedly, humiliating students, being defensive about teaching style, hurting the feelings of students, making students vulnerable to peer bullying, and allowing mockery of students in need of special education. Disciplinary refusal consists of the frequent dismissal of specific students from the teaching environment, the discontent with the whole class, the use of unnecessary force, allowing classroom disruptions, and the exclusion of minority students. Some researchers state that certain behaviors of teachers such as aggression, mocking, and unfair punishment against students should be defined as bullying (Papházy, 2005). However, teachers may have a tendency to defend bullying behaviors by justifying them as motivational, an appropriate part of teaching, an appropriate disciplinary response, or good classroom management (Sylvester, 2011).

Violence occurs when a person harms another person physically or with an object (Olweus, 1999). When bullying and violence are addressed together, it can be considered as physical bullying (Pişkin, 2002). Teacher violence is defined as the deliberate use of power by teachers against their students to harm, which can take place in many different ways such as physical, verbal, psychological and sexual (Pişkin et al., 2014). Behaviors considered as violence are examined under three sub-categories as physical violence, psychological violence and passive aggression. Physical violence occurs as behaviors such as beating children (individually or collectively); psychological violence occurs as behaviors such as contempt and mocking; and passive aggression occurs as behaviors such as low expectations from students and not being objective in assessment (Ünal & Gürsel, 2015). Behaviors such as locking students in a limited space, taking them out of the classroom inappropriately, keeping students in positions that are physically difficult to stand for a long time (standing, keeping them on one leg), forcing students to perform harmful physical exercises, forcibly eating inappropriate things (such as paper), and exposing them to harmful environmental influences are also included in the definition of passive aggression (SAM, 2003: 385; as cited in Greydanus et al., 2003). Teacher-to-student violence is mostly perpetrated by the teacher during the lesson. If there is a situation that prevents the teacher from using violence against the child in the classroom, the teacher sends the child to the school administration. According to the researches, the rooms of school principals are the places where violence is applied the most (Bulut, 2008).

According to the results of studies on the results of physical/emotional bullying and violence at school; the loss of self-esteem, excessive guilt and high anxiety behaviors are likely to be observed in students who have experienced or witnessed violence, and this negatively affects their psychosocial health and educational development. More importantly, about half of the children punished by physical violence were found to be more prone to the emotional disorder called EIPSD (Educationally Induced Post Traumatic Stress Disorder) (Hyman, Clark, and Zelikoff 1986; as cited in Bulut, 2008). The people with EIPSD suffer from a mixture of depression and anxiety indicators. Such students suffer from difficulty in sleeping, constant tiredness and boredom, sadness, low self-esteem, suicidal tendency, anxiety attacks, disruption of peer relations, decrease in academic success, antisocial behaviors, truancy from school, not attending school and other high risk-taking behaviors (Dubanoski et al., 1983).

BULLYING BEHAVIORS OF CHILDREN AGAINST CHILDREN (PEER)

Although rates and forms of bullying vary among countries, global surveys show that bullying is a worldwide problem. The latest global status report on school violence and bullying (UN Global Status Report) confirmed that bullying is the most common type of school behavior in Europe, Australia, Africa, and in some parts of the Middle East (UNESCO, 2017). In terms of forms of bullying, it is noteworthy that some forms are more common than others. Verbal and psychological bullying (picking nickname, mocking, threatening, and social exclusion) is the most common type of bullying worldwide (Haner & Lee, 2017). Male students are at a higher risk of being involved in physical bullying, and female students in verbal and relational bullying (Beran & Tutty, 2002). A meta-analysis of studies on peer bullying was conducted and 26 of 28 studies organized based on the situations that may pose a risk revealed a significant correlation between at least one contextual level variable and bullying behavior. Variables at the contextual level can be listed as: physical and social characteristics of the school (school size, class size, teacher-student ratio), socio-demographic characteristics (number of students per class/school, socioeconomic status, proportion of ethnic minorities, gender ratios, mean age), environmental/climate or social aspects of schools (existence/implementation of rules/regulations, safety, support/adaptation, relationship between teachers and students, teaching style, academic pressure and victimization rates), and the wider community context of the neighborhood, city, or country (poverty, inequality, gross domestic product, homicide rates, etc.) (Azeredo et al., 2015).

The NSW Department of Community Services (2007) presents the following situations involving risk and protective factors for being bullied as shown in Table 1.

Bullying often occurs when supervision is very poor and where the bullies may remain covert or anonymous. Social factors are critical in encouraging or allowing a behavior. When making evaluation, field experts should consider the family, peer group, school, society and all social factors that accelerate such behaviors (Vanderbilt & Augustyn, 2010). It has been determined that bullying behavior peaks in early adolescence and decreases within high school period (Nansel et al., 2001). This finding supports previous studies showing that a disordered school environment characterized by a negative school climate, high rates of student behavior problems, intense disadvantage, and student mobility is associated with a range of problematic outcomes for adolescents, including bullying (Bradshaw et al., 2009). While we should be careful in interpreting these school-based risk situations as a possible cause between children's victimization and experience of bullying, these situations reveal some links that should be considered when both aiming to prevent bullying and responding to bullying situations. For example, the association with recommending positive behavioral expectations suggests that programs using such social norm strategies may be a promising approach to preventing bullying. These findings identify potential designable targets for intervention (Bradshaw et al., 2015). Schools that have established rules and accepted regulations for anti-bullying and pro-victim attitudes, along with the capacity to respond to violence, have lower rates of bullying. This shows that violent behaviors can be reduced by changing the environmental factor of the school (Steffgen et al., 2013).

Table 1. Examples of risk and protective factors

Risk factors	Protective factors
Childhood factors	
• birth injury/disability/low birth weight • insecure attachment • poor social skills	• social skills • attachment to family • school achievement
Family factors	
• poor parental supervision and discipline • parental substance abuse • family conflict and domestic violence • social isolation/lack of support networks	• supportive caring parents • parental employment • access to support networks
School factors	
• school failure • negative peer group influences • bullying • poor attachment to school	• positive school climate • sense of belonging/bonding • opportunities for some success at school and recognition of achievement
Community factors	
• neighbourhood violence and crime • lack of support services • social or cultural discrimination	• access to support services • community networking • participation in community groups

Cited from http://www.community.nsw.gov.au

FACTORS CAUSING BULLYING

The reasons for the bullying behavior of children can be listed as drawing attention of their friends, proving themselves as the strong in their circles, and ensuring that their wishes are fulfilled (Mc Ginnis & Goldstein, 2003). Socioeconomic level stands as an important cause of physical and social peer bullying. The examination of bullying behaviors of girls and boys based on their socioeconomic level revealed that physical and emotional bullying behaviors are more common among boys in schools with low socioeconomic level. In schools with a high socioeconomic level, on the other hand, emotional and verbal bullying behaviors are more common among girls (Çetinkaya et al., 2009).

Bully and victim behaviors of children at school are greatly influenced by parental behaviors in the family environment. Domestic bullying and violence can continue through generations (Hazler, 1996). In other words, children's experiences with their parents have a significant impact on their future peer relationships and bully/victim role (Schwartz et al., 1997). Children who are insecurely attached, those with weak family relationships, those who grow up with strict discipline, children whose fathers are cold and indifferent, and children who are exposed to parental behaviors that include bullying and physical violence may be prone to the behaviors of their parents, who are the primary role models of their lives (Smith & Myron-Wilson, 1997). It is known that children with bullying behaviors experience more family problems than other children. By reflecting their negativities and anger to other children, these children become the performers of this bullying behavior (Beane, 2008; Gökler, 2009). Various familial characteristics such as socioeconomic status, emotional state and migration history are also highly effective in the formation of bully and victim roles. It is also known that the majority of bully children grow up in disciplined and authoritative home environments with strict rules (Perren, Stadelmann, and Klitzing, 2008). Children who are exposed to violence can use violence as an instrument, and some of them internalize their parents who are exposed to violence and display an introverted attitude instead. This may cause them to become victims for bullying children (Uysal & Dinçer, 2012). In one study, the reasons for bullying behaviors were asked to the teachers through a form and their answers were (from the most given answer to the least according to the frequency value) role modeling, domestic verbal-physical violence, application of wrong and incomplete discipline methods in the family, the media, and the family attitudes (Sezgin, 2018). In another study examining bullying behaviors in terms of family characteristics, the causes of bullying behaviors of children were stated as living in a broken family, being the only child, socioeconomic level, education level of parents, environment, number of siblings, and exposure to violence (Danacı & Çetin, 2016).

In the context of the concept of gender, it can be seen that the child-raising attitudes of the families influence boys to resort to physical bullying or aggression more. This type of behavior of boys may be tolerated and encouraged by the family. In fact, a boy with aggressive behavior is often considered strong, brave and assertive. In addition, children's problems in sharing toys, taking a leadership role in games and role-sharing, as well as weak social skills and being physically weak, are among the reasons for resorting to bullying or becoming a victim (Akduman, 2012).

It would be better to evaluate the causes of school bullying under two groups as physical and psychological reasons arising from the child, and reasons arising from the child's family and environment. It is possible to specify the reasons arising from the child as high/low self-esteem level, anger level and other personality traits (Koç, 2007). In addition, children who could not establish close friendships and do not feel part of the school are more likely to engage in risky behaviors (Thomas & Sandra, 2004). On the other hand, over-demanding teachers can cause emotional bullying among children with their attitude just like other factors. In a study in which attitudes towards violence were examined in terms of different variables, the reasons for children's tendency towards violence were listed as being male in terms of gender, being under the influence of media and friend groups, attributing some meanings to violence within the framework of social relations, having a low sense of belonging towards school, and low self-efficacy (Balkıs, Duru and Buluş, 2005). According to Arslan and Tuğrul (2013), the only child in the family exhibits relational bullying behavior more than children with siblings. Because they often do not favor sharing and delayed fulfillment of their wishes. According to Ünalmış (2010), children who use violence or have a positive attitude towards violence have been exposed to violence in their past.

Sexuality and aggression are instinctive actions that individuals born with. A certain stimulus or environment is sufficient for this energy to be released (Freud, 1950). It has been determined that the testosterone hormone secreted in males is associated with aggressive behavior. In addition, overall ill-tempered state, irregular eating and sleeping habits, negative mood states, difficulties in adapting to the new situations cause aggression, behavioral disorders; and therefore, bullying behaviors (Pearce, 1992). Bandura (1977), on the other hand, expressed the sources of aggression as observational learning, reinforced performance and structural determinants in his study "*Social Learning Theory of Aggression*". According to Bandura, people often engage in violent behavior because of their cognitive skills and self-control. In addition, the study addresses the influence of family, media elements and subculture on aggressive behaviors. Media elements can direct children to perform negative behaviors with factors such as imitation, desensitization, aggression and risk taking (Lewis, 2005).

In cases where parents focus only on their children's failures and mistakes, children, just like their parents, can focus only on their faults and deficiencies and feel incompetence and failure. This situation may cause damage to children's self-efficacy perception both academically and psychologically (Gander & Gardiner, 2010). External factors such as unemployment, poverty, death, alcohol addiction, stress, insufficient social support can also be observed in families where there is a risk of bullying. In addition, both the low educational levels of the parents and the lack education and care required for the development of the children are also causes of bullying. The isolation of the family and the lack of elements such as communication, sensitivity and tolerance in the family can also trigger this situation. The strict rules in the environment and the presence of a dominant character can also be one of the reasons (Mckinney et al., 2000; Potts and Mondleco, 2007). According to Celiloğlu (2018), the factors that cause bullying are gender inequality and social inequality, lack of family support services, low-income level, social approval of some elements of violence, and insufficient efforts to prevent abuse and neglect.

Psychological effects of emotional abuse can be summarized as an external locus of control and a more anxious nature, inability to establish good relations with peers, inability to form a unique identity, being on the side of both perpetrators and victims of violence in a close relationship in the future, decrease in self-esteem, and antisocial behaviors such as depression, obsession, psychosocial dwarfism, aggression, over passivity, stealing (Berzenski & Yates, 2008; Öztep, 2010; Durmuşoğlu & Doğru, 2016; Karakuş, 2006). The effects of exposure to emotional abuse on the body can be summarized as decreased cortisol (stress hormone) response, initiation of intravenous substance use, diseases such as bulimia nervosa and binge eating disorder, sleep disorders such as bedtime resistance, sleep anxiety, night terrors and daytime sleepiness (Carpenter et al., 2009; Monteleone et al., 2022; Pei et al., 2022).

CONCLUSION

In conclusion, emotional bullying is a type of bullying that is more difficult to observe compared other types of bullying. At this point, parents and teachers should observe the changes in children more systematically and distinguish well whether the possible psychological changes in the child are a natural result of their development. Once a problem is detected, necessary measures should be taken as quickly as possible.

FUTURE RESEARCH AND DIRECTIONS

Emotional bullying is a frequently consulting thing in every moment of life. People are exposed to different types of emotional bullying every day, but they fail to define it, because they are not aware of the situation. Recognizing this type of bullying that we face from our childhood period can be a guide to prevent it. Doing more work on this is very important topic, it will minimize this type of bullying in society.

REFERENCES

Acar, T. (2009). *Dokuzuncu sınıf öğrencilerinde akran zorbalığı ve psikolojik belirtiler* [Peer bullying and psychological symptoms in ninth grade students] [Unpublished master's thesis].Hacettepe Üniversitesi, Sosyal Bilimler Enstitüsü, Ankara.

Akduman, G. (2012). Okul öncesi dönemde akran zorbalığın incelenmesi [Investigation of peer bullying in preschool period]. *Gazi Üniversitesi. Toplum ve Sosyal Hizmet Dergisi, 23*(1), 121–138.

Aktay, M. (2020). İstismar ve ihmalin çocuk üzerindeki etkileri ve tedavisi [The effects and treatment of abuse and neglect on children]. *Gelişim ve Psikoloji Dergisi, 1*(2), 169–184.

Al-Bitar, Z. B., Al-Omari, I. K., Sonbol, H. N., Al-Ahmad, H. T., & Cunningham, S. J. (2013). Bullying among Jordanian schoolchildren, its effects on school performance, and the contribution of general physical and dentofacial features. *American Journal of Orthodontics and Dentofacial Orthopedics, 144*(6), 872–878. doi:10.1016/j.ajodo.2013.08.016 PMID:24286910

Archer, J., & Coyne, S. M. (2005). An integrated review of indirect, relational, and social aggression. *Personality and Social Psychology Review, 9*(3), 212–230. doi:10.120715327957pspr0903_2 PMID:16083361

Atış-Akyol, N., Yıldız, C., & Akman, B. (2018). Öğretmenlerin akran zorbalığına ilişkin görüşleri ve zorbalıkla baş etme stratejileri [Teachers' views on peer bullying and strategies for coping with bullying]. *Hacettepe Üniversitesi Eğitim Fakültesi Dergisi, 33*(2), 439–459.

Azeredo, C. M., Rinaldi, A. E. M., de Moraes, C. L., Levy, R. B., & Menezes, P. R. (2015). School bullying: A systematic review of contextual-level risk factors in observational studies. *Aggression and Violent Behavior, 22*, 65–76. doi:10.1016/j.avb.2015.04.006

Bandura, A. (1978). Social learning theory of aggression. *Journal of Communication, 28*(3), 12–29. doi:10.1111/j.1460-2466.1978.tb01621.x PMID:690254

Beane, A. L. (2008). *Protect your child from bullying expert advice to help you recognize, prevent, and stop bullying before your child gets hurt.* Jossey-Bass.

Benbenishty, R., & Astor, R. A. (2007). Monitoring indicators of children's victimization in school: Linking national-, regional-, and site-level indicators. *Social Indicators Research, 84*(3), 333–348. doi:10.100711205-007-9116-4

Beran, T. N., & Tutty, L. (2002). Children's reports of bullying and safety at school. *Canadian Journal of School Psychology, 17*(2), 1–14. doi:10.1177/082957350201700201

Berenbaum, H. (1996). Childhood abuse, alexithymia and personality disorder. *Journal of Psychosomatic Research, 41*(6), 585–595. doi:10.1016/S0022-3999(96)00225-5 PMID:9032722

Berenson, K. R., & Andersen, S. M. (2006). Childhood physical and emotional abuse by a parent: Transference effects in adult interpersonal relations. *Personality and Social Psychology Bulletin, 32*(11), 1509–1522. doi:10.1177/0146167206291671 PMID:17030892

Berzenski, S. R., & Yates, T. M. (2010). A developmental process analysis of the contribution of childhood emotional abuse to relationship violence. *Journal of Aggression, Maltreatment & Trauma, 19*(2), 180–203. doi:10.1080/10926770903539474

Besag, V. E. (1989). *Bullies and victims in schools. a guide to understanding and management*. Open University Press.

Boulton, M. J., & Hawker, D. S. (1997). Non-physical forms of bullying among school pupils: A cause for concern. *Health Education, 2*(2), 61–64. doi:10.1108/09654289710158393

Bradshaw, C. P., Waasdorp, T. E., & Johnson, S. L. (2015). Overlapping verbal, relational, physical, and electronic forms of bullying in adolescence: Influence of school context. *Journal of Clinical Child and Adolescent Psychology, 44*(3), 494–508. doi:10.1080/15374416.2014.893516 PMID:24738548

Bulut, S. (2008). Öğretmenden öğrenciye yönelik olan fiziksel şiddet: Nicel bir araştırma [Physical violence from teacher to student: A quantitative study]. *Abant İzzet Baysal Üniversitesi Eğitim Fakültesi Dergisi, 8*(1), 105–118.

Burns, E. E., Jackson, J. L., & Harding, H. G. (2010). Child maltreatment, emotion regulation, and posttraumatic stress: The impact of emotional abuse. *Journal of Aggression, Maltreatment & Trauma, 19*(8), 801–819. doi:10.1080/10926771.2010.522947

Carpenter, L. L., Tyrka, A. R., Ross, N. S., Khoury, L., Anderson, G. M., & Price, L. H. (2009). Effect of childhood emotional abuse and age on cortisol responsivity in adulthood. *Biological Psychiatry, 66*(1), 69–75. doi:10.1016/j.biopsych.2009.02.030 PMID:19375070

Çetin, H. (2020). Çocukların istismar ve ihmalden korunma hakkı. In Disiplinlerarası yaklaşımla çocuk hakları içinde [The right of children to be protected from abuse and neglect] (pp. 161-179). Ankara: Pegem Akademi.

Çetinkaya, S., Nur, N., Ayvaz, A., Özdemir, D., & Kavakçı, Ö. (2009). Sosyoekonomik durumu farklı üç ilköğretim okulu öğrencilerinde akran zorbalığın depresyon ve benlik saygısı düzeyiyle ilişkisi [The relationship of peer bullying with depression and self-esteem levels in three primary school students with different socioeconomic status]. *Anadolu Psikiyatri Dergisi, 10*, 151–158.

Coie, J. D., Watt, N. F., West, S. G., Hawkins, J. D., Asarnow, J. R., Markman, H. J., Ramey, S. L., Shure, M. B., & Long, B. (1993). The science of prevention: A conceptual framework and some directions for a national research program. *The American Psychologist, 48*(10), 1013–1022. doi:10.1037/0003-066X.48.10.1013 PMID:8256874

Dake, J. A., Price, J. H., & Telljohann, S. K. (2003). The nature and extent of bullying at school. *The Journal of School Health, 73*(5), 173–180. doi:10.1111/j.1746-1561.2003.tb03599.x PMID:12793102

Danacı, M. Ö., & Çetin, Z. (2016). Erken çocukluk döneminde görülen okul zorbalığı davranış eğilimlerinin çocukların kişisel/sosyal–dil–motor gelişimleri ile olan ilişkisi [The relationship between school bullying behavior tendencies in early childhood and children's personal/social-language-motor development]. *Hacettepe University Faculty Of Health Sciences Journal*, *3*(2), 53–72.

Dias, A., Sales, L., Hessen, D. J., & Kleber, R. J. (2015). Child maltreatment and psychological symptoms in a Portuguese adult community sample: The harmful effects of emotional abuse. *European Child & Adolescent Psychiatry*, *24*(7), 767–778. doi:10.100700787-014-0621-0 PMID:25270111

DoCS (NSW Department of Community Services). (2007). *Risk, protection and resilience in children and families, research to practice notes*. Author.

Dubanoski, R. A., Inaba, M., & Gerkewicz, K. (1983). Corporal punishment in schools: Myths, problems and alternatives. *Child Abuse & Neglect*, *7*(3), 271–278. doi:10.1016/0145-2134(83)90004-2 PMID:6686472

Durmuşoğlu, N., & Doğru, S. S. Y. (2006). Çocukluk örseleyici yaşantılarının ergenlikteki yakın ilişkilerde bireye etkisinin incelenmesi [Investigation of the effects of childhood traumatic experiences on the individual in close relationships in adolescence]. *Selçuk Üniversitesi Sosyal Bilimler Enstitüsü Dergisi*, (15), 237–246.

Eriksen, T. L., Nielsen, H. S., & Simonsen, M. (2012). *The effects of bullying in elementary school*. Academic Press.

Freud, S. (1950). *Beyond the pleasure principle*. Liveright.

Gander, M. J., & Gardiner, H. W. (2010). *Çocuk ve ergen gelişimi [Child and adolescent development]*. İmge Kitabevi.

Glaser, D., & Prior, V. (1997). Is the term child protection applicable to emotional abuse? *Child Abuse Review*, *6*(5), 315–329. doi:10.1002/(SICI)1099-0852(199712)6:5<315::AID-CAR361>3.0.CO;2-A

Gökler, R. (2009). Okullarda akran zorbalığı [Peer bullying at schools]. *Uluslararası İnsan Bilimleri Dergisi*, *6*(2), 511–537.

Gözün-Kahraman, Ö., & Şahin, D. (2018). Çocuk ihmal ve istismarı. In *Çocuk hakları içinde* [Child neglect and abuse]. (pp. 184–208). Academic Press.

Gürhan, N. (2017). Her yönü ile akran zorbalığı [Bullying in all aspects]. *Turkiye Klinikleri J Psychiatr Nurs-Special Topics*, *3*(2), 175–181.

Haner, M., & Lee, H. (2017). Placing school victimization in a global context. *Victims & Offenders*, *12*(6), 845–867. doi:10.1080/15564886.2017.1361675

Hart, S. N., & Brassard, M. R. (1991). Psychological maltreatment: Progress achieved. *Development and Psychopathology*, *3*(1), 61–70. doi:10.1017/S0954579400005095

Hazler, R. J. (1996). *Breaking the cycle of violence: interventions for bullying and victimization*. Taylor Francis.

Hedef, Basın, Greydanus, Pratt, & Spates, Blake-Dreher, Greydanus-Gearhart, & Patel, D. R. (2003). Corporal punishment in schools: Position paper of the Society for Adolescent Medicine. *The Journal of Adolescent Health, 32*(5), 385–393.

Hürler, Ş. (2018). Üniversite öğrencilerinin duygusal istismara ilişkin algılarının incelenmesi [Examination of university students' perceptions of emotional abuse] [Unpublished master's thesis]. Doğu Akdeniz Üniversitesi Lisansüstü Eğitim ve Araştırma Enstitüsü.

Iwaniec, D., Larkin, E., & Higgins, S. (2006). Research review: Risk and resilience in cases of emotional abuse. *Child & Family Social Work, 11*(1), 73–82. doi:10.1111/j.1365-2206.2006.00398.x

Kara, B., Biçer, Ü., & Gökalp, A. S. (2004). Çocuk istismarı [Child abuse]. *Çocuk Sagligi ve Hastaliklari Dergisi, 47*(2), 140–151.

Karakuş, F. T. (2006). *Ergenlerde algılanan duygusal istismar ile sosyal beceri arasındaki ilişki* [The relationship between perceived emotional abuse and social skills in adolescents] [Unpublished master's thesis]. Marmara Üniversitesi.

Kent, A., & Waller, G. (2000). Childhood emotional abuse and eating psychopathology. *Clinical Psychology Review, 20*(7), 887–903.

Kepenekçi, Y. K., & Çınkır, Ş. (2003). Öğrenciler arası zorbalık [Bullying between students]. *Kuram ve Uygulamada Eğitim Yönetimi, 34*(34), 236–253.

Koç, M. (2007). Şiddetin ortaya çıkardığı psikolojik travmayla baş etmede sporun işlevselliği [The functionality of sports in coping with the psychological trauma caused by violence]. *Ahmet Yesevi Üniversitesi Sosyal Bilimler Dergisi, 18*, 167–179.

Krugman, R. D., & Krugman, M. K. (1984). Emotional abuse in the classroom. The pediatrician's role in diagnosis and treatment. *American Journal of Diseases of Children, 138*(3), 284–286. doi:10.1001/archpedi.1984.02140410062019 PMID:6702775

Lee, M. A. (2015). Emotional abuse in childhood and suicidality: The mediating roles of re-victimization and depressive symptoms in adulthood. *Child Abuse & Neglect, 44*, 130–139. doi:10.1016/j.chiabu.2015.03.016 PMID:25890665

McGinnis, E., & Goldstein, A. P. (2003). *Skillstreaming in early childhood: new strategies and perspectives for teaching prosocial skills* (Revised ed.). Research Press.

McKinney, E., Ashwill, J., Murray, S., James, S., Gorrie, T., & Droske, S. (2000). Maternal-Child Nursing. Saunders Company.

Mevzuat Bilgi Sistemi. (2005). *Çocuk Koruma Kanunu*. https://www.mevzuat.gov.tr/MevzuatMetin/1.5.5395

Moeller, T. P., Bachmann, G. A., & Moeller, J. R. (1993). The combined effects of physical, sexual, and emotional abuse during childhood: Long-term health consequences for women. *Child Abuse & Neglect, 17*(5), 623–640. doi:10.1016/0145-2134(93)90084-I PMID:8221217

Monks, C. P., Smith, P. K., & Swettenham, J. (2005). Psychological correlates of peer victimisation in preschool: Social cognitive skills, executive function and attachment profiles. *Aggressive Behavior, 31*(6), 571–588. doi:10.1002/ab.20099

Monteleone, A. M., Tzischinsky, O., Cascino, G., Alon, S., Pellegrino, F., Ruzzi, V., & Latzer, Y. (2022). The connection between childhood maltreatment and eating disorder psychopathology: A network analysis study in people with bulimia nervosa and with binge eating disorder. *Eating and Weight Disorders, 27*(1), 253–261. doi:10.100740519-021-01169-6 PMID:33774786

Mynard, H., & Joseph, S. (2000). Development of the multidimensional peer-victimization scale. *Aggressive Behavior: Official Journal of the International Society for Research on Aggression, 26*(2), 169–178. doi:10.1002/(SICI)1098-2337(2000)26:2<169::AID-AB3>3.0.CO;2-A

Nansel, T. R., Overpeck, M., Pilla, R. S., Ruan, W. J., Simons-Morton, B., & Scheidt, P. (2001). Bullying behaviors among US youth: Prevalence and association with psychosocial adjustment. *Journal of the American Medical Association, 285*(16), 2094–2100. doi:10.1001/jama.285.16.2094 PMID:11311098

Norman, R. E., Byambaa, M., De, R., Butchart, A., Scott, J., & Vos, T. (2012). The long-term health consequences of child physical abuse, emotional abuse, and neglect: A systematic review and meta-analysis. *PLoS Medicine, 9*(11), e1001349. doi:10.1371/journal.pmed.1001349 PMID:23209385

Olweus, D. (1978). *Aggression in the schools: Bullies and whipping boys*. Hemisphere.

Olweus, D. (1993). *Bullying At School: What We Know and What We Can Do*. Blackwell.

Olweus, D. (1996). Revised Olweus bully/victim questionnaire. *Journal of Psychopathology and Behavioral Assessment.*

Olweus, D. (2005). A useful evaluation design, and effects of the Olweus Bullying Prevention Program. *Psychology, Crime & Law, 11*(4), 389–402. doi:10.1080/10683160500255471

Olweus, D., Limber, S., & Mihalic, S. F. (1999). Blueprints for violence prevention, book nine: Bullying prevention program. Boulder, CO: Center for the Study and Prevention of Violence.

Öztep, İ. C. (2010). *Duygusal istismar algılayan ve algılamayan ergenlerin kaygı düzeyleri ve denetim odaklarının karşılaştırılması* [Comparison of anxiety levels and locus of control of adolescents who perceive and do not perceive emotional abuse] [Unpublished master's thesis]. Maltepe Üniversitesi, İstanbul.

Öztürk, S. (2007). *Çocuklarda duygusal istismar* [Emotional abuse in children] [Unpublished master's thesis]. Fırat Üniversitesi, Elazığ.

Papházy, J. E. (2005). *Violence in schools*. Springer. doi:10.1007/0-387-28811-2_12

Pei, F., Yoon, S., Maguire-Jack, K., & Lee, M. Y. (2022). Neighborhood influences on early childhood behavioral problems: Child maltreatment as a mediator. *Child Abuse & Neglect, 123*, 105391. doi:10.1016/j.chiabu.2021.105391 PMID:34768072

Perren, S., Stadelmann, S., & Von Klitzing, K. (2009). Child and family characteristics as risk factors for peer victimization in kindergarten. *Schweizerische Zeitschrift fu¨r Bildungswissenschaften, 31*(1), 13–32.

Pişkin, M. (2002). Okul zorbalığı: Tanımı, türleri, ilişkili olduğu faktörler ve alınabilecek önlemler [School bullying: Definition, types, related factors and measures to be taken]. *Kuram ve Uygulamada Eğitim Bilimleri, 2*(2), 531–562.

Pişkin, M., Atik, G., Çınkır, Ş., Öğülmüş, S., & Babadoğan, C., & Çokluk, Ö. (2014). Öğretmen şiddeti ölçeği'nin geliştirilmesi ve doğrulanması [Development and validation of the teacher violence scale]. *Eurasian Journal of Educational Research, 56*, 1–24.

Potts, N., & Mandleco, B. (2007). *Pediatric nursing*. Delmar.

Remillard, A. M., & Lamb, S. (2005). Adolescent girls' coping with relational aggression. *Sex Roles, 53*(3), 221–229. doi:10.100711199-005-5680-8

Riggs, S. A., & Kaminski, P. (2010). Childhood emotional abuse, adult attachment, and depression as predictors of relational adjustment and psychological aggression. *Journal of Aggression, Maltreatment & Trauma, 19*(1), 75–104. doi:10.1080/10926770903475976

Rodkin, P. C., & Hodges, E. V. E. (2003). Bullies and victims in the peer ecology: Four questions for psychologists and school professionals. *School Psychology Review, 32*(3), 384–400. doi:10.1080/02796015.2003.12086207

Romeo, F. F. (2000). The educator's role ın reporting the emotional abuse of children. *Journal of Instructional Psychology, 27*(3), 183–186.

Sağlam, M., & Aral, N. (2016). Tarihsel süreç içerisinde çocuk ve çocukluk kavramları. *Çocuk ve Medeniyet Dergisi, 2*, 43-56.

Salmivalli, C. (2010). Zorbalık ve akran grubu: Bir inceleme [Bullying and the peer group: A review]. *Saldırganlık ve şiddet davranışı, 15*(2), 112-120.

Sanders, C. E. (2004). What is bullying? In *Bullying* (pp. 1–16). Academic Press. doi:10.1016/B978-012617955-2/50004-7

Schwartz, D., Dodge, K. A., Petit, G. S., & Bates, J. e. (1997). The early socialization of aggressive victims of bullying. *Child Development, 68*(4), 665–675. doi:10.2307/1132117 PMID:9306645

Smith, P. K. (2014). Understanding school bullying: Its nature and prevention strategies. *Sage (Atlanta, Ga.)*. Advance online publication. doi:10.4135/9781473906853

Smith, P. K., & Myron-Wilson, R. (1998). Parenting and school bullying. *Clinical Child Psychology and Psychiatry, 3*(3), 405–417. doi:10.1177/1359104598033006

Smokowski, P. R., Evans, C. B., & Cotter, K. L. (2014). The differential impacts of episodic, chronic, and cumulative physical bullying and cyberbullying: The effects of victimization on the school experiences, social support, and mental health of rural adolescents. *Violence and Victims, 29*(6), 1029–1046. doi:10.1891/0886-6708.VV-D-13-00076 PMID:25905143

Sneddon, H., Iwaniec, D., & Stewart, M. C. (2010). Prevalence of childhood abuse ın mothers taking part ın a study of parenting their own children. *Child Abuse Rewiev, 19*(1), 39–55. doi:10.1002/car.1078

Spertus, I. L., Yehuda, R., Wong, C. M., Halligan, S., & Seremetis, S. V. (2003). Childhood emotional abuse and neglect as predictors of psychological and physical symptoms in women presenting to a primary care practice. *Child Abuse & Neglect, 27*(11), 1247–1258. doi:10.1016/j.chiabu.2003.05.001 PMID:14637300

Steffgen, G., Recchia, S., & Viechtbauer, W. (2013). The link between school climate and violence in school: A meta-analytic review. *Aggression and Violent Behavior, 18*(2), 300–309. doi:10.1016/j.avb.2012.12.001

Sylvester, R. (2011). Teacher as bully: Knowingly or unintentionally harming students. *Delta Kappa Gamma Bulletin, 77*(2), 42.

Taner, Y., & Gökler, B. (2004). Çocuk istismarı ve ihmali: Psikiyatrik yönleri [Child abuse and neglect: Psychiatric aspects]. *Acta Medica, 35*(2), 82–86.

Thomas, S. P., & Smith, H. (2004). School connectednes, anger behaviors and relationships of violent and non-violet American Youth. *Perspectives in Psychiatric Care, 40*(4), 219–228. doi:10.1111/j.1744-6163.2004.tb00011.x PMID:15739755

Twemlow, S., Fonagy, P., Sacco, F. C., & Brethour, J. R. Jr. (2006). Teachers who bully students: A hidden trauma. *The International Journal of Social Psychiatry, 52*(3), 187–198. doi:10.1177/0020764006067234 PMID:16875191

Uğurlu, Z., & Gülsen, İ. A. (2014). Çocuk hakları ve hukuki bağlamda çocuğun ihmal ve istismardan korunması [Child rights and protection of the child from neglect and abuse in the legal context]. *Uluslararası Sosyal ve Eğitim Bilimleri Dergisi., 1*(1), 1–24.

Ünal, A., & Gürsel, M. (2015). Negative teacher behaviors from which teacher candidates are affected. In *Proceedings of Teaching and Education Conferences* (No. 2404066). International Institute of Social and Economic Sciences.

Ünalmış, M. (2010). *Lise 1. sınıf öğrencilerinin zorba, kurban olma durumlarına göre şiddete yönelik tutumlarının ve sosyal beceri düzeylerinin incelenmesi* [Examination of high school first year students' attitudes towards violence and social skill levels according to being bullied and victimized] [Unpublished master's thesis]. Gaziosmanpaşa Üniversitesi, Tokat.

Underwood, M. K., & Rosen, L. H. (2011). Gender and bullying. *Bullying in North American Schools, 33*(1), 13-24.

UNESCO. (2017). School violence and bullying: Global status report. Paris: United Nations Educational, Scientific and Cultural Organization.

Uysal, H., & Dinçer, Ç. (2012). Okul öncesi dönemde akran zorbalığı [Bullying in preschool]. *Kuramsal Eğitimbilim Dergisi, 5*(4), 468-483.

Vanderbilt, D., & Augustyn, M. (2010). The effects of bullying. *Paediatrics & Child Health, 20*(7), 315–320. doi:10.1016/j.paed.2010.03.008

Wagner, P. J., & Mongan, P. F. (1998). Validating the concept of abuse: Women's perceptions of defining behaviors and the effects of emotional abuse on health indicators. *Archives of Family Medicine*, *7*(1), 25–29. doi:10.1001/archfami.7.1.25 PMID:9443694

Whitted, K. S., & Dupper, D. R. (2008). Do teachers bully students? Findings from a survey of students in an alternative education setting. *Education and Urban Society*, *40*(3), 329–341. doi:10.1177/0013124507304487

WHO. (2006). *Preventing child maltreatment: A guide to taking action and generating evidence*. World Health Organization.

ADDITIONAL READING

Acosta, J., Chinman, M., Ebener, P., Malone, P. S., Phillips, A., & Wilks, A. (2019). Understanding the relationship between perceived school climate and bullying: A mediator analysis. *Journal of School Violence*, *18*(2), 200–215. doi:10.1080/15388220.2018.1453820 PMID:30778279

KEY TERMS AND DEFINITIONS

Comparing: Comparing children with each other, ignoring their different developmental characteristics.

Distinguishing Between Children: Children; to classify according to factors such as religion, language, race, sect, socio-economic level of the family.

Encouraging Crime: Provoking the child to behaviors that society will not accept. Ignoring his negative behaviors and setting an example for him with morally negative behaviors.

Giving Responsibility Beyond Its Capacity: Forcing the child (exaggerated religious duties, constantly preparing for competitions and pressure to win, etc.) can be given as an example.

Humiliation: It includes behaviors such as behaving by the adult that will humiliate the child and harm his dignity, being called by nicknames that will create a sense of inadequacy and saying insulting words that will damage his self-confidence and self-esteem.

Refusal to React Emotionally: It includes emotional deprivation such as indifference to the child's problems, not to hug, not kiss.

Self-Interest, Exploitation: It is the parent's use of the child for their own benefit. Include behaviors such as using the child as a marriage security.

To Witness Violence: In the educational setting, if other children witness this while they abuse any child, it also means indirectly exploiting them.

Chapter 22
Peer Bullying

Merve Şepitci Sarıbaş
https://orcid.org/0000-0001-6969-7203
Independent Researcher, Turkey

Gülümser Gültekin Akduman
Gazi University, Turkey

ABSTRACT

Bullying makes an appearance in various manners starting from the first years of life. Regardless of whether it is direct or relational, bullying negatively affects the bullies and the victims. In addition, bullying has destructive effects on societies as well. In this respect, it is highly important to know what bullying, types of bullying, characteristics of bullies and victims, bullying statuses, factors that affect bullying, and the short and long-term effects of bullying are. In this sense, it can be seen that all kinds of studies, activities, and programs that might be effective against bullying are necessary. Within this scope, the concept of bullying is dealt with in a detailed manner in the related section.

INTRODUCTION

Although bullying has not always been referred to as bullying, it has made an appearance in various ways since the birth of humanity. However, the use of the concept of bullying as we know today has started to be used and dealt with in written sources only in the 1500's. The concept of bullying has first been referred to in Germany, in 1538 in its current meaning (Volk et al., 2014). In the 1960's, Konrad Lorenz studied animal behavior and observed that animals acted in a systematic and organized manner in groups against other animals. Konrad Lorenz has coined this emerging behavior as "mobbing". At this point, the concept of mobbing has been approached as the first version of bullying (Leymann, 1996). With the increase of bullying, studies have been done in many parts of the world on the subject and the causes and consequences of bullying have been researched. The studies carried out in Scandinavian countries, which have a high welfare and income level, on bullying have become the pioneering studies in this area (Berger, 2007). Although other studies have been done in various countries on bullying as well, the event which brought the concept of bullying to the world agenda has been the suicide of three children

DOI: 10.4018/978-1-6684-5426-8.ch022

aged 10-14 in Norway, as a result of the pressure of their peers. As a consequence of the suicide of the children, actions have started to be taken at a national level in Norway to prevent peer bullying. In 1970, Dan Olweus's research project carried out in North European schools has become the pioneer of these studies (Olweus et al., 1999).

Bullying is observed in the structure of all societies, cultures, school types and grade levels regardless of language, religion, and race (Levine & Tamburrino, 2014; McDougall, 1999). As a result of UNICEF's study involving 100.000 adolescents from 18 different countries, it has been seen that two thirds of the participating adolescents were victims of bullying (United Nations Educational, Scientific and Cultural Organization, 2017). In the report published by World Health Organization in 2012, it was indicated that the incidence rate of bullying ranges between 1% and 32% (Currie et al., 2012). In the report on adolescent period risks published in 2011 in the USA, it was seen that the rate of bullying between adolescents ranges between 20% and 56% (Eaton et al., 2012). As a result of a study carried out in Brazil, it was determined that 18% of adolescents aged 13-15 was bullies, 5.5% was victims and 2,7% was bullies-victims (Serra-Negra et al., 2015). In a study carried out in Turkey, it was determined that 40% of 4th and 5th grade primary school students have been subjected to verbal, physical or emotional peer bullying at least once (Kapçı, 2004). Yıldırım (2001) has stated that 16,4% of adolescents is in the bully group, 26,2% is in the victim group and 23,8% is in the bully-victim group. Smokowski and Evans (2019) have reported that 16% of girls and 26% of boys in Belgium; 17% of girls and 13% of boys in Canada; 12% of girls and 13% of boys in France and 11% of girls and boys in Switzerland aged 13 are victims of bullying. Although their results are different, studies have shown that about 15-20% of students are affected by peer bullying experienced in the school environment (Ayas & Pişkin, 2011; Espelage & Swearer, 2003; Genç, 2007). In addition, there are studies which report that about 60-70% of adolescents experience bullying in daily life as well (Bradshaw et al., 2007; Rivers et al., 2009).

It can be seen that a majority of research done on bullying involve children/adolescents who are primary school, high-school and university students. However, it is known that peer bullying starts in the pre-school period. As a result of the study carried out by Gültekin-Akduman (2012), it was determined that the most frequently seen type of bullying among pre-school children is physical bullying and that verbal and relational bullying are also seen in this period. Metin-Aslan and Tuğrul (2013) have shown that children with higher relational bullying scores display more relational and physical bullying behaviors in their games. The results of the study showed that children with higher scores of physical bullying are subjected to more physical bullying. In addition, the researchers have found that pre-school children display bullying behaviors such as taking their friends' toys or belongings by force, pushing and threatening their friends, excluding them from their group/games, ignoring and being indifferent to them. It is expressed that children who are subjected to peer bullying in the pre-school period experience adaptation problems and psychological problems later in life (Szewczyk-Sokolowski et al, 2005). In addition, it is reported that children who display bullying behaviors and are victims in the first years of their lives have the potential to be bullies and victims in later years (Gillies-Rezo & Bosacki, 2003). This makes the pre-school period a risky period in terms of bullying behaviors which might be observed later in life.

Bullying acts appear in all age groups starting from the pre-school period and have been increasing all over the world. This affects individuals in the short-term and society as a whole in the long-term. It is considered that dealing with bullying which has destructive effects on individuals and societies is necessary and important. In this respect, the concept of bullying, bullying statuses, types of bullying, characteristics of bullies and victims, factors which affect bullying, and the short and long-term effects of bullying were given place to under the following headings.

The Concept of Bullying

The concept of bullying has started to be dealt with and defined more by researchers as its negative effects and increasing prevalence have been observed. When the literature is reviewed, it can be seen that there are numerous definitions on bullying. Bullying can be defined as the repetitious aggressive and derogatory behaviors of an individual or group towards a weaker individual (Salmivalli, 2010). According to another definition, bullying involves behaviors observed between a weak and a strong person or people, where the strong side continues to display bullying to harm the weak side (Smokowski & Evans, 2019). Polanin et al. (2012) expressed bullying as actions which involve aggressive, repetitious and compelling behaviors towards a weak victim.

Although bullying is related to the concept of aggression and violence, it carries different characteristics from these concepts. Bullying can be viewed as a type of aggression. Bullying can be expressed as certain behaviors displayed by an individual or group to hurt or harm others (Deptula & Cohen, 2004). The difference between bullying and aggressiveness is caused by the power of balance. While aggressiveness is accepted as the aggressive behaviors between two people who have equal power, there is a power imbalance between individuals in bullying (Pişkin, 2002). Violence is approached as a sub-category of aggression like bullying. Situations in which peer bullying takes place physically are regarded as violent behaviors as well. However, bullying can take place in a relational and verbal manner as well. For instance, although behaviors such as making fun, excluding, insulting, slandering are evaluated as bullying, they are not regarded as violence. Many violent actions carry characteristics of bullying as well. In fact, while fights between students can be seen as violent behaviors, it is not an accurate approach to define these actions as bullying (Pişkin, 2003).

Olweus (2003) expressed that bullying can be differentiated from aggressiveness in terms of its three characteristics. Bullying is similar to aggressiveness in the sense that it damages an individual emotionally and physically; however, since bullying is done in a conscious manner to take pleasure and have fun, it is separate from aggressiveness. While aggressiveness is a consequence of impulsive emotions, bullying does not take place in a random manner as it involves repetitious actions. Lastly, a person who commits bullying sees himself/herself as a stronger being compared to the other individual. Baldry and Farrington (2000) have expressed that bullying is quite different from school yard fights and the bantering, scuffling and quarreling seen between peers. Gülay (2018) has defined peer bullying as a problematic relationship type which is shaped by aggressiveness. At this point, it is considered that being aware of the differences between peer bullying and peer conflict is important to prevent problematic relationship types and to decrease the negative effects of bullying. The differences between peer bullying and peer conflict are given in the table below.

Bullying Statuses

Classifying bullying statuses only as bully and victim is not regarded as an accurate approach. In general, peer bullying statuses are classified under four groups as "bully", "victim", "bully-victim" and "onlooker" (Pişkin, 2002).

The concept of bully is used to define a person who continuously and consciously bothers peers who are weaker in terms of various characteristics (Camodeca et al., 2002; Pişkin, 2002). According to another definition, a bully is a person who plans or initiates bullying (Olweus & Limber, 2007).

Table 1. Differences between peer bullying and normal peer conflict

Peer Bullying	Normal Peer Conflict
There is a power imbalance.	There is equal power.
There is no friendship.	There is friendship.
Negative behaviors are repeated.	Negative behaviors are seen from time to time.
The consequences are serious. It causes physical and psychological destruction.	The consequences are not serious.
There is a search for obtaining control and power.	There is no search for obtaining control and power.
There is a search for making a gain (such as money and buying furniture).	There is no search for making a gain.
A person or people who display bullying do not feel emotions such as regret and sadness.	Regret and sadness are felt.
No effort is spent to solve the problem.	Effort might be spent to solve the problem.
Intense negative emotions are observed only in the victim.	

Source: Güvenir (2005)

The term victim status is used to define people who are subjected to peer bullying (Olweus & Limber, 2007). Victims can be classified under four groups as passive, provocative, volunteering and chronic. Victims who submit to all demands and meet these demands because they are physically weaker compared to the bully are defined as passive victims (Ayas, 2010; Storey & Slaby, 2013). Children who try to react by picking on others when they are subjected to bullying behaviors are defined as provocative victims. Children who assume the role of the victim to be included in friend groups, loved by peers and accepted by peers are defined as volunteering victims. Children who always wish to be victims are defined as chronic victims (Ayas, 2010).

Bully-victim status is used to define children who sometimes commit bullying and sometimes are victimized by bullies (Pekel, 2004; Perren & Alsaker, 2006; Solberg et al., 2007). When aggressive victims join bullies, they can also be classified as bully-victim (Storey & Slaby, 2013). Since children with bully-victim status do not exactly know when they will be bullies or victims, they are under greater risk compared to children with other bullying statuses. These children display bullying behaviors towards an individual or people they view as weak in order to raise their self-respect since they are victimized by bullies, are not able to establish healthy relationships with their peers and are alone and depressed (Gürhan, 2017).

The term onlooker status is used to define children who watch the bullying act without intervening (Ayas, 2010). Onlookers sometimes help bullies and sometimes resist bullies (Olweus, 2004; Olweus & Limber, 2007). Onlooker children can feel emotions such as taking revenge, desperation and anger since they help or resist bullies. In addition, these children can also feel guilt since they are afraid of being victims and they are unable to prevent the act of bullying (Ayas, 2010).

Types of Bullying

In general, types of bullying are dealt with under two groups as direct and indirect/relational (Craig et al., 2007; Mynard & Joseph, 2000).

The term direct bullying is used to define the type of bullying in which the bully and the victim have interaction. Direct bullying, which is a clear expression of power, can be dealt with under three sub-headings as verbal, physical and non-verbal/non-physical bullying (Gürhan, 2017; Lamb et al., 2009). In verbal bullying type, bullies wish to hurt their victims with the words they use (Uysal & Dinçer, 2012). Verbal bullying involves behaviors such as making fun, calling names, scorning, cursing, playing pranks, making someone angry by catcalling, shouting and making racist comments (Ayas, 2010; Lyznicki et al., 2004) and constitute 70% of bullying acts (Coloroso, 2003). Physical bullying consists of overt physical attacks which aim at harming the victim (Gillies-Rezo & Bosacki, 2003). In physical bullying, the bully attempts to gain superiority by kicking, punching, pushing the victim or stealing and harming the belongings of the victim (Berger, 2007; Ergül-Topçu, 2018). Besides these, behaviors such as spitting, slapping, tripping, pinching, biting and hair pulling are among physical bullying (Metin-Aslan & Tuğrul, 2014; Lyznicki et al., 2004; Schoen & Schoen, 2010). In non-verbal/non-physical bullying, it is observed that the bully makes obscene gestures and scares the victim through threats (Gürhan, 2017).

Indirect bullying expresses a type of bullying which is done secretly and through manipulation (Mynard & Joseph, 2000). Indirect bullying takes place when the bully harms the victim's social relationships and status in a secret manner or makes the victim suffer by ostracizing him/her (Metin-Aslan & Tuğrul, 2014; Burnukara & Uçanok, 2012; Lamb et al., 2009). Indirect bullying can be dealt with under three sub-headings as verbal, physical and non-verbal/non-physical bullying. Verbal bullying takes place when the bully gossips about the person he/she sees as the victim to hurt him/her. In indirect physical bullying type, the bully subjects the targeted person to physical bullying by provoking the people around them. In non-verbal/non-physical bullying, the bully ostracizes unwanted people, leaves them intentionally alone or provokes the people around them to isolate the individuals he/she sees as victims to hurt them (Gürhan, 2017; Karataş, 2011).

Some researchers have expressed that indirect bullying involves sexual bullying as well (Levine & Tamburrino, 2014), whereas a group of researchers have preferred to deal with sexual bullying as a separate category. Sexual bullying involves behaviors of sexual content such as groping, lifting skirts, taking photographs from under skirts and pulling down pants (Doğan, 2010; Topçu, 2008; Wong, 2009). In addition, sexual demands, sexually inviting attitudes, sexual messages, obscene talk, unwanted touch and hugs can also be considered examples of sexual bullying. Moreover, although making fun of an individual's sexual life and spreading rumors are not direct actions, they are also regarded as sexual bullying. Women are subjected to sexual bullying more than men (Cooper & Snell, 2003; Rigby, 2002). People who are subjected to sexual bullying can feel shame, display asocial behaviors, take a dislike to sexuality and experience emotional and psychological problems.

Another type of bullying known as cyber bullying other than direct and indirect types of bullying has come to the picture as a result of developing technology. Cyber bullying has emerged as a result of erroneous and unconscious use of technology by people (Horzum and Ayas, 2011). While cyber bullying is regarded by some researchers as a type of bullying in the category of indirect bullying (Lyznicki et al., 2004), it is classified separately by some other researchers. Cyber bullying is defined as a person's or group's intentionally harming another person in a repetitive and conscious manner through technological tools (Lamb et al., 2009). According to another definition, cyber bullying is the use of electronic communication tools against a vulnerable person in an intentional, repetitive and aggressive manner (Smith et al., 2008). A person's sending messages or e-mails using technological tools such as cell phones or computers with the intention of harming another individual; using another person's photographs on web pages without asking for permission and bothering others through social communication sites or instant messaging programs are regarded as a part of cyber bullying (Doğan, 2010).

Characteristics of Bullies and Victims

It is stated that bullies and victims have certain characteristics which distinguish them from others and that these characteristics pave the way to becoming bullies or victims or consolidate at the end of the bullying process. In the following paragraphs, the characteristics of children with bully-victim and on-looker status, besides the characteristics of bullies and victims are given.

Children who are under risk of becoming bullies are regarded as children who do not participate in social activities, act on impulse, are not academically successful, are abused, usually have fragmented families and are subjected to domestic violence or witness violence (Perry, 2001). It is observed that in general bullies resort to lying, do not feel regret as a consequence of bullying behaviors and are in search of power. In addition, children who are bullies act picky, have bad intentions, often deny their actions, act selfishly and prefer not to use kind words. Bullies, who can be defined as attractive and can be popular among their peers, are generally not mature individuals. In addition, bullies who do not trust their environment, usually act indifferently to what is happening around them (Alper-İlhan, 2008). While bullies can display asocial behaviors, they can also act sociably and efficiently among their peers (Gülay, 2018). Bullies, who have a tendency to externalize their problems and lack problem solving skills, like hurting their victims and making them suffer. Bullies, who lack empathic skills, justify their behaviors, claim that they are provoked and defend themselves. These children do not only display bullying behaviors towards their peers, but display negative behaviors towards adults as well. Bully children generally do not obey rules and have the tendency to reject rules (Gürhan, 2017).

Just like bully children, victim children also have characteristics which distinguish them from other children. It is observed that victims are generally introverted, passive, sensitive, obedient and self-blaming individuals. Victims, who do not know how to behave towards bullies, usually experience self-confidence problems, are more anxious compared to their peers who do not experience bullying and have difficulty trusting their environment. As a result of all these factors, victims tend to isolate themselves from their peer groups (Kaltiala-Heino et al., 2000; Pişkin, 2002). Since victim children think that they will be subjected to bullying, they become students who are afraid of going to school, are in general stressed and emotionally and physically weak (Selçuk & Güner, 2004). Victims see themselves as shy, anxious, helpless, timid, erroneous, needy individuals with a low sense of being (Çınkır & Karaman-Kepenekçi, 2003; Kavşut, 2009). With the worry that they will be subjected to bullying again and that adults will not be able to protect them, victims can rarely protect themselves in the face of bullying and act passively in terms of letting adults know what they are experiencing. Since they are unable to prevent bullying, these children feel angry, frustrated, sad, jaded, confused, shaken, puzzled, tired and hurt (Gürhan, 2017). Satan (2011) has studied the characteristics of passive and provocative victims separately and expressed that passive victims are individuals with low social skills, who are isolated from the school environment, have no self-confidence, are unable to defend themselves against bullying, whereas provocative victims are lonely, ostracized, have no self-confidence, irritable, do not get along with their friends and start fights, have learning difficulties, tend to continue conflicts, prefer to act as passive attackers in fights and are unable to defend themselves against bullying.

When the literature is analyzed, it can be seen that although in general there are studies which deal with the characteristics of bully and victim children, the characteristics of children with bully-victim status are given place to partially. However, since the risk of bully-victim children becoming psychopathological cases is higher compared to the children in other groups, there is a need for further studies related to these children to be done and their characteristics to be identified (Liang et al., 2007). It is stated that children with bully-victim status in general get angry easily, act aggressively, are hyperactive and experience communication problems (Wolke et al., 2000). In addition, it is expressed that these children have low ties with their schools, experience health problems, are not popular among their peers and spend time on their own (Atik &Kemer, 2008). Bully-victims view the world as an insecure place which is full of spite (Smokowski & Kopasz, 2005), experience emotional problems and have a higher level of emotional stress compared to other people (Pekel, 2004). Koç-Yıldırım (2003) have stated that they have observed characteristics such as not being liked, being easily provoked and provoking others, being unwanted in social environments and having low self-esteem in children with bully-victim status as well.

It is stated that individuals with onlooker status may have certain characteristics due to their behaviors. Onlookers generally prefer not to take any action in the face of bullying (Olweus, 2003). In some cases, onlookers are able to interfere with bullying and actively participate in bullying. Coloroso (2003) has stated that in cases where onlookers do not interfere with bullying feel fear and guilt and this may lower their self-confidence and self-esteem. At this point, it is possible to say that individuals with onlooker status do not interfere with bullying since they generally feel fear. This can cause them to feel inadequate and sad.

Factors which Affect Bullying

The factors with affect bullying can be dealt with under two categories as factors caused by the personal characteristics of the child and environmental factors (Açıkgöz, 2017). While the age, gender and personality traits can be accepted as personal characteristics which affect bullying, parental behaviors and school environment can be regarded as environmental factors which affect bullying.

It is expressed that as age increases, both the frequency of the bullying behavior and the type of bullying change (Aksu, 2019). While some researchers suggest that the frequency of displaying bullying behaviors decrease as age increases, some others state that power increases as age increases and the frequency of bullying behaviors increase for that reason. Englander and Muldowney (2007) have reported that the number of bullying incidents increased in the primary school level, reached peak level in the middle-school level and started decreasing in the high-school level. Rigby (2002) has expressed that the rate of being subjected to bullying decreases as age increases. In general, older children commit bullying against children who are younger than them. Younger children's being physically weaker has an effect in terms of being targeted as victims by bullies. This makes their initial years in school riskier in terms of becoming victims (Gürhan, 2017; Hanish & Guerra, 2000). Studies show that as age increases, the frequency of displaying bullying behaviors also increases (Wolke et al., 2001). As a result of Ayas and Pişkin's (2011) study involving secondary education institutions, it was found that junior students (11th grade) display bullying behaviors much more than freshmen students (9th grade). However, the results of the study showed that younger children resort more to physical bullying, whereas older children resort to and are subjected to verbal bullying more frequently. As a result of Akyol et al.'s study (2018), it was determined that younger children commit physical bullying the most. In addition, the results of the study showed that older children mostly commit psychological/emotional bullying and verbal bullying towards each other. Similarly, as a result of Gültekin Akduman's study (2010) involving children aged

7-14, it was determined that children aged 7-8 resort to physical violence more and while the incidence of physical aggressiveness decreases, the incidence of verbal bullying increases as age increases.

Another factor related to bullying is gender (Aksu, 2019). Mills (2001) has stated that male individuals take more part in violent acts since they are more interlaced with violence. Olweus (2003) has similarly underlined that in particular the characteristic traits of male children, behavior types and physical strength or weakness conditions are effective in terms of bullying. It is stated that in general boys are more involved with physical bullying acts in a direct manner compared to girls. It is observed that girls take place in indirect bullying acts such as ostracizing and spreading gossip rather than direct and physical bullying (Burnukara & Uçanok, 2012; Öztuna, 2018). In addition, girls defend victims more and participate in bullying acts less compared to boys. It is observed that boys mostly engage in groups which have an onlooker status and support bullies (Yıldırım, 2012). While girls' bullying acts decrease, male children's physical bullying acts increase as age increases (Gürhan, 2017). When the literature is reviewed, it can be seen that there are studies which show that boys display more bullying acts compared to girls (Metin-Aslan & Tuğrul, 2013; Salı, 2014; Veenstra et al., 2005). It is stated that people who are subjected to bullying are mostly males. In Hunter et al., (2004) and Pellegrini and Long's (2002) studies, the researchers have shown that males are subjected to bullying more frequently than girls. As a result of Ayas and Pişkin's study (2011), it was determined that in all other types except for verbal bullying, boys are subjected to bullying more than girls.

Another factor related to bullying is character (Selçuk & Güner, 2004). There is a close relationship between children's character traits and problematic behaviors (Essa, 2003). Children who are born with certain character traits give different reactions to events individually. Coloroso (2003) has suggested that some children are born with the tendency to impulsively display aggressive behaviors and that one of the factors which cause the individual to display aggressive behaviors towards the people around them is this tendency. Children who are easy going and have a compatible character are extroverted, sociable, compatible and optimistic, whereas children with a difficult character have difficulty in being compatible. In addition, while children with an easy going character in general form positive relationships with the people around them, children with a difficult character can have difficulty in forming relationships and maintaining the relationships they form (Berk, 2013; Berns, 2015). At this point, it can be suggested that children who have a difficult character display more bullying behaviors compared to easy going children. It is considered that this may create a risk for easy going children in terms of being subjected to bullying. In fact, the results of studies on this area support what is being told about the subject. In Erdal's study (2019), it was determined that besides psychiatric and environmental factors, genetic factors also affect victimization. When it is considered that genetic factors affect character, then it is possible to state that character affects bullying. As a result of Sakarya and Pekdoğan's study (2020), it was seen that character predicts character's activity sub-dimension in terms of the behaviors of child bullies and victims.

Another factor which has an effect on bullying is the attitude and behaviors of parents towards their children. Problematic attachment between the mother and the child causes the child to approach the people around him/her in a hostile, insecure and extremely suspicious manner. According to the Social Learning Theory, the problems experienced in the family negatively affect the relationships of children (Gürhan, 2017). Karaca (2018) has emphasized that the child's not having the supervision of his/her family, his/her negative behaviors being supported by his/her parents and having bully role models lead to bullying. Protogerou and Flisher (2012) have expressed that bullies' parents are individuals who are unable to set clear boundaries, unstable in terms of showing compassion, cold and indifferent. It is stated that children of oppressive and authoritative parents have a higher chance of both displaying bullying behaviors and being victims (Olweus, 1995). In addition, it is seen that children from fragmented families display bullying behaviors more. Since the relationship between bullies and their parents is based on power, this causes the bully child to display bullying behaviors towards other people as well (Güven, 2015). Some children take their violent parents as their role-models and harm their peers (Gürhan, 2017). In such cases, bullies are stigmatized with negative traits by their environment and identify themselves with these traits (Güven, 2015). As a result of Arslan's study (2008), it was determined that children who witness domestic violence are subject to violence by family members and have fragmented families display bullying behaviors more compared to children who do not have these characteristics. Numerous factors such as communication problems between parents, being inadequate in supporting their children emotionally, negative family environment, domestic violence and abuse can cause the child to become a victim as well (Cardona et al., 2015; Özyürek & Kurnaz, 2019; Swearer & Hymel, 2015). Parents of children with victim status protect their children more than necessary and attempt to solve every problem for their children since they think that their children are anxious, needy and defenseless. This behavior prevents their children from developing skills and abilities, learning the correct conflict resolution skills and causes them to become victims as they are unable to defend themselves (Güven, 2015). Children who take their violent victim parents as a role-model shrink back into their shell and are subjected to bullying as well (Gürhan, 2017). Gökler (2007) has also expressed that children with bully-victim status have domestic problems; their parents often display an overly protective or negligent attitude and sometimes display abusive behaviors. In addition, bullies-victims grow up in families where the parents do not show affection, are unstable in terms of raising children, indifferent, angry and frequently use physical punishments (Gürhan, 2017).

As the age of starting school has dropped, children started going to educational institutions at early ages. Children form their first long-term relationships after their parents with their peers in schools. The quality of the relationship formed with peers and the school environment are regarded as one of the factors which affect bullying. The primary target in schools is to protect children from the risks in the school environment throughout educational life. The leading danger in the school environment is bullying (Hamurcu, 2020). There are various reasons why bullying takes place in schools. The low morale of teachers, crowded classes, implementation of unstable and strict disciplinary rules, frequent change of teachers, not giving importance to the identity development of students, social comparison and competition seen between peers, teachers' and administrators' attitude towards bullying, unclear rules and behaviors expected of students are listed as factors which lead to bullying in schools (Açıkgöz, 2017; Ekşisu, 2008; Kabil, 2010). Participation of families in bullying acts in schools and weak student-teacher relationships also affect bullying (Swearer & Hymel, 2015). In this respect, it can be stated that today's teachers are more influential in students' developing a positive character (Hilliard et al., 2015). The quality of the relationship between peers affects bullying as well. Flisher and Protogerou (2012) have expressed that the primary reason which pushes students towards bullying is their desire to acquire a higher power, respectability and status among their peer groups. According to Pellegrini (2002), the characteristics of peer groups and the social structures in schools constitute the source of bullying. At this point, great responsibilities fall on the shoulders of school principals and teachers in terms of preventing violence and bullying in school environments (Hoşgörür & Orhan, 2017). In fact, the behaviors, attitudes and routines of administrators and teachers give clues as to the extent of bullying that takes place (at classroom level or school level) (Olweus, 2003). In institutions where success is taken as the basis and methods of preventing bullying are implemented as the school culture, bullying incidents are seen less (Acar, 2009).

Short and Long-Term Effects of Bullying

Bullying has negative effects on everyone with bullying statuses in the short and long-term. The emergence of bullying in all kinds of environments where people interact (Cardona et al., 2015) can increase the negative effects of bullying on individuals. Steinberg (2005/2007) has expressed that peers can contribute to each other's psycho-social development, however they can harm their psycho-social development as well with humiliating, exclusory, insulting and harmful behaviors. The act of bullying negatively affects children's psychological and physiological health (Flannery et al., 2004). Victims are harmed more from bullying acts compared to bullies. Victims can have difficulty in adapting, develop a low sense of being, feel depressed (Özyürek & Kurnaz, 2019; Smith & Brain, 2000; Yelboğa & Koçak, 2019) and display pain, sadness, insecurity, inferiority, anxiety and loss of self-confidence (Austin & Sciarra, 2009/2017). Bullying acts cause students to develop school phobia, display low academic performance, take a dislike to school (Beran & Li, 2007; Katzer et al., 2009; Üstündağ-Şener et al., 2015) and their quality of life to decrease (Gültekin & Sayıl, 2005). Although victims have social skills, they prefer to be alone because of the bullying acts they experience (Hisar, 2018) and have inadequate leadership and friend making skills (Storey & Slaby, 2013). These children avoid being in crowded places with the fear of being subjected to bullying (Genç, 2007). It is stated that both bullies and victims have a high level of suicidal thoughts and the tendency to commit suicide (Hinduja & Patchin, 2010; Romero et al., 2013). Gini and Pozzolli (2013) have stated that health problems such as sleep disorders, headaches or stomach aches are seen in both bullies and victims. Dake et al. (2003) have determined that bullying victims experience sleep and anxiety disorders, whereas bullies experience exhaustion. Rigby (2003) has underlined that the effects of bullying can emerge in four ways as, psychologically low level of wellbeing, feeling psychological pain, physically not being in good shape and low social adaptability. Krygsman and Vaillancourt (2019) have determined in their study on pre-school children that there is a positive relationship between depression and being subjected to bullying.

It is stated that the negative effects of bullying experienced early in life can be seen in adulthood as well (Ahmed & Braithwaite, 2004). Children who display bullying can carry their aggressive, impulsive, risky and anti-social behaviors into their future lives (Kaltiala Heino et al., 2000; Pearce & Thompson, 2009). These children are at higher risk of getting involved in crime compared to children who do not display bullying behaviors (Kaltiala-Heino et al., 2000). Experiencing peer bullying causes adaptation problems and psychological problems in the later stages of children's lives (Oexle et al., 2020; Szexczyk-Sokolowski et al., 2005). Bullying victims may experience mental problems in adulthood (Özada & Duyan, 2018). Bullying incidents negatively affect individuals' self-esteem (Gillies-Rezo & Bosacki, 2003) and sense of security (Sprague & Walker, 2002). This causes the duration bullying victims develop positive social relationships to be extended over a long period of time. Bullying results in physical injuries in students as well (Jan & Husain, 2015). In some cases, the scars of physical injuries are permanent. This causes bullying victims to repeatedly experience trauma as they see these physical damages. Regardless of bullying status, children who experience bullying are unable to focus on their lessons and experience academic failure (Whitted & Dupper, 2005). This causes individuals to be unemployed in the future and not having any goals in life. In addition, it is stated that bullying acts and problematic behaviors such as substance abuse are related (Ttofi et al., 2016). At this point, it can be stated that bullying poses a danger against a healthy life both in the present time and the future.

FUTURE RESEARCH DIRECTIONS

In this section, the concept of bullying, bullying statuses, types of bullying, characteristics of bullies and victims, factors which affect bullying and short and long-term effects of bullying have been dealt with. The appearance of bullying starting from the first years of life and its gradual increase over time has necessitated extensive studies to be done on bullying. At this point, there is a need for longitudinal and cross-sectional studies which make use of both qualitative and quantitative data collection tools which will present the causes and risk factors of bullying. It is considered that these studies will be effective in terms of the preparation of intervention programs and the fight against bullying. Based on this point of view, it is suggested to make the studies on the subject more detailed, expand these studies as to cover the pre-school period as well and prepare intervention programs.

CONCLUSION

Bullying is a type of aggression where a weaker individual is intentionally and continuously harassed by a stronger person. Bully and victim children are not the only ones who are affected from bullying, as children with other bullying statuses are also subjected to the destructive effects of bullying. Regardless of whether they are direct or indirect, bullying acts prevent children from developing in a healthy manner. Bullying does not only affect the first years of life and its influence continues throughout life.

There are certain characteristics which differentiate bully and victim children from others. In order to be able to prevent bullying which causes such destruction, children with the potential of becoming bullies and victims should be identified and intervention programs should be prepared. As long as the risk factors for bullying are not known and bully children are not prevented, the incidence and intensity of bullying behaviors will increase. Therefore, it is considered that there is a need for all types of researches, activities, studies and programs which might be effective in the fight against bullying.

REFERENCES

Acar, T. (2009). *Peer bullying and psychological symptoms among nineth grade students* (UMI No. 258374) [Master's dissertation, Hacettepe University]. Higher Education Council Thesis Center database.

Açıkgöz, T. (2017). *Bullying and attitude towards secondary school students: Sample of Kartepe district* (UMI No. 462314) [Master's dissertation, Sakarya University]. Higher Education Council Thesis Center database.

Ahmed, E., & Braithwaite, V. (2004). Bullying and victimization: Cause for concern for both families and schools. *Article in Social Psychology of Education, 7*(1), 35–54. doi:10.1023/B:SPOE.0000010668.43236.60

Alper-İlhan, S. (2008). *Bullying in elementary scholl* (UMI No. 221001) [Master's dissertation, Uludağ University]. Higher Education Council Thesis Center database.

Arslan, S. (2008). *The effect of family and self concept relation on peer bullying in high school students* (UMI No. 204019) [Doctoral dissertation, Istanbul University]. Higher Education Council Thesis Center database.

Atik, G., & Kemer, G. (2008). The role of problem solving skills state=trait anger and anger expression style physical self=efficiency in predicting bullying among middle school students. *Dokuz Eylül University the Journal of Buca Faculty of Education, 23*, 198-206. https://acikerisim.deu.edu.tr/xmlui/bitstream/handle/20.500.12397/264/182.pdf?sequence=1&isAllowed=y

Austin, V. L., & Sciarra, D. T. (2017). *Çocuk ve ergenlerde duygusal ve davranışsal bozukluklar* [Children and adolescents with emotional and behavioral disorders] (3rd ed., D. M. Özekes, Ed. & Trans.). Nobel Akademik. (Original work published 2009)

Ayas, T. (2010). *Okullarda yaygın sorun olan zorbalığı önlemek* [Preventing bullying a common problem in schools] (1st ed.). Maya Akademi.

Ayas, T., & Pişkin, M. (2011). Investigation of bullying among high school students with regard to sex, grade level and school type. *Elementary Education Online, 10*(2), 550-568. https://dergipark.org.tr/tr/pub/ilkonline/issue/8592/106821

Baldry, A. C., & Farrington, D. P. (2000). Bullies and delinpunts: Personal characteristics and parental styles. *Journal of Community & Applied Social Psychology, 10*(1), 17–31. doi:10.1002/(SICI)1099-1298(200001/02)10:1<17::AID-CASP526>3.0.CO;2-M

Beran, T., & Li, Q. (2007). The relationship between cyber bullying and school bullying. *Journal of Student Wellbeing, 1*(2), 15–33.

Berger, K. (2007). Update on bullying at school: Science forgotten. *Developmental Review, 27*(1), 90–126. doi:10.1016/j.dr.2006.08.002

Berk, L. (2013). *Child development* (9th ed.). Pearson.

Berns, R. (2015). *Child, family, school, community: Socialization and support* (10th ed.). Cengage Learning.

Bradshaw, C. P., Sawyer, A. L., & O'Brennan, L. M. (2007). Bullying and peer victimization at school: Perceptual differences between students and school staff. *School Psychology Review, 36*(3), 361–382. doi:10.1080/02796015.2007.12087929

Buhs, E. S., & Ladd, G. W. (2001). Peer rejection in kindergarten as an antecedent of young children's school adjustment: An examination of mediating processes. *Developmental Psychology, 37*(4), 550–560. doi:10.1037/0012-1649.37.4.550 PMID:11444490

Burnukara, P., & Uçanok, Z. (2012). How much overlap between traditional and cyberbullying in Turkish adolescents? *Turkish Journal of Psychology, 27*(69), 81–96. https://www.psikolog.org.tr/tr/yayinlar/dergiler/1031828/tpd1300443320120000m000084.pdf

Camodeca, M., Goossens, F. A., Meerum Terwogt, M., & Schuengel, C. (2002). Bullying and victimization among school-age children: Stability and links to proactive and reactive aggression. *Social Development, 11*(3), 332–345. doi:10.1111/1467-9507.00203

Cardona, R. S., Reyes, A. S., & Tangalin, M. M. (2015). The bullying experiences and classroom discipline techniques in an Urban National High School in the Philippines: A basis for an Anti-Bullying Program. *American International Journal of Contemporary Research, 5*(2), 49–52. https://www.researchgate.net/publication/321882096_The_Bullying_Experiences_and_Classroom_Discipline_Techniques_in_an_Urban_National_High_School_in_the_Philippines_A_Basis_for_an_Anti-Bullying_Program

Çınkır, Ş., & Karaman-Kepenekçi, Y. (2003). Bullyıng among students. *Educational Administration in Theory & Practice, 34*(34), 236-253. https://dergipark.org.tr/tr/pub/kuey/issue/10363/126858

Cooper, D., & Snell, J. L. (2003). Bullying: Not just a kid thing. *Educational Leadership, 60*(6), 22–25. https://pdo.ascd.org/lmscourses/PD11OC105/media/Bullying_M1_Reading_Kid_Thing.pdf

Craig, W., Pepler, D., & Blais, J. (2007). Responding to bullying: What works. *School Psychology International, 28*(4), 465–477. doi:10.1177/0143034307084136

Currie, C., Zanotti, C., Morgan, A., Currie, D., de Looze, M., Roberts, C., Samdal, O., Smith, O. R. F., & Barnekow, V. (Eds.). (2012). *Social determinants of health and well-being among young people.* WHO Regional Office for Europe. https://www.euro.who.int/__data/assets/pdf_file/0003/163857/Social-determinants-of-health-and-well-being-among-young-people.pdf

Dake, J. A., Price, J. H., & Telljhonann, S. K. (2003). The nature and extent of bullying at school. *The Journal of School Health, 73*(5), 173–180. doi:10.1111/j.1746-1561.2003.tb03599.x PMID:12793102

Deptula, D. P., & Cohen, R. (2004). Aggressive, rejected, and delinquent children and adolescents: A comparison of their friendships. *Aggression and Violent Behavior, 9*(1), 75–104. doi:10.1016/S1359-1789(02)00117-9

Doğan, A. (2010). Ecological systems model as a framework for bullying. *Turkish Journal of Child and Adolescent Mental Health, 17*(3), 149–162. https://cms.galenos.com.tr/Uploads/Article_27669/cogepderg-17-149.pdf

Eaton, D. K., Kann, L., Kinchen, S., Shanklin, S., Flint, K. J., Hawkins, J., Harris, W. A., Lowry, R., McManus, T., Chyen, D., Whittle, L., Lim, C., & Wechsler, H. (2012). *Youth Risk Behavior Surveillance - United States, 2011.* U.S. Department of Health and Human Services. https://www.cdc.gov/mmwr/preview/mmwrhtml/ss6104a1.htm

Englander, E. K., & Muldowney, A. (2007). Just turn the darn thing off: Understanding cyberbullying. In D. L. White, B. C. Glenn & A. Wimes (Eds.), *Proceedings of persistently safe schools: The 2007 National Conference on safe schools* (pp. 83-92). Hamilton Fish Institute, George Washington University.

Erdal, C. (2019). *Investigation of the relationship between cyberbullying / victimization and Monoamine Oxidase A enzyme gene polymorphism in university students* (UMI No. 615048) [Master's dissertation, Uskudar University]. Higher Education Council Thesis Center database.

Ergül-Topçu, A. (2018). A review of prevalence and nature of peer bullying at schools. *Crisis Journal, 26*(2). https://dergipark.org.tr/kriz/issue/41895/505251

Eşkisu, M. (2009). *Investigation of the relationship between the bullying grade, family functions and perceived social support among high school students* (UMI No. 270114) [Master's dissertation, Istanbul University]. Higher Education Council Thesis Center database.

Espelage, D., & Swearer, S. (2003). *Bullying in American schools: A social-ecological perspective on prevention and intervention* (1st ed.). Lawrence Erlbaum Associates.

Essa, E. (2003). *A practical guide to solving preschool behavior problems* (5th ed.). Delmar Cengage Learning.

Flannery, D. J., Wester, K. L., & Singer, M. I. (2004). Impact of exposure to violance in school on child and adolescent mental health and behaviour. *Journal of Community Psychology, 32*(5), 559–573. doi:10.1002/jcop.20019

Genç, G. (2007). *Peer bullying and its management in high schools* (UMI No. 226994) [Doctoral dissertation, Inönü University]. Higher Education Council Thesis Center database.

Gillies-Rezo, S., & Bosacki, S. (2003). Invisible bruises: Kindergartens' perceptions of bullying. *International Journal of Children's Spirituality, 8*(2), 163–177. doi:10.1080/13644360304628

Gini, G., & Pozzoli, T. (2013). Bullied children and psychosomatic problems: A meta-analysis. *Pediatrics, 132*(4), 720–729. doi:10.1542/peds.2013-0614 PMID:24043275

Gökler, R. (2007). *Examination of school bullying with regard to some variables among middle school children* (UMI No. 235698) [Doctoral dissertation, Ankara University]. Higher Education Council Thesis Center database.

Gülay, H. (2018). *Okul öncesi dönemde akran ilişkileri* [Peer relationships in the preschool period] (3rd ed.). Eğiten.

Gültekin, Z., & Sayıl, M. (2005). A study of the reliability and validity of the Peer Victimization Scale. *Turkish Psychology Articles, 15,* 47-61. https://toad.halileksi.net/sites/default/files/pdf/akran-zorbaligini-belirleme-olcegi-toad_1.pdf

Gültekin-Akduman, G. (2010). Peer bullying of 7-14 year old children and their proffers of solution. *Journal of Theoretical Educational Science, 3*(2), 13–26. https://dergipark.org.tr/tr/download/article-file/304137

Gültekin-Akduman, G. (2012). An investigation of peer bullying at preschool period. *Journal of Society & Social Work, 23*(1), 107–120. https://dergipark.org.tr/tr/pub/tsh/issue/48532/615984

Gürhan, N. (2017). All aspects of the bullying. *Turkey Clinics J Psychiatr Nurs-Special Topics, 3*(2), 175-181. https://www.researchgate.net/publication/319257215_Her_Yonu_ile_Akran_Zorbaligi

Güven, F. (2015). *An invastigation of bullying and being victim at 8th grade secondary school students, in relation with sex, parent education, socioeconomic status and emphaty level* (UMI No. 408926) [Master's dissertation, Toros University]. Higher Education Council Thesis Center database.

Güvenir, T. (2005). Okulda akran istismarı [Peer abuse at school] (1st ed.). Kök.

Hamurcu, S. (2020). Peer bullying in primary school students: The case of Ankara Pursaklar. *OPUS–International Journal of Society Researches, 16*(32), 5540–5564. doi:10.26466/opus.758653

Hanish, L. D., & Guerra, N. G. (2000). Children who get victimized at school: What is known? What can be done? *Professional School Counseling, 4*(2), 113–119.

Hilliard, L. J., Batanova, M., & Bowers, E. P. (2015). A positive youth development approach to bullying: Promoting thriving and reducing problem behaviors. In E. P. Bowers, G. J. Geldhof, S. K. Johnson, L. J. Hilliard, R. M. Hershberg, J. V. Lerner, & R. M. Lerner (Eds.), *Promoting positive youth development: Lessons from the 4-H study* (pp. 249–272). Springer. doi:10.1007/978-3-319-17166-1_13

Hinduja, S., & Patchin, J. W. (2010). Bullying, cyberbullying, and suicide. *Archives of Suicide Research, 14*(3), 206–221. doi:10.1080/13811118.2010.494133 PMID:20658375

Hisar, T. (2018). *The influence of family communication in the relationship among substance addiction, bullying and anger in individuals between 15 and 25 years old* (UMI No. 486087) [Master's dissertation, Üsküdar University]. Higher Education Council Thesis Center database.

Horzum, M. B., & Ayas, T. (2011). He examination of cyberbullying and victimlevels of highschool students according to school type and gender. *Journal of Educational Sciences & Practices, 10*(20), 139–159.

Hoşgörür, V., & Orhan, A. (2017). The causes of bullying and violence at schools and managing the prevention of it (the sample of Muğla province). *Journal of Bayburt Education Faculty, 12*(24), 859–880. https://dergipark.org.tr/en/pub/befdergi/issue/33599/292827

Hunter, S. C., Boyle, J. M. E., & Warden, D. (2004). Help seeking amongst child and adolescent victims of peeraggression and bullying: The influence of school-stage, gender, victimisation, appraisal, and emotion. *The British Journal of Educational Psychology, 74*(3), 375–390. doi:10.1348/0007099041552378 PMID:15296546

Jacobs, A. (2008). Compenents of evidence-based intervevtions for bullying and peer victimization. In M. Roberts (Ed.), *Handbook of evidence-based therapies for children and adolescents* (pp. 261–279). Springer. doi:10.1007/978-0-387-73691-4_15

Jan, A., & Husain, S. (2015). Bullying in elementary schools: Its causes and effects on students. *Journal of Education and Practice, 6*(19), 43–56. https://files.eric.ed.gov/fulltext/EJ1079521.pdf

Kabil, M. (2010). *Affects of number of students in classes on bullying behavior* (UMI No. 253402) [Master's dissertation, Sakarya University]. Higher Education Council Thesis Center database.

Kaltiala-Heino, R., Rimpela, M., Rantanen, P., & Rimpela, A. (2000). Bullying at school-an indicator of adolescents at risk for mental disorders. *Journal of Adolescence, 23*(6), 661–674. doi:10.1006/jado.2000.0351 PMID:11161331

Karaca, K. (2018). *Examining the prevalence of the peer bullying and levels of depression and anxiety of the bully-victims in the secondary schools* (UMI No. 497276) [Master's dissertation, Atatürk University]. Higher Education Council Thesis Center database.

Karataş, H. (2011). *Examining the effect of the program developed to adress bullying in primary schools* (UMI No. 304497) [Doctoral dissertation, Dokuz Eylül University]. Higher Education Council Thesis Center database.

Katzer, C., Fetchenhauer, D., & Belschack, R. (2009). Cyber bullying: Who are the victims? A comparison of victimization in internet chatrooms and victimization at school. *Journal of Media Psychology*, *1*(21), 25–36. doi:10.1027/1864-1105.21.1.25

Kavşut, F. (2009). *The research of the relationship betweeen peer bullying and emotional intelligence in adolescents* (UMI No. 241590) [Master's dissertation, Abant İzzet Baysal University]. Higher Education Council Thesis Center database.

Koç-Yıldırım, P. (2003). *Çıkmaz sokak: Okulda şiddet ve zorbalık* [Dead end: Violence and bullying at school]. Nobel.

Krygsman, A., & Vaillancourt, T. (2019). Peer victimization, aggression, and depression symptoms in preschoolers. *Early Childhood Research Quarterly*, *47*, 62–73. doi:10.1016/j.ecresq.2018.09.006

Lamb, J., Pepler, D. J., & Craig, W. (2009). Approach to bullying and victimization. *Canadian Family Physician Medecin de Famille Canadien*, *55*(4), 356–360. https://www.researchgate.net/publication/24278081_Approach_to_bullying_and_victimization PMID:19366941

Levine, E., & Tamburrino, M. (2014). Bullying among young children: Strategies for prevention. *Early Childhood Education Journal*, *42*(4), 271–278. doi:10.100710643-013-0600-y

Leymann, H. (1996). The content and development of mobbing at work. *European Journal of Work and Organizational Psychology*, *5*(2), 165–184. doi:10.1080/13594329608414853

Liang, H., Flisher, A. J., & Lomard, C. J. (2007). Bullying, violence, and risk behavior in south african school students. *Child Abuse & Neglect*, *31*(2), 161–171. doi:10.1016/j.chiabu.2006.08.007 PMID:17313977

Lyznicki, J. M., McCaffree, M. A., & Robinowitz, C. B. (2004). Childhood bullying: Implications for physicians. *American Family Physician*, *70*(9), 1723–1728. https://www.aafp.org/afp/2004/1101/p1723.html PMID:15554490

McDougall, L. (1999). A study of bullying in further education. *Pastoral Care in Education*, *17*(2), 31–37. doi:10.1111/1468-0122.00125

Metin-Aslan, M., & Tuğrul, B. (2014). The content analysis of preschool children's bullying and victimization behaviors in play. *Journal of Theoretical Educational Science*, *7*(1), 60–77. doi:10.5578/keg.6205

Metin-Aslan, Ö., & Tuğrul, B. (2013). Analyzing preschool children's bullying and play behavior during play. *Mediterranean Journal of Educational Research,* *7*(13), 27-41. https://mjer.penpublishing.net/makale_indir/330

Mills, M. (2001). *Challenging violence in schools: An issue of masculinities*. Open University.

Mynard, H., & Joseph, S. (2000). Development of the Multidimentional Peer Victimization Scale. *Aggressive Behavior*, *26*(2), 169–178. doi:10.1002/(SICI)1098-2337(2000)26:2<169::AID-AB3>3.0.CO;2-A

Oexle, N., Ribeiro, W., Fisher, H. L., Gronholm, P. C., Laurens, K. R., Pan, P., Owens, S., Romeo, R., Rüsch, N., & Lacko, S. E. (2020). Childhood bullying victimization, self-labeling, and help seeking for mental health problems. *Social Psychiatry and Psychiatric Epidemiology, 55*(1), 81–88. doi:10.100700127-019-01743-5 PMID:31324960

Olweus, D. (2003). A profile of bullying at school. *Educational Leadership, 60*(6), 12–17. https://www.researchgate.net/publication/279570438_A_profile_of_bullying_at_school

Olweus, D. (2004). *Bullying at school* (9th ed.). Blackwell.

Olweus, D., & Limber, S. (2007). *Olweus bully prevention program: Teacher guide*. Hazelden.

Olweus, D., Limber, S., & Mihalic, S. F. (1999). Bullying prevention program: Blueprints for violence prevention, book nine. Blueprints for violence prevention series. Center for the Study and Prevention of Violence.

Özada, A., & Duyan, V. (2018). Parent-child relationships and bullying. *Turkish Journal of Family Medicine and Primary Care, 12*(1), 49–55. doi:10.21763/tjfmpc.399941

Öztuna, A. (2018). *Relationship between physiological indications and performing peer victimization and being exposed to peer victimization and ninth and tenth grade students* (UMI No. 526005) [Master's dissertation, İstanbul University]. Higher Education Council Thesis Center database.

Özyürek, A., & Kurnaz, F. B. (2019). Evaluation form for bully and victim child behavior: Reliability and validity. *Mersin University Journal of the Faculty of Education, 15*(1), 246–261. doi:10.17860/mersinefd.401251

Paul, S., Smith, P. K., & Blumberg, H. H. (2013). Surveying bullying using peer nomination methods. *Paediatrics Today (Tuzla), 9*(1), 102–111. doi:10.5457/p2005-114.67

Pearce, J. B., & Thompson, A. E. (2009). Practical approaches to reduce the impact of bullying. *Archives of Disease in Childhood, 79*(6), 528–531. doi:10.1136/adc.79.6.528 PMID:10211002

Pekel, N. (2004). *The Examination of peer victimization groups in terms of sociometric status, loneliness and acedemic achievement* (UMI No. 144590) [Master's dissertation, Hacettepe University]. Higher Education Council Thesis Center database.

Pellegrini, A. D. (2002). Bullying, victimization and sexual harassment during the transition to middle school. *Educational Psychologist, 37*(3), 151–163. doi:10.1207/S15326985EP3703_2

Pellegrini, A. D., & Long, J. D. (2002). A longitudinal study of bullying, dominance, and victimization during the transition from primary school through secondary school. *British Journal of Developmental Psychology, 20*(2), 259–280. doi:10.1348/026151002166442

Perren, S., & Alsaker, F. D. (2006). Social behavior and peer relationships of victims, bully victims, and bullies in kindergarten. *Journal of Child Psychology and Psychiatry, and Allied Disciplines, 47*(1), 45–57. doi:10.1111/j.1469-7610.2005.01445.x PMID:16405640

Pişkin, M. (2002). School bullying: Definition, types, associated factors and precautions to take. *Educational Sciences: Theory and Practice*, *2*(2), 531–562. https://app.trdizin.gov.tr/makale/TWpFME1qST0/okul-zorbaligi-tanimi-turleri-iliskili-oldugu-faktorler-ve-alinabilecek-onlemler

Pişkin, M. (2003). A common problem in our schools: Peer bullying. In *7. National Psychological Counseling and Guidance Congress*. İnönü University.

Polanin, J. R., Espelage, D. L., & Pigott, T. D. (2012). A meta-analysis of school-based bullying prevention programs'' effects on by stander ıntervention behavior. *School Psychology Review*, *41*(1), 47–65. doi:10.1080/02796015.2012.12087375

Porter, L. (2007). *Bullying. Student behaviour: Theory and practice for teachers* (3rd ed.). Allen and Unwin.

Protogerou, C., & Flisher, A. J. (2012). Bullying in schools. In A. van Niekerk, S. Suffla & M. Seedat (Eds.), Crime, violence and injury in South Africa: 21st century solutions for child safety (pp.119-133). MRC-University of South Africa Safety & Peace Promotion Research Unit.

Rigby, K. (2002). Bullying in childhood. In P. K. Smith & C. H. Hart (Eds.), *Blackwell handbooks of developmental psychology. Blackwell handbook of childhood social development* (pp. 549–568). Blackwell.

Rigby, K. (2002). *New perspectives on bullying* (1st ed.). Jessica Kingsley.

Rigby, K. (2003). Consequences of bullying in school. *Canadian Journal of Psychiatry*, *48*(9), 583–590. doi:10.1177/070674370304800904 PMID:14631878

Rivers, I., Poteat, V. P., Noret, N., & Ashurst, N. (2009). Observing bullying at school: The mental health implications of witness status. *School Psychology Quarterly*, *24*(4), 211–223. doi:10.1037/a0018164

Romero, A. J., Wiggs, V. B., Valencia, C., & Bauman, S. (2013). Latina teen suicide and bullying. *Hispanic Journal of Behavioral Sciences*, 1–15. doi:10.1177/0739986312474237

Sakarya, S., & Pekdoğan, S. (2020). The predictive power of temperament traits on the bully and victim behaviors of the child. *International Journal of Euroasian Research*, *8*(23), 311–324. doi:10.33692/avrasyad.655616

Salı, G. (2014). An examination of peer relationships and exposure to peer violence among pre-school children in terms of different variables. *Cukurova University Faculty of Education Journal, 43*(2), 195-216. https://dergipark.org.tr/tr/download/article-file/46526

Salmivalli, C. (2010). Bullying and the peer group: A review. *Aggression and Violent Behavior*, *15*(2), 112–120. doi:10.1016/j.avb.2009.08.007

Satan, A. (2011). The relationship of between peer pressure self-esteem and alcohol use among adolescents. *Marmara University Atatürk Education Faculty Journal of Educational Sciences, 34*(34), 183-194. https://dergipark.org.tr/tr/pub/maruaebd/issue/376/2488

Schoen, S., & Schoen, A. (2010). Bullying and harassment in the United States. *The Clearing House: A Journal of Educational Strategies, Issues and Ideas*, *83*(2), 68–72. doi:10.1080/00098650903386444

Selçuk, Z., & Güner, N. (2004). *Sınıf içi rehberlik uygulamaları* [In-class guidance applications]. 4th ed.). Pegem A.

Serra-Negra, J. M., Paiya, S. M., Bendo, C. B., Fulgencio, L. B., Lage, C. F., Correa-Faria, P., & Pordeus, I. A. (2015). Verbal school bullying and life satisfaction among Brazilian adolescents: Profiles of the aggressor and the victim. *Comprehensive Psychiatry*, *57*, 132–139. doi:10.1016/j.comppsych.2014.11.004 PMID:25465652

Smith, P. K., & Brain, P. (2000). Bullying in schools: Lessons from two decades of research. *Aggressive Behavior*, *26*(1), 1–9. doi:10.1002/(SICI)1098-2337(2000)26:1<1::AID-AB1>3.0.CO;2-7

Smith, P. K., Mandavi, J., Carvalho, M., Fisher, S., Russell, S., & Tippett, N. (2008). Cyberbullying: Its nature and impact in secondary school pupils. *Journal of Child Psychology and Psychiatry, and Allied Disciplines*, *49*(4), 376–385. doi:10.1111/j.1469-7610.2007.01846.x PMID:18363945

Smokowski, P. R., & Evans, C. B. R. (2019). *Bullying and victimization across the lifespan: Playground politics and power* (1st ed.). Springer. doi:10.1007/978-3-030-20293-4

Smokowski, P. R., & Kopasz, K. H. (2005). Bullying in school: An overview of types, effects, family characteristics, and intervention strategies. *Children & Schools*, *27*(2), 101–110. doi:10.1093/cs/27.2.101

Solberg, M. E., Olweus, D., & Enderesen, I. M. (2007). Bullies and victims at school: Are they the same pupils? *The British Journal of Educational Psychology*, *77*(2), 441–464. doi:10.1348/000709906X105689 PMID:17504556

Sprague, J., & Walker, H. (2002). *Creating school wide prevention and intervention strategies*. Northwest Regıonal Educatıonal Laboratory. https://www.ojp.gov/pdffiles1/ojjdp/book1.pdf

Steinberg, L. S. (2007). Ergenlik. İmge. (Original work published 2005)

Storey, K., & Slaby, R. (2013). *Eyes on bullying in early childhood*. Education Development Center. http://www.promoteprevent.org/sites/www.promoteprevent.org/files/resources/Eyes%20on%20Bullying%20in%20Early%20Childhood_1.pdf

Swearer, S. M., & Hymel, S. (2015). Understanding the psyhology of bullying: Moving toward a social-ecological diathesis-stress model. *The American Psychologist*, *70*(4), 344–353. doi:10.1037/a0038929 PMID:25961315

Szewczyk-Sokolowski, M., Bost, K. K., & Wainwright, A. B. (2005). Attachment, temperament and preschool children's peer acceptance. *Social Development*, *14*(3), 379–397. doi:10.1111/j.1467-9507.2005.00307.x

Topçu, Ç. (2008). *He relationship of cyber bullying to empathy, gender, traditional bullying, internet use and adult monitoring* (UMI No. 227700) [Master's dissertation, Middle East Technical University]. Higher Education Council Thesis Center database.

Ttofi, M. M., Farrington, D. P., Lösel, F., Crago, R. V., & Theodorakis, N. (2016). School bullying and drug use later in life: A meta-analytic investigation. *School Psychology Quarterly*, *31*(1), 8–27. doi:10.1037pq0000120 PMID:25866866

United Nations Educational, Scientific and Cultural Organization. (2017). *School violence and bullying global status report*. UNESCO. https://unesdoc.unesco.org/ark:/48223/pf0000246970

Üstündağ-Şener, N., Başar, M., Şen, B., & Göncü, A. (2015). The teachers' views on student bullying behavior and investigation of learning environment. *Journal of Educational Sciences, 41*(41), 157–173. doi:10.15285/ebd.22661

Uysal, H., & Dinçer, Ç. (2012). Peer bullying during early childhood. *Journal of Theoretical Educational Science, 5*(4), 468–483. https://dergipark.org.tr/tr/download/article-file/304203

Veenstra, R., Lindenberg, S., Oldehikel, A. J., De-Winter, A. F., Verhulst, F. C., & Ormel, J. (2005). Bullying and victimization in elementary schools: A comparison of bullies, victims, bully/victims, and uninvolved preadolescents. *Developmental Psychology, 41*(4), 672–682. doi:10.1037/0012-1649.41.4.672 PMID:16060813

Volk, A. A., Dane, A. V., & Marini, Z. A. (2014). What is bullying? A theoretical redefinition. *Developmental Review, 34*(4), 327–343. doi:10.1016/j.dr.2014.09.001

Whitted, K. S., & Dupper, D. R. (2005). Best practices for preventing or reducing bullying in schools. *Children & Schools, 27*(3), 167–175. doi:10.1093/cs/27.3.167

Wolke, D., Woods, S., Bloomfield, L., & Karstadt, L. (2000). The association between direct and relational bullying and behaviour problems among primary school children. *Journal of Child Psychology and Psychiatry, and Allied Disciplines, 41*(8), 989–1002. doi:10.1111/1469-7610.00687 PMID:11099116

Wolke, D., Woods, S., Stanford, K., & Schulz, H. (2001). Bullying and victimization of primary school children in England and Germany: Prevalence and school factors. *British Journal of Psychology, 92*(4), 673–696. doi:10.1348/000712601162419 PMID:11762868

Wong, J. S. (2009). *No bullies allowed understanding peer victimization, the impacts on delinquency, and the effectiveness of prevention programs* [Unpublished doctoral dissertation]. Pardee RAND Graduate School, Santa Monica.

Yelboğa, N., & Koçak, O. (2019). Evaluation of some factors predicting peer bullying in adolescents. *OPUS International Journal of Society Researches, 13*(19), 2286–2320. doi:10.26466/opus.543567

Yıldırım, R. (2012). Peer bullying. *Manisa Celal Bayar University Journal of Social Sciences, 10*(2), 39-51. https://dergipark.org.tr/tr/download/article-file/45882

Yıldırım, S. (2001). *The Relationship of bullying, family environment and popularity* (UMI No. 105069) [Master's dissertation, Middle East Technical University]. Higher Education Council Thesis Center database.

ADDITIONAL READING

Camodeca, M., & Coppola, G. (2018). Participant roles in preschool bullying: The impact of emotion regulation, social preference, and quality of the teacher-child relationship. *Social Development*, *28*(1), 3–21. doi:10.1111ode.12320 PMID:29618853

Colorosso, B. (2003). *The bully, the bullied, and the bystander* (1st ed.). HarperResource.

Gür, N., Eray, Ş., Makinecioğlu, İ., Sığırlı, D., & Vural, A. P. (2020). The relationship of peer bullying with familial expressed emotion and psychopathology. *Anatolian Journal of Psychiatry*, *21*(1), 77–86. doi:10.5455/apd.43917

Kapcı, E. G. (2004). Bullying type and severity among elementary school students and its relationship with depression, anxiety and self esteem. *Ankara University. Journal of Faculty of Educational Sciences*, *37*(1), 1–13. https://dergipark.org.tr/tr/download/article-file/509200

Kovač, V. B., & Cameron, D. L. (2021). Are we talking about the same thing? A survey of preschool workers' attitudes and beliefs about bullying. *Child Care in Practice*, 1–15. doi:10.1080/13575279.2021.1951167

Ostrov, J. M., Kamper-DeMarco, K. E., Blakely-McClure, S. J., Perry, K. J., & Mutignani, L. (2018). Prospective associations between aggression/bullying and adjustment in preschool: Is general aggression different from bullying behavior? *Journal of Child and Family Studies*. Advance online publication. doi:10.100710826-018-1055-y

Şahin, M., & Akbaba, S. (2017). *Okulda ve sanal ortamda zorbalık ve empati* [Bullying and empathy at school and online] (1st ed.). Nobel.

Tanrıkulu, İ., Kandemir-Özdinç, N., & Besnili, Z. N. (2021). An Investigation of the Relationships between School Structure and Preschool Bullying. Erzincan University Journal of Education Faculty, 23(3), 857-873. doi:10.17556/erziefd.875930

Türk Kurtça, T., Ermağan-Çağlar, E., & Sanal-Özcan, Y. (2020). A review on the relationship between peer bullying and post-traumatic stress disorder. *Kastamonu Education Journal*, *28*(2), 584–595. doi:10.24106/kefdergi.693410

KEY TERMS AND DEFINITIONS

Aggressiveness: It covers all sorts of actions intended to harm others.

Bully-Victim: A bully-victim is a person who sometimes displays bullying behaviors and sometimes is victimized by bullies.

Direct Bullying: It is a type of bullying, which is openly directed at the victim, and the bully and the victim have interaction.

Indirect Bullying: It is a type of bullying intended to harm the social relationships of the victim in a secretive manner.

Peer Bullying: It is a type of aggression where a weaker individual is intentionally and continuously harassed by a stronger person.

Victim: A victim is a person who is targeted by a bully and is subjected to bullying.

Violence: It is the use of physical power to harm others.

Chapter 23
The Role of Teachers in Peer Bullying

Dicle Cantekin
Gazi University, Turkey

Gülümser Gültekin Akduman
Gazi University, Turkey

ABSTRACT

In addition to the school, family, and community, teachers also play a critical role in the prevention and intervention plans for peer bullying. The role of teachers in peer bullying will be explained. It is planned to create a framework for the arrangements that teachers should make in the prevention and intervention phases of peer bullying. Therefore, the components that teachers can apply to prevent peer bullying, education programs, classroom environments, and what needs to be done at the individual level, will be explained with sub-titles. Some suggestions will be made to help teachers support peer relationships.

INTRODUCTION

Peer bullying, which is accepted as a global health problem, is an important problem that draws attention to its worldwide prevalence by the World Health Organization (WHO) and the United Nations (UN). According to the WHO (2012) report, approximately 32% of children in 38 countries/regions are exposed to various forms of bullying. Bullying is an international problem that negatively affects prosperity (http://uis.unesco.org/en/news/new-sdg-4-data-bullying). Although studies on bullying concentrate on primary and high school students; It is seen that it starts in the pre-school period (Gültekin Akduman, 2012). In order to eliminate the development of bullying in the following years, it is important to monitor the aggressive behaviors of young children closely and to intervene by examining them at the earliest period.

Peer bullying is defined as the deliberate and negative behaviors of individuals that create verbal, psychological, physical, or social pain and stress on powerless people (Besag, 1989). Olweus (1993), on the other hand, defines peer bullying, as a sub-dimension of aggression, as the repeated use of violence by the strong child on the weaker without any provocative element. Bullying is considered as a

DOI: 10.4018/978-1-6684-5426-8.ch023

sub-genre of aggression. Bully children are usually those who are powerful or perceived as powerful by the abuser. Bully children can be active, sociable, popular, full of hostility and aggressive in their peer structure. It has been determined that bully children have aggressive, quarrelsome, destructive, negative self-esteem and low level of social competence. Children who resort to violence have more positive attitudes towards bullying than other children. These children may have different characteristics within the peer group. Some bully children have few friends and are lonely (Gillies-Rezo & Bosacki, 2003; Kartal & Bilgin, 2007).

Children who experience peer bullying in schools are more likely to face negative consequences in the future. Studies have shown that exposure to peer violence may be associated with depression, loneliness, behavioral disorders, low academic performance, school dropout, and substance use in the coming years. On the contrary, it has been revealed that children with higher peer acceptance are more successful in academic and emotional areas in their adult lives. (Boulton & Underwood, 1992; Audley- Piotrowski & Patterson, 2015; Ladd & Burgess, 2001).

Olweus and Limber (2010) formed the bullying cycle consisting of 7 types of student groups. Accordingly, the groups in the bullying cycle are bullies (students who bully), followers or henchmen, supporters or passive bullies, passive supporters or possible bullies, disengaged onlookers, possible defenders and defenders.

Figure 1. Bullying Circle (Olweus & Limber, 2010).

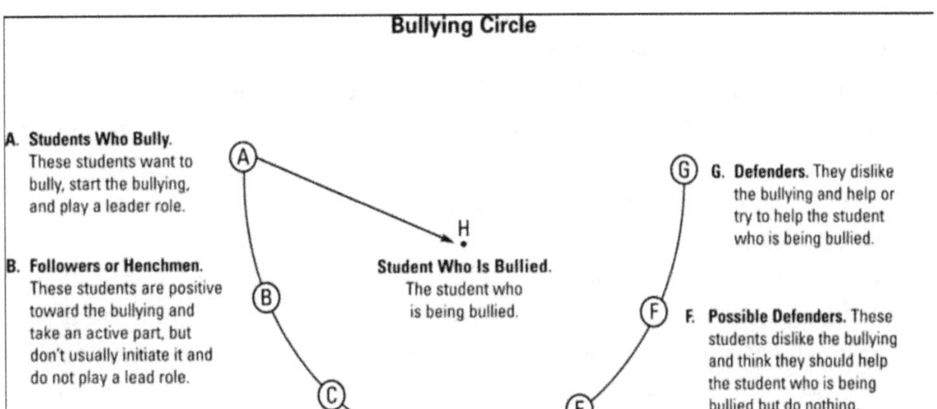

- The bullies initiate the bullying and take on the role of the leader.
- Followers or henchmens have a favorable attitude to bullying. But they usually do not initiate the bullying and do not take the leading role.
- Supporters or passive bullies explicitly support bullying. They do this by laughing or drawing attention to the action. But they do not engage in bullying.

- Passive supporters or possible bullies love bullying but they don't show their support openly.
- Disengaged onlookers do not engage in or take an active part in the act of bullying. They watch the events, saying 'it's none of my business'.
- Possible defenders do not like bullying but do not actively intervene even though they want to help the victim. Their dislike of bullying is just a word. They pay lip-service to bullying.
- Defenders dislike bullying and try to help the victim.

Peer bullying can start in the pre-school period. Children who show bullying behavior in the early years may continue these behaviors in the following years. Different classifications of peer bullying can be made. Olweus &Limber (2018) examine the types of bullying in 3 categories: direct, indirect and cyberbullying. Direct bullying includes physical and verbal behaviors. Physical bullying is openly exhibited behaviors such as attacking, hitting, pushing and damaging property against the targeted person. Verbal bullying, on the other hand, is openly displayed behaviors such as threatening, teasing, swearing, and nicknaming. Indirect bullying includes behaviors such as exclusion from the group, social pressure, gossip, damaging relationships, and isolating the targeted person socially. Cyberbullying, on the other hand, is a type of bullying that is used to harass, threaten or intimidate peers through computers, mobile phones and other electronic devices (Archer & Coyne, 2005; Bhat, 2008; Hinduja & Patchin, 2014; Scheithauer et al., 2006).

Nowadays, considering the short and long-term effects of bullying on children's physical and mental health, many programs have been developed to prevent peer bullying. Teachers, students, school administrators, parents and guidance services need to cooperate in the fight against peer bullying in schools (Smith et al., 2004; Ttofi & Farrington, 2008).

In these prevention and intervention plans, teachers play a critical role as well as school, family and society. It is very important for teachers to be aware of bullying and to know bullying comprehensively. Likewise, teachers' behaviors and attitudes will be determinative in preventing bullying and children's coping skills against bullying (Farrington & Ttofi, 2009; Smith & Shu, 2000; Van der Wal et al., 2003).

In the light of such information, the role of teachers in peer bullying will be tried to explain. It is planned to create a framework for the arrangements that teachers should make in the prevention and intervention phases of peer bullying. Therefore, the components that teachers can apply to prevent peer bullying; education programs, classroom environments and what needs to be done at the individual level will be explained with sub-titles. Some suggestions will be made to help teachers support peer relationships.

Teachers' Attitudes Towards Peer Bullying

In terms of peer relations, educational institutions are the first and only place where peers meet regularly. Teachers often face different kinds of problems in developing and supporting peer relationships among children. When peer relation problems are examined, it is seen that there are peer bullying, physical aggression, difficulties in cooperation, and turn-taking behaviors (Moon, 2001). Bullying is a problematic type of relationship formed by aggression. Teachers and school management are the people who witness the peer bullying of children the most. The attitudes of teachers, especially school management, towards peer bullying in classrooms and schools are a valuable criterion in creating a safe environment.

There are many studies examining teachers' attitudes towards peer bullying. In a study, 21% of the students stated that when they reported the bullying incident to their teachers, they would not be interested in the incident. In another study, it is seen that teachers do not have sufficient knowledge and equipment about peer bullying despite their professional experience (Bauman & Hurley, 2005; Glover et al., 2000; Ihnat & Smith, 2013; Kennedy et al., 2012). As a result of a study examining the teachers' coping strategies against peer bullying, it is seen that the students mostly use the strategies of ignoring, warning/threatening, verbal and physical violence, using a mediator, and trying to solve the situation fairly when they bully. In another study on teachers, it is determined that teachers give more importance to verbal bullying behaviors. In addition, it is emphasized that they intervene more directly in bullying situations than in indirect bullying situations (Duy, 2013).

These studies indicate that teachers have difficulty in recognizing or do not make appropriate interventions due to the indirect practice of peer bullying. Besides, when the views on when and where the bullying occurs are analyzed, it is seen that it takes place in the corridor, toilet and schoolyard where they are not under the supervision of teachers. This may cause some school administrators and teachers to think that bullying does not occur in their own schools. At the same time, educators believe that conflicts between students are natural and that they can be resolved among themselves (Bullock, 2002; Graham, 2011; Hunt, 2011; Başar & Çetin, 2013; Çınkır & Kepenekçi, 2003). Teachers are the key in all bullying incidents (Olweus & Limber, 2013). Therefore, teachers and other personnel should be positive role models. It is important that the teacher directly supports peer relations with his communication style, arrangements in the education program, close, warm and interested attitude (Gülay Ogelman, 2018).

In order to be a positive teacher, the following approaches should be internalized carefully.

- Being respectful and sincere
- Predetermining the rules and putting them into practice in a courteous and determined manner
- Creating classroom rituals, organizing enjoyable and peaceful activities
- Trusting the student and giving him/her responsibility and choice.
- Talking about the problems with the student privately at the end of the lesson, not during the lesson.
- Being open to cooperation
- Involving parents in the process
- Giving positive feedback to the student (Çevik, 2021)

Teachers' having sufficient and correct information in their efforts to prevent peer bullying, their comprehensive knowledge of intervention programs have an important role in preventing students from being exposed to bullying (Smith & Shu, 2000).

Relationships between teacher and student showed the effect of students on their roles in bullying (Chang, 2003). For this reason, the warm and positive nature of the relationship between teacher and student can enable students who experience bullying to express their problems more easily. In addition, teachers can intervene in bullying behaviors early by communicating better with students who are bullied (Okur Karahan, 2020). Teacher-student relationship should be positive and solid because teacher attitudes have an important place in peer bullying. Teachers' attitudes should be carefully examined and their roles should be emphasized. It should be noted that teacher reactions affect the behavior of bullies, victims, and bystanders in later life.

Components that Teachers Can Apply to Prevent Peer Bullying

Schools need to have a comprehensive anti-bullying policy. These policies will provide a framework for reducing bullying. An anti-bullying policy should include intervention planning for bullies, victims, and bystanders (Pepler & Craig, 2014). The school administration, teachers, parents and students responsible for the execution of the intervention plan should be detailed and the details of the policy should be specified.

Figure 2. The practices of teachers to prevent bullying behaviors are presented at three different levels as follows.

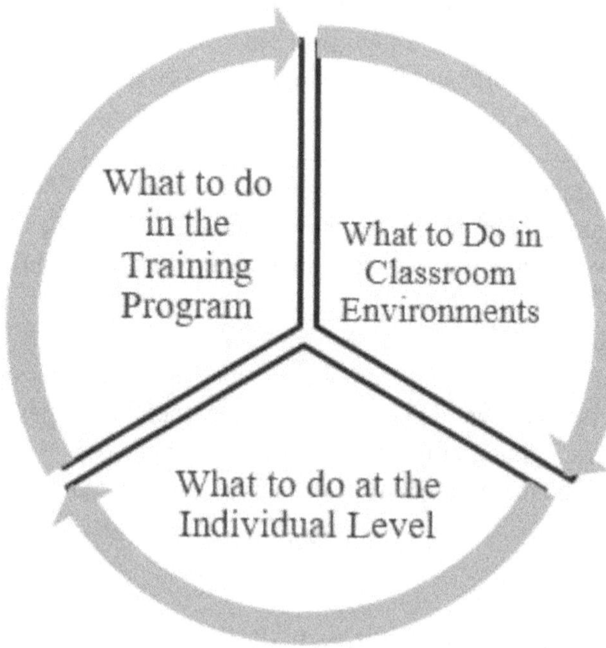

What to Do in the Training Program

Approaches to the prevention of bullying should be examined in a very broad framework, including assessment, prevention and intervention (Crothers & Levinson, 2004). For this reason, teachers have great responsibilities in preventing and intervening peer bullying in schools. It is especially important to plan an effective training program both in the prevention phase and in the intervention phase. It is necessary to support various social skills of students in order to contribute to peer relations.

Children who acquire these skills will have the opportunity to be in harmony with their peers and establish healthy communication before resorting to violence (Akay, 2019; O'Moore & Minton, 2004; Pişkin, 2006). Therefore, teachers should develop these skills that prevent bullying behaviors. Gaining these skills at an early age is important for establishing healthy relationships. Teachers, administrators, parents and students should work in coordination in order for the training programs to be implemented to yield positive results. These skills, which will support social skills and positive peer relations, will contribute to the prevention of peer bullying.

Table 1. Important social skills to be acquired by children to prevent peer bullying

Social and Emotional Skills Training	It is the process of acquiring necessary the knowledge, attitudes and skills and effectively applying to manage the emotions of children and adults, to set and achieve positive goals, to feel and show empathy for others, to establish positive relationships and to make responsible decisions. Social and emotional skills training involves five basic qualifications that can be taught in a variety of settings and methods. These are; self-awareness, self-management, social awareness, relationship skills, and responsible decision-making (Weissberg & Cascarino, 2013).
Communication Skills Training	Communication skills are the skills to use verbal and non-verbal communication together, to take responsibility for feelings, thoughts and behaviors using self-centered language, to express oneself, to ask questions and to react effectively (Cüceloğlu, 2001). Communication skills training will contribute to find constructive solutions against bullying and to receive support from their environment for children (Sönmezay, 2010). It is stated that negative behaviors and bullying will decrease in schools where positive communication is established (Heinrichs, 2003).
Respect for Diversity Training	Within the scope of training; First of all, it is ensured that children get to know themselves, show respect and tolerance to different cultures and work with different cultures, avoid prejudices and provide them with anti-discrimination education (Aykut, 2019).
Empathy Training	The aim of empathy education is to help individuals establish healthy interpersonal relationships with each other by improving the ability of empathy in people. Educational programs focus on the development of emotional and cognitive abilities that include empathetic responses (Yüksel, 2004). Jolliffe and Farrington (2006) found that bullying children had low empathy levels and explained the reason for these children's bullying behaviors as their inability to understand the emotions of the victims.
Assertiveness Skills Training	Assertiveness skills training contributes to the individual's ability to defend himself/herself, to express his/her feelings clearly and comfortably, to use his/her own rights by taking into account the rights of others (Alberti & Emmons, 2002). Assertiveness training has become important in order to prevent peer bullying. Assertiveness training will contribute to the self-esteem, decision-making skills and self-confidence of individuals (Eslami et al, 2016; Erdoğan & Uçukoğlu, 2011).
Emotional Awareness Skills Training	It is an individual's ability to recognize and describe their own and others' emotions. Emotional awareness is one of the psychological needs of the individual as well as being a social skill (Dizen et al., 2005). Emotional awareness skills training will contribute to the reduction of negative behaviors such as aggression and violence in peer relations (Ayas, 2008).
Social Problem Solving Skills Training	It is a skill defined as preventing or resolving social conflicts, generating the most effective response options, and applying the most effective of these options. The development of this skill has an important place in helping children cope with the problems they encounter in daily life (Berk, 2013; Dereli, 2008).

In addition to supporting social skills, preventive intervention programs for bullying should be developed. In this context, the establishment of the "Bullying Prevention Coordination Committee" is the first step. While dealing with the program about bullying;

- Definition of bullying
- Types of bullying
- How to take a stance in the face of bullying
- Short and long-term strategies
- Where and when the bullying occurred
- Advice to bully, victim and witnesses
- Which preventive activities will be included
- A detailed report should be prepared on information such as which groups are at risk of bully-victim (Olweus & Limber, 2010; Pepler & Craig, 2014).

What to Do in Classroom Environments

In order to prevent and identify bullying, it is necessary to develop an evaluation program for peer relations with reliable and appropriate techniques. The main evaluations are observation, interview techniques, questionnaires, sociometric techniques. Evaluation of bullying behaviors of children should be carefully planned by teachers and guidance service (Crothers & Levinson, 2004).

Teachers should regularly collect information about children from the moment they enroll in school. From the first day, peer relations should be evaluated regularly with different techniques. The information obtained from the techniques should be interpreted together (Ogelman, 2018).

It is important for teachers to determine the social position of children in cases of peer bullying they encounter in their classrooms. Traditional sociometry assessment methods are mostly preferred to determine peer preferences and peer relations problem situations among children. (Farmer et al., 2011). As a result of sociometry measurements, peer acceptance/rejection emerges. Rejection and negative position in the early years are among the determinants of behavior problems in the following years (Erwin, 1993). Rejection by peers, which emerged as a result of sociometric measurements, was associated with non-social behavior, committing crimes, dropping out of school, low academic achievement, and mental health problems in later years (Dodge et al., 2003; Zettergen, 2005). In addition to this evaluation, teacher evaluations also have an important place in determining the problems experienced among peers. This information should be shared with their families on a regular basis. Keeping in touch with the families of children with problems is vital. Family involvement can be achieved through phone calls, conferences, and events. Information should be provided to parents by asking their opinions, suggestions and observations about their children's social skills and peer relationships (Moon, 2001; Ogelman, 2018).

At the same time, teachers can make the following interventions, taking into account the characteristics of their classrooms:

- Students should be informed about what bullying is and why it is harmful, and teachers should be actively involved in designing classroom rules against bullying.
- In-class activities such as drama, role playing, circle time should be included that can help students learn how to deal with bullying better.
- A confidential "message box" that can not be opened by anyone other than the teacher can be used, where students can write and post their suggestions and thoughts on all subjects related to their classes.
- Conditions that contribute to bullying in the classroom should be identified.
- It is important to involve all students in classroom activities.
- Class rules against bullying should be specified.
- Regular weekly class meetings with students. should be done. Practices for positive skills such as empathy, perspective-taking, and problem solving skills should be created to help students in these meetings.
- Meetings with class families should be organized (Kanik, 2010; Salmivalli et al., 2009).

What to Do at the Individual Level

Bullying is common in certain areas such as the school garden, toilets and corridors. Teachers should monitor these areas frequently. Observation is important for teachers to understand the peer interaction and to be able to make the necessary interventions. It's important to have serious conversations with bully students and their parents. Attention should be paid not to impose hostile and harsh sanctions. Teachers should develop individual intervention plans for the students involved (Olweus & Limber, 2010)

Assertive skills training should be provided to talk to victims, provide support and help them learn by coping successfully with bullying. Interviews should also be conducted with victims' families. (Salmivalli et al., 2009).

It is important that teachers do not act nervous and anxious when they observe bullying. No use of sarcasm or threatening should be used. When there is a problem, it is necessary to label the behavior, not the child. Teachers should be shadow watchers of potential victims (Çevik, 2021).

It is of great importance that teachers convey the coping strategies they can use to the victims in order to prevent and reduce bullying. Coping skills have two important functions; problem-focused and emotion-focused coping skills. In problem-focused coping skills, instead of acting aggressively, it is necessary to be calm and rational to solve the problem. Emotion-focused coping skills includes self-alienation or self-control, asking for help, escape-avoidance, accepting responsibility and re-evaluating (Imran, 2020).

Teachers need to create a safe environment for children to report bullying. When children are bullied, the most prominent feelings are fear and shame. In this context, less than half of children report their bullying to adults. Below are strategies for creating a supportive and safe environment for teachers:

1. Teachers should thank the children for having the courage to come and report the bullying. Children's bullying should be paid attention to. Reflective listening should be used so that they can express their feelings and thoughts comfortably.
2. Embarrassment should be tried to be reduced so that children can easily explain the bullying they experience. An environment where everyone feels safe at school should be created. As a teacher, you should try to be determined by stating that you will do all the necessary help.
3. One should try to listen to the bullying incident without judging or criticizing. It should be tried to show empathy to the bullying incident.
4. It should be clearly stated that teachers will guides to ensure the elimination of bullying.
5. A friendly, warm, caring, loving approach should be formed with open communication.
6. Try to speak in a soft and low tone of voice.
7. Be a role-model to establish positive relationships with peers.
8. Opportunities should be created for students to express their feelings and thoughts. Listen carefully to what children say without interrupting them and by making eye contact (Pepler & Craig, 2014).

The activities that the committee can do in the prevention and intervention practices of peer bullying are explained:

- **Plan:** Establish a comprehensive plan to develop and implement bullying prevention initiatives. The plan should include setting goals. It is necessary to identify performance indicators and key activities. All prepared activities should be communicated to everyone.
- **Implement:** A bullying prevention plan should be implemented. Meetings should be held at the school to develop the plan and to discuss the obstacles experienced.
- **Education:** The entire school community (students, teachers, school administrators, parents and community members) should be trained.

- **Evaluation:** An environmental survey should be conducted on school-wide bullying and reviewing other available data (eg incident reports). Therefore, it is important to prevent the progression of bullying behaviors and to make the necessary improvements.
- **Review initiatives:** Based on the feedback from the assessments, the objectives and implementation plans should be reviewed.
- **Advocacy:** Communicate with the entire school community about preventing bullying and advocating for the problem.
- **Sustain:** A plan should be developed for the sustainability of bullying prevention initiatives over time.
- **Regular Meetings:** Meet at least three times a year (September, January, and June). Between meetings, teams should pay attention to active communication and cooperation (Pepler & Craig, 2014).

Various Approaches to Resolving Peer Bullying

Dan Olweus introduced a school-based intervention program for bullying for the first time. Olweus explains the basic principles of the school-based intervention program developed and evaluated by a national campaign against bully/victim problems in Norwegian schools as follows (Olweus, 1998)

- To raise awareness about the problem of bully/victim and to improve knowledge about the subject. It includes raising accurate information about bullying and its causes. It is important to implement the bully/victim questionnaire. In this way, more realistic information about the frequency of problems in schools can be obtained.
- It should be ensured that teachers and parents actively participate in all activities related to bullying. Adults have a responsibility to control to some extent what happens between children and young people at school. The only thing to do to achieve this is to ensure the necessary supervision during breaks and lunch breaks. At the same time, teachers need to prevent potential bullying situations. For this, they should give the message that bullying is absolutely unacceptable at school.
- At the same time, it is important for teachers to talk seriously with victims and bullies and their families when there is a bullying problem in their classroom. The core message should be "we do not tolerate bullying in our school and we will see it come to an end". Such observation and close supervision should be carried out continuously at school. If the necessary intervention is not taken, the situation may become worse for the victim.
- Rules for bullying should be clearly stated. Examples of these rules are "We should not bully other students", "We should try to help students who are bullied". Besides, school rules can form the basis for what bullying behavior is. Teachers should be careful to specify and apply sanctions in cases where the rules are not followed. To implement the determined sanctions is crucial. It is very important to give positive feedback when it is complied with.
- Teachers should provide support and protection for victims. Moreover, teachers should provide assistance to those students. Teachers should give victim students the opportunity to express themselves in the classroom. Teachers should help victim students feel valued in the eyes of their classmates. Parents of victim students should be given advice to help their children establish new friendships. In this regard, information should be obtained from the school guidance service about establishing and maintaining new friendships.

Various intervention strategies have been developed and implemented to prevent bullying. Eight approaches that have been implemented in some countries and reported positive results are summarized below (Smith et al., 2003):

- **Holistic School Approach:** According to this approach, the purpose and strategies of the school in terms of behaviors related to bullying at school are set forth in a written document. This written document should ensure that its objectives and strategies are implemented, monitored, maintained and reviewed. The holistic school approach mostly includes the democratic participation of all school staff in policy making.
- **Classroom Climate:** Anti-bullying practices to be carried out in the school environment should be conducted in order to improve and develop relations in the classroom. In a practice conducted in Norway, it was reported that bullying behaviors were greatly reduced. This program helps reduce the probability of bullying by restructuring the school environment. School members have responsibilities in promoting and implementing the program. In these policies, the duties and responsibilities of school administration and staff, teachers, students and families should be clearly stated.
- **Peer Support Systems:** It is emphasized that students make an effort to cope with bullying. Peer support methods are as follows:
  - Doing group work for cooperation in the classroom.
  - Taking time to evaluate relationships in the classroom, including anger, fighting, and bullying.
  - Creating a circle of friends who will work with vulnerable students and offer them peer support.
  - Establishing mutual aid groups in which students are assigned to help or be with their peers.
  - Selecting a group of students who can implement anti-bullying policies and counsel students in need. To ensure that the selected student group and the school support the policies to be followed.
- **School Courts:** In a school court, evidence of students involved in bullying is heard. Students are selected to decide what the sanctions or punishments will be as a result of bullying. It has been confirmed that there is a decrease in bullying behaviors with this method applied in Canada.
- **Playground Improvements:** Especially in primary schools, the places where bullying behaviors are most common are playgrounds and schoolyards. It is important to increase supervision and oversight in these areas. Arrangement of playgrounds is indicated as an important measure.
- **Curriculum Study:** In-class discussion environments can be created to increase students' awareness of bullying and to cope with bullying. In addition to these, teachers can implement activities through various specifically prepared videos, films, literary works and animations.
- **Working with Special Students:** Self-righteousness training is a work for victims or prospective victims. It is aimed to enable these students to cope with bullying without being passive and aggressive. This approach is a counseling-based system for students who have been bullied.
- **Bringing Together in the Community:** This strategy is to bring together people who are experiencing conflict in the community. The bully and the victim are brought together, accompanied one person for each. The bully apologizes to the victim. Thus, they settle the incident amicably. A pilot scheme was conducted in schools in Australia. It was reported that the participation was high and positive results were obtained in the study.

While preparing programs to prevent bullying in schools; It should not be forgotten that every school has its own problems. For instance, while there may be bullying behavior in the form of sexual abuse among male students in one school, in another school in the same region, there may be another problem such as students bringing guns to school. Prevention programs to be implemented for these two situations require absolutely different approaches (Astor et al., 2005). Therefore, it should be avoided to define and implement a single program for the whole country. Different programs should be implemented considering the needs and problems of each school.

CONCLUSION

Peer relationships have many functions in the social development of children. Through peer interactions, children learn to cooperate with others, solve problems, and cope with problems. From an early age, children spend most of their time with their peers in educational institutions. In educational institutions, teachers have an important role in developing children's peer relationships and preventing negative peer relationships. The fact that teachers are role-models for children with their positive behaviors determines the quality of peer relations in the classroom. Teachers have great responsibilities in recognizing and correcting peer bullying. It is important for teachers to develop and implement strategies to prevent bullying in their classrooms. At the same time, they can include activities that will increase teacher-student and student-student interaction in order to provide a positive classroom atmosphere in their classrooms. These activities can reduce bullying in classrooms.

As a result, studies show that peer bullying threatens the lives of children and adolescents in the short and long term, such as academic failure, behavioral problems, and withdrawal from school. For this reason, it is very important to determine the factors that cause peer bullying in groups of bully, victim and witness children. Learning individual and family factors will make it easier to put forward sensitive and effective intervention programs in order to reveal and solve the problems of peer bullying. Intervention programs should be designed considering all developmental characteristics of individuals. At the same time, the family structure of the countries, social norms, social and cultural values and the components of the education system should be taken into consideration.

FUTURE RESEARCH DIRECTIONS

It is important to create programs based on psychological foundations, including parents, teachers and institutions, in the prevention and intervention phase of peer bullying. In particular, teachers have important duties to support children's peer relationships in prevention plans. The prevention plan should include the definition of bullying, the types of bullying, the names responsible for the program, preventive activities and strategies to deal with bullying. Furthermore, recommendations should be stated clearly about what victims, bystanders and parents should do when bullied. Teachers can suggest reading advice through helpful books and websites on raising awareness of peer bullying. Teachers have an important role in planning all these points in detail. Comprehensive in-service training can be designed and the effectiveness of the training can be evaluated in order to inform teachers about peer bullying in every aspect. In addition, pre-service teachers can be informed about peer bullying in the courses they take during their undergraduate education. It is important that effective peer bullying prevention and intervention programs are not only in educational institutions, but also that these programs take place in the social policy practices of different countries. In this study, the role of the teacher in the fight against peer bullying was examined. At the same time, roles in terms of family and school management can be discussed. Intervention programs implemented in different education systems can be compared in future studies.

REFERENCES

Akay, Y. (2019). The effect of emotional awareness activities developed for primary school students in preventing peer bullying. *Education in Science*, *44*(200), 205–227.

Alberti, R., & Emmons, M. (2002). *Exercise Your Right to Assertiveness*. HYB Publishing.

Archer, J., & Coyne, S. M. (2005). An integrated review of indirect, relational, and social aggression. *Personality and Social Psychology Review*, *9*(3), 212–230. doi:10.120715327957pspr0903_2 PMID:16083361

Astor, R. A., Meyer, H. A., Benbenishty, R., Marachi, R., & Rosemond, M. (2005). School Safety Interventions: Best Practices and Programs. *Children & Schools*, *27*(1), 17–32. doi:10.1093/cs/27.1.17

Audley-Piotrowski, S., Singer, A., & Patterson, M. (2015). The role of the teacher in children's peer relations: Making the invisible hand intentional. *Translational Issues in Psychological Science*, *1*(2), 192–200. doi:10.1037/tps0000038

Ayas, T. (2008). *The effectiveness of the bullying prevention program based on the whole school approach* [Unpublished PhD Thesis]. Ankara University, Ankara.

Aykut, S. (2019). *Educational Problems of Syrian Children in Turkey: School Social Work Proposal with a Focus on Respect for Diversity Education* [PhD thesis]. Hacettepe University Institute of Social Sciences, Ankara.

Başar, M., & Çetin, Ö. (2013). A Study on Primary and Secondary School Students' Levels of Bullying Behaviors and Learning Environments for These Behaviors. *E-Journal of New World Sciences Academy*, *8*(4), 471–488.

Bauman, S., & Hurley, C. (2005). Teachers' Attitudes and Beliefs About Bullying: Two Exploratory Studies. *Journal of School Violence*, *4*(3), 49–61. doi:10.1300/J202v04n03_05

Berk, L. E. (2013). *Infants and children: Prenatal through middle childhood*. Nobel Publications.

Besag, V. E. (1989). Bullies and Victims. In *Schools. A Guide To Understanding and Management*. Open University Press.

Bhat, C. S. (2008). Cyber Bullying: Overview and Strategies For School Counsellors, Guidance Officers, and All School Personnel. *Journal of Psychologists and Counsellors In Schools*, *18*(1), 53–66.

Boulton, M. J., & Underwood, K. (1992). Bully/victim problems among middle school children. *The British Journal of Educational Psychology*, *62*(1), 73–87. doi:10.1111/j.2044-8279.1992.tb01000.x PMID:1558813

Çevik, B. (2021). *Bullying with Real Witnesses*. Sola Unitas Publications.

Çınkır, S., & Kepenekçi, Y. K. (2003). Bullying between students. *Educational Management in Theory and Practice*, *34*, 236–253.

Compass, B., Connor-Smith, J., Saltzman, H., Thomsen, A., & Wadsworth, M. (2001). Coping with stress during childhood and adolescence: Problems, progress, andpotential in theory and research. *Psychological Bulletin*, *127*(1), 87–127. doi:10.1037/0033-2909.127.1.87 PMID:11271757

Crothers, L. M., & Levinson, E. M. (2004). Assessment of bullying: A review of methods and instruments. *Journal of Counseling and Development*, *82*(4), 496–503. doi:10.1002/j.1556-6678.2004.tb00338.x

Cüceloğlu, D. (2005). *Human to Human Again*. Remzi Bookstore.

Dereli, E. (2008). *Social Problem Solving in Children*. Tablet Publications.

Dizen, M., Berenbaum, H., & Kerns, J. G. (2005). Emotional awareness and psychological needs. *Cognition and Emotion*, *19*(8), 1140–1157. doi:10.1080/02699930500260468

Dodge, K. A., Lansford, J. E., Burks, V. S., Bates, J. E., Pettit, G. S., Fontaine, R., & Price, J. M. (2003). Peer rejection and social information-processing factors in the development of aggressive behavior problems in children. *Child Development*, *74*(2), 374–393. doi:10.1111/1467-8624.7402004 PMID:12705561

Durlak, J. A., & Wells, A. M. (1997). Primary prevention mental health programs for children and adolescents: A meta-analytic review. *American Journal of Community Psychology*, *25*(2), 115–152. doi:10.1023/A:1024654026646 PMID:9226860

Duy, B. (2013). Teachers' attiudes toward different types of bullying and victimization in Turkey. *Psychology in the Schools*, *50*(10), 987–1002. doi:10.1002/pits.21729

Erdoğan, Ö., & Uçukoğlu, H. (2011). The relationships between primary school students' perceptions of parental attitudes and their assertiveness and fear of negative evaluation. *Kastamonu Journal of Education*, *19*(1), 51–72.

Erwin, P. (1993). *Friendship and Peer Relations in Children*. John Wiley & Sons Publishers.

Eslami, A. A., Rabiei, L., Afzali, S. M., Hamidizadeh, S., & Masoudi, R. (2016). The effectiveness of assertiveness training on the levels of stress, anxiety, and depression of high school students. *Iranian Red Crescent Medical Journal*, *18*(1), 1–10. doi:10.5812/ircmj.21096 PMID:26889390

Farmer, T. W., McAuliffe Lines, M., & Hamm, J. V. (2011). Revealing the invisible hand: The role of teachers in children's peer experiences. *Journal of Applied Developmental Psychology*, *32*(5), 247–256. doi:10.1016/j.appdev.2011.04.006

Gillies-Rezo, S., & Bosacki, S. (2003). Invisible Bruises: Kindergartens' perceptions of bullying. *International Journal of Children's Spirituality*, *8*(2), 163–177. doi:10.1080/13644360304628

Glover, D., Gough, G., Johnson, M., & Cartwright, N. (2000). Bullying in secondary schools: Incidence. *Impact and Intervention. Educational Research*, *42*(2), 141–156. doi:10.1080/001318800363782

Graham, S. (2011). *Bullying: A module for teachers*. Error! Hyperlink reference not valid.

Gülay Ogelman, H. (2018). *Peer Relations in Preschool Period*. Educational Book.

Gülay Ogelman, H., & Akman, B. (2009). *Social Skills in Preschool Period*. Pegem Academy.

Gültekin Akduman, G. (2012). An investigation of peer bullying at preschool period. *Society and Social Work, 23*(1), 121–138.

Heinrichs, R. R. (2003). A whole-school approach to bullying: Special consideration for children with exceptionalities. *Intervention in School and Clinic, 38*(4), 195–204. doi:10.1177/105345120303800401

Hinduja, S., & Patchin, J. W. (2014). *Bullying beyond the schoolyard: Preventing and responding to cyberbullying*. Corwin Pres.

Hunt, J. (2011). *Bullying should not be a teenage rite of passage*. https://www.americanprogress.org/wp-content/uploads/issues/2011/02/pdf /antigay_bullying.pdf

Ihnat, L., & Smith, D. (2013). Solutions for bullying: Intervention training for pre-service teachers. *Journal of Teaching and Learning, 9*(1), 1–13. doi:10.22329/jtl.v9i1.3604

Imran, A. (2020). *"I survived": Coping strategies for bullying in schools: A systematic literature review from 2009-2020* [Master Thesis]. Jönköping University.

Jolliffe, D., & Farrington, D. P. (2006). Examining the relationship between low empathy and bullying. *Aggressive Behavior, 32*(6), 540–550. doi:10.1002/ab.20154

Kanık, B. (2010). *Teachers' Perceptions of School Bullying* [Master Thesis]. Yıldız Technical University Institute of Social Sciences.

Kartal, H., & Bilgin, A. (2007). An anti-bullying program application for primary school students: School de-bullying program. *Theory and Practice in Education., 3*(2), 207–227.

Kempes, M., Matthys, W., de Vries, H., & Van Engeland, H. (2005). Reactive and proactive aggression in children: A review of theory, findings and the relevance for child and adolescent psychiatry. *European Child & Adolescent Psychiatry, 14*(1), 11–19. doi:10.100700787-005-0432-4 PMID:15756511

Kennedy, T. D., Kevorkian, M. M., & Russom, A. G. (2012). Teacher and administrator perceptions of bullying in schools. *International Journal of Education Policy and Leadership, 7*(5), 1–12. doi:10.22230/ijepl.2012v7n5a395

Ladd, G. W., & Burgess, K. B. (2001). Do relational risks and protective factors moderate the linkages between childhood aggression and early psychological and school adjustment? *Child Development, 72*(5), 1579–1601. doi:10.1111/1467-8624.00366 PMID:11699688

Moon, M. (2001). Teacher perspectives on peer relation problems of young children. *Asia Pacific Education Review, 2*(1), 22–31. doi:10.1007/BF03024929

Okur Karahan, Ş. (2020). *Examination of the roles of Turkish and Syrian students in the province of Kahramanmaraş in bullying and teachers' attitudes towards bullying* [Master Thesis]. Cerrahpaşa Institute of Forensic Medicine and Forensic Sciences.

Olweus, D. (1998). Bullying in the schools: How educators can help. *Education Digest*, (7), 30–34.

Olweus, D. (2013). School bullying: Development and some important challenges. *Annual Review of Clinical Psychology*, *9*(1), 751–780. doi:10.1146/annurev-clinpsy-050212-185516 PMID:23297789

Olweus, D., & Limber, S. P. (2010). Bullying in school: Evaluation and dissemination of the olweus bullying prevention program. *The American Journal of Orthopsychiatry*, *80*(1), 124–134. doi:10.1111/j.1939-0025.2010.01015.x PMID:20397997

Olweus, D., & Limber, S. P. (2018). Some problems with cyberbullying research. *Current Opinion in Psychology*, *19*, 139–143. doi:10.1016/j.copsyc.2017.04.012 PMID:29279213

Pepler, D., & Craig, W. (2014). Bullying Prevention and Intervention. In *The School Environment: Fact-sheets and Tools*. National Center for Injury Prevention and Control Devision of Violence Prevention.

Pişkin, M. (2006). School violence: Definition, prevalence and prevention strategies. *Social Policy in the Public*, *1*(2), 4–62.

Salmivalli, C., Karna, A., & Poskiparta, E. (2009). *From peer putdowns to peer support: A theoretical model and how it translated into a national anti-bullying program*. Academic Press.

Scheithauer, H., Hayer, T., Petermann, F., & Jugert, G. (2006). Physical, verbal, and relational forms of bullying among german students: Age trends, gender differences, and correlates. *Aggressive Behavior: Official Journal of The International Society For Research On Aggression*, *32*(3), 261–275. doi:10.1002/ab.20128

Smith, Peter K., Ananiadou K., Cowie, H. (2003). Interventions to reduca school bullying. *The Canadian Journal of Psychiatry-In Review*, *48*(9), 22–31.

Smith, P. K., Ananiadou, K., & Cowie, H. (2003). Interventions to reduca school bullying. *The Canadian Journal of Psychiatry-In Review*, *48*(9), 22–31.

Smith, P. K., Pepler, D., & Rigby, K. (2004). *Bullying in schools: How successful can interventions be?* Cambridge University Press. doi:10.1017/CBO9780511584466

Smith, P. K., & Shu, S. (2000). What good schools can do about bullying: Findings from a survey in english schools after a decade of research and action. *Childhood*, *7*(2), 193–212. doi:10.1177/0907568200007002005

Smith, P. K., & Shu, S. (2000). What good schools can do about bullying: Findings from a survey in english schools after a decade of research and action. *Childhood*, *7*(7), 193–212. doi:10.1177/0907568200007002005

Sözmezay, H. (2010). *Investigation of the Relationship of Bullying with Communication Skills and Perceived Social Support in High School Students* [Master Thesis]. Ankara University.

Ttofi, M. M., & Farrington, D. P. (2008). Bullying: Short-term and long-term effects, and the importance of defiance theory in explanation and prevention. *Victims & Offenders*, *3*(2-3), 289–312. doi:10.1080/15564880802143397

Uz Baş, A. (2019). School-based prevention: Characteristics of effective school-based prevention programs. *Journal of School Psychological Counseling*, *2*(1), 73–94.

Van Der Wal, M. F., De Wit, C. A., & Hirasing, R. A. (2003). Psychosocial health among young victims and offenders of direct and indirect bullying. *Pediatrics, 111*(6), 1312–1317. doi:10.1542/peds.111.6.1312 PMID:12777546

Weissberg, R. P., & Cascarino, J. (2013). Academic learning + social-emotional learning = national priority. *Phi Delta Kappan, 95*(2), 8–13. doi:10.1177/003172171309500203

Yüksel, A. (2004). The effect of empathy education program on empathic skills of primary school students. *Journal of Uludag University Faculty of Education, 17*(2), 341–354.

ADDITIONAL READING

Ansary, N. S., Elias, M. J., Greene, M. B., & Green, S. (2015). Best Practices To Address (Or Reduce) Bullying In Schools. *Phi Delta Kappan, 97*(2), 30–35. doi:10.1177/0031721715610088

Espelage, D. L., & Swearer, S. M. (2003). Research on school bullying and victimization: What have we learned and where do we go from here? *School Psychology Review, 32*(3), 365–383. doi:10.1080/02796015.2003.12086206

Fekkes, M., Pijpers, F. M. I., & Verloove-Vanhorick, S. P. (2005). Bullying: Who does what, when and where? Involvement of children, teachers and parents in bullying behavior. *Health Education Research, 20*(1), 81–91. doi:10.1093/her/cyg100 PMID:15253993

Flonnery, D. J., Wester, K. L., & Singer, M. I. (2003). Impact of exposure to violence in school on child and adolescent mental health and behaviour. *Journal of Community Psychology, 32*(5), 559–573. doi:10.1002/jcop.20019

Jackson, R. M. (2018). *Teachers' Perceptions of Bullying in a Rural School District* [Doctoral dissertation]. Walden University.

Kuntsche, E., Pickett, W., Overpeck, M., Craig, W., Boyce, W., & de Matos, M. G. (2006). Television viewing and foms of bullying among adolescents from eight countries. *The Journal of Adolescent Health, 39*(6), 908–915. doi:10.1016/j.jadohealth.2006.06.007 PMID:17116523

O'Moore, M., & Minton, S. J. (2004). *Dealing with Bullying in Schools: A Training Manual for Teachers, Parents and Other Professionals*. SAGE Publications. doi:10.4135/9781446211878

Zettergren, P. (2005). Childhood peer status as predictor of midadolescence peer situation and social adjustment. *Psychology in the Schools, 42*(7), 745–757. doi:10.1002/pits.20121

KEY TERMS AND DEFINITIONS

Aggression: It is defined as intentional and harmful behavior towards people or objects. Although it does not directly harm the source it targets, any behavior done for this purpose is considered as aggression.

Peer Bullying: It is a form of destructive interaction in which certain people aim verbal, physical aggression, or other forms of abuse

Peer Relationships: Communities that create unique values and standards for behaviors and create a social structure consisting of leaders and followers form peer groups

Prevention Training Program: It includes practices designed to reduce the possibility of future problems in individuals and societies and to improve mental health. It includes an approach to intervene in the problems observed in students and applications at different teaching levels based on increasing and strengthening competencies by taking into account the problems to be experienced in the future.

Social Position: Peer acceptance and rejection refer to the social position of children in the peer group. Social position is an indicator of peer relationships. Social position emerges according to the results obtained from sociometric measurements.

Social Skills: It is defined as verbal or non-verbal behaviors that initiate and maintain social relations, facilitate the solution of problems experienced in social relations

Teacher's Attitudes: Teachers' mentality, emotional reactions, various habits, and their inclusive personality affect their attitudes towards students. From this point of view, teacher attitudes are one of the strongest determinants of his/her behavior in his/her profession.

Using Strategies for Coping with Bullying: There are many coping strategies available to prevent peer bullying. Coping strategy is defined as purposeful, cognitive, and behavioral efforts undertaken to manage the internal and external demands of a stressor in order to resolve stress or alleviate emotional reactions.

Chapter 24
An Increasing Problem in Schools:
Peer Bullying

Asuman Bilbay
Sivas Cumhuriyet University, Turkey

Nevra Atış Akyol
Sivas Cumhuriyet University, Turkey

ABSTRACT

Peer bullying is when an individual is exposed to negative actions on his/her property, body, emotions, relationships, reputation, digital presence by a stronger peer or peers. In peer bullying, there are different roles such as bully, victim, bully/victim, bystander, and even these roles can change over time. Bullying is examined under five headings: physical, verbal, relational, sexual, and cyberbullying. Studies show that there are some differences in the types and frequency of peer bullying in schools according to age and grade. As a result, peer bullying is frequently experienced in schools. For this reason, many different intervention programs have been developed and implemented in the world.

INTRODUCTION

Peer bullying is the continuous exposure of the weaker person to the negative behavior of one or more stronger peers among unequally powerful peers. Bullying is a negative interaction between the bully and the victim in a social ecological context, including teachers and peers. Studies show that children who are bullied at an early age are more prone to problems such as academic failure, withdrawal from school, antisocial problems, violence and substance use.

Bullying behaviors occur in a variety of ways. physical bullying; verbal bullying, relational bullying, sexual bullying In addition to these bullying types, homophobic bullying and racist bullying are also defined in the literature. There are different roles in peer bullying; Apart from the bully and the victim, there can be both the bully and the victim, and bystanders.

DOI: 10.4018/978-1-6684-5426-8.ch024

School bullying, a type of aggression that occurs in schools, involves older or physically stronger students directly or indirectly harming and harassing children who are weaker than themselves. Bullying is common in schools. In schools, physical bullying is more common in younger age groups, and psychological/emotional and verbal bullying is more common in older age groups.

Early intervention programs are needed to prevent peer bullying from an early age. Although the types of bullying differ according to age, in general, the aspects of bullying and the victim need to be developed are similar. Contrary to the intervention strategies applied in the whole school in the fight against peer bullying, the potential power of education to target social-cognitive and moral factors that will less stigmatize students and give them individual needs is emphasized. Although the effectiveness of school-wide intervention programs is recognized, it is very important to expand these interventions to include individual applications.

What is Peer Bullying?

Known as the founder of peer bullying literature, Olweus started his studies in Norway in the 60s, when bullying became a problem in Scandinavian countries (Karaman Kepenekçi & Çınkır, 2006). Olweus (1994) defined peer bullying as the continuous exposure of the weaker individual among peers with unequal strength to the negative actions of one or more stronger individuals. According to another definition, the term bullying refers to a wide variety of behaviors that can have a negative impact on a person's property, body, emotions, relationships, reputation and social status (Beane, 2008).

For any behavior to be defined as bullying, it must have three basic components. These components can be listed as follows: the harmful behavior must be intentional and done with the purpose of causing harm, the harmful behavior must be repeated, and there must be a power imbalance between the bully and the victim as an asymmetric power relationship (Harris, 2009; Tarshis, 2010). The said power imbalance can be physical or psychological (Beane, 2008).

Types Of Peer Bullying

Bullying behaviors may occur in various ways, and their classification is done in different ways. As a general classification in the literature, bullying is examined under three headings as physical, verbal and social-relational bullying. In some studies, sexual bullying (Duncan, 1998; Fredland, 2008) and cyberbullying (Beale & Hall, 2007; Shariff, 2008) are included in the types of bullying. Accordingly, types of peer bullying are discussed under 5 categories in this study.

Physical Bullying

It is also called open (overt) bullying in the literature (Crick et al., 1997). It is quite common and is the most easily recognized type of bullying. Physical bullying describes situations in which the bully harms or hurts the target person through physical contact (such as hitting, slapping, kicking or punching, tripping, pushing, pulling, poking, pulling hair, attacking with a knife, etc.) (Gültekin, 2003; Karaman Kepenekçi & Çınkır 2006; Pişkin, 2002). Physical bullying does not necessarily include all undesirable physical behavior. For a behavior to be considered physical bullying, it must have the purpose of hurting, injuring, harming or intimidating the other person (Smith, 2016).

Verbal Bullying

It is a type of bullying that occurs through verbal expressions such as picking nicknames, mocking, open insult, sarcasm, belittling, teasing, annoying, implicating things and humiliating before people (Ayas, 2008; CDC, 2020). It is the most common type of bullying (Bilgin, 2007). Often, verbal bullying may accompany physical bullying, and sometimes verbal bullying can be more hurtful than physical bullying (Beane, 2008). In some cases, verbal bullying is approved and supported by the social environment or family. However, this destructive behavior can be seen as simple, and it is sometimes neglected that verbal bullying can have very serious costs and consequences (Tural Hesapçıoğlu & Yeşilova, 2015).

Relational Bullying

It is also called indirect bullying. Relational bullying is an indirect type of bullying that is used as an alternative when the direct bullying behavior is difficult to perform and the social position of the other party is desired to be lowered (Archer & Coyne, 2005). Although it is not a visibly harmful behavior, emotional bullying is a highly consuming one among bullying types. It is manifested by behavior patterns such as being hostile, ostracizing, gossiping, ignoring, and neglecting. Social exclusion is the occurrence of relational bullying in the social environment and the isolation of the individual (Soenens et al., 2008).

Sexual Bullying

Bullying can also occur through the performance of sexually offensive behaviors. Therefore, sexual harassment-like behaviors should also be considered in peer bullying studies (Rigby, 2003). Although it has similar characteristics in terms of the nature of the behavior, studies include sexual bullying as a sub-dimension, apart from the concept of sexual harassment (Ayas, 2008; Ayas & Pişkin, 2011). Sexual bullying may occur in various ways (Rigby, 2003). It can occur through physical means such as touching, through verbal means such as using offensive words or derogatory names with sexual meaning, and through indirect means such as hand gestures, throwing kisses, gossiping about sexual matters (Freadland, 2008; Rigby, 2003). Sexual bullying is one of the situations that people try to hide/conceal the most; thus, it is more difficult to reveal compared to other types of bullying. The reason behind this can be the intense feelings of sadness and guilt of the victim of sexual bullying or the fear of being labeled by other people. Sometimes, victims may not able to understand at first whether the situation they are exposed to is sexual bullying. Sexual bullying is an important problem that negatively affects the social relations and psychological well-being of individuals. In order for a behavior to be defined as sexual bullying, there must be an imbalance of power between the two parties, and it must consist of behaviors targeting one party/sex and including sexual aggression (Gruber & Fineran, 2015).

Cyber (Virtual) Bullying

The exponential increase in instant messaging on the internet and subscriptions to social networking sites in recent years has revealed a new type of bullying called cyberbullying. Unlike the classical or traditional types of bullying, in this new type of bullying, the bully uses communication technologies such as instant messaging, e-mail, chat rooms, websites, online games, social networking sites, and text messaging to degrade, humiliate, or deliberately harm the victim by insulting them (Hanhan, 2012; Kowalski et al.,

2014; Wang et al., 2009). Cyberbullying has some features such as the possibility of occurring at any time of the day and the possibility of the bullies not being known, and even being long-term and permanent because the offensive action is repeated on the internet (Tokunaga, 2010).

In addition to these types of bullying, the definitions of homophobic bullying, which expresses negative attitudes and aggressive behaviors towards homosexual individuals and racist bullying, which occurs when the individual is exposed to discriminatory behaviors due to his/her minority ethnic group have also started to take place in the bullying literature (Donnellan & Firth, 2006).

Types of peer bullying are also classified as direct and indirect bullying. Directly applied peer bullying describes open attacks directed at the person chosen as the target. In other words, physical violence, verbal insults and humiliations, derogatory facial expressions and gestures fall into this category. In direct bullying, the victim knows who the aggressor is because the aggressor and the target person are confronting each other face to face. Indirect bullying, on the other hand, is implicit, unlike direct bullying. It includes behaviors such as social isolation of the target person and deliberate exclusion from a group. Ignoring and/or encouraging others to do so, spreading malicious rumors, lies or gossip fall into indirect bullying. In this type of bullying, bullies resort to this method as they may be uncomfortable with their identities being known by the victim (Güvenir, 2008; O'Moore & Minton, 2004; Olweus, 2003; Pişkin, 2002).

In addition to these, in the classification made by Mynard & Joseph (2000), peer bullying was examined under four categories as verbal, physical, social manipulation and attacks on property. Here, the concept of social manipulation overlaps with the concept of relational bullying mentioned above. Attack on property that is not included in the previous classifications, on the other hand, includes behaviors such as damaging the target child's belongings and taking his/her belongings without permission by the bully.

Roles in Peer Bullying

There are different roles in peer bullying; apart from the bully and the victim, there can be persons both being bully and victim together and bystanders. Accordingly, the bullying child or group is defined as the bully, the bullied child as the victim (sufferer), the bullying and the bullied child as the bully/victim, and the children witnessing the bullying as the bystander.

Bully

A bully is defined as an individual who engages in harmful and irritating behaviors, treats the person he/she chooses as the victim cruelly, and does not care about victim being hurt (Cook et al., 2010). In studies on bullies, it has been determined that bullies have some common characteristics like being stronger than victims physically and psychologically, being insufficient in empathy, trying to get results through bullying due to lack of knowledge on how to cope with problems and develop problem-solving strategies, experiencing some difficulties in adapting to their environment and the society(Ayas, 2018). Even though bullies achieve their desired goals in the short term through violence and pressure, they suffer from their behaviors in the long term (Bilgiç, 2007).

Olweus (1993) states that bullying children perform these aggressive behaviors not only against their peers but also against adults, that they mostly exhibit antisocial personality traits, have difficulty in complying with the rules, and violate the rules, and that their anxiety levels are low although their self-esteem levels are high. At the same time, it has been revealed in various studies that bullies have positive attitudes towards violence, act impulsively, like to be dominant over others, and that boys use physical bullying more compared to girls (Korkut, 2007). According to Beale & Scott (2001), bullying children gain some rewards such as money and prestige among their friends as a result of their bullying behavior (Güven, 2015). It can be observed that bullies are more likely to continue to commit crimes and go to jail when they reach their twenties compared to their non-bully peers (Conn, 2004). An interesting finding about bullying is that although bullies seem to be rejected and isolated by their friends during childhood, they are more accepted and liked by their peers in their adolescence (Cook, et al., 2010).

Victim

Individuals who systematically become the target of aggressive behaviors, have difficulty in defending themselves, and are physically weak are called victims. Victim children are unpopular, more sensitive, more impatient, more obedient, more anxious and more sensitive compared to other children (Korkut, 2007; Menesini & Salmivalli, 2017). Children who are bullied have low self-confidence and social skills, and are unable to defend themselves due to previous traumas, abuses and physical weaknesses (Satan, 2011). Typically, victim children do not know how to stop the bully, and instead of informing on the bully, they choose to remain silent because they think they will be bullied more. What enables bullies to become stronger and continue their bullying behavior is that the victims do not engage in a struggle to prevent the bullying experience (Green, Collingwood & Ross, 2010; Olweus, 1995; Tarshis, 2010). Studies show that children who are bullied at an early age are more prone to problems such as academic failures, antisocial problems, violence and substance abuse (Costello, Foley & Angold, 2006; Egger & Angold, 2006). As victims encounter bullying, they lose their self-esteem and feel worthless and inadequate. What is more worrying is that bullied children have higher rates of depression, anxiety and suicidal thoughts (Tarshis, 2010). Victims can be divided into different categories based on their attitudes and behaviors. These are passive victims, voluntary victims, chronic victims and provocative victims (Ayas, 2018).

Bully/Victim

People who choose weak individuals as victims and bully them, but on the other hand, become victims by being bullied by individuals who are stronger than themselves, are categorized as bully/victim. Bully/victim individuals are prone to bullying, but they also fall victim to it. It can be said that the anger and hatred of the bully/victim individuals stems from their own victim experiences (Georgiou & Stavrinides, 2008; Tarshis, 2010). Both the victim and the bully are at risk for poor relationships later in their life (Conn, 2004). Bullies bully for reasons such as having a leader role, influencing others with their harsh reputation, having the attention of their peers. Victims, on the other hand, are selected target for bullying because they are powerless and unable to resist the bully. Bully/victim individuals are in a different position in this sense, they share some characteristics of passive victims and bullies because of their "dual identities" (Georgiou & Stavrinides, 2008).

Bystander

One of the parties to the bullying process is the bystanders. The audience reinforces the bully's desire to be watched and causes the bullying to continue; the bystanders can cause this by not preventing the bullying situation, or even by keeping silent and approving it. In some cases, the bystanders are in a fan-like position like spectators watching a match, and bullying behavior that would not occur in the absence of an audience, therefore, may occur due to the presence of the audience. The bystanders may try to gain the sympathy of the bully as they see him/her as strong, charismatic, and a leader. By ignoring or only watching the bullying behavior, in a sense, they approve of the bully and encourage him/her to continue the bullying. In this context, bystander bullying behavior is evaluated not as a passive spectatorship, but as a spectatorship that plays an active role in bullying and results in being cruel (Wet, 2005). In addition, bystanders may experience fear and anxiety since they witness bullying, even if they are not bullied (Salmivalli, Kaukiainen & Voeten, 1996).

Bullying in Schools

Today, with the active participation of women in business life, children from an early age spend most of their time in schools with their peers. In addition to the positive effects of experiences and learning with peers, peer bullying is also encountered at all levels from pre-school to university.

Bullying, which had been seen as a normal behavior in school life or as the same concept as peer pressure in previous studies, began to be accepted as a harmful and unacceptable behavior by researchers at the end of the 20th century (Slee & Skrzy, 2016; Tarshis, 2010).

Schools provide the ideal environment for bullying to occur. They are hierarchical institutions in terms of both staff and student status, and power dynamics influence almost everything in these institutions. In recent years, being a victim of school bullying has emerged as a serious health problem among children and young people (Connolly & Beaver, 2016).

Bullying is considered a more important problem compared to many other negative situations in school. Bully students take away the "right to benefit from education freely" by intimidating other students with their words and behaviors (Pişkin, 2002). Being exposed to bullying by peers is one of the factors that destroy the motivation of students and decrease their love for school and education (Öztürk & Atlı, 2014). Children who are bullied become gradually distant from school, from the place where the bullying takes place; they may develop tendencies such as refusing to attend school and using more absent days, carrying injurious equipment for self-protection; and depending on these situations, they become subject to risks such as being exposed to academic, personal and psychological problems (Gökler, 2009).

Bullying disrupts the school atmosphere and learning environment, leading to a decline in overall academic achievement. In addition, bullying cases often take place in the playground areas, which leads to socialization problems and isolation in victim children (Tsai & Gomba, 2012). Bullying and peer bullying have negative consequences for both the bully and the victim child. The victim is psychologically affected more negatively by the bullying process and experiences symptoms such as depression, headache, eating disorder, and insomnia. However, the bully is at even greater risk, the risk of being involved in crime and being exposed to judicial measures, as he/she continues the bullying behavior of adolescence in his/her adult life, by making it a lifestyle.

A study examining the prevalence and effects of bullying in schools found that the most common types of bullying reported were mocking, picking nicknames, using offensive words, spreading rumors, threatening, injuring physically, belittling, and social exclusion. In addition, it was concluded that students who failed the exams and failed the class easily bullied their other classmates (Kshirsagar et al., 2007). It has been determined that physical appearance features are subject to nicknames, harassment and mocking among students (Al-Bitar et al., 2013).

If there is no supervisory or preventive mechanism in the environment where the bullying takes place, at the school or in the playground area, the act of bullying may become widespread. This may lead to more complex problems with multiple aspects. The intervention of teachers is the most important element to prevent and fight against bullying. However, the inconvenient intervention of teachers may cause the bullying to intensify, the victims to be put under more pressure, or the bullies to resist and react. Teachers are people who are just outside the border of peer circles, close to the peer circle but still outside of it. During the intervention, it is necessary to increase the moral values of the students, to examine their social status and friendly relationships, and to be aware of their ongoing/occurring interpersonal problems (Rodkin & Hodges, 2003).

Peer bullying is more likely to occur in educational settings with students that have to take the class/grade again due to their failure in the exams or between students of different ages/grades. If older students have a tendency for bullying, they can also find the opportunity to apply it since they are physically more developed than the younger students. Examples of bullying that bully students inflict on victim students can be specifying/ordering obedience for everything he/she says, pressuring to enable his/her cheating in the exam, physical intervention, mocking and humiliating with verbal expressions, demanding from victim to buy something for himself/herself, to carry his/her bag, to be a subordinate of himself/herself, and bullying to reinforce these. Students who bully think that they are superior because of their pressure and dominance on their peers (Genç, 2007).

Bullying behaviors seen in schools may be directed from student to student, or may occur among teachers, other staff and students. Setting unrealistic goals for individual performance or group performance of students can be given as an example of bullying behaviors to which students are exposed by teachers at school. In addition, this type of bullying includes threatening to fail the test, punishing, mocking and humiliating before people for failure, trying to discipline children by exerting excessive authority without a clear justification for taking control of the class and maintaining it. The discrimination of teachers against students due to characteristics that they have little or no control over, such as personal appearance, speaking style, social background, and sexual identity, are also bullying types to which students are exposed in schools (Rigby, 2003).

Detecting bullying among preschool children may not always be as easy as it seems, because children at this age tend to perform aggressive behaviors due to limitations in their cognitive and verbal development (Douvlos, 2019). For this reason, while physical aggression is more common among preschool children in general, it has been found that physical aggression decreases in most of the children as they complete transition from preschool to primary school (Ilola et al., 2016).

In a study examining the bullying attitudes of high school students, it was concluded that the most common types of bullying are verbal bullying and physical bullying, respectively. In addition, it has been stated that the place where bullying occurs most frequently is the classroom (Tural Hesapçıoğlu & Yeşilova, 2015).

Bullying among college students may have various forms. These may include: spreading unwanted rumors about the person's race, disability, gender, religion, or sexual orientation, mocking or humiliating, ostracizing from society, performing undesirable sexual approaches, stalking, following, threatening directly or on the internet, disclosing personal information shared confidentially (Cowie & Myers, 2016).

It is very important that parents, teachers and adults have detailed information about peer bullying. Because the lack of knowledge of adults about peer bullying or their neglecting attitude towards the importance of the issue causes an increase in bullying behavior (Bayar & Uçanok, 2012).

When peer bullying in the school environment is prevented, students will feel more secure and feel themselves as a part of the school. In order to prevent peer bullying, it is necessary to carry out studies to improve the communication skills of students and to enable them to express themselves and their feelings verbally more easily. On the other hand, arrangements should be made within the school so that young people can do artistic, sportive or cultural activities; this will enable young people to become aware that there are alternative ways to attract attention and gain a higher place in society (Tural Hesapçıoğlu & Yeşilova, 2015). Because children in the school environment aim to know that they are accepted by their teachers, classmates and other individuals in the school, that they contribute to the school, that they are meaningful and important for the school, and thus feel that they are valuable. In order to achieve this, they aim to do things that will enable them to show themselves individually or to stand out in the group. Children who cannot experience this cannot feel themselves belonging to the school either, cannot love their class and cannot be happy at school. They may also suffer from excessive use of absent days, rejection from school, learning difficulties, or academic failure. (Tatlılıoğlu, 2016). One of the negative consequences of students not being happy at school, not feeling like they belong to the school and not being at the forefront with their positive characteristics is that the students may aim to show themselves through negative behaviors. In this case, they may try to bully and dominate other students to show that they are strong and superior against them. The main motivation here is that when some adolescents cannot stand out with their success, they prefer to continue the "success of standing out" that they have gained through negative behaviors (Yeşildal, 2016).

Interventions to prevent peer bullying should be structured to include the bully, victim, parents, friends, teachers and social environment. Because bullying is not limited to two people, even if it occurs between the bully and the victim. It is necessary to organize family training on the subject, to inform teachers through courses and seminars, to provide the victim with social skills, and to provide the bully individual with the ability to express himself/herself and manage his/her emotions. In addition, teachers should openly express their opposition to bullying behaviors in order to both discourage bullying students and encourage victim students to seek help (Menesini & Salmivalli, 2017).

RISK FACTORS IN PEER BULLYING

Bullying is an important social problem. It affects children and youth all over the world. Understanding the risk factors for bullying requires a close examination of the reciprocal relationship between the individual and the environment. Risk factors can be listed as individual factors, school-related factors, family-related factors and social factors (Álvarez-García et al., 2015). Individual factors include characteristics such as the individual's age, gender, physical characteristics, psychological characteristics, and mental characteristics. School-related factors include features such as the relationship of the individual with the teacher, with his/her peers, the school climate and characteristics. Family-related factors include features such as the socioeconomic status of the individual's family, its attitude towards the child, the mental health of the parents, the structure of the family, and domestic violence. Social factors include features such as mass communication means, media, and the country's economic situation (Álvarez-García et al., 2015).

Individual Risk Factors for Peer Bullying

When the risk factors constituting peer bullying are evaluated, it can be seen that gender is highly important. While both girls and boys experience bullying, most of the children who are bullied and perform bullying are boys (Cook et al., 2010; Farrington & Baldry, 2010; Scheithauer et al., 2006). When the gender variable was evaluated based on the types of bullying, it was seen that physical bullying was more common among boys and relational bullying was more common among girls (Atik & Güneri, 2013; Hamel et al., 2021; Monks et al., 2011; Rigby, 2003). Age is also an important individual risk factor for bullying. The prevalence and types of bullying differ among age groups (Menesini & Salmivalli, 2017). It has been reported that bullying behavior increases slightly with the increase in age (Cook et al., 2010). The frequency of bullying and being exposed to bullying increases especially during the transition from childhood to adolescence (OECD, 2020). Bullying behavior peaks in the middle school years and tends to decrease until the end of high school (Swearer & Hymel, 2015).

In terms of individual risk factors, studies have concluded that having physical differences, such as obesity, is a risk factor associated with being a victim (Lemstra et al., 2012; Reulbach et al., 2013). Similarly, Pauline et al. (2014) found in their study that overweight is a potential risk factor for peer bullying in late childhood and adolescence. Similarly, those who perform bullying are often bulkier than their peers (Olweus, 2003). Being with special needs is also a risk factor for being bullied. It is known that children who do not have the same physical or mental abilities as others, for example, who are diagnosed with ADHD or who have speech defects, are more likely to be bullied (Rigby, 2003). In addition, it has been determined that children with autism spectrum disorder are more likely to be bullied compared to their peers with normal development (Little, 2002). Similarly, Zablotsky et al. (2014) concluded that children with Asperger's Syndrome and autism spectrum disorder who attend fully inclusive classes are at high risk of being exposed to peer bullying. It is known that children with special needs are exposed to bullying almost twice as much as children with normal development (Malecki et al. 2020). Russell et al. (2014), on the other hand, state that lesbian, gay, bisexual and transgender (LGBT) people are in the risk group for peer bullying. In their study, Bannink et al. (2014) found that having different ethnic origins, educational status and experiencing mental health problems (e.g., intellectual disability) cause more bullying. Pitsia and Mazzone (2020) found that speaking a non-native language is a risk factor for being a victim in a study conducted on 9048 children and adolescents aged 10-15 years. As can be seen, many situations that are "seen or felt as different" for children and young people constitute risk factors for bullying. In UNICEF's Jamaica report, it was stated that children who are seen as not groomed physically, poor, and messy are more bullied (UNICEF Jamaica Report, 2015). Victims are generally children with high levels of anxiety, low self-esteem and self-confidence, low social skills, and that are shy and introverted. Corcoran et al. (2012) examined 876 adolescents between the ages of 12 and 16 and found that low self-esteem and neurotic personality traits are risk factors for being a victim of peer bullying. Poor social skills of the child are also a risk factor for peer bullying; because it is among the findings of studies that victims, bully-victims and some bullies show inadequacy in terms of social skills (Cook et al., 2010). The frequency of depressive and anxiety disorders is higher in bullied children (Güvenir, 2008; Olweus, 1994). It has been determined that students with behavioral disorder are more likely to bully (Rose et al., 2011). The most important risk factor leading to peer bullying is the psychological characteristics of the child. The most important risk factor leading to peer bullying is psychological characteristics. Children who practice peer bullying need to feel powerful and keep others under control (Pişkin, 2002). These children show anti-social behavior and do not care about the rules of society. Children who bully also have insufficient empathy skills (Arsenio & Lemerise, 2001; Gini et al., 2007; Köksal Akyol & Bilbay, 2018). In addition, it has been determined that bullies are disturbed by the success of the people around them, cannot accept defeat, generally experience intense rage and anger, and do not have good bilateral relations (Olweus, 1994). Such children perform anti-social behavior and do not care about the rules of society. In the literature, there is also a research that shows that risk factors originating from individual characteristics mediate risk factors arising from family characteristics. In the study, Bifulco et al. (2014) concluded that the relationship between childhood risk factors for bullying (childhood abuse and neglect, parental conflict, violence between parents, low or variable supervision) reveals through contextual risk factors (troubled peer group and being a victim of bullying with aggression).

Family-Related Risk Factors for Peer Bullying

Considering the family-related risk factors, it is stated that the socio-economic status of the family is determinant for the risk. It can be observed that peer bullying is more common in schools in regions with poor economic conditions (Özkan & Çiftçi, 2010). In addition, studies have shown that children with low socioeconomic status are more bullied (Due et al., 2009; Menzer & Torney-Purta, 2012). Parent attitudes are also an important variable that poses a risk for peer bullying. There is a significant positive correlation between punitive parental attitude and bullying (Baldry & Farrington, 2005). Tippett & Wolke (2015) concluded in their study that sibling aggression increases in children who are exposed to harsh attitudes, depending on the attitudes of the parents, and this significantly increases the risk of being a victim of peer bullying. In their study, Tanrıkulu and Campbell (2015) concluded that there is a correlation between sibling bullying and peer bullying. Wolke et al. (2015) found that parenting quality and parent behaviors are strongly associated with sibling bullying, and sibling bullying increases the risk of being involved in peer bullying. In many studies, it has been determined that violence in the family and the mental health problems of the parents are positively correlated to peer bullying (Nocentini et al., 2019). In addition, it was determined that bullies were disturbed by the success of the people around them, could not stand defeat, were generally in a state of intense anger, and their bilateral relations were not good (Olweus, 1994). Considering the risk factors of children who practice bullying, these children come from families where aggression and violence are common. Bullying is common among adults whom it can model in the family. (Sutton, 2001; Güvenir, 2008). Children who practice bullying cannot also empathize (Arsenio & Lemerise, 2001; Gini et al., 2007; Köksal Akyol & Bilbay, 2018). One of the major risk factors is being physically abused by parents (Laeheem et al., 2009).

Negative family factors such as interparental conflict and family separation are closely associated with bullying or being bullied (Jablonska & Lindberg, 2007). Focusing on children's relationships with their parents and the life at home in the context of peer bullying; Gürhan's (2017) study determined that anger and disappointment experienced at home, cold fathers who spend little time with their children, or having weak and overprotective mothers are important risk factors for both choosing violence and being a victim. The bond between the parent and the child (Walden & Beran, 2010) and the quality of the parent-child relationship (Davis & Koepke, 2016; Murray-Harvey & Slee, 2010) are important risk factors for peer bullying.

School-Related Risk Factors for Peer Bullying

School, another risk factor for peer bullying, is a key context for children's social development. In general, students learn to interact and form friendships that will last a lifetime through the social relationships that take place at school. However, sometimes some students are bullied by their peers, which can have a negative impact on their lives (Álvarez-García et al., 2015). Studies have shown that schools with high levels of bullying have a negative and punitive school climate (Swearer, 2011). When the risk factors at the class level were examined, it was determined that the class hierarchy was related to bullying behaviors. In other words, it was observed that children who are popular in the classroom, have leadership traits, etc. bully more (Garandeau, Lee & Salmivalli, 2014). In addition, the attitudes of teachers and other personnel at the school (concerned, indifferent, etc.) are associated with the risk of peer bullying (Olweus & Solberg, 2018). Marengo et al. (2021) stated in their study that rejections caused by negative student-teacher relationships increase the risk of bullying and being bullied. In the same study, it was determined that popular students who had a positive relationship with their teachers were more likely to engage in physical bullying than others. It is also seen that students from certain ethnic, racial or cultural minorities are exposed to more bullying at school (Larochette et al., 2010; Lovegrove et al., 2012; Low & Espelage, 2013). Saarento et al. (2013), in their study, simultaneously investigated the risk factors for being a victim at the student, grade, and school levels, and concluded that victimization is more common in classrooms and schools, where students perceive their teachers to have less disapproving attitudes towards bullying. They also found that the effects of student-level predictors differed among grades, and class size moderated the effects of social anxiety and peer rejection on being a victim. Children who fail in school, do not pay attention to personal hygiene and self-care, are silent, self-isolating and non-confrontational are also preferred targets of bullies (Tarshis, 2010). For students who are bullies/victims, that is, both bullying and being bullied; it has been found that among their friends, they are disliked, easily provoked and provoke others, hyperactive, restless, inattentive, neurotic and psychotic, and have low levels of social acceptance and self-esteem (Pişkin, 2002). As a result, school psychologists and social care specialists can help reduce bullying by working in cooperation with teachers to create a positive school climate (Smokowski & Kopasz, 2005).

Social Risk Factors for Peer Bullying

In terms of social risk factors, Elgar et al. (2013) found that income inequality among families in the country was positively correlated to bullying and being bullied in their study conducted with subjects from 37 countries. The greater the income inequality, the more likely the student is to become a bully or victim.

Laeheem et al. (2009) stated in their study that one of the risk factors for peer bullying is children's preferences for violent cartoons. In their study, Özen & Kartelli (2017) examined the elements of violence in cartoons broadcast on TV channels for children in Turkey and found that elements of violence were used very frequently. In line with this finding, children who are overexposed to these elements may experience frequent crying, aggression, sleep problems, low self-esteem, focusing problems, and a tendency to depression.

INTERVENTION PROGRAMS FOR PEER BULLYING

Although the school environment has the potential to provide opportunities for the child to develop social and academic skills, it may also create risky situations. The most important of such risks is the school environment open to peer bullying (Bayar & Uçanok, 2012). At this point, due to the fact that bullying is a very common problem in schools and students who experience bullying may experience potential problems both in the present and in the future, it is important to state that there is a need for more studies to closely examine children who are victims or bullies and studies on how to prevent bullying behaviors (Gökkaya & Tekinsav Sütcü, 2015).

The aim of the efforts to prevent peer bullying in schools is to prevent bullying, to intervene in the existing bullying behaviors and to support the children in the bullying cycle in the school environment (Erk, 2019). In this sense, special-purpose programs are developed for the target group, as well as general prevention/intervention programs to cover all students throughout the school (Nickerson et al., 2014).

The most frequently studied and used intervention approaches against bullying aim to develop positive behavior and to teach social-emotional skills at classroom level and school-wide. There are also intervention approaches that focus specifically on bullying behavior (Nickerson et al., 2014). In addition to these, free support lines in the USA, Europe and Scandinavian countries also provide services for peer bullying (Erk, 2019). All school intervention programs used to prevent and stop peer bullying mostly focus on students, school staff and families (Karatoprak & Özcan, 2017).

Some of the many intervention programs applied for peer bullying and targeting different age groups in the literature can be listed as follows.

Positive Behavioral Interventions and Supports

Peer bullying prevention programs with positive behavioral interventions and supports can be explained as a school-wide model that includes both staff and students. It is an approach that focuses on improving the overall quality of life through strategies that help develop appropriate social behaviors. It includes all students in the school. Small group activities are held especially on how to behave towards disadvantaged people who are vulnerable to being victims. The purpose here is to help students with supportive and corrective practices in eliminating behavioral problems rather than applying punitive methods (Caldarella, 2011). The implementation of positive behavioral interventions in secondary schools contributed to the reduction of disciplinary applications, the improvement of the school environment, the improvement of student-teacher relations, and the reduction of verbal and physical aggression (Caldarella, 2011; Nickerson et al., 2014).

Social-Emotional Support Programs

Bullying prevention programs aimed at teaching social-emotional skills are based on the fact that teaching and learning in schools has strong social, emotional and academic components. With this approach, interpersonal processes in peer bullying are addressed in a constructive manner (Nickerson et al., 2014; Durlak et al., 2011). After a series of studies conducted by Espelage et al., it was concluded that there was a decrease in various types of bullying as a result of the social-emotional learning (Espelage et al., 2013).

Olweus Bullying Prevention Program (OBPP)

It is one of the most comprehensive anti-bullying programs implemented and systematically evaluated in Norway following several suicides happened due to bullying. The program was first implemented by psychologist Dan Olweus in 1983 as part of a longitudinal study that followed up approximately 2500 students. The program is focused on long-term change that seeks to create a positive school climate. It is used in primary school, secondary school and high school levels. The aim of the program is to reduce bullying problems among children at school and to improve peer relationships at school. It has been found that the program reduces bullying among students, positively changes the classroom climate, and reduces antisocial behaviors such as truancy from school. The Olweus Program is implemented in many countries, as well as in thousands of schools in the USA (Olweus, 2022). The content of the program includes various measures to be implemented at school level, classroom level, individual level and social level. School-level measures include surveys, conferences on bullying at school, and better control during break times and lunch hours. Classroom-level measures include practices such as creating and applying classroom rules against bullying, cooperative learning, role playing, etc. Measures at the individual level can be summarized as having serious conversations with bullies, victims and parents of children involved in bullying (Olweus, 1993). Social level measures include community participation and partnerships to support the school programs (Wojcik & Helka, 2019).

Kiusaamista Vastaan (KiVa)

KIVA (Kiusaamista Vastaan), meaning anti-bullying, is an anti-bullying program funded by the Ministry of Education and Culture and implemented at the University of Turku, Finland since 2007. The effectiveness of KiVa is scientifically proven and it focuses not on the victim(s), but on the witnesses and bystanders instead, which is a key aspect of the program (Clarkson & Hutchings, 2015). KiVa addresses problems among students, class materials and teachers, uses discipline strategies where students can use their ability to prevent bullying, computer games, and deal with parent knowledge on fight against bullying. It has been stated that KiVa is an effective intervention program in reducing the victim cases caused by peer bullying among 1st-9th grade students (Williford et al., 2012; Garandeau et al., 2012; Haataja et al., 2014). KiVa is both a preventive program and an interventionist program enabling students to learn how to confront bullying through games and studies. For this, individuals take classes at the age of 7-10-13. Students learn to describe what their classmates are feeling and to understand what emotions they feel with just their voice or facial expressions (Clarkson et al., 2016; Clarkson et al., 2019). It has been determined that the KiVa program reduces bullying and victim cases, as well as anxiety, depression, and supports motivation, academic achievement, and a positive group climate. After the intervention, 98% of the victim's state that their condition improved positively (Gaete et al., 2017).

VISC Program

The VISC program is a primary preventive program developed, implemented and assessed as a component of the Austrian national strategy plan, designed to reduce aggressive behavior and bullying and to promote social and intercultural competences in schools. The VISC Program has a systemic perspective and is designed for secondary schools (grades 5-8) (ages 11-14). The initial implementation of the program requires one school year. The VISC program aims to empower the entire school to take action against bullying. During the implementation of the program, teachers are provided with training on how to recognize bullying cases, how to deal with acute bullying cases, and how to apply preventive measures at school and classroom levels. In addition, parent meetings are held for parents. At the classroom level, the program trains students to take responsibility when bullying continues and to react in ways that positively contribute to the situation. As part of the teacher's student-centered teaching, students actively work together to find ways to prevent aggressive behavior in their classrooms. Finally, students design a small project so they work together to achieve a positive, common goal. The VISC program includes various components. Accordingly, the program is expected to prevent cyberbullying and cyber victims as well (Arenliu et al., 2020; Gradinger et al., 2016; Strohmeier et al., 2012).

INCLUSIVE Program

Bonell et al. (2015) developed a bullying intervention program under the title of Initiating Change Locally in Bullying and Aggression through the School Environment (INCLUSIVE). This intervention program was first applied to students aged 12-13 in 8 secondary schools in the UK to see if the adoption of the INCLUSIVE intervention program was feasible and acceptable and to test the program. The INCLUSIVE restorative approach to addressing bullying and aggression, which is intended to be applied to the whole school, includes some standard processes. These include forming a school action group and reviewing needs assessment data, bringing in external managers to set priorities, plan and monitor actions at school level, training the staff, and creating a new social and emotional skills curriculum. As a result, it has been demonstrated that the INCLUSIVE intervention program is feasible and acceptable for dissemination and testing in secondary schools. Additionally, another study by Bonell et al. (2020) found evidence of multiple effects of the INCLUSIVE intervention program on health-related outcomes (reduction in e-cigarette use, cyberbullying, aggressive behaviors) and educational outcomes (reduction in participation in school disciplinary procedures and reduction in truancy).

Zero Tolerance Program

After three students committed suicide due to peer bullying in Norway in the 1980s, this event was reflected in the media and early intervention efforts were started to counter and prevent bullying in schools. One of these efforts is the Zero Tolerance Program. The Zero Tolerance Program is a school-based program and developed primarily to address issues such as violence, drugs, and weapons. It was later implemented in American schools to address bullying through the Gun-Free School Act (Martinez, 2009). In this model, every student who exhibits certain bullying behaviors is punished accordingly (Holloway, 2002). After the school administrators and teachers were informed about the subject, sanctions were applied to the students without any tolerance. This program predicts that students will avoid bullying behaviors because they know that they will be punished as a result of such behaviors (Daniel & Bondy, 2008). However, studies have revealed that the model is applied incorrectly and that school principals impose serious sanctions on certain students specifically (Martinez, 2009). This program, unlike the others mentioned above, was criticized for being a reactive program and its adoption remained more limited compared to preventive programs.

CONCLUSION

Peer bullying is when an individual is exposed to negative actions on his/her property, body, emotions, relationships, reputation, digital presence by a stronger peer or peers. In peer bullying, there are different roles such as bully, victim, bully/victim, bystander, and even these roles can change over time. Bullying is examined under five headings as physical, verbal, relational, sexual and cyberbullying bullying. Studies show that there are some differences in the types and frequency of peer bullying in schools according to age and grade. As a result, peer bullying is frequently experienced in schools. For this reason, many different intervention programs have been developed and implemented in the world.

Future Research and Directions

School age, which covers an important part of human life, is the years when children and adolescents are together with their peers. All types of peer bullying encountered in this period can be considered as negative experiences for well-being. For this reason, efforts should be continued to reduce or even eliminate bullying. However, importance should be given to studies that develop children's and adolescents' ability to cope with bullying. Especially in schools, from early childhood, practices on emotion regulation, resilience, and self-esteem should be increased. By emphasizing the importance of well-being at the social level, attention should be paid not to lag behind academic concerns. well-being programs should be increased, with which policy makers, educators, academics, psychologists and sociologists work together to reduce risk factors and improve protective factors in peer bullying.

REFERENCES

Al-Bitar, Z. B., Al-Omari, I. K., Sonbol, H. N., Al-Ahmad, H. T., & Cunningham, S. J. (2013). Bullying among Jordanian school children, its effects on school performance, and the contribution of general physical and dentofacial features. *American Journal of Orthodontics and Dentofacial Orthopedics*, *144*(6), 872–878. doi:10.1016/j.ajodo.2013.08.016 PMID:24286910

Alvarez-García, D., García, T., & Núnez, J. C. (2015). Predictors of school bullying perpetration in adolescence: A systematic review. *Aggression and Violent Behavior*, *23*, 126–136. doi:10.1016/j.avb.2015.05.007

Archer, J., & Coyne, S. M. (2005). An integrated review of indirect, relational, and social aggression. *Personality and Social Psychology Review*, *9*(3), 212–230. 10.1207%2Fs15327957pspr0903_2 PMID:16083361

Arënliu, A., Strohmeier, D., Konjufca, J., Yanagida, T., & Burger, C. (2020). Empowering the peer group to prevent school bullying in Kosovo: Effectiveness of a short and ultra-short version of the VISC social competence program. *International Journal of Bullying Prevention*, *2*(1), 65–78.

Arsenio, W., & Lemerise, E. A. (2001). Varieties of childhood bullying: Values, emotion processes and social competence. *Social Development*, *10*(1), 59–73. doi:10.1111/1467-9507.00148

Atik, G., & Güneri, O. Y. (2013). Bullying and victimization: Predictive role of individual, parental, and academic factors. *School Psychology International*, *34*(6), 658–673. doi:10.1177/0143034313479699

Ayas, T. (2008). *The effectiveness of preventing bullying behaviors one program based on whole school approach* [Unpublished Doctorate Thesis]. Ankara University, Institute of Educational Sciences, Ankara.

Ayas, T. (2018). *Okullarda yaygın sorun olan zorbalığı önlemek* [Preventing bullying, a common problem in schools]. Vizetek Yayıncılık.

Ayas, T., & Pişkin, M. (2011). Investigation of bullying among high school students with regard to sex, grade level, and school type. *Elementary Education Online, 10*(2), 550–568.

Baldry, A. C., & Farrıngton, D. P. (2005). Protective factors as moderators of risk factors in adolescence bullying. *Social Psychology of Education, 8*, 263–284. doi:10.100711218-005-5866-5

Bannink, R., Broeren, S., Van de Looij-Jansen, P. M., De Waart, F. G., & Raat, H. (2014). Cyber and traditional bullying victimization as a risk factor for mental health problems and suicidal ideation in adolescents. *PLoS One, 9*(4), 1–7. doi:10.1371/journal.pone.0094026 PMID:24718563

Bayar, Y., & Uçanok, Z. (2012). School Social Climate and Traditional / Cyberbullying: The Mediational Role of Peer Perception. *Turkish Journal of Psychology, 27*(70), 101–114.

Beale, A. V., & Hall, K. R. (2007). Cyberbullying: What school administrators (and parents) can do. *The Clearing House: A Journal of Educational Strategies, Issues and Ideas, 81*(1), 8–12. doi:10.3200/TCHS.81.1.8-12

Beale, A. V., & Scott, P. C. (2001). Bullybusters: Using drama to empower students to take a stand against bullying behavior. *Professional School Counseling, 4*(4), 300–305.

Beane, A. L. (2008). *Protect your child from bullying*. Jossey-Bass.

Bifulco, A., Schimmenti, A., Jacobs, C., Bunn, A., & Rusu, A. C. (2014). Risk factors and psychological outcomes of bullying victimization: A community-based study. *Child Indicators Research, 7*(3), 633–648. doi:10.100712187-014-9236-8

Bilgiç, E. (2007). *Investigation of the bullying observed at elementary schools in view of the perception of class variables and atmosphere* [Unpublished Master Thesis]. Çukurova University, Institute of Social Sciences, Adana.

Bilgin, A. (2007). The Views of Day and Boarding Students about Bullying. *Ege Journal of Education, 8*(1), 1–18.

Bonell, C., Dodd, M., Allen, E., Bevilacqua, L., McGowan, J., Opondo, C., Sturgess, J., Elbourne, D., Warren, E., & Viner, R. (2020). Broader impacts of an intervention to transform school environments on student behaviour and school functioning: Post hoc analyses from the INCLUSIVE cluster randomised controlled trial. *BMJ Open*, 1–11. doi:10.1136/bmjopen-2019-031589 PMID:32414817

Bonell, C., Fletcher, A., Fitzgerald-Yau, N., Hale, D., Allen, E., Elbourne, D., Jones, R., Bond, L., Wiggins, M., Miners, A., Legood, R., Scott, S., Christie, D., & Viner, R. (2015). Initiating change locallyin bullying and aggression through the school environment (INCLUSIVE): A pilot randomised controlled trial. *Health Technology Assessment, 19*(53), 1–109. doi:10.3310/hta19530 PMID:26182956

Caldarella, P., Shatzer, R. H., Gray, K. M., Young, R. K., & Young, E. L. (2011). The effects of school-wide positive behavior support on middle school climate and student outcomes. *Research in Middle Level Education Online*, *35*(4), 1–14.

CDC Centers For Disease Control And Prevention. (2020). *Preventing bullying*. https://www.cdc.gov/violenceprevention/youthviolence/bullyingresearch/fastfact.html

Clarkson, S., Axford, N., Berry, V., Edwards, R. T., Bjornstad, G., Wrigley, Z., Charles, J., Hoare, Z., Ukoumunne, O. C., Matthews, J., & Hutchings, J. (2016). Effectiveness and micro-costing of the KiVa school-based bullying prevention programme in Wales: Study protocol for a pragmatic definitive parallel group cluster randomised controlled trial. *BMC Public Health*, *16*(104). Advance online publication. doi:10.118612889-016-2746-1 PMID:26832736

Clarkson, S., Charles, J. M., Saville, C. W. N., Bjornstad, G. J., & Hutchings, J. (2019). Introducing KiVa school-based antibullying programme to the UK: A preliminary examination of effectiveness and programme cost. *School Psychology International*, *40*(4), 347–365. doi:10.1177/0143034319841099

Clarkson, S., & Hutchings, J. (2015). Introducing and piloting the KiVa bullying prevention programme in the UK. *Educational and Child Psychology*, *32*(1), 49–61.

Conn, K. (2004). *Bullying and harassment: a legal guide for educators*. Association for Supervision and Curriculum Development.

Connolly, E. J., & Beaver, K. M. (2016). Considering the genetic and environmental overlap between bullying victimization, delinquency, and symptoms of depression/anxiety. *Journal of Interpersonal Violence*, *31*, 1230–1256. doi:10.1177/0886260514564158 PMID:25535249

Cook, C. R., Williams, K. R., Guerra, N. G., Kim, T. E., & Sadek, S. (2010). Predictors of bullying and victimization in childhood and adolescence: A meta-analytic investigation. *School Psychology Quarterly*, *25*(2), 65–83.

Corcoran, L., Connolly, I., & O'Moore, M. (2012). Cyberbullying in Irish schools: An investigation of personality and self-concept. *The Irish Journal of Psychology*, *33*(4), 153–165. doi:10.1080/03033910.2012.677995

Costello, E. J., Foley, D. L., & Angold, A. (2006). 10-year research update review: the epidemiology of child and adolescent psychiatric disorders: II. Developmental epidemiology. *Journal of the American Academy of Child and Adolescent Psychiatry*, *45*(1), 8–25. doi:10.1097/01.chi.0000184929.41423.c0 PMID:16327577

Cowie, H., & Myers, C. A. (2016). What we know about bullying among university students. In H. Cowie & C. A. Myers (Eds.), *Bullying Among University Students* (pp. 3–14). Routledge.

Crick, N. R., Casas, J. F., & Mosher, M. (1997). Relational and overt aggression in preschool. *Developmental Psychology*, *33*(4), 579–588. doi:10.1037/0012-1649.33.4.579 PMID:9232373

Daniel, Y., & Bondy, K. (2008). Safe schools and zero tolerance: Policy, program and practice in Ontario. *Canadian Journal of Educational Administration and Policy*, *70*, 1–20.

Davis, K., & Koepke, L. (2016). Risk and protective factors associated with cyberbullying: Are relationships or rules more protective? learning. *Media and Technology*, *41*(4), 521–545. doi:10.1080/17439884.2014.994219

Donnellan, C., & Firth, L. (2006). *Bullying*. Independence Educational Publishers.

Douvlos, C. (2019). Bullying in preschool children. *Psychological Thought*, *12*(1), 131–142. doi:10.5964/psyct.v12i1.284

Due, P., Merlo, J., Harel-Fisch, Y., Damsgaard, M. T., Holstein, B. E., Hetland, J., Currie, C., Gabhainn, S. N., Gaspar de Matos, M., & Lynch, J. (2009). Socioeconomic inequality in exposure to bullying during adolescence: A comparative, cross-sectional, multilevel study in 35 countries. *American Journal of Public Health*, *99*(5), 907–914. doi:10.2105/AJPH.2008.139303 PMID:19299676

Duncan, N. (1998). Sexual bullying in secondary schools. *Pastoral Care in Education*, *16*(2), 27–31.

Durlak, J. A., Weissberg, R. P., Dymnicki, A. B., Taylor, R. D., & Schellinger, K. B. (2011). The impact of enhancing students' social and emotional learning: A meta-analysis of school-based universal interventions. *Child Development*, *82*(1), 405–432. doi:10.1111/j.1467-8624.2010.01564.x PMID:21291449

Egger, H. L., & Angold, A. (2006). Common emotional and behavioral disorders in preschool children: Presentation, nosology, and epidemiology. *Journal of Child Psychology and Psychiatry, and Allied Disciplines*, *47*(3-4), 313–337. doi:10.1111/j.1469-7610.2006.01618.x PMID:16492262

Elgar, F. J., Pickett, K. E., Pickett, W., Craig, W., Molcho, M., Hurrelmann, K., & Lenzi, M. (2013). School bullying, homicide and income inequality: A cross-national pooled time series analysis. *International Journal of Public Health*, *58*(2), 237–245. doi:10.100700038-012- 0380-y PMID:22714137

Erk, A. B. (2019). *Akran zorbalığı, okullarda akran zorbalığını önleme çalışmaları ve zorbalık döngüsündeki çocuklar için uygulamalar [Peer bullying, bullying prevention studies in schools and apps for children in the bullying cycle]*. Ekinoks Yayınevi.

Espelage, D. L., Low, S., Polanin, J. R., & Brown, E. C. (2013). The impact of a middle-school program to reduce aggression, victimization, and sexual violence. *The Journal of Adolescent Health*, *53*(2), 180–186. doi:10.1016/j.jadohealth.2013.02.021 PMID:23643338

Farrington, D. P., & Baldry, A. C. (2010). Individual risk factors for school bullying. *Journal of Aggression, Conflict and Peace Research*, *2*(1), 4–16. doi:10.5042/jacpr.2010.0001

Fredland, N. M. (2008). Sexual bullying: Addressing the gap between bullying and dating violence. *Advances in Nursing Science*, *31*(2), 95–105. doi:10.1097/01.ANS.0000319560.76384.8a PMID:18497586

Gaete, J., Valenzuela, D., Rojas-Barahona, C., Valenzuela, E., Araya, R., & Salmivalli, C. (2017). The KiVa antibullying program in primary schools in Chile, with and without the digital game component: Study protocol for a randomized controlled trial. *Trials*, *18*(1), 75. doi:10.118613063-017-1810-1 PMID:28219403

Garandeau, C. F., Lee, I. A., & Salmivalli, C. (2014). Inequality matters: Classroom status hierarchy and adolescents' bullying. *Journal of Youth and Adolescence*, *43*(7), 1123–1133. doi:10.100710964-013-0040-4 PMID:24129884

Garandeau, C. F., Poskiparta, E., & Salmivalli, C. (2014). Tackling acute cases of school bullying in the KiVa anti-bullying program: A comparison of two approaches. *Journal of Abnormal Child Psychology, 42*(6), 981–991. doi:10.100710802-014-9861-1 PMID:24615005

Genç, G. (2007). *Peer bullying and its management in high schools* [Unpublished Doctorate Thesis]. Ankara University, Institute of Social Sciences, Malatya.

Georgiou, S. N., & Stavrinides, P. (2008). Bullies, victims and bully-victims. *School Psychology International, 29*(5), 574–589. doi:10.1177/0143034308099202

Gini, G., Albiero, P., Benelli, B., & Altoè, G. (2007). Does empathy predict adolescents' bullying and defending behavior? *Aggressive Behavior, 33*(5), 464–476. doi:10.1002/ab.20204 PMID:17683107

Gökkaya, F., & Tekinsav Sütcü, S. (2015). Development and evaluation of psychometric characteristics of the ınventory of cognitions related bullying for children. *Anatolian Journal of Psychiatry, 16*(1), 54–63. doi:10.5455/apd.174346

Gökler, R. (2009). Bullying in schools. *International Journal of Human Sciences, 6*(2), 511–537.

Gradinger, P., Yanagida, T., Strohmeier, D., & Spiel, C. (2016). Effectiveness and sustainability of the ViSC Social Competence Program to prevent cyberbullying and cyber-victimization: Class and individual level moderators. *Aggressive Behavior, 42*(2), 181–193. doi:10.1002/ab.21631 PMID:26879896

Green, R., Collingwood, A., & Ross, A. (2010). *Characteristics of bullying victims in schools*. London Publishing.

Gruber, J., & Fineran, S. (2015). Sexual harassment, bullying, and school outcomes for high school girls and boys. *Violence Against Women, 22*(1), 1–23. doi:10.1177/1077801215599079 PMID:26270385

Gültekin, Z. (2003). *he Development of a peer victimization scale* [Unpublished Master Thesis]. Hacettepe University, Instutue of Social Sciences, Ankara.

Gürhan, N. (2017). All aspects of the bullying. *Türkiye Klinikleri J Psychiatr Nurs-Special Topics, 3*(2), 175–181.

Güven, F. (2015). *An invastigation of bullying and being victim at 8th grade secondary school students, in relation with sex, parent education, socioeconomic status and empathy level* [Unpublished Master Thesis]. Toros University, Instutue of Social Sciences, Mersin.

Güvenir, T. (2008). *Okulda akran istismarı(Peer bullying in schools)*. Kök Yayıncılık.

Haataja, A., Voeten, M., Boulton, A. J., Ahtola, A., Poskiparta, E., & Salmivalli, C. (2014). The KiVa antibullying curriculum and outcome: Does fidelity matter? *Journal of School Psychology, 52*(5), 479–493. doi:10.1016/j.jsp.2014.07.001 PMID:25267170

Hamel, N., Schwab, S., & Wahl, S. (2021). Bullying: Group differences of being victim and being bully and the influence of social relations. *Studies in Educational Evaluation, 68*(6). Advance online publication. doi:10.1016/j.stueduc.2020.100964

Hanhan, A. A. (2012). *Research on the effects of restorative discipline model on peer bullying and violence in high schools* [Unpublished Doctorate Thesis]. Dokuz Eylul University, Institute of Educational Sciences, İzmir.

Harris, M. J. (2009). Taking bullying and rejection (ınter) personally: benefits of a social psychological approach to peer victimization. In M. J. Harris (Ed.), *Bullying, Rejection, And Peer Victimization: A Social Cognitive Neuroscience Perspective* (pp. 3–23). Springer Publishing Company.

Holloway, J. H. (2002). The dilemma of zero tolerance. *Educational Leadership*, *59*(4), 84–86.

Ilola, A. M., Lempinen, L., Huttunen, J., Ristkari, T., & Sourander, A. (2016). Bullying and victimisation are common in four-year-old children and are associated with somatic symptoms and conduct and peer problems. *Acta Paediatrica (Oslo, Norway)*, *105*(5), 522–528. doi:10.1111/apa.13327 PMID:26741067

Jablonska, B., & Lindberg, L. (2007). Risk behaviours, victimisation and mental distress among adolescents in different family structures. *Social Psychiatry and Psychiatric Epidemiology*, *42*(8), 656–663. doi:10.100700127-007-0210-3 PMID:17522746

Karaman-Kepenekçi, Y., & Çınkır, Ş. (2006). Bullying among Turkish high school students. *Child Abuse*, *30*(2), 193–204. doi:10.1016/j.chiabu.2005.10.005 PMID:16460802

Karatoprak, S., & Özcan, Ö. (2017). Peer Bullying. *Turkiye Klinikleri J Child Psychiatry-Special Topics*, *3*(3), 195–203.

Köksal Akyol, A., & Bilbay, A. (2018). Examination of the Correlation between Peer Bullying, Exposed to Bullying, and Emphatic Tendencies of Adolescent. *Tarih Kültür ve Sanat Arastirmalari Dergisi*, *7*(2), 667–675. doi:10.7596/taksad.v7i2.1379

Korkut, F. (2007). *Okul temelli önleyici rehberlik ve psikolojik danışma [School-based preventive guidance and psychological counseling]*. Anı Yayıncılık.

Kowalski, R. M., Giumetti, G. W., Schroeder, A. N., & Lattanner, M. R. (2014). Bullying in the digital age: A critical review and meta-analysis of cyberbullying research among youth. *Psychological Bulletin*, *140*(4), 1073–1137. doi:10.1037/a0035618 PMID:24512111

Kshirsagar, V. Y., Agarwal, R., & Bavdekar, S. B. (2007). Bullying in schools: Prevalence and short-term impact. *Indian Pediatrics*, *44*(1), 25–28. PMID:17277427

Laeheem, K., Kuning, M., & McNeil, N. (2009). Bullying: Risk factors becoming 'bullies'. *Asian Social Science*, *5*(5), 50–57. doi:10.5539/ass.v5n5p50

Larochette, A., Murphy, A. N., & Craig, W. M. (2010). Racial bullying and victimization in Canadian school-aged children: Individual and school level effects. *School Psychology International*, *31*(4), 389–408. doi:10.1177/0143034310377150

Lemstra, M. E., Nielsen, G., Rogers, M. R., Thompson, A. T., & Moraros, J. S. (2012). Risk indicators and outcomes associated with bullying in youth aged 9-15 years. *Canadian Journal of Public Health*, *103*(1), 9–13. doi:10.1007/BF03404061 PMID:22338321

Little, L. (2002). Middle-class mothers' perceptions of peer and sibling victimization among children with Asperger's syndrome and nonverbal learning disorders. *Issues in Comprehensive Pediatric Nursing*, *25*, 43–57. doi:10.1080/014608602753504847 PMID:11934121

Lovegrove, P. J., Henry, K. L., & Slater, M. D. (2012). Examination of the predictors of latent class typologies of bullying involvement among middle school students. *Journal of School Violence*, *11*(1), 75–93. doi:10.1080/15388220.2011.631447 PMID:22606069

Low, S., & Espelage, D. (2014). Conduits from community violence exposure to peer aggression and victimization: Contributions of parental monitoring, impulsivity and deviancy. *Journal of Counseling Psychology*, *61*(2), 221–231. doi:10.1037/a0035207 PMID:24635595

Malecki, C. K., Demaray, M. K., Smith, T. J., & Emmons, J. (2020). Disability, poverty, and other risk factors associated with involvement in bullying behaviors. *Journal of School Psychology*, *78*, 115–132. doi:10.1016/j.jsp.2020.01.002 PMID:32178807

Marengo, D., Fabris, M. A., Prino, L. E., Settanni, M., & Longobardi, C. (2021). Student-teacher conflict moderates the link between students' social status in the classroom and involvement in bullying behaviors and exposure to peer victimization. *Journal of Adolescence*, *87*, 86–97. doi:10.1016/j.adolescence.2021.01.005 PMID:33545582

Martinez, S. (2009). A system gone berserk: How are zero-tolerance policies really affecting schools? *Preventing School Failure*, *53*, 153–158. doi:10.3200/PSFL.53.3.153-158

Menesini, E., & Salmivalli, C. (2017). Bullying in schools: The state of knowledge and effective interventions. *Psychology Health and Medicine*, *22*(1), 240–254. doi:10.1080/13548506.2017.1279740 PMID:28114811

Menzer, M. M., & Torney-Purta, J. (2012). Individualism and socioeconomic diversity at school as related to perceptions of the frequency of peer aggression in fifteen countries. *Journal of Adolescence*, *35*(5), 1285–1294. doi:10.1016/j.adolescence.2012.04.013 PMID:22633914

Monks, C. P., Palermiti, A., Ortega, R., & Costabile, A. (2011). A cross-national comparison of aggressors, victims and defenders in preschools in England, Spain and Italy. *The Spanish Journal of Psychology*, *14*(1), 133–144. doi:10.5209/rev_SJOP.2011.v14.n1.11 PMID:21568171

Murray-Harvey, R., & Slee, P. T. (2010). School and home relationships and their impact on school bullying. *School Psychology International*, *31*(3), 271–295. doi:10.1177/0143034310366206

Mynard, H., & Joseph, S. (2000). Development of the multidimensional peer-victimization scale. *Aggressive Behavior*, *26*(2), 169–178. doi:10.1002/(SICI)1098-2337(2000)26:23.0.CO;2-A

Nickerson, A., Singleton, D., Schnurr, B. L., & Collen, M. H. (2014). Perceptions of school climate as a function of bullying involvement. *Journal of Applied School Psychology*, *30*(2), 157–181. doi:10.1080/15377903.2014.888530

Nocentini, A., Fiorentini, G., Di Paola, L., & Menesini, E. (2019). Parents, family characteristics and bullying behavior: A systematic review. *Aggression and Violent Behavior*, *45*, 41–50. doi:10.1016/j.avb.2018.07.010

O'Moore, O., & Minton, S. J. (2004). *Dealing with bullying in schools a training manual for teachers, parents and other professionals*. Chapman Publishing.

OECD. (2020). Bullying. İn PISA 2015 Results (Volume III): Students' Well-Being. OECD Publishing. doi:10.1787/9789264273856-12-en

Olweus, D. (1993). *Bullying at school: What we know and what we can do understanding children's worlds*. Blackwell Publishing Ltd.

Olweus, D. (1994). *Bullying at school. long -term outcomes for the victims and an effective school-based intervention program. In Aggressive Behavior: Current Perspectives*. Plenum Press.

Olweus, D. (2003). *Bullying at school*. Blackwell Publishing.

Olweus, D. (2022). *Olweus bullying prevention program*. Clemson University. https://olweus.sites.clemson.edu/

Olweus, D., & Solberg, C. (2018). *Bullying among children and young people. Information and guidance for parents*. https://bibliotek.bufdir.no

Özen, Ö., & Kartelli, F. (2017). Analysis of violence in cartoons broadcasted on kids TV channels in Turkey. *Marmara İletişim Dergisi*, *27*, 81–93. doi:10.17829/midr.20172729523

Özkan, Y., & Çiftçi, E. G. (2010). Peer bullying in primary schools low socio-economic level. *Elemantary Education Online*, *9*(2), 576–586.

Öztürk, N., & Atlı, A. (2014). An investigation of bullying cases in middle school students in terms of some variables. *Inonu University Journal of The Faculty of Education*, *15*(3), 43–63. doi:10.17679/iuefd.15365258

Pauline, W., Verlinden, J. M., Berkel, A. D., Mieloo, L. D., Raat, H., Hofman, A., Jaddoe, W. V., Verhulst, F. C., Jansen, W., & Tiemeier, H. (2014). Teacher and peer reports of overweight and bullying among young primary school children. *Pediatrics*, *134*(3). Advance online publication. doi:10.1542/peds.2013-3274 PMID:25157018

Pişkin, M. (2002). School bullying, its definition, types, related factors and measures to be taken. *Educational Sciences: Theory and Practice*, *2*, 531–562.

Pitsia, V., & Mazzone, A. (2020). The association of individual and contextual variables with bullying victimisation: A cross-national comparison between Ireland and Lithuania. *European Journal of Psychology of Education*, *36*, 1095–1115. doi:10.100710212-020-00514-0

Reulbach, U., Ladewig, E. L., Nixon, E., O'Moore, M., Williams, J., & O'Dowd, T. (2013). Weight, body image and bullying in 9-year-old children. *Journal of Paediatrics and Child Health*, *49*(4), 288–293. doi:10.1111/jpc.12159 PMID:23530984

Rigby, K. (2003). *Stop the bullying: a handbook for schools*. ACER Press.

Rodkin, P., & Hodges, E. (2003). Bullies and victims in the peer ecology: Four questions for psychologists and school professionals. *School Psychology Review*, *32*(3), 384–400.

Rose, C. A., Monda-Amaya, L. E., & Espelage, D. L. (2011). Bullying perpetration and victimization in special education: A review of the literature. *Remedial and Special Education*, *32*(2), 114–130. doi:10.1177/0741932510361247

Russell, S. T., Toomey, R. B., Ryan, C., & Diaz, R. M. (2014). Being out at school: The implications for school victimization and young adult adjustment. *The American Journal of Orthopsychiatry*, *84*(6), 635–643. doi:10.1037/ort0000037 PMID:25545431

Saarento, S., Kärnä, A., Hodges, E. V. E., & Salmivalli, C. (2013). Student-, classroom-, and school-level risk factors for victimization. *Journal of School Psychology*, *51*(3), 421–434. doi:10.1016/j.jsp.2013.02.002 PMID:23816233

Salmivalli, C., Kaukiainen, A., & Voeten, M. (2005). Anti-bullying intervention implementation and outcome. *The British Journal of Educational Psychology*, *75*(3), 465–487. doi:10.1348/000709905X26011 PMID:16238877

Satan, A. (2011). Investigating the prevalence and impact of peer abuse (bullying) on the development of Jamaica's children report. *Marmara University Atatürk Education Faculty Journal of Educational Science*, *34*, 183–194.

Scheithauer, H., Hayer, T., Petermann, F., & Jugert, G. (2006). Physical, verbal, and relational forms of bullying among German students: Age, trends, gender differences and correlates. *Aggressive Behavior*, *32*(3), 261–275. doi:10.1002/ab.20128

Shariff, S. (2008). *Cyber-bullying: Issues and solutions for the school, the classroom and the home*. Routledge.

Slee, P. T., & Skrzypiec, G. (2016). *Well-being, positive peer relations and bullying in school settings*. Springer International Publishing.

Smith, P. K. (2016). Bullying: definition, types, causes, consequences and intervention: Bullying. *Social and Personality Psychology Compass*, *10*(9), 519–532. doi:10.1111pc3.12266

Smokowski, P. R., & Kopasz, K. H. (2005). Bullying in school: An overview of types, effects, family characteristics, and intervention strategies. *Children & Schools*, *27*(2), 101–109. doi:10.1093/cs/27.2.101

Soenens, B., Vansteenkiste, M., Goossens, L., Duriez, B., & Niemiec, C. P. (2008). The ıntervening role of relational aggression between psychological control and friendship quality. *Social Development*, *17*, 661–681. doi:10.1111/j.1467-9507.2007.00454.x

Strohmeier, D., Hoffmann, C., Schiller, E. M., Stefanek, E., & Spiel, C. (2012). ViSC social competence program. *New Directions for Youth Development*, (133), 71–84. doi:10.1002/yd.20008 PMID:22504792

Sutton, J. (2001). Bullies: Thugs of thinkers? *The Psychologist*, *14*(10), 530–534.

Swearer, S. M. (2011). Risk factors for and outcomes of bullying and victimization. *Educational Psychology Papers and Publications*, *132*, 1–9.

Swearer, S. M., & Hymel, S. (2015). Understanding the psychology of bullying: Moving toward a social-ecological diathesis-stress model. *The American Psychologist*, *70*(4), 344–353. doi:10.1037/a0038929 PMID:25961315

Tanrıkulu, I., & Campbell, M. A. (2015). Sibling bullying perpetration: Associations with gender, grade, peer perpetration, trait anger, and moral disengagement. *Journal of Interpersonal Violence*, *30*(6), 1010–1024. doi:10.1177/0886260514539763 PMID:25038224

Tarshis, T. H. (2010). *Living with peer pressure and bullying*. Facts On File.

Tatlılıoğlu, K. (2016). Violence and tyranny at schools: risk factors, services of protect, prevent and ınterfere: the sample of the Konya. *Bingöl Üniversitesi SBE Dergisi*, *6*(12), 209–231. doi:10.29029/busbed.328657

Tippett, N., & Wolke, D. (2015). Aggression between siblings: Associations with the home environment and peer bullying. *Aggressive Behavior*, *41*(1), 14–24. doi:10.1002/ab.21557 PMID:25187483

Tokunaga, R. S. (2010). Following you home from school: A critical review and synthesis of research on cyberbullying victimization. *Computers in Human Behavior*, *26*(3), 277–287.

Tsai, K. C., & Gomba, C. (2012). Effects of bullying in schools: The teachers' perspectives. *Journal of Society and Communication*, *1*, 161–179.

Tural Hesapçıoğlu, S., & Yeşilova, H. (2015). Feelings, thoughts and attitudes of high school students toward school bullying and the bullies. *Anatolian Journal of Psychiatry*, *16*(4), 284–293. doi:10.5455/apd.155780

UNICEF. (2015). *Investigating the prevalence and impact of peer abuse (bullying) on the development of Jamaica's children report*. https://www.unicef.org/jamaica/reports/investigating-prevalence-and-impact-peer-abuse-development-jamaicas-children

Walden, L. M., & Beran, T. N. (2010). Attachment quality and bullying behavior in school-aged youth. *Canadian Journal of School Psychology*, *25*, 5–18. doi:10.1177/0829573509357046

Wang, J., Iannotti, R. J., & Nansel, T. R. (2009). School bullying among US adolescents: Physical, verbal, relational, and cyber. *The Journal of Adolescent Health*, *45*(4), 368–375. doi:10.1016/j.jadohealth.2009.03.021 PMID:19766941

Wet, C. (2005). The nature and extent of bullying in free state secondary schools. *South African Journal of Education*, *25*(2), 82–88.

Williford, A., Boulton, A., Noland, B., Little, T. D., Kärnä, A., & Salmivalli, C. (2012). Effects of the KiVa anti-bullying program on adolescents' depression, anxiety, and perception of peers. *Journal of Abnormal Child Psychology*, *40*(2), 289–300. doi:10.100710802-011-9551-1 PMID:21822630

Wójcik, M., & Helka, A. M. (2019). Meeting the needs of young adolescents: ABBL anti-bullying program during middle school tansition. *Psychological Reports*, *122*(3), 1043–1067. doi:10.1177/0033294118768671 PMID:29652220

Wolke, D., Tippett, N., & Dantchev, S. (2015). Bullying in the family: Sibling bullying. *The Lancet. Psychiatry*, *2*(10), 917–929. doi:10.1016/S2215-0366(15)00262-X PMID:26462226

Yeşildal, Y. (2016). A general overview of violence in healthcare. *Journal of Health and Nursing Management*, *1*(3), 44–55. doi:10.5222/SHYD.2016.044

Zablotsky, B., Bradshaw, C. P., Anderson, C. M., & Law, P. (2014). Risk factors for bullying among children with autism spectrum disorders. *Autism*, *18*(4), 419–427. 10.1177%2F1362361313477920 PMID:23901152

ADDITIONAL READING

Alvarez-García, D., García, T., & Núnez, J. C. (2015). Predictors of school bullying perpetration in adolescence: A systematic review. *Aggression and Violent Behavior*, *23*, 126–136. doi:10.1016/j.avb.2015.05.007

Arënliu, A., Strohmeier, D., Konjufca, J., Yanagida, T., & Burger, C. (2020). Empowering the peer group to prevent school bullying in Kosovo: Effectiveness of a short and ultra-short version of the VISC social competence program. *International Journal of Bullying Prevention*, *2*(1), 65–78.

Lınes, D. (2008). *The Bullıes Understandıng Bullıes And Bullyıng*. Jessica Kingsley Publishers.

KEY TERMS AND DEFINITIONS

Cyberbullying: It is the exposure of an individual to negative actions, which uses communication technologies, by her peer or peers who are self-powerful.

Homophobic Bullying: Exposure to negative actions by a heterosexual peer or peers due to homosexual sexual preferences.

Peer Bullying: It is the exposure of an individual to negative actions by a peer or peers who are stronger than herself on her property, body, emotions, relationships, reputation, digital presence.

Physical Bullying: It is the exposure of an individual to negative actions by a peer or peers who are stronger than herself on her body.

Relational Bullying: It is the exposure of an individual to negative actions by a peer or peers who are stronger than herself in her relationships.

Sexual Bullying: It is the exposure of an individual to sexual harassment-like behaviors by a stronger peer or peers.

Verbal Bullying: It is the exposure of the individual to verbal negative actions by his peer or peers who are stronger than herself.

Chapter 25
A New Problem Emerging With the Internet and Digital Media: Cyberbullying

Gülin Tuğçe Söyleyici
Siirt University, Turkey

Adnan Kalkan
Burdur Mehmet Akif Ersoy University, Turkey

ABSTRACT

Today, with the developing technology, online social media and social network have emerged as a cultural reality. With the increase in the use of digital media, in the modern age where the real world and the virtual world can be experienced in a synchronized way, digital media offers many opportunities. However, the increase in the time spent on the internet also brings with it undesirable situations such as cyberbullying. Cyberbullying is an act of cyber aggression aimed at harassing or humiliating. Cyberbullying is the behavior that disrupts the social relations of those chosen as victims and aims to arouse negative emotions. Understanding how cyberbullying occurs is very important for the development of strategies to prevent and respond to this attack. In this chapter, the concepts of cyber violence, cyber bullying, traditional bullying, and cyber victimization are explained.

INTRODUCTION

In the twenty-first century, people live in a world where social media and the internet are active. Communication is now just a button click. With the development of technology, the use of digital media is increasing day by day (Perera and Fernando, 2021, p.605). Online social media has been very helpful in reconnecting people, building networks and providing a space for freedom of speech (Fortunatus et al., 2020, p. 613). People from all over the world use the internet to communicate with each other. Social networks such as Twitter, Facebook, WhatsApp and Instagram, websites and application programs are the

DOI: 10.4018/978-1-6684-5426-8.ch025

most popular and common online tools used especially by adolescents. These tools provide an ambient for people to share information and new ideas and interact with each other (Singh et al., 2020, p.1637).

In recent years, people have tended to share their experiences, ideas and opinions publicly by using social media platforms over the internet. However, the positive and negative consequences of social media services depend on how users use social media (Singh et al., 2020, p. 1636). People can spread hatred against any person in social networks (Perera and Fernando, 2021, p. 605). In addition, today's digital native adolescents are at risk of being bullied not only in the traditional offline social context, but also in the online social context (Kim et al., 2020, p. 1). Bullying can be defined as an aggressive, deliberate action or behavior performed repeatedly and over time by a group or individual against a victim who cannot easily defend himself (López-Vizcaíno et al., 2021, p. 219). On the other hand, Cyberbullying is aggressive, abusive behavior that intentionally and repeatedly harms a person or a group of people (Perera and Fernando, 2021, p. 606). Despite the great interest in bullying and cyberbullying in recent years, the problem of defining this phenomenon is still debated. Recently, this discussion has also been expressed in terms of how young people who are directly related to bullying and cyberbullying understand these concepts (Menin et al., 2021, p. 1).

BACKGROUND

An anti-bullying charity called Ditch the Label, which studies the prevalence of cyberbullying on social networking sites, has recently conducted a large-scale survey for those who had been bullied: 46% of the respondents stated that they have been bullied more than once, and 20% have bullied others on social networking sites (Chan et al., 2021, p. 1). In addition, there are findings that school bullying is not only related to psychological behaviors related to suicide, but also psychological behaviors related to murder (Guo-Bao et al., 2019, p. 7). Bullying on social networks can cause suicide. Because the person who is bullied is exposed to serious psychosocial harm (such as depression) and physical harm (such as self-harming behavior), as a result, he tends to commit suicide. For example, a young girl who was bullied on social networks shot herself, and the incident resulted in death (Chan et al., 2021, p. 1).

An effective cyberbullying detection method is needed to create a safe space for cyber communication (Fortunatus et al., 2020, p. 612). For the detection of cyberbullying; It started with user studies from the fields of social sciences and psychology, and recently moved to computer science, aiming to develop models for automatic detection, and extensively studied (López-Vizcaíno et al., 2021, p. 220). Cyberbullying Research Center conducted a survey of 5700 adolescents nationwide in the USA. According to the results of the survey; 33.8% of the respondents have been cyberbullied and 11.5% have cyberbullied others (Chan et al., 2021, p. 1).

MAIN FOCUS OF THE CHAPTER

Cyberbullying

Cyberbullying, cyber rudeness and cyber mobbing includes the misuse of technology (i.e. computers, mobile phones and other electronic devices) to humiliate, intimidate, threaten and harm by using platforms such as social media, instant messaging, messaging and e-mail (Clark and Luparell, 2020, p. 1).

Cyberbullying has also been called as internet aggression, internet bullying, online bullying and electronic aggression (Kim and Faith, 2020, p. 2). Harassment or aggression through emails, mobile phones, online games and social media can be considered as cyber aggression or cyber bullying (Fortunatus et al., 2020, p. 612). The concept of "bullying" in cyberspace is defined by different terms. These terms are; electronic bullying, internet bullying, internet harassment, online bullying and online social persecution. The most common term in the literature and the most widely used by researchers is cyberbullying (Chan et al., 2021, p. 2).

The growth of internet users over the years has brought both positive and negative developments. One of the most common problems is cyberbullying (Fortunatus et al., 2020, p. 612). The widespread use of new technologies has led to the rapid emergence of bullying and cyberbullying through electronic devices. (Calvo-Morata et al., 2020, pp. 1-2). Cyberbullying affects people in different ways (Perera and Fernando, 2021, p. 605). Being exposed to cyberbullying causes students to feel angry, worried, disappointed, anxious and embarrassed. It also affects their mental health and physical condition, which can lead to depression and suicide attempts (Tudkuea et al., 2019, p. 147). It does not only affect health, but also it has different aspects that can threaten life. Cyberbullying is a modern worldwide phenomenon that people cannot avoid one hundred percent, but can be prevented (Perera and Fernando, 2021, p. 605). Although there are many opportunities associated with digital media, people tend to abuse it (Perera and Fernando, 2021, p. 605). In online environments, the absence of parents facilitates the possibility of cyberbullying. Anonymity on the Internet also makes it difficult for adults to interfere (Kim et al., 2020, p. 2).

The perception of cyberbullying is an attitude that cyberbullying is dangerous and illegal, and the higher this perception, the less likely the crime of cyberbullying will also be. It is thought that recognizing that cyberbullying is harmful and illegal can help prevent cyberbullying on young people (Bae, 2021, p. 4). Significantly higher rates of substance use and risky consumption were found in roles involved in cyberbullying than those not involved (Pichel et al., 2022, p. 3). The way people deal with a stressful situation such as bullying or cyberbullying actually depends not only on the event itself, but also on how people evaluate it (Menin et al., 2021, p. 3).

Cyberbullying incidents often involve more than one party, the prominent ones being; bullies, victims and eyewitnesses (Balakrishnan, 2018, p. 1190). Cyberbully and cyber victim are two roles involved in cyberbullying events (Singh et al., 2020, p. 1637). The concept of bullying, which was initially limited to physical and verbal abuse, was expanded in the 1990s to include indirect and relational bullying (Menin et al., 2021, p. 2). The prevalence rates give an idea about the severity of the cyberbullying phenomenon. It is important to examine the emotional reactions of victims, bullies and bystanders and the estimates of the actions taken. Thus, when necessary, appropriate interventions such as awareness and counseling programs can be designed accordingly (Balakrishnan, 2018, p. 1191). In recent years, young people may be faced with "cyberbullying", which is a serious public health problem (Dennehy et al., 2020, p. 1). Negative consequences of cyberbullying include depression, abuse of psychoactive substances, post-traumatic stress disorder and suicidal ideation (Kapitány-Fövény et al., 2022). Additional adverse effects range from suicide to psychological disorders such as chronic depression and anxiety (Alsawalqa, 2021, p. 2). Risky digital behaviors are affected by individual psychological factors. That is, a link was found between the online risk experience and psychological difficulties and emotional problems. Emotional problems have been associated with cyberbullying experiences (Bedrosova et al., 2022, p. 4). Cyberbullying is associated with an increased risk of suicidal and self-harming behaviors. One way to reduce risk is to reduce cases of cyberbullying. However, it is unrealistic to believe that this behavior can be completely eliminated or even well controlled (Dorol-Beauroy-Eustache and Mishara, 2021, p. 10).

The use of offensive language has become one of the most popular topics in social networks (Khairy et al., 2021, p. 157). There may be no repetition of aggression in cyberbullying, because a single image or video can be enough to attract many views and reactions on social media (Alsawalqa, 2021, p. 2). Although there are different definitions of cyberbullying and abusive language, all studies agree that they are often used among users to harm others through electronic media (Khairy et al., 2021, p. 164). Most of the researchers and solutions considered only one key feature of cyberbullying: detecting abusive language/insulting words or identifying the role of cyberbullying. Cyberbullying cannot be detected by considering a single feature. Cyberbullying is difficult to detect and different from detecting offensive content. Detecting abusive language/insulting words or hate speech is not a valid reason to show that this is cyberbullying (Perera and Fernando, 2021, p. 607).

The reason behind the emergence of cyberbullying as an international health problem today is seen as the rapid growth in information and communication technology (Dennehy et al., 2020). Most of the existing systems are focused on ways or techniques to detect cyberbullying (Perera and Fernando, 2021, p. 607). The fact that young people are intertwined (7/24) with information and communication technologies can cause cyberbullying to occur at any time of the day or night (Dennehy et al., 2020, p. 7). The biggest challenge is that cyberbullying can spread rapidly and remain visible for a very long time because it has a large audience (Perera and Fernando, 2021, p. 606). Visual cyberbullying, which is the distribution of humiliating pictures or videos in the virtual environment, is perceived as particularly harmful (Dennehy et al., 2020, p. 7).

Intention to harm has been reported by many studies as a key element in the definitions of youth cyberbullying (Dennehy et al., 2020, p. 4).

The percentage of individuals who have been cyberbullied at some point of time in their lives has doubled from 18% in 2007 to 36% in 2019. Moreover, it is expected to continue to increase, given the high use of information technologies, social networks and mobile devices by children and youth (López-Vizcaíno et al., 2021, p. 219).

In order to determine the relationship between cyberbullying and ICT use, a number of studies have been conducted by considering the frequency and amount of ICT use (Kim and Faith, 2020, p. 2).

The likelihood of being cyberbullied increases with the increasing frequency of teens going online. Compared with those who access the Internet several times a day or less, young people who are almost always online are more likely to be cyberbullied (Kim and Faith, 2020, p. 2).

Bullying and cyberbullying often start at an early age. It is quite common in schools, which often lack the resources or strategies to take action (Calvo-Morata et al., 2020, p. 2). Bullying has been found to be a risk factor for students' academic achievement and success in school, including their sense of belonging to the school. Students who experience cyberbullying tend to have difficulty concentrating, miss school lessons more often, and show lower academic performance (Kim and Faith, 2020, p. 3). An increase in school belonging is also associated with a decrease in bullying levels, including cyberbullying (Kim and Faith, 2020, p. 3).

The Relationship Between Traditional Bullying and Cyberbullying

Bullying victimization occurs in two ways; traditional and cyberbullying victimization (Zhong et al., 2021, p. 322). A great deal of overlap has been noted between cyberbullying and traditional bullying

(Dennehy et al., 2020, p. 7). Therefore, cyberbullying has a relationship with traditional bullying (Tudkuea et al., 2019, p. 146).

Traditional forms of bullying have some characteristics associated with cyberbullying. Behaviors are used to threaten, reject, and exclude others, directly or indirectly. Although cyberbullying and traditional bullying show similarities, there is a distinction between them: Cyberspace is a platform and e-technology is an ambient that provides opportunities for bullying to happen (Carter, 2013, p. 1296). Cyberbullying is the online version of traditional bullying and can take various forms such as giving embarrassing and hostile information about the victim (Dynel, 2021, p. 31).

Traditional bullying has been common in society for generations. Many people can remember stories of themselves or someone they knew growing up being bullied in one way or another. Although the purpose of inflicting pain on others through bullying has not changed significantly, the method of bullying has undergone significant transformations since the beginning of the 21st century (Choi et al., 2019, p. 3). The negative effects of cyberbullying have many similarities with traditional bullying, but they can also cause more harm due to the frequency and high spread allowed by technology (López-Vizcaíno et al., 2021, p. 219).

Studies have reported that compared to traditional bullying, cyberbullying can lead to more negative consequences for young people in terms of depression, anxiety, absenteeism and suicidal ideation (Kim and Faith, 2020, p. 2). There is still ongoing debate about whether cyberbullying should be understood as an integrated part of traditional offline bullying or as a unique experience in itself (Kim et al., 2020, p. 2).

Cyber Victimization

Cyberbullying is the behavior that disrupts the social relations of those chosen as victims and aims to arouse negative emotions. It can be classified into five dimensions: fake attitudes, gossip or insults, spreading confidential information, slander, and blocking others in cyberspace. These behaviors cause cyberbullying victims to feel frustration, irritability, anxiety, and shame, as well as anger. In addition, it indirectly causes mental health problems and affects physical well-being, which is the fundamental cause of student depression and other problems in social relationships. As a result of being exposed to cyberbullying, there is a possibility that students will consider and attempt suicide. Since the consequences are likely to be serious if victims are exposed to cyberbullying, educational institutions are now focused on solving this problem (Tudkuea et al., 2019, p. 145).

Cyberbullying is positively associated with internet use. However, cyber victimization is not related to internet use (Hood and Duffy, 2018, p. 105). In terms of potential gender-related determinants of cyberbullying behaviors, anger rumination may increase the risk of cyberbullying among male cyberbullying victims (Kapitány-Fövény et al., 2022, p. 2). Anger aggression is more a cause of offline bullying than cyberbullying (Graf et al., 2022, p. 6). At the same time, there is no consensus on gender differences in cyberbullying. While there are studies showing that there is no significant gender difference for cyber victimization, other studies have revealed that girls are more victims of cyberbullying than boys (Coelho and Romao, 2018, p. 220).

Victims of bullying and cyberbullying exhibited higher levels of social anxiety than students who were not involved in bullying or cyberbullying (Coelho & Romao, 2018, p. 224). Studies have shown that older victims are embarrassed to report cyberbullying incidents. That's why it's important to encourage victims to come forward when a crime occurs. This can be done by raising awareness through education (Balakrishnan, 2018, p. 1195). In addition, victims of cyberbullying are more likely to experience problems such as low self-esteem, poor academic performance, digestive issues, headaches and bedwetting. Cyberbullying victims also experience loneliness, frustration, and distrust of people. They are also likely to harm themselves and engage in aggressive behavior towards their friends and family (Alsawalqa, 2021, p. 2).

The fact that victims of cyberbullying are exposed to cyberbullying or that the perpetrators engage in bullying and cyberbullying have a negative effect on their physical, psychological and social well-being (Dennehy et al., 2020, p. 1). Individuals who experience bullying are at increased risk for future health and social problems. Despite this, research shows that not all bullying victims have poor health, which highlights the importance of investigating protective factors that can counteract negative effects (Urano et al., 2020, p. 182). While cyberbullying victimization increases the intention to commit cyberbullying, self-control acts as a critical buffer that suppresses the tendency to cyberbully others (Alsawalqa, 2021, p. 10).

Cyberbullying is an important problem for societies and has great negative effects on victims. Therefore, early detection of cyberbullying in social networks becomes crucial to reduce the impact on victims (López-Vizcaíno et al., 2021, p. 219). Studies have associated cyberbullying with negative effects on psychological and physical health, academic performance, depression, and a higher risk of suicidal ideation (López-Vizcaíno et al., 2021, p. 219). Increasing evidence in recent years has shown that childhood bullying victimization affects not only the short-term but also the long-term well-being of victims, extending into their mid-twenties (Urano et al., 2020, p. 183).

Cyberbullying in Adolescents

The accessibility to social media and widespread use of social media has created new opportunities for online aggression. Every single time, adolescents spend on social media and talk to strangers online relates to cyberbullying and deserves public health intervention. Problematic use of social media poses the strongest and most consistent risk (Craig et al., 2020, p. 101). Cyberbullying is the use of technology (e.g. internet, computers, mobile devices) to engage in bullying. The short-and long-term negative consequences of both bullying and cyberbullying raise significant levels of concern in school environments. For example; anxiety and depression; low self-efficacy and self-esteem; poor academic performance and other school problems; and guilt, truancy, and the possibility of dropping out more (Mishna et al., 2017, p. 269). Cyberbullying has been identified as a major problem and documented as a national health problem due to the continuous growth of online communication and social media (López-Vizcaíno et al., 2021, p. 219).

Considering the emergence of technologies that provide new tools for bullying, researches are directed towards exploring cyberbullying among young people (Pascual-Sanchez et al., 2021, p. 1). The widespread use of information and communication technologies has brought about an increase in the risks related to the safety and health of adolescents (Pichel et al., 2022, p. 2). The routine uses of technology, the internet, and social networking sites -especially considering the importance in the daily functioning of young people's lives (school-age individuals need technology and the internet to complete their classroom assignments as part of their work/learning experience and also to participate in activities in their spare time) victimization of bullying can be said to increase the probability of survival. Under this premise, young people who trust technology are more at risk of being victims of cyberbullying than those who do not (Choi et al., 2019, p. 6).

Therefore, since online social media has become a common way of interacting with people, cyberbullying can be perceived as an extension of unacceptable social behavior in offline interpersonal relationships (Fortunatus et al., 2020, p. 613). While social networking sites are a productive area for online bullying, cyberbullying can also occur in different online channels and platforms (Chan et al., 2021, p. 1). The rates of cyberbullying among children are alarming and the consequences of cyberbullying can be harmful (Vlaanderen et al., 2020, p. 2).

Unfortunately, being the victim of bullying is quite common during adolescence, with about one in five 12–18-year-olds in the United States reporting having been bullied at school (Fowler et al., 2021, p. 60). The rate of cyberbullying is particularly high in adolescents (Bae, 2021, p. 1). University students, on the other hand, have a lower level of experience of being a cyberbullying actor than high school students (Suparli & Ramdhani, 2015, p. 206). According to the cyberbullying survey, 18% of 4779 Korean adolescents have been cyberbullied in the last year. In addition, according to a study conducted in 8 European countries (Bulgaria, Cyprus, France, Greece, Hungary, Italy, Poland and Spain), 17.7% of male students and 10.9% of female students have committed cyberbullying (Bae, 2021, p. 1). Most studies on bullying indicate that boys are more often the perpetrators and victims of bullying. As a result of the research, it has been revealed that especially men do physical and direct verbal bullying more frequently (Charalampous et al., 2018, p. 112). In addition, problem behaviors such as violence and committing crimes are more common in boys than in girls. Cyberbullying crimes decreased as students transitioned from primary school to secondary school and high school (Bae, 2021, p. 4). Frequency of contact with strangers may constitute a particularly important risk factor for girls' involvement in cyberbullying (Craig et al., 2020, p. 107). Many studies have shown a significant association between cyberbullying and suicidal and self-harming behaviors among children and adolescents. However, it is stated that only a small part of cyberbullying victims and perpetrators will engage in these behaviors (Dorol-Beauroy-Eustache and Mishara, 2021, p. 5).

Despite the benefits of social media such as establishing and maintaining positive social relationships for children, it also carries risks that will expose users to cyberbullying (Vlaanderen et al., 2020, p. 2). Young people's continuous desire for digital connection and fear of social disconnection increases their risk of being cyberbullied (Dennehy et al., 2020, p. 9).

Teens often do not conceptualize cyberbullying as it is defined. For example, their definitions almost always omit the components of intentionality and repetition. Because of this uncertainty, children may have difficulty interpreting an event as a call to action. To be more descriptive; it is possible that children did not perceive relevant cues (for example, hearing derogatory names) that might have prevented them from recognizing events as cyberbullying events (Vlaanderen et al., 2020, p. 8). At the same time, university students with high self-control have an important skill in preventing and coping with cyberbullying events, as they can detect dangers compared to others (Kokkinos and Antoniadou, 2019, p. 65).

Cyberbullying crime can be explained with social learning theory. Based on this theory, an individual can imitate aggressive behavior in cyberspace through learning by observing violent online content. Especially, adolescents are more likely to imitate aggressive behaviors because they lack self-control compared to adults (Bae, 2021, p. 2). Considering the high prevalence of cyberbullying among children and its negative consequences, it is of great importance to continue the development of intervention programs to reduce cyberbullying (Vlaanderen et al., 2020, p. 10). Various mobile applications have been developed to monitor interactions between adolescents and general internet users. Some apps even allow parents to have full access to their children's online chats with others. However, privacy issues pose a great challenge in managing and controlling cyberbullying (Thun et al., 2021, p. 1).

SOLUTIONS AND RECOMMENDATIONS

Understanding how offline and online cyberbullying occurs is very important for the development of effective prevention and intervention strategies (Graf et al., 2022, p. 1). Theoretically, repetition is seen as a key criterion for identifying face-to-face bullying incidents (Menin et al., 2021, p. 3). Like those who experience face-to-face bullying, individuals targeted in cyberspace may also feel anxiety (Clark and Luparell, 2020, p. 2). It is also claimed that frustration is a psychological condition that leads to cyberbullying behaviors (Tudkuea et al., 2019, p. 148). Social media users often have the ability to hide their identities, which helps to abuse existing features (Khairy et al., 2021, p. 157).

Cyberbullying mostly occurs in the relationships between young people and in the social groups they belong to. In addition to some advantages such as the majority of young people being integrated into technology and using technology widely in every field, there are also disadvantages such as the risk that many young people are exposed to cyberbullying (Dennehy et al., 2020, p. 9). Cyberbullying can produce shame, guilt and fear (Alsawalqa, 2021, p. 2). Cyberbullying is a huge phenomenon among young people as victims, predators or bystanders (Perera and Fernando, 2021, p. 606). Young people believe that cyberbullying can happen, with or without the intent to harm (Dennehy et al., 2020, p. 9). Educators should provide educational programs that provide appropriate coping skills for children and are specifically designed to prevent victimization or to deal effectively with bullying (Zhong et al., 2021, p. 327).

Cyberbullying is a worrying social problem considering the serious consequences on the mental and physical health of the victims (Rey et al., 2020, p. 136). Universities should have certain procedures and policies regarding cyberbullying, and all staff should be trained to understand the importance of cyberbullying (Kokkinos and Antoniadou, 2019, p. 66). The novelty of cyberbullying requires that young people, as digital natives, be at the center of efforts to understand and address it. This synthesis draws on the contributions of young people to develop a deeper perspective on this phenomenon; highlights how the complexity and uncertainty of the cyber world cannot be ignored because of the role of technology in the lives of young people (Dennehy et al., 2020, p. 10). With cyberbullying, threatening or humiliating texts, pictures or videos are sent over the internet without permission, other people are harassed, intimidated, threatened or tried to harm in another way (Rey et al., 2020, p. 136). Researchers around the world are applying machine learning as a method of detecting cyberbullying texts. The machine is trained using features such as differences in texts through interactions in the social networking environment. The machine can also identify and profile users through the use of gender or hate speech (Thun et al., 2021).

With the development of modern technologies, it has become possible to reveal cyberbullying (Khairy et al., 2021, p. 159). Considering the increasing popularity of social media communication, detecting cyberbullying is an important task (Fortunatus et al., 2020, p. 620). Because social networks blur the boundary between private and professional life (Chan et al., 2021, p. 12). There are several types of related apps that can be used to detect online cyberbullying. Table 1 presents a comparison between these applications (Thun et al., 2021, p. 3).

ReThink is a mobile application that sends a warning message to users when users try to send texts consisting of harmful words (Thun et al., 2021).

Cyberbully Blocker is a mobile application that provides two methods for detecting malicious messages

BullyBlocker is a mobile application focused on cyberbullying detection on Facebook. The application is designed for parents of adolescents. Adolescents monitored by the application must log in to their facebook account via BullyBlocker (Thun et al., 2021).

Table 1. Comparison between applications

Application Name	Method	Limitation
ReThink	Detects vulgar words	Keyboard setting need to be changed to allow the application to work
Cyberbully Blocker	Classifies test using a brute force search algorithm that is trained with language modelling methods, or Allows users to input texts and choose the cyberbullying detection method preferred	Developed to test the performance of used algorithms rather than to be applied to real-life scenarios
Bully Blocker	Computes based on indicators, and detects and evaluates offending words with factors such as children's gender, age, etc. Through TS algorithm	Only shows why someone is detected as a cyberbullying victim, and does not Show the text detected
AbuSniff	Suggests user action from the set {"unfriend", "unfollowing", "sandbox", "ignore"} for features such as common photo count, mutual friend count, and so on using supervised learning algorithm	To detect potential cyberbully perpetrator, users need to log into their facebook accounts in AbuSniff and manually fill out a questionnaire about a random person from their friends' list

Source: Thun et al. (2021: 3)

AbuSniff is a system that identifies Facebook friends who are perceived as strangers or abusive, and protects the user by unfriending, unfollowing, or restricting access to information for those friends. To use this system, users must log into their Facebook account at AbuSniff. The system allows users to fill out a questionnaire about a random person from their friend list (Thun et al., 2021).

FUTURE RESEARCH DIRECTIONS

Cyberbullying is a problem that is not only seen in a certain region of the world, but also gains global importance (Serin, 2012, p. 3). Therefore, it has been determined that studies on cyberbullying have increased in recent years (Whittaker and Kowalski 2015, p. 11). However, although there have been many studies on cyberbullying on children and adolescents in the country and abroad, few studies have been conducted investigating the exposure of adults to cyberbullying in working life. In the future, cyber bullying in different organizations and different business life should be investigated and thus more clear and precise inferences can be made on this subject.

CONCLUSION

Cyberbullying is a social problem emerging in the digital age (Chan et al., 2021, p. 1). Digital resilience is an important 21st century skill that enables young people to use information and communication technologies to take advantage of the opportunities offered by the cyber world, while avoiding the risks of cyberbullying.

Building digital resilience requires developing digital skills. Digital skills include information-navigation skills associated with the informational use of ICT. Information navigation skills are related to cognitive skills that enable users to search, identify, understand and evaluate online information (Kim and Faith, 2020, p. 9).

Bullying is a persistent aggressive behavior characterized by an imbalance of power and directed with the intent to harm (Fowler et al., 2021, p. 60). Appropriate online social behavior should therefore be incorporated into university curricula. On the other hand, university personnel at all levels should be knowledgeable about the use of information and communication technology (Kokkinos and Antoniadou, 2019, p. 65). Bullying, both in the real world and in the cyber world, is a major violation of norms (Suparli & Ramdhani, 2015, p. 203). Teens are critical to creating cyberbullying interventions. The forward road cannot be mapped without their contribution (Spears et al., 2018, p. 90).

REFERENCES

Alsawalqa, R. O. (2021). Cyberbullying, social stigma, and self-esteem: The impact of COVID-19 on students from East and Southeast Asia at the University of Jordan. *Heliyon*, *7*(4), e06711. doi:10.1016/j.heliyon.2021.e06711 PMID:33869877

Bae, S. M. (2021). The relationship between exposure to risky online content, cyber victimization, perception of cyberbullying, and cyberbullying offending in Korean adolescents. *Children and Youth Services Review*, *123*, 105946. doi:10.1016/j.childyouth.2021.105946

Balakrishnan, V. (2018). Actions, emotional reactions and cyberbullying–From the lens of bullies, victims, bully-victims and bystanders among Malaysian young adults. *Telematics and Informatics*, *35*(5), 1190–1200. doi:10.1016/j.tele.2018.02.002

Bedrosova, M., Machackova, H., Serek, J., Smahel, D., & Blaya, C. (2022). The relation between the cyberhate and cyberbullying experiences of adolescents in the Czech Republic, Poland, and Slovakia. *Computers in Human Behavior*, *126*, 107013. doi:10.1016/j.chb.2021.107013

Calvo-Morata, A., Alonso-Fernández, C., Freire, M., Martínez-Ortiz, I., & Fernández-Manjón, B. (2020). Serious games to prevent and detect bullying and cyberbullying: A systematic serious games and literature review. *Computers & Education*, *157*, 103958. doi:10.1016/j.compedu.2020.103958

Carter, M. A. (2013). Third party observers witnessing cyber bullying on social media sites. *Social and Behavioral Sciences*, *84*, 1296–1309. doi:10.1016/j.sbspro.2013.06.747

Chan, T. K. H., Cheung, C. M. K., & Lee, Z. W. Y. (2021). Cyberbullying on social networking sites: A literature review and future research directions. *Information & Management*, *58*(2), 103411. doi:10.1016/j.im.2020.103411

Charalampous, K., Demetriou, C., Tricha, L., Ioannou, M., Georgiou, S., Nikiforou, M., & Stavrinides, P. (2018). The effect of parental style on bullying and cyber bullying behaviors and the mediating role of peer attachment relationships: A longitudinal study. *Journal of Adolescence*, *64*(1), 109–123. doi:10.1016/j.adolescence.2018.02.003 PMID:29448185

Choi, K. S., Earl, K., Lee, J. L., & Cho, S. (2019). Diagnosis of Cyber and Non-physical Bullying Victimization: A Routine Activities Approach to Constructing Effective Preventative Measures. *Computers in Human Behavior*, *92*, 11–19. doi:10.1016/j.chb.2018.10.014

Clark, C. M., & Luparell, S. (2020). Cyber-incivility, cyber-bullying, and other forms of online aggression: A call to action for nurse educators. *Nurse Education Today*, *85*, 104310. doi:10.1016/j.nedt.2019.104310 PMID:31805415

Coelho, V. A., & Romao, A. M. (2018). The relation between social anxiety, social withdrawal and (cyber) bullying roles: A multilevel analysis. *Computers in Human Behavior*, *86*, 218–226. doi:10.1016/j.chb.2018.04.048

Craig, W., Boniel-Nissim, M., King, N., Walsh, S. D., Boer, M., Donnelly, P. D., Harel-Fisch, Y., Malinowska-Cieslik, M., Gaspar de Matos, M., Cosma, A., Van den Eijnden, R., Vieno, A., Elgar, F. J., Molcho, M., Bjereld, Y., & Pickett, W. (2020). Social Media Use and Cyber-Bullying: A Cross-National Analysis of Young People in 42 Countries. *The Journal of Adolescent Health*, *66*(6), 100–S108. doi:10.1016/j.jadohealth.2020.03.006 PMID:32446603

Dennehy, R., Meaney, S., Walsh, K. A., Sinnott, C., Cronin, M., & Arensman, E. (2020). Young people's conceptualizations of the nature of cyberbullying: A systematic review and synthesis of qualitative research. *Aggression and Violent Behavior*, *51*, 101379. doi:10.1016/j.avb.2020.101379

Dorol-Beauroy-Eustache, O., & Mishara, B. L. (2021). Systematic Review of Risk and Protective Factors for Suicidal and Self-Harm Behaviors among Children and Adolescents Involved with Cyberbullying. *Preventive Medicine*, *152*, 106684. doi:10.1016/j.ypmed.2021.106684 PMID:34538376

Dynel, M. (2021). Humour and (mock) aggression: Distinguishing cyberbullying from roasting. *Language & Communication*, *81*, 17–36. doi:10.1016/j.langcom.2021.08.001

Fortunatus, M., Anthony, P., & Charters, S. (2020). Combining textual features to detect cyberbullying in social media posts. *Procedia Computer Science*, *176*, 612–662. doi:10.1016/j.procs.2020.08.063

Fowler, L. A., Kracht, C. L., Denstel, K. D., Stewart, T. M., & Staiano, A. E. (2021). Bullying experiences, body esteem, body dissatisfaction, and the moderating role of weight status among adolescents. *Journal of Adolescence*, *91*(1), 59–70. doi:10.1016/j.adolescence.2021.07.006 PMID:34333320

Graf, D., Yanagida, T., Runions, K., & Spiel, C. (2022). Why did you do that? Differential types of aggression in offline and in cyberbullying. *Computers in Human Behavior*, *128*, 107107. doi:10.1016/j.chb.2021.107107

Guo-Bao, Z., & Geng-Fu, W. (2019). Association between different stages of precollege school bullying and murder-related psychological behaviors among college students in Anhui Province, China. *Psychiatry Research*, *282*, 112593. doi:10.1016/j.psychres.2019.112593 PMID:31630040

Hood, M., & Duffy, A. L. (2018). Understanding the relationship between cyber-victimization and cyberbullying on Social Network Sites: The role of moderating factors. *Personality and Individual Differences*, *133*, 103–108. doi:10.1016/j.paid.2017.04.004

Kapitány-Fövény, M., Lukács, J. Á., Takács, J., Kitzinger, I., Kiss, Z. S., Szabó, G., Falus, A., & Feith, H. J. (2022). Gender-specific pathways regarding the outcomes of a cyberbullying youth education program. *Personality and Individual Differences*, *186*, 111338. doi:10.1016/j.paid.2021.111338

Khairy, M., Mahmoud, T. M., & Abd-El-Hafeez, T. (2021). Automatic Detection of Cyberbullying and Abusive Language in Arabic Content on Social Networks: A Survey. *Procedia Computer Science*, *189*, 156–166. doi:10.1016/j.procs.2021.05.080

Kim, B. K., Park, J., Jung, H. J., & Han, Y. (2020). Latent profiles of offline/cyber bullying experiences among Korean students and its relationship with peer conformity. *Children and Youth Services Review*, *118*, 105349. doi:10.1016/j.childyouth.2020.105349

Kim, S., & Faith, M. S. (2020). Cyberbullying and ICT use by immigrant youths: A serial multiple-mediator SEM analysis. *Children and Youth Services Review*, *110*, 104621. doi:10.1016/j.childyouth.2019.104621

Kokkinos, C. M., & Antoniadou, N. (2019). Cyber-bullying and cyber-victimization among undergraduate student teachers through the lens of the General Aggression Model. *Computers in Human Behavior*, *98*, 59–68. doi:10.1016/j.chb.2019.04.007

López-Vizcaíno, M. F., Nóvoa, F. J., Carneiro, V., & Cacheda, F. (2021). Early detection of cyberbullying on social media networks. *Future Generation Computer Systems*, *118*, 219–229. doi:10.1016/j.future.2021.01.006

Menin, D., Guarini, A., Mameli, C., Skrzypiec, G., & Brighi, A. (2021). Was that (cyber)bullying? Investigating the operational definitions of bullying and cyberbullying from adolescents' perspective. *International Journal of Clinical and Health Psychology*, *21*(2), 100221. doi:10.1016/j.ijchp.2021.100221 PMID:33552165

Mishna, F., McInroy, L. B., Daciuk, J., & Duncan, A. L. (2017). Adapting to attrition challenges in multi-year studies: Examples from a school-based bullying and cyber bullying study. *Children and Youth Services Review*, *81*, 268–271. doi:10.1016/j.childyouth.2017.08.019

Pascual-Sanchez, A., Hickey, N., Mateu, A., Martinez-Herves, M., Kramer, T., & Nicholls, D. (2021). Personality traits and self-esteem in traditional bullying and cyberbullying. *Personality and Individual Differences*, *177*, 110809. doi:10.1016/j.paid.2021.110809

Pascual-Sanchez, D., Guarini, A., Mameli, C., Skrzypiec, G., & Brighi, A. (2021). Was that (cyber) bullying? Investigating the operational definitions of bullying and cyberbullying from adolescents' perspective. *International Journal of Clinical and Health Psychology*, *21*(2), 100221. doi:10.1016/j.ijchp.2021.100221 PMID:33552165

Perera, A., & Fernando, P. (2021). Accurate Cyberbullying Detection and Prevention on Social Media. *Procedia Computer Science*, *181*, 605–611. doi:10.1016/j.procs.2021.01.207

Pichel, R., Feijoo, S., Isorna, M., Varela, J., & Rial, A. (2022). Analysis of the relationship between school bullying, cyberbullying, and substance use. *Children and Youth Services Review*, *134*, 106369. doi:10.1016/j.childyouth.2022.106369

Rey, L., Neto, F., & Extremera, N. (2020). Cyberbullying victimization and somatic complaints: A prospective examination of cognitive emotion regulation strategies as mediators. *International Journal of Clinical and Health Psychology*, *20*(2), 135–139. doi:10.1016/j.ijchp.2020.03.003 PMID:32550853

Serin, H. (2012). *Cyberbullying/Cyber victimization experiences in adolescents and the opinion of teachers and education managers about this behaviours* [Ergenlerde Siber Zorbalık/Siber Mağduriyet Yaşantıları ve Bu Davranışlara İlişkin Öğretmen ve Eğitim Yöneticilerinin Görüşleri]. İstanbul University, Institute of Social Sciences.

Singh, S., Thapar, V., & Bagga, S. (2020). Exploring the hidden patterns of cyberbullying on social media. *Procedia Computer Science, 167*, 1636–1647. doi:10.1016/j.procs.2020.03.374

Spears, B. A., Taddeo, C., & Barnes, A. (2018). *Online social marketing approaches to inform cyber/bullying prevention and intervention: What have we learnt?* Reducing Cyberbullying in Schools, International Evidence-Based Best Practices.

Suparli, A. S., & Ramdhani, N. (2015). Does Moral Emotion Plays Role in Cyber-bullying? *Social and Behavioral Sciences, 165*, 202–207. doi:10.1016/j.sbspro.2014.12.623

Thun, L.J., Teh, P.L., & Cheng, C.B. (2021). CyberAid: Are your children safe from cyberbullying? *Journal of King Saud University – Computer and Information Sciences.*

Tudkuea, T., Laeheem, K., & Sittichai, R. (2019). Development of a causal relationship model for cyber bullying behaviors among public secondary school students in the three southern border provinces of Thailand. *Children and Youth Services Review, 102*, 145–149. doi:10.1016/j.childyouth.2019.05.013

Urano, Y., Takizawa, Y., Ohka, M., Yamasaki, H., & Shimoyama, H. (2020). Cyber bullying victimization and adolescent mental health: The differential moderating effects of intrapersonal and interpersonal emotional competence. *Journal of Adolescence, 80*(1), 182–191. doi:10.1016/j.adolescence.2020.02.009 PMID:32169718

Vlaanderen, A., Bevelander, K. E., & Kleemans, M. (2020). Empowering digital citizenship: An anti-cyberbullying intervention to increase children's intentions to intervene on behalf of the victim. *Computers in Human Behavior, 112*, 106459. doi:10.1016/j.chb.2020.106459

Whittaker, E., & Kowalski, R. M. (2015). Cyberbullying Via Social Media. *Journal of School Violence, 14*(1), 11–29. doi:10.1080/15388220.2014.949377

Zhong, M., Huang, X., Huebner, E. S., & Tian, L. (2021). Association between bullying victimization and depressive symptoms in children: The mediating role of self-esteem. *Journal of Affective Disorders, 294*, 322–328. doi:10.1016/j.jad.2021.07.016 PMID:34311332

Chapter 26
Cyberbullying:
An Overview of Cyberbullying

Sevgi Mestci Sunerli
https://orcid.org/0000-0003-0176-1592
Eskulap Danışmanlık Merkezi, Turkey

Füsun Gökkaya
Cyprus International University, Cyprus

Zahide Aliusta Denk
Bahçeşehir Cyprus University, Cyprus

ABSTRACT

Cyber bullying is the repetitive and intentional use of digital tools to harm another person in the digital environment. Researchers show that females tend to be more cyber victims than males. There are different characteristics of cyber bullies. These are relational aggression, cognitive-affective deficits, and power and control. Cyber bullying causes serious results for both bullies and for the victims. There are some different prevention methods which can be grouped as in three categories: firstly, law, rules, and policies to control the use of media; secondly, education programs about using safe internet for children and youths and teaching them how to avoid these kinds of situations on the internet; and lastly, technological approaches.

INTRODUCTION

Development of the internet has made people's life easier to reach information and communicate with each other, learn from what is going on across the world. On the other hand, it is an area that still has some complicated problems like control and regulation. It is a large area and controlling what goes on can be challenging. It is known that teenagers and young adults use internet for sharing data, fun, doing research, socializing, talking, chatting with friends, and making new friends (Beran & Li, 2005). With the help of internet, people easily exhibit behaviors which they may not choose to show in face-to- face interaction

DOI: 10.4018/978-1-6684-5426-8.ch026

or in a real relationship (Ybarra & Mitchell, 2004). The International Organization for Standardization (2012) defined cyber space as a complex environment formed because of the interaction of people, software, and services on the internet through technological tools and networks. Cyberspace consists of an electronic world where individuals interact, connected by information technology networks, and the information on these networks (Hinduja & Patchin, 2014; Public Safety Canada, 2010). Besides the positive advantages of cyber areas, there are also there occurs some unforeseen consequences of internet. Sometimes, individuals became insensitive to the usual social rules due to the nature of technology and tend to behave in unusually cruel ways in cyber areas (Bauman, 2007). Negative cyber behaviors that sometimes require legal sanctions have led to the need for new legal regulations and results ranging from criminal sanctions have been experienced with the scope of cyber-crime (Lastowka & Hunter, 2004). One of these cruel behaviors is cyber bullying: bullying between children and teenagers has moved beyond playgrounds and schools to the virtual space. Some of the problematic behaviors among teenagers such as aggressive behaviors that occur on streets and in schools have become possible to be executed anytime and anywhere through cyber areas (Law et al., 2012). As a result, cyberbullying emerges as a new concept of bullying in the field of internet.

The concept of cyberbullying was first introduced in 2004 by Canadian education-science researcher Belsey. Belsey (2004) defined the concept of cyberbullying as the use of information and communication technologies, individually or as a group, by individuals to threaten another individual or group. Cyber bullying is defined as intentionally hurting others by using information and communication technologies like cell phones, internet, e-mail, instant messaging, chat room, or website (Topçu, 2008). Cyber bullying is an aggressive and intentional act toward victims who cannot easily protect and defend themselves via using electronic forms of contact repeatedly over time (Smith et al., 2005). Olweus (2012) showed that spreading the embarrassing picture or the video on a website or something once is common for both perpetrator and targeted group are the most common ways of cyber bullying.

Cyberbullying is the repetitive and deliberate act of aggressive behavior aimed at harming another person in the digital environment with digital tools (Tokunaga, 2010). Cyberbullying is an extension of bullying (Shariff, 2005). However, the bully uses technologies such as web pages, text messages, instant messaging, chatrooms, social-networking sites, and e-mails to embarrass, humiliate, harass, intimidate, or threaten others (Anderson & Sturm, 2007; Healey, 2011). These acts of harm; It includes behaviors such as insulting, revealing, spreading, death threats, deception, mocking, embarrassment, nicknames, humiliation, exclusion from a social group (Bauman, Toomey, & Walker, 2013; Betts, 2016; Bhat, 2008; Mehari, Farrell, & Le, 2014; Raskauskas & Stoltz, 2007). Some researchers have suggested that cyberbullying is similar to relational aggression with the intention of humiliating, lying, harming social status and relationships (Chadwick, 2014). According to Vandebosch and Van Cleemput (2008), the measure of power in real life is physical strength or age, while the measure of technology-based power is knowledge of technology, such as the ability to be anonymous. For cyberbullying, content such as a message, picture, video should be sent using the internet or mobile phones to harm the other party, and this should include repetitive negative actions and a power imbalance in the bilateral relationship.

Cyber bullying is defined as virtualbullying (Nocentini et al., 2010), digital bullying (Privitera & Campbell, 2009; Vandebosch & Van Cleemput, 2008), online bullying (Akbulut, Şahin & Erişti, 2010; Freis, & Gurung, 2013; Mehari, Farrell & Le, 2014; Privitera & Campbell, 2009; Tokunaga, 2010), electronic bullying (Akbulut, Şahin & Erişti, 2010; Campfield, 2008; Kowalski & Limber, 2007; Mehari, Farrell & Le, 2014; Olweus, 2012; Privitera & Campbell, 2009; Tokunaga, 2010; Topçu, Erdur-Baker & Çapa-Aydın, 2008; Wang, Iannotti & Nansel, 2009), e-bullying (oppression) (Privitera & Campbell,

2009) and techno-bullying in the literature (Akbulut, Şahin & Erişti, 2010). In addition, the concepts of online harassment (Ybarra & Mitchell, 2004), internet harassment (Kiriakidis & Kavoura, 2010), and electronic aggression are concepts that can be used as a reference to cyberbullying (Mehari, Farrell & Le, 2014; Tokunaga, 2010).

As it is mentioned, cyber bullying, continuous, and general attacking, insulting, threatening, mocking, slandering, spreading rumors, inclusion, blocking, humiliating, removing visual materials, seizing and reviewing commonly used ones through the bully's internet-based communication applications will damage reputation together who clothe the preparation. While the owner of the aforementioned aggressive behaviors is defined as "cyber bully" (Betts, 2015), those who are the target of the behaviors of cyberbullies and who are harmed by their behaviors are called "cyber aggrieved-victim" (Aktürk, 2015).

The common expressions in the definitions of cyberbullying, such as the fact that the bullying takes place by electronic means that the bullying is intentional and continuous, and in addition to these, the power imbalance between the bully and the victim are considered as the criteria of cyberbullying in the literature (Betts, 2016; Kowalski, Giumetti, Schroeder & Lattanner, 2014; Langos, 2012). The first of these criteria is the realization of bullying through digital tools, the second; the bully's repetition of the behavior, third; the tyrant, who is expressed as power imbalance, is stronger than the victim in terms of technology use, opportunity, and competence, fourth; the ability of the bully to hide his identity, and finally, the bully's intention to cause physical and psychological harm to the person (İğdeli, 2018).

Another component of cyberbullying is the repetition of the behavior. Cyberbullying can take different forms repeatedly. While the victim is subject to repeated damaging behavior from a single person, a single damaging action may be sufficient for cyberbullying. (Betts, 2016). In addition, because negative texts shared online can be protected, the victim may be tempted to read these negative comments again, and each review can further harm the victim's mental health (Bauman, 2007).

Information and communication technologies provide great convenience for obscurity (Mehari, Farrell & Le, 2014). In addition, it is claimed that the digital world offers people the opportunity to show themselves differently by creating fake accounts, which makes bullying in the cyber world attractive (Akbulut, Şahin & Erişti, 2010). Slonje and Smith (2008) stated that cyberbullies engage in cyberbullying because they can hide their identities more easily with electronic means. However, compared to most traditional bullies, when cyberbullies hide themselves, they may be less aware of, or even unaware of, the consequences of their behavior (Slonje & Smith, 2008).

CHARACTERISTICS THAT DISTINGUISH CYBERBULLYING FROM TRADITIONAL BULLYING

Common components in both cyberbullying and traditional bullying are exposure to harmful behaviors, power imbalance, repetition of the behavior and doing it with the intention of harming (İğdeli, 2018). In addition, the criteria that distinguish cyberbullying from traditional bullying are that cyberbullying takes place in the digital environment and the bully can be anonymous. Smith (2012) listed the characteristics of cyberbullying that differ from traditional bullying as follows:

1. Requires a certain technology expertise. While operations such as sending e-mail and text messages can be easily done, opening an account as someone else and sending defamatory messages on a web page requires more technology knowledge and skills.

2. It is a type of bullying that takes place indirectly rather than face to face and therefore can be anonymous.
3. The bully does not see the reaction of the victim, at least in the short term, since direct feedback cannot be seen, empathy or regret may decrease.
4. The role of witnesses to cyberbullying is more complex than the role of witnesses to traditional bullying. When any action takes place, such as sending an e-mail, message, the witness may be with the bully; may be with the victim or, in both cases, receive the message from a different place or see the bullying on the relevant website.
5. In traditional bullying, one of the motives of bullying is thought to be status gained by demonstrating power in front of others. However, unless the experiences of cyberbullying are shared publicly, the bully cannot achieve such a result.
6. The potential audience is more common in cyberbullying. For example, when negative comments are published on a web page, the audience that can see these comments can be much larger.
7. It is difficult to escape from cyberbullying because there is no place to hide. A message can be sent to the victim from anywhere with a mobile phone or computer. While in traditional bullying, the victim may be away from the bullying until the next day when he returns home, in cyberbullying, it is more difficult to escape because the victim can view messages, e-mails, and malicious content published on web pages (Smith, 2012).

In brief explanation of what Smith (2012) mentioned, cyber bullying takes places in technological areas, it is indirect, the feedback of the victim is not clear or seen, the audience may be very wide and there is no place to escape from cyber bullying in the cyber areas.

According to Şahin and Akbaba (2017), the differences between traditional bullying and cyberbullying can be listed as follows:

1. In traditional bullying, the bully is known by the bullying victim and is usually someone close to him. However, in cyberbullying, there is no obligation for the bully to recognize the victim with the effect of communication tools.
2. While the bully is physically superior to the victim in traditional bullying, there is no such obligation in cyberbullying.
3. In traditional bullying, the bully and the victim must be in the same environment for bullying to take place, but this is not necessary in cyberbullying. It is also known that in traditional bullying, when friends environment of the bully and the victim change, the bullying situation disappears, but in cyberbullying there is no such a thing.
4. In traditional bullying, the physical impact is intense on the victim, while in cyber bullying, the number of people who see the victim being bullied increases, and its psychologically destructive effects also increase.
5. Cyberbullying is capable of confronting the victim in any environment where technology is available (Şahin & Akbaba, 2017).

There are similarities as well as differences between traditional bullying and cyberbullying. More than half of traditional bully students also bully online (Yaman et al., 2011). As in traditional bullying, the cyberbully cannot see the reaction of the victim instantly. Since there is no immediate feedback, it can often be seen that there is no empathy or remorse as in face-to-face bullying (Serin, 2012). Unlike traditional bullying, cyberbullying causes emotional harm rather than direct physical harm. It is spread through text messages, photographs, blogs, e-mail, instant messaging programs and similar tools spread online (Huang & Chou, 2010).

Along with these, cyberbullying; It has been stated that it can lead to more serious consequences than traditional bullying due to its features such as the inability to control online impulses that support persecution, the absence of nonverbal (visual or auditory) signs and clues indicating the intention of the message, and the persistence of the content in the online environment (Bauman & Yoon, 2014). Compared to traditional bullying, the damage caused by cyberbullying can be greater, Harmful content can be easily protected for a long time, and it can reach very large audiences very quickly, and many people who cannot harm the other physically or similarly may turn to cyberbullying (Li, 2010).

Cyber bullying is more common than traditional types of bullying, the bully and the victim do not need to share the same environment in cyber area, cyberbullying can occur at any time and place, and can reach an uncertain and large number from a single person or a group at a time (Srivastavaa, Gamble & Boey, 2013). People who are the target of cyberbullying and exposed to cyberbullying are considered as cyber victims. The damage of cyber victims is often greater than the damage of traditional victim, because the victims can experience negative experiences and humiliation in front of more people in the virtual environment compared to traditional victimization (Macaulay, Steer & Betts, 2020). Apart from the cyberbully and the cyber victim, there is another concept that emerged: The audience as in traditional bullying. Witnesses to cyberbullying can reach even further than their circle of close friends. Even if the cyberbully regrets what he has done, the bullying material that are the images, texts, sounds and photographs can be recorded by many different people (Eliçora, 2020).

THEORETICAL FRAMEWORK OF CYBERBULLYING

It has been stated that cyberbullying can be understood with three different theoretical frameworks; relational aggression, power and control model, deficiencies in emotional and cognitive empathy (Faucher, Jackson & Cassidy, 2014). In relational aggression, the person tries to disrupt or harm friendships, group participation or social status with tactics such as rumors, gossip, and slander (Crick et al., 1999). Deficiencies in emotional and cognitive empathy mean having low emotional and cognitive empathy. In a study, it was concluded that men and women with low emotional and cognitive empathy, regardless of gender, have high cyberbullying scores (Ang & Goh, 2010). A third perspective that should be considered when examining the dynamic of cyberbullying is the power and control model. It has been stated that this model uses elements such as age and class level difference that constitute abuse as power and control wheels. By using these elements, the bully keeps the victim under control and bullies him/her (Faucher, Jackson & Cassidy, 2014).

Kowalski, Giumetti, Schroeder, and Lattanner (2014), who examined 131 studies investigating the prevalence of cyberbullying and victimization, its relationships with other variables, and its consequences, explained cyberbullying with the help of an integrative model. In the model, cyberbullying is explained by using personal and situational factors, paths, proximate processes and distant consequences. Among the factors that cause cyberbullying, personal factors (such as demographic characteristics, values and perceptions), situational factors (such as provocation, school climate, perception of anonymity) and internal characteristics of the individual (such as cognition, emotion, arousal) have an effect on the individual about making an assessment and deciding whether or not to engage in cyberbullying (Kowalski et al.,

2014). The individual factors that facilitate the emergence of cyberbullying are listed as, desire to take revenge, being a cyber victim or a cyberbully before, to have technological skills, impulses like having fun or feeling strong, personality traits such as empathy and narcissism, anxiety and depression, easy access to the Internet and spending time on the Internet for a long time, behaviors such as a history of physical assault or theft, moral approval of bullying (Gulendam, 2020).

Cyberbullying, which is a problem that is more common than expected and can affect individuals of all ages, causes negative consequences in terms of emotions, behavior, health, education and communication for both the victim and the perpetrators of cyberbullying. When the literature about the subject is examined, it is seen that there are many etiological and descriptive studies about cyberbullying (Bhat, 2008; Cassidy et al., 2009; Hoff & Mitchell, 2009; Rivers & Noret, 2010; Smith et al., 2008; Vandebosch & Van Cleemput, 2009; Varjas, Henrich & Meyers, 2009; Willard, 2007). According to the results of these studies, cyberbullying mostly results from communication and relational problems such as separation, jealousy, lack of tolerance and ganging. The fact that jealousy, which is the main starting point of cyberbullying, is seen in narcissistic individuals and the high level of internet usage of cyberbullies has revealed the problem of being an effect mechanism between these three concepts (Hoff & Mitchell, 2009; Willard 2007). The most important characteristics of narcissistic individuals are that they believe that they have special rights and privileges, that they cannot empathize and that they are closed to criticism. Therefore, due to these characteristics, individuals' narcissism tendency levels can also affect their bullying levels (Twenge & Campbell, 2010).

PREVALENCE AND GENDER DIFFERENCES OF CYBER BULLYING

During these years, because of the development of the internet accessibility cyber bullying is a frequent and increasing problems (Olweus, 2012). Studies in some countries show that cyber bullying is a common problem. Different studies show different ranges, and the rates change between 4.1% and 62% (Kowalski & Limber, 2007; Li, 2006). Kowalski, and Limber (2007) found that 4% of the students are cyber bullies, 11% of them cyber victims and 7% of them are bully victims. The bullying rates changes in different studies like 9% (Williams & Guerra, 2007) to 15% (Ybarra & Mitchell, 2004). According to age, Juvonen, and Gross (2008) showed that among 12-17 aged students 72% of them victimized of cyber bullying at least once in previous year. Wright et al. (2009) found that 29.8% of the high school students reported that they were victimized and 14.9% of them reported that they were cyber bullied by someone else. According to gender, it is known that females show more victimization compared to men (Hinduja & Patchin, 2008) and men show more cyber bullying (Arıcak et al., 2008). Researchers show that females tend to be more cyber victims than males (Kowalski & Limber, 2007; Dilmaç, 2009; Calvete et al., 2010).

There are also different rates in Turkey for example, Topçu (2008) states the bullying rates as 48%. Erdur-Baker, and Kavşut (2007) found that 28% of the high school student are cyber bullies, and 30% of the students are cyber-victims. Taylan et al. (2017) found the rates as 7% to 28% in Turkey. According to age, it is 11% to -18% in primary school aged children (Ayas & Horzum, 2012), in secondary school, it is 10% to 23% (Peker, 2015), and it is 10% to 17% among high school students (Özdemir & Akar, 2011).

Lee and Shin (2017) stated the prevalence among 7 to 12th grade Korean adolescents, 6.3% of the population involved in cyber bullying as bullies, victims were 14.6% and 13.1% were both bully and victim. Additionally, boys were involved in cyber bullying as perpetrators more than girls. In New Zea-

Figure 1. Number of Studies and Median Prevalence of Cyber Bullying

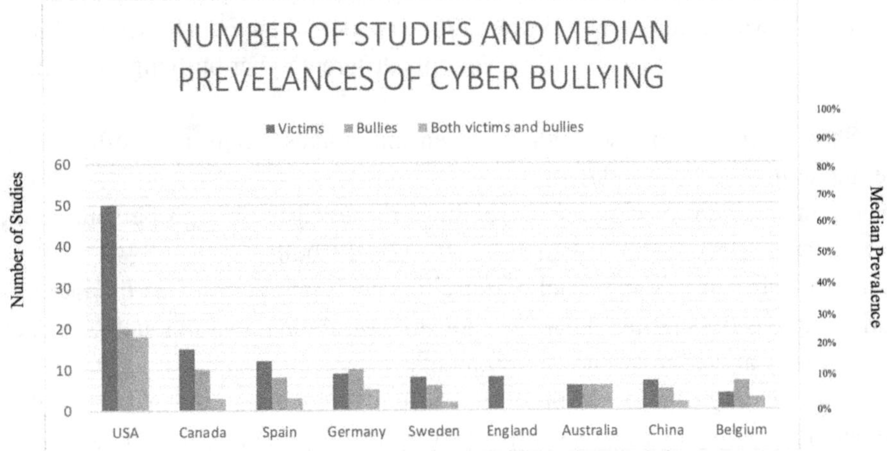

land, a study conducted with 20849 people, showed that 14.9% experienced cyber bullying as a victim, prevalence was higher among 18 to 25 years old than older and younger ages. Women experienced slightly more cyber bullying than men (Wang, et al., 2019). Popović-Ćitić, Djurić & Cvetković, (2011) stated the prevalence in Serbia among middle school students as 10% of the population found as cyber bullies, and 20% of them were victims. Additionally, the type of victimization was grouped as denigration, and harassment. According to gender, males reported much more bullying and victimization than females.

In a review among Spanish people, showed that cyber bullying is also a growing problem in Spain. However, the prevalence differed among the studies because of the cut-off points, different self-report instruments. Among the scales the prevalence of victimization was 26% and cyber bullying was 24%. The study stated that when the cyber bullying was assessed with multi-item instruments it was twice of the one-item instrument studies (Zych, Ortega-Ruiz & Marin-Lopez, 2016). Brochado, Soares and Frage (2017) prepared a review about cyber bullying prevalence among adolescents. 159 studies which were conducted in North America dn Europe were included in the study. The study showed that publication of cyber bullying studies had been increased over years. Firstly, in 2004 first papers were published and increased until 2010. Highest number of prevalence were showed in North American countries and then Europe. Figure in the below which showed the prevalence according to countries was taken from the study.

Reprinted from "A scoping Review Number of Studies of Cyberbullying Prevalence Among Adolescents" by S. Brochado, S. Soares & S. Fraga, 2017, *Trauma, Violence, & Abuse,* 18(5), p. 526. Copyright 2016 by Sage Publications.

To sum up, the results are different, the reason can be the instruments are different in different studies. Another reason is age range is different in the studies because it is known that age is an important variable in cyber bullying (Ayas & Horzum, 2012). Recall periods and perspectives also may be different such as victimization only, perpetration only or both may be focused in the studies (Brochado, Soares & Frage (2017). About gender, it is known that female students are more exposed to cyber bullying and male students are more engaged in cyber bullying (Kowalski & Limber, 2007; Hinduja & Patchin, 2008; Türkoğlu, 2013; Korkmaz, 2016; Taştekin & Bayhan, 2018).

TYPES OF CYBERBULLYING

Types of cyberbullying were examined by Willard (2007) under seven main headings. Although there is no sharp line between these titles, each section contains different cyber bullying in detail:

- *Flaming:* Short-lived heated discussion between individuals, often using offensive and obscene language, including insults and threats.
- *Harassment:* Intermittent or continuous sending of messages through personal communication channels to a target person who is seen as a victim by the bully.
- *Denigration:* Sharing of lies and cruel words about the victim chosen as the target, which harm him. In addition, it is the sharing of harmful information about the individual with fake photos that have been digitally altered in online environments.
- *Impersonation:* Sharing of information by a cyberbully, including information or photos that will harm the person's dignity by impersonating the person they are targeting, or harm their friendship by making them look bad.
- *Outing and Trickery:* Outing means revealing information or secrets or embarrassing images of the person chosen as the victim. Trickery is when the bully, who shows the victim that he is a good person, is actually deceiving him to reach his information.
- *Exclusion:* Exclusion is the intentional and deliberate removal of the person chosen as the victim from the group. It is exhibiting acts that exclude the victim, such as not participating in group games played on the Internet, not adding them to various social media accounts.
- *Cyber-stalking:* It is the constant sending of frightening or offensive messages to damage the reputation of the victim (Willard, 2007).
- Walker (2009) lists the types of cyberbullying according to the purposes of using technological tools in cyberbullying as follows:
- *Flaming:* Arguments made in a billingsgate and angry language in the virtual environment.
- *Cyber harassment or cyber stalking:* Sending offensive, vulgar, or insulting messages, calling and not speaking to the individual, using publicly accessible areas such as chat rooms to post threatening and frightening messages, engaging in other online activities that cause the individual to fear for their safety, and tracking the victim by sending viruses or using spyware.
- *Denigration:* To defame someone online, to spread insulting rumors online to damage the reputation of the individual among his friends.
- *Impersonation:* Hacking an individual's account and sending messages to other individuals on their behalf that will embarrass them, discredit them among their peers, and make them feel bad.
- *Outing/Tricking:* Sharing personal secrets or information that will cause embarrassment to the individual in the virtual environment, sending personal pictures and videos from one phone to another via local wireless connections (Bluetooth), uploading them to websites or sharing them on video upload sites that can be accessed by anyone.
- *Happy Slapping:* Recording physical attacks on mobile phones or other electronic devices and sending them to other people.
- *Exclusion:* Intentional exclusion of the individual in the virtual environment (for example, being removed from the friendship list or not included in online games played together).
- *Manipulation:* The cyberbully pressures the victim to reveal personal secrets and meet them face-to-face or provokes the victim with their words and actions.

- *Sexting:* Sending nude photos to others, receiving nude photos from others, and forwarding nude photos sent to him via mobile phone (Walker, 2009). Bullying behaviors observed in online environments were categorized as follows by Akça & Sayımer (2017); impersonation, exclusion, outing and trickery, cyber-stalking, flaming.
- Tamer and Vatanartıran (2014), on the other hand, defined the types of cyberbullying in the following ways:
- *Harassment:* Sending electronic messages in abusive and offensive language.
- *Cyberstalking:* Sending undesirable text messages repeatedly.
- *Denigration:* Spreading gossip, lies, or rumors about someone to discredit his friendships and/or the dignity of another person.
- *Impersonation:* To act like someone else.
- *Outing:* Revealing someone else's secrets or embarrassing information without their consent.
- *Trickery:* Talking to someone about their secret or embarrassing information and then revealing it online.
- *Exclusion:* Intentionally removing someone from an online group.
- *Cyber harassment:* Repetitive defamation or abuse including great fear or threat.
- *Sharing sexual content:* One of the subjects included in the types of cyberbullying is the sharing of sexually explicit images.

Cyberbullying is defined as behaviors that will harm another person in the virtual environment. Accordingly, those who distribute sexually explicit images can be counted as cyberbullies, and those who are exposed to these images can be counted as cyber victims. Behaviors such as sexual insults and humiliation, capturing personal images, and slandering are among the types of bullying encountered on social media (Dinç, 2020).

CHARACTERISTICS OF STUDENTS IN CYBERBULLYING STATUS PREDICTORS

There are many studies that show predictors of cyberbullying such as, Li (2007) stated that gender is an important predictor of cyber bullying; females are more exposed to cyberbullying and become victims (Calvete et al., 2010). Researchers show that females tend to be more cyber victims than males (Kowalski & Limber, 2007; Dilmaç, 2009; Calvete et al., 2010). Furthermore, in terms of the parental variables, having high-educated parents, low income (Syts, 2004) and parents who do not work were found as having a protection effect on cyberbullying and cyber victimization (Burnukara, 2009; Sengupta & Chaudhuri, 2011).

Characteristic of the people is also a predictor of cyberbullying, empathy is an important predictor, cyberbullies feel less empathy for the victims (Steffgen et al., 2011). Ildırım, Çalıcı, and Erdoğan (2017) showed that cyberbullying is positively related to anxiety, somatization, hostility, impulsivity, and internet addiction. Çelik et al. (2012) found that emotion instability is a predictor for being a cyberbully. Moreover, it is found that emotional dysregulation of anger is also related to being the perpetrator of cyberbullying (Johnson, 2015). Another personality characteristic which is a predictor of bullying is narcissistic personality which is linked to cyber bullying perpetration (Ang et al., 2009). Other predictors can be shown as attachment styles. Varghese, and Pistole (2017) stated that perpetrators are found to have more attachment anxiety than others. Moreover, Beran (2009) stated that parental rejection was found to be related with traditional peer victimization.

A study conducted by Sarak (2012) showed that high school students whose parents are literate of not educated, who are not academically successful in school, have 4 or more siblings, go to internet cafe, have psychiatric support were found to be more likely to be a perpetrator or victim of cyber bullying. It was found that being a perpetrator and victim of cyber bullying was increased by age. Addition to this, Türkoğlu (2013) found that mother, father education status, socio economic status, having private room, and having computer at home were related to cyber bullying among high school students. Among secondary school students it was found that male students engaged in cyber bullying more than female students. Students who are in private and selected by examination engaged in cyber bullying than students in government schools. Additionally, researchers showed that in schools which have only one gender students had less cyber bullying events than other mixed gendered schools (Horzum & Ayas, 2011). Korkmaz (2016) compared government, science, and private high school students, and found that cyber victimization was higher in government schools than science and private high schools.

Cyber victimization in university was higher than cyber bullying; gender, academic success, socio economic status of family, having internet connection at home, making anonymously calls, sending e-mails to others were found to be related to both cyber bullying and cyber victimization (Fırat & Ayran, 2016). Kılınç and Gündüz (2017) found that female students are more sensitive to cyber bullying. Students who have internet connection showed more internet addiction and cyber bullying sensitivity. Mestci (2021) found that parental status, daily internet usage and previous bullying and victimization status were related to being both cyber bully and victim among university students.

Furthermore, the frequency of internet and cell phone usage and joining the internet sites, chat rooms, and social media were found to be related to being cyberbully and cyber victim (Ybarra, 2004; Hinduja & Patchin, 2008; Erdur-Baker & Kavşut, 2007; Ekşi, 2012). Moreover, some studies show that individuals who had been bullied or victimized reported more bullying and victimization in their later lives (Olweus, 2012; Ybarra & Mitchell, 2004).

THE CONSEQUENCES OF CYBERBULLYING

Although there are many benefits of information and communication technologies, unlimited, and uncontrolled use has brought some negativities (Peker, Eroğlu & Ada, 2000). In recent years, the use of information and communication technologies has become quite common among young people. One of the consequences of this prevalence is the increase in the rate of being exposed to cyber bullying or engaging in cyberbullying (Erdur-Baker & Kavşut, 2007; Arıcak et al., 2008; Dilmaç, 2009; Peker & Eroğlu, 2010; Çetin, Pekeri, Eroğlu & Çitemel 2012).

Research show that people who are exposed to cyber bullying may show sleeping problems, afraid of being alone and going outside of the home, may have suicidal thoughts (Wong-Lo & Bullock, 2011; Kestel & Akbıyık, 2016), academic problems (Beran & Li, 2007), depression and anxiety (Erdur-Baker & Tanrıkulu, 2010; Johnson, 2011; Kowalski & Limber, 2013), aggression (Kestel & Akbıyık, 2016), low self-esteem (Zezulka & Seigfried-Spellar, 2016), psychosomatic problems like headaches (Olweus, 2012; Koh, 2013), frustration (Hinduja & Patchin, 2006).

Tokunaga (2010) states that cyber victims struggle with various problems such as loneliness, inability to socialize and engage in angry behaviors, and that the effect of cyberbullying on social relations is similar to traditional bullying, and that cyber victims cannot develop positive social behaviors just like traditional victims. Studies on cyberbullying show that cyber victimization negatively affects individuals in many ways. People who exposed to cyberbullying; depression, delinquency, and substance use have increased (Mitchell, Ybarra & Finkelhor, 2007). According to Beran and Li (2007), it was observed that they caused anger, anxiety, loss of motivation towards the lesson, academic failure, and absenteeism from school.

Arıcak (2009) found that the group that did not engage in cyberbullying and was not exposed to cyberbullying showed less psychiatric symptoms than cyberbullies and cyber victims. Hinduja and Patchin (2009) reported that cyber victimization, combined with stressful life conditions, causes victims to display behaviors that can even lead to suicide. Eroğlu et al. (2011) found that girls exposed to cyberbullying try to cope with cyberbullying by behaving submissively. Individuals exposed to cyberbullying are adversely affected in many ways. Individuals exposed to cyberbullying have serious problems such as sadness, anger, anxiety, academic failure, absenteeism, loneliness, low self-esteem, suicide, coping with by behaving submissively, and bringing a gun to school (Beran & Li, 2007; Hinduja & Patchin, 2009; Raskauskas & Stoltz, 2007; Willard, 2007; Eroğlu et al., 2011).

In cyberbullying, although it is thought that the victim is the injured ones, the individuals who do the bullying can also be negatively affected by this situation. Cyberbullies reported that they felt angry, sad and depressed after being bullied online, and they also felt popular and powerful when they were bullied, despite feeling guilty afterwards (Mishna et al., 2010). It is reported that cyberbullying has a negative impact on the school life and academic success of both the victim and the bully. It is noteworthy that cyberbullies and victims have problems in establishing social relations. The fact that cyber victimization is associated with social anxiety shows that cyber victims have difficulties in establishing social relationships (Aktepe, 2013). Hoertel, Le Strat, Lavaud, and Limosin (2012) determined that bullying causes more impulse control disorders and emotional disorders in women than in men. Exhibiting the state of depression as a result of cyberbullying was found to be almost half (49%). Hinduja and Patchin (2010) also stated that young people who are cyberbullied have more suicidal thoughts than those who do are not cyberbullied, and that they are also more likely to attempt suicide.

Batmaz and Ayas (2013) found that cyber bullying was positively corelated with hostility and agression, depression, psychotisicm, and interpersonal sensitivity among secondary school students in Turkey. Both cyber bullying and cyber victimization levels of secondary students was found to be related to somatization (Horzum & Ayas, 2014).

PREVENTION

As it is seen cyber bullying is a very common problem for different aged people and caused serious problems for both cyber bullies and victims. That's why prevention programs are very important about cyber bullying. It is known that cyber bullying has some common points with tradition bullying (Olweus, 2012). Thus, similar prevention programs may be applied because it is also known that mostly the traditional bullies are the cyber bullies (Juvonen & Gross, 2008). Aboujaoude et al. (2015) stated that parents have a great role in prevention in cyber bullying.

In the literature there are different ways of prevention most of them have similar non technological bases like in traditional bullying preventions, role plays, empathy training, discussing emotions, awareness raising whole school programs (Chaux, Velasques, Schultze-Krumbholz & Scheithauer, 2016; Ttofi &

Farrington, 2011; Tangen & Campbell, 2010; Ang & Goh, 2010). Providing information for youth, parents and whole school are the very common prevention techniques for cyber bullying (Cassidy, Faucher & Jackson, 2013). There was a prevention program named Kiva which was created to prevent traditional bullying however it was also effective for reducing cyber bullying (Salmivalli, Kärna & Poskiparta, 2011). On the other hand, the main difference between the cyber bullying and traditional bullying is the usage of technological areas. So, some prevention programs in the literature include technology usage education or limiting the technology for example in a study it is found that taking away the bully's access to technology is the most effective way of prevention cyber bullying (Kraft & Wang, 2009). There are also some programs which use technological tools like there are some computer programs which can detect cyber bullying (Dadvar, Jong, Ordelman & Trieschnigg, 2013). With the help of this program victims are also informed about what to the when the cyber bullying was detected. In a program, students are educated as cybermentors for virtual peer support and if it is needed these people can refer for mentors or counselors (Banerjee, Robinson & Smalley, 2010).

Topçu-Uzer and Tanrıkulu (2017) evaluated 3 prevention programs for cyber bullying in Turkey and stated that these are all for secondary and high school students, these have group counselling and do not have technological applications. Akça, Sayımer, Salı and Başak (2014) pointed out that media literacy is also important to prevent cyber bullying. Aydın (2016) found that cyber bullying awareness training program was effective on cyber bullying awareness on 6th grade students in Turkey.

As it is mentioned, there are some protective factors at individual, family, peer, school and community levels in cyber bullying however, there are still less research focused on protective factors among age groups than risk factors (Kowalski, Limber & McCord, 2019). It is known that there is still gap in prevention of cyber bullying (National Academies, 2016), however overlapping parts are very wide between cyber and traditional bullying (Olweus & Limber, 2018). This may be enlightening the research about cyberbullying prevention.

CONCLUSION

Increase in the internet usage changed many things in human beings' lives. Beside the positive effects of internet, many negative concepts are also occurred. One of the negative outcomes of the internet was cyber bullying. Cyber bullying has been defined with different concepts such as electronic bullying, online bullying, internet bullying, digital bullying, and online harming (Şahin & Akbaba 2017). Hinduja & Patchin (2009) define cyberbullying as using a computer, telephone, or other electronic devices for harmful and repetitive behaviors. Cyber bullying is a form of traditional bullying. There are both similarities and differences between them however, it is known that most of the bullies are also bullies in cyber areas (Yaman et al., 2011). There are some different types of cyber bullying as flaming, harassment, denigration, impersonation, outing and trickery, exclusion, cyber-stalking, flaming, happy slapping, exclusion, manipulation, and sexting (Willard, 2007). There are some different theoretical backgrounds of cyber bullying such as relation aggression theory, power and control model, and deficiencies in emotional and cognitive empathy (Faucher, Jackson & Cassidy, 2014).

Cyber bullying is an important concept because the prevalence rates change between 4.1% and 62% in different studies (Kowalski & Limber, 2007; Li, 2006). Research show that cyber bullying cause serios problems not only among children but also young adults, cyber bullying among university students are also high (Patchin & Hinduja, 2006; Ybarra & Mitchell, 2004). There are many cyber bullying studies all around the world, the problem is universal (Ybarra & Mitchell, 2004; Popović-Ćitić, Djurić, & Cvetković, 2011; Ayas & Horzum, 2012; Zych, Ortega-Ruiz & Marin-Lopez, 2016). There some predictors of cyber bullying, in this chapter some of them were discussed such as gender, and some characteristics of people. There are serious consequences of cyber bullying. It is known that not only cyber victims, but cyber bullies are also affected by cyber bullying (Horzum & Ayas, 2014). Cyber bullying should be handled because it is known that when it is not solved, it may also be seen in adulthood and in the workplace (Kota et al., 2014). Some prevention methods and studies were discussed in this chapter.

FUTURE RESEARCH DIRECTION

Since the technology era has started and people use technology nearly ever time in our every single time, problems have started to occur. Especially after the Covid-19 pandemic people were obliged to stay at home, schools, education, business, games, socialization, and many other things has become virtually done. Children forgot to play game, interacting with each other. So, education about social relations, cyber bullying awareness, and safe internet usage are important. Barlett, Simmers, Roth, and Gentile (2021) found that cyber bullying attitudes and perpetration were significantly increased during the pandemic. It is so easy to reach internet platforms, thus it cannot be controlled easily, a problem in the cyber area cannot solve easily. That's why policies should prohibit such behaviors (cyber bullying) in the internet platforms. In United States, there some states that prohibit electronic harassments (Hinduja and Patchin, 2012; United States Department of Education, 2011). All around the world, there should be some legal sanctions of cyber bullying to stop it.

REFERENCES

Aboujaoude, E., Savage, M. W., Starcevic, V., & Salame, W. O. (2015). Cyberbullying: Review of an old problem gone viral. *The Journal of Adolescent Health*, *57*(1), 10–18. doi:10.1016/j.jadohealth.2015.04.011 PMID:26095405

Akbulut, Y., Şahin, Y. L., & Erişti, B. (2010). Development of a scale to investigate cybervictimization among online social utility members. *Contemporary Educational Technology*, *1*(1), 46–59. doi:10.30935/cedtech/5961

Akça, E. (2017). Cyberbullying, it's types and related factors: An evaluation through the existing studies. *Online Academic Journal of Information Technology*, *8*(30), 1–20. doi:10.5824/1309-1581.2017.5.001.x

Akca, E. B., Sayımer, İ., Salı, J. B., & Başak, B. E. (2014). The causes and types of cyber bullying in school and role of media literacy in preventive services. *Electronic Journal of Occupational Improvement and Research*, *2*(1), 17–30.

Aktepe, E. (2013). Cyber-bullying and cyber-victimization in adolescents. *New Symposium Journal*, *51*(1), 31-36.

Aktürk, A. O. (2015). Analysis of cyberbullying sensitivity levels of high school students and their perceived social support levels. *Interactive Technology and Smart Education, 12*(1), 44–61. doi:10.1108/ITSE-07-2014-0016

Anderson, T., & Sturm, B. (2007). Cyberbullying from playground to computer. *Young Adult Library Services, 5*(2), 24–27.

Ang, R. P., & Goh, D. H. (2010). Cyberbullying among adolescents: The role of affective and cognitive empathy and gender. *Child Psychiatry and Human Development, 41*(4), 387–397. doi:10.100710578-010-0176-3 PMID:20238160

Ang, R. P., Ong, E. Y., Lim, J. C., & Lim, E. W. (2009). From narcissistic exploitativeness to bullying behavior: The mediating role of approval of aggression beliefs. *Social Development, 19*(4), 721–735. doi:10.1111/j.1467-9507.2009.00557.x

Arıcak, O. T. (2009). Psychiatric symptomatology as a predictor of cyberbullying among university students. *Eurasian Journal of Educational Research, 34*, 167–184.

Arıcak, O. T., Siyahhan, S., Uzunhasanoğlu, A., Sarıbeyoğlu, S., Çıplak, S., Yılmaz, N., & Memmedov, C. (2008). Cyberbullying among Turkish adolescents. *Cyberpsychology & Behavior, 11*(3), 253–261. doi:10.1089/cpb.2007.0016 PMID:18537493

Ayas, T., & Horzum, M. B. (2012). On being cyber bully and victim among primary school students. *Ilkogretim Online, 11*(2).

Aydın, F. (2016). *Effectiveness of the cyberbulling education on the sixth-grade students' cyberbulling awareness* (Unpublished Master theses). Sakarya University, Sakarya.

Banerjee, R., Robinson, C., & Smalley, D. (2010). *Evaluation of the Beatbullying Peer Mentoring Programme. Report for Beatbullying*. University of Sussex.

Barlett, C. P., Simmers, M. M., Roth, B., & Gentile, D. (2021). Comparing cyberbullying prevalence and process before and during the COVID-19 pandemic. *The Journal of Social Psychology, 161*(4), 408–418. doi:10.1080/00224545.2021.1918619 PMID:34128768

Batmaz, M., & Ayas, T. (2013). Predicting the cyber bullying levels of students ın second stage of primary school according to psychological. *Sakarya University Journal of Education, 3*(1), 43–53.

Bauman, S. (2007). Cyberbullying: A virtual menace. *National Coalition Against Bullying National Conference*.

Bauman, S., Toomey, R. B., & Walker, J. L. (2013). Associations among bullying, cyberbullying, and suicide in high school students. *Journal of Adolescence, 36*(2), 341–350. doi:10.1016/j.adolescence.2012.12.001 PMID:23332116

Bauman, S., & Yoon, J. (2014). Theories of bullying and cyberbullying. *Theory into Practice, 53*(4), 253–256. doi:10.1080/00405841.2014.947215

Belsey, B. (2006). Bullying. org: A learning journey. *Bulletin–Newfoundland and Labrador Teachers Association, 49*(4), 20.

Beran, T., & Li, Q. (2005). Cyber-harassment: A study of a new method for an old behavior. *Journal of Educational Computing Research, 32*(3), 265–277. doi:10.2190/8YQM-B04H-PG4D-BLLH

Beran, T., & Li, Q. (2007). The relationship between cyberbullying and school bullying. *The Journal of Student Wellbeing, 1*(2), 16–33. doi:10.21913/JSW.v1i2.172

Betts, L. R. (2015). Cyber bullying behaviours. In Encyclopedia of Information Science and Technology (pp. 6727–6735). doi:10.4018/978-1-4666-5888-2.ch661

Betts, L. R. (2016). *Cyberbullying approaches, consequences, and interventions*. Palgrave Macmillan. doi:10.1057/978-1-137-50009-0

Bhat, C. S. (2008). Overview and strategies for school counsellors, guidance officers and all school personnel. *Australian Journal of Guidance & Counselling, 18*(1), 53–66. doi:10.1375/ajgc.18.1.53

Brochado, S., Soares, S., & Fraga, S. (2017). A scoping review on studies of cyberbullying prevalence among adolescents. *Trauma, Violence & Abuse, 18*(5), 523–531. doi:10.1177/1524838016641668 PMID:27053102

Burnukara, P. (2009). İl ve Orta Ergenlikte Geleneksel ve Sanal Akran Zorbalığına Betimsel Bir İnceleme (Unpublished Master's Thesesis). Hacettepe University, Ankara.

Calvete, E., Orue, I., Estevez, A., Villardon, L., & Padilla, P. (2010). Cyberbullying in adolescents: Modalities and aggressors' profile. *Computers in Human Behavior, 26*(5), 1128–1135. doi:10.1016/j.chb.2010.03.017

Campfield, D. C. (2008). *Cyber bullying and victimization: Psychosocial characteristics of bullies, victims and bully/victims* (Unpublished master's thesis). Montana University, Missoula.

Cassidy, W., Faucher, C., & Jackson, M. (2013). Cyberbullying among youth: A comprehensive review of current international research and its implications and application to policy and practice. *School Psychology International, 34*(5), 575–612. doi:10.1177/0143034313479697

Cassidy, W., Jackson, M., & Brown, K. N. (2009). Sticks and stones can break my bones, but how can pixels hurt me?: Students' experiences with cyber-bullying. *School Psychology International, 30*(4), 383–402. doi:10.1177/0143034309106948

Çetin, B., Peker, A., Eroğlu, Y., & Çitemel, N. (2011). Siber zorbalığın bir yordayıcısı olarak ilişkilerle ilgili bilişsel çarpıtmalar: Ergenler için bir ön çalışma [Cognitive distorions related to relationships as a predictor of cyberbullying: A preliminary study for adolescents]. *International Online Journal of Educational Sciences, 3*(3), 1064–1080.

Chadwick, S. (2014). *Impacts of cyberbullying, building social and emotional resilience in schools. Springer Briefs in Education*. Springer., doi:10.1007/978-3-319-04031-8

Chaux, E., Velasquez, A. M., Schultze-Krumbholz, A., & Scheithauer, H. (2016). Effects of the cyber-bullying prevention program media hereos (Medienhelden) on traditional bullying. *Aggressive Behavior, 42*(2), 157–165. doi:10.1002/ab.21637 PMID:26879895

Crick, N. R., Werner, N. E., Casas, J. F., O'Brien, K. M., Nelson, D. A., Grotpeter, J. K., & Markon, K. (1999). Childhood aggression and gender: A new look at an old problem. In D. Bernstein (Ed.), *Gender and motivation* (pp. 75–141). University of Nebraska Press.

Dadvar, M., Trieschnigg, D., Ordelman, R., & de Jong, F. (2013). Improving cyberbullying detection with user context. In *Advances in Information Retrieval* (pp. 693–696). Springer. doi:10.1007/978-3-642-36973-5_62

Dilmaç, B. (2009). Psychological needs as a predictor of Cyber-bullying: A preliminary report on college students. *Educational Sciences: Theory and Practice*, *9*(3), 1291–1325.

Dinç, E. S. (2020). Cyber bullying in social media platforms: Examination of cyberbullying experiences among highschool students. *Journal of New Media*, *4*(1), 24–39.

Eliçora, R. (2020). *Investigation of the relationship between adolescents' cyber victimization and coping with cyberbullying skills and emotional intelligence* (Unpublished Doctoral Dissertation). Karabük University, Karabük.

Erdur-Baker, Ö. & Kavşut, F. (2007). Cyber bullying: a new face of peer bullying. *Eurasian Journal of Educational Researh,* (27), 31-42.

Erdur-Baker, Ö., & Tanrıkulu, İ. (2010). Psychological consequences of cyber bullying experiences among Turkish secondary school children. *Procedia: Social and Behavioral Sciences*, *2*(2), 2771–2776. doi:10.1016/j.sbspro.2010.03.413

Eroğlu, Y., Çetin, B., Güler, N., Peker, A., & Pepsoy, S. (2011). From cybervictimization to coping ways of stress: Gender as moderator. In *Proceedings of International Conference on Education and New Learning Technologies (EDULEARN11 Conference)* (pp. 2699-2707). Academic Press.

Faucher, C., Jackson, M., & Cassidy, W. (2014). Cyberbullying among university students: Gendered experiences, impacts and perspectives. *Education Research International*, *2014*, 1–10. doi:10.1155/2014/698545

Fırat, M., & Ayran, G. (2016). Cyberbullying among college students. *Turk Silahli Kuvvetleri Koruyucu Hekimlik Bulteni*, *5*(15), 322–329. doi:10.5455/pmb.1-1450776947

Freis, S. D., & Gurung, R. A. R. (2013). A Facebook analysis of helping behavior in online bullying. *Psychology of Popular Media Culture*, *2*(1), 11–19. doi:10.1037/a0030239

Gulendam, K. (2021). Children with Chronic Disease during COVID-19 Pandemic and Nurses' Roles. *International Journal of Caring Sciences*, *14*(3), 2058–2065.

Healey, J. (Ed.). (2011). *Dealing with bullying.* The Spinney Press. https://goo.gl/K8dCRZ

Hinduja, S., & Patchin, J. (2012). *School Climate 2.0: Preventing Cyberbullying and Sexting One Classroom at a Time*. Corwin Press. doi:10.4135/9781506335438

Hinduja, S., & Patchin, J. W. (2008). Cyberbullying: An exploratory analysis of factors related to offending and victimization. *Deviant Behavior*, *29*(2), 129–156. doi:10.1080/01639620701457816

Hinduja, S., & Patchin, J. W. (2009). *Bullying beyond the schoolyards.* Carwin.

Hinduja, S., & Patchin, J. W. (2010). Bullying, cyberbullying, and suicide. *Archives of Suicide Research, 14*(3), 206–221. doi:10.1080/13811118.2010.494133 PMID:20658375

Hinduja, S., & Patchin, J. W. (2014). Cyberbullying: An exploratory analysis of factors related to offending and victimization. *Deviant Behavior, 29*(2), 129–156. doi:10.1080/01639620701457816

Hoertel, N., Le Strat, Y., Lavaud, P., & Limosin, F. (2012). Gender effects in bullying: Results from an antional sample. *Psychiatry Research, 200*(2-3), 921–927. doi:10.1016/j.psychres.2012.03.036 PMID:22497957

Hoff, D. L., & Mitchell, S. N. (2009). Cyberbullying: Causes, effects, and remedies. *Journal of Educational Administration, 47*(5), 652–665. doi:10.1108/09578230910981107

Horzum, M. B., & Ayas, T. (2011). The examination of cyberbullying and victim levels of high school students according to school type and gender. *Educational Science and Practice, 10*(20), 139–159.

Horzum, M. B., & Ayas, T. (2014). The examination of cyberbullying and victim levels of high school students according to school type and gender. *Online Journal of Technology Addiction and Cyberbullying, 1*(2), 21–36.

Huang, Y. Y., & Chou, C. (2010). An analysis of multiple factors of cyberbullying among junior high school students in Taiwan. *Computers in Human Behavior, 26*(6), 1581–1590. doi:10.1016/j.chb.2010.06.005

İğdeli, F. (2018). *Investigating the university students' levels of cyberbullying, cybervictimization and cyberbullying sensitivity according to various variables* (Unpublished Master's Thesis). Eskişehir Anadolu University, Eskişehir.

Ildırım, E., Çalıcı, C., & Erdoğan, B. (2017). Psychological correlates of cyberbullying and cybervictimization. *The International Journal of Human and Behavioral Science, 3*(2), 7–21.

Johnson, C. L. (2011). *An Examination of the Primary and Secondary Effects of Cyber-Bullying: Development and Testing of a Cyber-Bullying Moderator/Mediator Model* (Unpublished Doctoral Thesis). Graduate School of Wayne State University, Detroit.

Johnson, P. (2015). *What Makes a Cyberbully/Victim? Factors Associated with The Perpetration of Cyberbullying By Cyber Victims* (Unpublished Master's Thesis). Macquarie University, Sydney.

Juvonen, J., & Gross, E. F. (2008). Extending the school grounds? Bullying experiences in cyberspace. *The Journal of School Health, 78*(9), 496–505. doi:10.1111/j.1746-1561.2008.00335.x PMID:18786042

Kestel, M., & Akbıyık, C. (2016). An ınvestigation of effects of cyber bullying on students' Academic, social and emotional states. *Mersin University Journal of the Faculty of Education, 12*(3), 844–859.

Kılınç, İ., & Gündüz, Ş. (2017). Investigation of high school students' cyber sensitivity, ınternet addiction and humanistic values. *Trakya University Journal of the Faculty Educaiton, 7*(2), 261–283. doi:10.24315/trkefd.304497

Kiriakidis, S. P., & Kavoura, A. (2010). Cyberbullying: A review of the literature on harassment through the internet and other electronic means. *Family & Community Health, 33*(2), 82–93. doi:10.1097/FCH.0b013e3181d593e4 PMID:20216351

Korkmaz, A. (2016). Comparing cyber bullying behaviors and being a victim of cyber bullying. *TRT Akademi, 1*(2), 620–639.

Kota, R., Schoohs, S., Benson, M., & Moreno, M. A. (2014). Characterizing cyberbullying among college students: Hacking, dirty laundry, and mocking. *Societies (Basel, Switzerland), 4*(4), 549–560. doi:10.3390oc4040549

Kowalski, R. M., Giumetti, G. W., Schroeder, A. N., & Lattanner, M. R. (2014). Bullying in the digital age: A critical review and meta-analysis of cyberbullying research among youth. *Psychological Bulletin, 140*(4), 1073–1137. doi:10.1037/a0035618 PMID:24512111

Kowalski, R. M., & Limber, S. P. (2013). Psychological, physical, and academic correlates of cyber-bullying and traditional bullying. *The Journal of Adolescent Health, 53*(1), 13–20. doi:10.1016/j.jadohealth.2012.09.018 PMID:23790195

Kowalski, R. M., Limber, S. P., & Agatston, P. W. (2012). *Cyberbullying: Bullying in the Digital Age*. Wiley Blackwell.

Kowalski, R. M., Limber, S. P., & McCord, A. (2019). A developmental approach to cyberbullying: Prevalence and protective factors. *Aggression and Violent Behavior, 45*, 20–32. doi:10.1016/j.avb.2018.02.009

Kraft, E. M., & Wang, J. (2009). Effectiveness of cyber bullying prevention strategies: A study on students' perspectives. *International Journal of Cyber Criminology, 3*(2), 513–535.

Langos, C. (2012). Cyberbullying: The challenge to define. *Cyberpsychology, Behavior, and Social Networking, 15*(6), 285–289. doi:10.1089/cyber.2011.0588 PMID:22703033

Law, D. M., Shapka, J. D., Hymel, S., Olson, B. F., & Waterhouse, T. (2012). The changing face of bullying: An empirical comparison between traditional and internet bullying and victimization. *Computers in Human Behavior, 28*(1), 226–232. doi:10.1016/j.chb.2011.09.004

Lee, C., & Shin, N. (2017). Prevalence of cyberbullying and predictors of cyberbullying perpetration among Korean adolescents. *Computers in Human Behavior, 68*, 352–358. doi:10.1016/j.chb.2016.11.047

Li, Q. (2010). Cyberbullying in High Schools: A Study of Students' Behaviors and Beliefs about This New Phenomenon. *Journal of Aggression, Maltreatment & Trauma, 4*(19), 372–392. doi:10.1080/10926771003788979

Macaulay, P. J. R., Steer, O. L., & Betts, L. R. (2020). *Factors leading to cyber victimization*. Emerging Cyber Threats and Cognitive Vulnerabilities. doi:10.1016/B978-0-12-816203-3.00001-0

Mehari, K. R., Farrell, A. D., & Le, A. T. H. (2014). Cyberbullying among adolescents: Measures in search of a construct. *Psychology of Violence, 4*(4), 399–415. doi:10.1037/a0037521

Mestci, S. (2021). *Exploring the link between object relations, narcissism, cyber bullying, and cyber victimization among university students* (Unpublished Master Thesis). University of Economics, İzmir.

Mishna, F., Cook, C., Gadalla, T., Daciuk, J., & Solomon, S. (2010). Cyber bullying behaviors among middle and high school students. *The American Journal of Orthopsychiatry, 80*(3), 362–374. doi:10.1111/j.1939-0025.2010.01040.x PMID:20636942

Mitchell, K. J., Ybarra, M., & Finkelhor, D. (2007). The relative importance of online victimization in understanding depression, delinquency, and substance use. *Child Maltreatment*, *12*(4), 314–324. doi:10.1177/1077559507305996 PMID:17954938

National Academies of Sciences, Engineering and Medicine. (2016). *Preventing bullying through science, policy, and practice*. The National Academies Press., doi:10.17226/23482

Nocentini, A., Calmaestra, J., Schultze-Krumbholz, A., Scheithauer, H., Ortega, R., & Menesini, E. (2010). Cyberbullying: Labels, behaviours and definition in three European countries. *Australian Journal of Guidance & Counselling*, *20*(2), 129–142. doi:10.1375/ajgc.20.2.129

Olweus, D. (2012). Cyberbullying: An overrated phenomenon? *European Journal of Developmental Psychology*, *9*(1), 520–538. doi:10.1080/17405629.2012.682358

Olweus, D., & Limber, S. P. (2018). Some problems with cyberbullying research. *Current Opinion in Psychiatry*, *19*, 139–143. doi:10.1016/j.copsyc.2017.04.012 PMID:29279213

Özdemir, M., & Akar, F. (2011). Examination of high school students' opinions on cyberbullying in terms of various variables. *Kuram ve Uygulamada Eğitim Yönetimi*, *17*(4), 605–626.

Patchin, J. W., & Hinduja, S. (2006). Bullies move beyond the schoolyard: A preliminary look at cyberbullying. *Youth Violence and Juvenile Justice*, *4*(2), 148–169. doi:10.1177/1541204006286288

Peker, A. (2015). The Investigation of Relationship Between Behavior Aggression and Cyber Bullying in Adolescents. *Ekev Akademik Dergisi*, *19*(61), 323–336.

Peker, A., Eroğlu, Y. & Şükrü, A. D. A. (2012). The investigation of predictors of cyberbullying and cybervictimization in adolescents. *Abant İzzet Baysal University Journal of Faculty of Education, 12*(2).

Popović-Ćitić, B., Djurić, S., & Cvetković, V. (2011). The prevalence of cyberbullying among adolescents: A case study of middle schools in Serbia. *School Psychology International*, *32*(4), 412–424. doi:10.1177/0143034311401700

Privitera, C., & Campbell, M. A. (2009). Cyberbullying: The new face of workplace bullying? *Cyberpsychology & Behavior*, *12*(4), 395–400. doi:10.1089/cpb.2009.0025 PMID:19594381

Public Safety Canada. (2010). *Canada's cyber security strategy: For a stronger and more prosperous Canada*. Retrieved from: https://www.publicsafety.gc.ca/cnt/rsrcs/pblctns/cbr-scrtstrtgy/ cbr-scrt-strtgy-eng.pdf

Raskauskas, J., & Stoltz, A. D. (2007). Involvement in traditional and electronic bullying among adolescents. *Developmental Psychology*, *43*(3), 564–575. doi:10.1037/0012-1649.43.3.564 PMID:17484571

Rivers, I., & Noret, N. (2010). Participant roles in bullying behavior and their association with thought's of ending one's life. *Crisis*, *31*(3), 143–148. Advance online publication. doi:10.1027/0227-5910/a000020 PMID:20573608

Şahin, M., & Akbaba, S. (2017). *Okulda ve Sanal Ortamda Zorbalık ve Empati*. Nobel.

Salmivalli, C., Kärna, A., & Poskiparta, E. (2011). Counteracting bullying in Finland: The KiVA Program and its effects on different forms of being bullied. *International Journal of Behavioral Development, 35*(5), 405–411. doi:10.1177/0165025411407457

Sarak, Ö. (2012). *Cyber bullying in high school students* (Unpublished Master's Thesis). Haliç University, İstanbul.

Sengupta, A., & Chaudhuri, A. (2011). Are social networking sites a source of online harrassment for teens? Evidence from survey data. *Children and Youth Services Review, 33*(2), 284–290. doi:10.1016/j.childyouth.2010.09.011

Serin, H. (2012). *Ergenlerde Siber Zorbalık / Siber mağduriyet yaşantıları ve bu davranışlara ilişkin öğretmen ve eğitim yöneticilerinin görüşleri* (Unpublished Doctoral Thesis). İstanbul Üniversitesi, İstanbul.

Shariff, S. (2005). Cyber-dilemmas in the new millennium: School obligations to provide student safety in a virtual school environment. *McGill Journal of Education, 40*(3), 467–487.

Slonje, R., & Smith, P. K. (2008). Cyberbullying: Another main type of bullying? *Scandinavian Journal of Psychology, 49*(2), 147–154. doi:10.1111/j.1467-9450.2007.00611.x PMID:18352984

Smith, B. W., Dempsey, A. G., Jackson, S. E., Olenchak, R. F., & Gaa, J. (2012). Cyberbullying among gifted children. *Gifted Education International, 28*(1), 112–126. doi:10.1177/0261429411427652

Smith, P., Mandavi, J., Carvalho, M., & Tippett, N. (2005). *An Investigation into Cyberbullying, Its Forms, Awareness and Impact, And the Relationship Between Age and Gender in Cyberbullying*. Goldsmiths College.

Smith, P. K. (2012). Cyberbullying: Challenges and opportunities for a research program—A response to Olweus. *European Journal of Developmental Psychology, 9*(5), 553–558. doi:10.1080/17405629.2012.689821

Smith, P. K., Mahdavi, J., Carvalho, M., Fisher, S., Russell, S., & Tippett, N. (2008). Cyberbullying: Its Nature and impact in secondary school pupils. *Journal of Child Psychology and Psychiatry, and Allied Disciplines, 49*(4), 376–385. doi:10.1111/j.1469-7610.2007.01846.x PMID:18363945

Srivastavaa, A., Gambleb, R., & Boey, J. (2013). Cyberbullying in Australia: Clarifying the problem, considering the solutions. *International Journal of Children's Rights, 21*(1), 25–45. doi:10.1163/157181812X637145

Steffgen, G., König, A., Pfetsch, J., & Melzer, A. (2011). Are cyberbullies less empathic? Adolescents' cyberbullying behavior and empathic responsiveness. *Cyberpsychology, Behavior, and Social Networking, 14*(11), 643–648. doi:10.1089/cyber.2010.0445 PMID:21554126

Syts, Y. (2004). *Beyond the schoolyard: Examining Electronic Bullying Among Canadian Youth (*Unpublished Master's Thesis). Carleton University, Ottawa.

Tamer, N., & Vatanartıran, S. (2014). Ergenlerin teknolojik zorbalık algıları [Adolescents' perception of technological bullying]. *Online Journal of Technology Addiction & Cyberbullying, 1*(2), 1–20.

Tangen, D., & Campbell, M. (2010). Cyberbullying prevention: One primary school's approach. *Australian Journal of Guidance & Counselling, 20*(2), 225–234. doi:10.1375/ajgc.20.2.225

Taştekin, E., & Bayhan, P. (2018). Examination of cyber bullying and victimization among adolescents. *Online Journal of Technology Addiction & Cyberbullying, 5*(2), 21–45.

Taylan, H. H., Aydin, F., & Topal, M. (2017). Investigation of secondary school students' cyberbullying situations in terms of several variables: Sakarya province sample. *Online Journal of Technology Addiction and Cyberbullying, 4*(1), 41–59.

Tokunaga, R. S. (2010). Following you home from school: A critical review and synthesis of research on cyberbullying victimization. *Computers in Human Behavior, 26*(3), 277–287. doi:10.1016/j.chb.2009.11.014

Topçu, Ç. (2008). *The Relationship of Cyberbullying to Empathy, Gender, Traditional Bullying, Internet Use and Adult Monitoring* (Unpublished Master Thesis). Middle East Technical University, Ankara.

Topçu, Ç., Erdur-Baker, Ö., & Çapa-Aydın, Y. (2008). Examination of cyberbullying experiences among Turkish students from different school types. *Cyberpsychology & Behavior, 11*(6), 643–648. doi:10.1089/cpb.2007.0161 PMID:18783345

Topçu-Uzer, Ç., & Tanrıkulu, İ. (2017). Cyberbullying prevention and intervention programs: A national systematic review. *Uludağ University Journal of Faculty of Education, 30*(1), 1–17. doi:10.19171/uefad.323367

Ttofi, M. M., & Farrington, D. P. (2011). Effectiveness of school-based programs to reduce bullying: A systematic and meta-analytic review. *Journal of Experimental Criminology, 7*(1), 27–56. doi:10.100711292-010-9109-1

Türkoğlu, S. (2013). *Ergenlerin Problemli İnternet Kullanımları ile Siber Zorbalık Eğilimleri Arasındaki İlişkinin İncelenmesi* [Investigation of the Relationshio between the Problematic Internet Use and Cyberbullying Tendencies] (Unpublished Master's Thesis). Marmara University, İstanbul.

Twenge, J. M., & Campbell, W. K. (2010). *Asrın vebası: Narsisizm illeti* (Ö. Köknar, Trans). İstanbul: Kaknüs Yayınları United States Department of Education, Office of Planning, Evaluation and Policy Development, Policy and Program Studies. https://www2.ed.gov/rschstat/eval/bullying/state-bullying-laws/state-bullying-laws.pdf

Vandebosch, H., & Cleemput, K. V. (2009). Cyberbullying among youngsters: Profiles of bullies. *New Media & Society, 11*(8), 1249–1371. doi:10.1177/1461444809341263

Vandebosch, H., & Van Cleemput, K. (2008). Defining cyberbullying: A qualitative research into the perceptions of youngsters. *Cyberpsychology & Behavior, 11*(4), 499–503. doi:10.1089/cpb.2007.0042 PMID:18721100

Varghese, M. E., & Pistole, M. C. (2017). College student cyberbullying: Self-Esteem, depression, loneliness, and attachment. *Journal of College Counseling, 20*(1), 7–21. doi:10.1002/jocc.12055

Varjas, K., Henrich, C. C., & Meyers, J. (2009). Urban middle school students' perceptions of bullying, cyberbullying, and school safety. *Journal of School Violence, 8*(2), 159–176. doi:10.1080/15388220802074165

Walker, J. L. (2009). *The contextualized rapid resolution cycle intervention model for cyber bullying* (Unpublished Doctoral Thesis). Arizona State University.

Wang, J., Iannotti, R. J., & Nansel, T. R. (2009). School bullying among adolescents in the United States: Physical, verbal, relational and cyber. *The Journal of Adolescent Health*, *45*(4), 368–375. doi:10.1016/j.jadohealth.2009.03.021 PMID:19766941

Wang, M. J., Yogeeswaran, K., Andrews, N. P., Hawi, D. R., & Sibley, C. G. (2019). How common is cyberbullying among adults? Exploring gender, ethnic, and age differences in the prevalence of cyberbullying. *Cyberpsychology, Behavior, and Social Networking*, *22*(11), 736–741. doi:10.1089/cyber.2019.0146 PMID:31697598

Willard, N. E. (2007). *Cyberbullying and Cyberthreats: Responding to The Challenge of Online Social Aggression, Threats, and Distress*. Research Press.

Williams, K. R., & Guerra, N. G. (2007). Prevalence and predictors of internet bullying. *The Journal of Adolescent Health*, *41*(6), 14–21. doi:10.1016/j.jadohealth.2007.08.018 PMID:18047941

Wong-Lo, M., & Bullock, L. M. (2011). Digital aggression: Cyberworld meets school bullies. *Preventing School Failure*, *55*(2), 64–70. doi:10.1080/1045988X.2011.539429

Wright, V. H., Joy, J. B., Christopher, T. I., & Heather, N. O. (2009). Cyberbullying: Using virtual scenarios to educate and raise awareness. *Journal of Computing in Teacher Education*, *26*(1), 35–42.

Yaman, E., Eroğlu, Y., & Peker, A. (2011). *Okul Zorbalığı ve Siber Zorbalık*. Kaknüs.

Ybarra, M. L., & Mitchell, K. J. (2004). Online aggressor/targets, aggressors, and targets: A comparison of associated youth characteristics. *Journal of Child Psychology and Psychiatry, and Allied Disciplines*, *45*(7), 1308–1316. doi:10.1111/j.1469-7610.2004.00328.x PMID:15335350

Zych, I., Ortega-Ruiz, R., & Marín-López, I. (2016). Cyberbullying: A systematic review of research, its prevalence and assessment issues in Spanish studies. *Psicologia dell'Educazione*, *22*(1), 5–18. doi:10.1016/j.pse.2016.03.002

ADDITIONAL READING

Çelik, S., Atak, H., & Erguzen, A. (2012). The effect of personality on cyberbullying among university students in Turkey. *Eurasian Journal of Educational Research*, *12*(49), 129–150.

Hinduja, S., & Patchin, J. (2012). *School Climate 2.0: Preventing Cyberbullying and Sexting One Classroom at a Time*. Corwin Press. doi:10.4135/9781506335438

Lastowka, F. G., & Hunter, D. (2004). Virtual crimes. *New York Law School Law Review. New York Law School*, *49*(1), 293.

Patchin, J. W., & Hinduja, S. (2012). *Cyberbullying Prevention and Response:Expert Perspectives*. Routledge. doi:10.4324/9780203818312

KEY TERMS AND DEFINITIONS

Audience: Audience is the witnesses to cyber bullying event.

Bully-Victim: People who are both engage in bullying but also a victim of cyber bullying event.

Cyber Bully: Cyber bully is the perpetrator of the bullying event who aimed to harm others in digital platforms.

Cyber Bullying: Cyber bullying is the repetitive and deliberate act of aggressive behavior aimed at harming another person in the digital environment with digital tools.

Cyber Victim: Cyber victim is the victim of the cyber bullying event who is suffered, affected by the event.

Prevention Program: Programs, trainings, and actions to avoid cyber bullying.

Traditional Bullying: It is the main form of bullying which is the having repetitive and deliberate act of aggressive behavior aimed at harming another person.

Chapter 27
Cyberbullying Issues

Amina Parveen
https://orcid.org/0000-0002-5092-0011
University of Kashmir, India

Shazia Jan
https://orcid.org/0000-0003-2849-4463
University of Kashmir, India

Insha Rasool
https://orcid.org/0000-0002-2046-8378
University of Kashmir, India

ABSTRACT

Bullying is the intentional harming and humiliation of others, particularly those who are smaller, weaker, younger, or more vulnerable than the bully. Cyberbullying is defined as bullying that happens via the use of modern technologies. The anonymous internet propagation of nasty remarks about a person is referred to as cyberbullying. Cyberbullying is a burning issue, and it's important to evaluate the implications of cyber aggression on individuals of all ages, particularly adolescents and emerging adults, and to provide some insight into how individuals cope with or handle cyberbullying. The aim of this chapter is to explore and discuss the idea of cyberbullying including its various forms and methods. The reasons for cyberbullying, cyberbullying consequences, prevalence of cyberbullying, and gender disparities in cyberbullying are also discoursed. Different prevention and intervention strategies are also be explored and discussed in order to combat cyberbullying.

INTRODUCTION

Digital era is the age of the internet where technology becomes more widely accessible to the general public, particularly students. While the internet has become a massive factor of millions of adults' ordinary activities, it has also become a key part of daily lifestyle of children also. Smartphone Internet connectivity has undoubtedly opened up new and fascinating possibilities. It allows young people, in

DOI: 10.4018/978-1-6684-5426-8.ch027

particular, to seek out social support, explore their identities, improve interpersonal and critical thinking skills, and benefit educationally from easy access to information. The Internet has become a prerequisite for information dissemination for children and individuals of all ages due to its ferocious ability to fetch information needed in a matter of seconds, making it an integral informational/educational tool that parents find challenging to deny. Unfortunately, technological advancements such as the Internet and Smartphones provide a potent weapon for antisocial behaviour. It introduces the child to all of the information on the web, which may or may not be appropriate for their developing minds, as well as to various social networking sites, where they are likely to encounter strangers who may have hidden agendas ranging from money to seeking sadistic/sexual pleasures. Befriending these people puts a strain on these young minds, diminishing their self-esteem and promoting depression (Anderson et al. 2014), and driving them to commit suicide on exceptional cases. It has introduced a new platform for bullying, which has switched from the physical world to the virtual cyber-world of school-aged children and teenagers. Some children are being exposed to unpleasant, threatening, or unsafe cyber interactions that jeopardise their safety and emotional well-being in this cyber-world (Li, Smith & Cross, 2012). Cyberbullying is an aggressive, intentional act committed by a group or individual, via electronic forms of contact, against a victim who cannot easily defend himself or herself, repeatedly or over time" (Smith et al. 2008). The anonymous electronic posting of despicable things about a person (such as a student) is referred to as cyberbullying (Merriam-Webster, 2017). Belsey (2004) defined it as the use of ICT to encourage deliberate, recurrent, and aggressive behaviour by a person or group with the intent to damage others. It can happen on social media sites, chat rooms, gaming platforms, and cell phones. Cyberbullying is more likely than other forms of bullying to go unnoticed by parents and administrators. This is due to victims' feelings that they needed to learn how to cope with it on their own, as well as their fear of their internet privileges being restricted or taken altogether if they told their parents. The existing literature consistently reveals that bullied teenagers do not report their experiences to others (Petrosino et al., 2010; Black et al., 2010; Mishna and Alaggia, 2005; Naylor and Cowie, 1999; Charach et al., 1995). For example, Ybarra et al. (2006) discovered that 33% of cyberbullying victims in their study did not acknowledge the incidence to anyone at all. Petrosino et al. (2010) work is especially relevant because their data was collected from a nationally representative sample of American schools and was based on data from the National Crime Victimization Survey School Crime Supplement (2007), which brought to light that 64% of adolescents aged 12 to 18 didn't disclose their experience. Cyberbullying is a real issue, and it's imperative to study the consequences of cyberaggression on people of all ages, particularly adolescents and emerging adults, as well as provide some insight into how individuals cope with or handle cyberbullying. This chapter will give an overview of the available literature on cyberbullying in order to explain and discuss the key areas:

- Difference between cyberbullying and traditional bullying.
- Different forms of Cyberbullying.
- Different means of cyberbullying
- Different Reasons behind Cyberbullying
- Consequences of cyberbullying
- Prevalence of Cyberbullying.
- Gender differences on Cyberbullying.
- Different prevention and intervention techniques for cyberbullying.

CYBERBULLYING VERSUS TRADITIONAL BULLYING

Bullying is a pattern of harming and humiliating others, especially those who are smaller, weaker, younger, or in any way more vulnerable than the bully. Bullying is a specific type of behaviour which is intended to harm, perpetrated by one or more individuals and carried out repeatedly over time (Nansel et al.2001). Furthermore, this form of behaviour entails an imbalance of power (physical or psychological), with the victim's ability to protect himself or herself being constrained.

Cyberbullying is defined as bullying that occurs via the use of digital technologies. It is known by a variety of names, such as electronic bullying, Internet bullying, Internet harassment, online bullying, and online social cruelty, with cyberbullying being the most used among researchers. It's a pattern of behaviour designed to frighten, enrage, or humiliate the people who are being targeted. Cyber bullying can be said to be an extension of traditional bullying where the perpetrator uses ICT to abuse their target. As little study has been undertaken to thoroughly explore the relationship between bullying at school and cyberbullying, its resemblance to traditional bullying is uncertain (Raskauskas & Stoltz, 2007; Beran & Li, 2007). There is no doubt that the online world has distinct qualities that may lead us to see cyberbullying as a different paradigm to offline bullying. 'Anonymity,' 'lack of physical and social cues,' 'breadth of potential audience,' and 'no place to hide,' are four major differences identified by Marczak and Coyne (2015) that may intensify the impacts of cyberbullying.

According to Hinduja and Patchin (2008), one major difference between these two types of harassment, is that, whereas physical strength is an essential element of conventional bullying, computer proficiency alone is vital to permit one to perform such crimes online. Brown, et al. (2006) agree with this belief while stating that since there is seemingly very little supremacy difference in cyberbullying, students who are disempowered in the real world or are victims of face-to-face bullying, may resort to aggression through anonymity or fake identities. Cyberbullying can happen at any time because it does not take place in person. Children's senses of vulnerability are heightened by the fact that electronic bullying communications can reach such a large audience in such a short amount of time (Kowalski & Limber, 2007). Electronic communications allow perpetrators to maintain anonymity, access to a wide audience and 24/7 attainability. Because the perpetrator cannot immediately see the reaction of their victim and their audience, and the victim may not be aware of the attack or the degree of the assault until later, the anonymity that comes with such distribution can be a difference for both the perpetrator and the victim (Bauman, 2009). Feinberg and Robey (2009) supported the statement, stating that because perpetrators cannot immediately see a reaction from their victims or audience, cyberbullying may be worse than face-to-face bullying because perpetrators frequently increase the intensity and frequency of their attacks without fully understanding the consequences of their actions. Furthermore, the secretive nature of the communication devoid of non-verbal quos differentiates cyber-bullying from traditional bullying. Perpetrators may feel less accountable and responsible, rendering victims more vulnerable (Huang & Chou 2010; Dehue, et al. 2008; Heirman & Walrave, 2008).

TYPES OF CYBERBULLYING

According to Willard (2004), cyberbullying can take different forms, with the main forms ranging from flaming, to harassment, to cyberstalking. The following list gives a formal definition for each form:

Flaming

This is usually a short-lived disagreement in which two or more young people exchange messages involving anger, violence, intimidation, insults, sarcasm, and the use of antagonistic tones and uncensored language (Turnage, 2008). Using all capital letters, numerous punctuation marks, and obscenity are all features of flaming communications. It is most common in public communication settings like a chat room, an online gaming forum, or a blog. According to Wallace (1999), because it is easy to identify someone with similar beliefs in virtual environments, group polarisation can be fairly strong in the Internet community. As a result, people may engage in prejudiced debates and assume that different viewpoints or attitudes are deserving of assault. However, it can also be defined as a sequence of private angry messages delivered via email or instant messaging.

Harassment

Harassment, unlike flaming, is the conveying of offensive messages to a single target on a regular basis (Willard, 2007). Personal multiple networks such as emails, instant messaging, and mobile text messages are commonly used to deliver these messages. Harassment lasts longer than flaming, and the harm is usually one-sided, with one person being the perpetrator and the other wishing the miscommunication to discontinue.

Cyberstalking

This is the repeated posting of destructive communications that contain threats of harm, they are highly intimidating or exceedingly offensive, and usually cause the recipient to fear for their safety.

Denigration (put-downs)

Denigration occurs when negative or inaccurate statements about another person are publicly disclosed online or communicated to others, as well as when gossip and rumours are propagated. The goal of denigration is usually to disrupt friendships or to undermine an individual's reputation. Because they do not always have access to the site where the false information was posted, the target of denigration may not be able to delete it.

Masquerade

Masquerading or impersonation is the act of pretending to be someone else online and posting anything that is disparaging to that person. Impersonation is relatively easy to do over the Internet because of its inherent anonymity. It can be hard to ascertain who has posted information and whether the information is genuine. Impersonating someone in a chat room is also possible. The exchanging of passwords, which is thought to be a sign of deep friendship among teenagers, particularly among girls, allows for impersonation.

Outing and trickery

Sharing sensitive, confidential, or embarrassing facts or photographs about another person without their permission is referred to as outing. The information can be shared with others by email, text messaging, chat rooms, or by posting it on web pages or blogs. Outing can happen in the context of a toxic relationship when one partner shares confidential information obtained while the relationship was still mutual. As part of the outing, there may be some deception. This occurs when a person is tricked into revealing personal information, which is then shared with others without their permission.

Exclusion

Excluding, removing, or barring someone from 'buddy' lists, chat rooms, Internet groups, or gaming platforms can lead to exclusion and ostracism. Exclusion from a 'buddy' list might feel like the ultimate humiliation for some teenagers.

MEANS

Cyberbully victims might be contacted in a number of ways. According to Willard (2006), sending harsh, angry, and occasionally frightening emails, creating web sites with information on the victim without the victim's knowledge, and uploading photographs online asking others to grade topics like who is the school's biggest loser are among these ways, . According to Beale and Hal (2007), the six main ways are email, instant messaging, chat rooms, bulletin boards, tiny text messaging, Web sites, and polling booths. Cyberbullies might use e-mail, instant chats, text messages, image messages, online bulletin boards, or social networking websites like Facebook or Myspace to carry out their acts (Juvonen & Gross, 2008; Hinduja & Patchin, 2009). Students can also create virtual worlds, vote on or rate websites, or hack other students' computers and share confidential material that was not intended for others to see (Hinduja & Patchin, 2009; Vandebosch & Van Cleemput, 2009). Text messaging has been the center of some research studies, with mixed findings. Whereas Cassidy, Jackson, and Brown (2009) argue that cyberbullying does not occur via text messaging, and Hinduja & Patching (2007) claim that less than 5% of cyberbullying episodes occur by mobile phone, other researchers have identified cell phones and text messaging as the principal way by which cyberbullying occurs. According to one study, the most common forms of cyberbullying were phone calls and text messages (Smith et al., 2008). Raskauskas and Stoltz (2007) examined 84 middle school children; they discovered that bullying via mobile phone was the most common kind of electronic bullying. Because the majority of teenagers own mobile phones and most of these phones have text, photo, and video capabilities, the opportunity to convey dangerous material by cell phone has greatly increased (Hinduja & Patchin, 2009). Unfortunately, modern cell phones have elevated cyberbullying to a new level, with more kids photographing or videotaping other students in the bathroom or locker room and then disseminating the images to other students at school (Raskauskas & Stoltz, 2007). Despite the widespread use of social networking sites like Facebook and Myspace, Bauman (2009) found that cyberbullying happens more frequently via text messaging than through other types of social networking sites.

REASONS BEHIND CYBERBULLYING

Cyberbullying is caused by the same factors leading to bullying in general. Bullies may succumb to peer pressure, seek revenge, and strive to elevate their social status in some way, or assert or display power over others. According to one study, 14% who cyber bullied did so because they disliked the individual, 13% did it because the person irritated them, 10% did it in retribution for being bullied, 9% did it because their friends did it, and 7% did it simply for the joy of it (Cassidy et al., 2009). The researchers examined at how teenagers regarded cyberbullying, as well as the motive for hiding behind a screen and the perpetrator's purpose. According to the focus groups Cyberbullies want to cause bodily discomfort, and are sometimes motivated by payback for traditional bullying at school, some cyberbullied anonymously in response to conflicts or disagreements with someone they meant to retaliate against in person. Boredom, as well as a sense of power or skill, was all suggested as causes for cyberbullying. The importance of anonymity as a predictor of cyberbullying was demonstrated by Barlett (2015) using a path model analysis. In the exchanging of IMs (instant messages) and cyberbullying, anonymity was discovered to be a mediating factor. Being anonymous also functioned as a mediator between a positive attitude regarding being a perpetrator and the frequency with which others were targeted. As a result, the harshness of punishment is minimized once anonymity is presumed, and cyberbullying becomes more common. Due to the difficulty of making communications confidential, e-mail usage was found to be negatively related to anonymity and a favourable attitude toward cyberbullying. These findings are important to consider, given the nature of new and ever-changing SNSs and applications. Even mobile applications designed for younger children may have functionality such as calling, messaging, or online chatting, and the ability to remain anonymous, if permitted, will inevitably lead to cyberbullying.

Cyberbullying is a source of entertainment for some people. They regard it as a leisure activity. Technology has put information at our fingertips, and our demands for constant entertainment are increasing. Teenagers who are dissatisfied with the web - based entertainment options may explore making their own. Then there's the matter of why people prefer cyberbullying to other types of bullying. It's pretty assured that cyberbullies will admit that it's easier to get away with. Many users who engage in cyberbullying presume they will not be identified or exposed because online interactions are difficult to monitor as there are no face-to-face confrontations. Because there are no face-to-face interactions, some cyberbullies are able to avoid at least some of the associated guilt. They are clueless to the immediate effects of their activities since they are not present to examine their victims' emotional states. When they commit cyberbullying, they can be emotionally alienated from their activities.

CONSEQUENCES OF CYBERBULLYING

According to the literature, Cyberbullied people are more likely to experience distress, loneliness, low self-esteem, school phobias, and social anxiety. Cyberbullying has also been correlated to psychological and cognitive difficulties like drinking, smoking, loneliness, and a lack of academic focus.

Bullying can lead to cognitive and psychosomatic distress, as well as serious emotional problems (Natvig, et al, 2001; Rigby, 2003; Roland, 2002; Seals & Young, 2003). Even a single incident of bullying at school can have negative consequences, with children experiencing anxiety, loneliness, sadness, insecurity, substance abuse, delinquent behaviour, post-traumatic stress disorder, sexual disorders, eating disorders, risky sexual behaviour, and the possibility of re-victimization (Nishina & Juvonene, 2005;

Frost, 1991; Hawker & Boulton, 2000; Saunders, 2003). As per Anderson, Bresnahan, and Musatics (2014), cyberbullying has negative consequences for victims, including reduced self-esteem and increased depression. It also creates a sense of powerlessness. Adolescents who report many types of victimisations (e.g., sexual abuse, physical abuse, peer victimisation) have been shown to have significantly greater rates of anxiety and depression symptoms than those who report only one type of victimisation (Finkelhor et al., 2007). Bullying can damage an adolescent's emotional and social development especially after they enter adulthood (Raskauskas & Stoltz, 2007). Traditional bullying increases the possibility of adults having suicidal thoughts to around 20% (Van der Wal et al., 2003), and it is firmly linked to other deviant behaviours including vandalism, shoplifting, dropping out of school, drug usage, and aggressive conduct like fighting (Ericson, 2001; Olweus et al., 1999; Patchin, 2002; Rigby, 2003). Cyberbullying has been shown to have severe consequences, including suicide and violence. The suicide brought on by bullying is referred to as "bullycide" (Marr and Field,2001).

Case Study

Megan Meier was a victim of cyberbullying that resulted in "bullycide." Megan, a 13-year-old female Missouri girl, was cyberbullied to the extent where she committed suicide in her closet in October of 2006. (Pokin, 2007). Megan mistook herself for chatting on MySpace with a 16-year-old boy named Josh. Megan's mother eavesdrops in on their conversation for the entire six weeks they were chatting. Megan received a message from Josh on MySpace on October 15th, 2006, saying, "I'm not sure if I want to be friends with you anymore because I've heard you aren't very polite to your peers." Students were posting bulletins about Megan following morning, and Josh had sent her another message that being said, "Everyone in O'Fallon is aware of your issue. You are a nasty person who is despised by everyone. Have a miserable rest of your days. Without you, the world would be a better place." Megan's parents found her hanging in her closet that day and brought her to the hospital, where she died the day after (Pokin, 2007). Megan's parents were aware of Josh and what he was saying to her, but there was no way of knowing that these messages would lead to Megan's death. Lori Drew, the mother of one of Megan's former friends, was revealed to have created the bogus MySpace account with her daughter. Drew was found guilty of three charges of misdemeanour cyber-crimes for her role in setting up the false account that deceived Megan, who ultimately committed suicide. This was the first cyberbullying conviction, which was handed out in New York on November 26th, 2008. (Steinhauer, 2008).

PREVALENCE OF CYBERBULLYING

Finkelhor, et al. (2000) were among the first to publish an article on cyberbullying. Since then, numerous studies on cyberbullying have been published all around the world. The prevalence of cyberbullying, its overlap with traditional bullying, its relationship with parenting and mediation techniques, coping strategies, health and (psychological) wellbeing, and other negative outcomes have all been extensively researched, with the majority of studies currently available focusing on the problem's prevalence. While the numbers vary, often significantly, it is obvious that cyberbullying is an extremely common occurrence in today's youth's social lives. In a study of 384 teenagers conducted by Hinduja and Patchin (2007), 30% said they had been victims of online bullying, 11% said they had bullied others online, and 47% said they had witnessed cyberbullying. Beren and Li (2007) conducted a study of 432 adolescents and discovered that 58% of them had been victims of cyberbullying at least once. In a study of 1,588 teenagers, Ybarra and Mitchell (2008) discovered that 33% had been harassed online in the preceding year. Despite the fact that these figures differ, there is some indication that the prevalence of cyberbullying is rising as adolescents become more accustomed to various types of technology communication. According to study conducted in 2001, just 11% of students reported being victims of cyberbullying, while 13% acknowledged being bullies themselves (Nansel et.al,2001). Cyberbullying was explored in 106 primary and secondary schools across Australia by Cross, Shaw, et al. (2012). According to the findings, 6.2% said they had been cyberbullied (repeatedly exposed – every few weeks or more frequently), while 23% said they had been exposed to cyberbullying behaviour at least once in the previous term. Sending obscene messages over the Internet or to someone's mobile phone, as well as intentionally ignoring or leaving someone out, were the most regularly reported behaviours.

Hinduja and Patchin (2015) conducted research on a random sample of kids aged 11 to 15 from a middle school in the Midwest of the United States. Approximately 43% of the pupils have been victims of cyberbullying at some point in their lives. 15% of students admitted to cyberbullying others.

Tippett and Kwak (2012) conducted study in South Korea and discovered that almost 10% of all pupils have been bullied using a cell phone. Only 77% had been targeted once or twice, whereas 13% had been targeted once a week or more frequently. Students' experiences of cyberbullying over the Internet were the least common, accounting for only 6.3%. In terms of percentages, 73% had been targeted once or twice, while 5% had been targeted once or twice a week or more frequently. Cyberbullying through online games was by far the most common form of cyberbullying, with 43% of all students reporting having been a victim. 46% had been cyberbullied once or twice, while 30% had been cyberbullied on a regular basis, at least once a week or more frequently. Mishna, Cook, Gadalla, Daciuk, and Solomon (2010) used a sample of 2,186 students aged 11 to 13 and 15 to 17 years to perform their research in Canada. According to this poll, over half of all students (49.5%) said they had been the victim of cyberbullying in the previous three months. The most common kind of cyberbullying was being called names, which accounted for 27% of all events. The survey employed in Cross, Piggin, et al. (2012) study included the opinions of nearly 4,600 secondary school pupils in the United Kingdom. There was no detailed information provided to the pupils about the questions they were asked or the alternative answers they may choose from. However, the results of the poll found that 28% of students had experienced cyberbullying in some way. Nearly a quarter (23%) of those who were continuously cyberbullied said it lasted for a year or more, while 19% said it lasted for a few months. The majority of cyberbullying occurrences appeared to be connected to the internet, with growing cyberbullying on social media sites (SNS).

According to Palfrey et al., (2008), differences in prevalence findings may be due to differing definitions employed by researchers; for example, studies that do not include characteristics like nuisance calls tend to indicate a lower incidence of cyberbullying. Furthermore, the rapid increase in internet use (Juvonen and Gross, 2008) and access to a broader range of electronic devices (Raskauskas and Stoltz, 2007) among children and young people may account for some of the differences in reported prevalence rates over time. Indeed, Rivers and Noret (2009) argue that it is critical to consider the timing of studies, citing a five-year study that revealed a considerable increase in prevalence year over year.

GENDER DIFFERENCES IN CYBERBULLYING

The research on gender differences in cyberbullying has been inconclusive. Some studies have identified significant gender differences, with girls being far more likely to be victims of cyberbullying, while others have concluded that gender has no influence on victimization. According to several studies, males and females have different patterns in bullying-related behaviours (Borg, 1999; Boulton & Underwood, 1992). Hinduja and Patchin (2008) revealed no significant differences between girls and boys as victims in a study of 1,378 students (32% of males and 36% of females were victims). Finkelhor, Mitchell, and Wolak (2005) discovered that Internet harassment was about equally targeted boys and girls. According to Kowalski and Limber (2007) boys and men prefer to indulge in more direct kinds of antagonism; girls are over-represented both as the victims and perpetrators of cyberbullying. In contrast to their 2008 study, Hinduja and Patchin (2009) investigated the issue of gender and discovered that because cyberbullying is primarily text-based so girls are more likely to cyberbully and be cyberbullied. According to a Pew Internet and American Life Project survey 2006 on cyberbullying, girls were more likely than boys to say they had been bullied online; 38% girls and 26% of online boys reported being bullied. In addition, girls aged 15 to 17 are the most likely to have been cyberbullied, with 41% of those in this age group reporting having been cyberbullied, compared to 34% of girls aged 12 to 14 (Lenhart, 2007). Furthermore, it was claimed that females may prefer to bully others via electronic communication means such as chat rooms and e-mail (Nelson, 2003; Thorp, 2004).

Hinduja and Patchin (2008) investigated why girls are more likely than males to engage in and experience cyberbullying. They discovered that because females are more verbal and cyberbullying is text oriented so females are more likely to engage in cyberbullying. Females are also more likely to bully in emotional and psychological ways, such as spreading rumours and gossiping, which is more akin to cyberbullying. Females are less confrontational in person, thus the anonymity of the online community may appeal to them more. Females are often culturally and socially confined when it comes to employing aggressiveness or physical violence, but they are not constrained while they are online- Hinduja and Patchin. Females are more likely to demand social support, and in order to obtain it, they frequently team together with other females. The online community is simple and rapid ways to gang up on other women and have a large number of people see it, contributing to the humiliation (Hinduja & Patchin, 2008).

The differences between girls bullying and boys bullying were addressed in the documentary *It's a girl's world*. Boys were more likely to employ physical bullying, but girls were more likely to disseminate rumours, exclude other girls from their social cliques, and use mocking or name calling. Female bullies are often manipulative, aggressive, and nasty, and use fear to manipulate their victims (Glazier, 2003).

PREVENTION OF CYBERBULLYING

Many professional groups, such as educators, teachers, and healthcare professionals, are aware of the negative effects of cyberbullying on health and well-being. These professionals, as well as hands-on experts, voice their concern and view that it is critical to fight cyberbullying and assist victims on the internet. There are numerous websites containing cyberbullying suggestions, advice, and recommendations, as well as a plethora of preventative and intervention programmes for both traditional and cyberbullying.

According to Willard (2006), schools, parents, and students can all play a role in preventing cyberbullying and intervening when it occurs. Increased awareness of cyberbullying problems; equipping educators, students, parents, and community members with knowledge of how to prevent and respond to cyberbullying; providing warnings to cyberbullies and their parents about the harmful consequences; and effective supervision and monitoring of online activities are all elements of Willard's recommendations for schools. Willard further mentioned that developing a plan of action to do effective threat analysis for any complaints of cyberbullying that raises worries about suicide or violence is crucial (Willard, 2006).

Willard recommended eight primary steps for dealing with cyberbullying. Participatory planning, assessment, guaranteeing an effective anti-bullying programme, and updating policies and procedures linked to the Internet and mobile communication devices are among them. Additionally, it is vital to conduct district-wide professional development, include parents in cyberbullying prevention and detection, educate students about cyberbullying and what to do about it, and assess the cyberbullying prevention and intervention plan on a regular basis to determine its effectiveness (Willard, 2006).

Kanayama and Kurihara (2018) from Japan reported on a variety of preventative measures implemented at one university to create a comprehensive multi-level support system for students. Following mandatory mental health screening for all new students, a personalised support plan is implemented, and a close working partnership with medical institutions is developed as needed. A peer support system was also created to help pupils acquire a sense of belonging. Two courses targeted at combating cyberbullying were created as part of the curriculum: "mobile phones and the law" (a required first-year course) and "cyber police" (connected to a branch of the police designated to address cyber-crimes).

Fryer (2006) outlined ten steps for dealing with cyberbullying in schools in his article Addressing Cyberbullying in Schools. Proactive collaboration, sponsorship of awareness events, hot spot surveys, anonymous drop boxes, inclusion of cyberbullying in the school district's computer use policy, and advance action team planning are among the steps. Encourage class meetings, put network security limits in place, and foster a culture of responsibility and accountability. It is proposed that schools work together with teachers, administrators, the educational community, and students to prevent high-profile incidents of bullying and cyberbullying.

There are a handful of cyberbullying prevention programmes available, including the Cyber Smart! Cyberbullying Package, which is available for free to schools across the country and is designed to be integrated into current curricula by classroom teachers. According to the CyberSmart! Education Company (2009), in collaboration with the National School Boards Association's (NBSA) Technology Leadership Network and the Character Education Partnership (CEP), the National Association of School Psychologists (NASP), and the National Cyber Security Alliance, Cyber Smart! launched the nation's first research-based cyberbullying prevention curriculum. CyberSmart! developed their Cyberbullying Package by "considering all current research findings and employing best practises from the disciplines of cyber security, school violence prevention, and character education to influence behavioural change" (CyberSmart! Education Company, 2009).

The CyberSmart! Cyberbullying Package allows students to have an open debate about cyberbullying and to develop a long-term cyberbullying prevention campaign that includes the entire school community. The Cyberbullying Package aims to assist students in developing critical thinking and decision-making abilities, as well as the ability to describe problems and situations on their own. The package also discusses research that indicates that most victims do not report online harassment to adults, the essential role of the bystander, and the ineffectiveness of "being harsh" on bullies.

One of the anti-cyberbullying programs is Netsmartz which was launched in partnership with Compaq, the Boys & Girls Clubs of America (B&GCA) and the National Center for Missing & Exploited Children (NCMEC). The Netsmartz Workshop was created in 2001 with the goal of reaching over 3.3

million adolescents serviced annually by the Boys & Girls Clubs of America to see if it was beneficial. Netsmartz Workshop includes engaging lessons and activities that teach children of all ages how to use the Internet properly and be safe while using it. Vice President Joseph R. Biden, who helped obtain financing for the Netsmartz programme, has applauded it (2001, Compaq).

Another programme is i-SAFE, which, in collaboration with i-LEARN, provides free Internet safety lessons. I-LEARN was previously only available in a classroom setting, but it is now open to the general public and divided into age categories. The initiative gives teachers and parents information that they may share with others to help them learn more about how to use the Internet safely and responsibly. The i-SAFE programme is made up of six online education streaming video courses that cover a variety of topics related to the online community and the risks that come with it. Personal safety, cyber-community issues, cyber-predator detection, cyber-security, intellectual property, and community outreach are among the modules covered. After seeing all modules, students who participate in the i-SAFE programme can become certified i-MENTORS. Cyberbullying, cyber-security, and cyber-predators are all issues that can be addressed by an i-MENTOR (Carlson, 2006).

FUTURE RESEARCH DIRECTIONS

More research is needed in the area of cyberbullying, particularly the effectiveness of proposed prevention and intervention strategies. In addition, it's important to keep tracking the prevalence of cyberbullying. Creating and using a student survey regarding cyberbullying for middle and high school students could help keep track of the incidence. Quantitative research should be carried out to see if there is a higher prevalence of cyberbullying based on demographic data such as race, language, socioeconomic status, and gender. Conducting a mixed-methods study can help researchers better understand cyberbullying among students with special needs and its impact on their academic progress, which the researcher discovered is uncommon in the literature.

CONCLUSION

To sum up, The Internet and mobile technology have clearly become an integral element of daily life. Young adults are increasingly linked to the Internet and communicating online than ever before, putting them at greater risk of experiencing a negative cyber incident. As children spend more time using technology that keeps them linked to people at all hours of the day, cyberbullying is becoming increasingly common. Cyberbullies communicate with their victims in a variety of ways, including instant messaging on the Internet, social networking websites, text messaging, and phone calls to cell phones. Harassment, impersonation, and cyberstalking are all examples of cyberbullying. It has been discovered that there are disparities between males and females in terms of not only the prevalence of cyberbullying, but also the ways in which males and females cyberbully. Cyberbullying, like bullying, is serious problems that can make the victim feel insecure and self-conscious, as well as increase the risk of suicide.

Students, administrators, parents, and members of the community should all be aware of and taught against cyberbullying. Victims of cyberbullying must understand how to report cyberbullying to adults, how to document emails, instant messages, or text messages received from a Cyberbully, and how to work with their parents and administrators to end the bullying. Parents should be aware that keeping an eye on their children's online activities and communicating with them about cyberbullying can all help to reduce cyberbullying in the home. School districts should create an anti-cyberbullying programme to promote awareness of the issue, enforce computer policies, and impose consequences for cyberbullies. Drop boxes may be installed throughout the school for students to anonymously report cyberbullying incidents that they have witnessed or participated in. Many professional groups, such as educators, teachers, and healthcare personnel, are well aware of the negative health and well-being consequences of cyberbullying encounters. These specialists, as well as hands-on experts, express their concern and believe that combating cyberbullying and assisting victims on the internet is vital. There are various websites with cyberbullying tips, guidance, and recommendations, as well as a plethora of traditional and cyberbullying prevention and intervention programmes.

REFERENCES

Anderson, Bresnahan, & Musatics. (2014). *Cyberpsychology, behavior and Social networking Combating weight-based cyberbullying on Facebook with the dissenter effect*. Academic Press.

Barlett, C. P. (2015). Anonymously hurting others online: The effect of anonymity on cyberbullying frequency. *Psychology of Popular Media Culture*, *4*(2), 70–79. doi:10.1037/a0034335

Bauman, S. (2009). Cyberbullying in a rural intermediate school: An exploratory study. *The Journal of Early Adolescence*, *10*(10), 1–31.

Beale, A. V., & Hall, K. R. (2007, September/October). Cyberbullying: What school administrators (and parents) can do. *The Clearing House: A Journal of Educational Strategies, Issues and Ideas*, *81*(1), 8–12. doi:10.3200/TCHS.81.1.8-12

Belsey, B. (2004). *What is cyberbullying?* Retrieved from: www.bullying.org/external/documents/ACF6F8.pdf

Beren, T., & Li, Q. (2007). The relationship between cyberbullying and school bullying. *Journal of Student Wellbeing*, *1*(2), 15–33.

Black, S., Weinles, D., & Washington, E. (2010). Victim strategies to stop bullying. *Youth Violence and Juvenile Justice*, *8*(2), 138–147. doi:10.1177/1541204009349401

Borg, M. G. (1999). The extent and nature of bullying among primary and secondary schoolchildren. *Educational Research*, *41*(2), 137–153. doi:10.1080/0013188990410202

Boulton, M., & Underwood, K. (1992). Bully/victim problems among middle school children. *The British Journal of Educational Psychology*, *62*(1), 73–87. doi:10.1111/j.2044-8279.1992.tb01000.x PMID:1558813

Brown, K., Jackson, M., & Cassidy, W. (2006). Cyber-bullying: Developing Policy to Direct Responses the are Equitable and effective in Addressing this Special Form of Bullying. *Canadian Journal of Educational Administration and Policy*, 57.

Carlson, E. (2006). *i-SAFE and Microsoft bring net safety to schools and parents*. i-SAFE Media. Retrieved November 22,2009, from http://www.isafe.org/imgs/pdf/outreach-press/iSAFE_MS YR-02-06.pdf

Cassidy, W., Jackson, M., & Brown, K. N. (2009). Students' experiences with cyber-bullying: Sticks and stones can break my bones, but how can pixels hurt me? *School Psychology International, 30*(4), 383–402. doi:10.1177/0143034309106948

Charach, A., Pepler, D. & Ziegler, S. (1995). *Bullying at school: a Canadian perspective*. Education Canada.

Cross, E.-J., Piggin, R., & Douglas, T. (2012). *Virtual Violence: Progress and Challenge in the Fight Against Cyberbullying*. Beat Bullying.

CyberSmart! Education Company. (2009). *CyberSmart! Cyberbullying awareness curriculum*. Retrieved April 1, 2009, from: www.nasponline.org/resources/cyberbullying/index.aspx

Dehue, F., Bolman, C., & Vollink, T. (2008). Cyberbullying: Youngsters' Experiences and Parental Perception. *CyberPsychology and Behavior, 11*(2), 217-223.

Feinberg, T., & Robey, N. (2009). Cyberbullying: School leaders cannot ignore cyberbullying but rather must understand its legal and psychological ramifications. *Education Digest, 74*(7), 26–31.

Finkelhor, D., Mitchell, K. J., & Wolak, J. (2000). *Online victimization: A report on the nation's youth*. National Center for Missing and Exploited Children.

Frost, L. (1991). A primary school approach: What can be done about the bully? In *Bullying: A practical guide to coping for schools*. Longman.

Fryer, W. A. (2006, November 20). Addressing cyberbullying in schools. *The TechEdge: The Journal of the Texas Computer Education Association*. Retrieved March 15, 2009, from: www.wtvi.comlteks/06 _ 07 _articles/cyberbullying.html

Hawker, D. S., & Boulton, M. J. (2000). Twenty years' research on peer victimization and psychosocial maladjustment: A meta-analytic review of cross-sectional studies. *Journal of Child Psychology and Psychiatry, and Allied Disciplines, 41*(4), 441–455. doi:10.1111/1469-7610.00629 PMID:10836674

Heirman, W., & Walrave, M. (2008). Assessing Concerns and Issues about the Mediation of Technology in Cyberbullying. *Cyberpsychology (Brno), 2*(2).

Hinduja, S., & Patchin, J. W. (2007). Offline consequences of online victimization: School violence and delinquency. *Journal of School Violence, 6*(3), 89–112. doi:10.1300/J202v06n03_06

Hinduja, S., & Patchin, J. W. (2008). Cyberbullying: An exploratory analysis of factors related to offending and victimization. *Deviant Behavior, 29*(2), 129–156. doi:10.1080/01639620701457816

Hinduja, S., & Patchin, J. W. (2009). *Bullying beyond the schoolyard: Preventing and responding to cyberbullying*. Sage Publications: Corwin Press.

Huang, Y. Y., & Chou, C. (2010). An analysis of multiple factors of cyberbullying among junior high school students in Taiwan. *Computers in Human Behavior, 26*(6), 1581–1590. doi:10.1016/j.chb.2010.06.005

Juvonen, J., & Gross, E. F. (2008). Extending the School Grounds? – Bullying Experiences in Cyberspace. *The Journal of School Health, 78*(9), 496–505. doi:10.1111/j.1746-1561.2008.00335.x PMID:18786042

Kanayama, K., & Kurihara, S. (2018). Preventive measures against cyberbullying at a university in Japan. In *Cyberbullying at university in international contexts* (pp. 168–172). Routledge. doi:10.4324/9781315189406-14

Kowalski, R. M., & Limber, S. P. (2007). Electronic bullying among middle school students. *The Journal of Adolescent Health, 41*(6), 22–30. doi:10.1016/j.jadohealth.2007.08.017 PMID:18047942

Li, Q., Smith, P. K., & Cross, D. (2012). Research into cyberbullying. *Cyberbullying in the global playground: Research from international perspectives, 1*.

Marczak, M., & Coyne, I. (2015). A focus on online bullying. In A. Attrill (Ed.), *Cyberpsychology*. Oxford, UK: Oxford University Press. https://www.merriam-webster.com/

Mishna, F., & Alaggia, R. (2005). Weighing the risks: A child's decision to disclose peer victimization. *Children & Schools, 27*(4), 217–226. doi:10.1093/cs/27.4.217

Mishna, F., Cook, C., Gadalla, T., Daciuk, J., & Solomon, S. (2010). Cyber Bullying Behaviours Among Middle and High School Students. *The American Journal of Orthopsychiatry, 80*(3), 362–374. doi:10.1111/j.1939-0025.2010.01040.x PMID:20636942

Nansel, T. R., Overpeck, M., & Pilla, R. S. (2001). Bullying behaviours among US youth: Prevalence and association with psychosocial adjustment. *Journal of the American Medical Association, 285*(16), 2094–2100. doi:10.1001/jama.285.16.2094 PMID:11311098

Natvig, G. K., Albrektsen, G., & Qvarnstrøm, U. (2001). School-related stress experience as a risk factor for bullying behavior. *Journal of Youth and Adolescence, 30*(5), 561–575. doi:10.1023/A:1010448604838

Naylor, P., & Cowie, H. (1999). The effectiveness of peer support systems in challenging school bullying: The perspectives and experiences of teachers and pupils. *Journal of Adolescence, 22*(4), 467–479. doi:10.1006/jado.1999.0241 PMID:10469511

Nelson, M. (2003). *School bullies going high tech*. Retrieved from http://www. canoe.ca/NewsStand/LondonFreePress/News/2003/09/02/174030.html

Nishina, A., & Juvonen, J. (2005). Daily reports of witnessing and experiencing peer harassment in middle school. *Child Development, 76*(2), 435–450. doi:10.1111/j.1467-8624.2005.00855.x PMID:15784092

Palfrey, J., Boyd, D., & Sacco, D. (2008). *Enhancing Child Safety and Online Technologies: Final Report of the Internet Safety Technical task Force on the MultiState Working Group on Social Networking of Sate attorneys General of the United States*. Harvard University: Berkman Center for Internet and Society.

Patchin, J. W., & Hinduja, S. (2015). Measuring cyberbullying: Implications for research. *Aggression and Violent Behavior, 23*, 69–74. doi:10.1016/j.avb.2015.05.013

Petrosino, A., Guckenburg, S., DeVoe, J., & Hanson, T. (2010). What characteristics of bullying, bullying victims, and schools are associated with increased reporting of bullying to school officials? Issues & Answers Report, REL 2010, No. 092, US Department of Education, Institute of Education Sciences, National Center for Education Evaluation and Regional Assistance, Regional Educational Laboratory Northeast and Islands, Washington, DC. doi:10.1037/e598622011-001

Pokin, S. (2007, November 13). Megan Meier story. *The St. Charles Journal.*

Raskauskas, J., & Stoltz, A. D. (2007). Involvement in traditional and electronic bullying among adolescents. *Developmental Psychology*, *43*(3), 564–575. doi:10.1037/0012-1649.43.3.564 PMID:17484571

Rigby, K. (2003). Consequences of bullying in schools. *Canadian Journal of Psychiatry*, *48*(9), 583–590. doi:10.1177/070674370304800904 PMID:14631878

Rivers, I., & Noret, N. (2009). 'I h8 u': findings from a five-year study of text and email bullying. *British Educational Research Journal*, *36*(4), 643–671. doi:10.1080/01411920903071918

Roland, E. (2002). Aggression, depression, and bullying others. *Aggressive Behavior: Official Journal of the International Society for Research on Aggression*, *28*(3), 198–206. doi:10.1002/ab.90022

Seals, D., & Young, J. (2003). Bullying and victimization: Prevalence and relationship to gender, grade level, ethnicity, self-esteem, and depression. *Adolescence*, *38*(152). PMID:15053498

Smith, P. K., Madhavi, J., Carvalho, M., Fisher, S., Russell, S., & Tippett, N. (2008). Cyberbullying: Its nature and impact in secondary school pupils. *Journal of Child Psychiatry*, *49*(4), 376–385.

Steinhauer, J. (2008, November 27). Verdict in MySpace suicide case. *The New York Times.*

Tippett, N., Houlston, C., & Smith, P. K. (2010). *Prevention and response to identity-based bullying among local authorities in England, Scotland and Wales.* https://www.equalityhumanrights.com/uploaded_files/research/64_identity_based_bull ying.pdf

van der Wal, M. F., de Wit, C. A. M., & Hirasing, R. A. (2003). Psychosocial health among young victims and offenders of direct and indirect bullying. *Pediatrics*, *111*(6), 1312–1317. doi:10.1542/peds.111.6.1312 PMID:12777546

Vandebosch, H., & Cleemput Van, K. (2008). Defining Cyberbullying: A Qualitative Research into the Perceptions of Youngsters. *Cyberpsychology & Behavior*, *11*(4), 499–503. doi:10.1089/cpb.2007.0042 PMID:18721100

Vandebosch, H., & Van Cleemput, K. (2009). Cyberbullying among youngsters: Profiles of bullies and victims. *New Media & Society*, *11*(8), 1349–1371. doi:10.1177/1461444809341263

Willard, N. (2004a). *An educator's guide to cyberbullying and cyberthreats.* Retrieved from http://cyberbully.org/docs/cbcteducator.pdf

Willard, N. (2004b). *Educator's guide to cyberbullying: Addressing the harm caused by online social cruelty.* Retrieved from https://www.asdk12.org/MiddleLink/ AVB/bully_topics/EducatorsGuide_Cyberbullying.pdf

Willard, N. B. (2007, March). *Cyberbullying legislation and school policies: Where are the boundaries of the "schoolhouse gate" in the new virtual world?* Center for Safe and Responsible use of the Internet. Retrieved from: http://csiru.org

Willard, N. E. (2006). *Educators guide to cyberbullying: Addressing the harm caused by online social cruelty.* Retrieved April 4, 2009, from: www.asdkI2.orglMiddleLinklAVBlbully_topics/ Educators Guide_Cyberbullying.pdf

Willard, N. E. (2006). *Educators guide to cyberbullying: Addressing the harm caused by online social cruelty.* Retrieved from: www.asdkI2.orglMiddleLinklAVBlbully_topics/ Educators Guide _ Cyberbullying.pdf

Ybarra, M. L., & Mitchell, K. J. (2008). How risky are social networking sites? A comparison of places online where youth sexual solicitation and harassment occurs. *Pediatrics, 121*(2), 350–357. doi:10.1542/peds.2007-0693 PMID:18227194

ADDITIONAL READING

Connolly, J., Hussey, P., & Connolly, R. (2014). Technology-enabled bullying and adolescent resistance to report: The need to examine causal factors. *Interactive Technology and Smart Education, 11*(2), 86–98. doi:10.1108/ITSE-04-2014-0003

Doumas, D. M., & Midgett, A. (2020). Witnessing cyberbullying and internalizing symptoms among middle school students. *European Journal of Investigation in Health, Psychology and Education, 10*(4), 957–966. doi:10.3390/ejihpe10040068 PMID:34542429

Raza Talpur, M. A., Touseef, T., Ahmed Jilanee, S. D., Shabu, M. M., & Khan, A. (2018). Effects of Cyber Bullying on Teenagers; a short review of Literature. *Jr Neurology Psy and Brain Res.*

Rodríguez-Álvarez, J. M., Yubero, S., Navarro, R., & Larrañaga, E. (2021). Relationship between socio-emotional competencies and the overlap of bullying and cyberbullying behaviors in primary school students. *European Journal of Investigation in Health, Psychology and Education, 11*(3), 686–696. doi:10.3390/ejihpe11030049 PMID:34563062

Saladino, V., Eleuteri, S., Verrastro, V., & Petruccelli, F. (2020). Perception of cyberbullying in adolescence: A brief evaluation among Italian students. *Frontiers in Psychology, 11*, 3112. doi:10.3389/fpsyg.2020.607225 PMID:33324303

KEY TERMS AND DEFINITIONS

Cyberbullying: The use of information and communication technologies to encourage deliberate, recurrent, and aggressive behaviour by a person or group with the intent to damage others **Bullycide-** Bullying which results in the victim's suicide.

Cyberstalking: Harassment that include threats of harm or is highly intimidating.

Denigration (Put-Downs): Sending or posting harmful, untrue, or cruel statements about a person to other people.

Exclusion: Actions that specifically and intentionally exclude a person from an online group.

Flaming: Sending angry, rude, vulgar messages directed at a person or persons privately or to an online group.

Harassment: Devious acts or unwanted actions of an individual or group, including threats, demands, and blackmail.

Instant Messaging: Software allowing users to chat online in "real time" from their computers or via wireless devices.

Masquerade: Pretending to be someone else and sending or posting that makes that person look bad or places that person in potential danger.

Outing and Trickery: Sending or posting material about a person that contains sensitive, private, or embarrassing information, including forwarding private messages or images. Engaging in tricks to solicit embarrassing information that is then made public.

Target: A person or object selected as the focus of a specific verbal or physical attack.

Text Messaging: The use of cell phone keypads to type short messages that can be instantly sent to other cell phone users.

Victim: A person attacked by another person, resulting in an unpleasant event.

Chapter 28
What Is Cyberbullying?

Rabia Şeyma Gün
https://orcid.org/0000-0001-5744-6917
Yalova University, Turkey

Gülümser Gültekin Akduman
Gazi University, Turkey

ABSTRACT

Cyberbullying, which internet users have faced especially in recent years, is a new type of bullying that has emerged with the widespread use of the internet. It is expressed as bullying using technological platforms with internet access. It includes repetitive behaviors aimed at intimidating, angering, or embarrassing target individuals. Since the number of victims of cyberbullying is increasing day by day, it is an important social problem that should be detected early, and precautions should be taken with protective strategies. In this chapter, there is information about cyberbullying, cyberbullying behaviors, cyberbullying tools, types of cyberbullying, the frequency of cyberbullying, the causes of cyberbullying, the roles of cyberbullying, the effects of cyberbullying, what to do when faced with cyberbullying, and precautions to be taken.

INTRODUCTION

With the rapid developments in the internet and technology, social media tools and internet applications have become a part of our lives. The unconscious use of these tools and applications brings with it many unknown, unforeseen, difficult to perceive dangers for individual and social life. One of these dangers is cyberbullying. Cyber bullying, which internet users have faced especially in recent years, is a new type of bullying that has emerged with the spread of the internet. It is expressed as bullying using technological platforms with internet access. It includes repetitive behaviors aimed at intimidating, angering or embarrassing target individuals. Since the number of victims of cyberbullying is increasing day by day, it is an important social problem that needs to be detected early and precautions should be taken with protective strategies. In this chapter, information on cyberbullying, cyberbullying behaviors, cyberbullying tools, types of cyberbullying, the frequency of cyberbullying, the causes of cyberbullying,

DOI: 10.4018/978-1-6684-5426-8.ch028

the roles of cyberbullying, the effects of cyberbullying, what to do when faced with cyberbullying and the precautions that can be taken against cyberbullying are given.

CYBERBULLYING

Internet and communication technologies, which continue to develop and become widespread at full speed today, have changed the social attitudes and behaviors of individuals (Li, Cross, & Smith, 2012). Changes have brought many innovations to individuals in accessing, storing and sharing information. One of these innovations is the transfer of communication between individuals to social networks, which are virtual environments. In this way, it makes it possible for individuals to communicate with each other very quickly, easily and in a different way, regardless of time and place (Bulunmaz, 2015). This situation brings with it some new dangers that we may encounter in real life. One of these dangers is cyberbullying. (Ekinci & Kayapalı Yıldırım, 2020; Gámez-Guadix, Orue, Smith & Calvete, 2013). Cyberbullying is a type of bullying that takes place using digital technologies. It is also expressed as bullying using technological platforms with internet access. The absence of barriers between people on technological platforms makes it possible for users to behave cruelly towards each other (Bulunmaz, 2015).

In cyberbullying, deliberate and repetitive harming the victim through electronic text comes to the fore (Patchin & Hinduja, 2006). It can be defined as the exposure of people to bullying or bullying practices through image and video broadcasts, e-mails, chat rooms, text messages, social media environments such as YouTube, Facebook, Instagram, Twitter, or electronic communication devices such as mobile phones (Ekinci & Kayapalı Yıldırım, 2020). The concept of cyberbullying was first used by Canadian pedagogue Bill Belsey in 2004. According to Belsey, "Cyberbullying is the use of information and communication technologies to support the deliberate, repeated and hostile behavior of an individual or group that aims to harm others" (Belsey, 2005). According to Willard, "it is a way of being cruel to others by sending or encouraging others to send harmful materials, engaging in other forms of social aggression using the internet or other digital technologies" (Willard, 2007). Kowalski and Limber (2007) define cyberbullying as "bullying via e-mail and instant messaging, in a chat room, on a website or via a text message sent to a mobile phone"; Hinduja and Patchin (2008) define cyberbullying as "intentional and repeated harm through the use of electronic devices such as computers and mobile phones". According to Smith et al. (2008) it is "an aggressive, deliberate act by a group or individual against a victim who cannot easily defend himself, using electronic forms of communication, repeatedly and over time". "Intentionally repetitive acts with the aim of threatening, harassing, embarrassing others through electronic means or devices" (Chun, Lee, Kim & Lee, 2020). "Cyberbullying is deliberate, cruel and repeated behavior among peers through electronic media" (Olweus, 2012). According to Campbell (2005), cyberbullying is also defined as "individuals torment and harm others by using various forms of technology such as e-mail, instant messages, chat rooms, and websites". When we look at the literature, it is seen that there are close and inclusive definitions of cyberbullying. Based on all these definitions, cyberbullying is the deliberate act of harming by using information communication technologies (ICT).

Cyberbullying Behaviors

It is possible to characterize malicious behaviors that can harm others in the digital environment as cyberbullying behavior. With the development of digital technology day by day, the fact that an unlimited number of people can be reached in the electronic environment increases the rates of cyberbullying (Selkie, Kota, & Moreno, 2016). With the decrease in the age of use of technological devices such as computers, phones, tablets, and the increase in the use of these devices, individuals may encounter cyberbullying behaviors at any time and become victims of cyberbullying. These behaviors include taking and sharing images of individuals without their consent, posting them by manipulating their photos, using their photos and posts to make fun of the individual, threatening to share some of their images or information, humiliating, mocking, insulting, threats, hatred through e-mail or mobile phone messages, sending messages containing sexual harassment or violence, shooting and posting videos containing fights and violence, sharing someone's personal information through social media without their knowledge and consent, spreading gossip about someone on social networks, creating defamatory and humiliating digital platforms about the individual, on behalf of another individual, opening a fake account and impersonating him, influencing common acquaintances, allowing them to delete and block the targeted individual from their friend lists, that is, to exclude them socially, to constantly make negative comments on their posts on social networks, to remove them from all social media accounts. It is possible to diversify the behaviors such as following persistently, sending messages to private message boxes, stealing the social media account and disclosing the information therein. In the research, it was determined that while girls encounter cyberbullying behaviors via e-mail, internet messages and text messages, boys encounter cyberbullying behaviors through online games (Brandtzag et al., 2009; Goebert et al., 2011).

Cyberbullying Tools

The means by which cyberbullying occurs is as important as cyberbullying behaviors in terms of intervention. Cyberbullying occurs by using mobile phones and computers, instant messaging, e-mail, text messages, forums and social networking sites (Kowalski, Limber & Agatston, 2012; Swartz, 2009). Instant messaging enables the individual to communicate simultaneously with the people on the friendship list in their social media accounts via the internet (Willard, 2007). The cyberbully uses instant messaging to send threatening and humiliating messages to the victim. In addition, cyberbullies can use instant messaging to create fake user images that allow them to hide their real identities, to exclude individuals by blocking them, or to share information about the private lives of others with large numbers of people (Kowalski, Limber & Agatston, 2008; Patchin & Hinduja, 2006). E-mail is a type of asynchronous communication that allows messages containing visual, verbal and/or audio materials to be sent to one or more recipients (Kowalski, Limber & Agatston, 2008; Willard, 2007). Text message sending services are provided by GSM operators and can be sent from a mobile phone to a computer as well as from a computer to a mobile phone (Willard, 2007). Forums are asynchronous communication environments where people interested in a specific subject area can discuss these issues among themselves, exchange ideas, and offer solutions to each other's problems. (Odabaşı, Kabakçı & Çoklar, 2007). Cyberbullies can mock the opinions of other individuals, humiliate them, threaten them, and damage their dignity through forums (Peker, 2013). Social networking sites are defined as applications where people create an account, create a profile about themselves, and communicate with people they know and do not know (Hinduja & Patchin, 2015). Examples of widely used social networking sites around the world are Facebook, Instagram and Twitter. These practices allow the cyberbully to hide his identity, create multiple accounts and approach the victim as if he were a different person (Rogers, 2010).

Types of Cyberbullying

Arıcak (2015) stated that there are two types of cyberbullying: technical-based electronic cyberbullying and communication-based cyberbullying. Technical-based electronic bullying is the actions taken by a single person or group, which occur due to technical situations such as the seizure of the websites, passwords, and e-mails of individuals or institutions and that can render the system out of use. Electronic communication bullying, on the other hand, is a psychological act that affects more emotions such as insulting people, making gossip, spreading images or videos without consent, mocking people through the use of information and communication technologies.

Willard (2007), on the other hand, discussed the types of cyberbullying in 7 groups:

1. **Humiliation:** It consists of untrue, humiliating and embarrassing, hurtful, cruel speech about the victim.
2. **Impersonation:** It is the conduct of damaging and embarrassing interventions such as sending inappropriate messages to others by hijacking an individual's account.
3. **Sharing Private Information:** It is mediating the dissemination of private conversations between individuals or sharing private images with others in the virtual environment.
4. **Entrapment:** It is deceiving an individual into revealing secrets and embarrassing information about himself, and then sharing them over the internet and victimizing them in this way.
5. **Exclusion:** It is the prevention/exclusion or restriction of an unwanted individual by a certain group from participating in activities in virtual environments.
6. **Virtual Tracking:** Sending repeated threats and intimidating messages to the targeted individual.
7. **Cyber Harassment:** It is the sending of repeated messages to the target people in an offensive manner.

As a result of the developments in the field of information and communication technologies, it is noteworthy that new concepts related to the types of cyberbullying have been added. These are sexting, griefing and trolling. Sexting, that is, obscene photo sharing online, is the sharing of sexually explicit photos in the virtual environment without the consent of the individual. Griefing is defined as online spoilsport, that is, intentional harassment of other players in online games. The aim of the individual who is a spoilsport online is to constantly disturb other players during the game, rather than to play or win the game (Kowalski, Limber, & Agatson, 2008). Trolling, on the other hand, means online provocation, sending insulting and provoking messages, diverting the individual from the purpose of the group or the focus of the discussion in the environment (Herring et al., 2002).

Frequency of Cyberbullying

In the 2020 data of the European Children Online Project (EU Kids Online), it was determined that the rate of cyberbullying that caused children in European countries to be upset and disturbed at least once in the last year was between 7-45% (Smahel et al., 2020). In Turkey data of the same project, between 2010 and 2015, it is seen that the age of children's first internet access decreased, the frequency of internet access and personal information shared on the internet increased, and the actions taken on the internet changed. Accordingly, in 2010, children frequently use the internet for studying and doing homework, and in 2015, they use the internet for socialization purposes such as accessing social media accounts, entering chat rooms, watching movies and listening to music. It has been reported that this change in internet use increases the risks children face over the internet and the rate of children who receive sexual messages or photographs has increased over the years (O'Neill, Livingstone & McLaughlin, 2011).

Causes of Cyberbullying

Determining the causes of cyber bullying and cyber victimization is very important in terms of developing solutions. One of the reasons for cyberbullying is that individuals who engage in cyberbullying behavior believe that they will not be caught because they can easily hide their identities in virtual environments (Willard, 2007). External factors such as family and individual characteristics, mass media and social environment are of great importance in the emergence and formation of cyberbullying (Alper, 2008). Cyberbullying is caused by reasons such as seeking success in the virtual environment, problems in or around the family, punishing others, being popular, and lack of self-confidence (Arıcak, 2015). One of the reasons for cyberbullying is family reasons. The attitudes and behaviors exhibited by the families directly affect the child. Children who grow up in a family environment devoid of love, who are exposed to physical violence by their parents and whose basic needs are not met, display bullying behaviors in virtual environments in the following years (Sönmezay, 2010). People who do not have healthy communication in the family turn to the internet and make friends with people they do not know in order to overcome this existing deficiency and establish new social relations (Eroğlu, 2011). According to the research conducted by Ybarra and Mitchell (2004), it was determined that adolescents and young people who have weak emotional bonds with their parents increase their use of cyberbullying. Among the causes of cyberbullying, individual characteristics are also of great importance. It has been determined that those who have weak social communication, substance and alcohol use, an aggressive and dominant character structure, and have difficulties in obeying the rules engage in cyber bullying behavior (Craig & & Pepler, 2003). At the same time, lack of empathy is among the causes of cyberbullying (Ybarra & Mitchell, 2004). Individuals who engage in cyberbullying are not aware of how hurtful they can be and how great the emotional discomfort they experience can be. Because of this lack of empathy, they do not have thoughts of ending their behavior (Willard, 2007; Fawzi, 2009). Among the causes of cyberbullying behaviors, motives such as taking revenge, having fun or satisfying their ego play an important role (Sharif, 2006). In addition, there is a linear relationship between the length of time an individual spends on the Internet and exposure to cyberbullying, and they have a higher risk of being exposed to cyberbullying compared to individuals who use the Internet less (Hinduja & Patchin, 2005). It has also been determined that the increase in the time children spend in virtual environments increases the probability of encountering cyberbullying (Ybarra & Mitchell, 2004). Mass media are also among the causes of cyberbullying. Developments in the field of technology have made it easier for children, adolescents and young people to access videos and pictures containing negative behaviors and cyberbullying without being controlled on computers, mobile phones and the internet. These videos and movies containing bullying and violence cause children to become desensitized to bullying and even internalize it (Sönmezay, 2010). The environment of the child in the school and neighbourhood environment and the socioeconomic level of this environment are seen as one of the reasons that push him to bullying in the real and cyber world (Genç & Aksu, 2010).

Cyberbullying Roles

In virtual environments, individuals probably correspond to cyberbullying in some way. When the literature is examined, it is seen that many different cyberbullying roles are defined, but the most prominent and most accepted one of these roles is the cyberbully and cyber victim role. Cyberbully is used to describe an individual who uses technology to carry out actions that will disturb, threaten or limit the freedom of the targeted individual. Cyberbullying disturbs or puts the targeted individuals in a difficult situation (Seçkin, 2017). Aggression (Ybarra & Mitchell, 2007), intense anger (Pornari & Wood, 2009), inability to communicate with parents, low academic success, high tendency to use substances, development in computer use knowledge and skills, high sense of revenge, low ability to empathize in cyberbullies (Özdemir, 2015), it is noteworthy that they often violate the rules and behave hostile towards other people around them, the intensity of showing behavioral problems and negative attitudes towards school (Arıcak, 2009).

Another side of the cyberbullying behavior is the cyber victim, who is used to characterize the individuals exposed to the act of bullying. A cyber victim is a person who is exposed to cyberbullying behaviors and feels uncomfortable with this behavior, is threatened, cannot respond to these behaviors and cannot defend oneself (Seçkin, 2017). Cyber victims experience this discomfort and threatening situation through cyberbullying channels and their freedom is restricted. According to a study carried out by him, it is seen that individuals in the role of cyber victims have extreme personality traits, are defined as too introverted or too extroverted, attention-grabbing and active. While introverts are chosen as victims because they are easy targets as they are in their physical environment, extroverts are chosen as victims in cyberspace in order to avenge physical jealousy due to their popularity (Topçu, Yıldırım, & Erdur Baker, 2012). In addition, cyberbullies are those who have low self-esteem and are generally unhappy, unable to interact and communicate with their social environment in a healthy way, have problems in adapting to the social environment, have emotional problems, low academic achievement, susceptibility to substance use or addiction. It has been stated that they are weak in using technological devices or social media platforms in general (Yaman, Eroğlu, & Peker, 2011).

Effects of Cyberbullying

Being exposed to cyberbullying causes intense anxiety, depression, loneliness, unhappiness, increased symptoms of physical illness, high levels of stress, social adaptation and self-confidence problems, which negatively affect the physical and psychological development of individuals. In cyberbullying, the development of not only the cyber victims but also the cyberbullies is negatively affected (Hinduja & Patchin, 2008). The effects of cyberbullying include depression, eating and drinking disorders, psychosomatic or chronic diseases, loafing at school or workplace, and loss of self-confidence (Mason, 2008). It has been concluded that adolescents exposed to cyberbullying show more depressive symptoms (Kowalski & Limber, 2013; Gámez-Guadix et al., 2013), excessive substance and alcohol consumption (Ybarra & Mitchell, 2007) and feel anger, stress, sadness, disappointment, and shame. (Özer, 2016). Cyberbullying causes long-term social, emotional, academic consequences and psychological problems on the individual (Baker & Kavşut, 2007). Kopecký and Szotkowski (2017) examined the effects of cyberbullying on victims in two groups as short-term (instant effects) and long-term (continuous effects). The short-term effects of cyberbullying on victims are anger, sadness and fear, feelings of helplessness, self-blame and crying right after the incident. The long-term effects of cyberbullying on the victim are sleep disturbance, headache, stomachache, loss of appetite, nausea, etc. and physical effects such as, frequent arguments with the people around the victim, frustration and aggression. According to Rigby (2003), the negative consequences of cyberbullying can be grouped under four headings: low psychological health, low social adjustment, psychological problems and physical discomfort. Low psychological health is unhappiness, low self-esteem, anger and sadness. Low social adjustment, discontent towards school, not going to school, feeling lonely and isolated. Psychological problems include high levels of anxiety, tendency to depression and suicidal thoughts. Physical discomfort can be listed as the presence of medically diagnosed physical disease symptoms and psychosomatic symptoms (Rigby, 2003).

What to Do When Faced with Cyber Bullying

Cyberbullying is a serious problem that is described as a crime today and cannot be ignored. When faced with cyberbullying, we should not forget that cyberbullying is not just a situation that happens to us, and in order to take the necessary precautions without ignoring the situation; to end communication with individuals who are cyberbullying and harassing them. Reporting these accounts or individuals who are cyberbullying. Making the necessary complaints on the platforms that one is exposed to cyberbullying. Securing personal accounts and not making them publicly accessible. If cyberbullying persists, it is absolutely necessary to tell trusted individuals and parents about the situation. Deleting or freezing accounts on bullied platforms. Making necessary complaints to official authorities. Parents, on the other hand, need to talk to their children, inform them about safe internet use, support them, and monitor their access in a controlled manner.

Precautions to be Taken in Cyberbullying

Preventive interventions against cyberbullying, which have devastating effects on children and adolescents, are important. These interventions can be examined in three groups as family-based interventions, school-based interventions and community-based interventions. Family-based interventions; This includes educating their children on the use of technology awareness, establishing an open communication environment for their children to share their experiences online, and seeking their legal rights when faced with this situation. School-based interventions; It includes organizing trainings on subjects such as cyberbullying types, harms and risks of cyberbullying, coping skills against cyberbullying, and digital literacy, in which all students are included in schools. Community-based interventions include informing the society about cyberbullying and cybercrime and thus raise awareness in the society about these issues (Karaçetin & Mutlu, 2020).

The conscious and safe use of internet and technology by children and young people should be encouraged instead of a prohibitive attitude in the measures that can be taken to combat cyberbullying. In this context, it is necessary to determine appropriate usage rules for parents, computers, mobile phones and other technological tools, for example, it should be clearly stated to their children's which sites they can visit and which ones you do not approve. It is also important to explain the reasons for unapproved behaviors related to internet use. In order for the rules to be easily adopted, it is also very important to listen to the child's objections to these rules and their reasons. Involving your children in the determination of these rules comes to the fore in order to ensure that these rules are adopted. Children should be helped to do their sharing wisely, that is, to avoid sharing that may harm themselves or others. Children should be guided as to who will see the content they share. It is very important to inform them about the risks of communicating with people they do not know, even on social networks. Some cases of cyberbullying are due to sharing passwords with friends. At this point, it should be emphasized that sharing passwords with children compromises their control over their identities and activities, and they should not share their passwords with anyone. It is seen as another important issue that parents cooperate with the school administration and teachers on the setting and implementation of the rules regarding the use of technology within the boundaries of the school. Educators as well as parents play an important role in raising awareness of children and youth about cyberbullying. Steps should be taken to make it easier for children and young people to share their cyberbullying experiences with school staff. For this, an understanding that embraces the right of children and young people to use the internet and encourages conscious use, not prohibitive, should be developed. Educators organize various seminars to increase the knowledge and awareness of parents about cyberbullying, explain what cyberbullying means and what behaviors are cyberbullying through activities without intimidation in order to inform children and young people about cyberbullying. Methods and practices such as determining the principles of combating cyberbullying with the participation of teachers, students and parents in order to develop a common understanding of cyberbullying in schools and acting in accordance with these principles are among the measures that can be taken to protect against cyberbullying.

FUTURE RESEARCH DIRECTIONS

In this section, what cyberbullying is, cyberbullying behaviors, tools, types, incidence, causes, roles, effects, what to do when faced and precautions that can be taken against cyberbullying are discussed. Since the number of victims of cyberbullying is increasing day by day, it is an important social problem that should be recognized early. Therefore, there is a need for extensive research on cyberbullying. It is recommended to conduct longitudinal and cross-sectional studies using both quantitative and qualitative data collection tools for cyberbullying.

The most effective way to deal with cyberbullying is to prevent it before it happens. At this point, families have a great responsibility to protect themselves from cyberbullying, to protect children from cyberbullying or to ensure that they are not cyberbullying. Although research on combating and coping with cyberbullying emphasizes the development of children and youth, the school climate and the importance of a tripartite structure consisting of families, there are very few studies on parents' internet use skills and their capacity to guide their children in internet use. Existing studies are mainly quantitative in nature and aim to understand what cyberbullying is and to explore the experiences of children and adolescents on this issue. For this reason, it is recommended to plan research on whether parental monitoring is beneficial, parents' knowledge and awareness about the issue, their approaches and reactions to their children who are victims or perpetrators of cyberbullying.

CONCLUSION

Cyberbullying is a type of bullying that takes place using digital technologies. It is defined as bullying using technological platforms with internet access. This type of bullying can be seen on social media, messaging and gaming platforms via mobile phones and computers. It includes repetitive behaviors aimed at intimidating, angering or embarrassing target individuals. Cyberbullying is the deliberate act of embarrassing rude behaviors, abusive speech and hostile online messages, threats, harassment and negative comments towards others, non-consensual photo sharing, e-mail, websites, social networks and messaging. Posting lies or embarrassing photos about the victim on the internet, sending insulting messages or threats on messaging platforms, sending controversial messages through the identity of someone else which is called a fake account are considered cyberbullying. Regardless of the age group observed, cyberbullying is a situation that causes long-lasting mental, psychological and emotional problems. Cyberbullying is a serious problem that is described as a crime today and cannot be ignored. When faced with cyberbullying; it is essential to end communications with the offending person, take the required measures, make the necessary complaints on the platforms through which it is exposed, make personal accounts protected, not make them publicly accessible, tell the trusted people/parents about the situation, and for parents to inform their children about safe internet use, support them, monitor their access in a controlled manner, and to make the necessary complaints to the official authorities instead of ignoring it. Since the number of victims exposed to cyberbullying is increasing day by day, it is an important social problem that needs to be noticed early and precautions should be taken with protective strategies. Cyberbullying, as a concept brought and spread by the age of technology, can cause quite devastating effects on individuals. The most effective way to deal with this is to know what cyberbullying is and to prevent it before it happens. At this point, families have a great responsibility.

REFERENCES

Alper, S. (2008). *İlköğretimde zorbalık* [Bullying in primary education] (Master Dissertation).

Arıcak, O. T. (2009). Üniversite öğrencilerindeki siber zorbalık davranışlarının bir yordayıcısı olarak psikiyatrik belirtiler. *Eğitim Araştırmaları, 34*, 167-184.

Arıcak, T. (2015). Siber alemin avatar çocukları. İstanbul: Remzi Kitapevi.

Baker, Ö., & Kavşut, F. (2007). Akran zorbalığının yeni yüzü: Siber zorbalık [The new face of peer bullying: Cyber bullying]. *Eurasian Journal of Educational Research, 27*, 31–42.

BelseyB. (2004). *Cyberbullying*. http://www.cyberbullying.org

Belsey, B. (2005). Cyberbullying: An emerging threat to the "always on" generation. *Recuperado el, 5*(5).

Brandtzag, P. B., Staksrud, E., Hagen, I., & Wold, W. (2009). Norwegian children's experiences of Cyberbullying when using different technological platforms. *Journal of Children and Media, 3*(4), 349–365. doi:10.1080/17482790903233366

Bulunmaz, B. (2015). Yeni Medyada Nefret Söylemi ve Üniversite Öğrencilerine Yönelik Bir Araştırma. *Uşak Üniversitesi Sosyal Bilimler Dergisi, 8*(1), 73-88.

Campbell, M. A. (2005). Cyber bullying: An old problem in a new guise? *Australian Journal of Guidance & Counselling, 15*(1), 68–76. doi:10.1375/ajgc.15.1.68

Chun, J., Lee, J., Kim, J., & Lee, S. (2020). An international systematic review of cyberbullying measurements. *Computers in Human Behavior, 113*, 106485. doi:10.1016/j.chb.2020.106485

Craig, W. M., & Pepler, D. J. (2003). Identifying and targeting risk for involvement in bullying and victimization. *The Canadian Journal of Psychiatry ın* Review, *48*(9), 577–582. PMID:14631877

Ekinci, O., & Kayapalı Yıldırım, S. (2020). *Siber zorbalık (Cyberbullying).* Nobel.

Eroğlu, Y. (2011). *Koşullu özdeğer, riskli internet davranışları ve siber zorbalık/mağduriyet arasındaki ilişkinin incelenmesi* [Examining the relationship between conditional eigenvalue, risky internet behaviors and cyberbullying/victimization] (Master Dissertation).

Eroğlu, Y., Peker, A., & Yaman, E. (2011). *Okul zorbalığı ve siber zorbalık [School bullying and cyberbullying].* Kaknüs.

Fawzi, N. (2009). *Cyber-mobbing: Ursachen und auswirkungen von mobbing im internet.* Nomos. doi:10.5771/9783845219813

Gámez-Guadix, M., Orue, I., Smith, P. K., & Calvete, E. (2013). Longitudinal and reciprocal relations of cyberbullying with depression, substance use, and problematic internet use among adolescents. *The Journal of Adolescent Health, 53*(4), 446–452. doi:10.1016/j.jadohealth.2013.03.030 PMID:23721758

Genç, G., & Aksu, M. B. (2010). Genel lise öğrencilerinin zorba-kurban davranıslarının çeşitli değişkenler açısından incelenmesi [Investigation of bully-victim behaviors of general high school students in terms of various variables]. *Gazi University Journal of Gazi Educational Faculty, 30*(2), 413–448.

Goebert, D., Else, I., Matsu, C., Chung-Do, J., & Chang, J. Y. (2011). The impact of cyberbullying on substance uses and mental health in a multiethnic sample. *Maternal and Child Health Journal, 15*(8), 1282–1286. doi:10.100710995-010-0672-x PMID:20824318

Herring, S., Job-Siuder, K., Scheckler, R., & Barab, S. (2002). Searching for safety online: Managing 'trolling' in a feminist forum. *The Information Society, 18*(5), 371–384. doi:10.1080/01972240290108186

Hinduja, S., & Patchin, J.W. (2005). *Research Summary: Cyberbullying Victimization. Preliminary findings from an online survey of Internet-using adolescents.* http://www.cyberbullying.us

Hinduja, S., & Patchin, J. W. (2008). Cyberbullying: An exploratory analysis of factors related to offending and victimization. *Deviant Behavior, 29*(2), 129–156. doi:10.1080/01639620701457816

Hinduja, S., & Patchin, J. W. (2009). *Bullying beyond the schoolyard: Preventing and responding to cyberbullying.* Corwin.

Hinduja, S., & Patchin, J. W. (2015). *Bullying beyond the schooyard: Preventing and responding to cyberbullying.* Corwin.

Karaçetin, G., & Mutlu, C. (2020). Siber zorbalık: Büyüyen bir problem [Cyberbullying: A growing problem]. In C. Evren (Ed.), *Davranışsal Bağımlılıklar [Behavioral Addictions]* (pp. 215–247). BAYT.

Kopecký, K., & Szotkowski, R. (2017). Cyberbullying, cyber aggression and their impact on the victim–the teacher. *Telematics and Informatics, 34*(2), 506–517. doi:10.1016/j.tele.2016.08.014

Kowalski, R. M., Limber, S. E., & Agatston, P. W. (2012). *Cyberbullying: Bullying in the digital age.* Wiley-Blackwell.

Kowalski, R. M., & Limber, S. P. (2007). Electronic bullying among middle school students. *The Journal of Adolescent Health, 41*(6), 22–30. doi:10.1016/j.jadohealth.2007.08.017 PMID:18047942

Kowalski, R. M., & Limber, S. P. (2013). Psychological, physical, and academic correlates of cyberbullying and traditional bullying. *The Journal of Adolescent Health, 53*(1), 13–20. doi:10.1016/j.jadohealth.2012.09.018 PMID:23790195

Li, Q., Cross, D., & Smith, P. K. (2012). *Cyberbullying in the global playground.* John Wiley & Sons. doi:10.1002/9781119954484

Mason, K. L. (2008). Cyberbullyıng: A preliminary assessment for school personnel. *Psychology in the Schools, 45*(4), 323–348. doi:10.1002/pits.20301

O'Neill, B., Livingstone, S., & McLaughlin, S. (2011). *Final recommendations for policy, methodology and research.* EU Kids Online.

Odabaşı, H. F., Kabakçı, I., & Çoklar, A. N. (2007). *İnternet, çocuk ve aile [Internet, child and family].* Nobel.

Olweus, D. (2012). Cyberbullying: An overrated phenomenon? *European Journal of Developmental Psychology, 9*(5), 520–538. doi:10.1080/17405629.2012.682358

Özer, G. (2016). *Ortaokul öğrencilerinin siber zorbalık yaşama düzeyleri ile siber zorbalığın öğrenciler üzerindeki etkileri ve öğrencilerin siber zorbalıkla baş etme stratejileri* [The cyberbullying levels of secondary school students and the effects of cyberbullying on students and their strategies for coping with cyberbullying] (Master Dissertation).

Patchin, J. W., & Hinduja, S. (2006). Bullies move beyond the schoolyard: A preliminary look at cyberbullying. *Youth Violence and Juvenile Justice, 4*(2), 148–169. doi:10.1177/1541204006286288

Peker, A. (2013). *İnsani değerler yönelimli psikoeğitim programının problemli internet kullanımı ve siber zorbalık üzerindeki etkisi* [The effect of human values-oriented psychoeducation program on problematic internet use and cyberbullying] (Doctoral Dissertation).

Pornari, D. C., & Wood, J. (2009). Peer and cyber aggression in secondary school students: The role of moral disengagement, hostile attribution bias, and outcome expectancies. *Aggressive Behavior, 36*(2), 81–94. doi:10.1002/ab.20336 PMID:20035548

Rigby, K. (2003). Consequences of bullying in schools. *Canadian Journal of Psychiatry, 48*(9), 583–590. doi:10.1177/070674370304800904 PMID:14631878

Rogers, V. (2010). *Cyberbullying: Activities to help children and teens to stay safe in a texting, twittering, social networking world.* Jessica Kingsley Publishers.

Seçkin, Z. (2017). *Örgütlerde mobbing ve siber zorbalık [Mobbing and cyberbullying in organizations].* Çizgi.

Selkie, E. M., Kota, R., & Moreno, M. (2016). Cyberbullying behaviors among female college students: Witnessing, perpetration and victimization. *College Student Journal, 50*, 278–287. PMID:28966413

Shariff, S. (2008). *Cyber-bullying: Issues and solutions for school, the classroom and the home*. Routledge. doi:10.4324/9780203928837

Smahel, D., Machackova, H., Mascheroni, G., Dedkova, L., Staksrud, E., & Ólafsson, K. (2020). EU *Kids Online 2020: Survey results from 19 countries*. Academic Press.

Smith, P. K., Mahdavi, J., Carvalho, M., Fisher, S., Russell, S., & Tippett, N. (2008). Cyberbullying: Its nature and impact in secondary school pupils. *Journal of Child Psychology and Psychiatry, and Allied Disciplines*, *49*(4), 376–385. doi:10.1111/j.1469-7610.2007.01846.x PMID:18363945

Sönmezay, H. (2010). *Lise öğrencilerinde zorbalığın iletişim becerileri ve algılanan sosyal destek ile ilişkisinin incelenmesi* [Examining the relationship of bullying with communication skills and perceived social support in high school students] (Master Dissertation).

Swartz, M. K. (2009). Cyberbullying: An extension of the schoolyard. *Journal of Pediatric Health Care*, *23*(5), 281–282. doi:10.1016/j.pedhc.2009.06.005 PMID:19720261

Topçu, Ç., Baker, Ö. E., & Çapa-Aydın, Y. (2008). Examination of cyber bullying experiences among Turkish students from different school types. *Cyberpsychology & Behavior*, *11*(6), 643–648. doi:10.1089/cpb.2007.0161 PMID:18783345

Willard, N. E. (2007). *Cyberbullying and cyberthreats: Responding to the challenge of online social aggression, Threats and Distress*. Research Press.

Ybarra, M. L., & Mitchell, K. J. (2004). Youth engaging in online harassment: Associations with caregiver–child relationships, internet use, and personal characteristics. *Journal of Adolescence*, *27*(3), 319–336. doi:10.1016/j.adolescence.2004.03.007 PMID:15159091

Ybarra, M. L., & Mitchell, K. J. (2007). Prevalence and frequency of internet harassment instigation: Implications for adolescent health. *The Journal of Adolescent Health*, *41*(2), 189–195. doi:10.1016/j.jadohealth.2007.03.005 PMID:17659224

ADDITIONAL READING

Morgan, N. (2018). *The teenage guide to life online*. Walker Books and Subsidiaries.

Patchin, J. W., & Hinduja, S. (2014). *Words wound: Delete cyberbullying and make kindness go viral*. Free Spirit.

KEY TERMS AND DEFINITIONS

Bullying: Aggressive behavior in which one person intentionally and repeatedly harms or causes discomfort to another.

Cyber: It is the reflection of the real world to the digital environment.

Cyberbullying: It is the repetitive act of aggressive behavior towards the cyber victim in a digital environment.

Digital Technology: It is a type of technology that works by itself without human touch as a result of programming technological products.

Information and Communication Technologies: All kinds of visual, audio, printed and written tools that enable access to information and creation of information.

Internet: It is a computer and information communication network, which has emerged as a result of the interconnection of computer networks in the world, without any limitations and administrators.

Social Media: It is a simple, easy, and digital way of access, conversion, interaction and connection (communication, sharing, messaging, information exchange, promotion, advertising, etc.) among people.

Technology: All of the knowledge, skills, methods and processes that develop, change and even transform the environment used to achieve the goal to meet the needs and desires of individuals.

Compilation of References

111th Congress (2009-2010). H.*R.1966 - Megan Meier Cyberbullying Prevention Act*. https://www.congress.gov/bill/111th-congress/house-bill/1966

A Doll Like Me – Every Child Should Feel Included. (2022). *Ability Magazine*. Retrieved February 24, 2022, from https://abilitymagazine.com/a-doll-like-me-every-child-should-feel-included/

Abbas, M. A., Fiala, L. A., Abdel Rahman, A. G., & Fahim, A. E. (2010). Epidemiology of workplace violence against nursing staff in Ismailia Governorate, Egypt. *The Journal of the Egyptian Public Health Association*, *85*(1-2), 29–43. PMID:21073846

Aboujaoude, E., Savage, M. W., Starcevic, V., & Salame, W. O. (2015). Cyberbullying: Review of an old problem gone viral. *The Journal of Adolescent Health*, *57*(1), 10–18. doi:10.1016/j.jadohealth.2015.04.011 PMID:26095405

Abreu, R. L., & Kenny, M. C. (2018). Cyberbullying and LGBTQ youth: A systematic literature review and recommendations for prevention and intervention. *Journal of Child & Adolescent Trauma*, *11*(1), 81–97. doi:10.100740653-017-0175-7 PMID:32318140

Acar, T. (2009). *Dokuzuncu sınıf öğrencilerinde akran zorbalığı ve psikolojik belirtiler* [Peer bullying and psychological symptoms in ninth grade students] [Unpublished master's thesis].Hacettepe Üniversitesi, Sosyal Bilimler Enstitüsü, Ankara.

Acar, T. (2009). *Peer bullying and psychological symptoms among nineth grade students* (UMI No. 258374) [Master's dissertation, Hacettepe University]. Higher Education Council Thesis Center database.

Açıkgöz, T. (2017). *Bullying and attitude towards secondary school students: Sample of Kartepe district* (UMI No. 462314) [Master's dissertation, Sakarya University]. Higher Education Council Thesis Center database.

Adams, E.A., Darj, E., Wijewardene, K., & Infanti, J.J. (2019). Perceptions on the sexual harassment of female nurses in a state hospital in Sri Lanka: a qualitative study. *Global Health Action*, *12*(1). doi:10.1080/16549716.2018.1560587

Adhikary Shubhra Tuhin. (2021). Bangladesh ICT Act: The trap of Section 57. *Dhaka Tribune*. https://www.thedailystar.net/frontpage/bangladesh-ict-act-the-trap-section-of-57-1429336

Adikaram, A. (2016). Not So Silent: How Social Support is Given and Received in Dealing with Sexual Harassment in Sri Lankan Work-Places. *NSBM Journal of Management*, *1*(2), 94–126. doi:10.4038/nsbmjm.v1i2.13

Aggarwal, S., Rai, S., Jaiswal, M. P., & Sorensen, H. (2016). Norm of reciprocity –Antecedent of trustworthiness in social media. In *Social media: The good, the bad and the ugly*. Springer.

Agnew, R. (1992). Foundation for a General Strain Theory of Crime and Delinquency. *Criminology*, *30*(1), 47–88. doi:10.1111/j.1745-9125.1992.tb01093.x

Agnew, R., Brezina, T., Wright, J. P., & Cullen, F. T. (2002). Strain, Personality Traits, and Delinquency: Extending general strain theory. *Criminology, 40*(1), 43–72. doi:10.1111/j.1745-9125.2002.tb00949.x

Ağralı, Ö., & Aydın, Ö. (2021). Tweet Classification and Sentiment Analysis on Metaverse Related Messages. *Journal of Metaverse, 1*(1).

Ahmed, E., & Braithwaite, V. (2004). Bullying and victimization: Cause for concern for both families and schools. *Article in Social Psychology of Education, 7*(1), 35–54. doi:10.1023/B:SPOE.0000010668.43236.60

Akay, Y. (2019). The effect of emotional awareness activities developed for primary school students in preventing peer bullying. *Education in Science, 44*(200), 205–227.

Akbulut, Y., Şahin, Y. L., & Erişti, B. (2010). Development of a scale to investigate cybervictimization among online social utility members. *Contemporary Educational Technology, 1*(1), 46–59. doi:10.30935/cedtech/5961

Akca, E. B., Sayımer, İ., Salı, J. B., & Başak, B. E. (2014). The Causes, Types And Media of Cyber Bullying in School. *Electronic Journal of Professional Development and Research (EJOIR),* 17-30.

Akça, E.B., & Sayımer, İ. (2017). Siber Zorbalık Kavramı, Türleri ve İlişkili Olduğu Faktörler: Mevcut Araştırmalar Üzerinden Bir Değerlendirme. *AJIT-e: Online Academic Journal of Information Technology, 8*(30).

Akça, E. (2017). Cyberbullying, it's types and related factors: An evaluation through the existing studies. *Online Academic Journal of Information Technology, 8*(30), 1–20. doi:10.5824/1309-1581.2017.5.001.x

Akca, E. B., Sayımer, İ., Salı, J. B., & Başak, B. E. (2014). The causes and types of cyber bullying in school and role of media literacy in preventive services. *Electronic Journal of Occupational Improvement and Research, 2*(1), 17–30.

Akca, M., & Kucukoglu Tepe, M. (2020). Relations Between Workplace Bullying, Conscientiousness And Counter-productive Work Behaviours: A Study At Logistics Company. *Beykoz Akademi Dergisi, 8*(1), 117–136. doi:10.14514/BYK.m.26515393.2020.8/1.117-136

Akduman, G. (2012). Okul öncesi dönemde akran zorbaliğin incelenmesi [Examination of peer bullying in preschool period]. *Gazi Üniversitesi. Toplum ve Sosyal Hizmet Dergisi, 23*(1), 121–138.

Akduman, G. (2012). Okul öncesi dönemde akran zorbalığın incelenmesi [Investigation of peer bullying in preschool period]. *Gazi Üniversitesi. Toplum ve Sosyal Hizmet Dergisi, 23*(1), 121–138.

Akers, R. L. (1990). Rational Choice, Deterrence, and Social Learning Theory in Criminology: The Path Not Taken. *The Journal of Criminal Law & Criminology, 81*(3), 653–676. doi:10.2307/1143850

Akman, Y. (2021). The Relationship between School Climate and Students' Aggressive Behaviors. *International Journal of Progressive Education, 17*(2), 430–448. doi:10.29329/ijpe.2021.332.26

Aksaray, S. (2011). Cyberbullying. *C. Finish. Journal of the Institute of Social Sciences,* 405-432.

Aktay, M. (2020). İstismar ve ihmalin çocuk üzerindeki etkileri ve tedavisi [The effects and treatment of abuse and neglect on children]. *Gelişim ve Psikoloji Dergisi, 1*(2), 169–184.

Aktepe, E. (2013). Cyber-bullying and cyber-victimization in adolescents. *New Symposium Journal, 51*(1), 31-36.

Aktürk, A. O. (2015). Analysis of cyberbullying sensitivity levels of high school students and their perceived social support levels. *Interactive Technology and Smart Education, 12*(1), 44–61. doi:10.1108/ITSE-07-2014-0016

Al Hosani, H., Yousef, M., Al Shouq, S., Iqbal, F., & Mouheb, D. (2019). A comparative analysis of cyberbullying and cyberstalking laws in the UAE, US, UK and Canada. *Proceedings of IEEE/ACS International Conference on Computer Systems and Applications, AICCSA*. 10.1109/AICCSA47632.2019.9035368

Alade Anuoluwapo. (2017, June). *The social media and the Nigerian society*. Academic Press.

Albdour, M., Hong, J. S., Lewin, L., & Yarandi, H. (2019). The Impact of Cyberbullying on Physical and Psychological Health of Arab American Adolescents. *Journal of Immigrant and Minority Health, 21*(4), 706–715. doi:10.100710903-018-00850-w PMID:30603837

Alberti, R., & Emmons, M. (2002). *Exercise Your Right to Assertiveness*. HYB Publishing.

Al-Bitar, Z. B., Al-Omari, I. K., Sonbol, H. N., Al-Ahmad, H. T., & Cunningham, S. J. (2013). Bullying among Jordanian schoolchildren, its effects on school performance, and the contribution of general physical and dentofacial features. *American Journal of Orthodontics and Dentofacial Orthopedics, 144*(6), 872–878. doi:10.1016/j.ajodo.2013.08.016 PMID:24286910

Alcantara, G. M., Claudio, E. G., & Gabriel, A. G. (2017). Prognosis of Workplace Bullying in Selected Health Care Organizations in the Philippines. *Open Journal of Social Sciences, 5*(9), 154–174. doi:10.4236/jss.2017.59012

Aleem, S. (2016). Bullying behavior among school students: A review. *Indian Journal of Health & Wellbeing, 7*(10).

Al-Hussain, S. M., Al-Haidari, M. S., Kouri, N. A., El-Migdadi, F., Al-Safar, R. S., & Mohammad, M. A. (2008). Prevalence of mistreatment and justice of grading system in five health related faculties in Jordan University of Science and Technology. *Medical Teacher, 30*(3), e82–e86. doi:10.1080/01421590801938845 PMID:18484446

Alim, S. (2016). Cyberbullying in the world of teenagers and social media: A literature review. *International Journal of Cyber Behavior, Psychology and Learning, 6*(2), 68–95. doi:10.4018/IJCBPL.2016040105

Alipan, A., Skues, J., Theiler, S., & Wise, L. (2015). Defining cyberbullying: A multiple perspectives approach. *Studies in Health Technology and Informatics, 219*, 9–13. https://ebooks.iospress.nl/publication/42114 PMID:26799870

Allen, P. F. (2003). Assessment of oral health related quality of life. *Health and Quality of Life Outcomes, 1*(1), 1–8. doi:10.1186/1477-7525-1-40 PMID:14514355

Allington, W. (2020). *Antisemitic Memes and Naïve Teens: Qualitative and Quantitative Impacts of the Internet on Antisemitism, the Evolution of Antisemitism 2.0, and Developing Adaptable Research Methodologies into Online Hate, Abuse, and Misinformation*. The University of Sydney. https://ses.library.usyd.edu.au/handle/2123/22444

Almeida, A. B. D., Leite, I. C. G., Melgaço, C. A., & Marques, L. S. (2014). Dissatisfaction with dentofacial appearance and the normative need for orthodontic treatment: Determinant factors. *Dental Press Journal of Orthodontics, 19*(3), 120–126. doi:10.1590/2176-9451.19.3.120-126.oar PMID:25162576

Alper, S. (2008). *İlköğretimde zorbalık* [Bullying in primary education] (Master Dissertation).

Alper, S. İ. (2008). *İlköğretimde zorbalık* [Bullying in primary education] [Unpublished master's thesis]. Uludağ Üniversitesi, Sosyal Bilimler Enstitüsü, Bursa.

Alper-İlhan, S. (2008). *Bullying in elementary scholl* (UMI No. 221001) [Master's dissertation, Uludağ University]. Higher Education Council Thesis Center database.

Alrawadieh, Z., Demirdelen Alrawadieh, D., Olya, G.T., Erkol Bayram, G., & Kahraman, O. C. (2021). Sexual harassment, psychological well-being, and job satisfaction of female tour guides: the effects of social and organizational support. *Journal of Sustainable Tourism*, 1 – 20. doi:10.1080/09669582.2021.1879819

Alsawalqa, R. O. (2021). Cyberbullying, social stigma, and self-esteem: The impact of COVID-19 on students from East and Southeast Asia at the University of Jordan. *Heliyon*, *7*(4), e06711. doi:10.1016/j.heliyon.2021.e06711 PMID:33869877

Al-Surimi, K., Al Omar, M., Alahmary, K., & Salam, M. (2020). Prevalence of Workplace Bullying and Its Associated Factors at a Multi-Regional Saudi Arabian Hospital: A Cross-Sectional Study. *Risk Management and Healthcare Policy*, *13*, 1905–1914. doi:10.2147/RMHP.S265127 PMID:33061722

Altiparmak, S., Yildirim, G., Yardimci, F., & Ergin, D. (2013). Annelerden alınan bilgilerle çocuk istismarı ve etkileyen etkenler [Child abuse and influencing factors with information obtained from mothers]. *Anatolian Journal of Psychiatry*, *14*(4), 354–361. doi:10.5455/apd.39819

Álvarez-García, D., Barreiro-Collazo, A., Núñez, J. C., & Dobarro, A. (2016). Validity and reliability of the Cyber-aggression Questionnaire for Adolescents (CYBA). *The European Journal of Psychology Applied to Legal Context*, *8*(2), 69–77. doi:10.1016/j.ejpal.2016.02.003

Alvarez-García, D., García, T., & Núnez, J. C. (2015). Predictors of school bullying perpetration in adolescence: A systematic review. *Aggression and Violent Behavior*, *23*, 126–136. doi:10.1016/j.avb.2015.05.007

Álvarez-García, D., Núñez, J. C., Collazo, A., & García, T. (2017). Validation of the Cybervictimization Questionnaire (CYVIC) for adolescents. *Computers in Human Behavior*, *70*, 270–281. doi:10.1016/j.chb.2017.01.007

Amado, J., & Freire, I. (2002). *Indisciplina e violência na Escola. Compreender para prevenir* [Indiscipline and violence at school. Understand to prevent]. Edições Asa.

Amira Nur Diana, A. H., & Safinaz, M. H. (2020). The effects of sharenting on children and its implications on a child's privacy rights in Malaysia. *Current Legal Issues*, *2*, 21–52.

Ammari, T., & Schoenebeck, S. (2015) Understanding and supporting fathers and fatherhood on social media sites. In *Proceedings of the 33rd Annual ACM Conference on Human Factors in Computing Systems* (pp.1905-1914). New York, NY: Association for Computing Machinery Press. 10.1145/2702123.2702205

Anderson, Bresnahan, & Musatics. (2014). *Cyberpsychology, behavior and Social networking Combating weight-based cyberbullying on Facebook with the dissenter effect*. Academic Press.

Anderson, C. A., & Bushman, B. J. (2002). Human aggression. *Annual Review of Psychology*, *53*(1), 27–51. doi:10.1146/annurev.psych.53.100901.135231 PMID:11752478

Anderson, T., & Sturm, B. (2007). Cyberbullying from playground to computer. *Young Adult Library Services*, *5*(2), 24–27.

Andersson, L. M., & Pearson, C. M. (1999). Effect of Tit for Tat? The Spiraling in the Workplace Incivility. *Academy of Management Review*, *24*(3), 452–471. doi:10.2307/259136

Andrews, M. E., Stewart, N. J., Morgan, D. G., & D'Arcy, C. (2012). More alike than different: A comparison of male and female RNs in rural and remote Canada. *Journal of Nursing Management*, *20*(4), 561–570. doi:10.1111/j.1365-2834.2011.01195.x PMID:22591157

Ang, R. P. (2022). Bullying Among Children and Youth in the Digital Age. In *Child Safety, Welfare and Well-being* (pp. 31–45). Springer. doi:10.1007/978-981-16-9820-0_3

Ang, R. P., & Goh, D. H. (2010). Cyberbullying among adolescents: The role of affective and cognitive empathy and gender. *Child Psychiatry and Human Development*, *41*(4), 387–397. doi:10.100710578-010-0176-3 PMID:20238160

Ang, R. P., Ong, E. Y., Lim, J. C., & Lim, E. W. (2009). From narcissistic exploitativeness to bullying behavior: The mediating role of approval of aggression beliefs. *Social Development*, *19*(4), 721–735. doi:10.1111/j.1467-9507.2009.00557.x

Antia, S. D., & Kreimeyer, K. H. (2001). The role of interpreters in inclusive classrooms. *American Annals of the Deaf, 146*(4), 355–365. doi:10.1353/aad.2012.0142 PMID:11816860

António, R., Guerra, R., & Moleiro, C. (2020). *Cyberbullying em Portugal durante a pandemia do Covid-19* [Cyberbullying in Portugal during the Covid-19 pandemic]. Centro de Investigação e de Intervenção Social (CIS-IUL, ISCTE-IUL).

Anwar, A., Kee, D. M. H., & Ahmed, A. (2020). Workplace Cyberbullying and Interpersonal Deviance: Understanding the Mediating Effect of Silence and Emotional Exhaustion. *Cyberpsychology, Behavior, and Social Networking, 23*(5), 290–296. doi:10.1089/cyber.2019.0407 PMID:32282237

APA Resolution on Bullying Among Children and Youth. (2004). Available from https://www.apa.org/about/policy/bullying.pdf

Aquino, K., & Bradfield, M. (2000). Perceived Victimization in the Workplace: The Role of Situational Factors and Victim Characteristics. *Organization Science, 11*(5), 525–537. doi:10.1287/orsc.11.5.525.15205

AraştırmasıÇ. B. T. K. (2021). Available from https://data.tuik.gov.tr/Bulten/Index?p=Cocuklarda-Bilisim-Teknolojileri-Kullanim-Arastirmasi-2021-41132

Archer, J., & Coyne, S. M. (2005). An integrated review of indirect, relational, and social aggression. *Personality and Social Psychology Review, 9*(3), 212–230. doi:10.120715327957pspr0903_2 PMID:16083361

Arendt, H. (2018). On violence (B. Peker, Trans.). İstanbul, Turkey: İletişim Yayınları.

Arënliu, A., Strohmeier, D., Konjufca, J., Yanagida, T., & Burger, C. (2020). Empowering the peer group to prevent school bullying in Kosovo: Effectiveness of a short and ultra-short version of the VISC social competence program. *International Journal of Bullying Prevention, 2*(1), 65–78.

Arias, E. (2019). How Does Media Influence Social Norms? Experimental Evidence on the Role of Common Knowledge. *Political Science Research and Methods, 7*(3), 561–578. doi:10.1017/psrm.2018.1

Arıcak, O. T. (2009). Üniversite öğrencilerindeki siber zorbalık davranışlarının bir yordayıcısı olarak psikiyatrik belirtiler. *Eğitim Araştırmaları, 34*, 167-184.

Arıcak, T. (2015). Siber alemin avatar çocukları. İstanbul: Remzi Kitapevi.

Arıcak, O. T. (2009). Psychiatric symptomatology as a predictor of cyberbullying among university students. *Eurasian Journal of Educational Research, 34*, 167–184.

Arıcak, O. T., Siyahhan, S., Uzunhasanoğlu, A., Sarıbeyoğlu, S., Çıplak, S., Yılmaz, N., & Memmedov, C. (2008). Cyberbullying among Turkish adolescents. *Cyberpsychology & Behavior, 11*(3), 253–261. doi:10.1089/cpb.2007.0016 PMID:18537493

Arif, M. (2021). A Systematic Review of Machine Learning Algorithms in Cyberbullying Detection: Future Directions and Challenges. *Journal of Information Security and Cybercrimes Research, 4*(1), 1–26. doi:10.26735/GBTV9013

Armitage, R. (2021). Bullying in children: Impact on child health. *BMJ Paediatrics Open, 5*(1), e000939. doi:10.1136/bmjpo-2020-000939 PMID:33782656

Arnarsson, A., & Bjarnason, T. (2018). The Problem with Low-Prevalence of Bullying. *International Journal of Environmental Research and Public Health, 15*(7), 1535. Advance online publication. doi:10.3390/ijerph15071535 PMID:30036943

Arseneault, L., Bowes, L., & Shakoor, S. (2010). Bullying victimization in youths and mental health problems: 'Much ado about nothing'? *Psychological Medicine, 40*(5), 717–729. doi:10.1017/S0033291709991383 PMID:19785920

Arsenio, W., & Lemerise, E. A. (2001). Varieties of childhood bullying: Values, emotion processes and social competence. *Social Development*, *10*(1), 59–73. doi:10.1111/1467-9507.00148

Arslan, S. (2008). *The effect of family and self concept relation on peer bullying in high school students* (UMI No. 204019) [Doctoral dissertation, Istanbul University]. Higher Education Council Thesis Center database.

Arslan, G., Allen, K. A., & Tanhan, A. (2021). School bullying, mental health, and wellbeing in adolescents: Mediating impact of positive psychological orientations. *Child Indicators Research*, *14*(3), 1007–1026. doi:10.100712187-020-09780-2

Arslan, M. (2001). *İş ve Meslek Ahlâkı*. Nobel Yayınları.

Arslan, S., Hallett, V., Akkaş, E., & Akkaş, O. A. (2012). Bullying and victimization among Turkish children and adolescents: Examining prevalence and associated health symptoms. *European Journal of Pediatrics*, *171*(10), 1549–1557. doi:10.100700431-012-1782-9 PMID:22735980

Asaoka, H., Sasaki, N., Kuroda, R., Tsuno, K., & Kawakami, N. (2021). Workplace Bullying and Patient Aggression Related to COVID-19 and its Association with Psychological Distress among Health Care Professionals during the COVID-19 Pandemic in Japan. *The Tohoku Journal of Experimental Medicine*, *255*(4), 283–289. doi:10.1620/tjem.255.283 PMID:34897160

Askew, D. A., Schluter, P. J., Dick, M. L., Régo, P. M., Turner, C., & Wilkinson, D. (2012). Bullying in the Australian medical workforce: Cross-sectional data from an Australian e-Cohort study. *Australian Health Review*, *36*(2), 197–204. doi:10.1071/AH11048 PMID:22624642

Astor, R. A., Meyer, H. A., Benbenishty, R., Marachi, R., & Rosemond, M. (2005). School Safety Interventions: Best Practices and Programs. *Children & Schools*, *27*(1), 17–32. doi:10.1093/cs/27.1.17

Ata, R. N., Ludden, A. B., & Lally, M. M. (2007). The effects of gender and family, friend, and media influences on eating behaviors and body image during adolescence. *Journal of Youth and Adolescence*, *36*(8), 1024–1037. doi:10.100710964-006-9159-x

Atayman, V. (2006). Şiddetin Mitolojisi. İstanbul, Turkey: Donkişot Güncel Yayınlar.

Atik, G., & Kemer, G. (2008). The role of problem solving skills state=trait anger and anger expression style physical self=efficiency in predicting bullying among middle school students. *Dokuz Eylül University the Journal of Buca Faculty of Education, 23*, 198-206. https://acikerisim.deu.edu.tr/xmlui/bitstream/handle/20.500.12397/264/182.pdf?sequence=1&isAllowed=y

Atik, G., & Güneri, O. Y. (2013). Bullying and victimization: Predictive role of individual, parental, and academic factors. *School Psychology International*, *34*(6), 658–673. doi:10.1177/0143034313479699

Atış-Akyol, N., Yıldız, C., & Akman, B. (2018). Öğretmenlerin akran zorbalığına ilişkin görüşleri ve zorbalıkla baş etme stratejileri [Teachers' views on peer bullying and strategies for coping with bullying]. *Hacettepe Üniversitesi Eğitim Fakültesi Dergisi*, *33*(2), 439–459.

Audley-Piotrowski, S., Singer, A., & Patterson, M. (2015). The role of the teacher in children's peer relations: Making the invisible hand intentional. *Translational Issues in Psychological Science*, *1*(2), 192–200. doi:10.1037/tps0000038

Austin, V. L., & Sciarra, D. T. (2017). *Çocuk ve ergenlerde duygusal ve davranışsal bozukluklar* [Children and adolescents with emotional and behavioral disorders] (3rd ed., D. M. Özekes, Ed. & Trans.). Nobel Akademik. (Original work published 2009)

Australia, S. W. (2022). *Workplace sexual harassment statistics and What to do if you are sexually harassed at work– new infographics*. Available at https://www.safeworkaustralia.gov.au/media-centre/news/workplace- sexual-harassment-statistics-and- what-do-if-you-are-sexually-harassed-work-new-infographics#:~:text=Social%20media-, Workplace%20sexual%20 harassment%20statistics% 20and%20What%20to%20do%20if%20you,harassed%20 at%20work%E2%80%93%20new%20 infographics&text=One%20in%20three%20people%20 (33,in%20the%20last%20five%20years.

Avşar, F., & Ayaz-Alkaya, S. (2018). Akran zorbalığının önlenmesinde okul sağlığı hemşiresinin rolü [The role of school health nurses in the prevention of peer bullying]. *Journal of Hacettepe University Faculty of Nursing*, *5*(1), 78–84.

Awai, N. S., Ganasegeran, K., & Abdul Manaf, M. R. (2021). Prevalence of Workplace Bullying and Its Associated Factors among Workers in a Malaysian Public University Hospital: A Cross-Sectional Study. *Risk Management and Healthcare Policy*, *14*, 75–85. doi:10.2147/RMHP.S280954 PMID:33447111

Ayas, T. (2008). *The effectiveness of preventing bullying behaviors one program based on whole school approach* [Unpublished Doctorate Thesis]. Ankara University, Institute of Educational Sciences, Ankara.

Ayas, T. (2008). *The effectiveness of the bullying prevention program based on the whole school approach* [Unpublished PhD Thesis]. Ankara University, Ankara.

Ayas, T. (2018). *Okullarda yaygın sorun olan zorbalığı önlemek* [Preventing bullying, a common problem in schools]. Vizetek Yayıncılık.

Ayas, T., & Horzum, M. B. (2012). On being cyber bully and victim among primary school students. *Ilkogretim Online, 11*(2).

Ayas, T., & Pişkin, M. (2011). Investigation of bullying among high school students with regard to sex, grade level and school type. *Elementary Education Online, 10*(2), 550-568. https://dergipark.org.tr/tr/pub/ilkonline/issue/8592/106821

Ayas, T. (2010). *Okullarda yaygın sorun olan zorbalığı önlemek* [Preventing bullying a common problem in schools] (1st ed.). Maya Akademi.

Ayas, T., & Pişkin, M. (2011). Investigation of bullying among high school students with regard to sex, grade level, and school type. *Elementary Education Online*, *10*(2), 550–568.

Aydemir, İ., Üçlü, R., & Aydoğan, A. (2020). Acil servis personeline göre şiddetin nedenleri [According to the emergency room staff the reasons for violence]. *Journal of Istanbul Faculty of Medicine*, *83*(1), 60–68. doi:10.26650/IUITFD.2019.0018

Aydın, F. (2016). *Effectiveness of the cyberbulling education on the sixth-grade students' cyberbulling awareness* (Unpublished Master theses). Sakarya University, Sakarya.

Aykut, S. (2019). *Educational Problems of Syrian Children in Turkey: School Social Work Proposal with a Focus on Respect for Diversity Education* [PhD thesis]. Hacettepe University Institute of Social Sciences, Ankara.

Aytaç, S., & Dursun, S. (2013). Çalışma hayatında kadına yönelik şiddet: sağlık sektöründe bir uygulama [Violence against women in working life: an application in the health sector]. *Journal of Istanbul University Law Faculty*, *71*(1), 67–78.

Azeredo, C. M., Rinaldi, A. E. M., de Moraes, C. L., Levy, R. B., & Menezes, P. R. (2015). School bullying: A systematic review of contextual-level risk factors in observational studies. *Aggression and Violent Behavior*, *22*, 65–76. doi:10.1016/j.avb.2015.04.006

Babanina, V., Tkachenko, I., Matiushenko, O., & Krutevych, M. (2021). Cybercrime: History of formation, current state and ways of counteraction. *Revista Amazonia Investiga*, *10*(38), 113–122. doi:10.34069/AI/2021.38.02.10

Babu, K. E. K., & Ullah, M. A. (2021). Cyber legislation and cyber-related legal issues in Bangladesh: Inadequacies and challenges. *International Journal of Electronic Security and Digital Forensics*, *13*(2), 180–196. doi:10.1504/IJESDF.2021.113379

Babvey, P., Capela, F., Cappa, C., Lipizzi, C., Petrowski, N., & Ramirez-Marquez, J. (2021). Using social media data for assessing children's exposure to violence during the COVID-19 pandemic. *Child Abuse & Neglect*, *116*, 104747. doi:10.1016/j.chiabu.2020.104747 PMID:33358281

Bacchini, D., Esposito, G., & Affuso, G. (2009). Social experience and school bullying. *Journal of Community & Applied Social Psychology*, *19*(1), 17–32. doi:10.1002/casp.975

Bae, S. M. (2021). The relationship between exposure to risky online content, cyber victimization, perception of cyberbullying, and cyberbullying offending in Korean adolescents. *Children and Youth Services Review*, *123*, 105946. doi:10.1016/j.childyouth.2021.105946

Bahar, A., Sahin, S., Akkaya, Z., & Alkayis, M. (2015). Acil Serviste Calisan Hemsirelerin Siddete Maruz Kalma Durumu ve Is Doyumuna Etkili Olan Faktörlerin İncelenmesi [Investigation of the Factors Affecting the Exposure to Violence and Job Satisfaction of the Nurses Working in the Emergency Service]. *Psikiyatri Hemsireleri Dernegi, 6*(2).

Bahji, A., & Altomare, J. (2020). Prevalence of intimidation, harassment, and discrimination among resident physicians: A systematic review and meta-analysis. *Canadian Medical Education Journal*, *11*(1), e97. doi:10.36834/cmej.57019 PMID:32215147

Bakaç, C., Chen, Y., Zyberaj, J., Kehr, H. M., & Quirin, M. (2022). Perceived intrinsic motivation mediates the effect of motive incongruence on job burnout and job satisfaction. *The Journal of Psychology*, *156*(1), 12–32. doi:10.1080/00223980.2021.1980758 PMID:34762556

Baker, Ö. E., & Kavşut, F. (2007). The New Face of Peer Bullying: Cyberbullying. *Eurasian Journal of Educational Research*, 31-42 .

Baker, Ö., & Kavşut, F. (2007). Akran zorbalığının yeni yüzü: Siber zorbalık [The new face of peer bullying: Cyber bullying]. *Eurasian Journal of Educational Research*, *27*, 31–42.

Bakırcı, K. (2000). *İş yerinde cinsel taciz ve Türk iş hukukuna ilişkin çözüm önerileri* [Suggestions for sexual harassment in the workplace and Turkish labor law]. http://www.turkhukuksitesi.com/makale_25.htm

Balakrishnan, V. (2018). Actions, emotional reactions and cyberbullying–From the lens of bullies, victims, bully-victims and bystanders among Malaysian young adults. *Telematics and Informatics*, *35*(5), 1190–1200. doi:10.1016/j.tele.2018.02.002

Baldo Moraes, R., Knorst, J. K., Brondani, B., Baldo Marques, B., de Sousa Reis, M., Henriqson, D., & Ardenghi, T. M. (2021). Relationship between gingival bleeding and associated factors with reports of verbal bullying in adolescents. *Journal of Periodontology*, *92*(2), 225–233. doi:10.1002/JPER.19-0745 PMID:32716571

Baldry, A. C., & Farrington, D. P. (1999). Brief report: Types of bullying among Italian school children. *Journal of Adolescence*, *22*(3), 423–426. doi:10.1006/jado.1999.0234 PMID:10462433

Baldry, A. C., & Farrington, D. P. (2000). Bullies and delinpunts: Personal characteristics and parental styles. *Journal of Community & Applied Social Psychology*, *10*(1), 17–31. doi:10.1002/(SICI)1099-1298(200001/02)10:1<17::AID-CASP526>3.0.CO;2-M

Baldry, A. C., & Farrıngton, D. P. (2005). Protective factors as moderators of risk factors in adolescence bullying. *Social Psychology of Education*, *8*, 263–284. doi:10.100711218-005-5866-5

Balkıs, M., Duru, E., & Buluş, M. (2005). Şiddete yönelik tutumların özyeterlik, medya, şiddete yönelik inanç, arkadaş grubu ve okula bağlılık duygusu ile ilişkisi [The relationship of attitudes towards violence with self-efficacy, media, belief towards violence, friendship group and sense of commitment to school]. *Ege Eğitim Dergisi*, *6*(2), 81–97.

Balwant, P. T., Odell, J., & Ramdeo, S. (2019). I've had enough!" Mental health as a mechanism in the relationship between sexual harassment and organizational commitment. *Work (Reading, Mass.)*, *64*(3), 1–13. doi:10.3233/WOR-193006 PMID:31683497

Bandura, A. (1978). Social learning theory of aggression. *Journal of Communication*, *28*(3), 12–29. doi:10.1111/j.1460-2466.1978.tb01621.x PMID:690254

Banerjee, R., Robinson, C., & Smalley, D. (2010). *Evaluation of the Beatbullying Peer Mentoring Programme. Report for Beatbullying*. University of Sussex.

Bangladesh Computer Council. (2019). *BGD e-GOV CIRT | Bangladesh e-Government Computer Incident Response Team*. Bangladesh Computer Council. https://www.cirt.gov.bd/

Bankers, C. J. (2013). Identifying Employers' Proxies in Sexual-Harassment Litigation. *Iowa Law Review*, *99*, 1785–1815.

Bannink, R., Broeren, S., Van de Looij-Jansen, P. M., De Waart, F. G., & Raat, H. (2014). Cyber and traditional bullying victimization as a risk factor for mental health problems and suicidal ideation in adolescents. *PLoS One*, *9*(4), 1–7. doi:10.1371/journal.pone.0094026 PMID:24718563

Barasuol, J. C., Soares, J. P., Castro, R. G., Giacomin, A., Gonçalves, B. M., Klein, D., Torres, F. M., Borgatto, A. F., Ramos-Jorge, M. L., Bolan, M., & Cardoso, M. (2017). Untreated dental caries is associated with reports of verbal bullying in children 8-10 years old. *Caries Research*, *51*(5), 482–488. doi:10.1159/000479043 PMID:28954260

Barboza, G. E., Schiamberg, L. B., Oehmke, J., Korzeniewski, S. J., Post, L. A., & Heraux, C. G. (2009). Individual characteristics and the multiple contexts of adolescent bullying: An ecological perspective. *Journal of Youth and Adolescence*, *38*(1), 101–121. doi:10.100710964-008-9271-1 PMID:19636795

Bargh, J. A., & McKenna, K. Y. A. (2004). The Internet and social life. *Annual Review of Psychology*, *55*(1), 573–590. doi:10.1146/annurev.psych.55.090902.141922 PMID:14744227

Barlett, C. P. (2015). Anonymously hurting others online: The effect of anonymity on cyberbullying frequency. *Psychology of Popular Media Culture*, *4*(2), 70–79. doi:10.1037/a0034335

Barlett, C. P. (2015). Predicting Adolescent's Cyberbullying Behavior: A Longitudinal Risk Analysis. *Journal of Adolescence*, *41*(1), 86–95. doi:10.1016/j.adolescence.2015.02.006 PMID:25828551

Barlett, C. P. (2017). From theory to practice: Cyberbullying theory and its application to intervention. *Computers in Human Behavior*, *72*, 269–275. doi:10.1016/j.chb.2017.02.060

Barlett, C. P., & Gentile, D. A. (2012). Attacking others online: The formation of cyberbullying in late adolescence. *Psychology of Popular Media Culture*, *1*(2), 123–135. doi:10.1037/a0028113

Barlett, C. P., Gentile, D. A., & Chew, C. (2016). Predicting cyberbullying from anonymity. *Psychology of Popular Media Culture*, *5*(2), 171–180. doi:10.1037/ppm0000055

Barlett, C. P., Rinker, A., & Roth, B. (2021). Cyberbullying Perpetration in the COVID-19 Era: An Application of General Strain Theory. *The Journal of Social Psychology*, *161*(4), 466–476. doi:10.1080/00224545.2021.1883503 PMID:33543673

Barlett, C. P., Seyfert, L. W., Simmers, M. M., Hsueh Hua Chen, V., Cavalcanti, J. G., Krahé, B., Suzuki, K., Warburton, W. A., Wong, R. Y. M., Pimentel, C. E., & Skowronski, M. (2021). Cross-cultural similarities and differences in the theoretical predictors of cyberbullying perpetration: Results from a seven-country study. *Aggressive Behavior*, *47*(1), 111–119. doi:10.1002/ab.21923 PMID:32853436

Barlett, C. P., Simmers, M. M., Roth, B., & Gentile, D. (2021). Comparing cyberbullying prevalence and process before and during the COVID-19 pandemic. *The Journal of Social Psychology*, *161*(4), 408–418. doi:10.1080/00224545.2021.1918619 PMID:34128768

Barlett, C., & Chamberlin, K. (2017). Examining cyberbullying across the lifespan. *Computers in Human Behavior*, *71*, 444–449. doi:10.1016/j.chb.2017.02.009

Barlett, C., Madison, C. J., Heath, J., & DeWitt, C. (2019). A correlational examination of technology access and time spent online in the Barlett Gentile Cyberbullying Model. *Computers in Human Behavior*, *92*, 250–255. doi:10.1016/j.chb.2018.11.013

Baron, R. A., & Neuman, J. H. (1996). Workplace violence and workplace aggression: Evidence on their relative frequency and potential causes. *Aggressive Behavior*, *22*(3), 161–173. doi:10.1002/(SICI)1098-2337(1996)22:3<161::AID-AB1>3.0.CO;2-Q

Başar, M., & Çetin, Ö. (2013). A Study on Primary and Secondary School Students' Levels of Bullying Behaviors and Learning Environments for These Behaviors. *E-Journal of New World Sciences Academy*, *8*(4), 471–488.

Bastiaensens, S., Vandebosch, H., Poels, K., Cleemput, K., Desmet, A., & Bourdeaudhuij, I. (2014). Cyberbullying on social network sites. An experimental study into bystanders' behavioural intentions to help the victim or reinforce the bully. *Computers in Human Behavior*, *31*, 259–271. doi:10.1016/j.chb.2013.10.036

Batmaz, M., & Ayas, T. (2013). Predicting the cyber bullying levels of students ın second stage of primary school according to psychological. *Sakarya University Journal of Education*, *3*(1), 43–53.

Bauman, S. (2007). Cyberbullying: A virtual menace. *National Coalition Against Bullying National Conference.*

Bauman, S. (2009). Cyberbullying in a rural intermediate school: An exploratory study. *The Journal of Early Adolescence*, *10*(10), 1–31.

Bauman, S., & Del Rio, A. (2006). Preservice teachers' responses to bullying scenarios: Comparing physical, verbal, and relational bullying. *Journal of Educational Psychology*, *98*(1), 219–231. doi:10.1037/0022-0663.98.1.219

Bauman, S., & Hurley, C. (2005). Teachers' Attitudes and Beliefs About Bullying: Two Exploratory Studies. *Journal of School Violence*, *4*(3), 49–61. doi:10.1300/J202v04n03_05

Bauman, S., & Pero, H. (2011). Bullying and cyberbullying among deaf students and their hearing peers: An exploratory study. *Journal of Deaf Studies and Deaf Education*, *16*(2), 236–253. doi:10.1093/deafed/enq043 PMID:20855432

Bauman, S., Toomey, R. B., & Walker, J. L. (2013). Associations among bullying, cyberbullying, and suicide in high school students. *Journal of Adolescence*, *36*(2), 341–350. doi:10.1016/j.adolescence.2012.12.001 PMID:23332116

Bauman, S., & Yoon, J. (2014). Theories of bullying and cyberbullying. *Theory into Practice*, *53*(4), 253–256. doi:10.1080/00405841.2014.947215

Bayar, Y., & Uçanok, Z. (2012). School Social Climate and Traditional / Cyberbullying: The Mediational Role of Peer Perception. *Turkish Journal of Psychology*, *27*(70), 101–114.

Bayer, J. K., Mundy, L., Stokes, I., Hearps, S., Allen, N., & Patton, G. (2018). Bullying, mental health and friendship in Australian primary school children. *Child and Adolescent Mental Health, 23*(4), 334–340. doi:10.1111/camh.12261 PMID:32677138

Bayrakci, E., & Dinc, M. (2020). Tersine Zorbalik (Mobbing) Eylemleri ve Tersine Zorbalikla Basa Cikma Stratejileri Uzerine Nitel Bir Arastirma [A Qualitative Study on Acts of Reverse Bullying(Mobbing) and Strategies for Coping with Reverse Bullying]. *Süleyman Demirel Üniversitesi Vizyoner Dergisi, 11*(27), 403–418.

Bayraktar, F., Machackova, H., Dedkova, L., Cerna, A., & Ševčíková, A. (2015). Cyberbullying: The Discriminant Factors Among Cyberbullies, Cybervictims, and Cyberbully-victims in a Czech Adolescent Sample. *Journal of Interpersonal Violence, 30*(18), 3192–3216. doi:10.1177/0886260514555006 PMID:25411234

Bayram, N., & Saylı, M. (2013). *Cyberbullying behavior among university students. İÜHFM.*

BC Gov News. (2022). *B.C. makes changes to better support francophone students, families.* BC Gov News. https://news.gov.bc.ca/releases/2022ECC0029-000644

Beale, A. V., & Hall, K. R. (2007). Cyberbullying: What school administrators (and parents) can do. *The Clearing House: A Journal of Educational Strategies, Issues and Ideas, 81*(1), 8–12. doi:10.3200/TCHS.81.1.8-12

Beale, A. V., & Scott, P. C. (2001). Bullybusters: Using drama to empower students to take a stand against bullying behavior. *Professional School Counseling, 4*(4), 300–305.

Beane, A. L. (2008). *Protect your child from bullying expert advice to help you recognize, prevent, and stop bullying before your child gets hurt.* Jossey-Bass.

Beane, A. L. (2008). *Protect your child from bullying.* Jossey-Bass.

Bedrosova, M., Machackova, H., Šerek, J., Smahel, D., & Blaya, C. (2022). The relation between the cyberhate and cyberbullying experiences of adolescents in the Czech Republic, Poland, and Slovakia. *Computers in Human Behavior, 126*, 107013. doi:10.1016/j.chb.2021.107013

Begotti, T., & Acquadro Maran, D. (2019). Characteristics of Cyberstalking Behavior, Consequences, and Coping Strategies: A Cross-sectional Study in a Sample of Italian University Students. *Future Internet, 11*(5), 120–131. doi:10.3390/fi11050120

Beitchman, J. H., Zucker, K. J., Hood, J. E., DaCosta, G. A., Akman, D., & Cassavia, E. (1992). A review of the long-term effects of child sexual abuse. *Child Abuse & Neglect, 16*(1), 101–118. doi:10.1016/0145-2134(92)90011-F PMID:1544021

Bell, M. E., Street, A. E., & Stafford, J. (2014). Victims' psychosocial well-being after reporting sexual harassment in the military. *Journal of Trauma & Dissociation, 15*(2), 133–152. doi:10.1080/15299732.2014.867563 PMID:24410254

Belsey, B. (2004). *What is cyberbullying?* Retrieved from: www.bullying.org/external/documents/ACF6F8.pdf

Belsey, B. (2005). Cyberbullying: An emerging threat to the "always on" generation. *Recuperado el, 5*(5).

Belsey, B. (2007). *Cyber bullying: An emerging threat to the 'always on' generation.* Retrieved June 11, from www.cyberbullying.ca

BelseyB. (2004). *Cyberbullying.* http://www.cyberbullying.org

Belsey, B. (2006). Bullying. org: A learning journey. *Bulletin–Newfoundland and Labrador Teachers Association, 49*(4), 20.

Bem, S. L. (1983). Gender schema theory and its implications for child development: Raising gender-aschematic children in a gender-schematic society. *Signs (Chicago, Ill.), 8*(4), 598–616. doi:10.1086/493998

Benbasat, I., & Wang, W. (2005). Trust in and adoption of online recommendation agents. *Journal of the Association for Information Systems*, *6*(3), 72–101. Advance online publication. doi:10.17705/1jais.00065

Benbenishty, R., & Astor, R. A. (2007). Monitoring indicators of children's victimization in school: Linking national-, regional-, and site-level indicators. *Social Indicators Research*, *84*(3), 333–348. doi:10.100711205-007-9116-4

Beran, T. N., Rinaldi, C., Bickham, D. S., & Rich, M. (2012). Evidence For the Need to Support Adolescents Dealing with Harassment and Cyber-harassment: Prevalence, Progression, and Impact. *School Psychology International*, *33*(5), 562–576. doi:10.1177/0143034312446976

Beran, T. N., & Tutty, L. (2002). Children's reports of bullying and safety at school. *Canadian Journal of School Psychology*, *17*(2), 1–14. doi:10.1177/082957350201700201

Beran, T., & Li, Q. (2007). The relationship between cyber bullying and school bullying. *Journal of Student Wellbeing*, *1*(2), 15–33.

Beran, T., & Li, Q. (2007). The relationship between cyberbullying and school bullying. *The Journal of Student Wellbeing*, *1*(2), 16–33. doi:10.21913/JSW.v1i2.172

Berdahl, J. L. (2007). Harassment based on sex: Protecting social status in the context of gender hierarchy. *Academy of Management Review*, *32*(2), 641–658. doi:10.5465/amr.2007.24351879

Berenbaum, H. (1996). Childhood abuse, alexithymia and personality disorder. *Journal of Psychosomatic Research*, *41*(6), 585–595. doi:10.1016/S0022-3999(96)00225-5 PMID:9032722

Berenson, K. R., & Andersen, S. M. (2006). Childhood physical and emotional abuse by a parent: Transference effects in adult interpersonal relations. *Personality and Social Psychology Bulletin*, *32*(11), 1509–1522. doi:10.1177/0146167206291671 PMID:17030892

Beren, T., & Li, Q. (2007). The relationship between cyberbullying and school bullying. *Journal of Student Wellbeing*, *1*(2), 15–33.

Berger, J., & Milkman, K. L. (2012). What makes online content viral? *JMR, Journal of Marketing Research*, *49*(2), 192–205. doi:10.1509/jmr.10.0353

Berger, K. (2007). Update on bullying at school: Science forgotten. *Developmental Review*, *27*(1), 90–126. doi:10.1016/j.dr.2006.08.002

Berger, L. M. (2005). Income, family characteristics, and physical violence toward children. *Child Abuse & Neglect*, *29*(2), 107–133. doi:10.1016/j.chiabu.2004.02.006 PMID:15734178

Berk, L. (2013). *Child development* (9th ed.). Pearson.

Berk, L. E. (2013). *Infants and children: Prenatal through middle childhood.* Nobel Publications.

Berkowitz, C. D. (2017). Physical abuse of children. *The New England Journal of Medicine*, *376*(17), 1659–1666. doi:10.1056/NEJMcp1701446 PMID:28445667

Berne, S., Frisén, A., Schultze-Krumbholz, A., Scheithauer, H., Naruskov, K., Luik, P., Katzer, C., Erentaite, R., & Zukauskiene, R. (2013). Cyberbullying assessment instruments: A systematic review. *Aggression and Violent Behavior*, *18*(2), 320–334. doi:10.1016/j.avb.2012.11.022

Berns, R. (2015). *Child, family, school, community: Socialization and support* (10th ed.). Cengage Learning.

Bernstein, J. Y., & Watson, M. W. (1997). Children who are targets of bullying: A victim pattern. *Journal of Interpersonal Violence, 12*(4), 483–498. doi:10.1177/088626097012004001

Berzenski, S. R., & Yates, T. M. (2010). A developmental process analysis of the contribution of childhood emotional abuse to relationship violence. *Journal of Aggression, Maltreatment & Trauma, 19*(2), 180–203. doi:10.1080/10926770903539474

Besag, V. E. (1989). *Bullies and victims in schools. a guide to understanding and management.* Open University Press.

Besag, V. E. (1989). *Bullies and victims in schools. A guide to understanding and management.* Open University Press.

Besag, V. E. (1989). Bullies and Victims. In *Schools. A Guide To Understanding and Management.* Open University Press.

Betts, L. R. (2015). Cyber bullying behaviours. In Encyclopedia of Information Science and Technology (pp. 6727–6735). doi:10.4018/978-1-4666-5888-2.ch661

Betts, L. R. (2016). *Cyberbullying approaches, consequences, and interventions.* Palgrave Macmillan. doi:10.1057/978-1-137-50009-0

Bhat, B. (n.d.). *The World's First Definition of "Cyberbullying".* https://cyberbullying.ca/

Bhat, C. S. (2008). Cyber Bullying: Overview and Strategies for School Counsellors, Guidance Officers, and All School Personnel. *Australian Journal of Guidance & Counselling, 18*(1), 53–66. doi:10.1375/ajgc.18.1.53

Bhat, C. S. (2008). Cyber Bullying: Overview and Strategies For School Counsellors, Guidance Officers, and All School Personnel. *Journal of Psychologists and Counsellors In Schools, 18*(1), 53–66.

Bhat, C. S., Chang, S. H., & Linscott, J. A. (2010). Addressing Cyberbullying as a Media Literacy Issue. *New Horizons in Education, 58*(3).

Bhat, C. S., Chang, S.-H., & Lınscott, J. A. (2010). Addressing Cyberbullying as a Media Literacy Issue. *New Horizons in Education, 58*(3), 34–43.

Bhushan, A. (2019). Understanding of Information Technology Act for E-Governance in India. *IIBM'S Journal of Management, 4*(2), 1–6. doi:10.33771/iibm.v4i1-2.138

Bifulco, A., Schimmenti, A., Jacobs, C., Bunn, A., & Rusu, A. C. (2014). Risk factors and psychological outcomes of bullying victimization: A community-based study. *Child Indicators Research, 7*(3), 633–648. doi:10.100712187-014-9236-8

Bigne, E., Andreu, L., Hernandez, B., & Ruiz, C. (2018). The impact of social media and offline influences on consumer behaviour. An analysis of the low-cost airline industry. *Current Issues in Tourism, 21*(9), 1014–1032. doi:10.1080/13683500.2015.1126236

Bilgiç, E. (2007). *Investigation of the bullying observed at elementary schools in view of the perception of class variables and atmosphere* [Unpublished Master Thesis]. Çukurova University, Institute of Social Sciences, Adana.

Bilgin, A. (2007). The Views of Day and Boarding Students about Bullying. *Ege Journal of Education, 8*(1), 1–18.

Black, S., Weinles, D., & Washington, E. (2010). Victim strategies to stop bullying. *Youth Violence and Juvenile Justice, 8*(2), 138–147. doi:10.1177/1541204009349401

Blum-Ross, A., & Livingstone, S. (2017). "Sharenting," parent blogging and the boundaries of the digital self. *Popular Communication, 15*(2), 110–125. doi:10.1080/15405702.2016.1223300

Bölükbaş, K., & Kırık, A. M. (2020). Twitter Phenomena in the Context of Cyberbullying. *Kahramanmaraş Sütçü Imam University Journal of Social Sciences, 17*(2), 944–966.

Bond, L., Carlin, J. B., Thomas, L., Rubin, K., & Patton, G. (2001). Does bullying cause emotional problems? A prospective study of young teenagers. *BMJ (Clinical Research Ed.)*, *323*(7311), 480–484. doi:10.1136/bmj.323.7311.480 PMID:11532838

Bonell, C., Dodd, M., Allen, E., Bevilacqua, L., McGowan, J., Opondo, C., Sturgess, J., Elbourne, D., Warren, E., & Viner, R. (2020). Broader impacts of an intervention to transform school environments on student behaviour and school functioning: Post hoc analyses from the INCLUSIVE cluster randomised controlled trial. *BMJ Open*, 1–11. doi:10.1136/bmjopen-2019-031589 PMID:32414817

Bonell, C., Fletcher, A., Fitzgerald-Yau, N., Hale, D., Allen, E., Elbourne, D., Jones, R., Bond, L., Wiggins, M., Miners, A., Legood, R., Scott, S., Christie, D., & Viner, R. (2015). Initiating change locallyin bullying and aggression through the school environment (INCLUSIVE): A pilot randomised controlled trial. *Health Technology Assessment*, *19*(53), 1–109. doi:10.3310/hta19530 PMID:26182956

Borg, M. G. (1999). The extent and nature of bullying among primary and secondary schoolchildren. *Educational Research*, *41*(2), 137–153. doi:10.1080/0013188990410202

Boulton, M. J., & Hawker, D. S. (1997). Non-physical forms of bullying among school pupils: A cause for concern. *Health Education*, *2*(2), 61–64. doi:10.1108/09654289710158393

Boulton, M. J., Macaulay, P. J. R., & Atherton, S. (2021). *Promoting Junior School Students' Anti-bullying Beliefs with the CATZ Cross-age Teaching Zone Intervention. Int Journal of Bullying Prevention.* doi:10.100742380-021-00111-9

Boulton, M. J., & Underwood, K. (1992). Bully/victim problems among middle school children. *The British Journal of Educational Psychology*, *62*(1), 73–87. doi:10.1111/j.2044-8279.1992.tb01000.x PMID:1558813

Bozbayındır, G. B. (2019). Cyberbullying and Criminal Law. *İstanbul Hukuk Mecmuası*, 425-450.

Bozkanat, E. (2020). Dijital İletişimin Karanlık Yüzü Siber Zorbalık: Kavramsal Bir Çerçeve. In Y. Akman (Ed.), *Dijital Dönüşüm ve Yenilik Yönetimi*. İskenderiye Book.

Bozyiğit, A., Utku, S., & Nasibov, E. (2021). Cyberbullying detection: Utilizing social media features. *Expert Systems with Applications*, *179*, 115001. doi:10.1016/j.eswa.2021.115001

Bradshaw, C. P. (2015). Translating research to practice in bullying prevention. *The American Psychologist*, *70*(4), 322–332. doi:10.1037/a0039114 PMID:25961313

Bradshaw, C. P., Sawyer, A. L., & O'Brennan, L. M. (2007). Bullying and peer victimization at school: Perceptual differences between students and school staff. *School Psychology Review*, *36*(3), 361–382. doi:10.1080/02796015.2007.12087929

Bradshaw, C. P., Waasdorp, T. E., & Johnson, S. L. (2015). Overlapping verbal, relational, physical, and electronic forms of bullying in adolescence: Influence of school context. *Journal of Clinical Child and Adolescent Psychology*, *44*(3), 494–508. doi:10.1080/15374416.2014.893516 PMID:24738548

Brady, W. J., Wills, J. A., Jost, J. T., Tucker, J. A., & Van Bavel, J. J. (2017). Emotion shapes the diffusion of moralized content in social networks. *Proceedings of the National Academy of Sciences of the United States of America*, *114*(28), 7313–7318. doi:10.1073/pnas.1618923114 PMID:28652356

Branch, S. (2008). You say Tomatoe and I say Tomato: Can we differentiate between Workplace Bullying and other Counterproductive behaviours? *International Journal of Organisational Behaviour*, 13.

Brandtzag, P. B., Staksrud, E., Hagen, I., & Wold, W. (2009). Norwegian children's experiences of Cyberbullying when using different technological platforms. *Journal of Children and Media*, *3*(4), 349–365. doi:10.1080/17482790903233366

Brewer, G., & Kerslake, J. (2015). Cyberbullying, self-esteem, empathy and loneliness. *Computers in Human Behavior*, *48*, 255–260. doi:10.1016/j.chb.2015.01.073

Brighi, A., Ortega, R., Pyzalski, J., Scheithauer, H., Smith, P. K., & Tsormpatzoudis, H. (2012). *European cyberbullying intervention project questionnaire – ECIPQ* [Unpublished questionnaire]. bullyingandcyber.net

Brochado, S., Soares, S., & Fraga, S. (2017). A scoping review on studies of cyberbullying prevalence among adolescents. *Trauma, Violence & Abuse*, *18*(5), 523–531. doi:10.1177/1524838016641668 PMID:27053102

Broder, H. L. (2007). Children's oral health-related quality of life. *Community Dentistry and Oral Epidemiology*, *35*(1), 5–7. doi:10.1111/j.1600-0528.2007.00400.x PMID:17615045

Brody, N., & Vangelisti, A. L. (2016). Bystander intervention in cyberbullying. *Communication Monographs*, *83*(1), 94–119. doi:10.1080/03637751.2015.1044256

Bronfenbrenner, U. (1979). Contexts of child rearing: Problems and prospects. *The American Psychologist*, *34*(10), 844–850. doi:10.1037/0003-066X.34.10.844

Brosch, A. (2016). When the child is born into the internet: Sharenting as a growing trend among parents on facebook. *The New Educational Review*, *43*(2), 225–235. doi:10.15804/tner.2016.43.1.19

Brosch, A. (2018). Sharenting – Why do parents violate their children's privacy? *The New Educational Review*, *54*(4), 75–85. doi:10.15804/tner.2018.54.4.06

Brown, J. M. (1998). Aspects of discriminatory treatment of women police officers serving in forces in England and Wales. *British Journal of Criminology*, *38*(2), 265–282. doi:10.1093/oxfordjournals.bjc.a014235

Brown, K., Jackson, M., & Cassidy, W. (2006). Cyber-bullying: Developing Policy to Direct Responses the are Equitable and effective in Addressing this Special Form of Bullying. *Canadian Journal of Educational Administration and Policy*, 57.

Buchanan, N. T., & Fitzgerald, L. F. (2008). Effects of racial and sexual harassment on work and the psychological well-being of African American women. *Journal of Occupational Health Psychology*, *13*(2), 137–151. doi:10.1037/1076-8998.13.2.137 PMID:18393583

Buelga, S., Martínez-Ferrer, B., & Cava, M. J. (2017). Differences in family climate and family communication among cyberbullies, cybervictims, and cyber bully victims in adolescents. *Computers in Human Behavior*, *76*, 164–173. doi:10.1016/j.chb.2017.07.017

Buhlmann, U., Cook, L. M., Fama, J. M., & Wilhelm, S. (2007). Perceived teasing experiences in body dysmorphic disorder. *Body Image*, *4*(4), 381–385. doi:10.1016/j.bodyim.2007.06.004 PMID:18089284

Buhs, E. S., & Ladd, G. W. (2001). Peer rejection in kindergarten as an antecedent of young children's school adjustment: An examination of mediating processes. *Developmental Psychology*, *37*(4), 550–560. doi:10.1037/0012-1649.37.4.550 PMID:11444490

Bulger, C. A. (2001). Union resources and union tolerance as moderators of relationships with sexual harassment. *Sex Roles*, *45*(11/12), 723–741. doi:10.1023/A:1015684202115

Bulunmaz, B. (2015). Yeni Medyada Nefret Söylemi ve Üniversite Öğrencilerine Yönelik Bir Araştırma. *Uşak Üniversitesi Sosyal Bilimler Dergisi, 8*(1), 73-88.

Bulut Serin, N. (2012). Erkek ergenlerin anne-baba ve genç yetişkinlerine yönelik duygusal istismar algıları [Perceptions of emotional abuse by male adolescents towards their parents and young adults]. *Türk Uluslararası Özel Eğitim ve Rehberlik ve Danışmanlık Dergisi*, *1*(2), 18–26.

Bulut, S. (2008). Öğretmenden öğrenciye yönelik olan fiziksel şiddet: Nicel bir araştırma [Physical violence from teacher to student: A quantitative study]. *Abant İzzet Baysal Üniversitesi Eğitim Fakültesi Dergisi*, *8*(1), 105–118.

Bureau of Justice Statistics. (2020). *Criminal Victimization.* https://bjs.ojp.gov/library/publications/criminal-victimization-2020

Burns, E. E., Jackson, J. L., & Harding, H. G. (2010). Child maltreatment, emotion regulation, and posttraumatic stress: The impact of emotional abuse. *Journal of Aggression, Maltreatment & Trauma*, *19*(8), 801–819. doi:10.1080/10926771.2010.522947

Burnukara, P. (2009). İl ve Orta Ergenlikte Geleneksel ve Sanal Akran Zorbalığına Betimsel Bir İnceleme (Unpublished Master's Thesesis). Hacettepe University, Ankara.

Burnukara, P., & Uçanok, Z. (2012). How much overlap between traditional and cyberbullying in Turkish adolescents? *Turkish Journal of Psychology*, *27*(69), 81–96. https://www.psikolog.org.tr/tr/yayinlar/dergiler/1031828/tpd1300443320120000m000084.pdf

Butler, J. (2012). Gender trouble: Feminism and the subversion of identity (B. Ertür, Trans.). İstanbul, Turkey: Metis Yayınları.

Butler, D., Kift, S., Campbell, M., Slee, P., & Spears, B. (2011). School policy responses to cyberbullying: An Australian legal perspective. *International Journal of Law and Education*, *16*(2), 7–28.

C., K. (2020). Social and Legislative Issues in Handling Cyberbullying in India. In *Research Anthology on Combating Cyber-Aggression and Online Negativity* (pp. 447–466). IGI Global. doi:10.4018/978-1-7998-4912-4.ch021

Caldarella, P., Shatzer, R. H., Gray, K. M., Young, K. R., & Young, E. L. (2011). The Effects of School-wide Positive Behavior Support on Middle School Climate and Student Outcomes. *RMLE Online: Research in Middle Level Education*, *35*(4), 1–14. doi:10.1080/19404476.2011.11462087

Caldarella, P., Shatzer, R. H., Gray, K. M., Young, R. K., & Young, E. L. (2011). The effects of school-wide positive behavior support on middle school climate and student outcomes. *Research in Middle Level Education Online*, *35*(4), 1–14.

Calvete, E., Gámez-Guadix, M., & Borrajo, E. (2019). Cyberbullying in Romantic Relationships: Cross-Cultural Issues. In Cyberbullying in Schools, Workplaces, and Romantic Relationships (pp. 150-183). Routledge.

Calvete, E., Orue, I., Estevez, A., Villardon, L., & Padilla, P. (2010). Cyberbullying in adolescents: Modalities and aggressors' profile. *Computers in Human Behavior*, *26*(5), 1128–1135. doi:10.1016/j.chb.2010.03.017

Calvo-Morata, A., Alonso-Fernández, C., Freire, M., Martínez-Ortiz, I., & Fernández-Manjón, B. (2020). Serious games to prevent and detect bullying and cyberbullying: A systematic serious games and literature review. *Computers & Education*, *157*, 103958. doi:10.1016/j.compedu.2020.103958

Çam, H. H., & Ustuner Top, F. (2021). Workplace violence against nurses working in the public hospitals in Giresun, Turkey: Prevalence, risk factors, and quality of life consequences. *Perspectives in Psychiatric Care*, 1–11. doi:10.1111/ppc.12978 PMID:34860413

Camodeca, M., Goossens, F. A., Meerum Terwogt, M., & Schuengel, C. (2002). Bullying and victimization among school-age children: Stability and links to proactive and reactive aggression. *Social Development*, *11*(3), 332–345. doi:10.1111/1467-9507.00203

Camodeca, M., & Nava, E. (2022). The long-term effects of bullying, victimization, and by stander behavior on emotion regulation and its physiological correlates. *Journal of Interpersonal Violence*, *37*(3-4), NP2056–NP2075. doi:10.1177/0886260520934438 PMID:32597723

Campbell, M. A. (2005). Cyber bullying: An old problem in a new guise? *Australian Journal of Guidance & Counselling, 15*(1), 68–76. doi:10.1375/ajgc.15.1.68

Campbell, R. (2008). The psychological impact of rape victims. *The American Psychologist, 63*(8), 702–717. doi:10.1037/0003-066X.63.8.702 PMID:19014228

Campfield, D. C. (2008). *Cyber bullying and victimization: Psychosocial characteristics of bullies, victims and bully/victims* (Unpublished master's thesis). Montana University, Missoula.

Cao, J., & Jin, Y. (2016). Theoretical interpretation on the communication power of internet strong language memes. *Chinese Journal of Journalism & Communication, 2*, 37–56.

Cao, Q., Xu, X., Xiang, H., Yang, Y., Peng, P., & Xu, S. (2020). Bullying victimization and suicidal ideation among Chinese left-behind children: Mediating effect of loneliness and moderating effect of gender. *Children and Youth Services Review, 111*, 104848. doi:10.1016/j.childyouth.2020.104848

Cappadocia, M. C., Craig, W. M., & Pepler, D. (2013). Cyberbullying: Prevalence, Stability, and Risk Factors During Adolescence. *Canadian Journal of School Psychology, 28*(2), 171–192. doi:10.1177/0829573513491212

Cara, M. J., & Moya, E. (2022). Cyberbullying in university students before and after COVID-19 lockdown. *Educación XX1, 25*(1), 67-91. doi:10.5944/educxx1.30525

Carballo-Diéguez & Dolezal. (1995, May 19). *Association between history of childhood sexual abuse and adult HIV-risk sexual behavior in Puerto Rican men who have sex with men*. Academic Press.

Cardona, R. S., Reyes, A. S., & Tangalin, M. M. (2015). The bullying experiences and classroom discipline techniques in an Urban National High School in the Philippines: A basis for an Anti-Bullying Program. *American International Journal of Contemporary Research, 5*(2), 49–52. https://www.researchgate.net/publication/321882096_The_Bullying_Experiences_and_Classroom_Discipline_Techniques_in_an_Urban_National_High_School_in_the_Philippines_A_Basis_for_an_Anti-Bullying_Program

Carlson Jones, D. (2004). Body image among adolescent girls and boys: A longitudinal study. *Developmental Psychology, 40*(5), 823–835. doi:10.1037/0012-1649.40.5.823 PMID:15355169

Carlson, E. (2006). *i-SAFE and Microsoft bring net safety to schools and parents*. i-SAFE Media. Retrieved November 22,2009, from http://www.isafe.org/imgs/pdf/outreach-press/iSAFE_ MS YR-02-06.pdf

Carney, A. G., & Merrell, K. W. (2001). Bullying in schools: Perspectives on understanding and preventing an international problem. *School Psychology International, 22*(3), 364–382. doi:10.1177/0143034301223011

Carpenter, L. L., Tyrka, A. R., Ross, N. S., Khoury, L., Anderson, G. M., & Price, L. H. (2009). Effect of childhood emotional abuse and age on cortisol responsivity in adulthood. *Biological Psychiatry, 66*(1), 69–75. doi:10.1016/j.biopsych.2009.02.030 PMID:19375070

Carrera, M. V., DePalma, R., & Lameiras, M. (2011). Toward a more comprehensive understanding of bullying in school settings. *Educational Psychology Review, 23*(4), 479–499. doi:10.100710648-011-9171-x

Carter, M. A. (2013). Third party observers witnessing cyber bullying on social media sites. *Social and Behavioral Sciences, 84*, 1296–1309. doi:10.1016/j.sbspro.2013.06.747

Carvalho, M., Branquinho, C., & de Matos, M. G. (2021). Cyberbullying and Bullying: Impact on Psychological Symptoms and Well-Being. *Child Indicators Research, 14*(1), 435–452. doi:10.100712187-020-09756-2

Casper, D. M. (2021). Types of traditional (offline) bullying. In P. K. Smith & J. O. Norman (Eds.), *The Wiley Blackwell handbook of bullying: A comprehensive and international review of research and intervention* (pp. 96–119). Wiley Blackwell. doi:10.1002/9781118482650.ch6

Cassidy, W., Jackson, M., & Faucher, C. (2016). Gender Differences and Cyberbullying Towards Faculty Members in Higher Education. *Cyberbullying Across the Globe*, 79-98.

Cassidy, W., Faucher, C., & Jackson, M. (2013). Cyberbullying among Youth: A Comprehensive Review of Current International Research and Its Implications and Application to Policy and Practice. *School Psychology International, 34*(6), 575–612. doi:10.1177/0143034313479697

Cassidy, W., Jackson, M., & Brown, K. N. (2009). Sticks and stones can break my bones, but how can pixels hurt me?: Students' experiences with cyber-bullying. *School Psychology International, 30*(4), 383–402. doi:10.1177/0143034309106948

Cava, M. J., Tomás, I., Buelga, S., & Carrascosa, L. (2020). Loneliness, Depressive Mood and Cyberbullying Victimization in Adolescent Victims of Cyber Dating Violence. *International Journal of Environmental Research and Public Health, 17*(12), 4269. doi:10.3390/ijerph17124269 PMID:32549276

CDC Centers For Disease Control And Prevention. (2020). *Preventing bullying*. https://www.cdc.gov/violenceprevention/youthviolence/bullyingresearch/fastfact.html

Çelik, T., & Tekin, Y. (2015). An Example of the Negative Effects of Social Media on Individuals: Cyberbullying. *The Journal of Academic Social Science Studies International Journal of Social Science*, 343-355.

Çetin, H. (2020). Çocukların istismar ve ihmalden korunma hakkı. In Disiplinlerarası yaklaşımla çocuk hakları içinde [The right of children to be protected from abuse and neglect] (pp. 161-179). Ankara: Pegem Akademi.

Cetin, Z., & Danaci, M. O. (2016). A multivariate examination of the child-abuse potential of parents with children aged 0-6. *Eurasian Journal of Educational Research, 16*(66), 71-86.

Çetin, B., Peker, A., Eroğlu, Y., & Çitemel, N. (2011). Siber zorbalığın bir yordayıcısı olarak ilişkilerle ilgili bilişsel çarpıtmalar: Ergenler için bir ön çalışma [Cognitive distorions related to relationships as a predictor of cyberbullying: A preliminary study for adolescents]. *International Online Journal of Educational Sciences, 3*(3), 1064–1080.

Çetinkaya, S., Nur, N., Ayvaz, A., Özdemir, D., & Kavakçı, Ö. (2009). Sosyoekonomik durumu farklı üç ilköğretim okulu öğrencilerinde akran zorbalığın depresyon ve benlik saygısı düzeyiyle ilişkisi [The relationship of peer bullying with depression and self-esteem levels in three primary school students with different socioeconomic status]. *Anadolu Psikiyatri Dergisi, 10*, 151–158.

Çevik, B. (2021). *Bullying with Real Witnesses*. Sola Unitas Publications.

Chadwick, S. (2014). *Impacts of cyberbullying, building social and emotional resilience in schools. Springer Briefs in Education*. Springer., doi:10.1007/978-3-319-04031-8

Chai, L., Xueb, J., & Hanc, Z. (2020). School bullying victimization and self-rated health and life satisfaction: The mediating effect of relationships with parents, teachers, and peers. *Children and Youth Services Review, 117*, 105281. doi:10.1016/j.childyouth.2020.105281

Chakraborty, A., Zhang, Y., & Ramesh, A. (2018). Understanding Types of Cyberbullying in an Anonymous Messaging Application. *Companion Proceedings of the The Web Conference 2018*, 1001-1005. 10.1145/3184558.3191530

Chan, A., Antoun, J. S., Morgaine, K. C., & Farella, M. (2017). Accounts of bullying on T witter in relation to dentofacial features and orthodontic treatment. *Journal of Oral Rehabilitation, 44*(4), 244–250. doi:10.1111/joor.12487 PMID:28128466

Chan, D. K., Chow, S. Y., Lam, C. B., & Cheung, S. F. (2008). Examining the job-related, psychological, and physical outcomes of workplace sexual harassment: A meta- analytic review. *Psychology of Women Quarterly*, *32*(4), 362–376. doi:10.1111/j.1471-6402.2008.00451.x

Chan, E. K. H., Lımoges, K. M., & Fung, T. S. (2010). Functional Social Support and Major Depression in Cancer Patients. *Psychology Journal*, *7*(2), 46–50.

Chang, V. (2021). Inconsistent Definitions of Bullying: A Need to Examine People's Judgments and Reasoning about Bullying and Cyberbullying. *Human Development*, *65*(3), 144–159. doi:10.1159/000516838

Chan, T. K. H., Cheung, C. M. K., & Lee, Z. W. Y. (2021). Cyberbullying on social networking sites: A literature review and future research directions. *Information & Management*, *58*(2), 103411. doi:10.1016/j.im.2020.103411

Charach, A., Pepler, D. & Ziegler, S. (1995). *Bullying at school: a Canadian perspective*. Education Canada.

Charalampous, K., Demetriou, C., Tricha, L., Ioannou, M., Georgiou, S., Nikiforou, M., & Stavrinides, P. (2018). The effect of parental style on bullying and cyber bullying behaviors and the mediating role of peer attachment relationships: A longitudinal study. *Journal of Adolescence*, *64*(1), 109–123. doi:10.1016/j.adolescence.2018.02.003 PMID:29448185

Charney, D. A., & Russel, R. C. (1994). An overview of sexual harassment. *The American Journal of Psychiatry*, *151*(1), 10–17. doi:10.1176/ajp.151.1.10 PMID:8267106

Chaudhuri, P. (2007). Experiences of Sexual Harassment of Women Health Workers in Four Hospitals in Kolkata, India. *Reproductive Health Matters*, *15*(30), 221–229. doi:10.1016/S0968-8080(07)30319-4 PMID:17938090

Chaux, E., Velasquez, A. M., Schultze-Krumbholz, A., & Scheithauer, H. (2016). Effects of the cyberbullying prevention program media hereos (Medienhelden) on traditional bullying. *Aggressive Behavior*, *42*(2), 157–165. doi:10.1002/ab.21637 PMID:26879895

Cheema, S., Ahmad, K., Giri, S. K., Kaliaperumal, V. K., & Naqvi, S. A. (2005). Bullying of junior doctors prevails in Irish health system: A bitter reality. *Irish Medical Journal*, *98*(9), 274–275. PMID:16300107

Chen, N., Zhang, M., Li, R., Wang, P., & Wang, Y. (2019). Investigation on workplace violence in a Grade 2A hospital - - A survey using the investing tool for workplace violence in hospitals developed by the World Health Organization. *China Occupational Medicine*, 157-162.

Chen, G., Kong, Y., Deater-Deckard, K., & Zhang, W. (2018). Bullying Victimization Heightens Cortisol Response to Psychosocial Stress in Chinese Children. *Journal of Abnormal Child Psychology*, *46*(5), 1051–1059. doi:10.100710802-017-0366-6 PMID:29196916

Cheng, J. C., & Yi, O. (2018). Hotel employee job crafting, burnout, and satisfaction: The moderating role of perceived organizational support. *International Journal of Hospitality Management*, *72*, 78–85. doi:10.1016/j.ijhm.2018.01.005

Cheng, L., Hu, X., Matulewska, A., & Wagner, A. (2020). Exploring cyberbullying: A socio-semiotic perspective. *International Journal of Legal Discourse*, *5*(2), 359–378. doi:10.1515/ijld-2020-2042

Chen, Q. Q., Lo, C. K. M., Zhu, Y., Cheung, A., Chan, K. L., & Ip, P.QiQi. (2018). Family poly-victimization and cyberbullying among adolescents in a Chinese school sample. *Child Abuse & Neglect*, *77*, 180–187. doi:10.1016/j.chiabu.2018.01.015 PMID:29407606

Chen, X., Luo, Y. J., & Chen, H. (2020). Body image victimization experiences and disordered eating behaviors among Chinese female adolescents: The role of body dissatisfaction and depression. *Sex Roles*, *83*(7), 442–452. doi:10.100711199-020-01122-4

Chiemela, Q. A., Ovute, A. O., & Obochi, C. I. (2015). The Influence of the Social Media on the Nigerian Youths: Aba residents experience. *Journal of Research in Humanities and Social Science*, *3*(3), 12–20.

Chikaodi, O., Abdulmanan, Y., Emmanuel, A. T., Muhammad, J., Mohammed, M. A., Izegboya, A., Donald, O. O., & Balarabe, S. (2019). Bullying, its effects on attitude towards class attendance and the contribution of physical and dentofacial features among adolescents in Northern Nigeria. *International Journal of Adolescent Medicine and Health*, *31*(2). Advance online publication. doi:10.1515/ijamh-2016-0149 PMID:28731856

China Internet Network Information Center. (2020). *The 46th China statistical report on Internet development.* https://cnnic.net.cn/hlwfzyj/hlwxzbg/hlwtjbg/202009/P020200929546215182514.pdf

Chipps, E. M., & McRury, M. (2012). The development of an educational intervention to address workplace bullying: A pilot study. *Journal for Nurses in Staff Development*, *28*(3), 94–98. doi:10.1097/NND.0b013e31825514bb PMID:22617778

Chisuwa, N., & O'Dea, J. (2011). Historical Perspective of Body Image and Body Image Concerns among Male and Female Adolescents in Japan. In Body image: Perceptions, interpretations and attitudes içinde (pp. 1-27). Nova Science Publishers.

Chisuwa-Hayami, N., & Haruki, T. (2017). Associations of body-related teasing with weight status, body image, and dieting behavior among Japanese adolescents. *Health Promotion Perspectives*, *7*(2), 80–87. doi:10.15171/hpp.2017.15 PMID:28326288

Choi, G. Y., & Lewallen, J. (2018). "Say Instagram, Kids!": Examining Sharenting and Children's Digital Representations on Instagram. *The Howard Journal of Communications*, *29*(2), 140–160. doi:10.1080/10646175.2017.1327380

Choi, K. S., Earl, K., Lee, J. L., & Cho, S. (2019). Diagnosis of Cyber and Non-physical Bullying Victimization: A Routine Activities Approach to Constructing Effective Preventative Measures. *Computers in Human Behavior*, *92*, 11–19. doi:10.1016/j.chb.2018.10.014

Cho, S., Park, C., & Kim, J. (2017). Leveraging consumption intention with identity information on sharing economy platforms. *Journal of Computer Information Systems*, *00*(00), 1–10. doi:10.1080/08874417.2017.1326295

Chowdhury, A. G., Sawhney, R., Mathur, P., Mahata, D., & Shah, R. R. (2019, June). Speak up, fight back! detection of social media disclosures of sexual harassment. In *Proceedings of the 2019 conference of the North American chapter of the Association for Computational Linguistics: Student research workshop* (pp. 136-146). 10.18653/v1/N19-3018

Chowdhury, A. G., Sawhney, R., Shah, R., & Mahata, D. (2019, July). # YouToo? detection of personal recollections of sexual harassment on social media. In *Proceedings of the 57th Annual Meeting of the Association for Computational Linguistics* (pp. 2527-2537). 10.18653/v1/P19-1241

Christian, C. W., & Block, R. (2009). Abusive head trauma in infants and children. *Pediatrics*, *123*(5), 1409–1411. doi:10.1542/peds.2009-0408 PMID:19403508

Christian, M. S., & Ellis, A. P. J. (2011). Examining the Effects of Sleep Deprivation on Workplace Deviance: A Self-Regulatory Perspective. *Academy of Management Journal*, *54*(5), 913–934. doi:10.5465/amj.2010.0179

Chudal, R., Tiiri, E., Brunstein Klomek, A., Ong, S. H., Fossum, S., Kaneko, H., Kolaitis, G., Lesinskiene, S., Li, L., Huong, M. N., Praharaj, S. K., Sillanmäki, L., Slobodskaya, H. R., Srabstein, J. C., Wiguna, T., Zamani, Z., & Sourander, A. (2021). Victimization by traditional bullying and cyberbullying and the combination of these among adolescents in 13 European and Asian countries. *European Child & Adolescent Psychiatry*, 1–14. doi:10.100700787-021-01779-6 PMID:33884501

Chun, J., Lee, J., Kim, J., & Lee, S. (2020). An international systematic review of cyberbullying measurements. *Computers in Human Behavior*, *113*, 106485. doi:10.1016/j.chb.2020.106485

Cilliers, L. (2021). Perceptions and experiences of cyberbullying amongst university students in the Eastern Cape province, South Africa. *The Journal for Transdisciplinary Research in Southern Africa*, *17*(1), 6. doi:10.4102/td.v17i1.776

Çınkır, Ş., & Karaman-Kepenekçi, Y. (2003). Bullyıng among students. *Educational Administration in Theory & Practice*, *34*(34), 236-253. https://dergipark.org.tr/tr/pub/kuey/issue/10363/126858

Çınkır, S., & Kepenekçi, Y. K. (2003). Bullying between students. *Educational Management in Theory and Practice*, *34*, 236–253.

Clark, S. J., Davis, M. M., Singer, D. C., Matos-Moreno, A., Kauffman, A. D., & Hale, K. (2015). *'Parents on social media: Likes and dislikes of sharen-ting: C. S. Mott children's hospital national poll', National poll on children's health.* Retrieved January 3, 2022, from https://mottpoll.org/sites/default/files/docu-ments/031615_sharenting_0.pdf

Clark, C. M., & Luparell, S. (2020). Cyber-incivility, cyber-bullying, and other forms of online aggression: A call to action for nurse educators. *Nurse Education Today*, *85*, 104310. doi:10.1016/j.nedt.2019.104310 PMID:31805415

Clarke, R. V. (2013). Situational Crime Prevention. In R. Wortley & L. Mazerolle (Eds.), *Environmental Criminology and Crime Analysis*. Willan., doi:10.4324/9780203118214

Clarke, R. V., & Cornish, D. B. (1985). Modeling offenders' decisions: A framework for research and policy. *Crime and Justice*, *6*, 147–185. doi:10.1086/449106

Clarkson, S., Axford, N., Berry, V., Edwards, R. T., Bjornstad, G., Wrigley, Z., Charles, J., Hoare, Z., Ukoumunne, O. C., Matthews, J., & Hutchings, J. (2016). Effectiveness and micro-costing of the KiVa school-based bullying prevention programme in Wales: Study protocol for a pragmatic definitive parallel group cluster randomised controlled trial. *BMC Public Health*, *16*(104). Advance online publication. doi:10.118612889-016-2746-1 PMID:26832736

Clarkson, S., Charles, J. M., Saville, C. W. N., Bjornstad, G. J., & Hutchings, J. (2019). Introducing KiVa school-based antibullying programme to the UK: A preliminary examination of effectiveness and programme cost. *School Psychology International*, *40*(4), 347–365. doi:10.1177/0143034319841099

Clarkson, S., & Hutchings, J. (2015). Introducing and piloting the KiVa bullying prevention programme in the UK. *Educational and Child Psychology*, *32*(1), 49–61.

Clough, J. (2012). The Council of Europe Convention on Cybercrime: Defining "Crime" in a Digital World. *Criminal Law Forum*, *23*(4), 363–391. doi:10.100710609-012-9183-3

Coelho, V. A., & Romao, A. M. (2018). The relation between social anxiety, social withdrawal and (cyber) bullying roles: A multilevel analysis. *Computers in Human Behavior*, *86*, 218–226. doi:10.1016/j.chb.2018.04.048

Cohen, S. V., & McKay, G. (1984). Social Support, Stress and the BufferingHypothesis: A Theoretical Analysis. Handbook of Psychology and Health, 253-267.

Cohen, J. S., Leung, Y., Fahey, M., Hoyt, L., Sinha, R., Cailler, L., & Patten, S. (2008). The happy docs study: A Canadian Association of Internes and Residents well-being survey examining resident physician health and satisfaction within and outside of residency training in Canada. *BMC Research Notes*, *1*(1), 105. doi:10.1186/1756-0500-1-105 PMID:18957136

Cohen, L. E., & Felson, M. (1979). Social Change and Crime Rate Trends: A Routine Activity Approach. *American Sociological Review*, *44*(4), 588–608. doi:10.2307/2094589

Coie, J. D., Watt, N. F., West, S. G., Hawkins, J. D., Asarnow, J. R., Markman, H. J., Ramey, S. L., Shure, M. B., & Long, B. (1993). The science of prevention: A conceptual framework and some directions for a national research program. *The American Psychologist, 48*(10), 1013–1022. doi:10.1037/0003-066X.48.10.1013 PMID:8256874

Collier, B. (2021). Infrastructural Power: Dealing with Abuse, Crime, and Control in the Tor Anonymity Network. In Cybercrime in Context (pp. 283–301). Springer. doi:10.1007/978-3-030-60527-8_16

Committee on Injury, Violence, and Poison Prevention. (2009). Role of the pediatrician in youth violence prevention. *Pediatrics, 124*(1), 393–402.

Compass, B., Connor-Smith, J., Saltzman, H., Thomsen, A., & Wadsworth, M. (2001). Coping with stress during childhood and adolescence: Problems, progress, andpotential in theory and research. *Psychological Bulletin, 127*(1), 87–127. doi:10.1037/0033-2909.127.1.87 PMID:11271757

Conn, K. (2004). *Bullying and harassment: a legal guide for educators.* Association for Supervision and Curriculum Development.

Connolly, E. J., & Beaver, K. M. (2016). Considering the genetic and environmental overlap between bullying victimization, delinquency, and symptoms of depression/anxiety. *Journal of Interpersonal Violence, 31*, 1230–1256. doi:10.1177/0886260514564158 PMID:25535249

Cook, C. R., Williams, K. R., Guerra, N. G., Kim, T. E., & Sadek, S. (2010). Predictors of bullying and victimization in childhood and adolescence: A meta-analytic investigation. *School Psychology Quarterly, 25*(2), 65–83.

Cook, C. R., Williams, K. R., Guerra, N. G., Kim, T. E., & Sadek, S. (2010). Predictors of Bullying and Victimization in Childhood and Adolescence: A Meta-analytic Investigation. *School Psychology Quarterly, 25*(2), 65–83. doi:10.1037/a0020149

Cooper, D., & Snell, J. L. (2003). Bullying: Not just a kid thing. *Educational Leadership, 60*(6), 22–25. https://pdo.ascd.org/lmscourses/PD11OC105/media/Bullying_M1_Reading_Kid_Thing.pdf

Cooper, G. D., Clements, P. T., & Holt, K. E. (2012). Examining childhood bullying and adolescent suicide: Implications for school nurses. *The Journal of School Nursing: the Official Publication of the National Association of School Nurses, 28*(4), 275–283. doi:10.1177/1059840512438617 PMID:22333524

Corcoran, L., Connolly, I., & O'Moore, M. (2012). Cyberbullying in Irish schools: An investigation of personality and self-concept. *The Irish Journal of Psychology, 33*(4), 153–165. doi:10. 1080/03033910.2012.677995

Corcoran, L., Guckin, C. M., & Prentice, G. (2015). Cyberbullying or Cyber Aggression?: A Review of Existing Definitions of Cyber-based Peer-to-peer Aggression. *Societies (Basel, Switzerland), 5*(2), 245–255. doi:10.3390oc5020245

Cornish, D. B., & Clarke, R. V. (2003). Opportunities, Precipitators and Criminal Decisions: A Reply to Wortley's Critique of Situational Crime Prevention. In Theory for Practice in Situational Crime Prevention, Crime Prevention Studies, Vol. 16. Criminal Justice Press.

Cornish, D. B., & Clarke, R. V. (1987). Understanding Crime Displacement: An Application of Rational Choice Theory. *Criminology, 25*(4), 933–948. doi:10.1111/j.1745-9125.1987.tb00826.x

Cortina, L. M., & Berdahl, J. L. (2008). Sexual harassment in organizations: A decade of research in review. Handbook of Organizational Behavior, 1, 469-497.

Cortina, L. M. (2004). Hispanic perspective on sexual harassment and social support. *Personality and Social Psychology Bulletin, 30*(5), 570–584. doi:10.1177/0146167203262854 PMID:15107157

Cortina, L. M., Lonsway, K. A., Magley, V. J., Freeman, L. V., Collingsworth, L. L., & Hunter, M. (2002). What's gender got to do with it? Incivility in the federal courts. *Law & Social Inquiry, 27*(2), 235–270. doi:10.1111/j.1747-4469.2002.tb00804.x

Cosma, A., Walsh, S. D., Chester, K. L., Callaghan, M., Molcho, M., Craig, W., & Pickett, W. (2020). Bullying victimization: Time trends and the overlap between traditional and cyberbullying across countries in Europe and North America. *International Journal of Public Health, 65*(1), 75–85. doi:10.100700038-019-01320-2 PMID:31844919

Costello, E. J., Foley, D. L., & Angold, A. (2006). 10-year research update review: the epidemiology of child and adolescent psychiatric disorders: II. Developmental epidemiology. *Journal of the American Academy of Child and Adolescent Psychiatry, 45*(1), 8–25. doi:10.1097/01.chi.0000184929.41423.c0 PMID:16327577

Cotler, J. L., Fryling, M., & Rivituso, J. (2017). Causes of Cyberbullying in Multi-player Online Gaming Environments: Gamer Perceptions. *Journal of Information Systems Applied Research, 10*(1), 4–14.

Council of Europe. (2021). *Full list*. Council of Europe. https://www.coe.int/en/web/conventions/full-list?module=treaty-detail&treatynum=185

Cowie, H., & Colliety, P. (2016). Who cares about the bullies? *Pastoral Care in Education, 34*(1), 24–33. doi:10.1080/02643944.2015.1119880

Cowie, H., & Myers, C. A. (2016). What we know about bullying among university students. In H. Cowie & C. A. Myers (Eds.), *Bullying Among University Students* (pp. 3–14). Routledge.

Coyne, I., Farley, S., Axtell, C., Sprigg, C., Best, L., & Kwok, O. (2017). Understanding the Relationship Between Experiencing Workplace Cyberbullying, Employee Mental Strain and Job Satisfaction: A Disempowerment Approach. *International Journal of Human Resource Management, 28*(7), 945–972. doi:10.1080/09585192.2015.1116454

Craig, W. M., & Pepler, D. J. (2003). Identifying and targeting risk for involvement in bullying and victimization. *The Canadian Journal of Psychiatry ın* Review, *48*(9), 577–582. PMID:14631877

Craig, W., Boniel-Nissim, M., King, N., Walsh, S. D., Boer, M., Donnelly, P. D., Harel-Fisch, Y., Malinowska-Cieslik, M., Gaspar de Matos, M., Cosma, A., Van den Eijnden, R., Vieno, A., Elgar, F. J., Molcho, M., Bjereld, Y., & Pickett, W. (2020). Social Media Use and Cyber-Bullying: A Cross-National Analysis of Young People in 42 Countries. *The Journal of Adolescent Health, 66*(6), 100–S108. doi:10.1016/j.jadohealth.2020.03.006 PMID:32446603

Craig, W., Harel-Fisch, Y., Fogel-Grinvald, H., Dostaler, S., Hetland, J., Simons-Morton, B., Molcho, M., de Mato, M. G., Overpeck, M., Due, P., & Pickett, W. (2009). A cross-national profile of bullying and victimization among adolescents in 40 countries, the HBSC Violence & Injuries Prevention Focus Group* and the HBSC Bullying Writing Group. *International Journal of Public Health, 54*(S2), 216–224. doi:10.100700038-009-5413-9 PMID:19623475

Craig, W., Pepler, D., & Blais, J. (2007). Responding to bullying: What works. *School Psychology International, 28*(4), 465–477. doi:10.1177/0143034307084136

Crawshaw, L. (2009). Workplace Bullying? Mobbing? Harassment? Distraction by a Thousand Definitions. *Consulting Psychology Journal, 61*(3), 263–267. doi:10.1037/a0016590

Creswell, J. W., Hanson, W. E., Clark Plano, V. L., & Morales, A. (2007). Qualitative research designs: Selection and implementation. *The Counseling Psychologist, 35*(2), 236–264. doi:10.1177/0011000006287390

Crick, N. R., Casas, J. F., & Mosher, M. (1997). Relational and overt aggression in preschool. *Developmental Psychology, 33*(4), 579–588. doi:10.1037/0012-1649.33.4.579 PMID:9232373

Crick, N. R., & Dodge, K. A. (1994). A review and reformulation of social information-processing mechanisms in children's social adjustment. *Psychological Bulletin, 115*(1), 74–101. doi:10.1037/0033-2909.115.1.74

Crick, N. R., Werner, N. E., Casas, J. F., O'Brien, K. M., Nelson, D. A., Grotpeter, J. K., & Markon, K. (1999). Childhood aggression and gender: A new look at an old problem. In D. Bernstein (Ed.), *Gender and motivation* (pp. 75–141). University of Nebraska Press.

Cross, E.-J., Piggin, R., & Douglas, T. (2012). *Virtual Violence: Progress and Challenge in the Fight Against Cyberbullying*. Beat Bullying.

Crosslin, K., & Crosslin, M. (2014). Cyberbullying at a Texas University-A Mixed Methods Approach to Examining Online Aggression. *Texas Public Health Journal, 66*(3), 26–31.

Crothers, L. M., & Levinson, E. M. (2004). Assessment of bullying: A review of methods and instruments. *Journal of Counseling and Development, 82*(4), 496–503. doi:10.1002/j.1556-6678.2004.tb00338.x

Cüceloğlu, D. (2005). *Human to Human Again.* Remzi Bookstore.

Cullen, F. T., Agnew, R., & Wilcox, P. (2006). *Criminological Theory: Past to Present: Essential Readings.* Oxford University Press.

cumhuriyet.com. (2021). *The sentence of the accused who harassed the Mine Brigade on social media has been announced.* Life News: https://www.cumhuriyet.com.tr/yasam/mine-tugayi-sosyal-medyadan-taciz-eden-sanigin-cezasi-belli-oldu-1891586

Cunningham, S. J., & Hunt, N. P. (2001). Quality of life and its importance in orthodontics. *Journal of Orthodontics, 28*(2), 152–158. doi:10.1093/ortho/28.2.152 PMID:11395531

Currie, C., Zanotti, C., Morgan, A., Currie, D., de Looze, M., Roberts, C., Samdal, O., Smith, O. R. F., & Barnekow, V. (Eds.). (2012). *Social determinants of health and well-being among young people.* WHO Regional Office for Europe. https://www.euro.who.int/__data/assets/pdf_file/0003/163857/Social-determinants-of-health-and-well-being-among-young-people.pdf

Cyberbullying Research Center. (2021). *Bullying and Cyberbullying Laws Across America.* Cyberbullying Research Center. https://cyberbullying.org/bullying-laws

CyberSecurity Malaysia. (2019). *CyberSafe Parenting: Ke Arah Kesejahteraan Siber* [Towards Cyber Wellness]. Cyberjaya, Selangor Darul Ehsan.

CyberSmart! Education Company. (2009). *CyberSmart! Cyberbullying awareness curriculum.* Retrieved April 1, 2009, from: www.nasponline.org/resources/cyberbullying/index.aspx

D'Ovidio, R., & Doyle, J. (2003). A Study on Cyberstalking: Understanding Investigative Hurdles. *FBI Law Enforcement Bulletin, 72*(3), 10–17.

Dadvar, M., Trieschnigg, D., Ordelman, R., & de Jong, F. (2013). Improving cyberbullying detection with user context. In *Advances in Information Retrieval* (pp. 693–696). Springer. doi:10.1007/978-3-642-36973-5_62

Dahlgren, G., & Whitehead, M. (1991). *Policies and strategies to promote social equity in health.* Institute for Futures Studies.

Dahlgren, G., & Whitehead, M. (2021). The Dahlgren-Whitehead model of health determinants: 30 years on and still chasing rainbows. *Public Health, 199*, 20–24. doi:10.1016/j.puhe.2021.08.009 PMID:34534885

Dake, J. A., Price, J. H., & Telljohann, S. K. (2003). The nature and extent of bullying at school. *The Journal of School Health, 73*(5), 173–180. doi:10.1111/j.1746-1561.2003.tb03599.x PMID:12793102

Damashek, A., Nelson, M. M., & Bonner, B. L. (2013). Fatal child maltreatment: Characteristics of deaths from physical abuse versus neglect. *Child Abuse & Neglect, 37*(10), 735–744. doi:10.1016/j.chiabu.2013.04.014 PMID:23768940

Danacı, M. Ö., & Çetin, Z. (2016). Erken çocukluk döneminde görülen okul zorbalığı davranış eğilimlerinin çocukların kişisel/sosyal–dil–motor gelişimleri ile olan ilişkisi [The relationship between school bullying behavior tendencies in early childhood and children's personal/social-language-motor development]. *Hacettepe University Faculty Of Health Sciences Journal, 3*(2), 53–72.

Daniel, Y., & Bondy, K. (2008). Safe schools and zero tolerance: Policy, program and practice in Ontario. *Canadian Journal of Educational Administration and Policy, 70*, 1–20.

Danvila, I., Sastre, M.A., & Marroquin, E. (2013). The importance of professional competencies in the development of emotional intelligence. *Revista Internacional De Organizaciones*, (10), 157. . doi:10.17345/rio10.157-179

Daugherty, S. R., Baldwin, D. C. Jr, & Rowley, B. D. (1998). Learning, satisfaction, and mistreatment during medical internship: A national survey of working conditions. *Journal of the American Medical Association, 279*(15), 1194–1199. doi:10.1001/jama.279.15.1194 PMID:9555759

Davenport, N., Distler, R. S., & Elliott, G. P. (2003). Mobbing, İşyerinde Duygusal Taciz [Mobbing, Emotional Harassment at Work] (O. C. Önertoy, Trans.). Istanbul: Sistem Yayincilik.

Davidson, M. J., & Cooper, C. L. (1992). *Shattering the glass ceiling: The woman manager*. Paul Chapman Publishing.

Davidson-Wall, N. (2018). *"Mum, seriously!": Sharenting the new social trend with no opt-out.* Paper presented at the 9th Debating Communities and Social Networks 2018 OUA Conference. Online Conference.

Davis, K., & Koepke, L. (2016). Risk and protective factors associated with cyberbullying: Are relationships or rules more protective? learning. *Media and Technology, 41*(4), 521–545. doi:10.1080/17439884.2014.994219

Dawkins, J. (1995). Bullying in schools: Doctors' responsibilities. *BMJ (Clinical Research Ed.), 310*(6975), 274–275. doi:10.1136/bmj.310.6975.274 PMID:7866165

Day, S., Bussey, K., Trompeter, N., & Mitchison, D. (2021). The impact of teasing and bullying victimization on disordered eating and body image disturbance among adolescents: A systematic review. *Trauma, Violence & Abuse*. Advance online publication. doi:10.1177/1524838020985534 PMID:33461439

De Judicibus, M., & McCabe, M. P. (2001). Blaming the target of sexual harassment: Impact of gender role, sexist attitudes, and work role. *Sex Roles, 44*(7/8), 401–417. doi:10.1023/A:1011926027920

De Oliveira, C. M., & Sheiham, A. (2004). Orthodontic treatment and its impact on oral health-related quality of life in Brazilian adolescents. *Journal of Orthodontics, 31*(1), 20–27. doi:10.1179/146531204225011364 PMID:15071148

deArimatéiadaCruz, J. (2020). The legislative framework of the European Union (EU) convention on cybercrime. In *The Palgrave Handbook of International Cybercrime and Cyberdeviance* (pp. 223–237). Palgrave Macmillan. doi:10.1007/978-3-319-78440-3_5

Deb, S. (2018). *Positive schooling and child development: International perspectives. In Positive Schooling and Child Development: International Perspectives.* Springer Singapore. doi:10.1007/978-981-13-0077-6

Dehue, F., Bolman, C., & Vollink, T. (2008). Cyberbullying: Youngsters' Experiences and Parental Perception. *Cyber-Psychology and Behavior, 11*(2), 217-223.

Deiss, D. M., Jr., & Savage, M. W. (2010). *Bridging the Gap in the Study of Cyberbullying: Placing the Study of Cyberbullying within the Dark Side of Interpersonal Communication Research.* Paper presented at the Annual Conference of the National Communication Association, San Francisco, CA.

Del Rey, R., Casas, J. A., Ortega-Ruiz, R., Schultze-Krumbholz, A., Scheithauer, H., Smith, P., & Guarini, A. (2015). Structural validation and cross-cultural robustness of the European Cyberbullying Intervention Project Questionnaire. *Computers in Human Behavior, 50*, 141–147. doi:10.1016/j.chb.2015.03.065

DeLongis, A., Folkman, S., & Lazarus, R. S. (1988). The impact of daily stress on health and mood: Psychological and social resources as mediators. *Journal of Personality and Social Psychology, 54*(3), 486–495. doi:10.1037/0022-3514.54.3.486 PMID:3361420

Demir, K., & Küçük, S. (2020). Akran zorbalığı önleme ve müdahale programlarında güncel yaklaşımlar ve hemşirelik rolleri [Current approaches and nursing roles in peer bullying prevention and intervention programs]. *Türkiye Sağlık Bilimleri ve Araştırmaları Dergisi, 3*(2), 87–102.

Demir, M., & Tokgöz, E. (2022). Snow Crash'ten Meta'ya, Metaverse'ün Kavramsal Ve Teknolojik Gelişimi. In N. Göker & G. Göker (Eds.), *İletişim ve Medya Alanında Uluslararası Araştırmalar IV*. Eğitim Publishers.

Demir, Ö., & Seferoğlu, S. S. (2016). Investigation of the Relationship between Information Literacy, Internet Addiction, Virtual Loitering and Various Other Variables with Virtual Bullying. *Online Journal of Technology Addiction & Cyberbullying, 3*(1), 1–26.

Dennehy, R., Meaney, S., Walsh, K., Sinnott, C., Cronin, M., & Arensman, E. (2020). Young people's conceptualizations of the nature of cyberbullying: A systematic review and synthesis of qualitative research. *Aggression and Violent Behavior, 51*, 101379. doi:10.1016/j.avb.2020.101379

DePaolis, K. J., & Williford, A. (2019). Pathways from Cyberbullying Victimization to Negative Health Outcomes among Elementary School Students: A longitudinal investigation. *Journal of Child and Family Studies, 28*(9), 2390–2403. doi:10.100710826-018-1104-6

Department for Education. (n.d.). *Bullying webpage*. http://www.education.gov.uk/schools/pupilsupport/behaviour/bullying

Deptula, D. P., & Cohen, R. (2004). Aggressive, rejected, and delinquent children and adolescents: A comparison of their friendships. *Aggression and Violent Behavior, 9*(1), 75–104. doi:10.1016/S1359-1789(02)00117-9

Dereli, E. (2008). *Social Problem Solving in Children.* Tablet Publications.

DeSouza, E., & Fansler, A. G. (2003). Contrapower sexual harassment: A survey of students and faculty members. *Sex Roles, 48*(11/12), 529–542. doi:10.1023/A:1023527329364

DeVellis, R. F. (2017). *Scale development: Theory and applications* (4th ed.). Sage.

Dhiraj, A. B. (2018). *Countries Where Cyber-bullying Was Reported The Most In 2018*. CEOWORLD Magazine. https://ceoworld.biz/2018/10/29/countries-where-cyber-bullying-was-reported-the-most-in-2018/

Diamanduros, T., Downs, E., & Jenkins, S. J. (2008). The role of school psychologists in the assessment, prevention, and intervention of cyberbullying. *Psychology in the Schools, 45*(8), 693–704. doi:10.1002/pits.20335

Dias, A., Sales, L., Hessen, D. J., & Kleber, R. J. (2015). Child maltreatment and psychological symptoms in a Portuguese adult community sample: The harmful effects of emotional abuse. *European Child & Adolescent Psychiatry, 24*(7), 767–778. doi:10.100700787-014-0621-0 PMID:25270111

DiBiase, A. T., & Sandler, P. J. (2001). Malocclusion, orthodontics and bullying. *Dental Update*, *28*(9), 464–466. doi:10.12968/denu.2001.28.9.464 PMID:11806190

Dictionary, C. (2022). *Cambridge University Press*. Retrieved May 24, 2022, from https://dictionary.cambridge.org/dictionary/english/

Dijilopedi. (2021). *2021 World Internet, Social Media and Mobile Usage Statistics*. https://dijilopedi.com/2021-dunya-internet-sosyal-medya-ve-mobil-kullanim-istatistikleri/

Dijk, T. A. V. (1988). *New Analysis: Case Studies of International and National News in the Press*. Lawrence Erlbaum Associates Publishers.

Dilmaç, B. (2009). Psychological needs as a predictor of Cyber-bullying: A preliminary report on college students. *Educational Sciences: Theory and Practice*, *9*(3), 1291–1325.

Dilmaç, J. A. (2020). Deviance in the Digital Environment: Cyber Bullying. *Turkish Studies - Social Sciences*, 1087–1099.

Dimberg, L., Arnrup, K., & Bondemark, L. (2015). The impact of malocclusion on the quality of life among children and adolescents: A systematic review of quantitative studies. *European Journal of Orthodontics*, *37*(3), 238–247. doi:10.1093/ejo/cju046 PMID:25214504

Dinç, E. S. (2020). Cyber bullying in social media platforms: Examination of cyberbullying experiences among high-school students. *Journal of New Media*, *4*(1), 24–39.

Dinçer, Ç. (2006). *İşyerinde cinsel tacizin bayan doktorlar ve hemşireler tarafından algılanmasına yönelik karşılaştırmalı bir alan araştırması [An empirical research about female doctors and nurses perception of sexual harassment at workplace]. Yayımlanmamış yüksek lisans tezi*. Hacettepe Üniversitesi.

Dingin, A. E. (2020). The Political Aspects of Identities Formed in the Face of Social Media. He. In *Kutlu, Decoupling from Advertising to Political Communication is an Interdisciplinary Study* (pp. 283–299). Detay Anatolia Akademik Yayıncılık Ltd. Şti.

Dingin, A. E. (2021). *The new Social Media Application is the "Tiktok" Application and Popular Culture. In A Calm, Critical View of Social Media 2- From Violence to Addiction, From Discrimination to Popular Culture*. Literatürk Academia.

Dizen, M., Berenbaum, H., & Kerns, J. G. (2005). Emotional awareness and psychological needs. *Cognition and Emotion*, *19*(8), 1140–1157. doi:10.1080/02699930500260468

Dobry, Y., Braquehais, M. D., & Sher, L. (2013). Bullying, psychiatric pathology and suicidal behavior. *International Journal of Adolescent Medicine and Health*, *25*(3), 295–299. doi:10.1515/ijamh-2013-0065 PMID:24006324

DoCS (NSW Department of Community Services). (2007). *Risk, protection and resilience in children and families, research to practice notes*. Author.

Dodge, K. A., & Coie, J. D. (1987). Social-Information-Processing Factors in Reactive and Proactive Aggression in Children's Peer Groups. *Journal of Personality and Social Psychology*, *53*(6), 1146–1158. doi:10.1037/0022-3514.53.6.1146 PMID:3694454

Dodge, K. A., Lansford, J. E., Burks, V. S., Bates, J. E., Pettit, G. S., Fontaine, R., & Price, J. M. (2003). Peer rejection and social information-processing factors in the development of aggressive behavior problems in children. *Child Development*, *74*(2), 374–393. doi:10.1111/1467-8624.7402004 PMID:12705561

Doğan, B. Ö., Ertürk, Y. D., & Aslan, P. (2018). The Transformation of Bullying-Oriented Cyber Harassment Directed at Facebook User Girls into Sexual Harassment: A Descriptive Evaluation via Newspaper News. *Journal of Interaction Üsküdar University Faculty of Communication*, 36-55.

Doğan, F. (2022). *Twitter has expanded the scope of its anti-cyberbullying Security Mode feature*. Social Media: https://shiftdelete.net/twitter-siber-zorbalik-karsiti-guvenlik-modu-ozelliginin-kapsamini-genisletti

Doğan, A. (2010). Ecological systems model as a framework for bullying. *Turkish Journal of Child and Adolescent Mental Health, 17*(3), 149–162. https://cms.galenos.com.tr/Uploads/Article_27669/cogepderg-17-149.pdf

Doko, E. (2022). *Alternatif Bir Dünya Arayışı: Metaverse*. https://www.lacivertdergi.com/dosya/2022/01/12/alternatif-bir-dunya-arayisi-metaverse

Dolgun, G. (2018). Akran zorbalığını önlemede hemşirenin rolü [Role of nurse in peer bullying prevention]. *Sağlık Bilimleri ve Meslekleri Dergisi, 5*(1), 95–101. doi:10.17681/hsp.335312

Donegan, R. (2012). Bullying and Cyberbullying: History, Statistics, Law, Prevention and Analysis. Elon Journal of Undergraduate Research in Communications, 3(1).

Donnellan, C., & Firth, L. (2006). *Bullying*. Independence Educational Publishers.

Donoghue, C., & Meltzer, L. J. (2018). Sleep it off: Bullying and sleep disturbances in adolescents. *Journal of Adolescence, 68*(1), 87–93. doi:10.1016/j.adolescence.2018.07.012 PMID:30067959

Dooley, J. J., Pyżalski, J., & Cross, D. (2009). Cyberbullying versus face-to-face bullying. *Zeitschrift für Psychologie. The Journal of Psychology, 217*(4), 182–188. doi:10.1027/0044-3409.217.4.182

Dorol-Beauroy-Eustache, O., & Mishara, B. L. (2021). Systematic Review of Risk and Protective Factors for Suicidal and Self-Harm Behaviors among Children and Adolescents Involved with Cyberbullying. *Preventive Medicine, 152*, 106684. doi:10.1016/j.ypmed.2021.106684 PMID:34538376

Doruk, Ö. (2013). Disiplin Toplumu Ve Haber Söylemi: Gökkuşağı Derneği'nce Yapılması Planlanan Yürüyüşün Engellemesine İlişkin Haberlerin Çözümlenmesi. *e-GİFDER, 2*(1).

Dougherty, T. W., Turban, D. B., Olson, D. E., Dwyer, P. D., & Lapreze, M. W. (1996). Factors affecting perceptions of workplace sexual harassment. *Journal of Organizational Behavior, 17*(5), 489–501. doi:10.1002/(SICI)1099-1379(199609)17:5<489::AID-JOB780>3.0.CO;2-6

Douvlos, C. (2019). Bullying in preschool children. *Psychological Thought, 12*(1), 131–142. doi:10.5964/psyct.v12i1.284

Draucker, C. B. (2019). Responses of nurses and other healthcare workers to sexual harassment in the workplace. *Online Journal of Issues in Nursing, 24*(1), 9. doi:10.3912/OJIN.Vol24No01Man03

Dredge, R., Gleeson, J. F., & De la Piedad Garcia, X. (2014). Risk Factors Associated with Impact Severity of Cyberbullying Victimization: A qualitative study of adolescent online social networking. *Cyberpsychology, Behavior, and Social Networking, 17*(5), 287–291. doi:10.1089/cyber.2013.0541 PMID:24611734

Duan, H., Li, J., Fan, S., Lin, Z., Wu, X., & Cai, W. (2021). Metaverse for social good: A university campus prototype. *Proceedings of the 29th ACM International Conference on Multimedia*. 10.1145/3474085.3479238

Duarte, C., & Pinto-Gouveia, J. (2017). Can self-reassurance buffer against the impact of bullying? Effects on body shame and disordered eating in adolescence. *Journal of Child and Family Studies, 26*(4), 998–1006. doi:10.100710826-016-0624-1

Duarte, C., Pinto-Gouveia, J., & Rodrigues, T. (2015). Being bullied and feeling ashamed: Implications for eating psychopathology and depression in adolescent girls. *Journal of Adolescence, 44*(1), 259–268. doi:10.1016/j.adolescence.2015.08.005 PMID:26318063

Duarte, C., Pinto-Gouveia, J., & Stubbs, R. J. (2017). The prospective associations between bullying experiences, body image shame and disordered eating in a sample of adolescent girls. *Personality and Individual Differences, 116*, 319–325. doi:10.1016/j.paid.2017.05.003

Dubanoski, R. A., Inaba, M., & Gerkewicz, K. (1983). Corporal punishment in schools: Myths, problems and alternatives. *Child Abuse & Neglect, 7*(3), 271–278. doi:10.1016/0145-2134(83)90004-2 PMID:6686472

Due, P., Holstein, B. E., Lynch, J., Diderichsen, F., Gabhain, S. N., Scheidt, P., ... Health, T. (2005). Bullying and symptoms among school-aged children: International comparative cross sectional study in 28 countries Behaviour in School-Aged Children Bullying Working Group. *European Journal of Public Health, 15*(2), 128–132. doi:10.1093/eurpub/cki105 PMID:15755782

Due, P., Merlo, J., Harel-Fisch, Y., Damsgaard, T., Scient Soc, M., Holstein, B. E., ... Lynch, J. (2009). Socioeconomic Inequality in Exposure to Bullying During Adolescence: A Comparative, Cross-Sectional, Multilevel Study in 35 Countries. *American Journal of Public Health, 99*(5), 907–914. doi:10.2105/AJPH.2008.139303 PMID:19299676

Duffy, M. (2009). Preventing Workplace Mobbing and Bullying with Effective Organizational Consultation, Policies, and Legislation. *Consulting Psychology Journal, 61*(3), 242–262. doi:10.1037/a0016578

Dukes, R. L., Stein, J. A., & Zane, J. I. (2010). Gender differences in the relative impact of physical and relational bullying on adolescent injury and weapon carrying. *Journal of School Psychology, 48*(6), 511–532. doi:10.1016/j.jsp.2010.08.001 PMID:21094396

Duncan, N. (1998). Sexual bullying in secondary schools. *Pastoral Care in Education, 16*(2), 27–31.

Durlak, J. A., Weissberg, R. P., Dymnicki, A. B., Taylor, R. D., & Schellinger, K. B. (2011). The impact of enhancing students' social and emotional learning: A meta-analysis of school-based universal interventions. *Child Development, 82*(1), 405–432. doi:10.1111/j.1467-8624.2010.01564.x PMID:21291449

Durlak, J. A., & Wells, A. M. (1997). Primary prevention mental health programs for children and adolescents: A meta-analytic review. *American Journal of Community Psychology, 25*(2), 115–152. doi:10.1023/A:1024654026646 PMID:9226860

Durmuş, E. (2013). Cinsel taciz: Üniversite öğrencilerinin algı ve tepkileri [Sexual harassment: university students' perceptions and reactions]. *İnönü Üniversitesi Eğitim Fakültesi Dergisi, 14*(1), 15-30.

Durmuşoğlu, N., & Doğru, S. S. Y. (2006). Çocukluk örseleyici yaşantılarının ergenlikteki yakın ilişkilerde bireye etkisinin incelenmesi [Investigation of the effects of childhood traumatic experiences on the individual in close relationships in adolescence]. *Selçuk Üniversitesi Sosyal Bilimler Enstitüsü Dergisi*, (15), 237–246.

Dursun, S. (2012). İşyeri şiddetinin çalışanların tükenmişlik düzeyi üzerine etkisi: Sağlık sektöründe bir uygulama [The effect of workplace violence on employees' level burnout: an application on health sector]. *Çalışma İlişkileri Dergisi, 3*(1), 105-115.

Dursun, S., & Aytaç, S. S. (2021). The prevalence of violence against healthcare workers in Turkey and employee job satisfaction. *Pakistan Journal of Medical & Health Sciences, 15*(6), 1607–1620. doi:10.53350/pjmhs211561607

Duy, B. (2013). Teachers' attiudes toward different types of bullying and victimization in Turkey. *Psychology in the Schools, 50*(10), 987–1002. doi:10.1002/pits.21729

Dye, T. D., Alcantara, L., Siddiqi, S., Barbosu, M., Sharma, S., Panko, T., & Pressman, E. (2020). Risk of COVID-19-related bullying, harassment and stigma among healthcare workers: An analytical cross-sectional global study. *BMJ Open, 10*(12), e046620. doi:10.1136/bmjopen-2020-046620 PMID:33380488

Dynel, M. (2021). Humour and (mock) aggression: Distinguishing cyberbullying from roasting. *Language & Communication, 81*, 17–36. doi:10.1016/j.langcom.2021.08.001

Eaton, D. K., Kann, L., Kinchen, S., Shanklin, S., Flint, K. J., Hawkins, J., Harris, W. A., Lowry, R., McManus, T., Chyen, D., Whittle, L., Lim, C., & Wechsler, H. (2012). *Youth Risk Behavior Surveillance - United States, 2011.* U.S. Department of Health and Human Services. https://www.cdc.gov/mmwr/preview/mmwrhtml/ss6104a1.htm

Eboibi, F. E. (2020). Concerns of cyber criminality in South Africa, Ghana, Ethiopia and Nigeria: Rethinking cybercrime policy implementation and institutional accountability. *Commonwealth Law Bulletin, 46*(1), 78–109. doi:10.1080/03050718.2020.1748075

Edison Research. (2018). *Sexual harassment in the workplace: A marketplace survey.* https://www.edisonresearch.com/sexualharassmentworkplace/

Egger, H. L., & Angold, A. (2006). Common emotional and behavioral disorders in preschool children: Presentation, nosology, and epidemiology. *Journal of Child Psychology and Psychiatry, and Allied Disciplines, 47*(3-4), 313–337. doi:10.1111/j.1469-7610.2006.01618.x PMID:16492262

Einarsen, S., Hoel, H., Zapf, D., & Cooper, C. L. (2011). The concept of bullying and harassment at work: The European tradition. *Bullying and harassment in the workplace: Developments in theory, research, and practice, 2*, 3-40.

Einarsen, S., Hoel, H., Zapf, D., & Cooper, C. (2010). *Bullying and harassment in the workplace: Developments in theory, research, and practice.* CRC Press. doi:10.1201/EBK1439804896

Einarsen, S., Hoel, H., Zapf, D., & Cooper, C. L. (2002). The concept of bullying at work: the European tradition. In *Bullying and Emotional Abuse in the Workplace* (pp. 21–48). CRC Press. doi:10.1201/9780203164662-6

Einarsen, S., Hoel, H., Zapf, D., & Cooper, C. L. (2003). *Bullying and Emotional Abuse in the Workplace: International Perspectives in Research and Practice.* Taylor and Francis. doi:10.4324/9780203278734

Einarsen, S., & Nielsen, M. B. (2015). Workplace bullying as an antecedent of mental health problems: A five-year prospective and representative study. *International Archives of Occupational and Environmental Health, 88*(2), 131–142. doi:10.100700420-014-0944-7 PMID:24840725

Eisenberg, M. E., Neumark-Sztainer, D., Haines, J., & Wall, M. (2006). Weight-teasing and emotional well-being in adolescents: Longitudinal findings from Project EAT. *The Journal of Adolescent Health, 38*(6), 675–683. doi:10.1016/j.jadohealth.2005.07.002 PMID:16730595

Eisenstadt, M., Stapley, E., Deighton, J., & Wolpert, M. (2020). Adolescent stressors and their perceived effects on mental well-being: A qualitative study. *Mental Health in Family Medicine, 16*, 992–1001.

Eker, H. H., Topcu, İ., Sahinoz, S., Ozder, A., & Aydin, H. (2011). Bir Egitim ve Arastirma Hastanesindeki Siddet Sikligi [Frequency of Violence in a Training and Research Hospital]. *Bidder Tıp Bilimleri Dergisi, 3*(3), 16–22.

Ekinci, O., & Kayapalı Yıldırım, S. (2020). *Siber zorbalık (Cyberbullying).* Nobel.

Elgar, F. J., Pickett, K. E., Pickett, W., Craig, W., Molcho, M., Hurrelmann, K., & Lenzi, M. (2013). School bullying, homicide and income inequality: A cross-national pooled time series analysis. *International Journal of Public Health, 58*(2), 237–245. doi:10.100700038-012- 0380-y PMID:22714137

Eliçora, R. (2020). *Investigation of the relationship between adolescents' cyber victimization and coping with cyberbullying skills and emotional intelligence* (Unpublished Doctoral Dissertation). Karabük University, Karabük.

Elsaesser, C., Russell, B., Ohannessian, C. M., & Patton, D. (2017). Parenting in a digital age: A review of parents' role in preventing adolescent cyberbullying. *Aggression and Violent Behavior, 3*, 62–72.

Engel, G. L. (1977). The need for a new medical model: A challenge for biomedicine. *Science, 196*(4286), 129–136. doi:10.1126cience.847460 PMID:847460

Englander, E. K., & Muldowney, A. (2007). Just turn the darn thing off: Understanding cyberbullying. In D. L. White, B. C. Glenn & A. Wimes (Eds.), *Proceedings of persistently safe schools: The 2007 National Conference on safe schools* (pp. 83-92). Hamilton Fish Institute, George Washington University.

Englander, E. K. (2020). *25 Myths about Bullying and Cyberbullying*. John Wiley & Sons. doi:10.1002/9781118747957

Equal Employment Opportunity Commission. (1980). Guidelines on discrimination because of sex (Sect. 1 604.1 1) Federal Register, 45,7 4676-1 4611.

Erdal, C. (2019). *Investigation of the relationship between cyberbullying / victimization and Monoamine Oxidase A enzyme gene polymorphism in university students* (UMI No. 615048) [Master's dissertation, Uskudar University]. Higher Education Council Thesis Center database.

Erdemir, F., Çıtak, E. A., Ulusoy, H., & Geçkil, E. (2011). Hemşirelerin hastalar tarafından cinsel tacize uğrama durumlarının belirlenmesi [Determination of sexual harassment of nurses by patients]. *Hacettepe Üniversitesi Hemşirelik Fakültesi Dergisi, 18*(2), 27–35.

Erdoğan, Ö., & Uçukoğlu, H. (2011). The relationships between primary school students' perceptions of parental attitudes and their assertiveness and fear of negative evaluation. *Kastamonu Journal of Education, 19*(1), 51–72.

Erdur-Baker, Ö. & Kavşut, F. (2007). Cyber bullying: a new face of peer bullying. *Eurasian Journal of Educational Researh,* (27), 31-42.

Erdur-Baker, Ö., & Tanrıkulu, İ. (2010). Psychological consequences of cyber bullying experiences among Turkish secondary school children. *Procedia: Social and Behavioral Sciences, 2*(2), 2771–2776. doi:10.1016/j.sbspro.2010.03.413

Ergül-Topçu, A. (2018). A review of prevalence and nature of peer bullying at schools. *Crisis Journal, 26*(2). https://dergipark.org.tr/kriz/issue/41895/505251

Eriksen, T. L., Nielsen, H. S., & Simonsen, M. (2012). *The effects of bullying in elementary school.* Academic Press.

Erk, A. (2019). *Peer bullying, peer bullying prevention studies in schools and applications for children in the bullying cycle*. Equinox Publishing House.

Erk, A. B. (2019). *Akran zorbalığı, okullarda akran zorbalığını önleme çalışmaları ve zorbalık döngüsündeki çocuklar için uygulamalar [Peer bullying, bullying prevention studies in schools and apps for children in the bullying cycle]*. Ekinoks Yayınevi.

Eroğlu, Y. (2011). *Koşullu özdeğer, riskli internet davranışları ve siber zorbalık/mağduriyet arasındaki ilişkinin incelenmesi* [Examining the relationship between conditional eigenvalue, risky internet behaviors and cyberbullying/victimization] (Master Dissertation).

Eroğlu, Y., Çetin, B., Güler, N., Peker, A., & Pepsoy, S. (2011). From cybervictimization to coping ways of stress: Gender as moderator. In *Proceedings of International Conference on Education and New Learning Technologies (EDULEARN11 Conference)* (pp. 2699-2707). Academic Press.

Eroğlu, Y., Peker, A., & Yaman, E. (2011). *Okul zorbalığı ve siber zorbalık [School bullying and cyberbullying]*. Kaknüs.

Er, T., Ayoglu, F., & Acikgoz, B. (2021). Saglik calisanina yonelik siddet: Risk faktorleri, etkileri, degerlendirilmesi ve önlenmesi [Violence against healthcare workers: Risk factors, effects, assessment and prevention]. *Turkish Journal of Public Health*, *19*(1), 69–78.

Erwin, P. (1993). *Friendship and Peer Relations in Children*. John Wiley & Sons Publishers.

Eşkisu, M. (2009). *Investigation of the relationship between the bullying grade, family functions and perceived social support among high school students* (UMI No. 270114) [Master's dissertation, Istanbul University]. Higher Education Council Thesis Center database.

Eslami, A. A., Rabiei, L., Afzali, S. M., Hamidizadeh, S., & Masoudi, R. (2016). The effectiveness of assertiveness training on the levels of stress, anxiety, and depression of high school students. *Iranian Red Crescent Medical Journal*, *18*(1), 1–10. doi:10.5812/ircmj.21096 PMID:26889390

Eslamipour, F., Afshari, Z., & Najimi, A. (2018). Prevalence of malocclusion in permanent dentition of Iranian population: A review article. *Iranian Journal of Public Health*, *47*(2), 178. PMID:29445627

Eslea, M., & Rees, J. (2001). At what age are children most likely to be bullied at school? *Aggressive Behavior*, *27*(6), 419–429. doi:10.1002/ab.1027

Espelage, D. L., & Swearer, S. M. (2010). A Social-Ecological Model for Bullying Prevention and Intervention: Understanding the Impact of Adults in the Social Ecology of Youngsters. In The Handbook of Bullying in Schools: An International Perspective Shane (pp. 61-72). Roultredge.

Espelage, D. L., Bosworth, K., & Simon, T. R. (2000). Examining the social context of bullying behaviors in early adolescence. *Journal of Counseling and Development*, *78*(3), 326–333. doi:10.1002/j.1556-6676.2000.tb01914.x

Espelage, D. L., Hong, J. S., & Valido, A. (2018). Cyberbullying in the United States. In *International Perspectives on Cyberbullying* (pp. 65–99). Palgrave Macmillan. doi:10.1007/978-3-319-73263-3_4

Espelage, D. L., Low, S., Polanin, J. R., & Brown, E. C. (2013). The impact of a middle-school program to reduce aggression, victimization, and sexual violence. *The Journal of Adolescent Health*, *53*(2), 180–186. doi:10.1016/j.jadohealth.2013.02.021 PMID:23643338

Espelage, D., & Swearer, S. (2003). *Bullying in American schools: A social-ecological perspective on prevention and intervention* (1st ed.). Lawrence Erlbaum Associates.

Espinoza, G., & Wright, M. (2018). Cyberbullying Experiences among Marginalized Youth: What do we know and where do we go next? *Journal of Child & Adolescent Trauma*, *11*(1), 1–5. doi:10.100740653-018-0207-y PMID:32318132

Essa, E. (2003). *A practical guide to solving preschool behavior problems* (5th ed.). Delmar Cengage Learning.

Estévez, A., Villardón, L., & Calvete, E., Padilla, P., & Orue, I. (2010). Adolescentes víctimas de cyberbullying: Prevalência y características [Adolescents viral from cyberbullying: Prevalence and characteristics]. *Psicología Conductual*, *18*, 73–89.

Estévez, A., Villardón, L., Esther Calvete, P. P., & Orue, I. (2010). Adolescentes víctimas de cyberbullying: Prevalencia, y características. *Behavioral Psychology. Psicología Conductual*, *18*(1), 73–89.

European Data Protection Supervisor. (2022). *Interoperability*. https://edps.europa.eu/data-protection/our-work/subjects/international-standards/cybercrime-convention_en

Evans, C., Fraser, M., & Cotter, K. (2014). The effectiveness of school-based bullying prevention programs: A systemic review. *Aggression and Violent Behavior*, *19*(5), 532–544. doi:10.1016/j.avb.2014.07.004

Eyuboğlu, M., Eyuboğlu, D., Pala, S. C., Oktar, D., Demirtaş, Z., Arslantaş, D., & Ünsal, A. (2021). Traditional school bullying and cyberbullying: Prevalence, the effect on mental health problems and self-harm behavior. *Psychiatry Research, 297*, 113730. doi:10.1016/j.psychres.2021.113730 PMID:33486274

Fabris, M. A., Badenes-Ribera, L., & Longobardi, C. (2021). Bullying victimization and muscle dysmorphic disorder in Italian adolescents: The mediating role of attachment to peers. *Children and Youth Services Review, 120*, 105720. doi:10.1016/j.childyouth.2020.105720

Family Lives. (2020). *What is cyber bullying? Being bullied online and advice on what to do*. Retrieved from https://www.bullying.co.uk/cyberbullying/what-is-cyberbullying/

Fan, C. Y., Chu, X. W., Zhang, M., & Zhou, Z. K. (2019). Are Narcissists More Likely to be Involved in Cyberbullying? Examining the Mediating Role of Self-esteem. *Journal of Interpersonal Violence, 34*(15), 3127–3150. doi:10.1177/0886260516666531 PMID:27565705

Farhat, T., Iannotti, R. J., & Simons-Morton, B. G. (2010). Overweight, obesity, youth, and health-risk behaviors. *American Journal of Preventive Medicine, 38*(3), 258–267. doi:10.1016/j.amepre.2009.10.038 PMID:20171527

Farik, Z. (2020). *Cosmetics businessman arrested over child abuse allegations*. Retrieved January 6, 2020, from https://www.thestar.com.my/news/nation/2020/03/06/cosmetic-businessman-arrested-over-child-abuse-allegations?fbclid=IwAR27Svkdq-BTz_rhtxd-TisbZZcA52J5N6eDXDvMcbtAWABzqafpAqgHNsU

Farkas, A. H., Scholcoff, C., Machen, J. L., Kay, C., Nickoloff, S., Fletcher, K. E., & Jackson, J. L. (2020). The experience of male physicians with sexual and gender-based harassment: A qualitative study. *Journal of General Internal Medicine, 35*(8), 2383–2388. doi:10.100711606-020-05695-4 PMID:32076981

Farley, L. (1978). *Sexual shakedown: The sexual harassment of women on the job*. McGraw-Hill.

Farmer, T. W., McAuliffe Lines, M., & Hamm, J. V. (2011). Revealing the invisible hand: The role of teachers in children's peer experiences. *Journal of Applied Developmental Psychology, 32*(5), 247–256. doi:10.1016/j.appdev.2011.04.006

Farouque, K., & Burgio, E. (2013). *The impact of bullying in health care*. The Royal Australasian College of Medical Administrators.

Farquhar, M. (1994). Quality of life in older people. In R. Fitzpatrick (Ed.), *Advances in Medical Sociology*. JAI Press Inc.

Farrington, D. P., & Baldry, A. C. (2010). Individual risk factors for school bullying. *Journal of Aggression, Conflict and Peace Research, 2*(1), 4–16. doi:10.5042/jacpr.2010.0001

Farrington, D. P., & Ttofi, M. M. (2009). School-Based Programs to Reduce Bullying and Victimization. *Campbell Systematic Reviews, 5*(1), i-148. doi:10.4073/csr.2009.6

Faucher, C., Jackson, M., & Cassidy, W. (2014). Cyberbullying among university students: Gendered experiences, impacts and perspectives. *Education Research International, 2014*, 1–10. doi:10.1155/2014/698545

Faucher, C., Jackson, M., & Cassidy, W. (2015). When online exchanges byte: An Examination of the Policy Environment Governing Cyberbullying at the University Level. *Canadian Journal of Higher Education, 45*(1), 102–121. doi:10.47678/cjhe.v45i1.184215

Fawzi, N. (2009). *Cyber-mobbing: Ursachen und auswirkungen von mobbing im internet*. Nomos. doi:10.5771/9783845219813

Feinberg, T., & Robey, N. (2009). Cyberbullying: School leaders cannot ignore cyberbullying but rather must understand its legal and psychological ramifications. *Education Digest, 74*(7), 26–31.

Fekkes, M., Pijpers, F. I., & Verloove-Vanhorick, S. P. (2005). Bullying: Who does what, when and where? Involvement of children, teachers and parents in bullying behavior. *Health Education Research*, *20*(1), 81–91. doi:10.1093/her/cyg100 PMID:15253993

Fellinger, J., Holzinger, D., & Pollard, R. (2012). Mental health of deaf people. *Lancet*, *379*(9820), 1037–1044. doi:10.1016/S0140-6736(11)61143-4 PMID:22423884

Feragen, K. B., & Stock, N. M. (2016). A longitudinal study of 340 young people with or without a visible difference: The impact of teasing on self-perceptions of appearance and depressive symptoms. *Body Image*, *16*, 133–142. doi:10.1016/j.bodyim.2016.01.003 PMID:26828822

Fernández-Bustos, J. G., Pastor-Vicedo, J. C., González-Martí, I., & Cuevas-Campos, R. (2020). Physical fitness and peer relationships in Spanish preadolescents. *International Journal of Environmental Research and Public Health*, *17*(6), 1890. doi:10.3390/ijerph17061890 PMID:32183282

Figueiredo, F. (2015). Redes sociais: Um suporte para a prática do self-cyberbullying [Social networks: A support for the practice of self-cyberbullying]. *Educação Sociedade & Culturas*, *44*, 107–129.

Filstrup, S. L., Briskie, D., da Fonseca, M., Lawrence, L., Wandera, A., & Inglehart, M. R. (2003). Early childhood caries and quality of life: Child and parent perspectives. *Pediatric Dentistry*, *25*(5), 431–440. PMID:14649606

Finkelhor, D., Mitchell, K. J., & Wolak, J. (2000). *Online victimization: A report on the nation's youth*. National Center for Missing and Exploited Children.

Fink-Samnick, E. (2016). The New Age of Bullying and Violence in Health Care: Part 2: Advancing Professional Education, Practice Culture, and Advocacy. *Professional Case Management*, *21*(3), 114–126. doi:10.1097/NCM.0000000000000146 PMID:27035082

Fırat, M., & Ayran, G. (2016). Cyberbullying among college students. *Turk Silahli Kuvvetleri Koruyucu Hekimlik Bulteni*, *5*(15), 322–329. doi:10.5455/pmb.1-1450776947

Fishbein, M. A., & Azjen, I. (1975). *Belief, attitude, intention and behaviour: An introduction to theory and research*. Addison-Wesley.

Fisher, H., Moffitt, T., Houts, R., Belsky, D., Arseneault, L., & Caspi, A. (2012). Bullying victimization and risk of self-harm in early adolescence: Longitudinal cohort study. *British Medical Journal*, *344*, 1–9. PMID:22539176

Fitzgerald, L. F., Swan, S., & Magley, V. J. (1997). But was it really sexual harassment? Legal, behavioral, and psychological definitions of the workplace victimization of women. In W. T. Donohue (Ed.), *Sexual Harassment: Theory, Research, and Treatment*. Allyn and Bacon.

Fitzgerald, L. F., Swan, S., & Magley, V. J. (1997). But was it really sexual harassment? Legal, behavioral, and psychological definitions of the workplace victimization of women. In W. O'Donohue (Ed.), *Sexual harassment: Theory, research and therapy* (pp. 5–28). Allyn & Bacon.

Flannery, D. J., Wester, K. L., & Singer, M. I. (2004). Impact of exposure to violance in school on child and adolescent mental health and behaviour. *Journal of Community Psychology*, *32*(5), 559–573. doi:10.1002/jcop.20019

Flannery, R. Jr, LeVitre, V., Rego, S., & Walker, A. (2011). Characteristics of Staff Victims of Psychiatric Patient Assaults: 20-Year Analysis of the Assaulted Staff Action Program. *The Psychiatric Quarterly*, *82*(1), 11–21. doi:10.100711126-010-9153-z PMID:20821050

Fleming, L. C., & Jacobsen, K. H. (2010). Bullying among middle-school students in low and middle income countries. *Health Promotion International*, *25*(1), 73–84. doi:10.1093/heapro/dap046 PMID:19884243

Folkman, S. (2013). *Stress: Appraisal and Coping*. Springer.

Foody, M., Samara, M., El Asam, A., Morsi, H., & Khattab, A. (2017). A Review of Cyberbullying Legislation in Qatar: Considerations for policy makers and educators. *International Journal of Law and Psychiatry*, *50*, 45–51. doi:10.1016/j.ijlp.2016.10.013 PMID:27837914

Forensic Statistics of the Ministry of Justice. (2020). *Judicial Statistics 2020.* Turkish Republic Ministry of Justice. https://adlisicil.adalet.gov.tr/Home/SayfaDetay/adalet-istatistikleri-yayin-arsivi

Forssell, R. (2016). Exploring cyberbullying and face-to-face bullying in working life – Prevalence, targets and expressions. *Computers in Human Behavior*, *58*, 454–460. doi:10.1016/j.chb.2016.01.003

Forssell, R. C. (2020). Gender and organisational position: Predicting victimisation of cyberbullying behaviour in working life. *International Journal of Human Resource Management*, *31*(16), 2045–2064. doi:10.1080/09585192.2018.1424018

Fortunatus, M., Anthony, P., & Charters, S. (2020). Combining textual features to detect cyberbullying in social media posts. *Procedia Computer Science*, *176*, 612–662. doi:10.1016/j.procs.2020.08.063

Fouché, A., Fouché, D. F., & Theron, L. C. (2020). Child protection and resilience in the face of COVID-19 in South Africa: A rapid review of C-19 legislation. *Child Abuse & Neglect*, *110*, 104710. doi:10.1016/j.chiabu.2020.104710 PMID:32938531

Fowler, L. A., Kracht, C. L., Denstel, K. D., Stewart, T. M., & Staiano, A. E. (2021). Bullying experiences, body esteem, body dissatisfaction, and the moderating role of weight status among adolescents. *Journal of Adolescence*, *91*(1), 59–70. doi:10.1016/j.adolescence.2021.07.006 PMID:34333320

fox19.com. (2012). *Lawsuit over 'sexting' suicide settled.* https://www.fox19.com/story/19766203/lawsuit-over-sexting-suicide-of-jessica-logan-has-been-settled/

Fox, A. K., & Hoy, M. G. (2019). Smart devices, smart decisions? Implications of parents ' sharenting for children ' s online privacy : An investigation of mothers. *Journal of Public Policy & Marketing*, *38*(4), 414–432. doi:10.1177/0743915619858290

Fox, S., & Stallworth, L. E. (2005). Racial/ethnic bullying: Exploring links between bullying and racism in the US workplace. *Journal of Vocational Behavior*, *66*(3), 438–456. doi:10.1016/j.jvb.2004.01.002

Francine, R., Pascale, S., & Aline, H. (2014). Congenital anomalies: prevalence and risk factors. *Mortality, 1*, 2.

Francioli, L. (2015). Workplace Bullying, Antecedents and Mechanisms. Università degli studi di Milano.

Franklin, J., Denyer, G., Steinbeck, K. S., Caterson, I. D., & Hill, A. J. (2006). Obesity and risk of low self-esteem: A statewide survey of Australian children. *Pediatrics*, *118*(6), 2481–2487. doi:10.1542/peds.2006-0511 PMID:17142534

Frazier, P., Berman, M., & Steward, J. (2002). Perceived control and posttraumatic stress: A temporal model. *Applied & Preventive Psychology*, *10*(3), 207–223. doi:10.1016/S0962-1849(01)80015-9

Fredland, N. M. (2008). Sexual bullying: Addressing the gap between bullying and dating violence. *Advances in Nursing Science*, *31*(2), 95–105. doi:10.1097/01.ANS.0000319560.76384.8a PMID:18497586

Freis, S. D., & Gurung, R. A. R. (2013). A Facebook analysis of helping behavior in online bullying. *Psychology of Popular Media Culture*, *2*(1), 11–19. doi:10.1037/a0030239

Freud, S. (1950). *Beyond the pleasure principle*. Liveright.

Friedman, L. S., Sheppard, S., & Friedman, D. (2012). A retrospective cohort study of suspected child maltreatment cases resulting in hospitalization. *Injury, 43*(11), 1881–1887. doi:10.1016/j.injury.2012.07.192 PMID:22901423

Frost, L. (1991). A primary school approach: What can be done about the bully? In *Bullying: A practical guide to coping for schools*. Longman.

Fryer, W. A. (2006, November 20). Addressing cyberbullying in schools. *The TechEdge: The Journal of the Texas Computer Education Association*. Retrieved March 15, 2009, from: www.wtvi.comlteks/06 _ 07 _articles/cyberbullying.html

Gadit, A. A., & Mugford, G. (2008). A pilot study of bullying and harassment among medical professionals in Pakistan, focussing on psychiatry: Need for a medical ombudsman. *Journal of Medical Ethics, 34*(6), 463–466. doi:10.1136/jme.2007.021832 PMID:18511621

Gaete, J., Valenzuela, D., Rojas-Barahona, C., Valenzuela, E., Araya, R., & Salmivalli, C. (2017). The KiVa antibullying program in primary schools in Chile, with and without the digital game component: Study protocol for a randomized controlled trial. *Trials, 18*(1), 75. doi:10.118613063-017-1810-1 PMID:28219403

Gaffney, H., Farrington, D., Espelage, D., & Ttofi, M. (2019). Are cyberbullying intervention and prevention programs effective? A systematic and meta-analytical review. *Aggression and Violent Behavior, 45*, 34–153. doi:10.1016/j.avb.2018.07.002

Galletta, D. (2014). Mobbing: From a Social Phenomenon to Psychopathology: Preliminary Data. *Journal of Psychiatry, 17*(5). Advance online publication. doi:10.4172/Psychiatry.1000137

Gámez-Guadix, M., Orue, I., Smith, P. K., & Calvete, E. (2013). Longitudinal and reciprocal relations of cyberbullying with depression, substance use, and problematic internet use among adolescents. *The Journal of Adolescent Health, 53*(4), 446–452. doi:10.1016/j.jadohealth.2013.03.030 PMID:23721758

Gander, M. J., & Gardiner, H. W. (2010). *Çocuk ve ergen gelişimi [Child and adolescent development]*. İmge Kitabevi.

Garandeau, C. F., Lee, I. A., & Salmivalli, C. (2014). Inequality matters: Classroom status hierarchy and adolescents' bullying. *Journal of Youth and Adolescence, 43*(7), 1123–1133. doi:10.100710964-013-0040-4 PMID:24129884

Garandeau, C. F., Poskiparta, E., & Salmivalli, C. (2014). Tackling acute cases of school bullying in the KiVa anti-bullying program: A comparison of two approaches. *Journal of Abnormal Child Psychology, 42*(6), 981–991. doi:10.100710802-014-9861-1 PMID:24615005

Garcia, A. C., Sousa, R., Varela, A., & Monteiro, L. (2021). Bullying, physical activity, and body image among Brazilian students. *Journal of Health Psychology, 26*(10), 1661–1673. doi:10.1177/1359105319884598 PMID:31674842

Garmy, P., Hansson, E., Vilhjálmsson, R. & Kristjánsdóttir, G. (2019). Bullying and pain in school-aged children and adolescents: a cross-sectional study. *SAGE Open Nursing. 10*, 5.

Gaskill, D., & Sanders, F. (2000). The Encultured Body: Policy Implications for Healthy Body Image and Disordered Eating Behaviours. Queensland University of Technology.

Gattario, K. H., Lindwall, M., & Frisén, A. (2020). Life after childhood bullying: Body image development and disordered eating in adulthood. *International Journal of Behavioral Development, 44*(3), 246–255. doi:10.1177/0165025419877971

Gatto, R. C. J., Garbin, A. J. Í., Corrente, J. E., & Garbin, C. A. S. (2019). The relationship between oral health-related quality of life, the need for orthodontic treatment and bullying, among Brazilian teenagers. *Dental Press Journal of Orthodontics, 24*(2), 73–80. doi:10.1590/2177-6709.24.2.073-080.oar PMID:31116290

Gelles, R. J. (2009). Child abuse. *Microsoft Encarta Online encyclopedia*. Retrieved from http://encarta.msn.com

Gelles, R. J. (2001). Child Abuse as Psychopathology: A Social Critique and Reformulation. *The American Journal of Orthopsychiatry*, *43*(4), 611–621. doi:10.1111/j.1939-0025.1973.tb00830.x PMID:4736790

Genç, G. (2007). *Peer bullying and its management in high schools* (UMI No. 226994) [Doctoral dissertation, Inönü University]. Higher Education Council Thesis Center database.

Genç, G. (2007). *Peer bullying and its management in high schools* [Unpublished Doctorate Thesis]. Ankara University, Institute of Social Sciences, Malatya.

Genç, G., & Aksu, M. B. (2010). Genel lise öğrencilerinin zorba-kurban davranıslarının çeşitli değişkenler açısından incelenmesi [Investigation of bully-victim behaviors of general high school students in terms of various variables]. *Gazi University Journal of Gazi Educational Faculty*, *30*(2), 413–448.

Georgiou, S. N., & Stavrinides, P. (2008). Bullies, victims and bully-victims. *School Psychology International*, *29*(5), 574–589. doi:10.1177/0143034308099202

Gerritsen, A. E., Allen, P. F., Witter, D. J., Bronkhorst, E. M., & Creugers, N. H. (2010). Tooth loss and oral health-related quality of life: A systematic review and meta-analysis. *Health and Quality of Life Outcomes*, *8*(1), 1–11. doi:10.1186/1477-7525-8-126 PMID:21050499

Gilbert, P., Clarke, M., Hempel, S., Miles, J. N., & Irons, C. (2004). Criticizing and reassuring oneself: An exploration of forms, styles and reasons in female students. *British Journal of Clinical Psychology*, *43*(1), 31–50. doi:10.1348/014466504772812959 PMID:15005905

Gilbert, P., & Irons, C. (2009). Shame, self-criticism, and self-compassion in adolescence. *Adolescent Emotional Development and The Emergence of Depressive Disorders*, *1*, 195–214.

Gillies-Rezo, S., & Bosacki, S. (2003). Invisible bruises: Kindergartens' perceptions of bullying. *International Journal of Children's Spirituality*, *8*(2), 163–177. doi:10.1080/13644360304628

Gini, G., Albiero, P., Benelli, B., & Altoè, G. (2007). Does empathy predict adolescents' bullying and defending behavior? *Aggressive Behavior*, *33*(5), 464–476. doi:10.1002/ab.20204 PMID:17683107

Gini, G., & Pozzoli, T. (2009). Association between bullying and psychosomatic problems: A meta-analysis. *Pediatrics*, *123*(3), 1059–1065. doi:10.1542/peds.2008-1215 PMID:19255040

Gini, G., & Pozzoli, T. (2013). Bullied children and psychosomatic problems: A meta-analysis. *Pediatrics*, *132*(4), 720–729. doi:10.1542/peds.2013-0614 PMID:24043275

Giorgi, G., Mancuso, S., Fiz Perez, F., Castiello D'Antonio, A., Mucci, N., Cupelli, V., & Arcangeli, G. (2016). Bullying among nurses and its relationship with burnout and organizational climate. *International Journal of Nursing Practice*, *22*(2), 160–168. doi:10.1111/ijn.12376 PMID:25825025

Girvan, C. (2018). What is a virtual world? Definition and classification. *Educational Technology Research and Development*, *66*(5), 1087–1100. doi:10.100711423-018-9577-y

Giumetti, G. W., & Kowalski, R. (2022). Cyberbullying via social media and well-being. *Current Opinion in Psychology*, *45*, 101314. doi:10.1016/j.copsyc.2022.101314 PMID:35313180

Glaser, D., & Prior, V. (1997). Is the term child protection applicable to emotional abuse? *Child Abuse Review*, *6*(5), 315–329. doi:10.1002/(SICI)1099-0852(199712)6:5<315::AID-CAR361>3.0.CO;2-A

Glasø, L., Nielsen, M. B., & Einarsen, S. (2009). Interpersonal Problems Among Perpetrators and Targets of Workplace Bullying. *Journal of Applied Social Psychology*, *39*(6), 1316–1333. doi:10.1111/j.1559-1816.2009.00483.x

Glew, G. M., Fan, M. Y., Katon, W., Rivara, F. P., & Kernic, M. A. (2005). Bullying, psychosocial adjustment, and academic performance in elementary school. *Archives of Pediatrics & Adolescent Medicine*, *159*(11), 1026–1031. doi:10.1001/archpedi.159.11.1026 PMID:16275791

Glover, D., Gough, G., Johnson, M., & Cartwright, N. (2000). Bullying in secondary schools: Incidence. *Impact and Intervention. Educational Research*, *42*(2), 141–156. doi:10.1080/001318800363782

Goebert, D., Else, I., Matsu, C., Chung-Do, J., & Chang, J. Y. (2011). The Impact of Cyberbullying on Substance Use and Mental Health in a Multiethnic Sample. *Maternal and Child Health Journal*, *15*(8), 1282–1286. doi:10.100710995-010-0672-x PMID:20824318

Gökkaya, F., & Tekinsav Sütcü, S. (2015). Development and evaluation of psychometric characteristics of the ınventory of cognitions related bullying for children. *Anatolian Journal of Psychiatry*, *16*(1), 54–63. doi:10.5455/apd.174346

Gökkaya, F., & Tekinsav Sütcü, S. (2020). Akran zorbalığının ortaokul öğrencileri arasındaki yaygınlığının incelenmesi [An investigation of the prevalence of peer bullying among middle school students]. *Hacettepe University Journal of Education*, *35*(1), 40–54.

Gökler, R. (2007). *Examination of school bullying with regard to some variables among middle school children* (UMI No. 235698) [Doctoral dissertation, Ankara University]. Higher Education Council Thesis Center database.

Gökler, R. (2009). Bullying in schools. *International Journal of Human Sciences*, *6*(2), 511–537.

Gökler, R. (2009). Okullarda akran zorbalığı [Peer bullying at schools]. *Uluslararası İnsan Bilimleri Dergisi*, *6*(2), 511–537.

Gökler, R. (2009). Okullarda akran zorbalığı [Peer bullying in schools]. *International Journal of Human Sciences*, *6*(2), 511–537.

Golos, D. B., & Moses, A. M. (2011). Representations of deaf characters in children's picture books. *American Annals of the Deaf*, *156*(3), 270–282. doi:10.1353/aad.2011.0025 PMID:21941877

Golos, D. B., Moses, A. M., & Wolbers, K. A. (2012). Culture or disability? Examining deaf characters in children's book illustrations. *Early Childhood Education Journal*, *40*(4), 239–249. doi:10.100710643-012-0506-0

Goodwin, K. (2017). *Sharenting- What parents need to consider before sharing pictures of their kids.* Retrieved January 3, 2022, from https://drkristygoodwin.com/sharenting-what-parents-need-to-consider-before-sharing-pictures-of-their-kids/

Gordon, J. U. (2018). *Bullying prevention and intervention at school: Integrating theory and research into best practices.* Academic Press.

Görgünbaran, A. (2008). Socialization and Quality of Life in Old Ages [Yaşlılıkta sosyalizasyon ve yaşam kalitesi]. *Yaşlı Sorunları Araştırma Dergisi*, *1*(2), 86–97.

Görzig, A., & Ólafsson, K. (2013). What makes a bully a cyberbully? Unravelling the characteristics of cyberbullies across twenty-five European countries. *Journal of Children and Media*, *7*(1), 9–27. doi:10.1080/17482798.2012.739756

Gottfredson, M. R., & Hirschi, T. (1990). *A General Theory of Crime.* Stanford University Press. doi:10.1515/9781503621794

Government Equalities Office. (2020). *2020 Sexual Harassment Survey.* IFF Research. https://assets.publishing.service.gov.uk/government/uploads/system/uploads/attac hment_data/file/1002873/2021-07-12_Sexual_Harassment_Report_FINAL.pdf

Government of India. (2022). *Home | Legislative Department | Ministry of Law and Justice | GoI.* https://legislative.gov.in/

Government, S. A. (2021). *Cybercrimes Act 19 of 2020 (English / Afrikaans)*. South African Government. https://www.gov.za/documents/cybercrimes-act-19-2020-1-jun-2021-0000

Gözün-Kahraman, Ö., & Şahin, D. (2018). Çocuk ihmal ve istismarı. In *Çocuk hakları içinde* [Child neglect and abuse]. (pp. 184–208). Academic Press.

Gradinger, P., Yanagida, T., Strohmeier, D., & Spiel, C. (2016). Effectiveness and sustainability of the ViSC Social Competence Program to prevent cyberbullying and cyber-victimization: Class and individual level moderators. *Aggressive Behavior*, *42*(2), 181–193. doi:10.1002/ab.21631 PMID:26879896

Graf, N. (2018). *Sexual harassment at work in the era of #MeToo*. Pew Research Center. Social and demographic trends. https://www.pewresearch.org/social-trends/2018/04/04/sexual-harassment-at-work-in-the-era-of-metoo/

Graf, D., Yanagida, T., Runions, K., & Spiel, C. (2022). Why did you do that? Differential types of aggression in offline and in cyberbullying. *Computers in Human Behavior*, *128*, 107107. doi:10.1016/j.chb.2021.107107

Graham, S. (2011). *Bullying: A module for teachers*. Error! Hyperlink reference not valid.

Grauerholz, E., & King, A. (1997). Prime time sexual harassment. *Violence Against Women*, *3*(2), 129–148. doi:10.1177/1077801297003002003 PMID:12294811

Greenberg, N. (2020). Mental health of health-care workers in the COVID-19 era. *Nature Reviews. Nephrology*, *16*(8), 425–426. doi:10.103841581-020-0314-5 PMID:32561871

Greenleaf, C., Petrie, T. A., & Martin, S. B. (2014). Relationship of Weight-Based Teasing and Adolescents' Psychological Well-Being and Physical Health. *The Journal of School Health*, *84*(1), 49–55. doi:10.1111/josh.12118 PMID:24320152

Green, R., Collingwood, A., & Ross, A. (2010). *Characteristics of bullying victims in schools*. London Publishing.

Grigg, D. W. (2010). Cyber-aggression: Definition and Concept of Cyberbullying. *Journal of Psychologists and Counsellors in Schools*, *20*(2), 143–156. doi:10.1375/ajgc.20.2.143

Grigg, D. W. (2012). Definitional Constructs of Cyber-bullying and Cyber-aggression From a Triangulatory Overview: A Preliminary Study into Elements of Cyber-bullying. *Journal of Aggression, Conflict and Peace Research*, *4*(4), 202–215. doi:10.1108/17596591211270699

Grogan, S. (2021). *Body Image: Understanding Body Dissatisfaction in Men, Women and Children*. Routledge. doi:10.4324/9781003100041

Gruber, J. E. (1990). Methodological problems and policy implications in sexual harassment research. *Population Research and Policy Review*, *9*(3), 235–254. doi:10.1007/BF00162837

Gruber, J., & Fineran, S. (2015). Sexual harassment, bullying, and school outcomes for high school girls and boys. *Violence Against Women*, *22*(1), 1–23. doi:10.1177/1077801215599079 PMID:26270385

Güçlü, D. M., & Acemioğlu, R. (2020). Erken çocukluk döneminde yaşanan fiziksel istismar: Nitel bir çalışma [Physical Abuse in the Early Childhood: A Qualitive Study]. *Uluslararası Anadolu Sosyal Bilimler Dergisi*, *4*(4), 97–111.

Gülay Ogelman, H. (2018). *Peer Relations in Preschool Period*. Educational Book.

Gülay Ogelman, H., & Akman, B. (2009). *Social Skills in Preschool Period*. Pegem Academy.

Gülay, H. (2018). *Okul öncesi dönemde akran ilişkileri* [Peer relationships in the preschool period] (3rd ed.). Eğiten.

Gulendam, K. (2021). Children with Chronic Disease during COVID-19 Pandemic and Nurses' Roles. *International Journal of Caring Sciences*, *14*(3), 2058–2065.

Gültekin Akduman, G. (2012). An investigation of peer bullying at preschool period. *Society and Social Work, 23*(1), 121–138.

Gültekin, Z. (2003). *he Development of a peer victimization scale* [Unpublished Master Thesis]. Hacettepe University, Instutue of Social Sciences, Ankara.

Gültekin, Z., & Sayıl, M. (2005). A study of the reliability and validity of the Peer Victimization Scale. *Turkish Psychology Articles, 15,* 47-61. https://toad.halileksi.net/sites/default/files/pdf/akran-zorbaligini-belirleme-olcegi-toad_1.pdf

Gültekin-Akduman, G. (2010). Peer bullying of 7-14 year old children and their proffers of solution. *Journal of Theoretical Educational Science*, *3*(2), 13–26. https://dergipark.org.tr/tr/download/article-file/304137

Gültekin-Akduman, G. (2012). An investigation of peer bullying at preschool period. *Journal of Society & Social Work, 23*(1), 107–120. https://dergipark.org.tr/tr/pub/tsh/issue/48532/615984

Gunn, J. F. III, & Goldstein, S. E. (2017). Bullying and suicidal behavior during adolescence: A developmental perspective. *Adolescent Research Review*, *2*(2), 77–97. doi:10.100740894-016-0038-8

Guo-Bao, Z., & Geng-Fu, W. (2019). Association between different stages of precollege school bullying and murder-related psychological behaviors among college students in Anhui Province, China. *Psychiatry Research*, *282*, 112593. doi:10.1016/j.psychres.2019.112593 PMID:31630040

Gürhan, N. (2017). All aspects of the bullying. *Turkey Clinics J Psychiatr Nurs-Special Topics, 3*(2), 175-181. https://www.researchgate.net/publication/319257215_Her_Yonu_ile_Akran_Zorbaligi

Gürhan, N. (2017). All aspects of the bullying. *Türkiye Klinikleri J Psychiatr Nurs-Special Topics*, *3*(2), 175–181.

Gürhan, N. (2017). Her yönü ile akran zorbalığı [All aspects of the bullying]. *Türkiye Klinikleri J Psychiatr Nurs-Special Topics*, *3*(2), 175–181.

Gürhan, N. (2017). Her yönü ile akran zorbalığı [Bullying in all aspects]. *Turkiye Klinikleri J Psychiatr Nurs-Special Topics*, *3*(2), 175–181.

Gürhan, N. (2017). Her yönü ile akran zorbalığı [Bullying in every aspect]. *Turkiye Klinikleri J Psychiatr Nurs-Special Topics*, *3*(2), 175–181.

Güven, F. (2015). *An invastigation of bullying and being victim at 8th grade secondary school students, in relation with sex, parent education, socioeconomic status and empathy level* [Unpublished Master Thesis]. Toros University, Instutue of Social Sciences, Mersin.

Güven, F. (2015). *An invastigation of bullying and being victim at 8th grade secondary school students, in relation with sex, parent education, socioeconomic status and emphaty level* (UMI No. 408926) [Master's dissertation, Toros University]. Higher Education Council Thesis Center database.

Güvenir, T. (2005). Okulda akran istismarı [Peer abuse at school] (1st ed.). Kök.

Güvenir, T. (2008). *Okulda akran istismarı(Peer bullying in schools).* Kök Yayıncılık.

Haataja, A., Voeten, M., Boulton, A. J., Ahtola, A., Poskiparta, E., & Salmivalli, C. (2014). The KiVa antibullying curriculum and outcome: Does fidelity matter? *Journal of School Psychology*, *52*(5), 479–493. doi:10.1016/j.jsp.2014.07.001 PMID:25267170

Hagan, J., Simpson, J., & Gillis, A. R. (1988). Feminist Scholarship, Relational and Instrumental Control, and a Power-control Theory of Gender and Delinquency. *The British Journal of Sociology*, *39*(3), 301–336. doi:10.2307/590481 PMID:3179640

Haley, K. (2020). Sharenting and the (potential) right to be forgotten. *Indiana Law Journal, 95*(3), 1006-1020. https://www.repository.law.indiana.edu/ilj/vol95/iss3/9

Hall, H. K. (2018). Oversharenting : Is it really your story to tell ? 33 oversharenting: Is it really. *The John Marshall Journal of Information Technology & Privacy Law, 33*(3).

Hall, D. L., Silva, Y. N., Wheeler, B., Cheng, L., & Baumel, K. (2022). Harnessing the Power of Interdisciplinary Research with Psychology-Informed Cyberbullying Detection Models. *International Journal of Bullying Prevention, 4*(1), 47–54. doi:10.100742380-021-00107-5

Ham, C. D., Lee, J., Hayes, J. L., & Bae, Y. H. (2019). Exploring sharing behaviors across social media platforms. *International Journal of Market Research, 61*(2), 157–177. doi:10.1177/1470785318782790

Hamel, N., Schwab, S., & Wahl, S. (2021). Bullying: Group differences of being victim and being bully and the influence of social relations. *Studies in Educational Evaluation, 68*(6). Advance online publication. doi:10.1016/j.stueduc.2020.100964

Hammond, J. W. (2019). *Parenting and working in the digital age: A qualitative examination of intensive parenting and ideal worker norms* (Doctoral dissertation). Washington State Univesity. https://research.libraries.wsu.edu/xmlui/bitstream/handle/2376/16735/Hammond_wsu_0251E_12635.pdf?sequence=1&isAllowed=y

Hammoud, M. M., Appelbaum, N. P., Wallach, P. M., Burrows, H. L., Kochhar, K., Hemphill, R. R., Daniel, M., Clery, M. J., & Santen, S. A. (2021). Incidence of resident mistreatment in the learning environment across three institutions. *Medical Teacher, 43*(3), 334–340. doi:10.1080/0142159X.2020.1845306 PMID:33222573

Hamurcu, S. (2020). Peer bullying in primary school students: The case of Ankara Pursaklar. *OPUS–International Journal of Society Researches, 16*(32), 5540–5564. doi:10.26466/opus.758653

Han, C.-B. (2018). Topologie der gewalt (D. Zaptçıoğlu, Trans.). İstanbul, Turkey: Metis Yayınları.

Hançerli Ekdal, S. (2011). *Çocuğun fiziksel istismari: Kuzey Kıbrıs Türk Cumhuriyeti örneği* [Physical abuse of the child: The case of the Turkish Republic of Northern Cyprus] [Unpublished master's thesis]. Polis Akademisi.

Haner, M., & Lee, H. (2017). Placing school victimization in a global context. *Victims & Offenders, 12*(6), 845–867. doi:10.1080/15564886.2017.1361675

Hanhan, A. A. (2012). *Research on the effects of restorative discipline model on peer bullying and violence in high schools* [Unpublished Doctorate Thesis]. Dokuz Eylul University, Institute of Educational Sciences, İzmir.

Hanish, L. D., & Guerra, N. G. (2000). Children who get victimized at school: What is known? What can be done? *Professional School Counseling, 4*(2), 113–119.

Hansen, H., Hasselgard, C., Undheim, A., & Indredavik, M. (2013). Bullying behaviour among Norwegian adolescents: Psychiatric diagnoses and school well-being in a clinical sample. *Nordic Journal of Psychiatry, 68*(5), 355–361. doi:10.3109/08039488.2013.845689 PMID:24161252

Hansson, E., Garmy, P., Vilhjálmsson, R., & Kristjánsdóttir, G. (2020). Bullying, health complaints, and self-rated health among school-aged children and adolescents. *The Journal of International Medical Research, 48*(2), 1–9. doi:10.1177/0300060519895355 PMID:32054367

Haraway, D. (2006). A cyborg manifesto: Science, technology, and socialist-feminism in the late twentieth century," in simians, cyborgs and women: The reinvention of nature (O. Akınhay, Trans.). İstanbul, Turkey: Agora Yayınları.

Harder, H. G., Rash, J., & Wagner, S. (2014). *Mental Illness in the Workplace: Psychological Disability Management.* Gower Publishing Limited.

Harned, M. S. (2000). Harassed bodies: An examination of the relationships among women's experiences of sexual harassment, body image, and eating disturbances. *Psychology of Women Quarterly*, *24*(4), 336–348. doi:10.1111/j.1471-6402.2000.tb00216.x

Harned, M. S., & Fitzgerald, L. F. (2002). Understanding a link between sexual harassment and eating disorder symptoms: A mediational analysis. *Journal of Consulting and Clinical Psychology*, *70*(5), 1170–1181. doi:10.1037/0022-006X.70.5.1170 PMID:12362967

Harris, M. J. (2009). Taking bullying and rejection (ınter) personally: benefits of a social psychological approach to peer victimization. In M. J. Harris (Ed.), *Bullying, Rejection, And Peer Victimization: A Social Cognitive Neuroscience Perspective* (pp. 3–23). Springer Publishing Company.

Harrison, K., & Hefner, V. (2006). Media exposure, current and future body ideals, and disordered eating among preadolescent girls: A longitudinal panel study. *Journal of Youth and Adolescence*, *35*(2), 146–156. doi:10.100710964-005-9008-3

Hart, S. N., & Brassard, M. R. (1991). Psychological maltreatment: Progress achieved. *Development and Psychopathology*, *3*(1), 61–70. doi:10.1017/S0954579400005095

Hawker, D. S., & Boulton, M. J. (2000). Twenty years' research on peer victimization and psychosocial maladjustment: A meta-analytic review of cross-sectional studies. *Journal of Child Psychology and Psychiatry, and Allied Disciplines*, *41*(4), 441–455. doi:10.1111/1469-7610.00629 PMID:10836674

Hay, C., Meldrum, R., & Mann, K. (2010). Traditional Bullying, Cyber Bullying, and Deviance: A General Strain Theory Approach. *Journal of Contemporary Criminal Justice*, *26*(2), 130–147. doi:10.1177/1043986209359557

Hazler, R. J. (1996). *Breaking the cycle of violence: interventions for bullying and victimization.* Taylor Francis.

Healey, J. (Ed.). (2011). *Dealing with bullying.* The Spinney Press. https://goo.gl/K8dCRZ

Health, M. D. o. (2019). *Public health interventions: Applications for public health nursing practice* (2nd ed.). Public Health. Retrieved from https://www.health.state.mn.us/communities/practice/research/phncouncil/wheel.html

Hedef, Basın, Greydanus, Pratt, & Spates, Blake-Dreher, Greydanus-Gearhart, & Patel, D. R. (2003). Corporal punishment in schools: Position paper of the Society for Adolescent Medicine. *The Journal of Adolescent Health*, *32*(5), 385–393.

Heinrichs, R. R. (2003). A whole-school approach to bullying: Special consideration for children with exceptionalities. *Intervention in School and Clinic*, *38*(4), 195–204. doi:10.1177/105345120303800401

Heirman, W., & Walrave, M. (2008). Assessing Concerns and Issues about the Mediation of Technology in Cyberbullying. *Cyberpsychology (Brno)*, *2*(2).

Hekim, H., & Başıbüyük, O. (2013). Siber Suçlar ve Türkiye'nin Siber Güvenlik Politikaları. *International Journal of Security and Terrorism*, *4*(2).

Heponiemi, T., Kouvonen, A., Virtanen, M., Vänskä, J., & Elovainio, M. (2014). The prospective effects of workplace violence on physicians' job satisfaction and turnover intentions: The buffering effect of job control. *BMC Health Services Research*, *14*(1), 19. doi:10.1186/1472-6963-14-19 PMID:24438449

Herring, J. (2021). Malicious Communications Act 1988. In Criminal Law Statutes 2011-2012 (pp. 103–105). doi:10.4324/9780203722763-40

Herring, S., Job-Siuder, K., Scheckler, R., & Barab, S. (2002). Searching for safety online: Managing 'trolling' ina feminist forum. *The Information Society*, *18*(5), 371–384. doi:10.1080/01972240290108186

Herschcovis, M. S. (2011). Incivility, Social Undermining, Bullying…oh My!: A Call to Reconcile Constructs within Workplace Aggression Research. *Journal of Organizational Behavior, 32*(3), 499–519. doi:10.1002/job.689

Hershcovis, M. S., & Barling, J. (2010). Towards a Multi-Foci Approach to Workplace Aggression: A Meta-Analytic Review of Outcomes from Different Perpetrators. *Journal of Organizational Behavior, 31*(1), 24–44. doi:10.1002/job.621

Heyman, R. E., Snarr, J. D., Slep, A. M. S., Baucom, K. J., & Linkh, D. J. (2020). Self-reporting DSM–5/ICD-11 clinically significant intimate partner violence and child abuse: Convergent and response process validity. *Journal of Family Psychology, 34*(1), 101–111. doi:10.1037/fam0000560 PMID:31328945

Hidalgo-Rasmussen, C. A., Ramírez-López, G., Rajmil, L., Skalicky, A., & Martín, A. H. (2018). Bullying and health-related quality of life in children and adolescent Mexican students. *Ciencia & Saude Coletiva, 23*(7), 2433–2441. doi:10.1590/1413-81232018237.16392016 PMID:30020395

Hilliard, L. J., Batanova, M., & Bowers, E. P. (2015). A positive youth development approach to bullying: Promoting thriving and reducing problem behaviors. In E. P. Bowers, G. J. Geldhof, S. K. Johnson, L. J. Hilliard, R. M. Hershberg, J. V. Lerner, & R. M. Lerner (Eds.), *Promoting positive youth development: Lessons from the 4-H study* (pp. 249–272). Springer. doi:10.1007/978-3-319-17166-1_13

Hinduja, S. (2021, October 21). Bullying During the COVID-19 Pandemic. *Cyberbyllying Research Center.* https://cyberbullying.org/cyberbullying-statistics-age-gender-sexual-orientation-race

Hinduja, S., & Patchin, J.W. (2005). *Research Summary: Cyberbullying Victimization. Preliminary findings from an online survey of Internet-using adolescents.* http://www.cyberbullying.us

Hinduja, S., & Patchin, J. (2012). *School Climate 2.0: Preventing Cyberbullying and Sexting One Classroom at a Time.* Corwin Press. doi:10.4135/9781506335438

Hinduja, S., & Patchin, J. W. (2007). Offline consequences of online victimization: School violence and delinquency. *Journal of School Violence, 6*(3), 89–112. doi:10.1300/J202v06n03_06

Hinduja, S., & Patchin, J. W. (2008). Cyberbullying: An exploratory analysis of factors related to offending and victimization. *Deviant Behavior, 29*(2), 129–156. doi:10.1080/01639620701457816

Hinduja, S., & Patchin, J. W. (2009). *Bullying beyond the schoolyards.* Carwin.

Hinduja, S., & Patchin, J. W. (2009). *Cyberbullying Fact Sheet: A brief review of relevant legal and policy issues.* Cyberbullying Research Center.

Hinduja, S., & Patchin, J. W. (2010). Bullying, cyberbullying, and suicide. *Archives of Suicide Research, 14*(3), 206–221. doi:10.1080/13811118.2010.494133 PMID:20658375

Hinduja, S., & Patchin, J. W. (2010). Cyberbullying Research Summary: Cyberbullying and Self-Esteem. *The Journal of School Health, 80*(12), 614–621. doi:10.1111/j.1746-1561.2010.00548.x PMID:21087257

Hinduja, S., & Patchin, J. W. (2011). High-tech Cruelty. *Educational Leadership, 68*(5), 48–52.

Hinduja, S., & Patchin, J. W. (2014). *Bullying beyond the schoolyard: Preventing and responding to cyberbullying.* Corwin Pres.

Hinduja, S., & Patchin, J. W. (2015). *Bullying Beyond the Schoolyard: Preventing and Responding to Cyberbullying* (2nd ed.). Sage Publications.

Hinduja, S., & Patchin, J. W. (2015). *Bullying beyond the schooyard: Preventing and responding to cyberbullying.* Corwin.

Hinduja, S., & Patchin, J. W. (2018). Connecting Adolescent Suicide to the Severity of Bullying and Cyberbullying. *Journal of School Violence*, *18*(3), 333–346. doi:10.1080/15388220.2018.1492417

Hinduja, S., & Patchin, J. W. (2020). *Bullying, Cyberbullying, and LGBTQ Students*. Cyberbullying Research Center.

Hisar, T. (2018). *The influence of family communication in the relationship among substance addiction, bullying and anger in individuals between 15 and 25 years old* (UMI No. 486087) [Master's dissertation, Üsküdar University]. Higher Education Council Thesis Center database.

Hlazo, N. I. (2018). *The legal remedies to protect minors against cyberbullying in South Africa*. Nelson Mandela University. http://vital.seals.ac.za:8080/vital/access/manager/Repository/vital:30914?site_name=GlobalView

Hobfoll, S. E. (1989). Conservation of resources: A new attempt at conceptualizing stress. *The American Psychologist*, *44*(3), 513–524. doi:10.1037/0003-066X.44.3.513 PMID:2648906

Hoel, H., & Vartia, M. (2018). Bullying and sexual harassment at the workplace, in public spaces, and in political life in the EU. In European, Parliament Directorate-General for Internal Policies of the, Union. European Parliament.

Hoertel, N., Le Strat, Y., Lavaud, P., & Limosin, F. (2012). Gender effects in bullying: Results from an antional sample. *Psychiatry Research*, *200*(2-3), 921–927. doi:10.1016/j.psychres.2012.03.036 PMID:22497957

Hoff, D. L., & Mitchell, S. N. (2009). Cyberbullying: Causes, Effects, and Remedies. *Journal of Educational Administration*, *47*(5), 652–665. doi:10.1108/09578230910981107

Holiday, S., Norman, M. S., & Densley, R. L. (2020). Sharenting and the extended self: Self-representation in parents' Instagram presentations of their children. *Popular Communication*, *18*(3), 1–15. doi:10.1080/15405702.2020.1744610

Hollon, S. D., & Kriss, M. R. (1984). Cognitive factors in clinical research and practice. *Clinical Psychology Review*, *4*(1), 35–76. doi:10.1016/0272-7358(84)90036-9

Holloway, J. H. (2002). The dilemma of zero tolerance. *Educational Leadership*, *59*(4), 84–86.

Holt, M. K., Greif Green, J., Tsay-Vogel, M., Davidson, J., & Brown, C. (2017). Multidisciplinary Approaches to Research on Bullying in Adolescence. *Adolescent Research Review*, *2*(1), 1–10. doi:10.100740894-016-0041-0

Holt, T. J., Bossler, A. M., & May, D. C. (2012). Low Self-control, Deviant Peer Associations, and Juvenile Cyberdeviance. *American Journal of Criminal Justice*, *37*(3), 378–395. doi:10.100712103-011-9117-3

Holubcikova, J., Kolarcik, P., Madarasova Geckova, A., Van Dijk, J. P., & Reijneveld, S. A. (2015). Is subjective perception of negative body image among adolescents associated with bullying? *European Journal of Pediatrics*, *174*(8), 1035–1041. doi:10.100700431-015-2507-7 PMID:25708851

Hong, J. S., & Espelage, D. L. (2012). A review of research on bullying and peer victimization in school: An ecological system analysis. *Aggression and Violent Behavior*, *17*(4), 311–322. doi:10.1016/j.avb.2012.03.003

Hood, M., & Duffy, A. L. (2018). Understanding the relationship between cyber-victimization and cyber-bullying on Social Network Sites: The role of moderating factors. *Personality and Individual Differences*, *133*, 103–108. doi:10.1016/j.paid.2017.04.004

Horzum, M. B., & Ayas, T. (2011). He examination of cyberbullying and victimlevels of highschool students according to school type and gender. *Journal of Educational Sciences & Practices*, *10*(20), 139–159.

Horzum, M. B., & Ayas, T. (2011). The examination of cyberbullying and victim levels of high school students according to school type and gender. *Educational Science and Practice*, *10*(20), 139–159.

Horzum, M. B., & Ayas, T. (2014). The examination of cyberbullying and victim levels of high school students according to school type and gender. *Online Journal of Technology Addiction and Cyberbullying*, *1*(2), 21–36.

Hoşgörür, V., & Orhan, A. (2017). The causes of bullying and violence at schools and managing the prevention of it (the sample of Muğla province). *Journal of Bayburt Education Faculty*, *12*(24), 859–880. https://dergipark.org.tr/en/pub/befdergi/issue/33599/292827

Hossain, A., Abdul Wahab, J., Islam, M. R., Khan, M. S. R., & Mahmud, A. (2022). *Cyberbullying Perception and Experience Among the University Students in Bangladesh*. IGI Global. doi:10.4018/978-1-7998-9187-1.ch012

Hosseini, H. R., Kaklamanos, E. G., & Athanasiou, A. E. (2017). Treatment outcomes of pre-surgical infant orthopedics in patients with non-syndromic cleft lip and/or palate: A systematic review and meta-analysis of randomized controlled trials. *PLoS One*, *12*(7), e0181768. doi:10.1371/journal.pone.0181768 PMID:28742129

Hosseinmardi, H., Mattson, S. A., Rafiq, R. I., Han, R., Lv, Q., & Mishr, S. (2015). *Prediction of Cyberbullying Incidents on the Instagram Social Network*. arXiv preprint arXiv:1508.06257.

Hossen, S. (2021). Nature and Aftermath of Cyberbullying with Female University Students in Bangladesh. *Journal of the Humanities and Social Sciences*, *26*(10), 45–53. doi:10.9790/0837-2610074553

Huang, Y., & Chou, C. (2010). An analysis of multiple factors of cyberbullying next term among junior high school students in Taiwan. *Computers in Human Behavior*, *26*(6), 1581–1590. doi:10.1016/j.chb.2010.06.005

Hughes, A. A. (2022). Cyberbullying: A qualitative analysis of perceptions of high school principals' mediation and intervention strategies. *Dissertation Abstracts International. A, The Humanities and Social Sciences*. https://www.proquest.com/dissertations-theses/cyberbullying-qualitative-analysis-perceptions/docview/2640072416/se-2?accountid=14744%0Ahttps://cbua-us.primo.exlibrisgroup.com/discovery/openurl?institution=34CBUA_US&vid=34CBUA_US:VU1&lang=es?url_ver=Z39.88

Hultin, M., Davidson, T., Gynther, G., Helgesson, G., Jemt, T., Lekholm, U., ... Tranaeus, S. (2012). Oral rehabilitation of tooth loss: A systematic review of quantitative studies of OHRQoL. *The International Journal of Prosthodontics*, *25*(6). PMID:23101034

Hunt, J. (2011). *Bullying should not be a teenage rite of passage*. https://www.americanprogress.org/wp-content/uploads/issues/2011/02/pdf /antigay_bullying.pdf

Hunter, S. C., Boyle, J. M. E., & Warden, D. (2004). Help seeking amongst child and adolescent victims of peeraggression and bullying: The influence of school-stage, gender, victimisation, appraisal, and emotion. *The British Journal of Educational Psychology*, *74*(3), 375–390. doi:10.1348/0007099041552378 PMID:15296546

Hürler, Ş. (2018). Üniversite öğrencilerinin duygusal istismara ilişkin algılarının incelenmesi [Examination of university students' perceptions of emotional abuse] [Unpublished master's thesis]. Doğu Akdeniz Üniversitesi Lisansüstü Eğitim ve Araştırma Enstitüsü.

Hurley, K. (2019). *Short Term and Long Term Effects of Bullying*. Remedy Health Media, LLC.

hurriyet.com. (2012). *A Turkish girl is a victim of a virtual bully*. https://www.hurriyet.com.tr/gundem/turk-kizi-seniz-sanal-zorba-kurbani-19693094

Husky, M. M., Delbasty, E., Bitfoi, A., Carta, M. G., Goelitz, D., Koç, C., Lesinskiene, S., Mihova, Z., Otten, R., & Kovess-Masfety, V. (2020). Bullying involvement and self-reported mental health in elementary school children across Europe. *Child Abuse & Neglect*, *107*, 104601. doi:10.1016/j.chiabu.2020.104601 PMID:32570185

Hutchinson, M., Vickers, M. H., Jackson, D., & Wilkes, L. (2005). "I'm gonna do what i wanna do." Organizational change as a legitimized vehicle for bullies. *Health Care Management Review*, *30*(4), 331–336. doi:10.1097/00004010-200510000-00007 PMID:16292010

Hutson, E., Kelly, S., & Militello, L. K. (2018). Systematic review of cyberbullying interventions for youth and parents with implications for evidence-based practice. *Worldviews on Evidence-Based Nursing*, *15*(1), 72–79. doi:10.1111/wvn.12257 PMID:28859246

Hu, Y.-Y., Ellis, R. J., Hewitt, D. B., Yang, A. D., Cheung, E. O., Moskowitz, J. T., Potts, J. R. III, Buyske, J., Hoyt, D. B., Nasca, T. J., & Bilimoria, K. Y. (2019). Discrimination, abuse, harassment, and burnout in surgical residency training. *The New England Journal of Medicine*, *381*(18), 1741–1752. doi:10.1056/NEJMsa1903759 PMID:31657887

Hymel, S., & Swearer, S. M. (2015). *Four Decades of Research on School Bullying An Introduction*. Academic Press.

Hymel, S., Schonert-Reıchl, K. A., Bonanno, R. A., Vaıllancourt, T., & Henderson, N. R. (2010). Bullying and Morality: Understanding How Good Kids Can Behave Badly. In The Handbook of Bullying in Schools: An International Perspective Shane (pp. 101-118). Roultredge.

Ifemeje, N. M. O. (2020). Protecting the privacy of data: Search and seizure of computer devices under the cybercrime (prohibition, prevention, etc.). *International Journal of Law and Clinical Legal Education, 1*. https://nigerianjournalsonline.com/index.php/IJOLACLE/article/view/2164

İğdeli, F. (2018). *Investigating the university students' levels of cyberbullying, cybervictimization and cyberbullying sensitivity according to various variables* (Unpublished Master's Thesis). Eskişehir Anadolu University, Eskişehir.

Ihnat, L., & Smith, D. (2013). Solutions for bullying: Intervention training for pre-service teachers. *Journal of Teaching and Learning*, *9*(1), 1–13. doi:10.22329/jtl.v9i1.3604

Ildırım, E., Çalıcı, C., & Erdoğan, B. (2017). Psychological correlates of cyberbullying and cyber-victimization. *The International Journal of Human and Behavioral Science*, *3*(2), 7–21.

Illia, L., Colleoni, E., Ranvidran, K., & Ludovico, N. (2022). Mens rea, wrongdoing and digital advocacy in social media: Exploring quasi-legal narratives during #deleteuber. *Journal of Public Affairs*, 1 – 16. doi:10.1002/pa.2805

Ilola, A. M., Lempinen, L., Huttunen, J., Ristkari, T., & Sourander, A. (2016). Bullying and victimisation are common in four-year-old children and are associated with somatic symptoms and conduct and peer problems. *Acta Paediatrica (Oslo, Norway)*, *105*(5), 522–528. doi:10.1111/apa.13327 PMID:26741067

Imai, H. (2020). Trust is a key factor in the willingness of health professionals to work during the COVID-19 outbreak: Experience from the H1N1 pandemic in Japan 2009. *Psychiatry and Clinical Neurosciences*, *74*(5), 329–330. doi:10.1111/pcn.12995 PMID:32105381

Imran, A. (2020). *"I survived": Coping strategies for bullying in schools: A systematic literature review from 2009-2020* [Master Thesis]. Jönköping University.

India Code. (2021). *India Code: Home*. https://www.indiacode.nic.in/

Ingelehart, M. R., & Bagramian, R. A. (2002). Oral health-related quality of life: an introduction. *Oral Health-Related Quality of Life*, 1-6.

International Labour Organization. (2016). *Fundamental Rights at Work*. Accessed January 29, 2022. http://www.ilo.org/caribbean/areas-of-work/ils/rights-at-work/lang--en/index.htm

International Labour Organization. (2019). *Sexual harassment at work: Insights from the global garment industry*. ILO.

İpek, Ö. (2019). İmgeler Arasında: Yeni Türkiye Sinemasının Düşünen İmgeleri Üzerine. İstanbul, Turkey: Doruk Yayınları.

Iwaniec, D., Larkin, E., & Higgins, S. (2006). Research review: Risk and resilience in cases of emotional abuse. *Child & Family Social Work, 11*(1), 73–82. doi:10.1111/j.1365-2206.2006.00398.x

Jablonska, B., & Lindberg, L. (2007). Risk behaviours, victimisation and mental distress among adolescents in different family structures. *Social Psychiatry and Psychiatric Epidemiology, 42*(8), 656–663. doi:10.100700127-007-0210-3 PMID:17522746

Jacobs, A. (2008). Compenents of evidence-based intervevtions for bullying and peer victimization. In M. Roberts (Ed.), *Handbook of evidence-based therapies for children and adolescents* (pp. 261–279). Springer. doi:10.1007/978-0-387-73691-4_15

Jacobs, N., Goossens, L., Dehue, F., Völlink, T., & Lechner, L. (2015). Dutch cyberbullying victims' experiences, perceptions, attitudes, and motivations related to (coping with) cyberbullying: Focus group interviews. *Societies (Basel, Switzerland), 5*(1), 43–64. doi:10.3390oc5010043

Jacobson, K. J. L., Hood, J. N., & Van Buren, H. J. III. (2014). Workplace Bullying across Cultures: A Research Agenda. *International Journal of Cross Cultural Management, 14*(1), 47–65. doi:10.1177/1470595813494192

Jadambaa, A., Thomas, H. J., Scott, J. G., Graves, N., Brain, D., & Pacella, R. (2019). Prevalence of traditional bullying and cyberbullying among children and adolescents in Australia: A systematic review and meta-analysis. *The Australian and New Zealand Journal of Psychiatry, 53*(9), 878–888. doi:10.1177/0004867419846393 PMID:31067987

Jain, S., & Agrawal, S. (2020). Perceived vulnerability of cyberbullying on social networking sites: Effects of security measures, addiction and self-disclosure. *Indian Growth and Development Review, 14*(2), 149–171. doi:10.1108/IGDR-10-2019-0110

Jain, V. (2021). Bullying and cyberbullying descriptions. *Asian Journal of Multidimensional Research, 10*(10), 854–859. doi:10.5958/2278-4853.2021.00970.8

Jakes, S. S., & Debord, K. (2010). The Interface of Family, School, and Community Factors for the Positive Development of Children and Youth. *Journal of Prevention & Intervention in the Community, 38*(3), 177–182. doi:10.1080/10852352.2010.486293 PMID:20603756

Jakobi, A. P., Martens, K., & Wolf, K. D. (Eds.). (2009). *Education in political science*. Routledge. doi:10.4324/9780203873311

Jan, A., & Husain, S. (2015). Bullying in elementary schools: Its causes and effects on students. *Journal of Education and Practice, 6*(19), 43–56.

Jang, H., Song, J., & Kim, R. (2014). Does the Offline Bully-victimization Influence Cyberbullying Behavior among Youths? Application of General Strain Theory. *Computers in Human Behavior, 31*, 85–93. doi:10.1016/j.chb.2013.10.007

Jennings, W. G., Song, H., Kim, J., Fenimore, D. M., & Piquero, A. R. (2019). An examination of bullying and physical health problems in adolescence among South Korean youth. *Journal of Child and Family Studies, 28*(9), 2510–2521. doi:10.100710826-017-0885-3

Jeong-Ju, Y., & Johnson, K. K. (2007). Effects of appearance-related testing on ethnically diverse adolescent girls. *Adolescence, 42*(166), 353. PMID:17849941

Jiang, F. (2011). Cyberbullying: Concept, origin and solutions—An analytical perspective based on risk society. *Zhejiang Academic Journal, 6*, 181–187.

Jimerson, S. R., Annan, J., Skokut, M., & Renshaw, T. L. (2009). Educational Psychology in New Zealand: Results of the 2006 International School Psychology Survey. *School Psychology International, 30*(5), 443–455. doi:10.1177/0143034309341617

Jimerson, S., Swearer, S., & Espelage, D. (2010). *Handbook of bullying in schools: An international perspective.* Taylor&Francis/Routledge.

Johal, A., Cheung, M. Y. H., & Marcenes, W. (2007). The impact of two different malocclusion traits on quality of life. *British Dental Journal, 202*(2), E6–E6. doi:10.1038/bdj.2007.33 PMID:17260428

Johanis, M. A., Bakar, A. R. A., & Ismail, F. (2020, April). Cyber-Bullying Trends Using Social Media Platform: An Analysis through Malaysian Perspectives. [). IOP Publishing.]. *Journal of Physics: Conference Series, 1529*(2), 022077.

John, A., Glendenning, A. C., Marchant, A., Montgomery, P., Stewart, A., Wood, S., Lloyd, K., & Hawton, K. (2018). Self-harm, suicidal behaviours, and cyberbullying in children and young people: Systematic review. Journal of Medical Internet Research, 20(4). doi:10.2196/jmir.9044

Johnson, C. L. (2011). *An Examination of the Primary and Secondary Effects of Cyber-Bullying: Development and Testing of a Cyber-Bullying Moderator/Mediator Model* (Unpublished Doctoral Thesis). Graduate School of Wayne State University, Detroit.

Johnson, P. (2015). *What Makes a Cyberbully/Victim? Factors Associated with The Perpetration of Cyberbullying By Cyber Victims* (Unpublished Master's Thesis). Macquarie University, Sydney.

Johnson, S. L., & Rea, R. E. (2009). Workplace bullying: Concerns for nurse leaders. *The Journal of Nursing Administration, 39*(2), 84–90. doi:10.1097/NNA.0b013e318195a5fc PMID:19190425

Jolliffe, D., & Farrington, D. P. (2006). Examining the relationship between low empathy and bullying. *Aggressive Behavior, 32*(6), 540–550. doi:10.1002/ab.20154

Jones, D. C., Vigfusdottir, T. H., & Lee, Y. (2004). Body image and the appearance culture among adolescent girls and boys: An examination of friend conversations, peer criticism, appearance magazines and Internalization of appearance ideals. *Journal of Adolescent Research, 19*(3), 323–329. doi:10.1177/0743558403258847

Joseph, B., & Joseph, M. (2016). The health of the healthcare workers. *Indian Journal of Occupational and Environmental Medicine, 20*(2), 71–72. doi:10.4103/0019-5278.197518 PMID:28194078

Jung, M. H. (2010). Evaluation of the effects of malocclusion and orthodontic treatment on self-esteem in an adolescent population. *American Journal of Orthodontics and Dentofacial Orthopedics, 138*(2), 160–166. doi:10.1016/j.ajodo.2008.08.040 PMID:20691357

Juvonen, J., & Gross, E. F. (2008). Extending the school grounds? Bullying experiences in cyberspace. *The Journal of School Health, 78*(9), 496–505. doi:10.1111/j.1746-1561.2008.00335.x PMID:18786042

Kabil, M. (2010). *Affects of number of students in classes on bullying behavior* (UMI No. 253402) [Master's dissertation, Sakarya University]. Higher Education Council Thesis Center database.

Kahsay, W. G., Negarandeh, R., Dehghan Nayeri, N., & Hasanpour, M. (2020). Sexual harassment against female nurses: A systematic review. *BMC Nursing, 19*(1), 1–12. doi:10.118612912-020-00450-w

Kaltiala-Heino, R., Rimpela, M., Rantanen, P., & Rimpela, A. (2000). Bullying at school-an indicator of adolescents at risk for mental disorders. *Journal of Adolescence, 23*(6), 661–674. doi:10.1006/jado.2000.0351 PMID:11161331

Kanayama, K., & Kurihara, S. (2018). Preventive measures against cyberbullying at a university in Japan. In *Cyberbullying at university in international contexts* (pp. 168–172). Routledge. doi:10.4324/9781315189406-14

Kanık, B. (2010). *Teachers' Perceptions of School Bullying* [Master Thesis]. Yıldız Technical University Institute of Social Sciences.

Kapçı, E. G. (2004). İlköğretim öğrencilerinin zorbalığa maruz kalma türünün ve sıklığının depresyon, kaygı ve benlik saygısıyla ilişkisi [The relationship between the type and frequency of being bullied in primary school students with depression, anxiety and self-esteem]. *Ankara Üniversitesi Eğitim Bilimleri Fakültesi Dergisi, 37*(1), 1–13. doi:10.1501/Egifak_0000000087

Kapitány-Fövény, M., Lukács, J. Á., Takács, J., Kitzinger, I., Kiss, Z. S., Szabó, G., Falus, A., & Feith, H. J. (2022). Gender-specific pathways regarding the outcomes of a cyberbullying youth education program. *Personality and Individual Differences, 186*, 111338. doi:10.1016/j.paid.2021.111338

Kaplan, A. M., & Haenlein, M. (2010). Users of the world, unite! The challenges and opportunities of social media. *Business Horizons, 53*(1), 59–68. doi:10.1016/j.bushor.2009.09.003

Kaplan, H. B. (1975). *Self-Attitudes and Deviant Behavior*. Goodyear.

Kara, B., Biçer, Ü., & Gökalp, A. S. (2004). Çocuk istismarı [Child abuse]. *Çocuk Sagligi ve Hastaliklari Dergisi, 47*(2), 140–151.

Karaca, K. (2018). *Examining the prevalence of the peer bullying and levels of depression and anxiety of the bully-victims in the secondary schools* (UMI No. 497276) [Master's dissertation, Atatürk University]. Higher Education Council Thesis Center database.

Karaca, M., Mutlu, T., & Gencer, G. (2021). Cyber victimization: A conceptual study. *Anadolu Akademi Journal of Social Sciences*,77-191.

Karaçetin, G., & Mutlu, C. (2020). Siber zorbalık: Büyüyen bir problem [Cyberbullying: A growing problem]. In C. Evren (Ed.), *Davranışsal Bağımlılıklar [Behavioral Addictions]* (pp. 215–247). BAYT.

Karakuş, F. T. (2006). *Ergenlerde algılanan duygusal istismar ile sosyal beceri arasındaki ilişki* [The relationship between perceived emotional abuse and social skills in adolescents] [Unpublished master's thesis]. Marmara Üniversitesi.

Karaman-Kepenekçi, Y., & Çınkır, Ş. (2006). Bullying among Turkish high school students. *Child Abuse, 30*(2), 193–204. doi:10.1016/j.chiabu.2005.10.005 PMID:16460802

Karatas, H. (2011). *Examining the effect of the program developed for bullying in primary schools* [Unpublished doctoral dissertation]. Dokuz Eylul University, Izmir, Turkey.

Karataş, H. (2011). *Examining the effect of the program developed to adress bullying in primary schools* (UMI No. 304497) [Doctoral dissertation, Dokuz Eylül University]. Higher Education Council Thesis Center database.

Karataş, H., & Öztürk, C. (2009). Sosyal bilişsel teori ile zorbalığa yaklaşım [Approach to bullying with social cognitive theory]. *Dokuz Eylül Üniversitesi Hemşirelik Yüksekokulu Elektronik Dergisi, 2*(2), 61–74.

Karataş, H., & Öztürk, C. (2011). Relationship between bullying and health problems in primary school children. *Asian Nursing Research, 5*(2), 81–87. doi:10.1016/S1976-1317(11)60016-9 PMID:25030257

Karatoprak, S., & Özcan, Ö. (2017). Peer Bullying. *Turkiye Klinikleri J Child Psychiatry-Special Topics, 3*(3), 195–203.

Karnowski, V., Leonhard, L., & Kümpel, A. S. (2018). Why users share the news : A Theory of Reasoned Action-based study on the antecedents of news- sharing behavior. *Communication Research Reports, 35*(2), 91–100. doi:10.1080/08824096.2017.1379984

Kartal, H., & Bilgin, A. (2007). An anti-bullying program application for primary school students: School de-bullying program. *Theory and Practice in Education.*, *3*(2), 207–227.

Kartal, H., & Bilgin, A. (2007). İlköğretim öğrencilerine yönelik bir zorbalık karşıtı program uygulaması: Okulu zorbalıktan arındırma programı [An implementation of an anti-bullying program for elementary school students: bully proofing your school]. *Journal of Theory and Practice in Education*, *3*(2), 207–227.

Kartal, H., & Bilgin, A. (2012). İlköğretim öğrencilerinin zorbalığın nedenleri ile ilgili algıları [The perceptions of elementary students about the reasons for bullying]. *Gaziantep Üniversitesi Sosyal Bilimler Dergisi*, *11*(1), 25–48.

Katsaras, G. N., Vouloumanou, E. K., Kourlaba, G., Kyritsi, E., Evagelou, E., & Bakoula, C. (2018). Bullying and suicidality in children and adolescents without predisposing factors: A systematic review and meta-analysis. *Adolescent Research Review*, *3*(2), 193–217. doi:10.100740894-018-0081-8

Katz, I., Keeley, M., Spears, B., Taddeo, C., Swist, T., & Bates, S. (2014). *Research on Youth Exposure to, and Management of, Cyberbullying Incidents in Australia*. Synthesis report.

Katzer, C., Fetchenhauer, D., & Belschack, R. (2009). Cyber bullying: Who are the victims? A comparison of victimization in internet chatrooms and victimization at school. *Journal of Media Psychology*, *1*(21), 25–36. doi:10.1027/1864-1105.21.1.25

Kaur, P., Dhir, A., Tandon, A., Alzeiby, E. A., & Abohassan, A. A. (2021). A systematic literature review on cyberstalking. An analysis of past achievements and future promises. *Technological Forecasting and Social Change*, *163*, 120426. doi:10.1016/j.techfore.2020.120426

Kavşut, F. (2009). *The research of the relationship betweeen peer bullying and emotional intelligence in adolescents* (UMI No. 241590) [Master's dissertation, Abant İzzet Baysal University]. Higher Education Council Thesis Center database.

Kavurucu, Ö., & Küçük, L. (2021). Çağın gelişen sorunu siber zorbalık: çocuk ve ergenlerde siber zorbalığı önleme [Cyberbullying, the emerging problem of the age: prevention of cyberbullying in children and adolescents]. *Medical Research Reports*, *4*(3), 50–56.

Kearl, H. (2018). *The facts behind the #Metoo movement: A national study on sexual harassment and assault.* https://web.archive.org/web/20201127111900/https://ncvc.dspacedirect.org/handle/20.500.11990/790

Kearl, H. (2018). *The facts behind the #metoo movement: A national study on sexual harassment and assault.* Stop Street Harassment. https://www.nsvrc.org/sites/default/files/2021-04/full-report-2018-national-study-on-sexual-harassment-and-assault.pdf

Kedar, T. (2021). Suicide and Suicide risk factors: A Literature Review. *Asian Journal of Nursing Education and Research*, *11*(3), 441–446. doi:10.52711/2349-2996.2021.00107

Keeley, P. W., Waterhouse, E. T., & Noble, S. I. (2005). Prevalence and characteristics of bullying of trainees in palliative medicine. *Palliative Medicine*, *19*(1), 84–85. doi:10.1191/0269216305pm968xx PMID:15690873

Keery, H., Van den Berg, P., & Thompson, J. K. (2004). An evaluation of the Tripartite Influence Model of body dissatisfaction and eating disturbance with adolescent girls. *Body Image*, *1*(3), 237–251. doi:10.1016/j.bodyim.2004.03.001 PMID:18089156

Keller, L. O., Strohschein, S., Lia-Hoagberg, B., & Schaffer, M. A. (2004). Population-based public health interventions: Practice-based and evidence-supported. Part I. *Public Health Nursing (Boston, Mass.)*, *21*(5), 453–468. doi:10.1111/j.0737-1209.2004.21509.x PMID:15363026

Keller, L. O., Strohschein, S., Schaffer, M. A., & Lia-Hoagberg, B. (2004). Population-based public health interventions: Innovations in practice, teaching, and management. Part II. *Public Health Nursing (Boston, Mass.)*, *21*(5), 469–487. doi:10.1111/j.0737-1209.2004.21510.x PMID:15363027

Kellij, S., Lodder, G., van den Bedem, N., Güroğlu, B., & Veenstra, R. (2022). The social cognitions of victims of bullying: A systematic review. *Adolescent Research Review*, *7*(3), 1–48. doi:10.100740894-022-00183-8

Kemp, S. (2020). *Digital 2020: October Global Statshot*. Data Reportal. https://datareportal.com/reports/digital-2020-october-global-statshot?rq=global%20social%20media%202020

Kempes, M., Matthys, W., de Vries, H., & Van Engeland, H. (2005). Reactive and proactive aggression in children: A review of theory, findings and the relevance for child and adolescent psychiatry. *European Child & Adolescent Psychiatry*, *14*(1), 11–19. doi:10.100700787-005-0432-4 PMID:15756511

Kennedy, K. (2019). *Positive and negative effects of social media on adolescent well-being* [Master of Science]. Minnesota State University.

Kennedy, T. D., Kevorkian, M. M., & Russom, A. G. (2012). Teacher and administrator perceptions of bullying in schools. *International Journal of Education Policy and Leadership*, *7*(5), 1–12. doi:10.22230/ijepl.2012v7n5a395

Kent, A., & Waller, G. (2000). Childhood emotional abuse and eating psychopathology. *Clinical Psychology Review*, *20*(7), 887–903.

Kepenekci, Y.K., & Çınkır, Ş. (2006). Türk lise öğrencileri arasında zorbalık [Bully Among Turkish High School Students]. *Çocuk istismarı ve ihmali, 30*(2), 193-204.

Kepenekçi, Y. K., & Çınkır, Ş. (2003). Öğrenciler arası zorbalık [Bullying between students]. *Kuram ve Uygulamada Eğitim Yönetimi*, *34*(34), 236–253.

Kestel, M., & Akbıyık, C. (2016). An ınvestigation of effects of cyber bullying on students' Academic, social and emotional states. *Mersin University Journal of the Faculty of Education*, *12*(3), 844–859.

Khairy, M., Mahmoud, T. M., & Abd-El-Hafeez, T. (2021). Automatic Detection of Cyberbullying and Abusive Language in Arabic Content on Social Networks: A Survey. *Procedia Computer Science*, *189*, 156–166. doi:10.1016/j.procs.2021.05.080

Khan, N., Begum, S., & Shaheen, A. (2015). Sexual harassment against staff and student nurses in tertiary care Hospitals Peshawar KP Pakistan. *International Journal of Innovative Research and Development*, *4*(1), 285–292.

Khine, A. T., Saw, Y. M., Htut, Z. Y., Khaing, C. T., Soe, H. Z., Swe, K. K., Thike, T., Htet, H., Saw, T. N., Cho, S. M., Kariya, T., Yamamoto, E., & Hamajima, N. (2020). Assessing Risk Factors and Impact of Cyberbullying Victimization among University Students in Myanmar: A cross-sectional study. *PLoS One*, *15*(1), e0227051. doi:10.1371/journal.pone.0227051 PMID:31967998

Kılınç, İ., & Gündüz, Ş. (2017). Investigation of high school students' cyber sensitivity, ınternet addiction and humanistic values. *Trakya University Journal of the Faculty Educaiton*, *7*(2), 261–283. doi:10.24315/trkefd.304497

Kilpatrick, D. G., Veronen, L. J., & Resnick, P. A. (1982). Psychological sequelae to rape: Assessment and treatment strategies. In D. M. Doleys, R. L. Meredith, & A. R. Ciminero (Eds.), *Behavioral medicine: Assessment and treatment strategies* (pp. 473–497). Plenum Press. doi:10.1007/978-1-4684-4070-6_19

Kim, B. K., Park, J., Jung, H. J., & Han, Y. (2020). Latent profiles of offline/cyber bullying experiences among Korean students and its relationship with peer conformity. *Children and Youth Services Review*, *118*, 105349. doi:10.1016/j.childyouth.2020.105349

Kim, J., Lee, Y., & Jennings, W. G. (2022). A Path from Traditional Bullying to Cyberbullying in South Korea: Examining the roles of self-control and deviant peer association in the different forms of bullying. *Journal of Interpersonal Violence, 37*(9-10). doi:10.1177/08862605211067022 PMID:35259313

Kim, S., & Faith, M. S. (2020). Cyberbullying and ICT use by immigrant youths: A serial multiple-mediator SEM analysis. *Children and Youth Services Review, 110*, 104621. doi:10.1016/j.childyouth.2019.104621

Kim, S., Kimber, M., Boyle, M. H., & Georgiades, K. (2019). Sex Differences in the Association Between Cyberbullying Victimization and Mental Health, Substance Use, and Suicidal Ideation in Adolescents. *Canadian Journal of Psychiatry, 64*(2), 126–135. doi:10.1177/0706743718777397 PMID:29783849

Kim, Y. S., Koh, Y. J., & Leventhal, B. (2005). School bullying and suicidal risk in Korean middle school students. *Pediatrics, 115*(2), 357–363. doi:10.1542/peds.2004-0902 PMID:15687445

Kim, Y. S., Koh, Y. J., & Leventhal, B. L. (2004). Prevalence of school bullying in Korean middle school students. *Archives of Pediatrics & Adolescent Medicine, 158*(8), 737–741. doi:10.1001/archpedi.158.8.737 PMID:15289244

Kim, Y. S., & Leventhal, B. (2008). Bullying and suicide: A review. *International Journal of Adolescent Medicine and Health, 20*(2), 133–154. doi:10.1515/IJAMH.2008.20.2.133 PMID:18714552

Kingma, M. (2001). Workplace violence in the health sector: A problem of epidemic proportion. *International Nursing Review, 48*(3), 129–130. doi:10.1046/j.1466-7657.2001.00094.x PMID:11558684

Kinzl, J. F., Mangweth, B., Traweger, C. M., & Biebl, W. (1997). Eatingdisordered behavior in males: The impact of adverse childhood experiences. *International Journal of Eating Disorders, 22*(2), 131–138. doi:10.1002/(SICI)1098-108X(199709)22:2<131::AID-EAT3>3.0.CO;2-G PMID:9261650

Kircaburun, K., Demetrovics, Z., Király, O., & Griffiths, M. D. (2020). Childhood Emotional Trauma and Cyberbullying Perpetration Among Emerging Adults: A Multiple Mediation Model of the Role of Problematic Social Media Use and Psychopathology. *International Journal of Mental Health and Addiction, 18*(3), 548–566. doi:10.100711469-018-9941-5

Kiriakidis, S. P., & Kavoura, A. (2010). Cyberbullying: A review of the literature on harassment through the internet and other electronic means. *Family & Community Health, 33*(2), 82–93. doi:10.1097/FCH.0b013e3181d593e4 PMID:20216351

Kirilmaz, H., Yorgun, S., & Atasoy, A. (2016). Saglik Calisanlarinda Psikososyal Risk Faktörlerini Belirlemeye Yonelik Bir Arastirma [A Study on Determining Psychosocial Risk Factors in Healthcare Professionals]. *Uluslararasi Kulturel ve Sosyal Arastirmalar Dergisi (UKSAD), 2*(1), 66-82.

Kirlioğlu, M., & Toygar, Ş. A. (2020). The effects of sexual harassment on quality of nurses' work life and turnover intentions: A sample of Ankara province. *OPUS Uluslararası Toplum Araştırmaları Dergisi, 16*(29), 1613–1627. doi:10.26466/opus.775992

Kisa, A., & Dziegielewski, S. F. (1996). Sexual harassment of female nurses in a hospital in Turkey. *Health Services Management Research, 9*(4), 243–253. doi:10.1177/095148489600900404 PMID:10162521

Kisa, A., Dziegielewski, S. F., & Ates, M. (2002). Sexual harassment and its consequences: A study within Turkish hospitals. *Journal of Health & Social Policy, 15*(1), 77–94. doi:10.1300/J045v15n01_05 PMID:12212934

Klinck, M., Vannucci, A., Fagle, T., & Ohannessian, C. M. (2020). Appearance-related teasing and substance use during early adolescence. *Psychology of Addictive Behaviors, 34*(4), 541–548. doi:10.1037/adb0000563 PMID:32039619

Kljakovic, M., Scheib, E., & Notter, O. (2012). The Joint Development of Traditional Bullying and Victimization With Cyber Bullying and Victimization in Adolescence. *Journal of Research on Adolescence, 22*(2), 301–309.

Knauss, C., Paxton, S. J., & Alsaker, F. D. (2007). Relationships amongst body dissatisfaction, internalization of the media body ideal and perceived pressure from media in adolescent girls and boys. *Body Image*, *4*(4), 353–360. doi:10.1016/j.bodyim.2007.06.007 PMID:18089281

Kocadaş, B. (2005). Kültür ve medya. *Bilig*, *34*, 1–13.

Koç, F., Halıcıoğlu, O., & Akşit, S. (2014). Hangi bulgular fiziksel istismarı düşündürür? [Which findings suggest physical abuse?]. *The Journal of Pediatric Research*, *1*(1), 1–5.

Kochenderfer, B. J., & Ladd, G. W. (1996). Peer Victimization: Cause or Consequence of School Maladjustment? *Society for Research in Child Development*, *67*(4), 1305–1317. doi:10.2307/1131701 PMID:8890485

Koç, M. (2007). Şiddetin ortaya çıkardığı psikolojik travmayla baş etmede sporun işlevselliği [The functionality of sports in coping with the psychological trauma caused by violence]. *Ahmet Yesevi Üniversitesi Sosyal Bilimler Dergisi*, *18*, 167–179.

Koç-Yıldırım, P. (2003). *Çıkmaz sokak: Okulda şiddet ve zorbalık* [Dead end: Violence and bullying at school]. Nobel.

Kokkinos, C. M., & Antoniadou, N. (2019). Cyber-bullying and cyber-victimization among undergraduate student teachers through the lens of the General Aggression Model. *Computers in Human Behavior*, *98*, 59–68. doi:10.1016/j.chb.2019.04.007

Köksal Akyol, A., & Bilbay, A. (2018). Examination of the Correlation between Peer Bullying, Exposed to Bullying, and Emphatic Tendencies of Adolescent. *Tarih Kültür ve Sanat Arastirmalari Dergisi*, *7*(2), 667–675. doi:10.7596/taksad.v7i2.1379

Kolawole, K. A., Otuyemi, O. D., & Adeosun, O. D. (2009). Nicknames and name calling among a population of Nigerian schoolchildren. *European Journal of Paediatric Dentistry*, *10*(3), 115. PMID:19761284

Kopeckya, K., Szotkowskia, R., & Inmaculada Aznar-Díazb, J.-M. R.-R. (2020). The phenomenon of sharenting and its risks in the online environment. Experiences from Czech Republic and Spain. *Children and Youth Services Review*, *110*, 104812. Advance online publication. doi:10.1016/j.childyouth.2020.104812

Kopecký, K., & Szotkowski, R. (2017). Cyberbullying, cyber aggression and their impact on the victim– the teacher. *Telematics and Informatics*, *34*(2), 506–517. doi:10.1016/j.tele.2016.08.014

Korkmaz, A. (2016). Comparing cyber bullying behaviors and being a victim of cyber bullying. *TRT Akademi*, *1*(2), 620–639.

Korkmaz, A. (2016). Cyberbullying: The new violence from physical to art. *Fiction*, *24*(2), 74–85.

Korkut, F. (2007). *Okul temelli önleyici rehberlik ve psikolojik danışma [School-based preventive guidance and psychological counseling]*. Anı Yayıncılık.

Ko, S. Y., Chung, H. K., Kim, J. I., & Shin, Y. (2021). A Study on the Typology and Advancement of Cultural Leisure-Based Metaverse. *KIPS Transactions on Software and Data Engineering*, *10*(8), 331–338.

Kota, R., Schoohs, S., Benson, M., & Moreno, M. A. (2014). Characterizing cyberbullying among college students: Hacking, dirty laundry, and mocking. *Societies (Basel, Switzerland)*, *4*(4), 549–560. doi:10.3390oc4040549

Kovler, M. L., Ziegfeld, S., Ryan, L. M., Goldstein, M. A., Gardner, R., Garcia, A. V., & Nasr, I. W. (2021). Increased proportion of physical child abuse injuries at a level I pediatric trauma center during the Covid-19 pandemic. *Child Abuse & Neglect*, *116*, 104756. doi:10.1016/j.chiabu.2020.104756 PMID:33004213

Kowalski, R. M., Giumetti, G. W., Schroeder, A. N., & Lattanner, M. R. (2014). Bullying in the digital age: A critical review and meta-analysis of cyberbullying research among youth. *Psychological Bulletin, 140*(4), 1073–1137. doi:10.1037/a0035618 PMID:24512111

Kowalski, R. M., & Limber, S. P. (2007, December). Electronic bullying among middle school students. *The Journal of Adolescent Health, 41*(6), S22–S30. doi:10.1016/j.jadohealth.2007.08.017 PMID:18047942

Kowalski, R. M., & Limber, S. P. (2013). Psychological, physical, and academic correlates of cyberbullying and traditional bullying. *The Journal of Adolescent Health, 53*(1), 13–20. doi:10.1016/j.jadohealth.2012.09.018 PMID:23790195

Kowalski, R. M., Limber, S. P., & Agatston, P. W. (2012). *Cyberbullying: Bullying in the digital age* (2nd ed.). Wiley-Blackwell.

Kowalski, R. M., Limber, S. P., & Agatston, P. W. (2012). *Cyberbullying: Bullying in the Digital Age.* Wiley Blackwell.

Kowalski, R. M., Limber, S. P., & McCord, A. (2019). A developmental approach to cyberbullying: Prevalence and protective factors. *Aggression and Violent Behavior, 45*, 20–32. doi:10.1016/j.avb.2018.02.009

Kowalski, R. M., Morgan, C. A., & Limber, S. P. (2012). Traditional Bullying as a Potential Warning Sign of Cyberbullying. *School Psychology International, 33*(5), 505–519. doi:10.1177/0143034312445244

Kowalski, R. M., & Toth, A. (2017). Cyberbullying among youth with and without disabilities. *Journal of Child & Adolescent Trauma, 11*(1), 7–15. doi:10.100740653-017-0139-y PMID:32318133

Kowalski, R., Morgan, C., Drake-Lavelle, K., & Allison, B. (2016). Cyberbullying among college students with disabilities. *Computers in Human Behavior, 57*, 416–427. doi:10.1016/j.chb.2015.12.044

Ko, Y. Y., Liu, Y., Wang, C. J., Liao, H. Y., Liao, Y. M., & Chen, H. M. (2020). Determinants of Workplace Bullying Types and Their Relationship With Depression Among Female Nurses. *The Journal of Nursing Research, 28*(3), e92. doi:10.1097/JNR.0000000000000367 PMID:31972730

Kraft, E. M., & Wang, J. (2009). Effectiveness of cyber bullying prevention strategies: A study on students' perspectives. *International Journal of Cyber Criminology, 3*(2), 513–535.

Kragt, L., Dhamo, B., Wolvius, E. B., & Ongkosuwito, E. M. (2016). The impact of malocclusions on oral health-related quality of life in children—A systematic review and meta-analysis. *Clinical Oral Investigations, 20*(8), 1881–1894. doi:10.100700784-015-1681-3 PMID:26635095

Krasnova, H., & Veltri, N. F. (2010). *Privacy calculus on social networking sites : Explorative evidence from Germany and USA.* Paper presented at 43rd Hawaii international conference on system sciences. 10.1109/HICSS.2010.307

Krejcie, R. V., & Morgan, D. W. (1970). Determining sample size for research activities. *Educational and Psychological Measurement, 30*(3), 607–610. doi:10.1177/001316447003000308

Krugman, R. D., & Krugman, M. K. (1984). Emotional abuse in the classroom. The pediatrician's role in diagnosis and treatment. *American Journal of Diseases of Children, 138*(3), 284–286. doi:10.1001/archpedi.1984.02140410062019 PMID:6702775

Krusell, M. K., Hohwü, L., Bjereld, Y., Madsen, K. B., & Obel, C. (2019). The impact of childhood bullying on the daily lives of Nordic children and young adolescents. *Acta Paediatrica (Oslo, Norway), 108*(6), 1096–1102. doi:10.1111/apa.14642 PMID:30421832

Krygsman, A., & Vaillancourt, T. (2019). Peer victimization, aggression, and depression symptoms in preschoolers. *Early Childhood Research Quarterly, 47*, 62–73. doi:10.1016/j.ecresq.2018.09.006

Kshirsagar, V. Y., Agarwal, R., & Bavdekar, S. B. (2007). Bullying in schools: Prevalence and short-term impact. *Indian Pediatrics*, *44*(1), 25–28. PMID:17277427

Kumar, P., & Schoenebeck, S. (2015). The modern day baby book. *Proceedings of the 18th ACM Conference on Computer Supported Cooperative Work & Social Computing- CSCW '15*. 10.1145/2675133.2675149

Kumar, V. L., & Goldstein, M. A. (2020). Cyberbullying and Adolescents. *Current Pediatrics Reports*, *8*(3), 86–92. doi:10.100740124-020-00217-6 PMID:33552702

Kunz, J., Jaynes, A., Seales, C., Calvert, W. B., Fei, K., & Griffioen, Z. (2003). The Metaverse - A networked collection of inexpensive, self-configuring, immersive environments. *Proceedings of the Workshop on Virtual Environments, EGVE'03*.

Kuş, O. (2021). Metaverse: 'Dijital Büyük Patlamada' Fırsatlar Ve Endişelere Yönelik Algılar. *Intermedia International e-Journal*, *8*(15). doi:10.21645/intermedia.2021.109

Kwok, R. P., Law, Y. K., Li, K. E., Ng, Y. C., Cheung, M. H., Fung, V. K., & Leung, W. C. (2006). Prevalence of workplace violence against nurses in Hong Kong. *Hong Kong Medical Journal*, *12*(1), 6–9. PMID:16495582

Ladd, G. W., & Burgess, K. B. (2001). Do relational risks and protective factors moderate the linkages between childhood aggression and early psychological and school adjustment? *Child Development*, *72*(5), 1579–1601. doi:10.1111/1467-8624.00366 PMID:11699688

Laeheem, K., Kuning, M., & McNeil, N. (2009). Bullying: Risk factors becoming 'bullies'. *Asian Social Science*, *5*(5), 50–57. doi:10.5539/ass.v5n5p50

Lamb, J., Pepler, D. J., & Craig, W. (2009). Approach to bullying and victimization. *Canadian Family Physician Medecin de Famille Canadien*, *55*(4), 356–360. https://www.researchgate.net/publication/24278081_Approach_to_bullying_and_victimization PMID:19366941

Lane, H. (2002). Do deaf people have a disability? *Sign Language Studies*, *2*(4), 356–379. doi:10.1353ls.2002.0019

Langos, C. (2012). Cyberbullying: The challenge to define. *Cyberpsychology, Behavior, and Social Networking*, *15*(6), 285–289. doi:10.1089/cyber.2011.0588 PMID:22703033

Larochette, A., Murphy, A. N., & Craig, W. M. (2010). Racial bullying and victimization in Canadian school-aged children: Individual and school level effects. *School Psychology International*, *31*(4), 389–408. doi:10.1177/0143034310377150

Larsen, S. E., & Fitzgerald, L. F. (2011). PTSD symptoms and sexual harassment: The role of attributions and perceived control. *Journal of Interpersonal Violence*, *26*(13), 2555–2567. doi:10.1177/0886260510388284 PMID:21156692

Larsen, S. E., Nye, C. D., & Fitzgerald, L. F. (2019). Sexual harassment expanded: An examination of the relationships among sexual harassment, sex discrimination, and aggression in the workplace. *Military Psychology*, *31*(1), 35–44. doi:10.1080/08995605.2018.1526526

Launer, J. (2013). Bullying in the health service. *Postgraduate Medical Journal*, *89*(1051), 307–308. doi:10.1136/postgradmedj-2013-131983 PMID:23596258

Law, D. M., Shapka, J. D., Hymel, S., Olson, B. F., & Waterhouse, T. (2012). The changing face of bullying: An empirical comparison between traditional and internet bullying and victimization. *Computers in Human Behavior*, *28*(1), 226–232. doi:10.1016/j.chb.2011.09.004

Lawler, M., & Nixon, E. (2011). Body dissatisfaction among adolescent boys and girls: the effects of body mass, peer appearance culture and internalization of appearance ideals. *Journal of Youth And Adolescence*, *40*(1), 59-71. doi:10.1007/s10964-009-9500-2

Lawson, M., Piel, M. H., & Simon, M. (2020). Child maltreatment during the COVID-19 pandemic: Consequences of parental job loss on psychological and physical abuse towards children. *Child Abuse & Neglect, 110*, 104709. doi:10.1016/j.chiabu.2020.104709 PMID:32893003

Lazard, L., Locke, A., Dann, C., Capdevila, R., & Roper, S. (2018). *Sharenting: Why mothers post about their children on social media*. Retrieved January 4, 2022, from https://theconversation.com/sharenting-why-mothers-post-about-their-children-on-social-media-91954

Lazarus, R. S., & Folkman, S. (1984). Coping and adaptation. In W. D. Gentry (Ed.), *Handbook of Behavioral Medicine* (pp. 282–325). Guilford Press.

Lazuras, L., Barkoukis, V., Ourda, D., & Tsorbatzoudis, H. (2013). A Process Model of Cyberbullying in Adolescence. *Computers in Human Behavior, 29*(3), 881–887. doi:10.1016/j.chb.2012.12.015

Leach, F. (2003). Learning to be violent: The role of the school in developing adolescent gendered behaviour. *Compare: A Journal of Comparative Education, 33*(3), 385–400. doi:10.1080/03057920302587

Lebrun-Harris, L., Sherman, L. J., Limber, S. P., Miller, B. D., & Edgerton, E. A. (2019). Bullying victimization and perpetration among U.S. children and adolescents: 2016. National Survey of Children's Health. *Journal of Child and Family Studies, 2*(9), 2543–2557. doi:10.100710826-018-1170-9

Lee, B., Jeong, S. & Roh, M. (2018). Association between body mass index and health outcomes among adolescents: the mediating role of traditional and cyber bullying victimization. *BMC Public Health, 18*(1), 674.

Lee, L. H., Braud, T., Zhou, P., Wang, L., Xu, D., Lin, Z., . . . Hui, P. (2021). *All one needs to know about metaverse: A complete survey on technological singularity, virtual ecosystem, and research agenda.* arXiv preprint arXiv:2110.05352.

Lee, S.-S., Song, H., & Park, J. H. (2021). Exploring risk and protective factors for cyberbullying and their interplay: Evidence from a sample of South Korean college students. *International Journal of Environmental Research and Public Health, 18*, 13415.

Lee, W. C., Periyayya, T., & Nair, G. V. (2017). Advent of the new media: The influence of intrinsic and extrinsic motivation in online photo sharing behaviours on facebook among young Malaysian adults. *SHS Web of Conferences 33*, 59. doi: 10.1051/ 73300059

Lee, C., & Shin, N. (2017). Prevalence of cyberbullying and predictors of cyberbullying perpetration among Korean adolescents. *Computers in Human Behavior, 68*, 352–358. doi:10.1016/j.chb.2016.11.047

Lee, G., & Sanchez, M. (2018). Cyber Bullying behaviors, anonymity, and General Strain Theory: A study of undergraduate students at a South Eastern University in the United States. *International Journal of Cyber Criminology, 12*(1), 84–96. doi:10.5281/zenodo.1467846

Lee, J. H. (2018). Victimization by Bullying and Physical Symptoms Among South Korean Schoolchildren. *The Journal of School Nursing: the Official Publication of the National Association of School Nurses, 34*(2), 149–155. doi:10.1177/1059840517696962 PMID:29512433

Lee, J., Chun, J., Kim, J., & Lee, J. (2020). Cyberbullying Victimisation and School Dropout Intention among South Korean Adolescents: The moderating role of peer/teacher support. *Asia Pacific Journal of Social Work and Development, 30*(3), 195–211. doi:10.1080/02185385.2020.1774409

Lee, K., Dale, J., Guy, A., & Wolke, D. (2018). Bullying and negative appearance feedback among adolescents: Is it objective or misperceived weight that matters? *Journal of Adolescence, 63*(1), 118–128. doi:10.1016/j.adolescence.2017.12.008 PMID:29289824

Lee, M. A. (2015). Emotional abuse in childhood and suicidality: The mediating roles of re-victimization and depressive symptoms in adulthood. *Child Abuse & Neglect*, *44*, 130–139. doi:10.1016/j.chiabu.2015.03.016 PMID:25890665

Lee, S., & Chun, J. (2020). Conceptualizing the Impacts of Cyberbullying Victimization among Korean Male Adolescents. *Children and Youth Services Review*, *117*, 105275. doi:10.1016/j.childyouth.2020.105275

Lee, S., Kim, C. J., & Kim, D. H. (2015). A meta-analysis of the effect of school-based anti-bullying programs. *Journal of Child Health Care*, *19*(2), 136–153. doi:10.1177/1367493513503581 PMID:24092871

Lee, Y., Kim, J., & Song, H. (2021). Do Negative Emotions Matter? Paths From Victimization to Cyber and Traditional Bullying From a General Strain Theory Perspective. *Crime and Delinquency*. Advance online publication. doi:10.1177/00111287211052439

legislationline. (2020). *Belgium - Criminal codes - Legislationline*. https://www.legislationline.org/documents/section/criminal-codes/country/41/Belgium/show

Lemstra, M. E., Nielsen, G., Rogers, M. R., Thompson, A. T., & Moraros, J. S. (2012). Risk indicators and outcomes associated with bullying in youth aged 9-15 years. *Canadian Journal of Public Health*, *103*(1), 9–13. doi:10.1007/BF03404061 PMID:22338321

Lereya, S. T., Copeland, W. E., Costello, E. J., & Wolke, D. (2015). Adult mental health consequences of peer bullying and maltreatment in childhood: Two cohorts in two countries. *The Lancet. Psychiatry*, *2*(6), 524–531. doi:10.1016/S2215-0366(15)00165-0 PMID:26360448

Lever, I., Dyball, D., Greenberg, N., & Stevelink, S. A. M. (2019). Health consequences of bullying in the healthcare workplace: A systematic review. *Journal of Advanced Nursing*, *75*(12), 3195–3209. doi:10.1111/jan.13986 PMID:30816567

Levine, E., & Tamburrino, M. (2014). Bullying among young children: Strategies for prevention. *Early Childhood Education Journal*, *42*(4), 271–278. doi:10.100710643-013-0600-y

Levinson, J. (2020, March 5). Why Diversity in Children's Media is so Important. *Psychology in Action*. https://www.psychologyinaction.org/psychology-in-action-1/2020/3/5/why-diversity-in-childrens-media-is-so-important

Levinson, J. A., Sarda, V., Sonneville, K., Calzo, J. P., Ambwani, S., & Austin, S. B. (2020). Diet pill and laxative use for weight control and subsequent incident eating disorder in US young women: 2001–2016. *American Journal of Public Health*, *110*(1), 109–111. doi:10.2105/AJPH.2019.305390 PMID:31751147

Lewis, D., Sheehan, M., & Davies, C. (2008). Uncovering Workplace Bullying. *Journal of Workplace Rights*, *13*(3), 281–301. doi:10.2190/WR.13.3.e

Lewis, M. A. (2006). Nurse bullying: Organizational considerations in the maintenance and perpetration of health care bullying cultures. *Journal of Nursing Management*, *14*(1), 52–58. doi:10.1111/j.1365-2934.2005.00535.x PMID:16359446

Leymann, H. (1996). The Content and Development of Mobbing at Work. *European Journal of Work and Organizational Psychology*, *5*(2), 165–184. doi:10.1080/13594329608414853

Leymann, H., & Gustafsson, A. (1996). Mobbing at work and the development of post-traumatic stress disorders. *European Journal of Work and Organizational Psychology*, *5*(2), 251–275. doi:10.1080/13594329608414858

Li, Q., Smith, P. K., & Cross, D. (2012). Research into cyberbullying. *Cyberbullying in the global playground: Research from international perspectives, 1*.

Liang, H., Flisher, A. J., & Lomard, C. J. (2007). Bullying, violence, and risk behavior in south african school students. *Child Abuse & Neglect*, *31*(2), 161–171. doi:10.1016/j.chiabu.2006.08.007 PMID:17313977

Lianos, H., & McGrath, A. (2018). Can the General Theory of Crime and General Strain Theory Explain Cyberbullying Perpetration? *Crime and Delinquency*, *64*(5), 674–700. doi:10.1177/0011128717714204

Library of Congress. (2015). *Brazil: New Law Creates Program to Combat Bullying Nationwide*. Library of Congress. https://www.loc.gov/item/global-legal-monitor/2015-11-13/brazil-new-law-creates-program-to-combat-bullying-nationwide/

Li, C. K., Holt, T. J., Bossler, A. M., & May, D. C. (2016). Examining the Mediating Effects of Social Learning on the Low Self-control-Cyberbullying Relationship in a Youth Sample. *Deviant Behavior*, *37*(2), 126–138. doi:10.1080/01639625.2014.1004023

Lieberman, M., Gauvin, L., Bukowski, W. M., & White, D. R. (2001). Interpersonal influence and disordered eating behaviors in adolescent girls: The role of peer modeling, social reinforcement, and body-related teasing. *Eating Behaviors*, *2*(3), 215–236. doi:10.1016/S1471-0153(01)00030-7 PMID:15001032

Lie, S. O., Ro, O., & Bang, L. (2019). Is bullying and teasing associated with eating disorders? A systematic review and meta-analysis. *International Journal of Eating Disorders*, *52*(5), 497–514. doi:10.1002/eat.23035 PMID:30706957

Li, L., Sun, N., Fei, S., Yu, L., Chen, S., Yang, S., & Li, H. (2021). Current status of and factors influencing anxiety and depression in front-line medical staff supporting Wuhan in containing the novel coronavirus pneumonia epidemic. *Japan Journal of Nursing Science*, *18*(2), e12398. doi:10.1111/jjns.12398 PMID:33258559

Lim, V. K. G., & Teo, T. S. H. (2009). Mind your E-manners: Impact of cyber incivility on employees ' work attitude and behavior. *Information & Management*, *46*(8), 419–425. doi:10.1016/j.im.2009.06.006

Lin, X., Featherman, M., & Sarker, S. (2013). Information Sharing in the Context of Social Media: An Application of the Theory of Reasoned Action and Social Capital Theory. *SIGHCI 2013 Proceedings*, 17. https://aisel.aisnet.org/sighci2013/17

Ling, M., Young, C. J., Shepherd, H. L., Mak, C., & Saw, R. P. (2016). Workplace Bullying in Surgery. *World Journal of Surgery*, *40*(11), 2560–2566. doi:10.100700268-016-3642-7 PMID:27624759

Li, P., Xing, K., Qiao, H., Fang, H., Ma, H., Jiao, M., & Liu, M. (2018). Psychological violence against general practitioners and nurses in Chinese township hospitals: Incidence and implications. *Health and Quality of Life Outcomes*, *16*(1), 117. doi:10.118612955-018-0940-9 PMID:29871642

Lipsitz, J. (2019). *Successful schools for young adolescents. Successful Schools for Young Adolescents* (1st ed.). Taylor and Francis. doi:10.4324/9781351318327

Lipu, M., & Siibak, A. (2019). 'Take it down!': Estonian parents' and pre-teens' opinions and experiences with sharenting. *Media International Australia*, *170*(1), 57–67. doi:10.1177/1329878X19828366

Li, Q. (2010). Cyberbullying in high schools: A Study of Students' Behaviors and Beliefs About This New Phenomenon. *Journal of Aggression, Maltreatment & Trauma*, *19*(4), 372–392. doi:10.1080/10926771003788979

Li, Q., Cross, D., & Smith, P. K. (2012). *Cyberbullying in the global playground*. John Wiley & Sons. doi:10.1002/9781119954484

Li, R., Lian, Q., Su, Q., Li, L., Xie, M., & Hu, J. (2020). Trends and sex disparities in school bullying victimization among U.S. youth, 2011–2019. *BMC Public Health*, *20*(1), 1583. doi:10.118612889-020-09677-3 PMID:33087087

Li, T. B. Q. (2005). Cyber-harassment: A Study of a New Method for an Old Behavior. *Journal of Educational Computing Research*, *32*(3), 265–277. doi:10.2190/8YQM-B04H-PG4D-BLLH

Little, L. (2002). Middle-class mothers' perceptions of peer and sibling victimization among children with Asperger's syndrome and nonverbal learning disorders. *Issues in Comprehensive Pediatric Nursing, 25*, 43–57. doi:10.1080/014608602753504847 PMID:11934121

Litwiller, B. J., & Brausch, A. M. (2013). Cyber bullying and physical bullying in adolescent suicide: The role of violent behavior and substance use. *Journal of Youth and Adolescence, 42*(5), 675–684. doi:10.100710964-013-9925-5 PMID:23381779

Liu, C. D. (2008). Current situation and development trend of network language research in China. *Shandong Social Science, 9*, 155–158.

Liu, Y. C., & Ning, F. M. (2004). Study on network language. *Journal of Armed Police Medical College, 4*, 75–79.

Liu, Y., Zhang, M., Li, R., Chen, N., Huang, Y., Lv, Y., & Wang, Y. (2020). Risk assessment of workplace violence towards health workers in a Chinese hospital: A cross-sectional study. *BMJ Open, 10*(12), e042800. doi:10.1136/bmjopen-2020-042800 PMID:33371045

Livingstone, S., Haddon, L., Görzig, A., & Ólafsson, K. (2011). *Risks and safety on the internet: The perspective of European children.* Full Findings. EU Kids.

Livingston, J. A., Derrick, J. L., Wang, W., Testa, M., Nickerson, A. B., Espelage, D. L., & Miller, K. E. (2019). Proximal association among bullying, mood, and substance use: A daily report study. *Journal of Child and Family Studies, 28*(9), 2558–2571. doi:10.100710826-018-1109-1 PMID:32269466

Li, W. (2020). The language of bullying: Social issues on Chinese websites. *Aggression and Violent Behavior, 53*, 101453. doi:10.1016/j.avb.2020.101453

Locker, D. (1988). Measuring oral health: A conceptual framework. *Community Dental Health, 5*, 3–18. PMID:3285972

Loh, J., & Snyman, R. (2020). The tangled web: Consequences of workplace cyberbullying in adult male and female employees. *Gender in Management, 35*(6), 567–584. https://doi.org/10.1108/GM-12-2019-0242

Longobardi, C., Gullotta, G., Ferrigno, S., Jungert, T., Thornberg, R., & Settanni, M. (2021). Cyberbullying and cybervictimization among preadolescents: Does time perspective matter? *Scandinavian Journal of Psychology, 62*(2), 259–266. https://doi.org/10.1111/sjop.12686

López-Vizcaíno, M. F., Nóvoa, F. J., Carneiro, V., & Cacheda, F. (2021). Early detection of cyberbullying on social media networks. *Future Generation Computer Systems, 118*, 219–229. doi:10.1016/j.future.2021.01.006

Lorenz, K., Wilson, M. K., & Huxley, J. (2005). On aggression. In On Aggression. Routledge. https://doi.org/10.4324/9780203994269.

Lovegrove, P. J., Henry, K. L., & Slater, M. D. (2012). Examination of the predictors of latent class typologies of bullying involvement among middle school students. *Journal of School Violence, 11*(1), 75–93. doi:10.1080/15388220.2011.631447 PMID:22606069

Low, S., & Espelage, D. (2014). Conduits from community violence exposure to peer aggression and victimization: Contributions of parental monitoring, impulsivity and deviancy. *Journal of Counseling Psychology, 61*(2), 221–231. doi:10.1037/a0035207 PMID:24635595

Lu, L., Dong, M., Wang, S. B., Zhang, L., Ng, C. H., Ungvari, G. S., & Xiang, Y. T. (2020). Prevalence of Workplace Violence Against Health-Care Professionals in China: A Comprehensive Meta-Analysis of Observational Surveys. *Trauma, Violence & Abuse, 21*(3), 498–509. doi:10.1177/1524838018774429 PMID:29806556

Luo, A., & Bussey, K. (2019). The selectivity of moral disengagement in defenders of cyberbullying: Contextual moral disengagement. *Computers in Human Behavior*, *93*, 318–325. doi:10.1016/j.chb.2018.12.038

Lyznicki, J. M., McCaffree, M. A., & Robinowitz, C. B. (2004). Childhood bullying: Implications for physicians. *American Family Physician*, *70*(9), 1723–1728. PMID:15554490

Macaulay, P., Betts, L., Stiller, J., & Kellezi, B. (2022). Bystander responses to cyberbullying: The role of perceived severity, publicity, anonymity, type of cyberbullying, and victim response. *Computers in Human Behavior*, *131*. doi:10.1016/j.chb.2022.107238

Macaulay, P. J. R., Steer, O. L., & Betts, L. R. (2020). *Factors leading to cyber victimization*. Emerging Cyber Threats and Cognitive Vulnerabilities. doi:10.1016/B978-0-12-816203-3.00001-0

MacGregor, F. C. (1970). Social and psychological implications of dentofacial disfigurement. *The Angle Orthodontist*, *40*(3), 231–233. PMID:5269955

Machackova, H. (2020). Bystander reactions to cyberbullying and cyberaggression: Individual, contextual, and social factors. *Current Opinion in Psychology*, *36*, 130–134. doi:10.1016/j.copsyc.2020.06.003 PMID:32668382

MacKinnon, C. A. (1979). *Sexual harassment of working women: A case of sex discrimination*. Yale University Press.

Maftei, A., Holman, A. C., & Merlici, I. A. (2022). Using fake news as means of cyber-bullying: The link with compulsive internet use and online moral disengagement. *Computers in Human Behavior*, *127*, 127. doi:10.1016/j.chb.2021.107032

Magley, V. J., Waldo, C. R., Drasgow, F., & Fitzgerald, L. F. (1999). The impact of sexual harassment on military personnel: Is it the same for men and women? *Military Psychology*, *11*(3), 283–302. doi:10.120715327876mp1103_5

Magsi, H., Agha, N., & Magsi, I. (2017). Understanding Cyber Bullying in Pakistani Context: Causes and Effects on Young Female University Students in Sindh Province. *New Horizons (Baltimore, Md.)*, *11*(1), 103–110.

Ma, J., Han, Y., & Kang, H. R. (2022). Physical punishment, physical abuse, and child behavior problems in South Korea. *Child Abuse & Neglect*, *123*, 123. doi:10.1016/j.chiabu.2021.105385 PMID:34800844

Malecki, C. K., Demaray, M. K., Smith, T. J., & Emmons, J. (2020). Disability, poverty, and other risk factors associated with involvement in bullying behaviors. *Journal of School Psychology*, *78*, 115–132. doi:10.1016/j.jsp.2020.01.002 PMID:32178807

Malta, D. C., Porto, D. L., Crespo, C. D., Silva, M. M. A., Andrade, S. S. C. D., Mello, F. C. M. D., Monteiro, R., & Silva, M. A. I. (2014). Bullying in Brazilian school children: Analysis of the national adolescent school-based health survey (PeNSE 2012). *Revista Brasileira de Epidemiologia*, *17*(suppl 1), 92–105. doi:10.1590/1809-4503201400050008 PMID:25054256

Marasli, M., Suhendan, E., Yilmazturk, N. H., & Cok, F. (2017). Parents ' shares on social networking sites about their children : Sharenting. *The Anthropologist*, *24*(2), 399–406. doi:10.1080/09720073.2016.11892031

Marcum, C. D., & Higgins, G. E. (2019). Examining the Effectiveness of Academic Scholarship on the Fight Against Cyberbullying and Cyberstalking. *American Journal of Criminal Justice*, *44*(4), 645–655. doi:10.100712103-019-09482-8

Marcum, C. D., Higgins, G. E., & Nicholson, J. (2017). I'm Watching Uou: Cyberstalking behaviors of university students in romantic relationships. *American Journal of Criminal Justice*, *42*(2), 373–388. doi:10.100712103-016-9358-2

Marczak, M., & Coyne, I. (2015). A focus on online bullying. In A. Attrill (Ed.), *Cyberpsychology*. Oxford, UK: Oxford University Press. https://www.merriam-webster.com/

Marengo, D., Fabris, M. A., Prino, L. E., Settanni, M., & Longobardi, C. (2021). Student-teacher conflict moderates the link between students' social status in the classroom and involvement in bullying behaviors and exposure to peer victimization. *Journal of Adolescence, 87*, 86–97. doi:10.1016/j.adolescence.2021.01.005 PMID:33545582

Marengo, D., Fabris, M. A., Prino, L. E., Settanni, M., & Longobardi, C. (2021). Student-teacher conlict moderates the link between students' social status in the classroom and involvement in bullying behaviors and exposure to peer victimization. *Journal of Adolescence*, 87. PMID:33545582

Margaret Brown, P., & Cornes, A. (2015). Mental health of deaf and hard-of-hearing adolescents: What the students say. *Journal of Deaf Studies and Deaf Education, 20*(1), 75–81. doi:10.1093/deafed/enu031 PMID:25237152

Martínez, I., Murgui, S., Garcia, O. F., & Garcia, F. (2019). Parenting in the digital era: Protective and risk parenting styles for traditional bullying and cyberbullying victimization. *Computers in Human Behavior, 90*, 84–92. doi:10.1016/j.chb.2018.08.036

Martinez, S. (2009). A system gone berserk: How are zero-tolerance policies really affecting schools? *Preventing School Failure, 53*, 153–158. doi:10.3200/PSFL.53.3.153-158

Marzano, G. (2019). *Setting Anti-Cyberbullying Legal Policies*. IGI Global. https://services.igi-global.com/resolvedoi/resolve.aspx?doi=10.4018/978-1-5225-8076-8.ch002

Mascheroni, G., Ponte, C., & Jorge, A. (2018). *The challenges for families in the digital age. In The International Clearinghouse on Children, Youth and Media at Nordicom (Nordic Information Centre for Media and Communication Research)*. University of Gothenburg.

Mason, K. L. (2008). Cyberbullyıng: A preliminary assessment for school personnel. *Psychology in the Schools, 45*(4), 323–348. doi:10.1002/pits.20301

Mason, W. A. (2001). Self-esteem and Delinquency Revisited (again): A test of Kaplan's self-derogation theory of delinquency using latent growth curve modeling. *Journal of Youth and Adolescence, 30*(1), 83–102. doi:10.1023/A:1005276905961

Matchen, J., & DeSouza, E. (2000). The sexual harassment of faculty members by students. *Sex Roles, 42*(3–4), 295–306. doi:10.1023/A:1007099408885

Mateu, A., Pascual-Sánchez, A., Martinez-Herves, M., Hickey, N., Nicholls, D., & Kramer, T. (2020). Cyberbullying and post-traumatic stress symptoms in UK adolescents. *Archives of Disease in Childhood, 105*(10), 951–956. https://doi.org/10.1136/archdischild-2019-318716

Matthiesen, S. B., & Einarsen, S. (2001). MMPI-2 configurations among victims of bullying at work. *European Journal of Work and Organizational Psychology, 10*(4), 467–484. doi:10.1080/13594320143000753

Matthiesen, S. B., & Einarsen, S. (2004). Psychiatric distress and symptoms of PTSD among victims of bullying at work. *British Journal of Guidance & Counselling, 32*(3), 335–356. doi:10.1080/03069880410001723558

Matthiesen, S. B., & Einarsen, S. (2010). Bullying in the workplace: Definition, prevalence, antecedents and consequences. *International Journal of Organization Theory and Behavior, 13*(2), 202–248. doi:10.1108/IJOTB-13-02-2010-B004

Maxfield J, Wells T (2003) Adverse effects of social pressure to be thin on young women: An experimental investigation of the effects of "fat talk". *Int J Eat Disord, 34*(1), 108–117. doi:10.1002/eat.10171

Mayer, B. A. (2022). *Why parents overshare on social media and when it might be dangerous*. Retrieved February 5, 2022 from https://www.parents.com/parenting/better-parenting/sharenting-meaning-and-when-it-might-be-dangerous/

McAvoy, B. R., & Murtagh, J. (2003). *Workplace bullying: The silent epidemic* (Vol. 326). British Medical Journal Publishing Group.

McCabe, M. P., & Ricciardelli, L. A. (2005). A prospective study of pressure from parents, peers, and the media on extreme weight change behaviours among adolescent boys and girls. *Behaviour Research and Therapy*, *43*(5), 653–668. doi:10.1016/j.brat.2004.05.004 PMID:15865919

McCarthy, M. (2021). Social Media, Students, and the Law. *Laws*, *10*(4), 81. https://doi.org/10.3390/laws10040081

McCrone, W. P. (2004). School Bullying: A Problem for Deaf and Hard of Hearing Students? Insights and Strategies. Odyssey. *New Directions in Deaf Education*, *5*(2), 4–9.

McDonald, P. (2012). Workplace Sexual Harassment 30 Years on: A Review of the Literature. *International Journal of Management Reviews*, *14*(1), 1–17. doi:10.1111/j.1468-2370.2011.00300.x

McDougall, L. (1999). A study of bullying in further education. *Pastoral Care in Education*, *17*(2), 31–37. doi:10.1111/1468-0122.00125

McGinnis, E., & Goldstein, A. P. (2003). *Skillstreaming in early childhood: new strategies and perspectives for teaching prosocial skills* (Revised ed.). Research Press.

McKenna, B. G., Smith, N. A., Poole, S. J., & Coverdale, J. H. (2003). Horizontal violence: Experiences of Registered Nurses in their first year of practice. *Journal of Advanced Nursing*, *42*(1), 90–96. doi:10.1046/j.1365-2648.2003.02583.x PMID:12641816

McKinley, N. M. (1999). Women and objectified body consciousness: Mothers' and daughters' body experience in cultural, developmental, and familial context. *Developmental Psychology*, *35*(3), 760–769. doi:10.1037/0012-1649.35.3.760 PMID:10380866

McKinney, E., Ashwill, J., Murray, S., James, S., Gorrie, T., & Droske, S. (2000). Maternal-Child Nursing. Saunders Company.

McLaughlin, H., Uggen, C., & Blackstone, A. (2017). The economic and career effects of sexual harassment on working women. *Gender & Society*, *31*(3), 333–358. doi:10.1177/0891243217704631 PMID:29056822

McLean, L., & Griffiths, M. D. (2019). Female gamers' experience of online harassment and social support in online gaming: A qualitative study. *International Journal of Mental Health and Addiction*, *17*(4), 970–994. doi:10.100711469-018-9962-0

McLuhan. (2008). Marshall McLuhan's Theory of Communication. Global Media Journal.

McWhinney, I. R. (1987). Health and disease: Problems of definition. *Canadian Medical Association Journal*, *136*(8), 815. PMID:3567791

Md. Salleh, A. S., & Mohd Noor, N. A. (2019). Sharenting: Implikasinya dari perspektif perundangan Malaysia. *Kanun: Jurnal Undang-undang Malaysia, 31*(1), 121-156.

me too. (2020). Available at: https://metoomvmt.org/about/

Mehari, K. R., Farrell, A. D., & Le, A. T. H. (2014). Cyberbullying among adolescents: Measures in search of a construct. *Psychology of Violence*, *4*(4), 399–415. doi:10.1037/a0037521

Menesini, E., & Salmivalli, C. (2017). Bullying in schools: the state of knowledge and effective interventions. *Psychol Health Med, 22*(sup1), 240-253. doi:10.1080/13548506.2017.1279740

Menezes, C., de Arruda, J. A., Silva, L. V., Monteiro, J. L., Caribé, P., Álvares, P., ... Bueno, D. F. (2018). Nonsyndromic cleft lip and/or palate: A multicenter study of the dental anomalies involved. *Journal of Clinical and Experimental Dentistry, 10*(8), e746. doi:10.4317/jced.54926 PMID:30305871

Menin, D., Guarini, A., Mameli, C., Skrzypiec, G., & Brighi, A. (2021). Was that (cyber)bullying? Investigating the operational definitions of bullying and cyberbullying from adolescents' perspective. *International Journal of Clinical and Health Psychology, 21*(2), 100221. doi:10.1016/j.ijchp.2021.100221 PMID:33552165

Menzer, M. M., & Torney-Purta, J. (2012). Individualism and socioeconomic diversity at school as related to perceptions of the frequency of peer aggression in fifteen countries. *Journal of Adolescence, 35*(5), 1285–1294. doi:10.1016/j.adolescence.2012.04.013 PMID:22633914

Meral, B., & Çağlar, S. (2021). Siber zorbalık: çocuklarda zorbalığın yeni dönemi ve hemşirelik yaklaşımları [Cyber bullying: the new period of childhood and nursing approaches in children]. *Dokuz Eylül Üniversitesi Hemsirelik Fakültesi Elektronik Dergisi, 14*(3), 261–267.

Mercurio, A. E., Hong, F., Amir, C., Tarullo, A. R., Samkavitz, A., Ashy, M., & Malley-Morrison, K. (2022). Relationships among childhood maltreatment, limbic system dysfunction, and eating disorders in college women. *Journal of Interpersonal Violence, 37*(1-2), 520–537. doi:10.1177/0886260520912590 PMID:32228345

Merkin, R. S., & Shah, M. K. (2014). The impact of sexual harassment on job satisfaction, turnover intentions, and absenteeism: Findings from Pakistan compared to the United States. *SpringerPlus, 3*(1), 1–13. doi:10.1186/2193-1801-3-215 PMID:24851198

Mestci, S. (2021). *Exploring the link between object relations, narcissism, cyber bullying, and cyber victimization among university students* (Unpublished Master Thesis). University of Economics, İzmir.

Meter, D. J., Budziszewski, R., Phillips, A., & Beckert, T. E. (2021). A Qualitative Exploration of College Students' Perceptions of Cyberbullying. *TechTrends, 65*(4), 464–472. https://doi.org/10.1007/s11528-021-00605-9

Metin-Aslan, Ö., & Tuğrul, B. (2013). Analyzing preschool children's bullying and play behavior during play. *Mediterranean Journal of Educational Research, 7*(13), 27-41. https://mjer.penpublishing.net/makale_indir/330

Metin-Aslan, M., & Tuğrul, B. (2014). The content analysis of preschool children's bullying and victimization behaviors in play. *Journal of Theoretical Educational Science, 7*(1), 60–77. doi:10.5578/keg.6205

Mevzuat Bilgi Sistemi. (2005). *Çocuk Koruma Kanunu.* https://www.mevzuat.gov.tr/MevzuatMetin/1.5.5395

Michelson, G. (2001). Whether victor or vanquished, we all lose to the office bully. *Sydney Morning Herald*, p. 1.

Migliaccio, T., & Raskauskas, J. (2016). *Bullying as a social experience: Social factors, prevention and intervention.* Ashgate Publishing Company. doi:10.4324/9781315570525

Milano, A. (2017). *Twitter.com.* Retrieved from: https://twitter.com/alyssa_milano/status/919659438700670976?lang=en

Milligan, B. (2022). Van Buren v. United States: Rogue Employees Avoiding Prosecution Under the CFAA Because the Court Said "So." *SSRN Electronic Journal.* doi:10.2139/ssrn.4030017

Mills, M. (2001). *Challenging violence in schools: An issue of masculinities.* Open University.

Milothridis, P. (2020). Bullying About Someone's Appearance and Interest in Cosmetic Surgery. In *Cosmetic Patient Selection and Psychosocial Background* (pp. 33–39). Springer. doi:10.1007/978-3-030-44725-0_4

Min, J. (2014). The relationships between emotional intelligence, job stress, and quality of life among tour guides. *Asia Pacific Journal of Tourism Research, 19*(10), 1170–1190. https://doi.org/10.1080/10941665.2013.839459

Mishna, F., & Alaggia, R. (2005). Weighing the risks: A child's decision to disclose peer victimization. *Children & Schools*, *27*(4), 217–226. doi:10.1093/cs/27.4.217

Mishna, F., Cook, C., Gadalla, T., Daciuk, J., & Solomon, S. (2010). Cyber bullying behaviors among middle and high school students. *The American Journal of Orthopsychiatry*, *80*(3), 362–374. doi:10.1111/j.1939-0025.2010.01040.x PMID:20636942

Mishna, F., Khoury-Kassabri, M., Gadalla, T., & Daciuk, J. (2012). Risk factors for involvement in cyber bullying: Victims, bullies and bully–victims. *Children and Youth Services Review*, *34*(1), 63–70. doi:10.1016/j.childyouth.2011.08.032

Mishna, F., Khoury-Kassabri, M., Schwan, K., Wiener, J., Craig, W., Beran, T., Pepler, D., & Daciuk, J. (2016). The contribution of social support to children and adolescents' self-perception: The mediating role of bullying victimization. *Children and Youth Services Review*, *63*, 120–127. doi:10.1016/j.childyouth.2016.02.013

Mishna, F., McInroy, L. B., Daciuk, J., & Duncan, A. L. (2017). Adapting to attrition challenges in multi-year studies: Examples from a school-based bullying and cyber bullying study. *Children and Youth Services Review*, *81*, 268–271. doi:10.1016/j.childyouth.2017.08.019

Mishna, F., Sanders, J. E., McNeil, S., Fearing, G., & Kalenteridis, K. (2020). "If Somebody is Different": A critical analysis of parent, teacher and student perspectives on bullying and cyberbullying. *Children and Youth Services Review*, *118*, 105366. https://doi.org/10.1016/j.childyouth.2020.105366

Mitchell, R.E., & Karchmer, M. (2004). Chasing the Mythical Ten Percent: Parental Hearing Status of Deaf and Hard of Hearing Students in the United States. *Sign Language Studies*, *4*(2), 138-163. https://www.jstor.org/stable/26190985

Mitchell, K. J., Ybarra, M., & Finkelhor, D. (2007). The relative importance of online victimization in understanding depression, delinquency, and substance use. *Child Maltreatment*, *12*(4), 314–324. doi:10.1177/1077559507305996 PMID:17954938

Modecki, K. L., Minchin, J., Harbaugh, A. G., Guerra, N. G., & Runions, K. C. (2014). Bullying prevalence across contexts: A meta-analysis measuring cyber and traditional bullying. *The Journal of Adolescent Health*, *55*(5), 602–611. doi:10.1016/j.jadohealth.2014.06.007 PMID:25168105

Moeller, T. G. (2001). *Youth aggression and violence : a psychological approach*. Lawrence Erlbaum Associates. doi:10.4324/9781410606488

Moeller, T. P., Bachmann, G. A., & Moeller, J. R. (1993). The combined effects of physical, sexual, and emotional abuse during childhood: Long-term health consequences for women. *Child Abuse & Neglect*, *17*(5), 623–640. doi:10.1016/0145-2134(93)90084-I PMID:8221217

Mogumder, A. (2022). Infringing upon our basic freedoms. *Dhaka Tribune*. https://www.dhakatribune.com/op-ed/2022/04/25/infringing-upon-our-basic-freedoms

Monks, C. P., Palermiti, A., Ortega, R., & Costabile, A. (2011). A cross-national comparison of aggressors, victims and defenders in preschools in England, Spain and Italy. *The Spanish Journal of Psychology*, *14*(1), 133–144. doi:10.5209/rev_SJOP.2011.v14.n1.11 PMID:21568171

Monks, C. P., Smith, P. K., Naylor, P., Barter, C., Ireland, J. L., & Coyne, I. (2009). Bullying in different contexts: Commonalities, differences and the role of theory. *Aggression and Violent Behavior*, *14*(2), 146–156. doi:10.1016/j.avb.2009.01.004

Monks, C. P., Smith, P. K., & Swettenham, J. (2005). Psychological correlates of peer victimisation in preschool: Social cognitive skills, executive function and attachment profiles. *Aggressive Behavior*, *31*(6), 571–588. doi:10.1002/ab.20099

Monteiro, A. P. (submitted for publication). Propriedades psicométricas da escala ECIPQ] [European Cyberbullying Intervention Project Questionnaire]. *Numa Amostra de Adolescentes Portugueses.*

Monteleone, A. M., Tzischinsky, O., Cascino, G., Alon, S., Pellegrino, F., Ruzzi, V., & Latzer, Y. (2022). The connection between childhood maltreatment and eating disorder psychopathology: A network analysis study in people with bulimia nervosa and with binge eating disorder. *Eating and Weight Disorders*, *27*(1), 253–261. doi:10.100740519-021-01169-6 PMID:33774786

Moon, M. (2001). Teacher perspectives on peer relation problems of young children. *Asia Pacific Education Review*, *2*(1), 22–31. doi:10.1007/BF03024929

Moores, D. (2001). *Educating the deaf: Psychology, principles and practices* (5th ed.). Houghton Mifflin.

Moxey, N., & Bussey, K. (2020). Styles of bystander intervention in cyberbullying incidents. *Int Journal of Bullying Prevention*, *2*(1), 6–15. doi:10.100742380-019-00039-1

Muhd. Zulfadli Hafiz, I., Nik Daliana, N. F., Rafzah, A. Z., Ramona Susanty, A. H., Elina, A. M. Edwan, M. A., & Aida, T. (2019). *Towards good cyber parenting- Exploring stakeholders' views in understanding parental digital security practice and online threat concerns in Malaysia.* doi:10.13140/RG.2.2.14431.30884

Muhonen, T., Jönsson, S., & Bäckström, M. (2017). Consequences of cyberbullying behaviour in working life: The mediating roles of social support and social organizational climate. *International Journal of Workplace Health Management*, *10*(5), 376–390. doi:10.1108/IJWHM-10-2016-0075 PMID:29721038

Murad, M. H. (2012). A Study of Digital Signature and Its Legal Implications in Context of Bangladesh. *IIUC Studies*, *6*(6), 111–122. doi:10.3329/iiucs.v6i0.12252

Murdoch, M., Bradley, A., Mather, S. H., Klein, R. E., Turner, C. L., & Yano, E. M. (2006). Women and war: What physicians should know. *Journal of General Internal Medicine*, *21*, 5–10.

Murphy, A. G. (2009). *Dealing with bullying*. Infobase Publishing.

Murray-Harvey, R., & Slee, P. T. (2010). School and home relationships and their impact on school bullying. *School Psychology International*, *31*(3), 271–295. doi:10.1177/0143034310366206

Murrhee, K. C. (2010). Squelching Student Speech in Florida: Cyberbullying and the First Amendment. *U. Fla. JL & Pub. Pol'y*, *21*, 307.

Myadvo. (2021). *What is Cyber Bullying or Anti-Bullying Laws in India.* https://www.myadvo.in/blog/must-read-what-is-cyber-bullying-or-anti-bullying-laws-in-india/

Myers, D. G., & Twenge, J. M. (2021). *Social psychology* (14th ed.). McGraw-Hill Education.

Mynard, H., & Joseph, S. (2000). Development of the multidimensional peer-victimization scale. *Aggressive Behavior*, *26*(2), 169–178. doi:10.1002/(SICI)1098-2337(2000)26:23.0.CO;2-A

Mynard, H., & Joseph, S. (2000). Development of the multidimensional peer-victimization scale. *Aggressive Behavior: Official Journal of the International Society for Research on Aggression*, *26*(2), 169–178. doi:10.1002/(SICI)1098-2337(2000)26:2<169::AID-AB3>3.0.CO;2-A

Nabe-Nielsen, K., Grynderup, M. B., Lange, T., Andersen, J. H., Bonde, J. P., Conway, P. M., & Hansen, Å. M. (2016). The role of poor sleep in the relation between workplace bullying/unwanted sexual attention and long-term sickness absence. *International Archives of Occupational and Environmental Health*, *89*(6), 967–979. doi:10.100700420-016-1136-4 PMID:27137811

Nabi, M. S. (2019). Unicef: 32% kids at risk of cyberbullying in Bangladesh. *Dhaka Tribune*. https://archive.dhakatribune.com/bangladesh/dhaka/2019/02/05/unicef-prevent-online-bullying-harassment-of-children-in-bangladesh

Nabi, H., Harley, S., & Murphy, E. (2013). The perils and triumphs of night surgical residents across South Australia. *Journal of Surgical Education, 70*(2), 265–272. doi:10.1016/j.jsurg.2012.09.004 PMID:23427975

Naidoo, S. (2000). A profile of the oro-facial injuries in child physical abuse at a children's hospital. *Child Abuse & Neglect, 24*(4), 521–534. doi:10.1016/S0145-2134(00)00114-9 PMID:10798841

Najafi, F., Fallahi-Khoshknab, M., Dalvandi, A., Ahmadi, F., & Rahgozar, M. (2014). *Workplace violence against Iranian nurses: A systematic review* [دنم ماظن رورم :ناریا رد ناراتسرپ هیلع راک لحم تنوشخ]. Retrieved from http://jhpm.ir/article-1-243-en.html

Najdowski, C. J., & Ullman, S. E. (2009). PTSD symptoms and self-rated recovery among adult sexual assault survivors: The effects of traumatic life events and psychosocial variables. *Psychology of Women Quarterly, 33*, 43–53.

Nakamoto, J., & Schwartz, D. (2010). Is peer victimization associated with academic achievement? A meta-analytic review. *Social Development, 19*(2), 221–242. doi:10.1111/j.1467-9507.2009.00539.x

Nalbant, K.G., & Uyanık, Ş. (2021). Computer Vision in the Metaverse. *Journal of Metaverse, 1*(1).

Nansel, T. R., Craig, W., Overpeck, M. D., Saluja, G., & Ruan, W. J. (2004). Cross-national consistency in the relationship between bullying behaviors and psychosocial adjustment. *Archives of Pediatrics & Adolescent Medicine, 158*(8), 730–736. doi:10.1001/archpedi.158.8.730 PMID:15289243

Nansel, T. R., Overpeck, M., Pilla, R. S., Ruan, W. J., Simons-Morton, B., & Scheidt, P. (2001). Bullying behaviors among US youth: Prevalence and association with psychosocial adjustment. *Journal of the American Medical Association, 285*(16), 2094–2100. doi:10.1001/jama.285.16.2094 PMID:11311098

Narin, B., & Ünal, S. (2016). Framing of News About Cyberbullying in the Turkish Print Media. *Akdeniz Journal of Communication*, 9 - 23.

Narin, B., & Ünal, S. (2016). Siber Zorbalıkla İlgili Haberlerin Türkiye Yazılı Basınında Çerçevelenişi. *The Journal of Akdeniz University's Faculty of Communication, 26.*

National Academies of Sciences, Engineering and Medicine. (2016). *Preventing bullying through science, policy, and practice*. The National Academies Press., doi:10.17226/23482

National Academies of Sciences, Engineering, and Medicine. (2018). *Sexual harassment of women: climate, culture, and consequences in academic sciences, engineering, and medicine*. Author.

National Center for Education. (2019). *Student Reports of Bullying Results from the 2017 School Crime Supplement to the National Victimization Survey*. Author.

National Deaf Children's Society. (2014, June). *Bullying Advice for Parents of Deaf Children.* Author.

National Legislative Bodies / National Authorities. (2003). Nigeria Act No. 26 of 2003, Child's Rights Act, 2003 Refworld | Nigeria: Act No. 26 of 2003, Child's Rights Act, 2003

Natvig, G. K., Albrektsen, G., & Qvarnstrøm, U. (2001). School-related stress experience as a risk factor for bullying behavior. *Journal of Youth and Adolescence, 30*(5), 561–575. doi:10.1023/A:1010448604838

Naveed, S., Waqas, A., Aedma, K. K., Tayyaba Afzaal, T., & Majeed, M. H. (2019). Association of bullying experiences with depressive symptoms and psychosocial functioning among school going children and adolescents. *BMC Research Notes, 12*(1), 198. doi:10.118613104-019-4236-x PMID:30940177

Naylor, P., & Cowie, H. (1999). The effectiveness of peer support systems in challenging school bullying: The perspectives and experiences of teachers and pupils. *Journal of Adolescence, 22*(4), 467–479. doi:10.1006/jado.1999.0241 PMID:10469511

Nche, G. C. (2012). The Social Media Usage Among Nigerian Youths: Impact on National Development. *International Journal of Advancement in Development Studies, 7*(5), 18-23.

Ndinojuo, Gbeneka, Diegbegha, & Eludu. (2016). Challenges in using contemporary Digital Tools in media relations practice in Nigeria. *Research on Humanities and Social Sciences.*

Nelson, M. (2003). *School bullies going high tech.* Retrieved from http://www. canoe.ca/NewsStand/LondonFreePress/News/2003/09/02/174030.html

Nesbitt, W. (2012). *Workplace bullying in the healthcare setting. SMSI Online Newsletter: The Hospital Reporter.* Security Management Services International and The Hospital Reporter.

Nesbo, E. (2021). *The Metaverse vs. Virtual Reality: 6 Key Differences.* https://www.makeuseof.com/metaverse-vs-virtual-reality/

Neto, A. P., & Barbosa, L. (2018). Bullying and cyberbullying: Conceptual controversy in Brazil. In The Internet and Health in Brazil: Challenges and Trends (pp. 225–249). Springer. https://doi.org/10.1007/978-3-319-99289-1_12.

Neumark-Sztainer, D., Story, M., Hannan, P. J., Beuhring, T., & Resnick, M. D. (2000). Disordered eating among adolescents: Associations with sexual/physical abuse and other familial/psychosocial factors. *International Journal of Eating Disorders, 28*, 249–258.

Nevelsteen, K. J. (2018). Virtual world, defined from a technological perspective and applied to video games, mixed reality, and the Metaverse. *Computer Animation and Virtual Worlds, 29*(1), e1752. doi:10.1002/cav.1752

Newman, M. L. (2014). Here we go again: Bullying history and cardiovascular responses to social exclusion. *Physiology & Behavior, 133*, 76–80. doi:10.1016/j.physbeh.2014.05.014 PMID:24858188

Ngo, A. T., Tran, A. Q., Tran, B. X., Nguyen, L. H., Hoang, M. T., Nguyen, T. H. T., Doan, L. P., Vu, G. T., Nguyen, T. H., Do, H. T., Latkin, C. A., Ho, R. C. M., & Ho, C. S. H. (2021). Cyberbullying Among School Adolescents in an Urban Setting of a Developing Country: Experience, Coping Strategies, and Mediating Effects of Different Support on Psychological Well-Being. *Frontiers in Psychology, 12*, 930. https://doi.org/10.3389/fpsyg.2021.661919

Nıckerson, A. B., Mele, D., & Osborne-Olıver, K. M. (2010). Parent-Child Relationships and Bullying. In The Handbook of Bullying in Schools: An International Perspective Shane (pp. 187-198). Routledge.

Nickerson, A. B. (2019). Preventing and intervening with bullying in schools: A framework for evidence-based practice. *School Mental Health, 11*(1), 15–28. doi:10.100712310-017-9221-8

Nickerson, A., Singleton, D., Schnurr, B. L., & Collen, M. H. (2014). Perceptions of school climate as a function of bullying involvement. *Journal of Applied School Psychology, 30*(2), 157–181. doi:10.1080/15377903.2014.888530

Nielsen, M. B., & Einarsen, S. V. (2012). Outcomes of Exposure to Workplace Bullying: A Meta-Analytic Review. *Work and Stress, 26*(4), 309–332. doi:10.1080/02678373.2012.734709 PMID:23236220

Nielsen, M. B., & Einarsen, S. V. (2018). What we know, what we do not know, and what we should and could have known about workplace bullying: An overview of the literature and agenda for future research. *Aggression and Violent Behavior, 42*, 71–83. doi:10.1016/j.avb.2018.06.007

Nikolaou, D. (2017). Does Cyberbullying Impact Youth Suicidal Behaviors? *Journal of Health Economics*, *56*, 30–46. doi:10.1016/j.jhealeco.2017.09.009 PMID:28968528

Nikolaou, D. (2022). Bullying, cyberbullying, and youth health behaviors. *Kyklos*, *75*(1), 75–105. doi:10.1111/kykl.12286

Nishina, A., & Juvonen, J. (2005). Daily reports of witnessing and experiencing peer harassment in middle school. *Child Development*, *76*(2), 435–450. doi:10.1111/j.1467-8624.2005.00855.x PMID:15784092

Nixon, C. L. (2014). Current Perspectives: The impact of cyberbullying on adolescent health. *Adolescent Health, Medicine and Therapeutics*, *5*, 143–158. doi:10.2147/AHMT.S36456 PMID:25177157

Nocentini, A., Calmaestra, J., Schultze-Krumbholz, A., Scheithauer, H., Ortega, R., & Menesini, E. (2010). Cyberbullying: Labels, behaviours and definition in three European countries. *Australian Journal of Guidance & Counselling*, *20*(2), 129–142. doi:10.1375/ajgc.20.2.129

Nocentini, A., Fiorentini, G., Di Paola, L., & Menesini, E. (2019). Parents, family characteristics and bullying behavior: A systematic review. *Aggression and Violent Behavior*, *45*, 41–50. doi:10.1016/j.avb.2018.07.010

Noetzel, S., Mussalem Gentile, M. F., Lowery, G., Zemanova, S., Lecheler, S., & Peter, C. (2022). Social campaigns to social change? Sexual violence framing in US news before and after# metoo. *Journalism*, 1–32. doi:10.1177/14648849211056386

Nor Hazlina, H., Yusniza, K., Marshina, M. H. J., & Nur Atikah, A. R. (2021). "Sharenting": A study of Malaysian parents' use of social media platforms. SEARCH. *Journal of Media and Communication*, *13*(3), 125–140.

Norman, R. E., Byambaa, M., De, R., Butchart, A., Scott, J., & Vos, T. (2012). The long-term health consequences of child physical abuse, emotional abuse, and neglect: A systematic review and meta-analysis. *PLoS Medicine*, *9*(11), e1001349. doi:10.1371/journal.pmed.1001349 PMID:23209385

Norton, P., Costa, V., Teixeira, J., Azevedo, A., Roma-Torres, A., Amaro, J., & Cunha, L. (2017). Prevalence and Determinants of Bullying Among Health Care Workers in Portugal. *Workplace Health & Safety*, *65*(5), 188–196. doi:10.1177/2165079916666545 PMID:28061740

Norwich, B., & Kelly, N. (2004). Pupils' views on inclusion: Moderate learning difficulties and bullying in mainstream and special schools. *British Educational Research Journal*, *30*(1), 43–65. doi:10.1080/01411920310001629965

Novitasari, N. F., Irma, N., & Hia, A. (2021). Cyberbullying in Movie Cyberbully : an Analysis From the Psychological Perspective. *Celtic: A Journal of Culture, English Language Teaching. Literatura y Lingüística*, *8*(1), 44–64. https://doi.org/10.22219/CELTIC.V8I1.16393

O'Brien, C., Benson, P. E., & Marshman, Z. (2007). Evaluation of a quality of life measure for children with malocclusion. *Journal of Orthodontics*, *34*(3), 185–193. doi:10.1179/146531207225022185 PMID:17761802

O'Brien-Pallas, L., Duffield, C., & Hayes, L. (2006). Do we really understand how to retain nurses? *Journal of Nursing Management*, *14*(4), 262–270. doi:10.1111/j.1365-2934.2006.00611.x PMID:16629840

O'Donohue, W., Downs, K., & Yeater, E. A. (1998). Sexual harassment: A review of the literature. *Aggression and Violent Behavior*, *3*(2), 111–128.

O'Hare, E., & O'Donohue, W. (1998). Sexual harassment: Identifying risk factors. *Archives of Sexual Behavior*, *27*(6), 561–579.

O'Higgins Norman, J. (2020). Tackling bullying from the inside out: Shifting paradigms in bullying research and interventions. *International Journal of Bullying Prevention*, *2*(3), 161–169. doi:10.100742380-020-00076-1 PMID:33005874

O'Moore, O., & Minton, S. J. (2004). *Dealing with bullying in schools a training manual for teachers, parents and other professionals*. Chapman Publishing.

O'Neill, B., Livingstone, S., & McLaughlin, S. (2011). *Final recommendations for policy, methodology and research*. EU Kids Online.

Obermaier, M., Fawzi, N., & Koch, T. (2016). Bystanding or standing by? How the number of bystanders affects the intention to intervene in cyberbullying. *New Media & Society*, *18*(8), 1491–1507. doi:10.1177/1461444814563519

Odabaşı, H. F., Kabakçı, I., & Çoklar, A. N. (2007). *İnternet, çocuk ve aile [Internet, child and family]*. Nobel.

OECD. (2020). Bullying. İn PISA 2015 Results (Volume III): Students' Well-Being. OECD Publishing. doi:10.1787/9789264273856-12-en

Oexle, N., Ribeiro, W., Fisher, H. L., Gronholm, P. C., Laurens, K. R., Pan, P., Owens, S., Romeo, R., Rüsch, N., & Lacko, S. E. (2020). Childhood bullying victimization, self-labeling, and help seeking for mental health problems. *Social Psychiatry and Psychiatric Epidemiology*, *55*(1), 81–88. doi:10.100700127-019-01743-5 PMID:31324960

Oksanen, A., Oksa, R., Savela, N., Kaakinen, M., & Ellonen, N. (2020). Cyberbullying victimization at work: Social media identity bubble approach. *Computers in Human Behavior*, *109*, 106363. doi:10.1016/j.chb.2020.106363

Okur Karahan, Ş. (2020). *Examination of the roles of Turkish and Syrian students in the province of Kahramanmaraş in bullying and teachers' attitudes towards bullying* [Master Thesis]. Cerrahpaşa Institute of Forensic Medicine and Forensic Sciences.

Olafsen, R. N., & Viemerö, V. (2000). Bully/victim problems and coping with stress in school among 10- to 12-year-old pupils in Åland, Finland. *Aggressive Behavior*, *26*(1), 57–65. doi:10.1002/(SICI)1098-2337(2000)26:1<57::AID-AB5>3.0.CO;2-I

Olweus, D. (1993a). Bully/victim problems among schoolchildren: Long-term consequences and an effective intervention program. In Mental disorder and crime (pp. 317-349). Academic Press.

Olweus, D. (2022). *Olweus bullying prevention program*. Clemson University. https://olweus.sites.clemson.edu/

Olweus, D., & Limber, S. P. (2019). The olweus bullying prevention program (OBPP): New evaluations and current status. *Making an Impact on School Bullying: Interventions and Recommendations*, 23–44.

Olweus, D., & Solberg, C. (2018). *Bullying among children and young people. Information and guidance for parents*. https://bibliotek.bufdir.no

Olweus, D., Limber, S., & Mihalic, S. F. (1999). Blueprints for violence prevention, book nine: Bullying prevention program. Boulder, CO: Center for the Study and Prevention of Violence.

Olweus, D., Limber, S., & Mihalic, S. F. (1999). Blueprints for violence prevention, book nine: Bullying prevention program. Center for the Study and Prevention of Violence, 12(6), 256–273.

Olweus, D., Limber, S., & Mihalic, S. F. (1999). Bullying prevention program: Blueprints for violence prevention, book nine. Blueprints for violence prevention series. Center for the Study and Prevention of Violence.

Olweus, D. (1978). *Aggression in the schools: Bullies and whipping boys*. Hemisphere.

Olweus, D. (1993). *Bullying at school: What we know and what we can do understanding children's worlds*. Blackwell Publishing Ltd.

Olweus, D. (1993). *Bullying at School: what we know and what we can do*. Blackwell Publishing.

Olweus, D. (1993). *Bullying at school: What we know and what we can do.* Blackwell.

Olweus, D. (1993). *Bullying at School: What we know and what we can do.* Blackwell.

Olweus, D. (1993). *Bullying At School: What We Know and What We Can Do.* Blackwell.

Olweus, D. (1993b). Bully/victim problems among schoolchildren: Long-term consequences and an effective intervention program. In P. Hodgins (Ed.), *Mental disorder and crime.* Sage Publications, Inc.

Olweus, D. (1994). *Bullying at school. long -term outcomes for the victims and an effective school-based intervention program. In Aggressive Behavior: Current Perspectives.* Plenum Press.

Olweus, D. (1994). Bullying at school: Basic facts and effects of a school based intervention program. *Journal of Child Psychology and Psychiatry, and Allied Disciplines, 35*(7), 1171–1190. doi:10.1111/j.1469-7610.1994.tb01229.x PMID:7806605

Olweus, D. (1996). Revised Olweus bully/victim questionnaire. *Journal of Psychopathology and Behavioral Assessment.*

Olweus, D. (1998). Bullying in the schools: How educators can help. *Education Digest*, (7), 30–34.

Olweus, D. (2001). Bullying at school: Tackling the problem. *The OECD Observer. Organisation for Economic Co-Operation and Development*, 24.

Olweus, D. (2003). A profile of bullying at school. *Educational Leadership, 60*(6), 12–17. https://www.researchgate.net/publication/279570438_A_profile_of_bullying_at_school

Olweus, D. (2004). *Bullying at school* (9th ed.). Blackwell.

Olweus, D. (2005). A useful evaluation design, and effects of the Olweus Bullying Prevention Program. *Psychology, Crime & Law, 11*(4), 389–402. doi:10.1080/10683160500255471

Olweus, D. (2012). Cyberbullying: An overrated phenomenon? *European Journal of Developmental Psychology, 9*(5), 520–538. doi:10.1080/17405629.2012.682358

Olweus, D. (2013). School bullying: Development and some important challenges. *Annual Review of Clinical Psychology, 9*(1), 751–780. doi:10.1146/annurev-clinpsy-050212-185516 PMID:23297789

Olweus, D., & Limber, S. (2007). *Olweus bully prevention program: Teacher guide.* Hazelden.

Olweus, D., & Limber, S. P. (2010). Bullying in school: Evaluation and dissemination of the olweus bullying prevention program. *The American Journal of Orthopsychiatry, 80*(1), 124–134. doi:10.1111/j.1939-0025.2010.01015.x PMID:20397997

Olweus, D., & Limber, S. P. (2018). Some problems with cyberbullying research. *Current Opinion in Psychology, 19*, 139–143. doi:10.1016/j.copsyc.2017.04.012 PMID:29279213

Omoteso, B. A. (2010). Bullying behaviour, its associated factors and psychological effects among secondary students in Nigeria. *Journal of International Social Research, 3*(10).

Oned, N., Peter, J., Kraaykamp, G., & Valkenburg, P. M. (2009). Research Note: Digital Divide Across Borders--A Cross-National Study of Adolescents' Use of Digital Technologies. *European Sociological Review, 25*(5), 551–560.

onedio.com. (2021). *Jess Davies, who works as a presenter at the BBC and is also a social media phenomenon, shared an incident of harassment she experienced over the internet.* https://onedio.com/haber/sosyal-medya-uzerinden-mustehcen-goruntulerle-taciz-edilen-bbc-sunucusunun-siber-saldirilara-karsi-isyani-1025414

Ooi, K. B., Lee, V. H., Hew, J. J., & Lin, B. (2019). Mobile social cyberbullying: Why are keyboard warriors raging? *Journal of Computer Information Systems*, *61*(4), 371–382. doi:10.1080/08874417.2019.1679685

Ordem dos Psicólogos, P. (2020). *Recomendações para pais, cuidadores e professores - Cyberbullying e segurança online*. Disponível em: https://www.ordemdospsicologos.pt/ficheiros/documentos/covid_19_cyberbullying_pais.pdf

Orpınas, P., & Horne, A. M. (2010). Creating a Positive School Climate and Developing Social Competence. In The Handbook of Bullying in Schools: An International Perspective Shane (pp. 49-60). Routledge.

Ostrosky, M. M., Mouzourou, C., Dorsey, E. A., Favazza, P. C., & Leboeuf, L. M. (2015). Pick a Book, Any Book: Using Children's Books to Support Positive Attitudes Toward Peers with Disabilities. *Young Exceptional Children*, *18*(1), 30–43. doi:10.1177/1096250613512666

Otero, P. (2017). Sharenting... should children's lives be disclosed on social media? *Archivos Argentinos de Pediatria*, *115*(5), 412–413. PMID:28895685

Ouvrein, G., & Verswijvel, K. (2019). Sharenting: Parental adoration or public humiliation? A focus group study on adolescents' experiences with sharenting against the background of their own impression management. *Children and Youth Services Review*, *99*, 319–327. doi:10.1016/j.childyouth.2019.02.011

Owens, T. J. (1994). Two Dimensions of Self-esteem: Reciprocal effects of positive self-worth and self-deprecation on adolescent problems. *American Sociological Review*, *59*(3), 391–407. doi:10.2307/2095940

Özada, A., & Duyan, V. (2018). Ebeveyn-çocuk ilişkisi ve zorbalık [Parent-child relationships and bullying]. *Turkish Journal of Family Medicine and Primary Care*, *12*(1), 49–55. doi:10.21763/tjfmpc.399941

Özdemir, M., & Akar, F. (2011). An Investigation of the Opinions of High School Students About Cyberbullying in Terms of Some Variables. *Educational Administration: Theory and Practice*, 605-626.

Özdemir, B. G. (2018). *A Film Toz Bezi Criticized by Within The Scope of Identification and Representation Facts Associated With Masquerade and Space in Academic Research in Social, Human and Administrative Sciences II*. Gece Kitaplığı.

Özdemir, M., & Akar, F. (2011). Examination of high school students' opinions on cyberbullying in terms of various variables. *Kuram ve Uygulamada Eğitim Yönetimi*, *17*(4), 605–626.

Ozdemir, M., & Stattin, H. (2011). Bullies, victims, and bully-victims: A longitudinal examination of the effects of bullying-victimization experiences on youth well-being. *Journal of Aggression, Conflict and Peace Research*, *3*(2), 97–102. doi:10.1108/17596591111132918

Ozen Col, S. (2008). Isyerinde psikolojik siddet: hastane calisanlari uzerine bir arastirma [Psychological violence at work: a study on hospital workers]. *Calisma ve Toplum Dergisi*, *4*(19), 107–134.

Özen, Ö., & Kartelli, F. (2017). Analysis of violence in cartoons broadcasted on kids TV channels in Turkey. *Marmara İletişim Dergisi*, *27*, 81–93. doi:10.17829/midr.20172729523

Özer, G. (2016). *Ortaokul öğrencilerinin siber zorbalık yaşama düzeyleri ile siber zorbalığın öğrenciler üzerindeki etkileri ve öğrencilerin siber zorbalıkla baş etme stratejileri* [The cyberbullying levels of secondary school students and the effects of cyberbullying on students and their strategies for coping with cyberbullying] (Master Dissertation).

Özer, Ö. (2001). *Haber Söylem İdeoloji: Eleştirel Haber Çözümlemeleri*. Literatürk Publishers.

Özkan, Y., & Çiftçi, E. G. (2010). Peer bullying in primary schools low socio-economic level. *Elemantary Education Online*, *9*(2), 576–586.

Özözen Danacı, M., Kavaklı, N., & Tıkız, G. (2018). The Effect of Narcissism Levels on Cyberbullying Sensitivity and Internet Addiction Levels of Pre-Service Teachers Studying at the Faculty of Education. *Journal of the National Academy of Education, 2*(2), 86–98.

Öztep, İ. C. (2010). *Duygusal istismar algılayan ve algılamayan ergenlerin kaygı düzeyleri ve denetim odaklarının karşılaştırılması* [Comparison of anxiety levels and locus of control of adolescents who perceive and do not perceive emotional abuse] [Unpublished master's thesis]. Maltepe Üniversitesi, İstanbul.

Öztuna, A. (2018). *Relationship between physiological indications and performing peer victimization and being exposed to peer victimization and ninth and tenth grade students* (UMI No. 526005) [Master's dissertation, İstanbul University]. Higher Education Council Thesis Center database.

Öztürk, S. (2007). *Çocuklarda duygusal istismar* [Emotional abuse in children] [Unpublished master's thesis]. Fırat Üniversitesi, Elazığ.

Öztürk, N., & Atlı, A. (2014). An investigation of bullying cases in middle school students in terms of some variables. *Inonu University Journal of The Faculty of Education, 15*(3), 43–63. doi:10.17679/iuefd.15365258

Özyürek, A., & Kurnaz, F. B. (2019). Evaluation form for bully and victim child behavior: Reliability and validity. *Mersin University Journal of the Faculty of Education, 15*(1), 246–261. doi:10.17860/mersinefd.401251

Padden, C., Humphries, T., & Padden, C. (2009). *Inside deaf culture*. Harvard University Press. doi:10.2307/j.ctvjz83v3

Paez, G. R. (2018). Cyberbullying Among Adolescents: A general strain theory perspective. *Journal of School Violence, 17*(1), 74–85. doi:10.1080/15388220.2016.1220317

Paksoy, N. (2007). Isyerinde Psikolojik Taciz-Yildirma (Mobbing) [Psychological Harassment-Intimidation (Mobbing) at Work]. Isletme Yuksek Lisans Projesi, Sosyal Bilimler Enstitusu, Kahramanmaras Sutcu Imam Universitesi.

Palfrey, J., Boyd, D., & Sacco, D. (2008). *Enhancing Child Safety and Online Technologies: Final Report of the Internet Safety Technical task Force on the MultiState Working Group on Social Networking of Sate attorneys General of the United States*. Harvard University: Berkman Center for Internet and Society.

Palmieri, P. A., & Fitzgerald, L. F. (2005). Confirmatory factor analysis of posttraumatic stress symptoms in sexually harassed women. *Journal of Traumatic Stress, 18*, 657–666.

Papanikolaou, M., Chatzikosma, T., & Kleio, K. (2011). Bullying at School: The role of family. *Procedia: Social and Behavioral Sciences, 29*, 433–442. doi:10.1016/j.sbspro.2011.11.260

Papházy, J. E. (2005). *Violence in schools*. Springer. doi:10.1007/0-387-28811-2_12

Pappa, S., Ntella, V., Giannakas, T., Giannakoulis, V. G., Papoutsi, E., & Katsaounou, P. (2020). Prevalence of depression, anxiety, and insomnia among healthcare workers during the COVID-19 pandemic: A systematic review and meta-analysis. *Brain, Behavior, and Immunity, 88*, 901–907. doi:10.1016/j.bbi.2020.05.026 PMID:32437915

Park, M. A., Golden, K. J., Vizcaino-Vickers, S., Jidong, D., & Raj, S. (2021). Sociocultural Values, Attitudes and Risk Factors Associated with Adolescent Cyberbullying in East Asia: A systematic review. *Cyberpsychology (Brno), 15*(1), 5. doi:10.5817/CP2021-1-5

Parzefall, M.-R., & Salin, D. M. (2010). Perceptions of and reactions to workplace bullying: A social exchange perspective. *Human Relations, 63*(6), 761–780. doi:10.1177/0018726709345043

Pascual-Sanchez, A., Hickey, N., Mateu, A., Martinez-Herves, M., Kramer, T., & Nicholls, D. (2021). Personality traits and self-esteem in traditional bullying and cyberbullying. *Personality and Individual Differences*, *177*, 110809. doi:10.1016/j.paid.2021.110809

Patchin, J. W. (2019, July 9). 2019 Cyberbullying Data. *Cyberbyllying Research Center.* https://cyberbullying.org/2019-cyberbullying-data

Patchin, J. W., & Hinduja, S. (2019). *Life time cyber bullying experiences.* https://cyberbullying.org/Cyberbullying-Research-In-Review.pdf

Patchin, J. W., & Hinduja, S. (2006). Bullies move beyond the schoolyard: A preliminary look at cyberbullying. *Youth Violence and Juvenile Justice*, *4*(2), 148–169. doi:10.1177/1541204006286288

Patchin, J. W., & Hinduja, S. (2006). Bullies Move Beyond the Schoolyard: A Preliminary Look at Cyberbullying. *Youth Violence and Juvenile Justice*, *4*(2), 148–169. https://doi.org/10.1177/1541204006286288

Patchin, J. W., & Hinduja, S. (2011). Traditional and Nontraditional Bullying Among Youth: A test of general strain theory. *Youth & Society*, *43*(2), 727–751. doi:10.1177/0044118X10366951

Patchin, J. W., & Hinduja, S. (2015). Measuring cyberbullying: Implications for research. *Aggression and Violent Behavior*, *23*, 69–74. doi:10.1016/j.avb.2015.05.013

Patchin, J. W., & Hinduja, S. (2022). Cyberbullying Among Tweens in the United States: Prevalence, Impact, and Helping Behaviors. *The Journal of Early Adolescence*, *42*(3), 414–430. doi:10.1177/02724316211036740

Patel, J. H., Moles, D. R., & Cunningham, S. J. (2008). Factors affecting information retention in orthodontic patients. *American Journal of Orthodontics and Dentofacial Orthopedics*, *133*(4), S61–S67. doi:10.1016/j.ajodo.2007.07.019 PMID:18407022

Patrão, I., & Sampaio, D. (2016). *Dependências online. O poder das tecnologias* [Online dependencies. The power of technology]. Pactor.

Patte, K. A., Livermore, M., Qian, W., & Leatherdale, S. T. (2021). Do weight perception and bullying victimization account for links between weight status and mental health among adolescents? *BMC Public Health*, *21*(1), 1–16. doi:10.118612889-021-11037-8 PMID:34088278

Pauline, W., Verlinden, J. M., Berkel, A. D., Mieloo, L. D., Raat, H., Hofman, A., Jaddoe, W. V., Verhulst, F. C., Jansen, W., & Tiemeier, H. (2014). Teacher and peer reports of overweight and bullying among young primary school children. *Pediatrics*, *134*(3). Advance online publication. doi:10.1542/peds.2013-3274 PMID:25157018

Paul, S., Smith, P. K., & Blumberg, H. H. (2013). Surveying bullying using peer nomination methods. *Paediatrics Today (Tuzla)*, *9*(1), 102–111. doi:10.5457/p2005-114.67

Pearce, J. (1992). What can be done about the bullying. In M. Elliot (Ed.), Bullying. A practical guide to coping for schools. Longman.

Pearce, J. (2002). What can be done about the bully. *Bullying a practical guide to coping for schools*, 74-91.

Pearce, J. B., & Thompson, A. E. (2009). Practical approaches to reduce the impact of bullying. *Archives of Disease in Childhood*, *79*(6), 528–531. doi:10.1136/adc.79.6.528 PMID:10211002

Pegis, J. (2013). *Straight Talk About Bullyıng*. Crabtree Publishing Company.

Pei, F., Yoon, S., Maguire-Jack, K., & Lee, M. Y. (2022). Neighborhood influences on early childhood behavioral problems: Child maltreatment as a mediator. *Child Abuse & Neglect*, *123*, 105391. doi:10.1016/j.chiabu.2021.105391 PMID:34768072

Pei, K. Y., Hafler, J., Alseidi, A., Slade, M. D., Klingensmith, M., & Cochran, A. (2020). National Assessment of Workplace Bullying Among Academic Surgeons in the US. *JAMA Surgery*, *155*(6), 524–526. doi:10.1001/jamasurg.2020.0263 PMID:32236505

Pekel, N. (2004). *The Examination of peer victimization groups in terms of sociometric status, loneliness and acedemic achievement* (UMI No. 144590) [Master's dissertation, Hacettepe University]. Higher Education Council Thesis Center database.

Peker, A. (2013). *İnsani değerler yönelimli psikoeğitim programının problemli internet kullanımı ve siber zorbalık üzerindeki etkisi* [The effect of human values-oriented psychoeducation program on problematic internet use and cyberbullying] (Doctoral Dissertation).

Peker, A., Eroğlu, Y. & Şükrü, A. D. A. (2012). The investigation of predictors of cyberbullying and cybervictimization in adolescents. *Abant İzzet Baysal University Journal of Faculty of Education, 12*(2).

Peker, A. (2015). The Investigation of Relationship Between Behavior Aggression and Cyber Bullying in Adolescents. *Ekev Akademik Dergisi*, *19*(61), 323–336.

Peker, A., & Nebioğlu-Yıldız, M. (2021). Mediating Role of Self-control in the Relationship Between Aggressiveness and Cyber Bullying. *Psychiatry and Behavioral Sciences*, *11*(1), 40–49. doi:10.5455/PBS.20210114051215

Pellegrini, A. D. (2002). Bullying, victimization, and sexual harassment during the transition to middle school. *Educational Psychologist*, *37*(3), 151–163. doi:10.1207/S15326985EP3703_2

Pellegrini, A. D., & Long, J. D. (2002). A longitudinal study of bullying, dominance, and victimization during the transition from primary school through secondary school. *British Journal of Developmental Psychology*, *20*(2), 259–280. doi:10.1348/026151002166442

Pennell, D., Campbell, M., & Tangen, D. (2022). The education and the legal system: Inter-systemic collaborations identified by Australian schools to more effectively reduce cyberbullying. *Preventing School Failure*, *66*(2), 175–185. https://doi.org/10.1080/1045988X.2021.2007835

Pepler, D., & Craig, W. (2009). Responding to Bullying and Harassment: An issue of rights. In W. Boyce, J. Roche, & D. Davies (Eds.), *Adolescent health: Policy, science, and human rights* (pp. 173–196). McGill-Queen's University Press.

Pepler, D., & Craig, W. (2014). Bullying Prevention and Intervention. In *The School Environment: Factsheets and Tools*. National Center for Injury Prevention and Control Devision of Violence Prevention.

Pereira, M., Fernandes, O. M., & Relva, I. C. (submitted). *Ciberbullying, ideação suicida e comunicação parental-filial em adolescentes e jovens adultos* [Cyberbullying, suicidal ideation and parent-affiliate communication in adolescents and young adults]. Academic Press.

Perera, A., & Fernando, P. (2021). Accurate Cyberbullying Detection and Prevention on Social Media. *Procedia Computer Science*, *181*, 605–611. doi:10.1016/j.procs.2021.01.207

Perren, S., Stadelmann, S., & Von Klitzing, K. (2009). Child and family characteristics as risk factors for peer victimization in kindergarten. *Schweizerische Zeitschrift fu¨r Bildungswissenschaften, 31*(1), 13–32.

Perren, S., & Alsaker, F. D. (2006). Social behavior and peer relationships of victims, bully victims, and bullies in kindergarten. *Journal of Child Psychology and Psychiatry, and Allied Disciplines*, *47*(1), 45–57. doi:10.1111/j.1469-7610.2005.01445.x PMID:16405640

Perren, S., & Alsaker, F. D. (2006). Social behavior and peer relationships of victims, bully-victims, and bullies in kindergarten. *Journal of Child Psychology and Psychiatry, and Allied Disciplines*, *47*(1), 45–57.

Perren, S., Corcoran, L., Cowie, H., Dehue, F., Mc Guckin, C., Sevcikova, A., ... Völlink, T. (2012). Tackling cyberbullying: Review of Empirical Evidence Regarding Successful Responses by Students, Parents, and Schools. *International Journal of Conflict and Violence*, *6*(2), 283–292.

Perren, S., Dooley, J., Shaw, T., & Cross, D. (2010). Bullying in School and Cyberspace: Associations with depressive symptoms in Swiss and Australian adolescents. *Child and Adolescent Psychiatry and Mental Health*, *4*(1), 1–10. doi:10.1186/1753-2000-4-28 PMID:21092266

Peter, I.-K., & Petermann, F. (2018). Cyberbullying: A concept analysis of defining attributes and additional influencing factors. *Computers in Human Behavior*, *86*, 350–366. doi:10.1016/j.chb.2018.05.013

Petersen, P. E. (2003). The World Oral Health Report 2003: Continuous improvement of oral health in the 21st century–the approach of the WHO Global Oral Health Programme. *Community Dentistry and Oral Epidemiology*, *31*, 3–24. doi:10.1046/j..2003.com122.x PMID:15015736

Petersen, P. E., Bourgeois, D., Ogawa, H., Estupinan-Day, S., & Ndiaye, C. (2005). The global burden of oral diseases and risks to oral health. *Bulletin of the World Health Organization*, *83*, 661–669. PMID:16211157

Petric, D. (2022). Psychology of Abusive Human Behavior. *Open Journal of Medical Psychology*, *11*(02), 29–38. https://doi.org/10.4236/ojmp.2022.112003

Petrosino, A., Guckenburg, S., DeVoe, J., & Hanson, T. (2010). What characteristics of bullying, bullying victims, and schools are associated with increased reporting of bullying to school officials? Issues & Answers Report, REL 2010, No. 092, US Department of Education, Institute of Education Sciences, National Center for Education Evaluation and Regional Assistance, Regional Educational Laboratory Northeast and Islands, Washington, DC. doi:10.1037/e598622011-001

Petska, H. W., Porada, K., Nugent, M., Simpson, P., & Sheets, L. K. (2019). Occult drug exposure in young children evaluated for physical abuse: An opportunity for intervention. *Child Abuse & Neglect*, *88*, 412–419.

Phillips, A. (1998). Terrors and experts (T. Erdem, Trans.). İstanbul, Turkey: Metis Yayınları.

Phillips, S. P., & Schneider, M. S. (1993). Sexual harassment of female doctors by patients. *The New England Journal of Medicine*, *329*(26), 1936–1939. doi:10.1056/NEJM199312233292607 PMID:8247058

Pichel, R., Feijoo, S., Isorna, M., Varela, J., & Rial, A. (2022). Analysis of the relationship between school bullying, cyberbullying, and substance use. *Children and Youth Services Review*, *134*, 106369. doi:10.1016/j.childyouth.2022.106369

Pigozi, P. L., & Jones Bartoli, A. (2016). School Nurses' Experiences in Dealing With Bullying Situations Among Students. *The Journal of School Nursing: the Official Publication of the National Association of School Nurses*, *32*(3), 177–185. doi:10.1177/1059840515613140 PMID:26502929

Pina, A., Gannon, T. A., & Saunders, B. (2009). An overview of the literature on sexual harassment: Perpetrator, theory, and treatment issues. *Aggression and Violent Behavior*, *14*(2), 126–138.

Pinar, T., Acikel, C., Pinar, G., Karabulut, E., Saygun, M., Bariskin, E., & Cengiz, M. (2017). Workplace Violence in the Health Sector in Turkey: A National Study. *Journal of Interpersonal Violence*, *32*(15), 2345–2365. doi:10.1177/0886260515591976 PMID:26124224

Pişkin, M. (2003). A common problem in our schools: Peer bullying. In *7. National Psychological Counseling and Guidance Congress*. İnönü University.

Pişkin, M. (2002). Okul zorbalığı, tanımı, türleri, ilişkili olduğu faktörler ve alınabilecek önlemler [School bullying: Definition, types, related factors, and strategies to prevent bullying problems]. *Educational Sciences: Theory and Practice*, *2*, 531–562.

Pişkin, M. (2002). Okul zorbalığı: Tanımı, türleri, ilişkili olduğu faktörler ve alınabilecek önlemler (School bullying: Definition, types, related factors and measures to be taken). *Kuram ve Uygulamada Eğitim Bilimleri*, *2*(2), 531–562.

Pişkin, M. (2002). Okul zorbalığı: Tanımı, türleri, ilişkili olduğu faktörler ve alınabilecek önlemler [School bullying: Definition, types, related factors and measures to be taken]. *Kuram ve Uygulamada Eğitim Bilimleri*, *2*(2), 531–562.

Pişkin, M. (2002). School bullying, its definition, types, related factors and measures to be taken. *Educational Sciences: Theory and Practice*, *2*, 531–562.

Pişkin, M. (2002). School bullying: Definition, types, associated factors and precautions to take. *Educational Sciences: Theory and Practice*, *2*(2), 531–562. https://app.trdizin.gov.tr/makale/TWpFME1qST0/okul-zorbaligi-tanimi-turleri-iliskili-oldugu-faktorler-ve-alinabilecek-onlemler

Pişkin, M. (2006). School violence: Definition, prevalence and prevention strategies. *Social Policy in the Public*, *1*(2), 4–62.

Pişkin, M., Atik, G., Çınkır, Ş., Öğülmüş, S., & Babadoğan, C., & Çokluk, Ö. (2014). Öğretmen şiddeti ölçeği'nin geliştirilmesi ve doğrulanması [Development and validation of the teacher violence scale]. *Eurasian Journal of Educational Research*, *56*, 1–24.

Pithon, M. M., Andrade, D., Fernandes, I., Mendes, J., Nunes, K., Michele, L., Ribeiro, A. V., & da Silva Coqueiro, R. (2014). Influence of malocclusion on social perceptions of adolescents at public and private schools. *European Archives of Paediatric Dentistry; Official Journal of the European Academy of Paediatric Dentistry*, *15*(1), 37–43. doi:10.100740368-013-0050-7 PMID:23797925

Pitot, M. A., White, M. A., Edney, E., Mogensen, M. A., Solberg, A., Kattapuram, T., & Kadom, N. (2022). The current state of gender discrimination and sexual harassment in the radiology workplace: A survey. *Academic Radiology*, *29*(3), 416–425. doi:10.1016/j.acra.2021.01.002 PMID:33495074

Pitsia, V., & Mazzone, A. (2020). The association of individual and contextual variables with bullying victimisation: A cross-national comparison between Ireland and Lithuania. *European Journal of Psychology of Education*, *36*, 1095–1115. doi:10.100710212-020-00514-0

Pokin, S. (2007, November 13). Megan Meier story. *The St. Charles Journal*.

Polanco-Levicán, K., & Salvo-Garrido, S. (2021). Bystander roles in cyberbullying: A mini-review of who, how many, and why. *Frontiers in Psychology*. https://www.frontiersin.org/article/10.3389/fpsyg.2021.676787

Polanin, J. R., Espelage, D. L., Grotpeter, J. K., Ingram, K., Michaelson, L., Spinney, E., Valido, A., El Sheikh, A., Torgal, C., & Robinson, L. (2022). A Systematic Review and Meta-analysis of Interventions to Decrease Cyberbullying Perpetration and Victimization. *Prevention Science*, *23*(3), 439–454. https://doi.org/10.1007/s11121-021-01259-y

Polanin, J. R., Espelage, D. L., & Pigott, T. D. (2012). A meta-analysis of school-based bullying prevention programs" effects on by stander intervention behavior. *School Psychology Review*, *41*(1), 47–65. doi:10.1080/02796015.2012.12087375

Polaschek, D. L. L., & Ward, T. (2002). The implicit theories of potential rapists: What our questionnaires tell us. *Aggression and Violent Behavior*, *7*(4), 385–406.

Polat, O. (2016). Şiddet [Violence]. *Marmara Üniversitesi Hukuk Fakültesi Hukuk Araştırmaları Dergisi, 22*(1), 15–34.

Ponte, C., & Batista, S. (2018). *EU Kids Online Portugal - 2018: Usos, competências, riscos e mediações da internet reportados por crianças e jovens (9 -17 Anos)* [EU Kids Online Portugal - 2018: Uses, competencies, risks and internet mediations reported by children and young people (9 -17 Years)]. EU Kids Online; NOVA FCSH. Disponível em: http://www.fcsh.unl.pt/eukidsonline/documentos/

Popović-Ćitić, B., Djurić, S., & Cvetković, V. (2011). The prevalence of cyberbullying among adolescents: A case study of middle schools in Serbia. *School Psychology International, 32*(4), 412–424. doi:10.1177/0143034311401700

Pornari, C. D., & Wood, J. (2010). Peer and Cyber Aggression in Secondary School Students: The role of moral disengagement, hostile attribution bias, and outcome expectancies. Aggressive Behavior. *Official Journal of the International Society for Research on Aggression, 36*(2), 81–94. doi:10.1002/ab.20336 PMID:20035548

Porter, C., Devaraj, S., & Sun, D. (2013). A test of two models of value creation in virtual communities. *Journal of Management Information Systems, 30*(1), 261–292. doi:10.2753/MIS0742-1222300108

Porter, L. (2007). *Bullying. Student behaviour: Theory and practice for teachers* (3rd ed.). Allen and Unwin.

Potts, N., & Mandleco, B. (2007). *Pediatric nursing*. Delmar.

Price, D., Green, D., Spears, B., Scrimgeour, M., Barnes, A., Geer, R., & Johnson, B. (2014). A qualitative exploration of cyberbystanders and moral engagement. *Australian Journal of Guidance & Counselling, 24*(1), 1–17. doi:10.1017/jgc.2013.18

Pricewaterhouse Coopers (PwC). (2012). *Health Research Institute. 2012. Social media "Likes" healthcare. From marketing to social business*. https://www.pwc.com/us/en/health-industries/health-research-institute/publications/pdf/health-care-social-media-report.pdf

Prino, L. E., Longobardi, C., Fabris, M. A., Parada, R. H., & Settanni, M. (2019). Effects of bullying victimization on internalizing and externalizing symptoms: The mediating role of alexithymia. *Journal of Child and Family Studies, 28*(9), 2586–2593. doi:10.100710826-019-01484-8

Privitera, C., & Campbell, M. A. (2009). Cyberbullying: The new face of workplace bullying? *Cyberpsychology & Behavior, 12*(4), 395–400. doi:10.1089/cpb.2009.0025 PMID:19594381

Promundo & UN Women. (2017). *Understanding Masculinities: Results from the International Men and Gender Equality Survey (IMAGES) – Middle East and North Africa, UN Women Headquarters*. https://www.unwomen.org/en/digital-library/publications/2017/5/understanding-masculinities-results-from-the-images-in- the-middle-east-and-north-africa

Protogerou, C., & Flisher, A. J. (2012). Bullying in schools. In A. van Niekerk, S. Suffla & M. Seedat (Eds.), Crime, violence and injury in South Africa: 21st century solutions for child safety (pp.119-133). MRC-University of South Africa Safety & Peace Promotion Research Unit.

Pryor, J. B. (1987). Sexual harassment proclivities in men. *Sex Roles, 17*(5), 269–290.

Pryor, J. B. (1995). The phenomenology of sexual harassment: Why does sexual behavior bother people in the workplace. *Consulting Psychology Journal, 47*, 160–168.

Pryor, J. B., & Stoller, L. M. (1994). Sexual cognition processes in men who are high in the likelihood to sexually harass. *Personality and Social Psychology Bulletin, 20*, 163–169.

Public Safety Canada. (2010). *Canada's cyber security strategy: For a stronger and more prosperous Canada*. Retrieved from: https://www.publicsafety.gc.ca/cnt/rsrcs/pblctns/cbr-scrtstrtgy/ cbr-scrt-strtgy-eng.pdf

Putri, S. A. R., & Prihandari Satvikadewi, A. A. I. (2017). A Critical Discourse Analysis Study of Cyberbullying in LGBTQ's Instagram Account. In *SHS Web of Conferences* (Vol. 33). Academic Press.

Pyżalski, J. (2013). Beyond Peer Cyberbullying: Involvement of Polish adolescents in different kinds of electronic aggression. *Studia Edukacyjne.*, *28*, 147–167.

Quick, J. C., & McFadyen, M. (2017). Sexual harassment: Have we made any progress? *Journal of Occupational Health Psychology*, *22*(3), 286–298. doi:10.1037/ocp0000054 PMID:27732009

Quine, L. (2002). Workplace bullying in junior doctors: Questionnaire survey. *BMJ (Clinical Research Ed.)*, *324*(7342), 878–879. doi:10.1136/bmj.324.7342.878 PMID:11950736

Rafferty, R., & Vander Ven, T. (2014). I hate everything about you: A qualitative examination of cyberbullying and online aggression in a college sample. *Deviant Behavior*, *35*(5), 364–377. doi:10.1080/01639625.2013.849171

Rajion, Z. A., & Alwi, Z. (2007). Genetics of cleft lip and palate: A review. *The Malaysian Journal of Medical Sciences: MJMS*, *14*(1), 4. PMID:22593645

Ramdeo, S., & Singh, R. (2020). Cyberbullying in the Workplace. In Encyclopedia of Criminal Activities and the Deep Web. IGI Global. doi:10.4018/978-1-5225-9715-5.ch047

Ramdeo, S., Balwant, P. T., Cowell, N., & Persadie, N. (2020). The moderated mediation model of bullying, support, justice, and organizational outcomes. *International Journal of Employment Studies.*, *28*(1), 48–81.

Ramdeo, S., & Singh, R. (2021). Out with the Old, in with the New: Innovative Work Practices for Navigating the Unknown. In B. Mehta (Ed.), *The Impact of COVID-19 on Human Resource Management* (pp. 57–67). Proud Pen. doi:10.51432/978-1-8381524-4-4_5

Raskauskas, J., & Stoltz, A. D. (2004). Identifying and intervening in relational aggression. *The Journal of School Nursing: the Official Publication of the National Association of School Nurses*, *20*(4), 209–215. doi:10.1177/10598405040200040501 PMID:15283614

Raskauskas, J., & Stoltz, A. D. (2007). Involvement in traditional and electronic bullying among adolescents. *Developmental Psychology*, *43*(3), 564–575. doi:10.1037/0012-1649.43.3.564 PMID:17484571

Rayner, C., & Hoel, H. (1997). A Summary Review of Literature Relating to Workplace Bullying. *Journal of Community & Applied Social Psychology*, *7*(3), 181–191. doi:10.1002/(SICI)1099-1298(199706)7:3<181::AID-CASP416>3.0.CO;2-Y

Reid Chassiakos, Y. L., Radesky, J., Christakis, D., Moreno, M. A., Cross, C., Hill, D., ... Swanson, W. S. (2016). Children and adolescents and digital media. *Pediatrics*, *138*(5), 1–18.

Remillard, A. M., & Lamb, S. (2005). Adolescent girls' coping with relational aggression. *Sex Roles*, *53*(3), 221–229. doi:10.100711199-005-5680-8

Research Service Member. (2018). *Victims Of Cyberbullying*. European Parliamentary Research Service Blog. https://epthinktank.eu/2018/10/28/victims-of-cyberbullying-what-europe-does-for-you/

Reulbach, U., Ladewig, E. L., Nixon, E., O'Moore, M., Williams, J., & O'Dowd, T. (2013). Weight, body image and bullying in 9-year-old children. *Journal of Paediatrics and Child Health*, *49*(4), 288–293. doi:10.1111/jpc.12159 PMID:23530984

Rey, L., Neto, F., & Extremera, N. (2020). Cyberbullying victimization and somatic complaints: A prospective examination of cognitive emotion regulation strategies as mediators. *International Journal of Clinical and Health Psychology*, *20*(2), 135–139. doi:10.1016/j.ijchp.2020.03.003 PMID:32550853

Riaz, A. (2022). *How Bangladesh's Digital Security Act Is Creating a Culture of Fear - Carnegie Endowment for International Peace*. Carnegie Endowment for International Peace. https://carnegieendowment.org/2021/12/09/how-bangladesh-s-digital-security-act-is-creating-culture-of-fear-pub-85951

Ricciardelli, L. A., & Yager, Z. (2015). *Adolescence and body image: From development to preventing dissatisfaction*. Routledge., doi:10.4324/9781315849379

Rideout, V., & Robb, M. B. (2019). *The Common Sense Census: Media Use by Tweens and Teen*. Academic Press.

Rigby, K. (1999). Peer victimisation at school and the health of secondary school students. *The British Journal of Educational Psychology*, *69*(1), 95–104. doi:10.1348/000709999157590 PMID:10230345

Rigby, K. (2002). Bullying in childhood. In P. K. Smith & C. H. Hart (Eds.), *Blackwell handbooks of developmental psychology. Blackwell handbook of childhood social development* (pp. 549–568). Blackwell.

Rigby, K. (2002). *New perspectives on bullying*. Jessica Kingsley Publishers.

Rigby, K. (2003). Consequences of bullying in school. *Canadian Journal of Psychiatry*, *48*(9), 583–590. doi:10.1177/070674370304800904 PMID:14631878

Rigby, K. (2003). *Stop the bullying: a handbook for schools*. ACER Press.

Riggs, S. A., & Kaminski, P. (2010). Childhood emotional abuse, adult attachment, and depression as predictors of relational adjustment and psychological aggression. *Journal of Aggression, Maltreatment & Trauma*, *19*(1), 75–104. doi:10.1080/10926770903475976

Ring, A. (2000a). Advertising and the Body as Ideal Image. In *The Encultured Body: Policy Implications for Healthy Body Image and Disordered Eating Behaviours*. Queensland University of Technology.

Ring, A. (2000b). Cosmetic Surgery and the Body as Work-in-Progress. In *The Encultured Body: Policy Implications for Healthy Body Image and Disordered Eating Behaviours*. Queensland University of Technology.

Rivara, F., & Le Menestrel, S. (2016). Preventing Bullying Through Science, Policy, and Practice - NCBI Bookshelf. National Academies Press (US).

Rivers, I., & Noret, N. (2009). 'I h8 u': findings from a five-year study of text and email bullying. *British Educational Research Journal*, *36*(4), 643–671. doi:10.1080/01411920903071918

Rivers, I., & Noret, N. (2010). Participant roles in bullying behavior and their association with thought's of ending one's life. *Crisis*, *31*(3), 143–148. Advance online publication. doi:10.1027/0227-5910/a000020 PMID:20573608

Rivers, I., Poteat, V. P., Noret, N., & Ashurst, N. (2009). Observing bullying at school: The mental health implications of witness status. *School Psychology Quarterly*, *24*(4), 211–223. doi:10.1037/a0018164

Rivituso, J. (2014). Cyberbullying Victimization Among College Students: An interpretive phenomenological analysis. *Journal of Information Systems Education*, *25*(1), 71.

Robert, E. (2021). Attempting a definition of cyber crime. *SSRN Electronic Journal*. doi:10.2139/ssrn.3830589

Roberto, A. J., Eden, J., Savage, M. W., Ramos-Salazar, L., & Deiss, D. M. (2014). Prevalence and Predictors of Cyberbullying Perpetration by High School Seniors. *Communication Quarterly*, *62*(1), 97–114. doi:10.1080/01463373.2013.860906

Robinson, R. K. (n.d.). Sexual harassment in the workplace: Guidelines for educating healthcare managers. *Journal of Health and Human Services Administration*, *27*(4), 501–530. PMID:16318016

Robson, C., & Witenberg, R. T. (2013). The influence of Moral Disengagement, Morally Based Self-esteem, Age, and Gender on Traditional Bullying and Cyberbullying. *Journal of School Violence, 12*(2), 211–231. doi:10.1080/15388220.2012.762921

Rodkin, P. C., Farmer, T. W., Pearl, R., & Van Acker, R. (2006). They're cool: Social status and peer group supports for aggressive boys and girls. *Social Development, 15*(2), 175–204. doi:10.1111/j.1467-9507.2006.00336.x

Rodkin, P. C., & Hodges, E. V. E. (2003). Bullies and victims in the peer ecology: Four questions for psychologists and school professionals. *School Psychology Review, 32*(3), 384–400. doi:10.1080/02796015.2003.12086207

Rodriguez-Rivas, M. E., Varela, J., González, C., & Chuecas, M. J. (2022). The role of family support and conflict in cyberbullying and subjective well-being among Chilean adolescents during the Covid-19 period. *Heliyon, 8*(4). doi:10.1016/j.heliyon.2022.e09243

Roelants, M., & Cameron, N. (2022). Adolescent growth. In *Human Growth and Development* (pp. 101–123). Academic Press., doi:10.1016/B978-0-12-822652-0.00015-8.

Rogers, V. (2010). *Cyberbullying: Activities to help children and teens to stay safe in a texting, twittering, social networking world.* Jessica Kingsley Publishers.

Roland, E. (2002). Aggression, depression, and bullying others. *Aggressive Behavior: Official Journal of the International Society for Research on Aggression, 28*(3), 198–206. doi:10.1002/ab.90022

Romeo, F. F. (2000). The educator's role ın reporting the emotional abuse of children. *Journal of Instructional Psychology, 27*(3), 183–186.

Romera, E. M., Ortega-Ruiz, R., Runions, K., & Camacho, A. (2021). Bullying perpetration, moral disengagement and need for popularity: Examining reciprocal associations in adolescence. *Journal of Youth and Adolescence, 50*(10), 2021–2035. doi:10.100710964-021-01482-4 PMID:34331660

Romero, A. J., Wiggs, V. B., Valencia, C., & Bauman, S. (2013). Latina teen suicide and bullying. *Hispanic Journal of Behavioral Sciences*, 1–15. doi:10.1177/0739986312474237

Romiszowski, A., & Mason, R. (2013). Computer-mediated communication. In D. Jonassen & M. Driscoll (Eds.), *Handbook of research on educational communications and technology* (pp. 402–436). Routledge.

Romito, P., Cedolin, C., Bastiani, F., & Saurel-Cubizolles, M. J. (2019). Disordered Eating Behaviors and Sexual Harassment in Italian Male and Female University Students. *Journal of Interpersonal Violence, 34*(14), 2960–2974. https://doi.org/10.1177/0886260516664315

Rosa, H., Pereira, N., Ribeiro, R., Ferreira, P. C., Carvalho, J. P., Oliveira, S., Coheur, L., Paulino, P., Veiga Simão, A. M., & Trancoso, I. (2019). Automatic cyberbullying detection: A systematic review. *Computers in Human Behavior, 93*, 333–345. doi:10.1016/j.chb.2018.12.021

Rose, C. A., Monda-Amaya, L. E., & Espelage, D. L. (2011). Bullying perpetration and victimization in special education: A review of the literature. *Remedial and Special Education, 32*(2), 114–130. doi:10.1177/0741932510361247

Rose, C. A., Swearer, S. M., & Espelage, D. L. (2012). Bullying and students with disabilities: The untold narrative. *Focus on Exceptional Children, 45*(2), 1–10. doi:10.17161/foec.v45i2.6682

Rosenberg, M. (1965). Rosenberg self-esteem scale. *Journal of Religion and Health.*

Rosenberg, M., Schooler, C., & Schoenbach, C. (1989). Self-esteem and Adolescent Problems: Modeling reciprocal effects. *American Sociological Review, 54*(6), 1004–1018. doi:10.2307/2095720

Rotundo, M., Nguyen, D. H., & Sackett, P. R. (2001). A meta-analytic review of gender differences in perceptions of sexual harassment. *The Journal of Applied Psychology, 86*(5), 914–922.

Rowell, P. A. (2005). Being a "target" at work: Or William Tell and how the apple felt. JONA. *The Journal of Nursing Administration, 35*(9), 377–379. doi:10.1097/00005110-200509000-00002 PMID:16200000

Rowe, M. M., & Sherlock, H. (2005). Stress and verbal abuse in nursing: Do burned out nurses eat their young? *Journal of Nursing Management, 13*(3), 242–248. doi:10.1111/j.1365-2834.2004.00533.x PMID:15819837

Royal College of Nursing (Great Britain). (2000). *Bullying and harassment at work: a good practice guide for RCN negotiators and health care managers.* Royal College of Nursing.

Runa, S. J. (2019). The Challenges of Freedom of Expression and the Digital Security Act 2018. *BiLD Law Journal, 4*(2), 75–92. https://bildbd.com/index.php/blj/article/view/20

Russell, D. E. H. (1984). *Sexual exploitation: Rape, child sexual abuse, and workplace harassment.* Sage.

Russell, S. T., Toomey, R. B., Ryan, C., & Diaz, R. M. (2014). Being out at school: The implications for school victimization and young adult adjustment. *The American Journal of Orthopsychiatry, 84*(6), 635–643. doi:10.1037/ort0000037 PMID:25545431

S, C. (2011). *Developing a framework for public health law in Europe.* Retrieved from http://www.euro.who.int/__data/assets/pdf_file/0004/151375/e95783.pdf

Saarento, S., Kärnä, A., Hodges, E. V. E., & Salmivalli, C. (2013). Student-, classroom-, and school-level risk factors for victimization. *Journal of School Psychology, 51*(3), 421–434. doi:10.1016/j.jsp.2013.02.002 PMID:23816233

sabah.com. (2022). *Cyber pervert! he has been harassed every day for 7 months.* https://www.sabah.com.tr/yasam/universite-ogrencisi-derya-kusa-sapik-kabusu-5860717

Sabak, M., Al-Hadidi, A., Oktay, M. M., Al, B., Kazaz, T., Kowalenko, T., & Hakmeh, W. (2021). Workplace violence in emergency departments in Turkey. *Avicenna Journal of Medicine, 11*(03), 111–117. doi:10.1055-0041-1732284 PMID:34646787

Sağlam, M., & Aral, N. (2016). Tarihsel süreç içerisinde çocuk ve çocukluk kavramları. *Çocuk ve Medeniyet Dergisi, 2*, 43-56.

Şahin, M., & Akbaba, S. (2017). *Okulda ve Sanal Ortamda Zorbalık ve Empati.* Nobel.

Sakarya, S., & Pekdoğan, S. (2020). The predictive power of temperament traits on the bully and victim behaviors of the child. *International Journal of Euroasian Research, 8*(23), 311–324. doi:10.33692/avrasyad.655616

Sa, L., & Fleming, M. (2008). Bullying, burnout, and mental health amongst Portuguese nurses. *Issues in Mental Health Nursing, 29*(4), 411–426. doi:10.1080/01612840801904480 PMID:18382918

Saleh, L., Niroumand, S., Dehghani, Z., Afshari Saleh, T., Mousavi, S. M., & Zakeri, H. (2020). Relationship between workplace violence and work stress in the emergency department. *Journal of Injury & Violence Research, 12*(2), 183–190. doi:10.5249/jivr.vol12i2.1526 PMID:32653889

Salı, G. (2014). An examination of peer relationships and exposure to peer violence among pre-school children in terms of different variables. *Cukurova University Faculty of Education Journal, 43*(2), 195-216. https://dergipark.org.tr/tr/download/article-file/46526

Salin, D. (2005). Workplace bullying among business professionals: Prevalence, gender differences and the role of organizational politics. *Perspectives interdisciplinaires sur le travail et la santé.*

Salin, D. M. (2003). Ways of Explaining Workplace Bullying: A Review of Enabling, Motivating and Precipitating Structures and Processes in the Work Environment. *Human Relations, 56*(10), 1213–1232. doi:10.1177/00187267035610003

Salmivalli, C. (2010). Zorbalık ve akran grubu: Bir inceleme [Bullying and the peer group: A review]. *Saldırganlık ve şiddet davranışı, 15*(2), 112-120.

Salmivalli, C. (2010). Bullying and the peer group: A review. *Aggression and Violent Behavior, 15*(2), 112–120. doi:10.1016/j.avb.2009.08.007

Salmivalli, C., Karna, A., & Poskiparta, E. (2009). *From peer putdowns to peer support: A theoretical model and how it translated into a national anti-bullying program.* Academic Press.

Salmivalli, C., Kärna, A., & Poskiparta, E. (2011). Counteracting bullying in Finland: The KiVA Program and its effects on different forms of being bullied. *International Journal of Behavioral Development, 35*(5), 405–411. doi:10.1177/0165025411407457

Salmivalli, C., Kaukiainen, A., & Voeten, M. (2005). Anti-bullying intervention implementation and outcome. *The British Journal of Educational Psychology, 75*(3), 465–487. doi:10.1348/000709905X26011 PMID:16238877

Salmivalli, C., Poskiparta, E., Ahtola, A., & Haataja, A. (2013). The Implementation and Effectiveness of the KiVa Antibullying Program in Finland. *European Psychologist, 18*(2), 79–88. doi:10.1027/1016-9040/a000140

Samnani, A.-K., & Singh, P. (2014). Performance-enhancing compensation practices and employee productivity: The role of workplace bullying. *Human Resource Management Review, 24*(1), 5–16. doi:10.1016/j.hrmr.2013.08.013

Sanders, C. E. (2004). What is bullying? In *Bullying* (pp. 1–16). Academic Press. doi:10.1016/B978-012617955-2/50004-7

Sanders, F., Gwynne, E., & Gaskill, D. (2000). Barbie Magazine: The First 12 Months. In *The Encultured Body: Policy Implications for Healthy Body Image and Disordered Eating Behaviours.* Queensland University of Technology.

Sarak, Ö. (2012). *Cyber bullying in high school students* (Unpublished Master's Thesis). Haliç University, İstanbul.

Sari, S. V., & Camadan, F. (2016). The new face of violence tendency: Cyber bullying perpetrators and their victims. *Computers in Human Behavior, 59*, 317–326. doi:10.1016/j.chb.2016.02.027

Sarmaşık, Ş. (2009). *İşyerinde cinsel taciz algılaması ve yönetim ilişkilerine etkisi hakkında bir araştırma [Detection of sexual harassment at work and the research about it effects on management relations].* Yayımlanmamış Yüksek Lisans Tezi, Pamukkale Üniversitesi.

Satan, A. (2011). The relationship of between peer pressure self-esteem and alcohol use among adolescents. *Marmara University Atatürk Education Faculty Journal of Educational Sciences, 34*(34), 183-194. https://dergipark.org.tr/tr/pub/maruaebd/issue/376/2488

Satan, A. (2011). Investigating the prevalence and impact of peer abuse (bullying) on the development of Jamaica's children report. *Marmara University Atatürk Education Faculty Journal of Educational Science, 34*, 183–194.

Sbraga, T. P., & O'donohue, W. (2000). Sexual harassment. *Annual Review of Sex Research, 11*(1), 258–285.

Schacter, H. L., Lessard, L. M., Kiperman, S., Bakth, F., Ehrhardt, A., & Uganski, J. (2021). Can friendships protect against the health consequences of peer victimization in adolescence? A systematic review. *School Mental Health, 13*(3), 578–601. doi:10.100712310-021-09417-x

Scheffel, D. L. S., Jeremias, F., Fragelli, C. M. B., dos Santos-Pinto, L. A. M., Hebling, J., & de Oliveira, O. B. Jr. (2014). Esthetic dental anomalies as motive for bullying in schoolchildren. *European Journal of Dentistry, 8*(01), 124–128. doi:10.4103/1305-7456.126266 PMID:24966759

Scheithauer, H., Hayer, T., Petermann, F., & Jugert, G. (2006). Physical, verbal, and relational forms of bullying among german students: Age trends, gender differences, and correlates. *Aggressive Behavior: Official Journal of The International Society For Research On Aggression, 32*(3), 261–275. doi:10.1002/ab.20128

Schoen, S., & Schoen, A. (2010). Bullying and harassment in the United States. *The Clearing House: A Journal of Educational Strategies, Issues and Ideas, 83*(2), 68–72. doi:10.1080/00098650903386444

Scholcoff, C., Farkas, A., Machen, J. L., Kay, C., Nickoloff, S., Fletcher, K. E., & Jackson, J. L. (2020). Sexual harassment of female providers by patients: A qualitative study. *Journal of General Internal Medicine, 35*(10), 2963–2968. doi:10.100711606-020-06018-3 PMID:32700219

Schoon, P. M., Porta, C. M., & Schaffer, M. A. (2018). Population-based public health clinical manual: The Henry Street model for nurses (3rd ed.). Sigma Theta Tau International Society of Nursing.

Schwartz, D., Dodge, K. A., Petit, G. S., & Bates, J. e. (1997). The early socialization of aggressive victims of bullying. *Child Development, 68*(4), 665–675. doi:10.2307/1132117 PMID:9306645

Schwartz, D., McFadyen-Ketchum, S., Dodge, K. A., Pettit, G. S., & Bates, J. E. (1999). Early behavior problems as a predictor of later peer group victimization: Moderators and mediators in the pathways of social risk. *Journal of Abnormal Child Psychology, 27*(3), 191–201. doi:10.1023/A:1021948206165 PMID:10438185

Seals, D., & Young, J. (2003). Bullying and victimization: Prevalence and relationship to gender, grade level, ethnicity, self-esteem, and depression. *Adolescence, 38*(152). PMID:15053498

Seçkin, Z. (2017). *Örgütlerde mobbing ve siber zorbalık [Mobbing and cyberbullying in organizations].* Çizgi.

Seefeldt, V. D., & Ewing, M. E. (1997). Youth sports in America: An overview. *President's Council on Physical Fitness and Sports Research Digest.*

Seehra, J., Fleming, P. S., Newton, T., & DiBiase, A. T. (2011). Bullying in orthodontic patients and its relationship to malocclusion, self-esteem and oral health-related quality of life. *Journal of Orthodontics, 38*(4), 247–256. doi:10.1179/14653121141641 PMID:22156180

Seehra, J., Newton, J. T., & DiBiase, A. T. (2011). Bullying in schoolchildren–its relationship to dental appearance and psychosocial implications: An update for GDPs. *British Dental Journal, 210*(9), 411–415. doi:10.1038j.bdj.2011.339 PMID:21566605

Seehra, J., Newton, J. T., & DiBiase, A. T. (2013). Interceptive orthodontic treatment in bullied adolescents and its impact on self-esteem and oral-health-related quality of life. *European Journal of Orthodontics, 35*(5), 615–621. doi:10.1093/ejo/cjs051 PMID:22843555

Segura, M. D., & Pecino, R. M. (2015). Cyberbullying Trough Mobile Phone and the Internet in Dating Relationships Among Youth People. *Comunicar. Media Education Research Journal, 23*(1).

Seixas, S., Fernandes, L., & Morais, T. (2016). *Cyberbullying – Um guia para pais e educadores* [A guide for parents and educators]. Plátano Editora.

Selçuk, Z., & Güner, N. (2004). *Sınıf içi rehberlik uygulamaları* [In-class guidance applications]. 4th ed.). Pegem A.

Selkie, E. M., Kota, R., & Moreno, M. (2016). Cyberbullying behaviors among female college students: Witnessing, perpetration and victimization. *College Student Journal, 50*, 278–287. PMID:28966413

Sengupta, A., & Chaudhuri, A. (2011). Are social networking sites a source of online harrassment for teens? Evidence from survey data. *Children and Youth Services Review, 33*(2), 284–290. doi:10.1016/j.childyouth.2010.09.011

Sentenac, M., Arnaud, C., Gavin, A., Molcho, M., Gabhainn, S. N., & Godeau, E. (2012). Peer victimization among school-aged children with chronic conditions. *Epidemiologic Reviews*, *34*, 120–128. doi:10.1093/epirev/mxr024

Sentse, M., Veenstra, R., Kiuru, N., & Salmivalli, C. (2015). A Longitudinal Multilevel Study of Individual Characteristics and Classroom Norms in Explaining Bullying Behaviors. *Journal of Abnormal Child Psychology*, *43*(5), 943–955. doi:10.100710802-014-9949-7 PMID:25370007

Serin, H. (2012). *Cyberbullying/Cyber victimization experiences in adolescents and the opinion of teachers and education managers about this behaviours* [Ergenlerde Siber Zorbalık/Siber Mağduriyet Yaşantıları ve Bu Davranışlara İlişkin Öğretmen ve Eğitim Yöneticilerinin Görüşleri]. İstanbul University, Institute of Social Sciences.

Serin, H. (2012). *Ergenlerde Siber Zorbalık / Siber mağduriyet yaşantıları ve bu davranışlara ilişkin öğretmen ve eğitim yöneticilerinin görüşleri* (Unpublished Doctoral Thesis). İstanbul Üniversitesi, İstanbul.

Serra-Negra, J. M., Paiya, S. M., Bendo, C. B., Fulgencio, L. B., Lage, C. F., Correa-Faria, P., & Pordeus, I. A. (2015). Verbal school bullying and life satisfaction among Brazilian adolescents: Profiles of the aggressor and the victim. *Comprehensive Psychiatry*, *57*, 132–139. doi:10.1016/j.comppsych.2014.11.004 PMID:25465652

Shadmanfaat, S. M. S., Howell, C. J. M., Muniz, C. N., Cochran, J. K., Kabiri, S., & Richardson, D. A. (2018). The Predictive Ability of Self-control and Differential Association on Sports Fans' Decision to Engage in Cyber Bullying Perpetration Against Rivals. *International Journal of Cyber Criminology*, *12*(2), 362.

Shafran-Tikva, S., Gabay, G., & Kagan, I. (n.d.). Sexual harassment of religious Jewish nurses by patients and its relation to the ward's listening climate, care avoidance and quality of nursing care. *Journal of Nursing Management*, 1-10. doi:10.1111/jonm.13515

Shalev, I., Moffitt, T. E., Sugden, K., Williams, B., Houts, R. M., Danese, A., Mill, J., Arseneault, L., & Caspi, A. (2013). Exposure to violence during childhood is associated with telomere erosion from 5 to 10 years of age: A longitudinal study. *Molecular Psychiatry*, *18*(5), 576–581. doi:10.1038/mp.2012.32 PMID:22525489

Shaon, A. I. (2018). The question of Section 57. *Dhaka Tribune*. https://www.dhakatribune.com/bangladesh/law-rights/2018/08/10/the-question-of-section-57

Shariff, S. (2005). Cyber-dilemmas in the new millennium: School obligations to provide student safety in a virtual school environment. *McGill Journal of Education*, *40*(3), 467–487.

Shariff, S. (2008). *Cyber-bullying: Issues and solutions for school, the classroom and the home*. Routledge. doi:10.4324/9780203928837

Shariff, S. (2008). *Cyber-bullying: Issues and solutions for the school, the classroom and the home*. Routledge.

Sharpe, H., Fink, E., Duffy, F., & Patalay, P. (2021). Changes in peer and sibling victimization in early adolescence: Longitudinal associations with multiple indices of mental health in a prospective birth cohort study. *European Child & Adolescent Psychiatry*, 1–10. doi:10.100700787-020-01708-z PMID:33432402

Shaw, W. C. (1981). The influence of children's dentofacial appearance on their social attractiveness as judged by peers and lay adults. *American Journal of Orthodontics*, *79*(4), 399–415. doi:10.1016/0002-9416(81)90382-1 PMID:6939333

Shaw, W. C., Addy, M., & Ray, C. (1980). Dental and social effects of malocclusion and effectiveness of orthodontic treatment: A review. *Community Dentistry and Oral Epidemiology*, *8*(1), 36–45. doi:10.1111/j.1600-0528.1980.tb01252.x PMID:6989548

Shen, L., He, F., Zhang, C., Jiang, H., & Wang, J. (2018). Prevalence of malocclusion in primary dentition in mainland China, 1988–2017: A systematic review and meta-analysis. *Scientific Reports*, *8*(1), 1–10. doi:10.103841598-018-22900-x PMID:29549346

Shigemura, J., Ursano, R. J., Morganstein, J. C., Kurosawa, M., & Benedek, D. M. (2020). Public responses to the novel 2019 coronavirus (2019-nCoV) in Japan: Mental health consequences and target populations. *Psychiatry and Clinical Neurosciences*, *74*(4), 281–282. doi:10.1111/pcn.12988 PMID:32034840

Ship, J. A., Inglehart, M. R., & Bagramian, R. A. (2002). Oral health-related quality of life in patients with oral cancer. *Oral Health-Related Quality of Life*, 153-168.

Shoham, N., Lewis, G., Favarato, G., & Cooper, C. (2019). Prevalence of anxiety disorders and symptoms in people with hearing impairment: A systematic review. *Social Psychiatry and Psychiatric Epidemiology*, *54*(6), 649–660. doi:10.100700127-018-1638-3 PMID:30547211

Shuhaiza Md Salleh, A., & Azlina Mohd Noor, N. (2019). Sharenting: Implikasinya dari perspektif perundangan Malaysia (Sharenting: Its implications from the Malaysian legal perspective). *Kanun: Jurnal Undang-undang Malaysia*, *31*(1), 121–156. doi:10.1108/13522751111163245

SignStation. (2022). https://signstation.org

Silverman, A. B., Reinherz, H. Z., & Giaconia, R. M. (1996). The long-term sequelae of child and adolescent abuse: A longitudinal community study. *Child Abuse & Neglect*, *20*(8), 709–723. doi:10.1016/0145-2134(96)00059-2 PMID:8866117

Simons, S. (2008). Workplace bullying experienced by Massachusetts registered nurses and the relationship to intention to leave the organization. *Advances in Nursing Science*, *31*(2), E48–E59. doi:10.1097/01.ANS.0000319571.37373.d7 PMID:18497581

Şimşek, T. (2019). Sosyal medyada mahremiyetin ifşası “instagram örneği”. *Sosyolojik Düşün*, *4*(1), 10–24.

Singh, S., Thapar, V., & Bagga, S. (2020). Exploring the hidden patterns of cyberbullying on social media. *Procedia Computer Science*, *167*, 1636–1647. doi:10.1016/j.procs.2020.03.374

Sischo, L., & Broder, H. (2011). Oral health-related quality of life: What, why, how, and future implications. *Journal of Dental Research*, *90*(11), 1264–1270. doi:10.1177/0022034511399918 PMID:21422477

Sivak, E., & Smirnov, I. (2019). Parents mention sons more often than daughters on social media. In *Proceedings of the National Academy of Sciences of the United States of America* (vol. 116, pp. 2039–2041). 10.1073/pnas.1804996116

Siyez, D., & Kaya, A. (2011). Akran zorbalığı gruplarında empatik eğilim [Empathic tendency in the peer bullying groups]. *Inonu University Journal of the Faculty of Education*, *12*(2), 23–43.

Skarstein, S., Helseth, S., & Kvarme, L. G. (2020). It hurts inside: A qualitative study investigating social exclusion and bullying among adolescents reporting frequent pain and high use of non- prescription analgesics. *BMC Psychology*, *8*(1), 1–9. doi:10.118640359-020-00478-2 PMID:33115532

Skelton, T., & Valentine, G. (2003). ‘It Feels Like Being Deaf is Normal.’: An Exploration into the Complexities of Defining D/deafness and Young D/deaf People’s Identities. *The Canadian Geographer. Geographe Canadien*, *47*(4), 451–466. doi:10.1111/j.0008-3658.2003.00035.x

Slade, G. D., & Spencer, A. J. (1994). Development and evaluation of the oral health impact profile. *Community Dental Health*, *11*(1), 3–11. PMID:8193981

Slee, P. T., & Skrzypiec, G. (2016). *Well-being, positive peer relations and bullying in school settings*. Springer. doi:10.1007/978-3-319-43039-3

Slonje, R., & Smith, P. K. (2008). Cyberbullying: Another main type of bullying? *Scandinavian Journal of Psychology*, *49*(2), 147–154. doi:10.1111/j.1467-9450.2007.00611.x PMID:18352984

Slonje, R., Smith, P., & Frisén, A. (2013). The nature of cyberbullying, and strategies for prevention. *Computers in Human Behavior*, *29*(1), 26–32. doi:10.1016/j.chb.2012.05.024

Smahel, D., Machackova, H., Mascheroni, G., Dedkova, L., Staksrud, E., & Ólafsson, K. (2020). EU *Kids Online 2020: Survey results from 19 countries*. Academic Press.

Smart, J., Cascio, J., Paffendorf, J., Bridges, C., Hummel, J., Hursthouse, J., & Moss, R. (2007). *A Cross-Industry Public Foresight Project. Metaverse roadmap 2007: Pathways to the 3DWeb*. Academic Press.

Smith, P. K. (2019). Research on Cyberbullying: Strengths and Limitations. In *Narratives in Research and Interventions on Cyberbullying among Young People* (pp. 9–27). Springer International Publishing. doi:10.1007/978-3-030-04960-7_2

Smith, A. M., & Ortiz, R. R. (2021). # Metoo social media engagement and perceived hypersensitivity in the workplace. *Communication Studies*, *72*(4), 531–546. doi:10.1080/10510974.2021.1953091

Smith, B. W., Dempsey, A. G., Jackson, S. E., Olenchak, R. F., & Gaa, J. (2012). Cyberbullying among gifted children. *Gifted Education International*, *28*(1), 112–126. doi:10.1177/0261429411427652

Smith, P. K. (2012). Cyberbullying: Challenges and opportunities for a research program—A response to Olweus. *European Journal of Developmental Psychology*, *9*(5), 553–558. doi:10.1080/17405629.2012.689821

Smith, P. K. (2013). Cyberbullying y ciberagresión. In A. Ovejero, P. K. Smith, & S. Yubero (Eds.), *El acoso escolar y su prevención: Perspectivas internacionales* [School bullying and its prevention: International perspectives] (pp. 173–190). Biblioteca Nueva.

Smith, P. K. (2014). Understanding school bullying: Its nature and prevention strategies. *Sage (Atlanta, Ga.)*. Advance online publication. doi:10.4135/9781473906853

Smith, P. K. (2016). Bullying: definition, types, causes, consequences and intervention: Bullying. *Social and Personality Psychology Compass*, *10*(9), 519–532. doi:10.1111pc3.12266

Smith, P. K., & Brain, P. (2000). Bullying in schools: Lessons from two decades of research. *Aggressive Behavior*, *26*(1), 1–9. doi:10.1002/(SICI)1098-2337(2000)26:1<1::AID-AB1>3.0.CO;2-7

Smith, P. K., del Barrio, C., & Tokunaga, R. (2013). Definitions of bullying and cyberbullying: How useful are the terms? In S. Bauman, J. Walker, & D. Cross (Eds.), *Principles of cyberbullying research: Definition, measures, and methods* (pp. 26–40). Routledge.

Smith, P. K., Madhavi, J., Carvalho, M., Fisher, S., Russell, S., & Tippett, N. (2008). Cyberbullying: Its nature and impact in secondary school pupils. *Journal of Child Psychiatry*, *49*(4), 376–385.

Smith, P. K., Madsen, K. C., & Moody, J. C. (2006). What causes the age decline in reports of being bullied at school? Towards a developmental analysis of risks of being bullied. *Educational Research*, *41*(3), 267–285. doi:10.1080/0013188990410303

Smith, P. K., Mahdavi, J., Carvalho, M., Fisher, S., Russell, S., & Tippett, N. (2008). Cyberbullying: Its nature and impact in secondary school pupils. *Journal of Child Psychology and Psychiatry, and Allied Disciplines*, *49*(4), 376–385. doi:10.1111/j.1469-7610.2007.01846.x PMID:18363945

Smith, P. K., Morita, Y., Junger-Tas, J., Olweus, D., Catalano, R. F., & Slee, P. (Eds.). (1999). *The nature of school bullying: A cross-national perspective*. Taylor & Frances/Routledge.

Smith, P. K., & Myron-Wilson, R. (1998). Parenting and school bullying. *Clinical Child Psychology and Psychiatry*, *3*(3), 405–417. doi:10.1177/1359104598033006

Smith, P. K., Pepler, D., & Rigby, K. (2004). *Bullying in schools: How successful can interventions be?* Cambridge University Press. doi:10.1017/CBO9780511584466

Smith, P. K., & Shu, S. (2000). What good schools can do about bullying: Findings from a survey in english schools after a decade of research and action. *Childhood*, *7*(2), 193–212. doi:10.1177/0907568200007002005

Smith, P., Mandavi, J., Carvalho, M., & Tippett, N. (2005). *An Investigation into Cyberbullying, Its Forms, Awareness and Impact, And the Relationship Between Age and Gender in Cyberbullying*. Goldsmiths College.

Smith, Peter K., Ananiadou K., Cowie, H. (2003). Interventions to reduca school bullying. *The Canadian Journal of Psychiatry-In Review*, *48*(9), 22–31.

Smokowski, P. R., David-Ferdon, C., & Stroupe, N. (2009). Acculturation and violence in minority adolescents: A review of the empirical literature. *The Journal of Primary Prevention*, *30*(3), 215–263. doi:10.100710935-009-0173-0 PMID:19387835

Smokowski, P. R., & Evans, C. B. (2019). *Bullying and victimization across the lifespan*. Springer International Publishing. doi:10.1007/978-3-030-20293-4

Smokowski, P. R., Evans, C. B., & Cotter, K. L. (2014). The Differential Impacts of Episodic, Chronic, and Cumulative Physical Bullying and Cyberbullying: The effects of victimization on the school experiences, social support, and mental health of rural adolescents. *Violence and Victims*, *29*(6), 1029–1046. doi:10.1891/0886-6708.VV-D-13-00076 PMID:25905143

Smokowski, P. R., & Kopasz, K. H. (2005). Bullying in school: An overview of types, effects, family characteristics, and intervention strategies. *Children & Schools*, *27*(2), 101–110. doi:10.1093/cs/27.2.101

Sneddon, H., Iwaniec, D., & Stewart, M. C. (2010). Prevalence of childhood abuse ın mothers taking part ın a study of parenting their own children. *Child Abuse Rewiev*, *19*(1), 39–55. doi:10.1002/car.1078

Sobba, K. N., Paez, R. A., & Ten Bensel, T. (2017). Perceptions of Cyberbullying: An assessment of perceived severity among college students. *TechTrends*, *61*(6), 570–579. doi:10.100711528-017-0186-0

Soenens, B., Vansteenkiste, M., Goossens, L., Duriez, B., & Niemiec, C. P. (2008). The ıntervening role of relational aggression between psychological control and friendship quality. *Social Development*, *17*, 661–681. doi:10.1111/j.1467-9507.2007.00454.x

Solberg, M. E., & Olweus, D. (2003). Prevalence estimation of school bullying with the Olweus Bully/Victim Questionnaire. *Aggressive Behavior: Official Journal of the International Society for Research on Aggression*, *29*(3), 239–268. doi:10.1002/ab.10047

Solberg, M. E., Olweus, D., & Endresen, I. M. (2007). Bullies and victims at school: Are they the same pupils? *The British Journal of Educational Psychology*, *77*(2), 441–464. doi:10.1348/000709906X105689 PMID:17504556

Song, H., Lee, Y., & Kim, J. (2020). Gender Differences in the Link Between Cyberbullying and Parental Supervision Trajectories. *Crime and Delinquency*, *66*(13–14), 1914–1936. https://doi.org/10.1177/0011128720912371

Sönmezay, H. (2010). *Lise öğrencilerinde zorbalığın iletişim becerileri ve algılanan sosyal destek ile ilişkisinin incelenmesi* [Examining the relationship of bullying with communication skills and perceived social support in high school students] (Master Dissertation).

Sourander, A., Klomek, B., Ikonen, M., Lindroos, J., Luntamo, T., Koskelainen, M., ... Hlenius, H. (2010). Psychosocial risk factors associated with cyberbullying among adolescents: A population-based study. *Archives of General Psychiatry*, *67*(7), 720–728. doi:10.1001/archgenpsychiatry.2010.79 PMID:20603453

Soyer, C. (2018). Okul yöneticisi ve öğretmenlerinin görüşlerine göre çocukların cinsel istismar ve ihmalinin değerlendirilmesi [Evaluation of children's sexual abuse and neglect according to the opinions of school administrators and teachers]. *Turkish International Journal of Special Education and Guidance & Counselling, 7*(2), 14-28.

Sözmezay, H. (2010). *Investigation of the Relationship of Bullying with Communication Skills and Perceived Social Support in High School Students* [Master Thesis]. Ankara University.

Spears, B. A., Taddeo, C., & Barnes, A. (2018). *Online social marketing approaches to inform cyber/ bullying prevention and intervention: What have we learnt?* Reducing Cyberbullying in Schools, International Evidence-Based Best Practices.

Spector, P. E., Zhou, Z. E., & Che, X. X. (2014). Nurse exposure to physical and nonphysical violence, bullying, and sexual harassment: A quantitative review. *International Journal of Nursing Studies*, *51*(1), 72–84. doi:10.1016/j.ijnurstu.2013.01.010 PMID:23433725

Spertus, I. L., Yehuda, R., Wong, C. M., Halligan, S., & Seremetis, S. V. (2003). Childhood emotional abuse and neglect as predictors of psychological and physical symptoms in women presenting to a primary care practice. *Child Abuse & Neglect*, *27*(11), 1247–1258. doi:10.1016/j.chiabu.2003.05.001 PMID:14637300

Spitzberg, B. H. (1999). An analysis of empirical estimates of sexual aggression, victimisation and perpetration. *Violence and Victims*, *14*, 241–260.

Sprague, J., & Walker, H. (2002). *Creating school wide prevention and intervention strategies*. Northwest Regıonal Educatıonal Laboratory. https://www.ojp.gov/pdffiles1/ojjdp/book1.pdf

Spriggs, A. L., Iannotti, R. J., Nansel, T. R., & Haynie, D. L. (2007). Adolescent bullying involvement and perceived family, peer and school relations: Commonalities and differences across race/ethnicity. *The Journal of Adolescent Health*, *41*(3), 283–293. doi:10.1016/j.jadohealth.2007.04.009 PMID:17707299

Springer, K. W., Sheridan, J., Kuo, D., & Carnes, M. (2007). Long-term physical and mental health consequences of childhood physical abuse: Results from a large population-based sample of men and women. *Child Abuse & Neglect*, *31*(5), 517–530. doi:10.1016/j.chiabu.2007.01.003 PMID:17532465

Sraboni, S. I. (2021). *Cyber Bullying is an alarming issue during Covid-19 situation in Bangladesh*. Lawyers Club Bangladesh. http://lawyersclubbangladesh.com/en/2021/08/03/cyber-bullying-is-an-alarming-issue-during-covid-19-situation-in-bangladesh/

Srabstein, J. C., & Leventhal, B. L. (2010). Prevention of bullying-related morbidity and mortality: A call for public health policies. *Bulletin of the World Health Organization*, *88*(6), 403–403. doi:10.2471/BLT.10.077123 PMID:20539848

Srivastavaa, A., Gambleb, R., & Boey, J. (2013). Cyberbullying in Australia: Clarifying the problem, considering the solutions. *International Journal of Children's Rights*, *21*(1), 25–45. doi:10.1163/157181812X637145

Stamate, I. F., Aimé, A., Gagnon, C., & Villatte, A. (2021). Association between Weight-and Appearance-related Bullying in High School and Postsecondary Academic Adaptation in Young Adults. *Journal of School Violence*, *20*(4), 1–12. doi:10.1080/15388220.2021.1952079

Stanhope, M., & Lancaster, J. (2019). *Public health nursing e-book: Population-centered health care in the community*. Elsevier Health Sciences.

Stapinski, L. A., Bowes, L., Wolke, D., Pearson, R. M., Mahedy, L., Button, K. S., Lewis, G., & Araya, R. (2014). Peer victimization during adolescence and risk for anxiety disorders in adulthood: A prospective cohort study. *Depression and Anxiety*, *31*(7), 574–582. doi:10.1002/da.22270 PMID:24788688

Star. (2020a). *Are you sharenting your children?* Retrieved May 25, 2022, from https://www.thestar.com.my/lifestyle/health/2020/06/12/are-you-sharenting-your-children

Star. (2020b). *Entrepreneur accused of abusing his two-year-old to create social media content*. Retrieved May 22, 2022, from https://www.thestar.com.my/news/nation/2020/03/05/report-lodged-alleging-entrepreneur-abused-adopted-child-2-for-online-content

Stark, S., Chernyshenko, O. S., Lancaster, A. R., Drasgow, F., & Fitzgerald, L. F. (2002). Toward standardized measurement of sexual harassment: Shortening the SEQ–DoD using item response theory. *Military Psychology*, *14*, 49–72.

Starling, S. P., Heller, R. M., & Jenny, C. (2002). Pelvic fractures in infants as a sign of physical abuse. *Child Abuse & Neglect*, *26*(5), 475–480. doi:10.1016/S0145-2134(02)00323-X PMID:12079085

Statistics, B. (n.d.). *PACER Center – Champions for Children with Disabilities*. Retrieved February 10, 2022, from https://www.pacer.org/bullying/info/stats.asp

Steffgen, G., König, A., Pfetsch, J., & Melzer, A. (2011). Are cyberbullies less empathic? Adolescents' cyberbullying behavior and empathic responsiveness. *Cyberpsychology, Behavior, and Social Networking*, *14*(11), 643–648. doi:10.1089/cyber.2010.0445 PMID:21554126

Steffgen, G., Recchia, S., & Viechtbauer, W. (2013). The link between school climate and violence in school: A meta-analytic review. *Aggression and Violent Behavior*, *18*(2), 300–309. doi:10.1016/j.avb.2012.12.001

Steinberg, L. S. (2007). Ergenlik. İmge. (Original work published 2005)

Steinberg, S. B. (2017). Sharenting : Children 's Privacy in the Age of Social Media. *Emory Law Journal*, *66*(839).

Steinhauer, J. (2008, November 27). Verdict in MySpace suicide case. *The New York Times*.

Steinmueller, W. (2000). Will new information and communication technologies improve the 'codification' of knowledge? *Industrial and Corporate Change*, *9*(2), 361–376. doi:10.1093/icc/9.2.361

Sticca, F., & Perren, S. (2013). Is cyberbullying worse than traditional bullying? Examining the differential roles of medium, publicity, and anonymity for the perceived severity of bullying. *Journal of Youth and Adolescence*, *42*(5), 739–750. doi:10.100710964-012-9867-3 PMID:23184483

Stinson, M. S., & Kluwin, T. N. (2003). Educational consequences of alternative school placements. In M. Marschark & M. E. Spencer (Eds.), *Deaf studies, language, and education* (pp. 52–64). Oxford University Press.

Stockdale, M. S., Visio, M., & Batra, L. (1999). The sexual harassment of men: Evidence for a broader theory of sexual harassment and sex discrimination. *Psychology, Public Policy, and Law*, *5*, 630–664.

Storey, K., & Slaby, R. (2013). *Eyes on bullying in early childhood*. Education Development Center. http://www.promoteprevent.org/sites/www.promoteprevent.org/files/resources/Eyes%20on%20Bullying%20in%20Early%20Childhood_1.pdf

Straus, M. A. (1994). State-to-state differences in social inequality and social bonds in relation to assaults, on wives in the United States. *Journal of Comparative Family Studies*, *25*(1), 7–24. doi:10.3138/jcfs.25.1.7

Street, A. E., Gradus, J. L., Stafford, J., & Kelly, K. (2007). Gender differences in experiences of sexual harassment: Data from a male-dominated environment. *Journal of Consulting and Clinical Psychology*, *75*(3), 464–474.

Strohmeier, D., & Gradinger, P. (2022). Cyberbullying and Cyber Victimization as Online Risks for Children and Adolescents. *European Psychologist*, *27*(2), 141–150. https://doi.org/10.1027/1016-9040/a000479

Strohmeier, D., Hoffmann, C., Schiller, E. M., Stefanek, E., & Spiel, C. (2012). ViSC social competence program. *New Directions for Youth Development*, (133), 71–84. doi:10.1002/yd.20008 PMID:22504792

Suler, J. (2004). Psychology of cyberspace – The online disinhibition effect. *Cyberpsychology & Behavior*, *7*(3), 321–326. doi:10.1089/1094931041291295 PMID:15257832

Sullivan, T. N., Farrell, A. D., Sutherland, K. S., Behrhorst, K. L., Garthe, R. C., & Greene, A. (2021). Evaluation of the Olweus Bullying Prevention Program in US Urban Middle Schools Using a Multiple Baseline Experimental Design The OBPP focuses on the prevention of bullying, which encompasses acts of aggression repeatedly directed toward. *Prevention Science*, *22*(8), 1134–1146. doi:10.100711121-021-01244-5

Sunday, S., Labruna, V., Kaplan, S., Pelcovitz, D., Newman, J., & Salzinger, S. (2008). Physical abuse during adolescence: Gender differences in the adolescents' perceptions of family functioning and parenting. *Child Abuse & Neglect*, *32*(1), 5–18. doi:10.1016/j.chiabu.2007.03.025 PMID:18082259

Süner, A. F., Emli Alpay, E., & Ünal, B. (2022). Akran zorbalığına kısa bir bakış: birinci basamak sağlık çalışanlarına tavsiyeler [A brief overview of peer bullying: Recommendations to primary care workers]. *Sürekli Tıp Eğitimi Dergisi*, *30*(6), 444–450.

Sun, L., Wong, H. M., & McGrath, C. P. (2017). Relationship between the severity of malocclusion and oral health related quality of life: A systematic review and meta-analysis. *Oral Health & Preventive Dentistry*, *15*(6), 503–517. PMID:28944350

Suparli, A. S., & Ramdhani, N. (2015). Does Moral Emotion Plays Role in Cyber-bullying? *Social and Behavioral Sciences*, *165*, 202–207. doi:10.1016/j.sbspro.2014.12.623

Sutton, J. (2001). Bullies: Thugs of thinkers? *The Psychologist*, *14*(10), 530–534.

Swartz, M. K. (2009). Cyberbullying: An extension of the schoolyard. *Journal of Pediatric Health Care*, *23*(5), 281–282. doi:10.1016/j.pedhc.2009.06.005 PMID:19720261

Swearer, S. M. (2011). Risk factors for and outcomes of bullying and victimization. *Educational Psychology Papers and Publications*, *132*, 1–9.

Swearer, S. M., & Hymel, S. (2015). Understanding the psyhology of bullying: Moving toward a social-ecological diathesis-stress model. *The American Psychologist*, *70*(4), 344–353. doi:10.1037/a0038929 PMID:25961315

Swearer, S. M., Wang, C., Berry, B., & Myers, Z. R. (2014). Reducing bullying: Application of social cognitive theory. *Theory into Practice*, *53*(4), 271–277. doi:10.1080/00405841.2014.947221

Swearer, S., & Espelage, D. (2010). *Expandıng The Socıal-Ecologıcal Framework Of Bullyıng Among Youth: Lessons Learned from the Past and Directions for the Future. Bullying in North American Schools*. Routledge.

Swearer, S., & Hymel, S. (2015). Bullying and Discrimination in Schools: Exploring Variations Across Student Subgroups. *School Psychology Review*, *44*(4), 504–509. doi:10.17105/15-0133.1

Sylvester, R. (2011). Teacher as bully: Knowingly or unintentionally harming students. *Delta Kappa Gamma Bulletin*, *77*(2), 42.

Symantec. (2012). *Norton Cybercrime Report*. https://icma.org/documents/2012-norton-cybercrime-report

Syts, Y. (2004). *Beyond the schoolyard: Examining Electronic Bullying Among Canadian Youth (*Unpublished Master's Thesis). Carleton University, Ottawa.

Szewczyk-Sokolowski, M., Bost, K. K., & Wainwright, A. B. (2005). Attachment, temperament and preschool children's peer acceptance. *Social Development, 14*(3), 379–397. doi:10.1111/j.1467-9507.2005.00307.x

Szutenbach, M. P. (2013). Bullying in nursing: Roots, rationales, and remedies. *Journal of Christian Nursing, 30*(1), 16–23. doi:10.1097/CNJ.0b013e318276be28 PMID:23495431

Tabachnick, B., & Fidell, L. (2013). *Using multivariate statistics*. Pearson Education Inc.

Tai, S.-Y., Lin, P.-C., Chen, Y.-M., Hung, H.-C., Pan, C.-H., Pan, S.-M., & Wu, M.-T. (2014). Effects of Marital Status and Shift Work on Family Function among Registered Nurses. *Industrial Health, 52*(4), 296–303. Advance online publication. doi:10.2486/indhealth.2014-0009 PMID:24909112

Takizawa, R., Maughan, B., & Arseneault, L. (2014). Adult health outcomes of childhood bullying victimization: Evidence from a five-decade longitudinal British birth cohort. *American Journal of Psychiatry, 171*(7), 777-784. doi:10.1176/appi.ajp.2014.13101401

Talas, M. S., Kocaoz, S., & Akguc, S. (2011). A survey of violence against staff working in the emergency department in ankara, Turkey. *Asian Nursing Research, 5*(4), 197–203. doi:10.1016/j.anr.2011.11.001 PMID:25030520

Tamer, N., & Vatanartıran, S. (2014). Ergenlerin teknolojik zorbalık algıları [Adolescents' perception of technological bullying]. *Online Journal of Technology Addiction & Cyberbullying, 1*(2), 1–20.

Tammam, A. H. (2022). Cyberbullying through social media And its relationship to achievement motivation among adolescent students. *International Journal of Instructional Technology and Educational Studies, 3*(3), 1–10. https://doi.org/10.21608/IHITES.2022.106649.1077

Taner, Y., & Gökler, B. (2004). Çocuk istismarı ve ihmali: Psikiyatrik yönleri [Child abuse and neglect: Psychiatric aspects]. *Acta Medica, 35*(2), 82–86.

Tangen, D., & Campbell, M. (2010). Cyberbullying prevention: One primary school's approach. *Australian Journal of Guidance & Counselling, 20*(2), 225–234. doi:10.1375/ajgc.20.2.225

Tangri, S., & Hayes, S. (1997). Theories of sexual harassment. In W. O'Donohue (Ed.), *Sexual harassment: Theory, research, and treatment* (pp. 112–128). Allyn & Bacon.

Tanrıkulu, T., Kınay, H., & Arıcak, O. T. (2013). The Scale of Sensitivity to Cyber Bullying: A Validity and Reliability Study. *Journal of the Faculty of Education of Trakya University*, 38-47.

Tanrıkulu, I., & Campbell, M. A. (2015). Sibling bullying perpetration: Associations with gender, grade, peer perpetration, trait anger, and moral disengagement. *Journal of Interpersonal Violence, 30*(6), 1010–1024. doi:10.1177/0886260514539763 PMID:25038224

Tarshis, T. P. (2010). *Living with peer pressure and bullying*. Infobase Publishing.

Taştekin, E., & Bayhan, P. (2018). Onl The Investigation of Cyber Bullying and Victimization among Adolescents. *Dec. ine Journal of Technology Addiction & Cyberbullying, 5*(2), 21-45.

Taştekin, E., & Bayhan, P. (2018). Ergenler arasındaki siber zorbalığın ve mağduriyetin incelenmesi [Examination of cyber bullying and victimization among adolescents]. *Online Journal of Technology Addiction & Cyberbullying, 5*(2), 21–45.

Taştekin, E., & Bayhan, P. (2018). Examination of cyber bullying and victimization among adolescents. *Online Journal of Technology Addiction & Cyberbullying*, *5*(2), 21–45.

Tatlılıoğlu, K. (2016). Violence and tyranny at schools: risk factors, services of protect, prevent and ınterfere: the sample of the Konya. *Bingöl Üniversitesi SBE Dergisi*, *6*(12), 209–231. doi:10.29029/busbed.328657

Taylan, H. H., Aydin, F., & Topal, M. (2017). Investigation of secondary school students' cyberbullying situations in terms of several variables: Sakarya province sample. *Online Journal of Technology Addiction and Cyberbullying*, *4*(1), 41–59.

Tehrani, N. (2012). *Workplace Bullying: Symptoms and Solutions*. Routledge.

Tekin, Y. E., & Bulut, H. (2014). Verbal, physical, and sexual abuse status against operating room nurses in Turkey. *Sexuality and Disability*, *32*(1), 85–97. doi:10.100711195-014-9339-7

teknosafari.net. (2021). *Turkey is the 5th in the World in Terms of Digital Kindness. Next up!* https://teknosafari.net/turkiye-dijital-nezaket-konusunda-dunyada-5-sirada retrieved from/

Temel, Z. F., Ekicİ, K. B. K., Kanat, K., & Şahin, E. N. (2018). 5-6 Yaş çocuklarinin fiziksel şiddete maruz kalma ya da tanik olmalari ile benlik algilari arasindaki ilişkinin incelenmesi [Examination of the relationship between 5-6 year old children being exposed to or witnessing physical violence and their self-perceptions]. *Sakarya Üniversitesi Eğitim Fakültesi Dergisi*, (35), 109-122.

Tepper, B. J. (2000). Consequences of Abusive Supervision. *Academy of Management Journal*, *43*(2), 178–190. doi:10.2307/1556375

Tepper, B. J. (2007). Abusive Supervision in Work Organizations: Review, Synthesis, and Research Agenda. *Journal of Management*, *33*(3), 261–289. doi:10.1177/0149206307300812

Terpstra, D. E., & Baker, D. D. (1989). The identification and classification of reactions to sexual harassment. *Journal of Organizational Behavior*, *10*, 1–14.

Testa, M. A., & Simonson, D. C. (1996). Assessment of quality-of-life outcomes. *The New England Journal of Medicine*, *334*(13), 835–840. doi:10.1056/NEJM199603283341306 PMID:8596551

Tharp-Taylor, S., Haviland, A., & D'Amico, E. J. (2009). Victimization from mental and physical bullying and substance use in early adolescence. *Addictive Behaviors*, *34*(6-7), 561–567. doi:10.1016/j.addbeh.2009.03.012 PMID:19398162

The Business Standard. (2022). Most DSA cases filed by ruling party people: Study. *The Business Standard*. https://www.tbsnews.net/bangladesh/most-dsa-cases-filed-ruling-party-people-study-408398

The Daily Star. (2022). Digital Security Act: 147 sued, 67 arrests a month. *The Daily Star*. https://www.thedailystar.net/news/bangladesh/news/detentions-under-dsa-recent-average-spikes-67-month-3010906

Thios, S. J., & Foster, S. B. (1991). *Changing Preschoolers' Attitudes toward Children with Disabilities*. Academic Press.

Thomas, A. M., & Kitzinger, C. (1997). *Sexual harassment. Contemporary feminist perspectives*. Open University Press.

Thomas, H. J., Connor, J. P., & Scott, J. G. (2015). Integrating Traditional Bullying and Cyberbullying: Challenges of definition and measurement in adolescents–a review. *Educational Psychology Review*, *27*(1), 135–152. doi:10.100710648-014-9261-7

Thomas, S. P., & Smith, H. (2004). School connectednes, anger behaviors and relationships of violent and nonviolet American Youth. *Perspectives in Psychiatric Care*, *40*(4), 219–228. doi:10.1111/j.1744-6163.2004.tb00011.x PMID:15739755

Thompson, N., & Brindley, J. (2020). Who are you talking about? Contrasting determinants of online disclosure about self or others. *Information Technology & People*. Advance online publication. doi:10.1108/ITP-04-2019-0197

Thomson, A. M., Cunningham, S. J., & Hunt, N. P. (2001). A comparison of information retention at an initial orthodontic consultation. *European Journal of Orthodontics*, *23*(2), 169–178. doi:10.1093/ejo/23.2.169 PMID:11398554

Thornberg, R., Halldin, K., Bolmsjö, N., & Petersson, A. (2013). Victimising of school bullying: A grounded theory. *Research Papers in Education*, *28*(3), 309–329. doi:10.1080/02671522.2011.641999

Thun, L.J., Teh, P.L., & Cheng, C.B. (2021). CyberAid: Are your children safe from cyberbullying? *Journal of King Saud University – Computer and Information Sciences.*

Tian, J. (2008). *A correlational study among workplace bullying and job vigor of cabin crew by using social support as moderating variable* [Unpublished master's thesis]. University of Technology Institute of Technical and Vocational Education and Human Resource Development.

Tippett, N., Houlston, C., & Smith, P. K. (2010). *Prevention and response to identity-based bullying among local authorities in England, Scotland and Wales.* https://www.equalityhumanrights.com/uploaded_files/research/64_identity_based_bull ying.pdf

Tippett, N., & Wolke, D. (2015). Aggression between siblings: Associations with the home environment and peer bullying. *Aggressive Behavior*, *41*(1), 14–24. doi:10.1002/ab.21557 PMID:25187483

Tıraşçı, Y., & Gören, S. (2007). Çocuk istismarı ve ihmali [Child abuse and neglect]. *Dicle Tıp Dergisi*, *34*(1), 70–74.

Toker, Y. (2016). İşyerlerinde cinsel taciz: kapsamı, öncülleri, sonuçları, kurumsal baş etme yöntemleri [Sexual Harassment in the Workplace: Scope, Antecedents, Consequences, Institutional Coping Methods]. *Türk Psikoloji Yazilari*, *19*(38), 1–19.

Toker, Y., & Sümer, H. C. (2010). Workplace sexual harassment perceptions in the Turkish context and the role of individual differences. *Applied Psychology*, *59*(4), 616–646. doi:10.1111/j.1464-0597.2010.00420.x

Tokunaga, R. S. (2010). Following you home from school: A critical review and synthesis of research on cyberbullying victimization. *Computers in Human Behavior*, *26*(3), 277–287. doi:10.1016/j.chb.2009.11.014

Tom, S. R., Schwartz, D., Chang, L., Farver, J. A. M., & Xu, Y. (2010). Correlates of victimization in Hong Kong children's peer groups. *Journal of Applied Developmental Psychology*, *31*(1), 27–37. doi:10.1016/j.appdev.2009.06.002

Topçu, Ç. (2008). *He relationship of cyber bullying to empathy, gender, traditional bullying, internet use and adult monitoring* (UMI No. 227700) [Master's dissertation, Middle East Technical University]. Higher Education Council Thesis Center database.

Topçu, Ç. (2008). *The Relationship of Cyberbullying to Empathy, Gender, Traditional Bullying, Internet Use and Adult Monitoring* (Unpublished Master Thesis). Middle East Technical University, Ankara.

Topçu, Ç., Erdur-Baker, Ö., & Çapa-Aydın, Y. (2008). Examination of cyberbullying experiences among Turkish students from different school types. *Cyberpsychology & Behavior*, *11*(6), 643–648. doi:10.1089/cpb.2007.0161 PMID:18783345

Topçu-Uzer, Ç., & Tanrıkulu, İ. (2017). Cyberbullying prevention and intervention programs: A national systematic review. *Uludağ University Journal of Faculty of Education*, *30*(1), 1–17. doi:10.19171/uefad.323367

Torshizi, L., & Ahmadi, F. (2011). Job stressors from clinical nurses 'perspective. *Iran Journal of Nursing*, *24*(70), 49–60.

Torun, N. K., & Torun, T. (2021). *Metaverse Kavramının İlk Çıkış Noktası: Snow Crash (Parazit) İncelemesi.* 14th International Conference of Strategic Research on Scientific Studies and Education, Antalya, Turkey.

Trades Union Congress. (2016). *Report on Sexual Harassment in the Workplace*. Available at https://www.tuc.org.uk/news/nearly-two-three-young-women-have-experienced-sexual-harassment-work-tuc-survey-reveals

Trépanier, S.-G., Fernet, C., & Austin, S. (2013). Workplace bullying and psychological health at work: The mediating role of satisfaction of needs for autonomy, competence and relatedness. *Work and Stress*, *27*(2), 123–140. doi:10.1080/02678373.2013.782158

Tristão, S. K. P., Magno, M. B., Pintor, A. V. B., Christovam, I. F., Ferreira, D. M. T., Maia, L. C., & de Souza, I. P. R. (2020). Is there a relationship between malocclusion and bullying? A systematic review. *Progress in Orthodontics*, *21*(1), 1–13. doi:10.118640510-020-00323-7 PMID:32869136

Trzesniewski, K. H., Donnellan, M. B., Moffitt, T. E., Robins, R. W., Poulton, R., & Caspi, A. (2006). Low Self-esteem During Adolescence Predicts Poor Health, Criminal Behavior, and Limited Economic Prospects During Adulthood. *Developmental Psychology*, *42*(2), 381–390. doi:10.1037/0012-1649.42.2.381 PMID:16569175

Tsai, K. C., & Gomba, C. (2012). Effects of bullying in schools: The teachers' perspectives. *Journal of Society and Communication*, *1*, 161–179.

Tsur, N., Katz, C., & Klebanov, B. (2021). "I don't have fur to protect me": Children's experience of pain as communicated in forensic interviews following parental physical abuse. *Children and Youth Services Review*, *120*, 105420. doi:10.1016/j.childyouth.2020.105420

Ttofi, M. M., & Farrington, D. P. (2008). Bullying: Short-term and long-term effects, and the importance of defiance theory in explanation and prevention. *Victims & Offenders*, *3*(2-3), 289–312. doi:10.1080/15564880802143397

Ttofi, M. M., & Farrington, D. P. (2011). Effectiveness of school-based programs to reduce bullying: A systematic and meta-analytic review. *Journal of Experimental Criminology*, *7*(1), 27–56. doi:10.100711292-010-9109-1

Ttofi, M. M., Farrington, D. P., Lösel, F., Crago, R. V., & Theodorakis, N. (2016). School bullying and drug use later in life: A meta-analytic investigation. *School Psychology Quarterly*, *31*(1), 8–27. doi:10.1037pq0000120 PMID:25866866

Tucker, J. (2022). *How parental oversharing on social media harms kids*. Retrieved May 23, 2022, from https://www.moms.com/how-parental-oversharing-on-social-media-harms-kids/

Tudkuea, T., Laeheem, K., & Sittichai, R. (2019). Development of a causal relationship model for cyber bullying behaviors among public secondary school students in the three southern border provinces of Thailand. *Children and Youth Services Review*, *102*, 145–149. doi:10.1016/j.childyouth.2019.05.013

Tukachinsky, R., Mastro, D., & Yarchi, M. (2017). The Effect of Prime Time Television Ethnic/Racial Stereotypes on Latino and Black Americans: A Longitudinal National Level Study. *Journal of Broadcasting & Electronic Media*, *61*(3), 538–556. doi:10.1080/08838151.2017.1344669

Tural Hesapçıoğlu, S., & Yeşilova, H. (2015). Feelings, thoughts and attitudes of high school students toward school bullying and the bullies. *Anatolian Journal of Psychiatry*, *16*(4), 284–293. doi:10.5455/apd.155780

Türkoğlu, S. (2013). *Ergenlerin Problemli İnternet Kullanımları ile Siber Zorbalık Eğilimleri Arasındaki İlişkinin İncelenmesi* [Investigation of the Relationshio between the Problematic Internet Use and Cyberbullying Tendencies] (Unpublished Master's Thesis). Marmara University, İstanbul.

Turktan, S. (2013). *The effects of peer support program for coping with bullying on middle school 6th and 7th grade students' ability to cope with bullying* [Unpublished doctoral dissertation]. Anadolu University, Eskisehir, Turkey.

Turner, D. W. III. (2010). Qualitative interview design: A practical guide for novice investigators. *Qualitative Report*, *15*(3), 754.

Turner-Moore, T., Milnes, K., & Gough, B. (2021). Bullying in Five European Countries: Evidence for Bringing Gendered Phenomena Under the Umbrella of 'Sexual Bullying' in Research and Practice. *Sex Roles*, *86*(1-2), 89–105. doi:10.100711199-021-01254-1

Tutar, H. (2004). Is yerinde psikolojik siddet sarmali: Nedenleri ve sonuclari [The spiral of psychological violence at work: Causes and consequences]. *Yönetim Bilimleri Dergisi*, *2*(2), 85–108.

Twemlow, S., Fonagy, P., Sacco, F. C., & Brethour, J. R. Jr. (2006). Teachers who bully students: A hidden trauma. *The International Journal of Social Psychiatry*, *52*(3), 187–198. doi:10.1177/0020764006067234 PMID:16875191

Twenge, J. M., & Campbell, W. K. (2010). *Asrın vebası: Narsisizm illeti* (Ö. Köknar, Trans). İstanbul: Kaknüs Yayınları United States Department of Education, Office of Planning, Evaluation and Policy Development, Policy and Program Studies. https://www2.ed.gov/rschstat/eval/bullying/state-bullying-laws/state-bullying-laws.pdf

Types of bullying. National Centre Against Bullying [NCAB]. (n.d.). Retrieved from https://www.ncab.org.au/bullying-advice/bullying-for-parents/types-of-bullying/

U.S. Equal Employment Opportunity Commission. (2022). *Charges Alleging Sex-Based Harassment (Charges filed with EEOC) FY 2010-FY 2021*. Available at https://www.eeoc.gov/statistics/charges-alleging-sex-based-harassment-charges-filed-eeoc-fy-2010-fy-2021

U.S. Merit Systems Protection Board. (1988). *Sexual harassment in the federal Government: An update*. Government Printing Office.

Ucak, A. (2009). *Saglik personelinin maruz kaldigi is kazalari ve geri bildirimlerinin değerlendirilmesi [Evaluation of occupational accidents and feedbacks of healthcare personnel] [Master]*. Afyon Kocatepe University, Institute of Health Sciences.

Uğurlu, Z., & Gülsen, İ. A. (2014). Çocuk hakları ve hukuki bağlamda çocuğun ihmal ve istismardan korunması [Child rights and protection of the child from neglect and abuse in the legal context]. *Uluslararası Sosyal ve Eğitim Bilimleri Dergisi.*, *1*(1), 1–24.

Ulusoy, H., Swigart, V., & Erdemir, F. (2011). Think globally, act locally: Understanding sexual harassment from a cross-cultural perspective. *Medical Education*, *45*(6), 603–612. doi:10.1111/j.1365-2923.2010.03918.x PMID:21501219

UN Women. (2021). *Research Brief - Intimate Partner Violence in Five CARICOM Countries: Findings from National Prevalence Surveys on Violence Against Women*. UNICEF. https://www.unicef.org/easterncaribbean/media/2926/file/Gen-U%20Trinidad%20Fact%20Sheet.pdf

Ünal, A., & Gürsel, M. (2015). Negative teacher behaviors from which teacher candidates are affected. In *Proceedings of Teaching and Education Conferences* (No. 2404066). International Institute of Social and Economic Sciences.

Ünalmış, M. (2010). *Lise 1. sınıf öğrencilerinin zorba, kurban olma durumlarına göre şiddete yönelik tutumlarının ve sosyal beceri düzeylerinin incelenmesi* [Examination of high school first year students' attitudes towards violence and social skill levels according to being bullied and victimized] [Unpublished master's thesis]. Gaziosmanpaşa Üniversitesi, Tokat.

Underwood, M. K., & Rosen, L. H. (2011). Gender and bullying. *Bullying in North American Schools, 33*(1), 13-24.

UNESCO. (2017). School violence and bullying: Global status report. Paris: United Nations Educational, Scientific and Cultural Organization.

UNESCO. (2020). *International day against violence and bullying at school including cyberbullying 2020*. Available from https://www.unesco.org/en/days/againts-school-violence-and-bullying-day

UNICEF. (2015). *Investigating the prevalence and impact of peer abuse (bullying) on the development of Jamaica's children report.* https://www.unicef.org/jamaica/reports/investigating-prevalence-and-impact-peer-abuse-development-jamaicas-children

UNICEF. (2016). Ending violence against children in Nigeria: A multi-sectoral response to the 2014 Nigeria Violence Against Children Survey. In *Ending violence against children in Nigeria.* UNICEF Nigeria.

UNICEF. (2019) Available from https://www.unicef.org/turkey/bas%C4%B1n-b%C3%BCltenleri/unicef-d%C3%BCnyadaki-gen%C3%A7lerin-yar%C4%B1s%C4%B1-okulda-ve-okul-%C3%A7evresinde-akran-%C5%9Fiddetine-maruz

UNICEF. (2019). Available from https://www.unicef.org/turkey/bas%C4%B1n-b%C3%BCltenleri/unicef-anketi-30-%C3%BClkedeki-gen%C3%A7lerin-%C3%BC%C3%A7te-birinden-fazlas%C4%B1-%C3%A7evrimi%C3%A7i-zorbal%C4%B1k

UNICEF. (2020). *Recomendações da Unicef têm como objetivo ajudar governos, empresas de TIC, educadores e pais a proteger as crianças em confinamento* [Unicef's recommendations aim at governments, ICT companies, educators and parents to protect children in people at the same time]. Disponível em: https://www.unicef.pt/actualidade/noticias/criancas-correm-maior-risco-desofrer abusos-online-durante-a-pandemia-global-de-covid-19/

UNICEF. (n.d.). *Cyberbullying: what is it and how to prevent it.* UNICEF. https://www.unicef.org/turkey/siber-zorbal%C4%B1k-nedir-ve-nas%C4%B1l-%C3%B6nlenir retrieved from

United Nations Educational, Scientific and Cultural Organization (UNESCO). (2019). *Behind the numbers: ending school violence and bullying.* Available from https://unesdoc.unesco.org/ark:/48223/pf0000366483

United Nations Educational, Scientific and Cultural Organization. (2017). *School violence and bullying global status report.* UNESCO. https://unesdoc.unesco.org/ark:/48223/pf0000246970

United News Bangladesh. (2020). 80% of cyberbullying victims are women. *United News Bangladesh.* https://www.unb.com.bd/category/Bangladesh/80-of-cyberbullying-victims-are-women/61781

United States Department of Justice. (2010). *Sexual assault definition.* https://web.archive.org/web/20191007043843/https://www.justice.gov/ovw/sexual-assault

Ünlüsoy Dinçer, N. (2012). *Hemşirelerin İşyeri Şiddetine Maruz Kalma Durumları ile İş Doyumları ve İşten Ayrılma Eğilimleri [The violence on nurses at workplace and the tendency to leave the job and job satisfaction of nurses]. Yayımlanmamış doktora tezi.* Hacettepe Üniversitesi.

Unnever, J. D., Cullen, F. T., & Pratt, T. C. (2003). Parental Management, ADHD, and Delinquent Involvement: Reassessing Gottfredson and Hirschi's general theory. *Justice Quarterly, 20*(3), 471–500. doi:10.1080/07418820300095591

Urano, Y., Takizawa, Y., Ohka, M., Yamasaki, H., & Shimoyama, H. (2020). Cyber bullying victimization and adolescent mental health: The differential moderating effects of intrapersonal and interpersonal emotional competence. *Journal of Adolescence, 80*(1), 182–191. doi:10.1016/j.adolescence.2020.02.009 PMID:32169718

Üstündağ-Şener, N., Başar, M., Şen, B., & Göncü, A. (2015). The teachers' views on student bullying behavior and investigation of learning environment. *Journal of Educational Sciences, 41*(41), 157–173. doi:10.15285/ebd.22661

Uysal, H., & Dinçer, Ç. (2012). Okul öncesi dönemde akran zorbalığı [Bullying in preschool]. *Kuramsal Eğitimbilim Dergisi, 5*(4), 468-483.

Uysal, H., & Dinçer, Ç. (2012). Okul öncesi dönemde akran zorbalığı [Peer bullying in the preschool period]. *Kuramsal Eğitimbilim Dergisi, 5*(4), 468-483.

Uysal, H. T. (2016). Calisanlarin liderlik algisi ve ters mobbing egilimi: Isgoren odakli liderligin etkisi [Employees' perception of leadership and reverse mobbing tendency: The effect of employee-oriented leadership]. *Journal of International Social Research*, *9*(47), 933–943. doi:10.17719/jisr.2016.1441

Uysal, H., & Dinçer, Ç. (2012). Okul öncesi dönemde akran zorbalığı [Peer bullying in the preschool period]. *Journal of Theoretical Educational Science*, *5*(4), 468–483.

Uysal, H., & Dinçer, Ç. (2012). Peer bullying during early childhood. *Journal of Theoretical Educational Science*, *5*(4), 468–483. https://dergipark.org.tr/tr/download/article-file/304203

Uz Baş, A. (2019). School-based prevention: Characteristics of effective school-based prevention programs. *Journal of School Psychological Counseling*, *2*(1), 73–94.

Vaiciunaite, R., Mitalauskiene, A., & Vasiliauskas, A. (2020). The relationship between congenital cleft lip and palate malformation, skeletal and dental occlusal anomalies, and the influence of its treatment on affected patients' oral health-related quality of life (OHRQoL). *Stomatologija*, *22*(4), 116–119. PMID:33847283

Vaillancourt, T., Hymel, S., & McDougall, P. (2003). Bullying is power: Implications for school-based intervention strategies. *Journal of Applied School Psychology*, *19*(2), 157–176. doi:10.1300/J008v19n02_10

Van den Berg, P., & Neumark-Sztainer, D. (2007). Fat¢ n happy 5 years later: Is it bad for overweight girls to like their bodies? *The Journal of Adolescent Health*, *41*(4), 415–417. doi:10.1016/j.jadohealth.2007.06.001 PMID:17875468

Van der Wal, M. F., De Wit, C. A., & Hirasing, R. A. (2003). Psychosocial health among young victims and offenders of direct and indirect bullying. *Pediatrics*, *111*(6), 1312–1317. doi:10.1542/peds.111.6.1312 PMID:12777546

Van Geel, M., Vedder, P., & Tanilon, J. (2014). Relationship between peer victimization, cyberbullying, and suicide in children and adolescents: A meta-analysis. *JAMA Pediatrics*, *168*(5), 435–442. doi:10.1001/jamapediatrics.2013.4143 PMID:24615300

Vandebosch, H., & Van Cleemput, K. (2008). Defining cyberbullying: A qualitative research into the perceptions of youngsters. *Cyberpsychology & Behavior*, *11*(4), 499–503. doi:10.1089/cpb.2007.0042 PMID:18721100

Vandebosch, H., & Van Cleemput, K. (2009). Cyberbullying among youngsters: Profiles of bullies and victims. *New Media & Society*, *11*(8), 1349–1371. doi:10.1177/1461444809341263

Vanderbilt, D., & Augustyn, M. (2010). The effects of bullying. *Paediatrics & Child Health*, *20*(7), 315–320. doi:10.1016/j.paed.2010.03.008

Vannucci, M., Nocentini, A., Mazzoni, G., & Menesini, E. (2012). Recalling unpresented hostile words: False memories predictors of traditional and cyberbullying. *European Journal of Developmental Psychology*, *9*(2), 182–194. doi:10.1080/17405629.2011.646459

Varela, J. J., Hernández, C., Berger, C., Souza, S. B., & Pacheco, E. (2022). To ignore or not to ignore: The differential effect of coping mechanisms on depressive symptoms when facing adolescent cyberbullying. *Computers in Human Behavior*, *132*, 107268. https://doi.org/10.1016/j.chb.2022.107268

Varghese, M. E., & Pistole, M. C. (2017). College student cyberbullying: Self-Esteem, depression, loneliness, and attachment. *Journal of College Counseling*, *20*(1), 7–21. doi:10.1002/jocc.12055

Varjas, K., Henrich, C. C., & Meyers, J. (2009). Urban middle school students' perceptions of bullying, cyberbullying, and school safety. *Journal of School Violence*, *8*(2), 159–176. doi:10.1080/15388220802074165

Vartia, M. A.-L. (2001). Consequences of Workplace Bullying with Respect to the Well-Being of Its Targets and the Observers of Bullying. *Scandinavian Journal of Work, Environment & Health, 27*(1), 63–69. doi:10.5271jweh.588 PMID:11266149

Veenstra, R., Lindenberg, S., Oldehikel, A. J., De-Winter, A. F., Verhulst, F. C., & Ormel, J. (2005). Bullying and victimization in elementary schools: A comparison of bullies, victims, bully/victims, and uninvolved preadolescents. *Developmental Psychology, 41*(4), 672–682. doi:10.1037/0012-1649.41.4.672 PMID:16060813

Veiga Simao, A. M. V., Ferreira, P., Francisco, S. M., Paulino, P., & de Souza, S. B. (2018). Cyberbullying: Shaping the use of verbal aggression through normative moral beliefs and selfefficacy. *New Media & Society*, (12), 4787–4806. Advance online publication. doi:10.1177/1461444818784870

Verswijvel, K., Walrave, M., Hardies, K., & Heirman, W. (2019). Sharenting, is it a good or a bad thing? Understanding how adolescents think and feel about sharenting on social network sites. *Children and Youth Services Review, 104*, 104401. Advance online publication. doi:10.1016/j.childyouth.2019.104401

Villegas, P. E., & Aberman, T. (2019). A double punishment: Post-secondary access for racialized migrant youth with precarious status in Toronto, Canada. *Refuge: Canada's Periodical on Refugees, 35*(1), 72–82. https://doi.org/10.7202/1060676ar

Vlaanderen, A., Bevelander, K. E., & Kleemans, M. (2020). Empowering digital citizenship: An anti-cyberbullying intervention to increase children's intentions to intervene on behalf of the victim. *Computers in Human Behavior, 112*, 106459. doi:10.1016/j.chb.2020.106459

Voelker, D. K., Reel, J. J., & Greenleaf, C. (2015). Weight status and body image perceptions in adolescents: Current perspectives. *Adolescent Health, Medicine and Therapeutics, 6*, 149. doi:10.2147/AHMT.S68344 PMID:26347007

Vogt, D., Pless, A. P., King, L. A., & King, D. W. (2005). Deployment stressors, gender, and mental health outcomes among Gulf War I veterans. *Journal of Traumatic Stress, 18*, 272–284.

Volk, A. A., Dane, A. V., & Marini, Z. A. (2014). What is bullying? A theoretical redefinition. *Developmental Review, 34*(4), 327–343. doi:10.1016/j.dr.2014.09.001

Vranjes, I., Farley, S., & Baillien, E. (2021). Harassment in the Digital World: Cyberbullying - Bullying and Harassment in the Workplace: Theory, Research and Practice. In *Developments in theory, research, and practice* (pp. 409–432). https://ebrary.net/131645/psychology/harassment_digital_world_cyberbullying

Vural, Z. B., & Bat, M. (2010). Social media as a new communication medium: A study for the faculty of communication of Ege University. *Journal of Yasar University*, 3348-3382.

Waasdorp, T. E., Mehari, K. R., Milam, A. J., & Bradshaw, C. P. (2019). Health-related risks for involvement in bullying among middle and high school youth. *Journal of Child and Family Studies, 28*(9), 2606–2617. doi:10.100710826-018-1260-8

Waasdorp, T., & Bradshaw, C. (2015). The overlap between cyberbullying and traditional bullying. *The Journal of Adolescent Health, 56*(5), 483–488. doi:10.1016/j.jadohealth.2014.12.002 PMID:25631040

Wachs, S., Bilz, L., Wettstein, A., Wright, M. F., Krause, N., Ballaschk, C., & Kansok-Dusche, J. (2022). The Online Hate Speech Cycle of Violence: Moderating Effects of Moral Disengagement and Empathy in the Victim-to-Perpetrator Relationship. *Cyberpsychology, Behavior, and Social Networking*. doi:10.1089/cyber.2021.0159

Wachs, S., Junger, M., & Sittichai, R. (2015). Traditional, cyber and combined bullying roles: Differences in risky online and offline activities. *Societies (Basel, Switzerland), 5*(1), 109–135. doi:10.3390oc5010109

Wagner, A., & Gasche, L. A. (2018). *Sharenting: Making decisions about other's privacy on social networking sites.* Retrieved February 10, 2020, from https://mkwi2018.leuphana.de/wp-content/uploads/MKWI_81.pdf

Wagner, P. J., & Mongan, P. F. (1998). Validating the concept of abuse: Women's perceptions of defining behaviors and the effects of emotional abuse on health indicators. *Archives of Family Medicine, 7*(1), 25–29. doi:10.1001/archfami.7.1.25 PMID:9443694

Walden, L. M., & Beran, T. N. (2010). Attachment quality and bullying behavior in school-aged youth. *Canadian Journal of School Psychology, 25*, 5–18. doi:10.1177/0829573509357046

Waldo, C. R., Berdahl, J. L., & Fitzgerald, L. F. (1998). Are men sexually harassed? If so, by whom? *Law and Human Behavior, 22*(1), 59–79.

Walker, J. L. (2009). *The contextualized rapid resolution cycle intervention model for cyber bullying* (Unpublished Doctoral Thesis). Arizona State University.

Walrave, M., & Heirman, W. (2011). Cyberbullying: Predicting victimisation and perpetration. *Children & Society, 25*(1), 59–72. doi:10.1111/j.1099-0860.2009.00260.x

Wang, B. C. (2004). Network language and the new trend of current social and cultural development. *Zhejiang Academic Journal, 6.*

Wang, L., & Ngai, S. S. (2021). Cyberbullying Perpetration Among Chinese Adolescents: The Role of Power Imbalance, Fun-seeking Tendency, and Attitude Toward Cyberbullying. *Journal of Interpersonal Violence.* doi:10.1177/08862605211062988

Wang, C. L., Huang, C. Y., Lu, K. Y., & Ho, M. Y. (2007). A study of the social support and job stress among nursing staff. *VGH Nursing, 24*(1), 59–68.

Wang, H. (2021). Big Data Security Management Countermeasures in the Prevention and Control of Computer Network Crime. *Journal of Global Information Management, 30*(7), 1–16. https://doi.org/10.4018/jgim.295450

Wang, J., Iannotti, R. J., & Nansel, T. R. (2009). School bullying among US adolescents: Physical, verbal, relational, and cyber. *The Journal of Adolescent Health, 45*(4), 368–375. doi:10.1016/j.jadohealth.2009.03.021 PMID:19766941

Wang, L., & Jiang, S. (2021). The effects of strain and negative emotions on adolescent cyberbullying perpetration: An empirical test of general strain theory. *Current Psychology (New Brunswick, N.J.)*, 1–11. doi:10.100712144-021-02426-8

Wang, M. J., Yogeeswaran, K., Andrews, N. P., Hawi, D. R., & Sibley, C. G. (2019, November). How common is cyberbullying among adults? Exploring gender, ethnic, and age differences in the prevalence of cyberbullying. *Cyberpsychology, Behavior, and Social Networking, 22*(11), 736–741. doi:10.1089/cyber.2019.0146 PMID:31697598

Wang, N. E., Baz, B., & Bechtel, K. (2007). Physical abuse of children: Identification. Evaluation, and management in the emergency department setting. *Emergency Medicine, 12*(9), 97–108.

Watts, L. K., Wagner, J., Velasquez, B., & Behrens, P. I. (2017). Cyberbullying in higher education: A literature review. *Computers in Human Behavior, 69*, 268-274.

Watts, C., & Zimmerman, C. (2002). Violence against women: Global scope and magnitude. *Lancet, 359*(9313), 1232–1237.

Wauters, L. N., & Knoors, H. (2008). Social integration of deaf children in inclusive settings. *Journal of Deaf Studies and Deaf Education, 13*(1), 21–36. doi:10.1093/deafed/enm028 PMID:17573356

WBI. (2015). *Mental health harm from workplace bullying.* Retrieved from https://www.workplacebullying.org/individuals/impact/mental-health-harm/

WBI. (2021). *U.S. Workplace Bullying Survey.* The Workplace Bullying Institute. https://workplacebullying.org/wp-content/uploads/2021/04/2021-Full-Report.pdf

Weibo. (2020). *Weibo Community Convention.* http://service. weibo.com/roles/gongyue

Weiler, B. L., & Widom, C. S. (1996). Psychopathy and violent behaviour in abused and neglected young adults. *Criminal Behaviour and Mental Health, 6*(3), 253–271. doi:10.1002/cbm.99

Weiner, M. T., Day, S. J., & Galvan, D. (2013). Deaf and hard of hearing students' perspectives on bullying and school climate. *American Annals of the Deaf, 158*(3), 334–343. doi:10.1353/aad.2013.0029 PMID:24133958

Weiner, M. T., & Miller, M. (2006). Deaf children and bullying: Directions for future research. *American Annals of the Deaf, 151*(1), 61–70. doi:10.1353/aad.2006.0021 PMID:16856647

Weissberg, R. P., & Cascarino, J. (2013). Academic learning + social-emotional learning = national priority. *Phi Delta Kappan, 95*(2), 8–13. doi:10.1177/003172171309500203

Welsh, S., & Gruber, J. E. (1999). Not taking it any more: Women who report or file complaints of sexual harassment. *Canadian Review of Sociology/Revue canadienne de sociologie, 36*(4), 559-583.

Welsh, S., Carr, J., MacQuarrie, B., & Huntley, A. (2006). "I'm not thinking of it as sexual harassment" understanding harassment across race and citizenship. *Gender & Society, 20*(1), 87–107.

Wendt, G., & Lisboa, C. (2013). Agressão entre pares no espaço virtual: Definições, impactos e desafios do cyberbullying [Peer-to-peer aggression in virtual space: Definitions, impacts and challenges of cyberbullying]. *Psicologia Clínica, 25*(1), 73–87. doi:10.1590/S0103-56652013000100005

Wet, C. (2005). The nature and extent of bullying in free state secondary schools. *South African Journal of Education, 25*(2), 82–88.

Wheeler, A. R., Halbesleben, J. R. B., & Shanine, K. (2010). Eating Their Cake and Everyone Else's Cake, Too: Resources as the Main Ingredient to Workplace Bullying. *Business Horizons, 53*(6), 553–560. doi:10.1016/j.bushor.2010.06.002

Whitney, I., & Smith, P. K. (1993). A survey of the nature and extent of bullying in junior/middle and secondary schools. *Educational Research, 35*(1), 3–25. doi:10.1080/0013188930350101

Whittaker, E., & Kowalski, R. M. (2015). Cyberbullying Via Social Media. *Journal of School Violence, 14*(1), 11–29. doi:10.1080/15388220.2014.949377

Whitted, K. S., & Dupper, D. R. (2005). Best practices for preventing or reducing bullying in schools. *Children & Schools, 27*(3), 167–175. doi:10.1093/cs/27.3.167

Whitted, K. S., & Dupper, D. R. (2008). Do teachers bully students? Findings from a survey of students in an alternative education setting. *Education and Urban Society, 40*(3), 329–341. doi:10.1177/0013124507304487

WHO. (2006). *Preventing child maltreatment: A guide to taking action and generating evidence.* World Health Organization.

WHO. (2006). The world health report: 2006: working together for health. World Health Organization.

WHO. (2017). *Violence and injury prevention - violence against health workers.* Retrieved from https://www.who.int/violence_injury_prevention/violence/workplace/en/

WHO. (2020). Basic documents. World Health Organization.

WHO. (2020). *Mental health and psychosocial considerations during the COVID-19 outbreak.* Retrieved from Geneva: https://apps.who.int/iris/handle/10665/331490

WHO. (March 9, 2021). *Younger women among those most at risk: WHO.* https://www.who.int/news/item/09-03-2021-devastatingly-pervasive-1-in-3-women-globally-experience-violence#

Whoqol Group. (1998). The World Health Organization quality of life assessment (WHOQOL): Development and general psychometric properties. *Social Science & Medicine, 46*(12), 1569–1585. doi:10.1016/S0277-9536(98)00009-4 PMID:9672396

Wickman, L. J. (2000). *A correlational study of the impact of media influence on the body image of adolescent females* [Master of Science Degree]. Wisconsin-Stout Üniversitesi.

Wiguna, T., Minayati, K., Kaligis, F., Ismail, I., Wijaya, E., Murtani, J., & Pradana, K. (2021). The effect of cyberbullying, abuse, and screen time on non-suicidal self-injury among adolescents during the pandemic: A perspective from the mediating role of stress. *Frontiers in Psychiatry, 12*, 743329. Advance online publication. doi:10.3389/fpsyt.2021.743329 PMID:34867535

Wilkinson, R. G., & Marmot, M. (2003). *Social determinants of health: the solid facts.* World Health Organization.

Willard, N. (2004a). *An educator's guide to cyberbullying and cyberthreats.* Retrieved from http://cyberbully.org/docs/cbcteducator.pdf

Willard, N. (2004b). *Educator's guide to cyberbullying: Addressing the harm caused by online social cruelty.* Retrieved from https://www.asdk12.org/MiddleLink/ AVB/bully_topics/EducatorsGuide_Cyberbullying.pdf

Willard, N. (2007). The authority and responsibility of school officials in responding to cyberbullying. *The Journal of Adolescent Health, 41*, 64–65.

Willard, N. B. (2007, March). *Cyberbullying legislation and school policies: Where are the boundaries of the "schoolhouse gate" in the new virtual world?* Center for Safe and Responsible use of the Internet. Retrieved from: http://csiru.org

Willard, N. E. (2006). *Educators guide to cyberbullying: Addressing the harm caused by online social cruelty.* Retrieved April 4, 2009, from: www.asdkI2.orglMiddleLinklAVBlbully_topics/ Educators Guide_Cyberbullying.pdf

Willard, N. E. (2006). *Educators guide to cyberbullying: Addressing the harm caused by online social cruelty.* Retrieved from: www.asdkI2.orglMiddleLinklAVBlbully_topics/ Educators Guide _ Cyberbullying.pdf

WillardN. (2005). https://cdn.ymaws.com/www.safestates.org/resource/resmgr/imported/educatorsguide.pdf

Willard, N. E. (2007). *Cyberbullying and cyberthreats: Responding to the challenge of online social aggression, Threats and Distress.* Research Press.

Willard, N. E. (2007). *Cyberbullying and Cyberthreats: Responding to The Challenge of Online Social Aggression, Threats, and Distress.* Research Press.

Williams, K. R., & Guerra, N. G. (2007). Prevalence and predictors of internet bullying. *The Journal of Adolescent Health, 41*(6), 14–21. doi:10.1016/j.jadohealth.2007.08.018 PMID:18047941

Williford, A., Boulton, A., Noland, B., Little, T. D., Kärnä, A., & Salmivalli, C. (2012). Effects of the KiVa anti-bullying program on adolescents' depression, anxiety, and perception of peers. *Journal of Abnormal Child Psychology, 40*(2), 289–300. doi:10.100710802-011-9551-1 PMID:21822630

Willness, C. R., Steel, P., & Lee, K. (2007). A meta-analysis of the antecedents and consequences of workplace sexual harassment. *Personnel Psychology, 60*(1), 127–162. doi:10.1111/j.1744-6570.2007.00067.x

Wilson, C., Sheridan, L., & Garratt-Reed, D. (2020). What is Cyberstalking? A review of Measurements. *Journal of Interpersonal Violence*, 1–21. PMID:33403888

Winkelman, S., Oomen-Early, J., Walker, A. D., Chu, L., & Yick-Flanagan, A. (2015). Exploring Cyber Harassment Among Women Who Use Social Media. *Universal Journal of Public Health*, *3*(5), 194–201. doi:10.13189/ujph.2015.030504

Wójcik, M., & Hełka, A. M. (2018). Meeting the Needs of Young Adolescents: ABBL Anti-Bullying Program During Middle School Transition. *Psychological Reports*, *122*(3), 1043–1067. doi:10.1177/0033294118768671 PMID:29652220

Wolke, D., Copeland, W. E., Angold, A., & Costello, E. J. (2013). Impact of bullying in childhood on adult health, wealth, crime, and social outcomes. *Psychological Science*, *24*(10), 1958–1970. doi:10.1177/0956797613481608 PMID:23959952

Wolke, D., & Lereya, S. T. (2015). Long-term effects of bullying. *Archives of Disease in Childhood*, *100*(9), 879–885. doi:10.1136/archdischild-2014-306667 PMID:25670406

Wolke, D., Tippett, N., & Dantchev, S. (2015). Bullying in the family: Sibling bullying. *The Lancet. Psychiatry*, *2*(10), 917–929. doi:10.1016/S2215-0366(15)00262-X PMID:26462226

Wolke, D., Woods, S., Bloomfield, L., & Karstadt, L. (2000). The association between direct and relational bullying and behaviour problems among primary school children. *Journal of Child Psychology and Psychiatry, and Allied Disciplines*, *41*(8), 989–1002. doi:10.1111/1469-7610.00687 PMID:11099116

Wolke, D., Woods, S., Stanford, K., & Schulz, H. (2001). Bullying and victimization of primary school children in England and Germany: Prevalence and school factors. *British Journal of Psychology*, *92*(4), 673–696. doi:10.1348/000712601162419 PMID:11762868

Women in News. (2021). *Sexual Harassment in the Media: African Report.* WAN-IFRA. https://womeninnews.org/wp-content/uploads/2021/07/20210712-Low-Res-Sexual-Harassment-Report.pdf

Wong, J. S. (2009). *No bullies allowed understanding peer victimization, the impacts on delinquency, and the effectiveness of prevention programs* [Unpublished doctoral dissertation]. Pardee RAND Graduate School, Santa Monica.

Wong-Lo, M., & Bullock, L. M. (2011). Digital aggression: Cyberworld meets school bullies. *Preventing School Failure*, *55*(2), 64–70. doi:10.1080/1045988X.2011.539429

Wong, N., & McBride, C. (2018). Fun over conscience: Fun-seeking tendencies in cyberbullying perpetration. *Computers in Human Behavior*, *86*, 319–329. https://doi.org/10.1016/j.chb.2018.05.009

Wood, C. L., Lane, L. C., & Cheetham, T. (2019). Puberty: Normal physiology (brief overview). *Best Practice & Research. Clinical Endocrinology & Metabolism*, *33*(3), 101265. doi:10.1016/j.beem.2019.03.001 PMID:31000487

World Health Organization. (1997, July). *Violence against women: A priority health issue.* https://web.archive.org/web/20201205103604/https://apps.who.int/iris/bitstream/handle/10665/63553/WHO_FRH_WHD_97.8.pdf

World Population Record. (April 14, 2021). *UNFPA Launches the State Of World Population Report, 2021: My Body Is My Own.* UNFPA. https://in.one.un.org/news/unfpa-launches-the-state-of-world-population-report-2021-my-body-is-my- own/#:~:text=Is%20My%20Own,UNFPA%20Launches% 20the%20State%20Of%20Wor ld%20 Population%20Report%2C%202021,My%20Body% 20Is%20My%20Own&text=Nearly%20half%20of%20all% 20women,Wednesday%2C%20April%2014%2C%202021

Wright, M. F. (2013). The Relationship Between Young Adults' Beliefs About Anonymity and Subsequent Cyber Aggression. *Cyberpsychology, Behavior, and Social Networking*, *16*(12), 858–862. doi:10.1089/cyber.2013.0009 PMID:23849002

Wright, V. H., Joy, J. B., Christopher, T. I., & Heather, N. O. (2009). Cyberbullying: Using virtual scenarios to educate and raise awareness. *Journal of Computing in Teacher Education*, *26*(1), 35–42.

Wu, Z. (2019). In search of the "middle ground": Rethinking the politics of othering in the "MeToo" movement. *Press Circles, 3*, 51–61. doi:10.15897/j.cnki.cn51-1046/g2.2019.03.007

Xiao, H., Gong, Z., Ba, Z., Doolan-Noble, F., & Han, Z. (2021). School bullying and health-related quality of life in Chinese school-aged children and adolescents. *Children & Society, 35*(6), 885–900. doi:10.1111/chso.12465

Xing, K., Jiao, M., Ma, H., Qiao, H., Hao, Y., Li, Y., & Wu, Q. (2015). Physical Violence against General Practitioners and Nurses in Chinese Township Hospitals: A Cross-Sectional Survey. *PLoS One, 10*(11), e0142954. doi:10.1371/journal.pone.0142954 PMID:26571388

Xu, Y. (2021). The invisible aggressive fist: Features of cyberbullying language in China. *International Journal for the Semiotics of Law - Revue internationale de Sémiotique juridique, 34*, 1041-1064. doi:10.1007/s11196-020-09746-1

Xu, W., & Zheng, S. (2022). Personality traits and cyberbullying perpetration among Chinese university students: The moderating role of internet self-efficacy and gender. *Frontiers in Psychology, 13*, 779139. Advance online publication. doi:10.3389/fpsyg.2022.779139 PMID:35391948

Yahya, A. S., Khawaja, S., & Chukwuma, J. (2020). COVID-19 and a potential rise in bullying behaviors. *The Primary Care Companion for CNS Disorders, 22*(3). doi:10.4088/PCC.20com02642

Yalçın, N. (2011). *Türkiye'de çocuk istismari ve çözüm önerileri* [Child abuse and solution proposals in Turkey] [Unpublished master's project]. Beykent Üniversitesi.

Yaman, E., & Sönmez, Z. (2015). Cyberbullying Tendencies of Adolescents. *Online Journal of Technology Addiction & Cyberbullying*, 18-31.

Yaman, E., Eroğlu, Y., & Peker, A. (2011). *Okul Zorbalığı ve Siber Zorbalık*. Kaknüs.

Yang, B., Wang, B., Sun, N., Xu, F., Wang, L., Chen, J., Yu, Z., Zhang, Y., Zhu, Y., Dai, T., Zhang, Q., & Sun, C. (2021). The consequences of cyberbullying and traditional bullying victimization among adolescents: Gender differences in psychological symptoms, self-harm, and suicidality. *Psychiatry Research, 306*, 114219. doi:10.1016/j.psychres.2021.114219 PMID:34614443

Ybarra, M. L., & Mitchell, K. J. (2004). Online aggressor/targets, aggressors, and targets: A comparison of associated youth characteristics. *Journal of Child Psychology and Psychiatry, and Allied Disciplines, 45*(7), 1308–1316.

Ybarra, M. L., & Mitchell, K. J. (2004). Youth engaging in online harassment: Associations with caregiver–child relationships, internet use, and personal characteristics. *Journal of Adolescence, 27*(3), 319–336. doi:10.1016/j.adolescence.2004.03.007 PMID:15159091

Ybarra, M. L., & Mitchell, K. J. (2007). Prevalence and frequency of internet harassment instigation: Implications for adolescent health. *The Journal of Adolescent Health, 41*(2), 189–195. doi:10.1016/j.jadohealth.2007.03.005 PMID:17659224

Ybarra, M. L., & Mitchell, K. J. (2008). How risky are social networking sites? A comparison of places online where youth sexual solicitation and harassment occurs. *Pediatrics, 121*(2), 350–357. doi:10.1542/peds.2007-0693 PMID:18227194

Yelboğa, N., & Koçak, O. (2019). Evaluation of some factors predicting peer bullying in adolescents. *OPUS International Journal of Society Researches, 13*(19), 2286–2320. doi:10.26466/opus.543567

Yeşildal, Y. (2016). A general overview of violence in healthcare. *Journal of Health and Nursing Management, 1*(3), 44–55. doi:10.5222/SHYD.2016.044

Yeşiltaş, M. (2005). İnsan kaynakları yönetimi açısından bir sorun olarak işyerinde cinsel taciz [Sexual harassment in the workplace as a problem for human resources management]. *Manas Üniversitesi Sosyal Bilimler Dergisi, 7*(13), 147–153.

Yetim, S. (2015). Cyberbullying, Comparison of Turkey and the USA ABD v. Drew Dosyası. *TBB Dergisi.*

Yiğit, M. F., & Seferoğlu, S. S. (2017). A Review on the Factors Related to Cyberbullying and Possible Solutions. *Online Journal of Technology Addiction & Cyberbullying*, 13-49.

Yıldırım, R. (2012). Peer bullying. *Manisa Celal Bayar University Journal of Social Sciences, 10*(2), 39-51. https://dergipark.org.tr/tr/download/article-file/45882

Yıldırım, S. (2001). *The Relationship of bullying, family environment and popularity* (UMI No. 105069) [Master's dissertation, Middle East Technical University]. Higher Education Council Thesis Center database.

Yildirim, D. (2009). Bullying among nurses and its effects. *International Nursing Review, 56*(4), 504–511. doi:10.1111/j.1466-7657.2009.00745.x PMID:19930081

Yildiz, S., & Yildiz, S. E. (2009). Bullying ve depresyon arasindaki iliski: Kars ilindeki saglik calisanlarinda bir arastirma [The relationship between bullying and depression: A study among healthcare workers in Kars province]. *Istanbul Ticaret Universitesi Sosyal Bilimler Dergisi, 8*, 133–150.

Yilmaz, E. (2013). *Mobbing davranisi ve Bandirma Ili kamu hastaneleri calisanlarina yonelik bir arastirma [A research on mobbing behavior and public hospital employees in Bandirma] [Master]*. Okan University Institute of Health Sciences.

Yoon, D., Shipe, S. L., Park, J., & Yoon, M. (2021). Bulling patterns and their associations with child maltreatment and adolescent psychosocial problems. *Children and Youth Services Review, 129*, 106178. https://doi.org/10.1016/j.childyouth.2021.106178

Yüksel, A. (2004). The effect of empathy education program on empathic skills of primary school students. *Journal of Uludag University Faculty of Education, 17*(2), 341–354.

Zablotsky, B., Bradshaw, C. P., Anderson, C. M., & Law, P. (2014). Risk factors for bullying among children with autism spectrum disorders. *Autism, 18*(4), 419–427. 10.1177%2F1362361313477920 PMID:23901152

Zapf, D. (1999). Organisational, work group related and personal causes of mobbing/bullying at work. *International Journal of Manpower, 20*(1/2), 70–85. doi:10.1108/01437729910268669

Zapf, D., Escartin, J., Einarsen, S., Hoel, H., & Vartia, M. (2011). Empirical findings on prevalence and risk groups of bullying in the workplace. In S. Einarsen, D. Hoel, D. Zapf, & C. Cooper (Eds.), *Bullying and Harassment in the Workplace* (pp. 75–106). Taylor and Francis.

Zhang, Z., Xiao, H., Zhang, L., & Zheng, J. (2021). Linking Cyberbullying to Job Strain: Roles of Ego Depletion and Self-Efficacy. *Journal of Aggression, Maltreatment and Trauma*. doi:10.1080/10926771.2021.1933288

Zhang, H., Chi, P., Long, H., & Ren, X. (2019). Bullying victimization and depression among left-behind children in rural China: Roles of self-compassion and hope. *Child Abuse & Neglect, 96*, 104072. doi:10.1016/j.chiabu.2019.104072 PMID:31319239

Zhang, M., McGrath, C., & Hägg, U. (2006). The impact of malocclusion and its treatment on quality of life: A literature review. *International Journal of Paediatric Dentistry, 16*(6), 381–387. doi:10.1111/j.1365-263X.2006.00768.x PMID:17014535

Zhang, R. (2010). Legal analysis of the characteristics of cyberbullying subject. *Seeker, 12*, 140–142.

Zhang, X., Sun, J., Wang, J., Chen, Q., Cao, D., Wang, J., & Cao, F. (2020). Suicide ideation among pregnant women: The role of different experiences of childhood abuse. *Journal of Affective Disorders, 266*, 182–186. doi:10.1016/j.jad.2020.01.119 PMID:32056874

Zhong, M., Huang, X., Huebner, E. S., & Tian, L. (2021). Association between bullying victimization and depressive symptoms in children: The mediating role of self-esteem. *Journal of Affective Disorders*, *294*, 322–328. doi:10.1016/j.jad.2021.07.016 PMID:34311332

Zhou, Z., Tang, H., Tian, Y., Wei, H., Zhang, F., & Morrison, C. M. (2013). Cyberbullying and its Risk Factors Among Chinese High School Students. *School Psychology International*, *34*(6), 630–647. doi:10.1177/0143034313479692

Zhu, C., Huang, S., Evans, R., & Zhang, W. (2021). Cyberbullying among adolescents and children: A comprehensive review of the global situation, risk factors, and preventive measures. *Frontiers in Public Health*, *9*, 634909. doi:10.3389/fpubh.2021.634909 PMID:33791270

Zi, W. (2018). *The discourse research of Feminist we media—based on sample analysis of Sina microblog* (Master's degree thesis). Guangxi Normal University. https://kns.cnki.net/KCMS/detail/detail.aspx?dbname=CMFD201901&filename=1018851076.nh

Zich, I., Farrington, D., & Ttofi, M. M. (2019). Protective factors against bullying and cyberbullying: A systematic review of meta-analyses. *Aggression and Violent Behavior*, *45*, 4–19. doi:10.1016/j.avb.2018.06.008

Zimmer-Gembeck, M. J., & Webb, H. J. (2017). Body image and peer relationships: Unique associations of adolescents' social status and competence with peer-and self-reported appearance victimization. *Journal of Adolescence*, *61*(1), 131–140. doi:10.1016/j.adolescence.2017.10.002 PMID:29080408

Zwickl, S., Wong, A. F. Q., Dowers, E., Leemaqz, S. Y. L., Bretherton, I., Cook, T., Zajac, J. D., Yip, P. S. F., & Cheung, A. S. (2021). Factors associated with suicide attempts among Australian transgender adults. *BMC Psychiatry*, *21*(1), 1–9. https://doi.org/10.1186/s12888-021-03084-7

Zych, I., Farrington, D. P., Llorent, V. J., & Ttofi, M. M. (2017). *Protecting Children Against Bullying and Its Consequences*. Academic Press.

Zych, I., Farrington, D. P., Llorent, V. J., Ribeaud, D., & Eisner, M. P. (2021). Childhood risk and protective factors as predictors of adolescent bullying roles. *International Journal of Bullying Prevention*, *3*(2), 138–146. doi:10.100742380-020-00068-1

Zych, I., Ortega-Ruiz, R., & Marín-López, I. (2016). Cyberbullying: A systematic review of research, its prevalence and assessment issues in Spanish studies. *Psicologia dell'Educazione*, *22*(1), 5–18. doi:10.1016/j.pse.2016.03.002

Zych, I., Ttofi, M. M., Llorent, V. J., Farrington, D. P., Ribeaud, D., & Eisner, M. P. (2020). A Longitudinal Study on Stability and Transitions Among Bullying Roles. *Child Development*, *91*(2), 527–545. doi:10.1111/cdev.13195 PMID:30566232

About the Contributors

Gülşah Sarı works as an Assistant Professor at the Department of Journalism, in Aksaray University, Turkey. She became a Ph.D. in İstanbul University, Department of Radio Television and Cinema in 2016. She holds a master's degree in Marmara University, department of Cinema in 2010. She has published several papers in journals and books including women's studies, gender, digital communication, communication studies.

* * *

Zaridah Abdullah is a senior lecturer at Faculty of Communication and Media Studies, Universiti Teknologi MARA (UiTM), Malaysia. Her research interest is Family Communication and Social Media.

Nevra Atış Akyol received B.S degrees in Preschool Education from Cumhuriyet University and M.A. degrees at Marmara University. She worked as a teacher at the Ministry of National Education between 2011 and 2015. She spent one year between 2013-2014 in the United States, and during this period, she worked as a volunteer teacher in three different schools, one of which was Headstart school. In 2015, she started her career in Cumhuriyet University Preschool Education Department. She completed her Ph.D. degree in Preschool Education from Hacettepe University. In addition, the author worked as a visiting researcher at Roehampton University in London for 6 months in 2019-2020. Her major research interests are school readiness, emotional and social development, peer relations, misbehaviors, gender, sexual development, and family involvement. She has authored or co-authored a lot of scientific publications, and books, and she has conducted many national and international projects

Hicabi Arslan is a Faculty Member at Adnan Menderes University, Faculty of Communication, Department of Journalism. He was born in 1967 in Erzurum. Arslan completed his B.A. at Istanbul University, Press and Broadcasting Vocational School, Department of Journalism and PR, his M.A. and Ph.D. degrees at Institute of Social Sciences, Department of Journalism at the same university. He worked as Anadolu Ajansı (1990), at Türkiye Denizcilik Bankası (1990-1992) and Türkiye Emlak Bankası (1992-2002), and Türkiye Cumhuriyeti Ziraat Bankası and he also undertook administrative duties. Arslan, who prepared many sectorial reports in the field of advertising, Finance and Insurance Turkey. He has several works and gives lectures on media management and organization, media critics , media economy, media ethics, marketing comm

Inês Carvalho Relva is a psychologist, Assistant Professor at the University of Trás-os-Montes and Alto Douro and an integrated researcher at the Research Center in Sport, Health, and Human Development, based at UTAD and a collaborating researcher at the Center for Research and Educational Intervention (CIIE) of the Porto University. PhD in Psychology from the University of Coimbra and post-doctorate from the Center for Social Studies also of the University of Coimbra (portugal). She has several national and international publications, being reviewer in journals with impact factor. Its areas of research have focused on family relationships, specifically the conflict between siblings, family functioning and psychosocial adjustment of children and young people. Other areas of interest are bullying, cyberbullying and cyberdating.

Yinyu Chen received her master degree in Integrated Marketing Communication from City University Of Hong Kong. Her work focuses on the area of cyberbullying language on social media. She is interested in the role of communication in maintaining democratic institutions.

Umut Çıvgın is an Assistant Professor in Bursa Technical University in Turkey. He has a Psychology Ph.D. from the Graduate School of Social Sciences at Dokuz Eylül University and a B.S. degree from Middle East Technical University. He gives courses such as Personality, Research Methods, Observation and Interview Methods, Supervision (CBT-based) and supervises students' master's theses. He continues to conduct research on psychological well-being, psychological resilience, coping with stress, and psycho-oncology.

Füsun Gökkaya, who completed her undergraduate education at Ege University, Department of Psychology in 1990, completed her master's degree in Developmental Psychology at the same university in 1994. She completed her PhD in Clinical Psychology in 2015. Füsun Gökkaya, who received the title of Associate Professor in 2020, works as a psychodrama therapist and family counselor at the Eskülap Counseling Center which she is a partner, in İzmir. She also teaches clinical psychology at the Cyprus International University. Füsun Gökkaya, who is the author of many scientific articles, chapters and books, conducts studies on peer bullying, psychodrama, cognitive behavioral therapies, anxiety disorder, OCD, couple therapy and family counseling.

Gülümser Gültekin Akduman completed her bachelor's degree in 2000, her master's degree in 2003 and his doctoral degree in 2007 at Ankara University. In 2008, she started to work as an assistant professor at Gazi University, Gazi Education Faculty, Department of Basic Education, Preschool Education Department. She received the Associate Professor in 2013 and Professor in 2019 in the same department. She is still working as a lecturer at Gazi University, Gazi Education Faculty, Department of Basic Education, Preschool Education Department. She has studied Child Mental Health, child neglect and abuse, children's rights, and social skills training.

Jingyi Guo has received the degree of Master of Arts in Integrated Marketing Communication from City University of HongKong in 2021.

Nor Hazlina Hashim commenced her Doctor of Philosophy in year 2010 at University of Wollongong (UOW), Australia. Earlier, Lina graduated Masters of Arts in Communication at Universiti Sains Malaysia (USM) in 2003 and Bachelors of Arts (in Public Relations) at Universiti of Techonologi

MARA (UiTM) in 1997. Lina also has 4.5 years of working experience as Supply Management Analysts (SMA) at Intel Technology Sdn. Bhd., Penang (1997-2001) and was a senior lecturer for 8 years at School of Communication, USM, Penang (2010-2018). Lina has taught Message and Design, and Digital Marketing for Master in Integrated Marketing Communication (IMC) at USM@KL, Wisma Sejarah, K.Lumpur from 2013 until 2018. Lina went for her Industrial Training at McCann-Erickson (M) Sdn. Bhd. and exposed on advertising and copy writing. Her research interest is on websites and online studies especially Integrated Marketing Communication (IMC), Digital Marketing, Product Development and Innovations and Q-Methodology.

Mehmet Kanak completed his undergraduate education at Cumhuriyet University, Faculty of Education, in the field of pre-school education in 2007. He received his master's degree from İnönü University Educational Sciences Institute in 2011 and his doctorate degree from Gazi University Educational Sciences Institute in 2015. He is still working as an associate professor in the department of pre-school education at Sivas Cumhuriyet University, Faculty of Education. Topics of the author's work; Child abuse is child rights and temperament.

Jin Liu is a master student from the Department of Media and Communication, City University of Hong Kong.

Sevgi Mestci Sunerli is a graduate of American Collegiate Institute (ACI'10) and completed her undergraduate education at İzmir University of Economics, Department of Psychology in 2014 as a High Honor Student. She completed Ege University Family Counseling Non-Thesis Master's Program in 2015 and became a Family Counselor. She has been accepted to Izmir University of Economics Clinical Psychology Master's Degree. During her education, she continued her sessions with adults and adolescents as part of psychoanalytic supervision. She has received long-term training in different approaches such as experiential play therapy and cognitive behavioral therapies and has been continuing her clinical interviews at Eskulap Counseling Center since 2014. She continues her individual therapy process and at the same time continues her group supervision.

Marshina Juliza Mohd Hasim holds a PhD in Interpersonal Communication from Universiti Sains Malaysia (USM) and is a freelance researcher currently collaborating with Faculty of Business and Accountancy, University of Malaya.

Ana Paula Monteiro is Assistant Professor at the School of Human and Social Sciences (Department of Education and Psychology) at the University of Trás-os-Montes and Alto Douro and member of the Center for Educational Research (CIIE) of the University of Porto. PhD in Social Psychology from the University of Santiago de Compostela. Certified trainer by the Scientific-Pedagogical Council for Continuing Education of the Ministry of Education of Portugal in the areas of psychology / psychosociology and group animation. Her research interests are conflict management, negotiation and mediation in different contexts, addition to the internet, bullying, cyberbullying, workplace bullying and rumour psychosociology. She has several national and international publications, and reviewer in journals with an impact factor.

Desmond Onyemechi Okocha, PhD, is a Social Scientist with specialisation in management and mass communication. He has over 15 years experience in consulting, Research and lecturing. He obtained his B.A degree in Management from the United Kingdom, holds a M.A and PhD in Journalism and Mass Communication, both from India. Additionally, has PGDs in Education Management and Leadership and another in Logistics and Supply Chain Management. He was the pioneer National Knowledge Management and Communication Coordinator for the International Fund for Agricultural Development project in the Niger Delta. He is presently, a Senior Lecturer, Department of Mass Communication, Bingham University, Nigeria. He is the Founder of Institute for Leadership and Development Communication, Nigeria. As an international voice, Dr. Okocha is a frequent speaker in conferences across continents. In 2018, he was invited to speak at Harvard University, USA, Vienna University, Austria, and at the MIRDEC-8th, International Academic Conference on Social Sciences, Portugal.

Sienne Okpor is currently a post graduate student in the department of Mass communication, Bingham University. She obtained her Bachelors Degree From University Of Mkar. She hails from Ukuwani local government area of Delta state.

Berceste Gülçin Özdemir is an associate professor at the Istanbul University. She completed her MA degree in Cinema and Television Department at Bahcesehir University and Ph.D. from Istanbul University. She did doctoral research at the L'Università degli Studi di Perugia. Her research concerns; feminist film theory, psychoanalytical film theory, Turkish cinema, independent cinema, digital cinema and characters' representation in film narratives, film philosophy. She is lecturing about cinema lessons. (Undergraduate and Ph.D. level) and works as a vice dean at Istanbul University, Faculty of Commuinication.

Seçil Özkan graduated from Ankara University, Faculty of Medicine in 1992. She served in Artvin / Yusufeli in 1992-1994 on compulsory duty. In 1999, she received her Public Health specialty from Gazi University, Faculty of Medicine, Department of Public Health. She served as the Head of Department for Health Centers under the General Directorate for Basic Healthcare Services in the Ministry of Health in 1999-2000. In 2002, she gained her Master's degree in "Educational Administration and Supervision" at Gazi University, Institute of Educational Sciences. She started to work as a lecturer at Gazi University, Faculty of Medicine, Department of Public Health in September 2000. She received the title of 'Professor' in 2011. She served as a Head of Public Health Institute in Turkey, Ministry of Health in 2013-2015 being assigned by the Ministry. Currently, she is working as a Professor at Gazi University, Faculty of Medicine.

Kadriye Özyazıcı is a lecturer at Sivas Cumhuriyet University Yıldızeli Vocational School Child Development Department. She graduated from Sivas Cumhuriyet University, Faculty of Education, Pre-School Teaching; She received her master's degree from Sivas Cumhuriyet University, Institute of Educational Sciences. As of January 2020, she is continuing her PhD in the Child Development Program of İnönü University. Child development and education are among his research areas.

Amina Parveen works as a senior Assistant professor in the Department of Education, University of Kashmir since 2007.

Serpil Pekdoğan completed her undergraduate education in the field of pre-school education in the Faculty of Education of İnönü University in 2009. She received her master's degree in 2011 from the educational sciences institute of the same university and his doctorate degree in 2015 from Gazi University's Educational Sciences Institute. She is still working as an associate professor in the department of pre-school education at the Inonu University Education Faculty. Topics of the author's work; Child abuse and neglect child rights and temperament.

Yuantao Peng is a graduate student at City University of Hong Kong.

Michael Prieler is a Professor in the Media School at Hallym University, South Korea. He has also been a Visiting Professor at the University of Illinois at Urbana-Champaign (USA) and at City University of Hong Kong. He is an expert on content analysis and his research focuses on advertising, health communication, new media, and diversity in the media (particularly representations of gender, race/ethnicity, and age). He has published in a variety of international journals on these topics, including Mass Communication and Society, Journalism & Mass Communication Quarterly, International Communication Gazette, Telematics and Informatics, Telecommunications Policy, African Journalism Studies, Sex Roles, and the International Journal of Cultural Studies, among others.

Monica Radu earned her Bachelor of Arts in Sociology and Master of Arts in Sociology from North Carolina Central University, and she received her Doctor of Philosophy from North Carolina State University. In August 2017, Dr. Monica Radu started as an Assistant Professor of Sociology in the Department of Criminal Justice, Social Work, and Sociology at Southeast Missouri State University. Her research interests include family inequality, intimate partner violence, bullying, and cyber bullying.

Shalini Ramdeo is an adjunct lecturer in the area of human resource management, and leadership and has teaching and research experience in the areas of organizational development and organizational behavior with the University of the West Indies, St Augustine, Trinidad. She holds a PhD in Business Administration with a specialization in Human Resource Management from the University of the West Indies and her research interests include workplace bullying, workplace cyberbullying, sexual harassment, organizational change, and human resource management.

Insha Rasool works as a research scholar in Department of Education, University of Kashmir.

Seda Sakarya completed her undergraduate education in the field of pre-school education at Gazi University Faculty of Education in 2007. She completed her master's degree in 2010 and PhD degree in 2015 at the Educational Sciences Institute of the same university. She is currently working as an associate professor at Kırıkkale University, Faculty of Health Sciences, Department of Child Development. Author's fields of study; visual literacy, the child's social emotional development and child rights.

Sinem Sarıçoban after graduating from Cumhuriyet University, Faculty of Health Sciences, Department of Health Management in 2013, she started her master's degree in Health Sciences Institute, Department of Health Management at the same university in 2014. In 2017, she completed her master's degree with her thesis on "Healthcare professions' exposure to violence and the effect of violence on intent to leave". In 2018, she started the Ankara University Health Sciences Institute Health Institutions

Management PhD and is currently working on her thesis. She has been working as a research assistant at Cumhuriyet University, Faculty of Health Sciences, Department of Health Management since 2014.

Merve Şepitci Sarıbaş was born in 1992 in the province of Isparta. In 2014, she graduated from Gazi University, Department of Preschool Teaching. In 2018, she received her master's degree from Gazi University Preschool Education Department. Between 2014-2018, she worked as a preschool teacher and Montessori teacher in private institutions in Ankara. In 2016, she graduated from Anadolu University Open Education Faculty, Department of Justice. Then again in 2016, she started her associate degree education at Anadolu University Open Education Faculty Social Services Department. In 2022, she received her doctorate from Gazi University Preschool Education Department. In addition, the author has studies on self-regulation skills, school adjustment, disadvantaged children, and children's rights.

Joshua T. Shadwick is an assistant professor at Southeast Missouri State University in the department of Criminal Justice, Social Work and Sociology. He teaches both undergraduate and graduate courses on topics ranging from research methods to gangs. His research interests include the justice system's response to social problems, police investigations, and wildlife crime. Dr. Shadwick's research has been published in peer-reviewed journals such as, Policing: An International Journal, Deviant Behavior, and Criminal Justice Policy Review.

Songyon Shin is an assistant professor at Southeast Missouri State University. Her research interest includes juvenile delinquency and comparative studies about how different societies affects individuals' criminal behaviors. her recent research was published in Policing: An International Journal, Deviant Behavior.

Margarida Simões is Assistant Professor at the University of Trás-Os-Montes and Alto Douro. PhD in Psychology from the University of Beira Interior and member of the Center for Educational Research (CIIE) of the University of Porto. Specialist in Clinical Psychology with advanced specialization in Justice Psychology. Coordinator of the Forensic Psychological Assessment Unit (U.A.P.F.) of UTAD, where she carries out psychological examinations for courts and other organs of justice. Researcher in the area of clinical psychology and justice, namely psychopathy in adolescence, cyberbullying and juvenile delinquency.

Riann Singh is a Lecturer at the UWI, St. Augustine Campus, Trinidad, and also serves as a Research Supervisor at the Master's and Doctoral Levels within the Caribbean. Her research interests include contemporary perspectives in employee turnover/embeddedness, workplace mistreatment/harassment and destructive work behaviors/psychological processes. Her teaching interests include organizational change/management and HRM. She is widely published in top International Journals and Books.

Hülya Şirin graduated Cukurova University, School of Medicine in 1992, worked as a general practitioner in the field of primary health care and completed PhD program in Public Health at Gazi University in 2011. Between the years of 2003 and 2005, she worked as a researcher at Center for Injury Research and Control, University of Pittsburgh. She got training on Newborn Screening Program Policies at U.S. National Newborn Screening and Genetics Resource Center, University of Texas. She has worked as a program manager in newborn screening program at the General Directorate of Mother and Child Health and Family Planning between 2006 and 2010, and as a senior advisor at the General Directorate of Public Health between 2014 and 2018, Ministry of Health. Dr Sirin created a great experience on public health science at almost every level including primary care, policy making and academy. At present, she enjoys sharing her knowledge and experience in Gulhane School of Medicine.

Kristen Sobba is an Assistant Professor at Southeast Missouri State University. Her research interests include victimology, cyberbullying, and juvenile delinquency.

Özge Tonbuloğlu Altıner was born in 1991 in Bolu, Turkey. She graduated from Bolu Science High School in 2009 and from Gazi University Faculty of Medicine in 2016. Between 2016-2017, she worked as a general practitioner at Bolu Refika Baysal Community Health Center. Between 2017 and 2021, she worked as an assistant physician in the Department of Pediatrics at Ankara Training and Research Hospital. She has been working as a research assistant at Gazi University Faculty of Medicine, Department of Public Health since July 2021.

Aslıhan Topal was born in Ankara in 1977 and completed his primary, secondary and high school education in Aydın. she graduated from Ankara University Faculty of Communication Department of Journalism in 2000 and completed her master's degree at Gazi University Institute of Social Sciences Department of Journalism in 2005. He works as a lecturer at Aydın Adnan Menderes University Aydın Vocational High School. He has academic works in the field of communication such as book section, article and conference statement.

Asiye Ugraş Dikmen graduated from Erciyes Medical Faculty in 2003. She completed her Public Health Specialization in 2010 from Gazi University and her PhD in Epidemiology in 2020 from Hacettepe University. Her studies are on epidemiology, biostatistics, violence and chronic diseases. And she is currently working as a hospital manager and dealing with the problems of healthcare workers.

Hatice Ulusoy completed her undergraduate education at the University of Cumhuriyet School of Nursing in 1986 in Türkiye. In the same year, she started to work as a research assistant at the same school. She completed her MSc degree at the University of Cumhuriyet Institute Health Sciences in 1989. She completed her PhD in nursing management at the University of Glasgow (Scotland-United Kingdom) with a YÖK scholarship. After working at Cumhuriyet University School of Nursing for 22 years, she was appointed as the founding head of the Department of Health Management, Faculty of Health Sciences, Cumhuriyet University in 2008. She is still working as a senior lecturer and Head of Department in the same department. She became an associate professor in 2012 and a professor in 2019. She has 42 articles published in scientific peer-reviewed journals (five of them SCI-SSCI), 80 papers presented in national and international scientific congresses, 12 book chapters, and a book editorship. Her scientific area of interests include organizational behavior in health services, quality and accreditation, patient and employee safety.

Tamara Wandel, a graduate of the State University of New York Albany and Indiana University, has taught at the collegiate level for two decades. Her research agenda has focused heavily on challenges to youth, from e-cigarette usage and legislation to handling the bereavement process of peer deaths to hurdles D/deaf individuals face. She is a 2022 Global Scholar and a 2021 Edward R. Murrow national award winner.

Caiwei Wang received a BA degree in Media Creativity from Communication University of China in 2014 and a MA degree in Integrated Marketing Communication from City University of Hong Kong in 2021. In 2014, she served with Jiangxi Radio and TV Station as a program director. In 2017, she joined Rocfly Co. as copywriter. She is now a freelance writer for a diverse array of organizations.

İlknur Yıldız is an assistant professor in Pediatric Nursing Department, Faculty of Health Sciences, Sivas Cumhuriyet University, Sivas, Turkey. Her research interests focus on infant, child, and adolescent health.

Index

J

K

L

M

N

O

P

Q

R

S

T

U

V

W

Y

Z

www.ingramcontent.com/pod-product-compliance
Lightning Source LLC
LaVergne TN
LVHW080618300926
849162LV00005B/1196